THAILAND

For Travellers By Travellers

Stuart McDonald

Danielle Karalus

Thailand - For Travellers By Travellers

1st Edition
> May 1997

Other books available in the Tales From the Other Side guidebook series
> Vietnam - For Travellers By Travellers

Published by
> Tales From the Other Side
> P O Box 743
> Hornsby NSW 2077
> Australia

> email: mcdonald@mail.enternet.com.au
> http://people.enternet.com.au/~mcdonald/

Printed by
> Proudly printed in Australia by
> McPhersons Printing Group, Australia

Distributed in Australia by
> Tower Books Wholesalers Pty Ltd

Text & Maps: Tales From the Other Side
Cover Design: Paula Garrod & Danielle Karalus.
Cover Photo: "Buddha caught by the sun", Tham Khao Luang, Phetburi Province, by
Stuart McDonald.
Photos: Stuart McDonald (SM), Danielle Karalus (DK), Mark Ord (MO)
Illustration: Ian Bowie

The writers and publishers have taken extreme care ensuring all the information is as up to date and accurate as possible and take no responsibility for any inconvenience, injury, loss or death as a result of using this guidebook.

National Library of Australia Cataloguing - in - Publication Data

> McDonald, Stuart, 1970-.
> Thailand: for travellers by travellers

> Includes index
> ISBN 0 646 31385 1

> 1. Thailand - Guidebooks. I. Karalus, Danielle, 1971-. II. Title

915.930444

Words from the Writers

Tales From the Other Side was established by Stuart McDonald and Danielle Karalus in 1995 based on the philosophy of travellers writing guidebooks for other travellers. The conception of this endeavour came about whilst on an arduous hitching journey through Asia. Unsatisfied with other available guides — their lack of coverage of out of the way places and unfocussed attention to the 'traveller' — we decided to pool our resources and publish the most comprehensive guide possible without all the waffle.

Travelling is about choice, and unfortunately choice is limited to the amount of information that you have available. With this in mind, we have endeavoured to provide you with a comprehensive coverage of Thailand enabling you to customise your trip to suit your own interests — whether they be soaking up the sun on a virtually deserted island, hiking side by side with the hilltribes, investigating untouristed ancient ruins, rockclimbing in cliff heaven or scuba diving in an underwater paradise — this is your perfect companion.

Thailand: For Travellers by Travellers is the second guidebook in the Tales From the Other Side travel guidebook series. This guide follows the successful publishing of our first guidebook, Vietnam, which has received amazing support and praise from travellers who took the chance of buying a guide that is new, fresh and a little different from the rest. Future guidebooks will continue to concentrate on Southeast Asia with Laos being the next off the rack. Now for a few words on your humble hosts.

Stuart McDonald

Although he calls Syndey, Australia home, Stuart has spent upwards of seven years bumming around the world — much of which has been spent in Southeast Asia and the subcontinent.

For this book, Stuart found himself all over Thailand, from the exotic far south to the back country of the north and northeast during which he developed a strong bond with both the Thai country and its people — along with yet another hundred reasons to go back. When in Sydney, Stuart continues to study Arts and run up the phonebill.

Danielle Karalus

At 19 Danielle set herself a personal quest to discover the world so packed her backpack and headed into the big wide world, concentrating in Asia and Europe. At the same time she also mastered the art of reducing the size of her backpack. After a spell of volunteer aid work in Costa Rica she returned to Sydney to complete a Business Degree at university. Danielle spent considerable time researching central, east and parts of northeast Thailand. Prepared to do anything, she found herself wrestling with a monkey, dodging exploding boat motors and surviving close encounters with motorcycles and comments about her hair!!

Mark Ord

Mark first came into contact with Tales From the Other Side on a tropical island in the far south. English born but Paris based, Mark contributed to the central, southern and far southern chapters as well as passing on volumes of his knowledge about Thailand from his all too frequent visits there over the years.

When not in Thailand, Mark works in the Parisian fashion industry and makes pancakes in Corsica. One of his long term goals is to run a guesthouse in Thailand which serves absolutely no pancakes or muesli!

Thankyou's

Editors: Richard McDonald, Samantha Milton, Peter Campbell, Grant Butler and Cassandra Sheridan.
Proofing: Kiernan Murphy, Sandra McDonald.
Final Glances: The Mission Impossible Crew of Erin, Gab & Wiiinnnnniiiiiiieeeeee.
Thai script: Cate Nagy

The authors would like to thank the following people for their invaluable help in compiling the guidebook: Mark Ord for his brilliant research, insight into Thailand and superb fishing prowess!!; Tanya for the lowdown on bugs, elephants and vegetarian restaurants; Michael Wright for saving us at the last minute and the Mardi Gras for bringing people together; our proofing and editing team for their long hours and corrections and John and Anna for their never failing support; many thanks to Amanda Tarlau for allowing us to use her mega machine, Cate Nagy for her efforts with the Thai script; Ian Bowie for his artwork in both this and the Vietnam book and all our friends for helping us get through this. We would like to thank Sandra, Richard and Erin for providing a bed, a roof, hot meals three times a day and an endless supply of coffee and support. Stuart would also like to give special thanks to Nici, Danke für die gute zeite, schlechte zeite und die schwere zeite. Wegen dir meine Gedächtnis sind die besten. Nicht ein wort diesen buch was geschrieben ohne denken über dich. Stu.

Stuart would like to dedicate this book to the memory of Maureen Smith, who always provided shelter from the Bangkok chaos.

Further thanks to:

Amanda Tarlau (Aust), Ian Bowie (Aust), Caroline Tran (Aust), Tanya (SA), Kristin Verhagan and Jaron (USA), Barry and Maureen Smith (Aust), Paula Jarrod (Aust), Tommy and Erica (Sw), Steve Finnis (E), Jum (J), Nelson (USA), Richard Oostinden (Neth), Sylvia (Arg), Dawn Johnstone (E), Noel Dalby (E), Matt (Aust) and Sophie (C), Jarrod Beaton (Can), Tim Bonnell (Can), Fiona Buckton (E),Emma (E), Ellen (E), Anne (E), Lauren McLoughlin (SA), Kimball Isaacson (Can), Shahar Bar-Itzhak (Isr), Andreas Blattner (S), Chris Blair (Aust), Eddie (TH), Samsen Tapmalipum (TH), Nantawan Prugsa (TH), Lompoo Jaichrendee (TH), Sontron Sreprodok (TH), Aki and June Yamashiki (J), Julian (E), Mao (TH) and Karla (US), Greg Robinson (Aust), Sarah Downs (Aust), Ben Bangs (USA), Jo, Con and Marg Ryan (Aust), Michael Wilson (USA)

We would like to thank everyone else who assisted in the compilation of this guidebook — you have not been forgotten!

Aust — Australia	USA — America	Sw — Sweden	E — England
J — Japan	Can — Canada	SA — South Africa	Isr — Israel
N — Netherlands	Arg — Argentina	S — Switzerland	TH — Thailand
C — Cambodia			

CONTENTS

A BACKGROUND TO THAILAND

Introduction	12	Entertainment	61
History	13	Country	62
Culture	26	Geography	62
The People	26	Climate and Temperature	63
Thai Cultural Characteristics	41	Flora and Fauna	64
Thai Ceremonies	46	Government	66
Thai Arts	49	Education	66
Calendar	53	Economy	66
Religion and Philosophy	55	General Information	68
Food	58	Currency	73
Drink	60	Weights and Measurements	75

TRAVEL LOGISTICS

Before You Arrive	81	What to Take	89
Visas	81	Documents	90
Overseas Royal Thai Embassies	83	Appropriate Clothes	90
Customs	84	How to Get Into and Out of Thailand	91
Health	85	Getting Around in Thailand	95

BANGKOK

Highlights	105	Entertainment	121
Vital Information	105	Things to Do Sights to See	127
Accommodation	115	Transport	142

AROUND BANGKOK

Highlights	105	Around Ayutthaya	174
Ratchaburi Province	156	Bang Pa-In	174
Ratchaburi (Ratburi)	156	Chachoengsao Province	175
Damnoen Saduak	159	Chachoengsao	175
Nakhon Pathom Province	160	Samut Prakan Province	177
Nakhon Pathom	161	Samut Prakan	177
Nonthaburi Province	165	Bang Phli	179
Nonthaburi	165	Samut Sakhon Province	181
Pathum Thani Province	166	Samut Sakhon	181
Pathum Thani	166	Samut Songkhram Province	182
Ayutthaya Province	167	Samut Songkhram	182
Ayutthaya	169		

CENTRAL THAILAND

Highlights	186	Chaloem Rattanakosin National Park	208
Kanchanaburi Province	187	Suphanaburi Province	208
Kanchanaburi	187	Suphanaburi	208
Sai Yok	196	Don Chedi	212
Sai Yok National Park	198	Ang Thong Province	214
Thong Pha Phum	200	Ang Thong	214
Thung Yai Naresuan Wildlife Reserve	201	Ban Bang Phae	215
Khao Laem National Park	201	Singburi Province	216
Erawan National Park	201	Singburi	216
Si Nakharin Dam and National Park	202	Chainat Province	219
Si Sawat	203	Chainat	219
Ban Thakradan	203	Uthai Thani Province	220
Sangkhlaburi	203	Uthai Thani	220
Three Pagoda's Pass	207	Lan Sak	222
Bophloi	208	Huay Kha Khaeng Wildlife Sanctuary	223

Nakhon Sawan Province	**224**	Nakhon Nayok	233
Nakhon Sawan	224	Khao Yai National Park	236
Lopburi Province	**226**	**Prachinburi Province**	**236**
Lopburi	226	Prachinburi	236
Around Lopburi	231	Thap Lan National Park	237
Saraburi Province	**231**	**Sa Kaew Province**	**238**
Saraburi	231	Sa Kaew	238
Khao Sam Lan National Park	232	Prang Sida National Park	239
Nakhon Nayok Province	**233**	Aranyprathet	240

EASTERN THAILAND

Highlights	244	**Chanthaburi Province**	**275**
Chonburi Province	**244**	Chanthaburi	275
Chonburi	244	Khao Kitchakut National Park	277
Bang Saen	246	Namtok Phliu - Khao Sabap	
Ko Loi	250	National Park	278
Ko Si Chang	251	**Trat Province**	**280**
Pattaya	253	Trat	280
Jomtien Beach	260	Coastline from Trat to Hat Lek	283
Ko Lan	261	Trat Beaches	283
Bang Saray	262	Khlong Yai	284
Sattahip	263	Hat Lek	285
Ko Samae San	264	Trip to Cambodia	285
Rayong Province	**264**	Laem Ngop (Back in Thailand)	288
Rayong	265	Ko Chang	289
Khao Chamao - Khao Wong		Ko Wai	298
National Park	266	Ko Mak	299
Man Islands	266	Ko Kham	303
Ban Phe	266	Ko Rayong-Nok	303
Ko Samet	268	Ko Kut	303

NORTHERN THAILAND

Highlights	309	Phu Hin Rong Kla National Park	346
Chiang Mai Province	**310**	Thung Salaeng Luang National Park	348
Chiang Mai	310	**Sukhothai Province**	**349**
Doi Suthep-Pui National Park	324	Sukhothai	349
Mae Sa Valley	325	Si Satchanalai-Chaliang Historical Park	353
Doi Inthanon National Park	326	**Uttaradit Province**	**355**
Tha Ton	326	Uttaradit	355
Kok River Trip	327	**Mae Hong Son Province**	**357**
Around Tha Ton	327	Pai	357
Fang	328	Soppong	360
Mae Doi Fang National Park	329	Pangmappa Village	360
Lamphun Province	**330**	Soppong to Mae Hong Son	362
Lamphun	330	Mae Lana	362
Pasang	332	Mae Hong Son	365
Doi Khun Tan National Park	332	Khun Yuam	368
Mae Ping National Park	332	Mae Sariang	368
Lampang Province	**333**	Mae Sam Laep	370
Lampang	333	**Tak Province**	**370**
Around Lampang	336	Mae Salid	371
Chae Son National Park	337	Mae Sot	371
Mae Ping National Park	337	Tak	373
Phichit Province	**338**	Taksin Maharat National Park	375
Phichit	339	Lan Sang National Park	375
Phetchabun Province	**341**	Waley	376
Phetchabun	341	Umphang	376
Khao Kho	342	Palatha	379
Nam Nao National Park	343	Mae Chan	379
Phitsanulok Province	**343**	Peung Kleung	379
Phitsanulok	343	Lae Thong Ku	380

Kamphaeng Phet Province	380		**Phrae Province**	399
Kamphaeng Phet	380		Phrae	399
Khlong Lan National Park	383		Phae Muang Phii	402
Mae Wong National Park	384		Wiang Kosai National Park	402
Khlong Wang Chao National Park	385		**Nan Province**	402
Chiang Rai Province	385		Nan	402
Chiang Rai	385		Pua	406
Kok River Trip	388		Doi Phu Kha National Park	406
Mae Sai	388		Sao Din	406
Doi Tung	391		**Phayao Province**	407
Doi Mae Salong	391		Phayao	407
Chiang Khong	393		Doi Luang National Park	409
Ban Hat Khrai	395		Ban Huak Border Market	410
Chiang Saen	396		Crossword	412
Sop Ruak (Golden Triangle)	399			

NORTHEAST THAILAND

Highlights	415		Nong Khai	455
Nakhon Ratchasima Province			Si Chiang Mai	460
(Khorat Province)	415		Sang Khom	461
Pak Chong	415		Ban Ahong	462
Khao Yai National Park	416		Around Ban Ahong	462
Nakhon Ratchasima (Khorat)	418		**Udon Thani Province**	462
Ban Dan Kwian	422		Udon Thani	463
Ban Pak Thong Chai	423		Ban Chiang	466
Ban Prasat	423		Phu Phra Bat Historical Park	466
Phimai	423		Na Yang-Nam Som Forest Park	467
Buriram Province	425		Phu Khao-Phu Phan Kham	
Buriram	426		National Park	467
Nang Rong	427		**Nong Bua Lam Phu Province**	467
Surin Province	429		Nong Bua Lam Phu	467
Surin	429		Tham Erawan	469
Ban Ta Klang	431		**Loei Province**	469
Si Saket Province	433		Loei	469
Si Saket	433		Phu Kradung National Park	473
Around Si Saket	436		Phu Rua National Park	474
Ubon Ratchathani Province	437		Phu Pha Man National Park	475
Ubon Ratchathani	437		Phu Luang Wildlife Sanctuary	475
Khong Chiam	440		Pak Chom	475
Pha Taem National Park	441		Chiang Khan	476
Chong Mek	441		Ban Tha Li, Ban Pak Huay and	
Phu Chong Nayoi National Park	441		Ban Nong Pheu	478
Yasothon Province	442		**Chaiyaphum Province**	479
Yasothon	442		Chaiyaphum	479
Ban Si Than	444		Tat Ton National Park	481
Amnat Charoen Province	444		Sai Thong National Park	481
Amnat Charoen	444		**Khon Kaen Province**	482
Mukdahan Province	446		Khon Kaen	482
Mukdahan	446		Chonabot	482
Mukdahan National Park	449		Phu Khao-Phu Phan Kham	
Phu Sa Dok Bua National Park	449		National Park	485
Sakhon Nakhon Province	449		Phu Wiang National Park	485
Sakhon Nakhon	449		**Mahasarakham Province**	485
Phu Phan National Park	451		Mahasarakham	485
Huai Huat National Park	451		**Roi Et Province**	488
Nakhon Phanom Province	452		Roi Et	488
Nakhon Phanom	452		**Kalasin Province**	490
That Phanom	454		Kalasin	490
Renu Nakhon	454		Muang Fa Daet	492
Nong Khai Province	455		Crossword	494

SOUTHERN THAILAND

Highlights	496	**Surat Thani Province**	**532**
Phetburi Province		Chaiya	532
(Phetchaburi Province)	**497**	Phun Phin	534
Phetburi (Phetchaburi)	497	Surat Thani (Ban Don)	534
Hat Chao Samran	500	Khao Sok National Park	538
Hat Puk Tian	500	Khlong Yan Wildlife Sanctuary	539
Cha Am	501	Kang Krung National Park	539
Kaeng Krachan National Park	502	Tai Rom Yen National Park	540
Pratchuap Khiri Khan Province	**504**	Ko Samui	540
Hua Hin	504	Ko Taen	563
Khao Sam Roi Yot National Park	508	Ang Thong National Marine Park	564
Aow Takiap	509	Ko Pha Ngan	564
Pratchuap Khiri Khan	509	Ko Tao	583
Bang Saphan Yai	511	Ko Nang Yuan	593
Thap Sakae	514	**Phuket Province**	**594**
Chumphon Province	**515**	Phuket	596
Chumphon	515	Khao Phra Taew National Park	607
Hat Sairee	518	**Nakhon Si Thammarat Province**	**608**
Thung Makham Yai and		Nakhon Si Thammarat	608
Thung Makham Noi	518	Khao Luang National Park	612
Hat Thong Wua Laen	520	Ban Khiriwong	613
Ranong Province	**520**	Nakhon Si Thammarat Beaches	613
Ranong	520	Namtok Yong National Park	614
Hat Chandamri	522	**Krabi Province**	**614**
Isthmus of Kra	523	Krabi	615
Ko Chang	523	Aow Nang	618
Laem Son National Park	524	Hat Khlong Muang	618
Phang Nga Province	**525**	Hat Nopphara Thara	618
Phang Nga	525	Hat Raileh	619
Aow Phang Nga National Park	526	Aow Leuk	622
Khao Lam Pi National Park	528	Khao Phanom Bencha National Park	622
Sri Phang Nga National Park	528	Than Bokkhoroni National Park	623
Kapong	528	Ko Phi Phi	623
Takua Pa	529	Ko Jam (Ko Pu)	627
Khao Lak National Park	529	Ko Poda	627
Khuraburi	530	Ko Hua Kwaan (Chicken Island)	628
Similan Islands National Park	530	Ko Si	628
Surin Islands National Park	531	Ko Lanta	628
Ko Yao Noi	532		

THE FAR SOUTH

Highlights	**634**	**Songkhla Province**	**646**
Trang Province	**634**	Songkhla	646
Trang	635	Songkhla Lake (Thaleh Sap Songkhla)	652
Hat Chao Mai National Park	638	Khao Khut Waterbird Sanctuary	652
Hat Pak Meng	638	Hat Yai	652
Ko Muk	638	Khao Nam Khang National Park	656
Ko Kradan	639	**Satun Province**	**656**
Ko Ngai (Ko Hai)	640	Satun	656
Ko Rok	641	Thale Ban National Park	659
Ko Libong	641	Wang Prajan	659
Khlong Lamchan Waterbird Park	642	La-Ngu	660
Phattalung Province	**642**	Pakbara	660
Phattalung	642	Ko Tarutao National Marine Park	660
Hat Lam Pan	645	Ko Lipe	663
Ban Sarnsuk Lam Pan	645	Ko Adang	664
Ban Chai Son	645	Ko Yang	664
Khao Poo Khao Ya National Park	646	Ko Bulon Lae	665
Thale Noi Waterbird Sanctuary	646	Yala Province	666

Yala	666	Budo-Sungai Padi Mountains		
Yala to Betong	670	National Park	681	
Betong	670	Hat Manao	682	
Pattani Province	**674**	Tak Bai	682	
Pattani	674	Ko Yao	682	
Hat Talor Kapor	677	Ban Taba	682	
Panare and Hat Khae Khae	677	Sungai Kolok	683	
Narathiwat Province	**678**	Crossword	687	
Narathiwat	678			

OTHER

Language	688	Index	697
Chart Index	695	Glossary	702
Photo Index	695	Puzzle Solutions	703
Map Index	696		

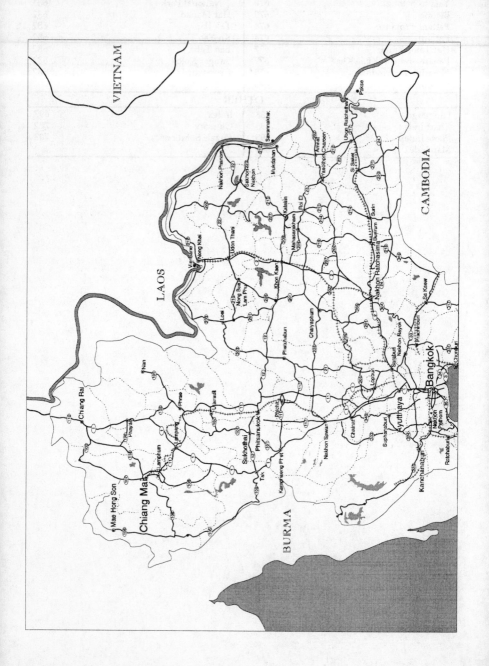

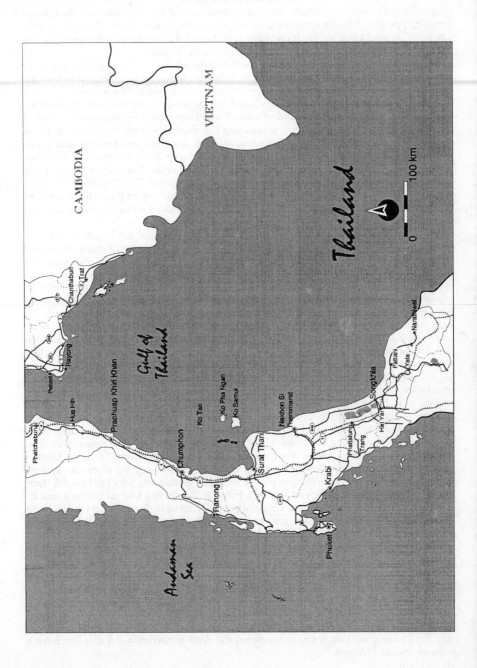

CAMBODIA

VIETNAM

Thailand

Gulf of
Thailand

Andaman
Sea

Trat
Chanthaburi
Rayong
Pattaya
Hua Hin
Prachuap Khiri Khan
Phetchaburi
Ko Tao
Ko Pha Ngan
Ko Samui
Chumphon
Ranong
Surat Thani
Krabi
Nakhon Si
Thammarat
Phattalung
Trang
Hat Yai
Songkhla
Pattani
Yala
Narathiwat
Phuket

0   100 km

Welcome to Thailand!

Characterised by very long hours, ridiculous schedules and the requirement to find every-thing, everywhere all the time, travel researching is certainly the kind of job, where, afterwards, you really do need a holiday. The funny thing is, at the end of my six month stint researching in Thailand, I did need a holiday, but I wanted to have it in Thailand!

For many years, I have found myself wandering through the arrivals section of Bangkok's Don Muang International Airport. When the immigration official flicks through my passport he notices that about ten pages are dedicated solely to Thailand entry and exit stamps, "So you like Thailand?" he says. I nod and, as always I get that great Thai smile.

They call Thailand the "land of smiles" and I can guarantee you that it is true — Thailand truly is a land of smiles. It was during this most recent trip that I came to know Thailand like never before. Up at the crack of dawn for some noodle soup and tea or coffee and right beside me monks slowly paced their way down the street as the locals lined up to fill their bowls with food. *Making merit* is what the Thais call it and for me it was one of the more fascinating daily rituals I would observe. For Thailand is a nation full to the brim with rituals. From simple things like the playing of the National Anthem in the cinema right through to the ritualised wai Thailand and the Thais certainly have the path laid out for them.

Many travellers appear to have the opinion that Thailand has become a victim of its own popularity. This is not the case. Thailand is so overloaded with things to do and sights to see that you could go there every month and see something different. Although places such as Ko Samui, Phuket, Chiang Mai and Chiang Rai have become very popu-lar, for each of these places there are another ten that no one seems to know about! Be adventurous, learn some Thai, look at a map, pick a place and go. Chances are you will have a great time. My strongest recommendation is to get off the trodden path. It's not hard to be adventurous in Thailand — the infrastructure is good and the people are al-ways willing to give you a helping hand. It is only by interacting directly with the Thai people that you will really begin to learn something about their culture and lifestyle. I think it is a shame that so few farangs have much to do with the locals.

Besides getting off the beaten track, learning the language and meeting the locals try to pick up some of the Thai lifestyle for yourself. Be sensitive to what is happening around you, be aware of their cultural norms and remember you are a guest in their country — act accordingly and you will gain the respect of the Thais.

Many of the people I met in Thailand this trip were farangs and it would often come up that I was researching the country. Just as Thailand attracts a wide range of visitors, these same visitors have widely differing opinions on the ethics of travel writing! Many a time I was physically threatened by farangs who thought I was going to give away their hideaways whilst on other occasions, people would be demanding why I did not tell them about this or that place! In the end, a story a friend in Ban Ahong told me comes to mind;

An old Laotion farmer and his young son decide to walk to the next village with their donkey. As they set off the man and boy walk beside the donkey. Before long a farmer coming the other way stops and declares "Old man get on the donkey, for you are too old to walk this distance" The old man obliges and they carry on. A second man appears and declares "Old man, get off that donkey and let the young boy ride upon him for otherwise he will collapse from the heat" The man and boy then swap places and continue only to meet a third man who says "Boy, get off the donkey for you are fit and can walk alone, do not burden the donkey with your weight"

I'm not sure exactly who was right, but it certainly reflects attitudes to travel writing, it does not matter how you do it, someone will always tell you to do it a different way. So I hope you think we have burdened the donkey correctly and that you have a fantastic trip in Thailand.

Travel Light
Stuart McDonald

HISTORY

Origins of the Thais

The origins of the Thai people are the subject of debate. Was Southeast Asia the birthplace of a civilisation or was it a gathering point for civilisations born elsewhere? Archeological evidence points towards the former with ground breaking discoveries in Ban Chiang and Ban Prasat yet a study of the origins of Thai language points to a far larger area and a far wider spectrum of people. Modern Thai holds little connection to the surrounding languages yet variations of the base language are spoken by Thai's, Lao's, Shan's and upland tribes such as Black, Red and White Thai. Today these people stretch from Burma through Thailand and Laos to southern China and far northern Vietnam thus providing a wide berth for cultural diversity and hence differing perceptions of their respective 'origins'.

There are two general positions held in this debate, one being that the peoples which are regarded as Thai initially migrated from either Mongolia or Northern China. Under the pressure of the expanding Chinese population these people became part of the kingdom of Nan Chao in 651 AD and over the next four hundred years, lived a somewhat tenuous life with their often aggressive northern neighbour — China. During this period, many Thai migrated south and established themselves in what is today northern Thailand and Laos. By 1000 AD their northern neighbours in Nan Chao were subjugated by the Chinese, severing this northern link.

The second position in the debate is that the Thai people did not originate in Northern China at all, but rather developed in the northeast of modern Thailand in the area of the Khorat plateau. This theory is supported by archeological finds at both Ban Chiang and Ban Prasat which date the region to at least 4000 BC. It is believed that these people lived in the northeast for the next four thousand years before migrating north into Yunnan, becoming part of the kingdom of Nan Chao before being forced back south by the expanding Chinese. Predating the establishment of Nan Chao, Thai society revolved around the idea of *muang*, a word which defies a literal translation to English. The muang could best be described as what began as a loose grouping of households relying on each other for shared labour and, in times of war, for mutual defence. The head of a muang was known as *Chao* and as time went on, as more households fell under the influence of a single Chao, the muang became a recognisable entity. To the larger regional powers of Vietnam and China, this was an improved system as it meant the rural administrators needed only to deal with a limited number of muangs as opposed to a limitless number of households. The Thai were regarded as river valley people and, as a result of this and the often inhospitable landscape of large mountain ranges and deep valleys, the muangs often developing fairly independently and diversely. The long term result of this is evident in the modern day dispersal of the Thai, with the Shans in Burma right across to Red Thai in northern Vietnam and a whole spectrum of peoples in between and holding little in common except for common ancestry.

The relation between the Thai and Nan Chao appears to have been one of mutual benefit. Although the rulers of Nan Chao were not Thai, many of the inhabitants of the southern realm of the kingdom were. For many of them, Nan Chao was to be their first contact with a sizeable foreign entity. The muangs were levied for taxes and in times of war for manpower, but were otherwise left to their own ends. However, there were two important results of Thai participation in Nan Chao. Firstly, the kingdom expanded across Burma to India serving to open some of the first trade links to the sub continent. Secondly, the kingdom of Nan Chao created an important buffer state between an expansionist China and the developing region of what was to become Thailand, Laos and Burma.

Following the establishment of Nan Chao in 651 AD, historians have divided the remainder of Thai history into four periods. The **Dvaravati period** from the 7th to the 11th Centuries, the **Sukhothai period** from 1238 to 1350, the **Ayutthaya period** from 1350 to 1767 and the **Bangkok period** which stretches to the present.

The kingdom with no capital - Dvaravati

This period is probably the darkest and least known of section of Thai history. It is believed that during this period Buddhist beliefs spread and Southeast Asia began to develop a cohesiveness which had never existed previously. It is not known where the Dvaravati capital was, nor even if there was one, and it is not known how far the 'empire' stretched. What is known is that most of the written records which were recovered were in Mon script and the location of Dvaravati towns would have allowed them to take good advantage of the trade routes which passed trough the area. Some of the larger sites were located in or nearby to the present day cities of Suphanaburi, Lopburi, Nakhon Ratchasima and further east at Muang Fa Daet (near present day Kalasin). To the north there was what appears to have been an offshoot outpost located in the Lamphun area. This last area came into prominence when the locals appealed to Lopburi for a leader and were sent Chamma Thewi who formed the kingdom of Haripunchai which was to last into the 11th Century. The most concentrated area of towns appears to have been around the Lopburi and Nakhon Pathom areas and it was in Nakhon Pathom that a coin was found with the inscription, 'Lord of Dvaravati' — the only such coin found.

Very little is known of the politics or culture of the Dvaravati period, and what is has been discerned from archeological finds. The towns were often quite large and generally walled in, often with an internal area as large as 10 sq km — pointing to large populations which probably relied on the people living outside the walls for food cultivation. As far as art and religion were concerned, the most interesting find has been stone carvings which were planted around the edge of sacred sites, most of which were Buddhist. Particularly fine examples of these boundary stones (or *bai sema*) can be found at both the Khon Kaen Museum and the site at Muang Fa Daet. A more common find were small clay tablets which bore the image of Buddha along with Mon script.

The connection between the Thai and Dvaravati is difficult to ascertain. As the Thai moved south from Nan Chao they may have come in contact with the Kingdom of Haripunchai whilst those further south may have come in contact with outposts in modern day Laos or northeast Thailand.

Enter the Khmers...

Unlike the Dvaravati Kingdom, the Kingdom of Angkor left volumes of inscriptions from which a comprehensive idea of its history can be ascertained. The capital, Angkor, was established in the 9th Century by King Jayavarman II and following this the empire rapidly expanded to both the north and west. It is not known as to whether the Khmers took the Dvaravati capital (if there was one) or if they took over the Dvaravati Kingdom piece by piece, but what is known is that by the end of the 9th Century the Dvaravati were history.

The Kingdom of Angkor was at that time the single most powerful empire in the region. Its sphere of influence stretched over most of modern day Thailand and it cemented its position in place through massive urban works and established religious centres throughout the region. The Khmer monuments have withstood time to an exceptional degree and today there are numerous well restored constructions in central Thailand, stretching from Kanchanaburi in the west to Phimai and Prasat Phanom Rung in the northeast. Religious centres were established throughout the region, with the main centres including That Phanom, Sakhon Nakhon, Phimai, Lopburi, Suphanaburi, Ratchaburi, Phitsanulok and Sukhothai.

How did the Khmer empire keep control of such a large area? It appears that in each of the provincial centres, Khmer upper class were installed as rulers and were held responsible for raising revenue in times of peace and battlefield fodder by slavery and indenture during periods of war. By 1200 the Khmer empire stretched south past Nakhon Si Thammarat, east to the Maekhong Delta, north to Luang Prabang and Chiang Saen and west to Kamphaeng Phet and Suphanaburi. Along with its taxes and manpower levies, the Khmers also brought with them religion, a strong influence of which can be seen in places such as Lopburi where Brahmanism, Theravada Buddhism and Mahayana Buddhism were mixed, and remain intermingled to this day. Lopburi, was one of the more troublesome vassal states, with frequent struggles for independence and religious prominence. It had been seen as a centre for religious study during the Dvaravati period and even attempted to receive diplomatic recognition from China at one stage. It was also probably in Lopburi that the name Siam first originated. A large bas relief from Angkor Wat displays a large number of Thai soldiers from Lopburi on parade in Angkor Wat walking past the Khmer King and they are referred to as *Syam* mercenaries.

One mans fiefdom - The Kingdom of Lan Na

By the late 13th Century, Southeast Asia had become the stage for monumental change. Both the Khmer Kingdom of Cambodia and the Pagan empire based in Burma were on the downhill slide as internal strife and conflict took their toll. When they did collapse they left in their place a power vacuum which the Thai acted rapidly to fill. In the far north of what is modern day Thailand, at the muang of Chiang Saen, the future founder of the Kingdom of Lan Na was born. Mangrai was born in October 1239 and succeeded his father as ruler of Chiang Saen in 1259. Once ruler, all Mangrai observed around him were Thai muangs which spent more time squabbling amongst each other rather than looking to the future for their people. It was this responsibility that Mangrai decided to take upon himself and over the next five years he embarked on a rapid expansion programme, which included the founding of a new capital at the site of modern day Chiang Rai. From there he went on to live at Fang and over the next 15 years established many treaties with his neighbours, resulting in a loose grouping of states which stretched from Luang Prabang, through Chiang Rai, Fang and Phayao to as far south as Sukhothai. He was also a skilful statesman, and through his efforts war was probably averted between Ngam Muang of Phayao and Ramkhamhaeng of Sukhothai (the later had seduced Ngam Muangs wife!). However, through all this wheeling and dealing, Mangrai's eye had never left the nearby principality of Hariphunchai. Back in 1274 he had sent off his scribe, Ai Fa, to the kingdom, to see what seeds of unrest could be sown to transform the state from a powerful kingdom, to one ripe for the picking.

Seven years later, Ai Fa let Mangrai know that his time had come, and after raising a colossal army he invaded and easily took the kingdom, then assumed the throne. Mangrai was now the ruler of a large kingdom which, via treaties, stretched over all of modern day northern Thailand. Following his taking of Lamphun (the modern day site of Hariphunchai) King Mangrai went touring the countryside and instigated a huge public works programme which included the founding of new cities and religious centres. Then in 1289 he embarked on an invasion of Pegu (situated in modern day Burma), however before he could attack, he met both the King of Pegu and his daughter, whose hand he accepted in marriage, thus sealing an alliance between the two states.

A decade later, Mangrai decided that the capital needed to be moved again, and on 27 March, 1292, he selected the site of his new city to be known, as it is today, as Chiang Mai. The construction did not begin for another four years as Lan Na's northern neighbour, China was becoming of major concern. Over the next 15 years there would be frequent fighting between the Chinese and Lan Na, but Lan Na appeared to be a thorn which the Chinese could not remove, and by 1312 they had turned to diplomacy.

By this stage, Mangrai was an old man, and upon his death, the throne was passed onto his second son (he had previously had his eldest son put to death for attempting to seize the throne). Although this son, Khum Kham, was to inherit a large and well organised state, the Kingdom rapidly fell into a power struggle amongst the descendents of Mangrai. It would not be until 1328, under the rule of Mangrai's great grandson Kham Fu, that some order was restored. Nevertheless in the space of sixty years a single man had managed to construct a Kingdom which even the Chinese had not been able to put down, setting the precedent for what was to be a series of powerful and influential kingdoms throughout Siam.

Rama the Bold - The rise of Sukhothai

As the Kingdom of Lan Na ruled the north, central Thailand was being transformed as the influence of the Khmer and Pagan empires of Cambodia and Burma ebbed. This change in influence was felt from the north of the country, through Lopburi to as far south as Nakhon Si Thammarat and perhaps even further south into the modern day Malaysian state of Kedah. The Kingdom of Lan Na had stepped into the power void of the north, and it was to be King Ramkhamhaeng, the third King of Sukhothai who was destined to fill the power vacuum in central Thailand.

During the reign of the Khmer empire, Sukhothai had played the role of a Khmer outpost and as the empire crumbled, Sukhothai became ripe for the picking. Sometime in the middle of the 13th Century the city was attacked and overrun by surrounding Thai rulers who then celebrated and crowned the first King of Sukhothai, King Sri Indraditya. For the next 20 to 30 years, the kingdom busied itself with setting a solid foundation as opposed to actively expanding. However it was during a battle with forces who had attacked the Sukhothai outpost at Tak that the shining star of the Sukhothai period announced himself. During this foundation period, one of Sukhothai's most troublesome neighbour had been a Thai prince based near the modern day city of Mae Sot. During a battle with this prince, the son of Ban Muang, the second King of Sukhothai, held his ground, and actually forced his way through the oppositions lines to the enemy commander and defeated him. This effort of grand valour earned him the title Ramkhamhaeng or Rama the Bold.

Rama the Bold was not to become King until 1279 and once he rose to power, he established Sukhothai as a force to be reckoned with. Rama the Bold was known for his lavish support of Buddhism and a famous inscription by him in 1292 details the work of a fair and just ruler, who created an empire not via the power of his armies but rather through treaties and the personal bonds of loyalty which he forged. Also during his reign there was a rapid growth in art and sculpture which has become known as the Sukhothai style. Potters were imported from China at this time, and it was their work which created the exquisite Sankholok ceramics.

At the peak of his reign, the Kingdom of Sukhothai stretched south as far as Nakhon Si Thammarat, west to Bago (in modern day Burma), east to Phitsanulok and Vientiane and north to border the Kingdom of Lan Na with whom he had signed a treaty. At this time the beginnings of a cohesive Thai nation were evident, with the Kingdom of Lan Na to the north, Sukhothai in the centre and south and Old Lopburi to the east, and although they were not partners to a bigger and brighter future, the Thai were beginning to make a mark on their land.

Rama the Bold died in 1298 and was succeeded by his son Lö Thai who proved to not be up to the task of running the state. Sukhothai rapidly disintegrated as many of the vassal states jumped ship or were overtaken by rival powers. Within 20 years, Sukhothai had regressed to its previous state, that of a small regional centre with next to no influence on the rapidly changing Thai world.

Ayutthaya

The rise of Ayutthaya was led by U Thong who was born in 1314 and founded his capital, Ayutthaya, on 4 March, 1351, not long after 9.00 am in the morning! This Kingdom was to stretch as far south as Pattani and raided the Khmer capital of Angkor on a number of occasions, the final sortie resulting in the Khmers fleeing to create a new capital which was to become Phnom Penh. Ayutthaya was also involved in frequent, prolonged and bloody warfare with the remnants of Sukhothai, finally attaining its vassal stature in 1438. Ayutthaya also fought the Kingdom of Lan Na, at one stage besieging Chiang Mai during a period of warfare which stretched on and off for over 100 years. Besides rapidly expanding, Ayutthaya was responsible for the establishment of what was to become the basis of Thai common law and, during the reign of King Boromtrailokant (1448-1488) the quite bizarre yet very important *sakdi naa* system was created. This called for a linking of ones social standing with a hypothetical land ownership and covered every possible position in life. For example a slave had a ranking of five, ordinary peasants were ranked 25 whilst officials had a ranking of between 50 and

400 with the highest officials being worth 10,000. This system was used in conjunction with the newly created common law methods to not only calculate the severity of the crime but also the punishment. For example if a person with a ranking of 5 attacked one who was ranked 50, then the assault was far more serious than if role of attacker was reversed. There were also detailed laws recorded for the royalty, one being that a King was only to be put to death by enclosing them in a velvet sack and beating them to death with sandalwood — so that no royal blood would hit the ground.

Despite the laws and bureaucracy which were created, the Ayutthayan's appeared to have been unable to come up with agreeable laws regarding royal succession. Blood ties were simply not sufficient, and it was not uncommon for following the death of a King, to have various ministers and houses of power vying to get their man or women into the hot seat. In the early days of Ayutthaya the most powerful houses were based in Lopburi, Suphanaburi and the newly established Ayutthaya and most royal successions were characterised by more than their fair share of intrigue, plotting and murder between these three centres. Nevertheless Ayutthaya was able to survive for over 400 years without being conquered, attesting to the strength of the kingdom regardless of the backroom wheeling and dealing.

One of Ayutthaya's most important assets was its location. Situated at the confluence of three rivers, Ayutthaya became an immensely important trading city, and it was here that the first Western traders arrived in the 16th Century. The Portuguese were the first to establish an embassy in the same century. However of more pressing concern than these roving salesmen was Ayutthaya's western neighbour, Burma. From the 16th to the 18th Centuries Burma invaded Ayutthaya a half dozen times often devastating the country on the way there, yet it would not be until 1767 that they finally succeeded in their goal of absolute destruction for Ayutthaya. Many of the early Burmese invasions appear to have been based on opportunism as a result of upheavals within Ayutthaya, however during the 17th and 18th Centuries, the warfare appeared to become almost personal. Many tales of bravery and spectacular battles exist from both the Thai and Burmese viewpoint.

In 1548 the Burmese attacked Ayutthaya with an army believed to number hundreds of thousands of men. They were hoping to take advantage of turmoil created by an unclear succession to the throne, and although they managed to surround the capital, they were unable to push home their advantage. The Burmese attacked again in 1564 and were assisted by the betrayal of the Siamese King's son-in-law, Maha Thammaracha. He had been installed as the ruler of Phitsanulok but sided with the Burmese for the final attack on Ayutthaya five years later in 1569. Ayutthaya fell on August 8, 1569 and after taking off with thousands of slaves and tonnes of booty, the Burmese installed Maha Thammaracha as a puppet king and returned to Burma.

Naresuan comes to Power
The period which followed the fall of Ayutthaya was one of growing instability and weakness. The Khmers invaded six times over the following 20 years and the Siamese were hardly able to defend themselves. However, as a result of these invasions, the Burmese allowed Ayutthaya to improve its defences and military strength so as to better resist the Khmer plunders.

King Maha Thammaracha had been forced by the Burmese to hand over his son, Naresuan to the Burmese to guarantee his good behaviour, and it was not till he was a teenager that Naresuan was returned to Thailand in exchange for one of his sisters. The King immediately put Naresuan in a position of power and Naresuan rapidly developed into a powerful and skilful military leader. His father died in 1590 after which relations with Burma rapidly deteriorated culminating in an attack by the Burmese on Ayutthaya in 1592. In spectacular recounts of the decisive battle, which took place in the region of Suphanaburi, King Naresuan and the Burmese Prince were both on elephant back and duelled. Naresuan quickly killed the Burmese Prince and subsequently the Burmese army broke ranks and fled. The Ayutthayans followed and caused heavy casualties. For the first time in over three decades, the tables of war between Burma and Ayutthaya turned.

During the reign of Naresuan he also forged a number of foreign treaties with China and the Spanish Philippines and further pushed back the frontiers with both Burma and Cambodia. International trade flourished as Portuguese and Chinese traders in particular had set a solid base within Siam. During his reign he had ruled almost jointly with his brother Ekathotsarot who became the King in 1605 upon the death of Naresuan. Although his move to the throne was relatively smooth, the series of successions following his death was anything but. A series of usurpions and 'untimely deaths' during the rise to power, culminated in the reign of King Narai which became a literal 'Greek tragedy'.

Narai and Phaulkon - A Siamese Greek Tragedy

King Narai came to the throne in 1656 at an important time in Siam's development. Western traders had set up a permanent camp, creating a new dynamic within the already active Siamese political model. During the same era the King also embarked upon ten years of war with Burma, ultimately capturing Rangoon, however the war was a heavy drain on Siam's manpower. In order to finance the war, the King imposed a Royal monopoly on all trade. This required that any goods destined for export from Siam had to first be sold to the crown. This served to seriously alienate the Western traders, with the Portuguese being the first to leave in 1663, however following protracted negotiations, they did return one year later, demonstrating to Siam just how important these Western traders had become. Other traders, including the English, French, Chinese and a whole bevy of independent traders had arrived in Ayutthaya by the late 17th Century and it was in this environment that a Greek adventurer by the name of Constantine Phaulkon became the Kings most influential advisor.

Constantine Phaulkon was born in 1647 and, before arriving in Siam courtesy of the English East India Company, had spent time in London. Upon arriving he became fluent in Thai and rose rapidly within the Royal service, often at the expense of others. Within a couple of years, he had the Kings ear, who relied on him more and more for advice. Phaulkon received missions from France and consequently pressed Narai to develop a closer relationship with France. Why France? Narai was Christian and his ultimate goal was to convert both Narai and the Siamese state to Christianity, he saw this as being quite a difficult mission, but also realised that if treaties were in place with France, once he had his foot in the door, France would probably step in to save the converts should things with Narai or the people go sour. The result of this was a mission by Chevalier de Chaumont in 1685 to 1686 which resulted in considerable trade concessions to the French along with the right to station French troops at Songkhla.

Whilst Narai was getting into bed with the French, Phaulkon was equally busy burning the bridges with the other traders. Relations with the English had been strained for a few years, and when Phaulkon basically installed two English friends at Mergui (in Burma) from where they acted as pirates, the English acted to blockade the port. Phaulkon's mates Burnaby and White then began to have second thoughts about their way of earning a living, especially when the English treatment of pirates was considered. Phaulkon seemed to sense betrayal was imminent and sent a Siamese force to Mergui with orders to kill every Englishman they could find. This was exactly what they did and Phaulkon subsequently declared war on the English East India Company. As this happened a second French mission arrived with six warships, over 500 troops and container loads of Jesuits who the French had decided would be installed at Bangkok rather than Songkhla so as to better allow them to control the trade of Siam.

This caused an outcry by the Siamese, particularly amongst the Buddhist monks who saw their king being advised by a Greek Christian as Jesuits and Christian priests increased in numbers throughout the city. Serious plots against Phaulkon arose during this time, and his response was always extreme, decimating sections of Ayutthaya in search of plotters. As public and private opinion rallied against Phaulkon, Narai fell ill in March 1688 and his time had come. The legal successors to Narai had all been discredited and just before Narais death on 11 July 1688 the opposition, led by Phetracha had Phaulkon arrested, charged with treason and executed immediately. Phetracha then had the other hopefuls for the throne murdered and assumed the throne on the day of Narai's death.

What followed was a period of rabid anti-French and anti-Christian feeling. The French troops were besieged at Bangkok by Siamese troops and agreed to get out of Siam whilst the missionaries were imprisoned and/or persecuted. Although trade with the English and Dutch continued, Siam appeared to feel it had been burnt by this foray into world politics and economics.

Ayutthaya's heydey and destruction
The height of the Kingdom of Ayutthaya is most often associated with the reign of King Borommakot who reigned from 1733 to 1758. During his reign public works and the erecting of Buddhist monuments were a priority as was the effective ruling of the largest Thai state so far. Amongst many, the most important action of Borommakot was the sending of an order of Siamese monks to Sri Lanka to support the order there which was suffering under the Portuguese. Sri Lanka had long been seen as a very important centre of Buddhist teaching, and for Siam to be seen supporting that order was of immense pride.

It was not all peace during Borommakot's reign, and although he was regarded as a fairly pious king, he certainly had his moments. When a disgruntled minister revealed that one of the King's sons was having an affair with one of the King's wives he had them both flogged — to death.

The last King of Ayutthaya was King Suriyamarin, unlike Borommakot who died with full regal ceremony (Borommakot means 'King in an urn (awaiting cremation))' this last king of Ayutthaya was destined to starve to death on a small boat adrift on the Chao Phraya River as his capital was being destroyed to the extent that it would never again be built.

The Burmese invaded in 1760 under the lead of the Burmese King Alaunghpaya and laid siege to Ayutthaya. It was only when one of the siege guns ruptured and exploded, critically injuring King Alaunghpaya that the Burmese forces withdrew. The King died on the way home. Within a couple of years the Burmese were on the warpath once again, raising a huge army and laying siege to Chiang Mai in 1763 which fell after six months. Although Chiang Mai later rebelled, the Burmese were quick to reimpose their power. From Chiang Mai they moved east, taking Luang Prabang in 1765 (with the aid of Vientiane) before making camp at Lampang where they bided their time for the end of the rainy season before attacking Ayutthaya. This massive army had been swelled by forces from the old Kingdom of Lan Na and as they moved south, two more Burmese armies made their move, one eastwards via Three Pagodas Pass and the other from the south via Phetburi and Ratchaburi. By February 1766, Ayutthaya was under a siege like no other it had ever faced. This was partially the result of particularly incompetent and uncoordinated resistance by King Suriyamarin. Once the siege was set, famine struck then there was a disastrous fire which destroyed thousands of houses.

The Siamese King, Suriyamarin realised that all was lost in early 1767 and offered to surrender to become a vassal state of the Burmese empire, but for the Burmese, nothing other than unconditional surrender and complete destruction was satisfactory. In early April, 1767 the walls of Ayutthaya were breached and the once brilliant city fell.

The savagery of the Burmese upon breaching the walls was to be unparalleled in the history of Siam. Anything that would burn was burnt, the inhabitants were raped and murdered and their possessions looted, the wats had their Buddhas melted down for the gold which was carted back to Burma, the surrounding fields were laid to waste, guaranteeing starvation in the future, the royalty was captured and imprisoned in Burma, whilst the last King of Ayutthaya, King Suriyamarin escaped in a boat but starved to death ten days later adrift on the Chao Phraya River.

King Taksin's Kingdom of Thonburi
Given the devastation of the final Burmese attack, it would have been understandable had the area remained in its devastated state, however it was only six months after the fall of Ayutthaya that a new capital was created as the head of a rapidly growing empire. The man responsible for this great turnaround was the son of a Chinese merchant and Siamese woman

and who took the name of Taksin. A skilled military strategist and tactician, he selected Thonburi as his new capital, was crowned King in 1768 and within three years had already brought together all of what had once made up the Kingdom of Ayutthaya.

Although a great military leader, some of Taksin's personality traits left a little to be desired, he regularly had his family flogged for fictional crimes and came to believe that he was the incarnation of Buddha. Withdrawing more and more from public life, he spent the vast majority of his time in meditation as he concentrated on learning how to fly. In 1782 rebels who could take no more of his increasingly bizarre rule seized him and called for Chaophraya Chakri to become King. As for Taksin, it was decided that he was to be put to death in the legally prescribed method. He was forced into a velvet bag and beaten to death with sandalwood clubs - so that no royal blood would touch the ground. His body was then spirited off and buried in a secret location.

King Ramathibodi, the origins of the Chakri Dynasty

Following the disposal of Taksin in 1782, one of his generals, Chaophraya Chakri became king under the name King Ramathibodi (King Rama I). One of his first actions was to move the capital to Bangkok, on the other side of the Chao Phraya River to make it less succeptible to attacks from Burma. The day he was coronated, 6 April, has become a public holiday in Thailand and is known as Chakri Day, the day that the Chakri Dynasty began, and has endured through to today. The reign of Rama I was dedicated to the creation of the base of what has endured through to today, and by the time of his death in 1809, even the threat of attack from Burma had receded.

Although the reign of Rama I's successor, Rama II was mainly just business as usual, the end of his reign was quite interesting. On 6 July, 1824, King Rama II assembled his ministers and informed them that upon the death of one of the royal white elephants, which was considered to be a particularly bad omen, he had decided to put his son, Prince Mongkut, into robes to serve his time as a monk. One week later, Rama II fell ill, and was speechless till his death a week later, aged 56. Following his death, his remaining son Prince Chetsadabodin (Rama III) was invited to take up the throne. It is believed that Rama II knew he was going to die in the near future so, in order to protect his son Mongkut, he opted for the saffron robes option rather than leave the throne open to public squabbling, which, so often in the past had been the downfall of the state. These actions by Rama II served to seal the idea of blood inheritance of the throne, a feature which has assisted in keeping the Siamese state stable.

In January 1827, during the reign of King Rama III, Lao forces, under the leadership of Chao Anu invaded Siam under the pretences of assisting the Siamese against the English campaign which was waging in Burma at the time. His forces reached as far south as Saraburi, which was only a few days march from Bangkok, however the tide then turned and the Siamese forces began to force him back, with the decisive battle being held in the remote northeastern province of Nong Bua Lam Phu. The Laotian forces were routed and Chao Anu fled first to Vientiane and then onwards to Vietnam. The Siamese then sacked Vientiane, leaving it in such a state that French explorers who reached in forty years later found only forest and ruins.

Following this action by the Laotians, Rama II acted to considerably shore up this region of his Kingdom by resettling large numbers of people from Laos in the area and created over 40 new muang. However as soon as the northeastern frontier was secured, trouble broke out in the far south.

Pattani, long a centre of strife for Siam, again rebelled and in league with Kedah attacked Songkhla who had to call on Bangkok for assistance. The upstarts were eventually defeated but this activity in the far southern states was to continue with distressing regularity. There was also a growing problem in Cambodia which the Siamese had attacked on a couple of occasions in an attempt to counter Vietnamese influence. None of the missions were standout successes, although they did achieve some degree of stability and removed some of the Vietnamese influence in the country.

Mongkut rises to Power

During the reign of Rama III, Mongkut spent his time in the cloth. By all accounts he proved to be a particularly able student and had received accolades from the royal court regarding his exceptional standard of knowledge. By the late 1830s he became abbot of Wat Bovornivet in Bangkok and became the head of a separate order within Siamese monkhood. By the time he left the monkhood to assume the throne in 1851, he was well versed in English and the Western sciences. Upon becoming King he immediately began to develop relations with the West with a view to creating a beneficial relationship whilst avoiding the Western tendency to colonise. The Siamese had seen the results of this colonisation on their neighbours with the British in Burma and the French incorporating Laos and Cambodia (through a double deal with the then young King Norodom) into their realm of French Indochina.

The immediate result of Mongkut's reforms in relation to the West was an explosion in trade. Junks were rapidly replaced by steam vessels and Bangkok was transformed into a modern trading port. Domestic reforms were fairly minor during the reign of Mongkut, and during the later days of his reign, his main preoccupation regarded the succession of his throne.

All the sons which Mongkut had sired before his sabbatical for 27 years, had died by this stage in his life, so he looked to his young son Chulalongkorn as his successor. This son was educated like no other Siamese King, and the movie "The King and I" supposedly records his tuition by Mrs Anna Leonowens — the film is banned in Thailand. Mongkut had planned to hand over the rule to his son when he came of age in 1873 however this was not to be. In 1868 father and son travelled south to view a solar eclipse but were both stricken with malaria, the King subsequently died on 1 October, 1868 and his son, who was only 15 years of age and in very poor health was poised to assume the throne. The end result was that Suriyawong served as regent until Chulalongkorn came of age.

King Chulalongkorn

Once Chulalongkorn became King, he embarked on a reformist agenda, decreeing the gradual abolition of slavery was one of his standout reforms. During his reign their was also a continued courting of foreign nations however it was to be the French who were to be the most troublesome. Irked by continuing Siamese influence in Laos, the French sought an excuse to 'punish Siam', and eventually found it in 1893. Following the death of the French consul in Luang Prabang, France laid claim to all of Laos east of the Maekhong River despite the fact that they had previously signed an agreement verifying Siamese suzerainty over some of the area. Then in April, 1893, when Siamese troops resisted French forces trying to take the territory, killing the Frenchman who was leading the attack, the French had their excuse. French gunboats forced their way up the Chao Phraya River after shelling the defences at Samut Prakan. Upon arrival at Bangkok the leader of the French pack delivered a set of outrageous demands to the Siamese, these included the withdrawal of all Siamese forces to the west of the Maekhong, an indemnity of three million francs and the occupation by the French of Trat, Chanthaburi and all of Siamese (western) Cambodia! These demands were essentially a punishment of Siam for defending its own territory, and faced with a threatened naval blockade by the French, to which the Siamese were defenceless, they had no choice but to accept the terms of the French demands. Notably, Siam was let down by the British, as they had expected the British to be of assistance in placating the French yet they were nowhere to be seen.

To Chulalongkorn, it became obvious that the French and British were not always as they seemed, and the behaviour of the colonial powers had made it clear that Siam was independent solely because it served their purposes. In 1897, both the French and the British made it clear that northeast Siam and western Cambodia and the Malay peninsula respectively were their spheres on influence.

By 1910, partially as a result of the situation in Europe, both the French and the British had settled down somewhat although in 1909 Thailand was forced to cede to the British the peninsular territories of Kelantan, Kedah, Perlis and Trengganu. The French had not completely removed themselves from Trat and Chanthaburi until 1906 which was closely followed by the ceding to France of the western Cambodian provinces of Battambang, Siem Riep and Sisophon. In essence the Siamese had retained their independence by selling off tracts of their land and the associated populations to the marauding French and British.

King Chulalongkorn died on 24 October 1910 and the period and depth of mourning which followed in the Siamese nation for this much loved and respected King had never before been seen.

The beginning of change

King Chulalongkorn was succeeded by Rama VI or King Vajiravudh. Educated at Oxford he emphasised the need for change and consequently made a number of fundamental changes to Thai society. The education system was reformed, the most important being the creation of compulsory education for almost half of Siam. He formed the Wild Tiger Corps which was a nationwide paramilitary group and also dedicated Siams first public holidays, in honour of King Chulalongkorn (23 October) and in honour of the Chakri Dynasty (6 April). However besides being a proponent of change he was also a big spender. His major coronation ceremony cost over five million baht, which at the time was almost ten percent of the states budget for the year! It was also during the reign of Rama VI that Siams first modern day coup surfaced. Although aborted, it heralded two important influences in modern Siam, the desire for the formation of a constitutional monarchy and the influence of the armed forces. Rama VI had a comparatively short reign dying at the age of 44 to be succeeded by his brother King Prajadhipok who was to be Siam's last absolute ruler.

Siam's last absolute monarch

Rama VII's reign was the shortest of the Chakri Dynasty lasting from 1923 to 1935. In the climate of the worldwide great depression, and the hangover of Rama VI's big spending, the battles which Rama VII fought were mainly economic ones. The price of rice (one of Siam's principal exports) dropped dramatically and all in Thailand, particularly the peasantry suffered tremendously. However, it was not to be economic hardship which brought an end to the rule, but rather political change. On 24 June 1932 whilst on holiday at Hua Hin, King Rama VII received notification of a coup in Bangkok, which had been led by disaffected students, the military and segments of Bangkok's elite. Rama VII accepted their terms under which he was to serve as a constitutional monarch. The event is referred to as the Revolution of 1932.

Rama VII attempted to rule within these new guidelines, but found it an uphill battle, and in particular had problems with the military forces. At the end of 1935 he abdicated in favour of his nephew Prince Ananda Mahidol who was only ten years old and in Switzerland at the time. Ananda was not to return until 1945 and in the interim period, Siam was run for the first time without serious royal interference by two men, Phibun and Pridi. Upon returning to Thailand, Ananda lasted only six months before being found dead, killed by a bullet to the head. To this day no satisfactory explanation has been given for the tragic event. Immediately after the shooting there were some short closed door trials of 'suspects' who were put to death, but no one really appears to know what happened and since open discussion of the shooting does not take place, and as books discussing it are banned, do not expect any rapid admissions explaining what really happened. Ananda was to be succeeded by his brother, Bhumibol Adulyadej, Rama IX who has ruled to this day.

Phibum and Pridi

Following the 1932 Revolution, Thai politics was dominated by two men. Phibun Songkhram had been one of the key instigators of the 1932 coup after working his way up through the military ranks and was considered fairly right wing and conservative. Pridi Panomyong had been the Prime Minister following the coup and had tried to push through social programmes and various socialist economic reforms which resulted in getting the military offside. Following the exile of Pridi to France in 1938 Phibun became Prime Minister and began to immediately shift the direction of Siam's development. Characterised by extreme nationalism, Siam became both more militaristic and xenophobic under his rule with the Chinese faring particularly badly. In 1939 he instigated the changing of Siam's name, to Thailand and much of Phibuns basis for this change centred around his desire to show that the nation was ruled by Thais, not Chinese.

World War II and afterwards

Following the early success of the Japanese forces in Southeast Asia, Prime Minister Phibun, sure that the Japanese would win sided with them and declared war on both Britain and the USA (although the Thai ambassador, Seni Pramoj, refused to pass on the message). He appeared to believe that by supporting the Japanese, Thailand would be able to reclaim some of the territories which Britain and France had previously taken. He allowed Thailand to be used by the Japanese as a staging base for their campaigns yet enjoyed little public support for his actions. Meanwhile Pridi had returned to the scene and in conjunction with the OSS (predecessor to the CIA) was training and leading the Free Thai Movement. As the war turned against the Japanese Phibun was forced to resign and Seni became premier.

One year after the end of the war, Seni's government was unseated in the general elections and Pridi once again came to power, changing the nations name back to Siam again! However, Pridi was thrown out again by his nemesis Phibun who managed to get Pridi implicated in the shooting of King Ananda who had been shot the same year. Phibun was then to remain premier until 1957 (although in name only after 1951), during which time the nations name was once again changed to Thailand, he suspended the constitution and led Thailand down an extreme anti-communist path, become an active supporter of both US and French imperialism in the region. During this period of his rule there was an attempted coup led by the Navy during which Phibun was captured and imprisoned on the navy's flagship the Sri Ayutthaya. The coup culminated with the attacking of the Sri Ayutthaya and as the ship sank, Phibun was able to swim to safety. During the fighting, over 1,200 people were killed and waves of suppression followed.

In 1951 another military coup took place with power being taken by Field Marshal Sarit Thanarat who did not get around to exiling Phibun until 1957. Sarit was even more right wing than Phibun and declared that Thailand was corrupt and needed reforming. He ruled the country effectively as a military dictatorship until 1963 when he died. Subsequent to his death it was revealed he had left a fortune of over US$150 million, a second wife and at least 50 other mistresses — so much for sorting out the corruption problems!

From Sarit's death until 1973, Thailand was ruled by two military officers Thanom Kittikachorn and Praphat Charusathien, who saw to it that Thailand played a vital role in the US campaigns against Vietnam, Cambodia and Laos. They allowed the US to establish huge airbases at Udon Thani, Ubon Ratchathani, Nakhon Phanom and U Tapao. The Thai military also sent ground forces to Vietnam totalling 11,000 by 1969 as well as waging their own campaign against the Pathet Lao in Laos, details of which little is known.

As the US began its gradual withdrawal from Vietnam, to let 'Asians' fight their own battles' students in Thailand became more outspoken about the lack of democracy in their country. This ill feeling came to a head in 1973 around Bangkok's Thammasat University where students rioted and the government responded with force - hundreds of unarmed students were killed. Demonstrating the power of the military, Commander in Chief General Krit Sivara refused to support further bloodshed as did the King and as a result both Thanom and Praphat were forced to leave Thailand.

Following this instability an elected government ruled until 1976. Then the military felt it was necessary to step in once again following more bloodshed at Thammasat University and installed Thanin Kraivichien as Premier, however he only lasted a year before being succeeded by Kriangsak Chomanan. During this period, the CPT (Communist Party of Thailand) had been gathering support in the provinces, and by the late 1970s the groups military wing, the PLAT (Peoples Liberation Army of Thailand) numbered over 10,000.

Based in many areas through Thailand there were a series of battles at the site of Phu Hin Rong Kla National Park between the PLAT and the military, and continued military strikes accompanied by offered amnesties eventually saw the CPT lose its support and fade away.

By 1980 the nation had yet another new leader, by the name of Prem Tinsulanond who led the country until his resignation in 1988. This is regarded as the most stable period of Thai history since World War II and many believed that the days of frequent military intervention and interference were done with, however that was not to be the case.

By the early 1990s under the lead of Chatichai Choonhavan Thailand had a sound economic base and there was considerable freedom of speech and of the press. Under his rule, foreign investment was particularly encouraged and this resulted in considerable economic growth, however corruption grew along with it. As the corruption grew, increasing numbers of the cabinet members were implicated in scandals. Despite these, Chatachai continued to lead Thailand until he began to attempt to downgrade the role of the military in the running of Thailand. This was a step which the military were unwilling to tolerate.

The 1991 Coup and onwards
On 23 February 1991 the Thai military overthrew the Chatichai government in a bloodless coup and handed power to a council more of their liking led by General Suchinda Kraprayoon. The first actions of the new government were to dissolve the parliament and abolish the 1978 constitution. The reason given for the coup was that the previous administration was guilty of vote buying, but the more likely reason is that the government was straying into policy areas which the military considered to be their own, namely foreign policy whilst simultaneously trying to cut out the military.

At the end of the year the military appointed their own man as Prime Minister, Ananda Panyarachun and a cabinet which was very biased towards the military. The unwritten rule being that Ananda was his own man as long as he did not cross the military. The military promised elections within six months of the coup and they were held in March of 1992 however the new constitution allowed Suchinda to wangle his way into the leadership at the head of a five party coalition which was very pro military.

The appointment of Suchinda was followed by large demonstrations in Bangkok and other urban centres involving hundreds of thousands of disgruntled Thais. Suchinda badly misjudged the feeling of the people and brutally put down the protests, resulting in over one hundred deaths. After being severely scolded by the King (on world television) for his lacklustre behaviour, Suchinda resigned and the military stated that the Prime Minister should be an elected MP. This resulted in the return to power of Ananda who lasted until the September 1992 elections. At this time Chuan Leekpai came to power at the head of a coalition government. Although vote buying was still a major problem, particularly in rural Thailand, Chuan was recognised as a sticker for the law and an upholder of democracy.

One of the platforms upon which Chuan had been elected was that of sorting out Bangkok's traffic problems. A huge task for the most apt of traffic engineers, Chuan floundered as a variety of offices responsible for different sections of the urban planning squabbled over the problem with the end result being a worsening of the traffic situation. If you think it is odd that solving traffic gridlock be a major political issue, visit Bangkok!

During 1994 Chuan's popularity surged as two major scandals unravelled. The first was that a number of opposition politicians were refused visas to the US due to their alleged drug trading activities and then during the Saudi gems scandal Chuan stepped in and had a number of senior police officers arrested and charged with ordering murders in order to cover the trail that the gems travelled along.

Corruption was to raise its ugly head again in 1995 when, following the withdrawal of one of the coalition members, Chuan was forced to dissolve parliament. In the ensuing campaign it came to light that during Chuan's land reform programme (a plan aimed at giving land to poor rural Thais) ten wealthy businessman (who by chance were mates of Chuan) were given tracts of beach front land on Phuket which was ideal for hotel development!

The July elections resulted in the Chart Thai Party which was led by Banharn Silpa-archa becoming the head of a new coalition. Despite his rhetoric regarding corruption, Banharn was often referred to as the 'walking ATM'! One of the most notable results of Banharn's rule was the effects on his home town of Suphanaburi. Any visitor there will be amazed by the high level of public works and monuments as Banharn attempted to lift its profile.

In late 1996, Banharn, after a string of scandals and alleged corrupt behaviour lost his position of leader of Thailand to the deputy Prime Minister Chavalit Yongchaiyudh. It will be interesting to see how he fares in the future. As the activity of the military in regard to politics in Thailand appears to be reducing, the biggest problem for stable government appears to be one of corruption. In an environment of high economic growth and development, many of the government ministers hold interests in the construction industry and appear to all too frequently get caught with their hands in the cookie jar. The planned construction of a second airport for Bangkok with its associated huge construction contracts should be a good test of Chavalit's stand on corruption.

CULTURE

THE PEOPLE

The Thai people are a very gentle, friendly and hospitable people. The population officially reached 60,000,000 on 2 November 1996 and is growing at a rate of 1.3% per annum. Due to the geographical location of Thailand it has become the home of many immigrants, so now, the 'typical' Thai person is a melting pot of cultures. Thai descendants include a mixture of Thai, Laotian, Chinese, Khmer, Malay, Mon, Indian, Persian, Japanese and Vietnamese. The only cultures that have resisted assimilation are the Muslim Malays of the Far South and various hilltribes. There are still regional differences between the people. An accurate breakdown of the total population is difficult due to the assimilation between cultures over hundreds of years. The largest minority group would have to be the Laotions who predominately live in the northeast and some reports state they make up around a third of the population. The Chinese are the next most populous minority making up around 11%.

Thai Origins

The origins of the Thai people are the subject of debate. This is partly due to a lack of sound archeological evidence, but also due to a basic disagreement as to whether Southeast Asia was the birthplace of a civilisation or the gathering point for civilisations born elsewhere. The other problem is that historians have only really traced the Thai people by their language group. Modern Thai holds little connection to the surrounding languages yet variations on the base language are spoken by Thai's, Lao's, Shan's and by upland tribes such as the Black Thai, Red Thai and White Thai. These people today stretch from Burma, through Thailand and Laos, to southern China and far northern Vietnam thus providing a wide girth for cultural diversity and hence differing perceptions of their respective 'origins'. For a more detailed look at the origins and early history of the Thai people, please refer to our history section at the beginning of this book.

HILLTRIBES

Hilltribe people is an all encompassing term referring to the ethnic minority groups that live mostly in the mountainous regions of the north, northwest and southwest of Thailand. In 1995 the total number of hilltribe people numbered around 695,000 who live across 20 provinces. The tribes are broken into nine major groups identified by their unique dress, culture, history, language, religion and architecture. Each tribe may be spread over regions, provinces or even countries, but are made up of smaller communities generally arranged in well established villages, some of which are still fairly nomadic.

The Karen (322,000) are the largest group making up 46% of the hilltribe population, followed by Hmong (Meo) (124,000), Lahu (73,000), Akha (48,500), Yao (40,500), H'tin (33,000), Lisu (28,000), Lawa (16,000) and Khamu (10,000). Two other tribes should be mentioned even though they hardly even register against the more populous tribes. The Palong have a population just under 500 people living in Chiang Mai Province and the Mlabri who number under 200 live in remote areas of Phrae and Nan Provinces. One of the major problems facing the hilltribe populations of Thailand is their population growth. Today the hilltribe population doubles every 20 years and this, combined with increasing environmental degradation and an unstable economic future, could become the tribe's biggest concern in the future.

Government Intervention

The Thai government more or less ignored the hilltribe people until the middle of the 20th Century. It was not until the 1960s, during the fighting against the PLAT, that the government realised that many hilltribes, particularly the Hmong and Mien were actively supporting the communist movement. The reasons for this include the fact that the tribes, particularly the Hmong, had become increasingly frustrated with continuing harassment in regard to their opium growing. The immediate result of the hilltribe allegiance with the communists was the napalming of selected hilltribe villages, which did nothing for the improving of relations. It would not be until the mid 1970s that the last of the Hmong would return to the mainstream fold. However it appears that the Hmong's relationship with the Thai government has gone full circle, as in recent times there have been accusations from the Lao government that the Thai's are now sheltering nationalist Hmong who are actively campaigning for a change of government in Laos - by peaceful or violent means.

The Thai government has taken an integrationist approach towards the hilltribes. Although it was not until 1976 that cabinet finally agreed on a policy of integration, albeit for reasons of national security as opposed to improving life for the hilltribes. The result of this is that the hilltribes are subject to Thai law and are only supposed to maintain their traditional life as long as it falls within the confines of the Thai legal system. The village headman is seen as a local representative in the local government and is responsible for matters such as registering voters and enforcement of the law.

One of the biggest problems for the integration of hilltribe populations into greater Thailand is that of agriculture and economic inconsistencies. The majority of the hilltribes pursue a agricultural system known as swidden or more commonly as slash and burn. This form of agriculture is ideal for small populations who have no major concern for environmental degradation. The method is to select a large swathe of land, cut down all trees and other vegetation then burn it. The aftermath of the burning is a layer of nutrients on the top layer of the soil which can then be utilised by shallow rooted crops such as dry rice. The slash and burn system does have a number of major disadvantages; the layer of nutrients lasts only a couple of seasons at best, after which the farmers must move on to a new parcel of land where the process is repeated whilst the previous area is left to regenerate — a process which can take up to 20 years in areas of poor soil. The second problem associated with swidden is that once the vegetation is removed, heavy rain washes the topsoil off the slopes down into the river beds. The result of this is threefold, the soil loses its productivity even quicker than by normal farming, the river beds become silted (two conditions which can lead to flooding further down river) and thirdly, and most importantly, in extreme cases the mountain slopes can lose their cohesiveness as the topsoil becomes extremely unstable and large scale avalanches can fall.

Perhaps the biggest problem with swidden agriculture is that there are simply too many hilltribes engaged in it. Any visitor to northern Thailand, especially around Chiang Mai and Chiang Rai, will be amazed by the huge swaths of land which have been completely deforested. Swidden agriculture, like logging, is a sustainable industry if done correctly and intelligently. But the problem is that the burgeoning hilltribe populations (present growth rate is around 5% per annum) will soon suffer from a lack of useful land if the present patterns continue.

Aside from the opium growing, the environmental degradation caused by the hilltribes is a cause of ongoing friction between the Thai government and the hilltribes. In regard to Thailand's National Parks, many hilltribes still live within certain park boundaries and still continue their slash and burn practice, often spending much of their remaining time running around the park shooting the animals! This ridiculous state of affairs has sparked some response from the various National Park offices leading to the relocation of some tribes to less 'valued' areas, unfortunately other tribes are still decimating National Parks as you read this.

From the Thai government's point of view, the hilltribes are standing in the way of furthering what has already been a very belated policy of environmental protection. In the future the remaining hilltribes will all have to be relocated outside the boundaries of the

National Parks if the conservation of these areas is to be taken seriously. From the hilltribes' point of view however, many of these National Parks are fairly recent creations, and in many cases the tribes have been living in the area for generations, a long time before the National Parks were gazetted. In other cases, those hilltribes not affiliated with the communists were encouraged to fight against them (during the fighting against the PLAT and CPT). But, as in the case of Phu Hin Rong Kla National Park in Phitsanulok Province, following the defeat of the CPT, the hilltribes who had supported the Thai government were kicked off the land they had lived on for generations when the area was rezoned a National Park - hardly a successful public relations exercise!

The other major grievance between the Thai government and the hilltribes is the subject of opium production. Under extreme pressure from the US DEA (Drug Enforcement Agency) and other anti drug bodies the vast majority of the opium production which once took place in Thailand has been pushed over the border into either Burma or Laos. Mark Ord gives his impressions of the success/failure of the Opium Eradication Programme.

THE OPIUM ERADICATION PROGRAMME

Opium poppy growing by hilltribes was, until recently, widespread throughout Northern Thailand, both as a cash crop (sold to the KMT and more recently SUA and Wa armies in Burma) and also for local consumption. Opium has played an important role in Hmong, Yao, Lisu and Lahu society as a recreational drug, important medicine and as a means to combat the fatigue and monotony of their daily hard physical work.

In recent years, under American pressure and with their financial backing, the Thai government has embarked on an intensive and effective poppy eradication programme.

Either through paid informants or helicopter spotting, the poppy fields are located and burned to the ground by field teams. Originally, the "unofficial" line was that smaller fields, purely for village consumption, would be "forgotten about" and small sections of the larger commercial plots ignored to prevent genuine hardship in the village. This is a gradual process with the intention of weaning villages off the growing habit and also hopefully leading to an intended 100% elimination over a short period of time. To be successful it must work in conjunction with the establishment of crop substitution programmes. As recently as five to ten years ago many poppy fields could easily be seen in Mae Hong Son, Chiang Mai, Chiang Rai and Nan Provinces, but they are now well hidden and few and far between. Isolated pockets still exist in Nan, Mae Hong Son and Tak Provinces in particular with the Hmong tribe being particularly persistent in its cultivation.

All very well you may say, but here is the rub. There are two major drawbacks to this process, one socio-financial and the other ecological. As stated, opium has been an important and traditional part of village life, for better or for worse, and many tribespeople cannot give it up "overnight". If local production becomes entirely eradicated then the hilltribes will be faced with the choice of finding and buying opium from elsewhere in Thailand which, with its increasing scarcity is becoming expensive, or buying imported Lao or Burmese opium which is equally expensive due to the risks and transportation involved. Secondly, substitute crops such as cabbages require a far larger area to be cultivated thus increasing the ecological damage to the surrounding environment.

Since opium is a relatively bulky product it is in fact easier and cheaper to import in its derivative form as heroin which is produced in the SUA or Wa factories over the border. Opium is generally smoked or eaten, whereas heroin is most effective and cheaper if it is injected leading to further problems. This practise manifests associated health problems such as Hepatitis and HIV and, as Hmong needle hygiene is not quite what it might be, these risks are becoming a very serious problem. Thus, instead of being a region for producing, Northern Thailand is now an importer, and instead of smoking opium, many hilltribes people are now injecting cheap Burmese heroin.

A further immediate consequence of the elimination of opium is the drastic rise of alcoholism in tribal villages with the cheap or home brewed rice liquors being an obvious substitute. Generally speaking, alcoholism has a far more destructive effect on family and village life than opium ever did and, along with heroin addiction, alcoholism is leading to serious social problems amongst hilltribes.

The financial aspect of the opium production issue is also of significance. Whilst crop substitution programmes and government aid may go some way to replacing opium revenue, money is still leaving the villages to pay for heroin, imported opium and alcohol.

This leads to the second major problem, the ecological one. Opium requires a very small amount of land for cultivation returning a high financial yield. All substitute crops such as fruit trees, tea plantations and cabbages demand a far larger surface area to reach anywhere near the same income level. Thus, previously where a forested hillside would contain one or two small hidden poppy plots, the same hill will now be covered with cabbages without a single tree in sight. The extensive tea and fruit orchids covering the once forested slopes around Mae Salong, or the hundreds of square kilometres of cabbage covered hills south of Mae Sot are good examples. Forest environments are a precious and essential part of the traditional lifestyles of the Akhas of Mae Salong and the Hmongs of Mae Sot yet they are obliged to destroy them to survive.

Should these villages be currently situated in designated "ecologically sensitive areas" then the Forestry and National Parks Departments will press for the tribes "relocation" due to their destructive presence, yet these hilltribes have traditionally lived in relative harmony with their forest environments for generation. The Thai government with US DEA assistance/insistence are creating major long term problems to a short sighted solution.

by Mark Ord

Hilltribe Trekking

Whilst in the north of Thailand, especially in the major centres of Chiang Mai and Chiang Rai, it is virtually impossible to miss the numerous establishments advertising hilltribe treks. Most guesthouses and travel agents offer a variety of one day or longer trips, many of which include a rafting and elephant riding experience. More recently the trips have also included a boat (longtail) or jeep ride to get tourists to more 'untouched' areas.

To enhance your experience and to reduce to possible effects of hilltribe trekking on their cultures, we wish to provide you with a little advice. Try and learn as much as you can about each of the hilltribe cultures that you intend to visit. The TAT offices can provide you with a list of authorised trekking companies - some of the better ones only hire guides that have studied the hilltribes in depth and will be able to answer most questions in relation to them. Often they will also be able to speak hilltribe dialects, as well as English, making your experience more informative. The trekking company that you use, must by law, register every trek into the hilltribe regions. Failure to do so means that they are not an authorised company. One of the most important features for ensuring an enjoyable trek is making sure the group you are trekking with is looking for a similar experience. Quite often it is possible to meet your group the day before departure and it is well worth your while to take advantage of this. There is nothing worse than going on a trek with a group with whom you have nothing in common, or worse, actively dislike. If you spend as much time investigating your group as you do looking out for the best price and itinerary, you are well on the way to an enjoyable trek.

Regarding your valuables, you can either take them with you or leave them at your guesthouse. If you opt for the latter, make sure you get an itemised list of everything that is there and exercise extreme care regarding credit cards, as there have been many cases where people have returned home only to receive a bill for their card that was run up to its limit whilst they were out on a trek. Talk to other travellers as the guesthouse situation in Chiang Mai is too fickle for us to list those with an 'impenetrable' safe. At the first suspicion of your goods being tampered with, go straight to the TAT and Tourist Police as this is something which the authorities are actively trying to clean up.

Whilst trekking you may be exposed to malarial mosquitos (however this is unlikely) hence take the necessary precautions including repellent and wear long pants and long sleeved shirts at dusk and dawn.

The last but most important point is to always respect the culture of the hilltribe village you are visiting. You are the visitor and should not impose or express your values onto them. Be aware of any religious areas, dress modestly, ask permission to take photographs and do not give sweets, clothing or medicine (more suitable gifts include donations, material for their handicrafts such as needles and cotton or educational items such as pens and paper). There are also a number of taboos which vary from tribe to tribe, these are detailed in the section on each tribe.

Independent Trekking
If you want to see a less touristy side of the hilltribe people, try organising your own trek through the mountains. The best way to do this is to decide on an area which you want to visit, then purchase a map which marks most villages in the chosen region. With this map in hand you should be able to design an itinerary according to which tribes you want to visit and you will be able to stay at a different village every night. For safety precautions, we would suggest that you organise a small group of people rather than going it along.

Quite often if you take the effort to communicate and learn about the hilltribe culture you will be offered a bed for the night. Otherwise indicate that you want accommodation for the night using the international sign for sleep. You will either be taken to the head of the village who will chose where you will sleep or you will be taken to a house commonly used for visitors. No special meal will be made but you are expected to eat with the family that you are staying with. The family will expect a small payment for the bed and food, much cheaper than what you would pay in a hotel, and for an unrepeatable cultural experience. Be aware of hygiene when staying with the highland hilltribes as they generally build their villages above the water level, so the sanitation and water sources may not be the cleanest.

The other option for observing hilltribe life is to hire your own motorcycle and visit the tribes by yourself. If the tribe is fairly easily accessed by road however, then you can expect that a great many people have visited the village before you, including tour groups. You will be accepted and respected for your individuality, and will get a more authentic experience if you get far away from sealed roads. A good map will note the hilltribes that are in easy access of sealed roads.

A good time to see hilltribes at their most colourful is during their celebration of New Year. Each hilltribe celebrates at a different time of year, but they generally fall between December and February. Be wary of the fermented alcohol which comes out by the gallon load at this time of year.

Effects of Tourism on Hilltribes
The hilltribes of Thailand are now as much a tourist attraction as the beaches of Ko Samui and Phuket. This has brought on both positive and negative effects. The positive effects can be seen in increased accessibility to health care, education and a new source of income in the form of the tourist dollar, unfortunately often at the expense of their own culture.

The villages seek out the tourist dollar often at the expense of their traditional lifestyle and particularly, in villages within striking distance of Chiang Mai, it is not uncommon to arrive at a village whose main street is lined with Pepsi vendors. As a result of some villages being visited on a daily basis (sometimes by more than one group) the villagers themselves now spend more time making handicrafts to sell to the visitors than they do tending their own crops. With frequent contact with outsiders, the younger generation start to move towards larger cities looking for work and the village may begin to lose its cohesiveness. Intermarriage, as hilltribes marry Thais, frequently cause another loss to the village, as it appears to be the accepted rule that the hilltribe half of the marriage is expected to shun his or her beliefs in favour of the Thai way of life. The most unfortunate aspect of frequent visits, is that over time, as the village becomes more oriented towards tourism rather than the traditional life, tourists may in fact lose interest in the village as it is seen as being too 'touristy', so people stop going there, and the village then finds itself stuck in a position where the new income source has evaporated, but the cultural damage is at a state of no return making it difficult to rekindle 'traditional' life.

Another by-product of frequent contact with Westerners is that the villagers, particularly the younger generation, begin to look more and more like us! The classic example was a Lisu male which one of the researchers saw in a remote village in Tak Province — he was adorned in a Perestroika T-shirt and a pair of Billabongs! Besides dissuading the locals from continuing with tradition, gifts of clothing also damage the local handicraft and weaving crafts, skills which until recently were highly valued.

Despite the contact with foreigners, the standard of living in the villages is still very poor. The children are often malnourished and an increasing number of the males in the village may be heroin addicts. Life expectancy in the villages is often very short with poor sanitation, lack of medical services and hard physical work all contributing towards an early death.

Many visitors to hilltribes use the common description that it is like a human zoo. Unfortunately, there is little that can be done to eradicate this part of the experience, as, just like a zoo, most visitors visit hilltribes out of curiosity to bear witness to a society less 'civilised' to that of the west and unfortunately, as in a zoo, people feel that a camera is a vital part of their equipment. There is nothing worse than observing Western visitors chase children around the village with a camera, not realising that the reason that the children are running away is because they are terrified of the camera, the tourist or both. If you honestly want to minimise your effect on the village, leave the camera at home and buy some of the readily available postcards instead. Many tribes do not mind having their photo taken, but always be sure to ask first.

Opium

In the past, the hilltribes were some of the biggest producers in Thailand although, in more recent times, a combination of Thai and US DEA policy has eradicated many of the crops. In the past the majority of the trade was run by the SUA, Wa and KMT armies who would visit the tribes, purchase their produce at low prices and continue to travel through the region in heavy armed 'drug caravans'. With the success of Thai and US DEA policies much of this has been eradicated and the tribes have become one of the major sources of tourism.

Many overnight visitors to the hilltribes actively look forward the opium sessions at the end of an evening and, although these sessions are relatively harmless to the user and often quite pleasant, few realise the damage they are doing both to themselves and their immediate surrounds. Besides the effects of opium on the smoker (nausea, lack of sleep, disorientation and in extreme cases death) the main detrimental effects are directly upon the state of affairs in the village and upon the tourist guide. In Chiang Rai in particular, opium and heroin (a derivative of opium) addicted trekking guides are a major problem. The problem is not that the guide is going to rob or harass you but rather that he will reach the first village, sit down for a smoke of opium or hit of heroin and leave three days later! If your trek is particularly cheap, and you are not interested in trying the opium, be very specific in requesting that you do not want to visit opium effected villages. You may be surprised that suddenly the price may jump up to a more standard price.

For the visitor, opium is generally a one off experience, something that is tried once or twice over a period of a few days generally without negative effects. However for the guide, the opium becomes a daily temptation, a temptation which many give in to. Within the villages themselves regular visits of opium seeking tourists greatly increase the demand and level of usage for the tribespeople. Within Hmong villages over 30% of males are addicted. A product which was once seen as a vice amongst the older members of the tribes is now becoming a debilitating scourge which can effectively cripple the village. Part of this can be directly associated to the Thai and US DEA policies which have reduced the supply of opium, hence encouraging the locals to often use imported Burmese heroin. The rest of the blame is on visiting Westerners who want to get high for a night.

Opium and opium consumption is illegal in Thailand, and if you are caught you can expect extreme penalties. *Tales From the Other Side certainly does not suggest that visitors to Thailand use, purchase or attempt to export opium.*

THE HILLTRIBES OF THAILAND

Karen
Population: 322,000

Subgroups: There are a four sub groups of the Karen in Thailand: Skaw (White Karen), Pwo or Plong (White Karen), Pa-O or Taungthu (Black Karen) and Bwe or Kayah (Red Karen) otherwise known as Padang.

Where did they come from?: Although in more contemporary times the Karen have been centred in modern day Burma, they are believed to have originated in central China over 2,500 years ago. The vast majority of their total population (almost 5 million) still reside in Burma, but in the face of continued SLORC (the illegitimate junta in Burma) oppression more and more are migrating to Thailand.

Where can they be found today?: Most Karen live along Thailand's western frontier with Burma, particularly in Mae Hong Son, Tak, Chiang Mai, Kamphaeng Phet, Kanchanaburi and Pratchuap Khiri Khan Provinces. Smaller groups can be found in Lamphun, Lampang, Phrae, Uthai Thani, Suphanaburi and Ratchaburi Provinces.

What do they wear?: The Karen traditional clothing is less distinctive than some other tribes' outfits. The shirts are simple hand woven cloth almost in the style of a short kaftan, and the pants are generally basic peasant sarongs. The men wear turbans made of cotton or sometimes silk, and they are generally red, although sometimes they are not dyed.

What are their beliefs?: The Karen have a number of different religious beliefs according to the relevant group. There are large groups of Buddhist Karens, but Christian missionaries have also had a large degree of success with the Karens in the past (the differences in religious beliefs between these two groups played a major role in the split between the KNU and DKBA in Burma). One of the reasons put forward for the success of the Christian missionaries is that the Karen also believe in a deliverance prophecy which states they will be led to a great palace by a messiah figure. A significant number of Karen also indulge in another spiritual belief which states there is a chief God who rules over the wilderness in the vicinity of the particular village. At important times of the year, such as harvest, new year and times of sickness, a ceremony is held where sacrifices are made to the God. After the ceremony the villagers depart for their homes but only after filling their ears with dirt so as to be invisible to the spirits. They also believe that the body is inhabited by a range of spirits which keep the body healthy. If one of these leave then the body becomes sick and if all leave the body dies. Children are apparently particularly susceptible to spirits, hence are never allowed to look upon a corpse in case the spirits of the dead carry away the child. The men of the village are also known to cover themselves with lavish tattoos which are believed to bring good luck.

The Karen also believe that it is the spirits who choose their headman as he is also seen as a holy man. However, once the first headman has been selected, the accession to this position runs in a hereditary pattern.

Taboos: Karen believe that fields which have been burnt out are protected by a Crop Goddess who sits on the stumps of the burnt trees and protects the fields. So that you do not squash the Crop Goddess you should never touch or damage the burnt top of the stumps.

Death: Upon a death in a Karen village, the corpse is washed by the family and dressed in their best clothes, although if the corpse is an unmarried woman, she is dressed in her wedding clothes to stop the spirits from taking advantage of her. The body can be either cremated or buried but, after the funeral, objects are laid on the path back to the village to make it difficult for the spirit to return to the village and haunt it.

Marriage, Sex & Children: Getting married in a Karen village can be quite a chore and, considering the rules and regulations, it is amazing that anyone ever meets! Unmarried couples are not allowed to be alone at any time and, although they may meet at various functions such as harvesting and other weddings, they are only allowed to court during funerals! As it is encouraged that people marry between villages rather than within villages, men often visit other villages with the purpose of checking out the talent and, although the women are not supposed to show any interest in the men, it is often the women who do the proposing! The marriage ceremony generally lasts a couple of days. The only gift giving is from the bride who presents her new husband with a shirt she made, however, the mother in law also gets in on the action and sprinkles his feet with water. Once the marriage is over, the new couple tend to live in whichever village offers the better land.

Once the Karen woman falls pregnant she has to abstain from alcohol and is not allowed to see a corpse or coffin in case the spirits take off with her child. She will generally give birth in her own home and the placenta is placed in a bamboo tube and hung either outside the village or buried under the house. The most important time for the child is when his or her ears are pierced so as to prove to the spirits that the child is not a monkey!

Pre marital sex is forbidden in Karen society and a fine is levied if couples are caught out - just because relatively few fines are levied does not mean it does not happen. Both divorce and adultery are rare and when they do occur, it really hits the fan! The guilty couple are required to perform a large sacrifice, after which they are often driven from the village.

What do their houses look like and where do they live?: Karen houses are simple wooden constructions as only the husband, wife and unmarried children can live in the same house. The house is generally built on stilts and the livestock are kept underneath the house. Karens live in mountainous areas, but not as high as some other tribes. Generally they are located between 500 m and 1,000 m above sea level.

What do they grow?: Wet rice, vegetables and occasionally opium. Larger villages may also grow fruit orchids.

Padang (Long Necks)

The Padang are part of the Bwe subdivision of the Karen hilltribe group. The Padang, or 'long necks' as they are known, are refugees from the mountainous region of the Kayah State of eastern Burma and have been conveniently located in Thailand by Shan businessmen. You have to pay a substantial amount in order to enter their villages, even if you go alone, and this money is supposedly used to assist the other Padang who remain in Burma. Maybe some of this money does go to help them, but the vast majority of it lands in the pockets of the Shan businessmen who run the place. In visiting here, you are essentially supporting a human zoo.

Neck rings are not traditional for this tribe. Normally only girls born under certain auspicious conditions (ie, on a full moon or when it is raining and albino elephants are cartwheeling over the river) have the dubious honour of wearing them. The rings are medically dangerous, yet more and more of the village women are being encouraged to wear the rings so that the tourists who visit continue to have something to take photos of, essentially women disfiguring themselves.

For those unfortunate enough to have to wear these rings, the ordeal begins at adolescence (between five to ten years old) with five loops placed around their necks to start with, and as the woman matures the ring is extended. The ring is not added to, but a completely new one replaces the old in a process that requires the head to be supported. Otherwise the woman may die as the muscles in the neck can no longer support the head on its own. Once the first ring has been placed the women lives with them for the rest of her life. Contrary to popular belief that the neck and vertebrae are extended, it is the collar bones and ribs which are actually compressed giving the illusion of a longer neck. The women also wear other jewellery over the rings. There are several theories as to why this is done. One is that it is a sign of beauty, another that long ago, the Padang angered the spirits so the spirits punished the people by sending tigers to the villages to eat the women. The Padang sought advise from their ancestors who suggested the women wear brass rings for protection. The third reason is that it was to stop the Burmese from wanting to take the women back to Burma as concubines, in essence to disfigure them. It is this third reason that seems the most truthful, although today's tradition has nothing to do with it as an inappropriate number of women are forced to wear the rings.

The first of the Padang camps is located on the border with Burma about 5 km northwest of Mae Hong Son. The second is south of there, accessible only by boat. Due to the 'uniqueness' of the Padang women or the ghoulish quality of the large numbers of visitors to the region, the Padang have become a popular tourist sight. The refugee camps can be visited for around 500B and, if you do decide to go, donations and supplies are greatly appreciated.

Hmong (Meo)
Population: (124,000)
Subgroups: Blue Hmong, White Hmong and Armband Hmong
Where did they come from?: The Hmong may have originated in Central Asia but more recently were found in Southern China.
Where can they be found today?: The Hmong are spread over a huge area from Burma to Laos and Northern Vietnam. Within Thailand they are found in pockets throughout northern Thailand, particularly in Chiang Mai, Chiang Rai, Nan, Phrae and Tak Provinces.
What do they wear?: The Hmong, in particular the women, are well known for their brilliantly embroidered clothing. Although they may not wear all their finery for a day of working in the fields, when they do put on their best clothes, the Hmongs are spectacular dressers. The men wear short shirts which are very brightly embroidered and baggy black pants. They also wear embroidered sashes around the waist and often shave their heads. The women dress even more extravagantly with silk and cotton blouses which are heavily embroidered around the cuffs and neck and, like the men, they wear brightly embroidered sashes. Blue Hmong women wear pleated short skirts whilst White Hmong wear plain white or un-dyed skirts. The Hmong keep much of their wealth in the form of silver jewellery, much of which is worn by the women. The quality of the silver can, at times, be amazingly high.
What are their beliefs?: The religion of the Hmong revolves around the spirits who, as long as they are appeased, serve to protect the village. Each village has an altar for the spirits and, during festival times, many sacrifices are made to keep the spirits well pleased. The village will also have a shaman who's role it is to call on the spirits in times of dire need.
Taboos: If visiting a Hmong village, remember that you cannot enter a house unless you are invited in by a male. If there are no males around then this taboo does not apply.
Death: One of the methods used to try and cure a Hmong villager when they fall ill is to build a bridge. The bridge is built over a nearby creek or river and the patient is led across with strings attached to their waist. If this method is not successful, a number of other tribal remedies will be tried before they turn to Western medicine. A Hmong funeral is a lavish affair since it is important that the person has a wealthy afterlife. After being washed by their children and grandchildren, the body is dressed in the finest clothes and the fingers are tied together with red string then the body is placed in a coffin. The coffin is carried to the cemetery and buried and, once in the grave, the carrying poles used to transport the body are broken so as to stop the spirit from returning to the village.
Marriage, Sex & Children: In comparison to the Karen, no tribe contrasts as much as the Hmong. Courtship amongst the Hmong is highly ritualised. Those of eligible age stand opposite each other, then the women throw a ball to the man of their choice, and the man has

the choice of accepting the ball or not. Premarital sex is very common and there are generally few refusals of the black ball! Once the couple are officially together, the haggling begins as the brides price must be decided upon. This often leads to the groom's family having to pay up to 10,000B in silver. Once this price has been paid (a process which can take years) the bride becomes the property of her husband and his family. If she decides in later life to leave her husband she needs to pay a fine to the husband. Wealthy Hmong men may take more than one wife and is limited only by how money he wants to spend.

When a Hmong baby is born, it is believed that the baby remains the property of the Baby Goddess for three days. After this time a celebration is held as the Goddess is seen to be relinguishing her hold over the child. Following birth the mother spends three weeks doing nothing but laying by the fire, after which it is back to work as usual. The placenta is buried outside the bedroom door.

What do their houses look like and where do they live?: Hmong houses are large and built on the ground, generally of hardwood logs. The houses have segmented bedrooms and a large living room, which is often dominated by an altar. Hmong live high up in mountain ranges, generally over 1,000 m, so as to be conveniently located for their opium growing. The houses are generally placed on the lee of a ridge, face downhill and are organised so that none of the houses are in line with each other, this would be an impediment for the entry of beneficial spirits.

What do they grow?: Opium is the main cash crop, with rice and corn being the main subsistence crops.

Lahu (Musur)
Population: 73,000
Subgroups: Lahu Nyi (Red Lahu), Lahu Na, Lahu Shehleh, Lahu Laba, Lahu Phu and Lahu Shi
Where did they come from?: The Lahu are believed to have originated on the Tibetan Plateau.
Where can they be found today?: The Lahu are concentrated in far northern Thailand, particularly in Chiang Rai and Mae Hong Son Provinces. There are also pockets of Lahu in Chiang Mai, Tak and Kamphaeng Phet Provinces.
What do they wear?: Lahu costumes differ widely from subgroup to subgroup. Lahu Nyi wear short red, white and blue edged jackets. The skirts have three horizontal panels, the top and bottom of which is red and the middle panel can be blue, black or red with additional thin black stripes in the centre. The men's clothing is generally loose fitting indigo coloured shirts and pants.

Lahu Sheh clothing is dominated by heavy black cotton and both men and women wear black turbans. The women wear tunics which are edged in yellow or white and the sleeves are deeply embroidered. The men wear loose fitting shirts and pants.

The Lahu Na wear ankle length tunics with a red trim, and the sleeves are also decorated with bands of colour along their length. A black sarong is worn under the tunic but is often decorated with colourful cloth. Lahu Na men wear black suits which are decorated with lines of black thread.

What are their beliefs?: Like the Karen, many of the Lahu have taken up Christian and Buddhist beliefs, but the majority are still very much ruled by the spirit world. Red Lahu villages often have a temple dedicated to the spirit world which is often decorated with coloured streamers. Twice a month celebrations are held at the temple where each family pours water into a central container symbolising the unity of the village.

Taboos: The sacred posts around the village temple should not be touched.

Death: Unlike other tribes, the Lahu tend not to heavily associate sickness to the spirits and hence are avid users of Western medicine as well as Thai and Chinese herbal concoctions. When someone dies, the body is dressed in white and placed in the main room of the house and food is served until the body is buried. When the body is placed in the coffin, a chicken leg and wing are placed in the coffin with the corpse. Lahu may bury or cremate the body although, if it is buried, the burial spot is chosen by throwing an egg - where ever the egg

breaks the body is buried. Following the burial, obstructions are placed on the path to the grave so as to hamper the spirits return to the village, and twelve days after burial a small house is built for the body's spirit, once again to dissuade it from returning into the village.
Marriage, Sex & Children: Courtship in Lahu society takes place during festivals, although the women are particularly forward and not ones to take a backward step when choosing their mate. Premarital sex is usual. Following the betrothal ceremony the boyfriend often lives with the girlfriend's family and works for them for a number of years before they marry. Divorce is fairly common in Lahu society and, if the male decides to leave the relationship, the woman retains custody of any offspring and he has to pay a fine.

During pregnancy the woman eats a clay substance which is rich in minerals and she gives birth in a kneeling position. The placenta is buried under the house and the mother will eat only rice and chicken for twelve days after the birth.
What do their houses look like and where do they live?: Lahu tend to live at high altitudes because, like the Hmong, they are still active opium growers. Their houses are built on stilts and each house is fenced in. The porch area is generally quite small and there is generally only one bedroom which is segmented as necessary.
What do they grow?: Opium, rice and corn are the three main crops on Lahu farms.

Yao (Mien)
Population: 40,500
Subgroups: None
Where did they come from?: The Yao originated in southern China around 200 years ago.
Where can they be found today?: Yao can be found in southern China, Vietnam, Laos and Thailand. Within Thailand they are most concentrated in northern Chiang Rai, Nan and Phayao Provinces.
What do they wear?: The Yao women wear elegantly embroidered tunics and trousers and, although there are a series of standard patterns, individual expression often adds to the design. The most popular patterns are made up of red, gold, blue and green cotton. Around the neckline of the shirt there is a ruff of bright red and fluffy wool which runs almost to the waist. This is the most stand-out characteristic of Yao clothing and is easily recognisable. The women also wear a turban which is often made up of red cloth. The men wear loose fitting pants and shirt, the latter of which is often decorated with red, blue and white edging. One of the most popular ways of displaying wealth amongst the Yao is to have gold capped teeth and, during festivals, large silver rings are also worn.
What are their beliefs?: The spirit world plays an important part in the life of the Yao. The spirits are deeply respected but also deeply feared. It is believed that during pregnancy spirits move from the house into the embryo, and that in the early years of childhood it is easy for their souls to be frightened away. The base religion for the Yao is Taoism, an ancient Chinese belief, and one of the biggest concerns for the older generation is that these beliefs are being seriously damaged by Western intrusions.
Taboos: When inside a Yao household, be sure not to touch or lean against the stove as it the home of the spirits. If taking photos of children, you should be sure that you have their consent.
Death: The Yao, like the Hmong, believe a bridge ceremony can be of assistance in curing ailing villagers - the more serious the illness, the bigger the bridge. They believe that the body is inhabited by a large range of spirits, and when a spirit is lost the body falls sick. Village shaman are the people responsible for dealing with the spirits in an effort to cure the sick.

After a death, the funeral service lasts for three days and involves a number of complex rituals. Once dead, a silver coin is placed in the body's mouth to stop the person from telling lies. Once the body is placed in the coffin a blue cloth leads from the coffin up and through the house roof, this is the path via which the soul leaves the body. Following this, the body and coffin are buried, and the eldest sons remains with the body for seven days. After this time the village priest returns and retrieves some bones which were buried separately from the rest of the corpse.

Marriage, Sex & Children: Yao do not practise any type of arranged marriage. As long as the partners come from different clans and they are of the right age, they may live together for a few years before they actually marry. Any children born before the marriage belong to the mother, whilst all those born after the wedding belong to the father. Before the wedding a price for the bride is agreed upon and a contract is signed between the two families. The wedding ceremony is quite a lavish affair with excessive feasting and drinking. When the bride arrives at the new village, the priest blesses the house and explains to the spirits that a new person is arriving to live in the village.

During pregnancy it is believed that the soul of the baby is residing in a variety of household appliances, such as the stove. As a result of this there are a complex set of rules regarding what can and cannot be done in the house during this period. For the month following childbirth the mother is not allowed to enter any other house. An extra door is also cut in the wall of the bedroom to the outside so she need not pass through any other areas of the house. Adoption from other tribes is a common happening in Yao families.

What do their houses look like and where do they live?: Yao homes serve to house extended families so they are both large and built on the ground. There are three doors in a Yao house, one for men on the men's side of the house, the second on the women's side of the house and the third doorway is used for ceremonies. Girls of a marriageable age have their own bedroom so that they can entertain suitors. Behind the house an area kept clear for the water dragon spirit.

What do they grow?: Dry rice and corn are the two most important crops to the Yao, but opium is also cultivated at times.

Akha

Population: 48,500

Subgroups: None.

Where did they come from?: General opinion puts the origin of the Akha in the Tibetan Highlands.

Where can they be found today?: Akha can be found in Chiang Rai, Chiang Mai, Tak, Kamphaeng Phet, Lampang and Phrae Provinces.

What do they wear?: Akha women are most easily recognised by their very ornate head dresses of which there are three basic kinds. The base of the U Lo-Akha head dress is a wide head band which has been decorated with all manner of silver paraphernalia. This base is topped by a bamboo cone which has been covered with cloth and then more silver ornaments. The second style is the Loimi-Akha head dress which is flatter than the U Lo-Akha and has strings of beads across the crown and down and over the shoulders. The Phami-Akha head dress is shaped more like a helmet and is completely covered with silver bits 'n pieces. It also has silver balls hanging down to the shoulders. Besides the head dress, Akha women's clothing is mostly indigo in colour with a variety of coloured embroidery. They often wear a midriff top with a sash wrapped around its base, heavily weighed down with even more silver. The men's clothing is much more sedate than the womens. Basic loose fitting black clothes are generally worn, although the front of the shirt is patterned with gold and red blocks of colour. The men will often also wear a wide black and white turban.

What are their beliefs?: The Akha have no word for religion, with the term 'The Akha Way' summing up their beliefs, and anyone who does not subscribe to their beliefs must leave the tribe. They practise ancestor worship and see themselves as a vital link between their ancestors and offspring. The Akha believe that there is a powerful being from whom all Akha people came. He taught them all they know including how to practise their beliefs. The Akha believe that at one time the spirit and human worlds lived in unison and peace, however because the humans and the spirits stole each other's belongings the only solution was to permanently separate the two. As a result whenever you enter an Akha village you will enter through a village gate - this gate separates the human world within the village from the spirit world outside in the forest. A new gate is constructed each year, so you may often enter through a series of older gates. The village is dominated by the Akha swing. Every year there is a four day swinging festival however, unfortunately over time, the significance of the festival has been forgotten. The dog is of particular importance to the Akha, and a soup made from dog bones is supposed to help the old and frail. To sacrifice a dog in an Akha village signals a big time event.

Taboos: Never touch the gates at the entrance to an Akha village. If you are offered food, drink or to enter someone's house, you must accept the offer. The greatest honour is to be offered (and accept) dog soup. Men should never enter the womens portion of an Akha household.

Death: Despite their indepth spiritual beliefs, Akha do not hesitate to use Western medicine to cure an affliction. If it is believed that a disease has been caused by crossing a spirit, then the best way to cure the ailment is to discover which spirit was involved and right the wrong. Upon death the corpse is cleansed and pieces of gold are placed in the mouth. This is to allow the soul to buy whatever is necessary in the next life. Until the actual burial takes place, a few days after death, a wake takes place involving many ceremonies including gambling. The Akha coffin is an impressive construction which resembles a boat. The body is placed inside and the family wipe down the eyes with cotton to pay their last respects. When it is buried the grave is dug in an east/west direction and a bag of food is left on a pole above the grave. One year after the full ceremony is complete, the spirit is invited back into the village to look over the household.

Marriage, Sex & Children: Akha villagers are free to marry who they want, although the initial courting takes place in the village 'courting ground' where the boys and girls perform for each other then pair off before heading off into the woods. The wedding takes place at the groom's village and the bride's family is not invited. At the ceremony prior to the actual marriage, an egg is passed between the couple three times and then eaten. At sometime through the festival both are given a long talking to regarding following the 'Akha Way'. Than at the end of the week, the rest of the village throws mud at the married couple to initiated them into married life! Divorce is common in Akha villages and the causes usually involve the husband's drug addiction, the wife's adultery or her inability to have male children. Men can also take second wives, although it is fairly uncommon.

Birth in Akha society is a process frought with taboos and disaster. If the new baby is deformed in anyway, even minor ailments like extra fingers or toes, or if the baby is a twin, then the baby is suffocated and buried a long way from the village. Even worse is death in childbirth, an event which creates the need for difficult ceremonies and sacrifices to attempt to keep the mothers soul at bay.

What do their houses look like and where do they live?: Akha villages tend to be found at heights of over 1,000 m generally along ridges. The houses are built on the ground and have very low eaves, which make it dark inside but keep it dry and sheltered.

What do they grow?: Their main crops are dry rice and corn, although opium is a major crop for the Akha.

Lisu

Population: 28,000

Subgroups: Hua Lisu (flowery) and the He Lisu (black).

Where did they come from?: Eastern Tibet.

Where can they be found today?: Lisu can be found in China, Burma, Northeast India and Thailand. Within Thailand they can be found in Chiang Mai, Phayao, Chiang Rai, Mae Hong Son, Tak, Lampang, Sukhothai, Kamphaeng Phet and Phetchabun Provinces

What do they wear?: Lisu women dress in particularly bright colours and the wealthier women supplement this with silver ornaments and jewellery. Although much of the material they wear is synthetic, it is still very attractive. Their shirts are predominantely either blue or green, have red sleeves and bands of bright colours running across the shoulders. Knee length pants are worn and the top is wrapped by a large black sash with coloured strings and pom poms. In times of ceremony, a brilliant black head dress is worn with coloured string hanging down and over the shoulders. In modern times the coloured string is quite often replaced by tinsel resembling something close to a Christmas tree. The men wear blue or green trousers and a black jacket with a red sash around the waist. Black turbans are also worn but are more often than not replaced with simple white towels!

What are their beliefs?: Like most of the other tribes, spirits play a vital role in every day Lisu life. There is the village guardian who looks over the village, as well as four other categories of spirits - ancestral, forest, owner and bad death. Of these four, bad death is the worst, as this kind of 'lost soul' tends to run around attempting to attack those still alive. Both the village priest and shaman play important roles in Lisu life and some of the ceremonies they oversee are spectacular to say the least. When someone is ill, an experienced older tribesperson will read the remains of chicken or pig bladders to determine what is wrong. Young Lisu children have their heads shaved to allow the evil spirits to escape from their body before their skull seals up.

Taboos: There are a few rules to abide by inside a Lisu household. Be sure never to stand in the doorway with a foot on each side of the doorway, men and women cannot sleep together in the guestroom, as this is where the altar is kept, and guests are forbidden from entering the bedrooms, touching the altar or sleeping with their head pointed towards the fire.

Death: The Lisu believe that sickness is caused by either loss of soul or by malicious evil spirits. In order to call back the soul, planks of wood are laid out resembling a bridge. The patient waits at home whilst the priest returns from the bridge, trying to encourage the soul to return. In the end of the ceremony strings are tied around the patient's neck in an effort to keep the soul within. As far as placating the evil spirits are concerned, this tends to involve copious (and often expensive) animal sacrifices. The Lisu believe that their God, Yelaun, has already written when they will die. When someone dies, grains of rice and pieces of silver are placed in their mouth and a gun is fired to inform everyone of the death. Once the body has been washed and the coffin made, a wake takes place involving drinking, feasting and gambling. When the burial takes place, the burial site is determined by tossing an egg (where the egg breaks is a good place to be buried) and above the grave a bucket of water is left suspended. This water is changed by the family every day for ten days and a month later the water is returned to the family shrine. The ritual and water indicates that the dead person has become an honoured ancestor. The wooden poles which are used to transport the coffin are also broken at the burial site so as to make it more difficult for the spirit to escape back to the village. Every year for the following three years, the family will sacrifice a pig and a couple of chickens at the site to honour both the dead and the 'Spirit of the Graves'.

Marriage, Sex & Children: Compared to other tribes, courtship amongst the Lisu is particularly informal - they just chat each other up when ever the opportunity arises. Whenever a couple hit it off, a stylised drama unfolds as the parents attempt to agree on the bride price. The couple will live together until the family has been able to gather the necessary bride price. When they are actually married, the groom bangs his head on the ground three times in front of his parents-in-law after which there is a big feasting session. At the end of the meal, guests drop money into a bowl, which is then emptied into the grooms hands who then gives it all to his bride. This money is seen to ensure healthy children. After a Lisu woman gives birth she lays by the house fire for month. The new child is given a temporary name for the first three days as it is only after the first three days that the child becomes human.

What do their houses look like and where do they live?: Lisu live in high altitudes. Their villages are placed at between 1,000 m and 1,600 m and are generally located not too far from a fresh water source. The houses can be built on either the ground or up on stilts. When a daughter reaches puberty she gets her own room.

What do they grow?: Opium is the big crop for the Lisu. Sold to traders and tourists alike they rely on this crop for the hard cash which they need to purchase the other necessities of life. Other crops such as rice and corn are grown at levels below the village at a subsistence level.

OTHER TRIBES

H'tin
Population: 33,000
Subgroups: None
Where did they come from?: Not big travellers, the H'tin are believed to have originated in Laos, although they have lived in Thailand for a considerable time.
Where can they be found today?: Nan Province.
What do they wear?: It is rare to see the H'tin women in their traditional dress, but when worn it consists of red, yellow and black banded cloth. The black jackets also carry considerable embroidery along the edges.
What are their beliefs?: Like the Akha, H'tin guard the entrance to their villages with spirit gates. Spirits play a very important part in their lives, although a considerable number have taken up some Christian and Buddhist beliefs.
Taboos: H'tin are particularly suspicious of foreigners, as they are believed to bring hosts of evil spirits into the villages. If you do plan to visit H'tin villages, be aware of this.
Marriage, Sex & Children: H'tin are monogamous (or most are anyway!) and until a couple has had a few children they live with the wife's family, after which they move to a new dwelling.
What do their houses look like and where do they live?: The houses tend to be built on stilts, are built from wood or bamboo and are often at an altitude of over 1,000 m. The houses are large as they play host to the extended family at times.
What do they grow?: Dry rice and tea are the two big crops for these people, although some H'tin do grow opium at higher altitudes.

Lawa
Population: 16,000
Subgroups: Lua and Kun
Where did they come from?: Thailand
Where can they be found today?: Mae Hong Son Province, to the east of the Salawin River. The Lawa also claim to be the original settlers of Chiang Mai before they were pushed out by the Thais. There is apparently some archeological evidence which supports this.
What do they wear?: The women wear white cotton shirts with some mild coloured edging, whilst the skirt is around knee length and is a colourful assortment of bright banded colours. You are only likely to come across Lawa in traditional dress in the most remote of areas. The older women are often seen puffing away on a pipe.
What are their beliefs?: They are generally Buddhist but there is a high level of underlying spiritualism thrown in as well. They frequently perform animal sacrifices and it is not unusual to see them wearing cloth bracelets around both the ankles and wrists to warn off evil spirits.
What do their houses look like and where do they live?: They tend to live between 1,000 m and 1,200 m and their houses are built in a straightforward Thai style.
What do they grow?: The Lawa are wet rice cultivators and are seen as being the most environmentally aware (for hilltribes that is).

Khamu
Population: 10,000
Subgroups: None
Where did they come from?: It is believed that they originated in Thailand, moved to Laos and have since moved back into Thailand.
Where can they be found today?: The Khamu are found only in the north of Nan Province.
What do they wear?: The Khamu are rarely seen in their traditional dress. When worn, the women adorn themselves in indigo shirts with red edging, and patterned red sarongs often with gold embroidery. Their head dress consists of an indigo happy hat with red embroidery on the front of it.

What are their beliefs?: Like the Lawa , the Khamu are predominantly Buddhist with an animist underlay. Spirit gates may still be made on occasion, whilst on the other hand, some have become Christian. Khamu shamans are supposedly top of their class and are often invited to participate in Laotian festivals.
What do their houses look like and where do they live?: Their houses tend to be built at around 1,000 m in a Thai style. They try to situate themselves within easy distance of a river.
What do they grow?: Wet rice and tea.

Mlabri
The Mlabri or *Phi Tong Luang* (Spirit of the Yellow Leaves) are one of the stranger tribes in Thailand. They are known as Spirit of the Yellow Leaves due to their nomadic lifestyle. In the past, when the leaves of their shelter turned yellow, they would move on. The Mlabri are the closest to hunter/gatherers you will come across in Thailand. It has only been in the past few years that the Mlabri have began to understand how to use money and, according to many, these people are one of the most 'primitive' in the world.
Population: Under 150.
Subgroups: None
Where did they come from?: Unknown.
Where can they be found today?: In Nan and Phrae Provinces.
What do they wear?: Nothing. It is not unusual for these people to get around in the forest stark naked, although when they work for others they tend to just wear a loincloth.
What are their beliefs?: The Mlabri appear to have no religious beliefs, although one group of them in Phrae Province live under the control of a US Christian missionary Eugene Long. If you want to let him know what you think of his activities with these people, he can be contacted by radio phone from Phrae GPO.
Death: When a Mlabri dies, there is no ceremony. The body is buried quickly and the remainder move on quickly.
What do their houses look like and where do they live?: Their 'houses' are better described as lean to's, often no more than a collection of cut branches over a low wooden floor.
What do they grow?: Nothing. Their culture excludes them from the growing of rice and in the past, they hunted their living in what were once Thailand's rich forests. Now, with the devastation of the forests, the Mlabri men work as labourers mostly for the Hmong. When one of our researchers visited a Mlabri family in Nan Province, the men were virtual slaves to the Hmong, who would work them into the ground and pay them with a bowl of rice.

THAI CULTURAL CHARACTERISTICS
National Dress
Thais really do not have a national dress as they have worn Western clothing for so long. During the Prime Minister Pibun's nationalistic era, all people were forced to wear hats and shoes, because the resemblance to Europeans was highly regarded. The closest thing women get to a national dress is the *phasin* which is a tubular skirt resembling a sarong, patterned with intricate and colourful designs. It is mostly worn with a shirt or blouse.

Thai Family
The Thai family is considered a special unit which extends far beyond the immediate nuclear family to include grandparents, aunts, uncles and cousins. Elder members of this family unit are treated with great respect and are looked after by the younger members of the family. Young children are encouraged to participate in family functions from an early age. In lieu of the social security net which is present in many Western countries, in Thailand it is to the children that the elderly need to look to find this net.

Thai Women

At a glance Thai culture may appear to be patriachial with most senior public positions dominated by men yet behind the scenes, and particularly in their 'traditional domain' of the family home, women exert significant influence. Men are traditionally the bread winners, but it is often the women who hold the reigns regarding family matters and financial transactions.

In times past, Thai women were seen as a possession of men. Whether it was the father arranging marriage, or the husband buying his wife, women and money changing hands seemed to go hand in hand. From early on in Thai history, the women's responsibility to the family was both vital and non negotiable. It took dramatic upheavals overseas to bring about the changes which were needed to impart more freedom unto Thai women. As Thai men were called to war, Thai women were forced to take on more responsibility. This was to include looking after the farms and business transactions which previously had been the domain of the men. The kings of the current dynasty have done more for women than any other, Rama IV eradicated the sale of women, and Rama VI made education compulsory for both males and females. The biggest turning point was when Thailand became a democracy in 1932 and changes to the constitution gave women supposedly equal rights.

Thai women are now experiencing a sense of independence as the wave of change continues to sweep through politics, economics, business and manufacturing. Although women now account for close to 50% of the employed population, as in many Western countries, the women are actively discriminated against, as they are paid less and offered fewer opportunities than their male counterparts. A positive sign is that more women are being employed in previously male dominated industries with many of them rising to influential positions. As in the West, now that many women are working, most are still expected to take on their traditional roles in the home as well, demonstrating that even though the seeds of change have been sown, there is still a long way to go in the furthering of women's rights in Thailand. As Thailand struggles to find a fair balance between its historical culture, Western influence and conservative elements it will be interesting to see what the future has to hold.

Thai Names

One distinct cultural difference between Westerners and the Thais is in the representation of peoples names. In the west where people are introduced by a prefix and surname, such as Mr Smith, the Thais use their first name. Their surnames are only used in official greetings, or to avoid confusion when another person has the same first name. In more social interactions, Thai people are referred to by their nicknames. Every person has a nickname that may either be a shortened version of their first name, or something they were called as a child.

In regard to first names, it would be virtually impossible to count all the possible variations as each child is specially named at birth. Often the names are invented and the special meaning of the name is only known to the mother or individual. Male names generally emphasise masculine characteristics, and female names the soft and beautiful things. Despite this there is quite a large collection of names that can be used for either sex.

The use of surnames in Thailand is only a recent invention, made compulsory by Rama VI in 1913. Surnames became common place when the king decided it would be easier for social interaction if everybody had surnames. He then started by individually naming noble families. Those that never received a royal name had to make up their own, hence every name has a special meaning. The king meticulously ensured that every unrelated family had a different name which to this day still holds true.

Business Practices

It is important to understand the Thai way of doing business if dealing with them on a business basis or even as a customer. The Thais have a more relaxed attitude than most Western nations. Deadlines are not made to necessarily be kept and things will happen eventually. Accepting this, and enjoying the change of pace, will save your sanity so do not let yourself get frustrated.

In Bangkok, meetings should be scheduled before 3.30 pm as Thais like to try and beat the peak hour traffic congestion. Thais also like to make business meetings as sociable as possible, therefore if you end up in a restaurant the person who invited you should pay, otherwise it is the eldest person or the foreigner at the table.

Customs

When visiting any country it is always important to step lightly to not offend cultures that may be different from your own, or to save your own embarrassment. To do this you must be aware of the differences. Below is a list of customs sacred to the Thai people. If you hope to earn the respect of the Thai people, try following these few simple rules and your stay in Thailand may become more than just a holiday - you can experience a way of life.

Many of the Thai customs, values, arts, lifestyle and temperament are based upon religious beliefs which often originate in their Buddhist beliefs. In general, the Thais are a very easy going nation, and exposure to foreigners through tourism has made them more accepting of Western social customs, although this has not always been accepted willingly.

SOCIAL GRACES

Monarchy and Religion

There are two things in Thailand that you never mock or criticise under any circumstance. These are the monarchy and religion. The Thais have such an enormous respect for both, especially the monarchy, and it is actually illegal to make any disrespectful comments towards the ruling family. If caught it can put you behind bars.

Losing Face

Part of the Thai non-confrontational culture is never to lose face, something Westerners find difficult to accomplish. Although the Thais are getting more used to Western forms of expression, you will lose their respect if you ever exhibit strong emotional scenes. A Thai will never show anger, disappointment or disgust to another person except in the most extreme situations.

You should never raise your voice, lose your patience or get angry as it is seen as a weakness and lack of control and this behaviour will get you nowhere. The Thais strive for harmony between all people and things, *Jai yen* is the term that means cool heart and is a term used to describe a person that has the ability to appear calm in every conceivable situation — a compliment hard to beat. For this reason, the Thai smile can mean an assortment of emotions from happiness through to anger.

The Elephant Icon

Ever wondered why elephants are so highly regarded in Thailand? Early in Thai history, elephants were a force to deal with in many aspects of life from their courage in combat, their strength in labour or for carrying supplies and commercial viability in exports to India. They are considered a sign of prosperity and power and hence as a sign of respect, elephants were well looked after. This belief has its origins in Brahmin beliefs.

Albino elephants are the most revered and associated with superstition. If one is discovered the country will prosper under the current ruler, but in the reverse, if one dies, then watch out. If any Thai national discovers an albino elephant they are required by law to offer it to the king before all else. The albino elephant stared on the Thai national flag up until King Rama VI's reign when it was changed to five stripes.

Wars have even been fought over white elephants. Around the mid 1500s, a Burmese king suffered a case of the Jones' and was jealous of the fact that King Chakkraphat of Siam owned seven white elephants and he had none. Since they symbolise and reflect power, he was determined to get his hands on them. He kindly asked for half, but when refused, marched his troops to Ayutthaya for battle. His ulterior motive may have been to extend his territorial domain, but the elephant excuse gives more colour the history books.

Respect

Politeness and signs of respect underline the Thai culture. This is carried out through something called *kreng jai*, a term denoting respect for the status hierarchy within the culture, and a behaviour of humility. This may be observed with Thais by way of them not accepting things on first go. For example, if offering a Thai a drink, they may be thirsty, but want to gain your respect, so will decline the offer a couple of times. So keep up the persistence when wanting to share your cigarettes, food, drinks or anything you have - the Thais may actually want it.

Elders are highly respected within the Thai culture in an undefined class structure. The position in Thai society is unwritten but is generally based upon a variety of factors including family, age, occupation and wealth with each Thai person knowing exactly where they stand. To show respect to an elder or another person is to put the word *phee* before their name. This is mostly used for the immediate family, and to a lessor extent the extended family. *Khun* is a word that any visitor to Thailand will surely hear, and when saying it before someone's name is a polite way to address an equal person. It replaces the Western use of Mr, Mrs or Miss. It is also used as a replacement for the word 'you' in conversation, or to attract someone's attention.

The idea of social superiority is applicable within Thai society. Therefore it is rude to stand over an older person or monk. More to the point, your head must never be on a higher level than a person of greater superiority. You will notice the Thais lowering their head when they pass others simulating a lower status as sometimes it is impractical to literally pass by an elder at a lower height to them.

Greetings

The common and traditional form of greeting in Thailand is a wai. This involves the palms of the hands being pressed together like in prayer, whilst bowing the head slightly. The higher your hands the more respect given, so when waiing a person of higher status or age, your hands should be raised to your nose (the tip of your thumbs should touch the tip of your nose) and only to your chest for someone of equal status. When waiing a monk or Buddha image, your thumbs should touch the section between your eyes. The person of the lower status should always wai first and the superior person can respond by waiing, or just acknowledging the wai by lifting a hand, or just a nod. It is not socially acceptable, or considered foolish or bad luck, if you wai a younger person first. A monk will not wai back to anyone unless they are religious, but instead they will acknowledge it in some way. Due to the larger foreign influence in Thailand the handshake is becoming a more accepted practice with foreigners.

Head and Feet

Never touch a Thai person on the head, even in an act of affection or friendship, as it is considered close to the most offensive act possible. They believe that the head is the most sacred part of the body for a couple of reasons. One is that the head is the home to a person's spirit that looks after their health. If not protected the spirit will leave the body bringing bad luck and health to that person. The other is that it is the closest part of the body to nirvana.

In the same vein, the feet are considered the lowest and dirtiest part of the body, so never point at anyone or anything with the soles of your feet. To keep yourself from doing this accidentally whilst sitting, practice using the mermaid position where your feet are to your side, and your feet facing behind you. You will notice many of the Thais sitting this way.

Even clothes worn by certain parts of the body are categorised in a similar way. Underwear and socks, and to a lesser degree, shorts, pants and skirts should not be hung in a high position, even when hanging up washed clothes. Due to this you will probably notice that many Thais possess two clothes lines. Quite often female clothes are also hung at a low height. This is to prevent any possibility of a male's head being touched by a female's article of clothing which could send his spirit out of his body. Lastly, never step across another person, whether it is a sleeping child, or the outstretched legs of a resting person, for the same reasons as above.

Modest Dress and Behaviour
The clothes you choose to wear in Thailand impact on the way the Thai people will respect you. As a general rule, try not to wear shorts as this is improper attire worn only by children or poor people. In more touristy areas, a slacker dress sense is accepted, and the Thais are used to the barely clad traveller. However, nudity and topless bathing at beaches is a blatant disrespect for the Thai culture. Rules also apply to appropriate attire for places of religious significance. See the religion section for details. Avoid all forms of amorous behaviour except for holding hands in public between males and females, as this is quite offensive.

Yes means No
When speaking to a Thai person in English, it is important to understand how they interpret questions. For instance, if you were to ask, "You are not coming", they will more than likely answer yes, in agreement with you, but really mean "No, I'm not coming".

National Anthem
Whenever the national anthem is played, all Thais will stand, and expect foreigners to stand also out of respect. The national anthem is played daily at 8.00 am and 6.00 pm on every radio and television station. It is not uncommon for whole towns to stop in their tracks for the duration of the anthem. Occasionally you will unexpectedly find it very easy to cross the road, only to realise that you have been oblivious to the fact that all the cars and pedestrians have stopped moving to pay their respects.

When Customs Fade Into Superstition
Here are just a few to chew over.

- No Thai will write their name in red pen, as it signifies death. When a person is awaiting cremation, their name is written in red on the coffin.

- Never wear anything black to a Thai wedding as it is a sign of mourning.

- Thais will not sleep with their head facing west as the setting sun also signifies death.

- Gifts should never have a sharp point, such as a knife, as this will be the beginning of the end of your friendship.

- Thais will try not to have their hair cut on Wednesdays as it will bring bad fortune.

- A single eyebrow signifies dishonesty - get out those pluckers!!!

RELIGIOUS OFFENCE
The following points should be memorised and applied for your entire stay in Thailand.

- It is highly offensive to have your photo taken with anything that resembles a Buddha, and a lighting bolt will probably strike you down if you go climbing over religious relics.

- A woman is never allowed to touch a Buddhist monk or even give anything to a monk. If a women wishes to give something the best method is to place it on the ground in front of or beside the monk.

- The respect for Buddhist monks extends even further. The rear seats on buses are generally reserved for them, so the seats must be vacated at the appropriate times. You should also never stand over a seated monk, as they should always be at a higher elevation than the average person. This is based on the belief that anyone of higher status should always have a higher place than you, and applies to elders as well.

- Buddhist monks should never handle money, so if offering a donation at a temple, or religious sanctuary, pass it over within an envelope, or place it in the donation box that is usually provided for this purpose (this comes from the rule that monks cannot handle gold or silver, but some monks do not regard money as precious metal, so may in fact freely handle it).

• When entering places of religious significance, wear conservative clothes such as long pants or skirt, and do not wear sleeveless shirts. It is compulsory practice to take off your shoes when entering visiting a Buddhist wat or Muslim mosque.

• In the mosques, you should be very aware of what your wearing. Women should have their heads covered, preferably with a scarf, and they need to be well covered with their long sleeved shirt buttoned to the neck. Women are not supposed to enter the mosque during their periods or during a service.

• Thais will always remove their shoes before entering a temple or private house, and Westerners are expected to also. It makes sense to bring a pair of slippers or slip on shoes if you plan on making many visits to these places - it saves having to do up your shoe laces over and over again.

THAI CEREMONIES

Following are just a few of the many ceremonies carried out by Thais and Buddhists. To cover them all would require a book in itself but, due to limited space, hopefully these will give you enough insight into the fascinating idiosyncrasies of the Thai culture.

Temple Donations
When visiting a Buddhist temple, you will notice a box or boxes placed around the entrance for making donations. The resident monks rely on these donations for general living expenses and for the upkeep of the temple. Thais, irrespective of their wealth, will usually donate something whenever they visit a temple. Donations are made this way for ease, as monks can not handle money directly. If passing money directly to a monk, make sure that it is contained within an envelope. Women cannot pass anything directly to a monk and, if necessary, must place the object on the ground in front of the monk.

Waiing to Buddha images
When Thais wai to a Buddha image it is performed with the highest respect. Both men and women kneel in front of the image (men with the bottom of their toes touching the ground and women with their feet flat and the tops of their toes touching the ground). You must bow three times from your hip, each time you reach the ground, the palms of your hands must lay on the ground either side of your head. On the rise bring your palms together positioning your thumbs to the middle of your eyes.

Buddhist ceremonies
Every Buddhist ceremony involves the use of a *sai sin*, a cord carried by a monk and used to keep evil spirits at bay.

Topknot Ceremony
One particularly interesting Thai, or more specifically Brahmin, custom is the cutting of the topknot (*pitti goan juk* in Thai). Next time you see a Thai child with a protruding tuft of hair coming out of an otherwise shaven head, you will know that it is a custom rather than an attempt to regenerate the punk era.

Originally all children shaved their heads and grew topknots until they reached the age of 11 or 13 when it is ceremoniously cut off. Now it is only grown as a cure for a sick child, whether male or female.

Riddle Neung

Nim owns a hotel. Everytime you stop outside Nim's hotel you must pay her $400. Why?

Amulets (*khruang*)

A popular tradition is for babies to have amulets tied around their wrists and, to a lessor degree, ankles and necks by Buddhist monks. In old times amulets consisted of silver or gold charms with Pali characters inscribed upon them (which brought good fortune). These were rolled into tubes and attached by a string. These days the gold and silver charms are missing leaving the string on its own. If the string breaks it is considered bad luck.

In adults, amulets are more popular amongst the males, especially amongst those who work in dangerous industries such as taxi drivers, coal miners and travel writers. Some amulets have been around for centuries and many people believe they retain certain powers. These are highly prized and tend to reach huge prices in the amulet market scene. Specific amulets can even be purchased which offer protection for specific occupations. Like a crystal, amulets should only be handled by the owner. The most popular form of amulet is the religious type (*phra khruang*) which is either a tiny Buddha or image of a highly regarded monk.

Tattoos

Like amulets, traditional tattoos are believed to offer protection and instill strength in the proud owner, especially if they depict religious themes, powerful animals, old Khmer script or mystical images. Monks also give themselves over to the power of the ink but only on higher parts of the body and with religious text or images. Criminals use tattoos to indicate gang membership. The gang's motif, usually a wild beast of some sort covers either their whole chest or back.

Death visits

When a Thai person dies, they will be taken back to the family house or to a temple for a religious rite. Quite often the ceremony will involve four monks chanting consistently for seven days, after which the body is cremated, releasing the spirit from the human body giving eternal freedom. Sometimes the body is kept for up to a year before being cremated, held in an embalmed state at the temple until the family can raise the money. However today it seems like only the wealthy Thais can afford to have the remains of their deceased cremated, the poor folk must stick to burial. The deceased is far from forgotten, as the family practice rituals 7, 50 and then 100 days after the cremation.

Placing the Bones

This is a Thai ceremony where the cremated remains of the head figure of a family is placed into a special vault within temple grounds. The ceremony itself is carried out by nine monks who perform chants and blessings for the deceased.

Making Merit

As part of the Buddhist faith, followers must earn merit to help clear their path to Nirvana. Making merit can happen via a number of ways but the most common is to provide food for monks on their daily alms rounds. Other recognised merit making actions include giving the monks new robes or essential items on special occasions.

Wai Kru Ceremony

Wai Kru is a ceremony designed to pay respect to teachers and is held at every educational institution at the beginning of the school year - something Western teachers would cry for. The ceremony dates back to a time before schools as we know them existed, and students were taught at temples. The ceremony involves the principal and head students saying prayers and offerings flowers and gifts to the teachers, in order to have a successful academic year.

Thai Marriage

Thai weddings are surrounded by many traditions, incorporating both Buddhist and Brahmin customs in the planning and the actual ceremony. Traditionally the ceremony is carried out over a few days with the grooms family paying for the event. The groom also has to give the bride's mother a dowry, traditionally of gold and money, called *nguan nom* (mother's milk money). Monks will bless everything associated with the wedding through chanting and prayers and keep away evil spirits using the *sai sin* cord. The wedding comes with a couple of varieties of water blessing. One form is by the monk who blesses the couple with a sprinkling of holy water. Later the couple are blessed by their guests with an old Brahim custom of having water poured over their hands. They also have chalk symbols marked on their foreheads and wear halo like ribbons on their heads.

Weddings are generally held during even numbered months of the lunar calendar for the simple reason that a multiple of two signifies the joining of two people. This is despite the fact that even numbers are generally thought of as bad luck. However the ninth month is preferred over the tenth or twelth for its association with prosperity and good health.

Spirit House
Virtually every Thai building has a special shrine placed outside, looking something like an extravagant and ornate bird house. This custom is not based on Buddhism, but derived from ancestor worship and has permeated virtually every Thai household, regardless of religious ties. This shrine is said to house the spirit of the dwelling, and to keep good fortune coming their way as long as the daily offerings of food, flowers and incense continue.

Traditional Medicine
Traditional medicine from both Thailand and China with influences from India, is a popular form of treatment for many ailments within the kingdom. If you need to stock up on some natural remedies, or just want to have a look, go for a wander around the Chinese quarter of Bangkok or any town for that matter. The herbal shops are hard to miss, just look for the obscure and dried animals displayed in various jars and containers.

Periods of Thai Art			
Period	Date	Location	Influences
Dvaravati	7th - 11th C	Central Thailand (Nakhon Pathom, U-thong)	Indian and Mon
Khmer/Lopburi	7th - 14th C	Northeast and Central Thailand (Phimai, Phanom Rung, Lopburi)	Khmer, Pala and local
Srivijaya	8th - 13th C	South Thailand (Chaiya, Nakhon Si Thammerat)	Indian, then Mon then Khmer
Chiang Saen (Lan Na)	13th - 18th C	North Thailand (Chiang Mai, Lampang, Lamphun)	Burmese, Lao and local styles
Sukhothai	13th - 14th C	Central/North Thailand (Sukhothai, Si Satchanalai, Phitsanulok, Kamphaeng Phet)	Local styles
Ayutthaya	1351 - 1767	Central Thailand (Ayutthaya)	Khmer then Ayutthayian
Thonburi	1767 - 1782	Central Thailand (Thonburi)	Local styles
Bangkok	1782 -	Central Thailand (Bangkok)	European

THAI ARTS

Buddhism has been the most influential force upon Thai arts over history. This, combined with the perishable materials used in past centuries, have not done the preservation of historical pieces any favours. There are not many 'famous' artists in Thai history due to the fact that Buddhism preaches anonymity, and individuals only started to be recognised once the Bangkok period began. Buddhism does not place importance in preserving ruins or honouring individuals, hence the disrepair of many of Thailand's ancient shrines, temples and buildings. Over time, the stones used in old temples have been reused to build more modern structures. It was not until European influence on Thailand began in the second half of the 1800s that preservation became practiced. King Mongkut (Rama IV) was the first king to show an interest in archaeology, and the first museum for the public was built in 1874. However it was not until the 1920s that official departments were established to research Thailand's archfeological history.

Sculpture

The most popular image in Thailand is the Buddha. Every wat or shrine abounds in them and every house is also bound to display a few. In Theravada Buddhism the statues are not created to be idolised, but rather as a reminder of the great teachings of Buddha. There are four basic poses in which the Buddha is depicted; standing (teaching), walking (leading), sitting (meditating) and reclining (death symbolising the passing of Buddha to Nirvana). The different hand positions (mudra) indicate additional variations and meanings to each of the four basic stances. The ancient set of rules that every Buddha pose must abide by also cover other things such as the direction of the hair and fall of the robe.

Bhumisparsa (touching the earth) is when Buddha has his left hand in his lap and the right hand over his knee. This is the position is also known as *Maravijaya* (victory over Mara or victory over Satan). This is taken from the most honoured part of Buddha's life when he was meditating under the Banyan tree and vowed to not budge until he attained enlightenment. In an effort to deter him, Satan sent all manner of distractions including floods, tempests and young floosies but Buddha touched the earth to call nature to witness his resolve. *Dhyana* is the pure meditation pose where both hands are in Buddhas lap and *Vitarka* (one hand) or *Dhammachaka* (two hands) means the turning of the karma wheel and represents the first Buddhist teaching. This pose is when either one or two hands have the index finger and thumb joined to form a circle.

The most common walking and standing stance is that of *Abhaya* (dispelling fear) where Buddha has either one or both hands extended in front of his body with the palms facing outwards. This position is one in which he offers protection to his followers. *Vara* (blessing or giving charity) is when one hand is extending downwards with the palm facing forward. *Buddha calling for rain* is when both arms are stiffly pointing downwards on either side of the body with the palms inward.

Sculptures are easily dated to the relevant period of its creation based on the style and decorations on the image. The Thais started to digress from Khmer style sculpture during the Sukhothai Period with more flowing artwork including rounded eye brows and nose, fatter lips and pointed chin. It was not until the Ayutthaya Period that Siamese art really stood out on its own. Where the Khmers worked in stone, the Thais preferred bronze, stucco and clay (especially since bricks were used instead of stone in constructions). Sculpture of things other than Buddhas became stylised as the Thais increased their use of moulds, essentially putting an end to individual expression. Apart from Buddha images, bronze casting occasionally produced the odd dragon or bell.

Traditional Painting

Ancient paintings found in Thailand are generally frescoes depicting the life of Buddha. Many of these were destroyed during the sacking of Thai cities in wars with Burma and other neighbouring countries. During the 15th Century, painting took on a more stylized form resulting in little individual expression. Artists did not create for the pure visual enjoyment, but rather for a purpose, and individuality was shown mainly through technical ability. Later the main topics of paintings were of ceremonies or historical events used for decorating the houses of the elite or royal palaces.

Other Arts and Crafts

Over time the Thai craftsmen have become skilled at a number of other crafts. Thais became quite proficient at making **jewellery** with precious metals and stones which were much favoured by European traders. **Wood carving** never gathered a huge following and was mostly used in decorating doors and pillars of buildings although some astounding wooden carvings can be seen in Chatuchak Weekend Market in Bangkok. The decorations mainly consist of floral arrangements and religious characters. **Ceramics** is another area where the Thais dabbled. The style and technique was brought to Thailand by the Chinese, however Thai designs permeated the ceramic making over time. By the Bangkok Period, imitations had inundated the market making the classification of ceramics difficult. **Weaving** was once a popular past time mainly in the north of the country. The costumes worn in the court of the royals were particularly colourful with intertwined silver and gold thread. Jim Thompson revived the silk industry after WWII. Other crafts include **lacquerware** (especially in the north), **mat weaving** and **basket making**.

    Batik is also widely available throughout Thailand and it is often the traveller's choice in clothing. If a traveller does not own a batik article of clothing when arriving in Thailand, they are more than likely to be swathed in it when they leave. Batik or rather bateh is a Javanese term referring to the combination of a style of dyed cloth and the technique associated with it.

Architecture

Notable Thai architecture can be divided into either ancient ruins, temples or domestic buildings. As for the ancient ruins, the earliest influences were of Khmer and Indian origin, however there was a definite progression to more local Thai styles from the time of the Sukhothai and Lopburi kingdoms. Laterite was often used for building in this time and the respective decorations were carved out of stone. Laterite is a porous stone which was popular with the Khmers. Laterite is actually a thick red soil when excavated making the soft blocks easy to carve. When the substance is exposed to the elements it sets into a hardy stone. In more recent ancient ruins, such as that of Ayutthaya, laterite was not as abundant and decorations and adornments were made of less durable materials.

    Ancient ruins occassionally possess similar characteristics. The lintel is an ornate stone placed above a doorway. Prasat and Prasada refers to an Indian influenced building for a king or god. Stucco is a heavy plaster that was easy to mould often covering walls.

    Many of Thailand's original domestic architectural structures no longer exist simply because they were made out of wood. Today the traditional wooden architecture is rarely seen, as easier methods of construction and material have become available. The design was based more on beliefs and religion than practicality. The carpenters job was certainly cut out for them as there were no right angles, not even in the windows which have non parallel sides. The north and central design differ in the slant of the walls. In the north, the walls slant outwards, whereas in the south they slant in. Also in the north the house orientation is north/south as a protective stance against the harmful winds. Teak was used in the construction due to its past abundance in the north of Thailand. The roof was often adorned with intricate carvings for decoration. The one practical part of the buildings is that they were made for moving with most of it made in prefabricated style. The walls were made of both vertical and horizontal planks which slid together with ease and only wooden pegs were used to keep it together.

Literature and Poetry

The Ayutthaya Period is often referred to as the Golden Age of literature, and one of the most reknowned pieces of literature from this time is *phra law*, a story similar to Romeo and Juliet, however most written works from this time were of religious content. Unfortunately for Thai culture, many works were destroyed and forgotten after the Burmese invasions of Thailand. Since then various kings have tried to rekindle the art of poetry and literature especially during the Bangkok period. Sunthon Phu was a well known writer in the early 1800s and one of his most famous pieces is *Khun Chang, Khun Phen* which is set during the Ayutthaya Period and tells of the lives of two men.

Ramakien

The Ramakien is an ancient epic story told through classical Thai dance. The tale originated in India (as the Ramayana) and there are many versions of it throughout Asia. The Thais have been telling this tale since before the 13th Century, but the most common version was written by King Taksin around 1785. It was later translated into classical Thai verse, and episodes of the Ramakien are still taught in Thai school, as it beautifully portrays much of the Thai culture.

In total the Ramakien has 138 episodes which are divided into 3 sections. In summary the story tells the tale of Rama and his love for his wife Sida who was also from a royal family. It begins at Rama's birth during the Ayutthaya period. Rama and Sida are married but shortly afterwards Sida is abducted by Totsakan a ten headed demon who takes her to a place called Longka. Rama goes to Sida's rescue and, after a long battle, defeats the demon, taking his wife back to the throne of the almighty Thai Kingdom.

Dance and Theatre

Traditional Thai dances are very highly regarded and are basically a combination of opera, drama and classic dance. The most famous Thai dance is the **khon** which originated in India and where the performers are masked, wear jewelled costumes and spiral crowns, with four specific characters including a male, female, monkey and demon. In this form of dance the script of the dancer, or more accurately actor, are voiced by singers in the orchestra. The dance has definite movements, many of which are interpreted by the audience who are already familiar with their meaning. Quite often the khon dance is based on the Ramakien. The traditional khon dance is rarely performed today, but can occasionally be seen at the National Theatre or at a restaurant catering to tourists.

Other similar traditional dances are the **lakhon** and **likay**. These dances are similar to the Khon, but do not use masks and the actors recite lines themselves. Put simply, a lakhon is a melodramatic play, whereas a likay is a historical romance incorporating comedy. The **fawn lep** is another form of Thai dance, which originated in Northern Thailand, where the female dancers wears long nails on their fingers.

Nang yai, also known as shadow plays, are large puppet like characters that are cut out of leather (often over 2 m high). The puppets are attached to a pole or two and are backlit onto a screen which is placed in between them and the audience. Puppeteers will move the characters so their shadows relate the relevant tale. Occasionally the nang yai directly perform to the audience and are intricately decorated with paints. The themes for the plays are generally classical stories or the Ramakien. Similar, but smaller, are the **nang thalung**. These puppets are slightly more complex often with an additional moving arm. The nang thalung originated in Indonesia and were developed to ward off evil spirits.

Music

Traditional Thai music is a combination of the classical Thai scale (an octave of seven full notes), and the Western scale which was introduced about 160 years ago. Thai instruments were influenced by Indian music in the Sukhothai Period, but the scale was developed independently. Traditional music is mostly played in conjunction with dance and theatre.

Orchestras consist of a variety of instruments including different sized wooden xylophones (*ranad*), a brass disc xylophone (*kong wong yai*), flutes (*phi nai*), drums, gongs and cymbals.

SPORT

Traditional sports are highly regarded in Thailand. Gambling always tends to be a part of sport which no doubt had a hand in the development of more obscure sports such as fish fights, cock fights and even goat fights in some areas. More recently, Western influence has introduced the popular sports of golf, tennis, bowling and snooker.

Kick Boxing (Muay Thai)

This is the national sport of Thailand and attracts large numbers of spectators country wide. Kick boxing actually originated from history when close contact fighting was a common form of battle strategy. In 1560 King Naresuan included it in Thailand's military training. It became the national sport after King Naresuan was captured by the Burmese. He was offered his freedom if he could beat Burma's best kick boxers which he did. Since then *muay thai* has spread from a weapon to a popular sport practised by a wide range of Thai people. Official boxing matches must receive written permission from the government.

Kick boxing allows participants to use gloved fists as well as their feet, elbows, knees, thighs and shoulders. Fighters gain points for each blow, and there are no restrictions in where you can hit. At the beginning of the match boxers partake in a prayer ritual whilst wearing a *mongkol* (a form of headband) to show respect, and eerie (some would say irritating) music is played to instigate the fighting. Each of the five rounds lasts for three minutes with two minute intervals. It is possible to view a match of *muay thai* at many festivals or in most provinces which have a boxing stadium. However two of the best known venues for fights in Bangkok are the Ratchadamnoen and Lumpini Stadiums.

Kite Fighting

This is an ancient sport still practised today. The sport has a huge following and has been patronised by the kings of Thailand for centuries. The main contest is held between March and April at Sanam Luang in Bangkok. Another popular place to observe this sport is at Bangkok's Phra Mane Ground. Some of the kites are very large requiring a number of people to fly them and can come in hundreds of varieties, in any form or colour. The kites are either males *chulas* or female *pukpaos*. The male kites come in the minimum size of five feet long, with five points, while the female is smaller reaching only two and a half feet long, but sporting a tail. The males and females are opponents and, using skilled techniques, the kite flyers aim to force the opposition's kite to land in their half of a marked field. Skilled techniques can mean trying to snag your opponents line in yours or ramming them to cause damage to the frame or cover.

Takraw

This game has a few variations and uses a *takraw* (a ball smaller than a volleyball) made of rattan. Net takraw is similar to volleyball, the players cannot use their hands but are allowed to utilise their head, feet, knees, elbows or any part of their body to hit the ball over the net without it touching the ground. Players demonstrate very difficult manoeuvres in an effort to show their skill and please the crowd. This version of the sport is an official sport at the SEA Games in Asia. Net Takraw can be seen in Bangkok at the National Stadium.

Another popular version of this sport in Thailand is *Hoop Takraw*. This involves a team of no less than six people who stand in a circle aiming to hit the takraw through the numerous hoops suspended above the circle for points. This style can be seen at Sanam Luang between February and April. Tossing Takraw involves either an individual or team of players keeping the ball off the ground for as long as possible, similar to the popular game of hacky sac in North America.

Fish Fighting
Fish fighting is a native sport of Thailand, although illegal within Bangkok, which can still be witnessed at the fringe of the city and in some rural areas. There are two types of Thai fighting fish, both of which exhibit brilliant colours and illuminate when the fish is angry, fanning their gills and fins, despite their relative small size, of around 5 cm long and 1 cm wide. The most aggressive fish, the *lukmoh*, is rarely found in its natural habitat of ponds and marshes, so is bred by professional breeders. The second species, the *likpah*, is not as rare, but cannot match up to the *lukmoh* in long battles. Only the male fish partake in the fighting, having more presence with more vibrant colours and larger fins and tails than the females.

The fish fight is to the death, often leaving the battle scene full of chewed fins, tails, scales and gills. The fish seem to have an innate aggressive nature, and delicately manoeuvre for position before attacking their opponent with sharp teeth. Observers bet on the fishes form before they are placed into the ring, and during the brutal battle

CALENDAR

Lunar Calendar
For traditional and religious purposes the lunar calendar is used within Thailand, however since Thailand has become affiliated with the West, for practical reasons, has adopted the Western calendar. In Thailand, the year may be referred to by one of two dating methods, either according to the Buddhist Era (BE) or the Christian Era (CE). The BE started 543 years before the BC, hence, 1996 AD is equivalent to BE 2539. Both references are commonly used and accepted within business and daily practices.

The lunar calendar originated in China and is based upon a 12 year cycle. Each year is affiliated with a different animal; Rat (Chuat), Ox (Chalu), Tiger (Kahn), Rabbit (Toh), Dragon (Marong), Snake (Maseng), Horse (Mamia), Ram (Mamae), Monkey (Wok), Rooster (Raga), Dog (Jor), Pig (Goon). Apart from this, each year also aligns to one of the five elements - earth, water, wood, metal, and fire.

FESTIVALS AND PUBLIC HOLIDAYS

National Public Holidays
* Date determined by lunar cycle

New Years Day	1 January
Makha Bucha Day (Full Moon Day)	* (March)
Chakri Day	6 April
Songkran Festival (Thai New Year)	12-14 April
National Labour Day	1 May
Coronation Day	5 May
Ploughing Ceremony	* (May)
Visakha Bucha Day (Full Moon Day)	* (May)
Asalha Bucha Day (Full Moon Day)	* (July)
Khao Phansa Day/Buddhist Lent Day	* (July)
H.M. the Queen's Birthday	12 August
Chulalongkorn Day	23 October
H.M. the King's Birthday	5 December
Constitution Day	10 December
New Years Eve	31 December

The fun loving and religious people of Thailand celebrate numerous festivals throughout the year. Many of these are localised, only celebrated within regional areas or towns in honour of local legends or past events. Festivals in Thailand take on a similar feel, whether they be in the north or south. They are often celebrated with bright colours, processions, markets and usually come with religious overtones. Inevitably, they often involve water as well.

In the south many of the local festivals are held around October for three practical reasons. Firstly, at this time the canals and rivers are full and in the past allowed easy access to neighbouring towns before modern infrastructure and roads were built. Secondly, the rice fields are not yet ready to harvest so the people have some spare time, and thirdly it is the end of the traditional three month period when Buddhist monks participate in meditation and study (Buddhist Lent). Some of the more popular and nationally celebrated festivals are as follows:

Songkran

Songkran is the lunar and traditional new year of Thailand celebrated between 12 and 14 April. For many Thais it is a time to pray for health and prosperity, however the most significant image of this festival is water. Buddha images are bathed, elders are shown respect through water ceremonies and, for the more fun loving Thais, Songkran is the perfect excuse for a water fight with everyone and anyone. The festivals held in the north of the country are generally more enthusiastic than the south. For the traveller, this means that often you are one of the main targets, especially if you have a backpack on as you are an easy target. So do not be offended if you get attacked by giggling children or adults throwing water bombs.

Loi Krathong

The festival of Loi Krathong is one of Thailand's most celebrated, taking place on the day of the full moon during the twelfth lunar month, between the end of October and through most of November. The festival runs parallel to the common floods that span the kingdom during this time. It is in honour of Mae Kong Ka (the goddess of water) for providing water, essential in Thai life whether for work in the fields, transport and simply drinking. This nation wide festival can be recognised by the specially produced *krathongs* that are religiously released on rivers, canals and waterways. The krathongs are small lotus blossom boats made out of banana leaves representing a lotus flower and each contains a small candle.

The modern day krathong was first introduced by a woman called Nang Nopamas, a daughter of a well respected priest during the Sukhothai Period. She designed the krathong based on her Brahmin heritage and presented it to the king during an early Loi Krathong celebration. Now, prior to the festival, the markets and shops are inundated with krathongs for everybody to purchase and celebrate Loi Krathong at their leisure.

If in Bangkok for this festival, make a special effort to visit the canals around the Chulalongkorn University for a spectacular view of the university procession. If not you can always purchase your own Krathong and release it onto one of Thailand's many waterways with the hope of having your sins forgiven and good luck bestowed upon you for the next year.

Monarch's Birthdays

The great respect and love for the monarchy by the Thai people is only accentuated through the public holidays in honour of their birthdays. The Queen's birthday represents a national holiday on 12 August, and the King's birthday is on 5 December. Many of the streets and government buildings in both Bangkok (especially around the Grand Palace) and throughout the country are decorated with banners and lights to celebrate this auspicious occasion.

Others

Makha Bucha Day celebrates the time when 1,250 of Buddhas followers spontaneously met. *Chakri Day* honours Rama I, the founder of the Chakri Dynasty. *Visakha Pucha Day* is a festival in honour of Buddha, his life, death and enlightenment whilst *Asalha Pucha Day* is more specific and commemorates Buddha's first teaching.

RELIGION AND PHILOSOPHY

Approximately 95% of Thais practice Buddhism, however they have also incorporated beliefs and rituals from other religions such as Brahmanism from Hinduism. The next most prominent religious group is Islam with a following of 3.8% of the population. The other religious beliefs in Thailand include Christian, Hinduism, and Animism which is adhered to by the majority of the hilltribes.

Buddhism

With such a large proportion of Thais being of the Buddhist faith, it is no wonder that their culture is virtually a reflection of this religion. Almost every significant act involves some kind of ceremony. The majority of Buddhists in Thailand are of the Theravada strain due to the outlawing of the Mahayana belief many centuries ago by royalty.

Buddhism first appeared in Thailand around 300BC when King Asoka from India, sent two missionaries, Sona and Uttara, to spread the word. The inhabitants of the land at the time were the indigenous Mons who embellished themselves in the religion, but they were also open to other religious influences and gods such as Brahma, Indra, Ganesh and Vishnu. The Khmers who dominated the land around the 11th to 13th Centuries followed Mahayana Buddhism, hence, when the Thais migrated south from China during this time, they encountered both forms, Mahayana as well as Theravada from both the Mons and Khmers.

Theravada is based on the pure teachings of Buddha which aims to restrain from all forms of desire leading you closer to Nirvana (a state of bliss) and personal enlightenment. Theravada Buddhism is mainly practiced in a large part of Southeast Asia including Thailand, Burma, Laos and Cambodia. The other form of Buddhism is Mahayana, whose followers also believe in Buddha's teachings but they have been revised and their belief praises religious idols additional to Buddha. In Mahayana Buddhism the aim is to personally reach the state of enlightenment, but then to try and lead others down the right path. The Mahayana strain eventually developed to a stage where monks were able to have greater community involvement rather than locking themselves away to reach their spiritual goals. Today, Mahayana Buddhism has based itself in Vietnam, China and Japan.

Both Buddhist strains practice the belief in reincarnation. Influenced by the laws of karma, people reincarnate, either progressing or regressing into human or animal forms depending on their previous life and the deeds they performed, with the ultimate goal being Nirvana itself.

There are no formal services in Buddhism. Instead believers practice personal examination and experience. They visit Buddhist temples to create conditions appropriate for self improvement. Every time a Buddhist enters a pagoda it is expected that they light and burn incense and pay their respects to Buddha. If you are non-Buddhist it would not hurt to also light incense. Note, however, that whenever you light incense it is always three or more.

Over the years, Thais have incorporated worship of other deities, gods and ancestors into their life as an addition to Buddhism. One such deity is Brahma, the god of the heavens - one of the most highly respected gods. The royals welcomed some Brahmin beliefs mainly since Buddhism preaches absolute freedom, and Brahmanism is quite happy with the idea of one man rule. So both religions worked side by side or rather in conjunction with each other for centuries. As a result, Brahmin rituals are still associated with religious ceremonies. As the Brahmin beliefs permeate royalty, animistic beliefs are commonly followed with the mass of the population. Other gods that are glorified include Vishnu and Indra. The deities are prayed to usually for the sole purpose of wanting a wish or favour granted through prayers and offerings.

Monks

Thai males are encouraged to become ordained as a monk at some stage in their life. The duration of their stay is purely up to the individual or their family, but can range from three months to life. In the past it was compulsory, but now it is personal choice, however most comply. This religious devotion gives the monk's parents credit for the years of relentless giving during the monks childhood and upbringing. Men that enter under 20 years of age are considered novices and cannot become fully fledged members until they are over this age and as long as they have no criminal tendancies. Many men choose to enter the monkhood during the Buddhist lent, Phansa. During the Buddhist lent, which last three months, monks are forbidden to join or leave the monkhood. They are also not allowed to sleep anywhere except their own resident temple. The lent ends in October on the full moon of the 11th lunar month.

Monks must shave their heads, give up all material possessions, wear the easily recognisable plain saffron robes and they live off the generosity of Buddhist followers. However, on a few occasions the modern monk has been spotted wearing a set of headphones or other modern wonders. The two types of monks in Thailand, the Mahayana and the Theravada, wear slightly different coloured robes, one orange and the other a reddy-brown. Their robes must be made up of scraps of material that are sewed together in a particular way. If a monk was to receive a complete piece of material, it must then be cut up into smaller pieces and sown back together. Monks are governed by many other rules for living a humble life including only eating twice a day (not after noon) but some only eat once a day, they cannot indulge in alcohol or entertainment, they cannot lie, have sexual intercourse, kill or steal. Followers of Buddhism make merit, in the hope of moving one step closer to Nirvana, by providing monks with everything they need including medicines, robes and so on and provide them with alms (food) at dawn every day.

Monks and their blessings are part of every occasion in Thailand including weddings, funerals, house warming and even buying new and expensive items. Monks are called *phra*, which is a term given to royalty or sacred things or people.

Nuns

Women are not permitted to become monks, so those that feel the strong call to spirituality become nuns. Nuns are not officially recognised within the religion but are regarded more as devout laypeople. They wear white robes, shave their heads, live on monastery grounds in very simple houses, basically living a very humble life. Nuns are not presented with alms by followers of the religion.

Parts of a Wat

A *wat* is simply a Buddhist monastery or temple. Monks live in the wat compound but generally are seen as the carers, as the wat belongs to the community. Hence, you can generally determine the communities wealth by how large, well kept and adorned the wats are. Thailand has over 30,000 wats spread throughout the country and are categorised depending on their use. The majority are fairly common community wats and the most revered are the royal wats of which there are around 190 in Thailand. Royal wats can be recognised by their name which, depending on their English translation, start with Racha, Rat or Raja.

Most wats are made in the same fairly standard layout, however some may also have regional or historical influences evident. Each wat has both an outer and inner wall, the former simply identifies the wat's grounds, and the latter, which often comes in the form of a gallery, surrounds the wat's most important buildings. The gallery is often enclosed and is often used for meditation, the perfect spot to hold a few more Buddha images. In between these walls, on the southern side of the compound, are the monks living quarters called **kutis** and, in large wats, the aministration and school buildings. Other buildings you may come accross include libraries (haw trai) containing Buddhist scriptures, rest pavilions (sala), study halls (sala kan parian) which are open sided buildings, a mondop which is a structure that houses important religious objects such as a Buddhas footprint, a bell tower (haw rakhang) and drum pavillion (haw kong).

Within the inner wall are a number of standard elements including the *bot, wiharn, chedis* and *prangs*. The **bot** (otherwise known as ordination hall or ubosoth) is the prayer hall and the most sacred part of a monastery. Entrance to the bot is quite often restricted to monks who use the bot for daily meditation and chants. The bot is usually a fairly large rectangular building with a sloping roof made of coloured tiles. Inside, facing the entrance at the end of the hall, will always be a large Buddha image, with his smaller counterparts, Sariputta and Moggallana statues beside him. The internal walls are often decorated with murals and the wooden doors are also often highly decorated with relief sculpture. The most sacred bot in Thailand is Wat Phra Kaew in Bangkok. The bot, as with the wiharn, is often placed in a position facing water, and quite often when there is not a natural source a pond is created. You will always be able to recognise a bot as it is surrounded by eight **bai semas** placed around its external perimeter. These are slabs of stone with an affinity to the shape of a leaf. The bai sema is always a give away to the wats age as its decorative attributes co-ordinate with periodical designs.

Also located inside the inner wall is the **wiharn** (assembly hall). Smaller wats may not contain a wiharn and larger wats may have more than one, but either way the wiharn looks very similar to the bot, recognisable by the lack of bai semas around its perimeter. The wiharn is one of the mosts widely used buildings and usually contains a collection of Buddha images.

A **chedi** (also called stupa) is basically a rounded tower which is very wide at the base and tapers off to a point, most are small reaching only a few metres high and can be found near the bot. Chedis traditionally carry the remains of either monks affiliated with the wat, dedicated followers or royalty. Some chedis claim to hold remains of the enlightened Buddha himself and those that do (which seem to be in almost every Thai town) hold the name Wat Mahathat, translated as 'the monastery of the great relic'. The largest chedi in Thailand is in Nakhon Pathom. A **prang** is simply a Khmer style chedi which are not as common as the average chedi. The most spectacular example in Thailand is Wat Arun in Bangkok.

Brahmanism and Hinduism

Certain Brahmin rituals and beliefs were assimilated into Thai life (in conjunction with Buddhism) so their kings could function, and rituals performed without breaking any Buddhist religious rules. Brahmanism, which is a part of Hindu rituals, was only open to a selected few. It was introduced by the Khmers who followed a mixture of Hindu and Mayahana Buddhism. Other Hindu deities absorbed into Thai beliefs include Indra. Hindu beliefs were restricted to royalty and the administrators of Siam.

These days Brahman rituals are part of many peoples lives. They exist in royal ceremonies, most festivals (except religious ones) and even the superstition associated with albino elephants has its origins in Brahmanism. The image of Brahma is a four headed god who is believed to have created the world.

Islam

The majority of the Muslim population lies in the far south of Thailand, mainly along the four most southern provinces that border with Malaysia, although speckles of the religion appear in other parts of the country such as some of the northern Shan and Chinese. Islam was introduced to Southeast Asia, and consequently parts of Thailand, by the Indian and Arab traders that visited these shores in earlier dynasties.

Christian

Christianity arrived on the shores of Thailand mainly through European missionaries in the 17th Century then again in the 19th Century when they were permitted to return again but they have never been overly successful converting the faithful Buddhist population. Many of the Karen hilltribe have been converted into Christianity by roving missionaries. Despite their small numbers, Christians have had a reasonable impact on Thai life, especially the schools which were always considered with high regard. You may see the odd cathedral during your travels.

Animism and Pantheism

Animisim and pantheism in varying degrees is adhered to by the various hilltribes populations. Even tribes that have a predominant Christian or Buddhist following, such as the Karen, manage to carry a number of animist and pantheist beliefs. Followers of animism maintain harmony with nature and believe that all things in nature such as clouds, trees, rivers and even stones possess souls and respect them accordingly. Pantheism is the belief that God is present in all things and is therefore very similar to Animism.

FOOD

Thai food is very distinct from that of the food of its neighbouring countries with the main influences coming from China and India, with other influences from Malaysia and even the Portuguese.

Thai dishes are rice based usually consisting of a soup, curry, side dishes and followed by dessert. Thai food is very distinctive, commonly using spices such as coriander, garlic, lemongrass, turmeric, pepper, pandanus, sweet basil, ginger, basil, vinegar and cardamun. A Thai dish would not be a Thai dish without a healthy portion of chilli, the hottest type is *phrik lueng*, in a deceiving yellow-orange colour. Meals are accompanied by shrimp paste, fish sauce (salt substitute), tamarind sauce, and often with coconut milk.

Dessert, and also breakfast, often consists of fresh fruit in Thailand due to the plentiful supply of succulent tropical fruits such as durians, rose apples (*com phu*), papayas (*malako*), longans (*lamyai*), guavas (*farang*), jackfruit (*khanun*), sapodilla (*lamut*), lychee (*linchi*) mangos, pineapples, coconuts (*maphrao* -young coconut), oranges and bananas (*kluai*). Other ingredients used in Thai sweets include eggs, mung beans, lotus seeds, cassava roots and rice flour. Sweets will often be impregnated with a pleasant fragrance for an aromatic appeal.

Besides the basic Thai cuisine, there are large regional variances. Basically the food differences can be divided into four specific tastes: the south is generally very hot, the north and northeast very spicy. In the south and central Thailand, normal rice is served, whilst in the north and northeast, sticky rice is a common accompaniment.

Street fare is quite varied, tasty, usually clean and cheap. If particularly worried about eating street food, make sure it is well cooked and is still hot. Better still, try and watch them cook it. Restaurant food is very good, often offering a wide choice of dishes, but a little more expensive than that sold on the street. Guesthouse food can range from good to quite often, very poor. Thai food in guesthouses is often made to the farang taste, resulting in poor imitations at a higher price than on the street.

The Price of Food

Below is an idea of what a typical single dish Thai meal (including rice) and a drink, in a street stall or cafe, will cost you around Thailand.

	Small Town	Medium Town	Large Town
Meal	10B - 15B	15B - 20B	20B - 35B
Soft drink	5B - 6B	7B - 10B	10B - 15B

Convenience stores, such as 7-eleven, are the cheapest places for water at 3B (but man cannot live on water alone!!).

Popular Dishes

Following are a few common Thai dishes that you can order when eating in restaurants that do not supply an English menu.

Khao Pat (Fried Rice) - Even a simple dish like this is good in Thailand. Fried rice comes with onions, pieces of vegetables and the choice of either chicken, pork, shrimp, squid and so on, according to your taste. Rarely very good in guesthouses, you will find this in just about any eating spot in Thailand. Try it with a Khai Dao (fried egg on top). Expect to pay 15B to 20B in a cafe or street stall, 30B to 35B in a restaurant or guesthouse.

Khao Niaw (pron. Neow) (Sticky Rice) - A Northeastern Thai specialty, it is a sweet in its own right. Sticky rice is eaten with your fingers and rolled into small balls to dip in sauces. You will also see it cooked in pieces of bamboo or banana leaves mixed with coconut milk, sugar, nuts or beans or other goodies. A large variety of deserts are made from sticky rice. It usually costs 5B to 10B.

Khao Naa Kai/Pet/Muu (Rice with Chicken/Duck/Pork) - Common staple dish found just about anywhere in Thailand. Consists of a plate of rice with slices of meat, a few bits of greenery and a spoon of sauce over the top. Generally comes with a bowl of clear soup. The pork will be either pork leg or red pork (muu daeng) the latter comes with a hard boiled egg. It is not spicy. Anywhere you see a duck or chicken hanging up or pig's legs stewing will sell you this for 15B to 20B including the soup. It is sold in food stands and cafes.

Phat Ka-Phrao Muu/Kai (Fried Basil with Pork/Chicken) - Generally cooked with minced pork but occasionally chicken, this is another staple Thai dish. Northern in origin but commonly found from Mae Hong Son all the way to the Malaysian border. Minced meat is fried with Chinese basil, onions and chillies in a tangy sauce. It is spicy and generally served sai khao (over rice). It costs 15B to 20B in markets or 30B to 40B in restaurants. Many guesthouses offer a variation on this without the chillies and veggies mixed in with the meat for 40B to 50B.

Tom Yam Kung/Kai (Spicy Lemmongrass Soup with Shrimp/Chicken) - A Thai culinary classic found in Asian restaurants all over the world. The soup contains ginger, chillies, mushrooms, lemongrass and so on and may be very spicy. Many guesthouses do reasonable versions of this without the chillies. Some smaller cafes serve it as do all restaurants. Prices depend on size at 40B to 50B up to 80B.

Tom Khao Kai (Chicken Coconut Soup) - This is a popular dish with farangs basically similar to tom yam but milder and creamier, not as common though. A restaurant dish costs 50B to 80B.

Khao Tom (Rice Soup) - Generally a plain rice soup with a few herbs floating in it. It is served with side dishes of pork slices, ginger, peanuts and dried shrimps for example which you add to taste. Filling and cheap, it is a popular late night or breakfast food. Thais recommend it for hangovers. It costs around 15B and some guesthouses do variations or will do if asked.

Laap (Spicy Meat Salad) - Usually made with pork but sometimes chicken. Minced meat is made with chillies, corriander, lemon juice and onions and served with fresh raw veggies. Originally a Northeastern dish, it is now a standard in Thai restaurants and drinking spots throughout the country. Some markets and street stalls make this spicy dish as do all restaurants and occasional guesthouses. Expect to pay 30B to 60B.

Kaeng Keow Waan (Green Curry) - This is another popular dish with Thais and farangs alike. It is a creamy coconut curry with a distinct green colour (from the crushed herbs and chillies) usually with chicken, served in Thai restaurants. It is also very common in guesthouses where they will add veggies and any meat you want to it. It is spicy and the many guest-house variations are good. It costs about 50B.

Kaeng Pet (Spicy Curry) - This dish is more common in street stalls and usually consists of pork and various beans in a thick red sauce. It is spicy, as the name indicates, and costs 20B to 40B. It is common in guesthouses but usually called red curry.

Kaeng Som (Orange Curry) - This Southern speciality is a firey fish curry with a distinct orange colour. It is more of a soup than a curry with large pieces of fish and vegetables floating in a hot sour stock. Common in southern Thailand but rare elsewhere. It is very spicy and costs 30B to 50B.

Kaeng Massamaan (Muslim Style Curry) - A milder, rich curry with a peanuty sauce and chicken, beef or goat. It's a Southern specialty served in cafes and street stalls.

Pad Thai (Noodles with Peanuts) - This dish is consumed in markets and cafes all over Thailand with only minor regional variations. It consists of thin rice noodles fried with dried shrimps, tofu, peanuts, onions, lemon juice and the occasional extra ingredient. Most guesthouses have this on their menus although they almost never resemble the real thing in price or taste. In English menus, Pad Thai usually means any kind of fried noodles. It is not spicy and costs 15B to 20B.

Raat Naa - This is another common noodle dish, made with wide rice noodles and greens, fried with pork and in a thick rich gravy. This is market food that is not spicy. It costs 15B to 25B.

Kuay Tiaw (pron. Kwy Teow) Nam - Literally translated as noodle water, this basic Thai rice noodle soup is sold in the smallest cafes in the smallest villages. Noodles are dunked in and served in a stock with various herbs, beansprouts and meatballs or sliced meat on the top. Point to what you want in it. Its hard to go wrong with this dish and add some condiments to spice it up. It is not spicy, and costs 10B to 15B.

Som Tam (Papaya Salad) - Along with noodle soup this is probably one of the commonest dishes throughout Thailand - Som Tam can be found everywhere. It consists of grated green papayas, mixed with peanuts, chillies, small tomatoes, pickled crabs or dried shrimps. Often very spicey the pickled crabs can give this dish an odd taste but you can always ask them to leave them out. Check out any stall where you see someone pounding a mortar and pestle, as chances are they are making Som Tam. It costs 10B to 12B.

Bah Jang - This is an item you will regularly see for sale. This is a steamed Chinese meal of rice, dried shrimp, sausage, mushrooms, eggs and pork. It comes in a pyramid shape, wrapped in banana leaves and string and is sold for anything up to 20B.

Eating Etiquette

Unlike many other Asian nations and popular belief, chopsticks are not traditionally used to eat Thai food, instead a spoon and fork is the more preferred method. The fork is used mainly to scoop food onto the spoon. If you place the fork in your mouth it is considered very rude (like sticking the knife in you mouth in the West). Chopsticks are used whenever a noodle dish is served. Knives are not required as the food is usually already cut into edible portions.

The Asian custom of having all dishes served at the same time is also practised in Thailand. When eating you usually have your own plate of rice and take only a spoonful of food at a time which you eat with some rice. Only then should you take a spoonful of another dish (rather than piling up your plate with a bit of everything first).

Thai food is not traditionally served with alcohol, however beer is acceptable at more informal meals. Also, never blow your nose or lick you fingers during a meal and only use your right hand to pick up food when required.

DRINK

Water

It is advisable to avoid tap water in Thailand unless you are staying at a reasonable hotel (and even then you cannot be sure), as you may otherwise find yourself spending your holiday over a toilet. Thais very rarely drink tap water themselves since they are just as likely to become ill as anyone else. Many tourists are very wary of the water in cafes, but there is no reason to be. The free water given in restaurants and cafes is drinking water. It comes from the large plastic bottles containing over 20 litres. If the water has a brownish tinge then it is boiled water, not dirty water, since it is usually boiled with a few tea leaves.

As for ice, it is usually manufactured, but unless you have proof, it may be best to avoid it as it could possibly be made out of tap water. Even if the ice is properly manufactured, often large blocks are transported in hessian bags or open coming into contact with the ground and possible disease. This type of ice is chipped away or crushed for use in drinks and stands out from the cubed ice sold in plastic bags.

Bottled water as well as soft drink is readily available and affordable. Bottled water costs between 3B and 10B for a litre, but make sure that the bottle is correctly sealed before purchasing. Cases are reported where entrepreneurs have collected empty bottles and filled them up with tap water, re-selling them to unexpecting tourists. One way to stop this trade is to put a hole in every bottle that you finish with.

Alcohol

Beer is readily available in Thailand and is very drinkable, however also puts a bit of a dent in your wallet, (especially if you enjoy regular consumption) due to the high government taxes. Beer usually comes in two sizes and the two most popular beers are Singha and Carlsberg. A small bottle costs between 25B to 30B, while a large one is between 40B and 50B in the markets, however in restaurants and guesthouses expect to pay around 40B for a small and around 60B for large bottles. In trendy bars and pubs small bottles may fetch a 100B tag.

If beer is not to your liking, then try the popular local cane whiskey, Mekong Whisky or Sang Thip Whisky which are quite affordable at around 60B for a hip flask, or 125B for a bottle. It is however a sweeter whiskey than most Western types. A local concoction known as Lao Cao is rather potent and is the kind of drink you will only consume once. Made from fermented rice, it contains a kick strong enough to send you all the way home and is very cheap.

ENTERTAINMENT

Cinemas

Thailand offers quite a large variety of both American and French films at selected cinemas along with a variety of local films. If you need a Western fix, try a movie with daily screenings and matinees on weekends and holidays. The tickets are reasonably cheap. The national anthem is always played prior to the screening of every film, so make sure that you stand.

Nightclubs

Major large towns in Thailand will have at least one. Characterised by very expensive drinks, a cover charge and blaring Thai music they may not be everyone's cup of tea. Although the patronage is mainly male, in the more progressive provinces the crowd is generally fifty fifty.

Live Music

Thailand has some outstanding local live music and is also becoming an increasingly popular destination for touring Western bands. One of the best ways to find out who is playing where is to peruse either one of the main English dailies or one of the popular "What's On?" style magazines. Cover charge (if there is one) is usually reasonable and, for international acts is way below what you would probably pay at home.

Bars

Even more prevalent than nightclubs, bars can be found virtually anywhere in Thailand. A common theme amongst the plusher bars is the polished wood feel, with wagon wheels and Mississippi numberplates hanging all over the place. The bars often serve food and live music is often thrown in for free. More popular with Thai men than women, the evenings in these places are characterised by huge drinking sessions with scotch being a particular favourite.

Go Go Bars

Generally restricted to farang orientated destinations, these bars are full of bikini clad (or naked) Thai girls dancing around in front of gawking foreigners. Those planning on visiting these kind of establishments should be aware that the girls are often not dancing willingly having been sold into the trade. Often a front for prostitution, the conditions that the sex workers endure in these places are scandalous. In the past, following a fire in a brothel in Bangkok, the charred remains of a couple of sex workers were found handcuffed to their beds. HIV is also a major problem amongst the sex workers of Thailand and as such one should always use protection (the best being not to visit).

COUNTRY

The kingdom of Thailand (*Muang Thai*) is commonly referred to as the 'Land of Smiles', however, literally translated it means 'Land of the Free'. The Prime Minister Phibun changed the name from Siam to Thailand on 24 June 1939 for two reasons. Firstly, to break any association with the history of the old country (the ruling powers changed to a constitutional monarchy from an absolute monarchy in 1932), and secondly, because 'Thai' is what they have called themselves for centuries rather than Siamese, a name inherited from their neighbours. Thailand was actually officially founded in 1238 and is the only country in Southeast Asia that has never been colonised by European powers although it was forced to cede large tracts of territory to both France and England.

GEOGRAPHY

Thailand covers an area of 514,000 sq km, with the land mass making up 511,770 sq km and the remainder made up of marine territory. Thailand's land mass is often compared to the shape of an elephants head, but to be more geographically useful, the terrain is divided into definable areas. The northern regions are mostly mountainous, the northeast is dominated by the semi arid Khorat plateau, central Thailand is extremely fertile with the plains surrounding the Chao Phraya Basin acting as the nations ricebowl and the southern peninsula which carries a spine of mountains down its length with plains leading down to the Gulf of Thailand.

From north to south Thailand stretches for 1,640 km, from west to east, its widest point measures 800 km and at its thinnest is the Isthmus of Kra which slims to around 25 km. Thailand's land bound perimeter stretches for a total of 4,863 km and shares four land borders: Malaysia to the south (506 km), Burma (Myanmar) to the west (1,800 km), Laos to the north and northeast (1,754 km) and Cambodia to the east (803 km). Thailand's southern coastline is also extensive, covering 3,219 km and it makes contact with two oceans; the Andaman Sea to the west and the Gulf of Thailand in the east. Currently 30% of the country is classified as forest and woodland and 34% of land is arable.

Waterways, Oceans and Islands

Thailand currently boasts 18 National Marine Parks with another 6 on the drawing board. The first to be established, Khao Sam Roi Yot, was opened in 1966. A separate division of the National Parks Authority was created to care for these marine parks so that specific issues regarding sustainability of local industry and the protection of marine environments could be dealt with effectively.

The Gulf of Thailand on Thailand's east coast and the Andaman Sea on Thailand's west coast are home to the almost 300 islands which Thailand lays claim to. The Gulf of Thailand forms part of a platform which only a few million years ago was a dry part of Southeast Asia's land mass, but rising sea levels have now immersed it. Despite its expanse, the gulf averages a depth of only 30 m, but reaches 86 m at its deepest point and the water temperature in this region averages 20° C to 26° C. There is an underwater ridge that runs between the southern point of Vietnam and the northern point of Malaysia which affects the Gulf's sealife and as a result, there is very little coral north of Rayong and large coral reefs do not exist until just south of Chumphon. The Andaman Sea in comparison boasts much better coral reefs from the Surin Islands near the Burmese border all the way to the Tarutao island group near Malaysia with clearer waters and deeper seabeds. If you are going to Thailand for diving or snorkelling the Andaman Sea is generally a more rewarding choice.

Unfortunately both local industry and tourism has had a devastating impact on the fragile underwater world. Local industry has created damage through a range of destructive fishing procedures. The worst of these is known as a 'push net', which runs right to the seabed and removes everything from the base including crabs and other crustaceans, coral and all manner of sealife in between. The result of this manner of fishing is complete devastation of the seabed, and could be not unfairly compared to a 'slash and burn' style of fishing, with the seabed often taking a long time to regenerate. A second problem is that the larger trawlers are running closer and closer to the coast, often impinging on the traditional fishing areas close to the coast, which in the past have served two vital roles, they served as a food source for small fishing villages who were effectively subsistence fishers, and thus fished at a much more sustainable level, and the area was also a vital area for fish stock regeneration. Other practises such as dynamite fishing have certainly done the stocks no favours.

The other major problems are based on the mainland. Removal of the mangrove forests for shrimp farms has had a critical effect on coastal species as the shrimp farms are effectively a monoculture, near which very little can survive. Another problem is the often ridiculous levels of pollution which simply runs off into the ocean. Areas such as Pattaya and Hua Hin have undergone high profile revivals, as their areas were cleaned up and rudimentary sewerage treatment was introduced, but for many other areas, which do not boast the high profile of Pattaya or Hua Hin, the problem is continuing.

Tourism has acted as the catalyst for more environmental damage through creating the need for luxury resorts in previously pristine areas such as Ko Phi Phi. However tourists are often also the culprits, walking on coral, breaking it off and taking it home. Once touched the coral die. Coral is not there to add to your personal collection, but rather is there for all to see.

CLIMATE AND TEMPERATURE

Thailand can best be described as tropical and humid for the majority of the country during most of the year. The area of Thailand from Bangkok northwards have its climate determined by three seasons whilst the southern peninsular region of Thailand has only two. In the northern area the seasons are clearly defined. From November to May the weather is mostly dry, however this is broken up into the periods November to February and March to May, the later of which has higher relative temperatures. Although the northeast monsoon does not directly effect the northern area of Thailand, it does cause cooling breezes from November to February. The other northern season is from May to November and is dominated by the southwest monsoon, during which time rainfall in the north is at its heaviest. The southern region of Thailand really has only two seasons, the wet and the dry although it is necessary to distinguish between the east and west coasts of the peninsula. On the west coast the southwest monsoon brings rain and often heavy storms from April to October, whilst on the east coast the most rain falls between September and December. The southern parts of the country get by far the most rain at around 2,400 millimetres every year, compared with the central and northern regions which both get around 1,400 millimetres.

The best time to visit Thailand is from November to February when the northeast monsoon is blowing cool, dry air which serves as a respite from the heat. During this cool season, the temperature ranges from 18° C to 32° C in Bangkok, however in the north and northeast it can get quite cool ranging from 8° C to 12° C with the occasional 20° C day. Nights are particularly chilly and at high altitudes the temperatures can easily drop below freezing.

The summer period, or hot and dry season, is from March to June with the temperature in Bangkok averaging around 34° C, but it is not uncommon to reach 40° C with the humidity often around 75%. Try and avoid April, unless you plan to be permanently submerged in the ocean, because this is the hottest month.

From July to October is the monsoonal or wet season when most of Thailand's annual rainfall is accumulated. The humidity averages just under 90%, with temperatures averaging around 29° C in Bangkok. The monsoons finish when the wind direction changes, bringing dry weather from the northeast. At best this season can be described as unpredictable and not the constant downpour of rain like you would expect. The middle months of this season may hold particularly heavy rains for the north of the country.

Bangkok												
	Jan	Feb	Mar	Apr	May	Jun	Jul	Aug	Sep	Oct	Nov	Dec
Temp ° C (max)	32	33	34	35	34	33	32	32	32	31	31	31
° C (min)	22	23	24	26	26	25	25	25	24	24	23	21
Rain (mm)	10	30	35	65	155	160	170	185	275	205	60	10

Chiang Mai												
	Jan	Feb	Mar	Apr	May	Jun	Jul	Aug	Sep	Oct	Nov	Dec
Temp ° C (max)	29	32	35	36	34	32	32	31	31	31	30	29
° C (min)	13	14	18	22	24	24	24	24	23	22	19	14
Rain (mm)	10	10	20	55	150	150	185	220	280	125	40	15

Phuket												
	Jan	Feb	Mar	Apr	May	Jun	Jul	Aug	Sep	Oct	Nov	Dec
Temp ° C (max)	31	32	33	33	32	31	31	31	30	31	31	31
° C (min)	23	23	24	24	25	25	25	24	23	23	23	23
Rain (mm)	40	35	60	130	270	240	220	235	295	290	180	80

FLORA AND FAUNA

The Environment

Conservation of natural environments is only a fairly recent undertaking in Thailand with the first National Park established in 1961. The forested regions of the country are steadily decreasing; in 1939, forest covered 70% of the country but in 1997 it is estimated that this figure is well under 20%. The total protected areas (including National Parks, wildlife sanctuaries, non-hunting areas, forest parks and other reserves and gardens) cover close to 13% of Thailand - this sounds better than reality. Despite the land being set aside for conservation, Thailand still has a long way to go to protect these areas — setting them aside is not enough. The main cause of the degradation has been the increase in population and need for more agricultural areas. Today, however, other major offenders include hilltribes practising slash and burn agriculture, illegal logging, poaching, residential and farming encroachment into protected land, irresponsible planning of infrastructure (which in some cases have carved highways through the middle of National Parks), golf courses and poor education of many visitors in conservation issues (hence the littering and souvenir collection). However an influential environmental movement is growing in Thailand, who in the past have had major victories including stopping plans to build a dam above Erawan waterfall in Kanchanaburi.

Currently there are 77 National Parks (with plans to increase it to around 115 by the year 2000), 35 wildlife sanctuaries and numerous other 'protected' areas. Wildlife sanctuaries differ from National Parks as they are areas set aside to preserve animals and natural habitats in an environment generally closed to the public, except for park officers.

Preservation

Thailand has a wonderful array of animals and wildlife, unfortunately Thailand also has many animals listed as endangered species. Wild animals are occasionally used to make souvenirs and trinkets, and even more are incorporated into some of the local cuisine. This is illegal in Thailand. Under no circumstances should wild animals be killed for food. The traveller can help stop the slaughter of hundreds of animals by refusing to eat at local restaurants that list wildlife on the menu. If you do come across such a place, you can report it to the Wildlife Conservation Division, Royal Forestry Department in Bangkok, ☎ (02) 579 1565. You can also help preserve many other aspects of Thailand such as refusing to purchase souvenirs made of animals or corals and be aware of your litter (and other people's).

Plant Life

Thailand's forests can generally be classified into varying degrees of deciduous forest (65%) and evergreen forest (35%). To date 15,000 different native plants have been identified in Thailand however this is a conservative number as it is estimated that only a quarter of the plant species that exist have been scientifically recorded.

Orchids are the symbol of Thailand, particularly the dendrobium orchid, a native species of Asia. There are over 1,000 species of orchid but the most common colour is the purple and white variety, but you will probably see them in yellow, pink, white and purple. They tend to grow in wild in the north, which turns into a sea of colour when the orchids flower in the middle of the dry season. An alternative sea of colour is in the flower markets located in regional areas, and in the Chatuchak Market in Bangkok, held on the weekends.

Orchids are used for commercial purposes as are other plants. Teak has, in the past, been a big revenue raiser, however it was heavily logged in a particularly short term period. This forced the government to bring about a complete ban on logging, including teak. Government permission is now needed even to used the wood from a teak tree which has fallen over.

Animal Life

Thailand boasts a considerable animal population, most of whose habitat is within natural preservation areas. Over the years and through lack of care, some have hit the extinct lists (as well as the dinner table) whilst many are listed as endangered. Areas where animal life is reasonably plentiful (in comparison to the worst areas), even with the larger and endangered species, include Khao Yai, Kaeng Krachan, Thap Lan, Mae Wong, Thap Lan, Prang Sida and Khao Sok National Parks as well as Thung Yai Naresuan and Huai Kha Khaeng wildlife sanctuaries. However in all of the above, poaching is still a major problem. Unless the Thai government bites the bullet (excuse the pun) and installs a similar penalty in regard to poachers as some African nations do, (shoot to kill policy) the future does not bode well for the wildlife.

Thailand's bird population includes over 920 identified species (including migratory birds) currently flying, roosting and squawking their way around the country. The large number exist due to the varied geographical features of the country from mountainous to coastal regions and also due to Thailands location which makes it a popular stop for migratory birds.

As for bigger beasts, 280 mammals have been recorded in Thailand but the most regal are now low in numbers. The elephant, which is associated with the nation's royalty and has been a national icon for years, has dwindling numbers in the wild. Many are retained in elephant camps and farms and others are used for labour or to hike the odd tourist around popular sights. The tiger's existence is in critical danger with only a few pockets of the animals known to officials and unfortunately it seems that the poachers are better at finding them than the park officials. Three of Thailand's hoofed animals have become extinct in the country including the Javan rhinoceros, Schomburgk's deer and the kouprey, whilst others on the endangered list include Eld's deer, wild buffalo and Sumatran rhinoceros. Other animals that are dramatically losing numbers include the Asiatic black bear, the clouded leopard, gaur and Fea's barking deer. Some of the animals face extinction due to peoples preference for them on the dinner table or as 'medical' enhancers rather than in the wild. Rhinoceros horns were sent to China in the thousands in past centuries whilst bears have been a Korean speciality for years.

Thailand's monkey population is in a somewhat healthier state with different species dominating a variety of areas around the country. If you are in the right place at the right time you can expect to see the pileated gibbon, white handed (lar) gibbon, pig tailed macaques and crab eating macaques and possibly others. However in areas such as Phuket, more monkeys are in captivity than live in the wild.

Marine Life

Thailand's varied marine life is spread throughout the Gulf of Thailand and Andaman Sea. Thailand is home to over 100 coral reef fish plus a huge variety of more commercial species. Besides the fish, there are the turtles, all of which are endangered. Four species can be seen nesting on some of Thailand's coastline and islands from November to January — Ridley's, leatherbacks, hawksbills and green turtles. Other sealife include up to 30 types of sea snakes, dolphins and the occasional whale. The dugong (sea cow) is facing extinction, but if you are lucky you may come across one around the Phang Nga to Satun Provinces.

The Andaman Sea possesses far more spectacular coral than the Gulf coast with over 200 species of hard coral recorded, the Gulf has only 80. You can add the plentiful soft coral to this list to contribute to a visual display unmatched in many parts of Asia.

Thailand's inland freshwater waterways also hold a substantial number of fish, the most well known being the endangered Maekhong River Giant Catfish. These fish are not called giant for nothing, when fully grown they can reach 3 m and weigh up to 300 kg.

Fishing has been the bread winner for many of the coastal villages in the past. Recently, farmers and large investors from Bangkok have found a lucrative trade in other forms of sealife including jellyfish farming (exported to Japan and Korea) and the increasingly destructive shrimp farming.

GOVERNMENT

As a constitutional monarchy since 1932, the King plays the role of the head figure for the state, armed forces and religion. The king maintains legislative and judicial power through the established system, but generally refrains from using it. All people of Thailand are eligible to vote for the government through the well established democratic system, however corruption, dishonesty and vote buying is still a major problem with political figures, as witnessed with the forced resignation of Prime Minister Banharn Silpa-archa at the end of 1996.

The sign of the Thai government is the garuda (*krut*), attained from Brahmanism. The government base is Bangkok, with more localised forms of government prevailing throughout the 76 provinces (*changwat*). These are divided into districts (*amphoe*), sub districts (*tambon*) and villages (*muuban*).

EDUCATION

The literacy rate in Thailand is high at 93% (1990) made up of 96% of males and 90% of females. Traditionally, education was taught by monks in the monasteries (known as the *sangha*), and since females were unable to become monks, were refrained from any kind of formal education. Due to this monastic education system the Thais developed a high literacy from very early on. All (male) walks of life had access to school as it was not segregated to cities alone, but every place where a wat existed. A modern system of education was developed during King Rama V's reign which encompassed Burmese, English and Japanese techniques however only the elite could go to these new schools, most of whom were in Bangkok.

Compulsory primary education was established in 1921, and now all children must attend school for this period. Even after the establishment of modern schools in Thailand, many Thais still had to rely on monastic schools for their education due to lack of funds to build European style schools throughout the country. After the change to a constitutional monarchy in 1932 there was a strong focus on providing decent schooling countrywide and funds were allocated accordingly. Today, English is taught to most school children.

Chulalongkorn University was established in 1917, the first time women had access to tertiary professional education. Thammasat University was founded in 1934.

ECONOMY

In 1990, 31 million Thais were eligible for the workforce. The breakdown of employees included 62% in agriculture, 13% in industry, 11% in commerce and 14% in services including government. This breakdown tells a story of its own regarding the structure of Thailand's economy. Thailand is positioned perfectly within Southeast Asia to prosper from economic activity and has prospered over the past 20 years.

International trade flourished in the Ayutthaya Period when the Chao Phraya River was successfully used with traders from China, Persia and Malaysia and later included the Portuguese and Dutch. Early on, the Thais mainly exported primary commodities and by the early 1900s rice cultivation was one of the major industry. In 1910, rice made up 80% of the countries exports with teak taking up another 10%. Economic reforms during this century have placed more focus on manufacturing industries. In the 70s and 80s things were looking good for Thailand through a global upswing in tourism, of which Thailand had become a popular choice. However the 1991 coup which threw out a democratically elected government on charges of vote buying shocked Thai-philes around the world. Although Thailand has since recovered from this coup and the economy is definitely a booming one, the fickleness of the political and economical system in Thailand had been demonstrated, as had the influence of the military.

The Military
Political unrest, including a series of coups in the 70s and 90s, slowed down economic growth, and served to highlight one of the major problems in Thailand, being that of the military. The Thai police and armed forces are chronically underpaid and are often corrupt. Partially as a result of this the armed forces wield an incredibly high level of control over Thai life and it is not unusual for those with a military background to hold influential positions within major industries. The relationship between THAI Airways and the Air Force are a fine example of this. The military's outlook on life in generally fairly rightwing, although they certainly are not ones prone to take a backwards step regarding meddling in Thailand's neighbours affairs. Alledged Thai military support of the Khmer Rouge, KMT, Hmong groups opposing the Pathet Lao government in Laos, and KNU forces in Burma fighting against the SLORC has long been suspected but certainly has not been admitted to. To expand its economic growth and to attract further foreign investment, which has been gradually declining, Thailand aimed to improve its infrastructure and produce more tertiary educated graduates with business and technical skills, a decision which is now paying off.

Recent Economic Activity
Traditionally a country relying on its agriculture and primary resources for survival, Thailand has now ventured into the more profitable manufacturing industries. Over the past decade, the increase in Thailand's GDP has been the result of development in a few key areas including textiles and precious stones. Thailand is also the worlds second largest rice exporter.

Thailand's huge growth has not come without its problems. In the attempt to adjust to its new prosperity, Thailand has had to face enormous infrastructure changes to cope with the increased productivity. Bangkok has had to undergo a transformation from a busy town to a seething metropolis. Urban migration, particularly from the northeast is creating a new class of poor in the bigger cities, and this problem is not just taking place in Bangkok, but other centres such as Chiang Mai and Nakhon Ratchasima. This urban migration is created partly through a lack of jobs and prospects in rural areas, but also because of the dream of making it big in the big smoke. The supply of telecommunications, transport, and water and power is still in dire need of development. The opening of the port at Laem Chabang as well as other smaller versions has made a huge difference reducing the load on the existing ports.

Besides urbanisation, Thailand lacks sets of strict and enforceable environmental guidelines, which has resulted in at times chronic pollution caused by the uncontrolled development of industry, this in turn can act to deplete natural resources and the wilderness. Another major problem regarding economic growth is corruption and a fairly short term view for quick profits rather than investments over longer periods. This can be seen all over Thailand, in situations such as golf courses being built in National Parks, refugee camps planned on tropical islands and dams planned in positions which will cripple local fishing industries.

GENERAL INFORMATION

THAI FLAG

The Thai flag has been in its current state since 1917. It possesses five horizontal bands, with red on the outside (representing the nation), then white (reflecting Buddhism), and blue in the centre, double in size of the others (depicting the monarchy). It was changed to this pattern after Thailand joined the allies in WWI under the rule of Rama VI. Previously it was red depicting a white elephant enclosed by a wheel. The king at the time, Rama II, owned three white elephants, denoting good luck.

BUSINESS HOURS

The business week is from Monday to Friday, as Saturday and Sunday are holidays. Normal business hours are listed below:

Banks are open from 8.30 am to 3.30 pm. They may close for one hour over lunch.
Government offices from 8.30 am to 12.00, then 1.00 pm to 4.30 pm.
Private offices from 8.00 am to 5.00 pm.
Department stores from 10.00 am to 9.00 pm.
Shops from 8.00 am to 8.00 pm. The tourist markets however usually do not open until the afternoon and trade up to midnight. These markets include Khao San Road, and Pat Pong.
Museums Most museums are closed on Monday and Tuesday.

TELEPHONE

Public telephone booths take 1B coins for calls, but some take up to 5B at hotels. In telephone directories Thais are listed by their first names and farangs by their surnames. For information on changed numbers call ☎ (02) 233 1199.

Thailand Country Code is 66. The provincial area codes are listed in each relevant section, however when making calls from overseas, do not dial the zero.

Directory Assistance with an English speaking operator, call the following:
Bangkok   13
Provinces   183
By calling these numbers you can get international access.

Trunk Calls for:
Domestic (including Malaysia and Vientiene)   101
Foreign Countries   100

Emergency Numbers
Police   191
Tourist Police   195
Fire   199
Ambulance in Bangkok   (02) 252 2171

Facsimile

Facsimile services are available at most post offices, large hotels and some guesthouses.

POST

The opening hours of post offices are generally from 8.00 am to 6.00 pm from Monday to Friday, and 8.30 am to 4.00 pm on Saturdays. Some post offices are open on Sundays and public holidays. Bangkok also uses agency post offices. These are indicated by a notice on a pole or the shopfront illustrating the Garuda emblem of the Thai Post and Telegraph Department as well as the opening hours. Often postal agencies are run from large hotels.

Post restante facilities are very reliable throughout Thailand and available at virtually every town, just remember that in towns with more than one post office, the mail will be kept at the main one. Mail is usually kept for a period of three months, after which it is returned to the sender or forwarding address. Your mail is generally filed under your last name, but occasionally filed by your first name, so check both.

Postage within Thailand is very inexpensive (2B for letter under 20g), however to destinations abroad the costs are relatively expensive. Aerogrammes cost 10B to any destination and postcards cost 9B to send. Letters sent by airmail under 10 grams cost 13B to Australia, New Zealand and Europe and 16B to Canada, USA and South America. Both airmail and seamail are priced according to destination and weight (which jumps every kilogram). International Express Mail (EMS) and registered mail facilities are also available. Packing supplies are available at most post offices in provincial capitals and larger towns.

TIME

The most important difference to remember is that Thailand is 7 hours ahead of Greenwich Mean Time. Since the world insists on so many variations on determining the time, Thailand is also 14 hours ahead of Eastern Standard Time, and 11 hours ahead of Pacific Standard Time. There is only one time zone in Thailand. What this means is that when it is midday in Bangkok, it is 1.00 pm in Perth, 3.00 pm in Sydney, 5.00 pm in New Zealand, 9.00 pm the previous day in Los Angeles, midnight the previous day in New York, 5.00 am in London, 6.00 am in Zurich and 10.00 am in Lahore.

TIPPING

Tipping is not a common practice in Thailand, unless you are in a large hotel. Often in more expensive hotels they save you the effort and charge a 10 to 15% service charge. Sometimes in restaurants a services charge is added to the bill. However tips will never go astray, especially since some Thais may need the small amount of money more than you.

ELECTRICITY

Most places in Thailand run at 50 Hz 220 volts. Often you should be careful of sub standard wiring, especially in cheap bungalows where the wiring can be nothing short of deadly.

BOOKS

An invaluable part of any traveller's luggage, it is easy in most major centres to find at least a rudimentary selection of English books. In the larger tourist centres such as Bangkok, Chiang Mai and Krabi there is also a large secondhand book business going on. Many guesthouses also offer a selection of books either for sale or on a swap basis. One place where the book bargains are not quite what they appear to be, is on Khao San Road, which is inhabited by some of the most unscrupulous book dealers known to humankind. These retailers often sell second hand books above and beyond their recommended retail price and offer rock bottom rates when buying these books back off you...nevertheless, they do a roaring trade.

Bangkok would have to be one of the best centres for new English books in South East Asia. There are a number of excellent chain stores including Asia Books and Bookazine amongst many others. Any large department store should have one of these stores.

For those who are interested in the country they are travelling in, rather than a decent fiction read, there are some excellent books available on most aspects of Thai society, history and pastimes. Below is a glance at some of the better reading options.

History
The Archaeology of Mainland Southeast Asia by Charles Highham an excellent read for anyone keen on investigating some of the many sites in Thailand. This book also offers a look at many of the sites in the surrounding countries, including the major site of Angkor Wat.

Thailand – A Short History by David K. Wyatt is just about the only easy to read book on Thailand's history that has been written recently. An excellent read for anyone interested in Thai history.

Southeat Asia – An Introductory History by Milton Osborne covers the whole of South East Asia and its coverage of Thailand is fairly brief, but if you are looking for a simple overview it is not a bad choice.

The People
Travellers' Tales Thailand by James O'Reilly and Larry Habegger. This book is one of the best books we have read regarding Thailand. A series of anecdotal stories about both the people and the country, this at times hysterical read is imperative both for those who have not yet been there and those who have returned and want to recharge the memories. Highly recommended.

Behind the Smile: Voices of Thailand by Sanitsuda Ekachai contains a series of short pieces mainly concerned with the people of the northeast. A fascinating read, this is definitely worth reading if you are planning to spend much time in the area.

Mai Pen Rai Means Never Mind by Carol Hollinger is a lightweight, light hearted look at the life of an expat in Bangkok.

The Hilltribes of Northern Thailand by John R. Davies contains an overview of all the major hilltribes and has some nice photos and rudimentary maps.

The Hilltribes of Thailand put out by the Tribal Research Institute has a basic look at all the main tribes.

Getting Around
David Unkovich in Chiang Mai has released a series of books specialising in motorcycle touring in Northern Thailand. His two most popular are the *Mae Hong Son Loop* and *Motorcycle Touring in North Thailand*. He has a third book, concerning the southern area of Northern Thailand, but it is quite difficult to find. The first two though are indispensable purchases for anyone considering touring the north.

Language
Robertson's Practical English-Thai Dictionary is the best pocket dictionary available and has the phonetics sounding and the Thai script for each and every word.

Regional Reads
Most tourist areas now have English publications concerned with the immediate area.

National Parks of Thailand. This very good, full colour, book has in depth information on some of Thailand's better National Parks as well as brief information on the remainder. Some great photos and interesting commentary regarding the environmental degradation which goes on in Thailand.

North

Welcome to Chiang Rai and Chiang Mai is a monthly publication which has interesting articles on the region as well as recommendations for eating, day trips and so on. They are also on the net at **http://www.infothai.com/wtcmcr/**

Trip Info coming out of Chiang Mai, is a monthly magazine which has loads of information including room prices, travel costs and timetables as well as information on sights and other things to keep you busy. Free and available at most travel agents and hotels in Chiang Mai.

Bangkok

Thaiways is touted as the guide for tourists and business people, and that is exactly what this is, with concise information of places to see, restaurants and loads of other bits and pieces. Free, this can be picked up in travel agents and some hotels. Updated monthly.

Bangkok Metro Magazine A must buy for anyone wanting to discover the night in Bangkok, find out about museum exhibitions etc etc In a similar format to a What's On type of guide, at 80B, indispensable reading.

Bangkok Guide by the Australian-New Zealand Women's Group is mainly concerned with those who are thinking of settling in Thailand. Some excellent information is within its covers, though it is a fairly bulky book and more suited to a suitcase than a backpack.

South

Krabi Holiday Guide by Ken Scott is a bargain at 90B and contains some excellent and up to date information on the Krabi area. It also contains a series of articles on matters such as mangrove ecosystems, bird watching and the national parks. Widely available in Krabi. 90B.

The Magic of Krabi by Morag McKerron, Craftsman Press 1990. This book explains the myths and legends behind Krabi's stunning landscapes. Distributed by Asia Books.

Maps

There are a large selection of maps available on Thailand, most are fairly good, though they all have their share of errors. One of the best sets of maps, particularly for those planning extensive touring by motorcycle or bicycle is a set put out by the *Department of Highways in Thailand*. Small, waterproof and easily fitted into a pocket, these maps are each dedicated to a separate area of Thailand, ie., North, Northeast, Central and South, are free and can be picked up at any large highway's office. All major towns have their name in Thai and Roman script, making getting directions a good bit easier for non Thai speakers. This appears to be something which most of the larger maps have overlooked.

Bartholomew's 1995 Thailand map at a scale of 1:1,500,000 is not a bad choice and does have relief although the distances between destinations are not marked and, unfortunately, the only detail on the map, of Bangkok, is fairly useless.

Thailand & the Internet

Coined as the information superhighway, anyone with access to the internet would be foolish not to have a peak at what is on the web about Thailand before embarking. The list below is far from comprehensive, but does list some of the more interesting sites, both for publications based in Thailand, as well as pages by those who have been to Thailand and want to share their experiances. So check out some of the homepages below and see what you find. If you know of other pages regarding Thailand which you think are useful, or have your own page, let us know and, if we agree with your opinion, we will list it in our newsletter, **el cuentista**. You can contact us on the net at: mcdonald@mail.enternet.com.au

Thailand Related Internet Pages

http://www.people.enternet.com.au/~mcdonald/ This is our page, so pop in and find out what is going on.

http://www.bangkokpost.co.th/horizons/horizons.html This is the Horizon section of the Bangkok Post which contains an archive or travel related stories. The address without the

horizons add on will take you to the Bangkok Post page with the latest news in Thailand.
http://www.tat.or.th is the official page of the Thai Tourist Authority.
http://www.infothai.com/wtcmcr/ this is the page to the Chiang Mai based paper, Welcome to Chiang Mai & Chiang Rai.
http://www.asiaway.com/thai/title.htm Comprised of information supplied by the TAT this page has basic shopping and travel advice.
http://www.thaiindex.com This excellent site contains complete and detaild information on most features of Thailand, including travel tips and a business directory.
http://www.phuket.com/island.sea.htm is mainly concerned with diving and other water sports activities in Phuket.
http://www.infohub.com/TRAVEL/TRAVELLER/ASIA/thailand.html is another excellent page about Thailand.
http://www.thailine.com/thailand/english/north-e/chmai-e/pai-e.htm is a detailed look at the north of Thailand, with particular attention given to Pai, Chiang Saen and Chiang Khong.
http://www.asiatravel.com/thaiinfo.html is another good source of Thai related material.
http://www.nectec.or.th/WWW-VL-Thailand.html is a page on Thailand, based in Thailand.
http://www.siam.net/goin/ This is from the Go Internet cafe at Chaweng Beach, Ko Samui.
http://www.ivr.net/samui/index.htm contains a look at Ko Samui.

Outside Thailand Pages
http://www.freeburma.org/ May be of interest to those wanting to find out the state of affairs in Burma.
http://www.globalpassage.com/ This is one of the standout pages on the net and it contains just about everything you would ever want to know about anything!
http://www.geocities.com/Yosemite/6241/backpackers_guide.htm This is a backpackers page with a lot of potential but is not frequently updated.
http://www.ozemail.com.au/~backpack/ is another backpackers page worth a glance.

Newspapers
There are a selection of English dailys available in Thailand of which the two best are *The Bangkok Post* and *The Nation*. These have a substantial world news section and also carry interesting local travel sections on a weekly basis. The Sunday editions of newspapers are a good source of information for activities in Bangkok, providing information on films, exhibitions and concerts. Another source of valuable information is a monthly magazine called *"Living in Thailand"* which provides a variety of activities for the month.

TELEVISION

Most television broadcasts are in the Thai language, however most channels provide an English translation on FM radio for selected international programs and news bulletins. There are five regular television stations in Bangkok as well as cable and satellite television. The list of programs and radio frequencies are published in the daily newspapers.

RADIO

Both local and overseas English language broadcasts are listed in the morning newspapers. Local stations come on FM band, and overseas broadcasts on the SW band. The Bangkok chapter lists some relevant frequencies.

PHOTOGRAPHIC FILM

Film is both cheap and readily available throughout Thailand. Slide film can be a little more difficult to get outside of the major cities but is readily available in the major centres such as Bangkok and Chiang Mai. Processing of slide and print film in Bangkok is easy and is ridiculously cheap when compared to Western prices, although with slide processing the quality can, on occasion, vary tremendously. The print processing is generally pretty good.

Photo development outside of Bangkok is usually poor even if there are Kodak or Fuji signs all over the shop. This possibly includes the larger cities such as Chiang Mai and Hat Yai and tourist spots such as Ko Samui, Phuket and Krabi . Khao San Road in Bangkok has good and cheap developing shops and you can ask for a discount if you are developing several rolls.

LAUNDRY

Cheap and easy, but the detergent is even cheaper at around 1B for enough detergent to wash a load, so it is time to get those hands wet! Most guesthouses offer a laundry service but prices vary tremendously. Generally it works out cheaper if you wash by weight rather than by piece. Forty to 50B per kg is not an unreasonable rate to pay at a guesthouse, whilst if you are paying by piece, the charge may be as high as 15B for a single pair of jeans.

CURRENCY

Cash

The Thai currency is called baht and is made up of both coins and notes. One baht can be divided into 100 satangs. The currency comes in various denominations: 25 and 50 satang (copper coins), 1, 2 and 5 baht, (siver coins), 10 (note and silver and copper coin), 20, 50, 100, 500, and 1000 baht (notes).

A wide range of foreign currency can be exchanged within Thailand.

Exchange rates (as at March 1997)

The Thai baht is pegged to a basket of foreign currencies which is heavily weighted to the US dollar and, as such, has been fairly stable for quite some time now, so do not expect great variances in these exchange rates.

Currency	Baht	Currency	Baht
Australian Dollar	20.59	Italian Lira	0.02
Austrian Dollar	2.18	Indonesian Rupiah	0.01
Belgian Franc	0.75	Japanese Yen	0.21
British Pound	42.1	Malaysian Dollar	10.51
Canadian Dollar	18.89	New Zealand Dollar	18.38
Danish Krone	4.05	Philippines Pesos	1.05
Dutch Guilder	13.73	Singapore Dollar	18.06
Finnish Markka	5.17	South African Rand	5.87
French Franc	4.58	Spanish Peseta	0.18
German Mark	15.48	Swedish Krona	3.41
Greek Drachma	0.10	Swiss Franc	17.90
Hong Kong Dollar	3.35	United States Dollar	26.06
Indian Rupee	0.73		

Changing Money

The tourist trade is established enough in Thailand for there to be a bank, currency exchange service, or authorised money changer in every decent sized town. Bank hours are usually 8.30 am to 3.30 pm from Monday to Friday, and closed on Saturdays, Sundays and Bank holidays. Currency exchange services have the best operating hours for the unorganised traveller. You can usually catch them open from 8.30 am to 10.00 pm everyday. Authorised money changers in the large and expensive hotels provide 24 hour service, but others operate at various times, the most common being from 9.00 am to 5.00 pm.

Warning: You may have trouble changing money (both foreign cash and traveller's cheques) at banks in towns that are not very popular with travellers. However the staff are likely to point you to a bank that does.

It is important to retain your transaction receipts as you may need them if you are changing large amounts of Thai baht back into foreign currencies upon departure.

The banks that you are likely to stumble across include the following: Asia Bank, Bank of Ayudhya, Bangkok Bank, First City Bangkok Bank, Krung Thai Bank, Siam City Bank, Siam Commercial Bank, Thai Farmers Bank and Thai Military Bank. We have tried to mark a selection of banks on most of the maps in this book, as not only are they needed for financial matters, but are also handy reference points when you are trying to find your way around.

Travellers Cheques
Travellers cheques are widely accepted throughout Thailand at most major banks and exchange booths. Often a 13B fee applies for each cheque changed, therefore it is better to use large denomination cheques.

Credit Cards
Major credit cards are accepted within Thailand at banks and money exchange offices as well as at large hotels, restaurants, department stores and other large shops. Not all types of credit cards are accepted at all banks. Those accepted include Mastercard, Visa, American Express and Diners Club.

If you need to report a lost or stolen card, contact the following:
Visa and Mastercard: Thai Farmers Bank, ☎ (02) 271 0234, daily between 7.00 am and 10.00 pm.
American Express: American Express Office, ☎ (02) 273 0022, daily 24 hour service.
Diners Club: Diners Club Office, ☎ (02) 238 2920, (Monday to Friday working hours), or ☎ (02) 233 5775 after hours or weekends.

Black Market
The black market in Thailand is far from being a profitable business. The currency is very stable, and you are more likely to be ripped of than get a better deal if using the black market. Access to authorised money exchange places is widespread.

Inflated Prices for Foreigners
This is an unfortunate phenomena in many Asian countries mainly due to the belief that visiting Westerners must be rich since they can actually afford to travel. Thailand's fairly long standing exposure to the Western world however makes this a minor problem as long as you do not mind paying more than what the locals do for the exact same service. The prices in this book should be seen only as a guide as prices do always fluctuate, but beware particularly of tuk tuk drivers who never hesitate to overcharge. Remember that if you are being overcharged, it is most likely that it is happening because the vendor realises that there is a good chance you do not know what the correct price is. The best way around this is of course to learn Thai so that you can find out the correct price, however if you do not have the time or inclination to do this, at least try to learn a few words to give yourself some chance of finding out what is going on. If you do know the correct price, offer the correct money, and chances are you will get it for the right price. Watch what others pay, and learn the numbers, and you should get by OK.

If you realise you are being overcharged a ridiculous amount, point this out to the vendor, and if you still have no luck then shop elsewhere. But most importantly, do not lose your temper, as this is certainly not going to alter the situation and it is not worth losing your cool over a few baht.

SHOPPING
Shopping in Thailand can be either fun or a frustrating experience. If you take a bit of advice, you will come away with many valuable memories of your trip as well as a few things to show for it. Some of the more popular items that tourists purchase in Thailand because of

their quality, craftsmanship, or price are silk, silverware, jewellery, leather goods, ceramics, wood carvings, and cotton clothes.

There are however a few scams that travellers get caught in time and time again that can leave a miserable taste in your mouth and hole in your wallet, possibly putting a downer on your Thailand adventure. Con artists are so good at what they do, that they can be very believable - you could swear that the lovely Thai person helping you make a purchase would never rip you off. But beware, that is how they make their money. When buying jewellery or precious stones, be careful of the following and read our section on Dangers, safety and Crime advice.

Beware of any stranger offering to help you make a purchase - they may be tuk tuk drivers, taxi drivers, hotel owners, ex-monks (most Thai men enter monkhood at one stage of their life), doctors, business people. If someone takes you to a jewellery store, the price of the merchandise will be at least 10% to 30% more expensive so that the person gets a commission. Make sure you compare prices in more than one shop, to ensure that you are getting a fair price.

Many shop owners will claim that they are a government store, or they have a deal with the government, and stipulate that you can get a refund of any purchase at any Thai embassy, consulate, or government agency around the globe. This is simply not true. It does not matter how official the receipt looks, even if it does have a stamp with an elephant on it, you will not get a refund. The general practice within Thailand is that no jewellery purchase can be returned for a refund. The more reputable shops may take a refund, but give you a time limit of around 30 days. Others may give you a refund, but take up to 30% off the price for 'damages'. If you still feel like making a purchase, be sure to get all relevant details in case there is a problem - the receipt, a quality certificate, credit card slip, prices in Thai and foreign currency, and the name and address of the shop and shop assistant.

Thailand also has a problem with endangered species being used for trinkets. Never purchase an item made from wild animals.

Bargaining

Bargaining in Thailand is a well established custom that has been the accepted form for transaction for many years. Quite often a Westerner will be quoted a ridiculously high price. A good rule of thumb is to offer back an equally ridiculous price, at half that first stated. Usually you will agree on a price in the middle. Many Westerners find it difficult to bargain as it is not a natural interaction for them, but the more you practice, the better you become, usually with great results.

Prices have however soared up over the past as more and more foreigners have visited Thailand. As a result of this, the locals know that they can get away with offering high prices because they are still relatively cheap compared to home prices and some tourists are willing to pay for the goods. If you do not accept their price, there is a good chance that the person behind you will. Most department stores follow a different policy and set fixed prices. Only small shops and street vendors will bargain with you.

WEIGHTS AND MEASUREMENTS

Generally, the measurement system used within Thailand is metric. This means that any reference to distances, weight, capacity or length will either be kilometres, kilograms and litres or any part of these. There are two variances to this rule, that is in the measurement of fabric where either metres or yards are used, and in the measurement of area (land) where the Thais utilise their own system using rai and wa. The term rai actually refers to the amount of land that could be ploughed in a typical working day using a buffalo. Compared to the more commonly used Western measurements of acre and hectare, the rai and wa rate as follows:

1 rai = 1,600 square metres (2/5 acre)	1 acre = 2.5 rai
1 hectare = 2.47 acres = 6.25 rai	1 rai = 400 square wa
1 wa = 2 square metres	

ACCOMMODATION

The choice of accommodation in Thailand is varied, catering to all tastes and price ranges. Within this guide book we try to provide as many alternative forms of accommodation that satisfy our preferred maximum price range of 250B. Often in areas where the high tourist activity has inflated the prices we will mention the hotels and guest houses that are more than this, but come close to this price. Quite often on the islands, we will list accommodation by location, usually beginning at the port of entry.

Other alternatives for accommodation are available in Thailand, although becoming more scarce than a few years ago. Buddhist temples will often provide basic accommodation and facilities for a small donation. The donation is at your discretion, and should be handed over in an envelope because monks should never touch any form of currency.

In the north it is quite acceptable to stay in hilltribe villages. If on an organised trek, this will usually be part of the package. If you are trekking the mountains on your own and you require accommodation, indicate this through the internationally known sleep gesture. The decision is usually made by the chief of the village who will allocate a hut. Food will be included, which will be the same as your host family's dinner. Hilltribe accommodation will cost you some money, but is relatively cheap at around 50B per person. Be careful of your health when staying at the Akha villages, as they prefer to live at fairly high altitudes, hence possibly above fresh water sources.

During the Chinese New Year many restaurants and a few guesthouses are closed. It can also be difficult getting a seat on a train.

DANGERS, SAFETY AND CRIME ADVICE

General

Overall, Thailand is a very safe country, particularly when compared to most Western nations. The authors have visited Thailand on numerous occasions, and the only hassle was when an American cut up the researchers face with a beer bottle! The Thai's are generally friendly and extremely hospitable people but, as anywhere, there are always the bad eggs. When going out at night, exercise the same level of caution and common sense that you would if you were in a different city of your home country.

Realistically, most hassles appear to be from other travellers rather than the locals, so thank the locals for this fact by respecting their customs and dressing appropriately. By far the biggest complaint that many Thais appear to have about farangs is their lack of suitable attire. Walking topless though a Muslim fishing village is not really breaking down barriers, but rather reinforcing them.

Although known as the 'Land of Smiles', there are a few things that travellers should be aware of whilst visiting Thailand.

Gems

Scams with jewellery and valuable stones are mainly practised in Bangkok, Chanthaburi and Chiang Mai. Guides and tuk tuk drivers may try to convince you to venture into a jewellery shop offering bargains (they get a commission if you purchase anything). Another common scam is to be approached by a 'well dressed man' who will start an innocent enough conversation which in the end may result in you buying ridiculously priced pieces of polished glass thinking they are priceless gems which you can sell at home for a packet. If it was really this easy do you think we would be writing guidebooks! Do not believe any promises that you can get your money back, whether from the shop, the police or from the Thai Embassy in your own country. Gem smuggling is illegal.

The Card Game

This is a fairly elaborate one! Be prepared to be chatted up for a period (in some cases of up to week) by an apparently friendly Thai man before the mention of a card game comes into play. The story goes that they want you to play a dummy hand in a game whilst they rip off someone else when in fact they are planning to rip you off. Some of the card games will go for hours and you may often find yourself ahead, but do not expect to be allowed to leave the table. Then the sting will come and you will be escorted to someone who will look after a large portion of your traveller checks plus any baht you have laying around.

The Thief
Be on constant guard for petty theft, particularly in popular tourist destinations. A good money belt which can be worn under your clothes is the best kind to ward off wandering hands. Bumbags and shoulder bags can be opened quite easily on crowded public transport or when you are asleep without your knowing.

Watch out for children with newspaper draped over their forearm, or groups of people who approach you, engage you in animated conversation, and rifle your pockets simultaneously. In Bangkok during our last visit, there were some Israeli travellers who were selling 'fashion accessories' which were supposedly a good alternative to money belts, however in both our opinion and that of the police in Bangkok, wearing these waist pouches is just inviting a visit from the thief.

Credit Cards
Credit card fraud is becoming an increasingly serious problem in Thailand. A big problem with credit card fraud is that often you do not know that someone has used your card until it is too late. There is no worse feeling than reaching the bank teller to get your last few pennies for the departure tax, only to find that some low life scumball has run your limit to hell and your card company has a hit squad looking for you! Be aware of leaving your credit cards in guesthouse safes, and report any lost cards immediately to stop all transactions. The best advice is to never leave your card out of your sight. Always double check the amount on the form and on the receipt when purchasing items with your card.

Druggings
Every year in Thailand there are reports of people being drugged and robbed whilst drinking in bars, clubs and restaurants. Generally you are befriended by a group of Thais who will at some stage of the evening buy a round of drinks and next thing you know you get to wake up in the gutter vomiting, dizzy headed and of course cashless — if not worse. Girlie bars seem to be a favourite of the druggers but the problem is by no means restricted to these, as there have been cases on Hat Chaweng and Hat Lamai on Ko Samui and Hat Rin on Ko Pha Ngan.

Trekking
The trekking industry in Thailand has been cleaned up big time compared to the three ring circus which was running full tilt a few years ago. There is still the occasional problem of a robbery whilst trekking, but a much more serious risk is your goods being pilfered whilst left in the care of a guesthouse during your trek. Best advice is to trek with a government approved trekking agency and get a fully itemised receipt of everything you leave in the care of a guesthouse. Better still, get a safety deposit box.

Please note, however unlikely it is that you will be robbed by bandits during a trek, if you are unfortunate enough to find yourself in that minority, *do what they say, give them what they want and live to see another day.*

Drivers
Be very wary of traffic on Thailand's roads, especially in larger cities. The danger may extend to the footpath, which impatient tuk tuk drivers and motorcyclists will not hesitate to use as an extra lane scattering pedestrians left, right and centre. We have heard stories of farangs being rundown by motorcycles on the footpath and being found at fault for not getting out of the way fast enough!

Hitch-hiking

Tales From the Other Side does not suggest hitch-hiking as a safe or advisable way to travel any country. You will never know who the local axe-murderer or rapist is until it is too late.

Hitch-hikers will want to stand well back off the road if they want to get to their destination in anything other than an ambulance (and a late running one at that!) — the middle of the shoulder is not a particularly bright place to stand. When hitching try to keep all your luggage with you rather than placing anything in the boot and 'if the ride just does not feel right' wait for another one.

The thumbing gesture used in the West is not widely recognised in Thailand. Instead, wave your hand face down towards the ground. For more information on hitching, refer to our section on hitching in the Getting Around Thailand chapter.

Border Fighting

Make sure you are aware of the latest problems (if any) along the frontiers with neighbouring countries, and steer away from the regions concerned if any fighting breaks out. In January 1995, artillery and soldiers spilled into the Mae Hong Son and Tak Provinces from the war of liberation between the Karen National Union (KNU) and the SLORC dictatorship. More recently in February 1997 SLORC backed Karen forces crossed the border in Tak Province and razed to the ground a number of Karen refugee camps, apparently at the prompting of the SLORC. A number of people were killed during the fighting, so visitors should exercise extreme caution and be sure to keep themselves informed of goings on in this region. The area is still considered fairly dangerous at times, so exercise care when travelling between Mae Sot and Mae Sariang along route 105 and keep an eye on the Bangkok Post, the television news and talk to other travellers before visiting.

Drugs

This book is certainly not the place for a debate on the legality of drugs, but the fact is, in Thailand, drugs are very illegal, and the penalties are very harsh- even for small amounts of marijuana. Foreigners appear to believe that drugs in Thailand are freely available and, if caught, you will just be able to pay off the police officer concerned. Nothing is further from the truth. If you are caught with drugs in Thailand your chances of being able to pay off the arresting officer or officers are low. Allegedly, 'fines' for one joint of marijuana can reach as high as 100,000B or 150,000B and do not expect the police to hang around while your parent's cheque clears - you will be expected to raise the *cash* within 24 hours. If you are able to pay your way out of a problem leave the country ASAP and buy a lottery ticket!

We recently heard of one alleged case where two Australians were caught in Bangkok with two grammes of cocaine after the guy who sold it to them dobbed them in. It cost AUD$12,000 to have the privilege of getting on the next plane out of the country (quite a step up from the 200B departure tax!) and they had 24 hours to raise the money. Luckily for them they had wealthy friends and family who were able to organise the funds, not everyone is so lucky.

At times such as the full moon parties at Hat Rin, Ko Pha Ngan where there is a wide belief that drug use is tolerated, the Thai Police allegedly have undercover cops (both Thai and Western) operating to find and arrest users and dealers of illegal drugs. Just because the man offering to sell you drugs is Western, long haired and smoking a joint himself does not mean he is not a cop. We would advise smokers to use *extreme* care and caution when lighting up. It is not unheard of for police to plant drugs on you, and anyone openly trying to sell you drugs should be dealt with extreme caution.

Do *not* carry your drugs with you when travelling. Searches of buses, cars and motorcycles are not unheard of, and if you are caught travelling with the drugs, then you are going to be in a whole new world of grief. In the North, particularly around Mai Sai, it is not unheard of for police to set up random road blocks which search each and every farang passing through, supposedly for opium. If you decide to smoke dope whilst in Thailand, do so at your own risk, but please at least take our advice, and do not carry it with you. Dump what is left when you move on. The dope is cheap in Thailand and certainly not worth a stint in the slammer for something that cost you a few dollars.

With regard to smoking opium on hilltribe treks please look into our section on hilltribe trekking. Opium consumption by foreigners is illegal in Thailand and there have been fatalities attributed to over indulgence. Heroin addiction amongst trekking guides is still a problem, particularly for operations working out of Chiang Rai. Please realise that when you ask to do a trek during which you want to smoke opium you are contributing to this problem and do not be surprised if on your first day out your guide gets so stoned that he cannot take you any further!

Foreigners are subject to the same laws and penalties as Thai nationals, and your home country will not be able to get you out of jail. Thailand has not signed the *Vienna Consular Convention* meaning that they are not required to inform foreign embassies of minor drug arrests, so if caught you may find yourself completely on your own, in jail, taking an elongated stay in Thailand courtesy of the Thai authorities. Always pack your own bag before entering and leaving the country, and never carry anything for anyone else.

Police

The police force in Thailand, as in many Asian nations, is underpaid and as in most countries worldwide has a corruption problem. Because of this and because of the perception of Westerners being walking bags of money, you may find yourself a prime target for extortion. This being said, over our many trips to Thailand we have never had any problems what so ever with the police force and have heard many reports of them being particularly friendly and helpful towards farangs in distress. The Thai police force, like any law enforcement agency around the world does have its bad eggs, and incidents such as drug plantings, extortion and robbery are not completely unheard of. If you or your luggage are being searched by the police (or anyone for that matter) keep a close eye on what they are doing.

Legend

1	Mae Hong Son	26	Surin	51	Rayong
2	Chiang Mai	27	Buriram	52	Chanthaburi
3	Chiang Rai	28	Mahasarakham	53	Trat
4	Phayao	29	Khon Kaen	54	Samut Prakan
5	Nan	30	Phetchabun	55	Bangkok
6	Lampang	31	Chaiyabphum	56	Nonthaburi
7	Lamphum	32	Nakhon Ratchasima	57	Nakhon Pathom
8	Phrae	33	Lopburi	58	Samut Sakhon
9	Tak	34	Nakhon Sawan	59	Samut Songkram
10	Sukhothai	35	Phichit	60	Ratchaburi
11	Uttaradit	36	Kamphaeng Phet	61	Phetchaburi
12	Phitsanulok	37	Uthai Thani	62	Prachuap Kiri Khan
13	Loei	38	Kanchanaburi	63	Chumphon
14	Nong Bua Lam Phu	39	Chainat	64	Ranong
15	Udon Thani	40	Singburi	65	Surat Thani
16	Nong Khai	41	Suphanburi	66	Phang Nga
17	Sakhon Nakhon	42	Ang Thong	67	Phuket
18	Nakhon Phanom	43	Saraburi	68	Krabi
19	Mukdahan	44	Ayutthaya	69	Nakhon Si Thammarat
20	Kalasin	45	Pathum Thani	70	Trang
21	Roi Et	46	Nakhon Nayok	71	Phathalung
22	Yasothon	47	Prachinburi	72	Satun
23	Amnat Charoen	48	Sa Kaeo	73	Songkhla
24	Ubon Ratchathani	49	Chachoengsao	74	Pattani
25	Si Saket	50	Chonburi	75	Yala
				76	Narathiwat

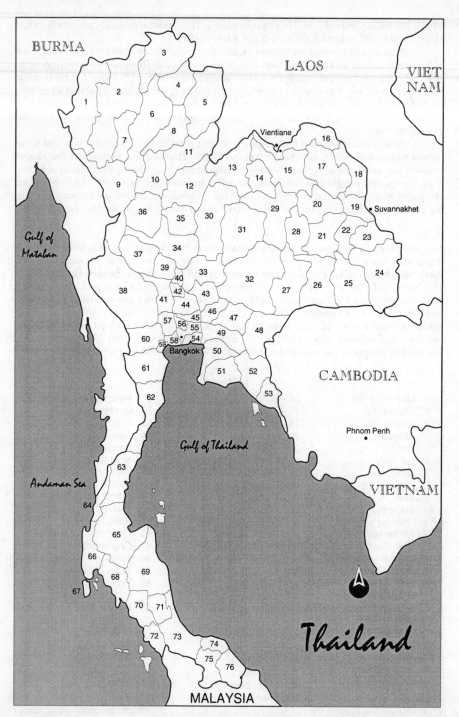

BEFORE YOU ARRIVE

VISAS

Thailand offers five different types of visas but you will probably only require a transit or tourist visa. When applying for the visa, you will need the following:

The Paperwork
Application requirements:

* A valid passport expiring not less than six months after your intended arrival
* 1 application form
* Two identical passport size photographs 4 x 6 cm (taken within 6 months of application)
  Those with diplomatic or official passports require two sets of photographs.

Rules
If you are planning on staying in Thailand for an extended period and want the appropriate visa, you should apply for a Thai visa before leaving home or at least before you arrive at the country's border. Otherwise you can apply for a transit visa at official entry points; Don Muang Airport (Bangkok), Chiang Mai Airport, Phuket Airport and Hat Yai Airport plus the overland crossings. In the south these include Wang Prajan in Satun Province, Sadao in Songkhla Province, Betong in Yala Province and Sungai Kolok and Tak Bai in Narathiwat Province. Whilst in the north and northeast of Thailand the official overland crossings are Chong Mek in Ubon Ratchathani Province, Mukdahan in Mukdahan Province, Nakhon Phanom in Nakhon Phanom Province, Nong Khai in Nong Khai Province, Chiang Khong and Mai Sai in Chiang Rai Province.
　　　If your visa runs out whilst you are still in Thailand, it can be extended for another 30 days at immigration offices throughout Thailand. If you need longer than 30 days the best advice is simply to leave the country and get another tourist visa or you can attempt to get another 15 day extension. If, for whatever reason, you decide to overstay your visa, anything up to a seven or eight day overstay should not create too many problems, but bear in mind that if you intend to work or live in Thailand in the future, long overstays are not viewed favourably. The fee for overstaying is applicable to both land and air departures and is 100B per day.

Health Restrictions
Officially, travellers are not required to have any inoculations or injections for entry into Thailand, unless arriving from a 'contaminated' region. Despite this, we recommend you read our health section before visiting Thailand. Before leaving home you should also check with your local health authorities to ensure health regulations have not changed and that there are no epidemics in Thailand.

TYPES OF VISAS

Transit Visa
This visa is allows you to stay within Thailand for up to 15 or 30 days depending on your country of origin. It is designed for transit purposes, flight connections and short visits to

Thailand. Officially this visa requires a confirmed plane ticket to another country within the 15 or 30 days (although you may not be asked to show your ticket) and a valid passport. Transit visas cannot be extended and are issued free of charge at all legal points of entry to Thailand.

Nationals of the following 55 countries are eligible for a 30 day transit visa. Other country nationals are allowed only a 15 day transit visa or require a visa upon arrival.

Algeria, Argentina, Australia, Austria, Belgium, Brazil, Bahrain, Brunei, Burma, Canada, Denmark, Egypt, Fiji, Finland, France, Germany, Greece, Iceland, Indonesia, Ireland, Israel, Italy, Japan, Djibouti, Kenya, Republic of Korea, Kuwait, Luxembourg, Malaysia, Mauritania, Mexico, Morocco, Netherlands, New Zealand, Norway, Oman, Papua New Guinea, Philippines, Qatar, Saudi Arabia, Senegal, Singapore, Slovenia, South Africa, Spain, Sweden, Switzerland, Tunisia, Turkey, United Arab Emirates, United Kingdom, United States of America, Vanuatu, Western Samoa, Republic of Yemen.

The countries which are only able to get a 15 day transit visa are;

Albania, Andorra, Antigua & Barbuda, Bahamas, Barbados, Belize, Bhutan, Bolivia, Botswana, Bulgaria, Burindi, Burkina Faso, Cameroon, Cape Verde, Central African Republic, Chad, Chile, Colombia, Comoros, Costa Rica, Cote D'Ivoire, Cyprus, Dominica, Dominican Republic, Equador, Equatorial Guinea, Ethiopia, Gabon, Gambia, Grenada, Guatemala, Guinea, Guinea Bissau, Haiti, Honduras, India, Jamaica, Kiribati, Liechtenstein, Lesotho, Liberia, Malawi, Mali, Malta, Mauritius, Maldives, Monaco, Naura, Niger, Panama, Paraguay, Peru, Rwanda, San Marino, Sao Tome & Principe, Seychelles, Sierra Leone, Soloman Islands, Somalia, St Christophor & Naviss, St Lucia, St Vincent & the Grenadinces, Surinam, Swaziland, Tanzania, The Vatican, Togo, Tonga, Trinidad & Tobago, Tuvalu, Uganda, Uruguay, Venezuela, Zaire, Zambia, Zimbabwe.

Tourist Visa
As its name states, this visa is issued to those who intend to visit Thailand for tourism purposes. The visa is valid for 60 days from the date of entry, is cancelled upon arrival and can be obtained from a Thai embassy or consulate before your arrival in Thailand. The cost is A\$18 for each entry, US\$15 in the USA. The tourist visa can be extended for another 30 days for a fee of 500 Baht.

It is possible to apply for a double entry visa on your original application, which allows you to leave Thailand and return to use up the remaining time left on your visa.

Non-Immigrant Visa
To obtain this visa, you must provide a letter of support from a Thai resident. It allows a stay for up to 90 days. If you require more than 90 days, the Thai Immigration authorities in Bangkok must approve your application, and the process takes close to three months. You must obtain a tax clearance before you leave the country. The cost is A\$30 for each entry.

Immigration Visa
Like the non-immigrant visa, you need prior authorization from the Thai Immigration authorities in Bangkok. Requirements include a guarantor and their address in Thailand. (This is for Australian nationals and other people whose country has a bilateral agreement with Thailand). This visa is based upon a quota system, so the length of processing will vary according to the quota. The cost will vary as all expenses incurred during the application process must be paid for by the applicant.

Official Visa
To obtain this visa you need to make an official request. Contact the Thai embassy in your country for details.

Lost Passports & Visas
If you are unfortunate enough to lose your passport or have it stolen, you must do the following. Report your loss to the tourist or local police and obtain a police report, take this

to your embassy or consulate and apply for another passport or equivalent documentation, and upon receiving it, take it to the Thailand Immigration Bureau to have your visa restamped. When you visit immigration take the police report, new passport and a document from your embassy verifying the reason for your new passport. If you do not have an embassy or consulate in Thailand, contact the Ministry of Foreign Affairs (Passport Division), ☎ (02) 503 3497.

Note that for some nationalities your replacement passport may only be a temporary one valid for a shorter time period. So if you want to get a proper passport, take a completed passport form from your home country and keep it with your other valuable paperwork.

Visas for Other Asian Countries
The following prices are quoted from travel agents, unless otherwise indicated, and there are plenty all over Khao San Road. Many farangs that live in Bangkok also use the travel agents in this area as it has a reputation of cheap prices which are difficult to beat. For sample airfare prices see the Bangkok section.
Burma - This visa takes one day, costs 300B to 400B and is valid for one month.
Cambodia - Takes two days to process, costs 850B and is valid for one month.
China - Takes four days to process, costs 1,200B and is valid for one month.
India - The visa takes five days to process, costs 1,150B and is valid for three months.
Laos - Expect it to take three to four days for a 1,400B fee which is valid for two weeks. Visas from the Lao Embassy take three days, cost 1,000B and are valid for either two or four weeks. You will need to visit the embassy three times though which may be an inconvenience. Visas at border crossings such as Nong Khai are much more expensive, with a 24 hour visa service costing 2,400B and a seven day service costing 1,500B.
Nepal - Takes two days to process, costs 850B and is valid for one month.
Vietnam - Takes four days to process, costs 1,250B and is valid for one month.

OVERSEAS ROYAL THAI EMBASSIES

Australia, 111 Empire Circuit, Yarralumla, ACT, 2600, ☎ (06) 273 1149, Fax (06) 273 1518.
Consulate - General, Thai Airways International Building, 2nd Floor, 75-77 Pitt Street, Sydney, NSW, 2000, ☎ (02) 9241 2542, Fax (02) 9247 8312.
Austria, Weimarer Strasse 68, 1180, Vienna, ☎ (01) 310 3423, Fax (01) 310 3935.
Burma, Ward No. 45, Pyay Road, Yangoon, ☎ (01) 35670.
Cambodia, No. 4 Boulevard Monivong, Sangkat Srass Chork, Khan Daun Penh, Phnom Penh, ☎ (23) 26124, Fax (18) 810 860.
Canada, Island Park Drive, Ottawa, Ontario, K1Y OA2, ☎ (613) 722 4444, Fax (613) 722 6624.
Denmark, Norgesmindevej 18, 2900 Hellerup, Copenhagen, ☎ 3162 5010, Fax 3162 5059.
France, 8 Rue Greuze, 75116, Paris, ☎ (01) 4704 3222, Fax (01) 4755 6713.
China, 40 Guang Hua Lu, Beijing 100600, ☎ 532 1903, Fax 532 1748.
Consulate - General, White Swan Hotel, Southern Street, Shamian Island, Guangzhou, ☎ (20) 888 6968 EXT. 3315, Fax (20) 887 9451.
Consulate - General, King World Hotel, (3rd Floor), 28 Beijing Road (South), Kunming, Yunnan Province, 650011, ☎ 341 2996, Fax 316 6891.
Czech Republic, Romaina Rollanda 3, 160 00, Prague 6 - Bubence, ☎ (2) 381 140, Fax (2) 370 646.
Germany, Ubeirstrasse 65, 53173, Bonn, ☎ (0228) 956 860, Fax (0228) 363 702.
Consulate - General, Podbielskiallee 1, 14195, Berlin, ☎ (030) 8312 715, Fax (030) 831 6587.
Hong Kong, Consulate - General, Fairmont House, 8th Floor, 8 Cotton Drive, Central, Hong Kong, ☎ 2521 6481, Fax 2521 8629.
India, 56-N, Nyaya Marg, Chanakyapuri, New Delhi, 110021, ☎ 605 679, Fax 687 2029.
Consulate - General, "Krishnabad", 2nd Floor, 43 Bhulabhai Desai Road, Mumbai, 400 026, ☎ (22) 363 1404, Fax (22) 363 2417.

Consulate - General, 18-B Manddeville Gardens, Ballygunge, Calcutta, 700 019, ☎ (33) 440 7836.
Indonesia, 74. Jalan Imam Bonjol, Jakarta, 10310, ☎ (21) 390 4052, Fax (21) 310 7469.
Italy, Via Bertiloni 26 B, 00197, Rome, ☎ 807 8955, Fax 807 8942.
Japan, 3-14-6, Kami-Osaki, Shinagawa-ku, Tokyo 141, ☎ (03) 3441 1386, Fax (03) 3442 6750.
Consulate - General, Kohnoike East Building, 4th Floor, 3-6-9, Kitakayahoji-machi, Chuo-ku, Osaka, 541, ☎ (06) 243 5563, Fax (06) 243 5597.
Korea, 653-7 Hannam-dong, Yongsan-ku, Seoul, ☎ (2) 795 3098, Fax (2) 798 3448.
Laos, Route Phonekheng, Vientiane, PO Box 128, ☎ (21) 214 582, Fax (21) 214 580.
Malaysia, 206 Jalan Ampang, 50450, Kuala Lumpur, ☎ (3) 248 8222, Fax (3) 248 6527.
Consulate - General, 4426 Jalan Peng Kalan Chepa, 15400, Kota Bharu, Kelantan, ☎ (9) 782 545, Fax (9) 749 801.
Nepal, Ward No. 3, Bansbari, Maharajgunj Road, PO Box 3333, Kathmandu, ☎ 420 410, Fax (1) 420 409.
Netherlands, 1 Buitenrustweg, 2517 KD, The Hague, ☎ (070) 345 2088, Fax (070) 345 1929.
New Zealand, 2 Cook Street, Karori, PO Box 17-226, Wellington, ☎ 476 8618, Fax (04) 476 3677.
Norway, Munkedamsveien 59 B, 0270, Oslo, ☎ 2228 3217, Fax 2283 0384.
Philippines, 107 Rada Street, Legaspi Village, Makati, Metro Manila. PO Box 1228, Makati Central Post Office, 1252 Makati, Metro Manilla, ☎ (2) 815 4219, Fax (2) 815 4221.
Republic of South Africa, 840 Church Street, Eastwood, 0083, Pretoria, ☎ (11) 342 5470, Fax (11) 342 4805.
Singapore, 370 Orchard Road, Singapore 1923, ☎ 235 4175, Fax 732 0778.
Spain, Calle del Segra, 29--2 a 28002, Madrid, ☎ 563 2903, Fax (1) 564 0033.
Sweden, Floragatan 3, 114 31, Stockholm, ☎ (08) 791 7351, Fax (08) 667 6251.
Switzerland, Eigerstrasse 60 (5th Floor), 3007 Bern, ☎ (031) 372 2281, Fax (031) 372 0757.
United Kingdom of Great Britain and Northern Ireland, 29-30 Queen's Gate, London, SW7 5JB, ☎ (071) 589 0173, Fax (071) 823 9695.
United States of America, 1024 Wisconsin Avenue, N.W., Washington DC, 20007, ☎ (202) 944 3600, Fax (202) 944 3611.
Consulate - General, 35 East Wacker Drive, Suite 1834, Chicago, Illinois, 60601, ☎ (312) 236 2447, Fax (312) 236 1906.
Consulate - General, 801 N. La Brea Avenue, Los Angeles, California, 90038, ☎ (213) 937 1894, Fax (213) 937 5987.
Consulate - General, 351 East 52nd Street, New York, NY 10022, ☎ (212) 754 1770, Fax (212) 754 1907.
Vietnam, 63-65 Hoang Dieu Street, Hanoi, ☎ (4) 235 092, Fax (4) 235 088.
Consulate - General, 77 Tran Quoc Thao Street, District 3, Ho Chi Minh City, ☎ (8) 222 637, Fax (8) 291 002.

CUSTOMS

Duty Free Allowances on Entry to Thailand
Cigarettes/cigars/tobacco: You cannot have more than 200 cigarettes or 250g of tobacco.
Wine/Spirits: Maximum of one litre.
Photographic Material: One still camera and five rolls of film or one video/movie camera and three rolls of movie camera film.

Prohibited Items
The usual items are refused entry into Thailand. These include narcotics, 'obscene' material, firearms (unless accompanied with a permit), stinger missiles and certain species of plants including fruit and vegetables. To check on restricted species, you can call the Agricultural Regulatory Division, Bangken, Bangkok, ☎ (02) 579 1581.

   Permission regarding the entry of animals by air can be obtained upon arrival. If animals are arriving by sea, permission must be arranged prior to arrival at the Department of Livestock Development, Bangkok, ☎ (02) 251 5136.

Prohibited Items for Export
Antiques (especially religious and Buddha figurines, including fragments of relics), art objects, the crown jewels and wild animal products are strictly forbidden to be taken out of the country unless a licence is first approved.

HEALTH

Travelling to Thailand poses many possible health problems, but none are insurmountable if you are prepared for them. You will need to see your local doctor before you go to receive the necessary vaccinations and prescriptions. Try and go as early as you can because some vaccinations require booster injections every four weeks. No inoculation are officially required when entering Thailand, unless arriving from a 'contaminated' region, however we recommend you take certain precaution before arriving.

Yellow fever, dengue fever, malaria and Japanese encephalitis are all transmitted by mosquitos. So protecting yourself against these little devils can cut down the risks considerably. Mosquitos commonly bite between dusk and dawn, so wear long-sleeved clothing and long trousers when going out at night. Colognes, perfumes, after-shaves and unfortunately dark clothes attract mosquitos, so avoid these during those critical moments and use insect repellent whenever possible. To reduce the risk even further, it is best to sleep in the most developed and maintained part of town and make sure you do not leave windows open at night. Use a mosquito net with the edges tucked under the bed. Increased protection can be obtained by impregnating the net with Permethrin. Make sure you check the nets for tears. You might also consider using mosquito coils in your bedroom. Also consider taking a bungalow with a share bathroom, as this will remove one source of stagnant water from where you sleep.

If you do require medical attention in Thailand, you will be expected to pay cash up front, even if you have medical insurance — something we strongly suggest you invest in. Keep all your receipts, and claim back any expenses incurred through your travel insurance company when you return home.

Food and Water
The golden rule is: If you cannot peel it, boil it or cook it — do not eat it.

• Tap water can be downright dangerous (although in large cities such as Bangkok and Chiang Mai the tap water in hotels and restaurants is generally OK), so do not drink it or even use it to brush your teeth. Purify all water by boiling for ten minutes. Purifying tablets are not as effective as boiling, but some protection is provided by adding Puratabs (chlorine) or iodine which is more effective than chlorine. Use four drops of iodine to one litre of water and let it stand for forty minutes. Do not use iodine for extended periods or if you have thyroid problems.

• There is a good chance that on a hot humid day you will crave some crushed ice in your drink and you will probably have it and never get sick, but be warned. Ice, although manufactured with clean water is open to contamination when it is transported as the large blocks come into contact with the ground. The ice cubes sold in plastic bags should be safe.

• Drink bottled water and make sure you check the seal is not broken. Bottled water is readily available in Thailand for 3B and up. Reputable brands of soft drink and other sealed drinks are readily available.

• Avoid fresh salads or raw vegetables as they may be washed with contaminated water.

• Avoid eating raw shellfish, crab and cold cooked meats.

Malaria

Malaria is transmitted by mosquitos in the dawn to dusk period. Plasmodium falciparum infection is the most serious and can be fatal. Some types of malaria may persist for forty years after infection. Prevention is therefore the best approach by protecting yourself against mosquito bites and by using prophylactic medication. Chloroquine is a commonly prescribed prophylactic, but there is a high degree of resistance to this medication. Mefloquine is another prophylactic which will protect you against these strains. Mefloquine should not be used in pregnancy and you should avoid falling pregnant for three months after finishing your course of Mefloquine. Doxycycline is an antibiotic that is sometimes used as protection against malaria. Your doctor will be able to prescribe the right type and dose for you.

Anti-malarials (such as Larium) may have side effects such as nausea, vomiting, amazing dreams, mental problems and diarrhoea. If you experience these symptoms seek medical help but do not stop taking the medications in infected areas. There is apparently a class action suit taking place in England against the producers of Larium, whose alleged side effects can be particularly nasty.

The symptoms of malaria develop ten to fourteen days after being bitten and consist of high fever with alternate shivering and sweating, intense headaches, and usually nausea and vomiting. Seek prompt medical attention if you develop these symptoms. (Anti-malarials are not 100% effective, so do not assume you cannot have malaria just because you are taking anti-malarials tablets). Please note that malarial prophylactics are relatively expensive in Thailand, pills such as Doxycycline can cost up to 20B per pill.

Malaria is not of major concern in Bangkok or most major tourist destinations, however it can be a problem in the following areas: Trat Province including Ko Chang (especially the inland area of the national park), possibly Ko Kut as well as rural areas in the province. Also be wary of Ko Samet, some border areas along the Burmese/Thai frontier and the mountainous areas in Phetchabun (Khaeng Krachan) and Kanchanaburi as well as the entire border region of Tak Province, the western parts of Kamphaeng Phet and Uthai Thani Provinces. If you are only venturing to Bangkok, Phuket, Ko Samui or other southern island resort areas, there is little point in taking the sometimes harmful anti-malaria pills.

Diarrhoea

There is nothing worse than squatting half your holiday away over a toilet, yet it is the most common medical problem that travellers face. Most can be attributed to a change in diet in which you are exposed to different strains of bacteria (E. Coli) which you are not used to. Other causes are food poisoning such as typhoid (a form of Salmonella), or amoebiasis or giardiasis or simply too much chilli.

Mild diarrhoea — Maintain fluid intake with diluted soft drink or rehydration mixture (Gastrolyte) if available. Use medication such as *Lomotil* or *Imodium* only if you need to travel.

Moderate diarrhoea — Maintain fluids, self-administer antibiotic such as norfloxacin 400mg twice a day for three days, avoid Lomotil or Imodium.

Severe diarrhoea with fever — As for moderate and seek medical attention if symptoms persist for more than 48 hours.

Persistent diarrhoea — May be due to amoebiasis or giardiasis (also known as dysentry). If you have a fever and have mucus or blood in your stools, suspect amoebiasis. If you have abdominal cramps, flatulence and bubbly, foul-smelling diarrhoea (not a nice thing to have) persisting beyond three days, suspect giardiasis. You may want to seek medical attention, but you can self-administer metronidazole (Flagyl) 750mg every eight hours for seven to ten days. Prevention is the best cure — so be careful of what you eat and drink. Activated charcoal can also provide much relief and is a time honoured treatment.

Rabies

Affected animals include dogs, cats, monkeys and feral (wild) animals. If you are bitten, scratched or even licked by an animal you should wash the site immediately with soap or a detergent (wash, do not scrub) and seek medical help. With proper treatment you should not have any trouble, however if the infection reaches the brain it has a 100% fatality rate. The incubation period for rabies depends on the site of infection. About ten days for the head and neck, forty days for the arms and sixty days for the legs.

Cholera

Cholera tends to occur in outbreaks, especially after floods. So if you find yourself in an epidemic area be very careful of what you eat and drink. Do not even brush your teeth with local water unless it has been boiled. Symptoms include profuse watery (rice-water) stools (e.g. one litre/hour), fever, vomiting and rapid dehydration. Rehydrate yourself with a rehydration solution such as Gastrolyte (the general rule is to drink the same amount that comes out). Get yourself to a good hospital as soon as possible.

Dengue Haemorrhagic Fever

This disease starts with a sudden onset headache, backache, muscle aches and pains, conjunctivitis and fever. Seek medical attention if you experience these symptoms. Dengue fever is still a problem in Ko Pha Ngan.

Schistosomiasis

This is a disease is contracted when you come into contact with contaminated fresh water (which include the larger flowing rivers). The larvae of flatworms in the water burrow through unbroken skin until they hit the bloodstream. The initial symptoms include a rash at the point of entry into the body, and after a couple of weeks once the larvae have hit the bloodstream, fever, pain when urinating, chills and night sweats, fatigue and possibly a rash over the body. If you have any of these symptoms, get suitable drugs from a doctor for treatment. If swimming or bathing in rivers or creeks that may be contaminated (mainly in the northeast) you can reduce the possibility of infection by immediately rubbing your skin with a towel.

Heat

Thailand is a prime location to suffer heat related illness from simple sunburn to the potentially fatal heat stroke. Fortunately the prevention of any discomfort is easy. Some people believe it is only possible to get **sunburnt** whilst sunny, but UV rays are just as potent in cloudy weather. Save your skin by staying out of the sun during the middle and hottest parts of the day, splashing on sun cream of at least 15 SPF (sun protection factor) and wearing light clothes that cover exposed skin. If you sunbathe sensibly you can still take a tan home. **Heat exhaustion** is basically dehydration and its symptoms include headaches, fatigue and light headedness. Treatment is simply getting out of the sun, taking it easy and drinking plentiful amounts of water. **Heat Stroke** is the next level on from heat exhaustion which is recognised by a rise in body temperature, painful headaches, very little sweating, convulsions, delirium and in more serious cases unconsciousness. Heat stroke victims should be taken to a hospital as soon as possible, but in the meantime, try and cool the person with wet towels and fanning.

Snake Bites

Always wear shoes when walking through forests or other potentially dangerous areas as Thailand has its share of poisonous snakes, the Cobra being the most famous. Sea snakes are also quite venomous and there are a number of species, so it is best to maintain your distance from all of them. If you are bitten by a snake — keep calm, apply a pressure bandage over the *whole* affected limb (not a tourniquet) and seek medical attention promptly.

Leeches

During the wet season, the damp National Parks and forests attract blood sucking leeches. To get rid of these slimy creatures from your skin, try rubbing them with salt, vinegar, a flame (such as a lighter or cigarette - any brand will do) or alcohol.

HIV/AIDS

HIV (Human Immunodeficiency Virus) in most cases eventually develops into the fatal AIDS (Acquired Immune Deficiency Syndrome). HIV and AIDS is a growing problem in Thailand and the main forms of infection is through heterosexual intercourse (which goes hand in hand with the busy prostitution trade) and through infected needles with intravenous drug users. The HIV virus can be caught a number of ways; through exposure to infected bodily fluids including blood, semen and vaginal secretions; through infected blood transfusions (all blood in Thailand is tested before use); through infected needles used for intravenous drugs but also tattoos, vaccinations, acupuncture and body piercing.

If you plan on sleeping with sex workers while in Thailand, the chances are very high that you may bring home something other than a tan and holiday snaps. It is estimated that in some brothels throughout Thailand, as many as 25% to 50% of the sex workers are HIV positive (higher in the north) — quite often without knowing it. One of the double standards in Thailand includes the acceptance of men sleeping around because 'they are naturally more promiscuous'. Many Thai men visit brothels increasing the risk of passing it onto their wives or lovers. As in the west, sex workers are often paid more to have sex without a condom thus increasing the chances of infection.

Vaccination Checklist

Note: This table is relevant for adults. Children may have different requirements.

Vaccination	Method
Diptheria/pertussis/tetanus	Booster injection
Polio booster	2 x booster injection - 4 weeks apart
Typhoid	2 x injection - 4 weeks apart
BCG (tuberculosis)	1 x injection
Hepatitis	Vaccine - 3 x injection - 4 weeks apart - the last booster
	should be left as late as possible (6 months)
Japanese Encephalitis	2 x weeks apart (not available in Australia or USA)
Malaria	Do not forget your maleria prophylactic tablets!

Travellers' Medical Kit

Generally you will be able to get medical attention and medicine throughout Thailand for most minor ailments, at local hospitals, medical clinics or pharmacies. Treatment costs are very reasonable (by Western standards). If you are looking at major surgery or get seriously ill, get yourself to Bangkok or home for treatment. It is a good idea to take a small medical kit. There is not a prescription system in Thailand, so medication can be bought over the counter.

Materials

band aids	elastoplast dressing strip	steristrips (butterfly strips)
sterile gauze	cotton wool	thermometer
safety pins	scissors and tweezers	

Medications

Antibiotics	Antacid tablets	Antimalarials
Flagyl	Laxative	Imodium or Lomotil
Paracetamol	Rehydration mixture	Strepsils

Tropical items

antifungal cream	cetrimide antiseptic (Savlon)
mosquito net	cream insect repellent (Muskol, Repellem, Rid)
UV anti-sunburn	repellent sol (Permethrin)

WHAT TO TAKE

We do not want to give you an itemised list of what to take to Thailand, but give you a few hints of things that may come in handy. The first thing you need to bring is an **open mind** and a **sense of humour**. Try not to come with too many **preconceived ideas** on what Thailand is like, as media and friend's experiences have a habit of distorting reality.

Whichever way you are going to travel around, you will appreciate a **light bag**, so take as little as possible. If you have forgotten something, you will be able to buy it in Thailand, or swap, beg or borrow from other travellers. You will be surprised what some people carry around with them. Take enough **padlocks** for every double zipper to stop those wandering hands, and lock up your sacred belongings, even in your hotel room. A **costume (bathers)** is a good idea if you are planning to swim. A **day pack** for day trips funnily enough comes in handy to carry this amazing guidebook, water and other things. If planning to travel in the rainy season, an **umbrella** is recommended, and, if visiting the north in the cool season, bring a **sweater** (jumper) and other warm clothes. You will only need two changes of clothes and do not worry about washing because you can get your clothes washed almost anywhere, but remember dark clothes do not need to be washed as often, as long as you do not have a BO problem or you sweat an ocean of water out every day. **Sandals** for when your hiking shoes are too hot and can be bought in Thailand.

Snorkelling gear is worthwhile taking or buying upon arrival if you plan to spend a lot of your time in the water, alternatively put up a notice looking for someone's gear who is just about to leave. A **tent** for camping if you are going to be exploring many National Parks or other unpopulated areas as well as a **compass** for those long walks. If you are a wildlife freak we suggest you include some compact **binoculars** for viewing the birdlife and monkeys. A good **map** of Thailand is handy.

Take **earplugs** to get away from those noisy bedroom fans or long bus rides. Take a **mirror** for shaving, as often there is not one around for days on end. **String** is very handy for hanging up washing and lynching annoying kids. **Travel scrabble** to keep you stimulated. **Cigarette papers** can be difficult to find (except in tourist centres). **Foreign cigarettes** are also a great present to the locals to show your appreciation. Climbing shoes for rock climbing are useful as Thailand has some of the best cliffs in Southeast Asia.

A **spare pair of prescription glasses** or contact lenses and a copy of your **prescription** is essential in case of an emergency, of course only for those who wear them. Unless you are flying, you may have very long trips ahead of you, so your **favourite book** will come in handy (you do not need five of them because you can always swap with other travellers or buy new ones at the bookshops). A **personal walkman and tapes** are a good idea to send you away down memory lane. **Slide film** and **high performance film** is only really available in Bangkok or popular tourist destinations. The sun will burn you unless you take some **sun protection cream**. **Insect repellent** and perhaps mosquito coils are also a good idea. A small pocket size **torch (flashlight)** will come in handy when the electricity goes out or investigating caves. A **Swiss army knife** comes in handy. For more intimate moments, make sure you bring along condoms as an STD or AIDS is not something you would want to bring home.

If you plan on trying to discover the culture and people, the Thais will appreciate looking at some **photos** of your family, and perhaps some national icons, such as pictures of kangaroos if you are Australian (kitsch meets kitsch). Some spare **passport photos** will come in handy especially if you are applying for another visa or visa extension. Small **gifts** can be useful to give to children such as pens and coins from your country. Try not to hand these out willy nilly but only to those children that you create a friendship with.

If you are planning to travel long distances by motorbike, you would be wise to purchase a good quality **helmet** which you can do in Thailand. Last but not least, pack your stuff in **plastic bags** to stop it from getting wet, especially when travelling in the rainy season or even on boats.

DOCUMENTS

Following is a list of documents that are either compulsory or useful when in Thailand.

Passport

In some hotels and most guesthouses you need to fill out your personal details including passport number. Bring a completed **passport application form** from home in case you lose your passport. This makes it easier to apply for a new one, and you will not be given a temporary one, but rather a completely new passport.

Travel Insurance

Get it. Simple as that. Anyone that travels without at least Medical Insurance is mad. If you have a mishap requiring hospitalisation get yourself to a good hospital in Bangkok, but you do not want to be stuck with the bill. Do not forget to retain all receipts for your insurance claim. As for cover for theft, cancellation, terrorist attack and alien kidnapping, always read the small print. Also read the fine print regarding activities such as SCUBA diving and bungy jumping.

Student Card

This can come in the form of a Student ID card or an International Student Identity Card (ISIC). If you are not a student you can pick up fake student cards in Bangkok for $4.

Blood donor card

Take a blood donor card with your blood type written on it. This is important in case you are required to have emergency medical treatment with a blood transfusion.

Next of kin card

For safety reasons you should always carry a contact name and number of somebody in a position to help you if you are struck with a sudden case of amnesia, or death.

Script for medicine

If you have a medical condition that requires an assortment of pills, make sure you get a letter from your doctor identifying your need for them. This is just a precautionary measure to save you from any trouble, and useful when visiting any country.

Photo ID

Something with your photo on it besides your passport, like a driver's license or a student card is useful for identification if required .

Photocopies

Besides a photocopy of your passport details, keep a copy of travellers cheque numbers and travel insurance information. Keep these in a safe spot separate from your other important documents, ideally with your companion (if you are travelling with one) as well. Photocopies can be readily made in Thailand.

APPROPRIATE CLOTHES

Due to the tropical and humid climate of Thailand, the most appropriate clothing is light cotton — loose pants, shirts, and dresses. These are widely available in Thailand. In fact it is quite feasible to arrive in Thailand with an empty bag, and buy your clothes as you need them. Sandals are highly recommended for their coolness, and ease of removal when visiting religious sites. Covered shoes should be worn if you plan on doing any trekking or motorbike riding.

Long sleeved pants and shirts should be worn whenever visiting a religious site, temple or wat. Clothing such as beach wear, miniskirts, bicycle shorts, tank tops, no tops or topless (you better believe it - we have seen it!) are inappropriate when visiting a wat.

HOW TO GET INTO AND OUT OF THAILAND

BORDER ENTRY POINTS

Thailand can be entered either by air or by ground transport. Only rarely do travellers arrive by boat, in which case you should visit the closest immigration office to have your visa validated. If contemplating arriving by sea, be sure to check with your closest Thai embassy or consulate that you will be arriving via a legal arrival point as otherwise you can end up in trouble.
Note:
All the prices below were taken from travel agents on Khao San Road or from foreign travel agents and are an estimate of price only. Check with your own travel agent regarding price, and always be prepared to shop around. Visa information collated below was correct at the time of print, but may change in the future.

TO/FROM ASIA

Burma

Aeroplane
Rangoon is connected to Bangkok by air with prices starting at 2,500B for a one way flight. If departing for Burma, be sure that you have a valid visa before departure.

Land
Land crossings to Burma are organised in a random fashion dictated by the whims of the SLORC and the security situation. When open, it is only possible to enter on a day trip, the exception being Mai Sai where it is possible to do trips as far as China (subject to the whims of the SLORC). The popular crossings for day trips to Burma are Three Pagodas Pass in Kanchanaburi Province, Mae Sot in Tak Province, and Mai Sai in Chiang Rai Province. A day trip 'visa fee' costs US$5 and you generally need to leave your passport at the border. Please be aware that the US$5 you give the SLORC will probably be used for bullets - not school pens.

Cambodia

Aeroplane
Phnom Penh is connected to Bangkok by daily flights with THAI and Royal Cambodge amongst others. Figure on around 3,200B for a one way flight.

Land and Boat
There are presently no legal land or sea crossing from Thailand to Cambodia although some farangs do cross via Hat Lek. This may change in the future dependent on the security and political situation in Cambodia. Please refer to the chapter on Eastern Thailand for details about crossing at Hat Lek.

China
Aeroplane
Bangkok is linked to a number of Chinese cities with Peking and Kunming being two of the more popular. One way fares are 8,000B and 2,500B respectively.

Land
There is no direct land crossing from Thailand to China. For those contemplating an overland trip, you will need to cross to Laos then to Vietnam via Lao Bao (see below) after which you can cross into China via either Lang Son or Lao Cai.

Hong Kong
Aeroplane
There are daily flights between Bangkok and Hong Kong. The price for a one way flight purchased on Khao San Road starts at around 3,800B. In the reverse direction, China Airlines are the cheapest, starting at about US$150. Other reasonably priced carriers include THAI International and Air Lanka.

Indonesia
Aeroplane
There are daily flights from Bangkok to Jakarta starting at around 6,000B. If you have the time, it is a far more interesting trip heading to Indonesia through Malaysia via land and boat.

Japan
Fares from Tokyo to Bangkok are quite reasonable in price, with All Nippon leading the pack priced at around US$300. Other cheap carriers include China Airlines and THAI International.

Laos
Aeroplane
There are daily flights from Bangkok to Vientiane

Land
There are five overland crossings from Thailand to Laos which are open to farangs. From south to north they are at Chong Mek (Ubon Ratchathani Province), Mukdahan (Mukdahan Province), Nakhon Phanom (Nakhon Phanom Province), Nong Khai (Nong Khai Province) and Chiang Khong (Chiang Rai Province). All of these crossings are by boat except for Chong Mek which is a land crossing and Nong Khai which is via the Friendship bridge. When you apply for your visa, be sure that you state which of these entry and exit points you wish to use. If you plan on crossing Laos as a cheap route to Vietnam, the crossings at Mukdahan and Nakhon Phanom are the closest points to the Vietnam/Laos crossing point at Lao Bao. At the time of print there were plans to build a second bridge over the river at Nakhon Phanom.

Malaysia
Aeroplane
There are daily flights from Bangkok to Kuala Lumpur starting at around US$75 to US$100 for a one way ticket.

Land
One of the more appealing albeit expensive ways to travel the continent is via the **International Express train** that connects Singapore to Thailand, without requiring a change. It leaves from Singapore every morning and arrives in Kuala Lumpur in the early evening. The train continues

north overnight to Penang (Butterworth) then onto Hat Yai and eventually Bangkok. There are daily connecting trains to take you to and from Singapore and Kuala Lumpur, but it only offers first and second class tickets. If you value your money more than your comfort this train trip can be done relatively cheaply on **third class trains** the entire way, although the Malaysian segment is significantly cheaper if you buy it in Johore Bharu rather than Singapore.

There are numerous land crossings between Thailand and Malaysia and there are always sufficient bus services running between the two countries. The main crossing points are Sadao in Songkhla Province, Betong in Yala Province, Sungai Golok and Ban Taba in Narathiwat Province and the little used Wang Prajan in Satun Province.

The Philippines
Aeroplane
Philippine Airlines have a particularly good deal with flights to Bangkok. If you have booked other international tickets with the airline, you can fly from Manila to Bangkok for as little as US$150. Other carriers such as THAI International and China Airlines start at around US$300.

Singapore
Aeroplane
Daily flights to Singapore are very reasonably priced. The cheapest are probably Bangladeshi Air (Biman) which start at around 2,000B.

Vietnam
Aeroplane
There are daily flights from Bangkok to both Hanoi and Ho Chi Minh City (Saigon). Prices from travel agents on Khao San Road start at 4,200B to Hanoi and 4,100B to Ho Chi Minh City 4,100. It is also worth investigating the circuit tickets that some travel agents offer. These generally fly Bangkok to Ho Chi Minh City after which you overland it to Hanoi then fly back to Bangkok. These are quite reasonably priced.

Land
If you plan on reaching Vietnam by land, the only route is via Laos. If you want to spend a minimal amount of time in Laos, the crossings at Mukdahan and Nakhon Phanom are the closest points to the Vietnam/Laos crossing point at Lao Bao. If you cross at Lao Bao you enter Vietnam around the area of Dong Ha in what was once the demilitarised zone.

TO/FROM AUSTRALIA & NEW ZEALAND
Australia
Aeroplane
The cheapest tickets from Khao San Road travel agents one way to Sydney and Melbourne start at around 10,000B whilst in the reverse direction the cheapest one way ticket (low season) is generally around A$500-550 with a carrier like Air New Zealand. For those looking at getting to the cheapest Australian port and are not interested in travelling through Indonesia, Perth is generally the cheapest port with Bangkok fares starting at around 8,000B.

New Zealand
Aeroplane
From Bangkok to New Zealand, prices start at around 14,000B. In the reverse direction, THAI International start at US$525 and Garuda are slightly cheaper.

TO/FROM EUROPE

Aeroplane
With the exception of the United Kingdom, most destinations within Europe are priced at around 9,000 to 12,000B from Khao San Road travel agents.

Tickets to London start a little bit higher at around 10,000-12,000B. In the reverse direction, fares from London to Bangkok start at £275 with Aeroflot, £262 with Qantas and £250 with Royal Brunei.

TO/FROM NORTH AMERICA

Canada

Aeroplane
From Vancouver the cheapest route is with Korean Air and JAL, both of which offer return tickets to Bangkok in the region of CAD$1000-1100. From Toronto the cheapest one way tickets to Bangkok are with Korean and Northwest at around CAD$750 and return tickets start at CAD$1175 with Canadian Airlines. From Montreal low season tickets with Korean Airlines start at CAD$1275 with the same ticket in high season starting as high as CAD$1619. In the opposite direction one way tickets to Canada, bought on Khao San Road start at 16,000B.

United States of America

Aeroplane
From Khao San Road one way tickets to Los Angeles and New York start at 12,000B and 16,000B respectively. In the reverse direction, from LA and San Francisco China Airlines are amongst the cheapest, starting at around US$520. China Airlines are also one of the better bets from New York with single fares starting at around US$625.

TO/FROM AFRICA

South Africa

Aeroplane
From Khao San Road one way tickets to Johannesburg start at 14,000B. In the reverse direction Malaysian Airlines has the cheapest fares starting at around US$575. Malaysian also has some good deals with *Asia circuit* tickets.

TO/FROM THE SUB-CONTINENT

From Khao San Road one way tickets to Bombay, Delhi, Calcutta and Kathmandu start at 4,800B. The cheapest is often with Biman (Bangladeshi Airlines) and if you are lucky you will be able to get a free stop over in Dhaka.

These prices were supplied by **The Travel Specialists** at Level 9 MLC Centre, 19 Martin Place, Sydney 2000, Australia ☎ (02) 9262 3555. **Bridge the World Travel Centre** at 47 Chalk Farm Road, Camden Town, London NW1 8AN, England, ☎ (0171) 911 0900. **Pawana Travel** 72 Khao San Road, Bangkok, Thailand. **Adventure Zone** 187 college Street, Toronto, Ontario M5T 1P7, Canada email: adventure@travelcuts.com.

GETTING AROUND IN THAILAND

Thailand's infrastructure is one of the better developed of Southeast Asia, easing considerably the chore of getting around. The choice of transportation is varied with popular tourist areas serviced by both the public and private sectors, meaning if you choose to go to the islands in the south then to the mountains in the north it is still very affordable. Out of the way towns are also accessible via public buses and trains, and the local sights and places of interest can usually be reached by local transport such as songtheaws, tuk tuk's or by hiring your own motorbike.

AEROPLANE

All major provincial centres within Thailand are serviced by domestic flights with THAI International Airways. Most of them are connected by direct flights to Bangkok, but there are also a range of inter provincial flights. Some of the larger cities such as Chiang Rai, Chiang Mai and Phuket are also serviced directly by international flights, making an overnight stop in Bangkok unnecessary. Other airlines within Thailand are available but have nowhere near the coverage of THAI. Bangkok Airways most popular flights are between Bangkok, Ko Samui and Phuket, and they also have a limited coverage of other destinations with the intention of growing. Other than this your other choice is to jump on a charter flight run by small private companies. At the time of going to print, bidding was underway for a second national carrier, which has just been approved by the Thai government.

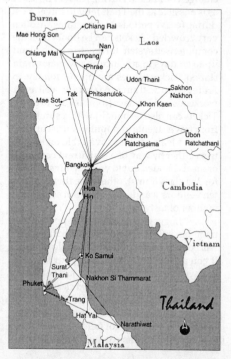

All destinations approachable by air have the necessary details mentioned in the relevant sections. There is also a detailed list of foreign carriers in the Bangkok section if you need to make changes or query your ongoing international flight.

Pricing of domestic flights are very reasonable and when combined with the time savings are often a worthwhile alternative to local buses of the train network.

There is a free THAI shuttle bus that regularly runs between the international and domestic terminals at Bangkok's Don Muang Airport. The terminals are only separated by a few hundred metres.

TRAIN

Thailand has an efficient and extensive railway system covering over 3,000 km. The network originates in Bangkok and heads north to Chiang Mai, north northeast to Nong Khai, east northeast to Ubon Ratchathani, east to Aranyprathet (with a spur down to Sattahip), west to Kanchanaburi and south to Hat Yai with a spur to Trang before leaving the country and extending onwards to Malaysia and Singapore. The eastern route once trekked all the way to Phnom Penh but has been closed for some time. In the future it may be reopen as a hint of peace once again settles upon Cambodia. The western route that extends to Kanchanaburi is once again being extended towards the Burmese border after being dismantled after WWII.

There are two railway stations in Bangkok, Hualumpong and Thonburi Noi. The former is the most used covering almost all destinations throughout Thailand whilst Thonburi Noi caters to some south bound trains as well as the short distance and regional services.

Trains seats are priced according to three distinct classes (1st, 2nd and 3rd) and to the speed of the train (ordinary, rapid and express). Class availability is dependent on the type of train, for example the slowest local trains may have only third class available whilst express super shiny trains tend to have only first and second available.

Many travellers find 3rd class trains sufficient as they are one of the cheapest forms of transport and can be a lot more comfortable than the ordinary buses. The seating generally consists of hard wooden benches where some extra weight on your tush is a definite advantage. Long trips on these seats are not recommended. On other types of trains the benches are padded, making the journey more bearable. If taking an overnight or very long trip it may be worthwhile paying for a 2nd class seat which is capable of reclining, or a 2nd class sleeper.

Tickets can be booked in advance, and for 1st and 2nd class it is recommended to book at least a day in advance if possible. Bookings can be changed and/or upgraded if seats permit. If you miss your train you have three hours after departure time to either refund or change your ticket. During festival times, such as Songkran in April, book as far in advance as is possible as the Thais tend to travel most during festive periods and the trains are often very crowded. Tickets can be booked on the computerised system for any trip in Thailand up to 60 days in advance at any major train station. Ticket offices are open Monday to Friday from 8.30 am to 6.00 pm as well as on weekends and holidays from 8.30 am to noon. Tickets can also be bought with a surcharge from travel agents in popular tourist areas.

Meals are often available on longer trips either by way of a restaurant carriage, or meals handed out to you in your seat (not for 3rd class trains), otherwise there are often vendors wandering the train selling all manner of tasty delights.

Luggage restrictions do apply on the trains but only the heaviest laden backpacker will be worried by the maximum allowances. If you are planning on taking your kitchen sink with you around Thailand, just be aware that the limits are as follows: 1st class (50 kg), 2nd class (40 kg), and 3rd class (30 kg).

Children between the ages of three and twelve who are not taller than 150 cm can travel on trains for half price. If you

have children under three years of age, and under 100 cm in height, they can travel for free as long as they do not take up a seat. Since children only pay half fare, they have half the luggage allowance as well. It is important to note that all train stations throughout Thailand have **luggage storing facilities**, generally for 5B to 10B per day for each item. This is handy if you are only planning to visit a town on your way to somewhere else and need a place to store your pack. Make sure you lock it tight if possible to keep it safe from wandering hands.

The State Railway of Thailand offers two types of 20 day rail passes. Pass A entitles you to unlimited access to all 2nd and 3rd class trains for 1,100B for adults and 550B for children. Pass B is for the same trains but includes facilities such as sleepers and express trains. This pass costs 2,000B for an adult and 1,000B for a child. This pass would only really be worth your while if you like to travel in style or have limited time and want to visit 101 places.

The Thai Railways also offer joint tickets, such as train and coach and in some cases train and express boats to specific islands (similar to the service offered by many private companies that run from Khao San Road). These tickets leave from Bangkok and service Phuket, Krabi, Ko Samui, Ko Pha Ngan, Chiang Mai and Ko Phi Phi amongst others. You can get further details from Hualumpong Station.

In Thailand the trains offer quite a variety of options for speed and comfort. The train type will determine the speed that you will arrive at your destination. The class is divided into three major categories with sub-groups, however as mentioned before, not all trains offer the same choice of classes for each journey.

Type of train	Surcharge	Description of train
Sprinter	70B	Seats only (2nd class sitting with A/C optional available)
Extra express	70B	Ordinary train that stops at most major stations
Express	50B	Ordinary train that stops at all major stations
Rapid	30B	Ordinary train stopping at every station except minor ones
Ordinary		Ordinary train stopping at all stations
Diesel Engine		Faster than ordinary trains
Suburban		Bangkok and immediate surrounds only
Combined		Same as ordinary train with cargo carriages

Train Classes		
1st Class		
1as	Sleeping	Seats change to a bed (2 seats per A/C room)
2nd Class		
2as	Sleeping	Seats change to a bed (carriage has A/C)
2s	Sleeping	Seats change to a bed
2a	Seat	Seat reclines (carriage has A/C)
2	Seat	Seat reclines
3rd Class		
3a	Seat	Non-reclining seat (carriage has A/C)
3	Seat	Non-reclining seat

Sleeping Berth Surcharges		
Cabin	**Cost**	**Train**
Double Cabin	520 B	Air Conditioned
Upper	250 B	Air Conditioned
Lower	320 B	
Upper	100 B	2nd Class in Rapid Train
Lower	150 B	
Upper	130 B	2nd Class in Special Express Train
Lower	200 B	
Upper	250 B	Air Conditioned 2nd Class in Special Express Train
Lower	320 B	

BUS

Travel by bus within Thailand is very regular, efficient, cheap and not too slow. Like the trains there are a number of different types of government buses from which you can choose, as well as a number of private operations. The cheapest and the slowest variety are the regular non air conditioned buses (referred to as ordinary buses). These may have a fan or two working to unsettle the dust when stopped or to aid the wind tunnel created by the open windows when moving. These buses, will stop at every town along a route as well as for anyone that waves their hand out, sometimes making the journey quite long. Despite the possible delays, this form of transport is one of the more interesting and cheapest forms, allowing you to meet many of the locals.

The next step up is a wide variety of air conditioned buses (referred to as A/C buses) which peak at the VIP style luxury coach which often include a complimentary meal and TV or movie. The air conditioned buses are not as regular as the ordinary buses. For long distance travel, ie. anything over six hours, the ordinary buses can become excruciatingly uncomfortable. We would advise an air conditioned bus as the cost is not much more than the regular bus and the extra legroom makes all the difference, particularly for Western legs.

Whenever monks board the bus, they tend to be seated at the rear. If the monk is standing, etiquette dictates that you should offer your seat to him and female travellers should try to avoid sitting beside a monk so as to avoid touching him during the bumpy ride. The rear is generally the best area to sit as there is sometimes more legroom and it is easier to keep your eye on your pack there. However it can get quite crowded with other peoples luggage as well. Smoking on the buses is generally frowned upon.

If contemplating booking a bus on Khao San Road or any other tourist centre for that matter, **be warned** that you may be promised free food, stops to stretch, air conditioning and early arrival time, but often this is just a ploy to get your business. Once you have paid your money and are on the bus it is difficult to complain about the lack of air conditioning, legroom, free meals and stops to stretch, and when you tell the driver what time you were told you would arrive, expect to be laughed at! On the other hand, you may get everything mentioned above but it is all guesswork. Anything an agent on Khao San Road says about bus travel can be taken with a pinch of salt.

WARNING There have been accounts of robberies on the buses at night when people are asleep. This appears to be particularly prevalent on the cheap buses from Khao San Road to Ko Samui and Ko Pha Ngan. One of the researchers has never caught a tourist bus along this route without someone being robbed on it! Do not be too quick in the finger-pointing either, the culprit is often a fellow traveller, attempting to prolong their trip with the cash value of your camera! The easiest place to lose your belongings is from bags stored below the chairs as would be thieves have easy access when everyone is asleep. So keep your most valuable items on your body and try to resist the temptations to drink a bottle of whiskey on the way down.

Just for interests sake if you happen to get stuck at a bus station for awhile, various bus stations around Thailand are participating in a graphic campaign displaying bus accidents and victims photographs on a board in a prominent place. We are not sure if it is to warn the drivers or passengers, but either way it makes you think more carefully about road transport in Thailand.

TAXIS

In Thailand there are two kinds of taxis, metered and unmetered. The majority of taxis within Bangkok use meters, but those elsewhere generally do not. Outside of Bangkok, if your taxi is metered, quite often the meter is 'asleep'. This is particularly the case in heavy traffic, late at night or if catching them from particular areas (bus stations, train stations etc.) Although the first taxi you approach may say the meter is asleep, ask at least four or five cabs before giving in and bargain for the fare.

In either an unmetered taxi or 'sleeping meter' taxi that is not working, you need to agree on the price before you go anywhere. When you do bargain, be prepared to bargain hard — it is not unheard of for taxi drivers to ask upwards of 400B for a fare which on the meter may come to 80B or 90B! If the first price is too much just ask other taxis and you will eventually get a reasonable price. As far as English speaking taxi drivers are concerned, air conditioned metered taxis are your best bet. If you can, always try and get an address or directions in Thai to show the driver and to save any confusion.

Motorcycle taxis are a very popular form of transport in both large and small towns. You will recognise them as the groups of people wearing matching coloured vests who often wait around street corners or bus and train stations. They generally charge similar prices to tuk tuks, but are very handy in traffic jams as they have no fear manoeuvring in between cars with the occasional turn onto a pedestrian sidewalk. Just watch out if you are the pedestrian.

For both car and motorcycle taxi's, make sure you take note of the official number of the vehicle or driver to recover anything you leave behind or for reporting any mishap that may happen along the way.

SONGTHEAWS

Literally 'two seats', songtheaws are basically a converted pick up truck with a roof over two benches in the back. They are often the cheapest form of local transport, following set routes within towns and to connect towns within a province. Usually you will never have to wait long as they constantly ply the roads, stopping anywhere along a route, all you have to do is wave it down. To get off, just press the buzzer attached to the roof or side walls. Journeys within towns are set at fixed prices usually around 3B to 5B, and anything out of town between 5B and 20B, usually paying after you get off. They can also be used as share taxis or chartered but always have your bargaining skills finely tuned. Comfortably seating around 10 passengers, occasionally you will see or be on one that is trying to break the world record for getting people onto a moving vehicle, with every inch (including the roof) taken up by a squashed body - certainly one way to get close to the Thai people.

TUK TUK AND SAMLORS

A tuk tuk is a three wheeled taxi used throughout Thailand. Particularly in the larger cities tuk tuk's are a fast way to get around and a convenient way to get carbon monoxide poisoning. In previous trips to Thailand we have found the tuk tuk drivers to be particularly unscrupulous and very eager to rip off all and sundry. This does appear to have been cleaned up considerably, especially in Chiang Mai, however they will still often ask for exorbitant rates to take you minuscule distances. Put your bargaining boots on. The actual price of tuk tuk's are comparable to taxi fares, but the fare needs to be decided before going anywhere.

A samlor is really another form of tuk tuk also with three wheels, but which is pedal powered rather than motorised. The seated area at the back will fit two people at a really tight squeeze and is pretty slow going, but they are generally cheaper than tuk tuks.

BOATS

Longtails are a common sight along rivers and waterways. Long wooden crafts that can sit from 10 to 20 people, they rely on an elevated motor on the back of the boat for both propulsion and manoeuvring. Commonly used to get to places along rivers or canals, longtails can also be used as tour boats to carry travellers to popular tourist destinations or chartered for your own explorations.

ON YOUR OWN

ROAD RULES

Outside of Bangkok, the roads are maintained fairly well and the traffic congestion is bearable. To make it even easier the road signs are often in English. It is illegal to drive in Thailand without a current international drivers license. We would suggest you invest in some insurance for the extent of your journey to cover you from any unexpected incidents.

Here is a basic summary of a few of the road rules in Thailand. If you are pulled over for speeding or some other 'irregularity' we would advise coming to an agreement with the first police officer (there is a good chance your wallet will talk better than your mouth).

a)   The maximum speed within city limits is 60 km/hr. Outside cities it is 80 km/hr. This counts for both cars and motorbikes.

b)   In Thailand you drive on the LEFT side of the road. On roads with more than one lane in each direction, slow vehicles should use the slow lane on the far left.

c)   GIVE WAY. In Thailand the working laws of giving way are regulated by size. The bigger you are the more leeway you are given. Motorcyclists are fairly low in the pile and should be prepared to be regularly run off the road (along with cyclists, people, water buffalo's and chickens!)

d)   When passing other vehicles, always do so on the right. It is usually the rule rather than the exception to overtake into oncoming traffic, if traffic coming towards you is overtaking in a dangerous manner, be prepared to get onto the shoulder, as they often will not yield but rather are waiting for you to get out of the way.

e)   The Thais love this one - either flash your headlights, or toot the horn when passing another vehicle on the same side of the road.

f)   Road signs are usually displayed on the side of the road and distances are in kilometres. Small concrete road side markers also line the road every kilometre with the route number, town name (in Thai only), town initials (in English) and kilometre number (counting from how far you have travelled from the last town).

g)   Thai drivers seem to have their own set of rules on the road. Despite the fact that roads look like absolute mayhem, once you get an understanding for it, the Thais are actually following some kind of organised chaos. Thais are generally observant and very aware of other vehicles on the road.

CAR

If you can afford it, a rented car in Thailand provides you with the opportunity to see and experience much of the diverse country that you may otherwise miss sticking to the main roads and train lines. The Bangkok section has some suggested car rental places and they are also available for rent in popular tourist towns. Make sure that the rental includes insurance to cover any potential disasters, as there are many of those on Thailand's roads. You also need a valid international drivers license for any insurance to be applicable. Expect the average daily rental to be around 1,000B for a small four door vehicle.

MOTORCYCLE

If a car is not your scene, then maybe a motorbike is, however before you leap on one, be sure to check that your travel insurance covers you in the advent of an accident. Many travellers hire motorbikes for day trips to see the outlying areas of popular towns or for prolonged periods to see more of the country. Expect to pay 100B to 250B per day for rental, less for longer periods, however prices may soar to as much as 400B per day on islands such as Ko Chang. The price of petrol is around 8B to 9B per litre. A valid drivers license is required, if not by the rental company or individual, by the police if they pick you up.

A law has been passed stating that all motorcycle drivers, including tourists, have to wear helmets. Although being a farang you can expect a bit of leeway in this regard, a helmet is a worthwhile investment anyway, especially when you see the Thai accident statistics. A good way to survive on Thailand's roads is to ride like the Thai's. If you see a gap fill it, make sure your horn is loud and use it at every possible occasion! Unlike in the west, where the horn is generally used to insult someone, in Thailand it is used to let vehicles and pedestrians know where you are.

Being a motorcyclist in Thailand is a little more risky than getting around by other methods, but it can be a very rewarding (or debilitating) experience. Here is a few pointers based on 3,000 km one of our researchers rode;

a) Thailand is not the place to learn how to ride a motorbike! Although many people learn how to ride a bike whilst there, some previous experience is always good.

b) Spend your time on the shoulder (if there is one) and always slow down when entering and passing through towns and villages, and especially before you hit a patch of sand or gravel.

c) Be prepared to be regularly run off the road.

d) Just because the bike in front of you has not signalled does not mean he or she is not going to turn, stop, slow down or fall off! Keep a decent distance back from other bikes as otherwise you can end up in a collision. The brakes and indicator lights on the bikes often do not work, so you should really drive with your eyes peeled.

e) Check the bike thoroughly before hire. Hire with insurance and helmet if possible. Check that the tires still have a lot of tread left, that the mirrors stand up to the pressure of the wind, that the horn works and is loud that there is oil in the bike and of course that the brakes work.

f) When planning to turn right (ie. across incoming traffic) be careful to indicate very clearly (preferably by pillion passenger waving) what you are planning to do so. The indication method used in the west to indicate a right turn is also used in Thailand to indicate it is safe to overtake, so if you are not very careful you will end up driving into the side of a car trying to overtake you!

g) If you are involved in an accident and no one is hurt, try to come to an agreement with the other parties concerned before the police show up. If you wait for the police to show up, it will cost you more.

h) Generally, when a farang is involved in an accident in Thailand, he or she is at fault, regardless of whose fault the accident really was.

i) As for what bike to hire, Honda Dream's (100cc) are fairly simple bikes that can cruise along at a comfortable 60km/h with a pillion passenger and can be taken virtually anywhere in Thailand. For any off road adventures, a larger 250cc dirt bike is recommended.

j) Wear sensible clothes. Motorcycling in shorts, sandals, T-shirt and no helmet is inviting disaster. People wear boots when they hike, why not wear them on a motorbike. Long pants, shirts and a helmet are simple, comfortable and sensible wear. Put that cheap pair of jeans you picked up in Bangkok to good use.

k) For those planning on hiring a bike for a longer period, it is worth considering purchasing your own helmet as they are reasonably priced and available throughout Thailand.

l) If you are carrying luggage, try to keep it to a minimum and attempt to keep the weight centred or towards the front of the bike.

m) Never leave anything unattended on your bike as it may not be there when you return.

n) It is illegal to ride motorbikes on beaches, and if caught you will be fined, plus it does not do much for the natural environment.

o) If you do not want to listen to us, listen to your mother.

BICYCLE

This is becoming an increasing popular way to travel around Thailand, either in full or in part. Usually people that plan to cycle around Thailand bring their own bike and equipment, including repair kit and tools. It is possible to purchase good quality brand name mountain bikes in Bangkok, but expect to take out a loan to afford them. They are one of the few things in Thailand that are more expensive than in the west. Many towns have bike shops but the spare parts usually only suffice for local or cheap brands.

Hiring bikes in tourist centres such as Ayutthaya, Mae Hong Son, Nong Khai and Kanchenaburi is a popular way of getting around. In these places guesthouses will usually have a supply or will know where you can get them from. Prices generally range from 30B to 50B per day, but check the bike over before renting.

HITCH

Hitching is a tricky one in Thailand: it is totally acceptable in remote rural areas and totally unacceptable elsewhere. In areas not at all or poorly served by public transport it is the usual and often only method of getting around. However, do not stand there with your thumb out — this is rather rude in Thailand, but either wait patiently in the shade or start walking in the right direction and if someone wants to stop they will do so. Do not try to stop vehicles yourself unless you are really desperate, as many Thais will find this an extremely embarrassing situation. If a pick-up or motorbike does stop, it is often an accepted practice to give a few baht for 'petrol' and regular drivers along rural routes will have a set tariff from one village to another. It is not necessarily easy to know whether they expect payment or not but if in doubt offer some and they can take it or leave it, as they often will do. We were never charged for our rides and were in fact often bought a meal, cigarettes or a drink, however we would shy from saying that you will not ever be charged for a ride. If you are charged, a price comparable to the bus fare is reasonable.

In areas with regular transport and on major roads, hitching is not an accepted practice. Thais do not do it and 'when in Rome . . .'. Public and taxi transport is so cheap and usually reliable in Thailand that most locals whizzing down the highway, seeing a backpacker standing at the side of the road with a thumb out are entitled to think that you could not be serious.

This said, people will stop, ie. those that want to practice their English or those that consider you must be in a really desperate situation (ie, your motorbike and/or passenger are lying wrecked in the ditch or that you will die in the next half an hour unless your dramatic tropical disease is treated immediately in the nearest hospital).

However if you are desperate or missed the last bus and do not want to sleep in the ditch (next to your wrecked bike and agonised passenger), do not stick your thumb out, but rather your right hand with palm and fingers hanging down and flap them around a bit.

Tales From the Other Side **does not suggest hitchhiking to be a safe method for navigating any country. You will never know who the local axe murderer or rapist is until it is too late.**

BANGKOK

Set astride the Chao Phraya River, Bangkok, known as Krung Thep (City of Angels) to the locals, became the capital of Thailand in 1782 and today represents everything both good and bad of a thriving Asian metropolis. Within Bangkok's city limits there are enough sights and experiences to keep one occupied for months and one of the best ways to grasp Bangkok is to wander (oxygen mask in hand) through its streets. The simple fact is that the city does not have enough streets for a city of its size and as a result, Bangkok's eight million inhabitants struggle for space, air and parking space. Throughout Bangkok, twenty four hours a day, the pedestrian plays second string to the thousands of taxis, buses, motorbikes, tuk tuks, bicycles and private cars that clog its streets as a heavy haze rises from the tar like steam from boiling water. Everywhere you turn new skyscrapers and condos are going up whilst simultaneous construction of more elevated roads and a railway continue at a hectic pace. There is no denying that the air in Bangkok is filthy and, when put alongside the crowds, traffic, noise and chaos, the result is an atmosphere which is way beyond most human's tolerance.

However, many find the above exhilarating, for in Bangkok rare are the quiet moments and rarer still are the moments when you fail to feel 300 percent alive. As you wander the streets be prepared to be accosted by thousands of tasty smelling food stalls, interrupted every few blocks by foul smelling khlongs (canals) and belching car exhausts. Wander the realm of Lumpini Park to try to escape it all or seek refuge in Bangkok's myriad selection of air-conditioned museums, temples and shopping centres. Catch the Chao Phraya River Express to observe the action from the water and to witness people being moved as only Bangkok can. Spend the evening out, trying to choose between some of South East Asia's best cuisine, good bars or a burgeoning live music scene. Go clubbing Thai style and attempt to figure out the latest in Thai bopping fashion. Last but not least, get up before most of the others and wander the streets when most of the locals are still only stirring. Watch the monks collecting their alms and the morning callisthenics from your hidden away noodle shop stall, sip the soup and strong coffee and wait for another day to explode upon your consciousness as Bangkok belts its way into the next century.

Bangkok is not only a city of man made extremes, but nature also plays a heavy part in making it as uncomfortable as possible. In the hot season you could almost fry an egg on the pavement (though you would not want to eat it!) and during the wet season, you could swim down some streets. Bangkok and its population also exist in the same world of extremes. Extreme wealth and abject poverty, young and old and ancient remnants and modern wonders live side by side. Bangkok is an urban sprawl that stretches for tens of kilometres in every direction and appears to have no limit.

With a population of between eight and ten million at any one time, up to one sixth of the country's population is living within the confines of Bangkok. The exact number is difficult to estimate due to the continuously fluctuating population and the ongoing problem of urban migration as poor peasants continue to make their way to the city in the hope of a better life.

As the city continues to grow the people in the know are grasping at straws looking for solutions to the growing disaster area which is commonly known as Bangkok. Upon arrival, give Bangkok a chance. Do not let the smog and crowds distract you from what can be a charming and very Thai city.

The Bangkok City Council have recently employed a very serious 'clean-up campaign'. Fines of up to 2,000B can be issued for littering. They have even even gone as far as driving police vans around Khao San Road and issuing warnings in English through loud speakers. So be careful where you throw away that next cigarette butt even though this only carries a 100B fine.

Krung Thep — City of Angels

Although known to the locals as Krung Thep, Bangkok actually has the longest name of any city in the world. Try and get your lips around this: Krung Thep Mahanakhorn Amornrattanakosin Mahinthara Ayutthaya Mahadilok Phobnopharat Rachathani Burirom Udomrachaniwet Mahasathaan Amornphimaan Awataan Sathitsawathapiya wisanukamprasit.

Highlights

Wat Phra Kaew and the **Grand Palace** are two of Bangkok's most impressive and are a definite highlight in any visit to Bangkok.

Wat Traimit contains the largest solid gold Buddha image in the world and weighs around five tons.

Jim Thompson's House was the home of Thailand's favourite farang and saviour of the Thai silk industry.

Vimanmek Teak Mansion is the resting place of much of Thailand's teak and offers a fascinating glimpse into the life of the Thai royals.

Wat Pho contains the oldest and largest reclining Buddha in Thailand which also has the biggest feet — inlaid with mother of pearl.

Orientation

Bangkok is split in two by the Chao Phraya River. Little visited Thonburi sits on the west bank and the 'centre' of town runs out from the east bank. Most of the sights along with the bulk of cheap accommodation and eateries are on the eastern side of the river. This eastern side of town can then be split into a number of segments. Between Krung Kasem Road and the Chao Phraya River are Banglamphu (backpackers' heartland) to the north, the Grand Palace and surrounds in the centre, and Pahurat (little India) and Chinatown to the south. This area is more or less split by Bamrung Muang Road running east to west and Maha Chai Road running north to south. Ratchadamnoen Road, north of Bamrung Muang forms an important link with the Phra Pin Klao Bridge to the west, whilst the east splits out to the northwest area of town.

East of Krung Kasem Road, you have Dusit (containing Vimanmek Teak Mansion and Chitralada Palace) to the north, Siam Square to the east and Lumpini Park further to the southeast, whilst more to the south the up-market and business area of Bangrak (containing the GPO, Silom Road, Patpong and many of the embassies and immigration office).

Further out along Sukhumvit Road (past Siam Square) is another up-market tourist and business area, whilst south of Lumpini Park you have Soi Ngam Duphli, another cheaper area to stay. These areas are best seen divided by the east-west running Rama IV Road, Rama I Road (becomes Sukhumvit Road), Phetchaburi Road and the north south running Phaya Thai Road and Withayu (Wireless) Road. Good Luck!!

Vital Information

Emergency Numbers

Unfortunately for the traveller, the emergency services in Bangkok and Thailand may not speak English, however the Tourist Police should. If you have to make an emergency call, get a Thai person to ring for you or call the Tourist Police to translate.

Police ☎ 191.
Tourist Police ☎ 1699 or ☎ (02) 221 6206-10.
Police Hospital for accidents only ☎ (02) 252 2171-5.
Missing Persons ☎ (02) 292 3892.

Tourist Authority of Thailand (TAT)

There are two main Tourist Information Offices in Bangkok, both with plentiful and essential information on Thailand, opening hours are daily from 8.30 am to 4.30 pm. The first is at 4 Ratchadamnoen Nok Road (which has a large sign out front saying "Tourist Information Office") only a 15 minute walk away from Khao San Road and the Democracy Monument, ☎ (02) 226 0060. The second is at 372 Bamrung Muang Road on the corner with Worachak

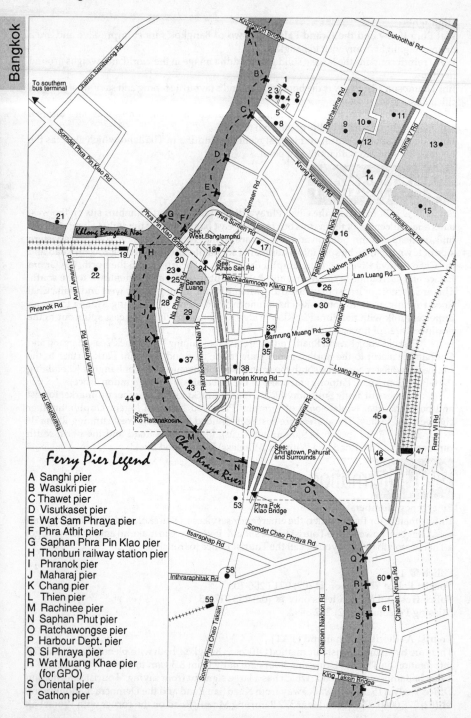

Ferry Pier Legend

A Sanghi pier
B Wasukri pier
C Thawet pier
D Visutkaset pier
E Wat Sam Phraya pier
F Phra Athit pier
G Saphan Phra Pin Klao pier
H Thonburi railway station pier
I Phranok pier
J Maharaj pier
K Chang pier
L Thien pier
M Rachinee pier
N Saphan Phut pier
O Ratchawongse pier
P Harbour Dept. pier
Q Si Phraya pier
R Wat Muang Khae pier
   (for GPO)
S Oriental pier
T Sathon pier

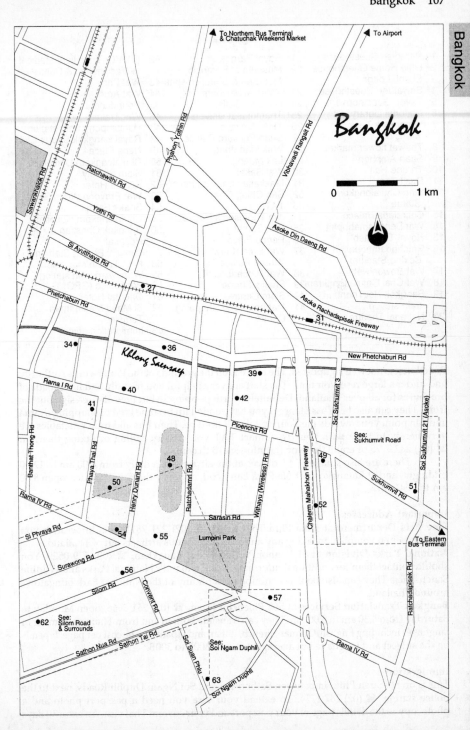

Bangkok

Legend

1	Paradise Guesthouse	21	Royal Barges	42	(TMVC) Travellers Medical & Vaccination & Centre
2	Little Home Guesthouse	22	Museum of Forensic Medicine & Siriraj Hospital	43	Wat Pho
3	Shanti Lodge	23	National Museum	44	Wat Arun
4	Sawatdee Guesthouse	24	National Gallery	45	Roundabout
5	Tavee Guesthouse	25	Thammasat University	46	Wat Traimit
6	National Library	26	THAI Airways	47	Hualumpong train station
7	Vimamnek Teak Mansion	27	Suan Pakkard Palace	48	Royal Bangkok Sports Club
8	Thawet flower market	28	Wak Mahathat	49	Nana Plaza
9	Suan Amphon	29	Lak Muang	50	Chulalongkorn University
10	Throne Hall	30	Wat Saket	51	Siam Society
11	Dusit Zoo	31	Makkasan train station	52	Atlanta Hotel
12	King Chulalongkorn Statue	32	Sao Ching Cha	53	Wat Prayoon Wong Sawat
13	Chitralada Palace	33	TAT	54	Snake Farm
14	Wat Benchamabophit	34	Jim Thomson's House	55	Chulalongkorn Hospital
15	Royal Turf Club	35	Wat Suthat	56	Bangkok Christian Hospital
16	Ratchadamnoen Boxing Stadium	36	Pantip Plaza	57	Lumpini Boxing Stadium
17	Wat Bowoniwet	37	Wat Phra Kaew and Grand Palace	58	King Taksin Monument
18	Wat Chai Chanasongkram	38	Wat Ratchabophit	59	Wongwian train station
19	Bangkok Noi/Thonburi train station	39	Phallis Shrine	60	Post office (GPO)
20	National Theatre	40	Siam Centre	61	Oriental Hotel
		41	Mahboonrong Shopping Centre	62	Si Maha Mariamman Temple
				63	Immigration office

Road but it is not well signposted. The office is on the grounds of the Waterworks Authority and under a large reservoir tank. The staff are very helpful and friendly and have loads of brochures for all over Thailand. Definitely worth popping in but how about a sign out the front! They can also be of assistance if you have ended up in some kind of shopping drama and can point you towards the Tourist Police if need be. Their bus and train timetables are very handy to have with you. To contact TAT you can try calling or faxing them on ☎ (02) 282 9775 or email them on (tatinfo@ksc15.th.com).

There are also smaller TAT offices at the airport open daily from 8.00 am to 12.00 midnight, and at Ratanakosin, 1 Na Phra Lan Road, opposite the Grand Palace, open 8.30 am to 7.30 pm.

Important Addresses
Fine Arts Department at 1 Na Phra That Road, ☎ (02) 221 7811. It is imperative you contact them if you plan on taking any antiques or religious artifacts out of Thailand.
National Parks Division at 61 Phahon Yothin Road, Bangkhen, ☎ (02) 579 0529. You should contact them for additional information on Thailand's National Parks and Wildlife Sanctuaries. They can also book accommodation for any of the National Park bungalows around Thailand.
Bangkok Translation Services at 562 Ploenchit Road, ☎ (02) 251 5666, open Monday to Saturday from 8.30 am to 8.00 pm. They can translate both to and from Thai to a number of languages including English, German, French, Italian and Japanese. The cost per page depends on the subject and language but averages around 300B to 500B.

Immigration
This is on Soi Suan Phlu, in between Sathon Tai and Soi Ngam Duphli Roads, next to the police station, ☎ (02) 287 1774. To extend your visa you need a passport photo and a photocopy of the details page of your passport and your current Thai visa. An extra 30 days

costs 500B and as long as it is your first extension, expect no hassles, but it does not hurt to dress in a 'presentable manner'. In theory after the initial 30 day extension you are supposed to be able to get a subsequent 15 day extension but we were refused this extension without explanation, so do not rely on being able to get it. The whole routine takes 15 minutes, depending on crowds. This is also the place for other Thai visa problems and some helpful brochures are available at the immigration office detailing most immigration hassles. They are open Monday to Friday from 8.30 am to 4.30 pm (break between 12.00 pm and 1.00 pm) and on Saturday for tourist enquiries only between 8.30 am and noon.

General Post Office and Telecommunications Centre
Bangkok GPO is located on Charoen Krung Road (Muang Khae or Si Phraya piers). There is a reliable Poste Restante at the far left hand side of the main building, enter and turn left. There is a 1B charge per piece of mail collected. Any registered post item or large parcel requires passport proof of your identity. There is also a packaging service at the GPO which is open 8.00 am to 8.00 pm weekdays. Within Bangkok, mail deliveries are twice a day from Monday through to Saturday and only once on Sundays and public holidays.

Next door to the GPO is the International Telecommunications Centre (building 16) which is open 24 hours. You can tend to any of your telecommunication needs here with telephone, fax and telex facilities. Phone calls can be made via direct dial to a foreign operator for over 20 countries. The public access fax number is 66 8 466 0140-3 and faxes will be held for you at a charge of 10B per page. To send a fax it will cost 100B (Australia, New Zealand and Northern America), and 110B (Europe and Africa). They can supply you with fax paper to write your message. Please see the introductory section for Home Direct numbers. International telephone facilities are also available at many guesthouses, hotels and travel agents throughout Bangkok.

At official 'Post and Telecom' centres, 30B is charged for collect calls, incorrect numbers and answering machine pick-ups. Sometimes they will also charge you if no-one answers. International phone cards can be purchased for 250B and 500B. Local phone cards are 50B with local calls costing 1B for three minutes.

If coming from Banglamphu or the National Library area, the quickest way to reach the GPO is aboard the Chao Phraya River Express. Get off at the Wat Muang Khae Pier (after Si Phraya), walk to the main road and turn left continuing for 50 m (it is on your left).

Khao San Road GPO
There are many places along Khao San Road where you can make overseas phone calls, send and receive faxes. Prices tend to be more expensive than the official GPO but they can get away with it due to the large volume of travellers passing through. One of the more popular and shops has a large blue GPO sign out the front and is located towards the police station. Phone call charges are comparable to the main GPO in Bangkok, but with a minimum call time of two minutes rather than one. Collect calls are 30B for 10 minutes and phone charges per minute are as follows: South America and Africa 53B, Europe and Israel 48B, USA, Canada, Australia and New Zealand 40B, Asia 38B, Singapore 25B, and Malaysia 50B.

Fax charges per page are exorbitant and are as follows: South America and South Africa 160B, Europe, Israel and Arab cities 140B, Australia and New Zealand 140B, Canada and USA 120B, Asia 110B, Malaysia 130B, and Singapore 70B. They will hold faxes for you and charge 30B per page to collect. The fax number is 66 2 281 1470. You will have to sift through the pile of faxes to find yours, however there is a place further down Khao San Road that writes your name on a board when you have a fax to collect.

There are very few places on Khao San Road, besides the hotels and guesthouses, where you can receive a phone call. One such place is Olavi Tours at the back of Chart Guesthouse which will charge you a high price per minute for a phone call but will let you chat to your friend or family when they return your call to the same place for a flat fee of 30B.

Codes

Bangkok's telephone area code is (02), and the central postal code is 10000, however the 36 districts each have different postal codes. The main codes for Bangkok are as follows:

Bangkok 1	(Pluphla Chai)	10100	Bangkok 7	(Bangkok Noi)	10700
Bangkok 2	(Ratchadamnoen)	10200	Bangkok 8	(Bang Sue)	10800
Bangkok 3	(Dusit)	10300	Bangkok 9	(Bangkhen)	10900
Bangkok 4	(Samsen Nai)	10400	Bangkok 10	(Lardprao)	10310
Bangkok 5	(Bangrak)	10500	Bangkok 11	(Phrakanong)	10110
Bangkok 5	(Pathumwan)	10330	Bangkok 12	(Yannawa)	10120
Bangkok 6	(Samleh)	10600	Bangkok 24	(Khlong Chan)	10240

Email and Internet

Email and the Internet has hit Thailand in a big way. Whilst researching, servers were opening up weekly in regional centres and expanding in Bangkok. A few internet cafes have opened up in popular tourist destinations such as Bangkok, Ko Samui and Phuket, but are still quite expensive. Fortunately the **Hello Pub and Restaurant** has a very cheap alternative offering the service of sending and receiving emails, but as yet you cannot browse the WWW. Their street address is 63-65 Khao San Road (opposite Chart Guesthouse). The email address is **hellopub@loxinfo.co.th** and costs 10B per page to receive and 30B per 30 lines to send with a limit to the time you can spend on the computers. There are more internet cafes throughout Bangkok, see restaurants for details.

Libraries

National Library located on Samsen Road is a brilliant place to do some extra research on your Thailand trip. They have an extensive section on Thai history and culture with a reasonable sized section in foreign languages. Membership is free. The Chao Phraya River Express Boat pier is Tha Thawet.

Siam Society Library at 131 Soi 21 (Asoke) Sukhumvit Road, ☎ (02) 259 4999 is open to members where they can find a wide range of references to Thai history, art and culture.

Bookshops

Asia Books has a number of shops spread around Bangkok, mainly in or around department stores. The main branch is at 221 Sukhumvit Road in between Sois 15 and 17.

DK Book House is the other large bookshop with branches widely spread around Bangkok.

The Bookseller at 81 Soi 1, Patpong Road has a large assortment of popular foreign titles including travel books as well as a variety of magazines and newspapers.

Elite Used Books at 593/5 Sukhumvit Road has used copies of a wide range of reading material.

Teck Heng Bookshop at 1326 Charoen Krung Road has many books on Thailand.

Language Schools

If you are planning on spending a bit of time in Thailand, you may want to participate in some Thai language classes to get you started. Below is a list of establishments you can try for both classes and private tuition, otherwise try and find a Thai person who may want to learn your language and swap notes.

AUA at 179 Ratchadamri Road, ☎ (02) 252 8170, for group lessons.

BIS International School at the Villa Theatre, 591/9 Soi 33/1, Sukhumvit Road, ☎ (02) 258 5099, for private or group lessons.

Nisa Thai Language School in the YMCA Building, Sathon Tai Road, ☎ (02) 286 9323, for group or individual tuition.

Union Language School, level 11, CCT Building, 109 Suriwong Road, ☎ (02) 233 4482, for intensive programmes.

Thai Cooking

So you have had a taste of the delectable Thai cuisine and you want to know how to do it yourself. Well it is possible to learn through Thai cooking classes. Those listed below are located in Bangkok, however other popular tourist towns also offer courses.

Thai Cooking School opposite the Oriental Hotel, across the Chao Phraya River, ☎ (02) 437 2918, has courses that run for five days giving you the basics.

Community Services of Bangkok at 19/2 Soi 33 Sukhumvit Road, ☎ (02) 258 5662.

UFM Food Centre Co Ltd at 593/29-39 Sukhumvit 33/1, Bangkok, ☎ (02) 259 0620, Fax (02) 2650530.

Radio

There are a few stations that you may want to tune into just to check out what English music the Thais are listening to. For the latest list of radio stations and their frequencies, look in the Bangkok Post, the Nation or the Bangkok Metro magazine.

SMASH 96 FM is the latest station to hit the air waves catering to the young Thais with tunes ranging from dance to British pop as well as a few old Thai and Western favourites.

95.5 GOLD FM plays music with English speaking presenters.

SMOOTH 105 FM plays easy listening music

EAZY FM 105.5 also plays those great easy listening tunes.

Chulalongkorn FM 101.5 plays classical music at night after 9.30 pm.

International Courier Services

Below are only a few companies that provide courier services, most with express facilities. For a more extensive list of companies that also provide freight services, visit the TAT office and ask for a copy of the latest Air-Sea Guide.

DHL Worldwide Express at 22nd Floor, Grand Amarin Tower, 1550 New Phetchaburi Road, ☎ (02) 207 600.

Emery Worldwide Courier Express, 142/23 Soi Sueksa Withayu Silom Road, ☎ (02) 233 6263.

FedEx, 8th Floor, Green Tower Building, Rama IV Road, ☎ (02) 367 3222.

Overseas Courier Service (OCS), 22 Soi 1 Sukhumvit Road, ☎ (02) 255 9957.

TNT Worldwide Express, 599 Chong Non See Road, ☎ (02) 249 5702.

WorldPak, 3/3 Sukhumvit Soi 24 Sukhumvit Road, ☎ (02) 258 6796.

Banks

There are banks everywhere. Any main road in Bangkok is liable to have at least a few banks which are open for regular bank hours (8.30 am to 3.30 pm weekdays). There are also some late opening banks. Popular tourist centres and shopping centres cater to those who need money at odd hours, with exchange counters opening well into the night. Popular banks which generally have branches all over Thailand include: Bangkok Bank, Bank of Ayudhya, Thai Farmers Bank, Thai Krung Bank, Thai Military Bank and Siam Commercial Bank. Occasionally their rates are a little different, but never substantially.

Hospitals and Medical Facilities

Bangkok has some of the best, if not *the* best medical care in South East Asia. If you are sick there are definitely worse places you could be. Some of the better hospitals in Bangkok include:

Bangkok Christian Hospital, 124 Silom Road ☎ (02) 233 6981/9.

Chulalongkorn University Hospital, Rama IV Road near the Dusit Thani Hotel, ☎ (02) 252 8131/9.

Bangkok Nursing Home, 9 Convent Road, Sathon Nua Road, ☎ (02) 233 2610/9.

Siriraj University Hospital, 2 Prannok Road, Thonburi, ☎ (02) 411 0241.

Bangkok Adventist Hospital, 430 Phitsanulok Road, ☎ (02) 281 1422.

Beside the hospitals there are private clinics spread all over the place set up by private doctors. You are likely to be treated fairly fast, but at a substantially higher cost. Just look for the green cross (usually illuminated in neon).

One of the best options for travellers with any kind of ailments or medical query is the **TMVC - Travellers Medical Vaccination Centre** set up and run by an Australian doctor. Here you will get expert medical attention and advice in an English speaking environment. The fees are generally expensive, but you are in good hands, and it is refundable if you have travel insurance. Many ex-pats and staff at the embassies and consulates use this centre for any ills they may have, and many will also recommend this place if you enquire for a doctor at your embassy. The staff are very friendly, they all speak English and will make you feel comfortable with conversation and coffee. Call for an appointment or just turn up and they will endeavour to fit you in. The centre is located at Level 8, Alma Link Building, 25 Soi Chidlom, Bangkok 10330 and the telephone number is ☎ (02) 655 1024-5, Fax (02) 655 1026. They are open from Monday to Friday from 8.30 am to 5.30 pm. If coming from Khao San Road, A/C bus 11 travels straight past Soi Chidlom.

For information on other English or foreign speaking doctors, call your embassy.

Traditional Medicine and Thai Massage
Wat Pho contains a **Traditional Medicine School** where you can be treated most afternoons. It also offers authentic Thai massage daily and they run classes teaching this ancient art which are open to foreigners.
Wat Bovornivet holds a **Centre for Herbal Medicine** and if you are interested in learning about special plants go and visit the wat compound where the herbs and trees are labelled.
Wat Mahathat sells raw traditional medicines on holy days only.
Along and around **Khao San Road** are a number of places offering traditional Thai massage and Swedish remedial massage.
There are also many traditional **Chinese and Thai herbal medicine shops** spread around Bangkok worth checking out for interest's sake because you would not dream of using most of the things they have displayed.

Tourist Police
The Tourist Police are there for you, hence they are helpful and generally speak good English. They tend to have booths or maintain a presence in most tourist areas around Bangkok (and around Thailand). If you are involved in an incident requiring police assistance contact the Tourist Police and if possible alert the regular police as well. Check regional information for details. Do not expect them to refund your money if you have been the victim of a scam, but it would be handy if you could provide them with any detailed information such as descriptions or addresses to help them find the culprits. The closest Police Station to Khao San Road is actually at the western end of Khao San Road, on the corner with Chakraphong Road.

FOREIGN EMBASSIES AND CONSULATES

Argentina at 20/85 Phrommit Villa, Sukhumvit Soi 49, ☎ (02) 259 0401/9198, Fax (02) 259 0402.
Australia at 37 Sathon Tai Road, ☎ (02) 287 2680, Fax (02) 287 2028.
Austria at 14 Soi Nandha, Sathon Tai, ☎ (02) 287 3970, Fax (02) 287 3925.
Bangladesh at 727 Sukhumvit Soi 55, ☎ (02) 392 9437, Fax (02) 391 8070.
Belgium at Silom Road, 44 Soi Phi Phat, ☎ (02) 236 0150, Fax (02) 236 7619.
Brazil at 23rd floor Lumpini Tower 1168/66 Rama IV Road, ☎ (02) 679 8567, Fax (02) 679 8569.
Brunei at 154 Soi Ekamai 14, Sukhumvit 63, ☎ (02) 381 5914, Fax (02) 381 5921.
Burma (Myanmar) at 132 Sathon Nua Road, ☎ (02) 233 2237, Fax (02) 236 6898.
Cambodia at 185 Ratchadamri Road, Lumpini, ☎ (02) 254 6630, Fax (02) 253 9859.

Canada at 11th Floor Boonmitr Building 138 Silom Road, ☎ (02) 237 4125, Fax (02) 236 7467.
Chile at 15 Sukhumvit Soi 61, ☎ (02) 391 4858, Fax (02) 391 8380.
China at 57 Ratchadaphisek Road, ☎ (02) 245 7030, Fax (02) 246 8247.
Czech Republic at 71/6 Ruam Ruedi Soi 2, Ploenchit Road, ☎ (02) 255 3027, Fax (02) 253 7637.
Denmark at 10 Soi Athakan Prasit, Sathon Tai Road, ☎ (02) 213 2021, Fax (02) 213 1752.
Egypt at 49 Soi Ruam Ruedi, Ploenchit Road, ☎ (02) 253 0161, Fax (02) 256 9310.
Finland at 16th Floor, Amarin Plaza, 500 Ploenchit Road, ☎ (02) 256 9306, Fax (02) 256 9310.
France at Soi 35 Rong Phaisi Kao, Charoen Krung Road, ☎ (02) 256 9306, Fax (02) 256 9310.
Germany at 9 Sathon Tai Road, ☎ (02) 213 2331, Fax (02) 287 1776.
Greece at 99 Rama IX Road, ☎ (02) 254 9729, Fax (02) 247 1068.
Hungary at 28 Soi Sukchai, Sukhumvit 42, ☎ (02) 661 1150.
India at 46 Soi Prasanmit, Sukhumvit 23, ☎ (02) 258 0300, Fax (02) 258 4627.
Indonesia at 600-602 Phetchaburi Road, ☎ (02) 252 3135, Fax (02) 255 1267.
Iran at 602 Soi Sukhumvit 22-24, ☎ (02) 259 0611, Fax (02) 259 9111.
Iraq at 47 Pradiphat Road, Samsen Nai, ☎ (02) 278 5335, Fax (02) 271 4218.
Ireland at 11th Floor United Flour Mill Building, 205 Ratchawong Road, ☎ (02) 223 0876, Fax (02) 224 5551.
Israel at 25th Floor, Ocean Tower, 11 Sukhumvit Road Soi 19, ☎ (02) 260 4854, Fax (02) 260 4860.
Italy at 399 Nanglinchi Road, ☎ (02) 285 4090, Fax (02) 285 4793.
Japan at 1674 New Phetchaburi Road, ☎ (02) 252 6151, Fax (02) 255 6999.
Korea (Republic) at 23 Thiamruammit Road, ☎ (02) 247 7537, Fax (02) 247 7535.
Laos at 502/1-3 Ramkhamhaeng 39, ☎ (02) 539 6678, Fax (02) 539 6678.
Malaysia at Regent House, 15th Floor, 183 Ratchadamri Road ☎ (02) 254 1700, Fax (02) 253 8970.
Mexico at 44/7-8 Convent Road, ☎ (02) 235 6367, Fax (02) 236 8410.
Nepal at 189 Soi Sukhumvit 71, ☎ (02) 391 7240, Fax (02) 381 2406.
Netherlands at 106 Withayu (Wireless) Road, ☎ (02) 254 7701, Fax (02) 254 5579.
New Zealand at 93 Withayu (Wireless) Road, ☎ (02) 251 8165, Fax (02) 256 0477.
Norway at 1st Floor, Bank of America, 2/2 Withayu (Wireless) Road, ☎ (02) 253 0390, Fax (02) 256 0477.
Pakistan at 31 Soi Nana Nua, 3 Sukhumvit Road, ☎ (02) 253 0288, Fax (02) 253 0290.
Philippines at 760 Sukhumvit Road, ☎ (02) 259 0139, Fax (02) 258 5358.
Poland at 8 Sri Yu Khon Building Sukhumvit, ☎ (02) 258 8891, Fax (02) 251 8895.
Portugal at 26 Soi Captain Bush, Chareon Krung Road, ☎ (02) 234 0372, Fax (02) 238 4275.
Romania at 150 Soi Charoenphon, 1 Pradiphat Road, ☎ (02) 279 7902, Fax (02) 279 7891.
Russia at 108 Sathon Nua Road, ☎ (02) 234 9824, Fax (02) 237 8488.
Saudi Arabia at 10th Floor, Sathon Thani Building, 90 Sathon Nua Road, ☎ (02) 237 1938, Fax (02) 236 6442.
Singapore at 129 Sathon Tai Road, ☎ (02) 286 2111, Fax (02) 286 2578.
South Africa at 6th Floor, The Park Place, 231 Soi Sarasin, Lumpini, ☎ (02) 253 8473, Fax (02) 253 8477.
Spain at 7th Floor, Diethelm Building, 93 Withayu (Wireless) Road, ☎ (02) 252 6112, Fax (02) 255 2388.
Sri Lanka at 89 Soi Ruamchai Sukhumvit 15 ☎ (02) 251 2788, Fax (02) 251 1960.
Sweden at 20th Floor, Pacific Place Building, 140 Sukhumvit Road, ☎ (02) 254 4954, Fax (02) 254 4914.
Switzerland at 35 Withayu (Wireless) Road, ☎ (02) 253 0156, Fax (02) 255 4481.
Taiwan at 10th Floor, 140 Kian Gwan Building, Wireless Road, ☎ (02) 251 9274, Fax (02) 254 9276.
Turkey at 61/1 Soi Chatson, Sutthisan Road, ☎ (02) 274 7262, Fax (02) 274 7261.

Bangkok

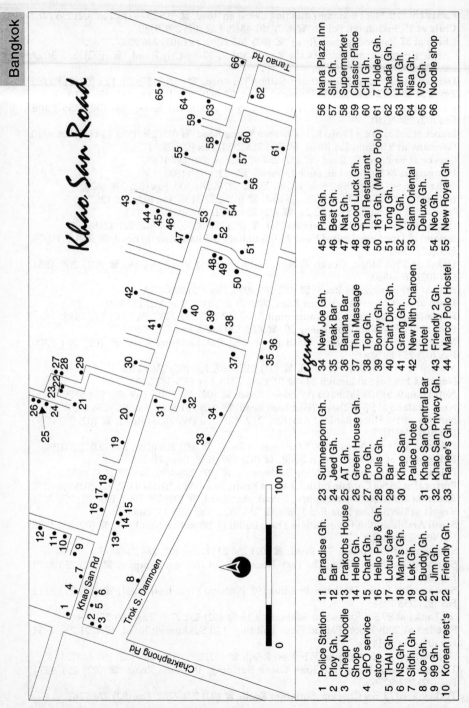

Khao San Road

Legend

1 Police Station
2 Ploy Gh.
3 Cheap Noodle
   Shops
4 GPO service
   store
5 THAI Gh.
6 NS Gh.
7 Sitdhi Gh.
8 Joe Gh.
9 99 Gh.
10 Korean rest's
11 Paradise Gh.
12 Bar
13 Prakorbs House
14 Hello Gh.
15 Chart Gh.
16 Hello Pub & Gh.
17 Lotus Cafe
18 Mam's Gh.
19 Lek Gh.
20 Buddy Gh.
21 Jim Gh.
22 Friendly Gh.
23 Sumneeporn Gh.
24 Jeed Gh.
25 AT Gh.
26 Green House Gh.
27 Pro Gh.
28 Dolls Gh.
29 Bar
30 Khao San
   Palace Hotel
31 Khao San Central Bar
32 Khao San Privacy Gh.
33 Ranee's Gh.
34 New Joe Gh.
35 Freak Bar
36 Banana Bar
37 Thai Massage
38 Top Gh.
39 Bonny Gh.
40 Chart Dior Gh.
41 Grang Gh.
42 New Nith Charoen
   Hotel
43 Friendly 2 Gh.
44 Marco Polo Hostel
45 Pian Gh.
46 Best Gh.
47 Nat Gh.
48 Good Luck Gh.
49 Thai Restaurant
50 161 Gh. (Marco Polo)
51 Tong Gh.
52 VIP Gh.
53 Siam Oriental
   Deluxe Gh.
54 Neo Gh.
55 New Royal Gh.
56 Nana Plaza Inn
57 Siri Gh.
58 Supermarket
59 Classic Place
60 CHI Gh.
61 7 Holder Gh.
62 Chada Gh.
63 Harn Gh.
64 Nisa Gh.
65 VS Gh.
66 Noodle shop

United Kingdom at 1031 Withayu (Wireless) Road, ☎ (02) 253 0191, Fax (02) 254 9579.
USA at 95 Withayu (Wireless) Road, ☎ (02) 252 5040, Fax (02) 254 2990.
Uruguay at 267 Charoen Krung Road, ☎ (02) 225 3718, Fax (02) 224 4139.
Vietnam at 83/1 Withayu (Wireless) Road, ☎ (02) 251 7201.

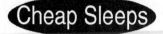

BANGLAMPHU

Most travellers spend their first night in Bangkok on the budget oriented and very busy Khao San Road. Situated in the heart of Banglamphu, Khao San Road is a hub of activity, providing enough guest houses to suit most budgets and travel agencies to accommodate virtually all imaginable travel needs throughout both the Kingdom and overseas.

Due to the incredible demand for rooms in this area, Khao San Road has split at the seams. Guesthouses have sprung up in a somewhat random fashion in and around a one kilometre circle of the road itself. Generally the rooms on Khao San Road are very noisy, cramped, often dirty and with an atmosphere not unlike a public toilet. The further you move from the road the better and the quieter your room is likely to be. For those who want to be within easy walking distance of Khao San Road, west Banglamphu (towards the river) is arguably your best bet, though for those who do not mind a bit of walking, the National Library area is far superior, both in tranquillity and room quality.

The standard of cheap guesthouses along Khao San Road does not vary significantly. Essentially you get what you pay for. The following rates are a general guide for the high season, in low season (April to November) prices are 20B to 30B lower. Dormitory 40B to 70B, single room 70B to 100B, double room 120B to 160B. For these prices you should get a share toilet and shower, and a ceiling or free standing fan. Do not expect to have your room cleaned or the linen changed until you leave.

For the sake of practicality we have split Banglamphu into five sections. Central Banglamphu consists of Khao San Road and immediate back alleys and sois. West Banglamphu is everything west of Chakraphong Road and south of Khlong Banglamphu. North Banglamphu is everything north of Khlong Banglamphu, East Banglamphu covers everything east of Tanao Road and towards the Democracy Monument, and the National Library area which is situated about 1½ km to the north of Khao San Road off Samsen and Si Ayutthaya Roads.

Central Banglamphu

Khao San Road is the 'big magnet' of the Asian backpacking scene. Either loved or despised we are constantly amazed by how many people visit Khao San Road and see no more of Thailand than this small street! (the present record that we know of is two English 'travellers' who spent 24 days here!) The street is lined with cafes, restaurants, tailors, travel agents and market stalls. The footpaths are always clogged with travelling fashion victims wandering the strip all day long.

Arrive with an open mind and you will probably leave with an entire one as long as you do not have too many nights on the Mekong Whiskey. Just do not expect too much of a Thai cultural experience here.

Traditional Thai massage is available on and around Khao San Road at reasonable rates, usually about 100B for an hour and 150B for Swedish Remedial massage. Many places are open until 12.00 midnight if you are looking for that night time relaxation after a hard day visiting the sights of Bangkok.

Most visitors arrive at Khao San Road with recommendations from other travellers, if you do not have one, here is the latest listing including our personal favourites and those which are frequently recommended.

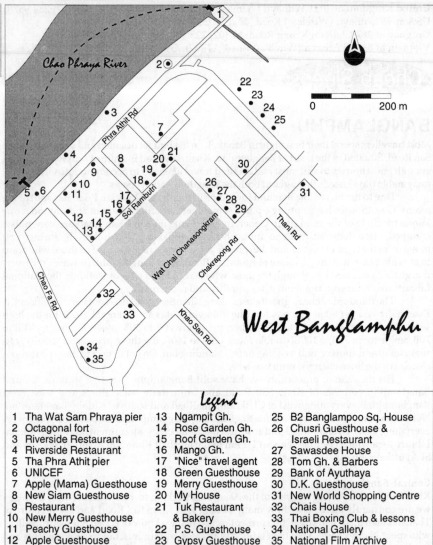

Chao Phraya River

West Banglamphu

Legend

1	Tha Wat Sam Phraya pier	13	Ngampit Gh.	25	B2 Banglampoo Sq. House
2	Octagonal fort	14	Rose Garden Gh.	26	Chusri Guesthouse &
3	Riverside Restaurant	15	Roof Garden Gh.		Israeli Restaurant
4	Riverside Restaurant	16	Mango Gh.	27	Sawasdee House
5	Tha Phra Athit pier	17	"Nice" travel agent	28	Tom Gh. & Barbers
6	UNICEF	18	Green Guesthouse	29	Bank of Ayuthaya
7	Apple (Mama) Guesthouse	19	Merry Guesthouse	30	D.K. Guesthouse
8	New Siam Guesthouse	20	My House	31	New World Shopping Centre
9	Restaurant	21	Tuk Restaurant	32	Chais House
10	New Merry Guesthouse		& Bakery	33	Thai Boxing Club & lessons
11	Peachy Guesthouse	22	P.S. Guesthouse	34	National Gallery
12	Apple Guesthouse	23	Gypsy Guesthouse	35	National Film Archive
		24	Gypsy bar		

Running from west to east on the northern side of Khao San Road are the following:

Sidthi Guesthouse has singles/doubles for 100B/140B and a good restaurant downstairs. Some of the rooms are reasonably quiet.

Paradise is up the soi, east of Sidthi, and rents rooms for 100B to 150B. The rooms are not much and the bar next door kicks later in the evening resulting in the rooms getting very noisy.

Hello is further east and rents singles/doubles for 90B/140B. Their restaurant is one of the more popular on Khao San Road.

Mam's has indifferent staff, only matched by their indifferent rooms starting at 140B for a double. The restaurant downstairs plays mediocre movies all night long.

Lek Guesthouse has singles/doubles for 100B/140B and is one of the quieter and friendlier

choices on the strip itself. They also do some of the best baguettes on Khao San Road.
Buddy Guesthouse has a good restaurant but toss the televisions.
Next is a laneway with four or five places (depending on demand). All are basic:
Doll, AT, Jeed, Greenhouse and **Sunneeporn** all have dismal rooms for 100B/150B for single/double, **Greenhouse** is probably your best bet and is often full.
Grand Guesthouse is back on the strip and offers fairly quiet rooms for 100B/140B for a single/double.
Nat has rooms starting at 100B/150B for singles/doubles.
Best Guesthouse is up the next soi and is a misnomer if there ever was one. This place is an absolute dump.
Marco Polo Hostel is further up and has overpriced rooms at 250B/300B and a comfortable restaurant downstairs.

Now going east to west on the south side of the road:
CH Guesthouse is 80B/120B for singles/doubles and the staff here are friendly.
Neo Guesthouse set back from the street is 90B to 160B, fairly quiet though a little cramped. The staff are friendly.
Marco Polo and **Good Luck** are both up the next soi and both charge 80B/120B for single/double. These are not too bad a choice with the rooms being pretty clean. The seafood cafe on this lane is good value.
Dior Guesthouse A personal favourite. Though the rooms are a bit cramped and the walls paper thin, there is a clean veranda area offering escape from outside. Particularly friendly staff offer luggage storage and travel agent facilities downstairs. Rooms are 80B/120B for singles/doubles with share shower and fan.
Bonny Guesthouse Another favourite. Set up the soi to the west of Dior, ordinary but fairly quiet rooms are set in a small common area with a large rocking chair swing thing to relax on. The staff may smile at you second time around. Mail held and message board available. Rooms rate at 90B/150B for singles/doubles and the dormitory is 50B. The new shower heads are a noted improvement! (It did take four years...)
Chart is towards the other end of the road and is 100B/150B as is **NS Guesthouse**.
Along Trok S Damnoen to the south of Khao San Road are a few places that are quieter and friendlier than the maelstrom just north. **Joe Guesthouse, Ranee Guesthouse** and **Joe II Guesthouse** are all in the 90B/150B range. About half way down the lane just past **Joe II** is the **Freak Bar**, a bit of a place to chill out and it is very popular with Japanese hippies. Next door is the minuscule and/or 'groovy' **Banana Bar**, but beware of police hassles.

West Banglamphu
Accommodation out this way is generally a little cheaper, better value and quieter than Khao San Road. As a result, some of the places are always full, but it is worth a look in if Khao San Road has driven you right round the bend. Starting at the northern end of Soi Rambutri:
Bangkok Guesthouse on tiny Soi Sulao, ☎ (02) 281 5278, clean rooms and friendly staff. Singles/doubles cost 120B/150B.
Terrace Guesthouse with passable singles starting at 100B.
Sawasdee House is next with singles for 130B and 200B with a balcony. The restaurant downstairs is nicely done but the service is pathetic and we have received fairly mixed reports about this place.
Chusri Guesthouse is next and is in the 60B/100B range for singles/doubles with share shower and fan. The restaurant has a Hebrew menu.
Roof Garden Guesthouse Four stories high and affords some nice views of the surrounds, but otherwise not much is going on here.
Chai's House quiet and secluded location, standard rooms here go for pretty standard prices.
Apple Mama Guesthouse Down a very narrow alley for about 100 m guarantees a bit of peace and quiet. Singles/doubles 100B/120B. Run by the same family as Apple Guesthouse.

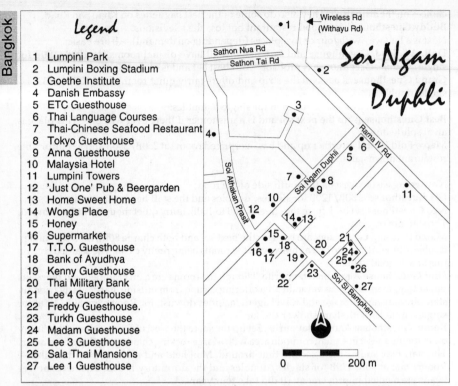

Legend

1   Lumpini Park
2   Lumpini Boxing Stadium
3   Goethe Institute
4   Danish Embassy
5   ETC Guesthouse
6   Thai Language Courses
7   Thai-Chinese Seafood Restaurant
8   Tokyo Guesthouse
9   Anna Guesthouse
10 Malaysia Hotel
11 Lumpini Towers
12 'Just One' Pub & Beergarden
13 Home Sweet Home
14 Wongs Place
15 Honey
16 Supermarket
17 T.T.O. Guesthouse
18 Bank of Ayudhya
19 Kenny Guesthouse
20 Thai Military Bank
21 Lee 4 Guesthouse
22 Freddy Guesthouse.
23 Turkh Guesthouse
24 Madam Guesthouse
25 Lee 3 Guesthouse
26 Sala Thai Mansions
27 Lee 1 Guesthouse

Merry V and **Green Guesthouses** are around the corner, heading south and have rooms for similar rates, 60B/120B for singles/doubles.

New Siam Guesthouse is a right turn up Soi Chana Songkhran. Very popular guesthouse with friendly staff. Charges 180B to 260B for small but clean rooms.

Once you reach Phra Athit Road, **New Merry V Guesthouse** has clean singles/doubles starting at 80B/120B then **Peachy Guesthouse** with singles/doubles for 90B/130B. The rooms here are quite large and even have furniture other than a bed. The garden area downstairs is nice and quiet.

Apple Guesthouse is left again down Trok Rong Mai. More often full than empty, rates here are 60B/100B for basic singles/doubles.

Rose Garden Guesthouse is around the corner from Apple on Soi Rambutri and costs 60B/100B for singles/doubles.

Mango Guesthouse is further to your left on the same soi and has a nice sitting area.

B2 Banglampoo Square House This place comes out a clear winner in the most unfriendly guesthouse of the area competition. Doubles with fan go for 280B, 380B with A/C.

East Banglamphu

Central Guesthouse, **PC Guesthouse** and **Srinthip Guesthouse** are on a small soi running parallel to the east of Tanao Road. They all have good clean rooms and a much quieter feel to them. Rates are all similar, 60B to 70B for a single, 120B for a double.

Nat II and **Sweety Guesthouse** are further south on the road parallel to Ratchadamnoen Road. Nat II charges 70B/100B for singles/doubles whilst Sweety charges 70B/120B for similar rooms. Clustered amongst these guesthouses are some decent street side eateries particularly near to **Nat II** and **Sweety** (both of which have their own restaurants as well.)

North Banglamphu

The accommodation up this way is a lot quieter and less congested with travellers than elsewhere. Many places are set down quiet Thai sois away from the hectic Bangkok traffic. **Home and Garden Guesthouse, Clean and Calm Guesthouse and River Guesthouse** are side by side on a soi off Soi 1, Samsen Road, a good five minute walk from Samsen Road. Rates are 80B/120B for singles/doubles and the people are pretty amiable. A quiet location.

Villa Guesthouse near Samsen Road is a green and quiet escape from Bangkok. Hammocks are supplied in the pleasant garden. Often full, rates start at 250B for a double.

Truly Yours Guesthouse has basic and noisy rooms starting at 140B and indifferent staff. **AP Guesthouse** rates start at 50B/100B for singles/doubles and is fairly quiet but tricky to find. It is east of Samsen Road and up off a branch on Soi 6.

NATIONAL LIBRARY AREA

This quiet area about 1½ km north of Khao San Road is a much nicer area to spend time in Bangkok if you want to get a bit away from the 'scene' on Khao San Road. The biggest hassle is trying to get a tuk tuk driver to understand where you want to go! But Thawet pier is five minutes walk away so a river boat is often a more affordable option. To reach the pier, walk through Thawet market (itself a fascinating area.) The accommodation is concentrated on two sois running north off Si Ayutthaya Road to the west of Samsen Road.

Tavee Guesthouse at 33 Si Ayutthaya Road, **Backpackers Lodge** at 35 Si Ayutthaya Road, **Sawatdee Guesthouse** and **Shanti Lodge** both of which lie on the same soi at 71 Si Ayutthaya Road. All of the above places have dorms for 40B to 60B, singles starting at 80B and doubles starting at around 120B to 150B.

Shanti Lodge is the most popular with no smoking, drinking or meat inside its doors! It has a nice garden and is often full. Fax facilities are available.

Sawatdee Guesthouse is opposite the Shanti Lodge, the staff here are friendly and relaxed although the food is a bit pricey.

Paradise Guesthouse was closed down at our last pass.

Tavee has particularly friendly staff and nicely decorated rooms. You cannot smoke inside as it burnt to the ground a few years ago. The rooms can be a bit noisy, especially when people show up at 4.00 am!

Backpackers Lodge is also very good and if times are busy is probably the best place to try for a bed.

Little Home Guesthouse is at 23 Si Ayutthaya Road and has had several good comments.

SOI NGAM DUPHLI

Before the great magnet was moved to Khao San Road, this is where it was kept and it was Soi Ngam Duphli which hosted the majority of first nighters to Bangkok for many years. Its popularity has dropped off considerably as Khao San Road now offers more facilities and a more central location for comparable and even cheaper accommodation. Soi Ngam Duphli however does still have its die hard loyalists who care about it and its more 'untourised' feel. If you do decide to stay here, bear in mind that it is not as central a location as Khao San Road and in the evenings it can get a bit sleazier and the traffic around here can drive you crazy.

ETC Guesthouse on Soi Ngam Duphli near the intersection with Rama IV Road has small rooms with share bathroom for 140B or 180B with private bathroom. This place is very popular with Japanese travellers and there is a travel agent downstairs.

Anna Guesthouse further down Soi Ngam Duphli has singles for 80B to 100B, doubles for 100B to 120B all with share bathroom or 180B if you want your own shower.

Home Sweet Home on a soi off Soi Si Bamphen. Rooms cost 120B and decent Indian food is available. The rooms here are some of the quieter ones in the area.

Further down the Soi Si Bamphen opposite the Thai Military Bank kiosk there are a couple of guesthouses including **Kenny** and **Turkh** as well as a couple of no name locations with basic and noisy rooms starting at 100B and a lively night trade is thrown in for free. Down the soi between **Kenny** and **Turkh** is **Freddy Guesthouse** with quieter rooms for 100B and 130B. Sometimes it's all shut up so you may have to ask around to get someone to open up.

Just past the Thai Military Bank kiosk there is a soi with a cul-de-sac running off it which contains the best accommodation in the area.

Lee 4 Guesthouse has quiet rooms with veranda shower and fan for 180B, discounts for longer stays though you may have to wake up the staff. Around the bend you have **Madam Guesthouse**, **Lee 3 Guesthouse** and **Sala Thai Mansion** all of which have good quiet rooms starting at 120B. Of the three, **Sala Thai** is probably the best value and has a nice common area. Further down Soi Si Bamphen you have **Lee 1 Guesthouse** which is only for the desperate with small noisy rooms starting at 100B.

Tokyo Guesthouse has friendly but small singles with fan for 100B.

T.T.O. Guesthouse has classier rooms for 250B for a single and 500B for doubles. Both of these places are particularly popular with Japanese travellers.

CHINATOWN, PAHURAT AND HUALUMPONG TRAIN STATION

Not many people choose to stay in this area due to the crowds, traffic and lack of other farangs but it is a fascinating area to stay if you want to get a glimpse of the multicultural side of Bangkok life.

Riverside Guesthouse Classier than average, with a great eating area floating on the river. Situated at the end of Soi Thanan Sanchao. Singles/doubles cost 300B/350B with fan and bath. Ask for a room on the river.

MY Guesthouse on the corner of Sang Sawat Road and Phat Road is probably the best budget bet in Chinatown. The manager speaks good English and has an OK restaurant downstairs. Rates are 150B with share bathroom, 180B with own bathroom. The rooms are clean and those on the roof have a good view. Centrally located in southern Chinatown.

Nine Storey Hotel just off noisy Yaowarat Road with basic rooms including shower and fan starting at 250B.

Dhaka Cafe and Guesthouse on Soi Wiwat Wiang off Ratchawong Road. This nice place has a decent Indian restaurant downstairs. Guests are almost exclusively Indian and Bangladeshi but all are welcome and English is spoken.

Tai Pei Hotel on Song Sawat Road, this huge hotel has rooms starting at 200B with shower and fan. Given its position, the rooms are fairly quiet and big.

Along Maitri Chit Road are a couple of **Chinese hotels** which are brothels first, hotels second. Only for the 'desperate' expect to pay 150B and up at an hourly rate! A place for the whole family!

Si Hualampong Hotel on Rong Muang Road just east of the train station, best and closest if you have just arrived by train. Rooms with shower start at 160B.

TT2 Guesthouse at 516-518 Soi Sawang 3, Si Phraya Road. It is a 10 to 15 minute walk from the station but it is worth it with decent doubles at 200B and dorms are available. A good place for tips on things to see but it is a bit out of the way. To get there from the station, take a left down Rama IV, right down Maha Nakhom, take Soi 8 to the left and it is just around the corner on Soi Sawang 3.

Golden Bangkok Guesthouse on the corner of Chakraphet and Yaowarat Roads. This one is popular with the Indian community and rates start at 250B fan, A/C is 350B.

Other Cheap Indian places Along the soi between Chakraphet and the khlong (canal) there are about 15 to 20 Indian guesthouses. The clientele is almost exclusively Indian but all are generally welcome. If you have just arrived from India or on the way and want to practice your Hindi, this is definitely a good area to stay. Rates are around 100B to 150B for a room with fan and share bathroom. Some of those guesthouses to choose from are: the **Evergreen**,

Bobby Guesthouse, Siam Guesthouse, Calcutta Guesthouse, Metro Guesthouse and **Amarin Guesthouse** (actually on Chakraphet Road). This area is also brimming with loads of cheap decent Indian restaurants.

SILOM

Madras Cafe and Guesthouse down on Soi 13 off Silom Road, this is the only real cheapy in this area. The clientele is almost uniformly Indian and is often full but worth a try. Doubles start at 250B and the food is not bad at all.

Hotel 27 down a soi near Patpong Road offers fairly decent rooms for 250B with A/C, but at times may have a prostitution overflow problem. However, it is definitely close to the Silom action.

SUKHUMVIT

Atlanta Hotel way down the end of Soi 2, Sukhumvit Road, this is your only budget option around. The rooms are not bad and the hotel has a nice garden area and pool. The restaurant is also not too bad. Rates start at 300B for a clean double.

S.V. Guesthouse located off Soi 19, rooms with shared bathroom start at 350B and A/C rooms start at 450B. The rooms are all clean and spacious.

Uncle Rey's Guesthouse situated off Soi Nana Tai, the nice and quiet rooms here are 400B/450B and all have bathroom and A/C.

Eat and Meet

RESTAURANTS, PUBS AND CLUBS

The section below is divided into areas of Bangkok and provides a variety of places to suit all budgets. Included are both cheap restaurants for those watching their pocket and expensive restaurants (in Thai standards) where you can eat in a beautiful setting and spoil yourself. A certain dress standard is expected in some of the more expensive restaurants. Also listed are some places where you can have a drink or a dance and be part of the Thai style nightlife.

Just a note to remember is if you are eating in an established restaurant or drinking in a pub where a service charge is not added (usually the more expensive restaurants) you should always give a tip from 10B to 100B depending on where you are as the waiting staff are often paid disgustingly low wages and rely heavily on tips.

KHAO SAN ROAD

The street is lined with tourist orientated restaurants, hence the choice of food is limited to guesthouse style food that is generally more expensive than any Thai food equivalent. Below area few places that have been tried and tested.

There are a few places that are not ruled by the video machine resulting in a burgeoning crowd. These include **Buddy, Khao San Central** and **Hello,** however the food is pretty average in all three. The first two are opposite each other half way up Khao San Road and often compete with heavy dance music well into the night.

The **Chart Guesthouse** always seems to have particularly friendly staff working making it a pleasant place for a drink.

A cheap and tiny place is the **Lotus Cafe**, and a good place for breakfast is **Prakorbs** offering a pleasant atmosphere, music and real coffee which you can sip whilst reading the daily newspapers they supply.

If you are seeking more choice in the real coffee stakes to help you kick start your day, there

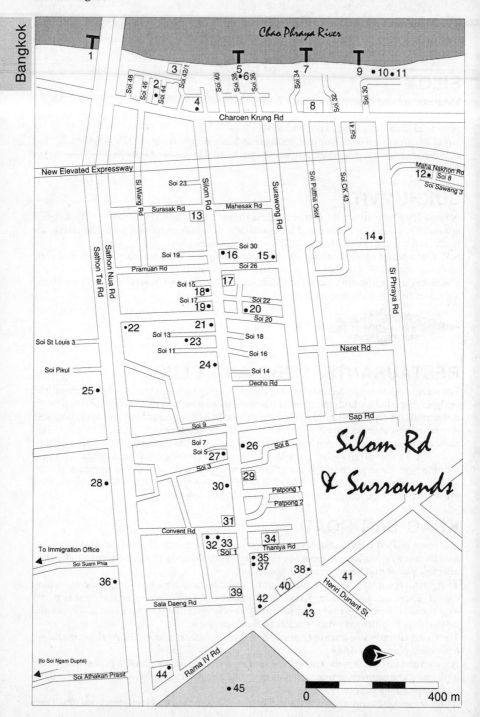

Bangkok

is a **coffee shop** in the alley just south of Khao San Road with a range of brews to choose from. This alley also has a few other gems of places to visit including a small restaurant that serves a variety of quiche and the **Freak and Banana Bar** are interesting places to check out late in the evening.

There are two **Israeli restaurants** in the soi just north of Khao San Road off Chakraphong Road.

For the **vegetarians** a tiny restaurant with a limited but delicious menu is located in the small street behind Tanao Road.

The **New World Department Store** has a food hall on the 8th floor with a wide range of dishes which average around 20B to 30B.

A cheaper choice is the open air street side places a block north on Rambutri Road and Chakraphong Road. There is also a **noodle bar** on the corner of Khao San and Tanao Roads and better ones just around the corner on Tanao Road.

A collection of restaurants also exists along the two sois immediately north of the khlong on the right off Chakraphong Road.

At night there are always food vendors along Khao San Road and the **chicken drumsticks** are one reason why you will always find yourself back on Khao San Road even though they are overpriced! You can also always pick up some freshly peeled fruit.

West Banglamphu

In the evenings there are a number of vendors on the street that serve decent food at good prices and across the road are a couple of restaurants on the Chao Phraya River. Along Soi Chana Songkhran is a lady who sells delicious barbecued whole chickens, a great cheap meal if you pick up a couple of baguettes on Khao San Road. Most of the previously mentioned guesthouses serve standard establishment food.

NATIONAL LIBRARY   หอสมุดแห่งชาติ

For almost 24 hour service there is a great **market** across the road from the bulk of the guesthouses on Si Ayutthaya Road. When one stall closes, another opens up. One food vendor located on the road past the bend does sensational curry dishes with sticky rice. The **Shanti Lodge** serves only vegetarian food if you do not feel like wandering across the road.

Legend

1 Sathon ferry pier	17 Silom Village Centre	34 Thaniya Plaza
2 Robinsons Dept Store	18 Thai Military Bank	35 Royal Jordanian Airlines
3 Shangri La Hotel	19 Hindi Temple	36 Australian Embassy
4 Cheap Muslim restaurant	20 Mosque	37 Body Shop
5 Oriental pier	21 Siam Commercial Bank	38 Jim Thompson Silk Shop
6 Oriental Hotel	22 Burmese Embassy	39 Central Dept Store
7 Wat Muang Khae pier	23 Madras Cafe & Restaurant	40 Charin Issara Tower
8 GPO	24 Tower Inn	41 Pasteur Institute and
9 Si Phraya pier	25 Bangkok Hospital	Snake Farm
10 Royal Orchid Sheraton	26 ITF Tower	42 Robinsons Dept Store
11 River City Shopping	27 Bangkok Bank HQ	43 Chulalongkorn Hospital
Centre & Korean BBQ	28 Embassy of Singapore	44 Front Page Pub
12 TT2 Guesthouse	29 Bangkok Christian Hospital	45 Lumpini Park
13 Holiday Inn/Crown Plaza	30 Malaysian Tourist Office	
14 St Joseph Hospital	31 CP Tower	
15 Maria Bakery & Rest.	32 Delaneys Irish Pub	
16 Bangkok Ban	33 Royal Nepali Airlines	

Bangkok

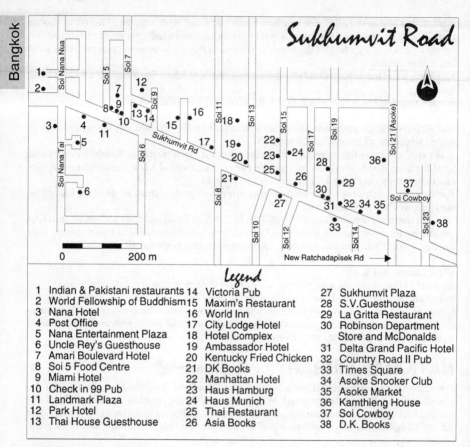

Legend

1	Indian & Pakistani restaurants	
2	World Fellowship of Buddhism	
3	Nana Hotel	
4	Post Office	
5	Nana Entertainment Plaza	
6	Uncle Rey's Guesthouse	
7	Amari Boulevard Hotel	
8	Soi 5 Food Centre	
9	Miami Hotel	
10	Check in 99 Pub	
11	Landmark Plaza	
12	Park Hotel	
13	Thai House Guesthouse	
14	Victoria Pub	
15	Maxim's Restaurant	
16	World Inn	
17	City Lodge Hotel	
18	Hotel Complex	
19	Ambassador Hotel	
20	Kentucky Fried Chicken	
21	DK Books	
22	Manhattan Hotel	
23	Haus Hamburg	
24	Haus Munich	
25	Thai Restaurant	
26	Asia Books	
27	Sukhumvit Plaza	
28	S.V.Guesthouse	
29	La Gritta Restaurant	
30	Robinson Department Store and McDonalds	
31	Delta Grand Pacific Hotel	
32	Country Road II Pub	
33	Times Square	
34	Asoke Snooker Club	
35	Asoke Market	
36	Kamthieng House	
37	Soi Cowboy	
38	D.K. Books	

SIAM SQUARE

Mahboonkrong Centre This centre will send your taste buds crazy with hundreds of food stalls on the 6th floor of the Mahboonkrong Shopping Centre. Virtually every shopping centre has a food hall with tasty and fairly inexpensive meals. Most dishes cost 25B to 30B and you must purchase coupons for the value of the meal which you need to hand to the vendor. Most large shopping centres have a food hall with a similar setup. After your meal, have a look around the shops - they are great if you have a thing for mobile phones, as every second shop seems to sell them (a sign of changing times in Bangkok).

Hard Rock Cafe If you have a tendency to visit every Hard Rock Cafe in every city that has one, then go to 424/3-6 Siam Square Soi 11, Rama 1 Road, open daily from 11.00 am to 2.00 am. You will see the same typical stuff and get a burger for 145B to 185B.

Chinese Restaurant in the Hilton at Nai Lert Park. It is open Sundays from 11.30 am to 2.30 pm. Here you can have unlimited food for a set price of 275B per head.

Whole Earth Restaurant at 93/3 Soi Lang Suan, Ploenchit Road, has both vegetarian and meat dishes with soothing guitar downstairs and relaxing cushions upstairs.

Round Midnight at 106/2 Soi Lang Suan, Ploenchit Road is a pub and restaurant that plays you the blues.

SILOM

Centrepoint, near Silom Road has a food hall on the 4th floor.

Cyberpub, ☎ (02) 236 0450. Internet users can get a fix at this futuristic pub located at the base of the Dusit Thani Hotel on the corner of Silom and Rama IV Roads. The clientele is either wealthy Thais or hotel guests from upstairs and the prices are set accordingly. It costs 150B for a membership card and then 300B per hour or 5B per minute to use the computers. Check out the toilets where the basin is meant to represent some kind of futuristic system, but we doubt its real functionality. The management also organises live bands and when they are not playing you can cruise the superhighway to the groovy tunes of the in-house DJ. Open from Monday to Saturday from 5.30 pm to late.

River City Barbecue on Charoen Krung Soi 30, is a Korean restaurant on the top floor (level 5) of the shopping centre next to the Sheraton. A meal will fill you up for around 250B per person. Here you can enjoy eating a meal with excellent views of the Chao Phraya River. Try and get there before the sun goes down so you can enjoy the sunset whilst eating. The third level of the shopping centre is full of antique shops, almost like a museum but does not cost you anything to have a look around.

Indian Restaurant in Holiday Inn Crown Plaza at river end of Silom Road. This restaurant is very expensive, but worth every penny. Expect to pay around 1,000B per person including heaps of alcohol.

Front Page at 14/10 Soi Saladaeng 1, near Rama IV Road in between Silom and Sathon Roads. It is a pub that has a variety of live music acts and is popular with ex-pats and journo's. Open weekdays from 10.00 am to 1.00 am and weekends from 6.00 pm to 1.00 am.

Molly's Jump If your are an Aussie, or live on the pulse of the music scene, you would have heard of Molly Meldrum. Well now he has his own club in Bangkok at 86/88 Silom Soi 4, open 7.00 pm until very late. It is quite a popular place for farangs and beer prices are reasonable at 70B, 40B at happy hour.

Silom Soi 2 is a very gay street and **Soi 4** is a little gay and both are filled with great clubs and bars where you can wiggle your tush to the latest dance tunes. Just take a wander around here and you will surely be enticed into one of the places, some are mere bars, whilst others are the most happening clubs in Bangkok. Expect to pay a cover charge of between 100B to 200B for some of the more popular clubs. Some places to start with are **DJ Station** at 8/6-8 Silom Soi 2, **Disco Disco** on Silom Soi 2, **Divine** at 98-104 Silom Soi 4 and **Sphinx** at 98-104 Silom Soi 4 (a street level bar).

SUKHUMVIT

Cabbages and Condoms at 10 Soi 12 Sukhumvit Road, has a nice outdoor setting with an awesome range of condoms. Oh, and you can eat here as well between 11.00 am and 10.00 pm. The Thai food is very good and reasonably priced for what you get. This is a very popular restaurant which is starting to branch out into other parts of Thailand. The profits go to anti-AIDS groups in Thailand.

L'Opera on Soi 39, Sukhumvit is Italian and meals cost around 300B per person.

Landmark Hotel on Sukhumvit Road is a great place for an after dinner coffee at around 80B per person, but you pay for the atmosphere.

Pan-Pan Italian Restaurant at 6-6/1 Soi 33 Sukhumvit Road. Meals here start at around 250B per person.

White Earth on Sukhumvit 26 is also worth checking out for a great meal.

Blue Moon Junction at 73 Sukhumvit 55 and open daily from 6.00 pm to 2.00 am. This is a live music venue with jazz and blues early on, followed by pop. They also have cabaret shows Fridays and Saturday for half an hour at 11.00 pm.

Cheap Charlies lives by his word in every sense of the word. This open air pub with no tables or chairs and is very popular with beers going for 30B. Check it out at 1 Sukhumvit Soi 11 every day from 3.00 pm to late.

Bangkok

Chao
Phraya
River

Sanam
Luang

Na Phra Lan Rd

Mahathat Rd

Thai Wang Rd

Charoen Krung Rd

Phra Phiphit Rd

Chetuphon Rd

Khlong
Bangkok
Yai

Ko Ratanakosin

0   200 m

Legend

1   Thawet flower market
2   National Gallery
3   National Theatre
4   National Museum
5   Thammasat University
6   Wat Mahathat
7   Maharaj pier
8   Silpakorn University
9   Chang pier
10 Lak Muang(City Pillar)
11 Wat
12 Royal Grand Palace
13 Saranrom Palace
14 Wat Ratchabophit
15 Thian pier
16 Wat Pho
17 Wat Arun
18 Police station
19 Rachinee pier

Utopia at 116/1 Sukhumvit 23 opposite Tia Maria is a meeting place for gay people open daily from noon to 2.00 am. It is open for both the girls and guys and consists of a shop and cafe, regular exhibitions as well as weekly video on Wednesdays at 8.30 pm. The Utopia Pub has a lesbian night every Friday.

CHINATOWN AND PAHURAT ROAD

Ped Tun Jao Thaa (Duck Noodle House) at 945 Soi Wanit 2. From Wat Traimit, cross Charoen Krung Road and walk up the tiny soi. The duck is exceptionally good, and the reasonable prices will put a smile on your face. It is open Monday to Saturday 5.30 pm till late.

The **Central Department Store** on Pahurat Road has a reasonably priced restaurant on the top floor in an air-conditioned setting.

OTHER AREAS

Clubs

Royal City Avenue, popularly known as RCA, it is off Rama IX Road. This street was once the place to be 'seen', and has to be seen to be believed. Originally there was a 1 km strip of nightclubs back to back, but now many have closed down leaving a strip of about 500 m where dance music pumps out of each doorway. It is quite a way from downtown Bangkok and a taxi there costs around 100B. Very few farangs make it out this far. Drinks are expensive at all the clubs, up to 150B for a small beer.

Saxophone Pub on Phahon Yothin Road near the Victory Monument has three floors where you can enjoy live jazz, reggae and blues. It is open every day from 7.30 pm to 2.00 am.

Party House on Rama IX Road is a gigantic entertainment complex complete with a variety of discos. It is the place to go to see how the more affluent Thais spend their weekends. **Abstract Fun Pub** If you need a thrash hit after doing some shopping, head to this pub at Sunday Plaza Soi 3, Chatuchak, behind the weekend market, open Saturday and Sunday only from noon to 10.00 pm. Bands play very loud covers of popular bands such as Green Day and Radiohead.

Visiting Wats and Royal Palaces

Many visitors that come to Thailand do so on short trips and unfortunately fail to gather a full understanding of the significance of religious and royal relics and buildings. Although we have pointed out social misnomers in our cultural section, we must insist on repeating a few points for those who intend to visit these places, especially after repeatedly seeing visitors abuse their welcome.

Absolute respect must be shown at all times in everything you do, but especially at wats, temples and royal palaces. Even though Thailand gets extremely humid and hot, always dress conservatively, with either long trousers or skirt and, at the minimum, a baggy T-shirt (shorts and singlets are out). Take your shoes off whenever you enter a place of worship, a building with royal connections, someone's house or any building that states you must do so (including most museums). Females should never touch or directly hand anything over to a monk and do not sneak around trying to get a photo of a Thai national or religious person - politely ask and you will more than likely be blessed with a perfect photo. These are the 'rules' that visitors tend to most abuse mainly due to ignorance. For a more extensive list, read our cultural section at the beginning of this guidebook. If you see someone acting disrespectfully, please politely make them aware of the correct way to act, as Thais will generally remain quietly offended.

Grand Palace   พระที่นั่งจักรี

The Grand Palace was constructed in 1782 to commemorate and house the most recent Thai dynasty royals. Most of the walled-in palace compound is still used by the royal family and as a result is closed to the public. A description of the buildings in the palace grounds allowing public access are mentioned below but one activity definitely worth doing is to walk through the grounds to soak up some of the regal extravagance. The magnificent buildings within the Grand Palace compound show a variety of Thai architectural styles as they were built over the reign of several kings.

Before the Dusit Hall is **Chakri Mahaprasat** which was designed by English architects. You are not allowed in, but the gardens are nice and make a nice photo. Before Chakri Mahaprasat is **Amarinda Hall** which is used for coronation ceremonies. The **Pavilion for Holy Water** is a traditional hall where priests used to attend a ceremony to swear their allegiance to the royalty. The **Royal Thai Decoration and Coin Pavilion** is open to the public and contains displays of Thai currency dating back as far as the 11th Century. As its name suggests, this pavilion also exhibits a variety of royal paraphernalia.

The admission fee is a steep 100B but this gives you entry to the Grand Palace, Wat Phra Kaew, Royal Thai Decorations and Coin Museum (too bad they do not have a stamp collectors hall to check out!!), the Vimanmek Mansion and the Dusit Throne. It is open daily from 8.30 am to 11.30 am and 1.00 pm to 3.30 pm. The Grand Palace is on Na Phra Lan Road, near Sanam Luang. You can get there via the Chao Phraya River Express Boat, alighting at Tha Chang Pier. There are also many buses that service this area including ordinary buses 1, 25, 44, 47, 53, 82 and 91, as well as A/C buses 3, 6, 8, 12 and 44.

Wat Phra Kaew (Temple of the Emerald Buddha)   วัดพระแก้ว

Adjacent to the Grand Palace and built in 1782 by King Rama I, Wat Phra Kaew (Temple of the Emerald Buddha) is home to the most sacred image in Thailand, the Emerald Buddha, which, just to fool you, is made of jade. Although the temple is the resident wat for the royal family, it is open to the public when it is not being used. The temple and chapel contain architectural styles from both the Ayutthaya and Ratanakosin Periods and detailed murals featuring the life of Buddha and the well known Thai Ramakien story. The Buddha image was moved from Chiang Mai, where it was found in 1464, to its current resting place but its origins are unknown.

Entry will be refused if you are not dressed appropriately, and photography, filming and recording is strictly banned within the bot. Please be sure to dress respectfully, remove your shoes upon entering the bot and if seated, turn the soles of your feet away so they are not facing the emerald Buddha. The wat is located on Na Phra Lan Road, near Sanam Luang and open every day from 8.00 am to 4.00 pm, ☎ (02) 2220094. To get there refer to the details above for the Grand Palace.

Vimanmek Teak Mansion   พระที่นั่งวิมานเมฆ

This incredible teak mansion is one of the 'must sees' of Bangkok. Although there is little traditional Thai to be seen here, the mansion is worth seeing just to stroll through and sample its amazing regal opulence and fine, mostly European, artefacts. The mansion is set to the north of downtown Bangkok in the vicinity of Dusit Throne Hall.

Vimanmek Mansion was originally constructed on Ko Si Chang in the mid 19th Century but following a trip to Europe in 1897, King Rama V decreed that the mansion be moved to Dusit Garden. On 27 March, 1901 the mansion was officially opened and King Rama V adopted it as his permanent place of residence. He lived there for five years before moving to Amporn Satern residence until his death in 1910. During the reign of King Rama VI, Her Majesty, Indhara Saksal, lived there until his death, after which the mansion remained unoccupied until 1982. Since 1982 the mansion has served as a museum of Thai National Heritage including some work of King Rama V.

The mansion displays an undeniably Western influence, reflected in the fact that much of the ornamentation originated in from Europe and North America. In all there are 31 rooms open to the public, though it is difficult to pick out favourites, as on the whole, they are all stunning. The bedroom, bathroom (including Thailand's first shower!!) dining room and 'throne room' deserve particular attention. The mansion is formed by two right angled wings each of three storeys and the octagonal residence of the King which is four storeys. The mansion is built entirely of teak wood (a resource of which Thailand now has precious little) and is said to be the largest teak palace in the world.

The mansion is open from 9.30 am to 3.15 pm and an English tour leaves every half hour starting at 9.45 am. The tours are very good, take about one hour and are free of charge. There are also two performances of Thai dancing and boxing - one at 10.30 am, the other at 2.00 pm (the performances are performed consecutively) Admission to the mansion is 50B if you do not have a Grand Palace ticket. To reach the mansion, buses 17, 18, 28, 58, 70 or A/C 10, 18 and 3 all pass within a reasonable walking distance - just get off by the park and walk.

Dusit Throne Hall   อภิเศกดุสิต

An area of great interest is **Dusit Hall** which is where the Queen Mother was kept in state for eight months. At the centre of the hall is a throne made of mother of pearl topped by a regal umbrella. If you are wondering why the umbrella is a bit tatty, it is because it can only be changed when the King changes (and the King has been reigning for over 50 years).

This building is to the east of Vimanmek Mansion and is now used to house an interesting collection of work crafted by members of SUPPORT (Promotion of Supplementary Occupations and Related Techniques Foundation) which is sponsored by the Queen. There is a large collection of handicrafts here including cloth, baskets, silverwork, glassware and sculptures made from beetle wings, topped off by the throne which is also here. The throne hall is open from 10.00 am to 4.00 pm every day and admission is 50B if you do not have a Grand Palace ticket.

As with Vimanmek Mansion, proper dress is necessary and there are no clothes for hire. Bags, shoes and photographic and filming equipment must be left in lockers.

Wat Pho (Temple of the Reclining Buddha) - Wat Phra Chetuphon วัดโพธิ์

This immense complex is the oldest and largest temple in Bangkok and has the reputation as the oldest learning centre in Thailand. Quite fittingly, it also contains the oldest and largest reclining Buddha in Thailand. The feet of the Buddha, which are over 3 m tall, have been inlaid with mother of pearl displaying 108 different characteristics of the Buddha. The gold plated statue is 46 m long and 15 m high, covered in gold leaf and represents the ascension of Buddha to Nirvana. The wall facing the Buddha is lined with collection cups into each of which you can drop a coin. Small change such as 25 satang pieces are available from the desk. You can purchase temple rubbings which are made from cement casts of marble reliefs removed from ruins at Ayutthaya.

One of the galleries in the northeastern corner of the compound houses 394 Buddha images mostly contained within glass boxes. The building itself is a three tiered temple, with Chinese rock sculptures at its entrance. The walls of another sanctuary are adorned with relief plaques that delicately retell stories from the Ramakien. You will also notice four chedis that were built to represent the first four kings who ruled during the current dynasty.

The original temple has been placed in the mid 16th Century, although the complex was entirely rebuilt in the late 18th Century, and the entire complex is in the process of a 50 million baht renovation (donations are gratefully accepted). Wat Pho is also home to a Traditional Medicine School and in the afternoons your ailments can be treated by traditional methods. There is also traditional massage available at the wat and classes are held for foreigners.

It is possible to hire English, German, French and Japanese guides on site for 150B for one, 200B for two, 300B for three to gain better insight into the Wat.

Wat Pho is situated to the south of the Grand Palace between Thai Wang Road, Sanamchai Road, Chetupon Road and Mahathat Road. It is about a five minute walk south of Sanam Luang and the entrance is on Thai Wang Road. It is open daily from 8.00 am to 5.00 pm. The closest pier for the Chao Phraya River Express is Tha Tien Pier, buses 1, 3, 6, 9, 12, 25, 48 and A/C 44 all run along Chetuphon Road.

Mural detail - Wat Phra Kaew

Wat Arun (Temple of Dawn)   วัดอรุณ

The story of Wat Arun states that in 1768 when King Taksin planned to move the capital from Ayutthaya to Thonburi he travelled down the Chao Phraya River by boat. At dawn he and his entourage arrived at an old wat and he came ashore to pay his respects. He later named the temple Wat Jang, meaning the Temple of Dawn. It was later renovated first by King Rama I and then later by King Rama III and the wat became known at Wat Arun whilst Thonburi was the Thai capital. Wat Arun played a central role and was temporarily home to the Emerald Buddha after which it was moved to its present site at Wat Phra Kaew.

The courtyard of the wat contains five prangs (stupas), with the most impressive and largest in the centre. The prangs are made in the Khmer style representing Mount Meru which is the home of the gods in Buddhist beliefs. Originally the middle prang was quite small at 16 m but it was considerably stretched to reach over 82 m by King Rama III in 1842. This elongation has given the prang a particular Thai style all of its own. The prangs are decorated all over with Chinese porcelain and the apex of the central prang is covered by a crown which was originally constructed for a different wat. It is possible to climb about half way up the prang from where fine views of Thonburi and the Chao Phraya River can be enjoyed. The prang has four mondops around it, each of which contains a Buddha image striking a different pose! The prang also has stone figurines built into its sides at the top level which you can climb to.

Back at ground level, the bot contains a seated Buddha image, the face of which was designed by King Rama II. At particular times of the year a light and sound show is held on the grounds in the early evening, spectacularly lighting up the main Prang.

To get to Wat Arun, catch the cross river ferry (1B) from Tha Tien pier at Thai Wang Road. The wharf is about a ten minute walk from to the Grand Palace entrance. Tha Tien can be reached by the Chao Phraya River Express ferry or buses numbered 44 and 91, or A/C comfort with 8 and 44. The entrance fee is 10B and it is open everyday from 8.30 am to 5.30 pm

Wat Traimit   วัดไตรมิตร

This small wat is located to the south of Chinatown on Traimit Road, a five minute walk from Hualumpong train station. The wat itself is fairly bland, but the Buddha on the site is incredible. The Buddha here is *solid gold* and weighs around five tons! It is almost 5 m high and nearly 4 m in diameter. It is the largest solid gold Buddha in the world and is one of Thailand's (and Buddhism's) greatest treasures. The Buddha is over 700 years old but it was not until 1955 that it was discovered to be solid gold! It had been encased in plaster at some time (probably to hide it from marauding Burmese) and it was not until it was chipped whilst being moved in 1955 that the true value was discovered! Some of the plaster is on display in a side cabinet to the main attraction. The wat is open from 9.00 am to 5.00 pm every day and admission is 10B.

Wat Mahathat (Temple of the Great Relic)   วัดมหาธาตุ

This wat is on Mahathat Road about five minutes walk from the entrance to the Grand Palace. The wat itself is fairly unremarkable but it is home to Mahachulalongkorn Buddhist University, one of the most highly esteemed sites of Buddhist learning in the country. During Buddhist holy days a busy market is held on the premises where, amongst other things, traditional medicines are sold in their raw form. Opposite the entrance, along Mahathat Road, is a sizeable amulet market which is worth a bit of a look in. It is possible to do Vipassana meditation courses here if you are interested, ask at the wat for details. The wat is open daily from 9.00 am to 5.00 pm, free of charge. The closest Chao Phraya River Express pier is Tha Maharaj.

Wat Saket and the Golden Mount (Wat Srakesa Rajavaramahavihara)   วัดเสก็ด

Before the rule of King Rama I, the wat was one of the most important around. After becoming king, King Rama I restored the wat and made it a Royal monastery. The most prominent feature of this temple is the Golden Mount set upon an artificial hill within the wat compound, however it was not added until the rule of King Rama III. The original chedi built on the spot at this time collapsed, creating the hill, but it was left as a pile of rubble until King Rama IV built the golden chedi at its peak reaching 100 m high. Additions were added by King Rama V and he placed a Buddha relic within the chedi. The relic that is now housed within the chedi originated from India. Final restoration work was made in WWII when the white concrete walls were added over the hill for support. These make a striking contrast to the golden chedi above. It is possible to walk up the 318 stairs to the top of the hill, but entrance to the Buddha relic and golden chedi above costs 10B, and is open from 7.30 am to 5.30 pm. The view from here is quite nice looking over the surrounding area.

The wat compound also houses some important Buddha statues. The main hall (uposatha), built in King Rama I's time, holds a meditating Buddha image from the early Chakri Dynasty. The Shrine Hall houses Phra Attharos, a 10.3 m high image from Phitsanulok, and Luangphor Dusit, a Buddha statue from the Dusit Palace. Unfortunately these are closed to the public except during the Songkran Festival. The entrance is on Boriphat Road and is a 15 minute walk from Khao San Road and the Democracy Monument.

Wat Bovornivet   วัดบวรนิเวศ

Just north of Khao San Road in Banglamphu is Wat Bovorn as it is better known, on Phra Sumen Road. The wat was built in 1826 and at that time was known as Wat Mai. Now within the walls exists Mahamakut Buddhist University, the second in Bangkok. Since its foundation, the wat has been home to a number of royals who entered the monkhood, but also many foreign monks reside here hence some of the religious ceremonies are spoken in English. The wat is worth a look if you are passing for its beautiful buildings and temples, and large golden stupa. The compound also contains ponds where giant turtles and catfish happily swim about.

Also within the compound is the Centre for Herbal Medicine where herbs and special trees with therapeutic elements are labelled. The closest Chao Phraya River Express pier is either Tha Athit or Tha Wat Sam Phraya.

Wat Benchamabophit (Marble Temple)   วัดเบญจมบพิตร

This wat of Italian marble was restored and enlarged in 1899 by King Chulalongkorn (Rama V) and according to his wishes, some of his ashes are now interred at the base of the central Buddha image. The wat has a huge collection of Buddha statues from different periods from all over the Buddhist world. The main attraction of the wat is the chanting hall. Construction began in 1901 but it was not completed before the death of Rama V in 1910. It is constructed entirely of white Italian marble and two large marble lions guard the front and rear entrance. Within the grounds is a canal full of turtles given to the wat by Thais wishing to make merit.

The chanting hall is surrounded by a gallery of 52 Buddha images and you may find it an interesting stroll to note the differences in style from period to period and region to region. The wat is situated by the intersection of Si Ayutthaya Road and Rama V Road to the south of Dusit. The wat is open daily from 8.00 am to 4.30 pm and admission is 10B. If you enter by one of the entrances on Si Ayutthaya Road there is no ticket booth so you can wander the grounds for free. A very informative and easy to read brochure (including map) is on sale at the ticket office for 20B. The sale of these maps provide funds for ongoing restoration work. Buses 5, 72 and A/C 3 stop nearby.

Wat Chai Chanasongkram

At the time of writing, the wat was being renovated. There are some very old shrines and all the vendors have been cleared out of the compound, though horses are still wandering about. Have a look at the huge old trees next to the wat's walls.

Wat Prayoon

The temple lies within a compound surrounded by lush trees on the Thonburi side of the memorial bridge. The most interesting feature of this place is not the temple itself, but the hill located within the grounds. Tradition tells that during King Rama III's reign, the King was awestruck by a particularly interesting mould left by the dripping of a candle. He was so inspired that he ordered an exact replica be built (the kind of thing you can get away with if you are a king). Reaching a height of over 10 m, the hill is surrounded by a moat containing turtles and pocketed with small vaults which contain the cremated remains of wealthy families.

Wat Suthat   วัดสุทัศน์

This wat stores some fine examples of murals and Buddha images, with the most prevalent being a large seated Sukhothai style one. It also contains a huge ordination hall. The wat is open daily from 9.00 am to 5.00 pm. It is easy to find, just look for the Giant Swing on Bamrung Muang Road which for interest's sake stems from Brahman tradition (see Giant Swing for details). The shops around this area are particularly useful if you plan on stocking up on religious paraphernalia.

Wat Rachanada and the Amulet Market   วัดราชนัดดา

This wat is well known amongst the Thais as the place to buy amulets. The purchasing of an amulet is taken very seriously involving time and effort in choosing the correct one. Each different design means different things and you can get one for almost any purpose. For instance, designs of images with a number of eyes to keep you safe from accidents and a Buddha covering his eyes is a general good luck one. Wat Rachanada is on Mahachai Road, on the other side of the khlong from the Golden Mount.

Temple guardian, Wat Phra Kaew

National Museum   พิพิธภัณฑ์แห่งชาติ

This impressive museum on the west side of Sanam Luang is just over 500 m north of the Grand Palace and was established in 1874 creating Thailand's first public museum. Some of the buildings architecture is 18th Century whilst the more recent addition of two storey concrete blocks were added in the late 1960s (concrete minimalism here we come!). This museum is the largest of its kind in Southeast Asia featuring fine examples of art from throughout the region, some dating back to Neolithic times, and is a fascinating place to visit, especially if you are planning to travel in northern and central Thailand.

Some of the highlights include Room 15 which has a large collection of musical instruments and recorded music so you can hear what you see. Room 17 contains the ornate Royal Funeral Chariots and room 13 displays some impressive wood carvings including an incredible set of 15 cm thick teak doors which were carved in the 19th Century (though partially damaged by fire in 1959). Rooms 1 and 2 display a collection of historical effects (some over 5,000 years old) which are well displayed to explain some of Thailand's heritage. There is also a room depicting Thai art from the Sukhothai Period, and a gallery dedicated to the Dvaravati and Khmer Periods.

All the exhibits carry English information displays and there are also free tours available. The English tours are on Wednesday and Thursday and depart from the ticket kiosk at 9.30 am - the Wednesday tour is for Buddhism, and Thursday for Thai culture and art. English literature is also available for 70B though it is organised in a bit of a random fashion. There is also a restaurant on the grounds so it is easy to spend two to three hours wandering the different pavilions.

Admission is 20B and the museum is open Wednesday to Sunday from 9.00 am to 4.00 pm. The museum is at 4 Na Phra That Road, within walking distance of Wat Mahathat, the Grand Palace and Wat Pho. Otherwise you can get there via bus 3, 6, 15, 19, 30, 32, 33, 39, 53, 59, 64 and 70, or A/C bus 39. The closest Express Boat pier is Tha Maharaj, a good 5 to 10 minute walk from the museum.

Jim Thompson's House   บ้านจิมทอมสัน

This site is often missed by travellers passing through Bangkok, but it is definitely worth a visit if you are interested in either Thai silk or architecture. Jim Thompson was born in Delaware, USA in 1906 and is widely recognised as the man responsible for the revitalisation of a waning Thai silk industry. He first visited Thailand as part of a planned 'liberation operation' in the late period of World War II, however the war ended before the operation began and Thompson (then in the employ of the Overseas Secret Service, predecessor to the CIA) moved back to the USA. After a stint in New York, he decided to return to Thailand. Over a long period of working tirelessly to promote Thai silk overseas, his efforts began to revive an ailing traditional Thai industry into what, today, has developed into a premier worldwide product.

In 1959, Jim Thompson's house was completed. The house is unique in appearance and style. It is actually constructed from six different traditional teak houses which were appropriated from as far away as Ayutthaya, but interestingly, the walls have been installed in reverse allowing windows to become niches for ornaments and also allowing high empty ceilings. His house has been decorated throughout with ancient relics from throughout Thailand, including some spectacular statues of Hindu deities. The house also contains works of art from Burma, China and Cambodia. There are some exquisite paintings and some of the furniture has been intricately carved. There are also some interesting pieces such as a cat shaped urinal (you pull the head off when nature calls) and a mouse house which could provide hours of entertainment.

Jim Thompson disappeared in the Cameron Highlands in Malaysia in 1967 in very mysterious circumstances and his body has never been found. Various theories have been suggested including a CIA plot, kidnapping by guerillas or being run down by a truck! None of these theories have ever been 'proved', and although his sister was murdered in the US the same year, Jim Thompson's death is sure to remain a mystery for a long time.

A shop in the grounds of his house sells all manner of Jim Thompson souvenirs including some very picturesque maps and postcards along with an interesting book on his life and times, "*Jim Thompson, the legendary American of Thailand*" (Jim Thompson Thai Silk Company, 1983, Bangkok) for 250B. It is also available outside of Thailand under the title of "*The Legendary American - The Remarkable Career and Strange Disappearance of Jim Thompson*" (Houghton Mifflin, 1970) by William Warren.

The house is on Soi Kasem San 2, Rama I Road, across from the National Stadium, and is open Monday to Saturday 9.00 am to 4.30 pm. Admission is 100B, under 25s (identification necessary) get in for 40B. A portion of this goes to the Bangkok School for the Blind. Watch out for touts on the soi who tell you the museum is closed, they are just dishonest low life, check for yourself. Buses 11, 15, 47, 48, 73, 93, 113, 204 and A/C 1 and 8 go by the soi to Jim Thompson House.

Suan Pakkard Palace   วังสวนผักกาด

This 'palace' houses a collection of fine traditional wooden Thai houses. Within each house there are antiques and traditional furnishing along with an art collection. Although set on busy Si Ayutthaya Road, the gardens do offer a fairly tranquil retreat from the Bangkok streets. It is also not too far from Jim Thompson's house and would form an excellent add-on to a visit to his house. Admission is 100B and it is open Monday to Saturday, 9.00 am to 4.00 pm. Ordinary buses 14, 17, 38, 77 and A/C 13 go past the entrance on Si Ayutthaya Road.

Museum of the Royal Barges   เรือพระที่นั่ง

The royal barges are used only a couple of times a year to carry the royal family in a royal barge procession down the Chao Phraya River. Although the procession consists of 26 boats in total, only a handful of these are designated as Royal boats and the others perform the roles of escorts, complimentary boats and a couple of 'Monkey Jar Barges' and 'Fabled Crocodile like Creature Barges.' Each royal barge is intricately decorated with coloured paint and metallic and reflective inlays, each sporting a different mythological figure or decoration at its head. The barges stretch for up to 50 m in length requiring over 60 crew per boat. The largest barge, Suphannahong, is used by the King himself and the oarsmen alone number 50 men. The sheds which contain the barges also hold somewhat shabby displays of other items such as the 'Royal Lean Pillow' and 'Royal Footrest' used on the royal barge throne.

The barges are located a short distance up Khlong Bangkok Noi, off the Chao Phraya River with the closest bridge being Phra Pin Klao. To get there, catch a ferry to the Railway Station pier which is just opposite Phra Athit near Khao San Road. Follow the road up to the first intersection, Arun Amarin Road, turn right and walk across the bridge for the canal, exiting at the stairs on the right. The entrance to the museum is inconspicuous, recognisable by a small sign and a couple of food vendors. The path is a 300 m labyrinth around local houses, but just keep going and follow the signs that pop up just as you think you have made a wrong turn. During this adventure look out for the house made of beer cans. The builder had a lot of fun making that!!

The museum is open daily from 8.30 am to 5.00 pm and admission is 10B, although it is closed on 31 December, 1 January and 12 to 14 April every year. You can also access the museum via the canal and most khlong tours will take you here at your request.

Lak Muang (City Pillar)   หลักเมือง

This pillar is considered to be the Bangkok's foundation stone and home of the city spirit. Its origins go back to 1782 when King Rama I erected a wooden pillar, but it has since been replaced with sturdier materials. It is now a site of considerable festivities and offerings by those who want to keep the city's guardian spirit well pleased. The pillar is at the southern end of Sanam Luang, close to Wat Phra Kaew. The nearest express boat pier is Tha Chang.

National Gallery   หอศิลปแห่งชาติ

Tha National Gallery on Chao Fa Road is worth a visit to catch a glimpse of both Thai contemporary and traditional art. The contemporary art section is on the ground floor in rooms to the left and right after the entrance, with the left being the better of the two. The artwork shows influences from cubism, impressionism, abstract and a touch of surrealism all with a slight oriental touch. The rooms upstairs are dedicated to traditional Thai art, most being tempura paintings in the Bangkok style of the 19th Century and the late Ayutthaya style of the 17th Century.

The rooms across the courtyard are used for temporary exhibitions of which there are usually one or two at any given time. Admission is 10B and the gallery is open from 9.00 am to 4.00 pm Wednesday to Sunday. The closest pier for the River Express is Tha Athit.

Kamthieng House   บ้านคำ เที่ยง

The house itself is around 100 years old and has been transported from Chiang Mai. The museum was set up to preserve and display elements of the northern Thai culture including folk arts, costumes, tools and other artifacts. It is located in the grounds of the Siam Society at 131 Soi 21 (Asoke) Sukhumvit Road, Bangkok and is open on Tuesdays to Saturdays from 9.00 am to noon, 1.00 pm to 5.00 pm. They give English tours on Saturdays at 9.30 am and admission is 20B.

Museum of the Department of Forensic Medicine

If you are after the bizarre or have an interest in medicine, then check out this museum, or more to the point, small room stuffed with all sorts of body parts. The main attraction are the mummified bodies of infamous Thai murderers. The rest of the crowded shelves contain skulls with bullet wounds, foetuses, an arm with a tattoo and other body parts whose identity (or rightful connection point to the rest of the body) we could not figure out. This museum is only one of ten on the grounds of Siriraj Hospital in Thonburi and is quite a challenge to find. It is located towards the northern end of the hospital, close to the anatomy building, though it would be best to ask directions once you get into the grounds of the hospital. The hospital is on the Chao Phraya River between the Railway Station pier and Tha Phrannok. Admission is free.

Chinatown   เยาวราช (สำเพ็ง)

'Created' in 1782 when a large Chinese population was moved from Ko Ratanakosin to make way for the seat of Royal Government, Bangkok's Chinatown is chaotic and clogged with pedestrians, shoppers and vendors in a manner which assaults one's senses. Buying and selling of just about everything imaginable surrounds you as you stroll through a huge variety of gold shops, textile merchants, tailors, autoshops and impressively cheap eateries all of which can be experienced within a few hours inside the tight confines of Chinatown.

Chinatown is worth visiting for a slightly different look at Bangkok, but do not expect a particularly 'authentic' experience. You will need to wander extensively before you find much in the way of an authentic 'Chinatown', especially along Soi Sampaeng you hear nothing but Thai spoken, and most of the food stalls seem to sell only Som Tam, Noodle soup and Pad Thai! The Chinatowns of Sydney, London, New York and San Francisco are probably a bit closer to the real thing. As far as shopping is concerned, you will be able to get some great bargains if you want to buy some plastic glittering garbage, snoopy T-shirts, squeaky sandals or reams of pseudo silk!

Be prepared though for unbelievably crowded lanes and alleys and also some fairly unpleasant smells and sights, such as the chicken plucker at the intersection of Mangkon and Charoen Krung Road. One of the better places to wander is Soi Wanit 1 (**Sampaeng Lane**) where, except for the occasional irritating motorcyclist, the only traffic is the human variety. Along this street do not expect to be needing to get your wallet out much as most of the vendors along here are selling absolute junk, but do be wary of pickpockets who are more than willing to take your wallet out for you. If you walk from south to north, Chakraphet Road marks the transition from Chinatown to Pahurat (little India). There are loads of cheap noodle shops along Mangkon Road, along with the Cathay Food Centre which has OK cheap food and is set slightly back from the road. If you walk north on Charoen Krung Road itself, it's easier to find the Thieve's Market (Nakhon Kasem) but is a lot noisier and no less crowded. Unsurprisingly the Thieve's market was known as such as it was once a popular source of goods which had 'fallen off the back of a truck.'

During the vegetarian festival, Chinatown is particularly lively and of course a great source of vegetarian food. To the south of Chinatown is Wat Traimit (Temple of the Golden Buddha) which can also be visited on the same trip.

Bus 53 goes along Yaowarat Road to Sanam Luang as does A/C 7 or else you can walk down to the Chao Phraya River and catch an express boat from Tha Saphan Phut.

Bangkok

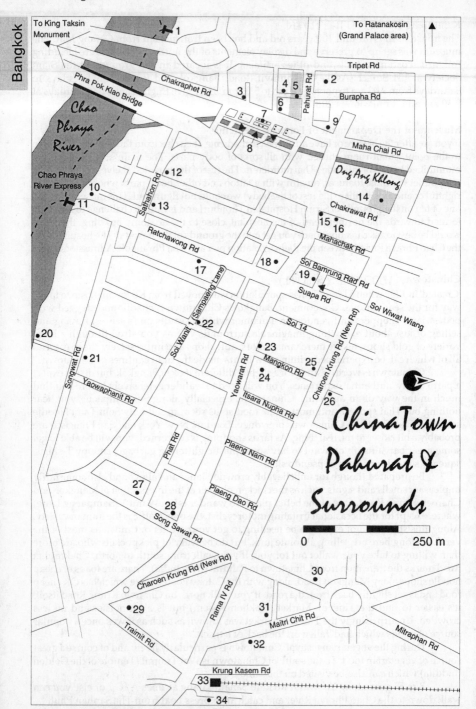

To King Taksin Monument

To Ratanakosin (Grand Palace area)

Tripet Rd

Chakraphet Rd

Pahurat Rd

Burapha Rd

Phra Pok Klao Bridge

Chao Phraya River

Maha Chai Rd

Chao Phraya River Express

Ong Ang Khlong

Chakrawat Rd

Sathorn Rd

Mahachak Rd

Ratchawong Rd

Soi Bamrung Rad Rd

Suapa Rd

Soi Wiwat Wiang

Soi 14

Soi Wanit 1 (Sampaeng Lane)

Charoen Krung Rd (New Rd)

Mangkon Rd

Yaowarat Rd

Itsara Nupha Rd

ChinaTown Pahurat & Surrounds

Songwat Rd

Yaowaphanit Rd

Phat Rd

Plaeng Nam Rd

Plaeng Dao Rd

Song Sawat Rd

0   250 m

Charoen Krung Rd (New Rd)

Rama IV Rd

Maitri Chit Rd

Mitraphan Rd

Traimit Rd

Krung Kasem Rd

Pahurat (little India)   พาหุรัด

This area was originally a Vietnamese centre within Bangkok but in the mid 19th Century a fire devastated the area. Following this catastrophe, the area was rebuilt and occupied by an Indian minority and was named after the dead daughter of Rama I, Pahurat. Pahurat is widely regarded as a centre for illegal immigrants from India, Bangladesh, Pakistan and Nepal, who are working illegally whilst trying to get to a Western nation. Police raids in this area are common, but often for a few hundred dollars those caught are back in Pahurat a few days later! The area north of Pahurat towards Wat Suthat supposedly has a large illegal weapons trade.

Like Chinatown, Pahurat seems to be experiencing a bit of a mid life crisis with the betel nut vendors the only real reminder that this is the Indian quarter. Thai pop music blares out everywhere, noodle shops and Pad Thai stalls rather than curry houses line the streets. For those wanting an interesting Indian area without visiting India itself, we would recommend the East End of London before Pahurat. The best area is the narrow stretch between Chakraphet Road and the khlong where you will find numerous guesthouses and Indian, Pakistani and even Nepalese food at very cheap prices (see Cheap Sleeps for details). From here footbridges cross over the canal into one of the more interesting areas of Chinatown. The cafes on the bridges themselves are good spots to sit and there are some good Chinese cafes on the opposite bank.

Illegal immigration and gun running apart, the main attraction within Pahurat is its sizeable cheap clothing market where, if you wander through the rear of the market, you can watch the seamstresses at work. This market is good for silk and some ready made clothes. If you are not after clothes, in Pahurat there is a good range of fish slicers and fake Tupperware sandwich containers (and much much more) available! The Central Department Store on Pahurat Road has a reasonably priced restaurant on the top floor in an air-conditioned setting.

At the intersection of Sampaeng and Mangkon Road are some examples of classic Bangkok architecture, both inside and outside the Bangkok Bank and the goldsmiths opposite. On the corner of Charoen Krung Road and Mangkon Road is **Wat Neng Noi Yee**, an interesting wat and temple complex. Very popular with the locals, this centre is part Chinese and part Tibetan. In the centre of the market is a **Sikh Temple** which is a little difficult to find. To reach it, take the soi next to the ATM on the riverside for about 50 m then take a left down the second soi. The temple looks great from outside and inside is cool and tranquil.

The closest River Express Boat pier for getting to Pahurat is Tha Saphan Phut.

Si Maha Mariamman Temple   วัดมหาอุมาเทวี (วัดแขก)

Located at the intersection of Silom and Pan Roads, this Hindu temple is worth a visit for the intricately decorated roofs of the main temple and surrounding shrines. Colourful statues of Hindu deities and idols compete for space as larger figures line the base of the roof gradually reducing in size as they approach the top. The main temple which opens to three decorated shrines has a stark white entrance with pillars made of mythical creatures and lotus leaves.

Legend

1 Saphon ferry pier	12 Wat Chakrawat	23 Nine Storey Hotel
2 Old Siam Plaza	13 Food stalls	24 Cathay Dept Store
3 Chinese Temple	14 Thieves market	25 Chicken Plucker
4 Sikh Temple	15 Bangkok Bank of Commerce	26 Wat Neng Noi Yee
5 Pahurat Market	16 Wat Chai Chana Songkhram	27 M.Y. Guesthouse
6 ATM Department Store	17 Irish Embassy	28 Siam City Bank
7 Royal India Restaurant	18 Krung Thai Bank	29 Wat Traimit
8 Cheap Indian Gh.	19 Dhaka Cafe and Gh.	30 Tai Pei Hotel
9 Golden Bangkok Gh.	20 Riverside Guesthouse	31 Post office
10 Rooks Snooker Club	21 Chinese Temple	32 Chinese Hotels
11 Ratchawongse ferry pier	22 Bangkok Bank	33 Hualumpong train station
		34 Sri Hualumpong Hotel

Dusit Zoo   สวนสัตว์ดุสิต (เขาดิน)

Dusit Zoo is worth visiting if only to escape Bangkok for a few hours or to seek motivation for writing letters to animal liberation groups. The zoo has a respectable number of reptiles, mammals and birds. Included amongst these are tethered elephants, giraffes, a few tigers, bears, crocodiles, gibbons and all manner of banana eaters, eagles and even one possum. The living conditions of all of these animals are deplorable. The crocodile tank water looks as though there has not ever been an attempt to clean it. Large eagles and monkeys are kept in small cages and the elephants are all tethered in a long line so you can throw bananas at them. The zoo is as much a funpark for Thais with river rides, merry go rounds and live music and on Sunday is packed with people. Entry is 20B or if you have your school uniform on it is only 10B. If you want to avoid the crowds pick a weekday. The zoo is open every day 9.00 am to 6.00 pm. To get there, bus 8 runs fairly close to it down Lam Luang and Wora Chak, whilst buses 18 and 108 run past the entrance.

Snake Farm (Pasteur Institute)   สวนงูเสาวภา

This is one of the popular sights for organised tours within Bangkok. There are glass encased displays of live and deadly snakes, a small museum with skins of enormous carcases, and an ampitheatre with a raised seating area where visitors can view the snake handlers tease the snakes and audience. On weekdays at 10.30 am and 2.00 pm there is a slide presentation with lecture, and at 2.30 pm and 11.00 pm a snake handling and venom extraction display. The venoms are collected for anti-venene, vaccines and for scientific work. In Southeast Asia alone, over 2,500 people die from snake bites every year.

The snake farm is in the scientific division of the Thai Red Cross Society in the Queen Saovabha Memorial Institute right next to the Chulalongkorn Hospital. When you enter the gate, follow the road around to the left, then straight ahead — you will see the farm on your right. Admission fee is 70B and its open on weekdays from 8.30 am to 4.30 pm, and weekends and holidays from 8.30 am to noon.

Chao Mae Tuptim (Goddess Tuptim Shrine) - Phallis Shrine

A strange shrine in a strange place. This tiny shrine is surrounded by penises of all sizes and shapes, some which would make a sex shop envious. The penises are one of the offerings left for the spirit which lived in the Sai tree above it. Other offerings include jasmine flowers, lotus flowers and incense. If you have a particular fascination for phallic objects, the shrine is located at the back of the Hilton International Hotel. Walk into the main driveway, past the lobby and continue straight ahead on ground level. Take a left through the carpark and when you get to the other end, you will see it on your right.

Lumpini Park   สวนลุมพินี

This large park, complete with canals, is a perfect escape from the hectic scene of the Bangkok streets around it with the traffic noise being reduced to only a quiet roar. It is a must for anyone seeking some solace and quiet time, an alternative to having to lock yourself in your hotel room. In the afternoons the internal roads are overrun with joggers imagining they are actually breathing in fresh air, and if you get there at the crack of dawn you can catch devoted Tai Chi practitioners doing their stuff. For some extra fun you can hire a paddle or row boat to part the water in the canal or buy a kite but only from mid February to April.

Sanam Luang Park   สนามหลวง

This park to the north of Wat Phra Kaew is traditionally used on royal occasions such as the ploughing ceremony when the King officially signals the commencement of the rice growing seasons and also royal cremations. In early March 1996, the Queen Mother was cremated here after lying in state at the Royal Palace for eight months.

In times long past, particularly nasty criminals were lined up and shot here, and the Chatuchak Weekend Market was originally held here, but nowadays kite flying is just about the most exciting pastime going on. During the competitions it is possible to hire your own kite and compete.

Sanam Luang is also a good transportation hub, with many buses circling, and it is also close to the river for the Chao Phraya Express.

Chulalongkorn University   มหาวิทยาลัยจุฬาลงกรณ์

The grounds of this university are huge, and like many of the largest city universities, the students are fairly conservative compared to the more colourful fine arts students of Silpakorn University. There are internet facilities available, but good luck in finding them or getting access. A few internet accessible computers reside in the libraries around the campus for free, and a lecture room is full of them at the Computer Education and Development Centre (CEDC). You may be able to rent them on an hourly basis when they are not being used for classes (usually in the mornings). You can get access to the WWW, but not email unless you have a password. This is the tricky part. To get one, go to the Centre Library and go through the motions of applying. You must be a student or teacher, but unless affiliated directly with the university, they may not grant one to you. If they do, it can take a couple of days. The general location of the central library and CEDC is to the west of the second walkway over Phaya Thai Road from Rama IV Road, but you will need to ask around for more specific directions.

Khlong Tour

Bangkok was once referred to as the 'Venice of the East' with its numerous canals creating both a way of life and a popular and convenient way to get around. The canals are mainly concentrated in Thonburi and its surrounds making it the most popular location for tours. The next most common way to tour the khlongs is to hire a longtail boat. The going rate is 300B per hour per boat, so it is best to gather a group together to reduce the cost. Try Tha Chang near the Grand Palace, or Tha Si Phaya and Tha Saphan Phut for a decent range of boats, or Tha Athit for a convenient pier close to Khao San Road. If you go to one of the piers not serviced by the Chao Phraya Express or deal directly with the boat driver you may be able to get a cheaper price as the front man always takes a cut, though you would have to be lucky.

The main longtail tour around Bangkok will take you to the floating market, snake farm, Wat Arun, Wat Pho, the Royal Barges, Orchard Farm and the Royal Grand Palace. Another choice for a longtail trip is to go exploring any major khlong. However a set route is often followed: up khlong Bangkok Noi, left into Khlong Chak Phra and left into Khlong Mon, back onto the Chao Phraya River and letting you off at Wat Arun if you so desire. This route is fairly uninteresting showing an industrial Bangkok background behind the jetties of private houses and an occasional wat. Only one small section is scenic when the river narrows and is bordered by lush green trees and quaint houses. We would suggest that you try to tailor your own khlong tour up some of the smaller canals for a more scenic journey. If you get off at a pier with a ticket attendant such as Tha Athit for Khao San Road, you will have to pay 10B to be let out. Trips can also be organised to visit destinations outside Bangkok including the crocodile farm at Samut Prakan, Ayutthaya (1,300B), River Kwai Bridge in Kanchanaburi (700B with lunch) or Damnoen Saduak Floating Market (400B).

For a more traditional, and cheaper, approach to exploring the khlongs catch the regular longtails that are used by the locals. Boats that travel Khlong Mon leave from Tha Tien every half an hour during the day for 4B one way. For Khlong Bang Waek, go to Tha Saphan Phut where longtails leave every 15 minutes for the same price, and for Khlong Om, catch a boat from Tha Phubul Songkram in Nonthaburi.

Exploding Kites
The kite flying that you often see around Sanam Luang was not always just for fun. The first kites in Thailand were filled with gunpowder and used as weapons of war!

Day Trips from Bangkok

If you only have a short time in Thailand and want to see some sights beyond Bangkok's busy metropolis, then there are day trips you can either organise on your own or with a tour.

Ayutthaya - Only an 1½ hour train ride away from Bangkok, you can explore this ancient city in a very full day - make sure you start early. The palace at **Bang Pa-In** is set in a more relaxed environment. Boat trips leave for the day from Bangkok every Sunday.

Damnoen Saduak - This is the sight of some of the most popular, but fairly touristy, floating markets around 100 km from Bangkok. They are easily visited by bus or boat trip from Bangkok.

Nakhon Pathom - The town located 58 km from Bangkok is busy and noisy, but its centrepiece is the highly revered Buddhist chedi, Phra Pathom Chedi, is the world's tallest. It is easily reached via train or bus.

Pathum Thani - If you want to get an authentic view of Thai life, head off to Pathum Thani for the day, only 56 km from Bangkok. Completely farang free, the town has not got much to see in terms of sights, but has an interesting market area.

Chachoengsao - Make sure you do this trip on a weekend to experience the activities around Wat Sothon. Accessible by bus or train.

Samut Prakan - Nearby are the Crocodile Farm and Ancient City. Quite a touristy outing and to fit them in a day you would be best going on an organised tour.

SHOPPING

Chatuchak Weekend Market   ตลาดนัดจัตุจักร

This market is huge, encompassing over 8,500 vendors selling everything imaginable, whilst dealing with over 100,000 hagglers a day. The bustling 28 acres making up Chatuchak are divided into 26 numbered sections. A clocktower identifies the centre of the market and sois lead off into the bargain bizarre. Unfortunately the market is not organised into sole product areas, however the map provides general areas where types of goods can be found. The area near to the bus station would be of most interest to visitors as it sells a variety of antiques and handicrafts. The northern end deals more with food, household goods and fresh produce. The market is only open on weekends from 8.00 am to 5.00 pm and is the perfect place to pick up the most obscure gift for your mother-in-law. Try and get there early before it gets too unbearably hot.

Pantip Plaza

Located on Phetchaburi Road, 100 m west of the Amari Watergate Hotel, and 200 m from the intersection with Ratchaprarop Road. The whole building is dedicated to computers and the large number of retailers ensures you will get a good prices for whatever you purchase,

however hardware tends not to be the cheapest around. The 'bargain' comes with the illegal pirated software where a CD with up to 40 programs will cost around 500B.

Pahurat Market
This is the Indian shopping centre. To get there from Khao San Road, take A/C bus number 6 from Chakraphong Road (do not cross street).

Banglamphu Market
If you are staying around Khao San Road, you are just an arm's length from one of the more popular markets in Bangkok. Banglamphu Market spreads itself around the streets to the north of Khao San Road mainly selling clothes and other fashion items.

River City Shopping Complex
This shopping complex sells some very expensive merchandise, but is the perfect place to go to check out some extraordinary antiques. Level 3 consists of shop after shop of antique shops, with enough artifacts to rival any museum.

ENTERTAINMENT

Kick Boxing
Thai boxing or *Muay Thai* is the world renowned national sport of Thailand. Ask any kick boxer and they will swear that the Thais are virtually unbeatable in this sport. While many kick boxing fighters train by kicking truck tyres or heavy boxing mats, the Thais train by kicking bamboo, killing all nerve endings in their shins and so making them formidable weapons. Thai boxing matches also tend to push beyond human limits with bouts continuing well after the towel would have been thrown in during Western boxing matches.

A Thai kick boxing match is best viewed in one of the main stadiums in Bangkok, either the Ratchadamnoen or Lumpini stadiums. **Lumpini Boxing Stadium** ☎ (02) 251 4303 is an old building set back from Rama IV Road next to the Military Academy and it holds matches every Tuesday and Friday at 7.00 am to 11.00 pm, and on Saturdays from 5.00 pm to 8.00 pm, then 8.30 pm to 12.00 pm. The cost is 230B, 460B and 920B for ringside seats. There are heaps of food stalls and a couple of Thai restaurants out the front to keep you going. The **Ratchadamnoen Boxing Stadium** ☎ (02) 2814208 is on Ratchadamnoen Nok Avenue, next to the TAT Office, a 15 minute walk from Khao San Road. Fights are held every Monday and Wednesday at 7.00 pm, Thursday at 5.00 pm and 9.00 pm, and Sunday at 2.00 pm and 6.00 pm. The cost is 230B for the cheapest seats about 20 m from the ring, and 800B for the most expensive ringside seats. Likit Restaurant is located next door and is a great place to start the evening although the food here is not the cheapest. Scrumptious charcoal chicken and sticky rice costs 80B, enough for two people.

Patpong Road and Market, Nana Plaza and Soi Cowboy
Patpong Road is infamous for its sleazy girlie bar and prostitute scene. Although you may be interested in visiting just for a look, by visiting you are supporting the prostitution that takes place. Not all the 'workers' there are dancing out of choice. Many are in bonded labour living and existing in virtual slave like conditions with there being documented cases of girls being chained to their beds. Child prostitution is also still a problem and is largely fuelled by demand from older, married Western men.

The market comes alive at night selling a large range of Thai market paraphernalia, including copies of top designer clothing, watches, bootleg music and jewellery.
Nana Plaza is situated off Sukhumvit road near the Atlanta Hotel. Nana Plaza is a four storey building packed with all manner of girlie bars and gogo bars, where Westerners sit in terraced seating and ogle young girls. Probably not as sordid as Patpong, Nana plaza does have some decent bars on the ground floor where you can go and have a drink without having to buy anything else.

Soi Cowboy in our opinion is probably the sleaziest of the three sex areas mentioned. On every occasion we have visited Soi Cowboy, the street has been full of drunk Westerners grabbing all flesh available, with frequent fighting, overpriced drinks and particularly disturbed looking girls. Only for the desperate — in all meanings of the word!

Cultural and Social Activities

For details on current films and other social activities at the locations below and more, check the 'What's On' section in the Bangkok Post on Sundays or various other magazines such as the Bangkok Metro which comes out monthly for 80B.

Cinemas Most main cinemas use English subtitles or have an English soundtrack. Movie times are generally the same in all cinemas: 12.00, 14.00, 17.00, 19.00, 21.00 and 10.00 on weekends.

Siam Society at 131 Soi 21 (Asoke) Sukhumvit Road, ☎ (02) 259 4999, is a club intent on promoting anything Thai, especially culture, history and art. They welcome visitors to partake in any events or trips that they organise. They are definitely worth checking out. They have a diverse library but it's only available to members.

Alliance Francaise is run by the Bangkok French connection at 29 Sathon Tai Road, ☎ (02) 213 2122. The alliance screens foreign films throughout the week as well as holding art exhibitions, concerts and cultural festivals.

British Council at 428 Soi 2, Siam Square, ☎ (02) 252 6136, is similar but with a British flavour.

Goethe Institute Bangkok at 18/1 Soi Athakan Prasit, Sathon Tai Road, ☎ (02) 286 9002, is for the Germans.

National Theatre at 1 Rachini Road near the National Museum, ☎ (02) 221 4885 holds theatre productions for Thai and foreign groups. They have regular showings of Thai classical dance and traditional music each month. Try the second Friday, Saturday and Sunday as well as the last Friday and Saturday of each month.

Thai Cultural Centre which is down a soi opposite Robinsons Department Store off Ratchdapisek Road does the same.

Call the **Cultural Information Service Centre**, ☎ (02) 247 0028, for detailed information on all the activities in Bangkok if you cannot find the details in the newspaper or local magazines.

◀ **Arriving and Departing** ▶

GETTING AROUND

Bangkok is a huge city and the heat and pollution seem to actively conspire against you if you plan to walk anything more than a couple of hundred yards. Luckily, there are a number of ways to get around. The Chao Phraya River Express is a great, quick and cheap way of getting from one end of the city to the other. Local buses (both A/C and non A/C) run up and down the streets throughout Bangkok, metered and non metered taxis abound (more of the former than the latter) as do motorcycle taxis and of course tuk tuks. Just for interest's sake, Bangkok's rush hour average speed is 12 km/hour, but has got some catching up to do to take the award for being the slowest. Tokyo and Delhi are two that beat it.

Bus

In October 1996, the Bangkok bus system came under a complete renovation with its 155 routes reduced to 86 routes to hopefully make the bus system a little more understandable, and reduce the number of unnecessary pollutants on the roads. Although changed, the buses are still very confusing and take most ex-pats at least a year or two to figure it all out. As long as you get to know a few routes you can generally use the buses quite efficiently, but occasionally they do try your patience when for no reason the bus you are used to catching suddenly goes a different route or it terminates at a different place.

Since the changes to the old bus system, many of the old and trusty bus maps are now invalid, so your best option for up-to-date information on the bus routes is to grab a free green Bangkok map from the TAT office. Although they do not consistently list all the bus routes, they give you a very good start. The more detailed area maps on the reverse side are handy.

The following maps have not been updated since the change of the bus routes, but once they are, they are bound to be a useful accessory for your Bangkok expeditions. "Tourist Map - Bangkok City" by Bangkok Guide have brief tips for the city and corresponding bus information. Periplus' Bangkok map carries some accurate bus routes, but it can take some deciphering. Thaiways provide detailed maps of Bangkok and although more of an advertorial, it does have some handy bus routes, and is free. Bangkok Thailand by Tour'n'Guide Map is the most widely available for 35B and not a bad effort either.

Bangkok's incredibly comprehensive public bus system is cheap, even if a little baffling to the novice. The main types of buses are air conditioned buses which are more expensive and run less routes, but are also less crowded, and thus more survivable. Fares range from 6B to 16B (more after hours) depending on destination and you pay as you board. Non air conditioned buses are as distinct as they are old, tatty, red in colour and belch exhaust fumes. The routes run all over the city but can get very crowded. Fares are 3.5B (5B after hours) for any distance. Keep your ticket as it is common for inspectors to board and check them.

To save you from ending up on a bus that travels a different route from what you are used to look out for the colour of the sign displayed in the front window and next to the door. A blue sign means that the bus will follow the normal route. If it is a red or yellow sign, the bus route has been changed and may terminate early or take a different road.

Green Mini Buses
Only for those seeking a little adventure as no one seems to know the routes of these buses. Their routing is a bit of a mystery as you can catch the same bus on different days and be taken to different places!! Apparently the routes are industry secrets with the conductor naming the destination of the bus when it approaches a bus stop. Rumour has it these are uninsured in every way, shape and feel! Every now and then, there is a story in the Bangkok Post along the lines of 'Bus Accident Driver Flees'.

Microbus
These are smart bright red and smaller than the usual buses, cost 15B flat rate and stop picking up passengers once full. They are a more comfortable way to get around town especially if caught in peak hour traffic for extended periods.

Taxis
There are two types, metered and non metered with the metered cabs always coming in cheaper. Flag fall changed as of 1 December 1996 and now the following charges apply: 35B for first 2 km, 4.50B for the 3rd to 12th km, 5B for the 13th to 20th km, and then 5.50B for any additional kilometre. A 1B per minute fee is also applicable if you're not going anywhere, great for those Bangkok traffic jams. The rates were changed because of the consistent complaints of taxi drivers refusing long trips.

Beware the taxi with a dodgy meter. Sometimes they will offer to run at a set price, that is, without the meter, but this is invariably more expensive. Non metered taxis are simply not worth wasting your time on. It seems that the drivers are all required to do a course in highway robbery before they get their licence. Be prepared to bargain hard.

Taking a taxi is a much safer and cleaner option than the dreaded tuk tuk, and actually works out at the same cost. It also means that you will probably be delivered fairly unscathed in air conditioned comfort rather than after breathing in the fumes of the vehicle next door and covered in an unidentified layer of grim. The more solid structure will also protect you from any encroaching psychopaths on the road.

If taking a taxi without a meter, agree on the fare before going anywhere as the fares can cover a ridiculous range, and if you do not agree to a fare, you will be expected to pay the quoted price at the end of the journey. Always bargain for your fare, as you can always get it for much cheaper. If you are still not happy with the price, another taxi driver will probably be more than happy to take you. Quite often when catching taxis from bus stations or train stations, the taxi driver will pick up more than one ride charging independently, so you may be better off finding a group of travellers heading in the same direction to reduce the fare.

If you want to call for a taxi, telephone ☎ (02) 319 9911 for an operator capable of speaking English. You will be given a taxi number when booking and charged an extra small booking fee on top of your fare.

Motorcycle Taxi

If you have already climbed Everest, bungy jumped and fought in the Angolan Civil War, you may want to take a motorcycle taxi in Bangkok just to get the adrenaline pumping. In price they are comparable to tuk tuks but are really fast! During the research for this guide, one of our researchers caught a motorcycle taxi down Sathon Tai Road when it was in gridlock. At one stage they were doing 70 km/hour between rows of stationary cars. Definitely a hair raising experience, and a quick one. The motorbike taxis that ply the roadways of Bangkok make a more versatile form of transport as they can dodge between the peak hour traffic and mount the kerbs. They usually hang around busy corners and are recognisable by their matching coloured and numbered vests. They are reasonably expensive compared to other forms of transport, however, they will certainly get you to your destination in time.

Tuk Tuk

Some will swear by them, others want to shoot them. These fume belching piles of scrap will take you anywhere in Bangkok but be prepared to bargain. These three wheeled open taxis, also known as samlors, are commonly used for small trips within Bangkok, and some regional centres. They are also a popular method of transport to see the sights of Bangkok, and most of the time the driver will wait while you check it out. Even though they are fairly dangerous, a trip to Thailand would not really be complete without going on at least one ride.

Beware tuk tuk drivers offering to take you to gem and jewellery stores. It's just a scam to lighten your wallet. Quite often the scam involves a tuk tuk driver trying to convince you to go to an 'authorised' or 'government' jewellery dealer where you will be guaranteed a bargain! You can usually tell the dodgy drivers as they will only charge you around 10B for a three hour city tour. The driver is usually paid a commission on any sales, and there is a very likely chance that the gems are not as authentic as you thought. Be careful unless you have experience recognising good quality or authentic jewellery.

The fare is usually around the same as a metered taxi and the journey is a lot more dangerous. The private tuk tuk's can charge whatever they want if they know they can get away with it. The government has set a standard rate of around 80B per hour, but some tourists have been known to pay exorbitant rates of up to 300B for a short journey within the city limits.

Car

If you are on a suicide mission, or a very bad driver, you can take up the wheel, rent a car, and feel right at home. Driving in Bangkok is not recommended, and you will see why when you try to cross the road. However, if you are planning on renting a car for an extended trip out of the capital then it can be very rewarding. There are a number of places to rent, some of which are located around Rama IV, Sathon and Sukhumvit Road.

AVIS, 2/12 Withayu (Wireless) Road, ☎ (02) 255 5300, or Dusit Thani Hotel, 946 Rama IV Road, ☎ (02) 236 0450.

HERTZ Rent A Car, 420 Soi 71, Sukhumvit Road, ☎ (02) 391 0461.

Highway Car Rent is on the corner of Rama IV and Sathon Nua Roads, ☎ (02) 235 7746.

Klong Toey Car Rent, 1921 Rama IV Road, next to the Bangkok Bank, ☎ (02) 250 1930.

Chao Phraya River Express (*rua duan*)

These run up and down the Chao Phraya River all day stopping to pick up and let off passengers along the way. Look for the long boat with the yellow flag and Thai flag on top and listen for the guy with the whistle. The boats with the red flag run a route along the alternate piers, and stop less often, meaning that you may not get to where you want to go. Rates run from 4B to 10B, you can pay on board or from a ticket vendor at some of the piers. It is a good idea to hang on to your ticket as they are sometimes checked by inspectors. If planning any trip between destinations on the river, this is definitely the quickest way. Jumping on and off at times is quite hair raising. They do not always stop at all piers as it depends if people are waiting to alight or embark and they have right of way over other boats along the Chao Phraya River.

The full route of the Chao Phraya River Express stretches from Nonthaburi in the north to Prayakrai in the south (Krung Thep Bridge) and takes about one hour to cover the full distance. You can explore further up and down river by taking slower connecting ferries. There is not much to see at Prayakrai (Wat Rajsingkorn pier) except yet another busy Bangkok street, but Nonthaburi in the north is well worth a visit for its large, authentic and interesting market.

Some of the more useful piers are (north to south): Thawet pier for the National Library and Dusit area, Phra Athit for Khao San Road, Thonburi Railway Station pier for the train station and royal barges, Chang and Thien piers for the Grand Palace, Wat Pho, Saphan Phut for Pahurat, Wat Muang Khae for the GPO and Sarawong Road, Oriental pier for Silom Road and Oriental Hotel.

Cross River Ferries (*rua kham fark*)

These barges that look like large floating matchboxes cost 1B and shuttle slowly back and forward over the river from most piers. They are useful for Wat Arun and the Royal Barges.

Canal Ferries

These oversized longtail boats run up and down a few of the accessible canals left in Bangkok. There are two main popular routes described below.

Hualumpong Train Station to Banglamphu Khlong

This canal is primarily used for public transport, but is well worth trying for a ride which appears to mimic what in the West can only be experienced at an amusement park.

The longtail boat leaves every half an hour and every fifteen minutes during peak hour and costs 6B (pay on board). For this 6B there is a choice of twelve piers at which you can hop on or off, although the entire journey only takes around ten minutes. During this ten minutes the speeding boat dodges dredgers, other boats and calculates some very tight corners. Waves from passing boats make it bumpy, but if it was not for the helper up at the front of the boat, who gives directions to the driver, whilst using his weight to manoeuvre the boat, it would never make it! - a job only for the experienced.

The journey ends (and starts) at the canal in front of and to the right of Hualumpong train station entrance. The other end is at Banglamphu, near Khao San Road. The Khao San Road stop is actually the second stop along the canal and you get on (and off) in the canal north of Khao San Road along Chakraphong Road.

Besides being a joyride, this 'ferry service' is a handy way to get to Hualumpong train station from Khao San Road and is much faster than any form of road transport in Bangkok. There are many other ferry services along Bangkok's many khlongs, but for the visitor this is one of the most handy.

Khlong Saensaep

This khlong ferry route is the longest, starting at the wharf by the Democracy Monument and travelling virtually 'off the map' east out of central Bangkok. It generally follows Lan Luang

Road, New Phetchaburi Road then Ramkhamheang Road. The more popular destinations are Jim Thompson's House, the World Trade Centre, and Siam Square — get off at Phaya Thai Road and walk the 50 m south to Rama I Road. The whole route is rarely done in one boat ride as the canal is blocked by gates maintaining varying water levels. This means that at certain stops you need to change into the connecting boat. Prices for the ferry depend on distance but cost between 5B and 15B for this very fast, efficient and fun form of transport. The boat stops are generally located under bridges.

Long Tails (*rua hang yao*)

The distinctive longtail boats are often seen hooning around the Chao Phraya River. Many travellers board a boat to do the popular sightseeing tours of some of the more popular Bangkok sights. These boat trips are advertised around the more widely used piers. The standard rate is 300B for the boat for an hour (regardless of how many people you have) which takes you to around five different destinations. You may be able to get the fare for less is you deal directly with a boat driver rather than through a middle man. For a more authentic canal experience you can hire your own to take you on an adventure around some of the many Thonburi backwaters. The boat can carry from 10 up to around 20 people, but since most people do not commonly travel with 19 other companions, you may want to grab a few other travellers to share the costs. Longtail boats are also often used as share taxis for the Thais to get them to the other side of the Chao Phraya River or along one of the many Thonburi canals, and many leave from Tha Chang pier.

AIR

Bangkok's Don Muang Airport is 22 km north of Bangkok on the Vibhavadi Rangsit Highway. The expressway linking the airport to the city has cut the travelling time dramatically making the trip into town only half an hour on a good run and three hours if traffic is bad. For international departure information call ☎ (02) 535 1254, and for arrival information call ☎ (02) 535 1301. For domestic flights call ☎ (02) 535 1253 for information. Airport tax is 200B on departure for international flights, and 20B for domestic flights.

THAI International and Bangkok Airlines cover the domestic market, flying to all Thailand's main regional centres. Khao San Road is one of the better places to look for cheap air tickets, but be warned, some of the travel agents here are unscrupulous. Best not to hand over the cash until the ticket is in your hands.

King Naresuan (1555 - 1605)

Also known as the 'Black Prince', King Naresuan is famed in Thai history for defeating the Burmese in their first successful invasion and regaining Thai independence on the land. As a prince he was taken by the Burmese to ensure that the king that they had installed would behave (King Maha Thammaracha). Whilst with the Burmese he studied military tactics with them and became a skilled tactician. After being returned to Ayutthaya under the rule of his father, he developed into a powerful and skilful military leader, and following the death of his father in 1590 he became King and relations with Burma rapidly deteriorated.

In 1592, the Burmese invaded Ayutthaya with massive forces. During the decisive battle King Naresuan found himself directly facing the Burmese prince and challenged him to a duel on elephant using swords. In spectacular accounts of the battle, King Naresuan killed the prince with a single stroke and the Burmese forced fled. This marked the turning point in Ayutthaya/Burmese relations. On the actual site of King Naresuan's victory, the *Don Chedi* has been constructed to commemorate his glorious win. After defeating the Burmese, King Naresuan led Siam through a period of considerable prosperity until his death in 1605.

International Flights
Below is a list of sample flights available from the travel agents around Khao San Road (which generally offer the cheapest flights out of Bangkok). All prices are one way and are a guide only. Quite often you will be able to find something a little cheaper, so look around.

Airfares					
Asia			Other		
Country	City	Price	Country	City	Price
Burma	Rangoon	2,500	Australia	Sydney	10,000
Cambodia	Phnom Phenh	3,200		Melbourne	10,000
China	Peking	8,000		Perth	8,000
	Kunming	2,500	Canada	Toronto	16,000
Hong Kong		3,800	England	London	10,000-12,000
India	Dehli/Bombay	4,800	Europe	Anywhere	9,000-12,000
Indonesia	Jakarta	6,000	New Zealand	Auckland	14,000
Nepal	Kathmandu	4,800	South Africa	Johannesburg	14,000
Singapore		3,000	USA	Los Angeles	12,000
Vietnam	Hanoi	4,200		New York	16,000
	Saigon	4,100			

AIRLINES

Air Canada, (GSA Airline Agency Ltd), 1053 Charoen Krung Road, Bangkok 10500, ☎ (02) 233 5900.

Air France, Ground Floor, Chart Issara Tower, 942/51 Rama IV Road, Bangkok, 10500, ☎ (02) 233 9477, open Monday to Friday 08.30 to 17.30, Saturday 08.30 to 12.00.

American Airlines, (Pacific Leisure Ltd), 6th Floor, 518/5 Maneeya Centre, Ploenchit Road, Bangkok, 10330, ☎ (02) 251 0806.

Air India, (S.S. Travel Service), S.S. Building, 10/12-13 Convent Road, Bangkok, 10500, ☎ (02) 235 0557, open Monday to Friday 08.15 to 17.00, Saturday 08.45 to 12.00.

Air New Zealand, 1053 Charoen Krung Road, Bangkok, 10500, ☎ (02) 237 1562, open Monday to Friday 08.30 to 12.00, 13.00 to 17.00, and Saturday 08.30 to 12.00.

Alitalia, 8th Floor, Boonmitr Building, 138 Silom Road, Bangkok, 10500, ☎ (02) 233 4000, open Monday to Friday 08.30 to 18.00, Saturday 09.00 to 13.00.

Bangkok Airways, Queen Sirikit National Convention Centre, New Ratchadapisek Road, Klongtoey, Bangkok, 10110, ☎ (02) 229 3456, open Monday to Sunday 08.00 to 17.00.

British Airways, 2nd Floor, Charn Issara Tower, 942/81 Rama IV Road, Bangkok, 10500, ☎ (02) 236 8655, open Monday to Friday 08.00 to 17.00 and Saturday 08.30 to 16.00.

Canadian Airlines International, 6th Floor Maneeya Centre 518/5 Ploenchit Road, Bangkok, 10330, ☎ (02) 251 4521, open Monday to Friday 08.30 to 17.00, Saturday 08.30 to 16.30.

Cathay Pacific Airways, 11th Floor, Ploenchit Tower, 898 Ploenchit Road, Patumwan, Bangkok, 10330, ☎ (02) 262 0606.

China Airlines, 4th Floor, The Peninsula Plaza, 153 Ratchadamri Road, Bangkok, 10330, ☎ (02) 253 4242.

Continental Airlines, 4th Floor Charn Issara Tower, 942/122 Rama IV Road, Bangkok, 10500, ☎ (02) 267 8135.

Delta Airlines, 6th Floor, Panjaphat Building, 1 Surawong Road, Bangkok, 10500, ☎ (02) 236 9513.

Egypt Air, 3rd Floor, C.P. Tower, 313 Silom Road, Bangkok 10500, ☎ (02) 231 0505, open Monday to Friday 08.30 to 17.00, Saturday 08.30 to 12.00.

Garuda Indonesia, 27th Floor, Lumpini Tower, Tungmahamek, Rama IV Road, Bangkok, 10120, ☎ (02) 285 6470, open Monday to Friday 08.30 to 17.30, Saturday 09.00 to 13.00.

Gulf Air, 15th Floor, Maneeya Centre Building, 518/5 Ploenchit Road, Bangkok, 10330, ☎ (02) 254 7931, open Monday to Friday 09.00 to 17.30, Saturday 09.00 to 16.00.

Japan Airlines, 254/1 Ratchadapisek Road, Bangkok, 10320, ☎ (02) 274 1400, open Monday to Friday 08.00 to 17.30, Saturday 08.00 to 17.00.

KLM Royal Dutch Airlines, 19th Floor, Thai Wah Tower II, 21/133-134 Sathon Tai Road, Bangkok, 10120, ☎ (02) 679 1100 ext 11, open Monday to Friday 08.00 to 17.00, Saturday 08.00 to 13.00.

Korean Air, Kongboonma Building, Silom Road, Bangkok, 10500, ☎ (02) 635 0465, open Monday to Friday 08.30 to 17.00, Saturday 08.30 to 16.00.

Lufthansa German Airline, 18th Floor, Q House Asoke Building, 66 Sukhumvit Road, Soi 21, Bangkok, 10110, ☎ (02) 264 2400, open Monday to Friday 08.30 to 17.00, Saturday 08.30 to 12.00.

Malaysia Airlines, 20th Floor, Ploenchit Tower, 898 Ploenchit Road, Bangkok, 10330, ☎ (02) 263 0565, open Monday to Friday 08.00 to 17.00, Saturday 09.00 to 13.00.

Northwest Airlines, 4th Floor Peninsula Plaza, 153 Ratchadamri Road, Bangkok, 10330, ☎ (02) 254 0789, open Monday to Friday 08.30 to 17.00, Saturday 08.30 to 12.00.

Philipine Airlines, Chongkolnee Building, 56 Surawong Road, Bangkok, 10500, ☎ (02) 233 2350, open Monday to Friday 08.00 to 17.00, Saturday 08.30 to 14.00.

QANTAS Airways, Ground Floor, Charn Issara Tower, 942/51 Rama IV Road, Bangkok, 10500, ☎ (02) 267 5188, open Monday to Friday 08.00 to 17.00, Saturday 08.30 to 16.30.

Royal Air Cambodge, 17th Floor, Two Pacific Place Building, room number 1706, 142 Sukhumvit Road, Bangkok, 10110, ☎ (02) 653 2261.

Royal Nepal Airlines, 9th Floor, Phaya Thai Plaza Building, 128 Phaya Thai Road, Bangkok, 10400, ☎ (02) 216 5591, open Monday to Friday 09.00 to 17.00, Saturday 09.00 to 12.00.

THAI Airways International - Bangkok			
Destination	Frequency	Time(hrs)	B (o/w)
Chiang Mai	Minimum 8 daily flights	1.10	1,650
Chiang Rai	Minimum 3 daily flights	1.20	1,940
Hat Yai	5 daily flights	1.25	2,280
Hua Hin (BA)	1.3.5.7 (11.20), .2.4.6. (18.20)	0.30	900
Khon Kaen	Minimum 3 daily flights	0.55	1,060
Lampang	2 daily flights (06.45, 15.00)	2.05	1,455
Mae Hong Son			1,865
Mae Sot			1,405
Nakhon Phanom	1...... (06.30), .2345.. (14.05), ...67 (15.20)	2.05	1,605
Nakhon Ratchasima	1....6. (06.55), Daily(08.30)	0.45	555
Nakhon Si Thammarat	1 daily flight (08.30)	1.55	1,770
Nan	1.3.5.. (09.10), .2.4.67 (09.10)	2.20	1,530
Narathiwat	1 daily flight (07.00)	2.55	2,575
Phitsanulok	5 daily flight	0.55	950
Phrae	1 daily flight (14.15)	2.10	1,325
Phuket	Minimum 9 daily flights	1.20	2,000
Ranong (BA)	1 daily flight (07.00)	1.20	1,980
Sakhon Nakhon	1....6. (06.30), .2345.. (14.05), ...7 (15.00)	1.10	1,530
Samui	12 daily flights	1.20	2,300
Sukothai	1.3.5.7 (07.30)	1.10	1,560
Surat Thani	2 daily flights (06.35, 17.30)	1.15	1,785
Trang	123.5.7 (07.30), ...4.6. (15.45)	1.20	2,005
Ubon Ratchathani	2 daily flights (06.40, 17.45)	1.05	1,405
Udon Thani	Minimum 2 daily flights (06.50, 17.30)	1.05	1,310
BA = Bangkok Airways			

Singapore Airlines, 12th Floor, Silom Centre, 2 Silom Road, Bangkok, 10500, ☎ (02) 236 0440.
South African Airways, 6th Floor Maneeya Centre Building, 518/5 Ploenchit Road, Bangkok, 10330, ☎ (02) 254 8206.
Swissair, 1 Silom Road, Bangkok, 10500, ☎ (02) 233 2930, open Monday to Friday 08.30 to 17.00.
THAI International Airways, 6 Lan Luang Road, Bangkok, 10200, ☎ (02) 280 0060, open Monday to Friday 07.00 to 18.30, Saturday 07.00 to 18.30.
United Airlines, 19th Floor, Regent House, 183 Ratchadamri Road, Bangkok, 10330, ☎ (02) 253 0558.
Vietnam Airlines, 578 - 580 Ploenchit Road, Bangkok, 10330, ☎ (02) 251 4242.

TRAIN

Bangkok has two train stations, the central station is Hualumpong, ☎ (02) 223 0341, in the centre of the city which serves most regional districts. The second is Thonburi Bangkok Noi, ☎ (02) 411 3102, which serves two of the train routes, one south to Malaysia and Singapore as well as west to Kanchanaburi Province. You have a choice of four main train lines leaving from Bangkok, the northern, northeastern, eastern and southern lines. For details and prices refer to the timetables for each of these regions at the end of the relevant chapter.

It is possible to purchase a Visit Thailand Rail Pass (similar in idea to Europe's Eurail). Unfortunately it would only offer a significant saving if you were rushing around to each destination. The passes must be used in 20 days and allow unlimited travel in that time. There are two passes available, the first allows rides on 2nd and 3rd class trains with no extra luxuries such as sleepers, or express trains. The second pass includes these extra bits. The cost, respectively is 1,100B for adults, 550B for children, and 2,000B adult and 1,000B child.

BUS (PUBLIC)

Bangkok has three main long distance bus stations. The north/northeastern terminal, the eastern terminal and the southern terminal. Generally these serve destinations in each direction but there are some exceptions for example; a bus to Pattaya can be caught from either the north/northeastern terminal or the eastern terminal.

When trying to get to these main bus stations, it is best to refer to them in their Thai name so the bus conductor or taxi driver will understand and will be able to inform you when to alight. The northern/northeastern bus terminal is *Molchit*, pronounced with a 'sh', the eastern bus terminal is *Ekamai*, and the southern bus terminal is *Sai Tai*.

When travelling by bus in Thailand, especially at night, watch your luggage and personal belongings. Theft on buses has not reached the epidemic proportions of buses from Khao San Road, but is certainly not unheard of.

North/northeastern Bus Terminal (*Molchit*), A/C ☎ (02) 279 4484, non A/C ☎ (02) 271 0101 on Phahon Yothin Road near the weekend market. This bus station is absolutely huge, and as such a second terminal is slowly beginning to emerge down the road. This may cause you some confusion when you are returning to Bangkok and get let off somewhere totally unfamiliar. The best way to get back into Bangkok central is to make your way to Phahon Yothin Road (the original terminal) where the bulk of local buses travel.

To get there catch the following buses: A/C bus 2, 3, 9, 10, 12, 13, 29, 38, 39, 136, 138 and 153. Non A/C buses 3, 8, 26, 27, 28, 29, 34, 38, 39, 44, 52, 59, 63, 74, 77, 96, 97, 104, 108, 112, 134, 136, 112, 145, 153 and 204. The best bus to get to Khao San Road is the A/C bus number 3 and 9 which travel along Ratchadamnoen Klang Road.

Bangkok

Eastern Bus Terminal, *(Ekamai)*, A/C ☎ (02) 392 9227 (or ☎ (02) 392 2521), non A/C ☎ (02) 391 2504 on Sukhumvit Road opposite soi 63.

To get there catch the following buses: A/C 1, 2, 8, 11, 13, 126 or non A/C 2, 23, 25, 38, 71, 72, 98. To Khao San Road there are a couple of fairly direct options. A/C bus 11, which you can catch from Sukhumvit Road, next to the bus station, all the way to Ratchadamnoen Road, past the Victory Monument. Another option is bus 23 from the street opposite and perpendicular from the station. From the end of the line, walk around the corner (left) and catch any bus that runs straight up this road, i.e. 3, 9, 30, 32, 33, 64. Khao San Road is about 1 km away.

Southern Bus Terminal 1, *(Sai Tai)*, A/C ☎ (02) 434 5558, non A/C ☎ (02) 435 1199 on Boromrat Chonnane Road. **Southern Bus Terminal 2** A/C ☎ (02) 435 1190, non A/C ☎ (02) 434 5558 on Pin Klao Nahkon Chaisri Road. There are actually two southern bus terminals, however most buses heading south and west leave from the first one.

To get to the first catch the following buses: A/C 3, 7, 11 and 17, non A/C 28, 30, 42, 57, 68, 79, 80, 91, 123, 124, 127, 146 and 203, or micro buses 8 and 18. To and from Khao San Road, the easiest is bus number 30.

Southern Departures				
	A/C Services		Non-A/C Services	
Destination	Cost	Departs Bangkok	Cost	Departs Bangkok
Chumphon	202B	14.00,21.40,22.00	112B	03.30,04.00,06.05,06.50
Bang Saphan	161B	08.00,10.20,13.30,17.30	125B	05.00,06.00,09.40,12.20
Cha Am	82B	07.00,08.20,11.00,14.20	45B	09.00,16.00
Hat Yai	500B	07.00.16.00.17.30.18.00	224B	05.30
Hat Yai		18.15.18.30.19.00.20.00		
Hua Hin	92B	Throughout the day	59B	Throughout the day
Krabi	347B	19.00,20.00	193B	19.00,20.00
Nakhon Si Thammarat	400B	Throughout the day	190B	06.40,17.00,19.00,21.30
Narathiwat	516B	18.30	281B	15.30
Pattani	464B	10.00	258B	16.30
Petchaburi	68B	Throughout the day	36B	Throughout the day
Phang Nga	346B	19.30	192B	07.00,16.00
Phattalung	376B	20.00	209B	20.30
Phuket	378B	18.50	210B	Throughout the day
Pranburi	107B	Throughout the day	59B	Throughout the day
Pratchuap Khiri Khan	130B	Throughout the day	72B	Throughout the day
Ranong	250B	09.00.20.20.21.00	139B	Throughout the day
Satun	427B	19.30	234B	19.30
Songkhla	425B	17.00,18.45,19.30	236B	14.30,19.30
Sungai Kolok	533B	18.30	282B	19.30
Surat Thani	285B	20.00,20.20,20.30	158B	09.20,23.00
Takua Pa	322B	18.50	N/A	
Trang	565B	19.00,19.50,20.00	203B	08.10,16.30
Yala	460B	10.30	255B	18.30
All of the above leave from the southern bus terminal on Pinklao Nakhonchaisi Road				
Where there are a selection of routes, the shortest route has been shown.				

Giant Swing

There used to be a swinging festival held at the giant swing every year where acrobatics were performed from a platform swung from a high bar, but this was stopped due to the number of accidents. In the old days, an official deputy would dress up as a mock king, and would lead a parade to the swing. Three teams of Brahmin priests would jump on the swing in

BUS (PRIVATE)

Many guesthouses and travel agents will offer private buses to popular tourist destinations.
Although words such as VIP and air conditioning are frequently bandied around, often they
never eventuate. The buses are often in poor condition and break down on a regular basis.
Theft on these buses is also common. But before you point the finger at the Thai's, watch out
for low life farangs extending their holiday with the help of your camera and walkman. Those
who board a bus to Surat Thani and drop off to sleep may well wake up 'sans walkman'.
These buses are bad.

Central & Eastern Departures					
		A/C Services		Non-A/C Services	
Destination		Cost	Departs Bangkok	Cost	Departs Bangkok
Ang Thong	*	N/A		29B	Throughout the day
Ayutthaya	*	38B	Throughout the day	28B	Throughout the day
Bang Saen	**	49B	Every 2 hours	N/A	
Ban Phe	**	90B	Every 2 hours	50B	Throughout the day
Chachengsao	**	50B	Throughout the day	28B	Throughout the day
Chainat	*	89B	05.30,08.00,12.10,17.10	49B	Throughout the day
Chanthaburi	**	108B	Throughout the day	48B	Throughout the day
Chonburi	**	40B	Throughout the day	26B	Throughout the day
Kanchanaburi	***	65B	Throughout the day	34B	Throughout the day
Lopburi	*	72B	Throughout the day	40B	Throughout the day
Nakhon Nayok	*	66B	Throughout the day	36B	Throughout the day
Nakhon Pathom	***	28B	Throughout the day	22B	Throughout the day
Nakhon Sawan	*	107B	Throughout the day	59B	Throughout the day
Pattaya (a)	**	66B	Throughout the day	37B	Throughout the day
Prachinburi	*	78B	Throughout the day	43B	Throughout the day
Ratchaburi	***	54B	Throughout the day	29B	Throughout the day
Rayong	**	85B	Throughout the day	47B	Throughout the day
Sa Kaew	*	133B	Throughout the day	74B	Throughout the day
Samut Sakhon	***	30B	Throughout the day	25B	Throughout the day
Samut Songkhram	***	40B	Throughout the day	25B	Throughout the day
Saraburi	*	41B	Throughout the day	29B	Throughout the day
Singburi	*	67B	Throughout the day	47B	Throughout the day
Sattahip	**	76B	Throughout the day	42B	Throughout the day
Si Racha	**	52B	Throughout the day	29B	Throughout the day
Suphanaburi	*	47B	Throughout the day	N/A	
Trat	**	140B	Throughout the day	78B	Throughout the day
Uthai Thani	*	97B	Throughout the day	57B	Throughout the day
* = bus departs from the northern bus terminal					
** = bus departs from the eastern bus terminal					
*** = bus departs from the southern bus terminal					
(a) Buses to Pattaya can also be caught from the northern bus terminal					
Where there are a selection of routes, the shortest route has been shown					

turns, and whilst dangerously sitting with their right foot balancing on their left knee, try and
catch a bag of money attached to a bamboo stick whilst swinging. If the priest touches the
ground whilst performing this he was disgraced. After the swinging, the Brahmin priests
perform a blessing by sprinkling holy water over everything and everyone.

Bangkok

Northern Departures				
	A/C Services		Non-A/C Services	
Destination	Cost	Departs Bangkok	Cost	Departs Bangkok
Chiang Mai	237B	Throughout the day	190B	Throughout the day
Chiang Rai	358B	Throughout the day	189B	17.30,19.10,20.30
Kamphaeng Phet	157B	12.00,22.30	87B	08.55,10.25,13.20,22.00
Lampang	262B	09.30,11.00,20.30,21.30	147B	08.00
Lamphun	292B	20.20,20.30	162B	19.00,22.00
Mae Hong Son	442B	18.00	245B	09.00,14.30,19.45
Mai Sai	365B	08.00.19.00.19.30.20.00	202B	14.00,15.00,16.20
Mae Sot	224B	21.00,22.15	124B	08.00,20.30,21.00,22.00
Nan	319B	08.00,20.10,20.30,20.45	160B	06.00,10.00,16.30,20.30
Phayao	302B	19.50,20.00	168B	07.00,11.00,20.00
Phrae	238B	20.30,20.45,20.50	132B	11.30,18.30,21.00
Phichit	149B	11.50,16.00,22.10	83B	Throughout the day
Phitsanulok	163B	Throughout the day	90B	08.10,12.00,15.20
Sukhothai	191B	14.40,22.20,22.40	106B	Throughout the day
Tak	183B	13.00,22.10,22.30	101B	06.50,09.20,11.30,22.20
Uttaradit	235B	10.40,11.00,16.00,21.45	115B	09.25,10.35
All of the above leave from the northern bus terminal on Phanon Yothin Road.				
Where there are a selection of routes, the shortest route has been shown.				

Northeastern Departures				
	A/C Services		Non-A/C Services	
Destination	Cost	Departs Bangkok	Cost	Departs Bangkok
Amnat Charoen	197B	09.30,21.00	137B	06.40,08.20,18.00,20.20
Buriram	179B	10.00,12.00,22.00,22.30	79B	09.00,21.00,22.45
Chaiyaphum	147B	Throughout the day	65B	Throughout the day
Chiang Khan	261B	08.15, 19.00	145B	05.32, 18.15
Chum Phae	188B	08.15,10.30,20.00,22.00	104B	Throughout the day
Kalasin	221B	20.40,21.30,21.45	123B	20.06,21.00,21.50
Khao Yai National Park	92B	07.00,09.00	N/A	
Khon Kaen	193B	Throughout the day	155B	Throughout the day
Loei	279B	09.00,12.30,20.30,21.00	128B	Throughout the day
Mahasarakham	203B	12.00,22.00,22.20,22.40	133B	20.10,20.50,21.45,22.45
Mukdahan	287B	07.00,20.20	164B	05.00,06.14,18.00
Nakhon Phanom	310B	08.30,19.30,20.00,20.30	172B	19.00,19.50
Nakhon Ratchasima	115B	Throughout the day	64B	Throughout the day
Nong Khai	263B	08.40,20.15,21.00	146B	Throughout the day
Roi Et	220B	Throughout the day	122B	Throughout the day
Sakhon Nakhon	271B	09.00,10.30,19.30,20.00	150B	12.25,17.41,19.15,19.45
Si Saket	245B	09.00,21.30	131B	07.40,19.45,20.45
Surin	195B	11.00,21.30,22.00,22.10	108B	Throughout the day
Ubon Ratchathani	290B	08.30,09.30,20.30,21.00	161B	Throughout the day
Udon Thani	241B	Throughout the day	134B	Throughout the day
Yasothon	179B	18.50,21.00,21.20,22.00	99B	09.00,17.00,18.00,19.20
All of the above leave from the northern bus terminal on Phanon Yothin Road				

GETTING TO THE CITY FROM THE AIRPORT

TRAIN

The train is one of the cheaper alternatives to get to Bangkok from the airport. The Don Muang train station is located a few minutes walking distance from the airport — across the main road via the pedestrian walkway. Purchase a ticket for 5B (ordinary train) asking for Hualumpong train station, Bangkok's central train station - it is the last stop. Catch the train on the train track closest to the airport between 03.00 and 20.00. It takes around 45 minutes. There is also a special A/C express train that travels between Don Muang Airport and Bangkok daily. It leaves Hualumpong at 07.35, 10.35, 13.35, 15.45, 17.55 and 20.45, costing 20B and taking around 35 minutes. From Hualumpong station the train leaves at 8.55, 12.10, 14.35, 16.55, 19.20 and 21.40. If you buy your ticket in the arrival hall of the airport you will have to pay 100B, and for the privilege you will get a 20 minute A/C shuttle bus ride to the train station!

A tuk tuk to and from Hualumpong train station to Khao San Road will cost you about 50B to 60B maximum. A cheaper way is to catch the canal boat that leaves from the canal in front and to the right of the train station entrance. For 6B the ferry will take you to Banglamphu in under 10 minutes. The closest stop to Khao San Road is the second last, but tell the conductor where you are going and hopefully you will be let off at the appropriate place. From here walk up and back over the bridge, following this road (Chakraphong Road) for a few hundred metres until Khao San Road appears on your left.

Taxi
This is another alternative for getting to and from the airport. Officials at the airport will recommend you catch official transport, but they tend to be more expensive and time consuming options. An airport taxi will cost from 350B to 400B to anywhere (counter 3), whereas a public taxi will only set you back 230B a car to anywhere in Bangkok (pick up a ticket from the public taxi counter at the exit next to counter 7). The authorities advise you not to catch a taxi from outside the airport as you will be ripped off.

Minibus
Travel agents on Khao San Road, some guesthouses and other popular tourist accommodation havens run minibuses to the airport generally every hour. Prices range from 50B to 80B depending on time and demand. Allow yourself about 2 hours as the bus has to do the rounds to pick up everybody.

Airport Bus
Three airport buses, aptly named A1, A2 and A3 will take you to different popular locations in Bangkok for a cost of 70B. The buses pass every 15 minutes between 5.00 am and 11.00 pm.
A1: Airport to Silom via Din Daeng, Pratunam, Racha Prasong, Lumpini Park and Silom.
A2: Airport to Sanam Luang via Din Daeng, Victory Monument, Phaya Thai Road, Phetchaburi Road, Lan Luang, Democracy Monument, Wat Phra Kaew, Sanam Luang (catch this bus to get to Khao San Road in Banglamphu).
A3: Airport to Phrakanong via Din Daeng, Sukhumvit, Ambassador, Eastern (Ekamai) Bus Terminal, Phrakanong.

Public Bus
This is another cheap way to get to and from the airport and the city. Although cheap, a public bus is not advisable during peak hour(s) 06.30 to 09.30 and 15.30 to 19.30 if you are loaded with gear due to the crowds. You may get on, but your bag won't!! Red buses cost 3.5B for any distance (5B after hours), A/C buses cost 6B for distances within 8 km (10B after hours), and up to 15B for any distance over that. It is possible to jump on the bus through any door, and the bus inspector collects the fare once you are on the bus. The green buses cost 2.5B.

Below are the main city routes from the airport:

Bus 59, Non A/C, cost: 3.5B, from 5.00 am to midnight.
Airport, Central Plaza Hotel, Northern bus terminal, Victory Monument, Ratchadamnoen Klang Road, Democracy Monument (close walk to Banglamphu and Khao San Road), Royal Hotel, the Grand Palace.

Bus 13, A/C, cost: 15B, from 5.30 to 20.00.
Airport, Rama Gardens Hotel, Central Plaza Hotel, Northern bus terminal, Victory Monument, Indra Hotel, Ratchaprasong Road, Le Meridien President Hotel, Sukhumvit Road, The Ambassador Hotel, Eastern bus terminal, Bang Na, Samrong.

Bus 29, A/C, cost: 15B, from 05.15 to 20.00, Non A/C, cost: 3.5B, runs for 24 hours.
Airport, Rama Gardens Hotel, Central Plaza Hotel, Northern bus terminal, Victory Monument, Asia Hotel, Siam Square, Mandarin Hotel, Rama IV Road, Hualumpong Railway Station.

Bus 4, A/C, cost: 15B, runs from 05.30 to 20.00.
Airport, Rama Gardens Hotel, Central Plaza Hotel, Vibhavadi Rangsit Road, Din Daeng, Pratunam, Ratchadamri, Indra Hotel, Rajaprasong Road, Regent Hotel, Lumpini Park, Dusit Thani Hotel, Silom Road, Narai Hotel, Bangrak, Charoen Krung Road.

Bus 10, A/C, cost: 15B, from 05.30 to 21.00.
Airport, Rama Gardens Hotel, Central Plaza Hotel, Northern bus terminal, Victory Monument, Ratchawithi and Samsen Road, Southern bus terminal, Wongwien Yai, Charan Sanitwong Road, Bang Pakaew.

Other

If you want to travel in style, you can catch a limousine for around 600B per car (counter 7). For a river view there is the express boat at 700B per person to any hotel on the river front, otherwise there is a helicopter available for those with some spare cash. If you want any more information regarding transport or Bangkok in general, visit the tourist information at counter 3.

Shuttle Bus

If you need to catch a connecting domestic flight, THAI International provides a free shuttle bus to the domestic terminal, enquire at counter 7. They also leave for the domestic terminal from 485 Silom Road every half hour between 06.30 and 21.00.

To Pattaya

To Pattaya from the airport in an A/C bus costs 180B per person and leaves the airport at 09.00, 12.00 and 19.00. You pick up your ticket from the limousine counter.

Royal Barge

The festival of kathin takes place just after the Buddhist lent. In this festival, the king takes a royal procession on the royal barge down the Chao Phraya River to principle wats and presents the monks with new saffron robes. All around the country, Buddhist followers do the same offering robes and other essential items to the monks.

The provinces described within this region are typically within a couple of hours of Bangkok and best visited on a day trip. Common day trips include the popular floating market of Damnoen Saduak near Ratchaburi, the tallest chedi in Thailand at Nakhon Pathom, the busy shipping towns on the Gulf of Thailand and Ayutthaya, the site of the ancient Thai capital, now an historical park.

The national capital, Bangkok and its associated huge urban sprawl, has made its presence felt in the bordering provinces, often to the extent that you cannot tell where one province ends and another begins. The route we have taken begins to the southwest of Bangkok and follows a circular clockwise direction around the capital. This chapter covers the following provinces: Ratchaburi, Nakhon Pathom, Nonthaburi, Pathum Thani, Ayutthaya, Chachoengsao, Samut Prakan, Samut Sakhon and Samut Songkhram.

Highlights

Visit the ancient Thai capital **Ayutthaya** (Ayutthaya Province).

Check out the tallest Buddhist monument in the world — the **Phra Pathom Chedi**. (Nakhon Pathom Province).

Observe an ancient Thai tradition — the **floating market** at Damnoen Saduak (Ratchaburi Province).

Catch the cable car to the top of **Khao Wang** and wander the Royal retreat (Ratchaburi Province).

Experience the chaotic atmosphere at **Wat Sathon** (Chachoengsao Province).

RATCHABURI PROVINCE

Ratchaburi Province marks the head of what forms the Thailand peninsula and eventually Malaysia. This strategic positioning has seen the province change hands many times in the past. Ratchaburi was a provincial centre of the Angkorian Kingdom and formed the thoroughfare for Burmese invasions during the Ayutthaya Period. The province is quite small, covering a total area of only 5,196 sq km and has little to entertain the casual visitor for more than a day. The most popular sight apart from the provincial capital is the nearby Damnoen Saduak Floating Market.

RATCHABURI (RATBURI)   ราชบุรี

Ratchaburi sits on the banks of the Mae Khlong River and despite the hustle and bustle, holds little of interest unless you are planning to visit Damnoen Saduak floating market or the surrounding caves. Ratchaburi is around 70 km north of Petchaburi, a bit over 40 km south of Nakhon Pathom and around 101 km from Bangkok.

Vital Information

Post Office is on the corner of Samut Sangrat and Amarinthra Roads.

Banks Krung Thai Bank has a branch on Amarinthra Road and most other banks have a branch somewhere in town. Check the map for details.

Hospital Ratchaburi's children hospital is about halfway between town and the bus station.

Police Station is on Amarinthra Road.

Codes The telephone code is (032) and postal code is 70000.

Thai Proverb

Fish eat ants during flood-tide. Ants eat fish at ebb-tide. (Every dog has its day)

Cheap Sleeps

Araiya Hotel, ☎ (032) 337 782, at 187/1-2 Krapetch Road has very noisy big rooms with fan, shower and TV for 250B.

Numsin Hotel, ☎ (032) 337 551, at 2/16 Krapetch Road has similar rooms starting at 250B.

Krong Hua at 202 Amarinthra Road in the market area. This friendly Chinese hotel has basic rooms starting at 100B.

Hong Fa, ☎ (032) 337 484, at 89 Ratsadonyindee Road is a friendly hotel that has a restaurant downstairs. It is quieter than the Krong Hua and basic rooms start at 170B.

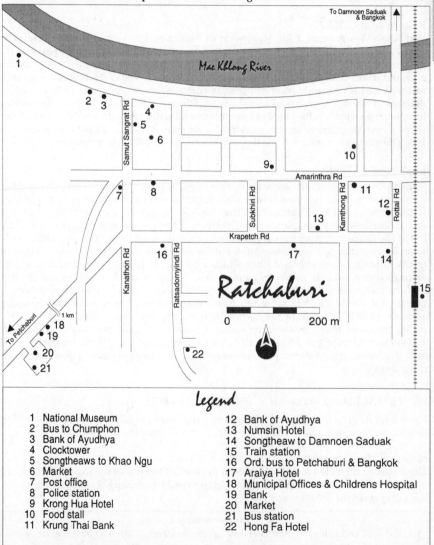

Ratchaburi

0   200 m

Legend

1 National Museum
2 Bus to Chumphon
3 Bank of Ayudhya
4 Clocktower
5 Songtheaws to Khao Ngu
6 Market
7 Post office
8 Police station
9 Krong Hua Hotel
10 Food stall
11 Krung Thai Bank
12 Bank of Ayudhya
13 Numsin Hotel
14 Songtheaw to Damnoen Saduak
15 Train station
16 Ord. bus to Petchaburi & Bangkok
17 Araiya Hotel
18 Municipal Offices & Childrens Hospital
19 Bank
20 Market
21 Bus station
22 Hong Fa Hotel

Around Bangkok

◀ **Eat and Meet** ▶

One thing Ratchaburi does have is good street side eating. **Cafes** line Amarinthra Road towards the railway and down the lane towards the river. There is also a lot of vendors along the Mae Khlong River come the evening as well as a large **market** in front of the police station and post office under the clocktower.

Things to do ◆ and ◆ Sights to See

Khao Wang   เขาวัง

Wat Khao Wang, some 2 km southwest of Ratchaburi town centre, was originally constructed as a palace for Rama V in the latter part of the 19th Century. Apparently the palace did not tickle his fancy or else he had other things to do, as he only ever used it once and it was actually converted into a wat by Rama VII. Today it has been completely restored and forms a pleasant hill temple complex overlooking the rather dubious delights of 'scenic' downtown Ratchaburi. Still the wat's buildings in a wooded setting have been painted a rather nice yellow colour and will come out well in your holiday snaps. Green songtheaws leave from in front of the police station and will take you there for 10B. If they take you up the low hill they will claim another 10B at the entrance.

Khao Ngu   เขางู

'Snake Mountain' is named more for its thin winding shape than anything else and lies 7 km to the west of town on Route 3087. It contains a series of caves including the locally renowned Phra Phutthachai Tham Reussii, previously a hermit's cave but now one of Ratchaburi's principle tourist attractions. The cave is a popular spot with Thais but at the time of writing the cave was rather run down. The main cave, with a large stone Buddha image is well looked after but the other caves, reached by semi-overgrown tracks, contain various ancient stone Buddha images, often in pieces piled on the floor amongst crisp packets and coke cans. A sala on top of the hill houses yet another Buddha footprint. Apart from that, the entire area is overrun by chubby monkeys. If you do not want to be hassled every two minutes to buy bananas for the charming animals, grab 5B's worth in the market before going and carry them clearly visible throughout your tour. Then you can decide if you want to give them to the monkeys! If you get bored looking at the caves, sit down somewhere and watch the frustrated local mongrels chasing the swarms of monkeys around. The monkeys have a good time even if the dogs do not.

Wat Phra Si Ratana Mahathat   วัดพระศรีรัตนมหาธาตุ

Known for its prang which is styled in ancient times after the Phra That in Angkor Wat, this wat is about a 1½ km walk to the west of town along the riverside.

National Museum

The museum is located on the riverside to the west of town past the market. This small museum contains a selection of ancient odds and ends, including skeletons which have been dug up in the local area.

Riddle Sawng
You are dead in the desert. There is a straw in your hand and a sandbag 50 feet away. How did you die?

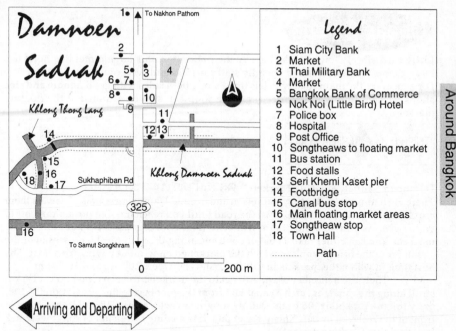

Damnoen Saduak

To Nakhon Pathom

Khlong Thong Lang

14

15
16
18   17   Sukhaphiban Rd

Khlong Damnoen Saduak

325

16

To Samut Songkhram

0   200 m

Legend

1 Siam City Bank
2 Market
3 Thai Military Bank
4 Market
5 Bangkok Bank of Commerce
6 Nok Noi (Little Bird) Hotel
7 Police box
8 Hospital
9 Post Office
10 Songtheaws to floating market
11 Bus station
12 Food stalls
13 Seri Khemi Kaset pier
14 Footbridge
15 Canal bus stop
16 Main floating market areas
17 Songtheaw stop
18 Town Hall
.... Path

Around Bangkok

Arriving and Departing

Bus
The bus station is about 1½ km out of town although it is never particularly busy. Most buses appear to leave from various points along Krapetch Road. From the bus station, a songtheaw into town costs 10B. A bus to **Petchaburi** is 30B and takes about an hour. Buses also run regularly to Nakhon Pathom, Bangkok and further afield. Minibuses/songtheaws leave from the intersection of Krapetch Road and Rottai Road to **Damnoen Saduak** costing 20B and taking about 1 hour dependent on traffic. Songtheaws for the surrounding destinations leave from around the clocktower eating area.

AROUND RATCHABURI

DAMNOEN SADUAK   ดำเนินสะดวก

Damnoen Saduak is situated just over 100 km to the southwest of Bangkok and is mainly visited for its floating markets as otherwise it is a fairly uneventful place. The floating market here get more than its fair share of tourists so it is best to start early if you want to avoid the hordes. There are a number of markets in town, all of which can be visited by boat in the space of about an hour or so.

Orientation

Upon arrival at Damnoen Saduak bus station when facing the river, you have the post office on the other side of the road, along with the lane to the 'Little Bird Hotel'. Ahead there is the bridge over the river. The turn off to the floating market is along this road, on the other side of the river.

Cheap Sleeps

Little Bird Hotel Down off the lane by the police box, this large motel like hotel has large rooms with shower and friendly staff for 150B and A/C rooms for 280B.
For a meal try the main road which is lined along both sides with good **noodle and rice shops**. Decent (though overpriced) noodle soup can also be sampled at the floating market.

Things to do and Sights to See

Damnoen Saduak Floating Market   ตลาดน้ำดำเนินสะดวก
There are a number of floating markets in and around Damnoen Saduak. To reach them cross the bridge and continue down the road until you reach the sign posted turn-off to your right. As you go along, there will be a number of signposts for boat hire to the markets. You can either take a boat or continue along the road until it crosses over the canal. From the bridge you can watch the market go on without paying for a boat. The best time to watch the markets in full flourish is between 7.00 am and 10.00 am.

There are a number of ways to get to the markets. You can either take a 1½ km stroll along the canal, or catch a canal taxi from the pier beside the bus station for 10B, or by tuk tuk for about 10B or the yellow songtheaw which costs 3B and leaves from in front of the 7-eleven by Seri Khemi Kaset pier. If travelling by tuk tuk or songtheaw, ask for *talaat nam* (floating market).

Once you get to the immediate surrounds of the market, there are a whole world of choices for boat hire and the price is completely dependent on your bargaining ability. Many will offer to take you to the market for 50B per person for around 30 minutes, if you get there early, this can be bargained down to 30B. If you arrive by tuk tuk, chances are you will be dropped at one of the agents where the tour buses normally arrive. Here, hire of a boat will cost between 100B to 300B for an hour in which time you will visit the market and the paddler's friend's soft drink stand!

◀ **Arriving and Departing** ▶

Bus and Songtheaw
A bus to **Samut Songkhram** costs 6B and takes about 30 minutes and a yellow songtheaw heading to **Ratchaburi** costs 20B and takes about 1 hour. A bus from Nakhon Pathom costs 21B and takes 1 hour. From **Bangkok** an ordinary bus costs 30B and takes around 2½ hours (from the southern bus terminal) depending on the traffic, an A/C bus costs 49B and takes 2 hours. This bus leaves every 20 minutes starting at 6.00 am. If you want to see the market in full action, you are probably best to stay in Damnoen Saduak overnight rather than getting up at 5.00 am for a 6.00 am bus from Bangkok.

NAKHON PATHOM PROVINCE

This region is where Buddhism was first introduced into Thailand. Over 2,000 years ago King Ashoka of India sent Phra Sona and Phra Uttera as missionaries to spread the Buddhist faith and Nakhon Pathom was one of their pitstops. Artifacts excavated from the province have demonstrated that it was a thriving city during the Dvaravati Period between the 7th and 11th Centuries. When the Khmer empire gained power in the

11th Century, Nakhon Pathom diminished in importance until eventually it was abandoned. King Rama IV prompted the resettlement of the city in the 19th Century, restoring both the town and the Phra Pathom Chedi.

The landscape of this province is predominantly very flat and set in an alluvial plain in what is mainly a rice producing region. The provincial capital has spread out to the west of the Chedi with a booming local economy. The province is particularly known for its cultivation of Som-O (Pomelo) which is regarded as being of exceptional quality. As a result of this, Nakhon Pathom is reportedly known as a land of 'Sweet Som-O, white rice, beautiful daughters and tasty Khao Lam'.

NAKHON PATHOM   นครปฐม

Nakhon Pathom is 58 km from Bangkok and home to the highly revered Phra Pathom Chedi. The town itself is nothing much to write home about being very busy and noisy and as a result most people pass through for the day, checking out the Chedi before moving onto the next destination. If you are planning on travelling out to Kanchanaburi, Nakhon Pathom makes a handy spot to break the trip as it is situated at roughly the halfway point between the two.

Vital Information

Post Office is about 200 m down the road that leads to Bangkok to the east of the chedi.
Banks There are plenty of banks surrounding the Chedi. See the map for details.
Hospital Nakhon Pathom Central Hospital, ☎ (034) 251 552, is not so central. It is located quite a long way down the road to Bangkok.
Police is on the north side of the chedi on Quapra Road, ☎ (034) 242 774.

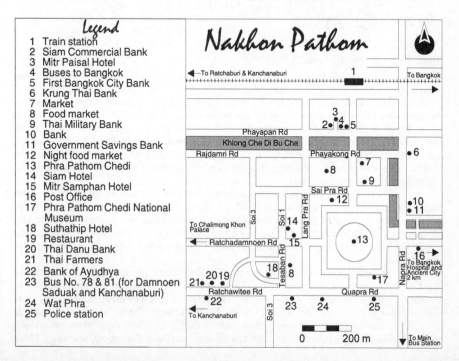

Legend

1 Train station
2 Siam Commercial Bank
3 Mitr Paisal Hotel
4 Buses to Bangkok
5 First Bangkok City Bank
6 Krung Thai Bank
7 Market
8 Food market
9 Thai Military Bank
10 Bank
11 Government Savings Bank
12 Night food market
13 Phra Pathom Chedi
14 Siam Hotel
15 Mitr Samphan Hotel
16 Post Office
17 Phra Pathom Chedi National Museum
18 Suthathip Hotel
19 Restaurant
20 Thai Danu Bank
21 Thai Farmers
22 Bank of Ayudhya
23 Bus No. 78 & 81 (for Damnoen Saduak and Kanchanaburi)
24 Wat Phra
25 Police station

Nakhon Pathom

To Ratchaburi & Kanchanaburi
To Bangkok
Phayapan Rd
Khlong Che Di Bu Cha
Rajdamri Rd
Phayakong Rd
Sai Pra Rd
Lang Pra Rd
To Chalimong Khon Palace
Sol 3
Sol 1
Ratchadamnoen Rd
Tesaban Rd
Napra Rd
To Bangkok Hospital and Ancient City 2 km
Ratchawitee Rd
Quapra Rd
To Kanchanaburi
Sol 3
To Main Bus Station

0   200 m

Around Bangkok

Cheap Sleeps

In Nakhon Pathom, all the hotels offer fairly similar rooms, though the noise factor is generally the deciding variable.

Suthathip Hotel, ☎ (034) 242242, on a street just off Tesaban Road. This hotel has no sign in English and is recognisable by the hotel like reception area. Rooms with a large bed, fan and bathroom cost 150B and are relatively protected from the din of the traffic.

Mitr Samphan Hotel on the street west of the Chedi. This hotel has similar rooms to those at the Suthathip for 160B, but is located next to one of the noisiest intersections in town so do not expect too much shut eye. Entrance is via Ratchadamnoen Road, but the office is in the furniture shop on the ground floor.

Siam Hotel around the corner at 2/1-5 Soi 1 offers large clean rooms with bathroom and TV for 220B.

Mitr Paisal Hotel, ☎ (034) 242 422, at 120/30 Phyapan Road near the railway station. Similar to the Siam Hotel, but not so clean for 250B.

Eat and Meet

The distinct lack of restaurants in Nakhon Pathom is made up for by the huge **nightly food market** held on the northern grounds of the Chedi. If you cannot find something to eat here then you are either in the wrong town or dead.

Restaurant This large Thai style eatery and bar on Ratchawitee Road has a good selection of food but little English is spoken. If you do not know any Thai dishes, pointing always works!

Things to do and Sights to See

Phra Pathom Chedi   พระปฐมเจดีย์

As you enter Nakhom Pathom you will see the Phra Pathom Chedi, the worlds tallest Buddhist stupa. Originally constructed over 1,000 years ago, it has undergone virtual rebuilding on a couple of occasions. The first structure, built during the Mon Empire was transformed into a 40 m high pile of rubble by the Burmese in the 11th Century. King Rama IV ordered restoration of the temple in 1853, replacing the original structure, but the inferior building fell down at a later date during a heavy storm. King Rama V finished it off, reconstructing it to its present state, and using imported golden Chinese tiles to cover the dome. A festival is held at the temple every November when the temple is adorned with lights and other paraphernalia.

Today, the Chedi is still the main feature of town as it towers above all else. And so it should, as it is the tallest stupa in Thailand and the highest Buddhist monument in the world, reaching a height of 115 m. The exterior of the Chedi is decorated with numerous evenly spaced Buddha images as well as a number of bell towers. Practising Buddhists circle the Chedi and ring each bell three times in a ritual which is believed to appease guardian spirits.

There are two museums within the Chedi grounds. The first is on the east side of the Chedi, down the stairs from Lab Lae Lane. This crowded display contains a variety of ceramics, statues, shells, weapons as well as notes and coins, all with no apparent connection. The second museum is the official tourist **Phra Pathom Chedi National Museum**, located within the grounds at the southern side of the Chedi. The display shows stone and metal Buddha images found on the site during the Ayutthaya Period, 600 years ago. There

metal Buddha images found on the site during the Ayutthaya Period, 600 years ago. There are also stucco motifs from the U-Thong Period (13th to 14th Century) and Buddha images from the Ratanakosin Period (19th Century). All have valuable descriptions in English. Entry is 10B and the museum is open Wednesday to Sunday 9.00 am to 12.00 am and 1.00 pm to 5.00 pm.

Sanam Chand Palace   พระราชวังสนามจันทร์

The palace is about 2 km to the west of the Phra Pathom Chedi and is the location of numerous royal palaces and residences from the reign of King Rama VI. The easiest way to get there is to catch a motorbike taxi or samlor.

Train

From **Bangkok**, trains leave Thonburi train station at 7.50 am and 1.50 pm and cost 10B. In the reverse direction, the train leaves Nakhon Pathom at 9.22 am and 4.46 pm. The trip takes about 1½ hours. If you are on your way to **Kanchanaburi**, the train leaves Nakhon Pathom at 9.00 am and 2.45 pm and takes around 1½ hours, costing 15B. The train in the reverse direction leaves at 7.31 am and 3.21 pm. If travelling south, the train to **Surat Thani** leaves at 11.40 am, 3.10 pm, 7.50 pm and 8.30 pm and the trip takes just under 10 hours. For detailed price and timetable information refer to the end of the chapter.

Bus

From **Bangkok**, numerous buses leave every hour from the southern bus terminal and cost 22B for the 1 hour trip. For buses to Bangkok, jump on a bus on the canal side of Phayapan Road, opposite the First Bangkok City Bank. Bus No 81 to **Kanchanaburi** leaves from Ratchawitee Road outside the camera shop every 30 minutes taking 1½ hours and costs 26B. It is possible to visit the floating market at **Damnoen Saduak** by catching bus No 78 from Ratchawitee Road for 21B. The bus passes every 30 minutes and takes one hour. When you alight at the last stop, take the local bus for 2 km and get off when you see the signs for the market. Ask for *talaat nam* (floating market) when you get to Damnoen Saduak. You would want to make a very early departure (6.30 am at the latest) if you

Phra Pathom Chedi at Nakhon Pathom

Around Bangkok

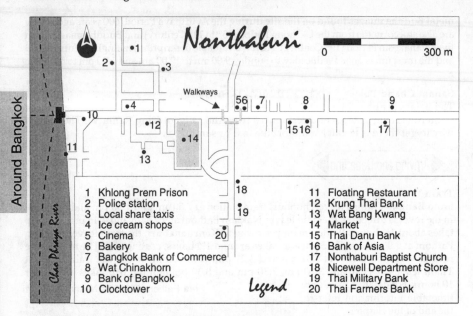

1	Khlong Prem Prison	11	Floating Restaurant
2	Police station	12	Krung Thai Bank
3	Local share taxis	13	Wat Bang Kwang
4	Ice cream shops	14	Market
5	Cinema	15	Thai Danu Bank
6	Bakery	16	Bank of Asia
7	Bangkok Bank of Commerce	17	Nonthaburi Baptist Church
8	Wat Chinakhorn	18	Nicewell Department Store
9	Bank of Bangkok	19	Thai Military Bank
10	Clocktower	20	Thai Farmers Bank

Legend

The Bangkok Hilton

The conditions in Klong Prem prison can be close to unbearable. Food rations per day consist of one bag of rice (which is often full of maggots) and a bowl of unappetising soup. Farangs are given no special privileges and an unwritten hierarchy exists according to the individual prisoners wealth. Prisoners need to buy everything they need to survive above a subsistence level. Farangs are not given much in the way of assistance from their embassy, hence they tend to rely on their family and visitors for survival.

Not all farang prisoners like getting visitors as they fear journalists writing articles which may result in harsher penalties and/or treatment as punishment. The embassies in Bangkok have lists of the prisoners who would like to be visited and occasionally you can pick up names from noticeboards in popular guesthouses. To make a visit, you will need to take your passport for admittance. Do not expect to see much in the way of the grotty conditions, as you will be led through neatly manicured gardens. The intimate meeting rooms consist of a six foot no mans land between you and the prisoner as well as two sets of bars. If there are more than a few visitors at anyone time, it is difficult to converse over the din. It is possible to bring gifts and food for the prisoners. These gifts will be searched and passed onto the prisoner later on. A small shop exists at the prison for this purpose. Visiting times are from 9.30 an to 11.30 am and 1.00 pm to 2.00 pm daily. Try to get there early to make the most of your time once the official procedures are over.

This is the prison that the movie "Bangkok Hilton" was based on, but conditions have not changed very much since that portrayal of prison life. In late 1996 an Australian prisoner escaped from here and as a result the prisoners were once again forced to wear shackles as punishment, as the authorities believe he had an accomplice. Nearby are the lighter security prisons, one for men and a separate one for women. In both of these prisons it is compulsory for the inmates to wear uniforms. The women suffer by far the worst conditions.

want to beat the tourist hordes at the market.

NONTHABURI PROVINCE

Located just north of Bangkok, the small province of 622 sq km became an independent province in 1946. It is easily accessible via land or river from Bangkok.

NONTHABURI   นนทบุรี

Situated at the last stop of the northern end of the Chao Phraya River Express, Nonthaburi is within an easy day trip distance from central Bangkok. There are a couple of activities worthy of your participation in Nonthaburi including visiting its interesting market or on a more serious note, visiting one of the foreign prisoners housed in one of the many prisons located here. Nonthaburi also has a famous fruit fair held annually between April and June where you can see processions, competitions and local handicrafts.

Vital Information

Banks All the major banks have a branch on the main road of Nonthaburi. See the map for details.
Police Station Upon leaving the wharf, take the first left and the police station is on the left.
Codes The telephone code for Nonthaburi is (02) and the postal code is 11000.

Things to do and Sights to See

Khlong Prem Prison
Nonthaburi is home to both the maximum security men's and women's prisons for Bangkok. Quite a few foreign prisoners are inmates of the Nonthaburi Prison, many of whom are serving life sentences for narcotics offences and many of whom would appreciate a visit and a fresh conversation to take them away from the atrocious conditions for a couple of hours.

The maximum security prison is located on the first street on the left after exiting the pier, and is easily recognisable by its high concrete walls and barbed wire. The prison is home to inmates serving sentences ranging from thirty years to one hundred years (which is to be replaced soon by a maximum sentence of forty years). Others spend their time here waiting on death row.

For those wanting to brighten an inmates otherwise fairly dull day, the embassies are a good place to start to get a list of those who would like to be visited. Visiting times are from 9.30 am to 11.30 am and 1.00 pm to 2.00 pm daily. Gifts are allowed to be given to the prisoners and are greatly appreciated.

Markets
It is well worth taking a trip to Nonthaburi to explore the authentic and very colourful markets. They are close to the ferry pier, just follow the road which leads from the pier for about 200 m to 300 m and they will appear on your right. Here, time can be spent slowly wandering around taking in the sights, colours and smells as you discover new, interesting and tasty foods.

Wat Chaloem Phra Kiat Worawihan   วัดเฉลิมพระเกียรติ
Quite a mouthful, so the locals call it Wat Chaloem. Located on the west bank of the Chao Phraya River. The area was once a fort in the Ayutthaya kingdom. King Rama III

Around Bangkok

The main temple comes complete with welcoming red carpet and photos of the King who visited in January 1993. The seated Buddha proudly wears a sash — a gift from the King. The detailed designs on the walls were hand painted by Chinese artists and the exterior doors and window shutters display cheerful rabbits. There are a few other Chinese influenced temples on the premises within the peaceful grounds. To get there, catch a barge across the river from the Nonthaburi pier for 1B, then jump on one of the many waiting motorbikes for 5B.

◀ Arriving and Departing ▶

The best way to visit Nonthaburi is via the Chao Phraya River Express Boat, Nonthaburi is the very last northern stop. From the pier in Nonthaburi it is possible to catch slower boats further up the river including Pathum Thani, however they leave in a very random fashion.

PATHUM THANI PROVINCE

Today Pathum Thani Province, separated from Bangkok only by the mini province of Nonthaburi (Pathum Thani is a mere 56 km from Bangkok), is an uneasy mixture of khlong/market gardening activities, old and new industry along the Chao Phraya River and new highways along with the encroaching Bangkok suburbia.

PATHUM THANI   ปทุมธานี

Pathum Thani was originally settled by Mon people migrating from the west during the Ayutthaya Period, and was known as Muang Sam Khok. 'Thai-ified' during the early 19th Century its name was changed to Pathum Thani and now little of the Mon heritage remains except for a few old stupas and some Mon style brick fabricatons in outlying villages.

A small but bustling town on the banks of the Chao Phraya River, Pathum Thani could make an interesting day trip from Bangkok because of its easy access and complete lack of farangs.

Vital Information

Post Office is on the other side of the market from the river. Refer to the map for details.
Banks Exchange facilities are on the main road, where the bus lets you off.
Police Station is situated beside the post office.
Codes Pathum Thani's telephone code is (02) and the postal code is 12000.

Legend
1   Wat Hong Pathum Mawas
2   Post office
3   Boat services
4   Bank
5   #33 Bus drop off
6   Police station
7   Eung Chua Kee Rest.
8   Bus & songtheaw station
9   Food stalls
10 Wat Sopharam
    Market Areas

Chao Phraya River

Pathum Thani

0   300 m

Eat and Meet

Plenty of market fare is available here, although the food is nothing exceptional. **Eung Chua Kee** is a good, centrally located seafood restaurant with reasonable prices and an English menu.

Things to do and Sights to See

There is not a lot to see in Pathum Thani except for its extensive riverside market area and a couple of interesting wats.

Wat Hong Pathum Mawas
A five minute walk from the centre of town heading north along the river, this wat spends more of its time in rather than by the river, outside of the dry season, and this is what makes it interesting. Thousands of large catfish swim in and around the chedis and shrines. Buy 5B worth of bread rolls for them and you have got a full scale catfish riot on your hands. Try to avoid falling in though. This is a good and shady spot to sit and watch the amazing variety of Chao Phraya River traffic cruising past. **Wat Sopharam** is another wat in town, but is nothing special, however is centrally located with a nice river bank location.

Wat Phailom   วัดไผ่ล้อม
For bird fans, a long tail boat taxi or regular ferry from one of the numerous market side piers, will take you the 15 km or so up river to this wat. This Sukhothai Period wat is noted for the annual migration from Siberia of open billed storks which breed in the trees in and around the wat from November through to May and June. The sight of hundreds of these large white birds perched amongst the tree tops is impressive.

Arriving and Departing

Bus
Pathum Thani is the terminus for the number 33 Bangkok city bus. Catch one on Samsen Road and do the 56 km's for 3½B! Note the drop off and hop on points in town are not at the same place. (See map for details).

Boat
Possible in theory, but this can be a little unreliable. You will need to catch the express boat to Nonthaburi and then wait around for the infrequent Nonthaburi to Pathum Thani service. Still, if you are not in a hurry, this is a nice way to reach town.

AYUTTHAYA PROVINCE

The sights of Ayutthaya Province are fairly few in number but central, located around the capital of the same name. The main attraction is Phra Nakhon Si Ayutthaya Historical Park in the midst of Ayutthaya city as well as the immediate surrounding area. Other sights worth seeing include Bang Pa-In and Bang Sai, but not much else. The ruins of the ancient city attract a devoted trail of tourists that are usually travelling north.

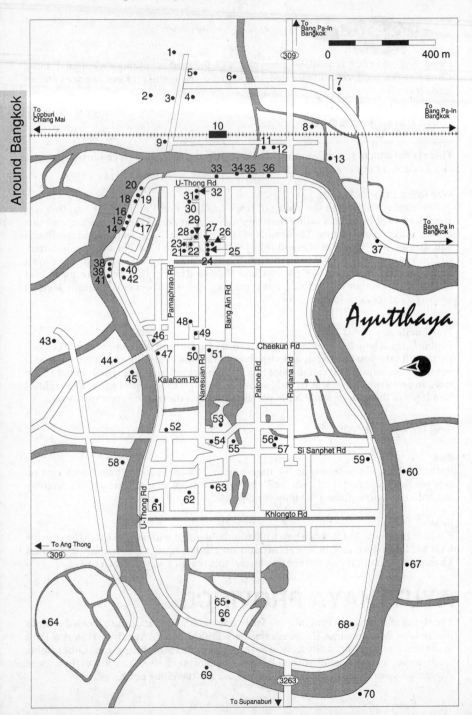

AYUTTHAYA พระนครศรีอยุธยา

Ayutthaya was the ancient capital of Thailand in the 15th Century, and its grandiose past can be re-experienced through the ruins that are scattered throughout the region. Unfortunately not much more than this can be relived as the relics and records from this period were destroyed during the Burmese rampage of 1767.

From 1350 to 1767, the beautiful city of Ayutthaya was the capital of what then was known as Siam. Surrounded by a 12½ km wall which was 5 m thick and 6 m high, the city had 99 gates, established brick and clay roads and canals to bring water into the city. Set at the meeting point of three rivers to make it central to trade, the city was founded in 1350 by King U-Thong and over the next 417 years, Ayutthaya would support 33 kings, 5 dynasties and repel 23 Burmese invasions, before being razed to the ground in 1767 after the Burmese finally succeeded in ransacking it. By all reports Ayutthaya was a fantastically beautiful city which would have rivalled most European capitals of the time. When the Burmese entered the town, they destroyed everything they came to, even to the extent of melting Buddhas for their gold.

Although Ayutthaya was once a truly beautiful city, the same cannot be said for the present town, located 76 km from Bangkok. It is worth spending a day here if time allows, to explore the many ruins around town, or two days if you want to also see Bang Pa-In, but other than that, there is very little to see, or do in the town except eat, sleep and sweat. If you had to choose between the historical parks of Ayutthaya or Sukhothai, the later is definitely the better choice.

Legend

1 Wat Maheyong
2 Wat Dusitaram
3 Wat Dusitaram school
4 Wat Pradoo Songtham
5 Wat Kudidao
6 Wat Wat Samanakot
7 Wat Yai Chaimongkol
8 Wat Kluay
9 Wat Pakho
10 Ayutthaya train station
11 Wat Thamniyom
12 Wat Phichaisongkarm
13 Wat Kokaew
14 Boat pier to Bang Pa-In and around the island
15 Food market
16 U Thong Hotel
17 Post office
18 Cathay Hotel
19 Bangkok Bank
20 Police station
21 Old BJ Guesthouse
22 PS Guesthouse
23 Ayutthaya Guesthouse
24 1st Bangkok City Bank
25 Bangkok Bank

26 Bus station
27 Siam City Bank
28 Sri Samai Hotel
29 Moon Cafe
30 Amporn Dept. store
31 Thai Farmers Bank
32 A/C minibus to Bkk
33 Bakery
34 Ferry crossing
35 Bangkok Metro. Bank
36 Ayutthaya Youth Hostel & Ruan Doem
37 Wat Phananchoeng
38 Hua Raw market
39 Thai Farmers Bank
40 Chan Kasem National Museum
41 Krung Thai Bank
42 Wat Sena Sanaram
43 Wat Sam Wiharn
44 Wat Intharam
45 Wat Wong Khong
46 Wat Ratpraditan
47 Wat Suwannawat
48 Thai Thai Bungalow
49 New BJ Guesthouse
50 Wat Ratburana

51 Wat Mahathat
52 Wat Thammikkarat
53 Folf Art Centre
54 Phra Chao U-Thong Monument
55 Wat Phraram
56 Chao Sam Phraya National Museum
57 TAT
58 Wat Na Phramane
59 Hospital
60 Wat Putthaisawan
61 Ancient Palace
62 Wat Phra Si Sanphet
63 Wihaan Phra Mongkhon Bophit
64 Wat Phu Khao Thong
65 Chedi Sisuriyothar
66 Wang Lang Royal Palace
67 St Josephs Cathedral
68 Somdej Park
69 Wat Kasittrathirat
70 Wat Chai Wattanaram

What's in a name?

Ayutthaya's name originates from the Sanskrit word Ayodhya which meant invincible. It was also the home of Rama, the hero of the Ramayana epic tale.

Around Bangkok

Orientation

Ayutthaya town is set on an 'island', and is surrounded by the meeting point of three rivers; the Lopburi, Prasak, and Chao Phraya Rivers. Strangely, Ayutthaya is a town of wide streets uncharacteristically not clogged with loads of traffic. There is little to see in Ayutthaya except for ruins and a couple of museums; all of which are best and most economically explored by push-bike, which can be hired at the guesthouses.

Vital Information

Tourist Office, ☎ (035) 246 076, is located on the grounds of Cham Samphraya National Museum. The staff are very friendly and an abundant source of information on the province. The office is open from 8.30 am to 4.30 pm daily.
Post Office is at the northeast corner of town on U-Thong Road. The telephone office is open from 7.00 am to 10.00 pm.
Banks These are abundant, mainly along U-Thong and Naresuan Roads.
Hospital The Phra Nakhon Si Ayutthaya Hospital, ☎ (035) 242 987, is on the corner of U-Thong and Si Sanphet Roads on the southern part of the island.
Police Station on U-Thong Road just north of Pamaphrao Road, ☎ (035) 241 001, although the tourist Police are on Si Sanphet Road ☎ (035) 242 352.
Codes Ayutthaya's telephone code is (035) and the postal code is 13000.

Cheap Sleeps

Ayutthaya has a decent selection of cheap guesthouses to choose from. Most are congregated around the bus station, but some further afield are also good options. Watch out for tuk tuk drivers seeking commissions, as most places are within walking distance if you are arriving at the bus station.
Old BJ Guesthouse, ☎ (035) 251 526, at 16/7 Naresuan Road has stock standard rooms for 80B/100B with shared bathrooms. Bicycles are 50B a day.
New BJ Guesthouse, ☎ (035) 246 046, at 19/29 Naresuan Road is located on a noisy road, the concrete rooms and shared bathrooms are pretty bad. The dorm starts at 60B with bigger rooms costing 120B.
Ayutthaya Guesthouse is just around the corner from Old BJ and is one of the best options in town. Set off the main road, it has been recently renovated with new bathrooms and mattresses. Wooden rooms cost 100B/120B or 60B if you do not mind sharing with a stranger. They also have bicycles for rent.
PS Guesthouse is a brand new guesthouse, opposite the Ayutthaya Guesthouse which charges 100B/120B for large clean rooms with mattresses on the floor.
Ayutthaya Youth Hostel, ☎ (035) 241 987, at 48 Mu 2 U-Thong Road. This place costs a little more but is really worth it. Huge rooms in an Old Thai house on the river cost 200B/250B with share bathroom, it is possible to lower the rate if they are empty. There is a great veranda overlooking the river and excellent restaurant on a boat set upon the river. The staff are very friendly.
Thong Chai Guesthouse, ☎ (035) 245 210. Friendly staff will rent you drab and dreary rooms with share bathroom for 120B. We recommend you invest in some earplugs if you intend on staying here.
Cathay, ☎ (035) 251 622, at 36/5-6 U-Thong Road. Pretty average hotel rooms on a busy road cost 170B/270B for singles/doubles with a fan and bath and 270B/300B for singles/doubles with A/C.

U-Thong Hotel, ☎ (035) 251 136, at 86 U-Thong Road. This large hotel has singles/doubles with TV and bath for 220B/280B and with A/C for 300B/400B. It is located on a noisy road, so try to get a room on the river side.

Si Samai, ☎ (035) 252 249, at 12 Mua 4 Tesaban 2 Road. The cheapest rooms here are 600B for a very clean hotel room with A/C and a real bath. It is set back from the busy streets.

Eat and Meet

Ruan Doem at 48 Mu 2 U-Thong Road is set on a romantic location on the river in front of the Ayutthaya Youth Hostel. It is great until the karaoke starts up. Excellent food costs 100B to 200B for two.

Markets There are two main markets in town; the **Chao Phrom Market** on the east side of the island is available for meals throughout the day at reasonable prices, whilst **Huaro Market** on the northeast corner is kicking in the evening.

Entertainment

There are two decent bars in town:

Moon Cafe is set on the same soi as Ayutthaya and Old BJ Guesthouses. A bit of a travellers haunt and under Japanese management. They play a good selection of CD's and it is not too expensive.

Rodeo Saloon on U-Thong Road, near the GPO is more of a Thai hang-out with live Thai music every night. The atmosphere builds up as the night progresses. Both food and drinks are available and it's not too pricey.

Things to do and Sights to See

If you are in Ayutthaya to see things, then you are talking ruins. Ruins are spread throughout the island and on the surrounding banks. Most of what is really worth seeing can be reached by bicycle in a day of cycling. Those with cash to spare can hire a boat for some of the more faraway spots. Besides ruins and wats, there are a number of museums worth checking out.

Chao Sam Phraya National Museum   พิพิธภัณฑสถานแห่งชาติเจ้าสามพระยา

This museum sits beside the cities temporary tourist office and houses a collection of various antiques, Buddhas and carved wooden panels. On the second floor at the east and west end are two rooms, the eastern one displaying gold treasures which were excavated from Wat Raturana, and the western room display similar wares from Wat Mahathat. The museum is located on Rotchana Road opposite the Ayutthaya Historical Study Centre and is open everyday from 9.00 am to 4.00 pm. It is worth a look.

Ayutthaya Historical Study Centre   ศูนย์ศึกษาประวัติศาสตร์อยุธยา

This centre, nearly opposite to the Chao Sam Phraya National Museum was funded by the Japanese government and contains an excellent exhibit dedicated to outlining what ancient Ayutthaya was like. The highlight is a model of Ayutthaya in all its former glory. Admission is 100B and the museum is open Wednesday to Sunday from 9.00 am to 4.30 pm.

Chan Kasem Palace National Museum   พระราชวังจันทรเกษม

Situated in the northeast corner of the island, there is really little see here which cannot be seen at the Chao Phraya Museum. What remains of the palace itself (like most nearly everything else in Ayutthaya, it was flattened by the Burmese) is worth a peek if you are around the post office anyway. Entry is 10B, and it is open Wednesday to Sunday from 9.00 am to 4.00 pm.

Once you get tired of museums, wait for the cooler part of the day, jump on your bicycle and visit some of the wats and ruins in town. Both are spread over a large area of town.

Wat Phra Si Sanphet   วัดพระศรีสรรเพชญ์

Wang Long Palace (Royal Palace) was built by King U-Thong upon the founding of the city. The palace was inhabited for another 98 years by a succession of Kings until the palace was moved, and this building was turned into a wat. In Ayutthaya's heyday, this was the largest wat in the city. There were eight forts around the palace and 22 gates. Little now remains except for the three chedis which once held the bones of Rama I, II, and III. Before the Burmese 24th foray, this wat contained a Buddha which was covered with over 250 kg of gold. The Burmese wasted no time melting that one down. Admission is 20B and gives you entry to the palace just to the north as well. The wat is at the northern end of Si Sanphet Road.

Wat Phra Mongkhon Bophit   วิหารพระมงครบพิตร

Just to the south of Wat Phra Si Sanphet, this wat contains one of the largest Buddha castings in Thailand. Cast in bronze the Buddha and its housing were badly damaged by fire. Photos inside the temple show how badly the image was damaged by fire and act as evidence of the immaculate restoration effort.

Wat Phra Mahathat and Wat Ratburona   วัดราชบูรณะ

These two wats are separated by Naresuan Road and were built on the command of King Borom Rachathirat II after his two elder brothers died during an elephant back duel to contest the crown. The ruins here are still in quite impressive condition and are well worth a look. Admission is 20B to each site.

Wat Yai Chaiya Mongkhon   วัดใหญ่ชัยมงคล

Located to the southeast of the island, this wat's chedi is visible from most of town. Built by King Naresuan in 1592 to commemorate his single handed victory on elephant back, the Chedi now has a distinct tilt, but still can be entered via the stairs. Those who make the effort will find themselves surrounded by meditating Buddhas in a peaceful environment. To get there cross the Preedee Thamrong Bridge then cross the train tracks and take a right down Route 3059. Admission is 20B.

Wat Phra Chao Phanan Choeng   วัดพนัญเชิง

Also to the southeast of the island, this wat can be reached by boat from the fortress ruins. It was built before Ayutthaya was established as the capital and it is believed to have been originally constructed by Khmers. The main sitting Buddha within is 10 m tall, and is highly revered by the residents of Ayutthaya. The ancient golden Buddha was made in 1344 and called Luang Po To. Amongst Chinese this statue is believed to impart protection to sailors and is known as Sum Po Hud Kong. This wat has never been deserted and hence has an interesting collection of artifacts and architectural styles from different periods.

Wat Phra Mane   วัดหน้าพระเมรุ

The most interesting fact about this wat is that it escaped destruction when the Burmese were burning everything down. Ironically, it was from the grounds of this wat that the Burmese King Chao Along Phaya decided to fire a cannon at the Grand Palace. The cannon exploded and he was grievously wounded and subsequently died on the way back to Burma. The wat itself is impressive with a vaulted ceiling and quite nice Buddha image. Admission is 10B and the wat is just over the bridge near Si Sanphet Road.

Wat Phu Khao Thong   วัดภูเขาทอง

This wat is about 5 km northwest of town and has a huge stupa which can be seen from the highway. The wat was built by King Ramesuan in 1387. When the Burmese arrived and put an end to the Kingdom of Ayutthaya, they built the stupa in front of this wat. It later collapsed, so King Boromakot rebuilt it in 1744 based on his own design. The climb to the highest platform of the stupa gives views of the surrounds and the distant city. The wat also contains a Buddha footprint from Saraburi.

Wat Lokayasutharam   วัดโลกยสุธาราม

The main feature here is a 29 m reclining Buddha made of brick and covered in white plaster. The wat itself is in a complete state of ruins showing a few hexagonal pillars and enough bricks to see where the buildings and rooms must have once stood. The ruins directly adjacent are Wat Chettharam, which was built by King Ekathotsarot in 1605 in honour of his brother. Neither site are much to write home about.

Wat Chaiwatthanaram   วัดไชยวัฒนาราม

This wat is still in remarkably good condition. It was built by King Prasat Thong in 1630 in honour of his mother, and the building served as a Royal monastery. The prangs and pagodas are similar in style to Khmer designs, purposely done so as to commemorate the victory over the Khmers. When the Burmese besieged the city in 1767, they used it as a army camp.

The wat consists of a main prang surrounded by four smaller prangs and then by eight merus. The gallery originally had 120 lacquered Buddha images around it. Twelve crowned Buddhas sit in each of the eight merus which are located at each of the cardinal points. A meru is a building specially built for royalty which has a multiple tiered roof imitating similar wooden structures. Stucco designs of Buddha's life can still partly be seen on the outside walls of the merus.

Directly opposite the wat on the other side of the river is the current Royal Palace where the current royal family occasionally visit by boat from Bangkok. Entry to the wat is 20B.

Other Wats and Ruins

If you are a true wat and ruin addict, pick up the tourist offices brochure of Ayutthaya which has an exhaustive list of wats and piles of rock. The above are the highlights.

Longtail Island Tour

Longtail boats are available to take you around the island, almost! Often there is not enough water to take you along Khlong Muang, the canal along the top of the island. A two hour trip with three stops (generally at Wat Phanachoeng, Wat Putthaisawan and Wat Chaiwattanaram) and back to the pier cost 400B per longtail. You may be able to haggle the price down to around 300B.

◀ **Arriving and Departing** ▶

Getting Around

Songtheaws within the island cost 3B and pass every few minutes, whilst a **tuk tuk** across the island will cost around 30B. Beware of tuk tuk drivers in Ayutthaya as they can be are very unscrupulous and may attempt to rip you off, the government rate of 150B per hour can be used as a guide for the hiring of tuk tuks for tours. The average price for a three hour tuk tuk tour is around 400B to 500B, but as it is possible to fit up to six people in the back of a tuk tuk, it need not be as expensive as it looks. It is also possible to travel by tuk tuk to Bang Pa-In and other out of town destinations, though you will need to bargain quite hard. One of the best ways to see the ruins outside of the island is by **bicycle**. The cost of renting a bicycle ranges from 20B to 50B and they are available from most guesthouses. The odd **mountain bike** can also be hired for 100B.

Longtail boats from the pier at the northeast side of the island charge around 200B per hour. To Bang Pa-In expect to pay a maximum of 600B for two hours travelling time and an hour to look around.

Train

Trains leave for Ayutthaya from **Bangkok** every hour between 4.20 am and 11.25 pm for 15B (3rd class) taking 1½ hours. The Bang Pa-In stop is 10 minutes earlier. Third class train to **Pak Chong** is 23B. The boat across to the train station in Ayutthaya costs 1B. For detailed price and timetable information refer to the end of the chapter.

Bus

Air conditioned buses leave **Bangkok's** northern bus terminal every 30 minutes between 6.00 am and 7.00 pm for 38B taking 1½ hours. Normal buses leave every 15 minutes between 4.30 am and 7.15 pm, cost 28B and take 2 hours. Returning buses to Bangkok run at the same times. Air conditioned minibuses leave every hour from the southern bus terminal and cost 35B, otherwise from the Victory monument for 25B.

You can catch a songtheaw to **Bang Pa-In** for 7B. Normal buses to **Saraburi** leave every half hour costing 18B for a 2½ hour trip, to **Ang Thong** every 40 minutes for 10B taking 1 hour, to **Suphanaburi** every half hour costing 18B and taking 1¾ hours, **Lopburi** every 30 minutes where for 19B you will travel for 2 hours.

AROUND AYUTTHAYA

Bang Pa-In   บางปะอิน

The Royal Palace at Bang Pa-In is just over 20 km south of Ayutthaya, but is only really worth visiting if you have half a day to kill in Ayutthaya. This site is very popular with tourists who arrive by tour bus or boat from Bangkok, so it can get a bit crowded.

King Prasat Thong had the Chumphon Nikayaram Temple built and later the palace on the island in the lake during his reign from 1630 to 1655. It was a popular country residence for Ayutthaya Kings and later for King Rama IV and V, the later who transformed it to its current state. The palace is surrounded by a 40 m wide lake, and there is also a pretty pavilion in the lake which is a popular subject for photos. The Palace consists of a number of halls and monuments, some of which are closed to the public, but it is an interesting and pleasant stroll amongst the buildings and elephant style gardens. It is open daily from 8.30 am to 3.30 am, and admission is 50B.

◀ Arriving and Departing ▶

Songtheaws from Chao Phrom Market in **Ayutthaya** to Bang Pa-In cost 7B. A bus from **Bangkok's** northern bus terminal costs 20B, and the train costs 15B and takes 1¼ hours. Boats also leave Bangkok every Sunday for a day trip to Bang Pa-In for around 250B. More expensive cruises are available at over 1,000B. If you have your own transport, take Phanon Yothin Road from Ayutthaya turning at the 35 km marker. From here its another 7 km to Bang Pa-In Palace.

Wat Nivet Thammaprawat   วัดนิเวศธรรมประวัติ

Outside the island itself, this wat is remarkable due to its gothic style, unlike anything else in Thailand. Not surprisingly it was built under the command of King Rama V in 1878.

Royal Folk Arts and Craft Centre at Bang Sai   ศูนย์ศิลปาชีพบางไทร

Operating under the guidance of the Queens SUPPORT Foundation, this centre facilitates the training of novices by Artisans in folk arts and craft. The centre is open for tourists to visit and it makes an interesting distraction from wats. The crafts taught here include: basketry, hand woven silk and cotton, silk dyeing, wood carving, Thai dolls, furniture making and other textile products. There is an annual fair here every January and they also put on a show for the Krathong Festival in November. The centre is open from Tuesday to Sunday from 8.30 am to 4.00 pm. Admission is 20B. A bus can be caught here from Bangkok's northern bus terminal for 25B (A/C) or 17B (non A/C) which leave every 30 minutes during the day.

CHACHOENGSAO PROVINCE

Chachoengsao Province is fairly small and reaps most of its income from the land through rice cultivation. The only worthwhile trip within the province is to the capital of the same name. Chachoengsao first made its way into the history books during the reign of King Maha Thammaracha. At that time, due to Burmese attacks, the country was in a fairly grim state of affairs, and a Khmer King, Phraya Lawaek attacked and took many of the citizens of Chachoengsao back with him as slave labour.

CHACHOENGSAO   ฉะเชิงเทรา

Also known as Paet Riu, the town located around 100 km from Bangkok makes a long day trip. The town was established around the mid 16th Century in the Ayutthaya era for the main purpose of recruiting armed forces. It is set upon the Bang Pakong River and most well known for Luang Pho Sothon, the town's revered Buddha image. The compound of Wat Sothon where is it kept is worth a visit of its own during the weekend. The views across the river are quite scenic showing a stark contrast from the busy town side and the opposite which has a lush green setting. Chachoengsao is nice enough as far as Thai towns go, however the residents are not particularly friendly and are a little suspicious of strangers. The town extends much further than the map which shows the market area.

Vital Information

Post Office is on the southeastern corner of the intersection of Chumpol and Mahachukapudi Roads. The telephone centre is open between 8.00 am and 8.00 pm.
Banks are around the market area, especially along Chumpol Road.
Hospital is on Chumpol Road about 500 m south of the intersection of Mahachukapudi Road.
Police Station is about 180 m up Chumpol Road north of Mahachukapudi Road.
Codes Chachoengsao's telephone code is (038) and the postal code is 24000.

Cheap Sleeps

The lack of accommodation in Chachoengsao around the market area means it is best to visit as a day trip or while passing through on your way to somewhere else.
River Inn Hotel, ☎ (038) 511 921, is a large hotel with unbelievably overpriced, small and stuffy rooms costing 370B/520B for fan/A/C. The address is 122/1 Narupong Road, but the reception is on Panich Road on the third floor. The first two floors are part of the attached department store.

Around Bangkok

Legend

1 Restaurant
2 Chinese Temple
3 Bangkok Bank
4 7-eleven
5 Siam Commercial Bank
6 Bank of Asia
7 Krung Thai Bank
8 Bank of Ayudhya
9 Restaurant
10 Thai Farmers Bank
11 Clothes Market
12 Expensive Restaurant
13 Police station
14 Food market
15 Department Store
16 River Inn Hotel
17 Bangkok Metropolitan Bank
18 Thai Military Bank
19 Post office
20 Bus station (3 km)
     Train station (2.5 km)
21 Hospital (400 m)
     City fort walls (700 m)
     Wat Sothon (2 km)

Eat and Meet

The large **market** has a variety of food stalls as does the grounds of Wat Sothon on the weekends. There are very few established restaurants.

Things to do and Sights to See

Wat Sothon Wararam Worawihan

More commonly called Wat Sothon, this wat contains one of the country's most sacred Buddha images, Phra Phuttha Sothon, or Luang Pho Sothon as it is known by the locals. The statue is fairly small, 198 cm high and 165 cm across its lap, and is sitting in the meditation position. According to legend three Buddha images floated down the river from Prachinburi, the largest one ended up at Ban Laem in Samut Songkhram Province, the smallest landed at Samut Prakan, but the middle sized statue found its way to Chachoengsao. On seeing the image the townsfolk tried everything to lift it from the river however did not succeed until they built a shrine and paid homage to the image. It has since been preserved within the wat.

On weekends, the wat is the place to be. People flood the compound from throughout the province and beyond to pay homage to Phra Phuttha Sothon. When we say flood, we mean flood. There are so many people that traffic jams are common and numbered parking attendants try to maintain some kind of order. Hundreds of people have to literally line up to take their turn in honouring the image. The weekend ritual has turned the grounds into a fair like display of lottery ticket sellers and food stalls (including tasty live fish and turtles in plastic bags, as well as the odd snake). The image and its associated statues are actually located in the large shed in front of the wat with a green tiled roof. Thai dancers also put on a constant show throughout the weekend festivities. The wat is certainly not short of cash - the numerous donation boxes are full and need to be consistently emptied, with the money paying for the huge new wat next door.

The Chinese temple next door is worth a look. The ground level holds a large laughing Buddha where you can try to throw 1B coins into a small slot in his generous belly. The next level holds a beautiful wooden shrine. To get here, jump on a blue songtheaw heading south along Chumpol Road for a few kilometres for 4B, and get off when you see the wat and huge chedi. Otherwise follow the traffic.

If you are a bit sick of the crowds, go and relax at **Somdet Phra Si Nakharin Park** located in front of Chachoengsao City Hall, or by the fitness park next to the river.

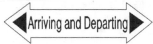

Arriving and Departing

Train

Trains travel between **Bangkok** and Chachoengsao almost hourly throughout the day. The train station is just off Mahachukapudi Road, just before the turn-off for the bus station. From here to the market area, walk to the road and catch a white songtheaw travelling east for 3B for around 2 km. For detailed price and timetable information refer to the end of the chapter.

Bus

Buses travel to Chachoengsao regularly from **Bangkok's** eastern bus terminal taking around 2 hours. The fare is 50B for an A/C bus which leaves every 1½ hours between 07.00 and 19.30, the last return bus is at 18.00. Ordinary buses cost 28B and leave every 30 minutes between 06.00 and 18.00 with the last returning to Bangkok at 18.10. Chachoengsao's town sprawl has caused the main bus station to move away from the market area. But to get to the centre of town, catch the white songtheaw that line up opposite the bus station for 3B and about 3 km.

SAMUT PRAKAN PROVINCE

Located to the south of Bangkok, Samut Prakan marks the end of the snaking journeys of the Chao Phraya River as it empties into the Gulf of Thailand. Like many provincial capitals, Samut Prakan has been moved in the past, with it arriving at its present position in 1819 by the orders of King Rama II. The move took three years to complete, but there is still little to keep you busy here. It was also here that French gunboats attacked up the Chao Phraya River in 1893, the final result being that Thailand was forced to cede an outrageous amount of territory (including all of Trat and Chanthaburi) to France for essentially defending its own territory.

SAMUT PRAKAN   สมุทรปราการ

Itself almost part of Bangkok's urban sprawl, Samut Prakan is located 30 km south of the Bangkok city limits on the Gulf of Thailand. The town is a hectic provincial capital with way too many people, but it is the town you must travel through if you are intent on visiting the nearby Crocodile Farm and Ancient City. The town is locally known as Pak Nam.

Orientation

The A/C bus station is on Sai Loud Road out of the centre of town. Once at the bus station, turn left (when facing the road) and walk or take a songtheaw for around 2 km and you will reach a roundabout with a clocktower in the centre. To get to the market area and songtheaw stations, walk up Pra Kone Chai Road (the road opposite Sai Loud Road) for a few hundred metres. The central Wat Pichai Songkhram is just past the market. The **market** is by far the best place for cheap and tasty Thai meals.

Vital Information

Banks Abound around the market area and at the roundabout end of Sai Loud Road.
Codes Samut Prakan's telephone code is (02) and the postal code is 10270.

Cheap Sleeps

The hotels in town are not of the highest standard and may suffer a cockroach problem.
Pak Num Hotel at 101/2-3 Naraiprapsuk Road, has fan and A/C rooms starting at 250B.
Nithra Swan is closer and cheaper with rooms with fan and bath starting at 150B. A/C rooms are also available.

◀ Arriving and Departing ▶

Bus and Songtheaw
There are a few buses that run from central **Bangkok** to Samut Prakan. The A/C bus number 11 costs 16B, (you can also catch A/C bus 7 and 8), and regular bus number 25 costs 5B (bus number 102 also travels here). Both can take up to 2 hours to cover the short distance, mainly due to heavy traffic congestion. Songtheaws around town and to the outlying sights cost 3B and a motorbike taxi costs 15B.

AROUND SAMUT PRAKAN

Samut Prakan Crocodile Farm and Zoo   ฟาร์มจระเข้สมุทรปราการ

This farm was originally set up in 1950 as an educational and research facility with the grand idea of protecting crocodiles foremost in the planning. Today the crocodile farm sells skins for commercial purposes. There are now over 40,000 crocodiles on the site and there is also a zoo containing an assortment of other animals. The farm offers a fine selection of tacky tourist pastimes, including crocodile wrestling on the hour between 9.00 am and 4.00 pm (not midday though) and elephant shows every hour between 9.30 am and 4.30 pm (excluding midday). Feeding Time is from 4.30 pm to 5.30 pm. There is also a dinosaur museum, elephant and camel riding, pedal boats, go carts, a shooting range and a mini train which covers most of the park. All of this costs 300B (200B for students and less if you are very persuasive). You can be the envy of your friends and spend even more of your loot in the shop which sells crocodile and fish skin products. Open 7.00 am to 6.00 pm. This park is also mentioned in the Guinness Book of Records as having the largest crocodile in captivity at 6 m long (9' 8") which weighs 1114.27 kg (2456 lb), but did you know that a crocodiles brain is smaller than your index finger.

Micro Bus number 13 travels directly to the crocodile farm via the Victory Monument in Bangkok. Otherwise catch a songtheaw from Samut Prakan.

Muang Boran (Ancient City)   เมืองโบราณ

This is Thailand's one stop historical park. It covers a total of 100 acres and is structured in the shape of Thailand with a canal running around its edge and around the main sights. There are currently 99 of Thailand's famous historical sights, ruins and monuments reproduced on site. A map and book are available at the information desk. Check out the elevated Prasat Hin Khao Phra Viharn (which is actually in Cambodia) for great views of the surrounding area and the Gulf of Thailand. You will need the better portion of an entire day to explore this park. Admission is 50B and the park is open 8.00 am to 6.00 pm.

The park is located on Sukhumvit Road at the 33 km mark. The entrance is a bridge over a canal on the left hand side of the road with a wooden archway with "Ancient City" inscribed in small white English and Thai text. Ask the songtheaw driver to let you off at *Muang Boran*.

◀ **Arriving and Departing** ▶

Both of the above points of interest can be reached by songtheaw from Samut Prakan and the songtheaw stations are 50 m apart near the market. From the roundabout, walk up Pra Kone Chai Road a few hundred metres. The blue songtheaws to the **Crocodile Farm** line up in the third street on the right hand side after the bridge and cost 3B. Be sure to verify the destination before you get on. It is a five minute trip, and you will know when you are there by the yellow archway and the entourage of tour buses.

White songtheaws to the **Ancient City** line up on the next street 50 m away. (There is a Bank of Ayudhya on one corner and a Chinese temple on the other). The trip takes ten minutes. To get to the Ancient City from the Crocodile Farm, turn right when facing the road, walk for ten minutes or catch a blue songtheaw to Sukhumvit Road. Once here, jump on a white songtheaw for the five to ten minute trip for 3B.

BANG PHLI

This non assuming town in Samut Prakan Province is set on the quiet Songram canal, near Phra Pradaeng. The time to visit is during the annual local festival held in late October (based on the lunar calendar) when the town changes personality, reliving its Mon heritage. Many of the local inhabitants can be traced back to Mon lineage, coming from Burma in the 18th Century after fleeing persecution in their native land. Although they have successfully mingled into Thai life, many are still characterised by the physical characteristics of the Mon.

The festival itself is based on local legend. In 1767, the Burmese empowered and later sacked the ancient capital Ayutthaya. In an effort to save their culture, local residents threw three gold Buddha images into the Chao Phraya River. Apparently they floated down river but years later were recovered. All three were found, two ending up in temples in Chachoengsao and Samut Songkhram Provinces, and the third and largest ended up in Bang Phli. The Buddha image is now know as Luang Pho Toh, and held at Wat Bang Phli Yai Nai, the main temple in the village.

During the festival, the seated Buddha image is placed onto a river boat, decorated in wreaths and brightly coloured cloth. It is the focus in a procession down the canal, when it is covered in a rain of pink and white lotus flowers from local residents. The festival also involves numerous competitions including the selection of the most beautiful boat in the procession and boxing matches whilst balancing on a pole.

Thai Proverb
If you enter the town of the crosseyed, cross your eyes (When in Rome . . .)

Around Bangkok

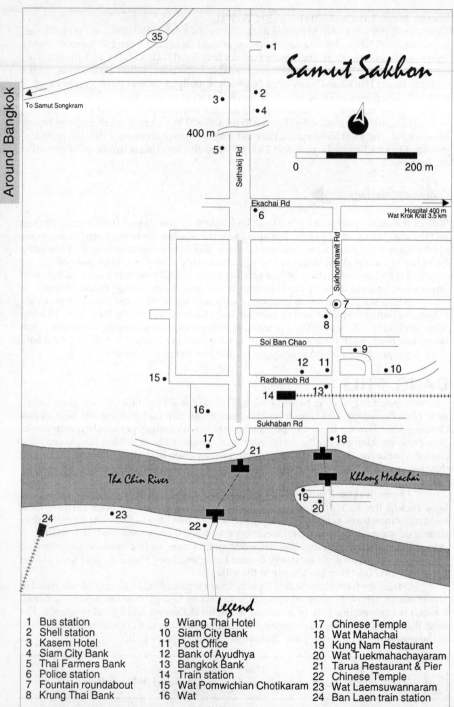

Samut Sakhon

To Samut Songkram

400 m

Ekachai Rd

Hospital 400 m
Wat Krok Krat 3.5 km

0   200 m

Sethakij Rd

Sukhonthawit Rd

Soi Ban Chao

Radbantob Rd

Sukhaban Rd

Tha Chin River

Khlong Mahachai

Legend

1 Bus station	9 Wiang Thai Hotel	17 Chinese Temple
2 Shell station	10 Siam City Bank	18 Wat Mahachai
3 Kasem Hotel	11 Post Office	19 Kung Nam Restaurant
4 Siam City Bank	12 Bank of Ayudhya	20 Wat Tuekmahachayaram
5 Thai Farmers Bank	13 Bangkok Bank	21 Tarua Restaurant & Pier
6 Police station	14 Train station	22 Chinese Temple
7 Fountain roundabout	15 Wat Pomwichian Chotikaram	23 Wat Laemsuwannaram
8 Krung Thai Bank	16 Wat	24 Ban Laen train station

SAMUT SAKHON PROVINCE

Originally known as Muang Tha Chin, this name is believed to have its origins in the vast number of Chinese trading junks which once visited. Later, during the reign of King Sua, work was begun on a new canal to the region after an unfortunate incident during which the King's coxswain was slaughtered for running into a tree. It is believed that he ran into the tree because the canal was so curvy, therefore a straight canal was the obvious solution. Once completed the canal met the Tha Chin River by the town of Mahachai, and although the town was later renamed Samut Sakhon, amongst the locals, it is still known as Mahachai.

Besides historical oddities, this province located to the south of Bangkok has little to interest the traveller. Its location next to the Gulf of Thailand has made it an important shipping centre, but the other money spinner is the large and numerous salt fields which generate more salt than anywhere else in Thailand.

Around Bangkok

SAMUT SAKHON สมุทรสาคร

Located 28 km south of Bangkok and a 'stone throw' from the Gulf of Thailand, Samut Sakhon is really just an extension of Bangkok's outer region. A hectic port and fishing town, Samut Sakhon sits on the Mahachai canal where it meets the Tha Chin River. Many of the townsfolk still call the town Mahachai as it was known during the reign of King Thaisa. The average traveller would have no real reason to visit as the sights are minimal and all the town has to offer is a market area and a municipal park which you can escape to, of which both have nicer versions in other towns.

Vital Information

Post Office In the heart of town on the corner of Sukhonthawit and Radbantob Roads open 8.30 am to 4.30 pm and 9.00 am till 12.00 am on Saturday.
Banks can be found around the post office and between the police station and the bus terminal.
Hospital 500 m east along the road cornered by the police station.
Police Station is 200 m up Sethakij Road from the pier.
Codes Telephone code is (034) and the postal code is 74000.

Cheap Sleeps

Kasem Hotel, ☎ (034) 411 078, at 927/28 Sethakij Road, close to the bus station, is an old hotel where the rooms really show their age. It is set on a noisy road, but rooms at the back may keep you sheltered from some of the traffic noise. Standard room with fan and bath is 200B and 350B with A/C.
Wiang Thai Hotel, ☎ (034) 411 151, at 821/5 Sukhonthawit Road, is located in the heart of downtown, but is surprisingly not too noisy. Rooms are small and well worn with fan and shower but no toilet and cost 200B. The hotel is up the small alley opposite the post office.

Eat and Meet

As usual the **market** sells a variety of cheap interesting meals and is located around the train station. Samut Sakhon is particularly well known for its seafood. Above the pier is **Tarva Restaurant** where you can grab a seafood meal from an English menu at a reasonable price. More pleasant due to its location and service, but more expensive is the **Kung Nam Restaurant,** ☎ (034) 423 107, on the southern side of the Mahachai canal with most meals in the price range of 60B to 150B.

Around Bangkok

Things to do and Sights to See

Wichan Chodok Fortress   ป้อมวิเชียรโชฎก

These ruins are all that remains of a fortress which was supposed to defend the coast from attack from marauding hordes, though it probably would have been of more use at Samut Prakan, where the French attacked in the late 19th Century. The remains of this fort are within the park, next to the pier. The cannons which once laid here, now sit by the city pillar shrine.

Khlong Pho Hak Floating Market   ตลาดน้ำหลัก5 (คลองโพธิ์หัก)

This market convenes every day between 6.00 am and midday except on Buddhist Sabbath days when the moon is full or new. The market is in Ban Phaew District, 30 km to the northwest of Samut Sakhon and can be reached by either bus or songtheaw along Route 35 (heading west) or Route 3079 (heading north). From here catch a longtail for 8 km up Pho Hak Canal, if you get a ride with some of the locals, chances are you will get a better price.

Wat Yai Chom Prasat   วัดใหญ่จอมปราสาท

The main attraction is the delicately carved floral designs on the wooden doors on the ubosoth. The monastery itself is fairly old, built in the Ayutthaya Period. The wat has a large standing Buddha out the front which is visible from the road. To get there, catch a songtheaw or bus heading along Route 35 towards Samut Songkhram for 10 minutes.

Salt Fields

One of Samut Sakhon's main industries is salt production. If you want to look at monotonous white piles of salt, visit one of the many sites along the Thonburi to Pak Tho Highway.

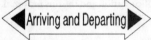

Arriving and Departing

Getting Around

Around town, motorbike taxis cost 15B and songtheaws 3B, cyclos are also available.

Train

Samut Sakhon is connected to **Bangkok's** Thonburi train station and is serviced four times a day taking around an hour for the trip. On the south side of town is Ban Laem train station from where trains to Samut Songkhram depart twice a day, at 10.00 am and 5.00 pm.

Bus

Buses leave from **Bangkok's** southern bus terminal. The A/C buses cost 30B and take 1 hour whilst the local buses cost 25B and take 2 hours, taking you on a tour of all the polluted and busy towns along the way. Coming back you can jump on a bus headed for Bangkok for 10B which lets you off at the west side of the memorial bridge. As the buses leave throughout the day, they are a better option than the train. A bus to Samut Songkhram will cost you 12B.

SAMUT SONGKHRAM PROVINCE

This province is quite low lying and is continually criss crossed with canals. This environment combined with frequent rain have made it a large fruit growing province with grapes, lychee and guava heading the list. Located to the southwest of Bangkok, Samut Songkhram is

Around Bangkok

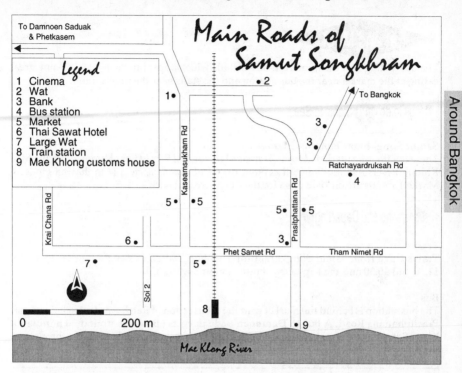

bordered to the south by Phetchaburi, Ratchaburi to the west and north and Samut Sakhon to the east with the Gulf of Thailand to the south.

SAMUT SONGKHRAM   สมุทรสงคราม

The capital of the province, Samut Songkhram sits astride the Mae Khlong River only a few kilometres from where it empties into the Gulf of Thailand. There is little to see in Samut Songkhram except for the sizeable Wat to the west of the train station. At night, the riverside and Phet Samet Road are transformed into lively night markets.

Vital Information

Banks The most central bank is on the corner of Phet Samet and Prasitphattana Roads, other branches are out on the road to Bangkok.
Codes Samut Songkhram's telephone code is (034) and the postal code is 75000.

Cheap Sleeps

The accommodation here is really difficult to find, you would be best to ask a tuk tuk driver to point you in the right way, if you have trouble finding a room.
Thai Sawat Hotel ☎ (034) 711 205, at 524 Phet Samet Road has noisy rooms for 150B. It is a bit of a challenge to find as there is no English sign but look for the cafe like rooms downstairs..
Two other choices are the **Alongklon 1 & 2 Hotels** on Kasem Sukham Road near the cinema.

Around Bangkok

Eat and Meet

The best eating is at the numerous street stalls which appear in the evening. Some great eating at the market near the bus station and the stalls near the train station.

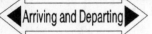

Samut Songkhram Floating Market

There is a floating market around 7 km or 8 km north of Samut Songkhram along the Mae Khlong River. Ask any longtail captain for *talaat nam amphawaa* (Amphawaa Floating Market) and figure on 100B or so for the ride there and back.

Arriving and Departing

Train

Trains leave from Samut Songkhram for Thonburi station in **Bangkok** at 06.20, 09.00, 11.30 and 15.30 and the trip takes about an hour costing 16B.

Bus

The bus station is behind the market near the intersection of Ratchayardruksah Road and Prasitphattana Road. A bus to **Damnoen Saduak** costs 6B taking around 30 minutes, a bus to **Samut Sakhon** costs 12B and a bus to **Bangkok** costs 25B. All buses leave throughout the day.

King Mongut or Rama IV (1804 - 1868)

King Mongut was the younger brother of Rama III, coming to power at the ripe old age of 46 and is fondly remembered by Thais as an innovative and humane ruler. King Mongut entered the monkhood at the age of 20 and remained there until his accession to the throne in 1851. He concentrated on accelerating contact with the west with a view to developing mutually beneficial relations and hopefully avoiding the colonialist experiences of their neighbours, Cambodia and Laos. He also had an inquisitive drive for scientific knowledge with which he paved the way for Siam to develop from a traditional country to one that was prepared to face the modern era. Notable developments of his include the issuing of paper currency and he was also the first monarch to be able to speak, write and read fluently in English.

His intellectual and scientific pursuits were to see the death of him when in 1868 he led an expedition to observe a solar eclipse. Unfortunately the area he chose for the viewing was swarmed by malarial mosquitos, and after one too many bites, died later in the year. His death left the country without an absolute ruler for five years until King Chulongkorn came of age. In this interim period, Siam was ruled by Chuang Bunnak (Chaophraya Sisuriyawong).

CENTRAL
THAILAND

Central Thailand is an extremely varied region spread across Thailand from the Burmese border to the Cambodian border, however the majority of it lies within the sweeping plains to the north of Bangkok. Much of the region rarely features on visitors' itineraries, but there are nevertheless pockets of interest and some highly worthwhile historical areas.

Kanchanaburi Province, located at the western reaches of Central Thailand and bordered with Burma, offers some particularly amazing scenery and varied National Parks. It also holds the ghosts of many military and civilian personnel who died during the construction of the Burmese Railway or 'Death Railway', as it was commonly called during WWII. At the eastern end of Central Thailand the landscape is also quite scenic at times with the central plains rising to the mountains, offering glimpses of natural phenomena such as waterfalls and wildlife living within the sporadically placed National Parks. In the central area the main point of interest is Lopburi which has a number of historical attractions, including evidence of some of the first Western presence in what was then the Kingdom of Siam.

For the purposes of this guidebook, Central Thailand covers from west to east the following twelve provinces; Kanchanaburi, Suphanaburi, Ang Thong, Singburi, Chainat, Uthai Thani, Nakhon Sawan, Lopburi, Saraburi, Nakhon Nayok, Prachinburi and Sa Kaew.

Highlights

Visit **Sangkhlaburi**, take a stroll over the **longest wooden bridge** in Thailand to the spectacular **Wat Mon** (Kanchanaburi Province).
Spend some time taking in the atmosphere along the **River Khwae** (Kanchanaburi Province).
Wander the ruins of **Lopburi** and visit the monkey fiefdom of the **Kala Shrine** and do a day trip out to **Wat Phra Phutthabat** (Lopburi Province).
Visit little visited **Uthai Thani** with a day trip out to **Lan Sak** (Uthai Thani Province).
Hike up all the steps of Thailand's favourite waterfall, **Namtok Erawan** (Kanchanaburi Province).

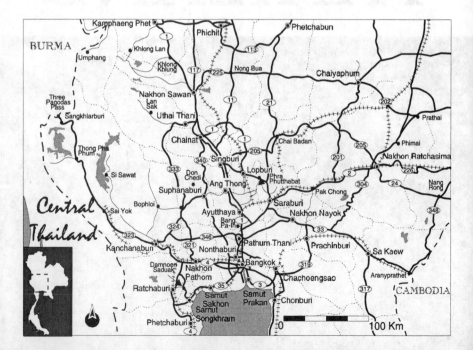

KANCHANABURI PROVINCE

The Thai government, TAT and the private sector are strong supporters of '1997 A Journey Year to Kanchanaburi' which is dedicated to strengthening and increasing tourism to the region. As a direct result of this many places which are presently difficult to reach, such as Thung Yai Naresuan National Park and Khao Laem National Park, should become more accessible - for better or for worse.

     The province is one of the most visually stunning in all of Thailand. The two major land routes, Route 323 and Route 3199, follow the banks of the Khwae Noi and Khwae Yai Rivers and allow access to most of the sights of Kanchanaburi. Khao Laem and Si Nakharin Dams have created two huge reservoirs in the northeast of the province with the latter, in particular, being very little visited by roaming farangs.

     The natural features of the province are plentiful with a good selection of National Parks, waterfalls and caves dotted throughout the densely forested karyst mountains. The northwest of the province is a juxtaposition of people with Burmese, Karen, Mon and Galeon minorities offering glimpses of different societies and cultures. Kanchanaburi Province also offers the opportunity of day trips into Burma for those who are interested, however the border crossing has been closed for some time now but may open on a random basis.

     Although a fairly popular destination amongst roaming farangs, Kanchanaburi's real success has been with the domestic tourists. In almost any household in Thailand, chances are you will find a poster of one of the many beautiful waterfalls in this province, and during the weekend, bus load upon bus load of tripping Thais descend into Kanchanaburi for a weekend of karaoke, eating, drinking and, of course, a visit to Erawan National Park.

     The province is bordered by Tak, Uthai Thani, Suphanaburi, Nakhon Pathon and Ratchaburi.

KANCHANABURI กาญจนบุรี

Famous as the location of the film 'Bridge over the River Kwai', Kanchanaburi is the provincial capital and is situated 128 km from Bangkok. A favourite for those who need to escape Bangkok or are just killing time waiting for a visa or flight, Kanchanaburi is also the kind of place which is ideal for commencing a trip in Thailand or as your final destination before heading off to another country. Sitting upon the Khwae Yai and Mai Klong Rivers, the town offers splendid riverside scenery, great sunsets, very good food and a few excellent guesthouses. All are capable of contributing to stretching a one night stay to a one week stay or, in some cases, a lifetime. Kanchanaburi has a reputation as a place to which many people return.

     On the other hand, Kanchanaburi is also well known for its 'Disco Ducks' which cruise up and down the river, blaring out Thai music at incredible levels till the very early hours. These, combined with ear piercing longtails, are the only real blights on an otherwise beautiful town whose road signs are shaped like fish just as the river is full of them.

Vital Information

Tourist Information The TAT Office is on Saeng Chuto Road, ☎ (034) 511 200, about a one minute walk from the bus station. Helpful staff are a good source of information about the province and have loads of brochures including helpful guides to accommodation and transportation.

Post Office is to the south of town, on Saeng Chuto Road about 1 km from the TAT. The telecom office is upstairs. A more central post office branch office is at the corner of Lak Muang and Pak Phraek Roads, just next to the city gateway. However, it has no international phone services, but is open normal working hours.

Central

Banks All the major banks have a branch or two in town with the most central being the Thai Farmers Bank and Thai Military Bank opposite each other by the bus station.

Hospital is on Saeng Chuto Road, south of the tourist office.

Police Station is located opposite and just north of the TAT on Saeng Chuto Road.

Immigration Office is open 8.30 am to 12.00 am and 1.00 pm to 4.30 pm, tourist visas can be extended here for 14 days for an exorbitant 500B. You need to bring your passport and two photos. The office is a fair way out of town, to get there follow the main road south out of town and go past the two hospitals and post office, and then take a right onto Maenam Maeklong Road. The intersection has traffic lights and City Hall is to the left. The immigration office is near the river on the left side.

Codes Kanchanaburi's telephone code is (034) and postal code is 71000.

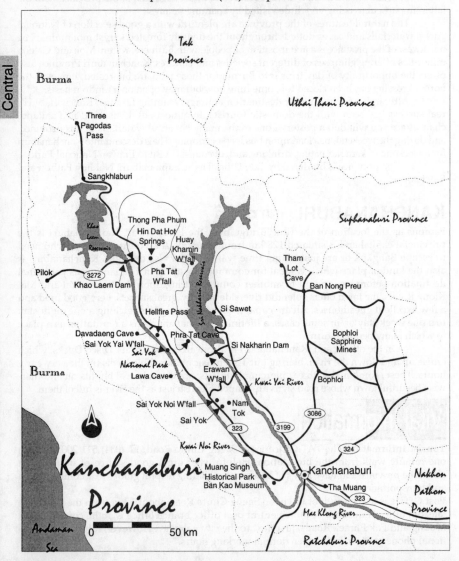

Cheap Sleeps

The riverside to the north of the centre of town is lined with both floating and land bound guesthouses. Although there are some hotels in town, your best bet is to head to the river first. If arriving by samlor or tuk tuk, **all** guesthouses pay commissions of around 20B, so do not pay more than 10B to 15B for a ride from the bus station.

River Guesthouse, ☎ (034) 512 491, is definitely the pick of the bunch for people on a budget. Expect a very friendly, family atmosphere, divine food (and reasonably priced) and a pleasant setting. Rooms for all budgets with great sunset views are available, but on the cheaper end of the scale, basic but functional singles/doubles with share bathroom are 40B/80B. Rooms with a private bathroom are 100B to150B. The only blow is the anti-cultural experience — the nightly video sessions. This guesthouse is highly recommended.

Bamboo House, ☎ (034) 512 532, is set on the river. It has a nice garden setting and well spaced bungalows. Rooms start at 100B/150B for single/double with shared bath to 300B with private bath. They also have a snooker table.

Mr Tees is at the end of Laos Road and has friendly staff with a riverside eatery. Rooms start at 150B with share shower, and 200B with private shower.

VN Guesthouse is just by River Guesthouse. It was looking a bit run down at our last pass, but the staff are still very helpful. Rooms are basic but clean, and watch out for people eating ants near the toilets. Rates are 40B/70B for singles/doubles with share bathroom, 100B to 150B for private bathroom. Larger concrete rooms are also available but cost more.

Jolly Frog Backpackers, ☎ (034) 514 579, More like a large motel than a guesthouse, this huge cash cow seems invariably full with all manner of good and bad travellers. The staff can be indifferent, but given what they have to put up with, it is understandable. The rooms are very clean and the food (both Western and Thai) is very good and reasonably priced. Their bikes however are not worth looking at. Room rates are 50B/80B with shared bath, 90B/120B with private bath (120B for the river side). Nice and very pretty garden.

Sam's Place, ☎ (034) 513 971, is closer to town than any of the above mentioned places and has a range of rooms with singles/doubles with share bathroom going for 80B/100B and 150B/200B with private bath. The main problem here is that a new bridge is under construction just by it and Sam's also receives a lot of noise from the floating discos.

Nita Raft House, ☎ (034) 514 521, was looking a bit run down but have nice enough staff. Singles/doubles here cost 40B/70B with share bathroom, and with a fan 100B, and with private bathroom 150B. It is also in noise range of the floating discos.

C&C River Guesthouse, ☎ (034) 624 547, at 265/2 Mae Nam Kwai Road, Soi England. This bungalow establishment at 265/2 Mae Nam Kwai Road is budget in price but not in location or facilities. This is a great place to stay with a large open garden separating clean bungalows costing only 100B to 150B with bathroom (80B in low season). At the time of writing a dorm was being built which will cost only 30B. Tents cost 30B to 50B.

VL Guesthouse, ☎ (034) 513 546, at 18/11 Saeng Chuto Road opposite the River Kwai Hotel. Large glistening rooms with starched sheets cost 150B for singles and doubles with fan and bathroom.

Sam's House Not to be confused with Sam's place. Rooms cost 80B without bathroom and larger rooms set back from the river cost 100B. Rooms with fan and private bathroom cost 150B. The staff are friendly and the eating area is elevated.

Bung Rung has small, old, ugly concrete rooms which are really only for the desperate. A room with bath and fan is 150B and A/C starts at 250B.

Thai Seri Hotel, ☎ (034) 511 128, at 142 Saeng Chuto Road. This hotel is pretty dingy and is only really being mentioned due to its proximity to the bus station, thus making it handy for very early departures or very late arrivals. Plain but adequate rooms start at 120B.

Central

Central

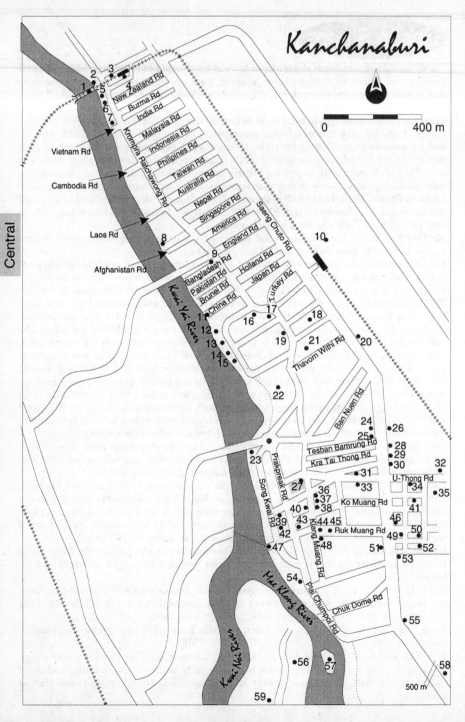

Kanchanaburi

0   400 m

New Zealand Rd
Burma Rd
India Rd
Krompra Ratchawong Rd
Malaysia Rd
Indonesia Rd
Philipines Rd
Taiwan Rd
Australia Rd
Nepal Rd
Singapore Rd
America Rd
England Rd
Bangladesh Rd
Pakistan Rd
Brunei Rd
China Rd
Holland Rd
Japan Rd
Turkey Rd
Saeng Chuto Rd

Vietnam Rd
Cambodia Rd
Laos Rd
Afghanistan Rd

Kwai Yai River

Thavorn With Rd

Ban Nuen Rd

Tesban Bamrung Rd
Kra Tai Thong Rd

U-Thong Rd

Prakpreak Rd
Song Kwai Rd
Klang Muang Rd

Ko Muang Rd
Ruk Muang Rd

Plai Chumpol Rd
Chuk Dome Rd

Mae Klong River

Kwai Noi River

500 m

Legend

1	Bridge over the River Kwai	21	Chinese Cemetery
2	Floating restaurants	22	Thai, Chinese
3	Tourist police		& Vietnamese temples
4	River Kwai train station	23	Sam's Place
5	WWII Museum	24	VL Guesthouse
6	Japanese War Memorial	25	Bookstore
7	Bamboo House	26	River Kwai Hotel
8	C&C River Kwai House	27	Day market
9	Sam's House	28	Siam Commercial Bank
10	Kanchanaburi train station	29	Bkk Bank of Commerce
11	Jolly Frog Guesthouse	30	Thai Farmers Bank
12	PS Gusethouse	31	Siam City Bank
13	Ricks Place	32	Bank of Ayudhya
14	VN Guesthouse	33	First Bangkok City Bank
15	River Guesthouse	34	Bangkok Bank
16	AS Mixed Travel	35	Department store
17	Bung Rung Bungalows	36	Bike rental
18	War Cemetery	37	Boonpong & Bros.
19	Catholic church	38	Chinese Temple
20	Luxury Hotel	39	Tourist police
		40	Aree Bakery

41	Market
42	Restaurants
43	Post office
44	City gate
45	Lak Muang Shrine
46	Thai Military Bank
47	Car ferry
48	Municipal office
49	Thai Farmers Bank
50	Minibus to Sangkhlarburi
51	Police station
52	Bus station
53	TAT Office
54	JEATH War Museum
55	Hospital
56	Chung Kai War Cemetery
57	Kasem Island Temple
58	GPO
59	Wat Tham Mongkhon Thong

Prasopsok Hotel, ☎ (034) 511 777, at 677 Saeng Chuto Road has bungalow style accommodation and large rooms with fan and bath start at 110B with A/C starting at 180B. **Luxury Hotel,** ☎ (034) 511 168, at 284/1-5 Saeng Chuto Road has dirty and drab hotel style rooms which certainly do not live up to the name! Singles/doubes start at 150B/180B and 250B/400B with A/C.

NOTE: The problem with staying on the river in Kanchanaburi is the prevalence of 'floating discos' more commonly referred to as 'Disco Ducks'. These barges (often a few are connected together) are dragged up and down the river until the very late hours pumping out some pretty abysmal tunes. Prevalent mainly on weekends, the music is not going to keep you up all night, but at times will drown out conversation. Very light sleepers may want to invest in some torpedoes. Another consideration with staying on the river is the possibility of flooding during monsoon. In heavy and consistent rainfalls river level bungalows and restaurants have been known to end up under water.

◆ Eat and Meet

Kanchanaburi has a number of good eating options. The best advice is to take a wander and see where the Thais eat which is always a good sign.

Night Market along Saeng Chuto Road, south of U-Thong Road. As always, the market is a good budget choice. Look out for the *phat thai* stall, about three vendors down from U-Thong Road - this is probably the cheapest meal you will find at 10B for a filling large plate. Opposite the bus station is a stall that serves delicious fruit and flavoured shakes.

River Guesthouse, although we are normally shy to mention guesthouses in the food section, the Thai food here is excellent and reasonably priced.

I-san Restaurant is popular with locals and fairly centrally located along Saeng Chuto Road. A comprehensive English menu, but the Kai Yaeng (BBQ chicken) can be a bit worn out. Expect to pay 100B to 150B for two.

River Kwai Hotel Restaurant is in front of the hotel and features live Thai bands. The tunes are not too bad, and the beef salad is mouth watering. They also serve ice cold beer.

Song Khwae Road The section of this road by the municipal garden has numerous food vendors who serve good food at decent prices. The gardens along the water are great for a picnic and many Thais take the opportunity to do just that. It is possible to hire mats to sit on. Opposite are a number of karaoke bars for those wanting to exercise their vocal chords.

Morning Market is in the centre of town. Get an early start to the day (around 6.00 am) to the view the market at its busiest and to grab some delectable cheap food such as a choice of curries for 10B (rice is another 5B).

Things to do and Sights to See

Kanchanaburi is mainly known for its place in history involving the construction of the infamous bridge over the River Khwae (it actually passes over the River Khwae Yai). Other than the museums and of course the bridge there are a few other things worth checking out.

Central

Death Railway Bridge   สะพานข้ามแม่น้ำแคว

The infamous bridge is not really particularly spectacular to look at but it is the history of the bridge which has made it so famous. Most people know it as 'The Bridge Over the River Kwai' from the popular book by Pierre Boulle and subsequent American movie. The original iron bridge was brought from Java by the Japanese armed forces and was reassembled by forced POW labour a few kilometres to the north of Kanchanaburi town over the Khwae Yai River. It consisted of eleven steel spans, with the remaining spans made of wood. Three of the spans were destroyed by Allied bombing and after the war were replaced with two angular steel spans. All the wooden spans were also replace by steel following the end of the war.

The bridge formed a part of the infamous 'Death Railway' which was planned to link Burma and Thailand by rail to form a vital supply link for the Japanese. The bridge was bombed by the allied forces on numerous occasions and was rebuilt following the end of the war in 1945. Today it is the curved spans of the bridge which are original and the bridge is still in use today for trains heading towards the northwest. The bridge is a pleasant place to wander to for sunset.

The length of the Death Railway to the Burma Base Camp is 415 km with 294 km in Thailand. Sixty thousand men were forced to build it in atrocious conditions between October 1942 and October 1943. The labourers included POWs, Indians, Burmese, Malaysians, Indonesians, Chinese and Thais. At the end of the war, 4 km of track on the Thai Burma border was dismantled. The State Railway of Thailand was handed the Thai section and ordered to dismantle it as far back as Nam Tok by the Thai government, which they did, but now regret it. Construction has already begun to rebuild the railway line.

There is a sound and light display held at the bridge every year in late November early December where the dazzling show replicates the bridge blowing up to the extent of a section of the bridge falling off!

JEATH War Museum

Set in a bamboo replica of the bamboo longhouses which housed allied POWs during WWII, the JEATH Museum (standing for Japan, England, Australia, America, Thailand & Holland) contains a moving photographic and artistic collection displaying the atrocious conditions under which the POWs existed. There is also a small collection of guns and bullets as well as other bits and pieces. Admission is 20B. By the river are longtails which can take you on tours of surrounding sights along the river at outrageous prices - save your money and hire a push-bike.

WWII Museum   พิพิธภัณฑ์สงคราม

Museum, art gallery, family shrine and much more!! This quite bizarre museum is worth a look and one could easily spend a few hours exploring it and making sense of all the strange historical interpretations. All manner of objects, from guns and swords to Buddha amulets and human remains are on display. Next door a smaller building contains a very disorganised photo display regarding death, destruction and depravity. Out the front of the museum are all the major war leaders with at times quite bizarre written histories besides them. At the time of our visit, the museum was being extended, so the display will surely be packed with more paraphernalia by the time you get there. The view from the roof (five floors up) offers a good view of the River Khwae Bridge. The WWII Museum is located to the north of town near the bridge over the Khwae River. Admission is 30B.

Kanchanaburi War Cemetery   สุสารทหาร

On Saeng Chuto Road, nearly opposite the train station, this very well kept cemetery contains the remains of 6,982 allied POWs who died during the construction of the Death Railway. All up an estimated 16,000 allied POWs and over 49,000 forced labourers died during its construction. The crosses were originally wooden, but have been replaced with stone memorial plaques.

Chung-Kai War Cemetery   สุสานช่องไก่

Around 2 km to the south of town on the far bank of the Khwae Noi River, this cemetery occupies the site of Chung-Kai POW camp. Around 1,750 POWs are buried here, most of whom died in the hospital. The cemetery is at the original site of the base camp hospital and a church which was built by the POWs.

About 12,000 people are buried around Kanchanaburi in various cemeteries and many more are remembered by memorials. A total of 61,000 Allied prisoners were transferred to Kanchanaburi from various camps in the region. All of these prisoners have been accounted for, but many visitors do not realise that tens of thousands of Malays, Chinese, Tamil and Burmese also died. The exact number of their dead is not known.

Japanese War Memorial

This small memorial is on the Khwae Yai River near to the WWII museum. A service is held here yearly in remembrance to those who died. Thailand's Japanese community holds a memorial service here each March.

Wat Tham Mongkon Thong   วัดถ้ำมังกรทอง

The 'Cave Temple of the Floating Dragon' has no floating dragon, but does have a floating nun. The current floating nun is about number five in a long list of past floating nuns. Past floating nuns still live here and can be seen walking (not floating) around the compound. Although very much a 'performance' it is worth seeing as the nun appears to float on top of the water whilst performing meditation and yoga positions. Sceptics have been known to jump in the water, but they have all sunk. After the show, the nun will bless and massage anyone with an illness or injury. If you are looking to partake in a truly strange experience try to filter into the amphitheatre-like 'viewing area' when a tour bus full of Thais shows up. The bell is rung when a show is about to start. It is surprising that there is not a video link up to the WWII museum from here. Entry is by donation.

There is a small museum near the nun's show that displays various artifacts found in the region. You can also visit the temple in a cave up the long stairwell and catch a view of the surrounds.

Wat Thum Khao Poon วัดถ้ำเขาปูน

This wat has a cave or more precisely eight caves which you can wander through as long as the monks are not using them for meditation. The caves have both stalactites and stalagmites but many have been broken so that tourists will not bang their head on them. Some of the formations resemble a crocodile, an elephant and a tooth. One section of the cave is only reached through a tunnel which you need to crawl through, so do not wear your tuxedo. At dusk thousands of bats fly out of the cave. Upon exiting the cave take the path which leads off to the left after the Chinese temple. The dirt road leads to a large outdoor sitting Buddha that cheerfully observes the pleasant view of the river and mountains. If you take the small path past the souvenir sellers you will come out at the death railway train track near a section where the POWs had to blast through a rock hill.

Train Trip
The TAT runs a special train from Kanchanaburi daily at 10.54 am for Nam Tok. For 100B you can jump on the special carriage and get coffee and drinks and a certificate from the TAT. Alternatively you can do the same trip without the TAT holding your hand for 17B.

Tours
Tours ranging from one day to four days and more can be arranged through tour operators in Kanchanaburi, two of the more popular agents are Jumbo Travel and AS Mixed Travel. Trips depart for a variety of sights throughout the province and often include rafting, elephant rides and walks. Cost ranges from 900B for a no frills tour to 3,000B and upwards for a top line luxury tour.

Arriving and Departing

Getting Around
Songtheaws around town cost 3B. Most travelling along Saeng Chuto Road stop at the bus terminal, so if you want to go to the post office, you need to catch another from the bus station. Motorbike taxis and tuk tuks cost 10B for short distances.

Train
From Kanchanaburi to **Nam Tok** (the end of the railway) it costs 17B. Work is currently under way to extend the railway tracks. A train to the **River Khwae Bridge** it costs 2B. For detailed price and timetable information refer to the end of the chapter.

Kanchanaburi Buses			
Destination	Bus Number	Depart Kanchanaburi	Fare
Bangkok 1st Class	81	04.00 to 19.00 every 15 minutes	65B
Bangkok 2nd Class	81	03.50 to 18.50 every 15 minutes	48B
Bangkok Ordinary	81	03.30 to 18.30 every 15 minutes	34B
Nakhon Pathom	81	03.30 to 18.30 every 15 minutes	20B
Ratchaburi	461	05.10 to 18.20 every 15 minutes	26B
Suphanaburi	411	05.00 to 18.00 every 20 minutes	25B
Bo Phloi	325	06.00 to 18.30 every 20 minutes	14B
Erawan Waterfall	8170	08.00 to 16.30 every 50 minutes	21B
Sai Yok Noi Waterfall	8203	06.45 to 18.30 every 30 minutes	18B
Sai Yok Yai Waterfall	8203	06.45 to 18.30 every 30 minutes	30B
Sangkhlaburi (VIP)	8203	09.30 to 14.30	120B
Sangkhlaburi (A/C van)	8203	07.30, 10.30, 11.30, 12.30, 13.30, 16.30	100B
Sangkhlaburi (ordinary)	8203	06.00, 08.40, 10.20, 12.00	70B

Central

Bus
Kanchanaburi bus station is located in the centre of town and is clearly laid out. The information booth also occasionally has English speaking staff there. An ordinary bus to **Nakhon Pathom** costs 20B, takes 1½ hours and leaves every 30 minutes.

AROUND KANCHANABURI

Kanchanaburi Province provides some of the most beautiful views, landscapes and natural phenomena in all of Thailand. Most of the popular destinations can easily be visited by local bus and day tours, but to explore some of the more out of the way places at your own pace, hiring a motorbike for a few days is definitely recommended. Due to the hot climate and the size of the province, trying to see all of the Kanchanaburi area by local transport is both uncomfortably hot and time consuming.

The following sights are structured around the three main roads leading out of Kanchanaburi. Route 323 follows the Khwae Noi River and extends as far as Sangkhlaburi and Three Pagodas Pass, with sights north of Tham Davadaeng covered in the Around Sangkhlaburi section. Route 3199 follows the Khwae Yai River to Erawan National Park, Si Sawat and beyond, whilst the less visited Route 3086 leads almost directly north, through Bophloi towards the provincial border with Suphanaburi. This area can be covered in a rushed 4 days, but more time is recommended to fully appreciate its beauty.

ROUTE 323

Ban Kao Museum   พิพิธภัณฑ์บ้านเก้า
Located 35 km from Kanchanaburi, the Ban Kao Museum displays evidence of prehistoric life in the region from about 4,000 years ago. During WWII a Dutch POW and archeologist, Mr H.R. Van Heekenen, discovered some prehistoric tools. After the war he organised a joint excavation between Thailand and the Netherlands at two sites, Bang and Lue. In total 50 human skeletons from the Neolithic Period were unearthed as well as various relics and tools. The museum contains some skeletal remains and artifacts from the burial sites as well as other evidence of prehistoric life from nearby caves. Next door to the museum is a small colourful wat with murals depicting the temptations of Buddha — definitely worth a look.

To reach the museum, follow Route 323 until you come to a turn-off on the left, take the turn-off and follow the English signs to the museum. By public transport, catch a local bus headed for Thong Pha Phum or Sangkhlaburi, getting off at the turn-off. From here you will need to walk or try to hitch a ride for the last few kilometres to the museum. You can also reach the museum by catching the train to **Tha Kilen** which is around 1 km from Prasat Muang Singh and about 9 km from the museum. The museum is open from 9.00 am to 4.30 pm Wednesday to Sunday.

Dangers of Kanchanaburi Province

Exploring Kanchanaburi Province by motorbike makes for a great journey. However, there are certain dangers that you need to be aware of. The province itself is relatively large so expect many long hot hours on the bike - which make the waterfalls and rivers a welcoming sight. The majority of the roads are fairly wide and carry heavy trucks, so ensure you stick to the shoulders of the road because the trucks have clearly got the right of way. One of the most stunning sections of road is in between Thong Pha Phum and Sangkhlaburi. Although the most beautiful, it is also the most dangerous section of road, reserved for only more experienced riders - it is very windy and very steep in parts where at times 10 km/hour seems a dangerously fast speed. Lastly, many of the roads that lead off Route 323 (closer to Sangkhlaburi) are restricted entry. If you explore too far you may find yourself out of police jurisdiction and if you were to have an accident in these places you may not get help for a very long time or you may be left in the hands of the local farmers.

Central

Prasat Muang Singh Historical Park อุทยานประวัติศาสตร์ปราสาทเมืองสิงห์

Situated off Route 323 about 43 km from Kanchanaburi and around 8 km from the Ban Kao Museum, this ancient town sits upon the banks of the Khwae Noi River and is over 800 years old. The site contains two excavated groups of ruins and another two which are not visible. Believed to have been built by the Khmers as an ancient trading town, it was known as Muang Singh or 'City of Lions' and formed the western most outpost of the Khmer Empire. A large variety of skeleton and other archeological remains have been unearthed at this site.

The main structure amid the ruins is that of Prasat Muang Singh (Tower of the City of Lions) and is contained within the better of the two excavated ruins. Like most Khmer monuments Prasat Muang Singh faces the east and thus to Angkor. Like most of the structures in the historical park, Prasat Muang Singh is made of laterite as are the ramparts and remaining walls. The town was originally made up of a number of sites but so far only the two have been excavated. The park is set in lush, green and peaceful grounds (when there is not a bus load of tourists ogling the ruins) and it is an enjoyable place to take in the atmosphere.

The park is well signposted from Ban Kao Museum and Route 323. If travelling by public transport, train is the better option with an hour trip from Kanchanaburi leaving at 6.10 am, 10.54 am and 2.25 pm and costing 10B. Once at the station, head towards the river, then follow the signs for around 1 km. To get to Ban Kao Museum or Route 323 you will need to hitch or walk about 8 km as the museum and Route 323 are in opposite directions from Prasat Muang Singh. If you plan on reaching the park by bus, be warned that bus number 8203 takes you the closest, but you will still be left around 7 km from the park. Admission to the historical park is 20B (5B for Thais) and it is open daily from 8.00 am to 4.00 pm.

Tham Kra Sae ถ้ำกระแส

This cave is one of many found in Kanchanaburi Province. It is advisable to get there by your own transport. From Prasat Muang Singh, turn left from the park, then straight ahead for 11 km and then follow the signs. You will need to take a torch.

Sai Yok

Sai Yok is located on Route 323, 60 km from Kanchanaburi. The highlight of this town is the waterfall, Namtok Sai Yok Noi, a popular destination for Thai day trippers. The impressive waterfall cascades over well worn rocks, however its presence is diminished by all the Thais clambering over it, trying to cool down from the often stifling heat.

To the right of the waterfall is a locomotive used on the Death Railway during WWII, and the beginning of a path which leads to a cave temple. Once well into the cave and past the shrines, look over your left shoulder to the far wall. The light reflection on the rocks creates the image of a human face. It is also possible to climb up the rocks outside the cave to the right for a view of the valley. A second deeper cave exists another 1½ km along the track. The path passes the source of the waterfall below.

Cheap Sleeps

Sai Yok Noi Bungalow, ☎ (034) 591 075, on Route 323 has dirty concrete bungalows with bath for 120B.
Cola Hotel Also on Route 323, has rooms with bath for 200B.
Kitti Raft, ☎ (034) 591 106, is just to the left of the Paksieng Pier on the river. Small rooms on the river are 400B without bathroom and 500B with bathroom.
River Huts About 100 m to the right of the pier cost 200B per room and each one has two large mats on the floor which can sleep up to four people.

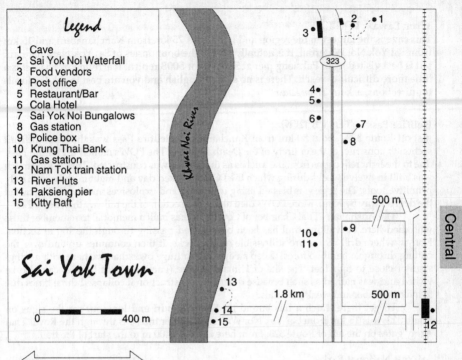

Sai Yok Town

Legend

1   Cave
2   Sai Yok Noi Waterfall
3   Food vendors
4   Post office
5   Restaurant/Bar
6   Cola Hotel
7   Sai Yok Noi Bungalows
8   Gas station
9   Police box
10 Krung Thai Bank
11 Gas station
12 Nam Tok train station
13 River Huts
14 Paksieng pier
15 Kitty Raft

◀ Arriving and Departing ▶

Sai Yok Noi Waterfall lies directly on Route 323, so any bus heading to Thong Pha Phum or Sangkhlaburi can let you off. From Prasat Muang Singh, turn left, then take the first right and follow for 8 km to reach Route 323, then turn left onto Route 323 and follow it for 37 km. A bus fro **Kanchanaburi** costs 18B.

You can reach Sai Yok by taking the train from **Kanchanaburi** to the final stop at Nam Tok (there are plans to extend the railway.) Trains leave from Kanchanaburi at 6.10 am, 10.54 am and 4.25 pm and take just over two hours, costing 17B. From the station, Route 323 is 1 km east and the waterfall is about 800 m north.

A less common but still possible method of reaching the waterfall is by boat from Kanchanaburi. This option is fairly expensive, and you are best to enquire at the ferry pier in Kanchanaburi about price. From Paksieng pier (2 km from the main road) it is possible to hire a longtail (for up to twelve people) to Lawa Cave for 500B return for the boat. The trips takes 40 minutes to get there and 30 minutes to return. Expensive accommodation up the river is available at Jungle Rafts, where rafts cost 600B for a return trip and if you want to also visit Sai Yok Yai Waterfall it is 1,200B one way or 1,500B return.

Reality or Hollywood?

Kanchanaburi is well known for the Death Railway and the infamous "Bridge on the River Kwai" which was made more famous by an American Film which stared William Holden and Alec Guinness. Although it is supposed to be set in Kanchanaburi Province, the film was actually shot in Sri Lanka.

Central

Tham Lawa   ถ้ำละว้า

This cave is the largest in the region and is situated 75 km from Kanchanaburi and 15 km from Sai Yok Noi Waterfall. It is actually within the boundaries of Sai Yok National Park but is best visited from Paksieng pier at Sai Yok for 500B return. If arriving by road, it is a little more difficult to reach. There is no sign in English and you are best to ask the locals for directions; ask for *Tham Lawa*.

Hellfire Pass   ช่อง เขาขาด

Just off Route 323, about 80 km from Kanchanaburi, Hellfire Pass was the most difficult section to construct of the entirety of the Death Railway. The POWs named it 'Hellfire Pass' due to the light reflections from the torches as the cutting was constructed. This 25 km stretch was built in twelve weeks during which the POWs worked day and night in shifts with only primitive tools. The rock was blasted using drill holes and explosives and the POWs carted the debris away by hand. More POWs died along this section of the railway than any other.

The Australian - Thai Chamber of Commerce has built a memorial to remember those who died here. A walking trail has been constructed passing through the 100 m section, Konyu, where drill marks are still visible on the rocks. It then continues up and over the cutting through a bamboo forest. Keep an eye out for huge owls that live here with a wing-span of close to four feet. The site of Hintack Bridge (Pack of Cards Bridge) can also be visited and was named as such because during its construction it collapsed three times due to inferior timber and weak materials.

To get there, catch a bus bound for Sangkhlaburi and look out for the signs on Route 323. It is 18 km from Sai Yok Noi Waterfall. The entrance is through the Royal Thai Army gates on the left of Route 323. From here it is only 400 m to the start of the trail.

Sai Yok National Park

Sai Yok National Park is a stunning 500 sq km reserve around 100 km from Kanchanaburi on Route 323. The turn-off from Route 323 will take you past a tollgate where foreigners must pay 25B. The road then meanders through an archway of forest trees for 2 km, passing the park guesthouses and finishing at the park headquarters where you will find the **Visitors Centre** which provides information on the park. Despite its size, most visitors only venture into a small section within range of the Park Headquarters. This allows them easy access to a couple of waterfalls, caves and springs. The park also encompasses the impressive caves, **Tham Lawa** to the south and the more popular **Tham Davadaeng**. Remains of prehistoric life dating back 4,000 years has been found within the park as well as the more recent Japanese presence during WWII.

The main attraction of the park is **Namtok Sai Yok Yai**, not to be confused with Namtok Sai Yok Noi further south. It is fairly small and unimpressive from the river view

Sign by the entrance to Sai Yok National Park

but has heaps of pools to swim in to cool down. This waterfall is the only one in Thailand that flows directly out of the mountains above into the Khwae Noi River. The name Sai Yok comes from a song written by Prince Narisaranvwattiwag who wrote the song "Khamane Sai Yok" after viewing the waterfall with King Rama V. A slightly more powerful waterfall, Namtok Sai Yok Yek is downriver a couple of hundred metres. Both waterfalls can be viewed by boat on the river or from the other bank which is accessible by the **suspension bridge** between the two. The height of both waterfalls is seasonal, depending on the level of the river at the time.

The main sights in the park are all signposted and within a couple of kilometres of the Park Headquarters. One path leads to the remains of **Japanese stoves used during WWII**, which comprise little more than a few bricks in the ground. The path behind this to the left leads to the cave **Tham Kaew** which has a tiny entrance, but can be explored if you have a torch. The path to the right leads to the **Natural Springs**. Two powerful streams gush out of the ground leading to the waterfalls.

Another path leads to three different caves. If you follow this path, you will come to a fork, the left fork leading to the better of the three caves, the **Bat Cave.** This is where the Kitti hog nosed bat was discovered in 1973 (the world's smallest mammal weighing in at two grams). It is only found in two other places in Thailand. At dusk, hundreds of bats swarm out of the cave creating a cloud of flying mammals. The cave extends fairly deep and is worth exploring. If you take the right fork in the path, you will first come across the remains of a **railway bridge** which is basically a mossy concrete block. After this the paved path turns into a single dirt trail leading to both caves **Tham Sai Yok** and **Tham Phra.**

Cheap Sleeps

It is worth staying the night at the National Park as bungalows are available for all budgets.
National Park Guesthouse There are eight sets of bungalows with showers on the road between the toll gates and Park Headquarters. These cost 800B and can sleep up to eight people. The National Park also has accommodation by the river for 500B.
Raft Accommodation The enterprising food vendors can supply a range of accommodation on the river. The cheapest is 150B per person which consists of a mat, pillow and blanket on the deck of a river raft, sleeping as many of the Thai workers in the park do. Other options are available here from 600B for a beautiful, clean and comfortable room with Western bathroom. Some of the rafts on the river have generators which are obtrusive to say the least. There are loads of food vendors here who offer cheap and tasty meals.

Tham Davadaeng   ถ้ำดาวดึงส์

Davadaeng Cave is a very impressive, eight chamber cave a few kilometres north of Sai Yok Yai Waterfall and is definitely worth making the effort to see it. The easiest way to visit is by a half hour boat ride from Sai Yok Yai Waterfall, this entails a 2 km walk uphill to the cave from where the boat drops you off.

If arriving by motorbike, it takes a bit of effort and by public transport, it would be extremely difficult. From the National Park entrance, the dirt track which leads to the cave is about 3½ km up Route 323, on the left. If you come across the Police Box, you have gone too far, so go back 1 km (and do not pass go or collect $300). There is a sheltered bus stop at the beginning of the track. A very weather worn road runs for 1 km to the river. At the time of writing, you could ferry yourself and the bike over the river on a small family boat for a few baht, but there is a new bridge under construction. Follow the small trail on the other side of the river for 300 m and turn left onto a more established dirt road. Follow this for 600 m until you reach Mr Samlee's place. Mr Samlee discovered the cave but does not seem to exist any more despite the sign stating that he can take you on a guided tour. Organise for someone else here to come up to the cave and provide you with some lanterns and a cave tour. Without the guide you may have some difficulty finding some of the caverns, plus the lanterns provide better lighting for the huge stalactites and stalagmites in the cave. Take a left turn up the street next to Mr Samlee's place, where you can ride a motorbike up for another kilometre, followed by a 500 m walk to the cave entrance. The mosquitos here invade your body in swarms. The caves are full of bats and your guide will point out various shapes created by the lime deposits including an elephant, pointing finger, Buddha and a lion. A lantern and cave tour will cost you about 100B per lantern. One lantern is sufficient for one to three people.

◀ **Arriving and Departing** ▶

Sai Yok National Park is 20 km along Route 323 from Hellfire Pass. If catching a local bus, get off at the turn-off and walk the 2 km to the park or try to hitch (although the traffic is pretty infrequent). Buses from **Kanchanaburi** cost 30B. It is possible to hire a boat from both Kanchanaburi and Paksieng pier at Sai Yok Noi Waterfall to reach Sai Yok National Park, although the price is excessive.

Namtok Pha Tat   น้ำพุร้อนหินดาด

This impressive three tiered waterfall is 130 km from Kanchanaburi and 30 km from Thong Pha Phum. Here you are almost guaranteed a refreshing swim in both the dry and wet season. The turn-off is on your right coming from Kanchanaburi and is signposted in English.

Hin Dat Hot Springs   น้ำพุร้อนหินดาด

The turn-off for the hot springs is a couple of kilometres further down Route 323. Once again the turn-off is signposted on the east side and the trail into the hot springs is 3 km long. Pools have been constructed here so that visitors can enjoy the natural heat.

THONG PHA PHUM   ท้องผาภูมิ

Located 147 km from Kanchanaburi, this town is emerging as a thriving destination. Thong Pha Phum can be used as a base for the surrounding region with a few of the sights easily accessible including the hot springs and waterfalls to the north and south along Route 323. Thong Pha Phum is actually 2 km off Route 323 on Route 3272 and another 4 km past town is the Khao Laem Dam, which created Khao Laem Lake above it. Thong Pha Phum has a hospital, police station and colourful food and clothing market. Another 60 km along the same road is Pilog Mine which is set on the Burmese border where tin was once extensively mined. Pilog Hill (32 km from Thong Pha Phum) is well known for its orchids and can also be visited. There are quite a few hotels in town including **S Boonyang Bungalow**, **Som Jai Nuk Bungalow**, **Si Thong Pha Phun Bungalow** and **Thanthong Hotel**. All have rooms ranging from 120B to 800B.

Buses travelling to Thong Pha Phum cost 40B, take 1½ hours and leave every 30 minutes from **Kanchanaburi** between 6.45 am and 6.30 pm. Buses and minibuses en-route to **Sangkhlaburi** also stop here for a five minute break.

Namtok Kroeng Krawia

This waterfall is located on the west side of Route 323, 33 km north of Thong Pha Phum. The entrance is clearly marked and you must pass through a boom gate.

Namtok Dai Chong

Dai Chong Waterfall is only a few kilometres further north of Namtok Kroeng Krawia, but is at the end of the trail running off from the east side of Route 323.

Thung Yai Naresuan Wildlife Reserve   เขตรักษาพันธุ์สัตว์ป่าทุ่งใหญ่นเรศวร

Thung Yai Naresuan Wildlife Reserve as well as Khao Laem National Park have their entrance off Route 323 in between Thong Pha Phum and Sangkhlaburi. Located in one of the most pristine and untouched regions of Thailand, these parks are yet to be developed as a tourist destination. The TAT is currently training tour operators and guides about the parks, advising them on areas soon to be opened and used for groups visiting the area. It is expected that limited areas of the parks will be accessible by 1997. Ask your guesthouse in Sangkhlaburi, Thong Pha Phum or Kanchanaburi for the latest information. Thung Yai Naresuan Wildlife Reserve is still pretty much inaccessible at this stage.

Khao Laem National Park   เขื่อนเขาแหลม

This National Park was declared in December 1991 and stretches for almost 150,000 hectares, but over time has borne the brunt of extensive logging and the hunting decimation of its wildlife. The best chance for viewing wildlife is in the area of the park closest to Thung Yai Naresuan Wildlife Reserve, as although the park was once abundant in large animals such as tigers, elephants and other mammals, those remaining have dwindled in numbers and now seek solace in the depths of the park. This, combined with a lack of trails, reduce the possibilities of seeing large mammals in the wild. The birdlife has also been hunted extensively and the best chance for seeing birdlife is in the further realms of the park.

Near the park headquarters a campsite has been established but campers will need to bring most of their own supplies. Around the Park Headquarters there is a small network of trails which at times link up with old logging trails and following these in the early morning will offer the best opportunities for seeing birdlife without having to delve further into the park. The lake created by the Khao Laem Dam is also part of the park and it is possible to arrange accommodation in bungalows beside it, however, there are a number of villages in this area so the chance of observing wildlife is low.

The Park Headquarters is located just under 150 km from Kanchanaburi off Route 323 and the closest jumping off point is Thong Pha Phum to which there are regular buses from Kanchanaburi.

ROUTE 3199

Erawan National Park   อุทยานแห่งชาติเอราวัณ

The first sight worth noting on Route 3199 is Namtok Erawan, 65 km from Kanchanaburi. Best known for this namesake waterfall, this would have to be one of the most popularly visited National Parks in Thailand. Erawan Waterfall is what people come to see despite the fact that the total area of the National Park stretches over 550 sq km and mainly consists of deciduous forest.

The waterfall is seven tiered, falling over 1,500 m and is at its most spectacular between August and October. The first tier is 700 m from the parking area, and the hike to the seventh step is around 1½ km from the park office and takes around 45 minutes to reach. A good set of shoes would be an asset. The seventh tier is the most spectacular and is where the waterfall's name comes from - the rock formation where the water passes over is meant to resemble the Hindu three headed elephant, Erawan. There are a few swimming holes along the way which are great places to cool off. The pool of water next to the giant Takhien tree and spirit house is believed to have medicinal powers. Also, if possible, weekdays are the best time to visit if you want to avoid hordes of Thai visitors and possibly get a chance to see some of the park's wildlife including rhesus monkeys and pig-tailed macaques, but the wildlife and birdlife living in the park extends much further than this.

The park office is by the parking area and dispenses volumes of information on the park in English. There are many food stalls here and bungalow accommodation is available as well as 10B beds in dormitory style rooms.

Central

Central

Buses go from **Kanchanaburi** bus station right to the National Park office for 21B, and take around 1½ to 2 hours, and leave every 50 minutes. If you could not be bothered to walk into town, a songtheaw runs daily past all the riverside guesthouses and picks up farangs and costs 70B round trip to the falls. Bus 8170 leaves for Erawan, the first at 8.00 am and the last returning bus leaves Erawan at 3.30 pm. If you are heading to Erawan Falls via Route 323 you can cut across at a point south of Sai Yok Noi on Route 3457. As you are about to cross the Khwae Yai River near Route 3199 you will pass an elephant park which is open to visitors.

Entry into the park is 25B, but only 5B for Thai nationals, and there are heaps of food stalls around the car park to grab some food.

Si Nakharin Dam and National Park   เขื่อนศรีนครินทร์

This is the first of two dams on the Khwae Yai River. When this dam was built, the huge lake above it was created by flooding much of the land in the Si Sawat area. It is possible to view the dam from its crest, which is accessible by a road a couple of kilometres from the Erawan National Park turn-off.

The Si Nahkarin Reservoir which makes up a large part of the 1,534 sq km National Park extends far to the north, beyond Si Sawat town. The waterfall, Namtok Huay Khamin, on the northwest bank is a popular destination as with Phra Cave which holds an old large Buddha statue and protected the Burmese army in the 18th Century. The park is home to a number of wildlife and birdlife species, but slash and burn agriculture and domestic grazing of farm animals has seen their numbers diminish greatly.

Caves

Tham Phra That is a cave a further 12 km beyond Erawan Falls on a pretty rough road. The 200 m deep cave is made of limestone displaying a variety of colours. **Tham Wang Baden** is another cave in the National Park where the narrow entrance opens into an expansive chamber and various side caves, and to help you get along, lights have been installed.

Si Sawat Lake

The drive along Route 3199 beyond Erawan Waterfall provides magical views of Si Sawat Lake, part of the Si Nakharin National Park, with a background of huge irregularly shaped mountain tops, a familiar sight from as far south as Kanchanaburi. There are many small towns either on this road or just off it which quite often are little more than a clump of houses. This, combined with the brilliant views and the non existence of farangs make this area worth a visit, for at least a day, but you will probably want to stay longer.

It is not advisable to visit the area unless you have your own transport to cover the vast distances with little in between. Infrequent buses do come from Kanchanaburi, but you will be restricted to the towns which are often quite a distance from the river.

The road beyond Erawan Waterfall climbs a very high pass and, at the time of writing, the first 14 km was under mass reconstruction, making the journey difficult. Route 3199 remains in fairly good condition until about 20 km beyond Dong Salao when it turns into gravel and then becomes virtually impassable unless using an off road motorbike or 4WD. The drive to this point is beautiful, over hilly terrain and a gradually thickening forest. If you plan on attempting the drive beyond this point, make sure you fill up with petrol at Dong Salao at the 40 gallon drum petrol station.

This region is unfortunately at risk of losing its beauty over the next few years as 1997 has been declared 'A journey year to Kanchanaburi' by the TAT. Worse still are plans to set up the 'Kanchanaburi Princess' luxury cruiser on the lake by 1997. This boat will be 60 m long, three stories high and its facilities will include three banquet rooms (each for 200 people), a convention hall (for 150 people), theatre, pool and bedrooms. Not only will Si Sawat be exploited, it will be catering only to the more affluent of travellers.

SI SAWAT   ศรีสวัสดิ์

Si Sawat is located 56 km after Erawan Waterfall on Route 3199 and boasts a hospital, police station, school, one restaurant and not much else. The locals play volleyball regularly in the afternoons on the school grounds if you feel like some exercise and stray farangs are more than welcome to join in. The houses are sparsely positioned and there is not even a shop - residents purchase everything they need from a man who sells everything off the back of his truck. Although there is no official accommodation in town, you could try the rafts on the lake or you may be fortunate enough to be asked to stay with a local family. The view down by the lake is beautiful, set in very tranquil surroundings.

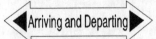 Arriving and Departing

To get to Si Sawat, follow Route 3199 until you see the turn-off for the ferry. The road actually continues around the bay to Si Sawat but is little used and has deteriorated substantially. The ferry costs 10B and takes you to a point from where it is still another 6 km to Si Sawat. The road from the ferry has completely eroded and is now a potholed dirt track, requiring extreme care.

BAN THAKRADAN

This is the last town of any size along Route 3199 which provides accommodation. Unfortunately the accommodation mainly caters to Thai tourists and is above the budget of many independent travellers. The town is nothing special itself, but borders with the stunning Si Sawat Lake.

Resort This place, like others on the waterfront, caters mainly to Thai tour groups which fill the place on weekends. Here, river huts with two beds, Western toilet, fan and balcony start at 700B. Follow the blue "resort" signs from the point where the main road in Ban Thakradan turns to gravel. The thin unsealed road continues on for a few kilometres. The derelict bamboo huts in the parking area are not the accommodation - follow the path down the hill. As with most places along the lake, they can organise fishing trips and overnight camping trips to Huay Khamin Waterfall.
Pha Klom Prai Resort is reached via the road to the right as the sealed road in town ends. Accommodation starts at 1,500B per night. The resort can organise longtail boat trips to Namtok Huay Khamin for 150B and the trip takes about a ½ hour.

SANGKHLABURI   สังขละบุรี

Virtually at the end of Route 323, the beautiful town of Sangkhlaburi cries out to be included on your travel itinerary. Little visited by farangs, Sangkhlaburi is a favourite weekend location for Thais and understandably so. Set on a large scenic lake created by the Khao Laem Dam in 1983 and separated from a Mon village by the longest wooden bridge in Thailand, Sangkhlaburi is the perfect location for relaxing and savouring life. Inhabited by a mix of Thai, Mon, Karen, Bangladeshi and Burmese an exciting cultural diversity can be experienced here, unlike any other town in Thailand.

Sangkhlaburi is 225 km from Kanchanaburi and about 70 km from Thong Pha Phum. The scenic view along this road of a lush, green and dense forest, karyst mountain tops and glimpses of the lake makes a visit to Sangkhlaburi more than worth the time it takes to reach it. Sangkhlaburi's higher altitude means that during monsoon, it gets more than its fair share of rain.

Central

Central *(vertical side text)*

Vital Information

Post Office A small and almost miss-able post office exits in Sangkhlaburi.
Bank Siam Commercial Bank is in the centre of town, open from 8.30 am to 3.30 pm.
Police Station is one block further east of the post office, on the right.
Immigration Office only really caters to Thai and Burmese Immigration queries. For farang hassles and extensions, you will need to go to Kanchanaburi.
Codes The telephone code in Sangkhlaburi is (034) and postal code is 71240.

Cheap Sleeps

P Guesthouse, ☎ (034) 595 061, fax (034) 595 139, located at 81/1 Tambon Nongloo around 2 km from the bus station. A motorcycle ride will cost 10B. Tiny singles/doubles with shared bath are 30B/50B, 100B with private bath. The guesthouse has friendly staff and a large nicely decorated restaurant with a grand view of the lake and Mon village. They can also provide valuable tourist information, jungle trekking and camping, elephant trekking, rafting, and motorcycle and canoe hire.

Burmese Inn is located about half way between the bus station and P Guesthouse. Rooms in a longhouse are 60B/80B with shared bath and 100B for clean bungalows with private bath. Nice garden and pleasant view from the restaurant of the wooden bridge and some of the lake and village. Friendly staff, good service and information on the surrounding area is available.

Phornphailin Hotel is around the corner and a block away from the Siam Commercial Bank, only for the desperate, rates start at 180B and A/C starts at 350B. The restaurant on the ground floor caters to farangs and offers meals ranging from 20B to 100B.

Forget Me Not House, ☎ (034) 595 013, offers resort rooms with the cheapest starting at 500B (with bath) up to 3,000B for a luxury room with a view of the river.

Ponnatee Resort, ☎ (034) 595 134, is a similar setup to Forget Me Not House with prices ranging from 500B to 700B

Sangkhla Garden, ☎ (034) 595 007, is on the corner down from P Guesthouse, offers individual wooden bungalows with A/C, bath, big bed, balcony and river views for 500B.

Resort Set at the end of the road to the wooden bridge, this resort has great views, but the cheaper rooms are in a barrack like set up and start at 500B with A/C.

Songkalia River Hut and Resort, ☎ (034) 595 023, is located on the town side of the concrete bridge and has large bungalows that can sleep up to four people for 400B and run down river rafts for 800B which can sleep eight people (or more if you are not fussy).

Things to do **and** Sights to See

Khao Laem Lake

Formed in 1983 by the damming of the Khwae Noi River near Thong Pha Phum, old Sangkhlaburi now rests at its depths. At the peak of monsoon, the lake almost reaches the top of the bridge. **Boat trips** to a variety of points of interest on the lake can be arranged from your guesthouse at reasonable prices. A trip generally visits the Mon village, some cliffs and, if the lake is low, the top of the submerged wat of Old Sangkhlaburi.

Mon Village

Home to neither refugees nor Thais, this friendly village at the far side of the wooden bridge can be visited in conjunction with a visit to **Wat Wang Wiwaekaram** (**Wat Mon**). Spread out across the far bank of the lake, this village has been formed by Burmese refugees

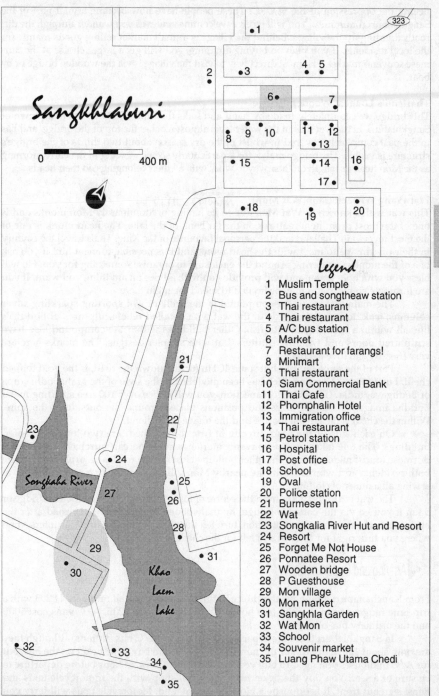

Sangkhlaburi

0   400 m

Songkalia River

Khao Laem Lake

Legend

1 Muslim Temple
2 Bus and songtheaw station
3 Thai restaurant
4 Thai restaurant
5 A/C bus station
6 Market
7 Restaurant for farangs!
8 Minimart
9 Thai restaurant
10 Siam Commercial Bank
11 Thai Cafe
12 Phornphalin Hotel
13 Immigration office
14 Thai restaurant
15 Petrol station
16 Hospital
17 Post office
18 School
19 Oval
20 Police station
21 Burmese Inn
22 Wat
23 Songkalia River Hut and Resort
24 Resort
25 Forget Me Not House
26 Ponnatee Resort
27 Wooden bridge
28 P Guesthouse
29 Mon village
30 Mon market
31 Sangkhla Garden
32 Wat Mon
33 School
34 Souvenir market
35 Luang Phaw Utama Chedi

Central

fleeing the oppression of the SLORC. These people have now become a vital part of the Sangkhlaburi community. You will receive welcoming smiles as you wander through the dirt roads dividing up the village. Behind the village is a small market selling goods mainly for the local residents. If you plan on buying anything, you will get a larger choice at the Burmese souvenir market. The most direct way to visit the village is via the wooden bridge or by boat.

Thailand's Longest Wooden Bridge
This bridge was completely made by hand and links the Mon village to the main town of Sangkhlaburi. In the wet season the water level almost reaches the top of the bridge, and has in the past completely covered it, whilst in the dry season about two thirds of the bridge's structure is visible. The bridge makes for a particularly scenic viewing in the early morning as the Mon tread its length on their way to work with all their belongings on their heads.

Wat Wang Wiwaekaram (Wat Mon)   วัดวังก์วิเวการาม
This wat is also known as Wat Mon due to its having predominantly Mon monks and is one of the most prominent features on the far bank of the lake. The head monk is one of the most revered in Thailand and the personal favourite of the King. Thais travel the country in their pilgrimage to meet with the head monk and it is possible to meet him if you ask one of the monks wandering around the enclosure to organise something for you. He will bless you with holy water and will provide you with advice on anything you want. If you are fortunate enough, you may be invited to spend the night there.

The main feature of the compound is the brilliant wat sporting sparkling silver columns, teak doors on each side of the wat with detailed relief sculptures of Buddha's life, all within a moat filled with fish. Other buildings within the compound also have sculptured doors and window shutters, but with simpler designs. The monks here are very friendly and love to chat.

Part of the same temple, but some 400 m further down the road, is the gold topped chedi, **Luang Phaw Utama**, which has been modelled in the style of the Mahabodhi stupa of Bodhgaya, India. Upon closer inspection, you will notice over 100 free standing metal Buddha images of varying sizes and positions placed around the outside of the spire. Within the chedi is the largest marble Buddha image in Thailand.

On each side of the road directly in front of the chedi are two long red roofed buildings. The one lakeside is a souvenir market where you can purchase a variety of Burmese tourist merchandise. The other building closer to the road is an orphanage where both residents and women from the nearby Mon village partake in a constant flow of sewing all manner of clothing.

The wat is around 2 km from the centre of town if you go via the wooden bridge or 5 km if you go via the concrete bridge. By the wooden bridge, follow the road after the bridge and when you reach a T junction, turn left then follow the road until the intersection where you turn right for the wat and left for the chedi.

◀ **Arriving and Departing** ▶

From **Kanchanaburi**, you have the choice of three forms of bus, all numbered 8203 with a trip time ranging from three to five hours. The VIP van costs 120B, A/C vans cost 100B and the ordinary bus costs 70B.

In Sangkhlaburi there are separate A/C and non A/C bus stations, although they are only about 150 m apart. For the non A/C bus, you can buy your ticket on the bus, but for A/C minibuses you need to buy your ticket early, at least an hour before departure to be sure of a seat. You buy the ticket from the small shop with the motorcycle taxis and Pepsi sign out front. It is opposite a block of vacant land. Motorcycle taxis will ferry you anywhere around town for 10B, but most sights are within walking distance.

AROUND SANGKHLABURI

It is possible to join the last leg of tours to this area which have run up from Kanchanaburi. The trips cost around 750B from Sangkhlaburi, more from Kanchanaburi, and include rafting the Runtee River, elephant rides in the National Park and the possibility of overnight camping. The availability of the trips is purely dependent on numbers and can be organised through P Guesthouse.

Three Pagoda's Pass   พระเจดีย์สามองค์
Just under 20 km from Sangkhlaburi, these diminutive 2 m high pagodas are almost guaranteed to disappoint - they are actually in the middle of a roundabout! For those who are not concerned about supporting the SLORC and are intent on visiting Burma, you can sometimes cross the border here for a few hours for US $5 or 130B. Whilst researching, the border crossing was closed to farangs and had been for some time, and there was no indication of when it would reopen. There is accommodation available at Three Pagoda's Pass but it is mainly geared to Thai tourists and most farangs choose to stay in Sangkhlaburi. If you do decide to cross to Burma, please be aware that your US $5 will most likely be used to buy bullets rather than school pens.

Cheap Sleeps

Three Pagodas Resort, ☎ (043) 595 316, is located about 500 m back up the road from the pass, this resort offers a variety of accommodation from 200B to 1,000B, however unless you are interested in doing some trading, there is little else to hold your interest for more than a day.

◀ Arriving and Departing ▶

Songtheaws leave regularly from **Sangkhlaburi** for 30B, and take 45 minutes to an hour. They leave from the non A/C bus station.

Things to do ◆and◆ Sights to See

Tham Wang Badon
This cave is about 1½ km from Three Pagoda's Pass back towards Sangkhlaburi. Catch a songtheaw heading back to Sangkhlaburi and hop off at the bus shelter on the left hand side about 1 km out of Three Pagoda's Pass. Walk down the track and at the end of the reservoir, turn right. The 'caves' are about 150 m down on your right and are reached by shoddy bamboo ladders and wooden bridges. The caves are a popular place for meditation, so be aware of this whilst wandering around. The top cave contains a skull and some bones. All of the caves are full of bats.

Cave Temple
This temple is built into a cave 5 km after the turn-off on the right hand side and it is 400 m short of the bridge over Songkalia River. The temple itself has a low roof made of stalagmite. Residents of the temple, besides the monks, are a couple of adorable monkeys who seem more at home in the monk's lap rather than in the trees. The access road is only a couple of hundred metres long and it is marked by an orange Buddhist flag and a bus shelter.

Central

Namtok Thaklien
Located 10 km up from the turn-off to Three Pagodas Pass, this waterfall is reached via a 9 km stretch of road. The road is barely passable in the wet season and you will need to walk the final 500 m as the road is blocked by a fast flowing stream. In the dry season the road is fine, but the waterfall may then not be worth the effort.

ROUTE 3086

An area little visited by roving farangs is north of Kanchanaburi along Route 3086. The main feature of this area is the **Bophloi Sapphire Mine** for gem freaks and **Chaloem Rattanakosin National Park** and its cave, **Tham Lot**, for the nature freaks.

BOPHLOI

Located 40 km from Kanchanaburi, just to the east of Route 3086 is Bophloi. Within this region you can visit the jewellery handicraft centre where the blue sapphires and other semi precious stones mined nearby are made into jewellery. Buses leave for Bophloi from **Kanchanaburi** every 20 minutes between 6.00 am and 6.30 pm and the trip takes 1½ hours.

Chaloem Rattanakosin National Park   อุทยานแห่งชาติเฉลิมรัตนโกสินทร์

Established in February 1980, this National Park covers 54 sq km and sits in the northern area of Kanchanaburi Province. The most visited location within the park is **Tham Lot**. The cave is close to the park headquarters and is 300 m deep. A river flows through the middle of it past the decorative stalactites and stalagmites which have formed over time. The path that leads beyond the cave reaches two waterfalls and another, less spectacular cave.

Within the park, bungalow accommodation is available and there is a camp ground but no gear is for hire. For those planning on spending a while in the park, you would be best to bring your own food and water as the closest restaurants and shops are in Nong Pru which is 15 km from the park.

The National Park is 97 km north of Kanchanaburi and is reached by catching the same bus which runs to Bophloi but jump off at the town of Nong Pru which is the closest point to the park. From here it is another 15 km to the National Park and it can be reached by motorcycle taxi from Nong Pru. The bus leaves Kanchanaburi every 20 minutes between 6.00 am and 6.30 pm and takes two hours.

SUPHANABURI PROVINCE

Suphanaburi has had as many location changes as name changes during its history. It was first founded in 877 and became prosperous during the Dvaravati Period. It started off as Panchum Buri on the left bank of the Tha Chin River. The next King named it Song Phan Buri ('City of Two Thousand' due to him making 2,000 city officials monks) and it moved to the right bank of the river. King U-Thong then named the town after himself and moved it to the west of the river. Its final resting place is on the east bank, named Suphanaburi by King Khun Luang Pha Ngua.

SUPHANABURI   สุพรรณบุรี

Suphanaburi is the provincial capital of the same named province which encompasses 5,358 sq km and the capital is located 109 km from Bangkok. The town's current claim to fame is that it is the birth place of the former Thai Prime Minister Banharn Silpa-archa. His love of his hometown has seen Suphanaburi receive what some would say a larger than fair slice of the budget. As a result of all this money, Suphanaburi is a beautifully manicured and remarkably clean place with developed infrastructure and public facilities — they even have real bins in the streets! The locals are not doing too badly either, as Suphanaburi is one of the more prosperous cities of its size in Thailand.

Mainly visited by travellers who are stranded between Lopburi and Kanchanaburi, Suphanaburi nevertheless has a fair bit to offer. Its quieter streets are tree lined and nice to wander along in the early hours. Although most Thais would say that there is little to see in Suphanaburi, the TAT is trying to change this with a tourism push predicted for 1997. If you are a wat fan, then there is plenty to keep you entertained, and for bird watchers, there is the nearby bird sanctuary. But whilst in town be prepared for prolonged stares as despite its size and proximity to Bangkok, the locals are still not too used to seeing farangs walking the streets.

Orientation

Most of the action in town occurs around the market area along the north/south running Phraphanwasa Road, on the right side of the bank of the river, between Nang Phim Road and Munhan Roads.

Vital Information

Tourist Office As yet there is no Tourist Office in Suphanaburi, but there are several 'one stop service centres', where you can get some very limited information. The main office is at 8/29 Munhan Road and the other two are on Phraphanwasa Road.

Post Office is along Nang Phim Road about ten minutes walk from the intersection with Phraphanwasa Road and almost opposite the Suphanaburi Tower. The post office is open 8.30 am to 4.30 pm weekdays, whilst the upstairs phone office is open until 9.00 pm.

Banks are lined along Phraphanwasa Road, see the map for details.

Hospital Supamitr General Hospital is open 24 hours and is located on Nen Kaeo Road, 100 m south of the King Pho Sai Hotel. Another hospital is located at the southern end of Phraphanwasa Road, just after the intersection with Munhan Road.

Police Station is on Phraphanwasa Road.

Codes Suphanaburi's telephone code is (035) and the postal code is 72000.

Cheap Sleeps

Suphan KAT Hotel, ☎ (035) 521 619, at 27 Phraphanwasa Road has clean singles/doubles costing 150B/180B with fan and shower. A/C doubles will set you back 230B. Parking is available.

Sunsunt Hotel, ☎ (035) 521 668, is at 113 Nang Phim Road opposite the post office, look for the big red painted building. Friendly staff have large clean rooms with fan and shower starting at 170B/180B for singles/doubles and 230B for A/C. The cafe downstairs in not too bad.

King Pho Sai Hotel, ☎ (035) 522 412, is almost opposite the bus station, on the other side of the main road and offers clean and functional rooms for 150B and 300B with A/C.

Valentine, ☎ (035) 521 836, at 195 Nen Kaeo Road is 200 m south of the bus station. Old and fairly small rooms with bath and fan cost 120B and 240B with A/C.

Phaitoon, ☎ (035) 521 411, at 2 Pratchathipatai Road is at the northern end of town, quite far from anything and nearby to a noisy factory. Dark dingy rooms with fan and bath are 200B, 300B with A/C. Only for the desperate.

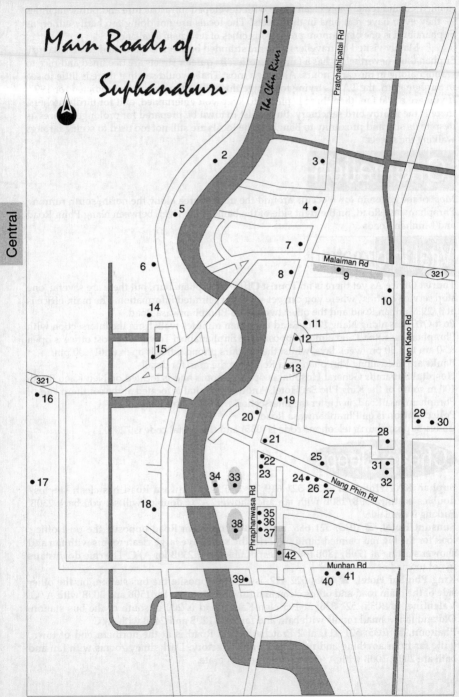

Main Roads of
Suphanaburi

Legend

1	Wat Phra Non	15	City Pillar	29	Bus station
2	Wat Phra Loi	16	Wat Pa Lelai	30	Godd restaurant
3	Hotel	17	Railway station	31	NASA mall
4	School	18	Wat Pharup	32	Hospital
5	Wat Khae	19	City Hall	33	Market
6	Wat Phra Si Rattana	20	Wat Suwannaphum	34	Outdoor restaurants
	Mahathat	21	Bangkok Metro. Bank	35	Bank of Ayudhya
7	Court	22	Police box	36	Thai Military Bank
8	Minimart	23	Siam City Bank	37	School
9	Outdoor restaurants	24	Banharn-Chaemsai Tower	38	Market
10	B'kok Bank of Commerce		(Suphanaburi Tower)	39	Hospital
11	Wat	25	Post office	40	Minimart
12	Statue	26	Outdoor restaurants	41	School
13	Suphan KAT	27	Suksunt Hotel	42	Street market
14	City Pillar Shrine	28	King Pho Sai Hotel		

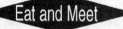

Eat and Meet

For an evening beer it is difficult to go past the **Nangpim Restaurant** at 32 Nang Phim Road. Look out for the cutout of a waving lady. This place is very popular with the Thais and meal prices range from 40B to 120B and you can expect to be waited on hand and foot.

Happy House is next to the King Pho Sai Hotel and does good Thai and Western food at fairly reasonable prices.

A popular eating place is by the market on the right bank of the Tha Chin River, north of the middle bridge. Other groups of outdoor eating restaurants include Malaiman Road (Route 321) between Pratchathipatai Road and Nan Kaeo Road, as well as on Nang Phim Road just east of the Suphanaburi Tower.

Things to do **and** Sights to See

Suphanaburi Tower หอคอยสุพรรณบุรี

Also known as Banharn - Chaemsai Tower, it sits in the immaculate Chalermphatara Rachinee Park on Nang Phim Road. The tower is the first to be built in Thailand and was built to honour the Queen's 60th birthday. The tower is 123.5 m tall and 30 m across at its widest point, although the highest viewing point is only at 72.75 m. The tower is the best place to get a good view of the surrounds and entry is 30B which is additional to the 10B fee to enter the park. The park itself is 'worth a visit' for its animal styled hedges and small waterslide facility. The park is open Tuesday to Sunday from 10.00 am to 7.00 pm, ☎ (035) 522 721.

City Pillar Shrine (Chao Pho Lak Muang)

The pillar itself is a crumbling concrete obelisk which is being renovated (like most things in Suphanaburi), whilst the shrine to the pillar is another 200 m up the road and is de-signed in the Chinese pavilion style with a golden dragon winding its way up the pole. Originally it was made of wood in a Thai design with two green stone Vishnu statues within. The temple is over 150 years old and now Chinese in every way shape and form - very decorative and colourful and much revered by the locals. The city shrine is located about 500 m west of the northern bridge, just off Malaiman Road.

Wat Suwannaphum (Wat Mai)   วัดสุวรรณภูมิ

Known as Wat Mai to the locals, the main attraction here is the Pun Punnasiri Museum. The museum contains two floors of artifacts including some from archeological digs, ranging from prehistoric times to the Sukhothai and Lopburi periods. Many of the displays are also of Chinese origin. There is also a photo display of significant monks with some starring the King and former Prime Minister Banharn.

The museum is the building with the red sign on the door, with red barred gates, doors and shutters and flags at the entrance. To visit is free, though you may need to ask to have it opened as the collection of dust and cobwebs is indicative of its use.

Wat Palelai (Wat Pa)   วัดป่าเลไลย

This wat is also known as Wat Pa. A huge seated Buddha dominates the temple with the white chedi and archway at its entrance. Originally it represented Buddha giving his first sermon, but after a renovation was changed to Buddha living a jungle life, referred to as Luang Pho To. People paying homage to Buddha have placed gold paper and coins up to Buddha's ankles as this was the highest point they could reach. The result is this Buddha is wearing glistening socks! An elephant and monkey guard the statue both as relief sculptures (now gold) on the walls either side of the image as well as in stone form outside the temple. Two festivals in honour of the Buddha are held in the 5th and 12th lunar months. Also within the compound is the proud statue of Rama V, just past the second building to the left. Further to the left is a wooden building housing a number of unlabelled items, most of Chinese origin. This wooden building is actually the home of Khun Chung, a figure who represents 'evil'. His opposite, Khun Phen represents 'good' and has a house dedicated to him in Wat Khae (see below).

Further left at the far end of the compound is a small decorative shrine with a red roof in honour of an important Suphanaburi monk. A statue of the monk sits in the middle in front of a box containing his remains. The statue to the right is King Thonburi. Wat Palelai is on Malaiman Road, 2 km west of the northern bridge.

Wat Phra Si Rattana Mahathat (Wat Prathat)   วัดพระศรีรัตนมหาธาตุ

On the west bank of the Tha Chin River, north of the northern bridge are more wats. The first worth seeing is Wat Phra Si Rattana Mahathat. A pavilion guarded by two reclining Buddhas contain rows of sitting Buddhas from the Ayutthaya Period, with a large Buddha in the middle. This wat is more than 600 years old and is known as Wat Prathat by the locals.

Wat Khae   วัดแค

Wat Khae has a sign out front with a picture of a tree draped with an orange sash. This represents the real tree which is found within the compound. The base of this magnificent tree has a circumference of no less than ten people with their arms outstretched. A modern version of Buddhist fortune telling sits in front of the tree for 1B but unfortunately your future is available in Thai only. The wooden house beyond the tree is the home dedicated to Khun Phen who represents 'good' (see Wat Palelai for the bad guy). Wat Khae is also home to another Buddha footprint which is displayed in an open pillared pavilion. To the left of this is an open pavilion with a Buddha statue for every day of the week. If making an offering, present it to the Buddha representing the day of the week you were born on. The statue on the left is Sunday, with the others following suit to the right (there are two spare statues.)

Wat Phra Loi   วัดพระลอย

The animals caged at this wat would give animal liberationists something to talk about. A bear and monkey are kept in tiny cages in terrible conditions. Not so for the fish in the river. If you go onto the raft you will see sacred fish who hang out waiting to be fed. The road leading into this wat has an entrance of large elephant and soldier statues. Wat Phra Loi is to the north of Wat Khae on the same side of the road.

Wat Phra Non   วัดพระนอน

The chapel by the river houses a statue of the deceased Buddha. It is fashioned in the Sukhothai style and is very similar to a statue which can be found at Kusinara, India where the Lord Buddha passed away.

The barge on the river in front is the feeding ground for thousands of fresh water fish and that is not an exaggeration. They just hang out, waiting for tourists to throw them food. Some are almost half a metre long, but budding fishermen need to keep their rods at bay as fishing is not permitted.

Wat Pharup   วัดพระรูป

The first temple to the right of the entrance houses a reclining stone Buddha known as 'Nen Kaeo'. The steps that lead to the top of the image are for use by men only. The main attraction of the wat however, is Buddha's footprint which is made of wood. It is the only wooden Buddha footprint in Thailand and there is speculation that it may well be the only one of its kind in the world. Both sides display relief carving. The back depicts Buddha within the box at the top and middle. The humans on the top level represent the good side of mortals and the lower level represents the evil side. The footprint is not openly on display and you have to ask to see it. Enter via the road entrance and turn left at the bridge, it is the second building, Buddha's footprint is on the second floor.

There are many more wats within Suphanaburi and its outskirts, but the collection above gives details on some of the more interesting ones. You could spend days visiting all the wats in Suphanaburi if you so desired.

◀ Arriving and Departing ▶

Suphanaburi has enough local buses, songtheaws, motorbike samlors and motorbike taxis to get you anywhere any time. Songtheaws within town cost 3B and the motorbike samlors cost 5B to 10B depending on distance.

Ban Bang Phae Drum Making Village

Train
Suphanaburi marks the beginning of the southern railway line and the station is 3 km west of the city centre. Refer to the end of the chapter for detailed price and timetable information.

Bus
The bus station is half way along Nan Kaeo Road. The bus to **Kanchanaburi** costs 25B, a bus to **Nakhon Pathom** costs 40B and a bus to **Lopburi** costs 25B taking 3 hours. A samlor to the bus station should cost 5B. The bus from **Lopburi** may drop you off at a random location outside of the centre of town.

Central

Central

AROUND SUPHANABURI

Don Chedi   ดอนเจดีย์

The Don Chedi monument was built to commemorate the victory of King Naresuan over King Maha Uparcha of Burma after a hand to hand, elephant to elephant battle in the late 16th Century (no one knows if there is a monument for the elephants - poor things). The triumph saved Ayutthaya from the tyranny of the Burmese Kingdom of Bago.

The site was rediscovered in 1913 as little more than a pile of rubble. However in 1952 a new chedi was built with the ruins in its belly. A statue of the triumphant King Naresuan on the back of an elephant has been erected out the front. A week long fair takes place here every year starting 25th January (Royal Thai Armed Forces Day).

Don Chedi is 31 km from Suphanaburi. To get there catch a songtheaw from the market area or jump on it at the intersection of Route 321 and Pratchathipatoi Road for 12B. If you have your own transport, English signs show the direction for the entire way.

Tha Sadet Bird Sanctuary   สวนนกท่าเสด็จ

Located 15 km from the city centre, this bird sanctuary will send birdwatchers crazy with its thousands of birds which include storks, a variety of heron, cormorant and white ibises. One of the best viewing times is around dusk when all the birds come home. Make sure you pack your camouflage and telephoto lens.

To reach the bird sanctuary, take Malaiman Road (Route 321) west for 3 km, then make a right turn onto Route 322 for another 12 km. One kilometre before the sanctuary entrance on the left side of the road is the Four Sacred Ponds, Sa Kaew, Sa Kha, Sa Yomana and Sa Ket. These are the source of sacred water used in special ceremonies even since Suphanaburi was known as U-Thong.

Wat Phai Rong Wua   วัดไผ่โรงวัว

Located quite a distance from Suphanaburi, on the southern border of the province, this wat is worth mentioning as it contains **Phra Phutta Khodom**. This is the largest Buddha statue to have been made from a metal cast in Thailand. It reaches 26 m in height and is 10 m wide at its widest point.

The wat is close to Song Phi Nong and can be reached via Route 321 then Route 3260 and finally Route 3422. It is also possible to visit the wat from Bangkok by boat. Every Sunday at 7.00 am a boat leaves from Tha Chang pier in Bangkok.

ANG THONG PROVINCE

The province is only tiny taking up 968 sq km beside the Chao Phraya River. It is only 108 km from Bangkok, set in a basin of fairly infertile soil. This puts the landscape in the same category as the assortment of uneventful towns - all very uninteresting viewing.

ANG THONG   อ่างทอง

Ang Thong is a small but busy town — capital of the same named province. The town is located 108 km from Bangkok and 33 km from Ayutthaya. The only real reason you may want to visit here is if you are on a mission to visit every province in Thailand. There is nothing to see in the town and all the attractions you may want to visit are spread over the province.

> According to a learned friend who studied at Thammasat University in Bangkok, the students there have dirty farang competitions. The aim of this is to first find the dirtiest farang and then guess their nationality! Just a thought for when you wander the streets.

Vital Information

Post Office From the centre of town, cross the bridge and turn right. When the street veers left after another 800 m take a sharp right and follow for 200 m.

Banks All of the major banks have a branch in town, on or just off the main street through town, cross the bridge and turn left.

Hospital is a few hundred metres from the police station on the road leading to Ayutthaya.

Police Station is on the south side of the bridge over the Chao Phraya River.

Codes Ang Thong's telephone code is (035) and postal code is 14000.

Cheap Sleeps

There are only two hotels of any substance in town.

Angthong Hotel, ☎ (035) 611 767, at 19 Ang Thong Road, is located right in the centre of town. A room with fan and bathroom is 180B, A/C starts at 260B and the VIP (with TV) costs 550B. Do not stay on the right hand side of the building as a noisy karaoke bar downstairs will keep you up until the wee hours of the morning.

Bua Lueng Hotel, ☎ (035) 611 116, is not marked by any English signs, so may be a little tricky to find. It is 2 km from the town centre, 250 m before the Suphanaburi turn-off when heading towards Ayutthaya. Rooms with fan and bath cost 140B, A/C 240B and VIP 380B.

Eat and Meet

The market, which is across the road and to the left of the Ang Thong Hotel, deals up some good and cheap meals.

Things to do and Sights to See

Ban Bang Phae Drum Making Village   หมู่บ้านทำกลองบ้านบางแพ

This village is well known for the **klawngs** (Thai Drums) made in a variety of shapes and sizes. To reach the village, take Route 309 between Ang Thong and Ayutthaya and take the turn-off to Pamok (18 km from Ayutthaya and 13 km from Ang Thong). The first semi sealed road on the right leads to the bus station and ferry. Catch a ferry to the opposite bank (1B per person, 3B for a motorbike). You will then need to ask the locals how to get to Ban Bang Phae, it is about 2 km from the bank of the river. The road passes the Municipality Office and follows Yang Mani Irrigation canal. Hopefully you will arrive when the drums are being made, otherwise it is not really worth going. A new bridge is under construction across the river 1 km towards Ang Thong.

Wat Phra Phuttha Saiyat Pa Mok   วัดพระพุทธไสยาสน์ป่าโมก

Near to the village of Ban Bang Phae, this wat is home to a large (22.5 m) reclining Buddha which was visited by King Naresuan before his historic battle against the Burmese. Another building within the grounds is home to a stone Buddha footprint which is guarded by a stuffed monkey. To reach the wat, follow the above directions for Ban Bang Phae, but instead of going ahead at the Municipality Office, take the left, and follow it for about 1 km.

Wat Sa Kaeo วัดสระแก้ว
Built in 1699, this wat serves as an orphanage for around 1,200 children and also as a cloth weaving factory. The mummified body of the monk who started up the orphanage is in a glass shrine. The wat is 1½ km down the right hand turn-off, 16 km from Ang Thong.

Wat Chaiyo Worwihan and Wat Khun Inthapramun   วัดไชโยวรวิหาร
วัดขุนอินทประมูล
Wat Chaiyo Worwihan is situated 18 km north of Ang Thong and is home to a large Buddha, whilst the latter wat, located 11 km to the north of town, is home to a 50 m reclining Buddha.

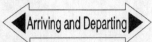

Buses and songtheaws can be caught to the nearby towns of Ayutthaya and Singburi, whilst any destination further afield is served by bus only. To **Ayutthaya** it costs 10B for a 1 hour trip and to **Chainat** a bus costs 17B. To reach the bus station in Ang Thong, turn right if coming into town by the bridge then turn right at the road 200 m up and follow your nose past the small market.

SINGBURI PROVINCE

The capital of this small province of only 822 sq km was formed by the combination of three smaller towns, Singburi, Inburi and Phromburi in 1895 during the reign of King Rama V. The new town, named Singburi, was established on the western bank of the Chao Phraya River.

SINGBURI   สิงห์บุรี

Situated 37 km to the north of Ang Thong, 48 km to the south of Chainat and 30 km to the west of Lopburi, this town is fairly uninteresting, busy, noisy and dirty. If you must spend the night here, the promenade by the river at the southern end of town is the most pleasant area. This is one of the few towns in Thailand where the entire town stops twice daily for the playing of the national anthem at 8.00 am and 6.00 pm.

If you happen to be in the region in September, it is worth keeping an eye out for the annual **longboat races** on the Chao Phraya River.

Orientation

Route 309 runs north/south through the western side of town. The distance from here to the river (east) is 300 m with Khun San Road in between and running parallel to both. This is the centre of the town activity.

Vital Information

Post Office On Nar Tan Road by the river, 200 m south of the end of the main road (Khun San Road). The telephone office is open 7.00 am to 10.00 pm.
Banks All the main banks have branch offices in Singburi, centred around Khun San Road.
Hospital There are two main ones in town. One on Route 309 just to the south of town and the other at the northern end of Khun San Road.
Police Station, ☎ (036) 511 213, is two buildings down from the post office.
Codes Singburi's telephone code is (036) and the postal code is 16000.

Cheap Sleeps

Singburi Hotel, ☎ (036) 511 653, at 882/18 Khun San Road, closest to the bus station (200 m away) with clean rooms for 190B with fan and bathroom and 290B for A/C.

Chao Phaya Hotel, ☎ (036) 511 776, on Khun San Road, only 30 m north of the Singburi Hotel, this hotel/brothel has the cheapest and nastiest rooms in town. Old, dirty rooms (including leaking pipes) cost 100B, 150B with television and 70B for those who only want to stay for a couple of hours (this is definitely a place to take the whole family!).

Chao Phaya Garden Hotel, ☎ (036) 511 348, at 184/13 Singburi-Lopburi Road. Large average rooms start at 150B for fan and 300B for A/C. The hotel is at the T junction at the northern end of Khun San Road, about 500 m from the bus station.

VST Hotel, ☎ (036) 511 732, at 249 Pho Khao Ton Road, this place is dodgy with a capital 'D'. Tucked away in the southern back alleys, their pride and joy is round 'love' beds with mirrored walls, but very dirty. They also have other rooms for 150B with fan, 260B and 300B with A/C.

City Hotel, ☎ (036) 511 189, at 151/30 Singburi - Lopburi Road, located 200 m to the left of the Chao Phraya Garden Hotel, this hotel has the cleanest rooms all of which are A/C and the cheapest starts at 200B.

Eat and Meet

Towards the southern end of town there are some good restaurants by the river. One particularly good one sets up tables on the promenade serving meals for between 20B and 60B. The market is half way up Khun San Road on the western side.

Money Pub and Coffee Shop Just around the corner of the southern end of Khun San Road, this is a modern club with two levels and a stage on the split level for Thai rock bands. This place pumps on the weekends, but rumour has it that it is run by the local mafia — beware of the management who seem particularly dodgy and one of the researchers reported being hassled here.

Things to do and Sights to See

There is not much in town as most sights are spread throughout the province, and even these will be pushing it to be mentioned in your diary.

Wat Sawang Arom   วัดสว่างอารมณ์

This wat contains a collection of around 300 Nong Yai, of which only about twelve are on display which you must ask to see. Nong Yai are leather caricatures held by sticks, otherwise known as shadow play caricatures, and are used in plays and performances. The wat is also meant to be a centre for Buddhist sculpture, but none other than the standard are laying around. The wat is 3 km to the south of town. A motorbike taxi costs around 20B or better still catch a songtheaw along Route 309 (the wat is on the left hand side) or walk along the promenade by the river and from where it finishes the wat is only another 400 m away.

Wat Phra Non Chaksi   วัดพระนอนจักรสีห์

This wat is around 3 km from town on Route 309 and is home to a 46 m long reclining Buddha image dating back to the Ayutthaya Period.

Central

Wat Phikum Thong   วัดพิกุลทอง

Another 9 km past Wat Phra Non Chaksi in Tha Chang is Wat Phikum Thong, with Thailand's largest outdoor sitting Buddha. To reach the wat, head south on Route 309 and take the turn-off to Phikum Thong town.

Inburi National Museum   พิพิธภัณฑ์สถานแห่งชาติอินทร์บุรี

To the north of Singburi on Route 311, this museum has a few artifacts to check out, including shadow play caricatures, religious fans and Buddha images.

Other Attractions

The Monument of Heroes in Khai Bang Raihan Park, located on Route 3032, 13 km south west of Singburi, commemorates the villager's efforts against the Burmese. **Wat Pho Kao Ton** is close by to the park. It has a sacred pond and the Mai Daeng (redwood trees dating back to the Ayutthaya Period). **Wat Pha Prang** and **Noi River Kiln Site** at Choeng Klat, 17 km from Singburi, has a prang 60 m high and 20 m wide dating back to the time of King Narai, a Buddha footprint and the remains of kilns from the Ayutthaya Period.

 Arriving and Departing

Bus

The bus station, ☎ (036) 511 064, is between Route 309 and Khun San Road at the southern end of town. Buses regularly leave for destinations within the province and further afield. To **Chainat** (52 km away) a bus costs 17B and takes 1 to 1½ hours and to **Uthai Thani** a bus costs 30B. Motorcycle taxis and tuk tuks cost 10B to 20B depending on distance.

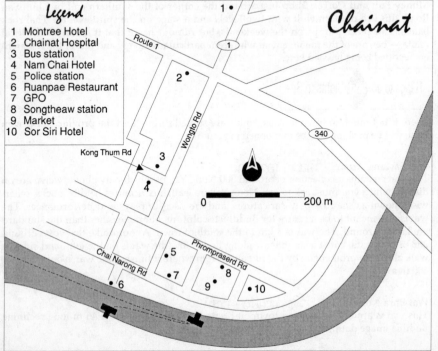

Legend

1 Montree Hotel
2 Chainat Hospital
3 Bus station
4 Nam Chai Hotel
5 Police station
6 Ruanpae Restaurant
7 GPO
8 Songtheaw station
9 Market
10 Sor Siri Hotel

Chainat

Route 1

Kong Thum Rd

Wongto Rd

Chai Narong Rd

Phrompraserd Rd

340

0   200 m

CHAINAT PROVINCE

Translated as 'Place of Victory', Chainat has played an important role in the past. The town is the site of numerous defeats for the marauding Burmese hordes. Established during the Ayutthaya Period, most visitors agree that Chainat's heyday has passed . . . a long time ago.

CHAINAT   ชัยนาท

Chainat is only a small town, but one best left off your travel itinerary. Although the town is nice enough, there is little to see and the local residents certainly do not go to much effort to improve matters. In Chainat there is a clear distinction between those who are doing all right for themselves and those who are just getting by, however both seldom wear a smile and both follow you around with suspicious eyes. The landscape here is much greener than that of the towns on the plains, as the foothills of the northern ranges start to make an appearance in this area.

Vital Information

Post Office is on Chai Narong Road.
Banks The banks in town are spread along Wongto, Kong Thum and Phrompraserd Roads.
Hospital is on Route 340 just outside town.
Police Station Just down from Chainorong Road on a side street.
Codes Chainat's telephone code is (036) and the postal code is 17000.

Cheap Sleeps

Sor Siri, ☎ (036) 411 580, on Chai Narong Road, this hotel is difficult to find, from the bus station turn right onto Wongto Road, left onto Phrompraserd road and right into Soi Phaisong 1 (the street after the songtheaw station and market), then turn left into a small street halfway up. This hotel offers the cheapest rooms in town in a fairly quiet location; 120B with fan/bath and 180B for A/C. The owners seem like they would much rather be somewhere else. The hotel is located about 500 m from the bus station.
Numchai, ☎ (036) 411 724, at 63/32 Khong Tham Road, directly opposite the bus station has rooms with fan and bath for 180B, and A/C starts at 380B/450B.
Montri, ☎ (036) 411 523, at 309/3 Phaholythin Road is 1 km from the centre of town. Turn left onto Wongto Road and keep going through the traffic lights. The hotel is on the left hand side a few hundred metres past this intersection. Rooms cost 220B with fan and 350B/450B for A/C.

Eat and Meet

Ruanpae Restaurant The restaurant is on a boat sitting in the river and serves delicious meals in the 40B to 200B price range and has an English menu. The restaurant is just to the west of the Post Office and Police Station — keep an eye out for the lights, it is not difficult to miss.
Chainat Market is situated just off Phrompraserd Road and is a good place for cheap meals, as are the food vendors that set up around the bus station in the evening.
Icecream Restaurant is in front of the Namchai Hotel.

Central

Chainat Muni National Museum   พิพิธภัณฑ์สถานแห่งชาติชัยนาทมุนี

The museum is in the grounds of **Wat Phra Borommathat** and displays artifacts excavated within the province. From Chainat, exit via Wonto Road and turn right at the traffic lights onto Route 340. After a few kilometres turn left onto Route 3183 and within a few hundred metres you will see a sign on the left hand side. Buses to Singburi pass by the turn-off.

Chainat Bird Park   สวนนกชัยนาท

Reputedly has the largest cage in Asia and has a whole range of other tacky tourist attractions. The park is worth a look for keen birdwatchers and for those who like giant bird statues decorating their gardens. The park is on Route 32, to the northeast of Chainat.

 ◄ Arriving and Departing ►

From Chainat, buses are generally heading north or south or to one of the nearby local towns. An old bus to **Singburi** costs 17B and takes around 1½ hours and a bus to **Ang Thong** costs 17B. Around town in a tuk tuk should cost 10B.

UTHAI THANI PROVINCE

This province of 7,700 sq km is situated in the southern region of northern Thailand. Very little visited by foreign visitors, the province is well forested and mountains dominate the landscape in the western reaches. Those who decide to visit this area of Thailand will not find themselves regretting their decision.

UTHAI THANI   อุทัยธานี

Situated on the banks of the Chao Phraya River, this extremely friendly town is some 220 km north of Bangkok and gets about half a farang a year judging by the 'Hey Farang' criteria. Although a little off the beaten track, Uthai Thani is still a nice place to relax in, with several interesting sights, and acts as a necessary base for the more adventurous who would like to explore the beautiful western part of the province with its many caves, waterfalls, mountains and the Huay Kha Khaeng Wildlife Reserve.

Vital Information

Post Office is about five minutes walk past the Piboonsuk Hotel on Si Uthai Road.
Banks are found around the interesting traffic circles, see the map for details.
Codes Uthai Thani's telephone code is (056) and the postal code is 61000.

Cheap Sleeps

Piboonsuk Hotel at 336 Si Uthai Road, singles/doubles are 150B/170B. The staff are friendly and the clean rooms have a fan and toilet although those on the street side can be very noisy. The hotel is a 20 minute walk or 15B samlor ride from the bus station.
Huay Thai Hotel at 37 Sakakrang Road, this is your only other choice in town and is situated within the market. Basic rooms are 60B per person. The hotel is not easy to find

and has no English sign. To find it, walk towards the river from the fish roundabout and take the second alley way on the right, after a few metres, you will emerge into the market. Take the first courtyard on the right.

Eat and Meet

There is an excellent **night market** which is very popular with the locals next to the footbridge, with tables overlooking the river. The equally good **day market** in the same area has a wide range of fascinating food where you can sit and eat freshly caught catfish, eels and terrapins, crunch on a few charcoal grilled beetles dipped in *nam phrik* sauce and watch the long tail boats carting their market wares with the lush Thepo island and its wat in the background. Brilliant!

Beside the **Sun Mart supermarket** is a place modelled on the Carte D'or chain which serves **great ice cream**.

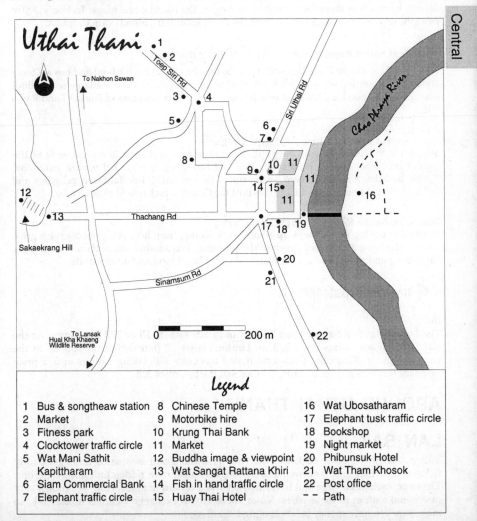

Legend

1	Bus & songtheaw station	8	Chinese Temple	16	Wat Ubosatharam
2	Market	9	Motorbike hire	17	Elephant tusk traffic circle
3	Fitness park	10	Krung Thai Bank	18	Bookshop
4	Clocktower traffic circle	11	Market	19	Night market
5	Wat Mani Sathit Kapittharam	12	Buddha image & viewpoint	20	Phibunsuk Hotel
6	Siam Commercial Bank	13	Wat Sangat Rattana Khiri	21	Wat Tham Khosok
7	Elephant traffic circle	14	Fish in hand traffic circle	22	Post office
		15	Huay Thai Hotel	– –	Path

Things to do **and** Sights to See

Wat Ubonsatharam   วัดอุโบสถาราม

Wat Bot to the locals, situated directly opposite the market area on Ko Thepo, a large wooded island in the middle of the Chao Phraya River. It is reached by a footbridge from where you could easily use up half a roll of film on the view of the town centre and market, the floating houses stretching out down the river and the wat itself nestled amongst the trees.

There are some interesting murals of scenes from Buddhas life, dating from the 18th Century, the best ones being inside the main shrine, which is usually locked. If you are dressed properly and ask politely, there should be no problems being let in. Otherwise there are several old chedis and stupas to be seen although the grotty aviary in front of the main temple and the felling of several of the islands ancient trees cannot be doing much for the abbot's karma. Still there are enough trees to give the island a real jungle feel only 200 m from the town centre, and a nice walk can be taken around the islands various tracks.

Wat Mani Sathit Kapittharam   วัดมณีสถิตย์กปิฏฐาราม

Known as Wat Thung Kaeo, this wat is next to the clocktower roundabout and has a Khmer styled prang housing some Buddha bits. Within the main shrine there is a large seated Buddha and a holy pond, the water of which was used in the coronations of Rama VI and Rama VII.

Wat Sangkat Rattana Khiri   วัดสังกัสรัตนคีรี

Situated at the foot of Sakae Krang Hill (*Khao Sakae Krang*) about a 20 minute walk or 15B samlor ride from the centre of town, this wat has a highly regarded bronze Sukhothai Period Buddha. It is also famous as the site of the colourful 'Tak Bat Devo' religious and folklore festival (meaning to fill the bowls of the Gods!) which is held each October.

Wat Khao Sakae Krang   วัดเขาสะแกรัง

Perched at the top of 400 steps up Khao Sakae Krang, from here you can observe a great view of the town and indeed much of the province. It is another one of those classic Thai, Meakhong and sunset spots, with plenty of well placed food and drink stands.

◀ Arriving and Departing ▶

Bus

The bus to **Nakhon Sawan** takes 1 hour and costs either 13B or 17B depending on the bus. To **Singburi** a bus costs 30B, to **Lopburi** costs 9B (but they drop you off at the turn-off) and to **Bangkok** by air-conditioned bus costs 97B, taking 4 hours or 57B in an ordinary bus which takes 5 hours. To **Lan Sak** the bus costs 20B.

AROUND UTHAI THANI

LAN SAK

This market town, some 60 km to the west of Uthai Thani is situated amongst paddy fields and orchids and is surrounded by jungle coated, cave ridden limestone outcrops. The town itself has a large and lively market and a certain remote feeling — farangs very rarely make it out to these parts. **Note:** There are no exchange facilities in Lan Sak, so make sure you have money before leaving Uthai Thani.

Cheap Sleeps

Lan Sak's is best visited as a day trip from Uthai Thani, but if you stay, there is the **Bunga-low Hotel**. Grotty rooms with fan and bath cost 200B. To find it, walk through the market, turn left in front of the supermarket then take the first right. When you see the malaria clinic on the right take the alleyway opposite and you will see an English sign reading "Bungalow".

Things to do ◆ and Sights to See

The surrounding cave systems are too numerous to list exhaustively and many are barely explored, but some of the more accessible are as follows:

Khao Phraya Phai Rua วัดพระยาพายเรือ

Get off the bus 2 km before Lan Sak on Route 3282 (there is a sign in English) and walk or hitch the 4 km of dirt track to **Wat Khao Phraya Phai Rua** at the foot of the Chinese junk shaped mount. The friendly monks have installed several kilometres of electric cable in the caves, which may ruin the cave for serious speliologists but makes life easy for the average tourist and they will be glad to guide you through for a donation to the temple fund. Do not bother trying to explore the cave alone, as even with all the lighting, chances are you will still get lost in the labyrinth. There are many large caverns with good stalactite and stalagmite formations interconnected by passages often less than one metre high! It would take all day to explore the entire cave system here. The donation box is at the foot of the staircase and, if it is too late to return to Uthai Thani, the monks will let you sleep at the wat.

Khao Khong Chai เขาฆ้องชัย

This also has some great caves and nice walks around the mountain. Get off the bus five kilometres before Lan Sak when you see the sign on your left. It's a short walk to the mount.

Khao Pha Raet

Around 8 km before Lan Sak, again on the left and again signposted in English. This mountain is close to the road and even has a small collection of food and drink stalls. Also around 8 km from Lan Sak is a turn-off to the left which leads to I-sa and Sai Boi Waterfalls and further cave systems. As usual the turn-off is signposted in English.

Huay Kha Khaeng Wildlife Sanctuary เขตรักษาพันธุ์สัตว์ป่าห้วยขาแข้ง

Continuing along Route 3282 for another 30 km or so after Lan Sak you will reach the entrance to Huay Kha Khaeng. This recently declared sanctuary has an area of just over 2,500 sq km and was declared a World Heritage Site on December 13, 1991. The park borders with Tak and Kanchanaburi Provinces and contains mountains, virgin forest, prairies and many species of wild animals, including elephants, tigers and gibbons. The facilities are as yet mainly undeveloped, and potential visitors would be best to contact the Royal Forestry Department before attempting to visit.

◀ Arriving and Departing ▶

Bus

Buses leave regularly from **Uthai Thani** bus station and the 1½ hour trip costs 20B. In Lan Sak the bus station is in front of the market.

NAKHON SAWAN PROVINCE

This province is regarded as one of the gateways to Northern Thailand and covers an area of just over 9,500 sq km. Located around 240 km from Bangkok, Nakhon Sawan at one stage played an important part in the timber trade with larger barges from further north being broken up and transferred onto smaller barges for the journey south. With the ban on logging which is now supposedly in force, this trade has dwindled off to nothing but the town continues to bustle along. There are a number of sights which could keep you busy for a day before proceeding further north or south and it does serve as a junction for those splitting off towards Tak to the west rather than heading straight north towards Chiang Mai.

NAKHON SAWAN   นครสวรรค์

This large city marks the confluence of four rivers, the Ping, Wang, Nan and Yom, which mix to form the Chao Phraya River which then snakes its way down to Bangkok. The provincial capital has little to tantalise the traveller except for a spectacular view from the nearby hilltop wat of Wat Cham Khiri Nak Phrot and an equally appealing waterfront market. The area surrounding the town has a number of interesting sights for those wanting to see a less touristy view of Thailand.

The one time of the year when Nakhon Sawan really goes off is during the Dragon and Lion Parade when the hotels are booked solid and everyone goes a bit mad for a while! See below for details.

Vital Information

Post Office is at the intersection of Kosi and Atthakawee Road.
Banks They line Suchada and Kosi Roads, see map for details.
Codes Nakhon Sawan's telephone code is (056) and the postal code is 60000.

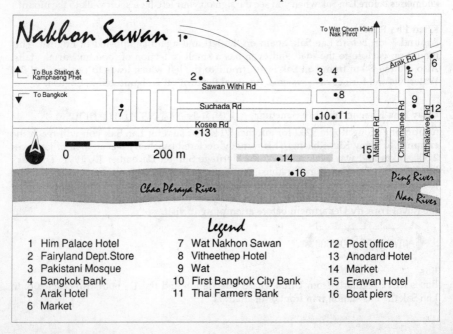

Legend

1 Him Palace Hotel	7 Wat Nakhon Sawan	12 Post office
2 Fairyland Dept.Store	8 Vitheethep Hotel	13 Anodard Hotel
3 Pakistani Mosque	9 Wat	14 Market
4 Bangkok Bank	10 First Bangkok City Bank	15 Erawan Hotel
5 Arak Hotel	11 Thai Farmers Bank	16 Boat piers
6 Market		

Cheap Sleeps

None of the hotels in Nakhon Sawan are especially great deals, but the cheapest has the best position - figure that one out!

Erawan Hotel is by the water towards the eastern end of the market — look for the large restaurant downstairs. Reasonably clean and tidy rooms start at 150B with fan.

Anondard Hotel at 473-479 Kosi Road, ☎ (056) 221 844, has A/C doubles for 260B. The rooms are clean and well kept.

Vitheethep Hotel at 159/1 Sawanwithee Road, ☎ (056) 222 733, has A/C rooms for 290B.

Eat and Meet

The best place for a cheap meal with atmosphere is the **market** by the river, open from early morning to late at night. The restaurant at the **Erawan Hotel** does passable food, and **Fairyland Mall** has a few good sit down options and Western junk food places. The **market** on Arak Road does decent pig skin soup for those interested.

Things to do and Sights to See

Wat Chom Khiri Nak Phrak   วัดจอมคีรีนาคพรต
Just to the north of town, the view from this monastery atop the hill is very nice, allowing one to see the town and Chao Phraya River. The steps lead up to a wat which was built by the Burmese following their sacking of Ayutthaya to demonstrate that they too believed in Buddhism. The start of the steps is a 15 to 20 minute walk from the centre of town.

Wat Woranat Banphot   วัดวรนารถบรรพต
This old monastery is located at the base of the Khop Mountain, was built during the Sukhothai Period and houses a replica of the Buddha's foot. Like Wat Chom Khiri Nak Phrak, the view from the top of the peak is well worth seeing for a scenic view of Nakhon Sawan and the surrounds. It is also a popular place for afternoon revelry and relaxing.

Utthayan Sawan   อุทยานสวรรค์
This park is located within the municipal area and is very popular amongst the locals seeking a bit of R&R. There is a small island located in the centre of the park and there are loads of food and drinks available around the park. This is an ideal place for a relaxing walk.

Bung Boraphet   บึงบอระเพ็ด
This is the largest source of freshwater fish in all of Thailand. Depending on the water levels, it is best described as a small lake or large swamp. By the side of the lake there is a small museum and an aquarium dedicated to the contents of the lake. Situated about 9 km from Nakhon Sawan, the best way to visit the lake is by the boat which departs from behind the market on the Chao Phraya River.

Dragon and Lion Parade   ประเพณีแห่เจ้า
This is an annual event held in the streets of Nakhon Sawan between 28 January and 3 February. The colourful Chinese celebration takes place to honour the revered golden dragon deity. During this time the streets are full of processions led by the appropriate dragon and lion dances, and filled with many images of other Chinese deities.

Central

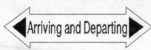

Train
The train station is 3 km out of town, and green songtheaw costs 5B to town. This stop marks the half way point between Bangkok and Chiang Mai. For price and timetable information, refer to the end of the chapter.

Bus
The bus to **Uthai Thani** costs 13B to 17B depending on the type of bus and the bus to **Lopburi** costs 13B. Yellow songtheaws around town cost 5B.

LOPBURI PROVINCE

Lopburi has made its way into the Thai history books on numerous occasions. The Khmer empire got their hands on it in the 10th Century, holding power in the region till the mid 13th Century. Then the Thais were eager to be recognised as an independent state and, moving south, defeated the Burmese and took control of the city. As a result, many of the ancient ruins in and around Lopburi possess distinct Khmer and Hindu characteristics, although over time many have been transformed into Buddhist monuments. Lopburi made the news again in 1664 when King Narai made it the second capital after Ayutthaya. At that time the French were roaming around and this influence can be seen, however slight, in some of the buildings in Lopburi. Although most visitors spend only an afternoon here before pushing onto Chiang Mai, you could easily justify spending a whole day or two exploring the ruins and sights of Lopburi Province.

LOPBURI   ลพบุรี

Lopburi town is split into two very distinct sections, the old and the new. The old town centres around the Kala Shrine and is generally completely overrun by monkeys, whilst the new town is out to the east, centred around a massive roundabout and is home to the bus station and arguably the worst placed tourist office in all of Thailand.

Vital Information

Tourist Office As stated above, this office is one of the worst located in all of Thailand. At around 4 km from the train station it is a must visit only for those who need it desperately. The indifferent staff do not increase the value. The TAT Office is best reached by tuk tuk or samlor and will cost about 10B to reach from the bus station.
Post Office The main post office and telephone centre is 200 m west of the pink roundabout heading towards the old city on Phra Narai Maharat Road. A second smaller post office is to the north of the old city on Prang Samyod Road, but it closes at 4.30 pm.
Banks Most of the banks are in the old city whilst in the new city there are a couple of branches around the first (pink) roundabout.
Codes Lopburi's telephone code is (036) and the postal code is 15000.

Monkey attacked by travel writer!
Watch out for the monkeys around the Kala Shrine in Lopburi. One of the researchers (who will remain anonymous) was bitten by a monkey after it refused to give back her headband. The worst offenders are kept in solitary confinement around the perimeter of the enclosure.

Cheap Sleeps

Your best bet for a bed is in one of the monkey infested places near the train station.
Asia Lopburi Hotel is the best with singles/doubles with fan and shower for 140B/190B.
Jukthip Hotel is near the station. It has no English sign, so keep an eye out for the hotel foyer. Dingy rooms start at 120B and the hotel has a busy night trade.
Nett Hotel has clean rooms and friendly staff. Single rooms with fan and shower cost 120B.
Supornphong Hotel is the closest hotel to the train station and has a definite monkey problem. Rooms start at 100B/120B and are small and dingy.
Rama Plaza Hotel, ☎ (036) 411 663, at 4 Ban Pom Road has rooms with fan for 250B and A/C for 320B.
Taipei Hotel at 24/6-7 Surasongkhram Road has large and very clean rooms starting at 140B for fan and 220B for A/C.
Muang Luang Hotel at 1/5-7 Prang Sam Yod Road has large noisy rooms for 120B.

◀ **Eat and Meet** ▶

Boon Baley is by the India Hotel. The staff seem to have a habit of getting out of the wrong side of the bed each day and serve breakfast and food for the rest of the day.
The best place to eat in town is the **open air eateries** by the train station, but be prepared to be deafened by passing trains and **rice and noodle shops** abound.
Ice cream There are quite a few ice cream restaurants around the old city. A couple of vendors by the train station sell mouth watering scoops of ice cream at 5B per scoop.

Things to do ◀and▶ Sights to See

Narai Ratchaniwet Palace   พระนารายณ์ราชนิเวศน์

Construction of this palace was commenced during the rule of King Narai of Ayutthaya in 1665 and was completed in 1677. Following the death of King Narai in 1688, the palace was used for the coronation of the King's successor and was then deserted until restoration works were undertaken by King Mongkut in 1863.

Although the buildings within the high walled-in enclosure are in a state of ruins, the grounds are still in a very well kept state and are pleasant to wander through. Within the grounds of the palace (which the King used as a summer retreat for up to six months of the year) there are the remnants of elephant and horse stables, a large water reservoir and a series of halls which King Narai once used to store all his goodies. At the southern end of the outer palace grounds is the remains of what was probably an audience hall used by King Narai to greet well regarded visitors.

Further into the palace enclosure you will reach the **Chantara Phisan Pavilion**. Originally built by King Narai as his own royal residence, it was transformed into another audience hall after King Narai moved his residence to the Suttha Sawan Pavilion in the southwest corner of the enclosure. This building is considered to be a fine example of classic Thai style architecture and was restored by King Mongkut in 1863 and now is home to a collection of Thai artifacts. Behind the pavilion in what was once part of the women's quarters is a display of rural Thai life and rural technology

To the south of the Chantara Phisan Pavilion is the **Dusit Sawan Thanya Maha Prasat Hall**. Built by King Narai for the reception of particularly important VIPs, this hall was where he probably greeted *Chevalier de Chaumont*, the representative of Louis XIV (b.1638 d.1715). Although the roof is long gone, it is believed that the original structure

Central

Central

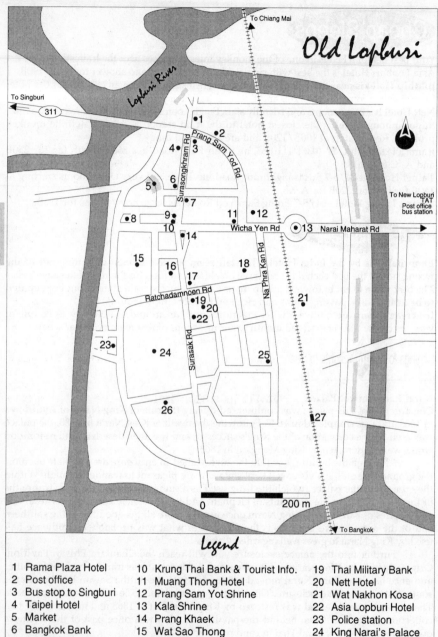

To Chiang Mai

Old Lopburi

To Singburi

Lopburi River

311

To New Lopburi
TAT
Post office
bus station

1 Rama Plaza Hotel
2 Post office
3 Bus stop to Singburi
4 Taipei Hotel
5 Market
6 Bangkok Bank
7 Bank of Ayudhya
8 Constantine Phaulkon's
  House
9 Thai Farmers Bank

Prang Sam Yod Rd
Surasongkhram Rd
Wicha Yen Rd
Narai Maharat Rd
Na Phra Kan Rd
Ratchadamnoen Rd
Surasak Rd

0   200 m

To Bangkok

Legend

1 Rama Plaza Hotel
2 Post office
3 Bus stop to Singburi
4 Taipei Hotel
5 Market
6 Bangkok Bank
7 Bank of Ayudhya
8 Constantine Phaulkon's
  House
9 Thai Farmers Bank
10 Krung Thai Bank & Tourist Info.
11 Muang Thong Hotel
12 Prang Sam Yot Shrine
13 Kala Shrine
14 Prang Khaek
15 Wat Sao Thong
16 Market
17 Siam Commercial Bank
18 Wat Indra
= Fortifications (old city walls)
19 Thai Military Bank
20 Nett Hotel
21 Wat Nakhon Kosa
22 Asia Lopburi Hotel
23 Police station
24 King Narai's Palace
   & National Museum
25 Supraphong Hotel
26 Wat Kawit
27 Train station

was formed by a multi-tiered roof topped by a tall spire similar in style to many Bangkok mondops. What is left of the building is considered to be a meld of Thai and French architectural styles.

In the far southwestern corner of the palace is the **Suttha Sawan Pavilion** which became King Narai's new residence when he moved from the Chantara Phisan Pavilion, and he lived here till his death on 11 July 1688. Before he died he dedicated both this pavilion and its immediate surrounding grounds to a monastery in order to protect it from plotters awaiting his death. The pavilion was recorded as originally being surrounded by beautiful gardens and fountains, some of the landscaping of which is still evident.

In 1856 during the reign of King Rama IV, the palace grounds were restored and the **Phiman Mongkut Pavilion** was built which was used as King Rama IV's residence whenever he visited. The three storey brick building is linked to three other buildings, all of which are now used as part of the Lopburi National Museum.

The **Lopburi National Museum** contains a good range of Lopburi Period sculpture and artifacts along with a range of historic goods relating to the visits by the French.

Admission to the grounds of King Narai's palace is 10B and the museum is open Wednesday to Sunday 9.00 am to 4.00 pm.

Central

Statue of King Narai the Great
This statue is situated at the entrance of town and was erected in honour of the same named King who has been credited with, amongst other things, being the first Thai monarch to establish diplomatic relations with France and to pursue a friendly policy towards foreigners, especially Europeans. The monument is at the centre of the large roundabout to the west of the historic centre of town.

Phra Prang Sam Yot   ปรางค์สามยอด
Translated to mean the 'Wat of Three Prangs', this structure is regarded as the landmark of Lopburi. Once a Hindu site, the structure is constructed of laterite and sandstone and the prangs are said to represent the Hindu Trinity of Brahma, Vishnu and Shiva. During the reign of King Narai the site was converted to a Buddhist temple and some ruined Lopburi Period Buddhas remain as evidence of this. The southern prang is probably the best kept of the three with decorative carving still visible. Like many sites in Lopburi, Phra Prang Sam Yot is at times overrun by monkeys. The shrine is near the Muang Thong Hotel, opposite the Kala Shrine.

San Phra Kan (Kala Shrine)   ศาลพระกาฬ
This shrine is not particularly old but highly revered. Built in 1951, the central shrine contains a stone statue of Vishnu with Buddha's head on it. The statue is completely covered in gold leaf but is still fairly unremarkable. What is more remarkable here is the number of monkeys. Monkeys here are such a problem that the entire area has had to be caged in to try and contain them and thus avoid too many flat monkeys on the road outside. Those who have a fear of monkeys may want to bypass this particular site as it is literally crawling in obese cheeky monkeys who will leap at you at every possible moment, and do not let any of your possessions lay unattended, as they will soon be claimed by one of the furry critters. The Kala Shrine in just west of the railroad tracks at the centre of the roundabout on Phra Narai Maharat Road, you cannot miss it.

Prang Khaek   ปรางค์แขก
This small ruin was, like Prang Sam Yot, originally a Hindu shrine and has been restored on a number or occasions. The site consists of three small brick prangs which are regarded as the oldest Khmer prangs found in Central Thailand. The site is on Vichayen Road near the Ratchaniwet Palace.

Central

Wat Nakhon Kosa   วัดนครโกษา

This wat was originally constructed by the Khmers and the Lopburi style prang out front was built in 1157. Once again this site may have originally been a Hindu site as U Thong Buddha images found here are believed to be predated by the rest of the structure. The shrine is fairly run down now and the restoration work has been somewhat haphazard. Wat Nakhon Kosa can be found just to the north of the railway station, near the Kala Shrine.

Wat Phra Si Rattana Mahathat   วัดพระศรีรัตนมหาธาติ

This historically and archeologically important site is believed to have been founded during the 12th Century whilst the Khmers were still in Lopburi. The prang is the tallest in Lopburi and is distinct from its northeastern contemporaries in that it is tall and slender. Built of laterite, much of the decorative work is eroded though some lintels and stucco work are still evident, allowing one to conjure up an image of what at one time must have been an impressive construction. The wat was restored by the Thai Fine Arts department and admission is 20B. The wat is directly across from the train station.

Constantine Phaulkon's Residence (Vichayen House)   บ้านวิชาเยนทร์

Originally constructed by King Narai as a residence for *Chevalier de Chaumont*, who was the first French ambassador to Thailand, its most famous resident was *Constantine Phaulkon* who maintained influence from 1675 to 1688. A Greek advisor who held the ear of King Narai, in 1688, as the King was on his deathbed, Phaulkon was assassinated by Luang Sorasak during a power struggle. The buildings are roofless but the grounds are very well kept and are worth wandering through to see the distinctly European style architecture. The grounds contain his residence to the left, a church in the centre and a reception hall on the right along with the remains of water tanks and fountains. Admission is a bit steep at 20B. Constantine's House can be found on Vichayen Road.

Wat Sao Thong Thong   วัดเสาธงทอง

This wat represents a meld of Buddhist and Gothic architecture. The wihaan and central Buddha image are of the Ayutthaya Period, however when King Narai restored the wat he altered the windows into a gothic style giving the building a quite bizarre appearance. The wat is to the north of the Royal Palace.

Lopburi Zoo   สวนสัตว์ลพบุรี

Situated to the rear of the Army theatre near the large roundabout this zoo has a small collection of animals (other than monkeys) and is a quiet and pleasant place to spend a few hours. Open Daily from 8.00 am to 6.00 pm, admission is 10B.

◀ **Arriving and Departing** ▶

Getting Around

Small green and blue buses travel Phra Narai Maharat Road between the old and the new town and cost 3B. Tuk Tuks and samlors cost between 10B and 20B depending on distance.

Train

Lopburi is on the main line to Chiang Mai, so if you are on a tight schedule, it is possible to leave Bangkok or Ayutthaya on an early train, spend the day in Lopburi, then hop on one of the night trains to Chiang Mai. You can leave your bags at Lopburi station for 5B. For detailed timetable and price information, refer to the end of the chapter.

Bus

The bus station in Lopburi is in the new city on the south side of the pink roundabout. If arriving from the old city, cross Phra Narai Maharat Road via the elevated footpath, take the street on your left and left again, then hey presto, you are there. A/C buses leave for Bangkok regularly from here, whilst most of the other regional destinations are served by non A/C buses. You may want to look at the grisly photographic display at the station, it supposedly acts as a deterrent to dangerous drivers.

Buses leave **Bangkok** for Lopburi every 20 minutes from the Northern bus station, cost 40B and take around 3 hours. From **Ayutthaya**, buses leave every 10 minutes and take 2 hours for 19B. Buses to **Nakhon Sawan** take 1 hour for 13B, to **Saraburi** cost 13B, to **Uthai Thani** cost 9B, to **Suphanaburi** the 3 hour trip costs 25B, and the buses are particularly bad, although the scenery is great. If you are planning on getting to Suphanaburi in time to make the connection to Kanchanaburi, it is imperative that you catch a bus from Lopburi by 12.00 noon if you want to have any chance of making the connection.

AROUND LOPBURI

Wat Phra Phutthabat   วัดพระพุทธบาท

Literally translated, this means 'Buddha Footprint' and that is exactly what this shrine houses. During the rule of King Song Kham of Ayutthaya, a Buddha's footprint was discovered and it is now considered to be one of the most significant discoveries in Thailand. The shape is unusual, looking more like a coffin than a footprint (Buddha must have had a heavy pack on the day he made this one). The footprint is kept in an exotic golden shrine decorated with thousands of glittering coloured glass pieces. The temple behind the shrine has a large sitting Buddha backed by a smaller reclining Buddha.

The shrine is within Saraburi Province (31 km from Saraburi) but it is just as easy to visit from Lopburi, and Lopburi makes for a more pleasant base than Saraburi. If you have seen all of Lopburi's sights in the morning, this makes for a fine afternoon excursion. A bus from either direction will let you off on Route 310 (5B normal bus, 20B for an A/C bus). From where you are dropped off, walk west (towards Lopburi) for a few hundred metres and turn left and walk for just under another kilometre (you will be able to see the shrine in the distance). A tuk tuk will cost 10B to 20B to get you there five minutes faster.

Wat Lai   วัดไลย์

This wat dates back to the Ayutthaya Period and the central shrine houses a statue of Phra Si Ariya. Further along the road on the front, back and inside walls of a crumbling pigeon infested wihaan are examples of well preserved and highly regarded stucco reliefs giving a visual interpretation of Buddha's life and first sermon. A small Buddha footprint also sits within the confines of the wihaan.

Located 24 km from Lopburi, catch a bus for 7B bound for Singburi along Route 311, getting off just after the town of Tha Wung. Take a right hand turn (Route 3028) for 6 km on the next bus, costing 3B and jump off at the fork in the road. Walk down the left fork for a few hundred metres to reach the wat's entrance. The effort needed to reach the wat is not really worth it unless you have some time to kill or just feel like wandering around.

SARABURI PROVINCE

This little visited province is no more than a train stop for most travellers who are heading further afield to the likes of Khorat and Nong Khai. Bordered to the west by Ayutthaya, Lopburi to the north, Nakhon Ratchasima to the east and Nakhon Nayok and Pathum Thani to the south, the province is probably best known as the home of the Tham Krabok Buddhist Monk Sanctuary.

SARABURI   สระบุรี

Saraburi is a ordinary large Thai city and the only reason you would want to visit would be to see what an ordinary large Thai city looks like. There are some sights in the province but these are more pleasantly and often more easily visited from elsewhere. The town is 108 km from Bangkok and was founded in the 16th Century.

Vital Information

Banks Plenty of banks are along both Phaholythin and Sutbanthat Roads.
Police Station is at the northeastern end of Phaholythin Road.
Codes Saraburi's telephone code is (036) and the postal code is 18000.

Cheap Sleeps

Saraburi Hotel is opposite the bus station on Sutbanthat Road and has rooms with fan for 230B/280B and A/C rooms for 320B/380B and the VIP rooms start at 500B.
Kaew Un Hotel on Phaholythin Road has rooms starting at 250B and is about 400 m from the bus station.
Sansuk Hotel If you are desperate, this hovel will give you a very noisy and dirty room for 100B/170B with fan. It also acts as a brothel and is located 800 m from the bus station.

Eat and Meet

Food vendors set up every night along Tesaban Road between Phaholythin Road and the railway station. During the day the **market** on Sut Banthat Road has plenty of food.

Things to do **and** Sights to See

Khao Sam Lan National Park   อุทยานแห่งชาติเขาสามหลั่น

Established in June 1981, this National Park 16 km from Saraburi has three waterfalls, Namtok Sam Lan, Namtok Pho Hin Dat and Namtok Ton Rak Sai. Due to its proximity to Bangkok, it is popular with Bangkok residents as a weekend retreat and also amongst birdwatchers who come to seek out the 80 odd species inhabiting the park. To reach the park, take the Bangkok road out of town for 6 km then turn right at the 102 km marker.

Wat Phra Phutthachai   วัดพระพุทธฉาย

This monastery is in the same direction as the above mentioned National Park and is known for the shadow of a Buddha image on a cliff. To reach the monastery, follow the Bangkok Road from Saraburi, take the right turn to the National Park and follow it for 4 km, then turn left for the monastery and follow the signs.

Tham Krabok Buddhist Monk Sanctuary   สำนักสงฆ์ถ้ำกระบอก

This is 25 km from town along Phaholythin Road, heading towards Lopburi. The monastery has been the cause of much controversy because it is a treatment centre for people with narcotics dependency problems, and the treatment, which involves herbal ingestion, is controversial to say the least, with the attendees often being virtually tortured in an effort to rid them of evil spirits. Nevertheless, the centre claims a staggering success rate amongst those who complete the treatment. The centre was established by a Buddhist nun, Mae-chii Mian, and has been run by Luang Phaw Chamrun Prachon for the past 37 years.

Wat Phra Phutthabat
See the Lopburi section for details on visiting this interesting wat.

◀ **Arriving and Departing** ▶

Train
For detailed price and timetable information, refer to the end of the chapter.

Bus
This large provincial centre services most major destinations. **Lopburi** costs 13B and takes about an hour, the bus to **Nakhon Nayok** is particularly ancient and costs 16B taking about 1½ hours and the bus to **Ayutthaya** costs 18B for 2½ hours.

NAKHON NAYOK PROVINCE

Nakhon Nayok Province covers an expanse of over 2,130 sq km, much of which is densely forested hills and mountains. Some parts of the province are covered by National Parks whilst other areas are dedicated to golf courses and botanical gardens. Little known to foreign visitors, Nakhon Nayok is quite popular amongst the more outdoor orientated Thais and you could easily spend a few days exploring the province.

NAKHON NAYOK   นครนายก

Established during the Dvaravati Period, the name Nakhon Nayok refers to a eastern garrison town of Ayutthaya during the reign of King U Thong. The provincial capital is some 106 km north of Bangkok making it an ideal weekend escape for holidaying Thais.

The town itself is fairly small and laid back and makes an ideal base from where to explore the nearby waterfalls, Khao Yai National Park and the botanical gardens. Prachinburi is 27 km to the southeast and Saraburi is 58 km to the northwest.

Vital Information

Tourist Office, ☎ (037) 312 282, a new office is at 84/23 Suwannasorn Road, 150 m left of the bus station (when facing the road). The staff here are very helpful.
Post Office The river end of Chaiapan Road. The phone office is open 8.30 am to 4.30 pm.
Banks more than enough to choose from, see the map for details.
Police Station on the corner of Banyai and Chaiapan Roads.
Codes Nakhon Nayok's telephone code is (037) and the postal code is 26000.

Cheap Sleeps

There are three hotels in town but most Thai tourists stay near the waterfalls in more expensive lodgings.
Kobkua Palace, ☎ (037) 311 633, at 420 Tongchai Si Muang Road. This hotel is the best choice in town with its sparkling, quiet rooms and it is also close to the market. Rooms with fan, large bathroom with balcony cost 200B whilst A/C starts at 600B.
White House Hotel on Suwannasorn Road is fairly new and is the closest to the bus station. Basic clean rooms cost 300B with A/C. They also have more expensive rooms.

Panchai Hotel, ☎ (037)311 399, at 342/1 Suwannasorn Road has rooms in the 350B to 500B range, but beware the noise from the road and the happening tunes pumping out of the karaoke bar downstairs.

North Bungalow, ☎ (037) 311 814, at 145 Mu 5 Sorika Road is located way out of town, 3 km up the road towards Nang Rong Waterfall. Rooms cost between 180B and 380B. Look for the white sign with red Thai writing.

Eat and Meet

Street vendors are spread out all over town and the market is a great place to pick up a tasty meal, though you may want to pass on the fried cockroaches. A **night food market** sets up on Tongchai Road every evening.

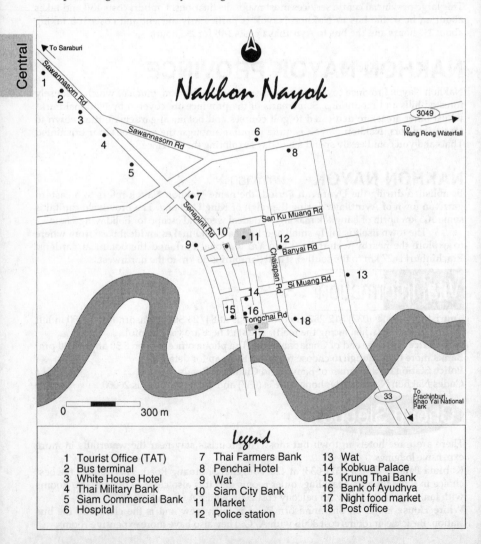

Legend

1	Tourist Office (TAT)	7	Thai Farmers Bank
2	Bus terminal	8	Penchai Hotel
3	White House Hotel	9	Wat
4	Thai Military Bank	10	Siam City Bank
5	Siam Commercial Bank	11	Market
6	Hospital	12	Police station

13	Wat
14	Kobkua Palace
15	Krung Thai Bank
16	Bank of Ayudhya
17	Night food market
18	Post office

Waterfalls Gardens and Canoeing
The waterfalls close to Nakhon Nayok are its main attraction and deservedly so. In the rainy season, to say they were impressive would be an understatement, in the dry season they are still worth looking at, but will not make your jaw drop. The best time to visit the falls is during the week, as the weekend can get very crowded.

Namtok Nang Rong   น้ำตกนางรอง
Located 19 km from town at the end of Route 3049, this waterfall passes through many levels, some of which have pools which are suitable to have a splash around in. From the entrance, which costs 5B (30B for a car), follow the road for another 500 m. You can cross a bridge here taking you to the other side and a path to gain a different perspective. A local bus leaves Nakhon Nayok bus terminal every 30 minutes and passes by the market near the bridge (it has pale yellow panelling on the side) for 7B, taking you to the gate.

Wang Takhrai   วังตะไคร้
This is a botanical garden 2 km before Namtok Nang Rong. The gardens cover a few hundred acres with a couple of waterways passing through. It offers a peaceful landscape that you can wander around by following one of the meandering roads or if you want to get wet, hire a truck innertube and float down the small rapids. Entry is 5B per person or 50B for a private car. There is expensive bungalow accommodation available as well as cheaper camping facilities for the budget traveller.

Canoeing
Sarika Canoe Club offers canoeing for all levels of expertise in and around the many waterways flowing into the Nakhon Nayok River. The club can fit you out with everything from canoe or kayak to tuition and advice, but unless you can speak Thai, the message may not be as clear as you had hoped. Set routes range in price from 250B to 400B covering from 2 km to 6½ km journeys in various degrees of rapids and difficulties. For larger groups they can arrange camping and canoeing trips. Sarika Canoe Club is located opposite the entrance to Wang Takhrai, just before the bridge.

Namtok Sarika   น้ำตกสาริกา
At the end of Route 3050, Sarika Waterfall flows over a cliff close to 100 m high. There are protected swimming holes both above and below the main fall. In the wet season the waterfall looks magical and in the dry season, the pools become little more than puddles. Entry is 2B! To get there, catch the local bus heading for Namtok Nang Rong and get off at the Namtok Sarika turn-off which is 12 km from town via Route 3050 and costs 7B. The waterfall is 3 km up at the end of the road. You can either walk, hitch or catch a songtheaw or motorbike taxi for 20B, but you will need to bargain.

Namtok Lon Rak
This waterfall flows over some fairly flat rocks which you can slide down. The turn-off is 7 km along Route 3049, with the waterfall another 5 km down a muddy potholed road. If you do not have your own transport, hitching is the only other option and it can be extremely difficult to get a lift. When you hit an intersection along the trail, take a right. Later on, the road has a well used left hand turn, but you need to keep going straight ahead. Although quite scenic, the waterfall is not really worth the effort required to reach it.

Namtok Wang Muang   น้ำตกวังม่วง
This waterfall is only small, but is set in very pleasant surroundings. Catch a bus headed for Prachinaburi (Route 33) and get off 8 km down the road. A 14 km sealed road to the falls is signposted on the left, and you will need to hitch the 14 km. It is best attempted on the weekend, when the traffic flow is heavier.

Khao Yai National Park
For more information on this excellent National Park, see Khao Yai National Park in the section on Nakhon Ratchasima, Northeast Thailand.

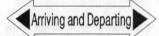
Arriving and Departing

Bus and Songtheaw
Buses leave regularly to most provincial destinations. Buses to **Bangkok** leave every 30 minutes and cost 36B, the bus to **Saraburi** costs 16B and the bus to **Prachinburi** costs 15B. Songtheaws around town cost 3B and motorbike taxis 10B, although Nakhon Nayok is so small that the only time you would really need these is during heavy rain.

PRACHINBURI PROVINCE

Situated about 130 km from Bangkok, this province of almost 5,000 sq km dates back to the 6th Century. Archeological evidence still remains of an ancient city, known as Muang Si Mahosot, in the form of moats, ramparts and both Khmer and Dvaravati artifacts. Today the province is best known for its fruit. Every year at the annual fruit festival, Prachinburi durian, jack fruit and bamboo shoots figure prominently in the awards.

The province is bordered to the south by Chachoengsao Province, to the east by Sa Kaeo, the west by Nakhon Nayok and the north by Nakhon Ratchasima.

PRACHINBURI   ปราจีนบุรี

Prachinburi, known as Prachin to the locals, is a very nondescript town unnecessarily spread over a few kilometres. The most exciting thing to do in town is watch 50 people squashed into a longboat practising their strokes up and down the Bangpakong River. If they are not practising when you are in town, you better have a good book, as there is little else to do.

Prachinburi is 134 km from Bangkok and 27 km from Nakhon Nayok. It can be used as a staging point to Khao Yai National Park, but Nakhon Nayok or Pak Chong (in Nakhon Ratchasima Province) would probably be a better option.

Vital Information

Post Office is 500 m north of the bus station on the main road that connects the railway station and the main bridge.
Banks These are unusually well spaced along both of the above mentioned roads.
Hospital A few hundred metres up the road to the north of the train tracks.
Police Station is 1 km west of the bridge on the main road running parallel to the river.
Codes Prachinburi's telephone code is (037) and the post code is 26000.

Wondering why white elephants are so highly revered? The legend goes that at the time of Buddha's conception, his mother dreamt that a white elephant entered her body bearing a lotus flower, hence symbolising the divine nature of white elephants.

Central

Cheap Sleeps

Bangprakong Hotel, ☎ (037) 211 363, has large clean rooms with wooden floorboards and away from the main traffic noise. Rooms with fan cost 170B, A/C 250B and VIP 300B. From the bus station walk west towards the main road for 150 m and turn right at the fire station (one street before the main road) and walk another 200 m. There is a nightclub and pool hall with full sized tables next door.

Hotel, ☎ (037) 211 012, has dirty, small, dreary rooms costing 80B for a box without a bath, 120B for fan and 350B for A/C. The hotel is on the east side of the main road between the bus station and bridge in the middle of the second block.

Kings Hotel, ☎ (037) 211 188, virtually sits on the north end of the bridge and has very noisy and equally ordinary rooms for 150B with fan and 360B with A/C.

Eat and Meet

There are two **markets** in town both offering cheap and tasty food. The **main market** is a few hundred metres along the road to the north of the train station, the other **market** is on the road parallel to the river, 300 m west of the intersection with the north south main road.

Things to do and Sights to See

Wat Kaeopichit   วัดแก้วพิจิตร
Built in 1879, the main feature of this wat, the ordination hall, was added in 1918. The temple is influenced by various styles including Thai, Chinese, European and Khmer. The outer front and back wall has a stucco relief sculpture of a section of the Ramakien. If you cannot find a monk to open the temple, do not bother, as you will only miss out on seeing some 'lovely' chandeliers. The wat is 1½ km east of the main road on the road north and parallel to the river.

Prachinburi National Museum   พิพิธภัณฑ์สถานแห่งชาติปราจีนบุรี
This museum has a display of ancient artifacts and sculptures which have been excavated within the province and its immediate surrounds. The museum is located 200 m south of the main bridge at the back of the wide boulevard, King Naresuan statue and Provincial Hall. The museum is open Wednesday to Sunday.

Sa Morakot   สะมรกต
If you are a history buff you may want to visit this ancient city where the largest and oldest Buddha footprints in Thailand are located. Carved onto laterite rock, each foot stretches to 3½ m in length and 1½ m in breadth. Each also has the 'Wheel of Dhamma' engraved into them. 'Buddha's first steps' are dated back to the 7th or 8th Century. Within the confines of the ancient city are a few other ruins, mostly little more than piles of rubble. To reach Sa Morakot, catch the bus heading to Chachoengsao along Route 319 for 23 km. There is an information booth there which is open daily and can provide detailed information on the particular sites.

Thap Lan National Park   อุทยานแห่งชาติทับลาน
Literally meaning 'palm', this is what you will find as most of the plants within this 2,240 sq km park are related to the palm family. Unfortunately the once abundant tree

cover has been heavily damaged by illegal logging with some estimates putting the loss of tree cover as high as 30%. The abundant talipot palm was once used to make Buddhist manuscripts. The usual wild animals also roam the park fairly free of human contact because the park is little visited and thus has few facilities. There are some waterfalls within the park boundaries but they are virtually unreachable.

The entrance to the park can be reached via Route 304 which leads to Nakhon Ratchasima (Khorat), the road leads to the north of Kabinburi and the park entrance is 32 km along here, so start hitching. There is no direct public transport to the park, so to reach it you will need to either have your own transport (possibly through the Forestry Department) or hitch in.

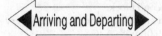

Bus
A bus from Prachinburi to **Nakhon Nayok** costs 15B and a bus to **Sa Kaew** costs 27B.

SA KAEW PROVINCE

This province was fairly recently established in 1993 and it extends all the way to the Cambodian border. The main reasons for visiting this region are the gem markets and the National Parks. At the time of writing it was impossible for foreigners to enter Cambodia at Aranyprathet.

SA KAEW   สระแก้ว

This town is little more than a glorified truck stop, but it leads the way to Pang Sida National Park, 27 km to the north of town. If you are planning to visit the National Park, there is no need to stay the night in Sa Kaew as accommodation is available in the park.

Vital Information

The highway runs through town in a southeast to northwest direction, and buses passing through stop 100 m to the southeast of the market (towards Aranyprathet).
Post Office is directly opposite the hospital and is open from 8.30 am to 4.30 pm.
Banks are spread along the highway.
Hospital is located 150 m southeast of the bus stop on the highway.
Codes Sa Kaew's telephone code is (037) and the postal code is 27000.

Cheap Sleeps

Kavee Hotel, ☎ (037) 241 216, at 43 Sa Kaew Aranyprathet Road is located on the highway 100 m southeast of where the bus lets you off. The rooms are clean, but unless you get an A/C room the noise will drive you crazy. A room with fan costs 200B with A/C 300B and VIP rooms start at 350B.
Sakow Hotel, ☎ (037) 241 024, at 704-5 Sa Kaew Aranyprathet Road. This is directly opposite the bus station on the highway and is recognisable by a red Thai sign with three flags on the top over the entrance to a small alley. As the hotel is not set directly onto the main road, the rooms are a little quieter. Rooms with fan start at 230B and A/C rooms start at 300B.
Chantra Hotel, ☎ (037) 241 711, at 16/2 Sa Kaew Aranyprathet Road. This upmarket hotel (they have a computer at reception) is 150 m southeast of the hospital. A/C rooms start at 400B and VIP rooms start at 550B.

◆ Eat and Meet ▶

The **market** is one block behind the Kavee Hotel, 100 m northeast of the bus stop. **Street vendors** and **shopfront restaurants** can be found along the highway and side streets.

Things to do ◆and◆ Sights to See

Prang Sida National Park   น้ำตกปรางสีดา

Prang Sida National Park has been the location of one of Thailand's more successful conservation programmes. Located 27 km to the north of Sa Kaew on Route 3462, this park covers 844 sq km and was officially opened in 1982. However between 1985 and 1993 the park suffered irreversible damage as the local people from 14 villages who lived within and around the park used illegal logging and poaching to earn their keep. Some of the logging gangs were heavily armed with machine guns and land mines to keep their operation clear of the Thai authorities. All illegal activities are now virtually eradicated as the families were moved out of the park and given land for agricultural use. Poachers were recruited as rangers to protect the park and the loggers were continuously arrested.

The National Park is now open to visitors and the two waterfalls and walks near the park headquarters make for a pleasant day trip whilst the walks and waterfalls further afield require a longer stay in the park. The closest waterfall is the 10 m high Namtok Prang Sida which is only 800 m from the park headquarters and visitors centre. From here two trails lead to Namtok Patakien which is just over 2 km away. Although it carries less water than Prang Sida, it is still picturesque. Both trails have markers inappropriately nailed to trees every 30 m and both are easy to follow except for the initial part where you need to cross the river. The lower trail (red A markers) follows the Klong Nam Khio stream whilst the other trail (yellow B markers) takes a higher route. It is possible to do a round trip using both trails with walking time taking around two hours. If you are lucky, you may stumble across some of the abundant wildlife still alive and well in the park. The visitors centre can provide a guide for 100B per person to take you around.

Cheap Sleeps

Bungalows are available for 600B for six people or you can pitch your own tent. If you do not have your own tent it is possible to hire one for 100B per night. Food and drink are available at the restaurant between the park office and visitors centre.

◀ Arriving and Departing ▶

This is the tricky bit. The National Park is easy to get to, but be prepared to stay the night if you spend too long soaking up the nature. Infrequent songtheaws leave from near the market in Sa Kaew. From the bus stop in Sa Kaew walk 150 m northwest and take the second street on the right. The songtheaws leave from the corner of the first street on the right. One leaves at 9.45 am and if the driver is in a good mood, will take you to the park headquarters for 20B and the trip takes around one hour. If not, the walk in from the turn-off is about 1½ km and the visitor centre is another 100 m up the road. Getting back to Sa Kaew is more difficult as songtheaws do not travel the road back to Sa Kaew in the afternoon, so you may need to hitch back. This is easier than it sounds but the traffic is not particularly heavy. If you are not having any luck, ask the park staff as some of them live in Sa Kaew.

Wildlife Feeding Centre
You may want to try this feeding centre if you have your own transport or are planning on leaving for there in the early morning. It is located 13 km along Route 3485 down the turn-off on your right, just to the north of Prang Sida National Park.

◀ Arriving and Departing ▶

Train
The train station is 1 km north east of the main road through to town. Take the street to the northwest of the bus station with a 7-eleven on the corner. Very slow trains pass twice a day in both directions. Train to Aranyprathet at 10.36 and 17.32 and to Bangkok at 07.29 and 14.36. For detailed price and timetable information refer to the end of the chapter.

Bus
The bus stop is on the main road through town, about 100 m to the southeast of the market. A Bus to **Prachinburi** costs 27B.

ARANYPRATHET   อรัญประเทศ

Aran, as it is affectionately known by the locals, is the most eastern district of Sa Kaew Province, borders with Cambodia and is 48 km from Sa Kaew. It was once a thriving border town profiting from the abundant trade (both legal and illegal) between the two countries, but the Khmer Rouge has put an end to that. Heavy fighting in the surrounding region in Cambodia has brought Aran to its knees as it awaits a breath of new life. Until this breath of fresh air arrives all you will find in town is more tuk tuks, samlors and motorbikes than you can poke a stick at, and a few antique shops. Thais and Cambodians can freely cross the border here, except during times of severe fighting, but foreigners are not allowed to cross (at the time of writing) so there is really little point in visiting here.

Vital Information

Post Office at the northern corner of Suwanasorn and Mahadthai Roads next to the clocktower. The telecom office is open until 10.00 pm.
Banks See the map for the details.
Hospital is opposite the post office on Suwanasorn Road.
Police Station at the northern end of Santiphap Road just past Mahadthai Road.
Codes The telephone code is (037) and the postal code is 27120.

Cheap Sleeps

Aran Garden 1 at the corner of Raduthid and Chitsuwan Roads. Small and average rooms (with a veranda overlooking a rusty roof if you are lucky) have rooms with fan and bath for 120B and 170B with A/C.
Aran Garden 2 at 110 Raduthid Road is a larger and newer version of its partner, but the only difference is that it looks like a hotel and charges more and the staff know how to smile. Rooms with fan and bath start at 160B and rooms with A/C start at 230B.
Inter Hotel, ☎ (037) 231 291, at 108/7 Ban Aran Road is the deluxe model hotel in town charging 400B to 500B for fully equipped rooms. The street is off Raduthid Road 30 m in the opposite direction from Aran Garden 1.

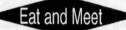

Eat and Meet

Most restaurants/bars will try to dazzle you with their flashing lights - you cannot miss them, but many are as concerned with providing carnal pleasures as a decent meal. **Chitsuwan Road** is home to a few legitimate restaurants and a small night food market. The **daily market** with a few nightly food vendors is on Weruwan Road at the end of Bumrungrad Road.

Things to do and Sights to See

Cambodian Market
Six kilometres from town at the border village of Ban Klong Lok is a market where you can purchase a variety of Cambodian products. Catch a tuk tuk, samlor or taxi to reach the village and you will need to haggle on price

Arriving and Departing

Train
Two trains a day stumble into Aran. Departures to **Bangkok** leave at 6.40 am and 1.45 pm and arrive in Bangkok at 11.30 am and 18.20 pm respectively. For detailed price and timetable information refer to the end of the chapter.

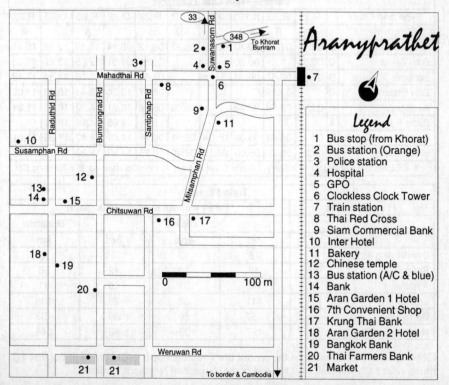

Aranyprathet

Legend
1. Bus stop (from Khorat)
2. Bus station (Orange)
3. Police station
4. Hospital
5. GPO
6. Clockless Clock Tower
7. Train station
8. Thai Red Cross
9. Siam Commercial Bank
10. Inter Hotel
11. Bakery
12. Chinese temple
13. Bus station (A/C & blue)
14. Bank
15. Aran Garden 1 Hotel
16. 7th Convenient Shop
17. Krung Thai Bank
18. Aran Garden 2 Hotel
19. Bangkok Bank
20. Thai Farmers Bank
21. Market

Central

Bus

Being at the end of the road before hitting the border buses are fairly infrequent but there is a way to get out. Buses arriving will either let you off on Bumrungrad Road or Suwanasorn Road, near the clocktower. Buses leave from both places as well. A/C and blue buses leave from Bumrungrad Road and pass the stop on Suwanasorn Road, whilst the orange local non A/C buses leave from Suwanasorn Road. Buses from Buriram and Khorat pass by on Route 348, just north of the orange bus station and you can get on or off here. Buses to **Chanthaburi** cost 55B and take 4 hours to complete the dusty but scenic trip.

Central Train Line Timetable											
Type and Class		R,23	O,23	X,2	O,23	R,23	X,123	R,23	X,12	R,23	R,23
Supplements				A		A,B	AB	A	A,B	B	B
Hualumpong	D	06.40	07.05	08.10	08.30	15.00	18.00	18.10	19.40	20.00	22.00
Don Muang Airport	D	07.27	07.51	08.52	09.19	15.47	18.45	18.57	20.25	20.44	22.47
Bang Pa-in	D		08.29		09.59			19.25			
Ayutthaya	D	08.09	08.42		10.12	16.26	19.24	19.35	21.04	21.24	23.27
Ban Phachi Jn	D	08.27	09.00		10.35	16.45		19.54			23.46
Lopburi	D	09.11	09.51	10.13	11.41	17.31	20.19	20.42		22.21	00.27
Ban Takhli	A	10.06	10.51		13.04	18.24	21.10	21.36			
Nakhon Sawan	D	10.53	12.01	11.35	14.21	19.10	21.56	22.18	23.31	23.54	02.06

X = Express, R = Rapid, O = Ordinary, (123) = Class of train, A = Air Conditioning, B = Sleeping Car

Central Train Line Timetable											
Type and Class		R,23	R,23	X,123	X,2	X,12	R,23	O,23	R,23	O,23	R,23
Supplements		B	B	A,B	A	A,B	B		A		A
Nakhon Sawan	D	00.13	01.13	00.10	02.48	05.37	06.12	08.44	11.16	12.18	15.41
Ban Takhli	D	00.55		00.20			06.59	09.51	12.05	13.22	16.23
Lopburi	D	01.58	02.57	00.30			07.58	11.23	13.06	14.34	17.12
Ban Phachi Jn	D		03.39				08.47	12.24	13.44	15.43	18.02
Ayutthaya	A	02.56	03.58	00.40		08.08	09.06	12.51	14.02	16.08	18.21
Bang Pa-in	A							13.05	14.14	16.21	
Don Muang Airport	D	03.41	04.42	05.09	05.34	08.51	09.46	14.01	14.42	17.03	19.01
Hualumpong	A	04.25	05.25	06.00	06.15	09.40	10.25	14.50	15.20	17.50	19.50

X = Express, R = Rapid, O = Ordinary, (123) = Class of train, A = Air Conditioning, B = Sleeping Car

Train Fares				
From Bangkok	Fares without supplements (baht)			
	Class			Distance
Station	1st	2nd	3rd	km
Don Muang Airport	18	10	5	22
Bang Pa-in	49	26	12	58
Ayutthaya	60	31	15	71
Lopburi	111	57	28	133
Ban Takhli	157	80	39	193
Nakhon Sawan	197	99	48	246

Please note that most trains on the central line continue north to Chiang Mai. For through trains, refer to the timetables at the end of the chapter on Northern Thailand.

EASTERN
THAILAND

Eastern Thailand is the smallest region in Thailand, made up of only four provinces, Chonburi, Chanthaburi, Rayong and Trat, but filled with a number of wonderful natural sights as well as numerous well developed and popular tourist destinations. The East's proximity to Bangkok has made it a popular holiday destination for Thais escaping the hectic city and students seeking a quiet piece of land to camp, sing and play their guitars.

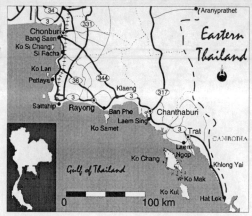

Today much of the coastline fills on weekends and holidays with growing numbers of wealthy Bangkok Thais and increasing numbers of farangs. The number of foreigners venturing further than Pattaya is also steadily increasing as islands like Ko Samet and Ko Chang, both of which are within a day's reach of Bangkok, become more accommodating and conducive to a relaxed stay.

Sinful Pattaya, one of Thailand's most visited holiday resorts amongst both package tourists and sex tourists, serves to sum up the results of ill thought and short sighted development. On the other side of the coin, the islands within Trat Province are considered by many as the last frontier in Thailand. Their deserted shores, limited accommodation and abundant nature serve to entrance all who visit. The stunning province is also one of the most beautiful as Khmer Rouge activity has delayed some development until now. The opening of the land border to Cambodia, as recent talks have suggested, may quickly change the whole region through the increase in economic and tourist traffic, but only time will tell.

This chapter covers the four provinces of Chonburi, Rayong, Chanthaburi and Trat.

Highlights

Ko Chang is a large and diverse island with something for everyone (Trat Province).
Ko Kut and **Ko Wai** are great getaways for absolute seclusion (Trat Province).
Chanthaburi town is a great place to kick back and pick up some gems while you are there (Chanthaburi Province).
Si Racha is another good place to hang out, particularly on the wharves over the ocean (Chonburi Province).
Cross to **Cambodia** from Hat Lek for an interesting (albeit illegal) day trip (Trat Province).

CHONBURI PROVINCE

Chonburi province stretches along the initial strip of eastern Thailand's coastline until it makes the dramatic western turn. Unfortunately, Chonburi's major claim to fame is the infamous Pattaya Beach, a sleazy den which most budget travellers are probably better off striking from their itinerary. There are however a number of other places within the province which are worth visiting if you are in the vicinity. Although Chonburi is best known for its seaside destinations, the province is also a major industrial and agricultural producer, with sugarcane fields particularly plentiful in this region of Thailand.

CHONBURI   ชลบุรี

This is the first major town you will reach when travelling down from Bangkok on Sukhumvit Road (Route 3). Little more than a large and busy provincial capital, Chonburi is important

Legend

1 Market
2 Chinese Temple
3 Thai Farmers Bank
4 Bangkok Bank
5 Rattana Chonburi Hotel
6 Thai Military Bank
7 Krung Thai Bank
8 Eastern Hotel & A/C buses
9 Audi Bakery
10 Thai Military Bank
11 Bangkok Bank of Commerce
12 The Forum Plaza
13 Swensens Ice Cream Shop
14 Wat Intharam
15 Bank of Ayudhya
16 Siam Commercial Bank
17 Chinese Temple
18 Bangkok Bank
19 Hospital
20 Sang Tong Hotel
21 Post office
22 Market
23 Bus to train station
24 Police station

mainly for its processing and canning of all the surrounding sugarcane, coconut and other crops. Chonburi is one of those provincial capitals where a bus ride through town is more than enough. The town's attractions are minimal but you may be interested in one of the outlying sites. If this is the case, you are probably better off staying at Si Racha and visiting them on a day trip.

East

Vital Information

Post Office is located on the corner of Vachira Prakorn Road and Soi Prai Sa Nee.
Banks see the map for details.
Hospital A small but central hospital is located on Soi Prai Sa Nee. Chonburi Hospital is at the southern end of Sukhumvit Road, after Vachira Prakorn Road joins it.
Police Station At the southern end of Vachira Prakorn Road.
Codes Chonburi's telephone code is (038) and the postcode is 20000.

Cheap Sleeps

Sang Tong Hotel at 108/4 Soi Prai Sa Nee, has rooms for 200B/300B for singles/doubles with fan, and also has pricier rooms starting at 450B.
Rattana Chonburi Hotel at 678/17-18 Sukhumvit Road, ☎ (038) 275 601, has rooms for all budgets, starting at 200B reaching a whopping 2,500B. The cheaper rooms are in the old building next door. Singles/doubles with fan cost 200B/250B but are not recommended by the staff. A/C rooms start at 320B/350B for singles/doubles. Check-out is noon.

Wat Intharam

Situated at the northern end of Chetchamnong Road and has a few statues around but all up is in a fairly dilapidated state. If you are in a religious mood, try the **Chinese Temple** on Pas Petra Road which is built in a pond and is worth visiting if you are bored out of your mind.

Water Buffalo Races　ประเพณิ่งควาย

Held annually every October, these races bring the town to a standstill, and even make the Bangkok evening news. The buffalo, which is traditionally a farming beast, is king for a day as they trade in their ploughs for a jockey, and race for the honour of crossing the line first. The day is filled with other exciting events including a local beauty contest (with the girls, not the buffalos). Check with TAT for the exact date in October as it changes every year.

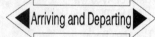

Buses leaving Bangkok for most eastern destinations usually pass through Chonburi, so you will never need to wait too long for a bus. Direct buses leave from **Bangkok's** eastern bus terminal with non A/C buses leaving every 15 minutes for 26B whilst the A/C buses cost 40B and leave every hour. There is a constant stream of songtheaws which connect Chonburi, Bang Saen, Nong Mon, Si Racha and Pattaya which travel along Sukhumvit Road.

AROUND CHONBURI

BANG SAEN　บางแสน

For many Thais who want to get away from the city, Bang Saen is a paradise full of fun, sand and ocean. To a traveller who may or may not have visited Thailand's true tropical islands, Bang Saen is a beach resort nightmare. The long grey beach is matched by grey water seemingly coming from places other than the ocean. Excited Thais carry on regardless making their claim on one of the hundreds of deck chairs and inner tubes available. There are also so many banana boats on the water you could start a plantation! Along the promenade, food vendors set up stalls en-masse, and if you happen to have forgotten your inflatable shark or bucket and spade, at Bang Saen, you have every colour under the sun to choose from.

Bang Saen is between Si Racha and Chonburi. From Sukhumvit Road (Route 3), the main road heads 3 km west to the beach, then takes a ninety degree turn to the right at the "Welcome to Bang Saen" sign and runs a few kilometres along the beach.

Vital Information

Tourist Information The TAT Office is on the beach road between Soi 2 and 3.
Post Office The GPO is on Sukhumvit Road to the right and opposite the main road that leads to the beach.
Police Station is on the road that runs parallel to the beach road at the end of Soi 5. A Police box also exists on the beach next to the TAT office.
Codes The telephone code is (038) and the postal code is 20130.

> At the time of going to press the final touches of the tallest Buddha image in the world were being carved into a cliff face in Chonburi Province.

East

Cheap Sleeps

Most accommodation in town is in the middle price range and located along the beach front catering to the status conscious Thais. For more budget priced beds, try the beach end of Soi 1 or on the road running parallel to the beach road, 500 m back. On weekends most places (even the cheap ones) increase their prices.

Eat and Meet

The food vendors on the beach are by far your best option, although if you do not fancy street fare there are a few more expensive restaurants along the beach road.

Things to do and Sights to See

Institute of Maritime Science Museum
Located within the grounds of Burapha University about half way along the main road which leads to the beach, this museum contains a well set out aquarium and a display of all manner of sea life from the rock beds to the deep ocean. The museum is open Tuesday to Sunday from 8.30 am to 4.00 pm and admission is 20B (10B if you put on your school uniform).

Khao Sam Muk เขาสามมุก
This promontory is 2 km from the northern end of the beach. Once you get there you will find a decorative Chinese temple and a bunch of expensive hotels and restaurants. Around the corner a few hundred metres to the east is a more interesting although less traditional Chinese temple containing numerous large, colourful and bizarre statues of Gods. Another 150 m around is a third Chinese temple not really worth a visit on its own, but just before it are some stairs. These lead up the mountain where the peak is topped by a Buddha footprint along with a great view of all the surrounding countryside including the offshore islands. Follow the stairs down the other side of the hill and you will come to a road and another viewing platform where a hotel has taken advantage of the position. A handful of spoilt monkeys that hang around here attract Thai tourists, but all they do is jump all over parked cars and grab any item or food carelessly left lying about. Take the road exit on your right (when facing the mountain) and after 1½ km you will be back at the beach. A motorbike taxi from the northern end of the beach, where the songtheaws stop, to Khao Sam Muk costs 20B.

Arriving and Departing

Songtheaw
A songtheaw from either **Chonburi** or **Si Racha** costs 7B. From Si Racha jump on a songtheaw in front of the Hua Hin Restaurant and ask to go to Nong Man and it will let you off on Sukhumvit Road after about a 25 minute ride. From there another songtheaw to the beach costs 5B, and any ride of a shorter distance costs 3B.

Riddle Sahm
You are in a concrete cell in the middle of the desert. There are no doors or windows in this cell. In the ceiling there is an opening covered by a metal grate. The only other object in the cell is an old woodle chair. How do you escape the cell, cross the desert and reach the town at the edge of the desert?

East

SI RACHA   ศรีราชา

It seems that Si Racha's days as a sleepy fishing village are finally over. Tourism and industrial development which has been growing to the north and south of the town, are complemented by huge condos and expensive hotels, themselves a result of opportunistic outsiders. Offshore, huge ships utilising the deep waterways, sit at anchor waiting to be used. Many of the locals, almost oblivious to this development, still make a living from the fishing industry, allowing the restaurants to offer delicious seafood.

Impending development aside, Si Racha still has a long way to go before tourism becomes a big money spinner. The town, despite sitting on the coast, is not particularly beautiful, but fortunately somehow still retains a small town atmosphere. The many wharves and houses over the water's edge trap truckloads of non-biodegradable rubbish and the water is far from crystal clear as raw sewage is dumped into the ocean.

Orientation

The main highway running between Bangkok and Pattaya (Sukhumvit Road) runs parallel to Si Racha's seaside Jermjompol Road about 1 km inland. The town sits on a bay with the tiny Ko Loi at the northern end and stretches south for about 1 km. Most roads leading off Jermjompol Road intersect with Sukhumvit Road.

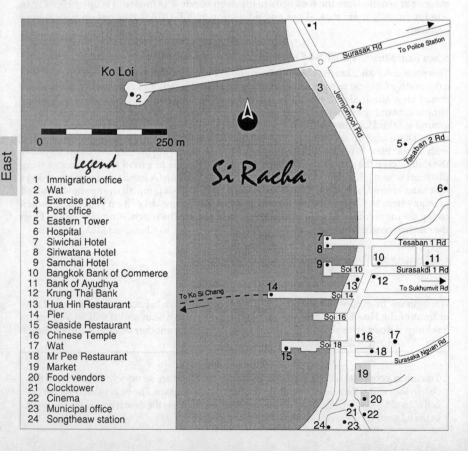

Legend

1   Immigration office
2   Wat
3   Exercise park
4   Post office
5   Eastern Tower
6   Hospital
7   Siwichai Hotel
8   Siriwatana Hotel
9   Samchai Hotel
10 Bangkok Bank of Commerce
11 Bank of Ayudhya
12 Krung Thai Bank
13 Hua Hin Restaurant
14 Pier
15 Seaside Restaurant
16 Chinese Temple
17 Wat
18 Mr Pee Restaurant
19 Market
20 Food vendors
21 Clocktower
22 Cinema
23 Municipal office
24 Songtheaw station

East

Vital Information

Post Office Is at the northern end of Jermjompol Road, 150 m before of the roundabout.
International Telephone There are a few international call facilities at the ocean end of Surasakdi 1 Road, however their rates are much higher than those of the GPO, and they will also hit you with an operator fee of 30B.
Banks A few banks are located on Surasakdi 1 Road as well as Sukhumvit Road.
Hospital There are two close by, one behind Eastern Tower in between Tesaban 2 and Surasak Road and the other is north of town 1 km past the roundabout on the road leading to Ko Loi.
Police Station is on Sukhumvit Road, just south of Surasak Road which leads to Ko Loi.
Immigration Office At the northern end of Jermjompol Road, past the roundabout.
Codes Si Racha's telephone code is (038) and the postcode is 20110.

Cheap Sleeps

Sriwatana Bungalows at 35 Jermjompol Road, ☎ (038) 311 037, down the soi opposite Tesaban 1 Road. This is the best place in town located on a wharf and is guaranteed to make your stay in Si Racha an enjoyable one. Rooms are 140B for a fan cooled room with bathroom.
Siwichai Right next door, ☎ (038) 311 212, virtually shares the same driveway as Sriwatana Bungalows. The rooms at the end of the pier are quite good for 200B, but the hotel lacks the atmosphere of next door. The rooms closer to the land are cheaper.
Samchai Hotel at 3 Jermjompol Road, ☎ (038) 311 134, down Soi 10 is another hotel on a wharf. The rooms are older and grubbier, although there is a marked difference between the cramped rooms at the land end and the open, balcony clad rooms that get the ocean breeze. Singles/doubles with fan and bath are 140B/200B and A/C rooms start at 350B.
If all the above are full, there are a couple of cheap hotels away from the waters edge, the Siripong Hotel and the Siracha Hotel, as well as a choice of new high-rise hotels on the outskirts of town.

Eat and Meet

Many would say that fishing towns have great seafood and this is definitely the case in Si Racha.
Seaside Restaurant, ☎ (038) 312 537, at the end of the wharf leading off Soi 18, this restaurant is located in a brilliant setting and the diligent staff attend your every need. The choice of food is extensive and very readable on an English menu with most meals costing between 60B and 120B. Open until 10.00 pm.
Hua Hin Restaurant, ☎ (038) 311 047, on Jermjompol Road, just south of Soi 10, opposite the Krung Thai Bank can satisfy most seafood cravings at a reasonable price. Open until 9.30 pm.
There are a few **Thai Restaurants** next door and across the road that have some seafood dishes as well as the more standard Thai dishes, but watch out for Chua Lee on Hua Hin's side of the road, they have great seafood, but your wallet may leave somewhat lighter.
Mr Pee Restaurant is down the small alley opposite Soi 18. A simple Thai menu as well as Western breakfasts, sandwiches and hamburgers, all priced between 20B and 40B. Open 6.00 am to 10.00 pm.
Both during the day and night, a few **typical Thai vendors** set up just to the south of the market, before the cinema.

East

Things to do and Sights to See

Ko Loi   เกาะลอย

This small island is connected to the mainland by a concrete jetty, to the north of town. It is a popular place for tour buses to drop a load of Thai tourists to fill in some time. Many locals visit to watch the sunset, go fishing, have a picnic, or just hang out, although plastic bags and bottles seem to be the catch of the day. There is a small Buddhist wat atop the rocky outcrop and a pool with giant turtles. Cruelly, the pool is concrete, painted blue and mildew covered and the turtles are not convinced they are in a natural environment. There are food vendors around who can satisfy your every hunger pang.

Khao Khieo Open Zoo   สวนสัตว์เปิดเขาเขียว

Claimed as Thailand's largest open zoo, it covers 1,200 acres. Whilst there you will be able to glimpse over 100 species including elephants, monkeys, deer and birds. The aviary is also huge, perfect for the budding birdwatcher. Visitors can wander the park at their own pace and explore forests, waterfalls and the wildlife with **Chan Ta Then Waterfall** located around 5 km from the entrance. The park is open 8.00 am to 6.00 pm, and admission is 20B.

To reach the zoo catch a songtheaw or bus north along Sukhumvit Road for 10 to 15 minutes to Bangphra, then make your way 11 km east down the well sign posted street next to the walkway.

Si Racha Farm   ศรีราชาฟาร์ม

If the open zoo was not enough, try the Si Racha Farm, 8 km from town on the same road leading to Si Racha International Golf Course. It is a small zoo with dangerous crocodiles, tigers and camels, hence the fences. Admission is 30B and the farm is open 9.00 am to 6.00 pm.

Arriving and Departing

Train

Si Racha has a train station, but irregular trains pass the very user unfriendly location to the east of Sukhumvit Road quite a long way out of town. To get there, go up Surasak 1 Road, turn left onto Sukhumvit Road for 200 m and take a right turn at the traffic lights.

Bus

Si Racha is on the Bangkok Pattaya Highway so buses pass through on a regular basis along Sukhumvit Road. It costs 10B to reach **Pattaya** (15B for A/C). From the stop on Sukhumvit Road, it is a 3B songtheaw ride down Surasakdi 1 Road or 20B in a tuk tuk to get to the seaside. A/C buses (52B) leave every 40 minutes to and from **Bangkok** until 20.00, and ordinary buses (29B) leave every 30 minutes up to 19.50 from Bangkok and 21.30 from Si Racha.

Songtheaw

The immediate area around Si Racha is best reached by songtheaw. Heading north, catch one in front of the Hua Hin Restaurant for Nang Man (jumping off point to **Bang Saen**, costing 7B), and to **Chonburi** it is the same price again. Going south 10B will take you to **Naklua** from where it is another 10B on another songtheaw to **Pattaya**. These songtheaws leave from the municipality office gate in Si Racha, next to the clocktower.

Ferry

Ferries leave virtually every hour out to Ko Si Chang, see Ko Si Chang for details.

KO SI CHANG   เกาะสีชัง

This island is certainly not the one which Thailand became famous for, but it is still a pleasant getaway from Bangkok. Located a short ferry ride from the coast of Si Racha, the island's eastern shores have become an accessory to the expanding shipping industry of the region. The western side however is a different place altogether, offering a tranquil setting of open bays and rocky coastline. Unfortunately access to the northern and southern sides of the island is restricted by a lack of roads, however they do not hold any deserted beaches, just high rocky cliffs falling to the ocean below. Most of the sights can be reached on foot or by samlor, but the western side requires a motorbike or bicycle. It is possible to see everything the island has to offer in a day if you are on a tight schedule.

One of the more interesting things about Ko Si Chang is the motorcycle taxis. These huge monsters have car engines in them with the passengers sitting in a chariot style construction behind the rider. Awesome speeds can be achieved in these. They are not seen anywhere else in Thailand.

Vital Information

Post Office At the northern end of Atsadang Road, just before the turn-off to Tha Tabon (pier).
Bank Thai Farmers Bank at 9-9/1-2 Atsadang Road is on the main road to the right of the pier.
Hospital Further north along Atsadang Road past the Thai Farmers Bank.
Police Station There is a small station just as you exit Tha Lang (pier) and a larger station on the road towards Tha Wong, near the gate to the Aquatic Resources Research Institute.
Immigration Office This office is about 500 m down a turn-off on the road to Tha Wang. Unfortunately travellers must go to the mainland to extend their visa.
Codes Ko Si Chang's telephone code is (038) and the postal code is 20120.

Cheap Sleeps

Tiew Pai Guesthouse, ☎ (038) 216 084, is on the southern end of Atsadang Road a few hundred metres to the left of the pier. This is the cheapest place on the island with accommodation ranging from simple two bed rooms with fan and toilet for 100B, to cosy A/C rooms for 500B, along with a range of rooms priced between these two. Motorbike hire is available from 150B per day.
Sri Pitsanuk Bungalow, ☎ (038) 216 024, is placed in a remote setting perched on a cliff overlooking the ocean, bungalows here cost 250B, 700B and 1,200B. The 1,200B bungalow sleeps seven people whilst the 700B room is a concrete room in the front part of a larger house.
Top Bungalow, ☎ (038) 216 001, is a couple of hundred metres back from the Sri Pitsanuk Bungalows where rooms are similarly priced, if you can find anyone to show you around. The bungalows are too far from the ocean for views.
Si Chang Villa Resort, ☎ (038) 216 210, is a more expensive option with a pleasant setting and tiny beach. Rooms with fan cost 500B and 800B for A/C.

Things to do ◆ and Sights to See

Chinese Temple
This temple is located at the northern end of Atsadang Road where a number of shrines embellish the hillside. In the middle level shrines are built into caves, with one containing a gold painted Buddha image created from mineral deposits over time, however the face has had some help from a chisel. The stairs (of which there are plenty) continue uphill to a small Buddha footprint and a stunning panoramic view of the town, island and mainland. During Chinese New Year, the temple is overrun with Chinese visitors.

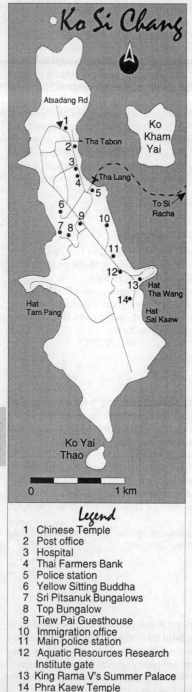

Legend

1 Chinese Temple
2 Post office
3 Hospital
4 Thai Farmers Bank
5 Police station
6 Yellow Sitting Buddha
7 Sri Pitsanuk Bungalows
8 Top Bungalow
9 Tiew Pai Guesthouse
10 Immigration office
11 Main police station
12 Aquatic Resources Research
   Institute gate
13 King Rama V's Summer Palace
14 Phra Kaew Temple

Yellow Sitting Buddha

On the other side of town is a small wat with a large yellow sitting Buddha. It stands out against the natural green setting of the hillside.

Hat Tha Wang and the Ancient Summer Palace

If you turn left at the pier and follow the road for about 2 km you will reach the unimpressive and rocky **Tha Wang Beach**. On the hillside to the right of this is the **Ancient Summer Palace of King Rama V**. There is not much to see here except for decrepit ruins, but restoration has been carried out on the paths, gardens and pools, although the pools are empty, as is **Wat Atsadangnimit** at the top of the hill.

Hat Sai Kaew

The road that leads through the Ancient Summer Palace takes you to Sai Kaew Beach on the other side of the promontory. On the way you will pass Phra Kaew Temple and a limestone cave. The beach itself is an outstanding improvement on Hat Tha Wang and attracts a family oriented crowd.

Hat Tam Pang

Located on the western side of the island, this small beach (where there are often more plastic bottles than sand) is set within a large bay. If you are able to visualise the beach without the rubbish, then this is a very tranquil location for a swim. Take the dirt road up the hill just before the Aquatic Resources Research Institute, then the concrete road (Chalerm Prakiart Road) that appears on your right. Do not bother exploring the dirt road any further as there is not much of interest further along except for huge white silos and a garbage tip. The concrete road ends at the far end of the bay at Tam Pang Promontory providing a very appealing view of the bay. To get to the beach, take the dirt track down the hill a few hundred metres from the end of the road. The other concrete road further along, that you would assume leads somewhere, actually peters out to a dirt track which becomes overgrown with shrubs, making access to the beach impossible.

Yai Phrik Vipassana Centre

Located on the road to Sri Pitsanuk Bungalows, this intensive meditation centre uses the surrounding caves for their silence. There are three caves in the near vicinity, Tham Pung, Tham Hadsai and Tham Yai Prik, so if you go exploring, consider the mortals trying to attain a higher state of mind nearby.

◀ **Arriving and Departing** ▶

Ferry

Ferries leave Si Racha pier at the end of Soi 14 at high tide and the 'pier' on Ko Loi at low tide. The ferry takes 40 minutes (as long as the engine does not blow up) and costs 20B. The ferry sometimes makes a stop at some of the anchored freighters sitting offshore. Once on the island, a motorbike taxi or samlor is never too far away. Two ferry companies do the trip between Si Racha and **Ko Si Chang** and working together, it is never too long a wait for a ride. The boats leave at 06.00, 06.40, 08.00 then every hour till 18.00. For ferries returning to the mainland, the first leaves at 07.00 then every hour until 20.00. There is no boat at 09.00, 13.00 or 17.00.

PATTAYA   พัทยา

Located a stone's throw from Bangkok (147 km), Pattaya has become a haven for wealthy Thais, package tourists and many unsavoury farangs overindulging in the sins of the flesh.

Catering to this market has produced an abundance of expensive accommodation, restaurants, sleazy bars and prostitutes. The budget traveller will find it difficult to stick to a budget here, but it can almost be done by staying at the limited range of budget accommodation and by eating at the restricted number of Thai eateries in town. The beaches are extremely crowded with deck chairs and travellers would be more rewarded on the better and more pristine beaches of Ko Samet or Ko Chang farther along the coast.

Central and South Pattaya is where most of the 'action' takes place, whilst North Pattaya and Jomtien Beach to the south of Pattaya Beach are only a little more bearable with cleaner beaches and a reduced sex scene (during the week).

It is almost worthwhile visiting for just a day to witness for yourself the degrading level that human beings can reduce themselves to after a few beers and an itch in the groin. Most will probably leave with more than this as it is estimated that one in four prostitutes in Pattaya have AIDS and other STD's. The most common sight in Pattaya is a Caucasian man (often grossly overweight) arm in arm with a young Thai girl - day and night. In December the place is overrun with wealthy Russians and there is even a Russian prostitution scene in town.

Orientation

Pattaya is divided into three areas, North, Central and South Pattaya. The beach runs for 4 km with Pattaya Beach Road stretching the entire length. Pattaya 2 Road runs parallel to this about 500 m inland and Sukhumvit Road (Route 3) is another kilometre east. North Pattaya Road, Central Pattaya Road and South Pattaya Road run perpendicular from the beach road through to Sukhumvit Road in their respective areas. Pattaya Beach Road and Pattaya 2 Road are also connected by numerous sois along the length of the beach.

Pattaya has excellent water sports facilities from catamarans to Scuba Diving, but the prices are higher than at many other excellent locations in Thailand.

Vital Information

Tourist Information The TAT have a temporary office set up on Pattaya Beach Road between Sois 7 and 8. The staff are extremely knowledgable and helpful with any queries you may have. The office is open daily 8.30 am to 4.30 pm.

Post Office at 183/21-23 Soi Post Office (Soi 15) in South Pattaya. International calls can be made here as well as regular postal services. The office is open Monday to Friday 8.30 am to 4.30 pm and Saturday 8.30 to midday.

East

Telecommunications Office on South Pattaya Road, east of Pattaya 3 Road also offers conveniently placed telephone facilities.

Banks There are banks sporadically spread along Pattaya Beach Road and Pattaya 2 Road with currency exchange branches all around South Pattaya's busier streets.

Pattaya International Hospital is on Pattaya Soi 4, just off Pattaya 2 Road, ☎ (038) 428 374.

Pattaya Memorial Hospital is on Central Road, near the corner with Pattaya 2 Road, ☎ (038) 427 751.

Police Station on Pattaya Beach Road in between Sois 8 and 9. There is also a police box on the beach road next to the pier and close to South Pattaya Road.

Immigration Office The Pattaya Immigration Office is located half way up Soi 8, in between Pattaya Beach Road and Pattaya 2 Road. It is possible to extend tourist visas here.

Codes Pattaya's telephone code is (038) and the postcode is 20260.

Cheap Sleeps

Most of the accommodation in Pattaya caters to the more affluent tourist or serve as brothels or at least a convenient place to take your latest catch (not that this is difficult). Below is a list of low end accommodation but includes a few mid range places as the cheapest are often little more than dog boxes or very dirty. Most of the cheaper places are on or around Pattaya 2 Road. The prices below may fluctuate wildly according to season.

South Pattaya

Honey House at 503/5-7 Soi Honey Inn (Soi 10), ☎ (038) 424 396, off Pattaya 2 Road. This place offers the most reasonable rates and rooms in town. A large very clean room with bath and fan costs 120B and A/C costs 200B. Both single and double rooms are available. You also have access to the pool across the road at Honey Inn.

Magic Guesthouse on Pattaya 2 Road on the corner of a road opposite and between Soi's 9 and 10, ☎ (038) 720 211. Under French management, these rooms are very clean, but the fan rooms are small. Singles and doubles are available, starting at 150B for a fan room and 250B, A/C.

U-Thumpharn on Pattaya 2 Road opposite Soi 10, ☎ (038) 421 350, also has rooms for 150B to 250B.

Cleans House at 519/52-53 Soi Prompan (Soi Skaw Beach) off Pattaya 2 Road, ☎ (038) 423 282, has standard hotel rooms which try to live up to their name but do not quite cut it. Rooms with fan and bath 150B, and 250B with A/C.

Jom House and **Lucky House** are also in this area on Pattaya 2 Road, although their cheap rooms are really only for the desperate. Tiny, filthy rooms with bath cost 150B with fan and 250B with A/C. Off season prices are 100B/200B, and you would be well advised to keep an eye on your belongings whilst here.

APEX on Pattaya 2 Road in between and opposite Sois 10 and 11, ☎ (038) 429 233, is a large hotel offering excellent rates for what you get. Clean rooms start at 250B including A/C, TV, fridge and hot water. There is a pool for when you get sick of the ocean.

Siam Guesthouse, Porn Guesthouse and **PS Guesthouse** as well as others are located on the busy Soi Yamato where there are heaps of shopfront bars and go-go shows, so do not expect too much sleep. Singles/doubles with fan and bath are 100B/150B and 200B/250B for A/C. Add on another 50B for high season. The staff here are unfriendly and security may be a problem.

Chris Guesthouse at 185 Soi 13, ☎ (038) 249 586 is located down a quiet Soi, is still close to the action yet retains a welcoming atmosphere. Large, comfortable rooms cost 400B, and some of the rooms have their own cable TV's, in addition to the usual A/C and hot water.

White House On Soi 13, ☎ (038) 426 222, next door to Chris Guesthouse, this Scandinavian place is very homely with high security. The rooms cost 500B with A/C, hot water and Mum's decorating touch.

Toi's Place is across the road from Chris' and the White House and rooms are similarly priced.

Honey Lodge On South Pattaya Road, ☎ (038) 429 133, has standard and well maintained rooms for 400B with A/C, hot water, fridge, telephone, and 450B gets you TV as well.
Victoria Guesthouse on Pattayaland Road, ☎ (038) 429 868, has friendly staff but very average rooms for 250B with A/C. This area is one of the busier hovels in South Pattaya. Other guesthouses on this street offer similar if not higher rates.

North Pattaya
In North Pattaya the beach is much cleaner and quieter and the night scene is toned down considerably, except on Soi Yodsak and a couple of other pockets. Unfortunately there is not much in the way of budget accommodation available.
Chez Rim Hotel on Soi 1, ☎ (038) 421 450, is run by a friendly old lady. Rooms are large, clean but very basic costing 200B for fan and 350B for A/C. There is a pool to hang out at and a restaurant serving reasonably priced food (by Pattaya's standards).
Welkom Inn Halfway down Soi 3, ☎ (038) 422 589, is a self contained entertainment area complete with bar, restaurant, pool and karaoke in Pattaya style. Rooms are priced from 400B.
Soi Yotsak has a few cheaper hotels for around 200B with fan but the busy street will keep you awake if the person with a prostitute next door does not. There is also some cheaper accommodation further north past North Pattaya in **Naklua**, but after the sex scene diminishes all you have is a busy Thai fishing town and a distinct lack of pleasant beaches as the coastline gets rocky.

Eat and Meet

Bakeries The international crowd attracted to Pattaya has lead to the creation of some delicious bakeries in town. **Montien Resort**, **Foodland** and **Big C** are all worth a sample.
     Budget priced food is mainly available on Pattaya 2 Road between Central and South Pattaya Road. Here you will be able to pick up a reasonably priced meal for 30B to 50B. A few **Thai eateries** are hidden amongst the more upmarket places for a standard meal, bank on around 20B. There is a small **Thai market** which sells a limited range of food on the corner of Central Pattaya Road and Pattaya 2 Road, but a much larger food market sets itself up at Naklua, and you can pick up **reasonably priced fruit** at the back of Mikes Shopping Centre on Pattaya 2 Road.
     If you want to splurge, Pattaya is the place to do it. Seafood is available almost anywhere, but be prepared to be stung by the price. The best method is simply to wander around and see what takes your fancy. There are also a few places which will complement your meal with a traditional Thai dance performance, but they are quite expensive.

Things to do and Sights to See

Nightlife
At most places in Pattaya you will be accosted by a prostitute and charged like a wounded bull for your drinks, but if you keep your wits about you, you will escape the debauchery fairly unscathed.
     The open bars are the safest option for a drink. There are often a few clustered together and some will have Thai Boxing matches on throughout the evening. The largest and most popular are in South Pattaya along Beach Road. Smiling girls will try to entice you to their bar, but if you let them know that you are only interested in a drink then you will be left alone (but they will make sure you always have a drink.) Be aware of any places where you must go upstairs through a closed door. These are pretty dodgy and you risk getting ripped off or seeing things that your mother never told you about.
Shamrock on Pattaya 2 Road is about the only place in town where you can go for a drink without a prostitute interrupting your conversation. It is popular with local ex-pats.

The Green Bottle Pub on Pattaya 2 Road between Sois 11 and 12 only has a few discreet prostitutes who will not approach you twice.

Las Vegas Bar If you must see a go-go show, try this small bar where the American owner prides himself on his not ripping you off on drinks. Like most similar bars, girls emotionlessly attempt to dance 'erotically' around silver poles on a stage, not unlike animals in a zoo, whilst desperate Caucasians sit around, picking out the girl to their taste.

The Palladium Disco is in North Pattaya at 78/33-35 Pattaya 2 Road. This huge disco has a capacity of around 6,000 and is open from 11.00 pm till late. It was once *the* place to go, however now the numbers are dwindling. Expect an expensive night out.

Transvestite Shows Two of the most popular shows are **Alcazar** and **Tiffany's**. Both are professional productions with three shows a night with some of the most feminine and believable transvestites you are ever likely to see. Alcazar's shows are 6.30 pm, 8.00 pm and 9.30 pm and on Saturdays at 11.00 pm as well. Tiffany's shows are 7.00 pm, 8.30 pm and 10.00 pm with an extra show at 5.30 pm on Fridays and Saturdays.

Marine Disco This huge 'disco' is a crazy scene, where on a busy night over 2,000 prostitutes are trying to outdo each other. Worth a look just to believe it.

Boys Town The few streets just to the north of South Pattaya Road is a predominantly gay area where the boys can visit one of the numerous establishments. Unfortunately the area is also tainted with paedophiles who hang around Boys Town and the ferry wharf. Lesbians will have a more difficult time finding an area to go out. Best to ask some of the locals for tips on this one.

The Million Years Stone Park and Pattaya Crocodile Farm

อุทยานหินล้านปี และฟาร์มจระเข้พัทยา

So named because the petrified trees in the park are over a million years old. Here you can see gardens and bonsai trees shaped in various ancient Thai Styles and the park also contains a variety of animals such as elephants, camels, lions, bears - you can even have your photo taken with a tame tiger! - one to show all your friends at home. The excitement does not stop there however, as the crocodile and magic show (these are separate events, not combined...) will attempt to mesmerise you. They are shown throughout the day. You will see the signs to the park from the northern end of Sukhumvit Road.

Legend

1 Bus to Bangkok	19 To train station	37 Chris Guesthouse
2 Tiffanys	20 Krung Thai Bank	38 White House
3 Palladium Disco	21 Pattaya Memorial Hospital	39 Siam Guesthouse
4 Bangkok Metropolitan Bank	22 Thai Farmers Bank	40 Post office
5 Chez Rim	23 Songtheaw and bus	41 Dolphin Diving Centre
6 Big C Shopping Centre	station	42 Royal Garden Plaza
and cinema	24 TAT	43 DK Bookstore
7 Welkom Resort	25 Immigration office	44 Victoria Guesthouse
8 Pattaya Int. Hospital	26 Made in Thailand Market	45 Thai Military Bank
9 Alcazar	27 Police station	46 Thai Farmers Bank
10 Suzie Massage Parlour	28 Magic Guesthouse	47 Shamrock Pub
11 Seafari Diving Centre	29 Paradise Scuba Divers	48 Honey Lodge
12 2nd hand bookshop	30 Mikes Shopping Mall	49 1st Bangkok City Bank
13 Bangkok Bank	31 Green Bottle Pub	50 Songtheaw to Jomtien
14 Macs	32 Honey House	51 Telecommunications Ctr.
15 Siam Commercial Bank	33 APEX Hotel	52 Sikh Temple
16 Market	34 Pattaya Scuba Club	53 Songtheaw station
17 Bus to Northeast	35 Toi's Place	54 Marine Disco
18 Songtheaw and bus station	36 PS Guesthouse	55 Big Buddha
		Gay area

East

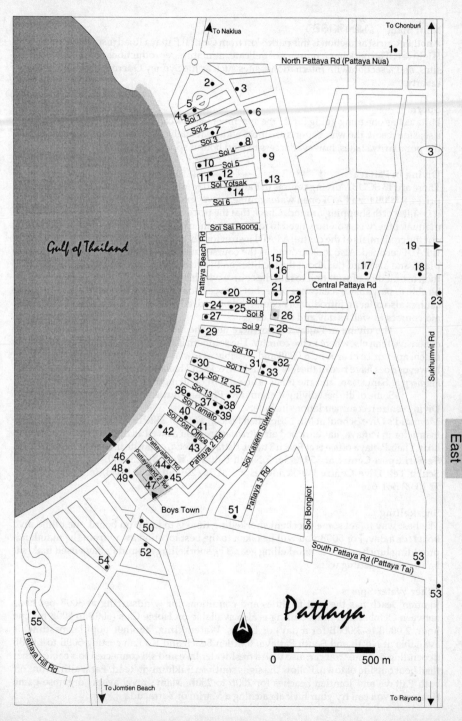

To Naklua

To Chonburi

North Pattaya Rd (Pattaya Nua)

Gulf of Thailand

Soi 1
Soi 2
Soi 3
Soi 4
Soi 5
Soi Yotsak
Soi 6
Soi Sai Roong
Pattaya Beach Rd

Central Pattaya Rd

Soi 7
Soi 8
Soi 9
Soi 10
Soi 11
Soi 12
Soi 13
Soi Yamato
Soi Post Office
Pattayaland Rd
Pattayaland 2 Rd
Pattaya 2 Rd
Soi Kasem Suwan
Pattaya 3 Rd
Soi Bongkot

Sukhumvit Rd

Boys Town

South Pattaya Rd (Pattaya Tai)

Pattaya Hill Rd

To Jomtien Beach

To Rayong

Pattaya

0   500 m

East

Mini Siam   เมืองจำลอง

Another tourist attraction is this park 3 km from Central Pattaya Road just off the Sukhumvit Highway. The park has a number of delicate, miniature reproductions of well known Thai sites, and a section with international sites such as the Sydney Opera House and Statue of Liberty.

Sports

Pattaya has one thing going for it - the sporting facilities can keep you busy for days. Being a seaside resort, the water sports are most widely available with ocean activities taking out the popularity stakes, however access to land bound sports also exists.

Diving in Pattaya

There are 13 SCUBA diving centres in Pattaya and Jomtien alone. They all charge the same prices, 9,000B for a PADI open water course, however each centre offers different perks, so it is still worth shopping around. Check that the prices include your own copy of the PADI manual, otherwise you may need to fork out another 1,100B for your own copy. Also check out the credentials of the centre. A PADI instructor does not necessarily mean that the centre is PADI certified. Also look around as the courses are structured differently from place to place, and also find out about the facilities on the boat and where they will be taking you, then use all this information to find the course which best suits you. In low season you may be able to bargain for a cheaper price, but cheaper does not always mean better. Most dive centres also offer an introductory course, advanced, advanced plus, rescue and medic first aid courses as well as day and night dives.

The diving in Pattaya is nowhere near the best in Thailand and it is also more expensive than elsewhere in the country. The southern islands have better conditions for the far cheaper price of around 6,000B and possibly as low as 4,500B in the low season. Pattaya however does have two of the few diveable wrecks in Thailand, one is at a depth of 20 m, the *Hardeep* at Samaesan, and the other is at a depth of 30 m, the *Bremen* at Sattahip.

Some of the best diving is around Ko Phai and further north around Ko Samae San. Diving centre recommendations include:

Mermaid's Dive School at Mu 12, Jomtien Beach,, ☎ (038) 232 219 with the only female dive instructor in Pattaya, has enriched air nitrox instruction as well as their own fully equipped boat. Their Pattaya office is at Beach Travel, Pattaya 2 Road, opposite the Royal Garden Plaza.
Seafari Sport Centre at 359/2 Soi 5 North Pattaya, ☎ (038) 429 060.
Scuba Tek Dive Centre Weekender Hotel at 78/20 Pattaya 2 Road, in North Pattaya, ☎ (038) 361 616.

Snorkelling

The best way to get some excellent snorkelling time is to jump on board one of the dive boats for a day. For 500B you will be taken to the best location away from the mainland, providing lunch as well as snorkelling gear. The snorkelling around Pattaya itself makes it hardly worth getting wet.

Other Water Sports

Jomtien Beach has the best facilities and conditions for **windsurfing** at 300B per hour between October and June. **Sailing** is also available on Hobie Cats (600B to 800B for one hour, 2,000B to 3,000B for a day) or Lasers. **Waterskiing**, another popular pastime, is available at North and South Pattaya, Jomtien Beach and Ko Lan costing 500B to 1,000B depending on time. You can also visit a freshwater lake and ski connected to a cable rather than boat outside of town. Follow the signs south on Sukhumvit Road. **Parasailing** runs off both Pattaya and Jomtien beaches for 200B to 250B. Many travel agents organise **game fishing** so you can try your luck at catching a Marlin or Barracuda.

East

Other Sports
Golf fanatics can play a round on one of the twelve courses around the area. Some are of an international standard. Over 14 hotels have **tennis courts** and a few also have **squash courts**. **Badminton** is available 24 hours a day at Soi 17 between 14.00 and 24.00 for 60B/hour, (20B racket rental, and 25B shuttlecock rental). You can throw some big balls around at one of the three **bowling alleys** for 30B to 40B per game. **Go Karts**, can be spun around a few tracks near town between 10.00 and 6.00 pm for 50B to 200B for 12 minutes, or for a more natural experience, try the **horse riding** option at the 11 km marker on Route 36 for 500B to 700B. Between Pattaya and Jomtien Beach **bungy jumping** is also available. Paintball has also hit town open every day except Monday from 2.00 pm and costing 500B for two hours.

Beaches
North Pattaya is the quietest and cleanest part of the beach in the Pattaya Bay area. It becomes dirtier and busier the closer you get to South Pattaya Beach. Deck chairs sometimes outnumber people and cost 20B a day and jet skis on the water will add to the sound of cars behind you.

Big Buddha
On the headland between South Pattaya and Jomtien Beach is a large Buddha image which also offers a great vantage point for viewing Pattaya. It is about 1½ km from the end of Pattaya 2 Road.

◀ **Arriving and Departing** ▶

Air
Bangkok Airways has a triple flight from Bangkok to Pattaya then onwards to Ko Samui which can be booked at most travel agents around town. A minibus to the airport at U-Tapao costs 200B to 250B depending on which agent you choose to use. A flight to **Ko Samui** costs 1,640B.

Train
A train leaves Hualumpong station at Bangkok and returns twice a day taking about 3 hours. The train station in Pattaya is just to the north of the intersection of Sukhumvit and Central Pattaya Road. Long distance prices include **Chiang Mai** 725B, **Hat Yai** 783B, **Surat Thani** 674B and **Butterworth** (Malaysia) 1,046B.

Bus
Both A/C (66B) and ordinary buses (37B) leave **Bangkok's** eastern bus terminal every 30 minutes between 05.00 and 22.30. They also return every 30 minutes up until 21.00. A/C buses also leave from Bangkok's northern bus terminal every 30 minutes (66B) taking you to Pattaya's A/C bus stop at the Sukhumvit end of North Pattaya Road. A bus also leaves for Bangkok airport every 2 hours for 180B between 07.00 and 17.00.

It is possible to jump on any passing bus running north or south along Sukhumvit Road from the end of North, Central or South Pattaya Roads. Buses along this route are similar in price to the songtheaws costing from 5B to 20B. A bus to **Si Racha** costs 10B and a bus to **Rayong** is 20B for 1½ hours. Some A/C bus fares to places further afield are; **Chiang Mai** 650B, **Khon Kaen** 425B, **Surat Thani** 850B, **Ko Samui** 850B, **Phuket** 850B, **Krabi** 850B and **Hat Yai** 1,100B.

A/C minibuses leave for Ban Phe (**Ko Samet**) daily at 08.00, 10.00, 12.00, and 15.30 daily for 120B from Malibu Travel at 485 Pattaya 2nd Road.

Minibus
Minibuses leave three times a day from **Bangkok** airport and cost 250B. From Pattaya they leave from next door to Alcazar. Other agents run minibuses to Bangkok for 180B.

Songtheaws

The Chonburi coastline is served by various songtheaws which cover different sections between Chonburi and Rayong. They only cost between 10B and 20B depending on distance.

Getting Around Town
Songtheaws

Songtheaws constantly ply the Pattaya circuit — down Pattaya Beach Road and up Pattaya 2 Road. Some also drive to Sukhumvit Road along North, Central and South Pattaya Road. Any trip within this region costs 5B. To Naklua it costs 10B as does a ride to Jomtien Beach, however a ride to the southern end of Jomtien Beach costs 20B. Any trip off the main route is considered to a charter and will cost much more. Many tourists in Pattaya complain about being charged much higher rates, but if a driver tries to pull one over you, pay them the correct amount and walk away. They will only continue to hassle you if they think they will get something from you.

Motorbike

Available motorbikes range from a 100cc Honda Dream to a powerful 1000cc Harley Davidson. The cheaper end will cost 150B to 250B per day going up to 700B per day for the beasts. You never need to walk too far before finding someone who hires them out. The cheaper places are along Pattaya 2 Road, but most exist on Pattaya Beach Road and Central Pattaya Road. Motorbike taxis around town should cost around 20B depending on distance.

Cars and Jeeps

Thais must think that farangs love large colourful jeeps because that is what you get, complete with bull bars and some with roll bars from 600B to 1,000B per day. More subdued cars are also available for rent, starting at around 800B per day for a tiny mobile, and more the larger you get. Insurance is usually extra. The rentals on Pattaya 2 Road offer slightly cheaper rates. Sie Car Rental at 216/59 Pattaya 2 Road, in South Pattaya offer cars for 800B fully insured.

Boat

Ferries leave for **Ko Lan** from the pier adjacent to South Pattaya road for 20B. The trip takes around 45 minutes unless the engine blows up and leaves you drifting towards oil rigs.

The travel agent one block south of the songtheaws to Jomtien arranges trips to Phu Quoc Island, Vietnam for 3 days and 2 nights for 7,200B and 4 days and 2 nights for 8,000B on Sunday, Tuesday and Friday. The Vietnamese visa costs an additional 1,000B.

AROUND PATTAYA

JOMTIEN BEACH   จอมเทียน

Just south of Pattaya, Jomtien Beach spreads itself out over a few kilometres. The sex scene here is small and more discreet and the beach is quieter - a welcoming sight after Pattaya. The beach caters more to Thai tourists and on weekends the place is overrun with Bangkokians fighting for deckchairs and cruising the long street in their cars. In the high season the road between Pattaya and Jomtien beach is reminiscent of Silom Road in Bangkok at peak hour. The further south along the beach you go, the quieter it gets along with less food vendors and the beach improves as well.

Post Office Down the third soi off the Beach Road along with the below mentioned budget accommodation.

Bank Thai Farmers Bank have a branch on the corner of Jomtien Beach Road and the third soi.

Cheap Sleeps

Accommodation is generally quite expensive, but there are a few grouped budget places available on the third street off Beach Road once you hit the beach after coming from Pattaya. **JB Guesthouse** is the first on this street, on the corner, ☎ (038) 231 581. Very small but clean rooms cost 200B for a fan and 300B for A/C.

Rainbow is the next along the street, ☎ (038) 231 856. It has no English sign except for a "Room 4 Rent" sign and the rooms are similarly priced to JB Guesthouse.

Hare and Hound House is run by an Aussie with a fascination for flags. It is on the same road after the Post Office, ☎ (038) 232 161. You cannot see the rooms unless you intend staying there 'for security reasons'. A room with A/C and TV costs 230B.

Moonshine Palace down the second street with the 7-eleven at the corner, has rooms with A/C, hot water and cable TV starting at 400B.

Things to do and Sights to See

Although quieter than Pattaya, Jomtien Beach can still get crowded. To escape the crowds go to the southern end of the beach where the beach is better and you will have less people bothering you. The northern end is the mecca of windsurfing in the area due to the more exposed beach and high strength offshore winds. Small sailing boats such as Hobie Cats are also for rent. See the Pattaya section for prices.

◀ Arriving and Departing ▶

Songtheaws leave Pattaya from just south of the intersection of South Pattaya Road and Pattaya 2 Road. It costs 10B to the beginning of the beach and 20B if you travel to the far end. Trips along Beach road cost between 5B and 10B.

KO LAN   เกาะล้าน

Ko Lan is the largest island off the coast of Pattaya and the only one which is accessible by local ferry. The island is quite beautiful offering considerably cleaner beaches than Pattaya and turquoise water. Unfortunately the best of the island's assets are overrun with merry holiday makers, noisy jet skis, banana boats and paragliding. Rumour has it the island is under the strict control of the local mafia who take pride in ripping off tourists with expensive hotels, restaurants and facilities. The snorkelling here is much better than on the mainland, but unfortunately there is no budget accommodation on the island, so it is best visited as a day trip from the mainland.

      Ta Waen Beach on the northwest side of the island is the most pristine and hence the most busy, thus best avoided. **Daeng Beach** is just around the northern end of the beach. It is smaller and has less people per square metre but has the addition of jet boats. **Thien Beach** is located on the southwest side of the island, it is long and more exposed than the others, but does not receive as many visitors, so is quieter. **Samae Beach** and **Nual Beach** are further south of Thien Beach and are more difficult to reach but do offer more privacy. The beaches can be reached by jumping on a motorbike taxi, but will cost 30B to Ta Waen Beach and 50B to Thien Beach, one way. **Ko Sak** and **Ko Krok**, the two small islands to the north and northeast of Ko Lan are accessible by chartered boat only.

Si Racha is known as the home of *nam phrik Si Racha*, the hot chilly sauce found on restaurant tables throughout the country.

East

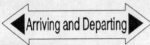

Arriving and Departing

A ferry leaves the pier near the southern end of South Pattaya Road at 08.00 and 10.00 and returns at 12.00, 14.00 and 17.00 for 20B. The trip takes about 45 minutes. You can also charter a boat for 120B without lunch or 280B with lunch, or a speed boat for a paltry 1,000B!

OTHER ISLANDS

Another set of islands exist further out from Ko Lan. The largest, **Ko Phai**, has the smaller **Ko Luam**, **Ko Klung Badan** and **Ko Manvichai** around it to the northwest and south. These islands are really only visited by dive boats so are virtually deserted except for the Royal Thai Navy who looking after them. Access to these islands, if not on a dive trip, is only by chartering a boat for anything between 1,000B and 5,000B per day and they are another 40 minutes out from Ko Lan. If you charter a boat it will cost you twice as much to go to Ko Phai than to Ko Lan even though you have the boat for the full day.

BANG SARAY   บางเสร่

Bang Saray offers a clean getaway from sinful and noisy Pattaya. In Bang Saray let your blood pressure ebb to the slow pace of a fishing village. The beach here is virtually deserted (during the week), and on weekends gets a Thai patronage. Deserted deck chairs occasionally interrupt a long clean stretch of sand, moored fishing boats replace ear shattering jet skis and you can actually hear the small waves lapping at the water's edge. The beach gets more pleasant the further away from town you go and, although the far northern end has a couple of huge luxury hotels, they are really too far away to bother you. Smouldering Pattaya dominates the far horizon - a reminder of where you could be - amongst the carnage.

Orientation

The road leading to the town and beach (Bang Saray Road) is a turn-off to the right shortly after the City Limit sign on Sukhumvit Road. It has an archway at the entrance stating "Bang Saray Fishing Village". This road heads for the ocean 2 km away and ends at the pier and, bar a few bends as it passes through town, the road is dead straight. To the right of the pier after a few houses and restaurants is the beach, and to the left is a 1 km road (Bang Saray Beach Road) with more houses, shops and restaurants. The second road in town runs parallel to Bang Saray Beach Road but about 30 m behind it.

Vital Information

Bank A Thai Military Bank branch is located on Bang Saray Road where there are two bends in close succession.
Police Station is on Bang Saray Road on the corner of the second road back from the pier.
Codes Bang Saray's telephone code is (038).

Cheap Sleeps

Bangsarae Villa Hotel at 24 Mu 2 Bang Saray Beach Road, ☎ (038) 436 070. This pool equiped hotel is 100 m from the beach and 300 m from the English "Hotel" signs on Bang Saray Road, just follow them to reach the hotel. All the rooms have A/C and cost 300B to 400B. You may be able to haggle the price down to 250B if business is slow.

East

There are two other hotels, but they are very expensive, the **Bang Sarae Fishing Lodge** on Bang Saray Beach Road and the **Bang Sarae Condo** at the end of the road parallel to the Beach Road with accommodation starting at 800B.

Eat and Meet

Despite its relatively small size, Bang Saray has a number of excellent seafood restaurants often visited by well-to-do Thais.

Ruantalay Restaurant on Bang Saray Beach Road, ☎ (038) 436 572, is 700 m to the left of the pier and next to the supermarket. Without a doubt the best and most expensive seafood restaurant in town, this eatery is located at the end of a long pot plant covered wharf and it offers an extensive and mouth watering menu with most dishes priced under 100B. The service is exceptional.

Bang Sa Re Restaurant is on the main pier with slightly less expensive meals, less variety and even less decor.

Rimhard Seafood Restaurant at 2/17 Bang Saray Beach Road, ☎ (038) 436 643, the last building before the beach. Large wooden tables look out over the beach with Pattaya in the distance. You can eat basic seafood dishes for 60B to 80B and more for delicacies, although *khao phat* (Fried Rice) is 25B. The English speaking waitress will recommend some gems of dishes and you can eat with romantic Thai music in the background.

Food vendors gather along the beginning of the beach during the day.

Arriving and Departing

Songtheaw
From Sukhumvit Road in Pattaya jump on a white songtheaw or regular bus heading south for 20 to 30 minutes and costing 10B. From the highway to the village either wait for a songtheaw which goes down the road every 15 to 30 minutes for 3B or catch a motorbike taxi for 10B to 20B. You can rent a motorbike at the taxi stand by the pier in the village.

SATTAHIP   สัตหีบ

Located 27 km south of Pattaya, this town is dominated by Thai Navy, Air Force and Army bases and their personnel. Although on the coast, the water in front of the town is polluted and the better beaches around it are owned by the armed forces, so foreigners cannot visit them. So there is really little point in sticking around.

Orientation

As you enter town you will hit a roundabout. To the left is the town's main street, Banna Road. If you continue through the roundabout for another 100 m you will reach Liab Chaitale Road which runs along the water parallel to Banna Road. Directly to the right, the road is accessible only to members of the armed forces. To the left it runs for 1½ km before it also becomes restricted access.

Vital Information

Post Office On Liab Chaitale Road just to the left once you enter via the roundabout road. The telecommunications centre is next door and is open 8.00 am to 8.00 pm.

Banks There are enough banks to choose from along Banna Road and Sai Klang Road, the first road that runs perpendicular to it, east of the roundabout.

Police Station on Liab Chaitale Road, 900 m east of the roundabout, after the small bridge. The **Marine Police** are next door.

Codes Sattahip's telephone code is (038) and the postal code is 20180.

Cheap Sleeps

Navy Hotel on Liab Chaitale Road, ☎ (038) 418 0320, outside the busy part of town, 1½ km east of the post office. Hang out here with Navy holidaymakers in uniform for 500B a night.

Koomdech Hotel at 474 Banna Road 70 m east of the roundabout. Rooms here cost 150B with a fan and two beds, 300B for A/C. This dump is really pretty dirty.

Fishing Trips

You can hire a fishing boat from the pier in front of the roundabout out to the nearby islands and try your luck at hooking a cheap meal.

Ko Samae San   เกาะแสมสาร

Just off the coast from Sattahip lies **Ko Samae San**, which is owned by the Navy, but it may be possible to organise a boat trip out to the island from Chong Samae San on the mainland. Dive centres in Pattaya bring some diving groups here as one of the only two diveable wrecks in Thailand lies nearby. They also come by land, then charter a boat. There is only one hotel in Chong Same San and no hotels on the island.

To get there (if you are not with a diving group) take a songtheaw or bus to the intersection of Route 3 and 33, 6 km to the east of Sattahip. From here you will have to charter a songtheaw for 100B or catch a motorbike taxi for 40B for the 10 km journey to Chong Same San, or hitch a ride if you are lucky, but many cars only go down as far as the airport.

◀ **Arriving and Departing** ▶

Bus

There is a bus station on Liab Chaitale Road opposite and to the east of Sai Klang Road.

Songtheaw

White songtheaws heading down Route 3 from Pattaya pass through town. From Pattaya and Bang Sarae it is 10B. Route 3 passes just to the north of town so if you are on a regular bus you will need to walk 100 m to the east side of Banna Road, but 1 km to the west end of the roundabout.

RAYONG PROVINCE

Rayong Province is best known for the popular Ko Samet island. The coast however is lined with beaches which are slowly being developed, mainly catering to Thai tourists. The beaches certainly are not the nicest around, but do exist. Besides Ko Samet, a number of other islands do sit offshore, including the Man islands south of Klaeng, that do not get the crowds, but facilities are very limited. There is also the Khao Chamao - Khao Wong National Park that borders with Chanthaburi Province.

> Rayong is famous for *nam plaa*, a fermented fish sauce and a common accompaniment to seafood.

RAYONG   ระยอง

Rayong is the capital of Rayong Province, 220 km from Bangkok. There is absolutely nothing to see in Rayong but you may have to pass through if you are heading to Ko Samet, which finds itself on the itinerary of many a wandering beach bum, or to one of the eastern seaboard beaches which are more popular with the Thai tourists.

Orientation

Sukhumvit Road (Route 3) runs east to west through the centre of town. The bus station is one block north of this road and the post office is at the western end of town. The cheaper hotels are 1 km east of the post office on Sukhumvit Road. The other main street in town, Taksin Maharaj Road turns right off Sukhumvit Road at the eastern end of town just past the hotels.

Vital Information

Post Office On Sukhumvit Road slightly east of the bus station. The telephone centre upstairs is open from 7.00 am to 10.00 pm.
Banks Plenty of banks reside on Sukhumvit Road and a couple on Taksin Maharaj Road.
Hospital On Sukhumvit Road in between the bus station and the hotels, right next to the overhead walkway crossing the main road.
Police Station is on Taksin Maharaj Road 500 m north of Sukhumvit Road just after the bridge over the septic Rayong River.
Codes Rayong's telephone code is (038), and the postal code is 21000.

Cheap Sleeps

Three of the cheaper hotels are grouped together 1 km east of the bus station on Sukhumvit Road. Two more expensive hotels are located at the western part of town.
Rayong Otani Hotel at 69 Sukhumvit Road, ☎ (038) 611 161. This huge hotel has clean and spacious rooms with fan for 230B.
Rayong Hotel at 65/3 Sukhumvit Road, ☎ (038) 611 073. The inconspicuous entrance is a white shopfront with dark tinted windows in the middle of the block. There is no English sign outside. Small, dark and hot rooms with fan are 200B/300B for singles/doubles. The A/C rooms are quite the opposite though at 350B/500B.
Asia Hotel Opposite the Rayong Otani down a small alley off Sukhumvit Road, look for the English sign and dodge the cockroaches. Cheap and nasty.
Rayong President Hotel located 50 m down Timtaron Road at 16/8 Timtaron Road, ☎ (038) 611 307, (Siam Commercial Bank on the corner of Sukhumvit Road marks the road) 100 m left of the Post Office, has A/C rooms starting at 550B.

Eat and Meet

The **night market** is on Taksin Maharaj Road, 150 m from Sukhumvit Road where you can pick up delicious Thai take away meals. The marinated and stuffed fish are difficult to walk by. The **day market** is just to the east of the bus station.

A few up-market restaurants exist on Taksin Maharaj Road opposite and to the north of the market. They tend to come complete with waiters in their black and whites. The cheapest restaurant of those in this area is the **Fill Up Restaurant** at 98/8 Taksin Maharaj Road.

East

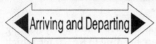

Bus and Songtheaw

Buses from **Bangkok** leave from the eastern bus terminal, A/C buses leave every 30 minutes between 05.00 and 22.00 for 85B, and non A/C buses leave every 30 minutes between 04.30 and 20.00 for 47B. A regular bus to **Pattaya** costs 20B and takes about 1½ hours or you can catch two songtheaws for the same price with the first to Sattahip. Buses to **Chanthaburi** are 30B. To **Ban Phe** (where you get the ferry to Ko Samet) you can catch a large blue songtheaw for 12B from the Rayong bus station. They line up on the eastern side with the destinations listed in English above the songtheaw stop.

AROUND RAYONG

Khao Chamao - Khao Wong National Park   อุทยานแห่งชาติเขาชะเมา

This small 84 sq km National Park is on the border of Rayong and Chanthaburi Provinces and is made up of two mountains of evergreen forest that rise up from the surrounding plains. The park is also connected to the two wildlife sanctuaries, Khao Soi Dao and Khao Ang Ru Nai which, in theory, should help to protect the wildlife. The National Park used to have large numbers of mammals roaming around, but only 22 species have been seen of late. There are also over 50 bird species flapping around.

Khao Chamao, meaning 'drunk', is the highest of the two mountains reaching 1,028 m, but the peak can only be reached if you plan on camping out for the night. A more popular sight is Namtok Khao Chamao, a waterfall 2 km from the park headquarters. Apparently if you eat the fish found in the pond you will become slightly intoxicated, due, it is said, to the effects of the fallen fruit which the fish feed upon. This fruit has also been used to treat leprosy. More arduous trails include one along the Khlong Phlu Valley, as well the trail from the north to the south of the park which follows some high ridges. Experienced trekkers, fully equipped, can also hike into Khao Soi Dao Wildlife Sanctuary. Other interesting sights worth visiting include the 80 Khao Wong caves at the base of Khao Wong Mountain, many of which are used by Buddhist monks, and four other waterfalls. There is accommodation in the park in the form of bungalows and one large dormitory for 80 people.

The park is around 70 km from both Rayong and Chanthaburi. From Route 3, turn off onto Route 3377 which is 7 km east of Klaeng and make your way 17 km along till you reach the village of Ban Nam Sai. From the village take the right hand turn-off for 1 km to the park headquarters. The caves can be reached by their own 12 km access road from Sukhumvit Road, another 14 km east of Route 3377.

Man Islands   เกาะมัน

These three islands, Ko Man Nai, Ko Man Klang and Ko Man Nok, are located south of Klaeng via the seaside resort area Laem Mae Phim. The last two islands each have one resort that offer package tours for 1,000B plus. The islands are accessible by hired boat from the Ma Kham Pom pier at Laem Mae Phim. The trip takes around 50 minutes, and costs 500B for a round trip.

BAN PHE   บ้านเพ

Ban Phe is about 25 minutes by songtheaw from Rayong. From here you can catch one of the many boats to Ko Samet. There are quite a few piers lined up along the water, but the main one is quite obvious, surrounded by travel agents, ticket sellers and touts even in the low season. The songtheaw may let you off at Sri Ban Phe Pier. This is not the correct pier and they charge exorbitant rates from here for a boat to Ko Samet. The main pier is about 400 m to your left (when facing the pier).

East

Vital Information

Tourist Information There is no official TAT Office but plenty of private travel agents will organise any travel arrangements for you. ST Travel which also has an office on Khao San road is opposite the pier and next to the 7-11.

Post Office is located about 350 m to the right of the main pier (when facing the pier).

Banks You can choose from a number of banks located to the right of the main pier and before the market.

Police Station is just to the left of the main pier and opposite the road (facing the pier).

Codes Ban Phe's telephone code is (038) and postcode is 21160.

Cheap Sleeps

If you get caught in Ban Phe there are a couple of accommodation choices, but try not to get stuck here as there is nothing to do except wait for a ferry or walk through the market which has a particularly strong aroma of drying fish.

Bungalow located next to the Thai Farmers bank a few hundred metres on the right of the pier when facing it. The office is an ice cream shop with tinted windows. Bungalows out the back go for 200B.

Queen Hotel, ☎ (038) 651 018, this is 200 m up the road opposite the pier. The hotel has rooms on both sides of the road costing 150B/250B for singles/doubles with fan or 350B/450B for A/C.

TN Place, ☎ (038) 651 824, is only about 100 m to the right (looking at the pier) of the pier but on the opposite side of the road. The office is in the Green Minimart downstairs and rooms are 200B for fan and 300B for A/C.

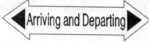 Arriving and Departing

Bus

A/C buses leave from **Bangkok** direct to Ban Phe every hour from 07.00 to 20.30 for 90B, and non A/C buses leave every hour between 05.15 and 18.30 for 50B.

A/C buses leave for Bangkok at 04.00, 07.00, 09.00 and every hour until 16.00, then 17.30 and 18.30. Ordinary buses leave at 05.00, 06.30, 08.30, 10.30, 12.30, 13.30, 14.30, 15.30 and 16.30. A/C minibuses travel to **Pattaya** for 120B at 10.00, 11.30, 13.30, 15.30 and 17.30.

Songtheaw and Minibus

The songtheaw to and from **Rayong** costs 12B each way from Ban Phe, just wave down the passing blue songtheaw. Travel agents at Ban Phe (including ST Travel across the road from the pier) can organise minibuses to **Bangkok** at 10.00 am and 2.00 pm for 150B or to Laem Ngop (**Ko Chang**) at midday for 200B.

Ferry

A number of boats leave for Ko Samet from the pier including regular boats and those that only leave when enough tickets have been sold. See the Ko Samet section for more details. You will be accosted by touts on the pier trying to get you to book accommodation on the island, however the best strategy is to find a place yourself as the island is small therefore making it easy to check out places. Also if you book through a tout, you will pay more for the room.

East

KO SAMET   เกาะเส็ด

Ko Samet island is a very convenient place to visit if you have a few days to kill in Bangkok and want to get away. Some of the places on the island are open year round whilst some of the other popular eastern seaboard islands, such as Ko Chang, are partially closed, making Ko Samet a good place to keep in mind. It is so named due to the dominance of the Samet tree on the island which displays white flowers, however all the growth on the island is secondary or scrub as the original primary trees were chopped down long ago. Ko Samet is part of the larger 131 sq km Khao Laem Ya - Ko Samet National Park encompassing Khao Laem Ya on the mainland, as well as various islands throughout the region. Although marine life has suffered over the recent years due to the waste from development on the mainland, reasonable snorkelling can still be had off Ko Samet's southern tip and off Thalu Island.

The island itself is within a National Park, but very built up with bungalows which line the popular beaches, although in line with National Park guidelines, the guesthouses remain behind the tree line. The abundance of accommodation is well and truly filled in the high season where relatively high rates are charged for a bed. However there are some beautiful areas left on the island as holiday makers very rarely visit the southern coastline which, even in the high season, remains unscathed by tourists. The eastern coast is the most beautiful, dotted with sandy beaches, coves and accommodation, but all parts are easy to visit as the island is only 6 km long and 3 km wide. Most of the accommodation is on the eastern side, but it is well worth a visit to Aow Phrao to watch the sunset.

On the notice board at the park entrance the rangers have placed a small sign requesting visitors not to use jet skis due to the damage they cause on the coral, but obviously the Thai and Korean holiday makers do not bother stopping long enough to read the sign. Jet skiing is now allowed off Sai Kaew and Aow Wong Duan so as not to create problems with the locals, but unfortunately the rangers do not prosecute offenders that ski out of these areas, the result being that the noisy beasts tend to scream up and down the east coast interrupting your quiet time. If you really want to get away from the crowds, try making it out to Ko Khudi. The National Parks have established a camping ground here but you need to bring your own tent, food, and organise your own transport.

WARNING

Malaria has not yet been eradicated from Ko Samet; although not as rampant as in past years, the threat is still very serious. The mosquitoes also tend to come out by the swarm load an hour before dusk after they have had all day to sharpen their teeth, often making you take refuge in your bungalow or on the beach with the sea breeze keeping them away. Make sure you take the necessary precautions in the form of medication, mosquito coils, insect repellent and long sleeves and pants to keep these beasties at bay.

Orientation

Ko Samet is a relatively small island making it easy to explore on foot. From the north to the south of the island it takes around two hours to walk, but a whole day is required if you want to walk along the coast and beaches including a few stops to enjoy the scenery, swims and snorkelling. The main pier is at Na Dan at the northern end of the island. An asphalt road goes through Ko Samet village and ends at the National Park entrance. From here a dirt road extends all the way to the islands southern point but cars can only travel as far as Wong Deuan; motorbikes can try and pass along the thinning road. Another road goes west to Aow Phrao from Thap Thim Beach. All the roads get a hammering in the wet season creating huge pot holes and in some cases the road is completely washed away. The park rangers will roughly fix them up in the dry season. Entry into the National Park has a farang rate of 50B.

Vital Information

Tourist Information There is no TAT Office on the island but most of the larger bungalow operations can provide you with information on the island, change money, organise telephone calls and organise fishing and snorkelling trips.

Post Office Naga Guesthouse on Aow Hin Khok is an authorised Post Office with mailing facilities, poste restante and a fax service (Europe 120B/minute, Asia 90B/minute, Thailand 20B/minute, and to receive a fax costs 20B per page. The number is 66 1 321 0732)

Banks Money exchange on the island offers poor rates and also swipes a 5% to 6% commission on credit card advances. For a large amount of money you are better off to go to the mainland. Ban Phe has plenty of banks with normal rates. Only a few places on the island will give credit card advances including Naga and Sai Khao Villa.

Hospital Ko Samet village, between Na Dan and Sai Kaew Beach has a small health clinic. Ban Phe has a larger clinic, and the closest hospital is at Rayong.

Police Station is next door to the health clinic is the police sub station.

Codes Telephone code is 038, but many places use mobile and or radio phones.

Cheap Sleeps

Ko Samet is a National Park so all bunga-lows must be behind the tree line however the 'tree line' gets closer to the beach the fur-ther south you go, where you may get one virtually on the beach. To avoid the mos-quitoes on the island make sure your bunga-low is completely sealed or has a mosquito net. The mosquitoes get worse, the further you go from the beach. Getting a room with-out a bathroom is good for keeping them away as it removes one source of still water from near your bed.

The accommodation on the island is not the cheapest around as it caters more to the Thai, Korean and Taiwanese tour groups or Western tourists with a few more baht to spend.

The most developed beaches worth avoiding are Sai Kaew and Wong Deuan. However the beaches between them and just south of Wong Deuan offer relatively quiet escapes and beautiful bays. The beaches on the south get very few visitors, even in the high season, making it worth the effort of get-ting there. Aow Phrao is the only beach on the west coast which also retains a peaceful at-mosphere in the high season, mainly due to its limited accommodation. At times at the peak of the high season and during public holidays you may very well find yourself

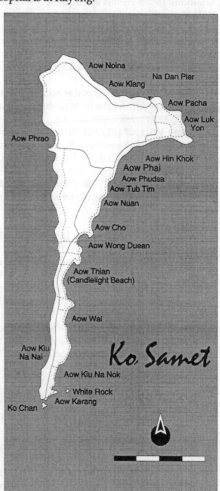

East

sleeping on the beach or on the floor of a restaurant, so booking ahead may be advisable, at other times its easy to find something once you're there. Camping is allowed anywhere on the island.

The following list of accommodation is categorised into respective beaches starting from the east coast. In the more popular beaches it is never more than a five minute walk to the closest exchange, overseas calls and travel facilities.

Hat Sai Kaew

Literally translated as 'white sand' beach, this is the longest and most beautiful of the island's beaches and as a result is the busiest. Reasonably expensive bungalow operations line up beside each other next to the karaoke bars, restaurants and shops and the beach itself is covered in deck chairs and inner tubes with jet skis and banana boats whizzing by. The Thais, Koreans and Taiwanese flock to the beach with their matching coloured towels by the boatload for day trips and weekends, but fortunately they do not often stray from this beach. Not many travellers stay on this beach.

Diamond Beach Resort is the quietest with the best location at the northern end of the beach. With daily BBQ's and videos this is often where the 'action' is. Rooms are a bargain in low season at 100B to 150B but jump to 700B plus in the high season.

Coconut Hut, ☎ (01) 943 2134, have rooms with two beds and bath for 150B low season and 350B in the high season.

Sinsamuk Bungalow has basic rooms with bathroom for 100B (120B in the high season). They have a pool table.

Toy Bungalow The owner of this establishment was shot in the back in the crowded restaurant last year, allegedly by the local mafia, because she refused to sell up. At the time of research Toy Bungalow was closed.

Sai Kaew Villa, ☎ (01) 321 1618, has huts with fan for 200B and with A/C for 500B in the low season. In high season the prices jump at least 100%.

Ploy Talay, ☎ (01) 321 1109, has huts with fan for 200B and 500B for A/C. The high season prices are not too much more.

White Sand Bungalows, ☎ (01) 321 1734, huts cost 150B at the back and 200B to 300B up front. In high season the prices rise to 200B and 400B to 500B respectively.

Aow Hin Khok

Separated from Hat Sai Kaew by a small rocky outcrop, adorned by a faded mermaid and prince statue, this beach retains the beauty of its northern neighbour, but on a smaller scale. Hin Khok is slightly less busy, but gets a lot of noisy jet skis cruising its shores. The statues are representations of a famous Thai epic, "Phra Aphai Mani", written by Sunthorn Phu (1786 to 1856) where a mermaid saved a prince from an underwater prison taking him to Ko Samet to live and be merry together. The prince killed the pursuing giant with his magic flute.

Naga Bungalow, ☎ (01) 321 0732, has been around for a while and the huts are showing their age. Small thatched very run down bungalows cost 80B, whilst slightly better ones are 100B. Naga is the official GPO and also does a good impression of a bakery, selling baguettes and other yummy tasties such as chocolate fudge. The restaurant (complete with ping pong table) sells pizza.

Tok's Little Hut has quite nice bungalows but they are fairly close together. The cheapest are at the back and for 150B are roomy, clean and have Western toilets. The 200B rooms are larger, have a fan and tiled floor and are closer to the beach. The restaurant here pulls in a dedicated crowd of video addicts on a nightly basis and also has chairs set up on the beach for a more pleasant eating atmosphere.

Jep's Bungalow is at the end of the small beach with huts for 200B. The food here is exceptionally good and worth checking out. They set up chairs on the beach but also have a restaurant on the other side of the road where they play a great selection of music instead of videos. At the end of the beach is a ramshackle construction where a woman named Chawalee lives with her dogs and extended family. She refuses to change her lifestyle as she has been living here for as long as anyone can remember, despite the fact that the land would be worth millions of baht.

Aow Phai
This beach is quite small, a pleasant size in the low season where you can go for a swim and find a patch of sand to dry off on, however in the high season gets quite crowded.
Aow Phai Hut, ☎ (01) 353 2644, is just before the small hill, but before the beach. This particularly friendly place is one of the best deals on the island. A screen sealed wooden room with Thai bathroom costs 100B (200B in high season) and more pricey bungalows have A/C. Electricity is from 5.00 pm to 7.00 am and there is water available 24 hours. The bungalows are set quite a way back from the beach, but are well spaced and shaded under native trees.
Seabreeze Bungalows The road travels up the side and behind Seabreeze Bungalows giving it clear access to the beach, but the squashed bungalows in a treeless compound get a bit of noise. Small bungalows go for 150B and ones with two beds go for 170B. The restaurant here plays a particularly good selection of films, try requesting one.
Silversand is at the end of the beach with bungalows for 150B/170B for singles/doubles and 300B to 350B for A/C. The bungalows are close together not allowing for much tree cover and the cheapest rooms are badly located.
Samed Villa, ☎ (01) 239 0223, is at the rocky end of the beach. Bungalows are 200B/250B for singles/doubles (more in the high season) and are very clean with real beds. The grounds are landscaped and well kept, providing a peaceful atmosphere.

Aow Phutsa (Aow Thap Thim)
Also known as Aow Thap Thim, this beach can be reached via either a turn-off from the main road or a small path that follows the coastline from Aow Phai. The beach is quite small but nevertheless nice, however the deck chair plague is beginning to make its presence felt here.
Pudsa Bungalow is the first on the beach. Some bungalows are quite close to the beach and generally well spread. Small bungalows with Thai bathroom come with mattress and not much more room for 150B. Slightly larger rooms go for 200B.
Rimtalay Express operates from here, catering for all your travel requirements.
Tub Tim Bungalow, ☎ (01) 321 1425, at the other end of the beach is a large operation with well spaced bungalows. Small huts are fully screened with raised bed and cost 200B. More stable wooden and concrete structures go for 400B and 500B. The best location on the far right of the hill costs 1,500B and sleeps 10 people. The beach bar here pumps out *great* hits such as "My Sharona!"

Aow Nuan
This tiny bay is one of the most secluded and romantic on the whole island accessible by a 10 minute walk from Aow Phutsa via the coastal route. The huts are easy to miss, but look for the roofs of the bungalows behind the trees. There is one bungalow operation here, **Aow Nuan Bungalows** that has large, open, oriental style bungalows going for 200B and more. The bay retains its ambience at night with the lack of electricity, relying on lamps to see your way around. A small atmospheric restaurant amidst a landscape of native plants arouses your taste buds.

Aow Cho
This beach is close by, but is open and dirty with few trees around the bungalows. There is a pier here with a boat leaving at 09.00, 11.00, 13.00 and 15.00.
Wonderland Resort has pretty old and dreary rooms, some with four rooms connected to each other. They cost 150B for the front and 100B out back, but the prices here are negotiable. They offer **sunset boat rides** from 4.00 pm to 7.00 pm.
Tarn Tawan has larger bungalows for 200B.

Aow Wong Duan

This is the second largest centre on the island after Hat Sai Kaew and is just as busy but lacks the beauty. The beach is lined with bars and restaurants and small shops all flashing their lights trying to entice you into their den. The only vaguely atmospheric place is Nice and Easy Restaurant in the middle of the beach, which plays decent music for lamp lit tables on the beach. Most of the accommodation here is fairly upmarket. In high season ferries depart from here at 08.30, 12.00, 14.00 and 16.00 for 30B.

Samet Cabana Bungalow provides ugly constructions with two small rooms and one shared bath for 150B per room. Larger bungalows with dirty bathrooms cost 200B, more in the high season.

Malibu Garden Resort the accommodation here is excessively expensive, but they do have a mini-mart.

Seahorse Bungalows At the cheaper end of the scale, the small bungalows cost 100B with decent bathrooms, but they are fairly exposed and do cost more in the high season.

Wong Duan Resort have bungalows priced in the 600B to 1,200B range, but offer a 50% discount in the low season.

Wong Duan Villa is next door and is also very expensive.

Aow Thian (Candlelight Beach)

On the coastal path you will be welcomed by a large wooden "Candlelight Beach" sign just over the hill, which is the name by which it is mostly referred to. The beach is long but narrow and broken up by rocky sections with deck chairs at the northern end and a rustic setting for beach lined bungalows at the southern end.

Candlelight Beach Bungalows Large bungalows sitting upon the hill overlooking the bay cost 400B, and although cheaper accommodation is available at 150B, if the wind picks up, your homely little bungalow may well blow over.

Bungalows The next place on this beach has bungalows virtually on the beach. Very basic huts with shared bath are 150B, whilst cute dog box like huts are 100B. The beds here are thin mattresses on the floor, but some of the huts have quite a bit of character.

Lung Dum Hut These sometimes unstable bungalows at the far end of the beach cost 100B and 150B with bath, and there is one small tree house available with a bird's eye view of the beach.

Aow Wai

This is a serene bay, sealed at both ends by tree covered headlands and calm blue green water. It is a fair walk down from Candlelight Beach and has one expensive resort, **Samet Villa**, ☎ (038) 651 681, which dominates the bay. Rooms with two beds go for 600B in the low season (when it is virtually empty) and slightly more in the high season (when it is still virtually empty). Even if you do not plan on staying here, it is still worth a visit. In the high season, it is possible to reach the beach by ferry.

Aow Kiu

A further 20 minutes walk over the rocks or via the road is Aow Kiu, a long stretch of unblemished sand backed by coconut trees. Very few people come here, even in the high season.

Ao Rin Coral Beach, ☎ (01) 321 1231, can supply you with a large and sturdy room with real beds, fan and Thai bathroom for 500B. They also have a couple of run down thatched huts around the place.

Aow Kiu Nanai

About 100 m walk from Aow Kiu, this offers fine **sunset** views and the best **snorkelling** on the island (about 50 m left and out to the ocean.)

East

Aow Karang
This is the rocky point at the far end of the island visible from Aow Kiu. There is one decrepit bungalow operation, **Bungalow Ao Pakarang**, which may blow right away in the next storm.

Northeast Coast
Aow Yon
Just over the hill behind Hat Sai Kaew are a couple of average places to stay, set back from a beachless coastline.

Banana Bungalow, ☎ (01) 321 0841, is the closest to Hat Sai Kaew with small bungalows with double bed, fan and Thai bath for 150B.

Pineapple Beach Bungalow, ☎ (01) 323 0714, have two bed bungalows with fan, bath and large balcony for 300B. Electricity is available from 6.00 pm to 6.00 am.

Aow Wiang Wan
Located to the west of Na Dan pier is a large bay where the locals have spread themselves out along the water's edge. The first lot of houses are set on stilts offshore where they breed large turtles and moor their fishing boats. Tours around the island often stop here for a look. There are a few bungalow operations along this stretch of coastline, but many have the look of failed ventures about them. At the far end of the bay between the piers is a sandy section of the beach. These resorts may only be open at the peak of the high season to capture the overflow of people from the nicer eastern coast resorts.

Samed Inn is positioned upon a hill and has very rustic, small and basic huts with shared bath for 150B.

Samed Resort is nearby, but was closed at the time of research. Prices would be around 400B.

Samed Cliff The dirt road suddenly becomes paved and long grass turns into manicured lawns. This is an expensive resort with orderly bungalows lined up by each other, each with their own private garden, but the 1,500B for a room makes it a bit hard on the pocket.

Samed Hut Small quaint bungalows line up facing each other in a V shape, each one has a bath and costs 300B plus.

West Coast
Aow Phrao
The road for Aow Phrao turns off behind Aow Phutsa, leading west to the only beach with accommodation and sunset view. The beach, Hat Sawahn, is fairly long and, due to the limited accommodation, it is always possible to find a quiet spot to relax or meditate, even in the high season. In high season Aow Phrao is also accessible by ferry.

Hat Sawahn Beach Bungalows A Swiss guy provides spacious wooden bungalows with mosquito nets, mattress on the floor and bathrooms for 150B in the low season, 450B in the high season. This is a pretty relaxed place with good music and a barge in the water from where you can catch the sunset. David from Holland is a **PADI instructor** who runs a diving school from the bungalows, but only does the open water course for 8,500B (without manual) over a leisurely five days and takes out both day and night dives.

Dome Bungalows, ☎ (038) 651 377, have concrete and wooden bungalows connected to each other, located on the hill. They come with proper beds, small bathroom and large balcony for 200B low season, 400B high season.

Aow Phrao Resort, ☎ (038) 651 156, this is an upmarket resort with the cheapest rooms starting at 1,400B. They hire excellent mountain bikes for 100B per hour and the restaurant makes good cappuccinos served by immaculately dressed waiters.

Ko Samet Village
The village at the north of the island spreads itself along the concrete road between Na Dan Pier and the National Park entrance. The street is lined with noodle shops, restaurants, grocery stores, pubs and karaoke bars, some which are open 24 hours catering to the

increasing tourist trade. The highlight of the town is the bakery where you can pick up large and small loaves of multigrain bread and chocolate treats. The art and tattoo shop sells original batik paintings and woodwork. Ask for Gai, the artist, and enjoy a chat over a coffee. Take any spare cloth badges or patches you may have for his jacket.

Eat and Meet

Every beach has restaurants attached to the bungalows, except for the remote Aow Karang and many of these do **nightly seafood barbecues**.

Jeps Inn at Aow Phai has particularly delicious cuisine and is complemented by digestible music rather than blaring videos.

The busier the beach, the wider the choice of restaurants, **Nice and Easy** on Aow Wong Duan gets a dedicated following and also plays good music.

Ko Samet has also been blessed with a couple of **bakeries**. **Naga** has been around the longest, but concentrates on baguettes. Another bakery is in Ko Samet village and bakes soft multigrain bread and, like Naga, has a selection of tempting treats like chocolate fudge.

In **Ko Samet village** there are a few 24 hour restaurants along with a few **noodle shops**.

Things to do and Sights to See

If you can tear yourself away from the beach and refreshing water, take a **hike with your mask and snorkel in hand to the south of the island** and escape the crowds. There are also some walks into the forest in the central and northern part of the island. The trails are thin and often overgrown and it is advisable to wear decent shoes and long pants in an attempt to keep the snakes at bay. The National Park officers are not of much help for information, so try your bungalow for the location of trails.

Arriving and Departing

Bus

To/From Bangkok

Coming from **Bangkok**, you are best to catch a bus direct to Ban Phe from the eastern bus terminal which will drop you off a few hundred metres from the pier to Ko Samet. From Khao San Road it is also possible to catch a minibus to Ban Phe and this tends to include the ferry cost in the price.

If arriving from elsewhere, catch a bus to **Rayong** then one of the large blue songtheaws which line up at the eastern side of the bus terminal to Ban Phe for 12B.

Ferry

In the low season boats to **Ko Samet** go only as far as **Na Dan** and depart four times daily, returning from the island at 07.00, 08.30, 12.30, 15.00 or when 18 people accumulate at the pier. The scheduled boats will leave earlier than planned if full, so you may want to get there a little early. The fare to Na Dan is 30B and takes 40 minutes. In the high season boats leave regularly between 06.00 and 17.00 for the same price.

In the high season many of the beaches can be reached directly from Ban Phe in boats owned by the individual resorts. Catch the boat to Na Dan if you want to stay anywhere at the northern end of the island or Sai Kaew, Aow Hin Khok, Aow Phai, Aow Thap Thin or Aow Phutsa. It is possible to walk from Na Dan to Aow Phutsa in around 20 minutes and less for the other beaches.

Aow Cho is serviced by a boat called "White Shark" for 30B and from here you can walk north to Aow Thian.

East

Aow Wong Duan has three boats, the "Seahorse", "Malibu" and "Wong Deuan Villa" which make the trip to Ban Phe for 30B. If you want to get to Aow Thian, catch the boat to Aow Wong Duan and walk south for 5 minutes.

For Aow Wai, catch the boat "Phra Aphai" for 40B and for Aow Kiu and Aow Karang catch "Thep Chonthaleh" for 30B.

The western beach, **Aow Phrao**, is also serviced by a boat for 30B.

If the boat to the beach of your choice is not full, you may be asked to pay more. If this is the case and you do not want to pay up, jump on one of the boats going to a more popular beach such as Aow Wong Duan and walk from there.

The pier at Ban Phe is full of touts trying to convince you to stay at their bungalow. Firstly, it works out cheaper if you find accommodation yourself and, secondly, these touts may mislead you on the quality of their establishment. So ask around at a few places, the travel agents which are not affiliated with a particular resort are your best bet for accurate information beside this book.

Getting Around

Once on the island songtheaws run to many of the beaches from Na Dan pier. Fares are as follows; Sai Kaew 10B (100B charter), Aow Phai, Aow Phutsa, Aow Thap Thin 20B (150B charter) Aow Phrao 30B (200B charter), Aow Wong Duan 30B (200B charter), Aow Thian 40B (300B charter), Aow Wai 40B (400B charter) and Aow Kiu 50B (500B charter). Before hopping on, always check the price to make sure you do not get charged the charter price. Occasionally in the wet season, the roads beyond Aow Wong Duan deteriorate and may be impassable. In the dry season a somewhat haphazard repair programme gets to some of the roads, the only indication that the 50B entry fee is being used wisely.

It is possible to rent **trail bikes** from one shop in Ko Samet Village, although they are quite expensive. Look for the motorbikes prominently displayed on the front porch. The best and cheapest way to get around is to walk. From north to south takes around two hours and is free. Mountain Bikes are available from Aow Phrao Resort at the beach on the west side of the island and are more expensive at 100B an hour plus passport.

CHANTHABURI PROVINCE

Little visited, this large province is best known for its gems and two large National Parks Namtok Phliu National Park and Khao Kitchakut National Park. The province's eastern side borders with Cambodia creating a mix of cultures in some areas.

CHANTHABURI   จันทบุรี

Chanthaburi, the city of the moon, located just under 300 km from Bangkok, is a mixing pot of different cultures seen in the faces of the inhabitants and the architecture that lines the streets. The most interesting part of town is the busy Chinese and Vietnamese quarter by the river. The Vietnamese, mostly Christians, arrived in droves on three separate occasions — during the persecution of Vietnamese Christians in the 1800s, during the treacherous rule of the French in the early 20th Century and in 1975 following the re-unification of Vietnam. The Chinese, as well as the Burmese and Cambodians, have ventured into Chan, as it is known by the locals, to partake in the lucrative gem and precious stone industry. Chanthaburi has long been the centre for ruby and sapphire mining in Thailand. The French, who ruled the town between 1893 and 1905, have left behind streets filled with hangovers from French architecture most prevalent around the river. On a tastier note, they have also influenced the local bakeries with the occasional croissant.

Chanthaburi is also known for its food, especially fruit. The tropical fruits grown here are amongst the best in Thailand and the noodles are famous worldwide.

East

Vital Information

Post Office On Benchamarachutid Road to the right of the end of Saritidet Road. Staffed by friendly English speaking staff with matching T-shirts! Open Monday to Friday 8.30 am to 4.30 pm, Saturday 9.00 am to 12.00 pm. The phone office is open 8.30 am to 4.30 pm.
Banks Spread around the market area, see the map for details.
Hospital The front entrance is on Saritidet Road by the bus station, but the hospital grounds take up the length of the block with a back entrance on Tha Luang Road.
Police Station is situated at the river end of Tha Luang Road.
Codes Chanthaburi telephone code is (039) and the postal code is 22000.

Cheap Sleeps

The cheapest and quietest accommodation is on the road by the river.
Arunsawat Hotel, ☎ (039) 311 082, at 239 Sukha Phiban Road is directly opposite the Chanthra Hotel and your best bet in town. There is no sign on the outside, but if you look inside, the hotel name is on the back wall. Rooms are the same price as at the Chanthra Hotel but are clean and well cared for. A/C rooms start at 150B.
Chanthra Hotel, ☎ (039) 312 388, at 248 Sukha Phiban Road has rooms with fan and a tiny bathroom for 120B and a cubicle without a bath for 100B. Unless you get one of the rooms overlooking the river (with small balcony) you have to be satisfied with dark rooms that could do with a scrub. The family who run it are very friendly though.
Kasem San 1 Hotel, ☎ (039) 311 100, at 98/1 Benchamarachutid Road, the very end of Saritidet Road has rooms with fan for 120B, A/C rooms for 200B and a good restaurant on the ground floor, although on a noisy street.
Kasem San 2 Hotel, ☎ (039) 311 173, at 23 Sirong Muang 2 Road is an associated branch of Kasem San 1 and has the same prices, but on a noisier street
S Sukchai Hotel, ☎ (039) 311 292, at 28 Tha Chaleb Road has old and noisy rooms for 100B.
Chanthaburi Hotel, ☎ (039) 311 300, at 42/6 Tha Chaleb Road, the entrance is on Naresuan 2 Road on a busy intersection. Rooms with fan start at 200B and A/C starts at 240B.
Kiatkachorn, ☎ (039) 311 212, at 27/28 Tha Luang Road, the road behind the bus station. Rooms are 150B for a fan and 250B for A/C, if they will let you stay.
Chai Lee, ☎ (039) 311 075, at 106 Kwang Road. Go down the driveway to find rooms with fan for 160B and A/C for 300B. Set back from a noisy road.

Eat and Meet

Chanthaburi is known for its fruit, and during the fruit fair in May or June you will get plenty of it. The large market has the usual abundance of food vendors, although it is not till night that the surrounding streets come alive with their mouthwatering aromas. Food stalls are set up in front of the market (by the roundabout), but as you make your way around to the west and southern sides, you will find more food stalls than you know what to do with. Many sell Thai deserts where you may be able to find the odd croissant.
Khon Tim Foodshop Directly at the end of the soi leading to the Chanthra Hotel, is this immaculately decorated small restaurant set overlooking the river. The front is a beauty salon. The English menu is basic and cheap (20B to 40B) whilst the Thai menu is more extensive with most meals costing 60B, so practice your Thai.
Seafood Restaurant is at the end of Awatha and Tesaban 2 Roads. Here you can get your Western style hamburger, pizza and ice cream cake fix as well as a number of other dishes. Decked out with underwater nostalgia it comes complete with a kids playground! Open 10.00 am to 9.00 pm weekdays and 10.00 am to 10.00 pm on weekends.

East

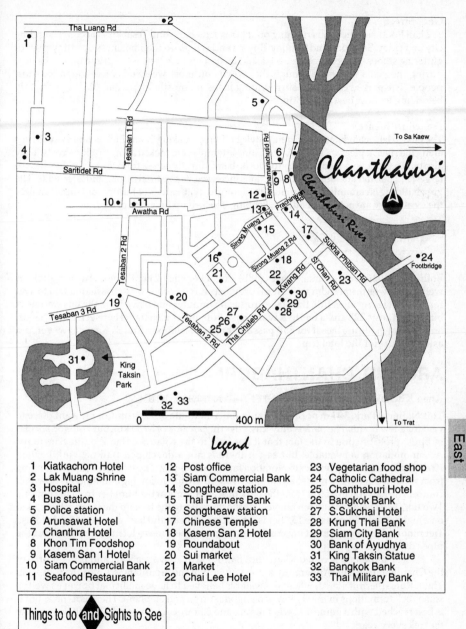

Legend

1 Kiatkachorn Hotel	12 Post office	23 Vegetarian food shop
2 Lak Muang Shrine	13 Siam Commercial Bank	24 Catholic Cathedral
3 Hospital	14 Songtheaw station	25 Chanthaburi Hotel
4 Bus station	15 Thai Farmers Bank	26 Bangkok Bank
5 Police station	16 Songtheaw station	27 S.Sukchai Hotel
6 Arunsawat Hotel	17 Chinese Temple	28 Krung Thai Bank
7 Chanthra Hotel	18 Kasem San 2 Hotel	29 Siam City Bank
8 Khon Tim Foodshop	19 Roundabout	30 Bank of Ayudhya
9 Kasem San 1 Hotel	20 Sui market	31 King Taksin Statue
10 Siam Commercial Bank	21 Market	32 Bangkok Bank
11 Seafood Restaurant	22 Chai Lee Hotel	33 Thai Military Bank

Things to do and Sights to See

King Taksin Park and Monument   อนุสาวรีย์สมเด็จพระเจ้าตากสินมหาราช

This fairly large man-made lake and islands offer a pleasant day or night escape. By day, fitness fanatics make themselves dizzy jogging around the statue of King Taksin and his charging horse. By night, the young folk make themselves dizzy on whiskey. You can hire paddle boats and swan boats from beside the clocktower for 30B per hour.

Gem Street
Si Chan Road and the roads running off it (Trok Krachang and Tesaban 4) become haggling city on Friday, Saturday and Sunday. Buyers and sellers do their business over tiny piles of glittering stones trying to get the best deal. The first week in June is the prime time to be here during the gems festival, although the crowds on most weekends are enough for most people. The parked cars in the surrounding lanes are mostly Mercs and BMWs, obviously belonging to those best at their trade.

French Influence
The French left behind dozens of French style buildings, making Sukha Phiban Road which runs along the river, a pleasant stroll. A few Chinese temples are tucked away up side streets. They also built a Catholic cathedral on the opposite bank, directly across from the footbridge. It is the largest in Thailand after four reconstructions increased its size to 60 m long and 20 m wide. The grey building is certainly not reminiscent of the great cathedrals of Europe and unfortunately the local clergy are not the friendliest, keeping it locked up for much of the time.

Bus
Both A/C (108B) and ordinary buses (48B) travel between Chanthaburi and **Bangkok**, as well as to towns throughout the eastern province. It is possible to catch a shared taxi to **Trat** for 40B that leave when full, they take around 45 minutes and leave from the bus station. A bus to Trat costs 22B and a bus to **Rayong** costs 30B. Buses also travel between Chanthaburi and **Khorat** in the northeast for 85B passing through Kabinburi and Sa Kaew however, put aside 5 hours for the total trip.

AROUND CHANTHABURI

Khao Kitchakut National Park   อุทยานแห่งชาติเขาคิชฌกูฏ
This National Park, 30 km north of Chanthaburi on Route 3249, is quite a pleasant place to visit for a few hours. The park is only tiny, covering an area of 59 sq km, but holds 53 species of birds, probably due to the fact that it lies next to the Khao Soi Dao Wildlife Sanctuary. Accommodation is available, but as yet there is not a developed trail network beyond **Krathing Falls**, making further exploration fairly challenging. The falls have 13 tiers, ranging from water rolling over a rock to an ear shattering 10 m drop following a continuous downhill course. The falls roll by 150 m from the park office, entering at the third tier from the bottom. Two tiers exist below it and ten above. It is worth making the trek up the steep hill for 1 km on a highly eroded path as the 13th tier is set amongst a beautiful background of dense forest. Tier nine and ten are the most impressive and the path becomes a lot more pristine once the pipes disappear.

The mountain is called Khao Phra Bat, 1,000 m above sea level and is the source of the Chanthaburi River. Apparently at the very top of the mountain is a Buddha footprint, Tham Ruesi (hermit's cave) where the water is believed to have medicinal power as well as some rock formations in the shapes of a pagoda, turtle and elephant. There is a track, but it is best reached with a guide and will take around 3 hours. A number of Thai pilgrims make the trek every year.

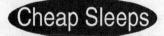

Accommodation comes in the form of bungalows starting at 600B for eight people to 1,200B for 14 people. Hiring a tent costs 40B and if you have your own it costs 5B. There have been cases of malaria reported in this park, so take insect repellent even if you are on malaria medication. Food is available in the park.

Arriving and Departing

Songtheaws run from the beginning of Prachiniyan Road in Chanthaburi opposite the Post Office every hour, and the driver may drop you at the boom gates for 20B, else it costs 15B to the turn-off, and a 1½ km walk to the park entrance. The road to the park is well used so hitching should not be too difficult.

Namtok Phliu - Khao Sabap National Park   น้ำตกพลิ้ว

Located 14 km from Chanthaburi, the highlight of this park is Phliu Waterfall which flows straight out of the side of the mountain into a large pool of water below where both Thais and fish frolic in the water. The park and waterfall, the fourth most frequently visited in Thailand are very popular with Thai visitors and, going by the size of the carpark and the army of Park Rangers, actually reaching the waterfall on weekends could be a struggle. There is wheelchair access for part of the way up but unfortunately the path does not lead to the best viewpoint of the falls. King Rama V built a bell shaped stupa to mark the spot where he and the Queen used to court and a pyramid shrine to hold her ashes after she drowned in 1876. Another trail leads to the top of the falls (which you cannot see) then dwindles into nothing.

The National Park takes up an area of 135 sq km, most of it a granite protrusion from the surrounding plains. The rainforest has been extensively logged over the years but still holds a few critters, with the most unique being the Siamese fireback, silver pheasant, the chestnut headed partridge and the blue rumped pitta.

There are three other waterfalls within the park boundaries, Makok, Khlong Nalai and Trok Nong Waterfalls, but they cannot be reached from the park office, but rather are reached from separate access roads along the park's boundary. Apparently there is a narrow road connecting Phliu and Trok Nong Waterfalls which would take a day to walk, but good luck in finding it as the park office and visitor centre seem fairly tight lipped about it.

Namtok Khlong Nalai is half way between Chanthaburi and Namtok Philiu and requires a 2½ km walk in from the main road. To reach Namtok Trok Nong catch a songtheaw to Klung town, then another for 10 km along the east side of the park. The turn-off to the falls is 3½ km along from the main road. Entry to the park is 3B.

Cheap Sleeps

Namtok Phliu has heaps of food vendors lining the street directly in front of the park entrance. There is no camping near the park headquarters but there are three bungalows, one for 600B which sleeps eight people and two for 800B also sleeping eight. Namtok Nong has a camping ground where amenities (showers, toilets and fireplaces) are provided but you must have your own tent and food.

Arriving and Departing

Songtheaws leave from the north of the market next to the roundabout in Chanthaburi. The driver will take you to the park entrance for 25B or to the turn-off for 10B, taking around 25 minutes, after which it is a 2½ km walk or hitch to the park headquarters. When you are leaving, unless you are particularly lucky, you will also need to walk back out to the turn-off. Songtheaws stop at 6.00 pm.

East

TRAT PROVINCE

Trat Province is the easternmost province of the eastern region of Thailand and includes numerous islands off its western coast, in the Gulf of Thailand. On the mainland it borders Chanthaburi to the west and north, and Cambodia to the east. The Khao Banthat Mountain Range extends along most of the eastern side creating a natural border, however this natural border was not enough to stem tens of thousands of refugees fleeing the terror and bloodshed in neighbouring Cambodia during the rein of Pol Pot. Up until the early 90s it was still possible to see the red glow from artillery in the evenings, closing the road south of Trat to the border when it was at its worst. The region on the Cambodian side of the border has been a Khmer Rouge stronghold for some time due to extensive natural resources in gems and timber which are smuggled into Thailand to allow the continued flow of funds to the Khmer Rouge. The border crossing between Hat Lek (Thailand) and Ko Kong (Cambodia) both officially and unofficially is a popular route for smuggled goods, drugs and prostitutes. Although closed to foreigners, it can unofficially be crossed for day trips and longer sorties into Khmer territory.

TRAT   ตราด

Trat is the provincial capital, situated around 400 km from Bangkok. Generally the town is only casually visited by foreigners heading out to the islands but is a pleasant town retaining a welcoming atmosphere, and the friendly inhabitants make a stop well worthwhile. There is not much to do in town, but it can be used as a base before going to Cambodia or for chilling out before or after visiting the islands.

Vital Information

Post Office On Tha Ruao Jang Road, out of the busy area of town but still close enough to walk. Phone facilities are open from 7.00 am to 10.00 pm.
Banks All along Sukhumvit Road, see the map for details.
Hospital Trat hospital is at the northern end of Sukhumvit Road, past the traffic lights. Trat Hospital has the reputation for the best malaria unit in Thailand and even patients from Bangkok are sent here for treatment. If you get any signs of malaria, as it is still a problem on the islands, get to the hospital as soon as you can.
Police Station is on the corner of Wiwitthana and Santisuk Roads at the northern end of the fitness park.
Codes Trat's telephone code is (039) and the postal code is 23000.

Cheap Sleeps

Foremost Guesthouse at 49 Thana Charoen Road, ☎ (039) 511 923, has been recently renovated offering rooms upstairs and a lounging around area downstairs which is A/C. Rooms are 60B with a large mattress, common bathroom and hot shower. Eddie, the owner, speaks excellent English and can provide you with up-to-date and detailed information about the province, islands and visits to neighbouring Cambodia.
Windy Guesthouse is also owned by Eddie, offering the same information and facilities in a more rustic setting upon the canal. The rooms are 60B with a bed, fan and most of the beds have mosquito nets. There is one single room for 50B. The rooms have been made from old shipping crates and some are so close to the toilets you can hear other guest's bodily functions, the relaxed outdoor environment makes your stay enjoyable, either on the small balcony, where you can watch the fireflies playing amongst the opposite palm trees, or in the small meeting area. Guests can use the hot shower at Foremost and all rooms have a common bathroom.

East

N.P. Guesthouse at 10 Soi Yai Ohn, ☎ (039) 512 270. This place has been completely renovated from an old wooden shopfront. There are twenty beds, ranging from 40B dorms (in the hallway), 80B singles and 120B doubles all with immaculate share bathroom facilities. They serve the standard Thai and Western food but it is cheaper to eat at the market. It is run by a friendly family that can also provide information on the region.

Trat Inn, ☎ (039) 511 028, the cheapest of the other hotels in town but it is also known as the busiest brothel in town. Rooms are 150B/190B for singles and doubles.

Trat Hotel is next to the hectic day and night market, rooms with fan 220B/370B for singles/doubles and 370B/500B for singles/doubles with A/C.

Thai Roong Roj Hotel is in the centre of Trat's night scene, fan rooms are 200B/250B for singles/doubles and 350B/400B for A/C singles and doubles.

Eat and Meet

The best and cheapest place for food is at the **night market** where you can choose from a variety of Thai delights. Ask Eddie from Foremost Guesthouse to show you the mouth watering curry stall that sets up in the night market after 9.00 pm. For dessert try the chocolate pancake with banana for dessert from the first stall off Sukhumvit Road.

Thai Restaurant A popular Thai restaurant is located on Tha Ruao Jang Road. They have some delicious vegetarian meals including an extraordinary baby eggplant dish, as well as Thai desserts out the front. One dish with rice is 15B and 5B for every scoop of another dish.

Sang Fah Restaurant A fairly sterile restaurant serving meals between 80B and 100B, although fried rice is 30B. It also acts as a bakery and serves ice cream.

Things to do **and** Sights to See

The nightlife in Trat caters solely to horny Thai men, so foreigners need to make their own fun.

Boat Trips

Eddie from Foremost and Windy Guesthouses is contemplating running overnight camping trips in the high season to the offshore islands where you will be able to fish, snorkel and camp under the stars. If you can get a group together he may run an interesting trip down to the border for you.

East

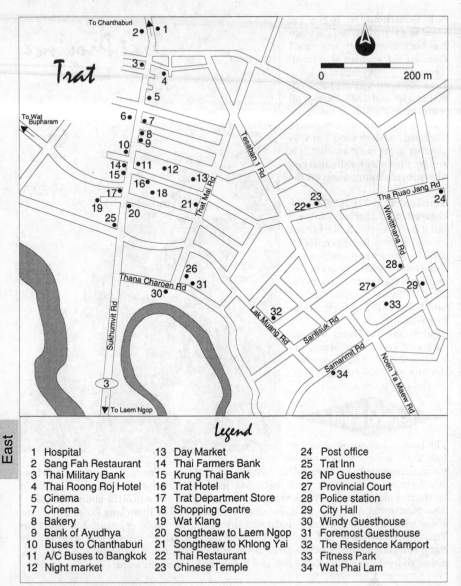

Trat

To Chanthaburi

To Wat Bupharam

To Laem Ngop

Tesaban 1 Rd

Tha Ruao Jang Rd

Wiwithana Rd

That Mai Rd

Sukhumvit Rd

Thana Charoen Rd

Lak Muang Rd

Santisuk Rd

Samanmit Rd

Noen Ta Maew Rd

0   200 m

Legend

1	Hospital	13	Day Market	24	Post office
2	Sang Fah Restaurant	14	Thai Farmers Bank	25	Trat Inn
3	Thai Military Bank	15	Krung Thai Bank	26	NP Guesthouse
4	Thai Roong Roj Hotel	16	Trat Hotel	27	Provincial Court
5	Cinema	17	Trat Department Store	28	Police station
6	Cinema	18	Shopping Centre	29	City Hall
7	Cinema	19	Wat Klang	30	Windy Guesthouse
8	Bakery	20	Songtheaw to Laem Ngop	31	Foremost Guesthouse
9	Bank of Ayudhya	21	Songtheaw to Khlong Yai	32	The Residence Kamport
10	Buses to Chanthaburi	22	Thai Restaurant	33	Fitness Park
11	A/C Buses to Bangkok	23	Chinese Temple	34	Wat Phai Lam
12	Night market				

East

The Residence Kamport

This building was used by the French officials when they seized Trat in 1904. They stayed until 1907. It was restored in 1928 and used as a medical centre. After this it was left to ruins, so now the crumbling walls make a wander through the building quite dangerous.

Wat Bupharam   วัดบุผาราม

This wat is 2 km from downtown Trat. Over 200 years old, the wat contains buildings constructed during the late Ayutthaya Period. It is worth visiting if you want to fill up a couple of hours whilst in Trat.

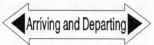

Bus

Buses leave **Bangkok's** eastern bus terminal and take around 6 hours. A/C buses cost 140B and non A/C buses cost 78B. A/C buses leave **Trat** for Bangkok at 06.00 then hourly until 23.30 and almost as regularly in the other direction. The ordinary buses run from Trat up until 23.00 in both directions.

Non A/C buses leave for **Chanthaburi** across the road but the actual non A/C bus station is about 1 km south of here, out of the centre of town. The bus leaves every half an hour between 05.30 and 14.30, then 15.45, 16.20 and 17.30 for 22B (1½ hours). Shared taxis also travel between Trat and **Chanthaburi** that leave when full taking 45 minutes and costing 40B.

Songtheaw

Songtheaws leave from the main road near the market in Trat to Laem Ngop (where the ferry leaves for Ko Chang). The songtheaw ride takes about 15 minutes and should only cost 10B, leaving when full. At slow times you may be charged more for the ride but the Thais are usually charged as well. The driver seems to want a minimum of 100B per trip, otherwise he will not leave.

AROUND TRAT

COASTLINE FROM TRAT TO HAT LEK

Namtok Saphan Hin

Located 32 km from Trat, the waterfall offers a bit of a change from the beach scene. The entry road passes an army base and after another 500 m you will reach the parking area where basic food and amenities are available. The actual falls are about 500 m up river and fall quite a distance. The area has only been open since 1989 as it was once scattered with land mines set up by the Cambodian army. Many refugees followed this river to make their way to Thailand to escape the reign of Pol Pot.

Trat Beaches

Many of the beaches along Trat's coast are not beautiful but you will be almost guaranteed to have them to yourself. They are a great place to camp but you will need to bring everything you need with you.

At the 31 km mark you will come across **Hat Lan Sai**. The resort on this pleasant beach has bungalows with fan for 300B and 700B for A/C. The bungalows are small but comfortable. The restaurant has a selection of dishes ranging in price from 50B to 100B. **Hat Sai Kaew** is just after the resort but has lost much of its charm.

Hat Sai Ngam is at the 37 km mark but the road does not go all the way to the beach. At the 41 km mark you will find **Hat Sai Ngaon** 500 m from the main road. There is nothing here and not much sand at high tide. It does however offer a fine panoramic view of the outlying islands.

Gold Hill Silvers and Resort at the 43 km mark at **Hat Paddodeng** is the first sign of the potential mass development of this coastline. The cheapest bungalows cost 1,200B for four beds.

Hat Thap Thim is at the 47 km mark and there are a few rustic local houses here which sell drinks in the dry season and it is a popular place for Thai students to come and camp out.

At 48 km from Trat is the **Red Cross Museum** at Khao Lan (Sala Ratchakarun). This was the site of one of the Cambodian refugee camps which once held about 10,000 people.

The Red Cross worked to set up an arts and crafts workshop which provided vocational training for the refugees once they could think about more than mere survival.

Many of the tens of thousands of refugees who started entering Thailand in 1978 walked over the Banthat Mountain Range. Most came from Siammarat, Si Saphan, Phra Tabong and Phailin. The largest refugee camp in Thailand was near Chonburi, the Phanat Nikhom Centre. Another large one which held nearly 200,000 refugees was located further south near Ban Mai Rut and was run by the Vietnamese. By the time many of the refugees arrived in Thailand after walking from their homes, they were beyond help, many died of starvation or were severely malnourished.

There are bungalows which are popular with Thai holiday makers available on the beautiful, long beach for 700B and 800B. You can camp for free or hire a tent for 100B.

Ban Khlong Manao at the 51 km mark is a fishing village built on a river just back from the ocean and is reached by taking the concrete road from the highway. The village farms jellyfish when they are in season and exports them to Japan and Taiwan. The morning glory vine leaves which grow on the beach are used to take the poison out of the jelly fish. To see them at work take the concrete pier which extends to the right and then walk across the wooden planks over the river to the beach side. There is one shop in town and a basic noodle restaurant on the entry road just before it comes to a T junction.

Ban Mai Rut (Root) is at the 53 km mark, 5 km in from the main road. You can take the turn-off with the Daungnapa Resort sign as it is only 1½ km from the village. This is a large and fairly wealthy fishing village. To reach **Daungnapa Resort,** ☎ (039) 581 363, take the concrete pier to the right (before the bridge) then a wooden plank path that leads off to the right. The cheapest rooms in a landscaped garden setting are 400B. The town has a few noodle shops for a meal.

The next beach is **Hat Ban Chuen** 60 km from Trat and 4 km from the main road and is locally known as **Hat Ma-Ro**. The Thais claim that this beach has the finest white powdery sand in the world but that may be a bit of an exaggeration. In the dry season you can get a motorbike taxi from the main road. The road passes the site of an old Cambodian refugee camp which once held 200,000 people. The only signs remaining of this are a few posts in the ground from the huts, an administration building and a triangle shaped assembly hall. The beach here is long and quite nice when compared with others on the coast. There are bungalows directly to the left for 250B with fan and bath. Half a kilometre to the right are more bungalows for 250B and 500B but they are a bit run down. This end of the beach is more shaded and has a few more restaurants. If you camp away from the main section of the beach you will escape the Thai crowds.

KHLONG YAI   คลองใหญ่

Travellers once came here to get visa extensions and now that the immigration office is at Laem Ngop there is no reason to visit. The town is surrounded by timber mills which receive truckload after truckload of primary forest cover smuggled over the border from Cambodia. The Thai and Cambodian governments deny that the illegal logging is happening so if you follow that theory, all the wood is simply magically appearing at the mills. Khlong Yai is 62 km from Trat. There are plenty of banks in town. The hospital is directly up from the pier and the bus and songtheaws leave from opposite the market.

Cheap Sleeps

Suksamran Hotel on the street that turns off the highway to the ocean. Rooms are 150B with fan and 250B with A/C.

Khlong Yai Bungalows is on the corner of the road and highway and has A/C rooms for 250B.

HAT LEK

A further 16 km from Khlong Yai is Hat Lek which is little except for a border crossing with shops and a pier. There is no town here however one may evolve fairly soon as a casino is being built on the Cambodian side of the border. The border crossing may not be open to foreigners for a while still but when it is eventually officially opened it will become a very popular gateway to Cambodia. There are a couple of immigration check points between Hat Lek and Khlong Yai and the actual border is open to Thais between 7.00 am and 5.00 pm (not that you need it).

TRIP TO CAMBODIA

Officially foreigners cannot cross the land border at Hat Lek into Cambodia however it is possible to cross unofficially by boat. The immigration officials are very aware that this is going on but turn a blind eye. This crossing point is one of the cheapest ways to get to Phnom Penh from Bangkok but since you do not get an exit stamp on your Thai visa you must either cross back at the same point or have no intentions of returning to Thailand on the same passport. If you come back another way, especially by flying into Bangkok, you will be arrested upon arrival and thrown into an immigration detention centre until help arrives.

We spoke to a French couple who did just that, unaware of the implications. Upon arrival at Bangkok the immigration officials separated them and threw them in jail. They spent twelve days in appalling conditions. Large but cramped rooms held a couple of hundred people where stretching or walking imposed on the other prisoners. The lights were never turned off and they were not given any blankets or pillows. They had to use sarongs to separate themselves from the cold hard concrete floors. One meal a day arrived at 5.30 am consisting of barely edible rice and they never received any clean water. Prisoners are only allowed one phone call a week and only then to a local Bangkok number. On their first call they contacted the French embassy in Bangkok who basically said, "Good Luck", and hung up. The only 'help' they received was by an external foreigner who systematically comes around and takes personal details. This may or may not have sped up the court hearing but after surviving for twelve days, a trial fined them 3,000B each and immediately deported them. If you do not have a flight out of the country then expect more delays while you find someone to organise one. American citizens rarely stay for more than a few days but some African inmates whose countries do not have an embassy in Thailand have been stuck there for months and in some cases years. The moral of the story is to *take immigration matters VERY seriously* or this story could be yours.

It is possible to visit Cambodia for the day or night without a Cambodian visa but for anything longer you have to go straight to Sihanoukville or Phnom Penh to have your visa validated (a Cambodian visa is available in Bangkok). When you return to Thailand, ensure that your Thai visa is still valid.

Travelling to Phnom Penh from Thailand this way will cost you as little as US$30 making it by far the cheapest way to see Cambodia from Thailand.

KO KONG (CAMBODIA)

Ko Kong is, by Cambodian standards, a large, busy and fairly well off town, just south of Hat Lek. Ko Kong's border town status has certainly helped it reach this size and level of affluence. The town itself is not really worth staying in, and if you can avoid it all the better, unless you just want to spend a night there for the Cambodian experience. It is possible to use Thai, Cambodian and US currency in town as is the case in Phnom Penh. Ko Kong receives heaps of smuggled goods from Singapore and is a busy thoroughfare for drugs and illegal prostitution rackets. Because of this, both Hat Lek and Ko Kong are great places to pick up whiskey, cigarettes and beer. A carton of Marlboro will cost around 130B and a bottle of decent whiskey around 150B. Budweiser, Grolsch and Tiger Beer, amongst many others, are also available by the carton at very reasonable prices.

East

There is an island directly opposite Ko Kong called Pak Khlong and another slightly to the south, Ko Khong Island. The boat from Hat Lek used to take you to Pak Khlong Island but now there has been a mass population exodus to the island so there is not much to see there except for a high immigration police presence. You can get a boat across for a small fee in Ko Kong.

Vital Information

Tourist Office on the road that runs parallel to the river, turn left from the sand pier past Kongken Hotel and the Police Station

Bank Pacific Commercial Bank is at the water end of the main street that runs perpendicular to the river. Expect the bureaucracy to take an hour. You will get better rates and have the cash in your hand in a minute if you change money at the market.

Police Station The building with the green fence right next to the Kongken Hotel. Depending where the speed boat lets you off walk left on the street running parallel to the river for either 100 m or 20 m.

Drugs Marijuana is semi legal in Cambodia and is priced at US$5 to US$10 per kilo! But do not bother trying to take a sample back to Thailand with you. As you should be well aware of the extremely harsh penalties applicable to this drug in Thailand.

Cheap Sleeps

The hotels in town have a busy prostitution scene but are bearable. They are also extremely expensive for Cambodian hotels but the border town status gives them the right to charge higher than other places in the country.

Khounchang Hotel To the right and close to the wharf on the road running parallel to the river. Rooms cost 150B with fan and bath and 250B with A/C. Be careful of electric appliances and the wiring or you may be the recipient of an electric shock which will knock you off your feet.

Kongken Hotel To the left of the wharf on the same road. Rooms are 100B with fan and shared bath, 150B for a fan room with bathroom. The rooms here are dirtier but the locals recommend this place over the Khounchang Hotel.

Kolabchaeyden Hotel Turn left at the wharf and take the second street on your right past the Kongken Hotel. Rooms with fan cost 150B and open up to a common driveway. When we visited the military were busy loading ammunition into the back of a truck from our adjoining room!

Bophakohkong Hotel Is a concrete monstrosity further down the same road. A/C rooms here cost 200B.

Eat and Meet

The **food market** here runs day and night. It is a few hundred metres from the river on the main road running at right angles from the water. The food is a mixture of Thai and Khmer.

Try one of the **street vendors** selling bread with a delicious filling of pork fat, cucumber, sprouts and sauce for 10B or 1,000 Riel. It is very similar to the Vietnamese version. Stock up on yummy crunchy baguette style bread which costs 5B or 500 Riel for a large one.

Khmer Restaurant The restaurant on the main road opposite the market sells rice and noodle dishes at expensive Thai prices. Expect to pay around 60B for a foreign beer and a meal.

◀ **Arriving and Departing** ▶

To/From Thailand
Boat and Bus
The route through Hat Lek to Ko Kong and on to Phnom Penh is one of the cheapest ways to enter Cambodia, costing overall around US$30 if going by land or just over $55 if you fly.

From Trat catch a songtheaw to Khlong Yai for 30B then another songtheaw to Hat Lek for 20B. Both leave when full. Hat Lek does not consist of anything more than a few shops selling smuggled goods and the immigration office. Take the road which leads down to the water where you will see a small pier, with small blue speedboats moored. There are actually two piers, the second which also has moored boats is off to the right. These boats will take you to **Ko Kong** in Cambodia in 20 minutes for 50B each as long as there are three or four people in the boat. The boats run from 07.00 to 17.00. The trip itself is quite scenic (once you get past the casino being built on the Cambodian side of the border) travelling along a wide river and past dense mangrove forest. There have been some reports of travellers being hassled by immigration police, probably if they had not got their quota of bribes for the day. So be wary even though the Thais travel this route without any problems, remember it is highly illegal.

To/From Phnom Penh
Air
There is an airport in Ko Kong with flights making a triangle three times a week flying **Phnom Penh**, Ko Kong, Kom Phom Som to Phnom Penh. From Ko Kong the flight to Phnom Penh costs US$50 plus US$4 airport tax and leaves at around 12.30 pm on Tuesday, Thursday and Sunday. A motorbike taxi to the airport costs 1,000 riel from the wharf as it is about 2 km away.

It is almost worth flying to Phnom Penh from Ko Kong as it only costs about US$20 more, and if you miss one of the boat or bus connections you will end up paying that money in hotels and lost time. Plus it is a far safer way to travel in Cambodia. As soon as you arrive in Phnom Penh get your visa stamped. The Cambodian visa is available in Bangkok for US$20.

Boat and Bus
The next step is to get to **Sihanoukville** from Ko Kong via boat since the roads are dangerous and impassable in places. An express boat leaves Ko Kong every day at 08.00 taking 3 hours and costs 500B. In the high season there are two boats every day. Sometimes slower boats leave between 06.30 and 08.00 and cost 400B but if you catch one of these you will miss the connecting bus to Sihanoukville. From Sihanoukville to Phnom Penh an express bus takes 3 hours and costs 100B or 1,200 Riel. Slower buses take 5 hours and the last leaves at midday. If you have time get your visa validated in Sihanoukville, otherwise as soon as you get to Phnom Penh

WARNING
Travel in Cambodia still carries very serious security risks. Despite the recent amnesties involving the Khmer Rouge, it still can be a very dangerous country and *Tales From the Other Side* strongly suggests you get up-to-date information from your embassy before planning any trip there.

Cambodian Refugees
During the Cambodian crisis, Trat and Sa Kaew Provinces were home to large camps of Cambodian 'refugees'. Quite often these 'refugees' were actually Khmer Rouge and the aid that was supposedly for the displaced people was actually feeding both the Khmer Rouge and their campaign in Cambodia.

LAEM NGOP (BACK IN THAILAND)   แหลมงอบ

Laem Ngop is the town from where the ferry to Ko Chang, Ko Mak and Ko Wai leave. An immigration office has also opened up here making it a convenient place to extend your visa. You will probably end up spending an hour or so in town either waiting for a ferry or for the immigration officer to finish talking to his mate, but there is little to see or do except hang out in one of the seafood restaurants on the pier. Laem Ngop is 17 km from Trat.

Vital Information

Tourist Information The TAT and Tourist police are on the right hand side of the pier just back from the water. The helpful staff have an abundant supply of information on both Trat and the surrounding provinces.

Post Office is located a few kilometres up the road from the pier on the left hand side. A songtheaw will cost you 5B each way or a motorbike taxi will cost 20B and he will wait while you do your business. They have phone facilities.

Banks Thai Farmers Bank have a branch about 250 m up the road from the pier.

Hospital is also a few kilometres up the road before the GPO but off to the right. Look for the sign. For anything serious go to Trat instead.

Police Station is 200 m straight up the road from the pier.

Immigration Office About 350 m from the pier on the right hand side of the road. It is the last shopfront in the large white building.

Roundabout In the middle of the roundabout by the pier you can get information on both tides and the time of sunrise and sunset.

Codes Laem Ngop's telephone code is (039) and the post code is 23120.

Cheap Sleeps

Chutkaew Guesthouse This guesthouse, just up from the Thai Farmers Bank about 280 m from the pier, caters to backpackers. Rooms are 60B/100B for singles/doubles. The restaurant serves Thai and Western food and will give you some tourist information on the islands if they can be bothered.

Eat and Meet

Saenchantr Restaurant serves seafood and other dishes. It is located at the beginning of the pier. Many travellers find themselves here waiting for the next ferry. There is another seafood restaurant further up the pier where the Thais tend to wait.

Laem Ngop Seafood is 300 m up the road leading to Ko Chang Islands National Park Headquarters. From the pier take the first street on the left. The setting is quite pleasant on the water and away from the pier. Meals cost between 50B and 100B and the staff will dig up the sole English menu in the place just for you! They also have bungalows for 300B.

Arriving and Departing

To/From Trat
Songtheaw
From Trat a songtheaw to **Laep Ngop** costs 10B (it leaves when full). If you are returning from Laem Ngop to Trat in the low season you will have to wait for a ferry to arrive before the songtheaw will fill up and hence depart. If the songtheaw still does not fill up, you will be asked to pay a little more for the ride. If you have booked a minibus to Bangkok they leave

from the pier but count on the ride taking at least two hours longer than what you were told it would take! It is quicker to get the songtheaw back to Trat and catch a bus to Bangkok from there rather than wait for the minibus which is often ridiculously overloaded. The A/C bus to Bangkok from Trat is 140B.

To/From the Islands
Boats
Ko Chang
Boats leave for the northern pier Aow Sarapot on **Ko Chang** at 09.00, 12.00, 13.00, 15.00, and 17.00 (more frequently in high season) taking 45 minutes. The cost depends on where you want to go. To Aow Sarapot it is 40B, but the price will usually include the taxi to the beach of your choice (70B to Hat Sai Kaew, 80B to Khlong Phrao, 90B to Hat Kai Bae). In high season the boat continues to Hat Sai Kaew (1½ hours), Khlong Phrao (2 hours) and Hat Kai Bae (2½ hours), just let the captain know where you want to go. The price will be the same as above.

There are a number of travel agents and shops that sell tickets for the boats just before the pier. If travelling in the low season, your ticket price includes the taxi ride from the wharf to the beach of your choice (you must tell them this when you purchase your ticket). Note that the taxi drivers will willingly accept a second payment if you offer, so just get off where you want. In the high season the boat will generally drop you off at your beach of choice so you need not worry about the taxi fare.

Ferries also travel to the less popular places on Ko Chang island: Tha Dan Mai at 13.00 for 35B taking 30 minutes (returns 07.00), Than Mayom at 13.00 for 30B taking 45 minutes (returns 07.00), Aow Salek Phet at 13.00 for 70B taking 2½ hours (returns 07.00), Khlong Son at 13.00 for 50B taking 1 hour (returns 07.00), Long Beach at 13.00 for 70B taking 2 hours (returns 07.00), Bang Bao Beach at 15.00 for 80B taking 3 hours (returns 07.00).

Other Islands
The boat to Ko Wai costs 100B, leaves at 15.00 and returns from Ko Wai at 08.00 taking 2½ hours. The boat to Ko Mak costs 150B, leaves at 15.00 and takes 3½ hours. To Ko Kham the boat costs 130B, leaves at 15.00 and takes 3 hours. In the rainy season boats can be fairly infrequent to these islands, but in the high season there should be at least one a day.

KO CHANG   เกาะช้าง

Ko Chang is part of the Laem Ngop - Ko Chang Marine National Park which covers 651 sq km and incorporates 52 islands and parts of the mainland. Ko Chang is the largest island in the region, second to Phuket in Thailand, stemming 30 km in length and close to 70% of it is covered in dense primary rainforest. Parts that were privately owned before it was designated a National Park remain so, hence parts of the north of the island and some of the smaller islands are used for farming where coconut and rubber tree plantations abound. Bungalow operations are also meant to stay behind the tree line which in most cases are virtually on the beach.

Ko Chang is also very mountainous with the highest peak reaching 744 m. This means the views from the ridges are spectacular, but it also means that any storms coming from the south dump their load in the hills leaving the more populated beaches on the west coast reasonably dry in the months approaching the high season. The region gets an exceptionally high rainfall with August where torrential downpours are common, so climate wise the best time to visit is between December and March, but the dry season is from November to May.

Only a few years ago, Ko Chang was very quiet and very little visited but a few seasons of heavy pushing by Khao San Road travel agents has changed that forever and now in peak season the beaches are covered with people sleeping, waiting for a room to become available.

The most popular beach is Hat Sai Kaew which is popular with Thai holiday makers and is known as 'white sand beach' but it is the greyest white sand we have ever seen.

East

The beach is nice but can get extremely congested. For those wanting to have a quieter time, you would be well advised to head further down the coast of the island to one of the other beaches. Although that said, Hat Sai Kaew does have the facilities of bars, restaurants, money exchange (at poor rates) and motorcycle hire (at exorbitant rates). Soon someone is going to have to come to terms with the development as human waste will become a very serious problem here if it is not addressed soon.

Ko Chang is a pleasant and convenient place to visit if you have a few days to spare in Bangkok as it is easily reached in a day. However be aware that at the height of the low season you will find it hard to get accommodation and a feed as the resorts and restaurants close down. Maybe you could try bringing a tent and a fishing rod!!

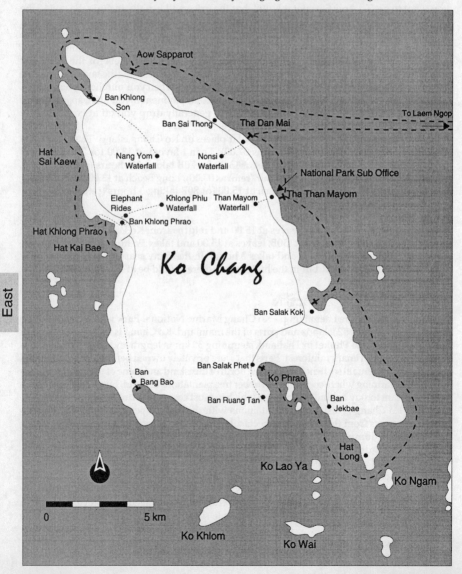

WARNING

There is a risk of catching malaria on Ko Chang island despite the fact that the recorded new cases seem to be diminishing. The malaria clinic on the island is not there for the sake of it. The locals take it seriously and so should you. Take the necessary precautions to prevent infection such as prophylactics and appropriate clothing at dawn and dusk. Another serious and uncomfortable problem on Ko Chang is the number of sand flies that preside on the beaches. Coconut oil is good to keep them away.

Vital Information

Tourist Office Many larger bungalow operations can deal with basic travel requests such as minibuses to Bangkok and reconfirmation of air tickets, as well as snorkelling trips from the island.

Post Office An authorised post office is located at Ban Salek Phet in a general store at the northern end of town. It is probably best to hold on to your mail until you get to a more convenient post office on the mainland. Laem Ngop GPO is a few kilometres up the road from the pier.

Hospital There are two health clinics, one at Ban Khlong Son and the other at Ban Khlong Phrao (where there is also a malaria clinic). If you suddenly come down with an unexplained fever, get to Trat on the next boat. The malaria unit at Trat hospital has the best reputation in the country.

Police Station A station exists just to the north of the main fishing village, Ban Salek Phet at the south east part of the island so hopefully you will not need them in a hurry. The police occasionally do the rounds of the island and word tends to get around when they are coming.

Codes The telephone code is (039) and the postal code is 23120.

Cheap Sleeps

Ko Chang beaches have become quite developed since being 'discovered' with all offering a range from budget to over the top bungalows. Some of the individual bungalows do not have electricity (however most of the more developed bungalow operations do), but you will be supplied with atmospheric lanterns. The popularity of the island means that prices are gradually increasing, so may be slightly more than the quoted price written below in the high season. In the height of the high season you may have to sleep on the beach until something comes up on Hat Sai Kaew. In the height of the low season you will be lucky to find anywhere to stay as much of the island closes down. The accommodation below is listed from north to south starting on the west coast, then the east coast.

West Coast
Ban Khlong Son
This is a small fishing village at the northwest of the island with a couple of places to stay but only worth it if you want to get away from farangs and observe the life of a small fishing village. There is no beach, only a large bay where houses are built over the water. Take the turn-off to the west at the intersection in between Aow Sapparot and Hat Sai Kaew for 400 m.

Manee Guesthouse has basic but sturdy boxes on stilts over the water for 80B. Take the road to the left just before the pier.

Khlong Son Resort, ☎ (039) 511 145, is opposite the wat on the water. A number of free standing bungalows with a view of a mangrove forest and a row of rooms with a view of a white wall cost 500B to 800B.

Hat Sai Kaew

The sand on this beach is far from its misnamed 'White Sand Beach', taking on much duller hues and is also far from deserted, but is the beach to head for if you are looking for a little action with an abundance of accommodation and a great selection of food. As the largest beach on the island it has also become the most popular with bungalows pressing against the ocean for almost the entire length of the beach. The following resorts run north to south.

White Sand Beach Resort is one of the best resorts in the area, spread out over 150 m of the far northern end of the beach. Small simple thatched bungalows with balcony, raised mattress and mosquito net line the beach. There is a second row of bungalows, some with bathrooms attached. It offers the deepest and most swimmable water just offshore and is backed by a heavily forested mountain where monkeys often play. The resort has its own entry road from the high mountain pass above. In the high season expect to pay between 100B and 120B, 450B with bath, and in the low season as little as 60B. The food is pretty dodgy.

Rocksand is 150 m down the beach set upon a rocky outcrop that juts into the water. Colourful creations on the hill with tin roofs cost 80B to 100B. It is better known for its friendly bar but plays loud music, which serves to hide the sounds of the forest behind it. Steer away from the food. They also have an overseas phone.

KC Bungalow is another 100 m down the beach. Comfortable sized bungalows with mattresses on the floor and balcony, lined up behind a row of shady palm trees, cost 100B in the high season, and 60B in the low. The bungalows to the north are the best, well spaced and more private. The new and spotless toilets get a gold star. This is the first place you see when you arrive via the steep and curvy road. They have trips to waterfalls and snorkelling trips to nearby islands. At the northern end of KC is **Pyramid Herbal Sauna and Massage** where you may feel lured towards the pyramid shaped hut to increase your natural energy flow.

Jinda Bungalow and Arunee Resort, ☎ (01) 219 3819, are on the opposite side of the road in a barren and hot landscape. Rooms in a row cost 200B and 250B (no bath/with bath), and 100B and 120B in the low season.

Yakah is a tiny establishment next to KC. Spacious bungalows cost 150B, 80B/100B in the low season but are placed quite close together. Their solo bungalow with bath costs more.

Ban Rung Rang Resort, ☎ (039) 597 184 is at the start of the busy centre of bungalow suburbia. Very cramped, solid bungalows line up in rows with the back ones getting a close view of the bungalow in front and noise from the road. Bungalows with/without bath are 150B/250B, and reduces to 120B in the low season. They have telephone, money exchange and basic travel services.

Cookie Brand new concrete and wooden bungalows come with bathroom, fan and mosquito net in an ugly surrounding. In the low season rooms are 200B (front row) and 150B to 180B (back rows) but excessively more in the high season. They organise boat trips.

Hut Hut also have newly constructed wooden huts with bath but a more visually pleasing environment for the same price.

MAC Bungalows are slightly smaller, better placed and in the same price range as Hut Hut.

Sai Kao Bungalows, ☎ (01) 211 6791, has some of the last rustic charm along the central beach. Three rows of well spaced, comfortable but basic bamboo and noisy wooden huts cost 80B. Three white Mediterranean looking concrete huts have been built at the end, probably with more to come. Electricity is from sundown to midnight. The restaurant is quite good.

Tan Ta Wan Bungalows have very squashed and old bamboo bungalows for 100B to 120B.

Apple have large wooden pleasant looking bungalows for 250B high season, 100B low season. They organise boat trips.

Sunsai Bungalows, ☎ (01) 211 4488, is the last place on the beach where the sand turns into a concrete retaining wall. They have a variety of well spaced bungalows spread over large grounds for 80B/150B/200B in the low season but double in the high season. There is a large restaurant, good food and service and a permanent volleyball net in place.

Plaloma Cliff Resort on the headland is an expensive resort with manicured lawns and stone paths. The cheapest rooms with bath are 600B in the high season, 300B in the low.

Aow Khlong Phrao

This is a long thin beach in a bay where the resorts are quite a distance from each other, but generally expensive. The few islands off the southern tip of the bay are good for snorkelling. The beginning of the bay is about 4 km south of Hat Sai Kaew. The bay and beach is divided by a fairly wide and deep inlet just south of Klong Plow Resort which can be crossed by a small boat when available.

Chaichet Bungalow is at the northern headland and has great views of the bay, but no beach. The huts are accessible via a wooden bridge past Coconut Beach Bungalows. Bamboo huts cost 120B, and concrete structures are 400B (300B low season).

Coconut Beach Bungalows have a grassy location without much shade but with nicely spaced solid wooden and concrete bungalows. They cost 200B (150B in low season) without bath and 450B plus with bath.

Ko Chang Resort, ☎ (039) 597 114, further down the beach is very expensive with the cheapest rooms going for 1,500B. Their banana boat and waterskiing facilities may create unwanted noise in the bay.

Klong Plow Resort, ☎ (039) 597 216, is another upmarket resort with accommodation set around a lake behind the beach. Bungalows cost 600B to 700B (400B to 500B low season). They also rent small two person tents for 100B per person.

Hobby Hut is the most secluded place on the island set on the inlet of the ocean. The four bungalows with bath are only rented by the month for 2,000B. It is a short walk to the beach.

P.S.S. Bungalows, ☎ (039) 597 159, are accessible via the small boat over the ocean inlet or turn off at Ban Khlong Phrao. Set on a nice beach in an open but shaded area, basic bungalows cost 150B. They organise fishing and overnight snorkelling trips to the nearby islands.

K.M. (Klong Makok) Bungalows Do not bother with this one as the bungalows were either never completed or left to ruins. It is on the river inlet, not the beach.

Erawan Bungalows is just off the road on a khlong, 100 m from the beach with bamboo bungalows for 100B.

The next two reasonably priced places are located at the southern point of the bay in beautiful locations with spectacular views of the bay but only just enough sand to call a beach. They are the pick of the budget accommodation on the beach and well worth the effort in getting to for a pleasant break from the crowds.

Magic Bungalows, ☎ (01) 329 0404, is across the bridge where bamboo bungalows cost 120B (80B low season) and are in slightly better condition than next door. The restaurant is set over the crystal clear water, a perfect location for an enjoyable meal. They organise boat trips.

Chok Dee Bungalows at the very end of the bay has very basic and small bamboo huts for 100B (70B low season) and concrete bungalows with bath for 300B.

Hat Kai Bae

This bay is smaller but beautiful with a panoramic view of three smaller offshore islands. Unfortunately the stunning bay has been overrun with bungalows, but still on a lower scale than Hat Sai Kaew. Accommodation is available for all price ranges. There is an absolutely stunning beach around the southern headland of the beach accessible by a narrow path, but be prepared for rocks and using ropes to pass.

Comfortable Bungalow better known for its bar than bungalows, this is a pretty chilled out place. Their bungalows are set behind Coral Resort's Bungalows and cost 150B with bath.

Coral Resort Bungalows, ☎ (01) 219 3815, have bungalows both with and without bathroom, lining the beach. They provide overseas phone facilities, money exchange and air ticket reconfirmation as well as the dreaded video monster at 7.00 pm every night. To get there, cross the two small bridges at the north of the beach. In the middle of the bridge is a noodle shop where a meal will set you back 15B.

Ngan Wong Bungalow have a few rows of basic huts away from the beach for 80B (50B low season). They rent hammocks, bikes and books.

East

Kai Bae Hut, ☎ (01) 329 0452, has a range of rooms with expensive ones at the front and cheaper ones behind them from 50B (no bath), 100B, 150B, 500B and 2,500B (with A/C). They can organise a car to the waterfall for 50B and snorkelling trips to Ko Wai. The **PADI Sea Horse Diving School** is behind the resort.

Kai Bae Beach Bungalows, ☎ (039) 597 105, also have a range of accommodation at 100B (80B low season), up to 1,000B (600B) but most are in the lower range. The cheapest bungalows extend along the beach to the south of the resort and are arguably set in the best location away from everything, hence quite a walk to the restaurant. They have phone and money exchange facilities.

Porns Bungalows is a nice place where the rooms are skewed at different angles to break up any kind of formality and close to each other but not obtrusive. They cost 150B (120B low season). The staff are very friendly and the restaurant is relaxed with mats and hammocks replacing chairs.

Sea View Resort, ☎ (01) 321 0055, this place has 200B cramped bungalows or 1,000B European style huts on a hill. This exclusive place comes with deck chairs and expensive restaurant complete with waiters in uniform and games room.

Siam Bay Resort at the end of the bay; has rooms for 150B (no bath), 200B (with bath) or 500B, but most look like they could do with a good repair job. Chances are you will break your neck walking around the uneven ground.

Ban Bang Bao

The village is at the southwest point of the island and has a few bungalows nearby. This part of the island is best visited directly by boat.

Bang Bao Blue Wave has rooms for 100B to 300B. The other resorts offer accommodation for 80B to 100B.

East Coast

The east coast lacks the beaches of the west and is not as picturesque, however accommodation is sparsely spread along the coast.

Aow Khlong Prao, Ko Chang

East

Ban Sai Thong
Sai Thong Bungalows is set on the beach where bungalows cost around 100B.

Ban Dan Kao
Koh Chang Cabana Although it has a picture of a backpacker on the sign, it must be referring to the Thai backpacker who can obviously spend the 600B for the cheapest room.

Than Mayom
This is the location of the Than Mayom Waterfall and there are a couple of accommodation choices available.
Ko Chang National Park Sub-Headquarters has a few bungalows for 500B. Another place just north of here charges 400B for small and basic bungalows.

Ban Ruang Tan
Just south of Ban Salek Phet at the west side of the large bay at the southeast point of the island there are a couple of places to stay. From here you can explore the fishing village of Salek Phet which is a busy and friendly town.
SP Resort and Seafood Restaurant is a rip off with box like rooms on a wharf for 150B. The next pier down will give you a similar room for 50B.

Ko Phrao
This island is located in Salek Phet Bay and has one expensive resort accessible via hired boat from the fishing village.

Hat Long
The beach itself is not that long but is a secluded and beautiful place to stay, however the future operation of its bungalow operation is questionable. The beach is virtually unreachable via an overgrown path from the closest village so you will have to arrive via boat from either Laem Ngop on its way to somewhere else or Ban Salek Phet. Ask around if it is open.
Long Beach Bungalow can give you a bungalow with electricity for 120B.
Tantawan House is further along amidst a rocky outcrop with rooms between 70B and 100B.

Eat and Meet

East

All bungalow operations on the island have restaurants attached but the food is quite often very average on the palette while still charging high island prices. There are a couple of great restaurants on Hat Sai Kaew and if you are near a village try the local noodle shops for a cheap feed. It may be a wise idea to stock up on a few things in Laem Ngop or Trat before leaving for the island as most things are quite expensive once you are surrounded by water. You may want to buy some fruit, water and cigarettes to save a few extra baht.

Hat Sai Kaew
My Friends Place This restaurant was established by John, an English lad, and delicate delights are prepared by Pen, the Thai restaurateur. They will make you feel at home with dim lights and pleasant conversation. The food (and you get plenty of it) is glorious especially the BBQ fish, crabs and curry dishes. The prices are extremely reasonable, set at the same as the bungalows. Next door is **Huk Hut** run by a young Dutch guy, but it may or may not be open. They are located across the road from the midway point of KC Bungalows and Ban Rung Rong Resort.
Thor's Place serves large portions of food that will melt in your mouth. All meals are cooked to perfection - try the Indian curry for a taste sensation. Low tables and cushions, enjoyable music, a good selection of books and games, and an atmospheric location on the beach brings back the same faces. The later you stay, the more people seem to appear. Next door is

Sundown Restaurant, but the food is disappointing compared to its neighbour. They are located in between Apple and Sunsai Bungalows just south of the rocky section at the southern end of the beach.

Aloha Bakery serves up some baked treats assured to satisfy your munchies. Get there in the morning for the best choice of goodies. It is located south of Sunsai Bungalows on the opposite side of the road. Next door is Manee Too Restaurant and another restaurant opposite.

Mini Marts There are a few grocery stores along the beach and road to stock up on supplies.

Things to do **and** Sights to See

Snorkelling

You can try your luck at snorkelling around Ko Chang but the best locations are around the smaller islands. Many of the bungalow establishments organise boat trips to the better islands.

Walking

The rainforest on Ko Chang is still very much intact and very accessible. Only two minutes walk from Sai Kaew Beach and you are in the thick of it. There are trails throughout the forest and along the ridges but most of the trails are overgrown through lack of use, especially after the low season. Make sure you wear the proper walking attire as there are various species of poisonous snakes sharpening their fangs in the underbrush. Ask the locals or bungalow staff for directions to the closest paths.

Laying on the Beach and Swimming

Always a good way to pass time.

Motorbike and Mountain Bike

Ko Chang is a large island and the only way to see a fair bit of it is to jump on a motorbike. The road is sealed between Ban Khlong Son and Hat Sai Kaew and be prepared for asphalt to Hat Kae Bae. At the southern end of Kae Bae the road becomes very rocky and hilly, whilst a thinner and more difficult trail leads to Ban Bang Bao. On the east coast the road is generally very good until Ban Salek Phet although some parts become mud pits after a heavy rainfall. Motorbikes are 400B for the day or 60B per hour.

     A fun half day can be spent riding a mountain bike along the valley inland from Ban Khlong Son. When you get the bike, take a songtheaw up the high mountain pass north of Hat Sai Kaew and take the turn-off to your right at Ban Khlong Son. The valley offers great views of the mountains and inland farms. The road which extends for around 5 km turns into a thin trail and is fairly flat.

Elephant Riding

You can jump on an elephant at the entrance to Khlong Phlu Waterfall and cruise around on its back for 250B for 40 minutes. It will take you along the path to the falls and will let you off at the National Park entrance.

Waterfalls

For a taste of fresh water instead of salt water, visit a waterfall and go for a refreshing dip. There are four that are fairly accessible.

Namtok Khlong Phu The entrance to this waterfall is on the east side of the road half way along Khlong Phrao Bay (look for the sign next to a shop and elephant waiting for its next tourist), and about 4 km from Hat Sai Kaew. The walk to the park entrance takes 30 minutes, then another 10 minutes to the actual falls, or ride your motorbike to the park entrance but you must cross a riverbed and dodge elephants. The waterfall is quite beautiful, falling about 40 m into a large pool, perfect for swimming and a cool refreshing break from the warm sea water.

Namtok Than Mayom is a larger waterfall located on the east coast by the Ko Chang National Park Sub Office. A short walk will take you to the falls and an hour's walk along a trail from here leads to the top ridge for a viewpoint. Nearby are the initials of King Rama VI and VII who left their mark after visiting. Just north of here, by the small village Dan Mai is the trail to **Namtok Nonsi**. This waterfall is easy to miss, so ask the locals, because it is less visited than the others on the island is quite stunning in the wet season.

Namtok Nang Yom this waterfall plunges for about 2 m - it is hardly worth a special trip, but there is a tiny pool at its base held together by a concrete retaining wall. It is located near the end of the 5 km road leading inland from Khlong Son. The trail is faint and quite difficult to follow.

Boat Trips

Various bungalow operations around the island offer snorkelling and fishing trips when they have enough people, however in the high season you never have to wait more than a couple of days. Popular trips include the following:

* Snorkelling day trips to a combination of nearby islands including Ko Wai, Ko Rang and others with lunch is 350B.

* Professional fishing for 3 days/2 nights with equipment is 1,500B (minimum six people).

* Ko Wai Island - a one way trip for 150B.

* Cambodian border trip costs 350B.

* Rent a large boat to anywhere costs around 4,000B plus fuel.

◀ Arriving and Departing ▶

The ferries that depart for Ko Chang leave the pier at Laem Ngop, 16 km and a 10B songtheaw ride from Trat. In the high season, ferries will go to all the beaches whether directly or after a few stops and the prices change accordingly. To the most popular beach, Sai Kaew, it is 70B (1½ hours), but in low tide you may have to pay another 5B for the small boat that meets the ferry and takes you to the shore. Ferries to the main pier at Aow Sapparot (40B) which may continue to the other beaches in the high season leave at 09.00, 12.00, 13.00, 15.00 and 17.00, although individual bungalows will run extra boats when it is busy. The return trip leaves at 07.00, 09.00, 12.00 and 16.00. In the low season when ferries only service this pier, you can purchase a ticket which includes the taxi ride to the beach of your choice which is 70B to Hat Sai Kaew, 80B to Khlong Phrao, 90B to Kai Bae.

A ferry also leaves at 17.00 on its way to Ko Chang from another pier 5 km north of Laem Ngop. If coming from Trat, the songtheaw driver will probably tell you when you reach Laem Ngop and take you to the other pier for no extra charge. This boat costs 50B to Aow Sapparot, then 30B for the taxi to Hat Sai Kaew.

Separate ferries leave at 13.00 for Dan Mai (35B, 30 minutes), Than Mayom (30B, 45 minutes), Khlong Son (50B, 1 hour), Aow Salek Phet (70B, 2½ hours) and Ban Bang Bao (80B, 3 hours).

When you buy your ticket tell them what beach you want to go to and they will let you know if the ferry will visit it.

Getting Around
Songtheaws

Transport around the island is very expensive, but is now more organised with fairly regular songtheaws passing along the main road in the high season. The songtheaws will always meet the ferries at Aow Sapparot to take you to the beach of your choice. If you go to Aow Sapparot and your ticket was more than 40B to 50B, then it includes the price of the taxi as well. Independent songtheaw rides around the island are quite expensive.

If you are going to the south of the island, such as Long Beach or Ban Bang Bao, you should organise to visit directly by ferry. If there is not one going there, then the resorts are not open.

Motorbike and Mountain Bike
Ko Chang is too large to really explore extensive parts of it on foot, so if you are interested in checking out a few places other than the beach, then you need some wheels. A motorbike costs 400B for the day (usually 8.00 am to 6.00 pm) or 60B per hour. A mountain bike is 80B for half day, but even if you get it for the whole day, you will only get to see a few things as you must stick to the roads through lack of trails to ride along. Surprisingly, when researching, a couple of bungalows had invested in a large number of racing bikes which probably will not last longer than a month before they are thrown on the scrap metal pile, as they will not even start to cope with the rough roads.

Boat
In the high season when the ferries visit more than one beach, you can jump on for a ride to the next beach for a fee similar to that charged by the songtheaws. Refer to the Laem Ngop section for ferry details to the island.

KO WAI   เกาะหวาย

Also known as Coral Island, Ko Wai is part of Ko Chang National Park. This tiny island to the south of Ko Chang is surrounded by some of the best coral and sea life that the eastern seaboard has to offer. It is a perfect place to escape to if you are searching for an island where there are no distractions from the natural beauty of the place and where you can relax and enjoy the view, turquoise water and a few but beautiful palm tree lined beaches. But do not expect much more, as snorkelling and collecting seashells are likely to be the most activity this island has seen and probably will see for a while. The view from the only two resorts on the island spans southern Ko Chang, the tiny Ko Lao Ya in the foreground, Ko Ngam to the right of Ko Chang, and then Ko Mai Si Yai further to the right. The island is privately owned by two families, so development is not likely to destroy its current peacefulness. Ko Wai is very popular in the high season so it may be difficult to get a room.

Cheap Sleeps

There are only two places to stay, both located on the north side of the island.

Ko Wai Paradise Beach Resort, ☎ (039) 597 031, is the newest resort which spreads itself along the longest and prettiest beach. Very basic bamboo bungalows with only enough room to fit a double sized thin mattress cost 60B, while more spacious and sturdy bungalows with roomy balconies go for 120B. The atmospheric restaurant, open until 9.00 pm serves the usual food at reasonable prices, similar to Ko Chang. The resort is sparsely lit by dim lights between 5.00 pm and 10.30 pm. Fresh water runs 24 hours. There is a tiny but private beach just around the point to the left (west) of the resort.

Ko Wai Coral Resort (Pakarung Resort) This is a larger and older establishment with an office in Laem Ngop catering more to Thai tour groups, but also offers reasonably cheap accommodation to individuals when they are not full. The setting is not as tranquil as the above and the beach is small with coarser and redder sand. When it is not busy a bungalow with bath costs 100B. At other times expect to pay 150B to 200B. Fresh water is limited to a couple of hours in the morning and evening, and electricity is out by 10.00 pm. The small restaurant is slightly more expensive than Paradise Beach.

Snorkelling

Both resorts rent mask and snorkel for 50B and fins for an additional 50B to explore the underworld. The best snorkelling for coral is on the north side of the island and for fish on the southern side. From Paradise Beach try the area approaching and just off the point to the left of the resort. Another good spot is to the right of Pakarung Resort. Start at the permanent buoy and swim around the point to the next bay with a private house. The further you go the more fish you will see. Underwater creatures that you may stumble upon include an assortment of solid coral formations and colourful fish, moray eels (be careful), barracuda, sea snakes, huge gropers and the odd shark.

Walking

It is not possible to walk around the island but there are a couple of trails leading to the opposite side of the island from the resorts. From just east of Paradise Beach the trail will take you on a 20 minute walk across the island to a small beach on the south side of the island, traverse east until you hit another beach, then head north again for 20 minutes over the horse saddle bringing you out just shy of Pakarung Resort. Let someone else walk first to clear the large spiders and webs and take a decent pair of shoes as the trail is not very clear. Just past the pier at Paradise Beach is a Burmese woman who offers massages for 100B. You may also run into a French guy who has made the island home with his Thai wife.

◀ Arriving and Departing ▶

Each resort has a boat ferrying passengers to the respective bungalows. The trip takes 2½ hours from **Laem Ngop** costing 100B. Paradise Beach's boat leaves the mainland at 3.00 pm and the island at 8.00 am. Pakarung is the opposite, leaving Laem Ngop in the morning and Ko Wai in the afternoon. If the boats are not running then the resorts are not open. Both close down in the low season. On a good day the dolphins will swim alongside the boat. In the high season it is possible to organise a boat from Ko Chang to Ko Wai for 150B or jump on one of the boats that venture to Ko Wai for snorkelling trips from Ko Chang for a similar charge. Alternatively you can try one of the fishing boats that pass Ko Wai from the nearby islands.

East

KO MAK   เกาะหมาก

Ko Mak is a fairly small island (but big for the region) located just south of the Ko Chang National Park boundaries. It is privately owned and most of the inhabitants can be traced back to one man, however inbreeding is only apparent in the domestic dogs and cats. The island is very flat and most of it is reserved for either coconut or rubber tree plantations. The beaches on the west and southwest side are very long and quite serene, however a large part of the underwater sand is riddled with dead coral. Ko Mak has a few tiny islands just offshore of which two have accommodation. The island is very popular in the high season, so reasonably priced accommodation may be difficult to find. Sandflies are a big problem on the island, so lie in a hammock instead of on the beach. There are also quite a few mosquitos, some of which may be malarial, so take precautions.

Tourist Statistics

1995 figures show that just under six million tourists arrived on Thailand's shores. The average stay was just over a week and 43% were on group tours.

Vital Information

Tourist Office A small information centre is located at the end of the pier on the southeast side of the island. Ask for Ung, if he is not there you may not find anyone else at the office who speaks English. All the bungalow owners carry a two way radio, so Ung can contact them at any time. This also means that everybody knows when a new farang has arrived.

Post Office is set up at the reception of the Koh Mak Resort, open from 8.00 am to 4.30 pm. A telephone service is available but quite expensive: USA, Canada, Asia, Australia and New Zealand are 60B per minute and Europe and the Middle East are 70B per minute. Within Thailand prices are as follows per minute: Bangkok 12B, Trat and Laem Ngop 6B, Pattaya and Rayong 8B, Phuket, Samui and Khorat 15B, Chiang Mai 18B. They have a fax for use.

Police Station There is a police box located at the centre of the island on the road leading north towards Ko Mak Resort.

Codes The telephone code is 039.

Cheap Sleeps

The accommodation on the island is generally expensive, however there are a couple of places for budget travellers. Below is a list of all bungalows according to their location.

Southeast Coast
There are a couple of places very close to the pier. The bay is quite nice, but busy, and has not really got a beach to write home about.

Ko Mak Guesthouse Just 50 m north of the pier, this guesthouse (affiliated with Koh Mak Resort) has large dormitory rooms built over the water for 80B, a pleasant restaurant and store. It is OK for a night if all else is full.

Sunshine Resort is a mid range Thai orientated resort with a few large wooden bungalows with bath 50 m south of the pier upon a hill overlooking the bay. When finished they will probably cost around 600B.

West Coast
This is definitely the prettiest and most swimmable beach on the island set within a large shallow bay looking out to Ko Kham. Just off the southern end of the bay is Ko Pee (Ghost Island), an ancient burial ground. The best time for spotting ghosts is at night time during a thunder storm.

Koh Mak Resort, ☎ (01) 327 0220, is a large bungalow operation located in the middle of the bay, but it lacks character. Bungalows cost between 300B and 600B for wooden and concrete bungalows lined up next to each other. The larger bungalows cost 1,000B for 4 people. This is the base for Afero II Scuba Diving School which works in conjunction with Paradise Divers at Aow Kao Resort. Diving costs 8,000B for the PADI Open Water Course and 1,350B for a day out with two dives. The GPO is also located here.

Fantasia is at the southern end of the beach, 50 m back from the sand behind a khlong. Your fantasies will be sparked by the different coloured triangle shaped wooden bungalows set upon a gradually sloping hill. Each bungalow has a mattress on the floor, but no mosquito net. The friendly staff can give you a coloured bungalow of your choice, when available, for 100B. Popular with Thais on weekends and holidays.

Southwest Coast
This is the longest beach on the island stretching for over 3 km in the wide and attractive Kathung Bay. Most of the beach has dead coral just offshore making swimming a hassle at times. Laem Tookata is the western most point on the island.

East

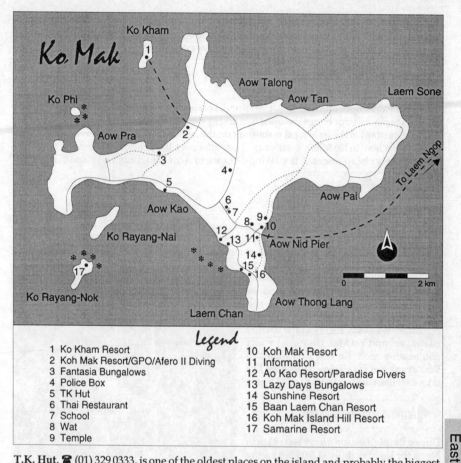

Legend

1 Ko Kham Resort
2 Koh Mak Resort/GPO/Afero II Diving
3 Fantasia Bungalows
4 Police Box
5 TK Hut
6 Thai Restaurant
7 School
8 Wat
9 Temple
10 Koh Mak Resort
11 Information
12 Ao Kao Resort/Paradise Divers
13 Lazy Days Bungalows
14 Sunshine Resort
15 Baan Laem Chan Resort
16 Koh Mak Island Hill Resort
17 Samarine Resort

T.K. Hut, ☎ (01) 329 0333, is one of the oldest places on the island and probably the biggest, set on the best part of the beach and popular with Thais. Bungalows cost 100B, 200B and 300B but slightly more in the high season. There are only two of the 100B bungalows, built apart from the others at the southern end of the compound.

Aow Khao Resort Located at the southern end of the beach, this place is managed by a very friendly German man and his brother, however caters predominantly to Germans, many of whom arrive directly from Patpong with their Thai 'girlfriends'. Solid bungalows with mosquito nets and fan cost 200B without bath and 650B for a huge one with bath. When it is not busy the rooms are very generously discounted as low as 100B to 300B, so it is worth checking out as it is one of the nicer places on the island. Meals, however, are extortionate costing 50B to 80B for basic meals and more for anything else but it is only a five minute walk to the islands sole Thai restaurant. They have a good bar and great music, organise snorkelling boat trips to nearby islands for 250B and offer scuba diving trips through their dive school Paradise Dive Centre.

Lazy Days Resort This popular and relaxed budget place, right next to Aow Khao Resort, is open one season and closed the next. Due to this, their spread out bungalows need major work, but some are livable. The family that run the restaurant live here all year, but the food is limited and not particularly cheap. Bungalows cost 100B, but ask around to find out if it is open.

Baan Laem Chan Resort is further on and has basic huts for 100B and rooms in the house for 50B. It is a friendly place but does not have a beach, only rocks. **Koh Mak Island Resort** is further south on a small beach and has expensive bungalows.

Eat and Meet

Every bungalow operation has a restaurant and, because the accommodation is a fair distance from other places, your bungalow operation and its closest neighbour may be the only options. **Thai Restaurant** is the only local restaurant on the island set on a street corner on the west side of the school in Ko Mak's 'main drag'. They offer over 100 delicious authentic Thai dishes for extremely cheap prices. It is walking distance to Aow Kao, Lazy Days and T.K. Hut.

Things to do and Sights to See

The island itself is not very interesting to explore because of the large tracts of rubber and coconut plantations, so if you do any walking try to avoid the inland routes. In a full day you will be able to walk around the island's perimeter along the beaches, roads and trails.

A few bungalows operations arrange snorkelling trips for 250B (including lunch and gear) and scuba diving can be organised through Koh Mak Resort and Aow Khao Resort. The PADI Open Water certificate is 8,000B. Plenty of the smaller islands around Ko Mak have clear water and healthy reefs. Ko Pee, Ko Kham and Ko Rayang Yai are all close by and Ko Kra is an excellent destination for day trips.

Arriving and Departing

During the high season a ferry leaves Laem Ngop for Ko Mak daily at 3.00 pm taking 3 to 3½ hours for 150B. A morning boat may also run on weekends and public holidays in the high season). The ferries work in a co-operative where two boats, "The Neptune" and the small "Loma" make the trip for two days in a row and then swap. Try and get a deck chair on the top level of the Neptune. The return ferry leaves at 8.00 am every morning.

Ask around Laem Ngop to find out if the ferry to Ko Mak is running. If it is not, then the resorts probably are not open. At the fringe of the high season, some resorts are open but the ferry may only run every few days. If you want to island hop, try one of the fishing boats to Ko Kut, Ko Wai, or Ko Chang, otherwise you will have to go back to Laem Ngop.

Coconut picker on Ko Mak

Tractor taxis or four wheel drives belonging to the various resorts chug slowly around the island. If they are going your way, the ride is free, otherwise you must rely on walking or hitching a ride from the islands one pick-up truck or dozen so motorbikes.

AROUND KO MAK

KO KHAM

This is a minuscule island is just 500 m off Ko Mak offering good coral, so the main activities apart from lying on the beach or hammock are obviously snorkelling. The resort runs a dive school as well. There is one place to stay where bungalows are 80B/100B for singles/doubles. The food is a bit on the pricey side and its popular with Thais on weekends and holidays. The boat to Ko Kham does the same daily route as the boat to Ko Mak, and they provide a long-tail connection to Ko Mak Resort for free.

Ko Kham Resort has fairly basic bamboo bungalows that cost 100B per night. They are set upon the only beach on the island stretching for about 40 m. A longtail boat can take you there from Koh Mak Resort for 100B.

KO RAYONG-NOK

This is the second island off the southwest beach with plentiful coral around its perimeter. Apparently it has one place to stay, **Samarine Resort,** set on a 30 m beach but mainly caters to package groups from Bangkok. Ask around at the tourist information if it is open and for the prices.

KO KUT   เกาะกูด

This island is often referred to as the last frontier in Trat Province and even Thailand. Despite the fact it is the second largest island to Ko Chang in the region, its lack of accessibility has kept it from being overrun. It has also meant that the natural beauty has been left intact with the stunning beaches and dense forest and two waterfalls all worth exploring. Namtok Klong Chao is fabulous and hiking through inland takes you through a nature freaks paradise. Unfortunately developers and farmers are starting to get their hands onto large tracts of land. A large section at the southern part of the island is owned by the navy but their presence is easy to avoid.

If you want to see an island in close to pristine state, then go now, but only if you have a real intent not to disturb, and not to be a tourist. There are several bungalow and potential bungalow owners, mostly from Bangkok, who are very intent on killing the place with tourism, making it similar to Ko Chang or Ko Samet, but hopefully this will be delayed for awhile. The island has huge potential but unfortunately dollar signs are blinding their eyes.

The beaches can get quite messy toward the end of the rainy season with as no-one feels the need to clean up the trash which is mainly trees and old nets and so on. Khlong Chao River dumps tons of jungle rubbish onto Khlong Chao Beach and the place can sometimes look like a disaster area. This is only the case until November when high tides come in and wash everything away.

Orientation

There are piers both at Ta Pho Beach and Aow Sa Lad (west and northeast side of the island respectively). Both these points are also joined overland by a road, however the road itself and the bridges are not always the most reliable, especially around the rainy season. The best beaches are on the west coast - try Hat Ta Pho, Hat Khlong Chao and Hat Khlong Yai Kii. On much of the island there is no electricity and only running water for some of the week.

Cheap Sleeps

Very little English is spoken on the island, especially the local families, so if you do not speak Thai, take a phrase book or be prepared to mime.

Bungalows There is accommodation on the island but the price will probably send you home from Thailand earlier than you expected. The five expensive resorts usually only deal with package tours.

Camping If you are interested in exploring the island, but do not want to get hit with huge accommodation costs, camping is freely available as long as you have your own tent. When you arrive on the island, head south from Hat Ta Pho to Hat Khlong Chao, about one hour's walk for a beautiful location. Namtok Khlong Chao is nearby, inland a short distance. The waterfall is also known as Tan Sanuk and are entered into the history books from when King Rama VI visited in 1911. Make sure you take enough food and water with you for your stay in case you cannot get food at the fishing villages or expensive resorts, however, the naturally supplied coconuts always make a great snack.

Other Accommodation Many travellers who have ventured to Ko Kut have stayed with one of the local families for a small price. Make sure you agree on the price for everything before take up an offer, this includes for accommodation as well as for food, as you will be charged for everything. Some travellers were charged by a woman to cut up a pineapple which was purchased in town and brought back to share with everyone!! You will certainly learn about Thai life when you live in the pockets of a Thai family, and it is well worth it.

Arriving and Departing

This is the tricky part as no-one on the mainland really knows when the ferries leave. They do not depart from Laem Ngop as they do for the other islands but from a place called Laem Sok south of Trat at the end of a peninsula. The journey takes 4½ to 5 hours. Several people agreed the boat leaves twice a week on the fringe of the high season, and possibly more in the high season but the days always differed. I was told Tuesday and Thursday as well as Tuesday and Friday, but this is not certain. Ask Eddie at Foremost Guesthouse in Trat for other options. One alternative is to try and get a ride with a fishing boat, either from the mainland or from one of the islands north of Ko Kut for a price. A very expensive alternative is to hire a boat from either Laem Ngop or Khlong Yai.

When catching the boat make sure you find out which side of the island it is going to, as the road crossing the island may be difficult to pass at times, and the bridges are a pretty scary experience.

OTHER ISLANDS

In and around Ko Chang National Park are a feast of islands, most uninhabited and tiny, many with deserted beaches and wild forest, and some with stunning coral, but only a few with accommodation, unfortunately they cater to expensive package tours.

Ko Lao Ya is located on the outskirts of Ko Chang's Salek Phet Bay towards the south of the island and is well known throughout the region for its coral. Many snorkelling trips from Ko Chang make a stop here for a dive. There is one resort on the island, Lao Ya Paradise Island Resort offering package tours for exorbitant prices.

Ko Ngam is just off the southeastern tip of Ko Chang Island and has a particularly beautiful sand spit lined with palm trees joining the two halves of the island. The ferry to Ko Wai passes close by, but the accommodation once again is for package tours and expensive at the one resort, Twin Island Beach Resort.

Ko Khlum is south of Ko Chang and west of Ko Lao Ya. It is a reasonably sized island but has no accommodation. The snorkelling is reasonable and the island gets a few visits from Ko Chang. There are heaps of fish and a stoneyard on the island.

Ko Kra Dad is just northeast of Ko Mak and is so named for the past abundance of Kradad trees. The island possesses a long beach with white sand and is also visited by boat trips from Ko Chang. Unfortunately it is privately owned by a wealthy family that has plans to make it an international resort.

Ko Rung is west of Ko Mak. The island has very little flat land, so no-one has built any bungalows. The lack of disturbance has enabled bird life to flourish and the coral is particularly stunning.

Eastern Train Line Timetable								
Type and Class	D,3	D,3	D,3	D,3	M,3	D,3	D,3	D,3
Train Number	109	151	203	183	251	187	185	181
Bangkok	06.00	07.00	08.05	09.40	11.20	13.10	15.05	17.25
Makkasan	06.12	07.12	08.17	09.53	11.41	13.21	15.17	17.37
Hua Mak	06.26	07.36	08.33	10.13	11.59	13.35	15.35	17.51
Hua Takhe	06.57	08.01	08.57	10.37	12.24	13.57	16.00	18.17
Chachoengsao	07.40	08.46	09.31	11.14	13.18	14.32	16.43	18.59
Prachinburi	08.55		10.41	12.25	15.27	15.52	17.59	20.10
Prachantakham	09.15		11.00		15.57	16.17	18.16	
Kabinburi	09.45		11.30		16.35	16.45	18.45	
Aranyprathet	11.30					18.20		
Chonburi		09.43						
Pattaya		10.45						
Plutaluang		11.30						
D = Special Diesel, M = Mix, (123) = Class of train								

Eastern Train Line Timetable								
Type and Class	D,3	M,3	D,3	D,3	D,3	D,3	D,3	D,3
Train Number	182	252	186	188	154	2.4	240	110
Plutaluang							14.15	
Pattaya							14.50	
Chonburi							15.40	
Aranyprathet				06.40				13.45
Kabinburi		05.05	07.05	08.14		12.30		15.26
Prachantakham		05.41	07.33	08.37		13.00		15.59
Prachinburi	05.00	06.08	07.50	08.59		13.19		16.20
Chachoengsao	06.09	07.53	09.09	10.17	12.30	14.33	16.25	17.33
Hua Takhe	07.00	09.00	09.51	10.50	13.10	15.08	17.28	18.19
Hua Mak	07.33	09.31	10.12	11.25	13.36	15.34	18.46	18.46
Makkasan	07.47	09.58	10.27	11.39	13.52	15.57	19.02	19.02
Bangkok	08.00	10.10	10.40	11.50	14.06	16.10	19.15	19.15
D = Special Diesel, M = Mix, (123) = Class of train								

East

Thai Proverb
To flee the tiger and meet the crocodile. (Out of the frying pan, into the fire)

Eastern Train Line Fares				
From Bangkok	**Fares without supplements (baht)**			
	Class			**Distance**
Station	**1st**	**2nd**	**3rd**	**km**
Makkasan	-	-	2	5
Hua Takhe	-	-	7	31
Chachoengsao	-	-	13	61
Prachinburi	-	-	26	122
Kabinburi	-	-	33	161
Aranyprathet	-	-	48	255
Chonburi	-	-	23	108
Pattaya	-	-	31	155
Platuluang	-	-	37	184

A Night Out at the Boxing

Professional and amateur Thai boxing (*Muang Thai*) can be seen around Thailand, but two of the most accessible and exciting stadiums are in the heart of Bangkok itself. Following is a description of what you are likely to encounter when watching a boxing match — because there is more to a bout than the boxing itself.

The atmosphere emanating from the stadium can be felt and witnessed as you approach. Outside, families line the footpath with food and mats, but these gatherings basically act as covers for gambling rings that swap money and bets with hopeful locals throughout the night. It is also just a place where Thai women can be part of all the fun, as you will be lucky to see a Thai female within the walls the stadium itself — strictly a male domain. The real excitement is inside. Within the walls the atmosphere is electric as the boxers prepare to fight. Ringside gambling becomes heated before every bout but more ecstatic as every round passes. The fact that gambling is illegal in Thailand is no deterrent.

To take part in the gambling is near impossible without years of intense study into the local lingo and sign language. The betting is in constant fury with hundreds of hand movements making perfect sense to everybody involved. Unbelievably the ring leaders remember them all, as well as the bets, taking and paying wads of notes after every round, and I mean wads (fistfuls of 1,000B notes are ceremoniously passed around).

The scene can be compared to something you only see in the movies. Each section of the seating, as well as the ring itself is divided by protective wire to the roof to stop the excited crowd from swarming the ring, and also to keep the fighters distant from any debris. Excited patrons try and sit the odd farang together, but it you don't fancy being herded into any particular section, change the subject to something interesting like the size of feet, which will suddenly make you friends for life (it helps if you drag along a friend with size 13 feet).

The boxing begins with a traditional prayer ritual. Each fighter wears special head-gear and kneels in prayer as he draws energy from the crowd around him which he plans to unleash upon his opponent. Once the fighting gets underway, you become quite content knowing that it's someone else up in the ring as the matches are often brutal encounters. Fighting tends to continue until someone is knocked out or the bell rings. It is rarely stopped, as no Thai fighter wants to lose face, but would rather deal with the punishing hands, legs, elbows and knees of the fearless warrior in front of them. Make sure you practice your 'oohs' to blend in with the crowd as each particularly debilitating blow is struck.

Each three minute round is followed by a two minute break, but the round is accompanied by traditional music consisting of a high pitched flute and bamboo xylophone, designed to spur on the fighters although the music can be grating to the untrained ear.

To see Thai boxing first hand will give you an experience that you will never forget and add to the memories of your Thailand adventure.   Danielle Karalus

NORTHERN
THAILAND

Northern Thailand differs considerably from other areas of Thailand. Extremely mountainous, and in some areas heavily wooded, visitors regularly comment on the stunning and very photogenic countryside. The north is probably best known for its trekking opportunities to hilltribe communities, but for those willing to get off the beaten track a little, this region has much more to offer. Although some regions have been exhaustively explored, there are still large tracts of quiet places where it is easy to slip off and relax, while still experiencing the unique northern culture.

Chiang Mai is the largest city in the north and the most popular place to use as a base for highland excursions, however, other secondary cities are increasing in size and popularity as many search for a subtler option to Chiang Mai. Mae Hong Son and Chiang Rai are probably the two most popular alternatives and both are easily reached from Chiang Mai.

Although trekking is the North's main claim to fame, many areas have now been more or less completely 'trekked out' and are really not worth visiting if you are looking for fairly traditional villages. Mae Hong Son, Chiang Rai, Pai and Nan are all far superior choices for trekking over Chiang Mai. For more information, refer to the section on trekking later in this chapter or in the Culture section in the introductory part of the book.

North Thailand

Due to the mountainous landscape, the temperature in the north can get quite cool. The cold season runs from the end of November to late February, with the coldest months being December and January. During this time the average temperature is 30° C, but nights average around 14° C. Nights can however drop to around freezing in higher altitudes. The hot season runs from early March to late May with the heat in April being particularly unbearable. During this period the average temperature is 35° C. The rainy season is from early June to late October with an average temperature of 31° C. If you are there in September take your wellies, raincoat and possibly even a boat, as the term 'wet' is an understatement.

Since the early 1980s the Thai government has concentrated on developing the roads in an extensive infrastructure program. As a result, the roads are generally very good when compared to other areas of the country.

Highlights
Trekking to **Thu-Lor-Sue Waterfall** in Umphang (Tak Province).
Trip to **Doi Mae Salong** (Chiang Rai Province).
Doi Phu Kha National Park (Nan Province).
Sukhothai Historical Park (Sukhothai Province).
A night at the **Brasserie** in Chiang Mai.
These are just good places to start, as there are literally hundreds of things to do and see in Northern Thailand which you should be able to find in the following chapter.

The Northern Loop
One very popular way to travel around the north is by hired motorcycle. A general high standard of roads combined with stunning scenery and fresh mountain air make the motorcycle an exhilarating, refreshing and reasonably priced way to see the area in depth. There are a number of different circuits which are becoming well worn in this region and all you really need is an accurate road map and a reliable motorbike (and of course this book!). Some sample circuits and minimum time length needed follows. Note that although we suggest a minimum time needed for a loop you could easily spend much longer doing the same thing.
a) Mae Hong Son Loop
Probably the most popular trip taken by motorbike out of Chiang Mai, this route takes you north out of Chiang Mai, through Pai and Soppong to Mae Hong Son. After this you head south via Khun Yuam to Mae Sariang then west via Hot and Chom Thong. You can probably take a deviation to the summit of Doi Inthanon before returning to Chiang Mai. This loop can be done easily in three days, although at least a week is needed to really enjoy the trip.
b) Samoeng Loop
This much shorter route takes you on a circuit around Doi Suthep and can be done in half a day, although if you take it in the anti clockwise direction you can spend your morning at the attractions in the Mae Rim and Mae Sa Valley area before pushing on to Samoeng. The scenery on this ride is particularly stunning.
c) Further Afield
Other areas in the north which offer particularly impressive rides are in and around Nan, between Chiang Khong and Chiang Saen, the ride up to Doi Mae Salong and between Mae Sariang and Mae Sot.
d) Longer Trips
Hired motorbike trips need not only be for short periods or just around the town where you hired the bike from. If you really want to see the north in depth and on your own terms we recommend you consider hiring a motorbike for an extended amount of time. Quite often this outweighs the cost of your own time plus catching buses, trains and local transport, and you are not confined to their timetables. Below we have an example of what you can do if you have the time and a hard tush, based on personal experience.

During the research of this book we did over 3,000 km on a hired motorcycle from Chiang Mai. The basic route ran as follows, but there were numerous side trips and points of interest along the way: Chiang Mai - Pai - Soppong - Mae Hong Son - Khun Yuam - Mae Sariang - Mae Sot - Umphang - Tak - Kamphaeng Phet - Sukhothai - Phrae - Nan - Phayao - Chiang Rai - Chiang Saen - Chiang Khong - Mai Sai - Doi Tung - Doi Mae Salong - Fang - Chiang Dao - Chiang Mai. The entire trip was on a 100cc Honda Dream with two passengers and luggage, and although the going was slow at times, the only time a bigger bike would have been really worthwhile was on the road to Umphang. This trip allowed us easy access to places which are otherwise difficult to get to, and with a couple of exceptions we were able to keep to secondary roads where the traffic was minimal. The above route is one of the many you could do in the northern region. For a circuit like the above, an absolute minimal amount of time would be three weeks, but do not blink because you will miss most of it. Six to eight weeks would allow you to get a real insight into all the places.

The **Thai Department of Highways** puts out laminated maps on each region which detail all the main roads. These maps are excellent and have been praised in particular by cyclists and motorbikers who want to avoid the heavier trafficked roads. They are available at any highway office and are in Thai and English. Another excellent purchase are the motorcycling guides put out by **David Unkovich** and widely available in Chiang Mai. These offer fairly accurate comments on road condition and elevation and are a veritable bonanza on out of the way points worth checking out along the way.

CHIANG MAI PROVINCE

Definitely the most popular tourist destination in the north of Thailand, Chiang Mai makes an interesting entry point to the north, although those seeking a less touristy feel may feel themselves being drawn further afield. The provincial capital, Chiang Mai, is particularly popular with middle aged European visitors, and you will notice the affect this has had on the tourist services available here. The city possesses enough attractions to keep most people busy for at least a few days, and the rest of the province is quite beautiful. The one pastime which is probably better done in areas other than Chiang Mai is the trekking. The trekking industry here has overtrekked the surrounds, and you will find better value for money elsewhere in the north.

Visitors planning to see Chiang Mai in depth should avail themselves to *Welcome to Chiang Mai and Chiang Rai* magazine which has great information not only on the sights but also serves to keep you abreast of what is happening once the sun goes down. A great way to explore the province is by motorcycle which can be hired at reasonable rates throughout the city. Pop motorcycle hire on Moon Muang Road is pretty reliable.

CHIANG MAI   เชียงใหม่

Chiang Mai is the second most visited city in Thailand, but in the real scheme of things it does not even compare to the capital, Bangkok. In fact, in comparison, Chang Mai is more like a small town with a population of around 200,000. Despite its smaller population, Chiang Mai still oozes a vibrant feel and an excellent nightlife. Because of its smaller size, Chiang Mai has a lot in its favour in regard to sightseeing as the centre of town is easily walked around and motorcycle hire shops abound, allowing you to reach the more out of the way sights. The city is packed with wats, some of which are particularly highly revered and well worth visiting.

Besides the wats, Chiang Mai is used by many people as a base for hilltribe trekking and it seems that virtually every bar, restaurant and guesthouse can act as a trekking agent. The Chiang Mai authorities have, in recent years, made a concerted effort to try to clean up what in the past has been a particularly problematic trekking industry, with mixed results. Now the problem seems to be how 'touristy' the trek is rather than how dodgy it is. We would still advise those who wish to see fairly traditional villages to try leaving from a different base, as the area around Chiang Mai has been more or less trekked out, and many of the tours now involve long car rides to get to the area that the travel agents claim to be a 'newly remote area'. See the **Trekking** section in the Culture chapter for more details.

Orientation

The centre of town is surrounded by the remnants of an ancient wall and moat originally built for defence purposes but which now serve only to confuse the traffic. Sections of the wall have been renovated successfully, giving an idea of how it must have once looked. There are a series of gates which provide entry into the old town, the highlight of Chiang Mai, with twisting little lanes and interesting wats which seem to pop out of nowhere. Once outside the city gates, the city transforms into a standard Thai city - dirty, concrete and ugly. One saving grace outside of the city gates is the Ping River waterfront bar area. This is one of our favourite areas in Thailand for splashing out on a nice bottle of wine and listening to an extremely high standard of live music. See **Entertainment** for more details.

Vital Information

Tourist Office, ☎ (053) 248 604, is on Route 106 on the east side of the Ping River, about a five minute walk from its junction with Charoen Muang Road. The staff are very helpful, and you will find informative transport and up to date accommodation brochures.
Post Office is inconveniently located out near the train station and there is a telecom office upstairs. For poste restante, be sure to ask for the packages box because anything not an exact standard letter size goes in there, and the staff do not volunteer this information. There is also a new post office along Samlan Road on the first block left off Pra Singh. They have an efficient packing service, facsimile and overseas telephone facilities.
Banks are all over town and exchange booths abound around Tha Phae Gate.
Hospital The McCormick Hospital is the best for English speaking staff and quick treatment.
Tourist Police are beside the tourist office.
Codes Chiang Mai's telephone code is (053) and the postal code is 50000.

Cheap Sleeps

There are three forms of information upon arrival at Chiang Mai regarding accommodation. There are TAT officers at the train station, there are touts who will tell you anything and everything to get you into dirty overpriced hotels and there is this book. If you have just come off the train or bus from Bangkok, you may be pretty tired and vulnerable, so be on your guard when bargaining. It is easy to lose your cool when you need sleep and you have a person annoying the hell out of you. Thankfully the hassling seems to have been cleaned up a little, and during our last visit we had to go and find a tuk tuk driver!

Most guesthouses also operate as travel agents, offering their own trekking trips from two to five nights. Almost all of them will guarantee you an authentic experience with a hilltribe village taking you to an area just opened to Westerners, often including an elephant ride and rafting. You may often have the opportunity to try opium, although this is not necessarily openly advertised and we suggest you read our section regarding trekking and opium beforehand. Because many of the guesthouses double as a trekking agent, it is often expected in high season that if you stay there you will be expected to go on their trek. If you refuse, or if you do not plan to go on a trek, guesthouses will often kick you out. We heard of one case where a couple who were doing a two week meditation course during high season had to change accommodation every other day because the guesthouses kept on throwing them out because they did not want to do a trek. Another problem is when one goes trekking, the valuables left in the 'safe' have been fiddled with. Be careful and listen to other travellers' recommendations.

The following accommodation listing is far from exhaustive, but lists the places which generally do not change name every year. There are so many places in Chiang Mai it would be ridiculous to write about them all. Below is the pick of the bunch, but generally shows the main

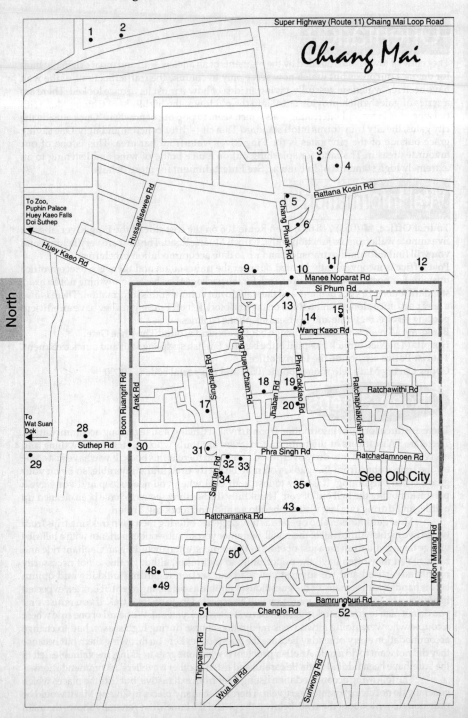

Chiang Mai

Super Highway (Route 11) Chaing Mai Loop Road

To Zoo,
Puphin Palace
Huey Kaeo Falls
Doi Suthep

Huey Kaeo Rd

Hussadisewee Rd

Chang Phuak Rd

Rattana Kosin Rd

Manee Noparat Rd

Si Phum Rd

Wang Kaeo Rd

Khang Puen Cham Rd

Singharat Rd

Arak Rd

Boon Ruangrit Rd

Phra Pokklao Rd

Inthan Rd

Ratchaphakinai Rd

Ratchawithi Rd

To
Wat Suan
Dok

Suthep Rd

Sam lan Rd

Phra Singh Rd

Ratchadamnoen Rd

See Old City

Ratchamanka Rd

Moon Muang Rd

Bamrungburi Rd

Changlo Rd

Thippanet Rd

Wua Lai Rd

Sunwong Rd

North

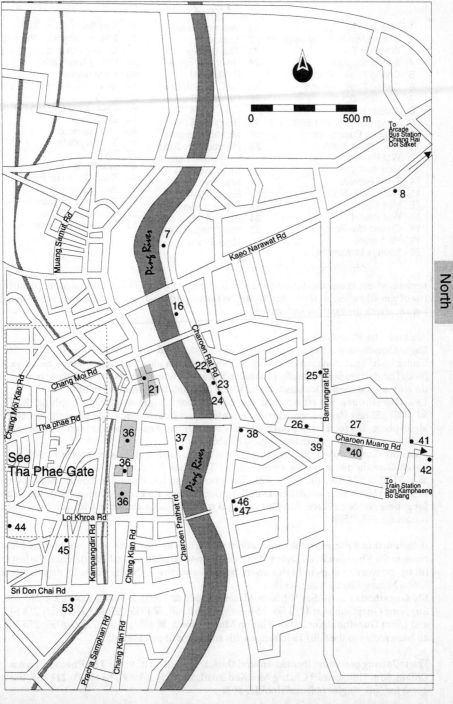

North

legend

1	Wat Jet Yot	21	Worarot market	37	Kim Gh.
2	Chiang Mai National Museum	22	Brasserie	38	Bus to Lamphun, Pasang,
3	Wat Kuu Tao	23	The Gallery		Chiang Rai and Lampang
4	Sports Stadium	24	Riverside Bar &	39	Krung Thai Bank
5	Chang Puak bus station		Restaurant	40	Food market
6	Chang Puak Hospital	25	C&C Teakhouse	41	Siam Commercial Bank
7	Je t'Aime Gh.	26	Bangkok Bank of	42	GPO
8	Arcade bus station		Commerce	43	Chiangmai Garden Gh.
9	Songtheaws to Doi Suthep	27	Bangkok Bank	44	DK Books
10	Chuang Puak Gate	28	Maharaj Hospital	45	Montha Hotel
11	Wat Chang Yuen	29	Hilltribes Products	46	Tourist police
12	Wat Pa Pao		Promotion Centre	47	TAT
13	Mountain View Gh.	30	Suandok Gate	48	Wat Phuek Hong
14	THAI Airways	31	Wat Phra Singh	49	Suan Buak Hat Park
15	Wat Chang Man	32	Krung Thai Bank	50	Wat Mangrai
16	Mee Gh.	33	Police station	51	Suan Prung Gate
17	Wat Prasat	34	Post office	52	Chiang Mai Gate
18	Chiang Mai Prison	35	Wat Chedi Luang	53	Suriwong Book centre
19	Post office	36	Night Bazaar		
20	3 Kings Monument				

regions where accommodation abounds. The map of Chiang Mai shows a more plentiful list of guesthouses, so if you are trying to find a particular guesthouse that is not listed below, check the map for its location.

Around Tha Phae Gate
Eagle Guesthouse at Soi 3, 16 Chang Moi Kao Road, ☎ (053) 235 387, fax (053) 216 368. Under Irish/Thai management, this guesthouse offers a pleasant garden setting and decent food. The staff are fairly friendly (doubly so if you trek with them). Rooms are basic but could do with a good scrub. Doubles with bath cost 100B and the dormitory is 40B.
Lek Guesthouse is just around the corner from Eagle at 22 Chaiyaphum Road, ☎ (053) 252 686. Particularly unfriendly staff detract from an otherwise pleasant courtyard atmosphere. The food is tasty but the staff here really leave a sour taste in your mouth. Fairly dirty rooms cost 80B/100B for singles/doubles.
Paocome Guesthouse is on the same lane as Eagle. Fairly quiet rooms cost 50B/80B.
Sarah Guesthouse is on the south side of Tha Phae Road at 20 Soi 4 Tha Phae Road, ☎ (053) 279 423, Fax (053) 279 423. The guesthouse has clean and comfortable rooms starting at 80B. Other nearby and similar priced places are **Living House**, **Mr John**, **Baan Jongcome** and **Nice Place**. Another standout is **Ratchuda Guesthouse** with quiet and clean rooms for 80B/150B.

In the **northeast** corner of the inner moat area there is another group of guesthouses. Most come in the Khao San Road style with large concrete buildings, but these are often the last to fill up, so worth a peek in high season, but it is a surprisingly quiet area to stay. Soi 9 off Moon Muang Road is your best bet.
SK Guesthouse at 30 Soi 9 Moon Muang Road, ☎ (053) 210 690, Fax (053) 210 690, **Supreme Guesthouse** at 44/1 Soi 9 Moon Muang Road, ☎ (053) 222 480, Fax (053) 218 545, and **Libra Guesthouse** at 28 Soi 9 Moon Muang Road, ☎ (053) 210 687, Fax (053) 275 324, all have rooms in the 80B/150B range with and without private bath.

The following places are located around the few sois just within the **Tha Phae Gate** area. **Chiang Moi House** at 29 Chiang Moi Kao Road, ☎ (053) 251 839, Fax (053) 214 337, has a dorm for 50B, singles 60B and doubles 80B.

Happy House is just south of Chiang Moi House and you will get similar rooms for 150B.
So Muang Guesthouse is across the moat and up Soi 2. Motel-like rooms cost 150B.
Moon Muang Golden Court is north of the intersection with Ratchadamnoen Road. It has pretty nice and clean rooms for 150B/180B.
Rendevous Guesthouse is located at 3/1 Soi 5 Ratchadamnoen Road, ☎ (053) 213 763, Fax (053) 217 229. To get here follow Ratchadamnoen past the USIS/AUA and take the marked Soi. Nice quiet rooms cost 120B/150B.
Kamil House is just a bit further up the Soi, and you will get a room for 120B/150B.
There are a few other places around this area, so the best advice we can offer is to just wander around, as some guesthouses come and go.

In the **southeast** corner of the inner moat area is another concentration of cheaper places to stay, some with considerable 'character'.
Banana Guesthouse, Phathai Guesthouse at 48/1 Ratpakinai Road, ☎ (053) 278 013, Fax (053) 274 075, **NAT Guesthouse** at 7 Soi 6 Phra Pokklao Road, ☎ (053) 277 878, and **Kent Guesthouse** at 5 Soi 1 Ratmanka Road, ☎ (053) 278 578, all have rooms in the 80B/150B range. The best way to find appropriate accommodation is to wander in following the

Legend

1 Miami Hotel
2 Night Market
3 Paocome Gh.
4 Eagle House
5 The Smiling Elephant
6 Lek House
7 Cheap Noodle Bar
8 New Happy House
9 Darets House
10 Tapae Gate
11 Police Box & ISD Phone
12 Roong Raeng
13 Firenze Restaurant
14 America Restaurant
15 Karaoke Bar Kawaii
16 Art Cafe
17 Wat Maharam
18 Tapae Place Hotel
19 Wat Burharam
20 Chiang Mai Books
21 Syntax Gh.
22 Living House
23 Home Place Gh.
24 Thapae Gh.
25 Midtown Gh.
26 Aroon Rai Restaurant
27 Mr John House
28 Sarah Gh.
29 Thana Gh.
30 Baan Jong Gh.
31 Ratchada Gh.
32 El Toro Pub & Restaurant
33 Flamingo Gh.
34 Little Home Gh.
35 Kaithong Restaurant
36 Wat

North

Legend

1	Money Guesthouse	31	Gap's House
2	Tanya Guesthouse	32	Aum Vegetarian Rest.
3	S.K. House	33	Domino Pub
4	Libra Guesthouse	34	Top North Hotel
5	Supreme House	35	Thai Way Guesthouse
6	Koon House	36	Saitum Guesthouse
7	Thongkoon House	37	Blues Pub, Legends Cafe,
8	Lanna Thai Cookery School		Johns Place
9	Wat Lam Chang	38	Library Service
10	Lam Chang Guesthouse	39	Golden Triangle Gh.
11	S.P. Hotel	40	Somwang Guesthouse
12	Somphet Market	41	Nice Sweet Place
13	Sumit Hotel	42	Andora Hotel
14	Your House	43	Rose Guesthouse
15	Your House	44	Nat Guesthouse
16	Family Trek Guesthouse	45	Muangtong Hotel
17	Irish Pub	46	Overlander Bar
18	Pop Motorcycle Hire	47	Jane Guesthouse
19	Rama Guesthouse	48	Pathara Guesthouse
20	Chiangmai Kristi House	49	Toy House
21	Rendevous House	50	Top North Guesthouse
22	Kavil Guesthouse	51	Topper Thai Guesthouse
23	AUA Language Institute	52	Mattana House
24	Post office	53	Chiangmai Guesthouse
23	AUA Language Institute	54	North Star Guesthouse
24	Post office	55	Thailand Guesthouse
25	J.J. Bakery	56	Kritsada House
26	Tapae Gate	57	Bus to Hang Dong
27	AUA Language Institute		Doi Inthanon, Hot
28	Siam Commercial Bank	58	Wat Sai Moon
29	Thai Cookery School	59	Youth Hostel
30	Police box & ISD Phone	60	Banana Guesthouse

Old City

0   300 m

plethora of signs, as quite a few places come and go in this area. These places are not listed because they may not be there when you go looking for them.

YHA members may want to check out the **Chiang Mai Youth Hostel** at 63 Bamrung Mai Road, ☎ (053) 272 169, south of the above mentioned places. It was unclear how mandatory a YHA membership was but if you flash it you should be given a discount in room rates. The dorm is 45B and singles/doubles cost 90B/130B. The staff are friendly and approachable.

East of the centre of town around the Ping River there are some decent places to stay.
C&C Teak House at 39 Bumrungrad Road, ☎ (053) 246 966, has cheap rooms in a atmospheric teak building for 60B/80B/120B, and the food is not too bad.
Cowboy Guesthouse is north of the river bars on Charoenrat Road. Friendly staff will offer you clean rooms in a pretty quiet setting for 80B with bath.
Mee Guesthouse is along the same road at 193/1 Charoenrat Road, ☎ (053) 243 534, and has basic rooms for 80B/100B.
Je T'aime Guesthouse is further north of Cowboy at 247-9 Charoenrat Road, ☎ (053) 241 912. It is located in a nice setting and has clean and large rooms, but is run by one of the grumpiest women to walk the streets of Chiang Mai. Rates are 70B/100B/140B.

Eat and Meet

Like the accommodation, Chiang Mai has restaurants to suit all budgets and tastes. The areas along Loi Khro Road, Chayapoom Road and Kotchasarn Road are abundant in restaurants catering to Westerners. Below are just a few choices, but more than likely, you will come across dozens of options down most streets.

AUM Vegetarian Restaurant Has a nice upstairs section - a covered patio with low tables and cushions on the floor. Delicious and interesting dishes, like fried marrow with Chiang Mai spicy sauce, chipi and ginger in coconut milk, all for a reasonable 25B and 7B extra for a generous portion of wild rice. The service is very friendly. Open 9.00 am to 2.00 pm and 5.00 pm to 9.00 pm, and located inside the Tha Phae Gate.

Aroon Rai is on Kotchasan Road, south of the Tha Phae Gate and has a good selection of tasty Thai dishes at reasonable prices.

Thanom Restaurant is just up from Aroon Rai and also does good food at fair prices. You will need to be politely dressed (no singlets) and no alcohol is served.

JJ's Bakery is on the other side of the moat, near the Tha Phae Gate, and has a huge menu of Western, Thai and Chinese favourites.

America Restaurant at 402-1-2 Tha Phae Road serves good Western food, though we would advise steering clear of the meatballs. **Internet Access**. There are a couple of computers here for those who want to browse the web or check their emails. This costs 180B per hour.

Thai Place is on Chang Moi Road and is a large open restaurant, very popular with locals for Thai and Chinese standards.

Night Bazaar has a huge adjoining section dedicated to good Thai seafood. Be sure to check the prices before you sit down or you will be charged a significant fortune. The main street of the night bazaar also has the normal selection of McDonalds and Burger King style places for the fast food junkies.

Noodle Shops are all over town. One central location is on Chaiyaphum Road, around the lane leading to Lek and Eagle Guesthouses.

Riverside Bar and Restaurant This place is more expensive than the other restaurants mentioned, but the food is worth it. It is a popular place with a river front setting. Other places line the river in this area and also serve good food.

Daret's House in the Tha Phae Gate area offers a large selection of Thai and Western food in Khao San Road style. You can buy cheap beer and it is popular with travellers.

Pubs Across the moat in the Tha Phae Gate area are a number of bars and eateries catering to the Western taste, but none are particular standouts.

Antique House at 71 Charoen Prathet Road. The setting lives up to its name, and although the prices are a little high, it is a nice place for a splurge.

Things to do and Sights to See

Tourism is the number one outside income earner for Chiang Mai, easily justifiable by the large number of attractions within a fairly confined area. At least three to four days could be allowed for seeing most of what Chiang Mai has to offer at a fairly relaxed pace. Most of the inner city sights can be reached easily by foot, whilst a motorcycle or bicycle is ideal for visiting the out of town sights. Many travel agents offer tours of the city at reasonable rates, although you are not always allowed the time to enjoy the sights at your own pace. Another option is to charter a tuk tuk for the day, if you let them take you out to Baw Sang and/or San Kamphaeng the price should be pretty reasonable as they get a free tank of gas out of it (and a commission on anything you buy).

Wat Chiang Man　วัดเชียงมัน

Located in the northeast corner of the old city (within the moat) this is the oldest wat in Chiang Mai. Built in 1296, by King Mangrai, Wat Chiang Man originally served as his home but is now inhabited solely by monks. The bot features classic Thai architecture with huge ornately decorated teak columns holding the roof up. Although the bot contains an impressive Buddha image, the true 'prizes' of this wat are contained within the smaller wihaan to the right. Two impressive Buddhas are stored behind glass in the centre of this wihaan. The larger of the two, **Phra Sila** (or stone Buddha) is a stone bas-relief which was imported from either India or Sri Lanka around 2,500 years ago! Its smaller counterpart, **Phra Sae Tang Kamani** (or crystal Buddha) stands to a height of only around 10 cm and is thought to have originally come from Lopburi around 1,800 years ago.

The Crystal Buddha has a very interesting history and, like many of the highly revered statues in the country, it has done more than its fair share of travelling. The story goes that there was a hermit named Phra Su-Tae-Wa who lived around 700 years after Buddha passed on. He was a disciple of Buddha's teachings and during a vivid dream, he met a god who told him that the King of Lawoh was busy building a Buddha image and that it needed to contain some relics of the Buddha. The hermit then ran off and organised to meet with the King where he successfully convinced the King to do just that. Once the statue was completed, it was believed that whoever conquered the town which possessed it could take it, as the losers did not deserve to retain it.

As a result of this belief, the statue moved house on a number of occasions. It first rested in the new city of Hariphoonsai (which itself was also built to house the image upon a dream had by another wandering hermit) until the city was destroyed by King Mangrai who installed it in his new capital of Chiang Mai. The statue remained for eleven generations after King Mangrai but was stolen by a monk of dubious character who spirited the statue off to Ayutthaya. When the King of Lan-Na found out the statue was gone, he initiated a campaign to Ayutthaya, needing to fully encircle the city with all his military might before the recalcitrant Ayutthayans agreed to hand it back. Then during the 16th Century, the King of Lan Chang (a kingdom which made up part of modern day Laos) overpowered Chiang Mai and took off with the statue. It was not until King Rama I was at war with Laos 225 years later that the statue was finally returned. Since then, the statue has only moved when carried around during the yearly Songkran festivities.

The wat is open to the public between 9.00 am and 5.00 pm daily. It is situated off Ratchaphakinai Road.

Wat Phra Singh　วัดพระสิงห์

Begun under the supervision of King Pha Vu in 1345, this large wat houses the highly revered yet controversial **Phra Singh Buddha**. Experts are not agreed as to whether this is the 'true' image, and identical statues can be found elsewhere in Thailand. Nevertheless, it is a very impressive statue, and the epicentre of the Songkran festival in mid-April. The large bot is particularly serene when not full of tour groups.

Located at the end of Phra Singh Road in the western centre of the old city, this is one place where one should keep an eye out for unscrupulous gem con men.

Wat Chedi Luang　วัดเจดีย์หลวง

Located in the centre of town on Phra Pokklao Road, this wat contains the ruins of what at one time must have been a huge chedi. Partially collapsed (due to either earthquake or cannon fire) the chedi was at one stage Chiang Mai's largest, and a definite impression of size can still be gained from seeing it today. Unfortunately, in attempting to restore the original structure the new naga gates, in particular, look crass and overly modern. The plan is for a complete restoration of the site - hopefully they will do a better job on the rest. The **Lak Muang** (city guardian pillar) is also located within the wat's grounds.

Wat Ku Tao   วัดกู่เต้า

The chedi was built in 1613 and is unique in style, but has the more traditional coloured porcelain decoration all over it. The chedi is supposed to represent the alms bowls of the Lord Buddha. It is located a bit out of town near the sports stadium.

Wat Chet Yot   วัดเจ็ดยอด

This wat was supposedly based on the Mahabodhi Temple in Bodhgaya, India, although those who have seen the 'original' may be a little nonplussed by some of the interpretations. The copy in Ubon Ratchathani is a finer copy. Each of the seven spires represent one of the seven weeks which Buddha spent in enlightenment in Bodhgaya. Constructed during the rule of King Tilokaraja in 1455, the wat hosted the 8th World Buddhist Council meeting in 1477 to revise the scriptures of Theravada Buddhism. Best reached by transport other than foot, a number 6 bus will take you right past. It is located out of central Chiang Mai, towards the national museum on the highway bypass road.

Wat Suan Dawk   วัดสวนดอก

Constructed by King Ku Nu in 1383, the bot in this compound contains a huge 500 year old bronze Buddha image which is surrounded by well preserved murals depicting Buddha's life. A variety of Buddhist amulets are sold within the grounds, around the wihaan (which was built in 1932). The whole complex was originally built as a garden for the Lan-Na Royal Family whilst now it serves as their (and others') graveyard. The wat is on the west side of Suthep Road around 1 km north of the Swan Dawk Gate.

Wat U Mong   วัดอุโมง

This forest wat was established during the reign of King Mangrai and is worth a visit to escape the often hectic madness of Chiang Mai. The wat's grounds are pierced by paths wandering through the trees and past the occasional bizarre sculptures. There is an art gallery by the entrance which contains an exhibition of work by various resident monks and the wat also has its own small library. A limited range of English books on Buddhism is available here. Occasional teachings are also given in English by resident foreign monks.

Wat Ram Poeng   วัดร่ำเปิง

This is the base for the Northern Insight Meditation Centre where many Westerners have studied vipassana. The courses are taught by resident monks with either Western students or English speaking Thais acting as interpreters. It is located about 2 km past Wat U Mong.

Chiang Mai National Museum   พิพิธภัณฑ์แห่งชาติ

Chiang Mai National Museum contains a good selection of the Buddha usuals as well as an extensive northern arts and crafts collection. Amongst the Buddha paraphernalia is a huge 15th Century Buddha head. The museum is open Wednesday to Sunday from 9.00 am to noon and 1.00 pm to 4.00 pm, admission is 10B. It is located out of town on the 'superhighway'.

Tribal Research Institute   ศูนย์ศึกษาชาวเขา

Located at the Chiang Mai University campus, this museum provides very detailed information on each of the hilltribe groups including traditional clothing and handicrafts as well as more factual information like farming cycle charts and festivals. It could be considered a 'must see' for anyone contemplating a hilltribe trek. If you want more information, you can access its library which contains books covering every aspect of hilltribe life. It is also possible to view films and slide shows. The institute is open on Monday to Friday from 8.30 am to 4.30 pm.

Chiang Mai University   มหาวิทยาลัยเชียงใหม่

The university is another quiet escape from Chiang Mai, and has a small bazaar of its own where you can buy some goodies. Not surprisingly, it is a good place to meet Thai students for a chat, and the **cybersurfers** amongst you may be able to gain some on-line time.

Chiang Mai Zoo   สวนสัตว์เชียงใหม่

More of a place for a quiet stroll rather than a zoological lesson (most signs are in Thai only). The zoo has many pretty gardens and a notable collection of gibbons. Admission is 20B. **Chiang Mai Arboretum** is nearby.

Night Bazaar   ไนท์บาซาร์

The main section of the night bazaar is in an enclosed building with many well established shops, however over the years it has spilled out onto the surrounding streets. Most of the streets around this area are overcrowded but this is one of the best (and largest) bargain shopping areas in town. Everything from T-shirts for 60B to ornate wood carvings for USD$15,000 is for sale here. The night market can be a good place for silver and hilltribe ware but, when shopping, be wary of rip-offs and be sure to give anything you buy a good look over as substandard goods are not uncommon. Bargain hard as the initial price may well be a mark-up of 300% plus and be prepared to walk away. If you are sick of shopping, sit back on the McDonalds terrace and watch the circus unfold.

If you are looking for antique silks and quality weaving and embroidery try the boutiques and small shops along Ratmankha (southeast end) and Loi Kroa Roads (near Sarah Guesthouse). You may pay a little more, but are guaranteed to find very knowledgeable shop owners. The markets are open until around 11.00 pm.

Suan Buak Park   สวนสาธารณะหนองบวกหาด

Unless there is an innovative horticultural scheme on the go where a beautiful park emerges from under vast expanses of concrete paving, you would probably be better off picnicking by the moat at Tha Phae Gate! A couple of palms remain and some marigolds, otherwise it really is a concrete jungle. The zoo is probably a better place for some peace and quiet.

Chiang Mai Prison   เรือนจำกลาง

Hardly a tourist attraction in itself, this grim walled-in building serves as a reminder for those contemplating purchasing a bit of dope off a tuk tuk driver. Many drugs are illegal in Thailand and the Westerners within these walls bear testament to that fact. The prison is near the centre of old Chiang Mai, off Ratwithi Road. You may like to visit prisoners from your country giving them some company and a break from this gruelling life for a short time. They would greatly appreciate any gifts such as cigarettes and books. The tuk tuk drivers in Chiang Mai are notorious for selling dope to foreigners then dobbing them into the police — smokers exercise caution.

Walking tour of Chiang Mai

One of the best ways to explore Chiang Mai is by foot and below is one suggestion of a route that you could take to see many of the sights within a kilometre circle of the Tha Phae Gate.

Beginning at the Tha Phae Gate, cross into the old city through the Tha Phae Gate and get some yummy breakfast at **JJ's Bakery**. Once energised, head down Ratchadamnoen Road, passing **Wat Sam Pao** on your right. Go to the intersection with Phra Pokklao Road and to your left on the other side of Phra Pokklao Road is the massive **Wat Chedi Luang**. After checking out the crumbling wat, head north up Phra Pokklao Road, past the monument to **King Mangrai** on your left and **Wat Duang Di** on your right and take a left down Inthawarorot Road to the impressive **Wat Phra Singh**. Across the road from the wat is a Thai restaurant which does great and spicy *som tam*. After a spicy lunch, head north up Singharat Road to just past the intersection with Wiang Kaeo Road. Around here there are some excellent **wood carving shops** you may be interested in. Continue north to Si Phum Road and turn right taking you to the Chang Puak Gate. From the other side of the moat here, you can get a **songtheaw up to Doi Suthep** if you feel like it. If not, continue east along Si Phum Road (taking in **Wat Chiang Yuen** on the other side of the moat) and turn right down Ratchaphanikai Road — **Wat Chiang Man** is on your right. After spotting the **Phra Sila** continue south to Ratwithi Road and take a left, this will take you back to Moon Muang Road. Cross to the other side of the moat and return to the Tha Phae Gate and take a left up Tha Phae Road. Along here you can visit **Wat Maharam** and **Wat Bupparam** on your right and **Wat Chettawan** on your left.

From here you can either continue east and head down Chang Klan Road to the **night bazaar**, or continue straight ahead and take a left up Wichayanon Road where there is a great **fresh produce market** (*talaat lam yai*). Once on Chang Moi Road, take a right to the river, cross the footbridge to **Wat Kate**, then head right down Charoen Rat Road and the **Riverside Bar and Restaurant** is on your right - no better place to finish up a long day of walking than here.

Hilltribe Trekking
For information relating to trekking, trekking etiquette, opium and the hilltribes, please refer to our section in the Culture chapter.

Day trips from Chiang Mai
The immediate surrounds of Chiang Mai contain enough points of interest to keep most busy for their entire stay in Chiang Mai. Convenient and interesting day trips can be done to the following destinations, either on an organised jaunt, or under your own steam.

Baw Sang and San Kamphaeng - These are the umbrella and silk/cotton cottage industries which are within 10 km of Chiang Mai. They are easily visited by either tuk tuk or local bus but be sure to shop around as the price and quality varies immensely.

Lamphun - The poor accommodation here makes it more attractive as a half day trip. Wat Phra That Hariphunchai and the National Museum are both worth seeing, and the trip from Chiang Mai is very scenic.

Doi Suthep/Doi Suthep National Park - Easily done in half a day, this is a must see for any visitor to Chiang Mai.

Doi Inthanon National Park - If travelling by public transport this is a long day, but under your own steam it can be easily done in a day. There are also scenic waterfalls in the same area.

Chiang Dao - An easy day trip for some spectacular caves.

Doi Ang Khang   ดอยอ่างขาง - A scenic area also known as Little Switzerland. Best visited with your own transport, if the weather is good this is a great area for a picnic. Located 20 km south of Fang.

Entertainment
Sick of kicking up your heels in front of the guesthouse TV? Head to the bars lining the Ping River for a welcoming cold drink and excellent live music. **Riverside Bar and Restaurant** is not a bad choice to start with for an excellent meal at reasonable prices, then crawl up through the nearby bars which get rowdier and rowdier until you hit **The Brasserie**. This place is open from 11.00 pm until 2.00 am and has live music sessions. If you like Dylan, The Doors, Clapton, Led Zepellin and Hendrix, then this is the place for you. No cover charge.

Bars
Along Moon Muang Road near the Tha Phae Gate area are a number of small bars. None are particular standouts and at times it is difficult to get in due the crowds of hookers out front.

What's in a name?
Chiang Mai — established in 1296 translates as 'new city'.

North

◀ **Arriving and Departing** ▶

Air

THAI Airways International - Chiang Mai			
Destination	**Frequency**	**Time(hrs)**	**B (o/w)**
Bangkok	Daily	1.10	1,650
Chiang Rai	Daily (07.40, 16.55)	0.40	420
Hat Yai	1.3.5.7 (11.30)	2.45	3,850
Hat Yai (OEA)			2,900
Khon Kaen	1.3.5.7 (17.30), .2.4.6. (18.30)	0.50, 1.30	2,700
Khon Kaen (OEA)			1,115
Mae Hong Son	Daily (10.00, 12.50, 15.30)	0.40	345
Mae Sot	.2.4.67 (07.20)	1.55	590
Nan	1.3.5.. (14.20)	0.45	510
Phitsanulok	.2.4.67 (07.20), 1.3.5.. (14.20)	0.50, 2.05	650
Phuket	.2.4.67 (07.20), 1.3.5.. (14.20), 1.3.567 (11.15)	1.55	3,455
Surat Thani	1.3.567 (10.10)	1.45	3,115
Surat Thani (OEA)			2,450
Ubon Ratchathani	1.3.5.7 (17.30)	1.50	3,045
Ubon Ratchathani (OEA)			1,950
Udon Thani	.2.4.6. (17.30)	0.50	2,950
Udon Thani (OEA)			1,300
International Flights			
Kuala Lumpur	..3...7 (13.40)	3.40	5,180
Kunming	.2.4..7 (14.25)	2.35	4,965
Singapore	....5.7 (12.40), .2..... (16.20)	4.10	6,400
Tokyo	..3.5.7 (20.15)	11.15	15,360
Vientiane	...4... (11.00), ...7 (15.30)	1.00	2,680
OEA = Orient Express Air, B (baht) = Full Price Fares			

Train

Second class sleeper is always a good choice as you can stretch out and because the trip is overnight you save on accommodation. However, this is about twice as expensive as the bus. For train timetable information, see the end of the chapter.

Waiting for the post...

Whenever asking for things in Thailand, be prepared to try all possible permutations before giving up. During the researching of this book, I was awaiting a package of notes at Chiang Mai GPO but the package had not shown up. After Sydney verified that the package had been sent, I returned to the GPO (again) to ask for mail - nothing there. This went on for six days, during which precious timetables were being revised and itineraries reordered.

Eventually the postmaster and I had a chat, during which I explained my frustration with the Thai mail system. The post master looked at me sympathetically and asked what it was I was waiting for. I explained (yet again) it was a large parcel full of papers. "Ah" he said, " full of work papers hey?", "then it is probably in the 'large parcels box'", walked off and returned with my mail — which had been postmarked as received eight days previously! I had asked for the package, parcel and mail boxes throughout my previous attempts, but never the 'large parcel box'.

Stuart McDonald

Bus
You can catch a bus to virtually anywhere in Thailand from the Arcade bus station at the northeastern end of town. For local buses or buses within Chiang Mai province you need to go to Chang Puak Bus (White Elephant) station to the north of town. Sample fares from the Arcade bus station are as follows:

From Chang Puak bus station, sample fares include; **Fang** 43B, **Chiang Dao** 20B, **Tha Ton** 53B, **Hot** 24B, **Chom Thong** 15B and **Mae Rim** 6B. Buses to **Baw Sang** and **San Kamphaeng** can also be caught from here for 5B. Other fares from Chiang Mai include **Lamphun** 7B, **Mae Sariang** 59B (A/C 106B), **Uttaradit** 87B, **Kamphaeng Phet** 88B and **Khun Yuam** 91B.

Chiang Mai Arcade Bus Station Tel (053) 242 664				
	A/C Services		**Non-A/C Services**	
Destination	**Cost**	**Departs Chiang Mai**	**Cost**	**Departs Chiang Mai**
Bangkok	237B	Throughout the day	190B	12.30
Chiang Rai (New Route)	102B	09.40,11.30,16.00	57B	Throughout the day
Chiang Rai (Old Route)	N/A		83B	Throughout the day
Chiang Saen	30B		73B	08.30
Chiang Khong	128B	09.00	91B	06.15,10.00,12.00
Khon Kaen	268B	08.00,18.00	192B	05.00,06.00,09.15,11.00
Lampang (a)	N/A		29B	Throughout the day
Mae Hong Son via Pai	175B	08.00	95B	Throughout the day
via Mae Sariang	206B	06.30,09.00,21.00	115B	08.00,11.00,13.30,20.00
Mai Sai	127B	Throughout the day	71B	Throughout the day
Mae Sot	172B	13.00	96B	07.40,09.45,11.10
Nakhon Ratchasima	324B	08.00,09.45,17.30,20.30	180B	03.30,06.30,19.00
Nakhon Sawan	N/A		115B	06.30,07.30,09.30
Nan	148B	10.00,14.00,22.00	83B	07.00,08.30,11.00,17.00
Pai	62B	08.30	45B	07.00,10.30,12.30,16.00
Pattaya	418B	13.45,16.15,17.00,19.00	232B	05.30,14.30
Phayao	71B	11.30,15.30	51B	Throughout the day
Phitsanulok (Old Route)	146B	08.45,10.00,12.00,15.00	104B	14.15
Phitsanulok (New Route)	N/A		86B	06.30,10.30
Phrae	76B	Throughout the day	55B	Throughout the day
Sukhothai	127B	Throughout the day	95B	05.00,06.00,14.15,15.00
Ubon Ratchathani	445B	12.15,17.45,18.30	247B	14.00,16.30
Udon Thani	N/A		170B	07.30,17.30,19.00
(a) The bus to Lampang leaves from near the Narawat Bridge.				

Songtheaw
If you catch a songtheaw along Chaiyapum or Tha Phae Road it will cost 20B to the bus station. But if you have arrived late at night or early in the morning expect to pay 50B to get into town. To get to the train station costs 20B, but only 10B in the reverse direction. The songtheaws to **Doi Suthep** are caught outside the Chang Puak Gate and cost 30B but only 20B to get back.

AROUND CHIANG MAI

Doi Suthep-Pui National Park   ดอยสุเทพ

This National Park was declared in 1981 but it is fighting to survive in the face of increasing urban sprawl from Chiang Mai, the continuing presence of hundreds of hilltribe families living within the its boundaries, and the encroachment of luxury holiday retreats. Luckily, a residents action group has sprung up in Chiang Mai in defence of the park and, hopefully over time, some of the damage will be allowed the breathing space it needs in order to repair itself.

Not all the blame for the degradation of the park lies in the hands of greedy developers. Continuing activities of the hilltribe villages and their slash and burn agriculture continue to devastate the park. The network of roads through the park continues to increase into previously untouched areas making it easier to reach both for poachers and illegal collectors of plant life.

This National Park can get quite busy as tour buses arrive and disgorge their loads of guided tourists. Urban myth has it that there are more package tourists on guided tours here (speaking German, French and English) per square metre than Phuket or the Grand Palace! Probably not true, but it can certainly seem that way.

Despite the tourist hordes, greedy developers and vandalising hilltribe villages, the park is still very nice to visit and is a veritable treasure trove of plant species. Almost 2,000 different varieties of flowering plants and ferns have been recorded, some set around quite scenic waterfalls. Although the vast majority of the animals have been tracked, trapped and tucked into, there is still a wide variety of birdlife which would keep most bird spotters more than content and there are hundreds of both butterfly and moth species in the park.

There are two main trails which can be walked including one to the peak of Doi Suthep. The trails can take you to most points of interest including a Hmong village, Phuping Palace and the scenic Khonthathan Waterfall. None of the walks are particularly strenuous and certainly beat driving around for atmosphere.

The entrance to the National Park is by the temple car park. If you can handle some extra steps, the entrance to the National Park Headquarters is on your left, a 10 minute walk up. There is an interesting photo and poster display on the reforestation programme at Doi Suthep at the seedling nursery - worth a visit for getting a perspective on destruction of natural resources and the hard work involved in reforestation.

Accommodation is available near the park office in the form of both bungalows and dormitories, and there are tents for hire for 40B or you can pitch your own for 5B. There is a small selection of eating places by the temple carpark and the Phuping Palace.

Yao hilltribe woman taking a break!

Wat Phra That Doi Suthep

For many this is a highlight of any visit to Chiang Mai. On a clear day, the views of Chiang Mai and its surrounds are unsurpassed. On the same clear day the gleaming golden chedi at **Wat Phra That Doi Suthep** can be seen from downtown Chiang Mai. Originally built in 1383 the wat has gone through a number of facelifts and extensions to reach its present state. The story behind the construction goes along the lines that the site of the temple was chosen in the late 14th Century as a storage place for local holy bits'n'pieces. All the goodies were placed on the back of a white elephant and they waited to see where the elephant went. After lumbering up the hill, the elephant reached the present site, jumped around in a circle three times, trumpeted and sat down. This was taken as a good indication of where to build a temple. Mmm...

It is around 300 steps to the wat from where you leave the road and the walk is not too strenuous. However if you are really struggling, catch the cable car. Ring the bells to bring yourself good fortune. Strict dress regulations apply if you want to get inside the wat - long sleeves and long pants. Accessories are available for people who are not respectable enough.

To get there catch the bus from the north of the Chang Phuk Gate for 30B up and 20B down. It is around 16 km from Chiang Mai.

Phu Phing Palace   พระตำหนักภูพิงค์

Around 5 km past the wat is the winter retreat for the royal family. Although the palace itself is off limits, lovely gardens are open to the public which you can wander through at your leisure. Again, you need to dress modestly, otherwise you can rent some pants for 10B. Songtheaws will charge another 20B each way from the wat.

Hmong Hilltribe Village   หมู่บ้านชาวเขาเผ่าม้ง (ดอยปุย)

Another 3 km past the palace is this well touristed village. It is worth visiting to see the destructive impact of over tourism on a fragile culture. At times visitors outnumber the locals. There are some bargains on the hilltribe wares.

To get there it costs another 20B by songtheaw each way from the palace. With the other sites, it makes a return trip fare to Chiang Mai cost an outrageous 130B, therefore the hiring of a motorbike (100B) becomes a reasonable alternative.

Baw Sang and San Kamphaeng   บ่อสร้าง, สันกำแพง

Baw Sang is also known as the umbrella village due to the fact that the entire street is lined with umbrella factories and retailers. Some stores offer good bargains, but shop around as quality varies tremendously. A big hit with package tours, you may have to fight your way through rude farangs at times. Tuk tuk drivers will offer to take you there because they get a free tank of gas (and commission) from the stores for taking you as a potential customer. It is around 9 km east on Route 1006 from Chiang Mai and a bus costs 5B. **San Kamphaeng** is the big area for cotton and silk. All the above rules also apply here, but there is also a discount for quantity.

Mae Sa Valley   ไร่แม่สาแวลเลย์

This village is a popular tourist destination, reached via Route 107 north of Chiang Mai. Just head up Route 107 for around 17 km, turn left and follow the signs. Elephant shows, feeding and rides are the highlights here with **Mae Sa Elephant Training Centre** getting the best reviews. The morning show starts at 9.30 am and costs 40B, after which short rides to 'Jungle trips' ranging in price from 50B to 250B are available. They are situated nearby to **Namtok Mae Sa** and only 10 km from the 107 turn-off at Mae Rim. Namtok Mae Sa is a ten tiered waterfall and is actually in Doi Suthep-Pui National Park. To get to Mae Rim from Chiang Mai costs 6B.

Samoeng Loop
This circuit trip is very popular for those wanting full day trips on a motorcycle from Chiang Mai. Best described in David Unkovich's handbook, *The Mae Hong Son Loop*, the trip is a combination of exhilarating motorcycling, some interesting sights, waterfalls and hilltribe villages. The basic route heads south from Chiang Mai to the junction with Route 1269 which you can then follow to Samoeng then head down Route 1096 to Mae Rim before turning south and returning to Chiang Mai. We suggest that anyone planning this trip pick up a copy of David Unkovich's book (available in Chiang Mai).

Doi Inthanon National Park   ดอยอินทนนท์
This National Park is home to Thailand's highest peak, Doi Inthanon Mountain, which climbs 2,595 m and offers superb views as well as stunning waterfalls and entertaining birdwatching. The park is best visited between November and February, but remember the high mountain air can get quite chilly at any time, and it is advised you take a pullover. There are three main waterfalls which can be fairly easily visited, **Mae Klang**, **Wachiratan** and **Siriphum**. Namtok Mae Klang is the largest of the three and the easiest to visit and with picnic and swimming possibilities it is a pleasant place to rest up. The next fall, Namtok Wachiratan, is nearly 21 km en-route to the top, and is supposedly the most powerful of the three but not as big as Mae Klang. Last but not least is Namtok Siriphum with a clear and serene fall, though hardly close to Niagara. It is probably the least visited of the three and the route takes you past a number of hilltribe settlements.

Last stop before the summit is **Napamaytanidol Chedi** which was built in 1989 to celebrate the King's 60th birthday. It is a very modern looking wat, worth a visit for something a bit different from the average wat. At the summit a large radar station mars the otherwise spectacular view. It is worth the ride up.

◀ **Arriving and Departing** ▶

The best and quickest way to get here is by hired motorbike or jeep. By public transport, catch a bus to Chom Thong 38 km from Chiang Mai and check out **Wat Phra That Si Chom Thong** for a well looked after Burmese style wat. From Chom Thong catch a songtheaw to Namtok Mae Klang (10B) or to the summit for 50B each way.

THA TON   ท่าตอน

The main reason people find themselves in Tha Ton is to catch the boat up the Kok River to Chiang Rai. Tha Ton itself has little of interest to the passer by and none of the guesthouses are particularly enticing. Not too far from town however, is **Asa's House**, a guesthouse in a Lisu village, which is an ideal place to get a look at hilltribe life, see **Around Tha Ton** for details.

Cheap Sleeps

Thip's Traveller House If you are arriving from Chiang Mai, this large guesthouse is on your left, just before the bridge over the Kok River. Rooms cost between 80B and 100B.
Chankasem Restaurant and Guesthouse is down the lane opposite Thip's. Room rates range from 70B to 350B. The cheapest rooms are small and characterless. The restaurant serves average food.
Apple Guesthouse is 100 m down the road on your right as you arrive from Chiang Rai (look for the sign). Large, clean, quiet and spacious bungalows with fan are 150B and concrete rooms in a longhouse style are 120B with fan and shower. There is also a restaurant here.

Along the lane by the river are a few **cafes** and **restaurants** mainly for people waiting for the river boat. All the above guesthouses have restaurants.

Things to do and Sights to See

Kok River Trip

The boat leaves at 12.30 pm and is a bit of a tourist trap (expect the only Thai person on board to be the driver), but still worth doing for the brilliant scenery and for a free shower from the spray. The boat passes by a number of hilltribe villages - all of which sell Pepsi or Coke, and you can get off at any of these and stay if you so desire. These hilltribe villages are well used to farangs, but you can use them as a base for visiting other outlying villages. Two of the most popular villages to use as a base are **Mae Salak** (Lahu) and **Ban Ruamit** (Karen). The fare from Tha Ton to Chiang Rai is 160B per person, 170B in the other direction, and the ride takes about four hours.

Wat Tha Ton   วัดท่าตอน

If you need to kill some time while waiting for the boat, you can take a hike up to Wat Tha Ton which offers a good view of the river and surrounding area.

Trekking and Rafting Trips

All of the guesthouses in Tha Ton can organise combined rafting and trekking trips for all budgets and time spans (between one and seven days). The cost is fairly reasonable. One day trips start at 400B to 500B per person, and three day trips cost around 1,000B to 1,200B per person. The kiosk in front of Chan Kasem Restaurant has a good display of photos taken on the trips which they run.

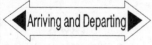

Bus

From Chiang Mai, catch an ordinary bus to Fang for 43B taking 3 hours, then a songtheaw to Tha Ton for 10B, taking another hour. Otherwise get a direct bus from **Chiang Mai** for 53B. From **Chiang Rai** there is a direct service via Mae Chan costing 75B (A/C). A bus from **Mae Sai** to Tha Ton costs 33B.

AROUND THA TON

The Lisu village of Louta is 14 km from Tha Ton towards Chiang Rai, and is home to the amazingly friendly **Asa's Guesthouse**. Rooms that are basic but clean and functional cost 150B including two meals and some flute playing by Asa's father - well worth it. Anyone wanting an insight into Lisu life would find this a wonderful experience, as Asa speaks very good English and is a great source of information. The trekking from here gets rave reviews from travellers. To get there, catch a yellow songtheaw from Tha Ton and tell the driver you are going to the Lisu village, the fare is 10B. It is a 1½ km walk or 20B motorcycle taxi ride to get there from the point where you are dropped off. If you walk it is easy to find as it is not very steep and is well signposted. Accommodation at Asa's can also be booked in advance by **email**, the email address is: asagh@infothai.com

FANG   ฝาง

Fang was founded by King Mangrai in the 13th Century as a trading centre. The original settlement is believed to predate this establishment by a further few hundred years. Today, Fang is little more than a place on a map that people pass en-route to Tha Ton, though it can be used as a trekking base or as a base from which to visit a couple of nearby sites including **Doi Fang National Park** and a selection of hilltribe villages.

Vital Information

Tourist Information The Fang Hotel has a limited range of information on the surrounds.
Banks Most major banks line Route 107 through the centre of town.
Police Station is on the left hand side of the main road as you walk towards Chiang Mai.
Codes Fang's telephone code is (053) and the postal code is 50110.

Cheap Sleeps

Fang Hotel is on the main road en-route to Tha Ton. Friendly staff will offer you clean rooms for 80B to 120B.
Wiang Kaew Hotel offers clean rooms with bathroom for 100B. To get there, turn right from Fang Hotel (facing the road) and take the first right. Follow the soi through and take the right bend, the hotel is about 50 m up the road past an intersection on your right.

Eat and Meet

As always, the cheapest and cleanest food can be found at the **market** in the centre of town. For a sit down meal, try the **Fang Restaurant** which is attached to the **Fang Hotel**.

Things to do and Sights to See

Hot Springs   บ่อน้ำร้อนฝาง

Located around 11 km west of Fang by the entrance to **Mae Doi Fang National Park** (see below) are a system of hot springs which are well worth visiting if you are in the vicinity. Wooden huts have been constructed over two of the hottest springs to create a couple of natural saunas. You may not come out–smelling too sweet and your silverware may be black for a few days, but they are free and good fun, so take a towel with you. There is one for men and one for women. The area is also a very popular place for picnics, with plenty of

Legend

1. Wiang Kaew Hotel
2. Fang Hotel
3. Bkk Bank of Commerce
4. Police station
5. Wat
6. Market
7. Thai Farmers Bank
8. Bangkok Bank
9. Market
10. Chok Thani Hotel

To Tha Ton

To Hot Springs

To Chiang Mai

Fang

0   200 m

food and drink stalls and regular songtheaws (during the weekend at least) from Fang. Ask for *baw naam rawn*.

Mae Doi Fang National Park
This park contains some fairly high mountains of over 2,000 m, great jungle hikes, waterfalls and several hilltribe villages. There are plenty of rarely visited hilltribe villages to the north and the west of Fang which are easily accessible. They can be reached by hiring a motorbike, by enquiring in the hotels about various songtheaws, hitching there or paying for a motorbike taxi. A couple of the taxi drivers in Fang speak very good English and can often be found hanging around at the Wiang Kaew Hotel. They propose tours to the National Park, the hot springs and a couple of villages (including either the Black Lahu, Chinese Muslim, Akha or Palang) for around 250B per day (if you cannot find them, and they do not find you, ask the hotel manager). These tours get very good reviews.

The **Palang** are very recent arrivals in Thailand from Burma and there are at least three villages in the Fang area. The whole community is very grateful to be there after escaping persecution in Burma and are therefore a lot more open and friendly than many other local tribes. The Palang are easily recognisable by their very brightly coloured clothes, plentiful silver jewellery and spectacular belts. Since their arrival, the Palang have been encouraged by the Thai government to grow a wide range of fruit crops as well as the traditional rice, corn, beans (and poppies). The Palang villages have small wats where Thai government loudspeakers try to entice them to become Buddhists, but the Palang do not understand much Thai and so the monks there get pretty bored. Both their culture and language are unique, though perhaps distantly related to the Karen ethnic group. Anyhow, they are very friendly and will willingly put people up for the night for a few baht.

◀ **Arriving and Departing** ▶

Bus and Songtheaw
Buses leave for **Chiang Mai** every 30 minutes, taking 3 hours, costing 43B and travelling 151 km. To **Tha Ton** a songtheaw will cost 10B taking 40 minutes and the bus is a bargain at 7B.

Tham Chiang Dao   ถ้ำเชียงดาว
This huge cave complex is a must see for your tour of North Thailand. The caves are partially lit and can be wandered through at your leisure or with a lantern equipped guide. The latter is a better choice as not all the caverns are lit.

One of the caves which is open to the public is **Tham Maa** which extends for over 6 km into the mountain. You will need a guide for this one as it is not lit. A more accessible cavern/tunnel is **Tham Phra Nawn** which is lit for all of its 300 m. Guides are mostly available on weekends. All the caves are marked and signposted and tracks often make the going fairly easy. Admission is 5B for the whole cave system.

The caves are located just over half way from Fang to Chiang Mai (72 km north of Chiang Mai, and around 90 km south of Fang), and 6 km west of the main road (Route 107). To get there take a bus from Chiang Mai or Fang/Tha Ton to the town of Chiang Dao where you can get songtheaws right to the cave complex. The bus from Chiang Mai costs 20B and takes 1 hour. Travel agents in Chiang Mai also arrange day trips to the caves. The caves close to the public at around 4.30 pm.

Taeng Dao Elephant Training Centre   ปางช้างแตงดาว
Located 56 km north of Chiang Mai, this centre puts on elephant shows for tourists in the morning. If you missed the show in Lampang Province, check out this one.

North

LAMPHUN PROVINCE

This province is believed to have been established in or around the 9th Century by a group of former Buddhist monks who had travelled north from Lopburi and founded the state of Haripunchai. Their first ruler, Chamma Thewi, arrived along with a sizeable collection of Mons and was one of the daughters of the ruler of Lopburi at the time. She established what was to become a dynastic succession for the next couple of hundred years. During this period, Lopburi was still seen as the centre of learning for the region, and young novices travelled south to Lopburi for instruction. The state of Haripunchai fell in 1281 as a result of some particularly sly 'behind the scenes' work by King Mangrai and his agents, and became incorporated into King Mangrai's growing Northern Kingdom.

Today the province has quietened down considerably, and although it may be a tempting place to relax for a few days outside of Chiang Mai, the lack of decent hotels makes it a better day trip destination. Like all places in Thailand, Lamphun has to be known for something, and in this case it is beautiful women and tasty longans. In August Lamphun is home to the tasty Longan Fair, where the best and tastiest are judged.

LAMPHUN   ลำพูน

Situated around 26 km to the southeast of Chiang Mai, Lamphun's quiet and provincial feel is enhanced by its lotus filled moats and some particularly old religious buildings. Most of the sights are easily visited on foot as they generally lie within walking distance of the centre of town. Considering its age and history, the monuments to attest to the past are fairly few and far between in Lamphun. The more contemporary Wat Phra That Hariphunchai and its associated National Museum are worth more than a cursory glance.

One of the highlights of any visit to Lamphun is the actual trip there from Chiang Mai. By taking the old way via Route 106 you will travel along a scenic route, 12 km of which is lined by beautiful 30 m tall Yang trees which are often wrapped in decorative cloth. Along this road, between Chiang Mai and Lamphun, are a selection of garden restaurants and the small town of Saraphi which is known as a centre for basketry and bamboo furniture. These can all serve as a pleasant break in the journey if arriving on your own wheels.

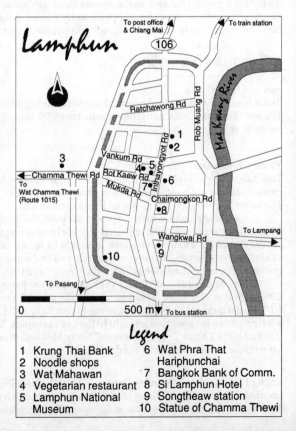

Legend

1	Krung Thai Bank	6	Wat Phra That Hariphunchai
2	Noodle shops	7	Bangkok Bank of Comm.
3	Wat Mahawan	8	Si Lamphun Hotel
4	Vegetarian restaurant	9	Songtheaw station
5	Lamphun National Museum	10	Statue of Chamma Thewi

Vital Information

Telephone Office is out of town along the road to Chiang Mai, on the right hand side when travelling towards Chiang Mai.

Banks A number of banks line the main road (Inthayongyot Road).

Codes Lamphun's telephone code is (053) and the postal code is 51000.

Cheap Sleeps

The one real option in town is the dingy **Si Lamphun Hotel** where disgusting, dirty and drab rooms make it a truly D class hotel. Singles/doubles go for 60B/100B.

Eat and Meet

Inthayongyot Road is lined with a few **rice and noodle shops**, none of which are particularly amazing. Behind the museum is a **vegetarian restaurant**.

Things to do and Sights to See

Wat Phra That Hariphunchai   วัดพระธาตุหริภุญชัย

Built during the reign of King Athittayarat in the 12th Century on the site of Chamma Thewi's Royal Palace, this wat has been repaired, renovated and renewed on numerous occasions. The pagoda is 46 m high and is topped by a solid gold, nine tiered umbrella weighing almost 6½ kg which, on a hot day, emanates a fair bit of heat. More interesting perhaps, is the intricately carved umbrella behind and to the right of the main pagoda. Also within the compound is a rare stepped pyramid chedi, a better example of which can be seen at Wat Ku Kut. Although the Buddhas that once were housed in the niches have long since wandered off, the niches still remain. On every full moon day of the sixth lunar month a festival is held within the grounds.

Hariphunchai National Museum   พิพิธภัณฑ์แห่งชาติลำพูน

Sitting almost opposite the rear entrance to the same named wat, this small museum contains a range of fine bronze pieces and Mon terracotta often characterised by fierce faces and Machiavellian grins. The terracotta display is characteristic of Hariphanchai art and is arguably the highlight of the artifacts. All of the displays were unearthed in the surrounding area. The museum is open from Wednesday to Sunday between 9.00 am and 4.00 pm, admission is 10B.

Wat Chamma Thewi   วัดจามเทวี

Also known as **Wat Ku Kut**, this wat was originally constructed by the Khmers around 755 then renovated by Mons during the Haripunchai Dynasty. The pagoda has been built with three Buddhas on each of four sides on five levels assuming the 'no fear' position (that is 60 Buddhas in total, if you were wondering). This mode of construction gives an impression of height, but the pagoda is actually quite small. The Buddhas within the niches are characterised by their long ears and generally wider faces and are Dvaravati in style. Within the pagoda are the remains of Queen Chamma Thewi. The name Ku Kut means 'pagoda without top', referring to the original pagoda top which was made of gold but 'disappeared'. Wat Chamma Thewi is located around 2 km from the museum down Chamma Thewi Road (Route 1015). To get there by foot takes 10 to 15 minutes from the museum or a samlor should cost 5B to 10B.

City Walls and Moats
Much of what once offered Lamphun protection is now in a state of ruins, but to the northwest and south the city's moats are still in good condition. To the east, the slow moving River Kuang offers a shady respite from the heat.

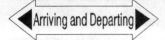
◀ Arriving and Departing ▶

Bus and Songtheaw
Lamphun bus station is about a 10 to 15 minute walk from the centre of town, south along Inthayongyot Road and on your left. A bus to the white elephant station in **Chiang Mai** costs 7B and take around ½ hour. The bus to **Lampang** is 21B and leaves every ½ an hour. Songtheaws to **Pasang** cost 5B.

AROUNG LAMPHUN

Pasang   ป่าซาง
Just over 10 km south of Lamphun, Pasang is well known for its cotton industry. Bargains can be had here, sometimes better than Chiang Mai rates, sometimes not, though large quantity buyers report Pasang to be *the* place to shop. Besides the cotton, Pasang is also supposed to be the epicentre of Lamphun's beautiful women. To get to Pasang, regular songtheaws leave from the bus station in Lamphun and cost 5B.

Wat Phra Phutthabat Taak Phaa   วัดพระพุทธบาทตากผ้า
Around 9 km further south of Pasang, this highly revered wat contains a shrine to the famous monk Luang Puu Phromma. The wat itself is nothing spectacular, though it is in a very nice setting with yet another footprint from Buddha. There is also an indentation in stone from where Buddha laid his robes to dry. From Pasang to the wat by songtheaw should cost around 5B to 10B.

Doi Khun Tan National Park   อุทยานแห่งชาติดอยขุนตาน
Established in March 1975, this park covers just over 250 sq km and is reportedly rich in flora, fauna and waterfalls in an evergreen mountain setting. Although popular with Thai visitors during the weekends, weekdays are particularly quiet and solitude is not difficult to find.

The highlight of a visit to this National Park is to hike up to the summit of Doi Khun Tan at over 1,300 m above sea level. The hike to the summit is a little over 8 km and takes around a day to reach, but the views once there are stunning. If attempting it at a relaxed pace, you would be best to stay at the bungalows about a quarter of the way to the summit, then strike out for it early the next day. Some of these bungalows are run by the Forestry Department and are available for hire at standard National Park rates. Camping is also allowed and tents can be hired from the park office.

The park is located around 52 km from Lampang and 18 km off Route 11 from the town of Mae Tha. Under the park is a 1,362 m railroad tunnel, the longest in Thailand. The park office is about a 1 km walk from the railway station at Khun Tan which sits at the northern end of the tunnel. The 1¼ hour trip from Chiang Mai to Khun Tan leaves at 06.30 and 07.00. From Bangkok, the trains leave at 15.00, 18.00, 19.40 and 22.00, arriving at Khun Tan at 03.44, 06.00, 06.52 and 10.39 respectively.

Mae Ping National Park   อุทยานแห่งชาติแม่ปิง
This National Park is better visited from Lampang rather than Lamphun, see the section on Lampang for more details.

LAMPANG PROVINCE

Lampang uses a horse carriage as its symbol, and indeed, Lampang is the only town in Thailand which still uses the horse carriage as a form of transport. Lampang was previously known as Kukutthanakorn, literally, 'city of the roosters'. This name was derived from a local legend. When the Lord Buddha visited Lampang, the God Phra Indra was worried that the locals would not wake up in time to give alms to Buddha, so Indra created a white rooster to crow at dawn to make sure everyone got up in time. This is why, in the centre of town there is a statue of a huge white rooster.

The province has a wide range of points of interest including a couple of National Parks, a baby elephant training centre and a range of interesting wats in both the Burmese and Lan-Na styles. The province covers just over 12,000 sq km and is bordered by Lamphun, Chiang Mai and Chiang Rai to the west, Phayao to the north, Phrae and Sukhothai to the east and Tak to the south.

LAMPANG ลำปาง

Lampang is the provincial capital laying claim to two 'unique' tourist 'attractions' in Thailand. In the town, horse drawn carts thrill the Thai tourists and foul the pavements for everybody else . . . they are indeed brightly painted and flower festooned if you like lumo paint work and plastic blooms. The other attraction is the world's only training school for baby elephants. Elephants and horsecarts aside, Lampang town has little to offer the independent traveller, although nearby is without doubt northern Thailand's **most** spectacular wat, Wat Phra That Lampang Luang.

The city centre has little intrinsic charm, being lined with endless shops selling plastic goodies and cheap clothes, rows of ageing concrete shop houses and the usual heavy traffic streaming past all day and most of the night. Even the river banks are concrete reinforced, although an evening stroll on the southern side is pleasant enough.

North

Vital Information

Tourist Information English speaking staff man the small desk inside the provincial head-quarters. Follow the signs on Boonyawat Road after the Si Chum Road intersection to find it.
Post Office is at the western end of town on Thipchang Road.
Banks There are many banks, refer to the map for their location.
Codes Lampang's telephone code is (054) and the postal code is 52000.

Cheap Sleeps

Lampang is supposed to have a couple of guesthouses. At our last pass, both appeared to be closed but in case they reopen here they are.
No 4 Guesthouse at 54 Thanon Phamai Road on the north side of the Wang River. Take the left turn before the Forestry Office and follow for about 150 m, it is on your right. When we visited it was closed but the close did not look too permanent. If it reopens, it would be a nice and quiet place to stay. Try asking at one of the other No 4 Guesthouses in Mae Sot or Sukhothai if you plan to stay here.
Riverside Lampang Guesthouse at 286 Tarat Kao Road, is a large house split up into decent sized rooms but was closed when we visited, however, it may reopen. It is in a nice, quiet and central position.
9 Mituna Hotel, ☎ (054) 217 438, at 285 Boonyawat Road, nearly opposite the Kim Hotel, has rooms that are clean but small. Singles are 150B, doubles 200B. All rooms come with both fan and bath. It has a lively night trade.

North

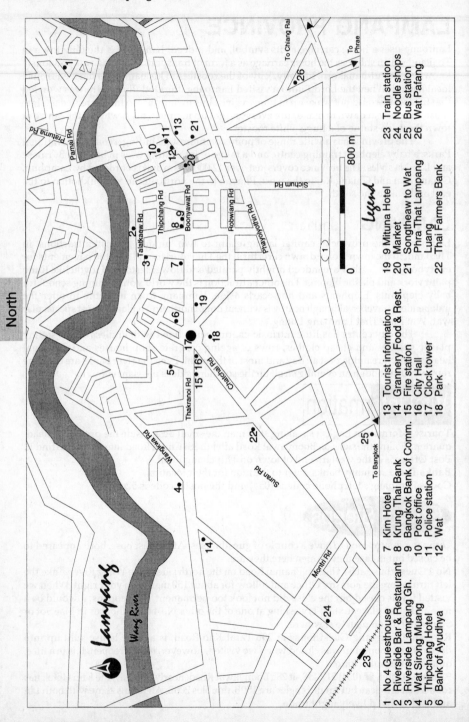

LAMPANG

Wang River

Legend

1 No 4 Guesthouse
2 Riverside Bar & Restaurant
3 Riverside Lampang Gh.
4 Wat Sirong Muang
5 Thipchang Hotel
6 Bank of Ayudhya
7 Kim Hotel
8 Krung Thai Bank
9 Bangkok Bank of Comm.
10 Post office
11 Police station
12 Wat
13 Tourist information
14 Grannery Food & Rest.
15 Fire station
16 City Hall
17 Clock tower
18 Park
19 Mituna Hotel
20 Market
21 Songtheaw to Wat
   Phra That Lampang
   Luang
22 Thai Farmers Bank
23 Train station
24 Noodle shops
25 Bus station
26 Wat Pafang

0   800 m

Romsri Hotel, ☎ (054) 217 054, at 142 Boonyawat Road, where friendly staff rent you clean rooms with fan and shower for an overpriced 220B for a double.

Siam Hotel, ☎ (054) 217 472, at Chatchai Road, a bit out of the centre of town, also has lively night trade. Rooms are 160B/220B for singles/doubles with fan and shower.

Other fairly dingy Chinese hotels are the **Lampang Hotel** (singles 170B, doubles 250B), **Sri Sanga Hotel,** ☎ (054) 217 070, (singles 100B), and the **Si Mutuna** (singles 160B, doubles 220B). There are plenty of medium and top range hotels available in town.

Nothing beats the **Riverside Bar and Restaurant** on Thipchang Road for a splurge. Very good food, a riverside setting and attentive service make the pricey dishes worthwhile, expect to pay 150B to 200B for two. There are a number of other restaurants lining the Wang River east of the Phatana Bridge that make good spots for an evening meal.

Grannery Food and Restaurant on the corner of Thakhrao and Suren Roads have great friendly staff who play good folk music and even yodel for you. They charge reasonable prices and no cover charge, open from 7.00 pm until late.

Booyawat Road and around the train station is the best area for **rice and noodle shops**. The **market** is on Boonyawat and Thipchang Road near the songtheaw stop to Wat Phra That Lampang Luang and is worth a visit, even if you aren't hungry, as this market really gets going. The spread out market does a brisk trade in plastic everything and occasional crispy disembowelled lizards (fresh from Thung Kwian Forest Market) are among the food stalls.

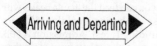

Wat Phra That Kaew Don Tao   วัดพระแก้วดอนเต้า
At the northeast corner of town, this wat was built during the reign of King Anantayot and at one stage housed the Emerald Buddha (now residing in Wat Phra Kaew, Bangkok). Today the main point of interest is the intricate carving within the wihaan. The pagoda out front shows Burmese influence, but is not the high point of any visit here. Wat Phra That Kaew Don Tao is a popular stop on most horse cart tours but to walk here is the most pleasant way of arriving as the streets are tree-lined and are fairly quiet. Within the wat grounds is a small museum containing a minor collection of exhibits.

Wat Si Rong Muang   วัดศรีรอง เมือง
This is worth a quick visit for the delicate Burmese style woodcarving, stained glass and gold gilt on the pillars of the wihaan.

Horse Cart Tours
The horse carts tend to congregate around the front of the City Hall and Thip Chang Road. A short ride will cost 20B to 30B whilst tours of the Wang River and a couple of wats will cost 80B to 100B. If business is slow you should be able to bargain them down.

◀━ Arriving and Departing ━▶

Getting Around
A songtheaw around town costs 10B. To the bus station it is 10B whilst to the train station it costs 20B.

North

Air

THAI Airways flies to **Bangkok** twice daily for 1,455B and **Phitsanulok** once daily for 485B.

Train

Lampang is on the main bus and train line on the Bangkok to Chiang Mai haul. Lampang train station is a good 20 minute walk from the centre of town, while a songtheaw into town should cost around 10B. See the timetable at the end of the chapter for detailed train information.

Bus

The bus station is even further out of the centre of town, sitting on Asia 1 Highway about a 25 to 30 minute walk from the town centre. A songtheaw into town costs around 10B. Virtually all buses from Chiang Mai to anywhere south make a stop here, the cost from **Chiang Mai** is 29B. A bus to **Lamphun** costs 21B.

AROUND LAMPANG

Wat Phra That Lampang Luang   วัดพระธาตุลำปางหลวง

This spectacular wat would have to be Northern Thailand's best. Around 20 km from downtown Lampang, this wat is best reached by motorbike or songtheaw from Lampang. The central wihaan was built in 1486 by the rulers of the time and is believed to be one of the oldest wooden buildings in Thailand. The central wihaan is open sided and has a three levelled roof which is supported by massive teak pillars. The entire complex is walled in by a high brick wall and the main entrance is via a large staircase, the arch of which is topped by beautiful and intricately carved lintels depicting intertwined dragon heads, supposedly dating to the 15th Century.

This wat is home to two very important Buddha images, **Phra Jao Lan Tang** which was cast in 1563 and is enclosed in a golden mondop towards the rear of the wihaan and **Phra Jao Tan Jai**, which sits behind it. The more recent (19th Century) wall panels depict court life. Whilst facing the wihaan, to your right is wihaan **Ton Kaew** which was built in 1476 (renovated around 25 years ago) and to the left and back a bit is wihaan **Phra Phut**, dating to the 13th Century. Behind the main wihaan is a small museum containing snaps of monks and a few Buddha bits and pieces.

Admission is 10B and it is open daily from 9.00 am to 12.00 noon and 1.00 pm to 5.00 pm. A direct songtheaw from Lampang (opposite the market) should cost around 30B each way though they ask for much more. It can be reached by taking a songtheaw first to the market at Ko Kha, then another to the wat, though it is quicker and not prohibitively more expensive to catch a direct one.

Baby Elephant Training Centre   ศูนย์อนุรักษ์ช้างไทย

Around 38 km to the west of Lampang is the Young Elephant Training Centre. Training for the babies begins at 5 years of age and they stick with the one master until they reach the ripe old age of 67!

Daily shows are held here at 9.30 am and 11.30 am where about 25 elephants are put through their paces as they line up obediently and demonstrate their strength and tolerance in log-hauling and lifting. After the interesting 30 minute show you can feed the gentle beasts with sugarcane or bananas (10B) and have a ride on one of these lumbering animals at 100B for 10 minutes or 400B for an hour's walk through the surrounding forest. Admission is 50B.

Allow 30 minutes for the longish walk to the show area, although you are more than likely to get a lift from one of the park officials. To get there catch a bus heading to Chiang Mai from Lampang Station for 20B and hop off at the centre - it is clearly signposted.

Thung Kwian Forestry Market   ตลาดป่าทุ่ง เกวียน

Only a few kilometres down the road from the baby elephant centre, this market sells a huge variety of forest products (both flora and fauna). Arrive in the early morning to secure your live water beetles, crispy larvae and eviscerated lizards. Vegetarians will appreciate the extensive fungi selection, while beef lovers can select their cow placentas with the locals. Apart from the core 'weird beast eats' section, the market is fairly touristy with curio shops on the fringe. For the unadventurous, there is grilled chicken and sticky rice as well as curry stalls. The market is not really worth a special mission but is open from 5.00 am to noon. To get there take a Chiang Mai bound bus from Lampang bus station for 20B.

Chae Son National Park   อุทยานแห่งชาติแจ้ซ้อน

Fairly recently declared in July 1988, this park has an area of just under 600 sq km and is best known for its namesake, the **Namtok Chae Son**. This waterfall has six levels and a pool suitable for swimming at each level. The park also has a collection of hot springs which are great for warming up in. Wildlife is reportedly not the highlight of a visit here, but the birdlife is plentiful. The park reaches altitudes of over 2,000 m and there are a number of trails. Camping is allowed and on weekends food is available.

Mae Ping National Park   อุทยานแห่งชาติแม่ปิง

This National Park of over 1,000 sq km was declared in July 1981, straddles Chiang Mai, Lamphun and Tak Provinces and was named after the Ping River which passes through the park. The most popular pastimes in the park are boat trips, which can be organised from both Chiang Mai and Bangkok as well as within the park itself. The park is easiest reached from Lampang.

North

The construction of the Bhumibol Dam has created **scenic lake side scenery** whilst at the same time destroying what was once riverside habitats. The park is also located near the wildlife sanctuaries of Omkoi and Ma Tun thus making it an important link in the chain for protecting Thailand's wildlife. There are two popular **boat trips** which can be organised, one heads southward from Doi Tao Reservoir to Bhumibol Dam, whilst the other strikes north from Sam Ngao in Tak Province. Both afford spectacular scenery and the opportunity of spotting the plentiful birdlife.

Besides the boat trips, the much snapped **Thung Kik-Thung Nangu meadows** are a favourite for campers and afford good views of the reservoir. There are a number of waterfalls within the park, including **Namtok Ko Luang** which is in seven steps. Both of these are best reached by your own transport as although there are roads to both, transport is rare.

The park headquarters is situated around 20 km from Li, a small town on Route 106. To reach Li from Lampang, take Route 1 south until you hit the junction

Buddha's hand, Wat Si Chum, Sukhothai

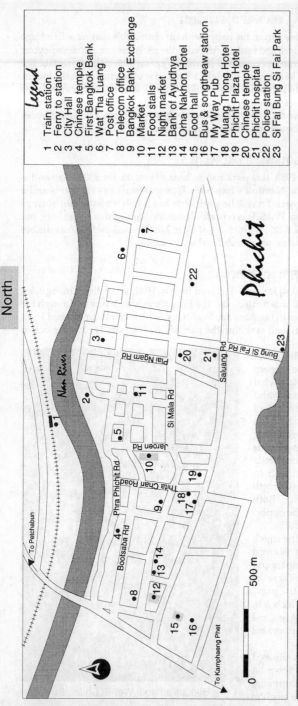

Legend

1 Train station
2 Ferry to station
3 City Hall
4 Chinese temple
5 First Bangkok Bank
6 Wat Tha Luang
7 Post office
8 Telecom office
9 Bangkok Bank Exchange
10 Market
11 Food stalls
12 Night market
13 Bank of Ayudhya
14 Orha Nakhon Hotel
15 Food hall
16 Bus & songtheaw station
17 My Way Pub
18 Muang Thong Hotel
19 Phichit Plaza Hotel
20 Chinese temple
21 Phichit hospital
22 Police station
23 Si Fai Bung Si Fai Park

with Route 106 (around 80 km), where you take a right and follow the road for another 15 km. Once at Li, take Route 1087 for the remaining 20 km to reach the park headquarters. Bungalows are situated near the park office along with a campsite, and the park officers can arrange accommodation on floating rafts should you so desire.

If you do not have your own transport, talk to one of the travel agents in Chiang Mai and you may be able to organise the transport down there on one of their trips and then make your own way back.

PHICHIT PROVINCE

Mention Phichit to any Thai and they will immediately reply crocodiles! However, wedged as it is between the Nan River on the east side and a large marsh to the west, mosquitos would nowadays be a more accurate term. The former swamplands, renowned for their crocs, have made way for paddy fields which constitute the region's major activity today.

Phichit gained provincial status during the reign of King Rama V, although it is believed that the original town was built in 1058. The province covers an area of just over 4,500 sq km and is bordered by Phitsanulok, Phetchabun, Nakhon Sawan and Kamphaeng Phet.

> **More than a scaly skin...**
> Looking for something to do on a hot day? Visit Bung Si Fai, the home of Phichit's giant crocodile. Thankfully it has an air conditioned stomach!

PHICHIT   พิจิตร

Virtually no farangs ever visit Phichit, and while this may have something to do with there being nothing to see, it is rather a shame, since the town is certainly one of the friendliest spots in Thailand. Located halfway between Bangkok and Chiang Mai, Phichit is not a bad place to while away a day or so if you happen to be passing.

Vital Information

Post Office is on Phra Phichit Road on the opposite side of the road to Wat Tha Luang.
Telecom Office is at the western end of town on Si Mala Road.
Banks Several exchange offices are on Si Mala Road near the bus station.
Police Station is at the eastern end of town on Si Mala Road.
Codes Phichit's telephone code is (056) and the postal code is 66000.

Cheap Sleeps

There is only one choice in the budget range, but no worries — it is a good one.
Muang Thong Hotel at 28 Thita Chari Road, ☎ (056) 611 128/611 671. This hotel is rather dilapidated but very clean with friendly and helpful staff. Rooms are spacious and all with bathroom, A/C and TV. Singles start at 130B, doubles at 200B.

Eat and Meet

There are plenty of **foodstalls** around the bus station and the market area, and there is a reasonable **night market** near the western end of Saluang Road. For those wanting to really cool down, pick up an ice cream or Thai snack in the air-conditioned and unusually named 'Fairy Cafe' across the road. For draught beer and live Thai Rock, try the **My Way Pub**, just around the corner from the Muang Thong Hotel on Saluang Road.

Things to do and Sights to See

Bung Si Fai   บึงสีไฟ
This large artificial lake, about 1 km west of Phichit town, has a park area, a freshwater aquarium and a 38 m long, 3 m high model crocodile! There are two smaller but live crocodiles also around and there are plenty of food and drink stands. This is a nice spot to sip a bottle of whatever you fancy and watch the sun set over the lake. A samlor from town will cost around 15B.

Old City Park (Muang Kao)   เมือง เก่า
This park contains the few remains of what was once 11th Century Phichit. The ruins are not particularly impressive, but the park is pleasant and there is an interesting wat next to the entrance on the main road. The ruins are located 3 km out of town, heading towards Kamphaeng Phet. Songtheaws go past from Phichit bus station, or samlors cost 50B if you are in a hurry.

Wat Tha Luang   วัดท่าหลวง
This wat is mainly interesting for its setting on the banks of the river and as the site of the annual Phichit boat races and pageant which are held in the first weekend of September. This wat also makes a good starting point for a stroll around town and along the quiet river bank road.

Wat Theva Prasat   วัดเทวปราสาท

Located in Amphoe Taphai Hin, about 20 km to the south of Phichit, this recently constructed wat contains a 24 m high sitting Buddha. The Buddha has a lap width of 20 m and is claimed as being the largest seated Buddha in Thailand.

Taphan Hin is on the bank of the Nan River on the Phitsanulok to Bangkok railway and can also be reached by songtheaw from Phichit bus station. The Buddha is . . . well you really cannot miss it, just look up!

Arriving and Departing

Train

There are numerous departures for Bangkok, Phitsanulok and Chiang Mai. Refer to the timetable at the end of the chapter for detailed train information.

Bus

Buses leave regularly for **Phitsanulok** costing 20B, and to most other regional destinations. Air-conditioned buses to **Bangkok** leave at 12.00, 14.30 and 22.30, take 5 hours and cost 149B whilst the ordinary buses take 6 hours and cost 83B.

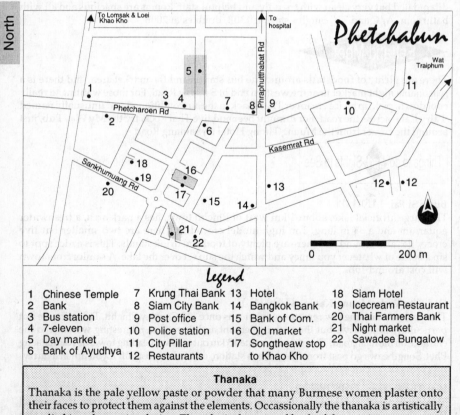

Legend

1	Chinese Temple	7	Krung Thai Bank	13	Hotel	18	Siam Hotel
2	Bank	8	Siam City Bank	14	Bangkok Bank	19	Icecream Restaurant
3	Bus station	9	Post office	15	Bank of Com.	20	Thai Farmers Bank
4	7-eleven	10	Police station	16	Old market	21	Night market
5	Day market	11	City Pillar	17	Songtheaw stop	22	Sawadee Bungalow
6	Bank of Ayudhya	12	Restaurants		to Khao Kho		

Thanaka

Thanaka is the pale yellow paste or powder that many Burmese women plaster onto their faces to protect them against the elements. Occassionally the thanaka is artistically applied in a decorative design. Thanaka is the ground bark of the acacia tree.

PHETCHABUN PROVINCE

This large province takes up a total of 12,668 sq km and is located almost in the middle of Thailand. Despite its size, the province is only now beginning to emerge as a tourist destination, but TAT is only currently catering to Thai nationals. The lack of tourism development is due to the past fighting with communist insurgents. The Thai army did not regain control of the area until the early 1980s after many fierce battles in the more remote hills of the province. Khao Kho, the amphoe north of Phetchabun town, is probably the most visited attraction in the province and shows many of the scars of the war years.

PHETCHABUN   เพชรบูรณ์

Phetchabun is not really a happening place and despite the fact that it is the provincial capital it is quite small, retaining a small town charm. There is not too much to do around town except walk the streets, but it can be used as a central point to explore the more remote parts of the province. If arriving in the town from the south you may notice the large golden tangerine placed alongside the road and this is what you will find being sold on most street corners.

Vital Information

Post Office is on the corner of Phetcharoen and Phraphuthabat Roads. The phones are open from 7.00 am to 10.00 pm.
Banks are spread around the central part of town, especially along Sankhumuang Road and on the road alongside the old marketplace.
Hospital is at the northern end of Phraphutthabat Road.
Police Station is on Phetcharoen Road, east of the centre of town.
Codes The telephone code is (056) and the postal code is 67000.

Cheap Sleeps

Siam Hotel, ☎ (056) 711 301, at 21 Sunkumuang Road, is located just a couple of hundred metres from the bus station and is run by a friendly family. The entrance is actually down a small street off Sunkumuang Road, it only has a Chinese sign out the front and the ground floor looks more like a warehouse. Rooms are comfortable and quiet for 120B with bathroom.
Sawadee Bungalow, ☎ (056) 721 850, at 54 Sunkumuang Road, is down a small street, the second east of the roundabout. Quietly located, it offers bungalows with bath starting at 170B and 220B with all the extras.
Hotel There is a cheap hotel on Phraphutthabat Road on the block north of Sankhumuang Road next to a small bus station. Although rooms only cost 100B, this place takes out the sleaze award. It is an obvious brothel with heaps of men hanging around, so you are advised to avoid it if possible.

Eat and Meet

Phetchabun has a great **night market** where you can pick up some northeastern delights. A large number of vendors and open restaurants as well as established restaurants open up at night down a street south of Sankhumuang Road, the first east of the roundabout. The **day market** gets an early start just north of Phetcharoen Road to the west of the bus station where you can get your hands on some cheap dishes. **Pickled tangerines,** which you will be able to pick up anywhere, seem to be the speciality of the town.

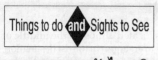

Wat Traiphum   วัดไตรภูมิ

This is quite a bland looking wat located on Phetcharat Road. It houses a Lopburi style Buddha image, **Phra Buddha Maha Thammaracha**, which is held sacred by the locals and was originally found in the Pa Sak River directly in front of the wat. Later, the image went missing, only to be found in exactly the same spot in the river. Now it is a tradition during the **Sart Festival** for the town's governor to dive into the river with the Buddha image to bring good fortune to the town and its inhabitants.

Bus and Songtheaw

Buses leave **Bangkok's** northern bus terminal regularly for Phetchabun and cost 100B. The bus station in Phetchabun is in the centre of town on Phetcharoen Road. Arriving buses may let you off 50 m before the actual station. Songtheaws to towns within the province leave from around the old marketplace and a songtheaw to **Khao Kho** costs 30B.

AROUND PHETCHABUN

KHAO KHO   เขาค้อ

Khao Kho is located 37 km north of Phetchabun. It is actually an amphoe of Phetchabun Province situated upon a mountain top plateau. Most of the sights on the plateau are related to the battles between the Thai Army and the PLAT (Peoples Liberation Army of Thailand) as this was a communist stronghold during the long running war.

A road circling the plateau takes close to an hour by songtheaw, but the rolling hills on the plateau offer great views virtually around every corner. The views down to the plains below are also quite majestic. Unfortunately, the sights in Khao Kho are spread out, and it is difficult to see them without your own transport, unless you plan to rely on songtheaws and a bit of leg power. The main sight is the old **army base** which has been turned into a small **museum** and just a little further up on the highest point of the plateau is a war monument that honours the Thai soldiers who died during the war with the communists. When open you can climb up inside the tower to a small viewing window for slightly better views of the surrounding area. Another sight is the fairly plain **royal palace** where the King and Queen stay whenever they are in this neck of the woods. There is the **Khao Khao Open Zoo** if you feel like visiting some animals. If you want to get back to nature, go and see the **waterfall** where large volumes of water fall over a 10 m drop.

The high plateau gets very cold in winter with the temperature dropping close to freezing, so any visits from mid November to mid February will require appropriate clothing. There is accommodation in Khao Khao, but currently this only caters for tour groups or people with their own transport. Bungalows are springing up, costing in the range of 500B and more. If you want to stay in Khao Kho for a night, try at the **Khao Kho Non-Hunting Area Office**, located back up the hill from the waterfall. Jump off the songtheaw when you see the waterfall sign. Here you may be able to stay in staff accommodation for around 100B a night. The other alternative is to pitch your own tent. The best location is around the waterfall as permanent food vendors are set up at the entrance, otherwise throw a fishing line into the river.

North

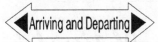

Songtheaws leave from the market in **Phetchabun** and do the one hour trip up the hill for 30B. The songtheaw continues on for another hour doing a circuit of the plateau. Going down only takes 45 minutes. From Khao Khao to the intersection with the highway it is 25B, and 10B for another songtheaw to **Lomsak**. The songtheaws can get very crowded, so you may want to jump on the roof for more space and to catch the great view.

Nam Nao National Park   อุทยานแห่งชาติน้ำหนาว

Nam Nao was one of Thailand's first National Parks, but rarely visited until recently due to conflicts with communists until the early 1980s. The park is 966 sq km and borders with the Phu Khieo Wildlife Sanctuary. The park was damaged considerably when Route 12 was constructed through its centre in 1975 and the animals now suffer as a result of the easy access.

The park mainly consists of open evergreen forests characteristically made up of sweeping stands of pines and it holds the source of three rivers, the Pa Sak, Loei and Phong. Animals which have settled in the park include elephants, deer, bears, tigers and monkeys. Bird fans will get a treat with over 200 species living within the confines of the park, many of which are uncommon in the rest of Thailand.

To get to the park headquarters take the 2 km road located at the 50 km marker on Route 12. It is 55 km from Lomsak and 103 km from Khon Kaen and buses leave daily from both of these towns for the park. There are a variety of fairly easy but long walks throughout the park as well as other sights. Many can be visited directly via the main roads that surround the park, otherwise visit the central headquarters.

A couple of walks start near the park headquarters. One goes to Phu Kum Khaw and is a round trip of 24 km over flat ground mainly through pine forests and fields of wild flowers. On a less strenuous note, a 4 km walk to a smaller pine forest or another 7 km walk may be more suitable. A popular walk is to the highest mountain, **Phu Phachit**, at 1,271 m. It is a steep 7 km walk starting off Route 12 from the 69 km marker — leave about 6 hours for the return trip. There is also a trail to another mountain viewing area, **Pha Lom Pha Kong**, which reaches 1,134 m, it also takes 6 hours. The park also has some caves and waterfalls which you can visit. It is possible to camp anywhere in the park, with the plateau of Phu Phachit being a particularly good spot, although you need to take all your supplies with you. Tents can be rented from the park headquarters and bungalows are also available for larger groups.

PHITSANULOK PROVINCE

Phitsanulok has retained an important role through much of Thailand's history. Centrally located, the provincial capital was, during the reign of King Trailoknat, the capital of Thailand. Its strategic positioning saw it used as both a training ground and recruitment area for forays against Burma. It was also the birthplace of King Naresuan and his brother Prince Ekathotsarot. Although marred by conflict with communists in the past, today it is a pleasant place to visit.

PHITSANULOK   พิษณุโลก

Phitsanulok is an ancient centre of Thai culture and politics. It is located 377 km north of Bangkok, sitting on the bank of the Nan River, where many of the locals still live a traditional lifestyle on floating houses. This sizeable city boasts a variety of interesting things to see and do. It served as the capital of Thailand for 25 years and was also the birthplace of King Naresuan and his brother Prince Ekathotsarot. Phitsanulok is also a transportation hub so it is very easy to go virtually anywhere in Thailand from here.

North

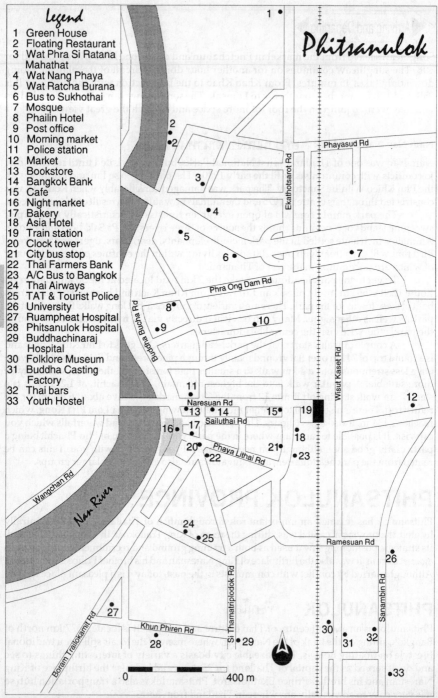

Legend

1   Green House
2   Floating Restaurant
3   Wat Phra Si Ratana Mahathat
4   Wat Nang Phaya
5   Wat Ratcha Burana
6   Bus to Sukhothai
7   Mosque
8   Phailin Hotel
9   Post office
10 Morning market
11 Police station
12 Market
13 Bookstore
14 Bangkok Bank
15 Cafe
16 Night market
17 Bakery
18 Asia Hotel
19 Train station
20 Clock tower
21 City bus stop
22 Thai Farmers Bank
23 A/C Bus to Bangkok
24 Thai Airways
25 TAT & Tourist Police
26 University
27 Ruampheat Hospital
28 Phitsanulok Hospital
29 Buddhachinaraj Hospital
30 Folklore Museum
31 Buddha Casting Factory
32 Thai bars
33 Youth Hostel

Phitsanulok

Phayasud Rd
Ekathotsarot Rd
Phra Ong Dam Rd
Buddha Bucha Rd
Wisut Kaset Rd
Naresuan Rd
Sailuthai Rd
Phaya Lithai Rd
Wangchan Rd
Nan River
Ramesuan Rd
Sanambin Rd
Khun Phiren Rd
Si Thamatriplodok Rd
Boram Trailokamit Rd

0   400 m

Vital Information

Tourist Office is at 209/7-8 Boram Trailokamit Road, ☎ (055) 252 742. The staff are particularly helpful, speak good English and have some very useful maps if you are planning to visit Sukhothai or Phu Hin Rong Kla National Park.
Post Office is on the bank of the Nan River a few minutes walk north of Naresuan Road.
Banks are concentrated along Naresuan Road.
Hospital Baddhachinnaraj Hospital is on Si Thamatriplodok Road.
Tourist Police are on the same road as the tourist office.
Codes Phitsanulok's telephone code is (055) and the postal code is 65000.

Cheap Sleeps

Green House formally Number 4 Guesthouse (which is what most of the tuk tuk drivers know it as) set to the north of the centre of town has nice rooms for 80B to 100B in an old wooden house. Friendly management are helpful and a good source of information.
Youth Hostel on Sanambin Road is nice enough but could be better. Lovely garden and dining areas are the highlights here as the rooms are small and full of savage mosquitoes. Rooms are 100B to 140B with old beds and share bathroom (dorm 50B), 50B more without membership.
Asia Hotel on Ekathotsarot Road south of the train station has large clean rooms with bathroom for 150B. It is in a central location so it is a good idea to get a room off the street.

Eat and Meet

Phitsanulok has some good choices for food. The **Youth Hostel** does a good selection of Thai food at reasonable prices. **Carte D'ior** near the train station is a popular place with young Thais and has the usual Carte D'ior cuisine. **Phan Si** is a good place for curries and other Thai and I-san standards. Prices are very reasonable. **Night Bazaar** by the river is home to the famous 'flying vegetable' where fried morning glory is prepared and then thrown up in the air for the waiters to catch. **Floating Restaurant** is near the Nan River serving reasonable food at not too inflated prices. North of the youth hostel are three or four **Thai style bar and restaurants** as well as a few noodle shops for those who could not be bothered walking into town.

Things to do and Sights to See

Wat Phra Si Rattana Mahathat   วัดพระศรีรัตนมหาธาตุ

Also known as **Wat Yai**, this famous wat is home to **Phra Buddha Chinnarat** which is regarded as one of the most beautiful Buddha images in Thailand. The wat was built in 1357 but it was not until 1631 that King Ekathotsarot applied the gold coating to the Buddha. The brilliance of this Buddha is accentuated by the huge black and gold pillars which support the roof. These act to draw the eyes to the image when you are seated on the floor. The beautiful mother of pearl inlaid doors were added by King Bornkot in 1756. Behind the wat is a 36 m prang with a staircase leading to the niche. Also on the grounds is the **Buddha Chinnarat National Museum** which contains a small Buddha and ceramics display. This is a highly revered site and those not wearing proper clothing will be refused entry.

> If you are looking for a guide to show you around Phitsanulok, ask for Dong at the front desk of the Phailin Hotel. It depends on if he has the time or not, but he gets great reports and speaks very good English. By chance the Phailin Hotel also delivers Pizza!

Shrine of King Naresuan the Great   ศาลสมเด็จพระนเรศวรมหาราช

Located within the Phittayakom School, the statue of the King is seated, whilst pouring water and declaring that Ayutthaya is indeed independent from Burma. The shrine was built in 1961 on the site of the Chandra Palace which was King Naresuan's birthplace.

Folk Museum   พิพิธภัณฑ์พื้นบ้าน

This interesting museum is on Wisutkaset Road not far from the youth hostel. It contains a display of exhibits from everyday rural life in Thailand and is well known for its basketry, pottery and other agricultural implements and tools. The museum is open every day.

Buddha Casting Factory   โรงหล่อพระ

Across the road from the folk museum (and under the same management) is the site of the casting of a huge range of bronze Buddha images made from the 'lost wax method'. During your visit here, you should be able to view some part of the manufacturing taking place and there is also a small shop on the premises which sells a range Buddha products.

Wat Chulamani   วัดจุฬามณี

Situated 5 km to the south of Phitsanulok, this wat was probably originally in the centre of town and in its heyday must have been quite an impressive structure. All that remains of the site is the Khmer style prang and bot whilst some of the walls have some nice lintels. To reach the wat, catch city bus number 4 down Barom Trailokamut Road for 2B.

◄ **Arriving and Departing** ►

Getting Around Town

Around town tuk tuks cost 10B to 20B whilst the city bus is 2B. City bus number 8 covers all interesting sights including the train and bus station.

Air

Thai Airways plane prices are as follows: **Bangkok** 950B with at least five flights a day, **Chiang Mai** 650B once a day, **Khon Kaen** 2,000B, **Lampang** 485B, **Nan** 575B, **Mae Hong Son** 800B, **Ubon** 2,345B and **Udon** 2,250B.

Train

Refer to the timetable at the end of the chapter for further detailed information.

Bus

Refer to the timetable on the opposite page.

AROUND PHITSANULOK PROVINCE

Phu Hin Rong Kla National Park   อุทยานแห่งชาติภูหินร่องกล้า

Situated at just over 120 km from Phitsanulok, this fairly recently (1984) declared National Park has a bloody history. From the late 1960s the Communist Party of Thailand had its headquarters in this area. Aided by rugged terrain, lack of roads and proximity to Laos the movement put its roots down and embarked on a campaign which drew it into direct conflict with the Thai government. The positioning of the camp was also ideal for recruiting members, as many of the hilltribes, sick of continuing government restrictions and interference with their opium growing, were more than willing recruits.

		Phitsanulok Buses	
Destination	**Duration**	**Depart Phitsanulok**	**Fare**
Bangkok (A/C)	5 hours	16.00 via Nakhon Sawan	163B
Bangkok Ordinary	6 hours	18 departures daily via Tak Fa	96B
Bangkok Ordinary	5 hours	09.00, 10.30, 13.00 via Nakhon Sawan	90B
Chiang Mai (A/C)	6 hours	07.25, 09.15 via Tak	146B
Chiang Mai Ordinary	6 hours	12 departures daily via Tak	104B
Chiang Mai Ordinary	5 hours	8 departures daily via Den Chai	86B
Chiang Rai (A/C)	6 hours	08.20, 10.40 via Uttaradit	146B
Chiang Rai Ordinary	6 hours	06.15, 07.10, 09.20 via Uttaradit	104B
Chiang Rai (A/C)	7 hours	08.00, 09.00 via Sukhothai	160B
Chiang Rai Ordinary	7 hours	06.25, 10.30 via Sukhothai	115B
Kamphaeng Phet		Throughout the day	32B
Khon Kaen (A/C)	5 hours	14.00, 01.30 - 166B for 01.30 departure	129B
Khon Kaen Ordinary	5 hours	11 departures daily	92B
Loei (A/C)	9 hours	23.30, 01.30 via Dan Sai	104B
Loei Ordinary	9 hours	7 departures daiy via Dan Sai	58B
Lomsak	2 hours	05.00 - 17.00 every hour	40B
Mae Sot A/C minivan	5 hours	08.00, 09.30, 10.30, 12.30, 14.00, 15.00	80B
Nakhon Ratchasima (A/C)	6 hours	09.30, 13.30, 22.30, 01.00 via Tak Fa	146B
Nakhon Ratchasima Ord.	6 hours	11.00, 15.00 via Tak Fa	82B
Nakhon Ratchasima Ord.	6 hours	05.45, 07.30, 11.00 via Nakhon Sawan	110B
Nakhon Thai	2 hours	06.30 - 18.00 every hour	28B
Phichit		Throughout the day	20B
Sukhothai	1 hour	05.40 - 18.00 every 30 minutes	16B
Tak Ordinary	3 hours	06.20 - 17.00 every hour	36B

Phu Hin Rong Kla National Park

Legend
1 Lin Haen Daek
2 Pachrin Waterfall
3 Visitors Centre
4 Restaurants & camping
5 Palad Waterfall
6 Tahd Pa Waterfall
7 Lan Hin Pum
8 Carpark
9 Flag Pole Cliff
10 Air Raid shelter
11 Communist HQ
12 Political & Military School
13 Romglao Waterfall
14 Air Raid shelter
15 Water wheel

In 1972, the Thai government launched a concerted military effort against the base, including air strikes, in an attempt to defeat them, but the effort failed. Following the student uprisings in Bangkok in 1976 during which hundreds of students were killed, the numbers in the insurgent's ranks swelled considerably as disaffected students headed for the hills. By the late 1970s their numbers had increased to over 5,000 and the conflict was becoming bloodier as the PLAT (People's Liberation Army of Thailand) became more organised. With the Pathet Lao taking power in Laos only 50 km away, communist cadres were being sent north of the border for military instruction and a field hospital and military school were set up.

In the early 1980s, the Thai government forces made renewed attacks and, although regaining some territory, the rebels remained in place. It was not until 1982 when the government offered an amnesty to all students who had joined the movement, that the numbers started to slip and following another attack in 1982, the PLAT surrendered and two years later in 1984 the area was declared a National Park.

Today a visit to the park is a fascinating journey into Thailand's bloody past. More frequently visited because of its history as opposed to natural beauty, there is a fascinating museum set up by the park office. This museum contains relics found at the PLAT camp including some impressive photos and a small display of military hardware. Out the front are some of the remains of a helicopter which the PLAT shot down during one of the battles. More interesting is the insight to the primitive conditions under which the students lived, allowing any visitor to empathise with their cause. Some of the other points of interest include Flag Raising cliff where the PLAT would raise a red flag following a victory as well as an air raid shelter and the military school. There are also a number of waterfalls within walking distance of the park office and an area known as Lan Hin Daek which means Million Broken Rocks. During air raids some of the PLAT would seek refuge in this area.

There is accommodation available by the park headquarters and there is also a camp ground, though you will need to bring your own tent. Food and drinks are also available beside the park office.

◀ Arriving and Departing ▶

From Phitsanulok, catch a bus to Nakon Thai (28B) which will take 1½ to 2 hours. The buses leave every hour from 06.30 to 18.00 and you will want to catch one of the first two or three if you want to visit here on a day trip. From Nakhon Thai, songtheaws leave at 09.30, 10.30, 14.00 and 15.00 and take about an hour to reach the park entrance and office for 20B. If you miss these, you will have to get to the park yourself and traffic along the road to there is rare after about 10.30. It's probably easier and quicker to visit the park by motorbike from Phitsanulok though you will need a decently powered bike as the road is very steep in places.

Sakunothayan Botanical Gardens   สวนรุกขชาติสกุโณทยาน

The park was named by the King in 1958 during a visit and is a very pleasant place to wander around. The highlight is the **Wang Nok Aen Waterfall** which falls around 10 m. This park is situated 33 km from Phitsanulok along Route 12. To reach the botanical gardens, catch any bus heading along Route 12 (eg bus to Loei) and hop off at the 33 km mark where you will see the sign to the gardens. The entrance is about 500 m down this road to the gardens.

Over the next 10 km or so from the Botanical Gardens are a collection of **riverside and forest resorts** that are well signposted off the road. Although they are priced with Thai tourists in mind, they are a pleasant place to break up a journey if you are travelling independently.

Thung Salaeng Luang National Park   อุทยานแห่งชาติทุ่งแสลงหลวง

One of Thailand's oldest National Parks, Thung Salaeng Luang National Park (Thung means meadow) has a peaceful feel but hides a bloody past. From the 1960s to the 1980s the park was used as an infiltration route by the PLAT (Peoples Liberation Army of Thailand) and was for a time sealed off by the army as they tried to eradicate the communists. However this area has not just been a staging area for people killing each other, but also for poaching. The positioning of Route 12 towards the northern area of the park has made for easy access for both poachers and illegal loggers and the park has suffered accordingly.

The park has a wide variety of both animal and bird life, although many of the larger animals have been hunted into the deepest parks of the park. The main natural highlight is the meadows. The namesake of the park, these meadows are situated quite deep in the park and are best reached by 4WD, but there is also a very nice waterfall, **Namtok Kaeng Sopha** easily reached from Route 12 and which is situated about 1½ km down the road near the 71 km mark.

The park office is well signposted on Route 12 at around the 80 km mark and is passed by all buses plying the Phitsanulok Lomsak route. Accommodation is available in the form of bungalows and dormitories and there are a number of camp grounds, although you will need to bring your own tent.

SUKHOTHAI PROVINCE

Sukhothai means 'dawn of happiness' and was the site of the capital of Thailand for around 120 years in a period which is seen as a Thai golden age. Thai arts and culture prospered throughout the reign of eight kings. Eventually a gradual decline began in 1365 and Sukhothai became a subservient state to the rising Ayutthaya.

SUKHOTHAI   สุโขทัย

This provincial capital is split in two. New Sukhothai is a typical modern Thai style city with virtually nothing of interest except places to stay and eat, and Old Sukhothai 12 km to the west. Unlike Ayuthaya, where the ancient ruins are spread throughout the town, Sukhothai's ruins are separate in an area of their own. Old Sukhothai Historical Park is a huge area full of ruins in various stages of restoration which is well worth a visit.

North

Buddha 'touches the earth' at old Sukhothai

North

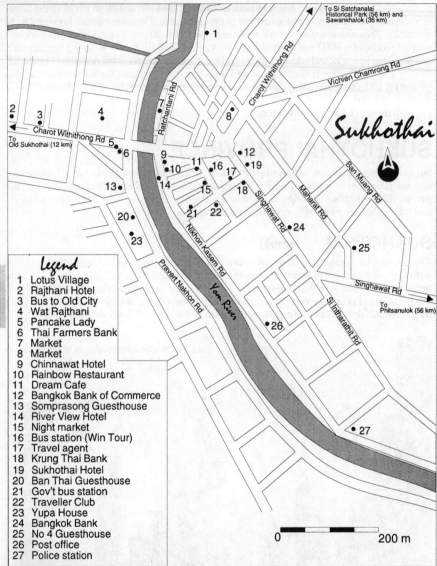

To Si Satchanalai Historical Park (56 km) and Sawankhalok (36 km)

Vichien Chamrong Rd

Charot Withithong Rd

Ratchantani Rd

Charot Withithong Rd

To Old Sukhothai (12 km)

Sukhothai

Ban Muang Rd

Mahahat Rd

Singhawat Rd

Nikhon Kasem Rd

Pravert Nakhon Rd

Yom River

Si Intharathit Rd

Singhawat Rd

To Phitsanulok (56 km)

Legend

1 Lotus Village
2 Rajthani Hotel
3 Bus to Old City
4 Wat Rajthani
5 Pancake Lady
6 Thai Farmers Bank
7 Market
8 Market
9 Chinnawat Hotel
10 Rainbow Restaurant
11 Dream Cafe
12 Bangkok Bank of Commerce
13 Somprasong Guesthouse
14 River View Hotel
15 Night market
16 Bus station (Win Tour)
17 Travel agent
18 Krung Thai Bank
19 Sukhothai Hotel
20 Ban Thai Guesthouse
21 Gov't bus station
22 Traveller Club
23 Yupa House
24 Bangkok Bank
25 No 4 Guesthouse
26 Post office
27 Police station

0   200 m

Vital Information

Tourist Information The Traveller Club is a bar, cafe, restaurant and video place which doubles as a source of everything you would ever need and want to know about Sukhothai and the surrounds. Free maps and other information are available.

Post Office is on the southeast side of the river about ten minutes walk from the main bridge.

Banks check map for details.

Police Station is on the same road as the post office, about five minutes walk further along. Codes Sukhothai's telephone code is (055) and the postal code is 64000.

Cheap Sleeps

Sukhothai has a good selection of accommodation and the competition keeps prices fairly low. **Somprasong Guesthouse** at 32 Pravert Nakhon Road has loads of rooms from 50B to 80B for singles and doubles with share bathroom and 140B with private bathroom. They hire motorbikes, serve basic food and have information on the surrounding area.

Lotus Village (at the old location of the No 4 Guesthouse) is a large wooden home with rooms for 100B/150B. The location is quiet and isolated but only a five minute walk into town.

Yupa House This family run place south of Somprasong has a dorm for 40B and singles/doubles for 60B/100B.

Nearby is **Ban Thai Guesthouse** with nice and quiet doubles for 150B with shower and fan. The restaurant here is very good and the staff friendly.

No 4 Guesthouse has moved from its old location and is now at 97/31 Soi Insee, ☎ (055) 610 165. They are a bit out of the way and it can be a challenge to find but nevertheless has a very loyal clientele. Rates range from 60B to 120B.

Sukhothai Hotel at 15/5 Singhawat Road, ☎ (055) 611 133, has 48 rooms with fan starting at 150B to 250B for singles/doubles.

Chinnawat Hotel on the river on Nikhon Kasem Road is a bit rundown and can be a bit noisy. Rooms with fan and bathroom start at 100B.

Eat and Meet

Normally we recommend the night market as first choice for cheap eating. Sukhothai now really has **two main markets,** one near the Travellers Club and the other on Charot Withithong Road, and we would definitely recommend the latter over the former. The market near the Travellers Club is very much geared to tourists with English signs and menus on most of the food carts and carrying inflated prices. The latter market is smaller but considerably cheaper. **Dream Cafe** has two branches packed with antiques and serving decent Thai food costing 30B to 50B per dish. **Rainbow Ice Cream and Restaurant** near the Chinnawat Hotel serves Thai and Western food at decent prices. **Travellers Club** is more of a cafe than a restaurant and screens videos in the evening for the video addicts. A friendly Thai lady sells *delicious* **pancakes** in the evening for next to nothing in front on the Thai Farmers Bank over the bridge.

Things to do **and** Sights to See

New Sukhothai has nothing of interest to visitors but is an ideal place from which to visit Old Sukhothai which can be reached by either songtheaw, motorcycle or bicycle.

Old Sukhothai Historic Park   อุทยานประวัติศาสตร์สุโขทัย

This fascinating park has been restored in co-operation between UNESCO and the Thai Fine Arts Department. The sites are still being restored in places but the vast majority are very well kept and suitable for long and relaxing strolls. Admission into the old city is 20B and a number of separate outlying sites also collect admission charges. Unfortunately, the map which is supplied is quite difficult to understand, however, at the entrance you can buy a brochure for 50B which contains an exhaustive look at all possible ruins and points of interest. Just remember that where you buy the tickets is already within the city walls and that should help your orientation.

The Ramkhamhaeng National Museum   พิพิธภัณฑ์แห่งชาติรามคำแหง

Built in 1960 and opened on January 25, 1964, this museum contains a collection of artifacts collected from the sites of Sukhothai and is a good place to begin your tour of the historic park. It is open daily from 9.00 am to 4.00 pm and admission is 20B. It is located to your left down the road before passing the entry office to the remainder of the park.

Wat Mahathat   วัดมหาธาตุ

Arguably the most impressive ruin within the park, this large wat is walled in and surrounded by a shallow moat. The ruined chedi is the most impressive part of the complex, which was built to contain Buddha relics brought to Sukhothai from Sri Lanka. The wat was rebuilt on many occasions during the Sukhothai Period and, as a result, carries different styles. If you walk down the main road after passing the ticket office, take the first main left and Wat Mahathat is on your right.

King Ramkhamhaeng Monument

To the north (right) of Wat Mahathat, this large bronze statue is flanked by four bas relief sculptures recording the King's life and exploits.

Wat Trapang Ngoen   วัดตระพังเงิน

Almost directly behind Wat Mahathat, this wat features a brick chedi and four Buddha images in the 'attitude of dispelling fear' stance facing four directions.

Wat Sra Si   วัดสระศรี

Located west of the King Ramkhamhaeng monument and situated on two connected islands, this wat is particularly beautiful and can be noted for its simplicity. A large and beautiful walking Buddha in Sukhothai style dominates the site along with one chedi in Sri Lankan style.

Outside the City Walls

Wat Si Chum   วัดศรีชุม

This famous and much photographed wat is definitely worth a visit, even if it does cost another 20B. The impressive mondop houses a larger Buddha 'touching the earth' which measures 11½ m from knee to knee. The walls of the mondop are 3 m thick. To get there follow

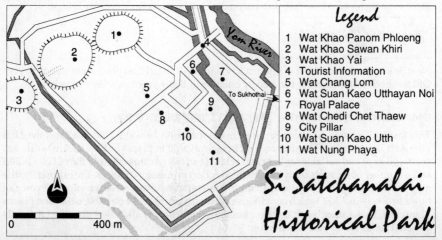

Legend

1 Wat Khao Panom Phloeng
2 Wat Khao Sawan Khiri
3 Wat Khao Yai
4 Tourist Information
5 Wat Chang Lom
6 Wat Suan Kaeo Utthayan Noi
7 Royal Palace
8 Wat Chedi Chet Thaew
9 City Pillar
10 Wat Suan Kaeo Utth
11 Wat Nung Phaya

Yom River

To Sukhothai

Si Satchanalai Historical Park

0   400 m

the road along the outside of the north city wall, and towards the end, turn-off to the right for Wat Si Chum. It is best done by motorbike or bicycle.

Wat Saphan Hin   วัดสะพานหิน
Two kilometres to the west of the main park, this wat is at an elevation of 200 m and affords good views of the historic park. There is not a lot here to see but it is worth the ride for the view.

Wat Phra Pai Luang   วัดพระพายหลวง
Originally a Khmer Hindu shrine, this wat was second in importance to Wat Mahathat. Of the three original prangs, only one remains and it is decorated with both Hindu and Buddhist designs. During excavations a Sivalinga (phallic symbol of Shiva) was discovered within the grounds of this wat.

Wat Chang Lom   วัดช้างล้อม
About 1 km to the east of the park entrance, this is the most important wat in the eastern area. The chedi is supported by a base of ruined elephants, although they are being restored.

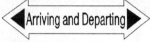

Arriving and Departing

North

Old Sukhothai
Old Sukhothai is 12 km from New Sukhothai and can be visited by motorbike, bicycle or songtheaw (5B). Once you get there a bicycle is the best way to tour the sights, otherwise it requires a lot of walking. Coming back to New Sukhothai from the historical park can be a nuisance if you do not leave early enough. The buses and songtheaws finish running just before sunset, leaving an expensive taxi or tuk tuk ride back to town. They will charge you a fortune because they know that you have no other alternative form of transport. This is a disappointment because the historical park is at its most beautiful silhouetted against a setting sky.

New Sukhothai
Air
Bangkok Airways flies Bangkok-Sukhothai-Chiang Mai and return every Monday, Wednesday, Friday and Sunday. A flight to **Bangkok** costs 1,170B and to **Chiang Mai** 540B.

Bus
The bus to **Uttaradit** is every hour, 40B taking 1½ to 2 hours; **Phitsanulok** is every half hour for 16B; **Chiang Mai** is every hour costing 95B (A/C is 127B); **Chiang Rai** is every hour for 105B; **Khon Kaen** costs 120B; **Sawakhalok** costs 10B taking 45 minutes; **Si Satchanckai** costs 20B and leaves every hour; **Phrae** costs 48B and **Kamphaeng Phet** is 24B. Private A/C buses to **Bangkok** and **Chiang Rai** leave from Win Tour or across the road from them.

AROUND SUKHOTHAI PROVINCE

Si Satchanalai-Chaliang Historical Park   อุทยานประวัติศาสตร์ศรีสัชนาลัย
Similar in style to those at Old Sukhothai, but much less visited, Si Satchanalai Historical Park can easily be visited on a day trip from Sukhothai. The ruins span from the 13th to the 15th Centuries and are set amongst scenic hills. There are 140 documented sets of ruins here including old walls, chedis, stupas, gateways, moats, kilns and much more. The sites are best toured by bicycle or motorbike (as with Sukhothai Historic Park), otherwise a lot of walking is required. Elephant tours are also possible to the prominent sights for 100B. At the ticket office a good brochure can be purchased for 5B with photos of most of the sights, although the map is a bit tricky to follow. Admission to the park is 20B.

An ideal place to start your tour is at the museum. Before you reach the ticket office a road turns off to the left. Follow this road for about one km and you will reach the museum. It contains a scale model of the park, some of the bits and pieces dug up there, some excellent photos and an interesting narrative from an early visitor to the area.

Wat Khao Panom Phloeng   วัดเขาพนมเพลิง

Sitting atop a hill in the north of the park, this wat has a chedi, some pillars and a damaged Buddha image. The view of the park from here is nice but a better viewpoint is at Wat Khao Sawan Khiri.

Wat Khao Sawan Khiri

All that remains here is a large chedi built on five tiers. The view however is excellent and well worth the climb. Situated in the northwest corner of the enclosure, the wat is best reached either from Wat Khao Panom Phloeng or by the path from the road to its west.

Wat Chang Lom   วัดช้างล้อม

Probably one of the most impressive of the ruins here. The huge chedi is supported by 39 elephants (though they are pretty rundown and look more like large fat dogs). The elephant tours generally start from in front of this wat.

Wat Chedi Chet Thaew   วัดเจดีย์เจ็ดแถว

Across the path from Wat Chang Lom, this wat has been quite well restored and some mural painting can still be seen. There are a few rows of chedis here, the largest being a copy of the one at Wat Mahathat.

Wat Suan Kaeo Utthayan Yai   วัดสวนแก้วอุทยานใหญ่

Just to the south of Wat Chedu Chet Thaew, this wat contains what was originally a sizeable hall. The wat is also known as Wat Kao Hong or 'Nine Room Temple'

Wat Nung Phaya   วัดนางพญา

This wat is well known for its reliefs on the northwestern wall of the seven room wihaan which dates back to the Ayutthaya Period. This wat is to the south of Wat Suan Kaeo Utthayan Yai.

Wat Suan Kaeo Utthayan Noi   วัดสวนแก้วอุทยานน้อย

This is unique in Si Satchanalai due to the brick building in front of the wat which looks not unlike a small church.

Wat Phra Si Rattana Mahathat   วัดพระศรีรัตนมหาธาตุ

Located a couple of kilometres south of the historic park in Chaliang, this large wat is the most impressive site in the area. The large chedi dates from the 15th Century and contains an excellent walking Buddha. Undoubtedly the most photogenic of the monuments, however electrical lighting wires have been strung around it, spoiling any chance of a decent photo. Admission is 10B but the ticket booth is often unattended. Nearby, stretching over the Yom River is a rope footbridge from which great photos of the river can be taken.

King Mangrai (1239 - 1317)

King Mangrai founded the Lan Na Kingdom of Northern Thailand which once extended into Southwest China and Northern Burma. The eventual capital was Chiang Mai and still today is regarded as the capital of the north. He developed a legal code and was highly regarded.

Celadon Kiln Site Study and Conservation Centre เตาไฟสวรรคโลก

A few kilometres to the north of the historic park, this centre contains a display of kilns, artifacts and excavated ceramics. Over 500 kilns have been excavated so far in the area of Sawankhalok town and there is evidence of the ceramics being shipped as far as China, Malaysia and Indonesia. The kilns are 7 m to 8 m wide, oval in shape with a curved roof. Admission to the centre is 20B and the centre makes for an interesting diversion from ancient piles of rocks.

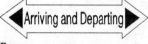

Cheap Sleeps

Si Satchanalai Historic Park can be visited on a day trip from Sukhothai, however accommodation is available at much closer Sawankhalok for those who want to spend more time there.

Muang Inn is at 21 Kasemrat Road, ☎ (055) 641 722. As you enter Sawankhalok from the south, this hotel is on your left. It has clean rooms with a fan for 160B

Sangsin Hotel at the northern end of town again on a road off to your left if you are coming from the south. It is well signposted and rooms with fan start at 180B.

 Arriving and Departing

Bus

To get to the historic park from Sukhothai catch a bus going to Si Satchanalai and ask to get off at the old town (*muang kao*), the bus costs 20B and takes around 1 to 1½ hours. The ruins are well signposted and if you take the southern most entry point (there are three) there is a bicycle hire place on your right a little down the road.

Motorcycle

Very simple. Follow Route 101 en-route to Uttaradit from Sukhothai and follow the signs. It should take you around 1½ hours

UTTARADIT PROVINCE

Known as a town of pretty ladies and widows, Uttaradit is a medium sized province of 7,838 sq km and is centrally located with Nan and Phrae to the north, Sukhothai to the west, Phitsanulok to the south and Laos to the east.

UTTARADIT อุตรดิตถ์

This provincial capital virtually never ends up on a farangs itinerary which is all the more reason to visit. Although the only remarkable point in town is the central wat, Uttaradit has some bustling markets, a pleasant river front and some decent hotels, making it a fine place to spend a day or so before heading onwards.

Vital Information

Post Office is north of the train station at the corner of Chareonchat Road and Muksada Road.
Banks Bangkok Bank has a branch on Chunrudee Road not far from the train station.
Police Station is on Chareonchat Road.
Codes Uttaradit's telephone code is (055) and the postal code is 53000.

Cheap Sleeps

Nam Chai Hotel, ☎ (055) 411 753, is good for those arriving by bus who only wanting a rest stop. This hotel has clean rooms with fan starting at 100/150B. Only five minutes from the bus station.

Pho Wanich 2 Hotel at 1-3 Si Uttra Road, **☎** (055) 411 499, is close to the train station and is the best deal in town. Clean and well kept rooms cost 100B/150B for singles/doubles.

Thanhothai Hotel, ☎ (055) 411 669, also on the river at the corner of Ploenrudee Road and the river, has clean rooms but smaller than the above two starting at 100B/150B.

Eat and Meet

For transients, there are some good **noodle shops** by the bus station, but for those staying longer than 15 minutes, the **market** at the start of Muksada Road is your best bet. There is another market towards the northern end of town along the river, whilst just south of the bridge over the bright green river is an open air **cafe bar restaurant** that is worth trying.

Things to do and Sights to See

Wat Tha Thanon   วัดท่าถนน

Opposite the train station, this large wat contains the very sacred bronze Buddha known as Luang Pan Phet which was cast during the Chiang Saen Period. It is considered to be the spiritual focal point of the town.

Monument of Phraya Phichai Dap Hak
อนุสาวรีย์พระยาพิชัยดาบหัก

Phraya Phichai was assigned to rule Uttaradit by King Taksin during his reign. This monument was dedicated on 20 February 1969.

Muang Lap Lae   เมืองลับแล

This district of Uttaradit Province is located only 6 km from town and is renowned for its natural beauty. It is also famed for its '*Teen Jog*' hand woven fabric, much of which can be purchased in the town.

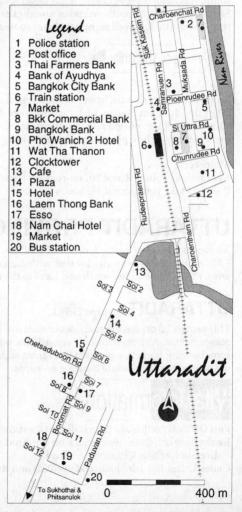

Legend

1 Police station
2 Post office
3 Thai Farmers Bank
4 Bank of Ayudhya
5 Bangkok City Bank
6 Train station
7 Market
8 Bkk Commercial Bank
9 Bangkok Bank
10 Pho Wanich 2 Hotel
11 Wat Tha Thanon
12 Clocktower
13 Cafe
14 Plaza
15 Hotel
16 Laem Thong Bank
17 Esso
18 Nam Chai Hotel
19 Market
20 Bus station

Uttaradit

To Sukhothai &
Phitsanulok

0   400 m

Ton Sak Yai (Big Teak Tree Forest Park)   วนอุทยานสักใหญ่

This forest reserve is home to the biggest teak tree in the world. It is located in Nam Pat District just over 90 km north of Uttaradit.

Getting Around
A samlor from town to the bus station is 20B. A ride within town costs 5B to 10B.

Bus
A bus to **Sukhothai** costs 40B taking 1½ hours, to **Chiang Mai** its 87B and takes 3 hours.

MAE HONG SON PROVINCE

Bordered by Chiang Mai to the east, Tak to the south and Burma to the west and north, this far flung province in Northern Thailand is becoming one of its most popular. With spectacular scenery, beautiful rivers and many hilltribe communities, Mae Hong Son has a lot to offer the independent traveller. The standard itinerary for exploring this province is to follow a loop, beginning and ending in Chiang Mai, passing through Pai, Soppong, Mae Hong Son, Mae Sariang and back to Chiang Mai. Although this loop can be done in three days or so, weeks can be spent exploring each region and town. The best way to do it is by motorbike (hired from Chiang Mai). This way you can stop when you want to take in the scenery or to explore side roads and tracks. The only problem is that some of the roads are very steep and windy, suitable only for more experienced riders. This area is also easily accessible (though less comfortable) by bus, or if you are rushed, you can fly to Mae Hong Son for only 345B from Chiang Mai.

PAI   ปาย

In peak season, Pai is packed with travellers and tourists alike. Well known for its easy going atmosphere, abundance of good, cheap guesthouses and many nearby hilltribe villages, some visitors will probably get no further on the loop than here.

WARNING: Pai does possess a pretty 'lively' drug scene, so be wary of both the police and the penniless addicts, both of whom can be quite eager to relieve you of your worldly possessions. If you are concerned about the penalties for use of illegal drug use in Thailand, you should be — they are extremely harsh.

Vital Information

Post Office is on the road leading out of town towards Chiang Mai.
Bank Krung Thai Bank has a branch in the centre of town, see the map for its position.
Hospital Pai Hospital is on Chaisongkran Road, to the left of the road to Mae Hong Son.
Police Station See map for location.
Codes Pai's telephone code is (053) and the postal code is 58130.

Cheap Sleeps

Pai has many cheap and friendly places to stay, though if you arrive in low season (highly recommended) some of the following places may be closed or cheaper.
Pai River Lodge From the name you may have guessed that it is located by the river. To get

there, follow the lane by the school. Friendly management have secluded A-frame huts costing 50B/70B for singles/doubles. Trekking is available from here. The lodge is a bit run down, but has a lot character.

PS Riverside Guesthouse This place is closer to the road than the Pai River Lodge, hence a little noisier, but still very nice. The prices are the same, but the rooms are in better condition.

Pins Huts are located down the lane between the two wats and will cost 50B to 70B. The location is nice and the staff amicable, and they specialise in strenuous trekking. They are known as 'No Mercy Trekking' - apparently they live up to their name.

Golden Huts are just by Pins Huts. The similar location offers similar ambience and price.

Charlies House is on the road in the centre of town. This very popular place has rooms for 80B with shared shower, 160B for a bungalow, or 40B for a room. It is often full, and can get a bit cramped, though the restaurant is good.

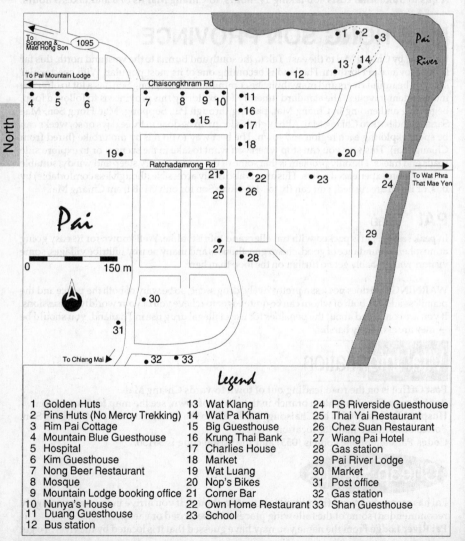

Legend

1 Golden Huts	13 Wat Klang	24 PS Riverside Guesthouse
2 Pins Huts (No Mercy Trekking)	14 Wat Pa Kham	25 Thai Yai Restaurant
3 Rim Pai Cottage	15 Big Guesthouse	26 Chez Suan Restaurant
4 Mountain Blue Guesthouse	16 Krung Thai Bank	27 Wiang Pai Hotel
5 Hospital	17 Charlies House	28 Gas station
6 Kim Guesthouse	18 Market	29 Pai River Lodge
7 Nong Beer Restaurant	19 Wat Luang	30 Market
8 Mosque	20 Nop's Bikes	31 Post office
9 Mountain Lodge booking office	21 Corner Bar	32 Gas station
10 Nunya's House	22 Own Home Restaurant	33 Shan Guesthouse
11 Duang Guesthouse	23 School	
12 Bus station		

Big Guesthouse is on a lane between Ratchadamrong and Chaisongkran Roads. The rates start at 40B/50B for singles/doubles.

Duang Guesthouse is a sizeable and central place with just about everything on offer. Rooms start at 40B/50B and 70B/80B for singles/doubles. The restaurant is not too bad either.

Pai Mountain Lodge is out of town, but more secluded than anything else on offer. Ask at their office on Chaisongkran Road before heading up. Roomy bungalows start at 100B/150B. If there are a few of you, they will arrange a ride to the lodge for you, otherwise you have got to get there yourself. This is done by hiring a motorbike, taking the road to Mae Hong Son, eventually reaching a sign on the left signalling Pai Mountain Lodge. Follow it for 8 km until the sealed road stops, then take a left which will lead to the lodge.

Peter and Vendee Hut, connected to Smiling Tiger Restaurant and Bar. This is a new place with friendly staff and gets good reports. They also offer Thai cooking lessons.

Eat and Meet

Most of the cuisine in Pai is glorified guesthouse food. Below are a couple of recommendations though many more abound.

Nong Beer offers Thai and Chinese food, certainly recommended for the taste, not the service. Not too pricey and it is very popular with the locals. It's located past the mosque on Chaisongkran Road. **Chez Suan** is a French restaurant which sometimes closes down in the low season, but when open it's a great place to pop into for cheese and wine amongst many other tasty bits 'n pieces. **Thai Yai Restaurant** is simply the place for breakfast in Pai. **Our Home Restaurant** is around the corner from Thai Yai and provides basic tourist food and more such as falafel, kebabs and lasagna. The prices are reasonable.

North

Things to do and Sights to See

Wat Phra That Mae Yen   วัดพระธาตุแม่เย็น

This nice wat is about a 30 minute walk from the centre of Pai, including the 300 plus steps to the summit. From the wat there is a great view of the surrounding area including Pai town.

Rafting, Trekking and Pachyderms

Like Chiang Mai and Mae Hong Son, in Pai it seems that virtually every shop front can put you on a raft or send you on a trek. The rafting is better in the later half of the year (June to December) and it is possible to do trips as far as Mae Hong Son. Some agencies offer combined rafting and trekking trips, generally with a day on rafts and the rest on foot.

On the whole, the trekking here is better value for money than Chiang Mai and prices range from 300B to 400B per day, including food and accommodation. Although most agencies here are also visiting 'new remote areas', it does not appear to be as heavily trekked as around Chiang Mai.

On the road to Chiang Mai, a kilometre or so from town is an 'elephant camp' where you can take a ride on a pachyderm.

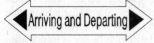

Arriving and Departing

Bus

Buses to **Chiang Mai** and **Mae Hong Son** leave regularly at 07.00, 08.30, 11.00, 12.30, 14.30, and 16.30 for 45B either way. An A/C bus to Chiang Mai costs 62B. A bus to **Soppong** is 22B.

AROUND PAI

Pai is surrounded by numerous **hilltribe villages**, **KMT villages** and **waterfalls**. Most can be visited on foot or bicycle. Ask at your guesthouse for the map which lays out the rough positions of most tribes. The biggest waterfall, **Namtok Maw Paeng**, is around 8 km from town — hire a bike to get there.

On Route 1095 between the Junction with Route 107 and Pai

Around 19 km along Route 1095 from its junction with Route 107 is **Namtok Mokfa**. It is about 2 km along a hilly and dusty/muddy (dependent on season) road, then about 300 m up a track where you can leave your bike. The waterfall itself is about 20 m high and the base provides a nice pool for a dip. It is best visited by motorbike.

At around 34 km from the junction is a turn-off to the south identified by Thai signs and a crossbar. This road goes for 11 km up a windy sealed road to a **spectacular vista** of the surrounding mountains. This is definitely worth a visit if travelling by motorbike.

A few kilometres west of this turn-off is the **Pangmappa Guesthouse**. It is ideally located if you are travelling slowly by bicycle or motorbike. Clean but concrete rooms are 250B and the food is good.

SOPPONG   สบป๋อง

This blip of a town is an ideal place to break the journey between Pai and Mae Hong Son. Soppong and the surrounding area have a lot to recommend as a destination in their own right. The scenery is stunning and numerous hilltribe villages are within easy walking distance. Soppong is actually two villages, Old Soppong is a sleepy Shan village bypassed by the main road because the buses stop at the newer Pangmappa village on the main highway. Soppong, a few years ago, was a lively little town with a couple of guesthouses and numerous hilltribe people coming to the market and selling their wares to farangs. However guesthouse and restaurant owners from Pangmappa village have allegedly bribed bus drivers to stop on the main highway instead, spelling immediate obscurity for the Old Soppong village. Consequently the more frequently visited shops and restaurants near the bus stop are invariably more expensive, less friendly and not as good as the ones in the 'Old Soppong high street', so it may be worth your while to walk the 1 km east down the highway to Old Soppong.

Vital Information

Both the **Post Office** and **Police Station** are on the main road of Pangmappa village. **Codes** Soppong's telephone code is (053) and the postal code is 58150.

Cheap Sleeps

Pangmappa Village   ปางมะผ้า

Kemarin Garden Lodge is situated down a lane at the east end of town (look out for the sign). Very nice wooden bungalows in a green garden setting go for 50B and 80B. Friendly staff can arrange trips to the surrounding caves and also supply useful trekking information. **Jungle Guesthouse** is about 1 km out of town on the road to Mae Hong Son. It has basic bungalows in a tranquil location for 50B. The friendly staff dispense heaps of information on the caves and trekking but, if you are waiting on food, make sure you have some rations to keep you going before it arrives. If the bungalows are full you can stay in the house. The shower is enticingly hot as is the fire in the restaurant area.

Lemon Hill Guesthouse is on the main road near the gas station. It was closed for renovations when we passed through, but would estimate room costs at around 50B to 100B.

Out of Pangmappa Village

Cave Lodge is around 9 km east of Pangmappa village at the end of a trail which runs off for 8 km from the small bridge at the end of Old Soppong's main road. If you like caves then this is the best place to stay. Situated near Tham Lot, they run treks to a wide variety of caves including one which is 14 km long (the longest in South East Asia) The friendly staff offer heaps of information and rooms are 80B, the dorm 40B. The hassle with this place is getting there. If you have your own wheels, just follow the signs — the last part of the road is rough and unsealed. If you don't have wheels, then expect a 1½ to 2 hour walk, otherwise hitch.

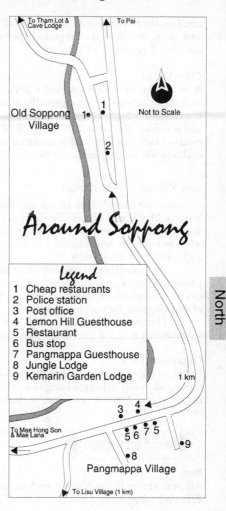

Around Soppong

Legend
1 Cheap restaurants
2 Police station
3 Post office
4 Lemon Hill Guesthouse
5 Restaurant
6 Bus stop
7 Pangmappa Guesthouse
8 Jungle Lodge
9 Kemarin Garden Lodge

Things to do and Sights to See

Tham Lot   ถ้ำลอด

This cave is well worth seeing despite the cost of a guide. Group up with other farangs and it can be very cheap. There is no point going on your own unless you are an experienced speleologist.

You will enter the cave through one side of the mountain and pass though several cathedral sized caverns as well as smaller ones with cave paintings and 2,000 year old coffins before emerging from the cave with a stream on the opposite side. It is at this exit that at around 5.00 pm to 6.00 pm there is a mass exodus of bats followed by the mass arrival of swallows. Spectacular to say the least.

Guides are available at the cave entrance and they will lead you through the caves for 100B. Make sure they are taking you to all caves if possible, although one is sometimes flooded. Be prepared to get wet, although there are bamboo rafts that will ferry you around for a 10B fee. The cave is open from 8.00 am to 5.00 pm.

Fog Lakes

There are a couple of points worth mentioning between Old Soppong and Tham Lot. Some 3 km to 4 km from Old Soppong is a large **Lahu village** (the first village you come to) and is of no real interest unless you want a meal, but this is where a track branches off to the right. Straight ahead is Tham Lot, whilst the right turn winds up a mountain from where you will get a fabulous view of the surrounding countryside. This is particularly beautiful in the early morning with the '**fog lakes**' in the valleys. The fog starts to disperse by 9.00 am and is generally all gone by 10.00 am. Continuing down the mountain on the other side, the track continues on through a **Lahu village** then a **Karen village** before forking west to reach Tham

Lot. This indirect route is about 15 km in all but get clued up beforehand in Soppong to make sure you know where you are going. If you do get lost, the villagers will point you in the right direction if you ask for Tham Lot.

Other Caves

A second, much smaller cave site that you can visit on your own and which is within easy walking distance of Pangmappa village are the coffin caves. This is a series of small caves in a cliff face which contain several wooden coffins (in varying degrees of disintegration) and which are more than 2,000 years old. From Pangmappa village walk for 4 km along the road to Mae Hong Son until you reach a banana grove on your right. Just behind this is the cliff face which contains the caves.

Lisu Village   หมู่บ้านลีซอ

A nearby and friendly Lisu village also makes for a good stroll from Pangmappa. Walking towards Mae Hong Son, take the first track on the left after Jungle Lodge and walk for 1 km until you reach the village. The village has a small store run by a Lisu lady called Alaima who can manage a little English and it is a good spot to sit, drink a soft drink, nibble a snack and watch the village go by.

    As in most frequented hilltribe villages, especially Lisu ones, you will come under pressure to buy various bracelets, bags and belts, but these people are very poor, so buy a couple of souvenirs to take home to Granny. The Lisus will be delighted and it is one way of thanking then for visiting their village.

    Numerous other Lisu and Karen villages, as well as caves, can be seen in the surrounding area. All guesthouses have maps and information on the area.

Organised Trips

For more organised treks over several days, Soppong is a good low key place to arrange these. Ask Sunny at **Jungle Lodge** for information on this one. Cave Lodge also organises caving trips of one to several days, including overnight camping in caves if that's your cup of tea.

Bus

All buses from Pai to Mae Hong Son stop in Soppong. The fare to **Mae Hong Son** is 25B, and takes 2½ to 3 hours. To **Pai**, 22B will take you on a 1½ to 2 hour ride.

SOPPONG TO MAE HONG SON

Most travellers blaze through this area but if you have got time, and preferably your own wheels, there are a number of places worth visiting.

MAE LANA   แม่ละนา

Around 10 km west of Soppong is a junction heading to the north and covered in signs in both English and Thai giving directions for all villages 'up-mountain'. Mae Lana village is around 8 km up this very spectacular road which follows the mountain crests for 25 km right to the Burmese border. After you pass through the first village which is a Black Lahu village, the road forks - take the right and this will take you to the village of Mae Lana. Mae Lana is a Shan settlement with a small shop selling essentials (ie, washing powder, cigarettes and whisky) and noodle shops.

Cheap Sleeps

The **Mae Lana Guesthouse** is just outside the village gate. Managed by Jack, his wife and young daughter, they will really make you feel at home. Jack spent quite a few years in Sydney, Australia and speaks excellent English — a very entertaining host. Spacious bungalows cost 100B and rooms in the longhouse go for 40B per person. Jack can take you on adventures to caves, nearby villages, the Burmese frontier and much more! Definitely worth a visit.
Tophill Guesthouse opposite Mae Lana Guesthouse is also nice, although it is not always open. Small huts with great views and shared bathroom cost 80B.

Things to do and Sights to See

Tham Mae Lana   ถ้ำแม่ละนา
As you walk into the village turn right at the temple and hike for 1½ hours to get to Mae Lana Cave. This cave is very spectacular with the Mae Lana River gushing from it but do not venture in too far, as it is really only for experienced speleologists.

Tham Lot   ถ้ำลอด
From Mae Lana village, a track leads east to Tham Lot passing through a couple of **Red Lahu villages**. This very spectacular route is around 12 km in length and is a bit tricky on a motorbike. If walking, allow for a day to fully take it in. Ask at either Cave Lodge, Soppong or Mae Lana Guesthouse for details. See the Soppong section for the full details on Tham Lot.

Other Caves
Alternatively hike up the mountain overlooking the village from the east side where, near the summit, are some smaller caves with a coffin and a Buddha. The view from here is brilliant and a local will guide you up here for a few baht.

Further North
Even more breathtaking is the northbound road from Mae Lana to the border. Climb back up the hill from Mae Lana and turn right. Approximately 4 km later you will reach a **small Shan village** perched on a mountain top. This friendly place with a shop may have a few pick-ups sitting around waiting for a fare back to the main road.

Further on up this road are two **Black Lahu villages,** the first of which has a **large cave**. Village children will show it to you for a sweet each (there is a small shop in the village which sells sweets - the kids will show you where this is too!). The second village, 14 km north of Mae Lana has a small church perched at the highest point in the village. The people here are not so friendly and the village is known as **Ban Huai Hea**. Despite rumours to the contrary, there is no guesthouse here. However, if you do find yourself stranded, for a contribution you can sleep comfortably in the village school (the teacher here speaks some English).

You can continue up the track to the border where there is another **Shan village** at some 30 km distance in total from the main road.

These villages are rarely visited and tracks lead off, particularly from the Black Lahu and cave village to remote and virtually never visited **Red Lahu villages**. Treks do not come this way because there are only Lahu villages, whereas south of the road there are a variety of tribes including Lisu, Lahu and Karen, which is more 'appealing' for trekking.

North

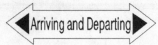

Arriving and Departing

If you do not have your own wheels, occasional motorcycle taxis head up from the junction with Route 1095 to Mae Lana. You are most likely to catch a ride in the mornings. When travelling along the main road by bus, let the driver know where you are going and he will make sure you get off at the right place. Once there, wait in the sala by the side of the road, and flag down anything with wheels passing by. You will be expected to make a contribution towards gas of 10B per person. **Warning** The road to get here tempts death in many places. In the wet season it may be close to impassable and in the dry season it is very dusty. This road is not recommended for novices just learning to ride a motorbike.

Wilderness Lodge

Just 23½ km west of Pangmappa village and 43½ km east of Mae Hong Son is a turn-off to the north beside a police box and numerous Thai signs. From here, the Wilderness Lodge is 1½ km up the road. It is very quiet, very isolated and, not surprisingly, set in the

Legend

1 Sang Tong Huts	10 Lucky Bakery	19 Jong Kham Guesthouse
2 Golden Hut	11 Mae Tee Hotel	20 Princes Guesthouse
3 Paradise Bungalows	12 Market	21 Johnnies Lodge
4 Mae Hong Son Guesthouse	13 Pen Porn House	22 Post office
5 Jeans House	14 Bangkok Bank	23 Rim Nong Guesthouse
6 Bus station	15 Thai Farmers Bank	24 Wat Chong Klang
7 Airport	16 Bank of Ayudhya	25 Wat Chong Kham
8 Alladin Restaurant	17 Holiday House	26 Joe Guesthouse
9 Sunflower Cafe	18 Friend House	

wilderness. Accommodation ranges from 50B to 100B for nice, well spaced bungalows with share bathrooms. You can do trips to various surrounding caves and hilltribe villages. A large map is on the guesthouse wall with details. From the main road it takes 20 to 30 minutes to walk to the lodge.

MAE HONG SON   แม่ฮ่องสอน

In peak season, Mae Hong Son is one of the 'travellers' centres' of Northern Thailand. If hordes of travellers are something you prefer to avoid, then Mae Hong Son is best visited in the low season. Although there is little of interest in the town itself, except the serene lake side views, it is a very good alternative to Chiang Mai for trekking and rafting. The prices are more competitive and the tribes are not too trekked out — yet. During the cool season (November to February), temperatures at night plummet and a sweater or jacket becomes a necessity.

Vital Information

Post Office is on Khunlumparaphat Road at the southern end of town.
Banks are spread throughout town, check map for their whereabouts.
Hospital is at the end of Singhanat Bamrung Road.
Tourist Police is on Singhanat Bamrung Road. They also distribute some travel information.
Codes Mae Hong Son's telephone code is (053) and the postal code is 58000.

Cheap Sleeps

This is not an exhaustive list of accommodation in Mae Hong Son. In low season some of the guesthouses may be closed, whilst in high season more will open up. All guesthouses in Mae Hong Son can and will organise trekking and rafting trips.
Jeans House at 6 Prachauthit Road, ☎ (053) 611 662, has friendly staff who can supply basic huts for 50B and rooms with bathroom for 80B. It can get a little noisy due to aircraft flying above, and thin walls allow you to hear everything that is going on next door.
Golden Hut at 253 Maksanthi Road has 15 rooms. These nicely placed bungalows with bathroom start at 150B. It is a little out of town but not too far.
Sang Tong Huts is further along the same road with similar good views and prices.
Mae Hong Son Guesthouse located at 18 Khunlumprapat Road, ☎ (053) 612 510. The no frills rooms are a bit cramped, but not too bad for 80B.
Pen Porn House at 16/1 Padungmuai Tor Road, ☎ (053) 612 577, is run by a very friendly lady, and is located off the main drag so it is fairly quiet. It is closer to Wat Phra That Doi Kong Mu than most other guesthouses. Clean rooms start at 150B.
Johnies Lakeside Lodge is run by a particularly entertaining elderly Thai guy. Rooms adjoining the lake cost 70B with a share hot shower.
Princess Guesthouse is beside Johnies. Nice and clean rooms over the lake cost 80B.
Jongkham Guesthouse at 7 Udomchaonithet Road, ☎ (053) 611 420, is next up from the Princess. This is quite a popular place to stay for no particular reason. Rooms cost 50B to 100B and they have a hot shower.
Friends Guesthouse is at the intersection past Jongkham Guesthouse. The noisy location is not compensated for by a cheap price. Rooms cost 100B.
Rimnong Guesthouse and Joe Guesthouse. These two places sit on the south side of the lake opposite each other. Rooms are a bit overpriced at 100B, but it is worth going there to ask and watch the two old guys (one from each place) eyeing each other out while you decide which to stay at. Rimnong has some larger share rooms at 50B per person.

Eat and Meet

Mae Hong Son is not known for its food and, with a couple of exceptions, you are probably best eating at your guesthouse (or someone else's).

Sunflower Cafe at 7 Singhana Thoumrung Road. Your hosts Fiona (Aussie) and La (Thai) make some delicious cakes and a variety of other light meals in a friendly atmosphere. Next door is **Lucky** which is also worth checking out.

Alladin Restaurant has food that is edible, but nothing to rave about.

Fern Restaurant is at the southern end of town on the road to Mae Sariang. They serve excellent food, although prices are a little high.

Night Market stalls have the unusual distinction of issuing English menus. Although this makes the ordering easier for those who do not know any Thai, the prices on these menus are at least double what the Thais are paying at the table beside you.

Things to do and Sights to See

North

Wat Pha That Doi Kong Mu   วัดพระธาตุดอยกองมู

Constructed by the first King of Mae Hong Son, Phraya Singhanatracha, this Burmese style temple dominates the landscape and affords great views of the town and surrounding area. The wat can be reached by motorcycle or bicycle, or via a long and steep staircase for those who want to walk.

Wat Chong Klang and Wat Chong Kham   วัดจองกลางและวัดจองคำ

These two wats sit on the southern side of Chong Klang Lake and are a stunning sight when mirrored onto the lake by the setting sun. Wat Chong Klang has a collection of Burmese dolls which were bought from Burma over 100 years ago and represent life stages of Buddha. Wat Chong Kham contains a highly revered Buddha image. They are both best seen in February when the immaculate garden is in full bloom.

Rafting

Rafting trips can be arranged to a variety of locations in Mae Hong Son including up towards Pai or west to the Burmese border to visit the longneck tribes. The best place to attempt to organise a boat trip is at Ban Huey Deua, 8 km to the southwest of town. From here a day trip will cost 400B to 500B per person. Longer and more involved trips can also be organised in Mae Hong Son. Ask around at the travel agents for details.

Visiting the 'Long Necks'

Many travel agents in Mae Hong Son advertise trips to visit these tribes, but before rushing off to see them, be aware that you may not be supporting as worthy a cause as you may think.

The 'long necks', or Padang as they are known, are refugees from Burma and have been conveniently located in Thailand by Shan businessmen. You have to pay a substantial amount in order to enter the village, even if you go alone, and this money is supposedly used to assist the other Padang who remain in Burma. Maybe some of this money does go to help them, but the vast majority of it lands in the pockets of the Shan businessmen who run the place. In visiting here, you are essentially supporting a human zoo.

Neck rings are not traditional for this tribe, contradictory to popular belief. Normally only certain girls have the dubious honour when born under certain auspicious conditions (ie, on a full moon or it is raining and albino elephants are cartwheeling over the river). The rings are medically dangerous, yet more and more of the village women are being encouraged to wear them so that the tourists who visit have something to take photos of, essentially women disfiguring themselves.

Arriving and Departing

Getting Around
Mae Hong Son is small enough that you can walk to most places. If you are feeling particularly lazy, a motorbike taxi costs around 20B, depending on destination. Many of the guesthouses hire motorbikes and bicycles which are ideal for exploring the surrounding area.

Air
THAI Airways has four daily flights to and from **Chiang Mai** for 345B which takes around 40 minutes. It is also possible to get flights to **Bangkok** (1,865B) and **Phitsanulok** (880B) from Mae Hong Son via Chiang Mai.

Bus
There are two bus routes from Chiang Mai to Mae Hong Son. One goes via Mae Sariang and the other goes via Pai. The former is the more comfortable of the two routes as the road is not as windy and larger buses are used making it better than the hillier and windier Pai route. However the route via Pai has spectacular scenery, so if you take this option, try your hardest to get a window seat.

From **Chiang Mai's** arcade bus station there are five ordinary and three A/C departures via Mae Sariang which cost 115B/206B respectively and take around 8 hours. Buses leave Chiang Mai at 08.00, 11.00, 13.30, 15.00 and 20.00 and the A/C buses leave at 06.30, 09.00 and 21.00. Via the **northern route (Pai)** there are six ordinary and one A/C departure a day which take around 9 hours. The fares are 175B for A/C to **Chiang Mai** and 95B for an ordinary bus, leaving Chiang Mai at 07.00, 08.30, 10.30, 12.30, 14.00 and 16.00. The A/C bus leaves at 08.00. To **Pai** an ordinary bus costs 45B and an A/C bus costs 85B taking 3 to 4 hours. To reach **Soppong** an ordinary bus costs 25B and to **Khun Yuam** the bus costs 35B. To **Mae Sariang** ordinary buses cost 61B and A/C buses cost 110B.

AROUND MAE HONG SON

Namtok Mae Surin National Park   อุทยานแห่งชาติน้ำตกแม่สุรินทร์

This National Park was declared in 1981 and incorporates many of the natural features of Mae Hong Son's mountainous landscape. The highlight of the park is the spectacular **Namtok Mae Surin** which is best reached from Khun Yuam to the south of Mae Hong Son. The waterfall is quite a challenge to reach as it is 25 km down a poor dirt road, which at times is probably impassable. Once there however, the waterfall is worth every ounce of effort used in getting there. Located in a scenic setting and plummeting for over 100 m down a sheer cliff, the waterfall is spectacular to say the least. See the Khun Yuam section for details on how to reach the waterfall. Other points of interest within the park include scenic settings on the Pai River, meadows and a series of other waterfalls, most of which are near Namtok Mae Surin.

Arriving and Departing

The main park office is about 8 km south of Mae Hong Son by the village of Ban Pang Mu, a little over 2 km from the turn-off. The bus from Mae Hong Son to Mae Sariang goes past the turn-off from where it is a simple hike. Accommodation is available in the form of bungalows and camping. There is also a camp ground near the southern falls of Mae Surin.

North

KHUN YUAM   ขุนยวม

For people doing the Mae Hong Son loop by bicycle or motorbike, Khun Yuam is the perfect halfway point. It is 70 km from Mae Hong Son and 99 km from Mae Sariang. Within the town itself there is not too much to see, but for those with a good motorbike, the spectacular waterfall of **Mae Surin** is within reach. This waterfall plummets over 100 m, reputedly the highest in all of Thailand. To get there, head north out of Khun Yuam for 2 km to the turn-off to the east. Follow this good sealed road for around 13 km, then take the dirt road turn-off to your left. The road is in very poor condition and in the wet season may be impassable. The waterfalls are along this road with Mae Surin, the most spectacular, the furthest down the road at 25 km away. There are camping facilities available and there are also a number of other waterfalls in the vicinity, although Mae Surin is by far the most spectacular.

Cheap Sleeps

Ban Farang is at the northern end of town at 29/5 Ratburana Road, just look for the big wooden sign. Clean and large rooms with shower cost 200B. The food is not too bad.
Mit Khunyuam Hotel is an older wooden hotel at 115 Ratburana Road, ☎ (053) 691 057. Rooms are clean and well kept at 60B to 100B.

Arriving and Departing

Bus
Buses stop in the centre of town, **Mae Sariang** costs 32B, **Mae Hong Son** costs 35B and **Chiang Mai** costs 91B (165B for A/C).

MAE SARIANG   แม่สะเรียง

This quiet town has a couple of excellent places to stay and straddles the Yuam River. Although little happens in Mae Sariang, it is a jumping off point for Mae Sam Laep on the Burmese border and a junction point between Chiang Mai, Mae Hong Son and Mae Sot. Not many people spend more than a night here, but there is plenty to keep you busy for a while. Most guesthouses organise **boat trips** on the Salawin River and, political conditions allowing, there are plenty of opportunities for **trekking** in this area where you can visit a number of easily reached **Karen villages**. It is supposedly even possible to organise combined rafting and hiking trips all the way to Umphang. We would be interested in hearing from anyone who has completed such a feat!

Vital Information

Post Office is on the road out of town to Chiang Mai near the New Mitaree Guesthouse.
Banks Thai Farmers and Krung Thai Banks both have branches in town. See the map.
Codes Mae Sariang's telephone code is (053) and the postal code is 58110.

Cheap Sleeps

Riverside Guesthouse at 85/1 Laeng Panit Road, ☎ (053) 681 188, has 10 huge rooms with share bathroom in a wooden house. Unfortunately the bathroom is two sets of stairs down from some of the rooms which cost 60B/80B for single/double rooms. The other down side is the rooms do not have nets and the bugs here can be a real problem. The food is not too bad. You will get enough *Cosmo* and *Vogue* magazines to last a lifetime and the

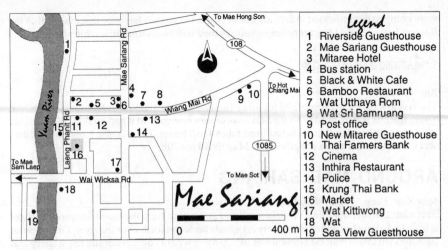

sitting area overlooking the river is pleasant.

New Mitaree Guesthouse at 34 Wieng Mai Road, ☎ (053) 681 109, just out of town en-route to Chiang Mai. Basic rooms cost 120B/200B for singles/doubles and the staff are friendly.

Sea View Guesthouse is more secluded on the other side of the river but still within easy walking distance of town. Longhouse style rooms with fan and bathroom cost 120B. The eating/bar area is nice.

Mae Sariang Guesthouse is in a central location and as such can get a bit noisy. Basic rooms cost 50B without bathroom and 80B with one.

Mitaree Hotel This is for those who hate staying in guesthouses. Large rooms with fan and bathroom cost 250B.

Eat and Meet

Inthira Restaurant has an extensive English menu accompanied by rapid fire service. The prices are reasonable and the food decent. **Black and White** is down the road towards the river from Inthira. It is a popular place for an evening beer but can get a bit sordid. The **market** is quite large with loads of assorted foods to eat at very low prices. This is the cheapest option in town. There is a small **night market** opposite the cinema.

Rafting

Rafting is the most popular pastime from Mae Sariang. Trips can be organised from any of the guesthouses in town and they generally raft down the Salawin River from Mae Sam Laep to Sop Moei where you can then relax on a small beach and take a refreshing swim. Longer trips can also be organised to as far as Tha Song Yang in Tak Province, or they can be combined with trekking for the more adventuresome. Ask at Riverside or Sea View Guesthouses for details.

Bua Tong Festival   งานวันดอกบัวตองบาน

This festival, named after the Bua Tong, a large particularly pretty flower which is also the symbol of Mae Hong Son Province, is held every November. These flowers only bloom for 15 days during which the landscape is stunning. At one stage it looked like these plants were going to be eradicated in favour of cash crops, but since it has been discovered that the flowers have certain insect repelling qualities they will be around for a while yet.

◀ **Arriving and Departing** ▶

Bus

The bus to **Chiang Mai** costs 59B for an ordinary bus, and 106B for A/C luxury. To **Khun Yuam** the bus is 32B, to **Mae Hong Son** an ordinary bus costs 61B and an A/C bus goes for 110B. A songtheaw to **Tak** costs 150B and takes 4 to 5 hours. There is also a regular minibus service to **Mae Sot** and a songtheaw to **Mae Salid** for 70B.

AROUND MAE SARIANG

Mae Sam Laep   แม่สามแลบ

This trading town sits above the Salawin River and across from the Burmese frontier. There is little to do here but watch boats ferrying goods back and forth over the river. One popular pastime is to take a boat ride downriver to Sop Moei where you can admire the scenery and cool off. Ask at the 'official' kiosk by the boats as to the cost, but figure on around 75B to 100B for a return journey depending on how busy the boatmen are.

Although there is very little to do in the village, it is quite a pretty place, set on the ridge of a hill. Many of the houses are interesting and there is also a fair sized Burmese style wat in town. There is a **guesthouse** in town with very basic rooms for 50B per person. It is about half way along the trail from the centre of town towards the boat pier on the left hand side.

◀ **Arriving and Departing** ▶

To get to Mae Sam Laep, take a morning songtheaw from Mae Sariang which, in the dry season, costs 50B. The road is sealed about half of the way (in total it is nearly 50 km) and in places the unsealed portion of the road is quite arduous, verging on treacherous. If visiting by hired motorbike, allow 1 to 1½ hours each way. In the wet season this road can be virtually impassable, although there were major road works under way at the time of writing so the travel conditions should improve in the near future.

TAK PROVINCE

This large province of over 16,000 sq km is seen by many as the future gateway to Burma. A high level of growing infrastructure and a good network of roads all seem to be working towards a final and firm opening of the border with Burma just to the west of Mae Sot on the Moei River. A bridge has been constructed here and political conditions allowing, the potential for trade is enormous. In the future, if the border was to open on a permanent basis, this would be the most likely place that farangs would be allowed to enter Burma by land.

On the other hand, Tak Province is also home to some of the very large **Karen refugee camps**. These camps are a direct result of the oppression of the present Burmese junta and a visit to one of these camps is an education in what is happening on the other side of the border.

At times it is possible to cross to Burma from Mae Sot on day trips, although the border officials sing a different tune every day so you are best to enquire at Mae Sot before heading to the border. Please be aware that the US$5 you pay to cross for the day will most likely be used to buy bullets rather than school pens.

Morbid Trivia
More people die from falling off mules every year than in air crashes.

MAE SALID

Mae Salid is a welcoming break in the journey between Mae Sariang and Mae Sot. Located around 114 km from Mae Sot and 112 km from Mae Sariang, Mae Salid is a small town with little to do. However some of the nearby villages can be explored as the surrounding guesthouses arrange various treks and river trips.

Cheap Sleeps

Mae Salid Guesthouse As you enter town from the north, this wooden guesthouse is up the lane to your left. Spacious rooms are 50B per person and there is a pleasant dining area. The staff can arrange trips to the surrounding villages and river trips at decent rates. English is spoken here and the staff appear to be a good source of information.

Chan Doi House is difficult to reach but worth the effort. Just south of Mae Salid Guesthouse is a dirt road heading east and Chan Doi House is 15 km up this road. Spacious A-framed bungalows are for rent for 250B per person including all meals. Check at the cafe on the other side of the road to be sure that the guesthouse is open before venturing the 15 km.

Mon Krating Resort offers incredible views and costs 350B per person including two meals. Rooms here can be arranged in advance at SP Tours in Mae Sot.

To get to the resorts, ask at the restaurant opposite the turn-off about arranging transport. In the past, the owner Mr Narong has met the first songtheaw from Mae Sot, but we are not sure if this is still the case. If travelling with your own wheels, the road is in pretty poor condition and in the wet season would be quite dangerous.

Due to low visitor rates both Chan Doi and Mon Krating resorts were closed at our last pass.

Eat and Meet

The **cafe** opposite the turn-off to Chan Doi House does OK food and food is also available at **Mae Salid Guesthouse**.

Arriving and Departing

Songtheaw
The songtheaw from **Mae Sot** costs 50B and leaves frequently taking around 4½ hours. The morning songtheaw from **Mae Salid** to **Mae Sariang** costs 70B.

MAE SOT   แม่สอด

This bustling trade centre has obviously benefited considerably from trade (legal and illegal) with neighbouring Burma and with the completion of the bridge over the Moei River, this should increase ten fold. The population here is a mix of Thai, Burmese, Karen and Muslims, resulting in a very multicultural town with a great selection of food. Not a town bursting at the seams with tourist attractions, it is nevertheless a pleasant enough place to stay and whenever it is finally allowed for foreigners to enter Burma by land, Mae Sot will boom overnight.

Vital Information

Post Office is on Intharakhiri Road beside the Mae Meoy Hotel.
Banks There are plenty of banks spread over Intharakhiri and Prasat Withi Road.
Police is on Intharakhiri Road.
Codes Mae Sot's telephone code is (055) and the postal code is 63110.

North

Cheap Sleeps

No 4 Guesthouse is on Intharakhiri Road to the west of the centre of town. This excellent guesthouse is a large wooden structure with equally large basic rooms. Friendly staff can supply you with informative details on Burma and can also assist in visiting the outlying refugee camps. The staff know very little about Thailand but the walls are layered in information. Rooms cost 40B for a dorm and 80B for a double room. Breakfast is available. **Mae Sot Guesthouse** on Intharakhiri Road is to the east of the centre of town. Ordinary rooms start at 100B and nicer A/C ones cost 200B. The dining room is very pleasant with cushions on the floor and very good and cheap Western and Thai food. The staff are amicable and can supply you with information. The Burmese manager is a pretty interesting guy and you can leave any spare clothes and medicines with him to pass on to the Karen refugees. Motorcycles are available for rent here for 180B per day.

SP House is out on Asia 1, just look for the 'tourist info' signs. Plain but large rooms cost 50B per person. They also have heaps of information on Mae Sot, Umphang and surrounds, and they are particularly eager to book you on their tours. If you are heading to Mae Salid from Tak, check here to find out whether Monkrating Resort is open or not. Check out their snaps of the views. They have friendly staff, but the guesthouse is a bit out of the centre of town.

Eat and Meet

Pim Hut is up Tang Kim Chiang Road. They serve decent Western and Thai food with an English menu. It is not too pricey at 25B to 30B per dish. Good Pizzas! **Fah Fah 2 Bakery** is across the road from Pim Hut and a good place for breakfast. **Myawaddy** mainly caters

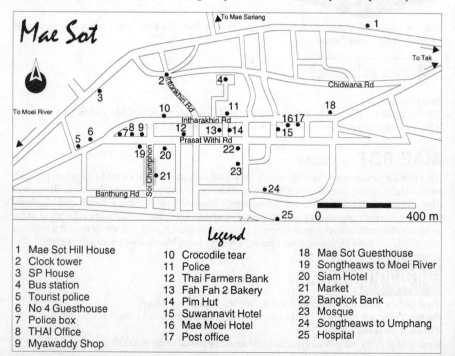

Mae Sot

To Mae Sariang
To Tak
Chidwana Rd
To Moei River
Intharakhiri Rd
Prasat Withi Rd
Banthung Rd
0   400 m

Legend

1 Mae Sot Hill House	10 Crocodile tear	18 Mae Sot Guesthouse
2 Clock tower	11 Police	19 Songtheaws to Moei River
3 SP House	12 Thai Farmers Bank	20 Siam Hotel
4 Bus station	13 Fah Fah 2 Bakery	21 Market
5 Tourist police	14 Pim Hut	22 Bangkok Bank
6 No 4 Guesthouse	15 Suwannavit Hotel	23 Mosque
7 Police box	16 Mae Moei Hotel	24 Songtheaws to Umphang
8 THAI Office	17 Post office	25 Hospital
9 Myawaddy Shop		

North

to Westerners working in the refugee camps. They serve overpriced but tasty food and icecream shakes (30B). This place also acts as an antique shop, bookswap and hands out free tourist information. Mae Sot's **night market** is hardly spectacular but there is a decent **Muslim eatery** opposite the mosque.

Things to do and Sights to See

Border Market
This market has some great specials to tempt your wallet including plastic compasses which do not work, plastic AK47 guns, girlie calendars and shoes with glowing lights on them. If you are planning to go to Burma you can exchange baht for kip (Burmese currency) here at fairly good rates. We have also heard of farangs crossing to Burma for the day here for a fee of 250B. They just hopped on a boat and waited to see what happened — a mild scolding from Thai officials was just about the extent of it on that occasion, but exercise caution if you plan to attempt to cross the border here illegally.

Refugee Camps
Due to the junta in Burma there are a number of Karen refugee camps in the vicinity of Mae Sot. They are definitely worth visiting, particularly if you are contemplating a trip to Burma. One of the most accessible camps is to the north of Mae Sot at Huaykalok (about an hour north on the road to Mae Sariang). If you decide to visit a camp, please do not go empty handed as clothes, blankets, medicine and more are all needed and much appreciated. If you cannot visit the camps in person, both No 4 Guesthouse and Mae Sot Guesthouses run collection services and you can leave the goods there. Both of these guesthouses can also supply information on how to get there and may be able to arrange a guide for you.

Arriving and Departing

Air
THAI Airways flies from Mae Sot to both **Phitsanulok** and **Chiang Mai** four times a week and the fare is 495B taking 35 minutes and 590B taking two hours respectively.

Bus and Songtheaw
The bus to **Tak** is 30B. There are also songtheaws and A/C buses to **Mae Sariang** and songtheaws to **Mae Salid** for 50B. There is an hourly A/C minibus service from the new market to **Tak, Sukhothai** and **Phitsanulok** (80B). Buses to **Chiang Mai** cost 96B for the 6 hour trip or 172B for A/C and to **Chiang Rai** it costs 147B or 264B for A/C.

TAK
Most travellers find themselves in Tak on the way to somewhere else. Nevertheless it is a nice enough place to spend a day or so, with a decent market and some nearby National Parks.

Vital Information

Tourist Office is on Charod Withi Road at the northern end of town. Friendly staff supply information on Tak, Phichit and Kamphaeng Phet.
Post Office is between Tesaban 1 and Charod Withi Roads, refer to the map for its location.
Hospital Taksin Hospital is on Phahon Yothin Road.
Police Station is on Tesaban 1 Road.
Codes Tak's telephone code is (055) and the postal code is 63000.

Cheap Sleeps

Tak only has a couple of cheaper hotels, all clustered in the centre of town. There are no signs in English, so follow the numbers and look for the foyer.

Mae Ping Hotel at 231/46 Mahat Thai Bamruang Road has numerous basic rooms which are at least clean, starting at 90B with shower.

Sanguan Thai Hotel at 619 Taksin Road is just down from the Bank of Ayudhya. Clean and fairly quiet rooms cost 180B with shower.

Eat and Meet

Opposite the Wiang Tak Hotel on Mahat Thai Bamruang Road is a good **Thai restaurant**. The **market** located a couple of blocks north is also good. At night **food stalls** are set up along the Mae Ping River.

Things to do and Sights to See

Very little! Go chat to the TAT staff for a few hours!

Shrine of King Taksin the Great   ศาลสมเด็จพระเจ้าตากสินมหาราช

This shrine houses a statue of King Taksin and early each year a festival is held here. The statue is slightly larger than life and he is sitting down with a sword on his lap. King Taksin was born in 1734 and died in 1782.

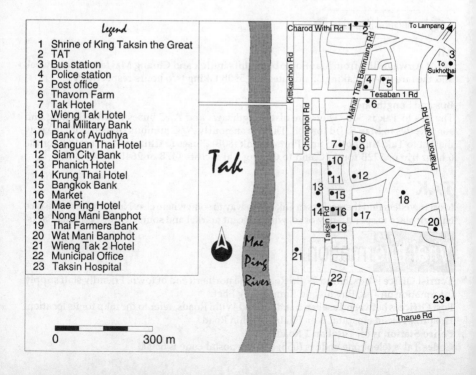

Legend

1 Shrine of King Taksin the Great
2 TAT
3 Bus station
4 Police station
5 Post office
6 Thavorn Farm
7 Tak Hotel
8 Wieng Tak Hotel
9 Thai Military Bank
10 Bank of Ayudhya
11 Sanguan Thai Hotel
12 Siam City Bank
13 Phanich Hotel
14 Krung Thai Hotel
15 Bangkok Bank
16 Market
17 Mae Ping Hotel
18 Nong Mani Banphot
19 Thai Farmers Bank
20 Wat Mani Banphot
21 Wieng Tak 2 Hotel
22 Municipal Office
23 Taksin Hospital

Tak

Mae Ping River

0   300 m

Mani Banphot Swamp

หนองน้ำมณีบรรพต

This swamp is located in the heart of Tak town and is presently undergoing redevelopment to transform it into an R&R facility for the good citizens of Tak. Nearby is **Wat Mani Banphot** home to the Saeng Thong Buddha image which was cast during the Chiang Saen Period.

Scenic Strolls

The river front area of Tak is particularly nice for late afternoon and evening strolls. As the afternoon rolls on, vendors set up a variety of food and drink stalls. You can purchase a meal and then go and eat it on the river bank and take a look at Tak's cable stayed bridge over the Ping River as the sun sets.

Bus

The bus station is a little out of town and a tuk tuk ride there costs 10B to 15B. The bus to **Mae Sot** costs 30B, ordinary buses every hour to **Phitsanulok** cost 36B (A/C 51B) taking 3 hours. A bus to **Kamphaeng Phet** costs 18B and one to **Mae Sariang** is 105B.

Sunset at Old Sukhothai

North

AROUND TAK

Taksin Maharat National Park   อุทยานแห่งชาติตากสินมหาราช

This small park's main claim to fame is a 50 m high dipterocarp tree, which is over 16 m 'around the waist', and the nine level Mae Ya Pa Waterfall. Unfortunately there is no information available in English and the staff are not particularly helpful. The park is 26 km from Tak en-route to Mae Sot, and after the turn-off the road winds for 1½ km to the park entrance.

Lan Sang National Park   อุทยานแห่งชาติลานสาง

Declared a National Park in 1979 this park is definitely the better of the two parks in this area and the friendly English speaking staff are eager to help and show you around. A couple of waterfalls are within easy walking distance of the office. By the office there is a large map detailing all the paths, tracks and attractions and copies of this are sometimes available. Food and accommodation is available with nice bungalows for 600B. The park turn-off is 17 km west from Tak on the road to Mae Sot, from the turn-off it is about 3 km to the park office, entry is 10B. This park is highly recommended both for the friendliness of the rangers and the easy accessibility of some of the sights.

WALEY   วะเลย์

This small and surprisingly sleepy border village is an important crossing point to Burma for smugglers and is also an important poppy cultivation area. The Burmese side of the frontier is at present firmly under government control as the KNU have been pushed to the south and north. So it unlikely that you will be allowed to cross the border, however you can always ask the Thai border guards (if you can find them and wake them up!). Other than the proximity to Burma, Waley holds little of interest apart from a wat and a couple of noodle shops, but it's the getting there that's the good part.

◀ Arriving and Departing ▶

The turn-off for Waley is Route 1206 off 1090 at Ban Saw-o, 36 km south of Mae Sot along the road to Umphang. From this turn-off it is another 25 km to Waley, with the final stretch of the road degenerating into a dirt track. Not far from this junction by the side of the road you will see a pretty waterfall and picnic area. The border police checkpoints en-route to Waley can be very strict, so make sure you have your passport with you before heading off. As you approach Waley, you will see a number of dirt tracks leading off, particularly to the south, with Thai signs. These all lead to various hilltribe villages, mostly Hmong and Karen, all of which are rarely visited by farangs. Some are quite close to the main road whilst others are a considerable distance off. It is really only feasible to visit these if you have your own wheels and you would be best advised to ask at your guesthouse beforehand for precise directions.

Waley is best visited as a day trip from Mae Sot and as there is no accommodation in Waley, be sure to catch the last songtheaw back to Mae Sot in the afternoon.

UMPHANG   อุ้มผาง

A small, very isolated town lying close to the Burmese border in the far south of Tak Province, Umphang has until recently been totally ignored by foreign visitors. However, as other areas further north begin to get severely over-faranged, a gentle trickle to Umphang is starting up. The nearest major town, bank and bus station is in Mae Sot, 165 km away on a road made up of hairpin bends. Also, since the road to Umphang is a dead end, there is no possibility of including Umphang in a round trip which puts some people off. However once there, Umphang is a tremendous spot and one which refreshes all who visit. A friendly, lazy little town, surrounded on all sides by tree covered hills, it is another nice hanging-out-doing-nothing place or a great and original starting point for treks into the vast, virgin forests to the south and west.

Vital Information

Post Office is out of the town centre on Mae Sot Road.
Hospital is next to the town hall.
Malaria Clinic is out of the town centre along Mae Sot Road.
Police Station is in the centre of town and is home to a very friendly policeman. The police station is a good place to watch takraw games at around 5 pm.
Note 1: There are no banks or money changing facilities in Umphang, so make sure you bring enough money with you from Mae Sot.
Note 2: The streets of Umphang at night time fill up with large packs of roaming hounds. Take a stick or fill your pockets with stones before you venture outside.

Words of Warning
If travelling to Umphang by motorcycle, remember to fill up your tank at the half way point as there is nowhere else that sells petrol (other than Umphang).

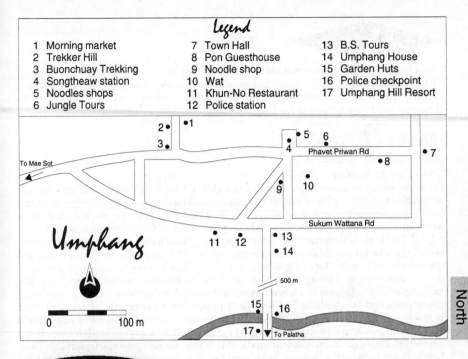

Legend

1	Morning market	7	Town Hall	13	B.S. Tours
2	Trekker Hill	8	Pon Guesthouse	14	Umphang House
3	Buonchuay Trekking	9	Noodle shop	15	Garden Huts
4	Songtheaw station	10	Wat	16	Police checkpoint
5	Noodles shops	11	Khun-No Restaurant	17	Umphang Hill Resort
6	Jungle Tours	12	Police station		

Cheap Sleeps

Umphang caters mostly for Thai tourists, so accommodation is more expensive than the farang frequented spots further north. However the situation is forever changing and new places in a more classic guesthouse style will be springing up.

Breakfast and Bed is out of the centre of town, just over 1½ km on the road heading towards Mae Sot. The management are friendly and the nice bungalows are 80B although there are only two or three of them.

Garden Huts on the river bank, by the bridge is about a five minute walk from the centre of town. Large, well kept huts in a garden setting are priced at 200B to 250B (negotiable). This is probably your best bet in town as it is run by a very friendly lady who cooks well, but does not speak a word of English. You can swim in the river in front of the huts.

Umphang Hill Resort is in a nice spot opposite the Garden Huts. As elsewhere in Umphang prices tend to fluctuate according to demand, but expect to pay a little more here than at Garden Huts.

Umphang Guesthouse and Restaurant has friendly and English speaking staff who will rent you a room for 50B per person or 150B for the room. Next door is **PM Travel** which organises treks and rafting.

Trekker Hill has clean and quiet bungalows for 150B and is located up the trail beside **Buonchuay Trekking** which organises raft and trekking trips.

Pon Guesthouse is behind the travel agent by the T junction. Grotty and run down huts cost an extortionate 50B per person. This place is only worth it if everything else is full.

Gift House is out of the centre of town about 1½ km back towards Mae Sot and about 100 m before Breakfast and Bed. Basic huts cost 60B per person.

Yai at the **Jungle Tours Office** can arrange free beds if you are going on one of his treks.

Eat and Meet

Other than the guesthouse restaurants, the **restaurant** by the 'petrol station' does decent Thai food, and the occasional stall is available for noodles, fried rice and other basics. **Garden Huts** does stand out though and can even do Western breakfasts. However, like the accommodation scene, the food choices should increase as demand does.

Things to do and Sights to See

Trekking and Rafting

There are plenty of interesting and stunning sights in Umphang District, but very few are accessible on your own. The roads are bad and few and far between, the distances concerned are often significantly long and certain areas can be a bit dodgy. A few regular songtheaws run to certain villages and some hitching can be done (see Around Umphang for details).

Trekking in Umphang can refer to anything from a one day tour by pick-up to a week long hike to Sangkhlaburi. Because most of the trekkers are Thai (they pay more) and the treks do take quite a bit of organisation (as this, unlike Chiang Mai, is a wild province) do not expect to pay Chiang Mai prices. The TAT are making a worthy effort to regulate trekking in this area (a good idea when the results of unregulated trekking in other provinces are considered), and as a result the TAT is partially responsible for setting the prices. At the time of research the official rate was 700B per day per person. As a result of this all guides should be TAT authorised, so do not make the mistake of going off with any old local cowboy. Prices are still open to negotiation, so ask around and take your time. A personal favourite is Yai at Jungle Tours, he is not the cheapest, but is great fun. Finally, several operators in Mae Sot and even as far as Mae Sariang propose treks in the Umphang District. However do not expect them to know the area around Umphang nearly as well as the local operators.

As for the treks themselves, do not expect 57 varieties of hilltribes. South of Umphang, there are only **Karen settlements**, but very traditional and unspoilt ones at that. The regions main attraction is its natural beauty. **Thu-Lor-Sue Waterfall** and the **Mae Khlong River** are the main high points, so treks generally involve a combination of hiking and rafting. **Elephant riding** can and often is included, but this will up the price of the trip (an elephant costs around 500B per day) since in these parts, elephants are used for work, not just carrying farangs around all day! The Mae Khlong River is a gem, cutting through limestone gorges, with overhanging stalactites, dense virgin forest, giant bamboo thickets, moss gardens and passing by numerous waterfalls. Some minor rapids make for good fun and there are even some hot springs and great bird watching to top it off. A **rafting trip** then back by pick-up is feasible in a day trip. However a typical three day trek would include a second day of hiking to reach the magnificent Namtok Thu-Lor-Sue, then a third day's elephant riding through Karen villages such as **Khota** or **Palatha**. For the lazy or rushed, Namtok Thu-Lor-Sue can also be reached by pick-up in a one day trip. For the above three day trip, an average price would be around 1,800B to 2,000B, but as already stated, both route and price are negotiable.

Arriving and Departing

Morning songtheaws leave **Mae Sot** for Umphang daily, every hour from 6.00 am until midday and take from between 4½ and 5½ hours. If travelling by songtheaw, try to get on the roof after Ban Saw Oh (36 km from Mae Sot) where you will be better able to take in the spectacular views. When leaving Umphang, songtheaws leave from the centre of town opposite the police station throughout the morning and the last one leaves at around 1.00 pm. These songtheaws will generally drop you off wherever you want in Mae Sot.

North

It is also possible to reach Umphang by motorbike. When we visited, we had two people on one 100cc Honda Dream and the trip almost killed the bike! If venturing there by motorbike, a trail bike would be a better option and watch your petrol. The half way mark at the Hmong village of Ban Rom Klao 4 (circa 80 km from Mae Sot) and Ban Saw Oh (36 km from Mae Sot) are the only places between Mae Sot and Umphang where you can get a refill. The ride takes four to five hours and some sections of the road are particularly dangerous, however nearly all of the road is sealed and the views are great and serve to take your mind off the road (for better or for worse). Also, if travelling by motorbike, a spare tyre, pump and puncture repair kit would be very handy!

En-route to Umphang are two waterfalls worth visiting if you are on a motorbike. **Namtok Thararak** (26 km from Mae Sot) and **Namtok Pha Charoen** (42 km from Mae Sot) are both around 700 m off the main road with Pha Charoen being the better of the two.

AROUND UMPHANG

At the time of writing, no bicycle or motorcycle rental service was available in Umphang unless you can find a local willing to oblige. However certain songtheaw services do exist to outlying villages. Enquire in your guesthouse for details, or if you can make yourself understood, ask at the songtheaw stand.

PALATHA

Palatha is a large **Karen village** 27 km due north of Umphang along a dirt road, on the bank of the Mae Khlong River, where and you can see working elephants. It should not be too difficult to find a room with one of the villagers if you cannot get back in one day from Umphang. Palatha should be feasible by motorbike and there is a certain amount of pick-up traffic for hitching.

For destinations to the west and southwest of town, you will have to double back on the Mae Sot Road to **Mae Khlong Mai** for 5 km. Numerous songtheaws head this way. From Palatha, numerous songtheaws and pick-ups head along a good and newly built dirt track to **Mae Chan** and even occasionally **Peung Kleung**.

MAE CHAN

The attraction of the otherwise nondescript town of Mae Chan is the nearby black market. This is actually situated in Karen held territory some 5 km to 6 km past Mae Chan, over the border in Burma. Political conditions allowing, there is frequent traffic from Umphang for Thais stocking up on cheap cigarettes, Chinese bric-a-brac or just on a day trip. If there are any problems in the area, Thai border police will stop you at one of the many checkpoints, otherwise anyone is welcome. You can sleep the night in the hospital and give a donation and/or medicines. Many of the wide variety of Karens, Muslim refugees and students speak English. You can visit here for just the day, which certainly makes for a fascinating trip. The cost of a bus from Doi Mae Salong is 12B.

Peung Kleung

Peung Kleung, a large mixed **Thai** and **Karen village** right on the border also makes an interesting destination. It is approximately 90 km from Umphang along a dirt track, but is worth reaching just for the fabulous scenery on the way.

At the entrance to the village is a **cave system** squatted by monks. The **Ekaracha Falls,** an hours hike further south, are also worth a look. The track to the village was only completed in 1995 so Peung Kleung has been isolated for a long time and has remained very traditional. There is no electricity in the village and many residents still use buffalo drawn carts to get around. Ask Mr Lem to let you sleep in the clinic or offer an English lesson in the local school for a nights sleep. There are even a couple of noodle shops in town.

North

Lae Thong Ku

Further south from Peung Kleung the going gets tough. The unique Lae Thong Ku village, with another **beautiful waterfall**, is only four hours walk in theory (there is no road) but is often off limits due to fighting between the KNU and the Burmese Army. NOTE: **Guides from Umphang may take you there, but under no circumstances should this trip be attempted alone.**

If you wait around in Peung Kleung long enough, occasional 4WDs make the trip down to Sangkhlaburi some 100 km (and 12 hours) to the south. This trip is done with armed Karen escorts as the track alternates between Thai and Burmese territory. You may have to wait for one hour or one week for this opportunity to arise, but it has been done.

KAMPHAENG PHET PROVINCE

Little visited by farangs, this historic city is an important place to visit for anyone interested in Thai history. The province is over 900 years old and the provincial capital is situated on the left bank of the Ping River. Originally known as Cha Kang Rao and Nakhon Chum, the province has a selection of fascinating ruins which lend support to what must have been a splendid past. The province is first mentioned in chronicles from 1004 when King Chaisiri had fled from enemies and settled in a new town called Kamphaeng Phet. However it is not clear as to on which side of the river this original development took place. This means that the founding of Kamphang Phet may even predate that of Sukhothai.

Over the following period, Kamphaeng Phet found itself in the bad lands between Chiang Mai, Ayutthaya and Sukhothai. For a period it paid treaty to Ayutthaya who used it as an outpost against forays from the Burmese side of the border. This mix of spheres of influence has resulted in the development of a unique Kamphaeng Phet style of sculpture which can be seen in the nearby historical park.

Although the provincial capital has little of interest other than the historical park, the surrounding province has a number of **National Parks** well worth visiting.

The province is medium sized at just over 8,500 sq km and the provincial capital is located 358 km from Bangkok. The province is bordered by Tak to the west, Nakhon Sawan to the south, Phichit and Phitsanulok to the east and Sukhothai to the north.

KAMPHAENG PHET   กำแพง เพชร

Split into two sections, the provincial capital, Kamphaeng Phet has a 'new' city which holds little of interest besides hotels (which double as brothels) and a quite strange restaurant, as well as the 'old' city which is jam packed with historic ruins of all descriptions. A day would allow you to see all the main sites but real history fans may want to spend longer.

Vital Information

Post Office is at the northern end of the new city at the end of Ratchadamnoen Road.
Banks Bangkok Bank has a branch at the corner of Ratchadamnoen and Chareonsuk Roads.
Hospital is at the far south of town on Ratchadamnoen Road.
Police Station is on Tesa Road 100 m north of the turn-off to the Kamphaengphet Bridge.
Codes Kamphaeng Phet's telephone code is (055) and the postal code is 62000.

Cheap Sleeps

Ratchadamnoen Hotel at the corner of Ratchadamnoen Road and Soi 4 is virtually the only cheap place to stay. Popular with Thai businessmen, in the evening the hallways are often clogged with Thai 'businesswomen'. Clean rooms with bathroom cost 120B/170B and the restaurant/cafe/karaoke bar is sufficient.

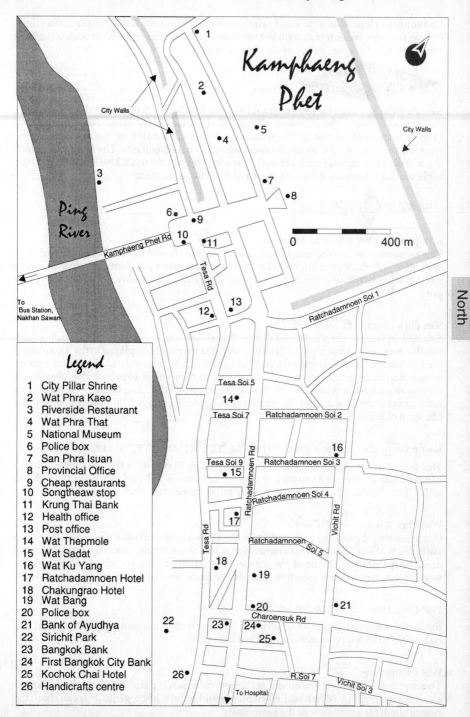

Kamphaeng Phet

City Walls

City Walls

Ping River

Kamphaeng Phet Rd

0   400 m

To
Bus Station,
Nakhan Sawan

Tesa Rd

Tesa Soi 5

Tesa Soi 7

Tesa Soi 9

Tesa Rd

Ratchadamnoen Soi 1

Ratchadamnoen Soi 2

Ratchadamnoen Soi 3

Ratchadamnoen Rd

Ratchadamnoen Soi 4

Ratchadamnoen Soi 5

Vichit Rd

Charoensuk Rd

R.Soi 7

Vichit Soi 3

To Hospital

North

Legend

1   City Pillar Shrine
2   Wat Phra Kaeo
3   Riverside Restaurant
4   Wat Phra That
5   National Museum
6   Police box
7   San Phra Isuan
8   Provincial Office
9   Cheap restaurants
10   Songtheaw stop
11   Krung Thai Bank
12   Health office
13   Post office
14   Wat Thepmole
15   Wat Sadat
16   Wat Ku Yang
17   Ratchadamnoen Hotel
18   Chakungrao Hotel
19   Wat Bang
20   Police box
21   Bank of Ayudhya
22   Sirichit Park
23   Bangkok Bank
24   First Bangkok City Bank
25   Kochok Chai Hotel
26   Handicrafts centre

Chakungrao Hotel is on Tesa Road just around the corner from the Ratchadmnoen Hotel. Rooms are more expensive at 300B but the rooms are A/C and clean. Next door is the **Mae Ping Cafe** which is quite an eye opener (see below).

Eat and Meet

Mae Ping Cafe is beside the Chakungrao Hotel. The food here is good and medium priced, but the main attraction is the floorshow. Scantily clad females screech their way through Thai 'classics' whilst a Thai Frank Sinatra will curl your hair and curdle your coconut soup. By the river (north of Mae Ping Cafe) are a couple of other **Thai restaurants**. The **market** is a block south of the Chakungrao Hotel. This is the cheapest place for the usual Thai standards and the **night market** is between the roundabout and the Provincial Office

Things to do and Sights to See

Kamphaeng Phet National Museum
This museum contains the usual collection of artifacts, Buddhas, terracotta and odds and ends, many of which were unearthed in the immediate surrounds. Not a standout museum but it costs only 10B to enter. It is open from Wednesday to Sunday from 9.00 am to 4.00 pm.

San Phra Isuan   ศาลพระอิศวร
Situated in front of the Provincial Office, this shrine has a sandstone base upon which stands a bronze cast (and copy) of the God Shiva. The original is displayed in the Kamphaeng Phet National Museum. During the reign of King Rama V, the hands and head of the statue were stolen by a German tourist who took them to Bangkok in 1886 with the intention of carting them back to Germany. It took a request from the King himself to have them returned and the Thai authorities graciously supplied a copy of the stolen goods to the Museum of Berlin.

Kamphaeng Phet Historic Park   อุทยานประวัติศาสตร์กำแพงเพชร
This large park stretches to the north of Kamphaeng Phet within the city walls and also further north of town in a separate enclosure. Entrance is 20B and this is valid for all the sights. The closest entrance is beside the city pillar shrine at the northern end of town.

Wat Phra Kaew   วัดพระแก้ว
Upon entering the historic park (20B) Wat Phra Kaew is the first site you reach. It is not a particularly stunning wat and is constructed solely of sandstone, hence the eroded state of much of the structure. Some of the surrounding Buddhas have become so eroded by the weather that they look like something out of *Close Encounters*. The chedi is Sri Lankan in style.

Wat Phra That   วัดพระธาตุ
Just to the southeast of Wat Phra Kaeo and built in classic Kamphaeng Phet style, this wat is dominated by a large sandstone and brick chedi.

Wat Chang Rop   วัดช้างรอบ
This wat is situated in the northern section of the historic park. The partially collapsed chedi is supported by 68 half bodied elephants and is quite photogenic. You can climb the ruined chedi for a nice view of the surrounds.

Wat Phra Non   วัดพระนอน

This site has been restored and is notable for its pillared entrance which gives a decent impression of the size of the original structure.

Wat Phra Si Ariyabot   วัดพระสี่อิริยาบถ

Also known as Wat Phra Yun, this site contains a large Buddha and the walls are decorated with Buddhas in each of the four stances (reclining, walking, standing and sitting). The standing Buddha is the most impressive.

Other Sites

The northern historic park contains many other sites, most of which are only foundations or piles of rocks. The best way to explore it is by motorbike or bicycle and all the sites are labelled in English and often have a brief history of each site. All the streets are signposted to the various ruins so it is fairly easy to find your way around.

Arriving and Departing

Bus

The bus to **Tak** costs 18B, to **Phitsanulok** 32B, to **Chiang Mai** 88B, to **Nakhon Sawan** 33B, and to **Sukhothai** 24B. To **Bangkok** an A/C bus costs 157B and an ordinary bus costs 87B and takes 5½ hours. The bus station is at the southwest end of town on the other side of the Ping River. To get there catch a songthaew from around the intersection of Kamphaeng Phet Road and Tesa Road which takes you over the Kamphaeng Phet Bridge to the bus station which is around 500 m past the end of the bridge.

AROUND KAMPHAENG PHET PROVINCE

The western part of the province is totally unexplored by farang tourists and has high mountains, forests, hilltribe villages and three National Parks, Khlong Lan, Khlong Wang Chao and Mae Wong. Trekking can be arranged from Umphang into some parts of this area.

Khlong Lan National Park   อุทยานแห่งชาติน้ำตกคลองลาน

This National Park was declared in 1982 and at one stage teemed with wildlife. However today the wildlife has suffered extensively from the effects of poaching and the forest has undergone considerable damage as a result of destructive agricultural practises of the hilltribes and opium cultivation. When the park was first declared, the hilltribes were allowed to remain in the park, but they have since been relocated in an effort to preserve the park.

The mountains in the western area of the National Park are the source of many of the streams which end up in the Ping River, and during and towards the end of the wet season the park is at its best offering some impressive waterfalls and pleasant walks through the forest.

Namtok Khlong Lan is easily the highlight of the park as it plunges almost 100 m down a cliff into a pool almost custom made for swimming. The waterfall is easily reached by a sealed road from the park headquarters. Other points of interest include **Namtok Khlong Nam Lai** about 25 km from the park headquarters and the **Kaeng Kao Roi rapids**. By the entrance to Namtok Khlong Lan there is also a small handicrafts centre which sells goods produced by the surrounding hilltribes.

Accommodation is available near the park office in the form of the standard National Park bungalows and camping is also allowed, although you will need to bring your own tent.

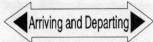

Arriving and Departing

The best way to reach the park is under your own steam. The closest provincial capital is Kamphaeng Phet. From there you can take Route 1 for just over 10 km south till you reach the turn-off for Route 1117, from where it is another 45 km to the turn-off to the park office. Occasional minibuses from the market in Kamphaeng Phet head out this way for 25B or else it is best done by hired motorbike.

Mae Wong National Park   อุทยานแห่งชาติแม่วงก์

This National Park is one of the few in Thailand without human settlers. In the past this

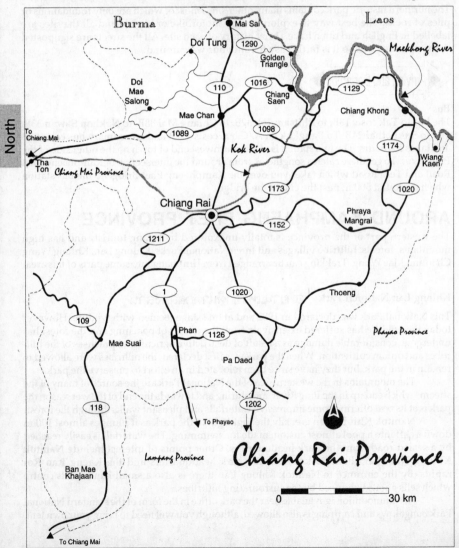

National Park incurred excessive damage at the hands of resident hilltribes whose slash and burn agriculture decimated the environment. These villages have since been relocated and the Park is beginning to show encouraging regeneration. Like Khlong Wang Chao National Park, visiting the park is not encouraged, although it is possible, and accommodation by the park headquarters is available. Visitors are not encouraged, partially to protect the environment, but also because poaching and illegal logging are still a problem and may present a security risk.

◄ **Arriving and Departing** ►

Travel south from Kamphaeng Phet to **Khlong Khlung**, from where you will need to take a right turn onto Route 1242 for around 60 km. The way to the park office is clearly signposted.

Khlong Wang Chao National Park
This park straddles Tak and Kamphaeng Phet Provinces and was established in 1990. The attractions of this park include waterfalls, caves and hot springs, however there is apparently not much in the way of amenities. The main attraction of the park is the waterfall, **Namtok Wang Chao**, which is accessible by road.

CHIANG RAI PROVINCE

This province is Thailand's northernmost and is predominantly mountainous. Bordered to the north by Burma and Laos, this province has in the past had a bit of a wild west feel to it, but the only cowboys you are likely to see up there now are the Texan variety as they get off their tourist buses.

Founded in 1262 by King Mangrai, Chiang Rai was at one stage the capital of Lan-na and also spent a period in Burmese hands before coming back to the Thai fold in 1786, becoming a province in 1910. The province boasts a huge assortment of things to do and sights to see and you could easily spend a couple of weeks exploring the province to its fullest.

In the past Chiang Rai was seen as a fine alternative to Chiang Mai as it was quieter and had less of a tourist feel to it. More popular today, Chiang Rai is still a good alternative trekking area to Chiang Mai as the hilltribes throughout the province have not been completely trekked out — yet. Opium is still cultivated in Chiang Rai and for this reason some areas can still be a little dangerous. The police here also seem to maintain a high level of exposure, so Chiang Rai is not the place to do much dabbling in the local produce.

CHIANG RAI   เชียงราย

Seen by many as a smaller and quieter version of Chiang Mai, Chiang Rai is both of these but still has enough within its urban boundaries to keep visitors busy for a day or so. Once finished here, we would suggest that those looking for quieter escapes head further north or east to places such as Mae Salong, Chiang Khong or Chiang Saen which are all interesting in their own right and even quieter than Chiang Rai.

Vital Information

Tourist Office, ☎ (053) 717 433, is at the northern end of town on Sing Hakai Road.
Post Office is located on Uttarakit Road in the centre of town.
Banks There are many banks in town, check the map for details.
Tourist Police, ☎ 1699 (emergency) or ☎ (053) 717 779, is beside the tourist office.
Hospital The **Chiang Rai Hospital,** ☎ (053) 711 300, is on the corner of Satharn Payabarn and Sanambin Road. The **Overbrook Hospital** is on Sing Hakai Road, ☎ (053) 711 366.
Codes Chiang Rai's telephone code is (053) and the postal code is 57000.

North

Cheap Sleeps

Mae Hong Son Guesthouse of Chiang Rai This is one of the best options in town with particularly friendly and reliable staff. Willhelm (Dutch) is a great source of local know-how and a great host. Rooms are basic but clean costing 60B/90B for singles/doubles with shared bathroom (hot showers). The guesthouse also hires out motorcycles and bicycles.

Chat House, ☎ (053) 711 481, at 3/2 Soi Saengkaew Trirat Road is fairly quiet and atmospheric and has friendly staff. They have rooms to suit all budgets, the dormitory is 40B, singles/doubles are 50B/80B and 100B with a private bath.

Ben Guesthouse on Soi 1, Ratchayotha Road. This is a beautiful building, however you may have to wake up the staff to get service. Doubles with fan and hot shower are 120B and singles cost 90B.

Mae Kok Villa is on Sing Hakai Road, west of the tourist office. A fresh produce market assembles in the carpark, so you do not need to go too far for a feed. The dormitory is 40B, singles 120B and doubles 150B.

Lek Guesthouse on Ratchayotha Road has friendly staff and clean simple rooms with food available (great muesli). Rooms cost 80B for a single with shower and 120B for a double.

Pintamorn Guesthouse is separated from town by a canal and the isolated location makes for quiet evenings. There is a gym and snooker table on site. Clean bland rooms with fan and hot shower costs 100B.

Chiang Rai Hotel is at 519 Suksathit Road, ☎ (053) 711 226. Basic hotel rooms cost 120B/140B for singles/doubles.

Siam Hotel at 531/6-8 Banphrapakan Road, ☎ (053) 711 077, has rooms for 140B/180B.

Boonbundan Guesthouse at 1005/13 Jet Yot Road, ☎ (053) 712 914, has a range of accommodation to suit most budgets at 80B/120B/250B with amenable staff.

Eat and Meet

For **breakfast** you cannot get much better than the morning market south of the post office. **Ban Khun** at 474/6 Sing Hakai Road has a comprehensive and good selection of reasonably priced cuisine. **Muang Thong Restaurant** at 889/1-2 Phahon Yothin Road has a decent selection of Thai and Chinese food with a good selection of frog dishes at reasonable prices.

Dee Dee Restaurant has an extensive Thai and Italian selection of food and is not too pricey. **La Cantina** at 528/20-21 Banphrapakan Road is an Italian restaurant and has huge breakfasts which are well worth the cost. **Bierstule** at 897/1 Phahon Yothin Road serves German cuisine. **Napoli Pizza** on Phahon Yothin Road. The name says it all, beer and pizza and it is not too pricey. The **Mae Hong Son Guesthouse of Chiang Rai** does some great Western food.

Things to do **and** Sights to See

Wat Phra Kaeo วัดพระแก้ว

This is the most highly revered wat in Chiang Rai. Legend has it that in 1434 the stupa was struck by lightning and fell apart revealing the emerald Buddha (the emerald Buddha is made of Jade and is now displayed in Bangkok in the temple of the same name). An almost but not exact replica was made from Canadian jade in celebration of the Queen Mother's 90th birthday and it is now housed on site.

Wat Phra Singh วัดพระสิงห์

Believed to have been constructed some time during the 15th Century this wat is regarded as a fine example of Lan-na style architecture. The wat once contained the Phra Phutthasihing, an important Theravada Buddha image, but it is now stored at Wat Phra Singh in Chiang Mai. This wat is located on Singhaclai Road.

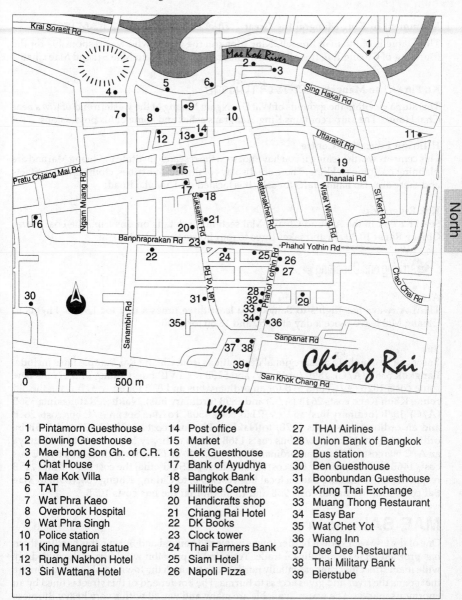

North

Legend

1	Pintamorn Guesthouse	14	Post office	27	THAI Airlines
2	Bowling Guesthouse	15	Market	28	Union Bank of Bangkok
3	Mae Hong Son Gh. of C.R.	16	Lek Guesthouse	29	Bus station
4	Chat House	17	Bank of Ayudhya	30	Ben Guesthouse
5	Mae Kok Villa	18	Bangkok Bank	31	Boonbundan Guesthouse
6	TAT	19	Hilltribe Centre	32	Krung Thai Exchange
7	Wat Phra Kaeo	20	Handicrafts shop	33	Muang Thong Restaurant
8	Overbrook Hospital	21	Chiang Rai Hotel	34	Easy Bar
9	Wat Phra Singh	22	DK Books	35	Wat Chet Yot
10	Police station	23	Clock tower	36	Wiang Inn
11	King Mangrai statue	24	Thai Farmers Bank	37	Dee Dee Restaurant
12	Ruang Nakhon Hotel	25	Siam Hotel	38	Thai Military Bank
13	Siri Wattana Hotel	26	Napoli Pizza	39	Bierstube

Wat Phra That Doi Chom Thong   พระธาตุดอยจอมทอง

Located further west of Wat Doi Ngam Muang, this wat is located by the banks of the Kok River upon a small hill and is pleasant enough to wander around. The stupa here predates the founding of Chiang Rai and following King Mangrai's founding of the city he organised renovations to be carried out on the stupa.

Monument to King Mangrai the Great   อนุสาวรีย์พ่อขุนเม็งรายมหาราช

This statue is of the man himself, King Mangrai the Great, who was responsible for the founding of Chiang Rai. It is situated at the start of the road to Mae Sai and Mae Chan

Ku Phra Chao Mangrai   กู่พระเจ้าเม็งราย

This stupa is within the grounds of Wat Doi Ngam Muang at the western end of town near Chat House. The stupa contains King Mangrai's ashes and some of his possessions.

Hilltribe Education Centre

This centre is worth visiting if you have not seen the research institute in Chiang Mai and are planning on going trekking. There are displays of the various tribes' clothing and artifacts and there are also handicrafts for sale. It is located on Thanalai Road.

Kok River Trip

See **Tha Ton** in the Around Chiang Mai section for details on this trip. The boat leaves Chiang Rai at 10.30 am and takes three to four hours to reach Tha Ton.

◀ **Arriving and Departing** ▶

Air

THAI Airways has flights to Bangkok at least three times a day for 1,960B. Flights to Chiang Mai leave twice a day at 08.50 and 18.50 for 420B.

Bus

Buses can be caught to most regional destinations from Chiang Rai. Sample fares include; **Bangkok** 358B (A/C), 189B (ordinary) and 525B for a VIP bus. **Chiang Mai** via the new route costs 102B (A/C) and 57B for an ordinary bus and 83B for an A/C bus via the old route. **Khon Kaen** costs 264B (A/C) and 189B (ordinary bus), **Nakhon Ratchasima** 356B (A/C), 198B (ordinary bus) and a VIP bus costs 450B, To **Mae Sot** an A/C bus costs 264B and an ordinary bus costs 147B, to **Nakhon Phanom** costs 442B (A/C) and 245B by ordinary bus, to **Nan** an A/C bus costs 136B and an ordinary bus costs 97B. To **Pattaya** an A/C bus costs 420B and an ordinary bus costs 230B. To **Phichit** via Uttaradit an A/C bus costs 146B and an ordinary bus costs 104B whilst via Sukhothai the cost is 160B and 115B respectively. To **Chiang Saen** a local bus costs 17B, to **Chiang Khong** costs 39B, to **Mae Sai** costs 18B, to **Phayao** costs 26B and to **Sukhothai** the bus costs 105B.

MAE SAI   แม่สาย

One of the few well known border towns between Thailand and Burma, this bustling town has profited on legal and illegal trade. Your first impression would be of the incredibly wide main street that runs essentially north-south through the town finishing at the bridge that spans the river and gives access to Burma. The border end of this street is lined by an enormous market. The wares available are many and varied with a very heavy Burmese influence - clothes, gems, you name it they have got it.

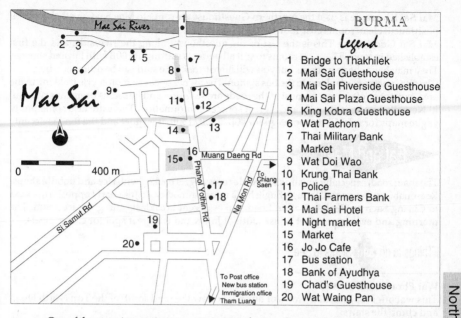

One of the more interesting pursuits in town for travellers is to watch the action up river from the bridge that spans the Sai River. Throughout the day, boats ferry people and goods back and forth between Burma and Thailand. Goods including alcohol and cigarettes pass under the dull gaze of the border guards and can be had for rock bottom prices. Apart from Mae Sai's close proximity to Burma and the Golden Triangle there is really nothing appealing about the town. The one saving grace is the large and diverse market mentioned above. There are some well placed guesthouses overlooking Burma in which you could concentrate on doing little for a few days and from which you could explore some of the surrounds.

Vital Information

Post Office has been moved to well out of town about 600 m south of Chads Guesthouse.
Banks There are quite a few lined along Phahon Yothin Road, see map for their locations.
Police Station is on Phahon Yothin Road.
Immigration is on the left hand side of the bridge over to Thakhilek town in Burma.
Codes Mae Sai's telephone code is (053) and the postal code is 57130.

Cheap Sleeps

Your best option for beds is along the riverside road which goes left (when facing Burma) at the river. Many are placed with excellent views of Burma.
King Kobra Guesthouse is along the riverside between the Mai Sai Plaza Guesthouse and the main road. It is run by a friendly American, rooms with shower are 200B and it also has decent food. You may be uninspired by the tasteless photos on the wall. There is also SKY TV, but whatever you do, do not touch *anything*.
Mai Sai Plaza Guesthouse is past the King Kobra Guesthouse on the riverside road. This place has loads of rooms with rates to suit all budgets. The staff are friendly and the cheapest rooms with shared bath cost 80B/120B for singles/doubles.

Mai Sai Riverside is past the Northern Guesthouse en-route to Mae Sai Guesthouse. Well positioned, clean rooms cost 150B/200B with fan and shower.

Mai Sai Guesthouse This is the last of the guesthouses along the riverside, and the first established in town. There are rooms to suit all budgets starting at 100B with fan and shower. They may have cheaper rooms but you will have to ask - the staff can be quite secretive.

Chad's Guesthouse is closer to the bus station. The owner once ran motorcycle trekking in the area, but not so often now as most of the roads are sealed — and he seems pretty angry about it! Nevertheless he is friendly and a great source of information. There are also some pretty vague maps for sale. Clean rooms go for 80B/120B/150B. It is quiet and the food is decent.

◀ Eat and Meet ▶

The main road, especially towards the border crossing, is packed with **rice and noodle shops**. Reasonable prices prevail though English is a rare commodity. **Jo Jos** nearly opposite the road to Chiang Saen on Phahon Yothin Road makes decent breakfasts and great icecream. The **morning and evening market** is just south of Jo Jos and is a great spot for cheap meals.

Things to do ◀and▶ Sights to See

Wat Phra That Doi Wao
This wat offers spectacular views of Burma. Follow the road south of the Top North Hotel and climb the stairs.

Trips to Burma
At the time of research it was possible for foreigners to enter Burma for the day for US$5 at the Mae Sai crossing. All you need is your passport and US$5. The town on the other side, Thakhilek, has been beautified by the Burmese 'authorities' so that all looks fine and well in sunny Burma. The town itself is no different, from what we have heard, to anything in Thailand, except perhaps for the Burmese style wat, similar versions of which you can see in Mae Hong Son Province anyway. If you want a more authentic view of Burma, save your $5 and visit a refugee camp. We would strongly advise anyone contemplating a visit to Burma to look at the bigger picture. Your $5 will go directly to the SLORC which in all likelihood will use it to buy bullets to maintain its reign of terror — every $5 counts. Better still donate your $5 to a Free Burma Organisation and do your bit for restoring the democratically elected government, and the lives of the Burmese.

Tham Luang (Great Cave)   ถ้ำหลวง
Around 6 km south of Mae Sai there is a turn-off to the west to Tham Luang which winds for nearly 3 km to the cave. Set in an idyllic, quiet and luscious green setting, this cave is huge with well formed stalactites and loud echos. Bring your own torch (you will need it) as there is not always an entrepreneur around from whom to hire one. If you are lucky you will see an English speaking guide with a lantern. To get there catch a bus bound anywhere south, but keep your eyes peeled for the sign. Once alighted, walk or hitch to the cave, otherwise you can easily get there by hired bike or motorcycle.

◀ Arriving and Departing ▶

Bus
The bus to **Chiang Rai** is 18B, to **Chiang Mai** 71B (ordinary) and 127B (A/C) and to **Tha Ton** 33B and a private bus to **Bangkok** is 202B without A/C and 365 with A/C.

AROUND MAE SAI

DOI TUNG   ดอยตุง

The main reason for going here is getting here. The windy (though completely sealed) road offers spectacular views as it snakes its way up to the peak, passing through numerous hilltribe villages and a royal residence. At the summit, at over 1,800 m, is a decent sized wat, **Wat Phra That Doi Tung**. The wat is not that special and it is not too easy to get a view from here, but a short hike down the trail nearby goes to a viewing area with better views. However the views from the road are the best. On the way up, Akha and Lisu hilltribes have set up markets with a variety of hilltribe wares at reasonable prices (you will need to bargain though).

Doi Tung is best visited by motorbike. If coming by public transport, catch a songtheaw from Mae Sai to the turn-off at **Ban Huay Khrai** for 8B. Once there, catch an occasional songtheaw to the summit (18 km away) for 30B. Otherwise you could try hitching.

WARNING: The road to Doi Tung at one stage was considered dangerous due to opium growing. In the past, late afternoon travel along here was not the greatest of ideas. Ask in Mae Sai for advice.

For those touring by motorcycle, there is an interesting, scenic and little travelled road which runs from near the royal retreat across to Route 1234 en-route to Doi Mae Salong. It is a more scenic trip than backtracking to Route 110 (and quicker). See Doi Mae Salong, Arriving and Departing, for details.

DOI MAE SALONG   ดอยแม่สลอง

This small town is unlike any other you are likely to see in Thailand. Originally settled by KMT fugitives who were chased out of Burma, the town feels like it would be better placed in North Vietnam, Northern Laos or even China. Night classes held here to teach the adult population Thai is an indication of just how un-Thai the town is.

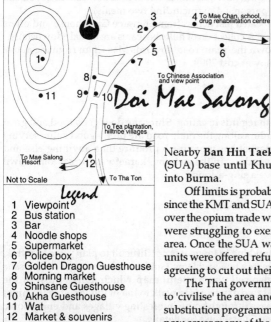

Ancient looking KMT combatants can still be seen on horseback in their uniforms, whilst Akha ladies flock into town to sell their wares and pick up a few necessities. Several Akha villages are within easy walking distance of town. Doi Mae Salong was very isolated until recently and was a pretty wild place by all accounts. Nearby **Ban Hin Taek** was a major Shan United Army (SUA) base until Khun Sa's forces were finally forced into Burma.

Off limits is probably a better description than isolated since the KMT and SUA had frequent and violent struggles over the opium trade with the Thai government forces who were struggling to exercise some sort of control over the area. Once the SUA was finally ousted, remaining KMT units were offered refugee status in Thailand in return for agreeing to cut out their opium trade.

The Thai government has made an important effort to 'civilise' the area and has introduced a variety of crop substitution programmes, principally tea and fruits which now cover many of the surrounding hillsides. A variety of

Legend

1 Viewpoint
2 Bus station
3 Bar
4 Noodle shops
5 Supermarket
6 Police box
7 Golden Dragon Guesthouse
8 Morning market
9 Shinsane Guesthouse
10 Akha Guesthouse
11 Wat
12 Market & souvenirs

North

North

locally grown products are sold in stalls around the town, the tea (a variety of Formosa Oolong) is highly regarded and there are also a range of herb and insect flavoured local liquors. Most stalls and shops will allow you to taste them - try the one with the giant centipede in it, it is excellent and just what you may well need to warm you up during the cold winter nights.

Doi Mae Salong stretches over a mountain crest. The mist, which normally disappears by mid morning, can hang around all day. Surprisingly, Mae Salong has several large, new and very expensive up-market resorts which seem to filling up with Taiwanese tourists. Perhaps they are catching up with their old KMT mates or perhaps they are all just Formosa Tea Sales Representatives, but what ever it is, Mae Salong is becoming a very popular place to visit amongst the more well heeled.

Set up in the hills to the northwest of Chiang Rai, it is an ideal retreat for those wanting to escape the heat and the tourists. Trekking around here is good, though one should exercise caution as a large quantity of opium is still grown in the vicinity - hence the drug rehabilitation centre in town. Ask at Shinsane Guesthouse for present conditions and any possible no go areas. Apparently in certain areas there are left over live mines from Sñr Khun Sa. Most of the trekking in the area is the do it yourself variety but some organised trekking and pony trekking (US$6 per day) is available at both Shinsane and Akha Mae Salong Guesthouse. There is no money exchange in Doi Mae Salong, so bring enough cash with you.

Cheap Sleeps

Shinsane Guesthouse is probably the best value in town, clean rooms with share hot shower are 60B/80B and there are nicer bungalows out back costing more. The restaurant serves good and inexpensive food and the staff are very friendly - the banana shakes are great! There is plenty of information on the walls and the staff can point you in the right direction for trekking as the same family owns a house out in the boonies which you can stay at - **Jha Ju village** at 65B per person a day (including two meals).

Akha Mae Salong Guesthouse is located just across from Shinsane Guesthouse and offers the same deal, but with less character. A collection of hilltribe wares are for sale downstairs.

Golden Dragon Guesthouse is down the 'main road' towards Mae Chan from the above guesthouses. Clean rooms with shower cost 200B.

Eat and Meet

Your options are pretty limited with regards to eating. **Shinsane** does good food and great banana shakes and the **noodle vendors** along the main road are pretty good value serving tasty meals. The early **morning market** has more fresh produce than anything else and there are a few soup and noodle vendors. In the evening, **karaoke** is the sell out crowd pleaser, so pick up a mike and have a sing-a-long.

Things to do and Sights to See

Trekking

Although there is little organised trekking in town, it is not difficult to plan your own trek, though the language barrier may create a few problems. Guides can be arranged at Shinsane at a reasonable rate. They can also sell you a useful map which marks most of the surrounding villages on it. A good two day trip is to walk to Jha Ju village, stay the night (or longer) and return. You will pass through some interesting villages and enjoy some wonderful scenery. Ask at Shinsane Guesthouse for details.

Viewpoint
At the top of the hill behind central Mae Salong is a wat which offers spectacular views of the surrounding area. It is most accessible via motorcycle and a winding steep though circular road taking about 10 to 15 minutes to get to the top. The view is particularly worthwhile in the early morning when mist often fills the valley. The wat itself is far from spectacular.

Morning Market
From about 5.00 am to 7.00 am a small market convenes between the Shinsane and Akha Mae Salong Guesthouses. Most of the goods are sold by Akha tribespeople but all sorts are doing the buying. The market is worth getting up for - if you are in the cheap rooms at Shinsane you need not bother using your alarm as the ruckus will wake you.

Arriving and Departing

Bus
From **Chiang Rai** and **Mai Sai**, get a bus to Ban Basang which is around 2 km north of Mae Chan on Route 110. From the intersection with Route 1130 there are songtheaws which run all the way to Doi Mae Salong for 50B (40B coming back). The bus to **Mae Chan** is 12B.

Motorcycle
The road to Mae Salong is sealed and in good condition in both directions (to Mae Chan and Tha Ton). If you plan on visiting Doi Tung, a little travelled road runs between Routes 1234 and 1149 although the turn-off can be a little difficult to find. If coming from Doi Mae Salong after around 23 km or so you come to a three way intersection, take the left turn. After that follow the road all the way until you reach Route 1149. The road meanders down through a deep valley with many steep switchbacks both ways. A challenge, but worth it.

If coming from Doi Tung, when coming back down from the summit take the right split before the palace but after the Lisu village. Follow this past the royal gardens and the military post until you reach a right turn with a couple of Thai road signs, this is the way.

One other point, when riding up to Doi Mae Salong on Route 1234, you come to a three way junction with an Akha gate at the centre (there is an English sign saying so) when facing the gate you need to take the left road. If going the other way, when facing the gate, you need to take the road on your right. It is excellent motorcycling all around here.

CHIANG KHONG   เชียงของ
For most visitors Chiang Khong is little more than a getaway to **Huay Xai** in Laos. But for those with a bit of time on their hands, it is worth a visit for its good guesthouses, spectacular river front scenery and the nearby village of **Ban Hat Khrai**, famous for its extra large Maekhong River Giant Catfish.

Thais flock to Chiang Khong during the weekend and public holidays for day shopping trips to Huay Xai and at this time the guesthouses can fill up very quickly. If all the guesthouses are full, then the Chiang Khong Hotel is your best bet.

Vital Information
Post Office is opposite Soi 6 on the river side of the main road.
Banks Thai Farmers Bank has a branch between Sois 7 and 9 on the river side of the main road.
Immigration Office is at the southern end of town, opposite the police station.
Codes Chiang Khong's telephone code is (053) and the postal code is 57140.

North

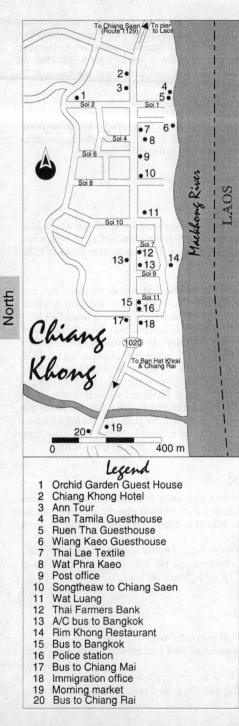

Legend

1. Orchid Garden Guest House
2. Chiang Khong Hotel
3. Ann Tour
4. Ban Tamila Guesthouse
5. Ruen Tha Guesthouse
6. Wiang Kaeo Guesthouse
7. Thai Lae Textile
8. Wat Phra Kaeo
9. Post office
10. Songtheaw to Chiang Saen
11. Wat Luang
12. Thai Farmers Bank
13. A/C bus to Bangkok
14. Rim Khong Restaurant
15. Bus to Bangkok
16. Police station
17. Bus to Chiang Mai
18. Immigration office
19. Morning market
20. Bus to Chiang Rai

Cheap Sleeps

Ban Ta Mila Guesthouse is down Soi 1 at the north end of town. It has a lovely garden and well positioned restaurant. Here you will meet friendly staff who hire clean bungalows for 100B.

Reun Thai Sophapham is next door to Ban Ta Mila Guesthouse. It has clean rooms in a large wooden house and also with a well positioned restaurant. Rooms range from 100B to 300B, though in low season you can get the rooms cheaper.

Orchid Garden Guesthouse is up the far end of Soi 2 and the newly constructed bungalows go for 80B with share shower whilst the rooms in the house go for 60B/100B. Some people have also been able to organise Laotion visas here in 1½ hours for 1,600B although this price is the exception rather than the rule.

Chiang Khong Hotel is only really worth it if everything else is full. Clean rooms with hot shower and fan cost 120B.

Eat and Meet

Rim Khong Restaurant is on the river between Sois 7 and 9. The good food comes at a reasonable price and has a limited English menu. The restaurant at **Ban Ta Mila Guesthouse** is not too bad. The other alternative is to try the **rice and noodle places** along the main road.

There is not much to do in town except to wait for a Laotian visa. There are a number of nearby Akha and Hmong hilltribes which you could wander to. If interested, ask at your guesthouse about getting a guide.

Wat Luang   วัดหลวง

The wat was once a very important wat in Chiang Rai Province but is now concentrating on fading into mediocrity. The chedi is over 600 years old.

Ban Hat Khrai   บ้านหาดไคร้

This small village is well known as a site for catching the infamous Giant Maekhong River Catfish and as a result the restaurants are often well stocked. This fish holds the record as being the largest fresh water catfish in the world and in the past great fanfare has accompanied the hunting and catching of these fish.

Today, however, the Giant Catfish is becoming rarer and rarer as a combination of over fishing and destructive dam construction hamper its life cycle. Construction of dams down river and up river on tributaries of the Maekhong are believed to be hampering the attempts of many fish to reach their spawning grounds, the result being that the fish often die without spawning. This is a problem which is not unique to the Giant Catfish and is one which is not being dealt with in an effective manner by the damming authorities. Thailand is an incredibly power hungry nation and it will be most unfortunate if one of the many victims of that hunger is the Giant Maekhong River Catfish.

In an attempt to alleviate the situation there is a fertilisation programme and mass release of fish hatchlings from here. Regardless of their rarity there is still mass celebration when one is caught as they fetch a very good price for the fisherman talented enough to catch one. The fisheries office can be visited by the river in Ban Hat Khrai a few kilometres south of town.

Motorcycle Day Trip
See the Chiang Saen section for the details of this highly recommended trip.

Boat Trip
If you have still got time to spare after ogling at fish, it is possible to hire a boat to take a ride up river to Chiang Saen. Ask at Ban Ti Mila Guesthouse for details and start getting people together. It can cost as much as 1,200B for the boat one way - ouch!

Crossing to Laos
Visas are now available in Chiang Khong for 1,700B at Ann Tour (near the Chiang Khong Hotel) and take seven days to be processed. The boat to Huay Xai regularly leaves from a couple of kilometres to the north of town and costs 20B. Have a nice trip!

If you are thinking of doing a day trip to Laos forget it. You probably will not be allowed to cross, and Huay Xai is by far one of the least interesting towns in all of Laos. Virtually all that you can buy there comes from Thailand except perhaps for the sapphires, which are Huay Xai's claim to fame (along with the AK47s).

◀ **Arriving and Departing** ▶

Bus
The bus to **Chiang Rai** takes 3 hours costing 39B, to **Chiang Mai** an ordinary bus is 91B, A/C is 128B, and VIP is 165B and the bus to **Chiang Saen** costs 25B. To **Bangkok** an A/C bus costs 371B and an ordinary bus costs 289B.

Motorbike
To really appreciate the scenery en-route from Chiang Rai, hire a motorbike and take the following Route: 110, 1209, 1098, 1271 then 1129. Whilst on 1129 you are given a choice of mountain top and river front roads (look for the sign). Try taking a different route each way as the scenery is spectacular on both.

Roadside snackstalls

If travelling around by motorcycle, always keep an eye out for the fruit vendors by the side of the road. Often the cheapest source of good and fresh fruit, there are often ten or so vendors in a row, so by shifting from one to the other you should get a great price.

North

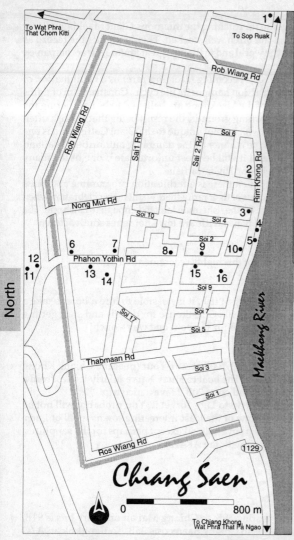

Legend

1 Gin Guesthouse
2 Siam Guesthouse
3 Siam Guesthouse
4 Food Vendors
5 Boats to the Golden Triangle
6 Old Tourist Office
7 Post office
8 Siam City Bank
9 Buses to Chiang Rai
10 Police station
11 New Tourist Office
12 Wat Pa Sak
13 Chiang Saen National Museum
14 Wat Chedi Luang
15 Bus to Chiang Mai & Bangkok
16 Market

CHIANG SAEN

เชียงแสน

Just south of the Golden Triangle tourist hell hole is Chiang Saen, a quiet and very historic town that sits by the Maekhong River and was once an independent kingdom. Archeological finds in the area have placed development here in prehistoric times. More recent communities have been placed in the region of the 13th to 14th Centuries when one of the sons of King Mangrai, Saen Pu, on his father's orders commenced construction of a walled city with the Maekhong River being one of those borders. In its heyday the walled-in city had an area of 2½ sq km and contained 76 temples within its walls and another 63 outside creating what must have been a spectacular city. Unfortunately, development and looting have taken a disastrous toll on many of these ruins and precious little remains. Following King Mangrai's unification of Northern Thailand, Chiang Saen became a frontier town of the Kingdom of Lan-na until the entire Kingdom was conquered by the Burmese. It was not until 1782 that Chiang Saen returned to the Thai fold and it became a district of Chiang Rai Province in 1957.

There are enough historic sites and wats around town to keep you busy for a couple of days (if you take it slowly) and it is also close enough to Sop Ruak (the point where the borders of Thailand, Laos and Burma meet) that you can pop up at dawn, take your photo and get out before anyone you know sees you there.

Vital Information

Tourist Information The small and friendly TAT office has moved to behind Wat Pa Sak. Both the old and new positions are marked on the map. They have a few bits of information on Chiang Saen.

Post Office is on Phahon Yothin Road about half way down the main road.

Bank Siam Commercial Bank are on the main road, towards the river from the post office.

Codes Chiang Saen's telephone code is (053) and the postal code is 57150.

Cheap Sleeps

All of the below should be able to arrange motorcycle hire.

Gin's Guesthouse is about 1½ km north of downtown Chiang Saen. This quiet escape is one of the more pleasant places to stay. Rooms in the house go for 150B (dorm 50B) and the nice bungalows out the back with bathroom are 120B. The bungalows are widely spread and quiet. Breakfast is available at the terrace adjoining the main house.

Siam Guesthouse is closer to town. Basic rooms in a longhouse style with shared bathroom are 60B/80B, whilst bungalows with bathroom are 100B and 120B for a nicer one. Food is available and reasonably priced. The staff are friendly and bicycles are available for hire.

Chiang Saen Guesthouse This is the cheapest in town, though a little noisy and pretty basic. However, they provide plenty of travel information. Rooms with shared bath start at 50B/70B.

Eat and Meet

There is not much to speak of in terms of restaurants in town. On the corner of Phahon Yothin Road and Rim Khong Road is a pleasant place for an evening meal. Around evening, **a good selection of noodle and fish vendors lay out mats on the pavement** along the river side of Phahon Yothin Road. Many of the locals eat here and it is a popular place for the younger Thais to gather over a meal, a few bottles of grog and a singing session.

Things to do and Sights to See

National Museum

This small museum is at the western end of town and has a small collection of artifacts which have been unearthed in the surrounding area. It is worth a look if you have got time to spare, or you want to tick off every museum in Thailand. It is open from Wednesday to Sunday, 9.00 am to 4.00 pm and admission is 10B.

Wat Phra That Chedi Luang   วัดพระธาตุเจดีย์หลวง

Behind and to the east of the museum is Wat Phra That Chedi Luang which was built in the 14th Century. It was originally established as the main monastery of town. Now, somewhat overgrown, it stands at almost 90 m and is well worth a look.

Wat Pa Sak   วัดป่าสัก

To the west of the museum (take a left at the end of Phahon Yothin Road, then your first right and follow the trail - the ruins are on your left), this site has undergone a hefty restoration and thus entails a hefty entrance fee (20B).

Wat Phra That Chom Kitti   วัดพระธาตุจอมกิตติ

This wat is to the northwest of town and can be reached from a number of directions including parachute. The walk or ride up the hill and/or steps is worth it for good scenic views. If you make a wish at the wat it is supposed to come true. Admission is free but donations are appreciated.

Wat Phra That Pa Ngao   วัดพระธาตุผาเงา

Located a few kilometres to the south of town, this wat at the base of the hill is definitely worth visiting to view the intricate carvings (especially on the doors) and interesting murals. After visiting the wat make your way up the long circular road to the chedi at the top to observe spectacular views of the surrounds far exceeding those of Wat Phra That Chom Kitti. To get there head south from Chiang Saen until you reach the big sign and bigger archway, enter and accept free lychees if you are lucky. The wat is on your right and the road that goes on past the wat leads up to the chedi.

Boat Rides

It is possible to take a boat to the official Golden Triangle at Sop Ruak for 400B one way or 500B return. The trip takes about 30 minutes each way. If the tourist buses are not around you may be able to bargain this down considerably. The boat to Chiang Khong is 1,200B and takes about 1½ hours.

Bung Chiang Saen   ทะเลสาบเชียงแสน

About 7 km out of town this lake is a very quiet and relaxing spot where it is easy to kick back and escape the hectic life of travelling for a few hours. The turn-off for the lake is 5 km out of Chiang Saen at the 27 km marker and the road leads off for another 2 km before reaching the lake.

Motorcycle Day Trip

A great day trip by motorcycle from Chiang Saen is to ride down to Chiang Khong and back using different routes. From Chiang Saen, take Route 1129 all the way to Chiang Khong. Part of this goes up and over a very high viewpoint from where the vista is breathtaking. Have lunch in Chiang Khong and perhaps have a look at the Fisheries Station then return. Instead of taking Route 1129 all the way back, take it only as far as the village of **Ban Huai Yen**, where you then take the right turn-off and follow this road until it links back up with Route 1129. The pristine riverside scenery along here is absolutely stunning. This trip is easily done on a Honda Dream and is highly recommended.

◀ Arriving and Departing ▶

Bus

The bus to **Chiang Rai** is 17B and takes 1½ hours, to **Chiang Mai** an ordinary bus costs 73B taking 5 hours and the A/C bus is 130B. The bus via Chiang Rai is the fastest route to Chiang Mai. To Chiang Khong a bus costs 25B. An ordinary bus to **Bangkok** costs 216B, taking 14 hours and an A/C VIP bus costs 600B.

King Taksin
King Taksin prominently rose to power, but fell hard, at least his head did. King Taksin, former governor of Tak, was a military leader that brought Thailand out of Burmese hands after the fall of Ayutthaya in 1767. He moved the capital of Siam to Thonburi. His militaristic leadership failed in maintaining a cohesive administration, and was eventually beheaded by General Chakri.

SOP RUAK (GOLDEN TRIANGLE)   สามเหลี่ยมทองคำ

Have you ever walked over the equator? Stood at the North Pole? Seen the leaning tower of Pisa and walked over the equator again? — loved it all and got the T shirts? Then this place is for you. The Golden Triangle actually refers to a large area of northern Thailand, Burma and western Laos but a scam is running here in that, like the Isthmus of Kra, a geographical area has been localised to a specific point solely for commercial purposes. So Sop Ruak is not really the Golden Triangle, but rather just where you buy the T-shirt and take the photo.

This place is more interesting as a study into mass tourism than anything else, though the view of the three rivers (or two rivers and a creek) is nice. This is the point where the borders of Thailand, Laos, and Burma meet and the tourist souvenir and trinket shops try and get your business, charging outrageous prices.

The **House of Opium** is worth visiting (admission is 10B) for its interesting collection of smokeables and smoking utensils and provides a detailed description of the growing and harvesting of the crop, although no samples are given out. If you go up to the wat on the hill next to the House of Opium, a break in the foliage provides better views of the 'meeting of the rivers'.

WARNING
In the area around Sop Ruak, especially on the road to Mae Sai and Chiang Saen, the police set up check points and, on occasion, stop and search everyone — with particular attention to farangs on motorbikes. They are supposedly looking for opium, but if you are found with anything illegal, even the tiniest bit of dope, you are in a whole new world of trouble. If you are on a motorbike, expect to be pulled over and have your pockets emptied before you can even take the motorcycle out of gear. Smokers beware — you will not have time to dump your stash as the police are numerous, very thorough, very mean and very serious.

PHRAE PROVINCE

This province located in the centre of far Northern Thailand has a number of attractions making it well worth your time to visit. The area is steeped in history and natural beauty. The provincial capital, Phrae, is one of the oldest cities in Thailand and the surrounding area of the province possesses large stretches of **teak forests** (which are now protected), a **National Park** and the bizarre soil pillars at **Phae Muang Phi**. The province is fairly small at only just over 6,500 sq km and is surrounded by Lampang to the west, Phayao to the north, Nan and Uttaradit to the east and Sukhothai to the south.

PHRAE   แพร่

This town is little visited, but worth the effort. 'Made in Phrae' is a well known phrase for the indigo dyed cotton shirts you see all over Thailand - Phrae is where the best originate. Phrae is one of the oldest centres in Thailand and was recorded as paying tribute to King Ramkhamhaeng in the 13th Century. But like many northern Thai capitals, Phrae appears to have changed hands on numerous occasions including a stint under Burmese influence. As a result of these long gone wars, Phrae still has large sections of its walls and moat remaining and the old city is fascinating to wander around.

Like many Thai cities, Phrae is split into the old and the new. The new holds little to keep your attention but the old is packed with traditional Thai architecture in the form of beautiful teak houses, some interesting wats, quiet sois and alleys. There are also more contemporary temptations with buildings made in less classic material, such as a pink house which looks as if it would better suit Pippi Longstocking.

Vital Information

Post Office is in the centre of the old city on Charoen Muang Road.
Banks are all over Charoen Muang Road in the new city.
Police are on Charoen Muang Road, just past the intersection with Rong Sor Road.
Codes Phrae's telephone code is (054) and the postal code is 54000.

Cheap Sleeps

Finding a hotel in Phrae can be a real hassle as none use roman script names. Follow the numbers and see how you go or just ask for directions.
Themviman Hotel at 226-8 Charoen Muang Road. This hotel has friendly staff with heaps of clean rooms with bathroom and cost 80B/140B for a single/double.
Thung Si Phaibun Hotel is at 84 Yantarakitkosin Road. Dingy rooms get mixed reviews but cost 80B/120B.
Sawatdikan is near the Thung Si Phaibun Hotel and is similar but even dingier.

North

Phrae

To Nan, Phayao

Yam River

Rob Muang Rd
Kham Saen Rd
Chai Boon Rd
Ban Mai Rd
City Walls
Rop Muang Rd
Nam Khue Rd
Yantarakitkosin Rd
Kham Lue Rd
Kham Doen Rd
Wichaira Chan Rd
Phra Ruang Rd
San Muang Luang Rd
Charoen Muang Rd
Rong Sor Rd
Rasadamnoen Rd
Choe Hae Rd
Muang Hit Rd

To Ban Prathap Chai House
To Lampang
To Den Chai & Uttaradit
To Airport, Wat Phra That Cho Hae & Phraya Chaiyabun Monument

0   400 m

Legend

1 Wat Jom Sawan	10 Post Office	19 Thepwiman Hotel
2 Bus station	11 Buddhist college	20 Relax Pub & Restaurant
3 Wat Sa Baw Kaew	12 Corner Road Pub	21 Bangkok Metro. Bank
4 Wat Luang	13 Wat Phra Ruang	22 Bangkok Bank
5 Wat Phra Non	14 Night market	23 Thung Si Phaibun Hotel
6 Vongburi House	15 Police station	24 Sawatdikan Hotel
7 Wat Phong	16 THAI Airways	25 Thai Farmers Bank
8 Park	17 Cinema & Nightclub	
9 Provincial Office	18 Bars & restaurants	

◀ **Eat and Meet** ▶

Phrae has a wide variety of places to have a munch. **Corner Road Pub** is at the corner of Kham Doen and Lak Muang Roads. Good food is served for fair prices and it is a nice place for an evening lager. **Malakaw Restaurant** is on Ratsadamnoen Road and serves a wide range of food and drink and, to make matters easier, some English is spoken. This is a pleasant eating area and very popular with the locals. The not huge but good **night market** is at the entrance of the old city. **Relax Pub and Restaurant** is on a Soi running off Charoen Muang Road and is very popular with younger well heeled Thais, and understandably so.

Things to do ◆ Sights to See

Ban Prathap Chai (impressive house)   บ้านประทับใจ

This huge teak house was built on 130 enormous teak logs with intricately carved bases. The house is full of everything imaginable which could be made out of teak and much of it is for sale. Although really just a large shop, it is still worth a visit. You will have to pay 10B to get in, twice what the Thais pay, but you get a tacky elephant souvenir for your generosity — a perfect gift for the mother-in-law.

The impressive house is 2 km west of the intersection of Muang Hit and Ratsadamnoen Roads. On the way you will pass another beautiful wooden house on your right (look for the fence posts). It is worth a peek over the fence and is far less over the top than Ban Prathap Chai with its own collection of spectacular carvings standing around in the garden.

Wat Luang   วัดหลวง

The oldest wat in town, Wat Luang was established in the 12th Century, and is particularly known for its Lan-Na style chedi which is often wrapped with Thai Lü silk. In the grounds of the wat there is also a museum which the monks will show you through. The snap of the beheading is worth seeing.

Vongburi House

Located on Pranonnur Road, this pink house, which looks like it has fallen out of the sky, was closed when we visited, but we were wondering whether Pippi Longstockings lives there!

Phraya Chaiyabun Monument   อนุสาวรีย์พระยาไชยบูรณ์

This monument is located around 4 km from the centre of town and is dedicated to the memory of Phraya Chaiyabun who was the ruler of Phrae during the reign of King Rama V. During the Ngiew rebellion of 1902 he refused to agree to their terms and as a result lost his life.

Wat Phra That Cho Hae   วัดพระธาตุช่อแฮ

This spectacular wat sits atop a teak covered hill 9 km to the southeast of town. The chedi is 33 m high and coated in gold sheets. The name of the wat (Cho Hae) is derived from a kind of satin which devotees wrap around the chedi.

Wat Jam Sawan   วัดจอมสวรรค์

Situated about 1 km northeast of the centre of town, this particularly beautiful wat was commissioned by Rama V and designed by a Burmese architect. Ask one of the monks on the premises to show you the Buddhist scripture carved into ivory. The Burmese design of the wat makes for a nice change from many of the other wats in Thailand.

North

◀ **Arriving and Departing** ▶

Air
THAI Airways fly from Phrae to Nan and Bangkok daily. The flight to **Nan** takes around 30 minutes and costs 300B. The flight to **Bangkok** takes 1½ hours at a cost of 1,325B. Phrae airport is 9 km out of town on the same road that leads to Wat Phra That Cho Hae.

Train
The closest train station is Den Chai 13 km south of town. Songtheaws run from outside the station entrance to Phrae costing 15B whilst the fare to Nan is 39B. See the timetable at the end of the chapter for complete train details.

Bus and Songtheaw
The bus to **Chiang Mai** costs 55B for an ordinary bus, 76B for an A/C one and 98B for first class. The bus to **Nan** costs 33B, an ordinary bus to **Sukhothai** costs 48B and a blue songtheaw to **Den Chai** (for the railway station) costs 15B. To **Bangkok** an A/C bus costs 238B taking 8 hours, and an ordinary bus costs 132B.

AROUND PHRAE

Phae Muang Phii   แพะ เมืองผี
Located about 18 km from Phrae town, this basin area is full of bizarre soil towers which have been caused by soil erosion. There is a similar area further north in Nan Province which is supposed to be even better. The park is best reached by motorbike, otherwise catch a bus en-route to Nan and hop off at the signposted turn-off with Route 1134. From the turn-off catch one of the occasional songtheaws which can take you 6 km closer after which it is a 2½ km walk or hitch. Phae Muang Phii means 'ghost land' and drinks are available on site.

Wiang Kosai National Park   อุทยานแห่งชาติเวียงโกศัย
This small National Park straddles Phrae and Lampang Provinces and was established in 1981. The park's main claims to fame are a series of **waterfalls** and the **Mae Jok Hot Springs** which reach 80° C. Accommodation is available near the park office. The National Park is around 80 km from Phrae town. To reach it, travel along Route 101 and take a right at km 10 after passing through Den Chai onto Route 11. Follow Route 11 for about 40 km then take a left at the sign post for another 13 km to reach the park office.

NAN PROVINCE

Among the most remote (if not *the* most remote) province of Thailand, Nan was until fairly recently off limits to most foreign visitors due to security concerns. However with the construction of good roads and a higher degree of positive attention from the Thai government, the security concerns of the past are considered to have been eradicated.

NAN   น่าน

This northern province has only really been 'open' to tourism for the last ten years and is still pretty undeveloped and 'backward'. As a result, Nan is very rural with few roads and a large hilltribe population. **Yao** are particularly prominent with plenty of them to be found in the Nan market. There are also many **Hmong**, **H'tin** and **Khamu**, the last two of which are only found in Nan Province.

North

Nan is very laid back and friendly and there are still few travellers who make it out here. There are plenty of wats, if that is your thing, and there are also some remnants of the old city wall heralding a period not all that long ago when Nan was still an independent Kingdom.

Vital Information

Tourist Information Both the Doi Phukha Guesthouse and the Nan Guesthouse have an excellent range of free information on Nan and Nan Province.
Post Office is on Mahawong Road and there is a phone office upstairs.
Banks are concentrated along Sumon Thewarat Road.
Police Station is on the corner of Suriyaphong and Sumon Thewarat Roads.
Codes Nan's telephone code is (054) and the postal code is 55000.

Cheap Sleeps

Doi Phukha Guesthouse at 94/5 Sumon Thewarat Road, Soi 1, ☎ (054) 751 517 is your best choice of resting in Nan. There is loads of information available for everything you would ever hope to see in Nan. Clean rooms are 80B/100B for single/double with share bathroom.
Nan Guesthouse is located down a soi opposite the THAI Airways office on Mahaphrom Road. Clean spartan rooms are 60B/80B and there is tourist information available.
Wiang Tai House is very central on a soi running off Sumon Thewarat Road. Clean rooms with shared bath are 100B/120B.
Amorn Si Hotel at 97 Mahayot Road is very central with 22 extremely noisy rooms. For the privilege you will pay 100B/120B for singles/doubles.
Suk Kasem Hotel at 29-31 Ananworaritdet Road, ☎ (054) 710 141, is almost as central as the Amonsi Hotel, but with cleaner, quieter and more expensive rooms at 150B/170B.

Eat and Meet

Night Market This is not the largest night market you will ever see, but it certainly serves its purpose. It is found along Ananworaritdet Road. Opposite the market, near to the Suk Kasem Hotel, is a large open **restaurant** with an English translated menu. They serve good and reasonably priced food. **Tanaya Kitchen** is nearby to the Suk Kasem Hotel and has reasonable food and good coffee. **Suan Issan** is down the soi by the Bangkok Bank. This would have to be the best place in town for I-san food at reasonable prices. **De Dario** This Swiss restaurant is located at the northern edge of town and can be quite difficult to find as it is situated at the end of a long soi. Ask at your guesthouse or Phu Travel for directions.

Things to do **and** Sights to See

Wat Phra That Chae Haeng   วัดพระธาตุแช่แห้ง

Over 600 years old, this is the most highly revered wat in Nan. The central gold sheeted Lao style chedi is 55 m high and on a hot day is uncomfortably warm to approach. On the full moon of the first lunar month, a festival with fireworks and processions takes place. The wat is 3 km southeast of town and is best visited by bicycle or motorcycle.

Wat Phumin   วัดภูมินทร์

Originally built in 1596, this wat has undergone many face-lifts. Unusual, due to the fact that both the bot and wihaan are in the one structure, the inside walls are decorated with incredible murals depicting all manner of 'life and times' including the arrival of Westerners to Thailand, hell and people boiling in a pot. The central Buddha, facing four ways, each in the position of subduing Mara, is strange yet captivating as are the nagas stretching from one side of the wat to the other. The wat is in the centre of town not far from the National Museum.

National Museum

Once the home of the Nan Royal Family, this museum is a must see for any visitor to Nan. The collection is quite impressive and thankfully has more than just Buddhas and hunks of rock. The centrepiece is a black elephant tusk measuring almost 1 m in length and believed to have magical powers. The museum is open 9.00 am to 12.00 pm and 1.00 pm to 4.00 pm from Wednesday to Sunday, admission is 10B.

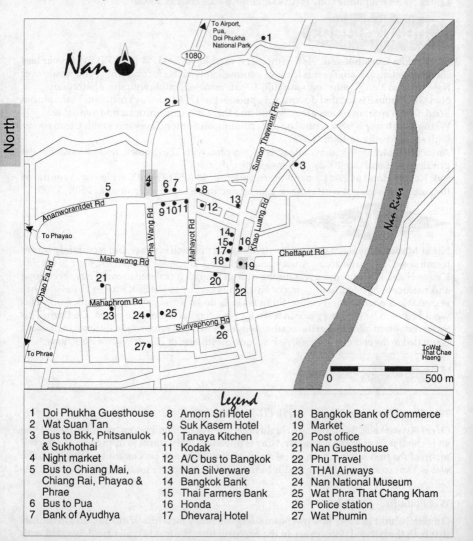

Legend

1	Doi Phukha Guesthouse	8	Amorn Sri Hotel	18	Bangkok Bank of Commerce
2	Wat Suan Tan	9	Suk Kasem Hotel	19	Market
3	Bus to Bkk, Phitsanulok & Sukhothai	10	Tanaya Kitchen	20	Post office
4	Night market	11	Kodak	21	Nan Guesthouse
5	Bus to Chiang Mai, Chiang Rai, Phayao & Phrae	12	A/C bus to Bangkok	22	Phu Travel
6	Bus to Pua	13	Nan Silverware	23	THAI Airways
7	Bank of Ayudhya	14	Bangkok Bank	24	Nan National Museum
		15	Thai Farmers Bank	25	Wat Phra That Chang Kham
		16	Honda	26	Police station
		17	Dhevaraj Hotel	27	Wat Phumin

Wat Phra That Chang Kham   วัดช้างค้ำ

The second most important wat in Nan (after Wat Phumin) is undergoing restoration on its murals which appear to have been painted over at some stage. The chedi behind the wihaan is supported by elephant statues and was also in the process of being restored when we visited.

Wat Phra That Khao Noi   พระธาตุเขาน้อย

The view from this wat is spectacular, encompassing Nan town and valley. It is located a few kilometres to the southeast of town and is easily visited by bicycle or motorbike.

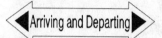
Arriving and Departing

Getting Around
Samlors cost 10B to 20B around town but most of the city is easily explored on foot.

Air
THAI Airways flies twice daily to **Bangkok** for 1,530B and **Phitsanulok** for 575B. There are also flights to **Chiang Mai** for 510B and **Phrae** for 300B.

Bus
Nan is well connected to northern Thailand by regular bus services. VIP buses to **Bangkok** cost 445B and leave at 19.00 and 20.00, A/C buses leave at 08.00, 18.30, 18.45 and 19.10 via the new route and cost 289B, whilst there are two A/C buses a day (08.30 and 18.00) via the old route for 319B. Ordinary buses leave at 08.00, 09.00, 19.30 and 20.00 via the new route and cost 160B, whilst via the old route there are departures at 08.30, 17.00, 17.30, 18.00 and 18.30 which cost 177B.

To **Chiang Mai** an ordinary bus costs 83B and takes 7 hours whilst the A/C bus costs 148B and takes about 6 hours. To **Chiang Rai** there is an A/C departure at 09.00 which costs 136B and the ordinary bus costs 97B. The bus to **Phayao** (via Song Khwae village) leaves at 08.00 and 13.30 and costs 52B (A/C 72B). There are buses throughout the day to **Phrae** which cost 33B, and a bus to **Den Chai** (for the train station) for 39B.

AROUND NAN

Tham Pua Tuub Complex   ถ้ำผาตูบ

Located in a small forestry park are a number of easily reached caves, many of which are full of Buddha images. The trails to each cave are not marked but are easy to find. What is more difficult to find is the cave complex itself. There are no English signs on the way there, so follow these directions. The caves are located 10 km north of town, so head north on Route 1080 past the km 10 marker where you will see a green wooden sign in Thai on your left, take this turn-off. From the road it is about 100 m to the caves.

Wat Nong Bua   วัดหนองบัว

This wat is at Nong Bua around 30 km north of Nan just off Route 1080. It is decorated by the same artist responsible for Wat Phumin but the murals are fairly faded. The town is also a good source for Thai Lue material which is wrapped around religious relics.

Although best visited by motorbike, you can reach Nong Bua by songtheaw from Nan. Catch a songtheaw (12B) to **Tha Wang Pha** and hop off a few kilometres beforehand - tell the conductor you want to go to Wat Nong Bua and he will yell when you must get off. From here it is a 2½ km walk to the wat. Pick up a map at Nan or Doi Phukha Guesthouse for some directions.

Pua

This town is little more than a place to fill your stomach and petrol tank but it is nearby to **Ban Pa Klang**, a must for all budding silver merchants. Situated by a scenic lake it is a great place to buy excellent silver at wholesale prices - expect to pay 40% to 50% of what you would pay at Chiang Mai.

To reach Ban Pa Klang from Pua take the turn-off to the National Park at Ban Hua Doi. You will reach a sharp right turn after which there is a concrete road off to the right and slightly up hill. Take this road for 2 km and you will come to a pretty lake, the silver shops are around the far side of the lake. It is best to go here via motorbike.

Doi Phu Kha National Park   อุทยานแห่งชาติดอยภูคา

This National Park is most accessible by motorbike from Nan town. It promises and delivers stunning mountain scenery and unspoilt forest along with numerous waterfalls. A number of different loops can be done of the National Park and it is best to pick up a map at either Doi Phukha or Nan Guesthouses beforehand deciding what you want to do. Basic accommodation is available at the National Park headquarters although it was closed for repairs at our last pass. There are no organised trails in the park but the ride through it is a highlight in itself.

Apart from spectacular scenery and exhilarating motorcycling, the park is also home to **'ancient' palm trees.** These are very tall palms which sit on each side of the road not far past the cafe and rest stop half way through the park. Their position is well marked by a sign just before you reach them. From **Pua** there are rare songtheaws to the headquarters for 40B.

Sao Din   เสาดิน

Translated as 'earth pillars' this area is similar to that of Phrae Muang Phii in Phrae Province, but covers a larger area. Situated around 30 km south of Nan it is best visited by motorcycle or bicycle as public transport will take you a year and a day to reach it.

Trekking

Phu Travel offers a trekking trip for 600B per person per day for four people. Phu Travel are the only trekking operator in Nan and can do one, two, three and four day treks. Obviously the longer the trek the better the experience and the less time you'll need to spend in Mr Phu's jeep.

Mr Phu is a fascinating guy himself. Of Chinese origin, his parents walked from Yunnan to Nan about 50 years ago to escape persecution. For a long time he earned his living riding motorcycles, but now he drives his jeep instead. Because there is not a high demand for trekking in Nan, if you can get a group together, it is possible to tailor make your trek to a degree which is simply not possible in other areas.

Treks can be organised into **Doi Phukha National Park** and the various hilltribe villages including visits to the **H'tin** and **Khamu** tribes as well as the particularly remote **Mlabri** tribe (if possible). The treks are organised in a manner whereby you leave your gear in the jeep when you start walking, and the jeep then meets you at pre-agreed points to pick you up and ferry you to another destination where you start to walk again. Mr Phu says it is also possible to organise long trips to visit the Mlabri tribes under the control of the American missionary Eugene Long.

As with all trekking do not rush into anything and make sure you have a cohesive group before heading off. There is nothing worse than trekking with people you would rather be on the other side of the world from.

> Occasionally certain hilltribes employ other tribes to work their land. Rumour has it that wages are sometimes paid in opium — an indication that drug abuse among some hilltribes is rife and that the opium eradication programme may not be as good as first thought.

PHAYAO PROVINCE

Phayao Province was split from Chiang Rai Province on 28 August 1977, but in the past has also been an independent municipality. The town was believed to have been first built by the King of Chiang Saen around the turn of the 12th Century and has now grown into another bustling provincial centre.

PHAYAO   พะเยา

The provincial capital of Phayao virtually never makes it on to the itinerary of travellers, but for those who want to get away from the tourist hordes but retain some classic Thai scenery, Phayao is not a bad choice. The city itself has been built in the classic concrete blockhouse style, but the attraction here is not so much in the architecture as the scenery. Phayao sits upon the stunning Kwan Phayao, a natural and beautiful lagoon, which is surrounded by a hilly landscape and filled to the brim with fish. Lining the banks on the city side of the lake are numerous excellent seafood restaurants from which the sunset view is spectacular.

Phayao, depending on route taken, is between 600 km and 700 km from Bangkok, 90 km from Chiang Rai, 140 km from Chiang Mai and 137 km from Nan. This positioning makes Phayao a pleasant stop to break the journey of those travelling between Nan and Chiang Mai or Chiang Rai. The province is bordered by Nan, Phrae, Lampang and Chiang Rai Provinces and it also shares a border with Laos.

Vital Information

Post Office is 3 km out of town on the road to Chiang Rai. A more convenient branch is at 887 Phahon Yothin Road at the eastern end of town. The phone office is on Pratoochai Road.
Banks are along Phahon Yothin Road, check the map for details.
Hospital is opposite the post office on the road to Chiang Rai.
Codes Phayao's telephone code is (054) and the postal code is 56000.

Cheap Sleeps

Wattana Hotel at 69 Donsanam Road, ☎ (054) 431 203, has clean and quiet rooms with fan and bath for 90B/110B. It is a popular place for travelling businessmen.
Tharn Thong Hotel at 55-59 Donsanam Road, ☎ (054) 431 302, is also a popular place with businessmen and rooms are much the same as Wattana but cost more at 150B/180B.
Bungalow Siriphan This is the only place on the lake but was closed for repairs when we visited. If it re-opens we guess it would charge around 150B/250B. It is the best location in town as it sits on the side of the lake and is separated from the hectic centre of town by a five minute walk. It is also the closest to the bus station.

Eat and Meet

Night Market stretches along Robwieng Road for about 250 m and serves the best bargain priced cuisine in town. **Thai restaurants** line Chai Kwan Road serving delicious seafood and standard Thai meals. The prices are not as inflated as you would imagine. As you wander along the lakeside in an easterly direction the bars begin to outnumber the restaurants.

Things to do and Sights to See

Wat Si Khom Khan   วัดศรีโคมคำ

This is one of the more bizarre wats in Thailand. It houses an impressive 17 m sitting Buddha, but what may turn the head a bit more is the strange sculpture garden full of sinners just to the right of the wat. This sculpture garden sits amongst trees just to the north of the temple entrance and the theme appears to be 'whatever you do, do not sin!' According to our calculations, the man whose tongue has been pulled out and dragged to his knees was probably a liar, the woman with her stomach ripped out and her intestines clearly visible may have had an abortion (or was it a really bad case of alien ingestion?) and the two nude people climbing the tree whilst having their ankles torn and snapped at by howling dogs may have been guilty of adultery (or was it nude bathing?) Some of the other sculptures are somewhat more cryptic — the boiling vat of people a bit mystifying to say the least. Anyway, check it out and let us know what you think is going on here. An annual fair takes place here in May. Also on the wat grounds is a small museum with a collection of artefacts and literary transcripts both old and new from the Phayao area.

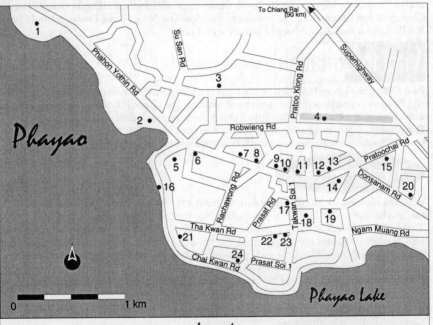

Legend

1	Wat Si Khom Kham	9	Bangkok Bank
2	Siriphan Bungalows	10	7-eleven
3	Bus station	11	Hotel
4	Night market	12	Than Thong Hotel
5	Statue of King Ngam Muang	13	Wattana Hotel
6	Thai Farmers Bank	14	Police station
7	Krung Thai Bank	15	Telecom office
8	Bangkok Bank of Commerce	16	Paddleboat hire

17	Bank of Ayudhya
18	City pillar
19	Wat Ratcha Krue
20	Post office
21	Restaurants
22	Wat Si U-Mong Kham
23	School
24	Mackenna Restaurant

King Ngam Muang Monument   อนุสาวรีย์พ่อขุนงำเมือง

This statue was erected in the memory of King Ngam Muang, a former ruler of Phayao. Born in 1238, Ngam Muang was educated in Lopburi and returned to take over his father's role as ruler of Phayao in 1258. Eighteen years later, when the expansionist ruler, King Mangrai (who is credited with the foundation of the Kingdom of Lan-Na) marched on Phayao, King Ngam Muang went out and met him, and instead of fighting cut a deal which gave some territory to Mangrai but averted war.

Kwan Phayao   กว๊านพะเยา

This large natural lagoon is fresh water and performs an important role in the local fisheries industry.

Phayao Fishery Office   สถานีประมง

Located at the far eastern end of the town, this fisheries station plays an important role in fish breeding programmes and some specimens are on display. The office is open daily.

Paddle Boats

For the thrill seekers, for next to nothing you can hire decrepit paddle boats to paddle around the waters of Kwan Phayao, as long as you do not mind the risk of swimming back to shore. You can rent them from the stalls in front of the Princess Mothers Park.

Doi Luang National Park   อุทยานแห่งชาติดอยหลวง

Declared a National Park in 1990, this park stretches over Lampang, Phayao and Chiang Mai Provinces. It is best known for its resident **Namtok Wang Kaeo** through which water cascades down 110 tiers. Besides this waterfall, the park has a number of others including **Namtok Champa Thong** which is in a very pleasant setting. There are also some caves. A number of hilltribe villages are also within the park's boundaries and wildlife is reported to be quite plentiful.

To reach the park under your own power, head north out of Phayao en-route to Chiang Rai on Route 1 for just under 20 km. The turn-off is on your left and clearly marked. From here it is about another 7 to 8 km down Route 1127 to Namtok Champa Thong.

◀**Arriving and Departing**▶

Getting Around

Phayao town is small enough to get around on by foot but a samlor ride within the town boundaries will cost around 10B.

Bus

The bus station is at the western end of town. To reach it follow Phahon Yothin Road and take the right turn just past Bungalow Siripan. The bus to **Nan** costs 72B for A/C and 52B for an ordinary one. To **Chiang Mai** it costs 71B for the A/C luxury and 51B for the regular bus and to **Chiang Rai** the ordinary bus costs 26B and takes around 2 hours. To **Bangkok** an ordinary bus costs 168B and takes 11 hours and an A/C bus costs 302B and takes 10 hours.

Picturesque Phayao

If you arrive in Phayao at the right time you will witness the beautiful purple coloured water hyacinth filling the lake. Locals use the stems to produce hats and baskets which can be purchased in the market.

AROUND PHAYAO

There are a number of sights worth visiting around this province, although if you do not have your own wheels the irregular public transport can make it a challenge.

Ban Huak Border Market   ฮวก

Around 100 km to the northeast of Phayao on the Laotion frontier, this bustling market is held only on the 10th and 30th of each month. It is mainly concerned with consumer goods, though you never know what you might pick up. To reach Ban Huak, catch a bus from the bus station to **Chiang Kham**, then catch a songtheaw the remainder of the way. It is only really worth trying to get here on the market days as otherwise it is a long trip with little reward except the scenery. If travelling under your own steam, leave Phayao heading south and take the left onto Route 1021 (which heads north). Follow this to **Chun** and continue along it to **Chiang Kham**. From Chiang Kham you will need to take Route 1210 and then right onto Route 1093 to reach the village. En-route you will pass **Phu Sang Waterfall** which has an 8 m drop and is 5 km shy of the village.

Thai Lua Tribes   ไทยลื้อ

The areas of Chiang Kham and Chiang Muan are both known for the Thai Lua tribe. These people create particularly impressive hand woven silk and cotton products which can be purchased at the villages or in the above mentioned towns. Outside of Chiang Kham the villagers have set up their own cultural centre where goods are available for purchase. Ask in Phayao for more details.

Northern Train Line Fares				
From Bangkok	**Fares without supplements (baht)**			
	Class			**Distance**
Station	**1st**	**2nd**	**3rd**	**km**
Don Muang Airport	18	10	5	22
Bang Pa-in	49	26	12	58
Ayutthaya	60	31	15	71
Lopburi	111	57	28	133
Nakhon Sawan	197	99	48	246
Phichit	266	131	63	347
Phitsanulok	292	143	69	389
Uttaradit	356	172	82	485
Den Chai	389	188	90	534
Lampang	463	221	106	642
Khun Tan	490	233	111	683
Lamphun	520	247	118	729
Chiang Mai	537	255	121	751

The Bus Blues

Thought you were safe in that bus? Well think again. Many Thai bus companies pay their drivers on a speed basis, ie, they are paid by the number of trips they can make in a day. This encourages dangerous and irresponsible driving, which too often manifests itself by the all too common sight of a bus rolled over on the side of the road. Hang on or close your eyes!!

Northern Train Line Timetable

Type and Class	R,23	O,3	S,2	S,2	R,23	S,2	X,23	R,23	X,123	S,2
Train Number	35	101	907	901	37	903	7	53	5	905
Supplements			A	A	A,B	A	A,B	A	A,B	A
Hualumpong	06.40	07.05	08.10	10.55	15.00	16.35	18.00	18.10	19.40	23.10
Don Muang Airport	07.27	07.51	08.52	11.33	15.47	17.13	18.45	18.57	20.25	23.49
Bang Pa-in		08.29								
Ayutthaya	08.10	08.42			16.27		19.25	19.35	21.05	
Lopburi	09.11	09.51	10.13		17.31		20.19	20.42		
Nakhon Sawan	10.53	12.01	11.35	14.14	19.10	20.05	21.56	22.18	23.31	03.08
Phichit	12.21	13.50	12.45	15.37	20.47	21.22	23.18	00.11		04.35
Phitsanulok	12.59	14.49	13.18	16.10	21.48	22.00	00.02	00.47		05.10
Uttaradit	14.32	16.47	14.21		23.02		01.24	02.21		
Den Chai	15.34	17.50	15.12		00.18		02.46	02.25	03.55	
Lampang	17.44		17.03		02.49		05.00		05.52	
Khun Tan	18.32				03.50		05.59		06.45	
Lamphun	19.15				04.35		06.45		07.34	
Chiang Mai	19.35		18.50		05.00		07.10		07.55	

X = Express, R = Rapid, O = Ordinary, (123) = Class of train, A = Air Conditioning, B = Sleeping Car

Northern Train Line Timetable

Type and Class	S,2	R,23	X,23	S,2	X,123	S,2	O,3	S,2	R,23	S,2
Train Number	906	38	8	908	6	902	102	930	36	904
Supplements		A,B	A,B	A	A,B	A		A		A
Chiang Mai		15.30	16.40	19.40	21.05			07.15	06.35	
Lamphun		15.51	17.01		21.21			07.36	07.02	
Khun Tan		16.39	17.55		22.17				07.55	
Lampang		17.46	18.59	21.15	23.04			08.56	08.41	
Den Chai		20.07	21.15	23.14	01.14		06.00	11.05	10.42	
Uttaradit		21.16	22.19	00.04			07.30	11.55	11.46	
Phitsanulok	22.45	22.53	23.34	01.07		08.50	09.24	13.16	13.32	16.55
Phichit	23.19	23.35	00.10	01.39		09.22	10.07		14.10	17.28
Nakhon Sawan	00.47	01.13	01.41	02.48	05.37	10.51	12.18	14.53	15.41	18.48
Lopburi		02.57	03.23				14.34	16.13	17.12	20.20
Ayutthaya		04.00	04.28		08.09		16.09		18.22	
Bang Pa-in							16.21			
Don Muang Airport	04.02	04.42	05.09	05.34	08.51	13.42	17.03	17.33	19.01	21.44
Hualumpong	04.45	05.25	06.00	06.15	09.40	14.20	17.50	18.10	19.50	22.25

X = Express, R = Rapid, O = Ordinary, (123) = Class of train, A = Air Conditioning, B = Sleeping Car

North

Crossword 1

Across
1 Buddhist belief / Wheel of _____
6 Ancient capital city from 1350 - 1767
7 Fruit with red hairy exterior
9 Also known as the Northeast
10 Other name for Khorat
13 Vendors sell from boats here
15 Celebration on 5 December
17 This king has a university named after him
18 Buddha sat under one when enlightened
19 Border crossing with Burma. Three __/__
22 Where the monarchy live in Bangkok
23 City pillar
24 English newspaper
25 Ayutthaya prospered under this king's rule and developed strong international links
26 Point where three countries meet

Down
1 Smelly but tasty fruit
2 Capital of Cambodia
3 Stone plaques placed around bot
4 Form of Thai drama
5 Translated Indian epic tale
8 King Rama IX's name
11 Collective term for people living in the mountains
12 Body of water to the east of Thailand
14 Bangkok wat with gold coloured chedi
20 Festival involving water fights
21 Thai word for canal

Answers at the back of the book

NORTHEAST THAILAND

Often ignored by the independent traveller to Thailand, the northeast region of Thailand, also known as I-san, is a wildly colourful and interesting area which is well worth exploring. Although lacking in some of the stronger tourist magnets such as beautiful beaches and large mountain ranges, I-san has a more subtle appeal, no better demonstrated than by the vista of the winding Maekhong River which lines much of the border area. The lack of tourism and tourists in this area is all the more reason to go, especially for those interested in a better look at a more unadulterated version of Thai *life and times*.

I-san covers almost one third of Thailand and some areas are bursting with worthwhile points of interest. Khao Yai National Park in Nakhon Ratchasima Province is viewed by many as being one of the best National Parks in the world and the spectacular ruins at Prasat Phanom Rung are arguably the best restored Khmer ruins in all of Thailand. The quaint sleepy riverside scenery along I-san's frontier with Laos is ideal for cyclists who can easily traverse much of the predominantly flat landscape. Festivals also play a big role in the area with Yasothon's Rocket Festival, Surin's elephant roundup, Phimai's boat racing, Ubon Ratchathani's Candle Festival and the highly regarded Songkran Festival celebrated throughout the province, each being a great reason for visiting the region.

The Northeast is made up of nineteen provinces: Amnat Charoen, Buriram, Chaiyaphum, Kalasin, Khon Kaen, Loei, Maha Sarakham, Mukdahan, Nakhon Ratchasima (Khorat), Nakhon Phanom, Nong Bua Lam Phu, Nong Khai, Roi Et, Sakhon Nakhon, Si Saket, Surin, Ubon Ratchathani, Udon Thani and Yasothon. All of these provinces are

easily visited and the provincial capitals each have a selection of hotels and restaurants as do many of the smaller towns. In some of the smaller, less visited provinces it can be difficult to find English speakers but that is just all the more opportunity to practise your Thai!

Highlights
Visiting **Prasat Hin Khao Phanom Rung** (Buriram Province).
A trip to That Phanom to see **Wat Phra That Phanom** (Nakhon Phanom Province).
Ban Chiang (Udon Thani Province).
Travelling around **Tha Li district** (Loei Province).
Khon Kaen Museum (Khon Kaen Province).

NAKHON RATCHASIMA PROVINCE (KHORAT PROVINCE)

Also known as Khorat, this province is Thailand's largest and the provincial capital, Nakhon Ratchasima (Khorat), is Thailand's second largest city. Regarded as the gateway to the northeast if arriving from Bangkok, Khorat province is generally the first place visitors stop within I-san as it is home to enough points of interest to keep most visitors busy for at least a few days. Best known for its high quality silk products, Nakhon Ratchasima Province is also home to the spectacular **Khao Yai National Park**, some well restored Khmer period ruins at **Prasat Phanom Rung** and **Phimai**, archeological digs and the famed pottery at **Dan Kwian**.

PAK CHONG   ปากช่อง

Pak Chong is little more than a collection of buildings on each side of Route 2 and holds virtually nothing of interest to the traveller. Despite this, Pak Chong gets a steady trickle of visitors who use it as a base for visiting nearby Khao Yai National Park, which is widely considered as one of the best National Parks in the world.

A word of warning, there are a number of different agents running tours of the park from Pak Chong and the quality of tours vary immensely. We have had first hand experience at the hands of the high profile Jungle Adventures mob and would advise that if you are looking for a serious look at the park, you consider looking elsewhere. If you arrive by train, expect to be met by touts who, despite all they say, are paid commission if you go with them.

Cheap Sleeps

Khao Yai Garden Lodge, ☎ (044) 313 567, this place is a bit out of town but they will organise free transport if you give them a call from the train station. They also have an office by the station (which you cannot miss) and if they are open you save 5B on the phone. The management is German and their rooms start at 100B. Their tour of Khao Yai National Park gets very good reviews.
Phubade Hotel is just up the road from the station and has noisy rooms for 200B.
Guesthouse on Tesaban 19, located up the grimy stairs on the right hand side. This 'on again off again' place has rooms that match the stairs for 80B.
Jungle Adventures and Guesthouse is at 63 Tesaban 16, Soi 3, and is run by some of the most unscrupulous and deceptive people you will meet in Thailand. If you do not do their tour, expect to be refused a room, "No tour - No room" was what they said to us. Their rooms are dingy, uncomfortable and generally neglected. It costs 80B per person including a generous breakfast. We have heard reports of the management here turning away single travellers at 2.00 am because the visitor was unwilling to book and pay for a trip on the spot!

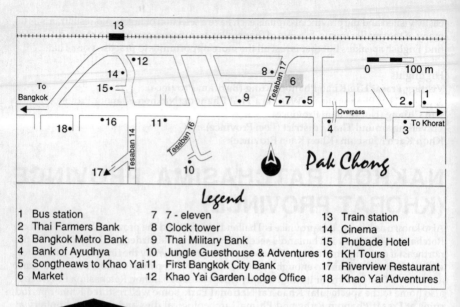

Legend

1	Bus station	7	7 - eleven	13	Train station
2	Thai Farmers Bank	8	Clock tower	14	Cinema
3	Bangkok Metro Bank	9	Thai Military Bank	15	Phubade Hotel
4	Bank of Ayudhya	10	Jungle Guesthouse & Adventures	16	KH Tours
5	Songtheaws to Khao Yai	11	First Bangkok City Bank	17	Riverview Restaurant
6	Market	12	Khao Yai Garden Lodge Office	18	Khao Yai Adventures

Eat and Meet

Tesaban 17 has a large night market if you are after a cheap feed. If you want to spend a little more, try **Riverview Restaurant** down a soi off Tesaban 14. It has good food with English menus and the price ranges from 25B to 200B.

Arriving and Departing

Train

The train station is one block back from the main road through town. A 3rd class seat on a regular train to **Ayutthaya** costs 23B and to **Bangkok** 36B. For detailed price and timetable information refer to the end of the chapter.

Bus

Buses pass through town and can be waved down easily or you can go to the bus station, which is at the eastern end of town, just past the Thai Farmers Bank. A bus to **Nakhon Ratchasima (Khorat)** is 24B and to **Bangkok** 80B. To Khao Yai National Park, songtheaw number 1317 departs from near the intersection with Tesaban 19 every 30 minutes and costs 15B.

AROUND PAK CHONG

Khao Yai National Park   อุทยานแห่งชาติเขาใหญ่

Khao Yai National Park is Thailand's second largest National Park, covering 2,168 sq km along the Panomdongrak Mountain Range and straddling four provinces, Nakhon Ratchasima, Nakhon Nayok, Saraburi and Prachinburi. Khao Yai was Thailand's first National Park, established on 18 September 1962. Within the park's boundaries are the sources of five important waterways, over 300 species of birds, 2,500 varieties of fauna including wild elephants, tigers, gibbons, pig tailed macaques, serows, sambar deers, horn bills and bats. The landscape of the park includes grassland on its fringe and everything up to dense tropical rainforest in its centre. The park also has numerous waterfalls, with **Namtok Heow Narok** and **Namtok Heo Suwat** undoubtedly two of the highlights of the park.

This stunning park is easily accessible if you have your own transport or join a tour. Hitching into the park can be frustrating and time consuming as the traffic into the park is light at times. If you do try to hitch in, the weekends are your best bet as the weekend Thai visitors will increase your chances of a lift.

The park headquarters is in the middle of the heavily pot-holed road which extends from near Pak Chong in the north to between Nakhon Nayok and Prachinburi in the south. The office is 40 km from Pak Chong, 61 km from Nakhon Nayok and 46 km from Prachinburi. It is worth using this road if you are travelling in between any of the above destinations as it passes some magnificent forest along the way. Admission is payable upon entrance to the park at either end and is 25B per person and 100B for private cars.

Cheap Sleeps

Khao Yai National Park has various levels of accommodation around the park headquarters ranging from camping through to comfortable bungalows.

Camping Two person tents can be hired from the park headquarters for 80B per night, three person tents cost 150B and four person tents cost 160B. You will need to bring a sleeping bag and blanket as it can get quite cold at night. In the rainy season you are almost guaranteed some rain during the day and night. The only problem is that the official camping ground is 8 km from the park headquarters towards Namtok Heo Suwat and can be reached by hitching there via the road or by a 7 km walk along the main trail.

Longhouses Basic bunkers are available at a few camps in the park. The closest is 200 m from the park office and costs 10B per person. There are others about 1 km from the park headquarters which cost 20B per person. No pillows or blankets are available so come prepared.

Lodges A few lodges are run by the National Park authorities which cost 1,200B and can sleep up to twelve people.

Eat and Meet

Food is available at the park headquarters, at Heo Sawat and Heo Narok. If you are camping or staying in bunkers or lodges and lack your own transport, take your own food to keep the hunger pangs away.

Things to do and Sights to See

Walks

Walking trails have been made around the park headquarters and police station which is 3 km down the road. These range from trekking trails and 'eco-tourism' trails to more developed mass tourism trails. Most lead to one of the many waterfalls and range from a few hundred metres to 8 km in length.

Mountain Bikes

Basic mountain bikes with Shimano gears and accessories can be rented from the park headquarters for 40B per hour for the first three hours, 20B per hour after that or 250B for the whole day. The bike offers a very interactive way to experience the beauty of the park, however they can only be used on the roads. This creates a problem because most sights are well off the road. For those sights that are actually close to the road, they are located quite far from the park headquarters where you hire the bikes and only accessible via many hilly roads, thus transforming your enjoyable 'pedal cruise' into sweat induced torture.

Namtok Heo Suwat   น้ำตกเหวสุวัต

Located 13 km from the park headquarters on its own very hilly access road, this waterfall is one of the park's better attractions. In the rainy season a raging torrent of water gracefully pours over a 30 m cliff, plummeting into a pool of whitewash and spray. A path leads to both the top and bottom of the waterfall and any attempt at swimming in the wet season would be dealt with by the laws of nature.

Namtok Heo Narok   น้ำตกเหวนรก

This waterfall is the highlight of the park. Literally translated it means 'chasm of hell' and once you see it in the flesh, you will realise how appropriate this name is. A 1 km path leads through the forest from the car park which takes you to the waterfall's base. Bring some soap and on a good day have a shower as the spray from the falls will have you dripping in seconds. The top of the falls gives no indication of the power of the falls below, as the river falls about 50 m in a single drop and then cascades down another 150 m. In the dry season the waterfall loses much of its impact but is impressive nevertheless. The scenery here is particularly beautiful with the river continuing on through dense forest.

Namtok Heo Narok is at the southern end of the access road, 24 km from the park office or 16 km from the turn-off along the southern entry road on Route 3077, 11 km past the boom-gates.

Treks and Tours

Most farangs visit the park from Pak Chong where a number of travel agents organise tours. Enquire at Khao Yai Garden Lodge or Jungle Adventures (if you are really desperate) for details. (See Pak Chong Cheap Sleeps for contact details). Overnight treks are also available in the dry season from December to June for one and two nights, starting at Nang Rong Waterfall. For more details contact the Tourist Authority of Thailand (TAT) at Nakhon Nayok on ☎ (037) 312 284. From the park headquarters you can go wildlife spotting at night for 300B per songtheaw. These short excursions last about an hour.

◄ **Arriving and Departing** ►

From Nakhon Nayok and Prachinburi

Access to Khao Yai National Park is easiest with your own transport. If you do not have your own wheels and do not go by organised tour, then it will likely become quite expensive to reach this spot. From Nakhon Nayok catch a bus to the turn-off at the large roundabout on Route 3077, 16 km from Nakhon Nayok and 11 km from Prachinburi. From here songtheaws can be rented for a minimum of 300B for the 40 km trip into the park office. If you can, try to get the songtheaw to take a break at Heo Narok Waterfall on the way in. If you cannot afford the songtheaw, hitching can be very slow with weekends offering the best opportunity for frequent traffic.

From Pak Chong

If trying to reach the park by public transport, songtheaw number 1317 departs from near the intersection with Tesaban 19 every 30 minutes and costs 15B. Or you can hire your own songtheaw for around 300B to 400B.

NAKHON RATCHASIMA (KHORAT)

นครราชสีมา (โคราช)

This bustling city is one of Thailand's largest and is well on its way to becoming the major industrial centre of the region. During the Vietnam War, Khorat was the site of one of the large US Air Bases from where missions over Laos, Cambodia and Vietnam were flown.

Today there is little of the American influence remaining, however, there is still the VFW Cafe and a small group of retired Vietnam veterans hanging around town. Within Khorat there is little to see which would keep you busy for more than a day, but there are a number of places around Khorat which are worth visiting and for this Khorat makes an ideal base.

The **Thao Suranari Fair** is an annual event that takes place for almost two weeks at the end of March. The fair is in memory of a local heroine who in the 1800s gathered the local residents to successfully ward off foreign invaders. The townsfolk celebrate with processions through the streets and cultural exhibitions.

Vital Information

Tourist Office, ☎ (044) 243 751, is on Mittaphap Road, a good hike out from the centre of town. The helpful staff can supply you with brochures on Khorat and the surrounding provinces. It is open daily 8.30 am to 4.30 pm and the tourist police are just around the corner.
Post Office There are two central post offices in Khorat. One on Atsadang Road, the other on Chomsurangyat Road. The office on Atsadang Road has ISD call facilities.
Banks Are mainly located along Mittaphap and Chomphon Roads. See the map for details.
Hospitals There is a hospital on Suranari Road and health clinics spread throughout town.
Codes Khorat's telephone code is (044) and the postal code is 30000.

Cheap Sleeps

There is a wide range of fairly cheap hotels in the centre of Khorat and one guesthouse a way out of town near the tourist office.
Doctors House at 78 Soi 4, Seup Siri Road, this fairly quiet guesthouse has large doubles with fan and share bathroom for 160B and breakfast is available. Take an upstairs room if you can to avoid being woken early by the nattering staff. Take a yellow songtheaw out to here and get off just before Cabbages and Condoms - look for the small blue sign on your right.
Siri Hotel at 167-8 Phoklang Road, ☎ (044) 242 831, this large hotel is fairly central and pretty quiet (by Khorat's standards). The higher you go, the cheaper it gets. Singles/doubles with fan and shower are 130B/150B and every room has complimentary soap, towels and condoms. The VFW Cafe is next door.
Patong Hotel on Ratchadamnoen Road is very central and very noisy. Liveable rooms cost 150B for a single, 200B for a double.
Fah Sang Hotel at 112-114 Mukkhamontri Road, ☎ (044) 242 143, has double rooms with fan starting at 200B. The Siri Hotel has better rooms, though the staff are friendlier here.
Thai Phokaphan Hotel on Atsadang Road is fairly central and not too noisy. Rooms with fan here are 150B.
Tokyo Hotel 1 & 2 are both on Suranari Road, and offer clean rooms with fan starting at 200B.
Muang Thong Hotel is on Chumphon Road near the market and museum. The building is nice, the rooms are not and 90B will get you a noisy and dingy one. This place is really only for the real budgeters.

Eat and Meet

One thing Khorat does have to offer is good and affordable food. Both the **Hua Rot Fai Market** (near the train station) and the **Manat Road Market** are good sources for cheap tasty evening meals.
Kai Yang Wang Fa on Ratchadamnoen Road has a cheap (though limited) menu and is a great place for people watching.
For **I-san Food**, there is a good place on Seup Siri Road, nearly opposite the soi to the Doctors

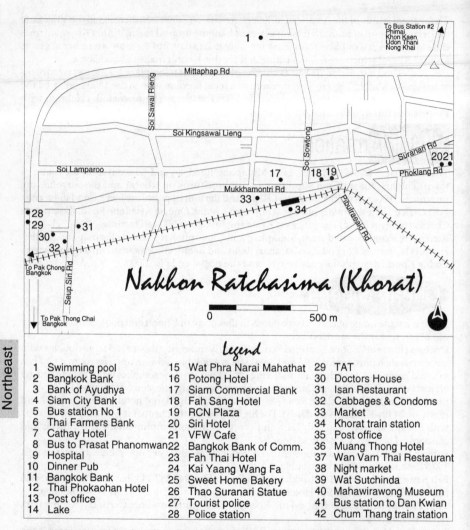

Nakhon Ratchasima (Khorat)

Legend

1	Swimming pool	15 Wat Phra Narai Mahathat	29 TAT
2	Bangkok Bank	16 Potong Hotel	30 Doctors House
3	Bank of Ayudhya	17 Siam Commercial Bank	31 Isan Restaurant
4	Siam City Bank	18 Fah Sang Hotel	32 Cabbages & Condoms
5	Bus station No 1	19 RCN Plaza	33 Market
6	Thai Farmers Bank	20 Siri Hotel	34 Khorat train station
7	Cathay Hotel	21 VFW Cafe	35 Post office
8	Bus to Prasat Phanomwan	22 Bangkok Bank of Comm.	36 Muang Thong Hotel
9	Hospital	23 Fah Thai Hotel	37 Wan Varn Thai Restaurant
10	Dinner Pub	24 Kai Yaang Wang Fa	38 Night market
11	Bangkok Bank	25 Sweet Home Bakery	39 Wat Sutchinda
12	Thai Phokaohan Hotel	26 Thao Suranari Statue	40 Mahawirawong Museum
13	Post office	27 Tourist police	41 Bus station to Dan Kwian
14	Lake	28 Police station	42 Chum Thang train station

House. The *laap kai* is very nice, and the chef speaks excellent English.

Cabbages and Condoms is also on Seup Siri Road. It is a branch of the original in Bangkok, offering excellent food and is not excessively expensive with the profits of the restaurant going to AID's awareness, research and help. The staff are very helpful and meals cost 100B to 150B per head including a beer.

Wan Varn Thai on Mahat Thai Road has very good Thai food in a relaxed atmosphere. It is pricey but not exorbitant.

VFW Cafe on Phoklang Road is the place to come to step into a time warp for a while. Vietnam vets huddle in the centre whilst surly staff throw cheap but not bad Western food at you. The portions are generous and the burgers are decent. This place is straight out of the sitcoms – grease and all. If you want to swap books here, "CIA mission to Burindi" was available during our last visit!!

Other **Western food** such as KFC and Dunkin Donuts can be found in the big department stores in the centre of town.

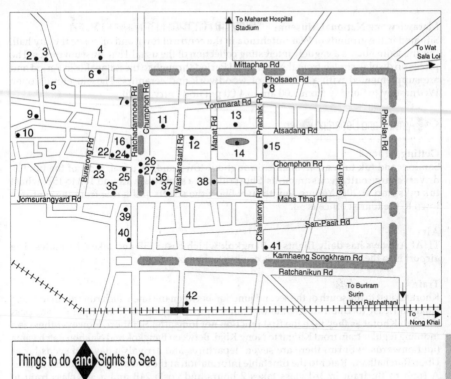

Things to do ◆ and ◆ Sights to See

Thao Suranari Memorial   อนุสาวรีย์ท้าวสุรนารี

This shrine at the Chumphon gate was built in 1934 and is dedicated to the Thai woman, Khun Ying Mo, who, in 1826 during the reign of King Rama III, led the locals into battle against the marauding Laotian forces of Prince Anuwong. Her actions helped to save the city. The shrine is highly revered and many people place offerings at its base and drape the statue with ribbons in the hope of good luck. From 23 March to 3 April there is a celebration in honour of Khun Ying Ho which attracts thousands of people.

Wat Phra Narai Maharat   วัดพระนารายณ์มหาราช

The wat is on Prachak Road to the east of the main drag and houses the city pillar and an image of the Hindu God Narayana, both extremely highly revered in Khorat. The wat is set in the centre of an artificial lake and is particularly photogenic in the late afternoon when it is beautifully reflected by the lowering sun. Just to the south of the entrance to the wat is a four storey mural representing the history of Khorat which has been made from tiles manufactured in nearby Dan Kwian.

Wat Sala Loi   วัดศาลาลอย

This wat, built in 1973, is a little out of town but is worth a visit if you want to see a different style wat. While most modern wats in Thailand repeat the tried and tested style of design, Wat Sala Loi dares to be different. Shaped like a Chinese junk symbolising the passage of devotees to Nirvana, the wat certainly succeeds in looking more stable than your average longtail. The wat sits on the banks of the Lam Takhong River and has been the recipient of several design awards.

Marawirwong National Museum   พิธิภัณฑ์สถานแห่งชาติมหาวีรวงศ์

Situated in the grounds of **Wat Sutchinda** in the centre of town and opposite the city hall, this museum houses a vaguely interesting collection of the usual Thai museum pieces. The pieces on display stretch from the Dvaravati Period through to the Ratanakosin Period and are supplemented with a selection of woodwork and ceramics. The museum is open Wednesday to Sunday from 9.00 am to 4.00 pm and entry is 10B.

Getting Around

Samlors and tuk tuks are available throughout town and, as usual, most of the tuk tuk drivers charge outrageous amounts. Short rides in a samlor are around 10B to 15B, whilst tuk tuks start at 20B. Yellow songtheaws blaze the streets and a ride from the centre of town to the tourist office is 3B.

Air

THAI Airways has daily flights to **Bangkok** which cost 555B and take 40 minutes. The airport is to the south of town and is easily reached by tuk tuk.

Train

Khorat is just to the south of the second junction between the line which runs north to Nong Khai and east to Ubon Ratchathani. Trains from Bangkok to Nong Khai do not pass through Khorat as they take the first junction not long after Saraburi. However there is a morning regular train from Khorat to Nong Khai. Between Bangkok and Nakhon Ratchasima (and onwards to Surin) there are seven departures and arrivals a day and six as far as Ubon Ratchathani. Refer to the timetable information at the end of the chapter for details. A train to **Buriram** in 3rd class takes 2 hours and costs 24B and a 3rd class train to **Bangkok** costs 50B and takes around 5 hours. For more detailed price and timetable information refer to the end of the chapter.

Bus

Khorat has two main bus terminals. Bus terminal 1 on Burin Road serves Bangkok and nearby provinces as well as the far north. Bus Terminal 2 located out of town on Route 2 serves northern I-san. Check with your hotel or ask a tuk tuk driver before deciding on which terminal to head for. Sample fares include: **Bangkok** 64B, **Phimai** 16B, **Surin** 45B, **Khon Kaen** 40B, **Pak Chong** 24B, **Chaiyaphum** 33B, **Loei** 95B, **Si Chiang Mai** 95B, **Udon Thani** 85B and **Buriram** 40B - buses to these places leave throughout the day. An A/C bus to **Bangkok** costs 115B and takes about 3½ hours.

There are a number of smaller bus stops in town, notably servicing **Dan Kwian** and **Prasat Phanom Wan**. See the particular section or the map for details.

AROUND NAKHON RATCHASIMA

Dan Kwian   บ้านด่านเกวียน

If you are interested in Thai ceramics, this is the place you need to visit. Dan Kwian apparently translates to 'by-pass area of bullcarts' and sits around 14 km to the north of Khorat. This ceramics village has been producing pottery for hundreds of years, its main claim to fame being the unique texture of the clay used which is supposedly super tough. Much of the ceramics produced is exported and what is left behind is available to you at very reasonable prices. Just remember anything you buy you will have to carry or post! Lots of ceramic jewellery and nick-nacks are available as well as bowls, plates and six foot high pots. A packing service is also available.

Ban Pak Thong Chai   ปักธงชัย

If pottery is not your go, then how about silk? Pak Thong Chai is well known for turning out top notch silk, and even if you are not a buyer it is still worth visiting simply to observe the whole silk production system at work. There are over 70 silk factories working away in this area and much of the silk produced is earmarked for export. If you are a buyer, prices are not too expensive — not dissimilar to the prices in Khorat itself, although Pak Thong Chai is becoming a bit of a tourist centre.

To get there jump on bus number 1303 from bus terminal 1 on Burin Road. It takes about 45 minutes to reach Ban Pak Thong Chai and costs 11B. If you were really cooking, you could visit both Ban Dan Kwian and Ban Pak Thong Chai in a day (including a break in Khorat for lunch and a change of bus).

Ban Prasat   บ้านปราสาท

This archeological dig has a fascinating display on site of various skeletons and pottery items which have been excavated in the surrounds. Six hundred year old skeletons have been found at a depth of between 1½ m to 2 m, whilst truly ancient bones going back as far as 3,000 years have been found at a depth of 3½ m to 4 m. The museum on site is open 9.00 am to 4.00 pm from Wednesday to Sunday.

To get there catch a bus bound for Khon Kaen or Phimai (number 1305) and leap off at Ban Prasat for 10B. From there catch a motorcycle taxi to the site which is a couple of kilometres away.

PHIMAI   พิมาย

If you are in Khorat, this is one place you should not miss. The town itself is a fairly sleepy hideaway graced with some nice restaurants and cheap guesthouses. However it is the very impressive ruins of Prasat Hin Phimai which steal the show. It is relatively easy to visit Phimai on a long day trip from Khorat, but for those wanting to experience the town in a little more depth, an overnight stay is both easy and pleasurable.

Vital Information

Tourist Information The Bai Toey Restaurant on Chomsudasapet Road has a few maps and tips which would be of interest. All is free.
Post Office is on Vonprang Road to the east of the ruins. ISD facilities are available.
Codes Phimai's telephone code is (044) and the postal code is 30110.

Cheap Sleeps

The first two listed guesthouses are hidden down a short soi towards the ruins from the Bai Toey Restaurant.
Old Phimai Guesthouse, rooms here are 90B/120B for a single/double with share bathroom. The staff are very friendly and the wall on your left as you enter is a great source of information.
S & P New Phimai Guesthouse has similar rooms for 80B/100B for a single/double with share bathroom.
Hostelling International Guesthouse at 125/1 A-Raksuksit Road is past the post office. It is very easy to wander up and down the road without seeing this place. Dorms cost 60B, singles are 80B, doubles are 100B and normal hostel restrictions apply.
Phimai Hotel is beside the bus station and has basic hotel rooms that start at 120B for a single, 180B double and 220B with shower. The guesthouses are a better deal.

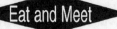

Eat and Meet

Bai Toey Restaurant on Chomsudasapet Road offers a reasonably priced English menu in fairly quiet surroundings. Try the Phimai fried noodles — tasty!

Things to do and Sights to See

Prasat Hin Phimai Historical Park   ปราสาทหินพิมาย

Thought to have been at one time a provincial capital of the Kingdom of Angkor, this large sandstone sanctuary has been very well restored and gives the visitor a true impression of how splendid it must have once appeared. It is believed that the Khmers were not the first to settle in Phimai, and considering its placement on the bank of the Mun River, its strategic positioning was not overlooked by the original settlers. At one time linked by road to the magnificent site of Angkor Wat, Phimai is believed to have been originally constructed upon a Hindu site during the reign of the Khmer King Jayavarman VII.

The site is enclosed within two red sandstone walls which are split by four gates, one at each of the cardinal points, north, south, east and west. Somewhat strangely for an

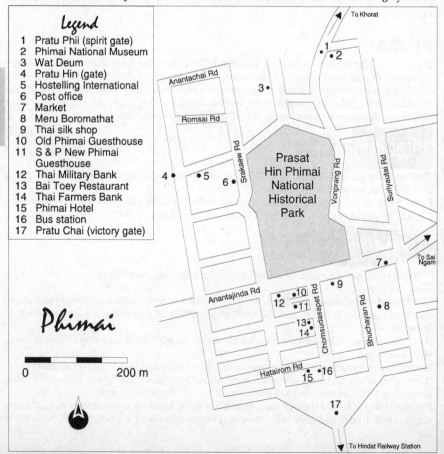

Legend

1. Pratu Phii (spirit gate)
2. Phimai National Museum
3. Wat Deum
4. Pratu Hin (gate)
5. Hostelling International
6. Post office
7. Market
8. Meru Boromathat
9. Thai silk shop
10. Old Phimai Guesthouse
11. S & P New Phimai Guesthouse
12. Thai Military Bank
13. Bai Toey Restaurant
14. Thai Farmers Bank
15. Phimai Hotel
16. Bus station
17. Pratu Chai (victory gate)

Phimai

0   200 m

Northeast

Angkor period monument, Phimai sanctuary faces to the south whilst most Angkorian constructions face the east. Dominating the scene is a 28 m high white sandstone prang, flanked to its left by a smaller laterite prang and to its right by a red sandstone prang. The main sanctuary has some stunning lintels carved with decorative Hindu reliefs, whilst the interior carvings have a more Buddhist flavour to them. Perhaps a site of mingling but not always coexisting beliefs. Within the grounds of the park is a small museum with a selection of archeological remains found in the area. The park is open daily from 7.30 am to 6.00 pm, admission is 20B.

Phimai National Museum
Opened in 1993, Phimai National Museum was originally an open air collection of relics which had been recovered from archeological sites located all over the surrounding areas including Prasat Phanonwan, Phanom Rung, Ban Prasat and Phimai. There is also a small bookstore on the premises. Admission is 20B and it is open Wednesday to Sunday.

Sai Ngam   ไทรงาม
'Beautiful Banyan Tree' is 2 km out of town, approachable by bicycle, foot or samlor. Intricately entwined banyan trees create oodles of shade for those hot days. Great place to sink a few Singha beers, but you have to take them with you.

Prasat Phanomwan   ปราสาทหินพนมวัน
If you plan to visit here it is best done before visiting Phimai as you may otherwise find yourself disappointed at the partially restored pile of rubble resting here. Although a restoration project here is still ongoing, Prasat Phanomwan certainly does not rival Phimai for its outstanding structures and many find the nearby wat to be more interesting. The ruins have been dated back to the 11th Century and were originally dedicated to Shiva although it is suspected that the ruins have been renovated on a number of occasions before ending up in their present state.

◀ Arriving and Departing ▶

Phimai and Prasat Phanomwan can easily be visited in a day from Khorat as long as you are willing to make an early start. Go to Phanomwan first then continue onto Phimai.
    Catch songtheaw number 4139 from the Pratunam city gate (on Phonsaen Road). This truck goes directly past Phanomwan, leaving Khorat at 07.10, 07.50 and 10.00, the fare is 7B. After surveying the ruins and the nearby wat, you will need to hitch back to Route 2 (most of the locals are eager to pick you up because farangs are crazy). Once back on Route 2, flag down a bus going north to Phimai, the fare from Khorat is 16B, expect all sorts of weird permutations as they calculate the farang rate for a shorter distance, anything from 10B to 16B. The bus takes 1½ hours to reach Phimai leaving you heaps of time to check out the ruins and museum before catching the last bus back to Khorat at 6.00 pm.

BURIRAM PROVINCE
Buriram is one of the Northeast's more populous provinces. Although predominantly rural, Buriram played an important part in the ancient Kingdom of Angkor and this role is reflected by an abundance of Khmer period sites in the province. The provincial capital of the same name contains precious little of interest to the traveller, but is a convenient jumping off point for the province's top attraction - the fantastic Angkor monuments of Prasat Hin Khao Phanom Rung and Prasat Muang Tham. Besides these two outstanding monuments, the province is littered with smaller secondary sites which, as restoration efforts continue, may become worth visiting. If you are in the vicinity around April, try to get to the Phanom Rung Festival at Prasat Hin Khao Phanom Rung (see below for details).

Northeast

BURIRAM   บุรีรัมย์

Little more than a small provincial centre, Buriram or 'City of Happiness', has little to offer unless you are specifically searching for plain country life, Thai style. Arguably the most 'interesting' thing to see in Buriram is the clocktower which stands in front of the train station. It has four clock faces at the top, each of which show a different and incorrect time.

Once you get over the amazing clock face the best thing to do is jump on a bus bound for the not too far away site of Prasat Hin Khao Phanom Rung. If you are in the area around mid April you will be able to participate in the Phanom Rung Festival. A light and sound show is the highlight of the whole day dedicated to merit making and festivities at the ancient Khmer site. The celebration is held on the full moon day of the 5th lunar month, during which the site is packed to the rafters. Highly Recommended.

Vital Information

Post Office is on Romburi Road just to the south of the clocktower.
Banks All the major banks have branches on Thani Road and Sontornthep Road.
Codes The area code for Buriram is (044) and the postcode is 31000.

Cheap Sleeps

The choice of hotels in Buriram is limited and they are generally of a very low standard.
Thai Hotel at 38/1 Romburi Road, ☎ (044) 611 112, is definitely the pick of the bunch. Clean and quiet rooms with fan and shower on the fourth floor (no elevator) start at 170B.
Grand Hotel at 137 Niwas Road, ☎ (044) 611 089, has doubles with A/C and shower starting at 250B but the staff are decidedly unfriendly.
Prachasamakkee Hotel on Sunthonthep Road, ☎ (044) 611 198, opposite the Thai Farmers Bank. Basic rooms with fan start at 80B.

Eat and Meet

Ploy Restaurant at 37/1-5 Romburi Road, south of the Thai Hotel on the other side of the road has a comprehensive English menu with reasonable prices. There is a swimming pool out back.
Night Market on Thani Road has a good selection of noodle and rice vendors as does the market to the left (on exiting) of the train station.

Things to do and Sights to See

Khao Kradong
This extinct volcano lies around 6 km from town and is the site of Khao Kradong Park. It is possible to drive to the peak, or the more energetic can hike up the 265 stairs which lead to the Phra Suphatthara Bophit image, a large shining white Buddha sitting at the top, as well as Prang Ku. At the base of the extinct volcano is a lake which is a popular place amongst the locals for chilling out and lying around. It is possible to reach the site by tuk tuk or songtheaw from the bus station.

Festivals
Buriram is home to a number of festivals which, if you are in the vicinity, are worth popping in to see. The **Buriram Kite Festival** is held in the second week of December and features kites of a minimum size of 2 m wide as well as a kite parade at the end of the day. The festival also features a beauty pageant and a procession of all the signs of the zodiac.

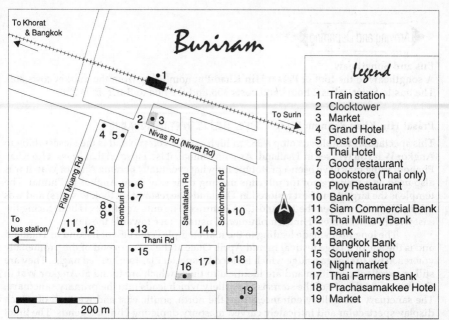

Buriram

To Khorat & Bangkok

To Surin

To bus station

Nivas Rd (Niwat Rd)

Plad Muang Rd

Romburi Rd

Samatakan Rd

Sontornthep Rd

Thani Rd

Legend	
1	Train station
2	Clocktower
3	Market
4	Grand Hotel
5	Post office
6	Thai Hotel
7	Good restaurant
8	Bookstore (Thai only)
9	Ploy Restaurant
10	Bank
11	Siam Commercial Bank
12	Thai Military Bank
13	Bank
14	Bangkok Bank
15	Souvenir shop
16	Night market
17	Thai Farmers Bank
18	Prachasamakkee Hotel
19	Market

0   200 m

The **Buriram Regatta** is held during the first weekend of November on the Moon River in Satuk District to the northeast of Buriram town. The awards after this race are given by the King himself and there is also a parade of boats which takes place after the race.

The biggest and most spectacular festival is the **Phanom Rung Festival** held at Prasat Hin Khao Phanom Rung on the full moon day of the 5th lunar month (around April). During this festival thousands pack the site for a parade and brilliant light and sound show at night.

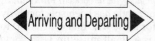

Arriving and Departing

Train

The train station is at the centre of town and there are 7 through trains each way a day between Surin and Bangkok and 6 a day through to Ubon Ratchathani. Refer to the timetable at the end of this chapter for details. A third class train to **Nakhon Ratchasima** is 24B and takes 2 hours.

Bus

The bus station is a ten minute samlor ride from the train station. A bus to **Khorat** costs 40B and takes 2 to 2½ hours, **Bangkok** is 79B and **Nang Rong** is 20B. An A/C bus to **Bangkok** costs 179B and takes about 6½ hours.

AROUND BURIRAM

Nang Rong   นางรอง

If Buriram does not tickle your fancy, go to Nang Rong. Little more than a crossroads, Nang Rong has even less attractions than Buriram but is much closer to Prasat Hin Khao Phanom Rung. Although keep an eye out for the crazy guitar playing Thai guy who loves The Eagles and is always willing to play his tunes for you at 3.00 am. For accommodation try the no name **Hotel**, two blocks back from the main road. It has big, fairly clean rooms with fan and shower for 120B but not a word of English is spoken here. The road leading up to the main road has a few noodle and rice shops which all do good and tasty cheap food for 10B to 15B.

Northeast

◀**Arriving and Departing**▶

Bus and Songtheaw

A songtheaw to the foot of **Prasat Hin Khao Phanom Rung** from the market costs 30B. The bus to **Surin** takes 2 hours and costs 30B and the bus to **Buriram** is 20B.

Prasat Hin Khao Phanom Rung   อุทยานประวัติศาสตร์พนมรุ้ง

This spectacular temple sits atop a 383 m high extinct volcano and is the closest thing to Angkor Wat you will see in Thailand. As with Phimai, it is suspected that Prasat Hin Khao Phanom Rung may have been a prototype for what eventually became Angkor Wat. It was also used as a resting spot for pilgrims making their way from Angkor to Phimai. The temple is the largest and best restored in Thailand (the restoration took 17 years) and was originally built between the 10th and 13th Centuries. The entire complex is built facing the east which, as with most Hindu monuments, usually face towards the dawn.

The long promenade leading to the main temple is the best of its kind in Thailand and is the site of a large festival in mid April. Once at the western end of the promenade you reach the first naga bridge which is sided by spectacular five headed nagas. They are still in excellent condition and are identical to those which are found at Angkor Wat in Cambodia. At the top of the stairs is the gallery which leads into the primary sanctuary. The sanctuary has gallery entrances from the north, south, east and west, all of which display spectacular and intricately carved masonry depicting Hindu legends. The lintel above the eastern entrance is the most famous. After being stolen in the 1960s it resurfaced in a display at the Art Institute of Chicago where it looked like it was going to stay, but thankfully it was eventually returned to its rightful home in 1988. Only after supporters of the cause had raised over $200,000 to 'facilitate' its return and had mounted a high profile campaign, the highlight of which was the album released by the band Carabao titled *Thap Lang* (Lintel). On the cover of the album was a picture of the Statue of Liberty holding the lintel and the song went along the lines of '*Take back your Michael Jackson, just give us back our Phra Narai*!'.

The central prang although built in a typical Khmer style has been spectacularly restored and is particularly photogenic in the mornings for those who make the effort to beat the tours and get there early. Near the site, there is a small museum with some sculpture from the site along with an interesting photographic essay of the restoration and a small selection of literature.

During early April a festival, the Phanom Rung Festival, is held here with traditional dance and fireworks along with a spectacular light and sound show in the evening. The site is open every day and admission is 20B.

It is a bit of an effort to get to Prasat Hin Khao Phanom Rung, but well worth it. If possible avoid weekends when the whole area is packed with Thais and not particularly conducive to a quiet appreciation of the site - 'Hey Farang!' During the festival in April it is packed solid (but the festival is worth seeing). Early morning (before 10.00 am) offers the best light for photography.

◀**Arriving and Departing**▶

Phanom Rung can be approached from Khorat, Buriram, Surin or nearby Nang Rong. From **Khorat**, **Buriram** or **Surin** catch a bus to Tapek which is 11 km to the east of Ban Ta Ko. It is well signposted as the turn-off to Phanom Rung. Get off the bus there and wait for a songtheaw which runs to the foot of the hill and costs 15B. The songtheaws can be quite infrequent (especially on weekdays) so if your patience gets the better of you, catch a motorcycle straight to the ruins which will cost 100B to 150B for a round trip including waiting for you - do *not* pay up front. If you get a songtheaw to the foot of the hill you can then get a motorbike taxi up and back for 50B to 100B. On weekends, songtheaws will take you up for 10B each way.

If you come from **Nang Rung**, catch a songtheaw straight to the foot of the hill. These leave from the market and cost 30B, most are clearly marked as running to Phanom Rung. Once at the bottom of the hill you will have to catch another songtheaw or motorbike to the top.

Prasat Muang Tam   ปราสาทหินเมืองต่ำ

Situated about 6 km or 7 km to the south of Prasat Hin Khao Phanom Rung, this site is in average condition although restoration work is ongoing. As with Prasat Hin Khao Phanom Rung there are some excellent examples of stone carvings, especially naga heads. The entire site has been dated to the 10th Century and despite its somewhat rundown state, it serves as a good example of what Prasat Hin Khao Phanom Rung must have looked like before restoration began. Admission is 20B. If you plan to visit, it is probably better seen before Phanom Rung to avoid disappointment. If travelling by motorcycle to Prasat Hin Khao Phanom Rung, a motorcycle taxi should take you the extra distance for an extra 40B to 50B.

SURIN PROVINCE

Bordered by Buriram, Si Saket, Roi Et and Cambodia, this province is best known as the home of the world famous elephant roundup. Besides the roundup, Surin is also home to numerous silk villages and the atmospheric ruins of Prasat Ta Meuan. The people here are a mix of Thai, Khmer, Lao and Suay and as long as you are not in town during the elephant roundup, you have a good chance of being just about the only farang around.

SURIN   สุรินทร์

Surin town is a nice town inhabited by very friendly people. Of particular note within the town itself is Surin's excellent market which is quite large and runs virtually 24 hours a day reaching its peak just before dawn.

During this century the need for elephants as labourers has steadily declined from figures of around 100,000 at the turn of the century to around four to five thousand today. This decline accelerated dramatically with the decision to ban logging in Thailand, as the elephants would serve as labourers, pulling out the trees. When this decision was made it was claimed that Thailand would become burdened with many redundant elephants! Nevertheless, the yearly elephant roundup (in late November) is still a huge event in Surin Province. More of a tourist show nowadays, the roundup was once dressed up in considerable ceremony and tradition. It is definitely worth getting to if you are anywhere near Surin, though you may find it difficult to find a room. Once the elephants go, so do most of the tourists, and Surin is returned to the sleepy little town it normally is during the rest of the year.

Vital Information

Tourist Information The Tarin Hotel on Sirirat Road has available a free and useful map of Surin town and province.

Post Office is on the corner of Tesaban 1 Road and Thonsarn Road.

Banks Krung Thai Bank and the Bank of Ayudhaya both have branches on Thonsarn Road.

Police Station is on Lak Muang Road, around the corner from Chitbamrung Road.

Motorcycle hire is available for 200B per day - ask at your hotel for details.

Codes Surin's telephone code is (044) and the postal code is 32000.

Northeast

Cheap Sleeps

Krung Sri Hotel at 185 Krung Si Nai Road, ☎ (044) 511 037, has large clean doubles with fan and shower for 120B. It is very quiet except for the dogs, and the staff are welcoming. **Country Roads Cafe and Guesthouse** at 165 1-2 Sirirat Road, a 5 to 10 minute walk from the train station. Run by Ron (Texan) and Chamnong (Thai) they have a couple of rooms for 100B. They are very friendly and helpful and are worth visiting just to check out their menu. **Pirom's House** at 242 Krung Si Nai Road, is a bit out of the centre of town but worth it. Clean rooms are 70B/120B for singles/doubles and a dorm is 50B. Make sure you get a net because the mosquitos are savage here. Pirom occasionally runs well regarded tours of the surrounding area including Ban Ta Klong, Ban Khaosinarin and some local ruins.

Surin

Legend

1	Bus station	8	Phetkasem Hotel
2	Train station	9	Country Roads Cafe
3	Elephants		& Guesthouse
4	New Hotel	10	Tarin Hotel
5	Wai Wat Restaurant	11	Post office
6	Bank of Ayudhya	12	Wat Nong Bua
7	Krung Thai Bank	13	Bangkok Bank
		14	Night market
		15	Pirom's House
		16	Krung Sri Hotel
		17	Government Savings Bank
		18	Police station

New Hotel at 6-8 Thonsarn Road, ☎ (044) 511 341, right by the station on Thonsarn Road. Single rooms are 100B and doubles cost 150B. Be aware of the train noise, a room off the street would probably be the quietest option.

Eat and Meet

Surin has an excellent and almost **24 hour market** set off Krung Si Nai Road. Good cheap meals of virtually any description can be had here at rock bottom prices.

Country Roads Cafe and Guesthouse at 165 1-2 Sirirat Road serves expensive but high standard Western food and a limited range of 25B to 35B Thai meals. Very friendly staff.

Along **Thonsarn Road**, away from the train station are a number of decent restaurants doing good and cheap I-san food.

Wai Wan Restaurant is on Sanitnikomrat Road. Turn left on leaving the train station — look for the wooden panelling. They have an English menu which is not too expensive.

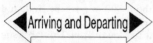

Things to do and Sights to See

Elephant Roundup   งานช้างสุรินทร์

Held every year on the third weekend of November, this huge festival attracts thousands of people during the two day event. Two hundred elephants compete for the right of being the *National Animal* and the highlight is a mock elephant battle. The festival attracts many tourists, both Thai and foreign, and is well worth getting to. If arriving by train at this time of year, book in advance for anything above a hard seat.

Arriving and Departing

Train

The train station is to the north of town. There are seven though trains each way a day between Surin and Bangkok and six through to Ubon Ratchathani. Refer to the timetable at the end of the chapter for details. The 3rd class train to **Si Saket** costs 20B and takes 2 hours. To **Bangkok** on 3rd class costs 73B. For more train details refer to the timetable at the end of the chapter.

Bus

The bus station is to the west of the train station on Thep Surin Road. A bus to **Khorat** costs 45B, to **Nang Rong** 30B, to **Ubon Ratchathani** 45B (A/C 80B), **Bangkok** 108B (A/C 195), **Roi Et** 45B and **Prasat** 10B.

AROUND SURIN PROVINCE

Ban Ta Klang

With the advent of more modern methods of labour, the humble elephant is being retired to the paddocks and is brought on show only at the annual roundup. However it is not a case of simply picking up your pachyderm the day before the show as training is a continual requirement to keep the elephant sharp, attentive and responsive. As a result of this, visitors to Ban Ta Klang may be able to visit the Suay training the elephants year round, and although not as spectacular as the roundup itself, it is nevertheless interesting.

Probably best described as a tribe of professional elephant catchers, the Suay are today suffering due to the serious reduction in the number of working elephants in Thailand. It was the Suay who in the past captured and trained the elephants to become the hard working and terribly underpaid labourers they were and for some, continue to be today.

◀**Arriving and Departing**▶

Ban Ta Klang is just under 60 km from Surin and is best reached by local bus. Buses run every hour from the bus station and take around 2 hours.

Silk Villages

Ban Khao Sinarin, about 20 km north of Surin on Route 214, was once best known as a cloth producing village but is now equally well known for its silver. Not a bad place to visit for those seeking upcountry bargains. Songtheaws run from the soi off Thonsarn Road between the roundabout and the train station to Ban Khao Sinarin throughout the day.

Khmer Ruins

Surin Province is dotted with many Khmer ruins, many of which are little more than rock piles which are presently on the receiving end of very little attention from the Fine Arts Department. One exception to this is Prasat Ta Meuan.

Prasat Ta Meuan

This series of three ruins is a long day trip from Surin, but is worthwhile visiting if you want to see jungle enclosed ruins in fairly decent condition. The ruins virtually sit upon the Cambodian border and if there is intense fighting on 'the other side', the ruins may be closed to tourists. Ask in Surin for details beforehand if you are concerned of any dangers.

The site consists of three separate areas, all situated in clearings surrounded by dense forest. The first site, Prasat Ta Meuan, dates from the 12th Century and was used as a rest stop for pilgrims. It is quite a simple structure and the roof is long gone, but it is still worth a look. The second site, Prasat Ta Meuan Tot, is about 500 m past the first, and probably acted as a hospital of sorts. There is a depression in front of it which may have been a bathing pool. The third and most impressive is Prasat Ta Meuan Tom. This large site has been partially renovated (though apparently lacking in skill - check the decorative block stuck in half way up a blank wall), and is now in a condition about half way between Prasat Phanomwan and Prasat Hin Khao Phanom Rung. The temple is nevertheless impressive and the noise from the birds and monkeys can be deafening. Apparently at times fire fights from the other side of the border can be heard. **WARNING - MINES are also a problem in this area, so DO NOT LEAVE THE CLEARED PATHS.**

◀**Arriving and Departing**▶

It is not as difficult as it might seem but it does involve a lot of time on buses. You will need to catch a bus to the village of Ban Kruat via Route 2121 and thus past the turn-off to the ruins (where a motorcycle will take you the remainder of the distance). Buses occasionally leave from **Surin**, cost 25B and will take 2½ to 3 hours to reach the turn-off. If no bus appears to be leaving from Surin, catch a bus to Prasat bus station, 30 km south of Surin, and catch another from there. The fare to **Prasat** is 10B, catch any bus to Khorat and it will pass through Prasat bus station. From Prasat to the turn-off, buses leave every one or two hours and take 1½ to 2½ hours to reach the turn-off. Once on the bus be at pains to repeat over and over again where you are going so that they can let you know when to get off.

The turn-off itself is not very well signposted, so our best advice is to get off at around the 25 km marker (i.e. 25 km from Ban Kruat, 48 km from Kap Choeng). Nearby there is a bunch of signs, all in Thai, with one green one reading "F.P.T.3.". This marks the turn-off! Motorcycles will ferry you from here along the 10 km to the site. About 8 km down this road you will reach a military checkpoint where you need to sign in and maybe leave your passport. If fighting in Cambodia is heavy you may be turned away here. After the checkpoint you pass a few soldiers' bunkers and other dug-in positions before reaching the site. These soldiers are very serious and are not there for stupid tourists to take their photos, please be aware that you may be only a kilometre or so from a war zone.

If coming here yourself by motorcycle follow Route 214 from Surin. At Prasat go straight across Route 24 and follow the signs for Prasat Ta Meuan Tom and when you come to a right for Route 2121 take it and follow for about 48 km. At the above mentioned turn by the "F.P.T.3." sign, take a left up the dirt road. Follow this road and you will reach a big statue in the middle of the road, go right here and follow the dirt road for around 8 km after which you reach the army checkpoint. Here they may ask you to leave your motorbike or accompany you the remainder of the distance. Regardless, you just follow the main track to the sights.

If you take a motorcycle taxi from the turn-off to the sites, count on 70B to 150B return fare, including waiting time. The taxis know how far you have already come so you may need to bargain hard to get a reasonable price.

WARNING - This can be a dangerous area. The army positions here are not for show and this is not a place to go bushwalking - STICK TO THE CLEARED PATHS and try your hardest not to step on LAND MINES.

Other Khmer sites

Other ruins you may want to look at include **Prasat Hin Ban Phluang** located 30 km south of Surin and within motorcycle taxi distance of Prasat. **Prasat Sikhoraphum**, has five prangs, the highest being 32 m and some good carvings are still evident here. The site is about 35 km east of Surin, on Route 2080. **Prasat Hin Chom Phra** is 28 km north of Surin on Route 214 and has a large Buddha image enshrined out front. All three can be visited by bus from Surin, with motorcycle taxis ferrying you to and from the bus stations in the nearest towns. These are Prasat, Sikhoraphum and Chom Phra respectively.

SI SAKET PROVINCE

Si Saket Province seldom finds its way onto many travellers itineraries. Except for the spectacular Khmer ruins at Khao Phra Wiham (which is actually in Cambodia) there is little to explore or do in this province. The province is bordered by Yasothon and Roi Et to the north, Surin to the west, Ubon to the east and Cambodia to the south.

SI SAKET   ศรีสะเกษ

The lack of tourism in Si Saket serves as an attraction for those wanting to see authentic I-san life but, for those wanting to see sights, you will rapidly realise why so few people visit here. Si Saket is also the jumping off point for Khao Phra Vihaan and other Khmer ruins. To visit Khao Phra Vihaan requires a full day in itself but some of the others can be visited in less time though they are nowhere near as spectacular.

Vital Information

Tourist Information A small Tourist Information Office is situated at the corner of Taepa Road and Lak Muang Road. The staff are helpful but do not speak much in the way of English. This is a good place to enquire about the current situation regarding Khao Phra Vihaan.
Post Office is on Taepa Road near the Tourist Information Centre.
Banks Most banks have a branch in Si Saket, see the map for positions.
Hospital, ☎ (045) 611 503, is at the western end of town on Kasikam Road and a new hospital is under construction on Ubon Road.
Codes Si Saket's telephone code is (045) and the postal code is 33000.

Cheap Sleeps

Si Saket Hotel at 384 Si Saket Road, this centrally located hotel about two minutes from the train station has plain basic double rooms for 120B.

Phrom Phiman Hotel at 849/1 Lak Muang Road, ☎ (045) 612 677, is a large hotel with big clean rooms containing a fan, bathroom and TV (Sky) starting at 240B. Try to get a room facing away from the train tracks if you do not want to be regularly woken all night, and check the plumbing.

Gessiri Hotel, ☎ (045) 614 007, on Khu Khan Road is next to the Thai Farmers Bank and costs 300B for a double.

Eat and Meet

By the train station there is a large **night market**. A smaller market is on Wan Luk Sua Road across from Suen Heng Plaza. The **day market** is off Khu Khan Road.

Suen Heng Plaza has a decent department store style restaurant on the ground floor which is great for people watching.

There is a **Carte D'or** branch on Ubon Road serving the usual fare.

Mr Hagen Pizza on Ubon Road does pizza, steak and beer if that is what you are after whilst **Food House Better Better** does decent food and the prices are even better!

There are many **street vendors** selling all and sundry wandering the streets of Si Saket.

Things to do and Sights to See

Princess Mother Park (Somdet Phrasinakarin Park)   สวนสมเด็จพระศรีนครินทร์
Around 1½ km from town, this park was constructed to honour the Princess Mother on her 80th birthday. The park is very pleasant and has been nicely landscaped allowing for a pleasant stroll for a few hours in the late afternoon to wind down.

Lam Duan Flower Festival
This festival is celebrated in Si Saket during March. This three day event provides the perfect opportunity to experience the many aspects of the Northeastern Thai culture including dance, food and handicrafts. Displays, performances and markets are set up with the best the Northeast has to offer.

Arriving and Departing

Train
Si Saket train station is in the centre of town and has six through trains each way every day between Ubon Ratchathani and Bangkok. Refer to the timetable at the end of the chapter for more details on trains throughout the region. The train from Surin to **Si Saket** takes up to 2½ hours, depending on the type of train you catch, and a 3rd class seat costs 20B. To and from **Bangkok** on 3rd class costs 87B.

Bus
The ordinary bus station is a way out of town on Kuang Heng Road and A/C buses leave from near the Si Saket Hotel to the north of the train station. An ordinary bus to **Ubon Ratchathani** costs 20B and to **Bangkok** it costs 131B (A/C 245B) taking just under 9 hours.

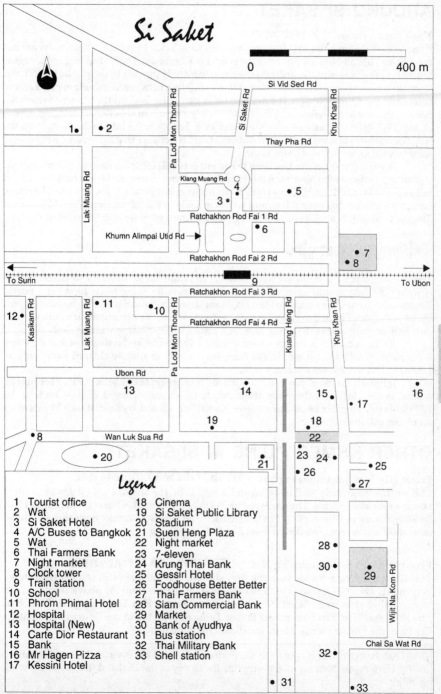

Si Saket

0   400 m

Legend

1	Tourist office	18	Cinema
2	Wat	19	Si Saket Public Library
3	Si Saket Hotel	20	Stadium
4	A/C Buses to Bangkok	21	Suen Heng Plaza
5	Wat	22	Night market
6	Thai Farmers Bank	23	7-eleven
7	Night market	24	Krung Thai Bank
8	Clock tower	25	Gessiri Hotel
9	Train station	26	Foodhouse Better Better
10	School	27	Thai Farmers Bank
11	Phrom Phimai Hotel	28	Siam Commercial Bank
12	Hospital	29	Market
13	Hospital (New)	30	Bank of Ayudhya
14	Carte Dior Restaurant	31	Bus station
15	Bank	32	Thai Military Bank
16	Mr Hagen Pizza	33	Shell station
17	Kessini Hotel		

Northeast

AROUND SI SAKET

Khao Phra Vihaan   วัดพระวิหาร

Khao Phra Vihaan is the highlight of any visit to Si Saket Province. These ruins are not actually in Thailand but are just over the border in Cambodia. Due to fighting in the region (and a lengthy bureaucratic process) the ruins were only opened to the public in 1991, but since then have sporadically been closed due to fighting between Cambodian government forces and the Khmer Rouge. The dry season in particular is a bad time to try to reach the ruins as this is when offensives by the Cambodian government are often undertaken. Check at any TAT office for advice or ask around in Si Saket on the latest situation. With the recent sentiments towards peace in Cambodia there is a chance that these ruins will become safer to visit in the not to distant future.

A partial restoration has been made but it is still far from its original splendour. According to those who have seen it (every time we have attempted it has been closed) do not expect the standard of Khao Hai Phanom Rung, but rather a 'ghost' of it. The entire complex stretches for over 800 m and sits atop a 600 m hill of the Dong Rok Mountains. There are many fine carvings present though some of the towers are in dire need of restoration.

◄ Arriving and Departing ►

To get there catch a songtheaw from Si Saket to Phum Saron which is 10 km shy of the temple. The ride should cost 15B to 20B. If you miss the songtheaw then get a bus to Kantharalak from where you can then get a songtheaw to Phum Saron. The bus should cost about 10B. From Phum Saron you get a motorcycle taxi to the ruins and back but expect to pay 200B to 300B as it is the going rate for a round trip including waiting time.

At the border crossing you need to pass a Thai and Cambodian post and the entry fee is 200B. **WARNING- Once in the complex, be sure to stick to cleared paths only as LAND MINES are a very serious risk.**

If the site is closed you can still visit the border and take a look at **Pha Mor Idaeng** where, in the cliff face, there are stone reliefs which are believed to date back to the 10th Century. From here you can also see Khao Phra Vihaan in the distance - binoculars would be a definite asset.

OTHER KHMER RUINS IN SI SAKET

Prasat Hin Wat Sakamphaeng Yai   ปราสาทหินวัดสระกำแพงใหญ่

This site has been fairly well restored and is well kept. It is worth a visit if you are a ruins addict or are killing time. The site is about 50 km to the west of Si Saket on the edge of Ban Sa Kamphaeng in Uthumphon Phi Sai District. The best way to visit both sites would be motorbike either from Si Saket or from Ban Sa Kamphaeng.

Prasat Hin Wat Sa Kamphaeng Noi   ปราสาทหินวัดสระกำแพงน้อย

This site is more ramshackle than the previous one but there are still some nice carvings evident. Its about 40 km west of Si Saket and about 10 km from the above site.

Other sites in Si Saket Province include **Prasat Phu Fai, Prang Ki, That Ban Prasat, Prasat Hin Ban Samor** and **Prasat Tamnak Sai**. Ask at the Tourist Information Centre or the Phrom Phimai Hotel in Si Saket for more details.

The Thai dialect which is spoken in the northeast of Thailand is virtually Lao. Although many Thais mock them for this, it supports the theory of the Thai and the Lao being 'one family'.

UBON RATCHATHANI PROVINCE

This large province is situated in the southeast corner of I-san, bordered to the south by Cambodia, the east by Laos, the north by Amnat Charoen and the west by Yasothon and Si Saket. Settled by Laos in the late 18th Century, this province retains a distinct ethnic mix along with a substantial Khmer population.

UBON RATCHATHANI   อุบลราชธานี

Towards the western side of the province is the capital Ubon Ratchathani commonly referred to as Ubon. This large city is over 600 km from Bangkok by road and is considered to be the trading and communications centre of Eastern I-san. Other than a few wats and a good museum there is little to keep people here for more than a day or so, though the surrounding area could be explored over a period of a few days. During the Vietnam War, Ubon served as a US base for air strikes into Vietnam and Laos and, although much of the American presence has disappeared, this is still a town which at times can seem quite Western.

Vital Information

Tourist Information The TAT office is at 264/1 Khuan Thani Road, ☎ (045) 243 770, (near the GPO). The staff here are helpful and English is spoken.
Post Office is on Si Narong Road. The telecom office is open 7.00 am to 11.00 pm.
Banks There are many banks in town - check the map for their positions.
Hospital Supasit Hospital on Supasit Road is your best bet.
Tourist Police The Tourist Police are on Si Narong Road, opposite the park.
Codes Ubon's telephone code is (045) and the postal code is 34000.

Cheap Sleeps

Tokyo Hotel at 360 Uparat Road is the best bet in town where clean medium sized double rooms with fan and shower cost 150B. Some of the rooms get really hot! They also have free maps of town available.
Sri Issan 1 & Sri Issan 2 on Ratchabut Road. These hotels face each other and are almost within the market. Decent rooms with fan range from 100B to 150B.
Suriyat Hotel at 302 Suriyat Road have dark singles/doubles with fan and shower going for 130B/150B. The above three are better.
Racha Hotel at 19 Chayangkum Road is like a huge motel. They charge 200B for clean rooms with fan and shower.
Krung Thong Hotel at 24 Si Narong Road, right near the post office in a good central location. The hotel is big and fairly flash but still has some rooms with fan and shower for 250B.

Eat and Meet

Noodle and rice stalls abound throughout town. For really cheap eats try the **night market** by the river and bridge or the other market north of the Racha Hotel on Uparat Road. **Chiokee Restaurant** is on Khuan Thani Road and has good food at reasonable prices - if you are choosy. The English menu has just about everything you could think of and breakfast is especially good. **Villa Pizza** at 115 Polpan Road has, without a doubt, the best crispy pizza in Thailand! It costs 200B for a pizza for two with SKY TV thrown in for free. Good for a splurge. **Restaurant** at 172 Si Narong Road, opposite and to your right as you leave the post office. They serve good cheap Thai food.

To: Wat Nong Bua
Ordinary bus station
Buses to Mukdahan,
Sakhon Nakhon, Udon Thani

Bus to Amnat Charoen,
Yasothon, Roi Et
and Khon Kaen

Chayangkum Rd

Legend

1 Siam Commercial Bank
2 Krung Thai Bank
3 Candle Pub for Health
4 7-eleven
5 Market
6 Racha Hotel
7 Bakery
8 Bank of Ayudhya
9 Airport
10 Swing Party
11 Thai Farmers Bank
12 Thai Military Bank
13 Suriyat Hotel
14 Noodle & curry shops
15 1st Bangkok City Bank
16 Wat Jaeng
17 Police station
18 Supasit Hospital
19 7-eleven
20 Siam Commercial Bank

21 Tokyo Hotel
22 Wat Payai
23 Villa Pizza
24 Market
25 Bus to Khong Chiam
26 Park
27 A/C buses
28 City Hall
29 Wat Thung Si Muang
30 Cafe
31 Krung Thong Hotel
32 Tourist police
33 National Museum
34 TAT
35 Post office
36 Chiokee Restaurant
37 Wat Supattanaram
38 Night Market
39 Sri Issan Hotel
40 Sri Issan 2 Hotel

U-Palesan Rd

Suriyat Rd

Supasit Rd

Pha Daen Rd

Nakorn Bai Rd

Phichit Rangsan Rd

Thepyotee Rd

Polpan Rd

Burapha Nai Rd

Palorangrit Rd

Uparat Rd

Si Narong Rd

Ratchabut Rd

Khuan Thani Rd

Luang Rd

Supat Rd

Prom Rach Rd

Prom Tap

Moon River

Ubon Ratchathani

0   300 m

To Warin Champhap & Train station (3 km)

Northeast

Ubon Ratchathani National Museum

This excellent museum is housed in the former governor's office which was built in 1873 and is widely accepted as being one of the best museums in Thailand. It is a great place to visit before travelling further into I-san as it covers the scientific and cultural aspects of the region. Most of the exhibits are labelled bilingually so it is easy to find out what you are actually looking at. There are some reproductions of the cave paintings at Pha Taem which are worth viewing if you do not plan on heading right out to the site. The museum is on Khuan Thani Road, open from 9.00 am to midday and 1.00 pm to 4.00 pm, Wednesday to Sunday and admission is 10B.

Wat Thung Si Muang   วัดทุ่งศรีเมือง

Situated off Luang Road, this wat was constructed during Rama III's reign and is considered to be a blend of Lao and Ratanakosin style architecture. There is a pretty teak library built on stilts in the centre of the lake here and the interior of the wat is decorated with beautiful wall paintings which tourist literature terms as being 'somewhat erotic!'.

Wat Supattanaram   วัดสุปัฏนาราม

Sitting on the bank of the Mun River, this wat is a mix of Thai, Khmer and European styles, and is also home to the largest wooden bell in Thailand. It is probably worth a glance if you are down this way to eat at the night market.

Wat Maha Wanaram   วัดมหาวนาราม

Built in 1807, this is regarded as the principal wat in Ubon. It contains the highly revered **Phra Chao Yai Indra Plang**, a Buddha image in the 'victory over Satan' position.

Wat Nong Bua   วัดหนองบัว

Located a bit out of town, on the road to Amnat Charoen, this sizeable wat was modelled on Budhakhaya Chedi in India and has important Buddha relics kept within. It is definitely worth a trip to see a wat which dares to be different and a bus out to it (2B) is cheaper than an air fare to India, although the similarities to the chedi in India are somewhat vague.

Wat Si Ubon Ratanaram (Wat Si Thong)   วัดศรีอุบลรัตนาราม

This wat has its main hall modelled on Wat Benchama Bophit in Bangkok. The Buddha image is made of topaz and is believed to be the largest single piece of topaz in Thailand. The Buddha was brought to Thailand from Vientiane in Laos at the same time as the Emerald Buddha.

Wat Nong Pa Pong

Located 12 km south of Ubon in Warin Chamrap District is this peaceful forest wat which was founded by Ajaan Chaa. The grounds contain a small museum dedicated to Ajaan Chaa, and a chedi contains his ashes. This wat is a popular place for Westerners to come to study meditation. To get there catch a number 3 bus which goes right by the turn-off to the wat.

Wat Pa Nanachat   วัดป่านานาชาติ

This is another wat which is very popular with Westerners wanting to study meditation. Both men and women are welcome, but men will be expected to shave their heads after three days and the sexes are strictly segregated. The wat is well signposted off the road to Si Saket, so the easiest way to get there is to hop on a Si Saket bus and hop off when you see the signs.

Northeast

Candle Festival   งานแห่เทียนพรรษา

This annual event is held at the beginning of Buddhist lent in July. The candles, made of bees wax, form the centrepiece of a variety of parades and processions before being presented to local wats. Beside the processions there is folk dancing and a general festive feel to the town.

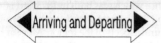

Getting Around

Ubon has a comprehensive and cheap local bus system. Pick up a bus route map from the TAT or your hotel (if they have one) and just follow the numbers. The fare is 3B and the buses run from 6.00 am to 6.00 pm. Tuk tuks should be around 10B for a ride within the city limits.

Air

There are two direct THAI Airways flights a day between Ubon Ratchathani and **Bangkok** for 1,405B one way. The airport is at the northern end of town.

Train

Ubon's train station is south of the river in Warin Chamrap, a ten minute tuk tuk ride away. This is the eastern terminal of the rail line with six departures a day to Bangkok. A 3rd class fare to **Bangkok** costs 95B and can take up to 13 hours. Refer to the timetable information at the end of the chapter for details.

Bus

Ubon is well served by buses to all and sundry destinations, though depending on destination they do leave from different parts of town, most of which are a tuk tuk ride away.

For Yasothon, Roi Et, Khon Kaen and Udon Thani they leave from a small station way out to the northwest of town. Catch a tuk tuk or number 1 bus and tell the conductor where you eventually want to get to: e.g. Udon, and they will drop you at the station. The bus to **Yasothon** costs 28B and takes 2 hours, **Roi Et** costs 44B and takes 3½ hours, Amnat Charoen costs 22B and **Khon Kaen** costs 75B and takes 5½ hours.

For Mukdahan, Nakhon Pathom and Sakhon Nakhon the terminal is again way out of town on Chayangkun Road, catch bus number 2 or 3 to reach it. The bus to **Mukdahan** costs 45B and takes 2½ to 3 hours, the bus to **Sakhon Nakhon** costs 70B, to That Phanom an A/C bus costs 99B and an ordinary bus costs 54B and the bus to **Nakhon Phanom** costs 60B and takes 3½ to 4 hours.

For Si Saket, Surin and Ubon Ratchathani (Khorat) the terminal is in Warim Chamrap District. Catch a tuk tuk or number 6 bus to the terminal which is located behind the market. **Si Saket** costs 20B and takes 1½ hours and **Surin** costs 45B for a 3 hour trip.

The **Bangkok** bus leaves from the terminal on Chayangkum Road near the Regent Palace Hotel. Bus numbers 2, 3 or 7 will take you past it. An ordinary bus costs 161B and takes 10½ hours and an A/C bus costs 290B and takes just under 10 hours.

AROUND UBON RATCHATHANI

KHONG CHIAM   โขง เจียม

Around 60 km to the east of Ubon at the confluence of the Mun and Maekhong Rivers, this sleepy town offers a quiet escape from the big smoke of Ubon. The point where the two rivers meet is called 'Two Colour River', because of the differing sediment levels in each river. A distinct difference in colour is evident from the river's edge. The far side of the river is Laos and other than this there is nothing to see in Khong Chiam except quiet rural life and a nice town.

Cheap Sleeps

Apple Guesthouse is just up the road from the bus station - look for its numerous signs. They do cheap good food and have clean rooms for 90B. They also hire motorbikes for 150B and bicycles.

GIO Guesthouse is closer to the bus station and has similar rates. The two colour river is a ten minute walk from here and there are some nice floating restaurants by the shore.

Eat and Meet

Besides the **guesthouse restaurants** there are a few **basic stalls** around the bus station. A far better eating stall selection exists **by the river** in the area of the two coloured river. Both seafood and standard Thai dishes are available here at reasonable prices.

Arriving and Departing

The bus from **Ubon** costs 30B depending on which way you go. Sometimes they go via Phibin Mangsaham, the quick way, or else via Trakan Phut Phon which takes twice as long and costs more! The last bus from Khong Chiam is at 3.30 pm. If you leave Ubon early (say 7.30 am) you can do this as a long day trip, but it is much more pleasant if you spend a night or so in Khong Chiam. Buses leave from Ubon from the bus station at the corner of Sanphasit Road and Burapha Nai Road.

AROUND KHONG CHIAM

Pha Taem National Park   อุทยานแห่งชาติผาแต้ม

Located about 25 km north of Khong Chiam is Pha Taem National Park where brilliant cliff side views of Laos can be had. About a 500 m walk to the base of the cliffs (follow the Thai signs with '500' on them) are some prehistoric cave paintings which are over 3,000 years old and depict such things as elephants, fish traps and outlines of Michael Jackson's hand. Well worth a look! Food and drinks are available in a shaded area by the car park.

On the way to the park entrance you will pass **Sao Chaliang**, an area with bizarre stone formations similar to those in Mukdahan. The park is best visited by motorbike from Khong Chiam, and is well signposted except for the final turn-off! When you are about 6 km from the entrance you will pass two turn-offs to the right about 50 m apart. These are the turn-offs, take the second one as each is a one way road in opposite directions.

CHONG MEK   ช่อง เม็ก

This is the only place in Thailand where foreigners are permitted to cross to Laos by land. To do so you need a visa endorsed for entry at Chong Mek/Pakse. The bus to Pakse from the border takes 3 hours. You can get to Chong Mek by bus or songtheaw from both Khong Chiam and Ubon.

Phu Chong Nayoi National Park

This park is little visited despite its size of just under 690 sq km, taking up the southeast corner of the Northeast region. Views from **Pha Phung** look over the area surrounding the tri-border where Cambodia and Laos meet Thailand. Other things within the park include the 40 m high **Bak Tew Yai Waterfall**, natural springs and rock formations.

YASOTHON PROVINCE

At one time a district of Ubon Ratchathani, Yasothon gained provincial status in 1972 and for the majority of the year, retains a very quiet atmosphere. During the second weekend of May however, Yasothon literally explodes with life as the annual Rocket Festival kicks off. Although rockets are let off throughout the country, Yasothon is the place to be for those into big rockets.

YASOTHON   ยโสธร

This sleepy provincial capital is about as quiet a place as you are likely to see in this area of Thailand, except of course during the Rocket Festival. Set to coincide with the end of the dry season, the festival has its roots in animist beliefs, believing that the firing of the rockets will appease the god of rain who will make sure that it pours down. Over time the festival has incorporated Buddhist beliefs and today, as per usual, the state has got its hand in its pocket to make sure the event is good, safe and publicly acceptable. This has lead to a degree of sanitising of the event with the public wearing of phallic symbols being outlawed. Meanwhile the rockets have got bigger and bigger with some carrying up to half a ton of gunpowder! The thought behind it — the bigger the better. Gambling is rife during the ceremony as people bet on the various rockets because the one which goes the highest wins.

1 Post office	6 Thai Farmers Bank	11 Bus station
2 Wat Mahathat	7 Nakhon Hotel	12 Clock tower
3 Krung Thai Bank	8 Siam Commercial Bank	13 Hotel
4 Bangkok Bank	9 A/C Buses to Bangkok	14 Wat Tai
5 Handicrafts store	10 Market	

Legend

Vital Information

Post Office is on the road out of town going to Roi Et (Chaengsamit Road).
Banks There are many banks in town. See the map for details.
Codes Yasothon's telephone code is (045) and the postal code is 35000.

Cheap Sleeps

Nakhon Hotel is on Uthairamit Road about 5 minutes from the bus station. Look for the wooden front restaurant. Rooms are 180B with fan, shower and TV.
Hotel There is another hotel at the Ubon end of town on Chaengsamit Road which probably charges similar rates but was closed at our last pass.

Eat and Meet

Noodle and rice shops are all there is in town - take your pick! The highest concentration of places is around the bus station and on Uthairamit Road. In the hot season try for the **food vendors** a little out of town on the banks of the Chi River.

Things to do and Sights to See

Wat Maha That or Wat Phra That Yasothon
Other than the Rocket Festival, Wat Maha That on Wareratchadet Road is worth a look if you are waiting for a bus or revelation. The chedi is believed to be around 1,300 years old and is similar in style to the one at Nakhon Phanom. Next to it is an ancient scripture hall which is built over a small pond. The ashes of Phra Ananda, who was a prominent follower of Buddha, are stored on site.

Phaya Thaen Public Park
This park is located within the municipal boundaries and is a popular place for the locals to relax. The park is geared up for a variety of pastimes including concerts, plays and boat racing and is also the centrepiece during the rocket festival.

Chi River แม่น้ำชี
During the dry season and about 1 km south of town, food vendors will sell their goodies along the banks of the Chi River. Nice on a really hot day (Yasothon gets a lot of these).

Shopping
Yasothon is a great place for picking up rock bottom priced axe pillows. The prices here are far cheaper than elsewhere in Thailand, especially Bangkok.

Rocket (Bung Fai) Festival งานประเพณีบุญบั้งไฟ
Yasothon's Rocket Festival is a spectacular event, definitely worth seeing if you are in the vicinity. Held in early May, the festival attracts pyromaniacs from all over the country as they all attempt to blow up bigger objects than each other. Rooted in a rain making ceremony, this is a must see if you are around.

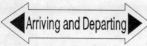

Arriving and Departing

Bus

The bus station is centrally located behind the clocktower. The bus to **Ubon Ratchathani** costs 28B and takes 2 hours, to **Amnat Charoen** it costs 20B and takes 1 hour, to **Mukdahan** the bus costs 45B and the bus to **Roi Et** costs 20B taking 1 to 1½ hours. To **Bangkok** an ordinary bus costs 99B and takes 8 hours and an A/C bus costs 179B.

AROUND YASOTHON

Ban Si Than   บ้านศรีฐาน

This small village, 20 km to the east of Yasothon towards Amnat Charoen on Route 202, is well regarded for its **axe pillows**. To get there take a bus bound for Amnat Charoen and ask for *Ban Si Than*. The bus should drop you at the turn-off to the village which is between the 18 km and 19 km markers. Once at the turn-off it is about another 3 km to the village itself, you can either walk the 3 km or hitch a ride.

AMNAT CHAROEN PROVINCE

This new province was only split off from Ubon Ratchathani in 1993 and the split was certainly not done because of some kind of tourist overload! Although lacking in riveting points of interest, the people here are especially friendly and eager to be of assistance.

AMNAT CHAROEN   อำนาจเจริญ

There is very little to see here except one big Buddha and loads of violent movies at the cinema! The people are great though and this place rates the highest 'Hey Farang' rating in Thailand. If you can figure out how the street numbers work here, let us know.

Vital Information

Post Office is on Anek Amnat Road, opposite the school.
Banks are along Chayangkun Road.
Hospital is on Arunprasert Road, heading towards Yasothon.
Codes Amnat Charoen's telephone code is (045) and the postal code is 37000.

Cheap Sleeps

Amnat Charoen Hotel at 288/267 Wichitsin Road, ☎ (045) 451 092, there is no English sign so look for the phone number sign near the roof situated opposite the cinema. This place has dumpy rooms for 80B to 100B and there is a restaurant on the lower floor.

Eat and Meet

For **eating**, the market around the bus station is not too bad a choice nor are some of the restaurants by the bus station. One even has English speaking staff. There are a couple of **restaurants** on the main road, although none are particularly highly recommended.

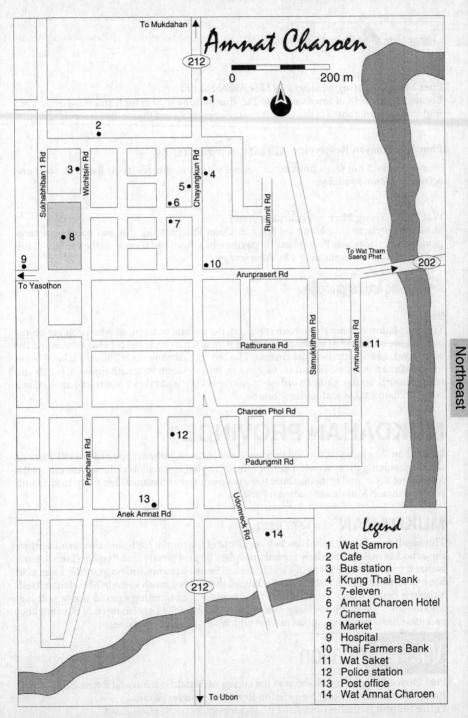

Amnat Charoen

0   200 m

To Mukdahan
To Yasothon
To Wat Tham Saeng Phet
To Ubon

Sukhabhiban 1 Rd
Wichitsin Rd
Chayangkun Rd
Rumnit Rd
Arunprasert Rd
Samukkitham Rd
Amnuaimat Rd
Ratburana Rd
Charoen Phol Rd
Pracharat Rd
Padungmit Rd
Udomreck Rd
Anek Amnat Rd

212
202

Legend

1 Wat Samron
2 Cafe
3 Bus station
4 Krung Thai Bank
5 7-eleven
6 Amnat Charoen Hotel
7 Cinema
8 Market
9 Hospital
10 Thai Farmers Bank
11 Wat Saket
12 Police station
13 Post office
14 Wat Amnat Charoen

Northeast

Phra Monkhan Ming Muang   พระมงคลมิ่ง เมือง

Located 3 km north of town on Route 212, this Buddha is 20 m high and was cast in 1965. Buddha is resisting Satan in this pose. It is quite impressive and the location is scenic and quiet.

Phuttha Utthayan Reservoir   อ่าง เก็บน้ำพุทธอุทยาน

Situated only 3 km from downtown Amnat Charoen, this reservoir has both food and accommodation available.

Wat Tham Saeng Phet   วัดถ้ำแสง เพชร

Similar in style to Wat Nong Pa Pong in Ubon Ratchathani, this wat contains a large pavilion known as Sala Phan Hong or 'pavilion of a thousand rooms'. In the vicinity of this wat there is a cave containing a Buddha image.

◀ **Arriving and Departing** ▶

Bus

The bus station in Amnat Charoen is right in the middle of town, so when you get off the bus you are surrounded by the market. The Amnat Charoen Hotel is between you and the main road, nearly opposite the cinema. The bus to **Yasothon** costs 20B and takes 1 hour, to **Mukdahan** it costs 24B and takes 2 hours, and to **Ubon Ratchathani** it costs 22B and takes 2 hours. To **Bangkok** an ordinary bus costs 137B and takes 9 hours and an A/C bus costs 197B and takes just under 7 hours.

MUKDAHAN PROVINCE

Mukdahan Province was formed from a slice of Nakhon Pathom Province in 1980. Famous for its Maekhong River scenery, this provincial capital is situated on the widest part of the Maekhong River, and from the shore there is a nice view of Savannakhet. Only 16 km south of Mukdahan is Mukdahan National Park.

MUKDAHAN   มุกดาหาร

This small provincial capital catches very little of the tourist trade and as a result visitors can expect to meet particularly friendly people. The provincial capital's main claim to fame is that it was the home town of Field Marshall Sarit Thanarat. Unless your life's aim is to have your photo taken outside Sarit's house, there is not much to do in Mukdahan itself, although that does not mean it is not a fine place for bumming around doing nothing. Mukdahan is gaining popularity as a crossing point to the Laotian town of Savannakhet and itself has a thriving Laotian market which sells absolute garbage.

Vital Information

Post Office is by the roundabout at the corner of Phitak Santirat and Route 2029.
Banks are mostly on Song Nang Sathit Road, see map for details.
Police Station is almost opposite Pith Bakery on Phitak Santirat Road.

Northeast

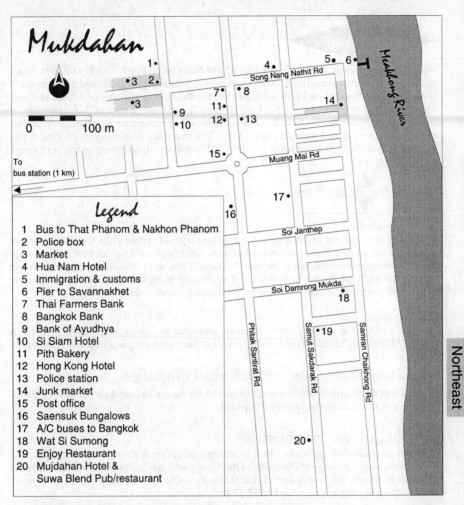

Mukdahan

0 ___ 100 m

To
bus station (1 km)

Song Nang Nathit Rd

Mekhong River

Muang Mai Rd

Soi Janthep

Soi Damrong Mukda

Phitak Santirat Rd

Samut Sakdarak Rd

Samran Chaikhong Rd

Legend

1 Bus to That Phanom & Nakhon Phanom
2 Police box
3 Market
4 Hua Nam Hotel
5 Immigration & customs
6 Pier to Savannakhet
7 Thai Farmers Bank
8 Bangkok Bank
9 Bank of Ayudhya
10 Si Siam Hotel
11 Pith Bakery
12 Hong Kong Hotel
13 Police station
14 Junk market
15 Post office
16 Saensuk Bungalows
17 A/C buses to Bangkok
18 Wat Si Sumong
19 Enjoy Restaurant
20 Mujdahan Hotel &
    Suwa Blend Pub/restaurant

Northeast

Immigration is by the pier at the corner of Song Nang Sathit and Samran Chaikhong Road.
Codes Mukdahan's telephone code is (042) and the postal code is 49000.

Cheap Sleeps

Hua Nam Hotel at 20 Samut Sakdarak Road, has rooms with fan and share shower for
120B. The central location can get a bit noisy though.
Mukdahan Hotel at 8/8 Mu 3 Samut Sakdarak Road, has plain rooms with fan and share
bathroom for 150B. The out of town location makes this place a bit overpriced for what you get.
Saensuk Bungalows is on Phitak Santirat Road and has concrete side by side bungalows
for 300B with A/C and bathroom.
Hong Kong Hotel at 161/1-2 Phitak Santirat Road, has rooms with fan for 150B. Not a
bad central choice but it does fill up fast.

Eat and Meet

Night Market is beside the City Hall Park on Song Nang Sathit Road. This has the best choice of cheap food in town including fried chicken, barbecued fish, spring rolls and much more.
Siwa Blend Restaurant and Pub is beside the Mukdahan Hotel on Samut Sakdarak Road. The menu has some Western dishes for 35B to 100B and there is also MTV by satellite.
Pith Bakery at 102 Phitak Santirat Road, does divine cakes, real coffee (Brazilian, Colombian, espresso and so on) and delicious breakfasts. The treats are a little expensive but if you have spent a while in the northeast you probably deserve a treat. Some of the staff speak excellent English.

Things to do and Sights to See

Indochine Market
If you have ever wanted to buy a plastic bonsai tree, a broken compass, a sock with Michael Jackson's face on it, a Thai speaking calculator, some broken ceramics or a six foot high plastic thermometer - then this is the place to pick up a bargain. Most of the buyers here are looking for a gift for the mother-in-law - it is absolute junk, but worth a look to see how local entrepreneurs can survive solely by selling crap to each other.

Phu Manorom
This hill is only 4 km south of town and from here you can enjoy scenic views of the town and the Maekhong River. At the top there is a pavilion with a replica Buddha Footprint.

Chao Fa Mung Muang Shrine ศาลเจ้าพ่อเจ้าฟ้ามุงเมือง
Regarded as the guardian of the town, this sacred shrine can be found on Song Nang Sathit Road and it also houses the former city pillar.

Wat Si Mongkon Tai วัดศรีมงคลใต้
This wat is situated by the river, close to where you get on to the boat to visit Laos. It is home to the revered image of **Phra Chao Ong Luang** which is believed to be older than the town itself. Beside the wat is an old bodhi tree at the base of which you can have your fortune told (as long as you understand Thai).

Wat Yod Kaew Siwichai
This wat is remarkable for its Lao style lotus bud chedis. Further south at **Wat Si Sumong**, more examples of the Lao style can be seen, along with a somewhat peculiar blend of colonial and eastern architecture.

Arriving and Departing

Bus
For buses to Ubon, Amnat Charoen and Yasothon, the bus station is quite a way out of town on Route 2029. A tuk tuk to the bus station costs 5B. The bus to **Yasothon** costs 45B, to **Amnat Charoen** it costs 24B and to **Ubon Ratchathani** it costs 45B.

For buses to Nakhon Pathom, the stop is beside the police box on Wiwit Suraken Road. The bus to **Nakhon Phanom** costs 30B and to **That Phanom** it costs 15B. For A/C buses to Ubon Ratchathani and Bangkok, they leave from Samut Sakdorak Road near the intersection to Route 2029. An A/C bus to **Bangkok** costs 287B and takes around 10½ hours.

AROUND MUKDAHAN

Mukdahan National Park   อุทยานแห่งชาติมุกดาการ

Established in 1984, this National Park is well know for its bizarre shaped rocks, not unlike what you would see in a 'Road Runner' cartoon. Besides the strange formations there are also caves, prehistoric rock art (as at Pha Taem in Ubon Ratchathani Province) and considerable wildlife. In the wet season there are some waterfalls. There are a few trails for hiking and a trail map is available from the park office. The park turn-off is between kilometre checks 14 and 15, and is about a 20 minute walk to your right - look for the signs in English. To get there, catch a songtheaw from south of the Mukdahan Hotel, they are generally blue and cost 5B.

Phu Sa Dok Bua National Park   อุทยานแห่งชาติภูสระดอกบัว

The title of this park comes from the same named mountain which when translated means 'Mountain of the Lotus Basin'. This name comes from the large bowls with water and lotus plants held at the base of the mountain. The park has some stunning natural features but also holds a few secrets of the past. Prehistoric paintings are scattered over the Phu Pha Taem cliff face, but are over 7 m above ground level, so bring your binoculars. You can view a beautiful sunset from Phu Pha Hom just as the insurgents of the defunct communist party used to. They once used the park and the caves as a hide out.

SAKHON NAKHON PROVINCE

This little visited province is bordered by Nong Khai to the north, Nakhon Phanom to the east, Mukdahan to the southeast, Kalasin to the southwest and Udon Thani to the west. It is best known for Wat Phra That Choeng Chum and Bung Nong Han (Thailand's largest natural lake) and both of these are within the provincial boundaries of the capital, Sakhon Nakhon.

SAKHON NAKHON   สกลนคร

This is a bustling market town and urban centre. The town's main claim to fame is the very sacred Wat Phra That Choeng Chum, which is the second most important Lao style chedi in the region after the one at That Phanom. Other than this wat and Bung Nong Han (the largest parasite infested natural lake in Thailand), Sakhon Nakhon has little to hold your attention for more than a day, although if you are here for the Wax Castle Festival (held at the end of Buddhist lent) be prepared for a pretty lively festival along with boat races on Bung Nong Han.

Vital Information

Post Office is on Jai Phasock Road, about a five minute walk from the roundabout.
Bank Krung Thai Bank have a branch on the corner of Charoen Muang Road and Sukkasem Road and Thai Farmers bank have a branch on the corner of Pratcharat and Sukkasem Roads.
Codes Sakhon Nakhon's telephone code is (042) and the postal code is 47000.

Cheap Sleeps

Krong Thong Hotel at 645/2 Charoen Muang Road, ☎ (042) 711 235, has decent rooms with fan for 100B and with A/C for 300B.
Somkiert Bungalows at 1348 Kamchat Phai Road, ☎ (042) 711 044, has basic rooms with fan for 150B and inside parking is available.
Araya 1 Hotel at 1432 Prem Prida Road, ☎ (042) 711 097, has basic rooms with fan for 150B.
Araya II Hotel and **Kitti Hotel** on Kamchat Phai Road are similarly priced.

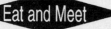

Eat and Meet

The main cuisine in Sakhon Nakhon is **rice and noodle shops** which are spread throughout town. The **market** is off Pratcharat Road near the bus station and there is a **restaurant** on the corner of Sukkasem Road and Kamchat Phai Road which does a variety of Western dishes.

Things to do and Sights to See

Wat Phra That Choeng Chum   พระธาตุเชิงชุม

The 24 m chedi in this wat was built over an originally much older Khmer prang. This wat has become an important pilgrimage point for Thais and is recognised as being the second most important site to visit in the region after the wat at That Phanom. The present chedi was built during the Ayutthaya Period and is worth a glance if you have to wait for a bus. A sizeable festival is held in the wat grounds in January. The wat is situated at the eastern end of town about a ten minute walk from the bus station.

Wat Phra That Narai Cheng Weng   พระธาตุนารายณ์เจงเวง

Around 5 km from town in Ban That, this Khmer style prang is 12 m high and was built between the 10th and 11th Centuries. It was originally built as a Hindu temple and as such has nicely carved lintels depicting Vishnu and Shiva. To get there from town catch a songtheaw on Sai Sawang Road and tell the driver you want to go to Wat Phra That Na Weng. Where you get dropped is a ten minute walk through the village to the wat.

Wat Pa Suthawat   วัดป่าสุทธาวาส

This wat is opposite the town hall and was where one of Thailand's most revered monks, **Ajaan Man** (1871-1919), lived and died. A small museum in the grounds displays a collection of his personal possessions.

Bung Nong Han   หนองหาร

This is Thailand's largest natural lake covering an area of 32 sq km. Boats can be hired to do trips on the lake, but do not bother going for a swim as it is infested with liver flukes which can cause you all sorts of horrible health problems.

Arriving and Departing

Air
THAI Airways flies from Sakhon Nakhon to **Bangkok**, **Khon Kaen** and **Nakhon Phanom**. One way fares are 1,530B, 445B and 300B respectively.

Bus
The bus station is at the southwest corner of town, about a five to ten minute walk from most of the hotels. To **That Phanom** the bus costs 20B, to **Nakhon Phanom** it costs 26B, **Ubon Ratchathani** 70B, **Kalasin** 35B and **Udon Thani** costs 42B. To **Bangkok** an A/C bus costs 271B and an ordinary bus costs 150B.

> The northeastern region is known for its sticky rice. The land is the least arable of Thailand so normal rice is difficult to cultivate. Only small portions of sticky rice are needed for the consumer to feel like they have a full belly (compared to wet rice).

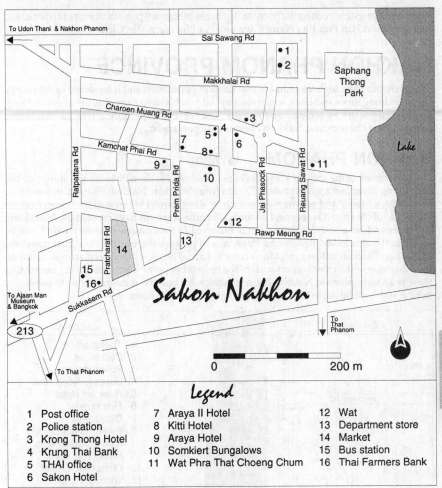

Legend

1	Post office	7	Araya II Hotel	12	Wat
2	Police station	8	Kitti Hotel	13	Department store
3	Krong Thong Hotel	9	Araya Hotel	14	Market
4	Krung Thai Bank	10	Somkiert Bungalows	15	Bus station
5	THAI office	11	Wat Phra That Choeng Chum	16	Thai Farmers Bank
6	Sakon Hotel				

AROUND SAKHON NAKHON

Phu Phan National Park   อุทยานแห่งชาติภูพาน

This National Park straddles Sakhon Nakhon, Nakhon Phanom and Kalasin Provinces and takes up 666 sq km. Established in 1972, this park was once a stronghold for communist insurgents and during the Japanese occupation of the area, the Free Thai stored some of their weapons in a cave within the present park's boundaries. Considerable wildlife has been seen here in the past including elephants, monkeys, bears, and very occasionally tigers. There is also plentiful birdlife. Two waterfalls, **Namtok Tat Ton** and **Kham Hom,** along with a natural rock bridge are the main natural attractions of this park. The park is about 25 km south of Sakhon Nakhon on Route 213 heading towards Kalasin.

Huai Huat National Park   อ่าง เก็บน้ำห้วยหวด

This National Park borders the eastern side of Phu Phan National Park and is slightly larger covering 830 sq km. The parks main feature is the reservoir of the same name as the park.

There are interesting rock formations on one bank, otherwise you can venture further afield and check out **Hip Phu Pha Nang Cave** and **Na Pha Nern Hin Cliff**.

NAKHON PHANOM PROVINCE

This province has a high Vietnamese and Laotian population and is bordered to the east by the Maekhong River and Laos, to the west by Sakhon Nakhon Province, the north by Nong Khai and the south by Mukdahan Province. The scenery, especially across the Maekhong River at That Phanom and Nakhon Phanom, is spectacular.

NAKHON PHANOM   นครพนม

Once the centre of the ancient kingdom of Si Kotrabun, Nakhon Phanom sits alongside the Maekhong River and approximately 735 km from Bangkok. Nakhon Phanom translates as 'City of Mountains' and was named as such by King Rama I because of the scenery on the other side of the river. Over time, Lao and other ethnic groups have crossed the Maekhong River around here and this migration is reflected in the cultural diversity which can be found in the area today. Besides the lively mix of peoples there is little to attract travellers to Nakhon Phanom unless you plan to cross to Laos. The view of the Laotian mountains on the other side of the river is spectacular. The only other point worth remarking here is that there is a tourist office in Nakhon Phanom which is a bounty of information - that is if you get the staff's attention in their seemingly soundproof TV room.

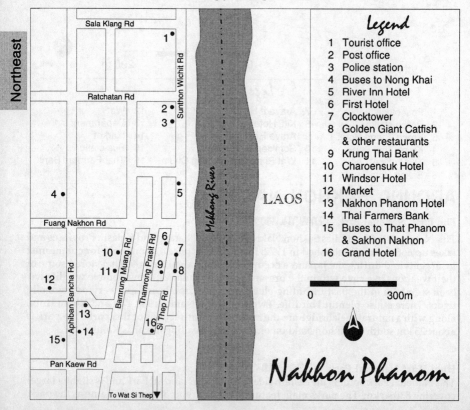

Legend

1   Tourist office
2   Post office
3   Police station
4   Buses to Nong Khai
5   River Inn Hotel
6   First Hotel
7   Clocktower
8   Golden Giant Catfish
    & other restaurants
9   Krung Thai Bank
10 Charoensuk Hotel
11 Windsor Hotel
12 Market
13 Nakhon Phanom Hotel
14 Thai Farmers Bank
15 Buses to That Phanom
    & Sakhon Nakhon
16 Grand Hotel

Nakhon Phanom

Vital Information

Tourist Information is on the corner of Sala Klang and Sunthon Wichit Road. Once you get their attention they can be quite helpful.
Post Office is on the corner of Ratchatan and Sunthon Wichit Road beside the police station.
Banks See the map for their location.
Police Station is beside the post office.
Codes Nakhon Phanom's telephone code is (042) and the postal code is 48000.

Cheap Sleeps

First Hotel at 16 Si Thep Road, ☎ (042) 511 253, is not a bad choice, if a bit pricey. Try for a third or fourth floor room if you want a view (shame about the unattractive building in front which partially obscures it). Doubles with shower and fan are 160B.
Charoensuk Hotel at 250 Bamrung Muang Road, ☎ (042) 511 130, this hotel has rooms with shower and fan for 150B, the staff speak a little English and are very friendly.
Grand Hotel at 210 Si Thep Road, ☎ (042) 511 526, is fairly classy but still has some cheap rooms, 160B with fan and shower.
River Inn Hotel on Sunthon Wichit Road has fairly grimy rooms but with a view and a fan going for 150B, with A/C 300B.

Eat and Meet

As long as you do not want to eat seafood, the seafood restaurants along the river serve cheap Thai food. As soon as you say fish, the price rockets.
The **Golden Giant Catfish** is opposite the clocktower and does good dishes on rice. The giant catfish is tasty but pricey at 250B for two. Besides this restaurant, there are a number of other seafood places along the promenade.
Along Si Thep Road and Bamrung Muang Road there are numerous **noodle and rice shops** all with stock standard 10B to 15B meals.

Things to do **and** Sights to See

Along Si Thep Road there are a few cheap **silver shops** if you are after some jewellery, but the only other 'attraction' is **Wat Si Thep**. Inside the wat are murals depicting stories about Buddha and the Chakri Kings.

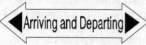
Arriving and Departing

Air
THAI Airways fly to **Bangkok** and **Sakhon Nakhon** from here. One way fares are 1,605B and 300B respectively.

Bus
The bus to **Sakhon Nakhon** takes 2 hours and costs 26B, to **Mukdahan** it costs 30B, to **Ubon Ratchathani** it costs 60B, to **That Phanom** it costs 15B, to **Beung Kan** it costs 45B and takes 5½ hours, to **Nong Khai** it costs 80B and takes 7½ to 8 hours via Beung Kan and to **Udon Thani** it costs 95B. To **Bangkok** an A/C bus costs 310B and an ordinary bus costs 172B.

THAT PHANOM   ธาตุพนม

This small town, 55 km from Nakhon Phanom, is a far preferable place to stay to Nakhon Phanom. Friendly people, beautiful scenery and Wat Phra That Phanom can keep you busy for a day or two. The archway at the entrance to town is a small replica of the huge arch in Vientiane, Laos.

Cheap Sleeps

Niyana Guesthouse is a large old wooden house on a soi off Phanom Phanarak Road (follow the signs). Niyana runs the guesthouse herself and uses the old **Esam Guesthouse** as an overflow. The rooms are large and have shared bathroom for 90B, singles for 70B.
Rimkhong Bungalows consist of large concrete adjoining bungalows with shower for 200B.
Chai Von Hotel on Phanom Phanarak Road has rooms with bath for 80B, or 60B for an upstairs room without bathroom.
Saeng Thong Hotel is south of the archway on Phanom Phanarak Road and offers basic rooms with share bath for 60B. The common area in the centre of the hotel is a nice spot to relax.

Eat and Meet

The **night market** at the intersection of Route 212 and Kuson Ratchadamnoen Road does good cheap and usual market fare, but it is all closed by 9.00 pm. For a later meal try one of the **restaurants** near the archway, but the English menus carry ridiculously inflated rates. There is a **floating restaurant** near the pier if you want to eat on the river.

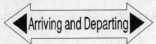

Things to do and Sights to See

Wat Phra That Phanom   วัดพระธาตุพนม

This is one of the most revered wats in I-san and is estimated to be over 1,500 years old. The apex is 57 m high and after collapsing in 1975 was rebuilt and is now a very impressive structure — especially at night. At the full moon of the third lunar month (February to March) a huge festival is held here and thousands of people descend upon the site. The wat is located on Chayangkun Road and is impossible to miss.

Renu Nakhon   เรณูนคร

About 10 km north of town is a small silk and cotton weaving village where reasonably priced fabrics are available. On Saturdays there is a market here where traditional dance is also performed. It is worth a visit if you are in That Phanom for a while. To get there take a songtheaw to the turn-off at km 44 and catch another for the 7 km to the village. There are occasional direct ones or visit it by bicycle - a long way, but it will keep you fit.

Arriving and Departing

Bus

The bus station is on Route 212 south of the archway. The bus to **Nakhon Phanom** costs 15B, **Mukdahan** 15B and to **Sakhon Nakhon** its 20B. To **Udon Thani**, A/C buses cost 105B and leave at 10.45 and ordinary buses cost 62B, leaving at 10.15, 11.30, 12.30 and 13.30. To **Ubon Ratchathani**, A/C buses cost 99B leaving at 07.45, 10.00, 14.45, and ordinary buses cost 54B leaving at 07.00, 07.20, 08.10, 10.05, 12.10 and 14.10. The **Kalasin** A/C bus costs 301B. To **Bangkok** an A/C bus leaves at 17.30 for 301B and the ordinary bus leaves at 08.00 for 167B.

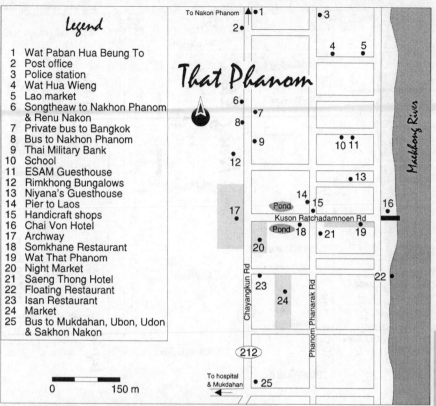

Legend

1. Wat Paban Hua Beung To
2. Post office
3. Police station
4. Wat Hua Wieng
5. Lao market
6. Songtheaw to Nakhon Phanom & Renu Nakon
7. Private bus to Bangkok
8. Bus to Nakhon Phanom
9. Thai Military Bank
10. School
11. ESAM Guesthouse
12. Rimkhong Bungalows
13. Niyana's Guesthouse
14. Pier to Laos
15. Handicraft shops
16. Chai Von Hotel
17. Archway
18. Somkhane Restaurant
19. Wat That Phanom
20. Night Market
21. Saeng Thong Hotel
22. Floating Restaurant
23. Isan Restaurant
24. Market
25. Bus to Mukdahan, Ubon, Udon & Sakhon Nakon

That Phanom

Maekhong River

0   150 m

212

To hospital & Mukdahan

Northeast

NONG KHAI PROVINCE

The long thin province of Nong Khai stretches across the top of I-san, bordered to the north by the Maekhong River and Laos. With the opening of the Thai-Lao Friendship Bridge in 1994, Nong Khai Province is a fitting farewell to Thailand for those heading to Laos, as it contains stunning riverside scenery, some excellent guesthouses and a couple of standout wats. **Wat Sala Kaew Ku** would have to be one of the most bizarre sights in Thailand - if not Asia.

NONG KHAI   หนองคาย

For foreigners, Nong Khai would have to be one of the most visited towns in I-san. This is partially due to it being a popular crossing point to Laos, but also because it has a wealth of its own attractions to offer the visitor. Look through any guesthouse book and you will see the same names repeating every year or so. Whether it is the quaint feel of the town, the slow river front scenery or the particularly friendly locals, Nong Khai gets a lot of repeat visitors.

Vital Information

Tourist Information Many of the guesthouses carry plentiful information on the area.
Post Office on Meechai Road has poste restante facilities and the phone office is upstairs. The phone office hours are 7.00 am to 10.00 pm but 5.00 pm to 6.00 pm is set aside for dinner!
Banks are plentiful — see the map for their location. The Bangkok Bank has an exchange

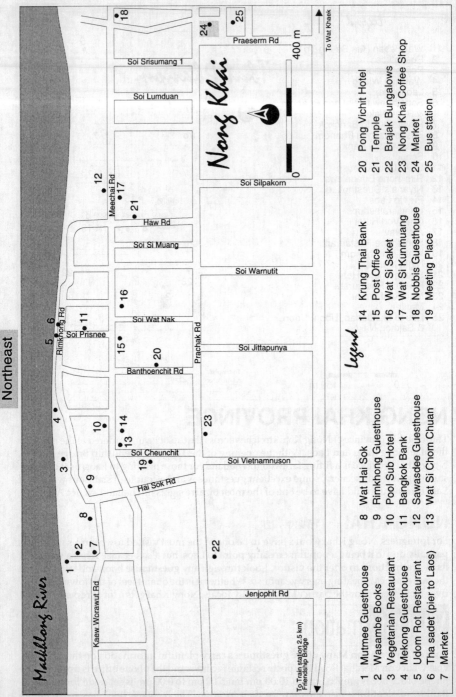

Nong Khai

To Wat Khaek

Maekhong River

Soi Srisumang 1

Soi Lumduan

Meechai Rd

Haw Rd

Soi Si Muang

Rimkhong Rd

Soi Prisnee

Soi Wat Nak

Banthoenchit Rd

Soi Cheunchit

Hai Sok Rd

Kaew Worawut Rd

Praeserm Rd

Soi Silpakorn

Soi Warnutit

Prachak Rd

Soi Jittapunya

Soi Vietnamnuson

Jenjophit Rd

To Train station 2.5 km/
Friendship Bridge

0   400 m

Legend

1 Mutmee Guesthouse
2 Wasambe Books
3 Vegetarian Restaurant
4 Mekong Guesthouse
5 Udom Rot Restaurant
6 Tha sadet (pier to Laos)
7 Market
8 Wat Hai Sok
9 Rimkhong Guesthouse
10 Pool Sub Hotel
11 Bangkok Bank
12 Sawasdee Guesthouse
13 Wat Si Chom Chuan
14 Krung Thai Bank
15 Post Office
16 Wat Si Saket
17 Wat Si Kunmuang
18 Nobbis Guesthouse
19 Meeting Place
20 Pong Vichit Hotel
21 Temple
22 Brajak Bungalows
23 Nong Khai Coffee Shop
24 Market
25 Bus station

Northeast

desk open seven days on the soi leading to the customs office and wharf.
Police on Meechai Road.
Codes Nong Khai's telephone code is (042) and the postal code is 43000.

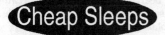

Cheap Sleeps

Mutmee Guesthouse at 1111/4 Kaeworawut Road, run by Julian (British) and his wife, Pon (Thai). This is one of the standout guesthouses in Thailand. Set on the Maekhong River, good and fairly reasonably priced food is served by the river and hammocks are available! Some of the rooms are a bit rundown in a bamboo longhouse whilst others are in good condition in a wooden house. All are very comfortable and rates run from 100B to 120B for a double with fan, nets and share toilet. If you want to splurge, ask for Room 1, the 'Honeymoon Suite', which is a divine room with private bath and your own sitting area looking over the river. At 200B it is worth every penny! The Mutmee also has loads of information (and mosquitos) on the area and Julian is friendly and very helpful. Mutmee also run a two day bike trip to discover rural Thailand which gets very good reviews. Individual hire is available but check the bike over before agreeing to hire it. On the same soi as the Mutmee is **Wasambe Books** which has a limited but interesting selection of new and used books. Email is available for 150B as well as fax, yoga and Tai Chi classes. The owner, Richard, runs the classes and also has some interesting Peace Corp experience.

Sawasdee Guesthouse at 402 Meechai Road is set in an old shophouse style building. The guesthouse has been renovated and is a very nice place to stay. There is an inner court area which is pleasant and the staff are very helpful. The rooms are a bit small but very well kept. Rates are 80B to 120B for singles and doubles with fan but it is best to get a room off the street if you want to sleep.

Mekong Guesthouse on Rimkhong Road has its entrance beside the Mekong Restaurant. Basic and clean rooms here start at 70B/80B for singles/doubles and the restaurant is good.

KC Guesthouse located at the head of the soi leading to Mutmee. Large basic rooms here cost 150B to 200B. This place really only deals with the overflow from Mutmee.

Rimkhong Guesthouse is also near the river on the other side of the same named road where singles are 80B and doubles 150B. There is a comfortable common area though the mosquitoes are rabid.

Nobbis Guesthouse is towards the eastern end of town on Meechai Road with a bar and restaurant downstairs. Rooms here are and are negotiable for longer stays.

Prajak Bungalows (sign reads Brajak), a bit back from the river on Prajak Road so the traffic can become quite noisy. The rooms are a decent size and clean and cost 250B to 300B for rooms with fans.

Phongwichit Hotel on Banthoengchit Road is stock standard material. It has unimpressive rooms which start at 200B with fan and bathroom.

Pool Sub Hotel on Meechai Road, when we asked here for a room, the staff wanted to know why we wanted to stay there rather than a guesthouse. Once you see the rooms you will understand why they asked! Basic and grimy at 150B with fan and bath.

Eat and Meet

Nong Khai has a number of taste tantalising places worth sampling. Along the waterfront by the immigration pier there are a few **waterside restaurants** which serve good food. **Udom Rot** is probably the best choice. Another good place in the area is the **Rim Nam Khong** situated by the Mekong Guesthouse.

The **night market,** at the intersection of Haisook Road and Meechai Road, is very good for both day and night cheap meals - the barbecued chicken is excellent. There is also a selection of vendors around the bus station. Next to the Phongwichit Hotel is a decent

Thai restaurant for all the standard restaurant fare. For more Western orientated food, **Mutmee's** restaurant does good food, and excellent **baguettes** (though they are a little pricey) and **Nobbis Guesthouse** has a decent restaurant downstairs. **Meeting Place** at 1117 Soi Si Chomchuen is a popular place for an evening beer, though the atmosphere can get a bit sleazy at times. Along Meechai Road there are also a few **convenience stores** such as the 7-eleven which is handy (and expensive) for chocolate and ice cream cravings.

Sunset cruises

The much touted sunset river cruises from Nong Khai can be very pleasant, though you will quite often see most of the sunset whilst waiting on the quay for the boat to leave.

Wat Pho Chai   วัดโพธิ์ชัย

This is home to a highly revered Buddha image which dates back to the Lan Chang Empire and part of the statue is solid gold. It is believed to be one of three statues made at the request of the daughters of the King of Lan Chang. In 1778 the images were taken to Vientiane in Laos and were subsequently carried to Nong Khai during the reign of King Rama III. However, during the move, one of the boats sank in a storm sending the Buddha on board hurtling to the bottom but was later recovered. The remaining two were interred in Thai Wats, the recovered statue now resides in Wat Ho Klong.

Wat Sala Kaew Ku (Wat Khaek)   วัดแขก

One of the stranger sights you will see on any trip in Thailand is this bizarre sculpture garden cum religious site cum festival garden. There is an equally bizarre story that goes with the wat. The main motivator behind this strange garden, a Laotian born artist and mystic by the name of Boun Leua Sourirat, went for a stroll in the mountainous lands of his homeland only to fall through a hole in the ground. He landed in the lap of one Keoku, an odd hermit who was living in the cave which Leua fell into. Keoku then went on to teach Leua the ways of Buddha, the underworld, and one assumes, the best way to mix concrete. Because, as the story goes, once Leua left the hermit he got building quick smart. First in Laos, then with the takeover by the communists, he decided to move to somewhere where he believed his hobby would be better tolerated, Thailand.

The sculpture garden is one of those places which is incredibly difficult to describe. It is big and full to the brim with concrete statues of deities from all manner of religions. The standout statue would have to be the seated Buddha with the naga heads behind it, the statue must be close to 35 m high. All of the sculptures are accompanied by a massive sound system which blares out Thai pop and disco music all day long, the final touch in quite a bizarre place.

The story goes on to say that all the constructions you will see there have been constructed by unskilled volunteers who live on the grounds and work for free. Concrete is used solely because it is the cheapest material available for constructions of this size. The wat is open daily and entrance is 5B. The wat is located a ten minute bicycle ride from central Nong Khai, the turn-off (to the right) is opposite a large arch on the left side of the road.

Phra That Nong Khai   พระธาตุหนองคาย

This partially submerged Lao chedi slipped off the bank of the river nearly 150 years ago and is now only visible when the river is low, usually in the dry season. It is quite a long walk from downtown Nong Khai and not really worth the effort, though a late afternoon stroll down the riverside promenade makes it pleasant enough. Once it surfaces, flags are tied to it to make it easier to spot. It is about a 20 to 30 minute walk east along the river promenade to get there.

Northeast

Prap Ho Monument   อนุสาวรีย์ปราบฮ่อ

Built to honour those who died in the crushing of the Ho rebellion of 1886, this monument was built on the orders of Prince Prachak Silpakhom. Originally it was positioned behind Nong Khai Police Station. In 1949 it was moved to its present location at the intersection of Prachak Road and the main road to Udon Thani.

Village Weaver Handicrafts Self Help Project

First established in 1982, this self help project has been established to promote weaving as an income generating activity in the hope of slowing the urban migration which takes place in rural I-san. Seen as an educational facility as well as a community one, all visitors are more than welcome to visit and observe the weaving processes. There is also a decent range of woven goods on sale. The weaving centre is on Prachak Road towards the eastern end of town.

Friendship Bridge   สะพานมิตรภาพ

Australians wanting to see their taxes at work may want to visit this bridge. Unfortunately it is not possible to walk over the bridge and tourists are only allowed to cross it in little minibuses. The Bridge was built jointly by Thailand, Australia and Laos and was opened on 8 April 1994.

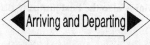

Arriving and Departing

Train

Nong Khai is the end of the line for trains running up the Udon Thani line. The train station is out of town on the way to the Friendship Bridge and has daily departures and arrivals to Bangkok from here. Trains also run from here to Nakhon Ratchasima. A third class fare to **Bangkok** costs 103B. See the timetable at the end of the chapter for details.

Bus

The bus station is centrally located in Nong Khai and has a clear English departures board over the ticket office. Buses to **Udon Thani** leave every 30 minutes, taking 1 hour and cost 15B, to **Loei** seven departures a day take 7 hours and cost 60B, to **Nakhon Phanom** the bus costs 80B. To **Tha Bo** buses leave throughout the day for 10B, **Si Chiang Mai** costs 13B, a bus to **Ban Phu** leaves every 30 minutes until 2.00 pm (last bus back at 4.00 pm) taking 2 hours and costing 20B, **Beung Khan** costs 36B and takes 2½ hours, **Khon Kaen** costs 79B, **Sangkhom** costs 25B and leaves every 50 minutes and buses to **Chiang Khan** cost 65B, though you may need to change at Pak Chom.

AROUND NONG KHAI

Wat Phra That Bang Phuan   วัดพระธาตุบังพวน

This very old pagoda is believed to date back to the early centuries AD. As per usual there have been a number of rebuilding and renovation botch jobs on this place. The most spectacular was in 1559 when the Laotian King extended his capital over the river and built a new Lao style chedi over the original. This lasted for a few hundred years, but with the rain the chedi began to develop a certain lean, a la leaning tower of Pisa, and in 1970 it toppled over. In the late 1970s the Thai Fine Arts Department restored the chedi, the most direct result being that the smaller remaining 16th Century Lao style chedis are now more interesting to the casual onlooker. There is also a small museum on site which is open to the public and admission is free, although donations are always gratefully accepted.

To reach the wat catch any bus from Nong Khai bus station bound for Si Chiang Mai and ask for Wat Phra That Bang Phuan. Hop off at the wat as it is easily seen from the

Northeast

bus. If travelling on your own wheels take Route 2 south until the junction with Route 211. Take the right turn up Route 211 for around 10 km before you reach the wat.

Wat Nam Mong

This is the home to the largest gold Buddha image in Nong Khai, the Luang Pho Phra Chao Ong Tu. Stone inscriptions maintain that this image was built in 1562 by King Chai Chettha. The King and his direct entourage employed 500 men to mould the image using a mixture of gold, brass and silver. Apparently as they were finishing it off, the God Indra showed up with 108 angels in tow to help out. The story also says that a person's sadness will be dispelled if they look at the image. To reach the wat you need to catch a bus from Nong Khai to Tha Bo. All buses from Nong Khai to Si Chiang Mai pass through this town. Once there, the wat is about 3 km from the centre of town, an easy walk or ride away.

SI CHIANG MAI   ศรีเชียงใหม่

This is the spring roll capital of Thailand. Everywhere you look, spring roll wrappers can be seen drying in the sun. Other than taking photos of spring roll wrappers it is a fairly uneventful place though it offers lovely views of Vientiane in Laos on the other side of the river. A promenade and dike are currently undergoing construction and, once finished, should allow for nice strolls by the riverside. Si Chiang Mai is also the best jumping off point for the historical park in Udon Thani Province.

Cheap Sleeps

There is only one place to stay in Si Chiang Mai. **Tim Guesthouse** is run by a Swiss guy and his Thai wife and their guesthouse is a goldmine of information about the area. They also hire bikes and arrange boat trips along the river for those interested. Once the dike is completed they plan to build a number of floating rooms on the river. Rooms are currently 80B/100B for single/doubles and good and reasonably priced food is available. The guesthouse is on the river and to get there wander down soi 16 or 17 to the river and you will see the signs. Currency exchange facilities are available on the main road through town.

Things to do and Sights to See

Wat Hin Mak Peng   วัดหินหมากเป้ง

This wat is a meditation centre and is worth visiting just to observe the scenery and lifestyle in this area of Nong Khai Province. The wat is particularly known for its monks who take a series of ascetic vows as well as the usual ones. The wat's grounds are both scenic and peaceful and visitors should be aware that **modest attire is required.** To reach the wat catch a songtheaw from Si Chiang Mai en-route to Sang Khom and ask for Wat Hin, it should cost around 10B.

Arriving and Departing

Bus

Buses to **Nong Khai** take 1½ hours and cost 13B, **Udon Thani** takes 1½ hours and costs 24B, **Khon Kaen** takes 3 hours and costs 52B, **Pak Chong** takes 2½ hours for 35B, **Sang Khom** takes 1 hour at a cost of 10B, **Loei** takes 5 hours and costs 60B, **Bangkok** takes 12 hours and costs 153B and the bus to **Nakhon Ratchasima** (Khorat) takes 6 hours at a cost of 95B.

SANG KHOM   สังคม

Situated about half way between Nong Khai and Chiang Khan, Sang Khom is an ideal place to break your journey to once again sample village life. In either direction from here the riverside scenery is magnificent. The 20 km or so in each direction from Sang Khom is best explored by bicycle or motorbike. In the surrounding area there are a number of waterfalls and caves and an impressive lookout, all of which can be visited by bicycle or motorcycle. The guesthouses in Sang Khom offer information on the area and a rough map is generally supplied on booking in. Other than the waterfall, caves and lookout, there is little to do in Sang Khom but sit on your riverside bungalow veranda and watch the river just slide by, which is the real beauty of the place.

Cheap Sleeps

Bouy Guesthouse is probably the best in town and is located off the main road, on the river. To get there hop off the bus and walk a little west of the T-intersection — you will see the sign. Run by friendly Ms Toy, the guesthouse is well situated with bungalows costing 50B to 90B with share bathroom. International calls can also be made and the food is good and reasonably priced. Tour groups occasionally stay here, so it can get a bit cramped.

River Huts Guesthouse When looking at the river, River Huts is to the right of Buoy and is run by a friendly Israeli guy and his Thai wife. Identical bungalows, a family atmosphere, a sizeable book shop, an excellent restaurant (try the jungle curry) and comparable prices to the Buoy make this a worthy and quieter alternative

TXK Guesthouse   Again looking at the river, TXK is to the left of Buoy. Bungalows go for 50B to 100B and are probably the most secluded of the three guesthouses.

All guesthouses rent bikes.

Things to do and Sights to See

Namtok Than Thip   น้ำตกธารทิพย์
This pretty waterfall is good for relaxing and bathing. It is a short bus ride to the west of town then a 4 km to 5 km hike to the falls. Ask at your guesthouse for details on how to reach it.

Hill hike
Climb up the hill at the eastern end of town to where there is a small wat with a brilliant view of the surrounds. From the top, a road leads down the other side to the main road and **Namtok Tha Thong**. It is a bit of a long walk and the Tha Thong Waterfall, which is on the main road, are very busy and a bit grubby, but it is a very pleasant walk.

Naga heads at Nong Khai

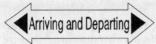◀ Arriving and Departing ▶

A bus from **Nong Khai** costs 25B and takes 2½ to 3 hours, and the bus **Pak Chom** costs 20B.

BAN AHONG

Over 100 km east of Nong Khai along the Maekhong River, this small village is a great place to stay for a quiet escape. The village is fairly uneventful but does have an interesting wat (which is decorated with wagon wheels!) and the abbot cooks up a daily herbal concoction which is definitely worth a taste. The scenery here is pretty and is an ideal jumping off point for the spectacular **Wat Phu Thawk**.

Cheap Sleeps

Hideaway Guesthouse, to get here jump off the bus that passes along the main road by the school (near the 115 km marker if coming from Nong Khai). Walk to the back of the school and turn right and eventually you will reach the guesthouse even though it is poorly signposted. Saksil (Thai) runs this place, is very friendly and fancies himself as a guitar playing Beatles fan! The huts are run down but acceptable. Singles are 50B and doubles 80B. Communal meals are available and hammocks are available.

◀ Arriving and Departing ▶

A bus to **Nong Khai** is 36B, **Beung Khan** is 7B to 10B and **Nakhon Phanom** costs 45B.

AROUND BAN AHONG

Wat Phu Thawk   วัดภูทอก

This spectacular wat is set atop a huge rocky outcrop. To get to the top you climb seven levels of often treacherous staircases (mimicking the seven levels of enlightenment). The views from the top are well worth the strenuous climb. Some of the cool caves are great for relaxing in and are a favourite for meditating monks. The wat is closed during Songkran but you may be able to wangle your way in. It is best visited by motorbike from Ban Ahong, making a nice day trip. By public transport catch a bus to Beung Kan, then a songtheaw south on Route 222 to Ban Similai (10B), then look out for the sign reading Wat Phu Thawk. From here hop on a songtheaw on the road leading east for 20 km to Phu Thawk (10B). Best to do this in the early morning as rides become quite infrequent. The alternative from Ban Similai is to hire a tuk tuk to the wat and back for 150B to 200B.

UDON THANI PROVINCE

This huge province of over 15,000 sq km forms a transportation hub as well as a commercial and agricultural centre for northern I-san. It is bordered to the north by Nong Khai, the west by Loei, the southwest by Nong Bua Lamphu, the south by Khon Kaen and Kalasin and the east by Sakhon Nakhon. Situated on a plateau, Udon Thani Province gradually slips downhill till it runs into Nong Khai Province. The provincial capital, Udon Thani, has little of interest to the traveller but the surrounding area may be of definite interest.

Northeast

UDON THANI   อุดรธานี

Following the establishment of a USAF base during the Vietnam War, this bustling centre became a boom town overnight and to this day there is still a US presence (although greatly reduced). Udon's (also known as Udorn) main role now is as an industrial base and transportation hub to throughout the Northeast and further afield. Although the city itself is not overflowing with things to see, it serves as a handy base from which to visit some of the surrounding sites.

Vital Information

Tourist Office is on Mukkhamontri Road, ☎ (042) 241 968, this new office has friendly and helpful English speaking staff and the usual load of free brochures.
Post Office is also on Mukkhamontri Road just north of the tourist office.
Hospital Wattana Hospital is at 70/7-8 Suphakit Janya Road near the US Consulate.
Police Station is on Si Suk Road.
American Consulate at 35/6 Suphakit Janya Road on the north side of Nong Prajak can issue replacement American passports. It is open from Monday to Friday, 7.30 am to 4.30 pm.
Codes Udon Thani's telephone code is (042) and the postal code is 41000.

Cheap Sleeps

Sri Sawat Hotel at 123/1-3 Prachak Silpakorn Road has clean singles/doubles with fan and shower for 100B/140B. The rooms get pretty hot but they are quiet.
Queen Hotel at 6-8 Udondudsadee Road has singles and doubles with fan and shower for 100B to 200B. They are noisy and the beds are very uncomfortable but the staff are friendly.
Prachapakdee Hotel at 156/8 Prachak Silpakorn Road has clean, comfortable and quiet singles and doubles with bath for 170B to 190B. Watch out for the crazy dog.
Malasrisangden Hotel on Prachak Silpakorn Road near the train station. Rooms with fan cost 140B but they can get noisy.
Chai Porn at 209-211 Mak Khaeng Road has clean singles/doubles with fan and bath for 200B/290B.

Eat and Meet

For those who crave a bit of Western cuisine after too long in the Northeast, Udon is not too bad (though Khon Kaen is better). Udon also has some great local food worth sampling. **Kai Yaang (BBQ Chicken)** near the cinema on the corner of Prachak Silpakorn and Mukkhamontri Road, this no name place does delectable barbecue I-san style chicken and great spicy salads. **Mandarin** next door to the Chai Porn Hotel serves good Thai fare at rapid speed and decent prices (35B to 60B per meal), though the staff really like to stare. Good ice cream is available but the menu is one of the most bizarre you are likely to see. First reader explaining to us what meal 'number 3902-Angry Ocean' is gets a free book! (you will need to include a photo of the dish!) Good pastries are also available.

There are a few decent **rice and noodle places** near the A/C bus pick-up and along Mak Khaeng Road there are innumerable and cheap Thai places. The **night market** is at the intersection of Udondusadee and Pho Si Roads. For **Western food**, your best bet is **Charoensi Plaza** for KFC and others of that ilk.

Northeast

Northeast

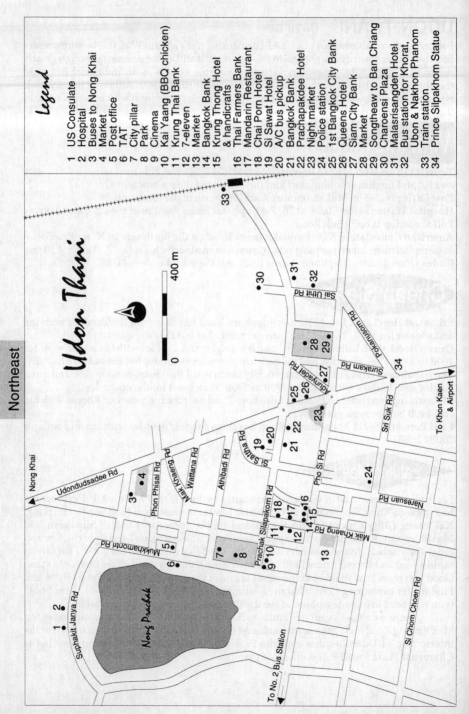

Udon Thani

legend

1   US Consulate
2   Hospital
3   Buses to Nong Khai
4   Market
5   Post office
6   TAT
7   City pillar
8   Park
9   Cinema
10   Kai Yaang (BBQ chicken)
11   Krung Thai Bank
12   7-eleven
13   Market
14   Bangkok Bank
15   Krung Thong Hotel
     & handicrafts
16   Thai Farmers Bank
17   Mandarin Restaurant
18   Chai Porn Hotel
19   Si Sawat Hotel
20   A/C bus pickup
21   Bangkok Bank
22   Prachapakdee Hotel
23   Night market
24   Police station
25   1st Bangkok City Bank
26   Queens Hotel
27   Siam City Bank
28   Market
29   Songtheaw to Ban Chiang
30   Charoensi Plaza
31   Malasrisangden Hotel
32   Bus station for Khorat,
     Ubon & Nakhon Phanom
33   Train station
34   Prince Silpakhom Statue

0   400 m

Things to do and Sights to See

Bung Nong Prachak   หนองประจักษ์

Other than visiting the tourist office just about the most exciting thing you can do in Udon Thani is to wander around Bung Nong Prajak, the large lake to the northwest, which is immensely popular with the locals for afternoon and evening strolls, meals and Mekong Whisky sessions. Named after Prince Prachak Silpakhom, this lake was revamped in 1987 to celebrate King Bhumibol's 60th birthday.

Prince Prachak Silpakhom Statue   อนุสาวรีย์กรมหลวงประจักษ์ศิลปาคม

This monument was erected in the heart of Udon Thani in commemoration of the city's founder, Major General Prince Parchak Silpakhom. Born in 1856 to King Rama IV and his wife Sangwan, he ruled the Northern Province from 1894 to 1900 and established Udon Thani in 1894.

Udon Sunshine Fragrant Orchid Farm   สวนกล้วยไม้อุดรแสงตะวัน

Around 2 km from the city limits, this orchid farm is always filled with the flowers' delicate fragrance. Both the flowers and their perfumes are on sale here.

Pu-Ya Shrine   ศาลเจ้าปู่-ย่า

This shrine near the railway station is home to the Mercy and Pu-Ya deities. Highly revered by the poor, unlucky and generally disadvantaged, the shrine is flanked by Chinese style pagodas.

Wat Pa Ban Tat

Set within a heavily forested area, this wat is regarded as a decent choice for those wishing to practise meditation. Fenced in by a heavy set concrete wall (apparently to keep all the wild beasts at bay) this wat is highly regarded as it is the monastery of Phra Maha Bua Yanasampanno, a follower of Phra Achan Man Phurithatto. To reach Wat Pa Ban Tat you will need to hire a motorbike and travel along Route 2 towards Khon Kaen for about 7 km, then turn right at the Ban Dong Kheng crossroads which you then follow for another 9 km.

Shopping

Udon is a good place for picking up goodies such as **woven rice holders, axe pillows, silk and loads of silver handicrafts**. One of the best handicraft stores in town sits on Prachak Silpakorn Road near its intersection with Mak Khaeng Road - check the map for details.

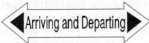
Arriving and Departing

Getting Around

It seems that all samlor and tuk tuk drivers are required to do a particular course in how to best rip off a farang. You will need to bargain furiously for decent rates but figure on 10B to 20B for short distances.

Air

THAI Airways has two flights a day to **Bangkok** which cost 1,310B one way and take one hour. There is also a flight to **Chiang Mai** which costs 2,950B one way. The airport is to the south of town, a tuk tuk ride away.

Northeast

Train

Udon Thani is on the Nong Khai to Bangkok line and there are three through trains in each direction daily. The train station is at the far eastern end of town, a ten minute walk from the centre of town. A 3rd class ticket to **Bangkok** costs 95B. Refer to the end of the chapter for price and timetable information.

Bus

Depending on your destination, there are a couple of different bus stations you need to report to. **Bus Terminal 1** off Sai Uthit Road services Khon Kaen, Roi Et, Nakhon Phanom, Sakhon Nakhon and Khorat. The bus to **Khon Kaen** takes 2½ hours and runs every half hour for 35B, to **Roi Et** costs 35B to **Nakhon Ratchasima (Khorat)** costs 85B, **Nakhon Phanom** costs 95B (every 40 minutes), **That Phanom** 105B (A/C) or 62B for an ordinary bus, **Nong Bua Lam Phu** costs 13B and **Sakhon Nakhon** costs 42B (every 25 minutes).

   Bus Terminal 2 which is way out of town services Loei, Nakhon Phanom, Nong Khai, Chiang Mai, Chiang Rai and Bangkok (note there are some overlaps to destinations between the two terminals). To get there catch the yellow number 2 bus which goes from downtown to the station. If you are unsure of which bus terminal to use, it is best to try at bus station 1 first and if they say no, then make the trek to 2. Buses to **Loei** cost 40B leaving every ½ hour, ordinary buses to **Chiang Mai** cost 160B leaving at 07.30, 17.00, 19.00 and 20.30 whilst A/C buses cost 320B leaving at 19.00 and 20.00. For **Chiang Rai** ordinary buses leave at 18.15 and 20.15 costing 200B and A/C buses run at 16.15 and 20.15 costing 350B. Buses to **Nong Khai** take 1½ hours and cost 15B and to **Si Chiang Mai** the bus costs 24B. To **Bangkok** an ordinary bus costs 134B taking 9 hours and an A/C bus costs 241B.

AROUND UDON THANI

Ban Chiang National Museum   พิพิธภัณฑ์สถานแห่งชาติบ้านเชียง

Declared a UNESCO World Heritage site in December 1992, this splendid museum is split into two sections. One half is a proper museum displaying pottery and artifacts dating back as far as 7,500 years, whilst the second section displays the actual excavation pits where skeletons, burial objects and other artifacts are displayed very much as they would have been found.

   Set near to the junction of three small streams, it was not until the 1960s that excavation of the sites began after a number of visitors had reported finding large pots of immense beauty. The first serious dig in 1967 unearthed a complete skeleton including bronze and iron relics, pottery and an assortment of glass beads. This early result encouraged further digging and by 1973, 30 sq m had been unearthed and due to this it was thought that the original settlement had once stretched for 3½ hectares. A huge range of relics had been unearthed and it was realised that the site was immensely important. By the early 1970s however, looting had become a very serious problem as private (and often foreign) collectors did their best to pillage the natural history of the region. The amount of damage done by these looters is immeasurable and it became difficult for the archeologists to work in areas which had not already been damaged. Tragically, one of the original instigators of the early research and excavations, Chester Gorman, died in 1981 as summarising investigations were being undertaken. Although Chester was never to see the results of his and many other's work, you can.

   Ban Chiang is within easy day trip distance of Udon Thani with any bus to Nakhon Phanom or Sakhon Nakhon passing by the turn-off to the site. There are also direct buses from Udon Thani throughout the day for 25B.

Phu Phra Bat Historical Park   อุทยานประวัติศาสตร์ภูพระบาท

This park is well worth a visit and is accessible from either Nong Khai or Udon Thani. Next to the park entrance is a steep climb to a wat which offers good views over the surrounding area. This park contains quite a bizarre collection of sights including ancient cave paintings carved out of rock shelters, caves and strangely shaped rocks. To wander through all the points of interest would take two to three hours at an easy pace. The trails are fairly well sign posted and pretty easy to follow, though the only trail map in English available when we visited was a huge fixed one, so you need to memorise everything! Some of the highlights include **Usar's tower**, **Temple of Father in Law (Wat Poh Ta)** and numerous cave paintings. The best way to see it is just to wander around.

To get there, the easiest method is by motorbike from either Nong Khai, Si Chiang Mai or Udon Thani. If going by bus and songtheaw you need to catch a bus to Ban Pheu (18B from Udon, 20B from Nong Khai), then from Ban Pheu catch a songtheaw (5B) to the village closest to the park. From here you will need to either walk, hitch or hire a motorbike for the last 2 km to the entrance. The last ride back to Nong Khai is at 2.30 pm and Si Chiang Mai at 4.30 pm. There is a 20B entrance fee and it is open every day from 8.30 am to 5.00 pm.

Na Yang-Nam Som Forest Park   วนอุทยานนายูง-น้ำโสม

This forest park is situated in the far northwest corner of the province and is home to the large **Namtok Yung Thong**. The waterfall cascades 40 m and is particularly spectacular during the wet season. Situated 103 km from Udon Thani the park is best reached by motorcycle. Follow the road through Ban Phu then through Ban Nam Som. When you reach the village of Ban Nam Som take the branch of the road for another 17 km.

Phu Khao-Phu Phan Kham National Park   อุทยานแห่งชาติภูเก้า-ภูพานคำ

This park stretches over 320 sq km, partially in both Udon Thani and Khon Kaen Provinces, and borders the northeastern side of Phu Wiang National Park. The main feature of the park is the Ubol Ratana Dam and Reservoir. See the Around Khon Kaen section for more details.

NONG BUA LAM PHU PROVINCE

Nong Bua Lam Phu was declared the 76th province of Thailand on December 1, 1993 and has an area of almost 4,000 sq km. It is bordered to the north and east by Udon Thani, Khon Kaen to the south and Loei to the west. Very little visited by foreign visitors, Nong Bua Lam Phu is predominantly rural with large forested areas and little development, all of which serve as attractions for those looking for rural unspoilt Thailand.

NONG BUA LAM PHU   หนองบัวลำภู

The provincial capital's history stretches back over 900 years. In 1574, King-to-be, Naresuan, and his father, King Maha-Dharmaracha, rested by Nong Bua Reservoir and used it as a staging point for their invasion of Laos. However King Naresuan fell ill with smallpox and had to return to Ayutthaya. A shrine has been erected in his honour. Two hundred years later, a group of Laotians fled the capital, Vientiane, to Nong Bua Lam Phu where they then erected a fort. However it was to no avail as the Laotian forces promptly visited Nong Bua Lam Phu and forced them to return to Laos. Sections of the stone wall of the fort can still be seen today.

Following that event, Nong Bua Lam Phu has waded around the waters of obscurity, indeed the designation as provincial capital has been the most exciting thing that has happened here in a good while. The city now has a very prefabricated feel to it, full of new shops that seem pretty empty. There is little of interest in town though the artificial lake is a popular evening strolling place.

Northeast

Northeast

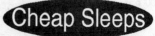
Vital Information

Post Office is on Wisai Udonkit Road.
Hospital is in the centre of town on Loei Street.
Police Station is on Wisai Udonkit Road.
Codes Nong Bua Lam Phu's telephone code is (042) and the postal code is 39000.

Cheap Sleeps

Srisompon Hotel on Po Chai Road has 10 rooms with the basics starting at 100B.
Swangchit Hotel on Wichanrangsan Road has 11 rooms with fan for 80B to 100B.

Eat and Meet

Most of the main restaurants are concentrated to the north side of town along Route 210. More central are **rice and noodle places** clustered around the hotels.

Things to do **and** Sights to See

Monument to King Naresuan
อุทยานแห่งชาติภูเก้า-ภูพานคำ
Located by the side of Nong Bua Reservoir, just north of the centre of town, this monument was made to commemorate King Naresuan and every year on 25 January people congregate to honour him and propitiate his spirit via ritual sacrifices.

Namtok Thao To   น้ำตกเฒ่าโต้
Around 3 km from the centre of town this park and waterfall offer a shady and peaceful escape. It is an interesting place to wander around for its wide variety of flora and rock formations. To get there follow Route 210 towards Udon Thani for around 3 km.

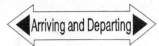

Arriving and Departing

Bus

Buses to **Udon Thani** cost 13B and take 1 to 1½ hours, buses to **Loei** leave every hour for 25B, to **Chaiyaphum** buses cost 45B to **Bangkok** the bus costs 154B (230B A/C) and **Chiang Mai** costs 160B (285B A/C).

AROUND NONG BUA LAM PHU

Tham Erawan   ถ้ำเอราวัน

This huge cave is on Route 210, approximately 45 km from Nong Bua Lam Phu towards Wang Saphun (west). Reached by a set of 600 stairs, the cave sits atop a mountain and has a large Buddha sitting in its entrance. The view from the top is magnificent. To get to Tham Erawan, catch a bus to Loei and jump off near the village Hong Phu Thawang, take a look for the cave which you can see from the road and start walking.

Wat Tham Klong Pane

This is the most famous and most highly revered wat in Nong Bua Lam Phu Province. At one time a place of meditation for the famous monk of meditation, Luang Pu Khaw Analayo, the wat now contains a museum dedicated to the man himself including a life size wax replica and a collection of his possessions. The wat is set in an area of forest, rocks and cliffs and is a very peaceful place. The wat is 15 km off Route 210 between Nong Bua Lam Phu and Udon Thani.

Ban Khong Sawan   โค้งสวรรค์

Famed for its pottery handicrafts, the inhabitants of this village are known for making clay pots and ornaments using ancient traditional methods. The village is on Route 210 en-route to Udon Thani, approximately 17 km from Nong Bua Lam Phu.

LOEI PROVINCE

For many visitors, Loei Province forms the vital junction point from the north to the northeast of Thailand and this positioning is felt here. More hilly than any other province of I-san, Loei retains an unspoilt rural atmosphere and a distinctly wild west ambience along its northern frontier with Laos. Although the provincial capital, Loei, is a bit of a pit, it can be used as a launching pad to Loei's excellent National Parks or merely as a place to spend the night before heading further afield. Loei Province is bordered to the east by Nong Khai, to the south by Nong Bua Lam Phu and Khon Kaen, by Phetchabun and Phitsanulok to the west and by Laos to the north. The province's landscape is breathtakingly beautiful in parts with rolling hills and lush green farmland and forests.

LOEI   เลย

This small provincial town is really not worth mentioning except as a place to sleep or to use as a launching point for other points of interest. For some reason, however, the town has become inundated with bakeries, nightclubs, bands and large and powerful motorbikes, making any venture across the street a dangerous one as the young hoons of the town try to impress their friends with their noisy machines.

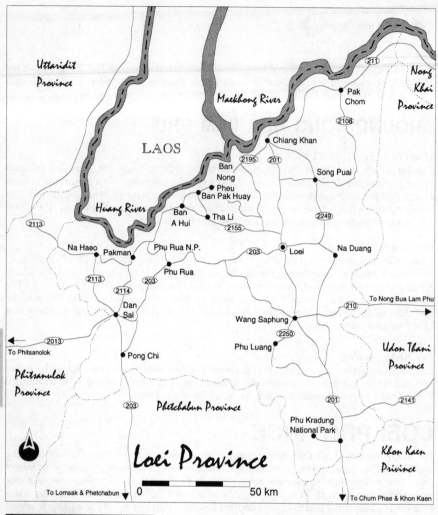

Vital Information

Post Office is on Chareonrat Road at the southern end of town, a few hundred metres after the suspension bridge. The telecommunications centre is located next door and open from 7.00 am to 10.00 pm.

Banks are concentrated along Chareonrat, Uaari, Ruamchit and Ruamchai Roads.

Hospital at the intersection of Maliwan and Nok Kaew Roads.

Police Station is at the intersection of Charoenrat Road and Phipatana Mongkot Roads.

Codes Loei's telephone code is (042) and the postal code is 42000.

Danielle's Poetic Prowess
Loei is lovely , Loei is nice, come and try their sticky rice.

Cheap Sleeps

Muangloei Guesthouse has moved a soi closer to the bus station and is now located in a brand new apartment block. Enquire at the restaurant where the sign tells you it is 30 m to the left. The owner will take you down the gap next to the restaurant to the hidden street behind and show you the second very sterile apartment with white walls, tiles and fluorescent lights. A bed will cost you 60B with fan, but try for one upstairs as every noise travels. The room downstairs has been split into two, so one room gets the door opening into the tiny garden, but the other has the light switch!! The owner can give the latest information on the surrounding area and National Parks. Australian, French and English men be warned, the owner is on a personal vendetta against you! If possible do not disclose your nationality. She used to rent motorcycles, but one too many came back damaged, although she may be able to find someone else willing to rent you theirs.

Sarai Thong Hotel, ☎ (042) 811 582, on 25/5 Ruamchit Road, has 56 decent sized rooms with fan and bathroom for 120B. The manager here prefers to try to speak French rather than English or Thai so checking in can be a bit of a struggle (if you are not French) but it is your best bet in town after the guesthouse.

Si Sawat Hotel, ☎ (042) 811 574, at 18 Ruamchit Road is 80B to 100B if they let you stay.

Thai Udom Hotel, ☎ (042) 811 763, is at 122/1 Charoenrat Road, on the corner with Uaari Road. It is located on a busy intersection but is large and central with friendly staff. Rooms with fan and one/two beds are 200B/280B, with A/C 300B/400B, and VIP 500B/600B. Try for a room at the back for a quiet sleep.

Phu Luang Hotel, ☎ (042) 811 570, at 55 Charoenrat Road, only has A/C rooms from 500B.

Eat and Meet

Jim Bakery at 12/3 Ruamchit Road, just south of the cinema is the best bakery in town attracting the more affluent Loei crowds in the A/C, non-smoking environment. Western style cakes and pasteries are divine, pizzas and steaks will fill you up, the treats like chocolate cake, almond cake and banana splits will keep you satisfied, and the De Loei white wine, happy. Open from 7.00 pm until 10.00 pm.

Sawita Bakery at 137-139 Charoenrat Road, has a decent selection of both Thai and Western food and ice cream all at reasonable prices. Great pastries! There is also the **Bakery House** located near the cinema on Uaari Road which does more delectable cream pastries and coffee.

Sor Ahan Thai Restaurant on Nok Kaew Road has a wide variety of Thai and Chinese cuisine in a nice outdoor wagon wheel setting. The price for meals is around 60B and up, and the service is good and friendly.

Chinatown Fast Food Restaurant on Uaari Road towards Charoenrat Road and has a wooden front covered with stickers. They serve standard Thai and Chinese fare with an English menu and reasonable prices. Some of the food is quite tasty though the service is indifferent.

Nid's Kitchen Thai Food Restaurant on Ruamchit Road, nearly opposite the Phu Luang Hotel has so many health department certificates that it will appease the most paranoid stomach. They serve very cheap I-san and Thai dishes for between 15B and 25B.

Tom's Cabin is more a place for beer than food but they do both. Its a great pub with live music most nights and is often full of Thais hoeing into the whiskey. A very entertaining place and highly recommended. The beer garden is also nice on quiet dry evenings.

Pegasas Music Hall on Ruamphattana Road is an impressive night club with karaoke bar on the ground floor and band room and nightclub on the first floor complete with two resident DJs, starting around 10.00 pm. Next door is **Robot** which also attracts a large number of the young social crowd in town.

Queen Pub is a small pub with a gothic theme. They have bands and it is open from 7.00 pm

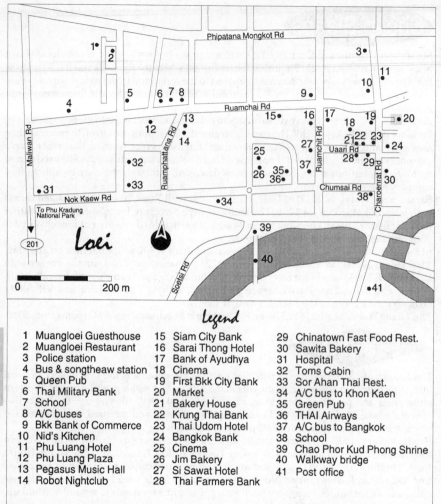

Legend

1	Muangloei Guesthouse	15	Siam City Bank	29	Chinatown Fast Food Rest.
2	Muangloei Restaurant	16	Sarai Thong Hotel	30	Sawita Bakery
3	Police station	17	Bank of Ayudhya	31	Hospital
4	Bus & songtheaw station	18	Cinema	32	Toms Cabin
5	Queen Pub	19	First Bkk City Bank	33	Sor Ahan Thai Rest.
6	Thai Military Bank	20	Market	34	A/C bus to Khon Kaen
7	School	21	Bakery House	35	Green Pub
8	A/C buses	22	Krung Thai Bank	36	THAI Airways
9	Bkk Bank of Commerce	23	Thai Udom Hotel	37	A/C bus to Bangkok
10	Nid's Kitchen	24	Bangkok Bank	38	School
11	Phu Luang Hotel	25	Cinema	39	Chao Phor Kud Phong Shrine
12	Phu Luang Plaza	26	Jim Bakery	40	Walkway bridge
13	Pegasus Music Hall	27	Si Sawat Hotel	41	Post office
14	Robot Nightclub	28	Thai Farmers Bank		

to 1.00 am. Another pub/club is the **Green Pub** on Chumsai Road.

Night Market sets up on Charoenrat Road where food stalls line up at night, instead of the clothing shops which are there during the day, selling a variety of local delights including eggs on sticks. They usually have a wide range of Thai desserts. There are also Thai food vendors who set up at night around both the cinemas for a **late night feed**.

Things to do and Sights to See

There is not too much to keep you enthralled within Loei town but if you have a few hours to kill you can go for a walk. Try crossing the suspension bridge and wandering past the farms on the other side of the river or along the khlong on the south side of town. There is the small **Chao Phor Kud Phong Shrine** on Soetsi Road and next to it is a walking bridge over the khlong to the other side where the fitness fanatics in town work their way around the park.

◀ **Arriving and Departing** ▶

Air

The THAI Airways office is located up a soi just off Chumsai Road, next door to PR House, look for the sign. The airport is 6 km along Route 2015, south of the roundabout. Enquire at the THAI Airways office for their shuttle bus to the airport. Flights to **Bangkok** cost 1,490B.

Bus

A/C buses to Phitsanulok, Chiang Rai and Chiang Mai leave from the other side of Ruamchai Road from the main bus terminal. To **Phitsanulok** the bus costs 58B at 10.00, 11.30, 14.30, 18.30, 19.30, to **Chiang Mai** costs 136B, **Chiang Rai** costs 156B and **Nakhon Ratchasima** (Khorat) costs 95B. The ordinary buses to Phitsanulok and Chiang Mai leave the bus station at 10.00, 12.00, 19.30, 21.30, 22.00. The bus to **Udon Thani** costs 40B, **Nong Khai** costs 60B, **Si Chiang Mai** costs 60B, **Pak Chom** costs 25B, **Chaiyaphum** costs 57B and **Nong Bua Lam Phu** costs 25B. Air conditioned buses to **Khon Kaen** leave from Nok Kaew Road, west of the roundabout at 06.30, 12.30 and 16.30.

Buses to **Bangkok** leave regularly from a couple of places, both A/C and ordinary buses leave from Ruamchai Road, east of the bus station for 279B/128B, and A/C VIP buses leave from Ruamchit Road with five between 07.00 and 12.30, and seven between 18.00 and 20.50.

Songtheaw

Songtheaws from the bus station to **Chiang Khan** cost 14B and to **Tha Li** cost 15B.

AROUND LOEI

Surrounding Loei are the three main reasons to visit Loei town, Pha Kradung National Park, Phu Luang Wildlife Sanctuary and Phu Rua National Park. All are within a very long day trip distance of Loei town, though to best appreciate them you will need to spend a night or so in each. The frontier around the Laos border is also worth a visit around Tha Li District, however details are under Around Chiang Khan.

Phu Kradung National Park   อุทยานแห่งชาติภูกระดึง

At an elevation of 1,360 m, and covering 349 sq km, the highlight of this National Park rests upon the summit of a large bell shaped sandstone mountain. The mountain top plateau covers 60 sq km, most of which is fairly open grassland with the odd pine tree. A range of different wild flowers bloom from September to December and in March and April the rhododendrons come to life. The views down to the rolling hills and plains below are spectacular and many of the trekkers make an effort to see the sunset or sunrise. The National Park is also home to a wide range of wildlife including the Asian wild dog, wild pigs, black giant squirrel, gibbons, barking deer, Asiatic black bear, elephants, langur and macaques as well as a variety of birdlife with 130 species found at last count.

The National Park is one of the best organised and most popular within Thailand and was officially declared a park in 1962. In 1996, over 10,000 people visited the park just during the New Year period! The park contains over 50 km of well marked trails through a variety of temperate vegetation. The temperature at the top is usually around 6° C less than at the base, in December dropping to freezing and in March it soars into the 30s. The walk from the headquarters to the top of the mountain is 9 km up a fairly steep incline that takes around 3 hours, however locals have set up rest stops and food stalls along the way. Porters sporting muscles on muscles can carry your bag for a per kilo fee — some of the weights they carry are almost inhuman. From here to the campsite is another 3 km on flat ground. At the end of 1996 a cable car project to the summit had just been approved by the government, which should make the trip to the summit considerably easier.

The highlights include views from numerous cliffs such as **Yiap Mek, Pa Nok Aen** (2 km from campsite) on the eastern side for sunrise and **Lomsak cliff** (9 km from campsite) an overhanging rock on the southern side for the sunset, as well as the waterfalls spread around the park. A big non event includes the small Buddha image, 500 m from the camping ground which has had its housing destroyed by lightning on numerous occasions, but the image itself has never been damaged. The park closes from June to October as the rainy season makes the trails treacherous and landslides can become a problem. Admission into the park costs 25B.

Cheap Sleeps

Accommodation is available at the park, though camping is by far the cheapest option. Tents are 40B for a tiny two person tent, and you can hire blankets for 10B each, otherwise it costs 5B to put up your own tent. The camping site is huge, often filled with Thai students and their guitars, but fortunately camping is allowed anywhere in the National Park, so you can get your own quiet time by seeking out another location if you have your own tent. You can also avoid some of the crowds by visiting during the week. There are also around 15 bungalows available that cost 500B, contact the National Park's Office in Bangkok for reservations, ☎ (02) 579 0529. **Restaurants and shops** are abundant at the camping ground where you can pick up virtually anything and you are also likely to find a Thai food vendor at any of the main sights. There are a couple of resorts in Phu Kradung town, most are expensive but the cheapest, at around 200B, is located near the bus station.

Arriving and Departing

It is best to stay overnight within the park to see it at its best, at sunrise or sunset, but also because a day trip will leave you an exhausted wreck. To get there from Loei catch a bus to Phu Kradung town 82 km from Loei, the first leaves Loei at 6.00 am, and the last returning bus leaves Phu Kradung bus station at around 5.45 pm. From the bus station, songtheaws run to the park entrance for 7B when full, otherwise a motorbike taxi will take you the 5 km for 20B. From the south you can catch a train to Khon Kaen from Bangkok then jump on a bus to Phu Kradung. If you are on the Bangkok to Loei bus that leaves from Bangkok's northern bus terminal get off at Pa Nok Khao and onto another bus heading down the road branching to Phu Kradung town. If in a car or motorbike, take Route 201, then turn onto Route 2019 for 8 km.

Phu Rua National Park   อุทยานแห่งชาติภูเรือ

Set at 1,365 m above sea level and covering 121 sq km, the prominent mountain within this park, Phu Rua, has a cliff jutting out which looks like a Chinese junk. Highlights in the park are the **Hin Tao rock formation** which resembles a turtle, **Pha Sap Thong cliff** covered in gold coloured lichen, the 30 m high **Huai Phai Waterfall** (2 km from headquarters), **Pa Lon Noi viewpoint** (3 km from headquarters) and the **Buddha image** (at the summit) which is a known pilgrimage site and offers views of Laos and the Maekhong River and stunning sunrise views. It is possible to drive all the way to the summit, alternatively there is a hiking trail which takes about two hours. The flora varies from tropical to evergreen but the wildlife is not as rich as in other parks in this region as authorities have had problems with local villagers over illegal logging and poaching.

Accommodation within the park is available with camping (bring your own or hire one) being the cheapest option. There are also seven National Park bungalows available and one dormitory for up to 50 people. Temperatures within the park have been known to reach below freezing in December.

◀**Arriving and Departing**▶

To get to the park catch a bus to the town of Phu Rua from where you will need to arrange your own transport to the park office itself. It is easy to get to Phu Rua but, as with most National Parks in Thailand, the last bit is always a challenge. Catch a bus from Loei bound for Lomsak or Phitsanulok along Route 203 and jump off at Phu Rua town (50 km from Loei) where you will see a sign to the park. If you are in luck there will be a tuk tuk waiting to whisk you up to the park office for 15B. If not perhaps a motorcycle taxi or hitching might be useful. Alternatively, you can follow the signs and walk the 4 km to the National Park headquarters, then another 5 km to the top of the mountain which can be reached via road.

Phu Pha Man National Park   อุทยานแห่งชาติภูผาม่าน

Covering 350 sq km this National Park was established in 1991 and encompasses parts of Loei and Khon Kaen Provinces. The temporary park headquarters is located on Route 201 at the 264 to 265 km marker, close to Pha Nok Khao town. Near the temporary office are **Tham Phothiyan, Tham Kled Kaew,** and **Tham Sakaew,** caves with a variety of stalactites and stalagmites. Pre-historic wall paintings exist on the walls at **Tham Lai Thaeng** and a number of waterfalls can cool you down - **Namtok Tat Hong, Tat Fa,** and **Khao Sam Yot.** Since the park has only been open a short time, facilities have not really been established. Accommodation is only possible in the camping ground for which you will need to bring your own tent.

Phu Luang Wildlife Sanctuary   เขตรักษาพันธุ์สัตว์ป่าภูหลวง

Also known as the 'Emerald of I-san' this park is at an elevation of 1,550 m. Although wildlife is abundant within the park boundaries, it is seldom visited and is strictly controlled by the National Parks Authority and is quite a difficult park to visit independently. Muangloei Guesthouse in Loei can be of assistance in arranging visits to the National Park or you can make a reservation by calling the Loei Administration and Service Office on ☎ (042) 812 033. The park is closed between June and September.

◀**Arriving and Departing**▶

Catch a bus from Loei 20 km south to the town of Wang Saphung. From there take Route 2250 to the southwest for 26 km until you reach the National Park Office, after which it is a further 9 km south by car, then 3 hours walk to the accommodation.

PAK CHOM   ปากชม

If travelling west from Nong Khai Province, Pak Chom is the first place you will reach within Loei Province which has accommodation. There is little to do in the town itself but sit around and chew the fat, though you can arrange boat trips from here along the Maekhong River.

Cheap Sleeps

Pak Chom Guesthouse is the only guesthouse in town. They have four bungalows with share bathroom for 50B/70B for singles/doubles. The restaurant here is decent and reasonably priced. The staff are friendly, speak passable English and can arrange boat trips for a decent rate along the Maekhong River. Not a bad choice if you are after some solitude. The guesthouse is at the western end of town. From the bus station walk out along the road to Chiang Khan till just before the 147 km marker. To your right there is a dirt track signposted to Pak Chom

Northeast

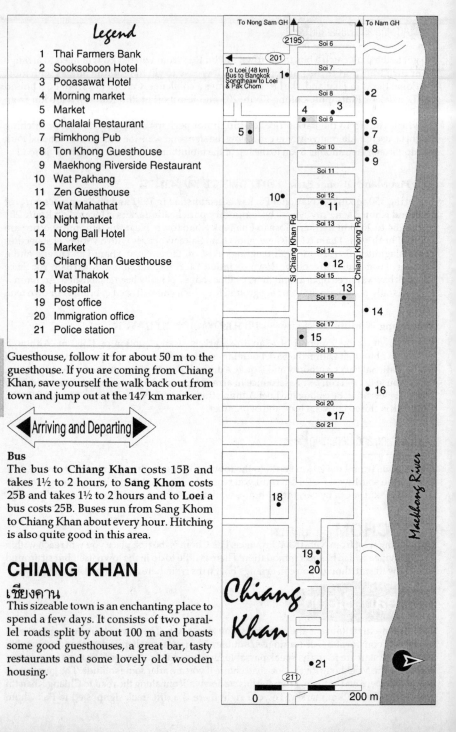

Legend

1 Thai Farmers Bank
2 Sooksoboon Hotel
3 Pooasawat Hotel
4 Morning market
5 Market
6 Chalalai Restaurant
7 Rimkhong Pub
8 Ton Khong Guesthouse
9 Maekhong Riverside Restaurant
10 Wat Pakhang
11 Zen Guesthouse
12 Wat Mahathat
13 Night market
14 Nong Ball Hotel
15 Market
16 Chiang Khan Guesthouse
17 Wat Thakok
18 Hospital
19 Post office
20 Immigration office
21 Police station

To Nong Sam GH
To Nam GH
2195
Soi 6
201
To Loei (48 km)
Bus to Bangkok
Songthaew to Loei
& Pak Chom
1
Soi 7
Soi 8
2
4   3
Soi 9
6
5
7
Soi 10
8
9
Soi 11
10
Soi 12
11
Si Chiang Khan Rd
Soi 13
Chiang Khong Rd
Soi 14
12
Soi 15
13
Soi 16
14
Soi 17
15
Soi 18
Soi 19
16
Soi 20
17
Soi 21
18
19
20
21
211
0   200 m
Maekhong River
Chiang Khan

Guesthouse, follow it for about 50 m to the guesthouse. If you are coming from Chiang Khan, save yourself the walk back out from town and jump out at the 147 km marker.

◄ Arriving and Departing ►

Bus
The bus to **Chiang Khan** costs 15B and takes 1½ to 2 hours, to **Sang Khom** costs 25B and takes 1½ to 2 hours and to **Loei** a bus costs 25B. Buses run from Sang Khom to Chiang Khan about every hour. Hitching is also quite good in this area.

CHIANG KHAN

เชียงคาน
This sizeable town is an enchanting place to spend a few days. It consists of two parallel roads split by about 100 m and boasts some good guesthouses, a great bar, tasty restaurants and some lovely old wooden housing.

Vital Information

Post Office is at the eastern end of town down the soi near and opposite the **hospital**.
Banks Thai Farmers Bank are on Si Chiang Khan Road opposite and between soi's 7 and 8.
Hospital is opposite the post office.
Police Station is at the eastern end of town.
Immigration Office is near the post office. Visas can be extended here.
Codes Chiang Khan's telephone code is (042) and the postal code is 42110.

Cheap Sleeps

Note that in slow periods all guesthouse rates here are very negotiable.
Chiang Khan Guesthouse, ☎ (042) 821 029, is where friendly Ong will set you up in a large twin room with fan and nice views for 50B to 80B. Food, boat trips and motorcycle hire (25B per hour) are all available. The place is a little run down but has a lot of character.
Tongkhong Guesthouse is opposite soi 10 on Chai Khong Road with lovely river views. Friendly management have clean but small rooms for 150B but will take 100B.
Zen Guesthouse is off the river on soi 12. This do-it-yourself guesthouse has signs everywhere telling you what to do! "Please leave your rent in the envelope. Thanks!" Clean double rooms go for 100B and they also have herbal steam baths, bicycles, library and much more available.
Phunsawat Guesthouse Hotel on soi 9 has basic rooms for 60B to 80B and motorcycles, bicycles and boat trips are available.
Nong Sam Guesthouse about 1 km west of town in an isolated location makes for a nice quiet retreat. Bungalows here are 80B to 150B with fan though you will need to go into town for food.

Eat and Meet

For a cheap feed go no further than **soi 9** which has a good selection of cheap I-san eateries.
Maekhong Riverside Restaurant is a friendly place on the river past soi 10. It has good food on an English menu and at reasonable prices. The **Rimkhong Pub** is a great place for an evening out in Chiang Khan and also has voluminous tourist information and traveller tips. If you want to do anything in Loei Province, Pascal is the man to talk to. English and French is spoken and boat trips and breakfast are available. **Chalalai Restaurant** is just west of Rimkhong Pub offering good fare that is not overly expensive with nice decor and amiable staff.

Things to do and Sights to See

Kaeng Khut Khu   แก่งคุดคู้

These rapids, about 4 km downstream from Chiang Khan, are worth spotting on a day trip. It is possible to hire boats to visit the rapids, else sit on the shore and munch out on great food. Particularly tasty is the *kung ten* (live prawns in a lime and chilli sauce) and *kung thawt* (prawns fried into large batter like biscuits and served with a chilli dip). The river here is lined with sit-down places and you could easily spend a few hours here. For those who are really taken by it, accommodation is available. The easiest way to get here is to hire a bicycle or motorbike, although hitching is not difficult especially on weekends. It is also possible to get there via boat from Chiang Khan and most guesthouses can arrange it.

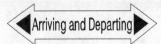

Bus and Songtheaw

To **Loei** there are dead slow songtheaws which leave every 20 minutes during the day at 14B. To **Sang Khom** buses leave every hour for 40B and to **Pak Chom** it costs 15B.

AROUND CHIANG KHAN

For those wanting to get further afield in this remote area of Thailand, we would suggest you pop into Rimkhong Pub and take a look at their notes on Chiang Khan. They have over 50 pages of bicycle trips, motorcycle trips and river and walking treks and are always keen to be of help. Motorcycle trips west towards Tha Li and Ban Pak Huay are particularly beautiful and highly recommended. There is no direct public transport to Tha Li District from Chiang Khan, although Route 2195 is sealed. At the moment all public transport goes via Loei. This is why a motorcycle trip is recommended. Traffic further west of Chiang Khan can be light and hitching could be difficult.

Ban Tha Li, Ban Pak Huay and Ban Nong Pheu   ท่าลี่

These border villages are in a fairly remote and little visited area of Thailand, yet are quite remarkable for the stunning scenery which surrounds them and the definite wild west feel which still exists. Bordering with Laos, the two countries are divided by the 40 m wide Heuang River (which joins the Maekhong River just west of Chiang Khan), however it is not enough to stop the constant trading of goods by small powered boats. Large amounts of contraband crosses the border from Laos and can be observed at the border market in the village of **Ban Nong Pheu** as boats loaded with just about everything imaginable criss cross the river. The best place to witness this is in the wat grounds where the market takes place on random dates which rotate according to the lunar calendar. Best to ask at OTS Guesthouse or in Chiang Khan first to find out whether the market is on before making the trip.

Tha Li District is set predominantly in a valley, surrounded by rolling hills and spotted with forest and farms varying from bananas to cotton. The Laotian side of the border tempts your adventurous side with larger mountains, sweeping forests and a touch of the unknown, but any attempt to cross may result in meeting with some unsavoury characters as the other side of the border can be quite lawless at times. If you arrive in Loei via Dan Sai (to the west) you will get a taste of the region, but the border road has a distinctly remote feel.

Tha Li is the most developed town within the general region, as it is the central point for the three other towns A Hui, Pak Huay and Nong Pheu. A Hui is fairly non descript, Pak Huay is the prettiest of them with the spacious town made up of old wooden houses, whilst Nong Pheu has the market which is the spot to view border trade.

Cheap Sleeps

OTS Guesthouse is located in Ban Pak Huay by the river. The three rustic bamboo bungalows cost 80B with a share bathroom, mosquito net and fan, but there may be a few holes in the roof so pray it does not rain. The friendly family make you feel at home and promise 'a quiet and peaceful stay with an atmosphere full of love'. Food is available as well as bicycle hire. A perfect place to lose yourself for a few days. There are a few noodle restaurants in town for variety.

To find OTS coming from Chiang Khan follow the road through Ban Pak Huay (do not take the turn-off to Tha Li) and continue straight when the road turns right (about 100 m). Continue down the dirt road and the guesthouse is on your left. If coming from Tha Li, take the left at the crossroad in Ban Pak Huay (right to Chiang Khan) and follow the above. If you get lost ask anyone there.

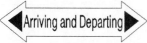

The border road extends for the whole district from Pak Chom in the east to Na Haew in the west (as well as into neighbouring provinces) and is asphalted the whole way. The best way to explore the region is by motorbike from Loei or Chiang Khan so you can stop at your leisure. Ban Nong Pheu is only 50 km away from Chiang Khan but songtheaws do not travel this route. Songtheaws do however visit Tha Li from **Loei** every half hour between 7.20 am and 5.30 pm for 15B, taking between 1 to 1½ hours (46 km). The last songtheaw back to Loei from Tha Li is at 4.00 pm. On weekends the songtheaws get very full, so you may want to jump on the roof. If you have your own transport take Route 201 heading north, after 8 km turn left onto Route 2115. When you get to a T-junction, Tha Li is 1 km left and Pak Huay 9 km to your right. Nong Phu is another 5 km on. Turn left after the boom gate to get to Nong Phu and when you hit a T-junction at the beginning of town, turn left to get to the wat. The Laotian village on the other side of the river is quite large at around 1,000 houses.

Songtheaws leave hourly between 7.00 am and 4.00 pm from Tha Li for **A Hui** and **Pak Huay** for 7B with some continuing onto Nong Phu.

CHAIYAPHUM PROVINCE

This province sits more or less in the centre of Thailand and has an area of just under 13,000 sq km. Approximately 50% of the province is either mountainous or forested and the remainder is plateau country. Despite its central location, Chaiyaphum rarely features on the traveller itinerary. In fact on arrival at Yin's Guesthouse the owner declared us to be a dying breed! The low exposure may make Chaiyaphum worth a visit for the outlying silk villages and Nam Nao National Park.

CHAIYAPHUM   ชัยภูมิ

Generally a quiet town with nothing much going on, but whilst we were there an LPG tanker exploded spraying shrapnel all over the place! Other than explosive activity there is not much else of interest but it does make a good base for exploring the surrounding province.

The city does have a long and interesting history. Chaiyaphum is believed to have first surfaced as a Khmer vassal state during the peak of the Angkorian Empire and this is evidenced by a series of ruins throughout the province. During the reign of King Narai the city was under the administration of Nakhon Ratchasima but was later abandoned. Later still, during the reign of King Rama II and then King Rama III a Laotian nobleman by the name of Lae wandered around in this area with his people. When he finally broke with his Laotian overlords and began to pay offerings to Rama III, he was given the city of Chaiyaphum. In response to this the Laotian forces attacked and took Nakhon Ratchasima. When they decided to retreat they attacked and took Chaiyaphum and, after failing to convince Lae to join the Laotian rebellion, killed him under a tamarind tree. A shrine to Lae still stands 3 km from town.

Vital Information

Post Office is on the corner of Bannakaan and Non Muang Roads.
Banks Krung Thai is on Yutitham Road and the Bangkok City Bank is on Yutitham Road.
Hospital is on Bannakaan Road.
Police Station is by the roundabout with the statue of Phraya Phakdi Chumphon.
Codes Chaiyaphum's telephone code is (044) and the postal code is 36000.

Northeast

Cheap Sleeps

Yin's Guesthouse is about a five minute walk from the bus station. Large basic rooms with a share bathroom in a big wooden house go for the bargain price of 40B per person. It is run by a friendly Norwegian and his Thai wife and tours to nearby silk villages can be organised here. They are also a good source of information on the area.

Charoen Hotel, ☎ (044) 811 194, at 196/7 Nong Muang Road, has rooms with fan for 120B.

Sirichai Hotel, ☎ (044) 811 461, at 565 Non Muang Road, has 102 rooms. This large hotel has rooms with fan for 150B but the bulk are A/C and start at 300B.

Eat and Meet

The **night market** cannot be surpassed for bargain priced and excellent food. If you stay at Yin's there is a good **noodle shop** on your left hand side as you walk back to the main road. Opposite the Ratanasiri Hotel is a **good restaurant** for both Thai and Chinese cuisine.

Things to do **and** Sights to See

Phraya Phakdi Chumphon Monument   อนุสาวรีย์พระยาภักดีชุมพล

Located in the centre of town, this monument is dedicated to the above mentioned Lae, the Laotian nobleman who, after refusing to join a Laotian rebellion, was killed under a tamarind tree 3 km from the centre of town (see below). The monument was made in 1975.

Chao Pho Phraya Lae Shrine   ศาลเจ้าพ่อพระยาแล

This shrine is 3 km to the west of town along Route 205. This shrine has been built to honour Lae and is built more or less on the spot where he was executed for refusing to join a Laotian rebellion.

Silk Villages

There are a number of silk villages around Chaiyaphum town which are worth visiting if you are interested in observing the silk making process. In most of these villages little, if any, English is spoken so you would be best to organise a trip with a guide. Yin's Guesthouse is your best bet for this. The most visited village is **Ban Kwao,** and although much of this village is dedicated to retail outlets some weaving can still be seen. If you want to buy silk this is the place. Prices are about half that of Bangkok or Chang Mai. The village of **Ban Sai Ngam** is probably the best choice to watch the silk making process but the shopping area here is very limited.

To get to **Ban Kwao** songtheaws leave from a block south of the Ratchatham Non Muang intersection. The ride takes about 45 minutes and costs 6B to 7B. The last songtheaw back leaves Ban Kwao in the early afternoon so it is best if you do this trip in the morning.

To get to **Ban Sai Ngam** catch a bus heading to Chumphae and jump off around 10 km up the road. The village sprawls out off the sealed road running off to your right. Tell the conductor where you want to get off so you do not miss it. Buses heading back to Chaiyaphum run throughout the day so just give them a wave. The cost is 10B and takes 20 minutes.

Prang Ku   ปรางค์กู่

This Khmer prang was constructed in the 12th Century as a kind of hospital for travellers en-route to Angkor Wat. The prang is highly venerated by residents of Chaiyaphum and is often surrounded by offerings. The prang is on the outskirts of town near the end of Bunnakan Road.

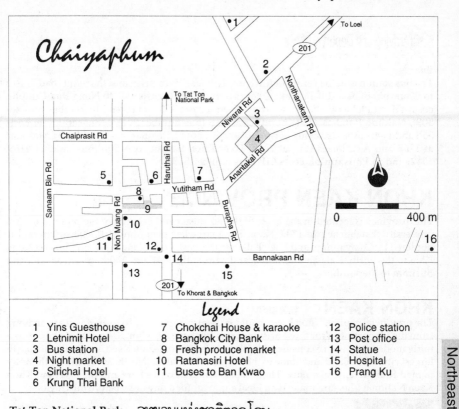

Chaiyaphum

Legend

1 Yins Guesthouse	7 Chokchai House & karaoke	12 Police station
2 Letnimit Hotel	8 Bangkok City Bank	13 Post office
3 Bus station	9 Fresh produce market	14 Statue
4 Night market	10 Ratanasiri Hotel	15 Hospital
5 Sirichai Hotel	11 Buses to Ban Kwao	16 Prang Ku
6 Krung Thai Bank		

Northeast

Tat Ton National Park   อุทยานแห่งชาติตาดโตน

This National Park was declared in 1980 and stretches to just under 220 sq km, however a vast majority of it is situated on a plateau over 500 m above sea level. It is located 21 km from Chaiyaphum and is best known for the same named **Tat Ton Waterfall**, which features a 50 m wide terrace and 6 m drop. This is also a popular picnic location for Thais during the weekends. Near the waterfall is the **Chao Pho Tat Ton Shrine** which is dedicated to Chao Pho Tat Ton, a Khmer man who moved to Thailand around the same time as Chao Pho Phraya Lae (the Laotian prince). He became a hermit who practised strict meditation and was believed to have healing powers. Upon his death a number of shrines were erected in his honour.

Accommodation at the National Park is available with bungalows which sleep six people starting at 250B. Small two person tents are also available for 30B or, if you bring your own tent, it costs a mere 5B per night. There is no direct public transport to the park but on weekends hitching would not be too tricky. Otherwise the best way to get there would be by motorbike.

Sai Thong National Park
This park is located to the southeast of Tat Ton and covers 319 sq km. There are a couple of low level mountain ranges passing through the centre of the park, Phang Ye and Phra Ya Fo, with the highest peak reaching just over 1,000 m. The parks' highlights consist of a few caves, waterfalls and gardens.

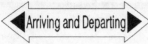

Bus

The bus station is in the centre of town just between the market and the main road. Buses to **Chumphae** costs 20B and take 2 hours but with A/C costs 45B, to **Nong Bua Lamphu** costs 45B and takes 4½ hours, to **Khon Kaen** it costs 35B and takes 2 hours (bus number 509), **Nakhon Ratchasima** (Khorat) costs 33B (bus number 204), **Mahasarakham** costs 35B and **Loei** costs 57B taking between 4 and 5½ hours. Regular buses to **Chiang Mai** start at 125B and A/C buses start at 220B. To **Nakhon Sawan** costs 50B (bus number 4165, 1542) and to **Phitsanulok** costs 61B (bus number 565).

KHON KAEN PROVINCE

This province is located in the heart of the northeast and is home to the region's largest university. Established in 1783, Khon Kaen stretches over almost 11,000 sq km and is bordered by Chaiyaphum and Phetchabun to the west, Loei, Nong Bua Lam Phu and Nong Khai to the north, Kalasin and Mahasarakham to the east and Nakhon Ratchasima and Buriram to the south.

KHON KAEN   ขอนแก่น

The provincial capital, Khon Kaen, could be seen as a gateway to I-san if you are arriving from the far north and for those arriving from further east, Khon Kaen may strike one as a fairly modern city with a considerable Western influence. Khon Kaen is actually the fourth largest city in Thailand and home to the largest university in Northeast Thailand, the aptly named Khon Kaen University. There is also a tourist office here and the excellent Khon Kaen National Museum make it an ideal stopover for a day or so before moving on.

Vital Information

Tourist Office, ☎ (043) 244 498, is well staffed and is located on Pratchasamosorn Road about a five minute walk from the bus station.

Post Office is on the corner of Si Chan and Klang Muang Road.

Banks most of the major banks have branches on Si Chan Road.

Lao Consulate This new consulate is a 15 minute tuk tuk ride away, in the south of town on Potisan Road, off Bung Kaen Nakhon. If you have trouble explaining to a tuk tuk driver where you want to go, ask the TAT to write down directions for you.

Police Station is beside the Tourist Office.

Codes Khon Kaen's telephone code is (043) and the postal code is 40000.

Cheap Sleeps

CoCo Guesthouse, ☎ (043) 241 283, at 58/1 Pimpasut Road, has the nicest rooms in town. Large rooms with two double beds and share shower cost 200B all in a nice old wooden building and 300B for A/C. This guesthouse can be a bit difficult to find, follow the soi up from 'First Choice' and it is through the gate to the left of the bar where the lane turns right.

Saen Samram Hotel, ☎ (043) 239 611, at 55/9 Klang Muang Road, has 52 rooms and the friendly staff here will give you a single room with fan for 160B.

Roma Hotel, ☎ (043) 236 276, at 50/2 Klang Muang Road, this large, impersonal hotel has 109 rooms and it is centrally located. Prices range from 200B to 250B for rooms with fan.

Northeast

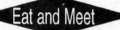

Eat and Meet

If you have been in the northeast for a while and craving some Western food, look no further than Khon Kaen.

First Choice opposite the glitzy Khon Kaen Hotel on Pimpasut Road has a huge menu of Thai and Western food, all of which is good and reasonably priced (though the steaks are really only for the desperate). **Pizza and Bake** is just around the corner on Klang Muang Road and has an extensive menu of Thai and Western food. **Tiam An Hue** is opposite the Pizza and Bake restaurant. This excellent Vietnamese restaurant was closed on our last visit but in the past we have found the food to be excellent and not too expensive. Near the **San Samran Hotel** is a large popular open air place where there is good food at reasonable prices.

Things to do and Sights to See

Khon Kaen is not a place full of eye popping sights. The only sight worth seeing (and it *really* is worth seeing) is the excellent Khon Kaen Museum.

Khon Kaen National Museum   พิพิธภัณฑสถานแห่งชาติขอนแก่น

Situated at the northern end of town this excellent museum contains various relics and finds from around the surrounding archaeological digs. The two storey museum contains some very impressive pieces including a carved stone lintel depicting the Indian deity, Indra, on the back of an elephant. On the ground floor there is a particularly fine carved stone bai sema displaying Buddha's journey to the city of Kabilabhasadu. An informative

Northeast

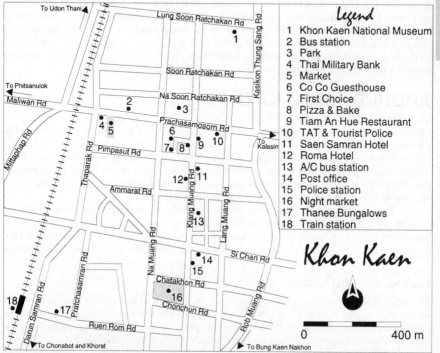

Legend

1 Khon Kaen National Museum
2 Bus station
3 Park
4 Thai Military Bank
5 Market
6 Co Co Guesthouse
7 First Choice
8 Pizza & Bake
9 Tiam An Hue Restaurant
10 TAT & Tourist Police
11 Saen Samran Hotel
12 Roma Hotel
13 A/C bus station
14 Post office
15 Police station
16 Night market
17 Thanee Bungalows
18 Train station

Khon Kaen

0   400 m

brochure can be purchased at the museum entrance which takes you through the displays. Aerial photos of regional towns may be of interest to budding town planners or archeology fans. The museum also displays a number of finer pieces from the dig at Muang Fa Daed in Kalasin Province. Check them out here and save yourself the trip to Muang Fa Daed. The museum is open daily 9.00 am to 4.00 pm and admission is 10B.

Bung Kaen Nakhon   บึงแก่นนคร

This pleasant lake is situated to the south of town and is a popular place with the locals for eating and wandering around. There is a large variety of food stalls selling a wide range of typical I-san food. On the northern banks of the town is Wat That, a typically I-san style wat.

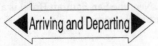
◀ Arriving and Departing ▶

Air

THAI Airways has four flights a day to **Bangkok** costing 1,060B, three flights a week to **Chiang Mai** for 2,700B and two a day to **Phuket** for 2,700B. Other flights include **Hat Yai** for 3,325B, **Phitsanulok** 2,000B, **Sakhon Nakhon** 445B and **Surat Thani** 2,835B. The airport is a few kilometres to the west of town and can be reached by a THAI shuttle bus.

Train

Khon Kaen sits on the Bangkok to Nong Khai line and there are three trains a day in each direction. See the timetable section at the rear of this chapter for details. A third class fare to **Bangkok** costs 77B.

Bus

A bus to **Udon Thani** takes between 2 to 2½ hours and costs 35B, to **Kalasin** takes 1½ hours and costs 15B, to **Chiang Mai** costs 195B, to **Chaiyaphum** costs 35B, to **Si Chiang Mai** costs 52B, to **Ubon Ratchathani** costs 75B, to **Mahasarakham** costs 22B, to **Roi Et** costs 30B and **Nakhon Ratchasima** (Khorat) costs 40B. A/C buses run from the terminal off Klang Muang Road and a bus to **Nong Khai** costs 79B. It is easy enough to walk around most of the town and a tuk tuk should not cost more than 10B.

AROUND KHON KAEN

Chonabot

This weaving centre to the southeast of Khon Kaen is worth a visit if you are interested in viewing the silk making process or want to buy silk products. There is also a handicrafts centre which contains a good display of silk and other handicrafts which is open from 9.00 am to 6.00 pm. The best way to observe the silk making processes is to wander around the villages themselves and witness the processes first hand. It is a good idea to have a Thai speaker with you though as just about nobody speaks English.

To reach Chonabot, catch a bus heading to Nakhon Sawan and get off at Chonabot (1 hour and 15B). Otherwise catch a direct songthaew to Chonabot for 15B which leave every hour or so, though the last one leaves Chonabot in the early afternoon. If you cannot find the songthaew to Chonabot say 'Chonabot' to anyone at the bus station and they will sort you out.

Koo Puai Noi   กู่เปือยน้อย

This ancient Khmer ruin is worth visiting if you want to see all the ruins in Thailand but, for the lay person who does not know much about ruins, this site may disappoint if they have already seen Phanom Rung or Phimai. The complex consists of a central sanctuary and a number of gates. Some of the gates still have impressively carved lintels.

The quickest way to get there is definitely by motorbike as it is straightforward but 75 km away. Follow Route 2 south to Ban Phai then take a left on Route 23 which is signposted to the town of Borabeu. Proceed for around 10 km until you hit the junction to Route 2297 and follow this for around 25 km to the town of Puai Noi where the ruins are situated.

Using public transport is a bit more of a challenge. Get a bus or train from Khon Kaen to Ban Phai, then a songtheaw direct to Puai Noi though the last ride from Puai Noi to Ban Phai leaves early afternoon, so you will have to leave Khon Kaen in the early morning if you were to get there in one day. If you get stuck in Ban Phai there is accommodation available.

Wat Phra That Kham Kaen   พระธาตุขามแก่น

This wat and its 19 m high chedi are the namesake of nearby Khon Kaen and are situated around 30 km from the centre of town. Legend has it that two monks en-route to That Phanom carrying a variety of Buddha relics stopped at this spot to spend the night and noticed that there was a dead Tamarind tree. The next day they pushed on to That Phanom only to find out that there was no accommodation for them. They then turned and returned to Khon Kaen only to find that the tree had miraculously come back to life. They then instructed the local villages to construct a chedi on the site and gave it the name 'Kham Kaen' (Hardwood Log).

Phu Khao-Phu Phan Kham National Park   อุทยานแห่งชาติภูเก้า-ภูพานคำ

This park covers 320 sq km, in both Udon Thani and Khon Kaen Provinces, and borders the northeastern side of Phu Wiang National Park. The park is dominated by mountains which provide great views of Ubol Ratana Dam and Reservoir, the main feature of the park, named after the King and Queen's eldest daughter. The reservoir can be explored by boat or you can go on walks looking for more evidence of prehistoric existence in the area. Camping is available at the park headquarters, around 5 km from the dam. The park is 54 km to the southeast of Nong Bua Lam Phu via Route 2146 or 50 km from Khon Kaen and best reached by hired motorbike.

Phu Wiang National Park   อุทยานแห่งชาติภูเวียง

Established in 1991 and situated around 80 km to the northwest of Khon Kaen, this National Park contains a number of important archeological sites including the 'Red Palm' cave. The walls of this cave have been decorated with wall paintings of red hand palms. At the park office fossil remains of vegetarian dinosaurs are on display. There is a network of trails which you can wander around on, including a trail to the beautiful **Phukti meadow**. There are also a number of waterfalls and a Buddha carved into the rock face. All are fairly easily visited from the park headquarters which is 15 km from the town of Phu Wiang to the west of Khon Kaen.

MAHASARAKHAM PROVINCE

Bordered by Kalasin to the northeast, Roi Et to the east, Surin and Buriram to the south and Khon Kaen to the west, Mahasarakham is located in the lower centre of I-san. Regarded as a centre for education, it is also known as 'Taksila of I-san'. The province is mainly comprised of rolling hills and its occupants are principally concerned with cultivation and animal raising. The hand woven silk of this province receives particular recognition.

MAHASARAKHAM   มหาสารคาม

This provincial capital is little more than a large town and has little to hold the traveller for more than a day. The points of interest are few and far between and the city is otherwise fairly bleak. Amongst Thais the city is most known for its music and as a fabrication centre for northeastern handicrafts.

Northeast

Mahasarakham

Legend

1 Lak Muang
2 Wat Mahathai
3 Post office
4 Police station
5 Thai Farmers Bank
5 Suthorn Hotel
7 Night market
8 Wasu Hotel
9 Thai Military Bank
10 Somphart Pohana Rest.
11 Bus station
12 Pattana Hotel

Vital Information

Post Office is by the clocktower at the intersection of Nakhon Sawan and Padung Withi Roads.
Bank Thai Farmers Bank have a branch on Worayut Road and Thai Military Bank are on Padung Withi near the canal.
Codes Mahasarakham's telephone code is (043) and the postal code is 44000.

Cheap Sleeps

Your accommodation choices in Mahasarakham are both limited and poor.
Sunthorn Hotel, ☎ (043) 711 201, at 1157 Worayut Road, has 15 rooms with share shower and fan for 80B, although A/C rooms are available.
Wasu Hotel, ☎ (043) 723 075, at 1096/4 Damnoen Nat Road, has A/C rooms with shower for 330B.
Phattana Hotel, ☎ (043) 711 473, at 1227/4-5 Somtawin Road, is on the bus station side of the canal with 72 rooms. It is grubby but has functional rooms with fan for 80B/120B.

Eat and Meet

Decent **rice and noodle shops** abound around the bus station. There is a large **night market** on Nakwichai Road. The **Somphort Pohana Restaurant** near the intersection of Somtawin and Worayut Road gets rave reviews for good and cheap food. **M & Y** on Nakhon Sawan Road is a bit out of town but does good seafood at reasonable prices in an open air setting.

Things to do and Sights to See

Wat Mahachai วัดมหาชัย
This wat is home to the **Northern Culture Museum** which houses an interesting collection of literature and regional art including Buddha images and door panels. It is often locked but ask in the wat and they may open it up for you.

I-san Cultural and Art Centre
Set on the grounds of Mahasarakham Teachers College, this centre has an exhibition of various handicrafts and a small historical display. The Teachers College is at the far eastern end of town along Si Sawat Damnoen Road, about a 15 to 20 minute walk from the centre of town.

Kaeng Loeng Chan แก่งเลิงจาน
Also within the boundaries of the Teachers College, this is a reservoir which is looked after by the fish hatchery. The pleasant setting makes this area quite popular with the locals.

Arriving and Departing

Bus
The bus station is located at the southern end of town on the other side of Khlong Samthawip. Buses to **Roi Et** cost 14B, to **Chaiyaphum** cost 35B, **Khon Kaen** cost 22B and **Ban Phai** will set you back 17B.

AROUND MAHASARAKHAM

Tambon Kwao

Approximately 5 km out of town on the road to Roi Et is this sizeable village engaged in pottery making. To get there follow Route 208 for 4 km then take a left turn for another kilometre. Buses run from the bus station to the village. Most of the production is large pots and bowls but some smaller pieces are available.

ROI ET PROVINCE

Roi Et Province is situated in the centre of the northeast in one of the most arid areas of Thailand. Government programs are currently underway in an attempt to increase the productivity of the area, but many people still leave the area every year in an attempt to find work in Bangkok and other urban centres.

ROI ET   ร้อยเอ็ด

Dominated by a huge walking Buddha and a large artificial lake, Roi Et plays the part of an oasis in the desert. The town is part of Thung Kula Rong Hai which means 'Crying Field of Kula'. Established over 200 years ago, the city was once a grander affair operating under the name of Saket Nakhon, but time has levied a toll on Roi Et and today it is just another Thai city. There is little worth eyeing off in town but it is a pleasant enough place nevertheless.

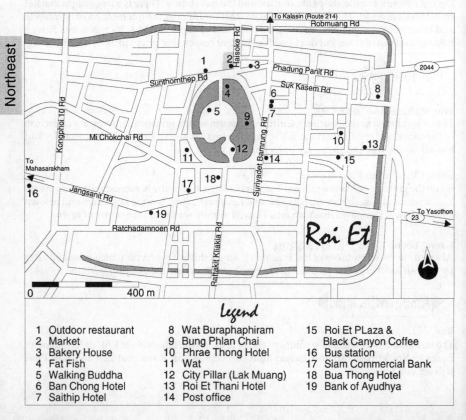

Legend

1 Outdoor restaurant	8 Wat Buraphaphiram	15 Roi Et PLaza &
2 Market	9 Bung Phlan Chai	Black Canyon Coffee
3 Bakery House	10 Phrae Thong Hotel	16 Bus station
4 Fat Fish	11 Wat	17 Siam Commercial Bank
5 Walking Buddha	12 City Pillar (Lak Muang)	18 Bua Thong Hotel
6 Ban Chong Hotel	13 Roi Et Thani Hotel	19 Bank of Ayudhya
7 Saithip Hotel	14 Post office	

Vital Information

Post Office is on Suriyadet Bamrung Road. The telecom office is beside the post office.
Banks are scattered throughout town. Check the map for details.
Codes Roi Et's telephone code is (043) and the postal code is 45000.

Cheap Sleeps

Banchong, ☎ (043) 511 235, at 99-101 Suriyadet Bamrung Road, has 30 basic rooms with fan and shower for 100B to 120B.
Phrae Thong Hotel on Ploenchit Road has basic rooms with fan for 140B.
Saithip Hotel at 133 Suriyadet Bamrung Road also has basic rooms for 120B to 160B.
Bua Thong Hotel, ☎ (043) 511 142, at 40 Rattakit Kliaka Road, has 36 plain rooms for 100B.

Eat and Meet

Along the northeast side of the lake and up Haisoke Road are loads of **rice and noodle places,** whilst a good **night market** by the post office does all the usual from dusk till 10.00 pm. On the northwest side of the lake is a large **outdoor sit-down place** with an English menu. The food is good and not too expensive.
Roi Et Plaza near the Phrae Thong Hotel has a large food hall and is also home to **Black Canyon Coffee** which offers loads of coffee varieties for the coffee buff as well as mixed drinks. **Bakery House** is on Sunthornthep Road at the northeast side of the lake.

Things to do and Sights to See

Bung Phlan Chai   บึงพลาญชัย

This large artificial lake is pleasant for a stroll and slightly cooler than the rest of town. Within the confines of the lake are a number of points of interest including the city pillar shrine, the large walking Buddha and a miniature zoo-like compound. There are also a number of islands which you can sit around on and where you can view some of the fattest, most over-fed fish you may ever feast your eyes on. Buy them some food for 5B and watch the feeding frenzy.

Wat Buraphaphiram   วัดบุรพา

This is home to the world's tallest Buddha image which measures 68 m. You can climb part of the way up the statue to enjoy a view of Roi Et. The wat is at the eastern end of town along Phadung Phanit Road and is difficult to miss. The statue is made of reinforced concrete and below the base are a number of museum chambers.

Wat Klang Ming Muang   วัดกลางมิ่งเมือง

This wat sits upon a small knoll in town and is believed to predate the foundation of Roi Et. Today it is used as a Buddhist teaching school, but in the past has been used as an office in which oaths to Roi Et were sworn.

Wat Sa Thong

This wat is home to the Luang Pho Sangkatchai (the Happy Buddha). First found in 1782 by the first ruler of Roi Et, the image was enshrined in Wat Sa Thong and officials of Roi Et must swear an oath to it to demonstrate their intentions to be honest to Thailand.

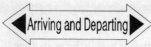

Arriving and Departing

Bus
The bus station is located to the southwest of town, a 10B tuk tuk ride away. Buses to **Kalasin** cost 15B and take an hour, **Udon Thani** cost 35B, **Khon Kaen** cost 30B and take 2 to 2½ hours, **Surin** cost 45B, **Ubon Ratchathani** cost 44B, **Yasothon** costs 20B and **Mahasarakham** is 14B.

AROUND ROI ET

Prang Ku/Prasat Nong Du
Located 8 km from town on the road to Yasothon, this is the site of a festival held during Songkran. The site has been partially restored by the Fine Arts Department and there are some nice carvings evident. The site consists of a three-tiered central prang and dates to the 11th Century. To get there catch a songtheaw heading towards Yasothon from beside Wat Buraphaphiram, the trip takes about 15 minutes and costs 4B. From where you are dropped off, follow the dirt road running off on the right hand side of the road for about 1 km until you reach the sign which says Prang Ku. Follow this into Wat Si Ratanaram, and Prang Ku is in the wat compound. If you get lost ask anyone for Prang Ku and they should help you out.

Ku Kasing   กู่กาสิงห์
These ruins are undergoing continued restoration work but still lack any kind of roof and possess only partial walls. On the whole the ruins are in a similar state to those at Prasat Phanomwan in Nakhon Ratchasima Province near to Phimai.
          To visit this site would involve a long day trip from Roi Et. The ruins are located in Ban Ku Kasing and are reached by taking Route 215 via Suwannaphum to the south well towards Surin. Any bus from Roi Et to Surin would ply this route, so it should not be too difficult to reach Suwannaphum. Once there you will need to organise transport to the village of Ban Dong Yang where the ruins are located.

KALASIN PROVINCE

This small province almost never gets onto the itinerary of travellers and, given the lack of things to do and see in town, this is understandable. However, for those looking for authentic I-san life and no tourists, Kalasin is not a bad choice. There are some outlying sights such as Muang Fa Daed and silk villages which could justify a couple of nights stay in Kalasin town.

KALASIN   กาฬสินธุ์

Kalasin town is fairly small and easily explored on foot. Other than a couple of wats (Wat Klang and Wat Si Bamruang) there is little of interest in town.

Vital Information

Post Office is at the intersection of Pirom Road and Kalasin Road.
Banks are along Pirom Road, towards the post office there are branches of Thai Farmers and Bangkok Banks.
Hospital sits on the northern end of Kalasin Road.
Codes Kalasin's telephone code is (043) and the postal code is 46000.

Northeast

Cheap Sleeps

Phaiboon Hotel, ☎ (043) 811 661, at 125/1-2 Somphamit Road, has 46 rooms and has large clean rooms with fan and shower for 160B.

Sai Thong Bungalows has clean rooms with fan and shower for 200B. Not a word of English is spoken.

Saeng Thong Hotel, ☎ (043) 811 555, at 100-102 Kalasin Road, has 31 basic rooms with share shower for 100B.

Eat and Meet

By the bus station there is a **market** with stock standard rice and noodle dishes. On Panna Road there is a good **curry shop** with plates for 10B and further along to the east is a **larger restaurant**, but no English is spoken.

Carte D'or at the intersection of Panna Road and Pirom Road offers standard Carte D'or food and prices — not a bad choice for a Western breakfast.

Legend

1	Wat Sribamruang	7	Phaiboon Motel	13 Restaurant
2	Wat Klang	8	Statue	14 Carte Dior
3	Krung Thai Bank	9	Post office	15 Market
4	Hospital	10	Thai Farmers Bank	16 Bus station
5	Saeng Thong Hotel	11	Bangkok Bank	
6	Sai Thong Bungalows	12	Good curries	

Things to do and Sights to See

Wat Klang   วัดกลาง

To the north of town on Kalasin Road this wat is most remarkable for its concrete murals depicting everyday life in Kalasin. The wat is primarily a teaching wat, though it does contain a large bronze Buddha image which, during the dry season, is paraded down the street in the hope that this highly regarded image will bring rain.

Wat Si Bamruang

Northwest of Wat Klang is this smaller wat containing a number of markers which were found in Muang Fa Daet. They can be seen sticking out of the surface throughout the wat's grounds.

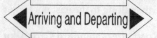

Arriving and Departing

Bus

The bus station is at the southern end of town, a five to ten minute walk from the centre. Buses to **Khon Kaen** and **Roi Et** both cost 15B and take about one hour. To **Sakhon Nakhon** the bus costs 35B and an A/C bus to **That Phanom** costs 310B.

AROUND KALASIN

Muang Fa Daet   เมืองฟ้าแดด

Regarded as one of the most important archaeological digs in the northeast region, the ancient town of Muang Fa Daet has been dated back to the 8th Century. It has been a regular treasure trove of old goodies, many of which can be seen in the Khon Kaen Museum. It is probably only of interest to budding archaeologists as many of its more impressive pieces have been removed. To get there take a bus heading to Roi Et and jump off 13 km down the road at the village of Ban Sema. From here you will need to hire a motorbike taxi or samlor for the 6 km journey to the site. Tell the bus driver at Kalasin where you are going so they do not forget.

Northeastern Train Line Fares				
From Bangkok	Fares without supplements (baht)			
	Class			Distance
Station	1st	2nd	3rd	km
Don Muang	18	10	5	22
Bang Pa-In	49	26	12	58
Ayutthaya	60	31	15	71
Saraburi	96	50	26	113
Pak Chong	146	74	36	180
Nakhon Ratchasima	207	104	50	264
Buriram	286	140	67	376
Surin	312	153	73	420
Si Saket	376	182	87	515
Ubon Ratchathani	416	200	95	575
Khon Kaen	333	162	77	450
Udon Thani	413	198	95	569
Nong Khai	450	215	103	624

Northeast

Northeastern Train Line Timetable

Type and Class	R,23	O,3	D,3	O,3	R,23	X,123	R,23	O,3	R,23	R,23	X,123
Train Number	31	75	213	63	39	1	51	245	33	29	3
Supplements					B	A,B	B			A,B	A,B
Hualumpong	06.50		11.45	15.25	18.45	21.00	22.45		06.15	19.00	20.30
Don Muang Airport	07.39		12.26	16.16	19.31	21.45	23.29		06.58	19.45	21.15
Bang Pa-In			12.57	16.51							
Ayutthaya	08.22		13.10	17.04	20.12	22.27	00.07		07.38	20.25	21.57
Saraburi	09.03		14.00	18.03	20.54	23.06	00.49		08.18	21.05	22.35
Pak Chong	10.24		15.48	19.39	22.19	00.36	02.31				
Nakhon Ratchasima	11.48	15.15	17.42	21.28	23.54	02.03	04.07	06.00			
Buriram	13.30		20.04	00.06	01.45	03.41	05.33				
Surin	14.21		20.45	00.57	02.38	04.24	06.40				
Si Saket	15.48			02.49	04.09	05.51	08.24				
Ubon Ratchathani	16.45			03.55	05.05	06.50	09.25				
Khon Kaen		18.54							09.18	14.08	03.12	04.43
Udon Thani		21.15							11.15	15.57	05.15	06.25
Nong Khai									12.05	16.50	06.15	07.20

X=Express, R=Rapid, O=Ordinary, D=Diesel, (123)=Class of train, A=Air Conditioning, B=Sleeping Car

Northeastern Train Line Timetable

Type and Class	O3	O,3	R,23	R,23	X,123	D,3	R,23	O,3	R,23	X,123	R,23
Train Number	76	66	52	40	2	214	32	73	30	4	34
Supplements					B				A,B	A,B	
Nong Khai	12.30								17.40	19.00	07.40
Udon Thani	13.22						06.35		18.39	19.55	08.35
Khon Kaen	15.28						08.53		20.40	21.41	10.33
Ubon Ratchathani		13.55	16.50	17.55	19.00	06.55					
Si Saket		15.03	17.50	19.06	20.05	07.56					
Surin		16.59	19.18	20.47	21.44	05.05	09.33				
Buriram		17.57	20.05	21.38	22.29	05.55	10.22				
Nakhon Ratchasima	18.55	20.26	21.49	23.24	00.14	08.16	12.28	12.45			
Pak Chong		22.18	23.19	01.00	01.43	10.03	13.52				
Saraburi		00.09	01.04	02.27	02.59	11.40	15.09		02.52	04.00	16.28
Ayutthaya		01.12	01.47	03.11	03.43	12.39	15.54		03.35	04.41	17.12
Bang Pa-In		01.27				12.51					
Don Muang		02.03	02.29	03.52	04.25	13.19	16.36		04.14	05.21	17.55
Hualumpong		02.55	03.20	04.35	05.15	14.00	17.25		05.00	06.10	18.40

X=Express, R=Rapid, O=Ordinary, D=Diesel, (123)=Class of train, A=Air Conditioning, B=Sleeping Car

Northeast

What is an Axe Pillow?

Axe pillows can be found throughout the Northeast region of Thailand. They are the triangular pillows made up of circular rolls. Found in homes, restaurants, bars and other public places, they are best suited to general chill out areas. Their material is distinctly colourful and designed in a unique fashion. The Northeast is one of the cheapest places to pick one up, but it is often difficult to find one without stuffing. Unless you know how to ask for a pillow without stuffing, you are the one that is stuffed!

Crossword 2

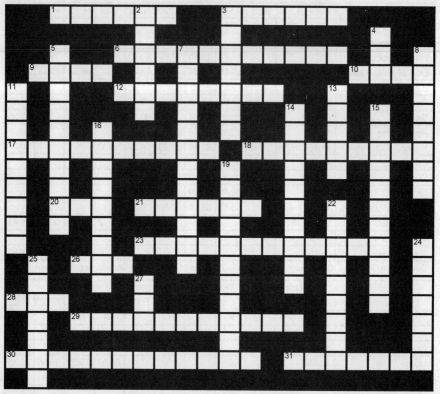

Across

1 Popular National Park in Kanchanaburi Province
3 Thailand's largest island
6 Located outside every Thai house
9 Country bordering Thailand
10 Hilltribe with traditional pastal coloured clothes
12 Name of Bangkok Airport
17 Play using characters made of leather
18 Thailand's earliest period
20 Thai word for beach
21 A god honoured by royalty
23 Province bordering Burma
26 Thai word for village
28 English for Thai word Aow
29 Largest baht note available
30 Sport played in the air
31 Location of the monkey infested Kala Shrine

Down

2 Thai word for district
3 Popular east coast holiday destination for tourists
4 Thai form of greeting
5 Bangkok district popular with backpackers
8 Religion of Thailand
11 National Park near Chiang Mai
13 A nun does this in wat near Kanchanaburi
14 River running through Bangkok
15 Social group interested in Thai culture
16 Popular form of transport
19 Remembered as the father of the silk industry in Thailand
22 Thai name for the capital city
24 Boxing stadium in Bangkok
25 Stomach bug
27 Main section of wat

Answers at the back of the book

SOUTHERN THAILAND

Southern Thailand extends as far as the Malaysian frontier along a narrow peninsula. When Thailand first started to seriously contend for the tourist dollar, the south, with its tropical islands and beautiful beaches, became one of the focal points. Now, it is one of the most popular destinations in the region and rightly so as its beaches and islands compete with the world's best. The number and variety of islands allow for world class resorts, isolated and deserted hideaways and everything in between. This chapter covers the provinces of Phetburi, Pratchuap Khiri Khan, Chumphon, Ranong, Phang Nga, Surat Thani, Phuket, Nakhon Si Thammarat and Krabi. The southernmost provinces are covered in the Far South chapter.

Highlights
Quiet and secluded, **Ko Chang** on the west coast offers one of the most secluded get aways in this region (Ranong Province).
The **Similan and Surin Island groups** are regarded as the best diving sites in Thailand — check them out (Phang Nga Province).
Kaeng Krachan National Park is a nature lovers paradise (Phetburi Province).

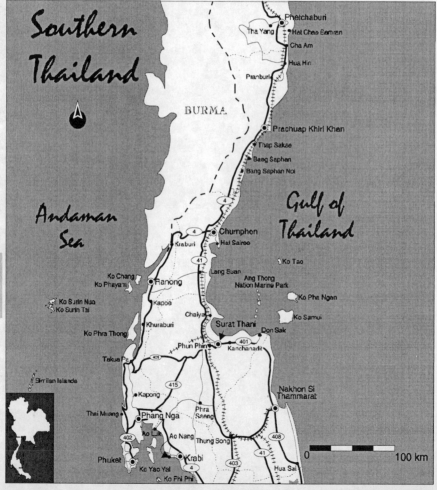

Stay in a tree house in **Khao Sok National Park** between wanders into the dense rainforest (Surat Thani Province).
Hugely popular and rightly so, **Ko Tao** still has its quiet and secluded bays — get there while they still exist (Surat Thani Province).

PHETBURI PROVINCE (PHETCHABURI PROVINCE)

This province borders Pratchuap Khiri Khan to the south, Burma to the west, Ratchaburi to the north and the Gulf of Thailand to the east. The provincial capital, Phetburi (also known as Phetchaburi) has a number of wats worth peeking at and the massive Kaeng Krachan National Park (Thailand's largest at 3,000 sq km) making a stopover of at least a few days worthwhile.
        This province is characterised by thick jungle covered mountains towards the western frontier with Burma that run down to the plains by the Gulf of Thailand. The majority of the population are involved in the agricultural and fisheries industries.

PHETBURI (PHETCHABURI)   เพชรบุรี

This old town has gone through a number of name changes in the past including Phripphri, Phripphli and Phetchaphli. Despite all the names, no one seems to be too sure as to the source, although the nearby Phetburi River seems to have had some influence on the matter. Depending on the route taken, this thriving provincial capital is either a 166 km or 121 km journey south of Bangkok, and 66 km north of Hua Hin. Amongst the sights worth seeing in and around town there are over 40 wats making it a real hit with wat freaks.

Orientation

Phetburi is split by the Phetburi River and the majority of sights are within walking distance of its banks. To the west of the river is Khao Wang, whilst most of the interesting wats are on the east side of the river. The centre of town is quite small and easy to navigate.

Vital Information

Post Office is on Ratchavithi Road near the A/C bus terminal. The telecommunications office is open from 7.00 am to 10.00 pm daily.
Banks are spread throughout town, particularly on Phongsuriya Road and Phra Song Road.
Codes Petchaburi's telephone code is (032) and the postal code is 76000.

Cheap Sleeps

One thing Phetburi certainly does not suffer from is an oversupply of hotels.
Rabieng Restaurant and Guesthouse This excellent guesthouse is set in an old teak building on Phongsuriya Road overlooking the river from the western side. It has small but comfortable rooms and there is a nice sitting area as well. The only problem is that it is noisy. Rooms with fan and shared bathroom go for 120B for a single and 240B for a double. The adjoining restaurant is excellent.
Chom Klao Hotel at 1-3 Phongsuriya Road has 31 rooms and friendly staff. Located on the Phetburi River by the bridge, rooms with shower are 130B and without for 100B. A lovely view can be had from the veranda of Wat Mahathat Worawihan at dusk.
Khao Wang Hotel at 174/1-3 Ratchavithi Road, this hotel is a bit of a hike from the centre

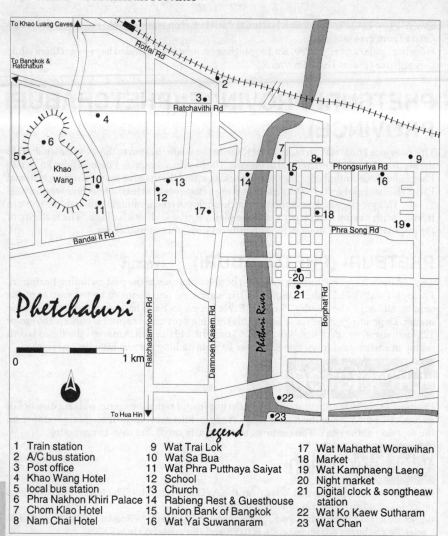

Phetchaburi

0 |————————————| 1 km

Legend

1 Train station
2 A/C bus station
3 Post office
4 Khao Wang Hotel
5 local bus station
6 Phra Nakhon Khiri Palace
7 Chom Klao Hotel
8 Nam Chai Hotel
9 Wat Trai Lok
10 Wat Sa Bua
11 Wat Phra Putthaya Saiyat
12 School
13 Church
14 Rabieng Rest & Guesthouse
15 Union Bank of Bangkok
16 Wat Yai Suwannaram
17 Wat Mahathat Worawihan
18 Market
19 Wat Kamphaeng Laeng
20 Night market
21 Digital clock & songtheaw station
22 Wat Ko Kaew Sutharam
23 Wat Chan

of town but closer to Khao Wang. Large uninteresting rooms with fan and television cost 200B and with A/C they are 300B. There are 56 rooms to choose from.

Nam Chai Hotel at 49 Phongsuriya Road has 22 rooms. This hotel has no English sign and can be difficult to find. Follow the street numbers, go through the open shop front and the desk is at the back. It has noisy rooms for 100B.

Eat and Meet

Rabieng Restaurant serves high quality food at very competitive prices (25B a dish). You will be entertained with the great decor and music, friendly staff and a nice view of the river. Watch out for the one metre lizards swimming past as you chow down! There are some **noodle shops** on Damnoen Kasem Road and also between Surinleuchai Road and Matayawong Road.

Things to do and Sights to See

Khao Wang and Phra Nakhon Khiri Palace   เขาวัง

This small series of hills (the highest of which is 92 m high) is the site of a Royal Palace which was constructed on the orders of King Rama IV as a site for his picnic trips. Completed in 1860, the palace was named Phra Nakhon Khiri, but is commonly known as Khao Wang. There are three areas of interest on the hilltops. On the eastern hill is Wat Maha Samanaram and Wat Phra Kaeo which bears a resemblance to the Temple of the Emerald Buddha in Bangkok. On the centre hill, there is a chedi, Phra That Cham Phet, from where a good view of Phetburi can be enjoyed, and on the western hill sits the Royal Residence. The Royal Residence is now a museum and is well worth a look. Some of the intricately carved furniture, especially the Kings' are quite impressive.

To get there, walk down Bandai It Road and take the right past Wat Chang. The walk up the hill is very strenuous so a cable car has been installed to whisk you up. Return fare on the cable car is 20B and entry to the museum is 20B. A samlor ride to Khao Wang from the centre of town costs 10B.

Wat Mahathat Worawihan   วัดมหาธาตุ

This old wat has a spectacular white prang which can be seen from throughout town. The central prang is particularly impressive at night, not unlike a floodlit Soviet rocket ready for takeoff! Each of the surrounding smaller prangs has a Buddha replica at its apex.

Wat Kamphaeng Laeng   วัดกำแพงแลง

The most dominant feature of this ancient wat is its sandstone prangs and although only one has been restored, they are in remarkable condition. Parts of the original wall which date to the 13th Century still remain from when it was originally a Khmer religious site constructed in accordance with Khmer protocol. The arrival of Buddhism to the area saw it transformed into a Buddhist place of worship.

Wat Yai Suwannaram   วัดใหญ่สุวรรณาราม

This wat has been renovated on a number of occasions but is still worth a peek. Some of the buildings here are made entirely of teak which has impressively borne out time. The pond in the centre of the area is full of large sacred fish so do not even think of bringing a fishing line.

Tham Khao Luang   ถ้ำเขาหลวง

These caves are well worth a visit and are fairly accessible, located only 5 km from the centre of Phetburi. The caves contain a number of Buddhas in a variety of stances. The best time to visit is around 5.00 pm when light through a hole in the ceiling falls directly on one of the Buddhas making for a superb photo. Legend has it that the entrance to the cave will send you through a twilight zone to a cave inhabited by young maidens!!

There is a secondary cave for which you will need a torch running off from near the head of the reclining Buddha. Down the passage are loads of monkeys playing amongst the various oddities including waterfall like stalactites, stones which look like faces and much more! There is a kid who speaks passable English who will guide you around (he will find you, do not worry) charging 10B to 15B per person.

A cycle rickshaw there and back will cost 50B to 150B depending on your bargaining skill, whilst a samlor will cost 50B. The songtheaw is the cheapest form of transport for 10B and it leaves from the clocktower.

South

◀ **Arriving and Departing** ▶

Getting Around
A samlor ride within town is 5B. A samlor to **Khao Wang**, **Khao Luang Caves** and your pick of wats will cost 100B to 200B depending on your bargaining skill. This is a great way to see the sights and some of the samlor drivers speak some English, so you get a commentary gratis.

Train
Phetburi train station is a bit out of town on Rotfai Road, going towards the Khao Luang Caves. A third class ticket to **Bangkok** costs 34B For detailed price and timetable information, refer to the tables at the end of this chapter.

Bus
The local bus station is located behind the far side of Khao Wang and is a 5B samlor ride or 15 minute walk from town. The bus to **Ratchaburi** is 30B and takes an hour whilst to **Cha Am** it is 22B and takes ½ hour. Ordinary buses also leave regularly to **Bangkok** for 36B, **Hua Hin** for 25B, **Pratchuap Khiri Khan** for 60B and **Bang Saphan** for 80B.
        When arriving in Phetburi the bus may drop you off at the corner of Bandai It Road and Ratchadamnoen Road without taking you closer to town. If they turn down Bandai It, get off! The A/C bus station is near the post office on Rotfai Road where the A/C bus to **Bangkok** goes for 65B and takes 5½ hours. There is also a cheap A/C service to Bangkok for 50B, but you get no hostess or toilet!

Songtheaws
Songtheaws leave from opposite the digital clocktower near the market area. A songtheaw to **Hat Chao Samran** costs 10B for the 15 km ride and **Hat Puk Tian** costs 15B to travel 25 km. At Hat Puk Tian change songtheaws for **Bang Ket** a further 10 km on (for 10B) and **Cha Am** which is 20 km away for 15B.

AROUND PHETBURI PROVINCE

Hat Chao Samran   หาดเจ้าสำราญ
Being the closest beach to Phetburi, Hat Chao Samran enjoys immense popularity amongst the Thais, so if you are after a quite day at the beach, weekdays are your best bet. Slightly nicer than Hat Puk Tian (see below) the beach here is in better shape and the town is not quite as desolate. There are loads of eateries and they offer some excellent seafood which will tantalise your taste buds. There is also a beach wat, a police station and a few small supermarkets here. A songtheaw from Hat Chao Samran to **Phetburi** or **Hat Puk Tian** cost 10B. For **birdwatchers**, try the expansive marshy land (competing with the inevitable shrimp farms and half constructed condominiums) between Hat Puk Tian and Hat Chao Samran.

Hat Puk Tian
This tiny coastal town is very popular with Thais during the weekend but remains virtually deserted during the week. The coastline is straight, flat and not particularly interesting but fine for a quick dip if you are staying in Phetburi town and there is a multitude of places to eat in the area. A songtheaw to **Phetburi** costs 15B to cover the 25 km, whilst songtheaws to both **Hat Chao Samran** and **Cha Am** cost 10B. Accommodation is also available.
        Puk Tian can get quite busy, partly due to its unusual statues of Thai mythological characters who are protagonists in the Thai epic 'Phra Aphaimai'. One of the more spectacular is 'Emerging from the Sea' where, some 10 m off the beach, the gruesome looking 6 m high figure of Pee Seua Samut (a female aquatic demon) waits whilst a flute playing prince is

poised on a nearby pile of offshore rocks. They are surrounded by other mermaids, wizened old men and other characters from the same tale which look out from the beach. All of this is done in the 'best possible taste'.

CHA AM   ชะอำ

This small town is only 20 minutes by bus to the north of Hua Hin. If you visit during the week it is a pretty quiet place but on weekends the usual hordes of Thai tourists crowd it to capacity despite its mediocrity.

Vital Information

Tourist Office is about 1 km south of town on Route 4, ☎ (032) 471 502. Friendly English speaking staff can give you enough brochures to fill any backpack.
Post Office on Narathip Road is between Route 4 and the train station .
Banks Siam Commercial Bank has a branch on Ruamchit Road.
Hospital is on Klongtien Road, at the northern end of town.
Police Station is on Narathip Road next to the post office and towards the train station .
Codes Cha Am's telephone code is (032) and the postal code is 76120.

Cheap Sleeps

If visiting during the week you should be able to get a discount on the following prices:
Samaan Guesthouse on a soi off Ruamchit Road has big rooms with shower, fan and cable television for 300B whilst smaller rooms are 200B.
Sims and **Sunrise** are both on the same soi located on the other side of the bus kiosk. They offer similar prices.
Cha Am Guesthouse has large rooms starting at 450B.
Jitravee Resort, ☎ (032) 471 382, has decent rooms with shower starting at 200B.
Cha Am Villa, ☎ (032) 471 241, has rooms that start at 300B with shower.

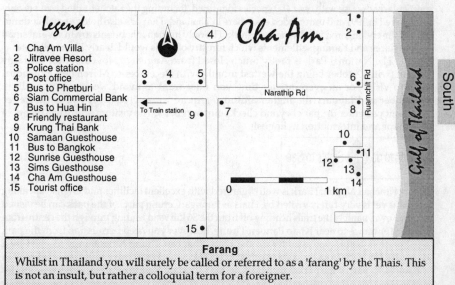

Legend

1   Cha Am Villa
2   Jitravee Resort
3   Police station
4   Post office
5   Bus to Phetburi
6   Siam Commercial Bank
7   Bus to Hua Hin
8   Friendly restaurant
9   Krung Thai Bank
10 Samaan Guesthouse
11 Bus to Bangkok
12 Sunrise Guesthouse
13 Sims Guesthouse
14 Cha Am Guesthouse
15 Tourist office

Cha Am

Narathip Rd

To Train station

Ruamchit Rd

Gulf of Thailand

South

0   1 km

Farang
Whilst in Thailand you will surely be called or referred to as a 'farang' by the Thais. This is not an insult, but rather a colloquial term for a foreigner.

Eat and Meet

The beach is lined with seafood restaurants and food vendors. The restaurant on the corner of the road back to town has good and reasonably priced Thai food and the staff are friendly.

Arriving and Departing

Bus
A bus to **Hua Hin** costs 15B taking 20 minutes and to **Phetburi** it costs 22B and takes ½ hour.

Kaeng Krachan National Park   อุทยานแห่งชาติแก่งกระจาน

Covering a total of 2,915 sq km, Kaeng Krachan is Thailand's largest and certainly one of its most beautiful National Parks. Its western border adjoins Burma and the park's northern border sides with Mae Nam Wildlife Sanctuary. Due to the region's inaccessibility and rugged terrain very little logging or settlement has taken place with the result that primary forest dominates, and covers 95% of the vast area. A nature lovers paradise.

The park is situated on the eastern slope of the Tenasserin Mountain Range, where the highest mountain, Khao Panoen Thung, reaches 1,207 m but the main peaks are actually over the border in Burma. The terrain in this part of the park is covered by steep, rugged slopes with numerous caves, waterfalls and river gorges. A large part of the park also extends into the watershed area of the Phetburi and Pranburi River systems. Kaeng Krachan has some of Thailand's highest rainfall so as a result, the forest is exceptionally lush, adding to its appeal.

Kaeng Krachan National Park contains a wide variety of flora and fauna. Its location at the 'junction' of continental Southeast Asia and the Malayan Peninsula has created a haven for several unique species. Thus northern deciduous forest, with its accompanying wildlife, meets the tropical evergreen jungle typical of the Malayan/Sumatran region. Large mammals are abundant in the park where elephants and tigers have been seen along with the Asian black bear, panthers, leopards, a variety of monkeys and the very rare Fea's barking deer. Birdlife is particularly diverse with over 400 species identified, including the ratchet-tailed tree pie only discovered in 1991 and unrecorded elsewhere in Thailand. The park also holds a small community of the endangered woolly-necked stork. The only human inhabitants are in several small mixed Karen and Karang settlements which forestry officials would dearly like to relocate.

The National Park is pretty much closed from August to November for the rainy season (with October being the wettest month) with December to March being the ideal time to visit. For an even quieter time you may want to avoid weekends as well. In December and January the higher altitudes require warm clothes. A 50B entrance fee applies if you enter the park beyond checkpoint number 9. The visitors centre has plenty of free maps and information in English.

Things to do and Sights to See

Kaeng Krachan National Park is well organised with excellent facilities and English speaking wardens yet is very rarely visited by Thais or farangs. Certain parts of the park can be visited on your own, namely the trails heading off from the 36 km road leading through the centre from the park entrance to near **Khao Panoen Thung**, however you need permission from the park headquarters before you wander up the road. Phanoen Thung Mountain is reached by a difficult 6 km track from the road starting at the 27 km marker. There is only one other road in the southern part of the park which leads to the waterfall, **Namtok Pala-u**. Otherwise guides can be hired from the park headquarters at 200B per day. You will be expected to provide your own food (and the guide's food) and tents (can be hired). A two or three day hike should work out reasonably cheap. For a supplement, rafting is available on the walk and boat trips on the reservoir can be organised through the National Park headquarters. A more destructive 4WD and a guide goes for 800B per day. If you are only here for a day try the **Tortip Waterfall**, which is a three hour walk from the 33 km marker off the road. The final section is very steep.

The 45 sq km artificial lake known as **Kaeng Krachan Reservoir**, formed in 1965 by the damming of the Phetburi River, is part of the park as well as being a tourist destination in itself. The dam is 2½ km past the Kaeng Krachan village checkpoint and is home to many bird, fish and reptile species including the Malayan Giant Frog which can grow up to 30 cm long. Former peaks now form wooded islands dotting the scenic lake. The King of Thailand is a regular visitor and has had a pavilion constructed for himself so he can enjoy the beautiful surroundings. Boat trips can be organised from the park office and the village of Ban Tha Rua.

If you are doing it on your own, do not stray off the track. You will still see some stunning scenery and plenty of wildlife and several campsites have been established along the way with washing facilities for your convenience. A tremendous advantage of the walks is that stream water is plentiful and drinkable so you do not need to weigh yourself down with water. However mosquito repellent and nets are essential — this is a malarial area. Leeches can also be a problem, so take some matches, a lighter or cigarettes to burn them off (any brand will do!)

Cheap Sleeps

The park has excellent lake side bungalows, some 500 m past the visitors centre for 100B per person, otherwise take a tent. There are camping facilities along the 36 km road to Khao Panoen Thung at kilometre markers 15, 27 and 30, camping is also allowed at other areas but you need to take everything with you.

Eat and Meet

There is a reasonable **restaurant** next to the visitors centre, though watch out for the giant hornbill which hangs out there. This bird is a thug, who's only aim in life is pecking farangs ankles, trying to land on their heads or crapping in their noodle soup. Plans are afoot to 'relocate' the bird, along with the Karens who are much more hospitable!

Cheaper fare including noodle soup and *pad thai* can be had in **Ban Tha Rua**, 1 km before the Park Headquarters.

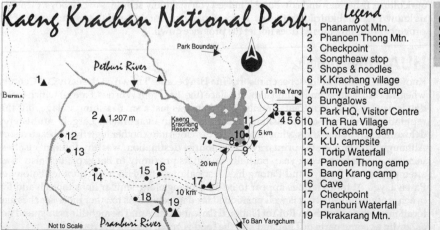

Kaeng Krachan National Park

Legend
1 Phanamyot Mtn.
2 Phanoen Thong Mtn.
3 Checkpoint
4 Songtheaw stop
5 Shops & noodles
6 K.Krachang village
7 Army training camp
8 Bungalows
9 Park HQ, Visitor Centre
10 Tha Rua Village
11 K. Krachang dam
12 K.U. campsite
13 Tortip Waterfall
14 Panoen Thong camp
15 Bang Krang camp
16 Cave
17 Checkpoint
18 Pranburi Waterfall
19 Pkrakarang Mtn.

South

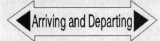
Arriving and Departing

From Phetburi

There are two main routes to the park. From Phetburi drive or ride 20 km south towards Tha Yang, take the indicated right and then follow the signs for the next 38 km. Otherwise drive through Tha Yang and Cha Am to Hua Hin, then follow the signs for the 60 odd kilometres into the park. Direct songtheaws leave from Matayawong Road near the digital clocktower. These stop in Tha Yang for 20 minutes then continue the remaining 40 km to Ban Kaeng Krachan. Once you reach Ban Kaeng Krachan, you will need to either walk, hitch or take a motorbike taxi for the remaining 5 kms to the park headquarters. This trip takes all up around 1½ hours and costs 30B. Otherwise you can get a songtheaw from Phetburi or Cha Am to Tha Yang (10B) and from there pick up another songtheaw to Ban Kaeng Krachan for another 20B. Rabieng Guesthouse in Phetburi plans to run organised trips to the park from January 1997, and can also organise more expensive minibus transport to the park, enquire at the guesthouse for details.

From further afield, all buses plying the Bangkok to Pratchuap Khiri Khan route stop at Tha Yang. There is even a direct A/C bus to Tha Yang from Bangkok.

From Hua Hin

The best way to reach the park from Hua Hin is by hired motorcycle via Route 3219. Follow the signs to the park ranger's office some 60 km away. You will enter via the southern reaches of the park, and Namtok Pala-u is 4 km further on. There is no accommodation available in this area yet, but there are a number of other waterfalls you can visit. By public transport your best bet is to get a songtheaw to Ban Nong Phlab, though we would suggest that Phetburi is a better approach point for those entering by public transport.

PRATCHUAP KHIRI KHAN PROVINCE

This province is long and thin, bordered to the north by Phetburi, the south by Chumphon, the west by Burma and the east by the Gulf of Thailand. The coastline is 225 km in length and is lined by many very pleasant beaches. Although Pratchuap Khiri Khan is the provincial capital, Hua Hin further to the north is Pratchuap's better known and more commonly visited centre. Tourist literature lists the occupations of people in this province as being agriculture, fisherman and cowboys! If indeed you make any sightings of cowboys, please let us know. Prachuabkhirikhan means 'Land of many mountains' and the western area of the province bordering Burma does not let the province down.

HUA HIN   หัวหิน

Known as Thailand's oldest beach resort, Hua Hin became 'known' in the early 20th Century when, in 1928, King Rama II built a royal palace (the 'Far From Worries' Palace) which to this day is used as a royal retreat. Initially Hua Hin was just a small fishing village, but this reputation (and most of the fishing boats) has all but evaporated. Largely multistorey deluxe hotels now mar the skyline as Hua Hin develops into another high flying beach resort. Although Hua Hin is still primarily a Thai tourist destination, wealthy foreign jetsetters increase in numbers every year, partially due to its proximity to Bangkok, but also in an attempt to avoid Pattaya and Patong like destinations. Hua Hin is not another Patong or Pattaya, yet. At times it does appear to be developing along similar lines though and the beach is often quite dirty. It is well positioned for day excursions to other nicer beaches and locations such as Khao Sam Roi Yot National Park and Cha Am. The nightlife is busy and not as sordid as some parts of Thailand and the food is good, though overpriced.

South

Mass erosion to the beach is occurring due to the trawler pier built in 1969 as well as the 200 houses, restaurants and guesthouses built on the beach. Both trawler and beach communities pass untreated waste into the water as the small waste water treatment plant stopped working a few years ago. There is a rumour that a new one will be built after the King recently visited the area and was appalled by the problem.

Vital Information

Tourist Office Open seven days and on the corner of Damnoen Kasem and Phetkasem Roads.
Post Office is on Damnoen Kasem Road, just towards the beach from the tourist office.
Tourist Police have a booth on Damnoen Kasem Road near to the beach and vendors.
Immigration It is *not* possible to extend your visa in Hua Hin. Bangkok, Surat Thani or Ko Samui are your best bets.
Codes The telephone code for Hua Hin is (032) and the postal code is 77110.

Cheap Sleeps

We would advise you walk to your hotel as several places pay commission to samlors and you end up really 'paying'!! As a general rule expect to pay anywhere from 50B to 75B more for a room here than in other regional towns in Thailand.
Pattana Guesthouse Definitely the pick of the bunch! On a soi off Naretdamri Road, this lovely old wooden building has decent sized and quiet rooms for 170B with share bathroom and friendly management.
Usuah Guesthouse/Amsterdam Bar on a soi off Naretdamri Road has rooms for 100B.
Maple Leaf Guesthouse is on the same soi as Usuah. Rooms here are 150B with shower. Other places similarly priced on this lane include **Moti Mahal**, **MR Guesthouse** and **MP Poo Guesthouse**.
Dangs House on Naretdamri Road has smallish rooms starting at 150B.
On the waterfront, **Seabreeze and MOD,** ☎ (032) 512 296, are interchangeable both for price, friendliness and quality and are built over the water. Dark rooms with fan and shower are 300B to 350B whilst those not actually over the water are 200B to 250B.
Thancote Guesthouse and **Karoon Huts** both have rooms with shower for 200B as does **Chomakhom Restaurant** and **Guesthouse**. All three are just north of Seabreeze and MOD on Naretdamri Road.
Bird Guesthouse just south of Seabreeze and MOD has small rooms for 200B going back from the beachfront
All Nations on Dechanuchit Road is a Kiwi run guesthouse and bar with huge rooms, all with veranda and massive share bathroom (two rooms to a bathroom) for 250B with friendly and helpful staff.
Suphamit Hotel on Amnuaysin Road has rooms with fan and shower for 250B, A/C, 450B.
Sri Phetkasem, ☎ (032) 511 394, on Srasong Road set behind a tourist office (which only sells religious amulets!?) Rooms with showers cost 200B.
Damrong Hotel, ☎ (032) 511 579, on Phetkasem Road has noisy rooms for 150B/200B.
Memory Guesthouse on a soi off Naretdamri Road has rooms with fan and shower for a staggering 350B, but it is quiet.
21 Guesthouse up from Memory (just follow the signs!) has rooms with fan and share bathroom for 150B.

South

The origins of the royal retreat
One of the earliest 'famous' visits to the area around Hua Hin was by King Mongkut (Rama IV) in 1868. He arrived to witness a solar eclipse which he had correctly predicted. However, it was to be his son, King Rama V who took the lead by building a royal retreat here.

Eat and Meet

Many of the restaurants in Hua Hin offer Western food such as pizza, steak, Swiss, German and Italian food. The **night market** on Dechanuchit Road offers a selection of rice and noodles and other Thai market food if you can barge your way past the watch buying tourists. Along Naretdamri Road, there is quite a few **seafood places**, all with the fish menus on display. **Moti Mahal** on Naretdamri Road serves good Indian food and the prices are not too steep. **All Nations, Kiwi Corner** and **Headrock** all have *meatpies* and the Kiwi Corner does a decent Sunday roast (all you can eat for 120B though it is not a bad idea to book as this is popular). There are also some popular Western eateries on Damnoen Kasem Road, including **'The Villa'** on Poonsuk Road which does excellent pizza.

Entertainment
Naretdamri Road, Damnoen Kasem Road and Poonsuk Road are the centre for Western bars. **Headrock** is probably one of the better, whilst **All Nations** is quieter and has much more of a pub feel to it. **Kiwi Corner** is a bit away from the 'scene' but still popular. The **Hurricane Pub** off Phetkasem Road and the **Rock Walk Pub** off Dechanuchit Road have live bands of varying quality.

Things to do **and** Sights to See

Hotel Sofitel Central Hua Hin
Originally the Hua Hin Railway Hotel, this impressive hotel is out of most budgets, but is definitely still worth a wander through. Large and superbly kept gardens surround a grandiose 'old colonial style' hotel. The staff do not mind you walking around, and it is a great place to have a drink and soak up the atmosphere. The hotel was also used as the set for the 'Hotel Le Phnom' in the award winning film, "The Killing Fields".

Hat Hua Hin
If you have a fetish for deck chairs and umbrellas, obese tourists, ponies, out of control horses and fashion shoots, then Hua Hin central beach is definitely the place for you. If they took all the crap off it, the beach would be very nice or if you are willing to walk along it for a bit (mind you do not trip on a leg jutting out from under an umbrella!) you will find somewhere to catch a bit of sun, but watch out for the horses. If you go for a swim, keep an eye out for the jet skis. Aside from these sights (and dangers), Hua Hin also has a golf course for those in need of such a sporting fix.

Arriving and Departing

Getting Around
Anything within town by samlor should not cost more than 10B to 15B. Motorcycles can be hired from 150B to 250B, as well as bicycles for 70B along Damnoen Kasem Road, opposite the bazaar.

Air
Hua Hin Airport is around 5 km north of town. Bangkok Airways flies daily to **Bangkok**. THAI Airways also has at least one flight a day to Phuket and Samui.

South

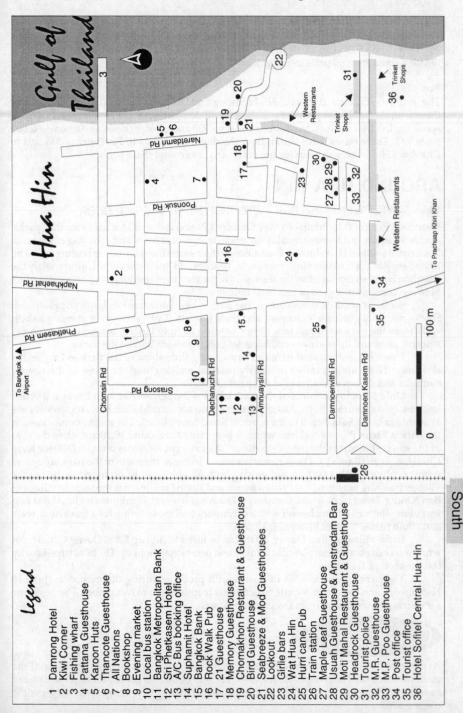

Hua Hin

Gulf of Thailand

Legend

1 Damrong Hotel
2 Kiwi Corner
3 Fishing wharf
4 Pattana Guesthouse
5 Karoon Huts
6 Thancote Guesthouse
7 All Nations
8 Bookshop
9 Evening market
10 Local bus station
11 Bangkok Metropolitan Bank
12 Sri Phetkasem Hotel
13 A/C Bus booking office
14 Suphamit Hotel
15 Bangkok Bank
16 Rock Walk Pub
17 21 Guesthouse
18 Memory Guesthouse
19 Chomakhon Restaurant & Guesthouse
20 Bird Guesthouse
21 Seabreeze & Mod Guesthouses
22 Lookout
23 Girlie bars
24 Wat Hua Hin
25 Hurri cane Pub
26 Train station
27 Maple Leaf Guesthouse
28 Usuah Guesthouse & Amsterdam Bar
29 Moti Mahal Restaurant & Guesthouse
30 Headrock Guesthouse
31 Tourist police
32 M.R. Guesthouse
33 M.P. Poo Guesthouse
34 Post office
35 Tourist office
36 Hotel Sofitel Central Hua Hin

Train
The train station is at the end of Damnoen Kasem Road. The train to and from **Bangkok** is 44B (3rd class), 92B (2nd class) and 182B (1st class). Refer to the end of the chapter for detailed timetable and price information.

Bus
The local bus station is at the corner of Srasong and Dechanuchit Road. There is an office there with timetable and price information for all destinations from Hua Hin and the staff speak English well. An A/C bus to **Bangkok** costs 92B and takes 3½ hours and a non A/C bus costs 59B. These buses leave throughout the day. A local bus to **Phetburi** is 20B and to **Cha Am** 15B. Keep an eye out for the crazy drivers around these parts!

AROUND HUA HIN

Khao Sam Roi Yot National Park   อุทยานแห่งชาติเขาสามร้อยยอด

Khao Sam Roi Yot (Mountain of Three Hundred Peaks) is one of Thailand's smaller parks, at only 98 sq km, but boasts arguably the widest range of scenery and activities of them all. It is located south of Hua Hin and in addition to the mountainous backdrop soaring to 600 m, Khao Sam Roi Yot contains numerous caves, beaches and limestone cliffs. Unfortunately the coastline has been damaged by the incursion of prawn farms resulting in continued conflict between conservation groups and local industry.

As far as wildlife is concerned, the park is best known for its large population of Serow, a kind of goat antelope cross, and these can usually be seen every evening a short walk from the park headquarters. Other wildlife include langur, macaque, mongoose, squirrel, civet and there are over 300 species of birds which inhabit the park.

Upon request the staff here can show you a slide show of the park as long as it a slow day. There are a number of clearly marked walking trails to some of the nearby summits and a map is available at the park office.

Only 5 km to the north of the park office is the serene **Hat Sam Phraya**, a beach lined by cool casaurina trees. Although there is no accommodation here, bungalows are available at **Laem Sala Beach** to the north of Sam Phraya Beach. The most popular cave in the park is **Tham Phraya Nakhon** which is best visited at around 10.30 am when the rays of the sun hit the top of the pavilion within. The cave pavilion was built in 1890 for King Chulalongkorn (Rama V). **Tham Kaew** is around 16 km to the north of the park office and is best explored with a lantern and guide - both of which can be arranged at the nearby village. Halfway between Sam Phraya Beach and Laem Sala Beach is the seaside village of **Ban Khung Tanot** from where the nearby **Tham Sai** is about 20 minutes walk. About half way along the trail it branches off with a secondary trail meandering for a three hour walk and climb to reach Tham Phraya Nakhon.

In the village of **Ban Daeng**, boats can be hired to ride up Khao Daeng Canal from where you can observe the plentiful birdlife and occasional monkey. The boat trips usually last for around 1½ hours.

The park can have a bit of a mosquito problem during the monsoon (June to November), and the ocean is quite treacherous from August to November. The best time for viewing the birdlife is from December to March.

Cheap Sleeps

At the park headquarters there are three bungalows, one holding eight for 500B and the other two each hold twelve people for 600B. The bungalows on Laem Sala Beach are priced as follows: 20 people for 1,000B, 16 people for 800B and two bungalows for 8 people costing 500B.

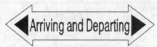
Arriving and Departing

Get a bus from Hua Hin to **Pranburi** (7B) and get them to drop you at the market on the main road. Then catch a songtheaw from there to the National Park office. The last one leaves Pranburi at midday and the last one from the National Park office leaves at 1.00 pm, after which it is very difficult to get back to Pranburi.

If you have your own wheels, take the left at the market in Pranburi and follow it until you reach the police box (about 25 km or so) then turn right and this road leads all the way to the National Park. It is fairly well sign posted.

Aow Takiap   อ่าวตะเกียบ
Located around 10 km to the south of Hua Hin, this bay has two hilltop temples. At the southern end of the bay is Wat Khao Takiap which is a well known monastery for meditation. The view from the top of the hill is very good and worth the climb. To get there, take a regular songtheaw from Hua Hin. If you have your own wheels, the turn-off is well signposted about 4 km to 5 km south of town.

PRATCHUAP KHIRI KHAN   ประจวบคีรีขันธ์

Originally known as Bang Nangrom, the town was abandoned during the fall of Ayutthaya, but a new town was established at the mouth of the Khlong I Ron and by 1845 the name became Pratchuap Khiri Khan. This small yet bustling town is the capital of the same name province and is situated on the Gulf of Thailand, 93 km south of Hua Hin and 176 km north of Chumphon. If you are taking your time heading north or south, Pratchuap Khiri Khan is not a bad place to spend a day or two. Although the beach is not great, the view from the top of Khao Chong Krachok is magnificent. Another reason to stay here is the seafood which is superb.

Cheap Sleeps

Yutichai Hotel on Kong Kiet Road, a few minutes walk from the train station. This hotel is the cheapest in town. A small room with share shower is 100B, with private shower 150B. The rooms are a bit noisy.

Inthira Hotel on Phitak Chat Road is the best deal in town. A huge room with two comfortable double beds, leather chairs and bathroom cost 200B and are much quieter than those at the Yutichai Hotel.

Suksan Hotel is a large multistorey hotel providing rooms with fan and shower starting at 240B. Beware the lively night trade!

Thetsaban Bungalows are overshadowed by Wat Thamikaran and the roomy bungalows with shower start at 500B which accommodate four people.

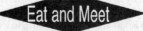
Eat and Meet

There is a **market** on Kong Kiat Road but a better option is the seafood vendors along the beachfront offering a huge variety of reasonably priced and tasty seafood. There is a **night market** near the Had Thong Hotel which is a bit smaller than the market on Kong Kiat Road.

Pan Phochana on Sarachip Road has divine food at reasonable prices. Try the *haw mok*, a mixed seafood dish done in a hot curry sauce - an absolute treat and at 70B it will feed two.

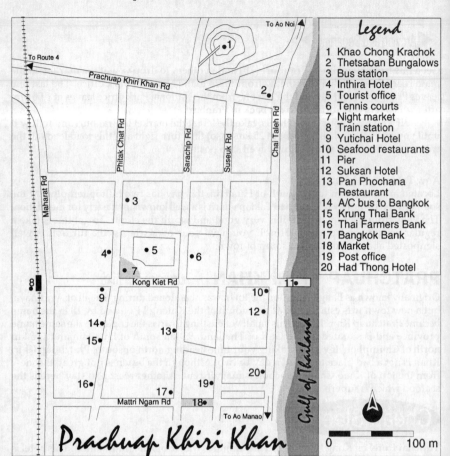

Legend

1 Khao Chong Krachok
2 Thetsaban Bungalows
3 Bus station
4 Inthira Hotel
5 Tourist office
6 Tennis courts
7 Night market
8 Train station
9 Yutichai Hotel
10 Seafood restaurants
11 Pier
12 Suksan Hotel
13 Pan Phochana
   Restaurant
14 A/C bus to Bangkok
15 Krung Thai Bank
16 Thai Farmers Bank
17 Bangkok Bank
18 Market
19 Post office
20 Had Thong Hotel

Prachuap Khiri Khan

0   100 m

Things to do and Sights to See

Khao Chong Krachok

Situated on a hill at the northern end of town, this hill offers good views of the coastline to the north and south. At the top of the 395 steps is **Wat Thamikaran,** a revered monastery and within its stupa is a sacred relic of Buddha. There is a tunnel in the hill which appears to reflect the sky, hence the name 'Mirror Tunnel Mountain'. The tunnel can be reached from the wat grounds. This wat and hill are completely overrun by monkeys who will not shy from leaping at you and chasing you around. Definitely not an experience for those with a phobia of monkeys. To get there, walk north along Sarachip Road and you will come to the stairs running up to your right.

Aow Manao   อ่าวมะนาว

This bay is actually part of the airforce base (no photos permitted) and is found 5 km to the south of Pratchuap Khiri Khan. You are allowed to visit, but you need to check in at the gates. The beach here is much nicer than that at Pratchuap Khiri Khan. To get there, just catch a songtheaw to the base gates from where you may need to walk the rest of the way to the beach.

Aow Noi

A few kilometres from Pratchuap Khiri Khan or a 10B songtheaw ride is Aow Noi. The beach here also betters the beach at Pratchuap Khiri Khan and there is also an interesting little village where basic accommodation is available.

Hat Wanakorn National Park   อุทยานแห่งชาติหาดวนากร

This is a tiny National Park at 38 sq km and the highlight is its namesake, **Wanakorn Beach**. Just offshore are two small islands, Ko Jan and Ko Thaisri where birdlife is plentiful.

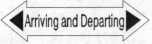

Arriving and Departing

Train

A train from Pratchuap Khiri Khan to **Bang Saphan Yai** costs 16B and takes about 2 hours. Ordinary trains also run to **Lang Suan** (via Surat and Chumphon) and north to **Hua Hin**, **Phetburi** and **Bangkok**. For detailed price and timetable information, refer to the timetable section at the end of the chapter.

Bus

The local bus station is on Phitak Chat Road near the Chow Ocha Restaurant. A bus to **Hua Hin** costs 30B, takes 2 to 2½ hours leaving every 30 minutes, to **Chumphon** a bus costs 50B.

BANG SAPHAN YAI   บางสะพาน

This small town some 80 kms south of the provincial capital and 100 kms north of Chumphon has several nice beaches, plenty of caves and waterfalls in its surrounding area. It offers some good snorkelling from February onwards and forms an all round 'nice kind of place to hang out for a few days' location. It is a low key resort area, too far for the Bangkok mobile phone set and well off the Surat Thani, Ko Pha Ngan, Ko Samui route so it is very quiet and has several bungalow resorts.

A word of warning, many of the buses running from Chumphon to Pratchuap Khiri Khan and reverse only stop outside of Bang Saphan Yai and Noi along Route 4. From here it is 10 km east to the towns and the coast and the only way to do it is by occasional songtheaw or motorbike taxi costing up to 80B. A better option is to catch either the train (which stops at Bang Saphan Yai) or a local bus going into the actual town from where a taxi to your guesthouse should only cost 20B to 30B.

Orientation

Towards the northern end of the beach is the town of Bang Saphan Yai and at the southern end is Bang Saphan Noi. Bang Saphan Yai is small enough that you can walk through the entire town in no time. To the west, Route 3169 runs out the 10 km to Route 4, a road leads off to the east for 4 km to a beach, and Route 3374 to the south leads to Bang Saphan Noi 15 km away.

Between these two towns there are a number of attractions apart from the beach including caves, fresh water lakes, waterfalls and goldfields! There is also an offshore island Ko Thalu which has good snorkelling and diving. Most of the bungalow operations can give you some information on these surrounding sights.

Vital Information

Tourist Information Your place of lodging will be the best source of information on this area.
Post Office is located on the road out to Route 4, a few hundred metres from the train tracks.

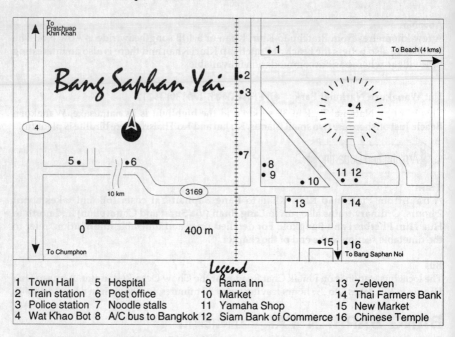

Legend

1	Town Hall	5	Hospital	9	Rama Inn	13	7-eleven
2	Train station	6	Post office	10	Market	14	Thai Farmers Bank
3	Police station	7	Noodle stalls	11	Yamaha Shop	15	New Market
4	Wat Khao Bot	8	A/C bus to Bangkok	12	Siam Bank of Commerce	16	Chinese Temple

Banks Both Thai Farmers Bank and Siam Bank of Commerce have branches in Bang Saphan Yai, see the map for details.

Hospital on the road to Route 4 a few hundred metres from the intersection with route 4.

Police Station is beside the train station.

Motorcycle Hire Yamaha on the main road in Bang Saphan Yai hire 100cc motorbikes for 200B per day.

Codes Bang Saphan Yai's telephone code is (032) and the postal code is 77140.

Cheap Sleeps

If you arrive late and cannot get to one of the beach resorts, most of which are several kms out of town, do not fret, there is the **Rama Inn** with rooms for 250B with fan and shower. If you are really broke then try the **Rest Huts** for 70B. The staff are friendly but the huts are rudimentary to say the least, and tend to fill up rapidly once Bang Saphan's bars close!

Eat and Meet

The best places in town for a cheap meal are the **noodle and rice stalls** around the market and alongside the railway. There are also several **cheap restaurants** on the main road.

Arriving and Departing

Train

Bang Saphan has a train station and they are proud of it, so buses are frowned upon in these parts. Numerous trains head south to **Chumphon** for only 20B and there are two **Bangkok** trains daily. Refer to the end of the chapter for detailed price and timetable information.

Bus
If you absolutely have to take a bus, you will need to catch one of the irregular songtheaws from the market to Route 4 where the buses stop, or else catch a motorcycle taxi for 50B. A bus to **Chumphon** costs 35B and leaves every hour from the local bus station taking between 2 and 3 hours. The last bus north from Bang Saphan Yai town to **Pratchuap Khiri Khan** leaves at 12.00 noon and costs 20B.

All buses pass the bus stop on Route 4 and can generally be waved down unless they are express buses. There are several A/C arrivals and departures for the 6 hour **Bangkok** trip everyday which cost 161B and an ordinary bus costs 125B. All buses heading north and south will pass so you should not have to wait too long for something to come by.

AROUND BANG SAPHAN

South of Bang Saphan
To the south stretches **Hat Bang Saphan**, a quiet, unspectacular beach with several rocky islands close offshore towards its southern end. These form the protected **Koh Thalu National Marine Park** which has some good coral and can be reached on boat trips from Suang Luang Resort. Also to the south of Bang Saphan and near the resorts is a limestone, hilly area featuring numerous **caves**, some **nice jungle** and a very **pretty lake**. One of the most accessible caves is **Tham Manrong** containing several spectacular chambers, lined with dozens of Buddha images in varying poses and sizes and lit by green and blue neon strips. Sounds weird and it is. There is also a sacred spring inside, the water of which is sold at the entrance by the monks from **Wat Khao Tham Mahrong**. The water is believed to have healing qualities. The wat is at the foot of the hill and the monks will turn on the lighting system as you arrive. The donations box is alongside the flasks of holy water outside the cave.

To the west of Route 4, wooded hills stretch up to the Burmese border (Thailand is a mere 25 km wide at this point) and these contain numerous other cave systems and waterfalls as well as a **gold field** where anyone can try their luck.

To the north of Bang Saphan Yai is **Ban Krut** and **Hat Khiriwong**. The tiny village of Ban Krut is 20 km from Bang Saphan Yai town and its only significant feature is the train station. The beach is nothing to write home about except for the **Giant Buddha image** on the headland at the northern point. The Buddha is 15 m tall and situated in a small park from where the view of the coastline and inland to the Burmese border is, to say the least, stunning.

Cheap Sleeps

Bang Saphan's budget accommodation is found grouped together amongst the palm groves, 6 km south of the village.
Suang Luang Resort, ☎ (01) 212 5687, fax (032) 691 054. This friendly and efficiently run resort has comfortable, spotlessly clean bungalows in a garden setting for 200B with a shower or 500B with A/C. The owners, a Franco-Thai couple, Paulo and Kong, provide bicycle and motorcycle hire services for 50B and 200B respectively if you want to explore the area on your own and can supply you with reams of information. They can also organise day trips to the border, waterfalls and caving expeditions for the reasonable price of 300B per day including food and drinks. From February to June overnight camping or day snorkelling trips to Ko Thalu are also on offer. The restaurant attached to the resort is very good and offers a wide range of Thai and Western food.
Karol L's is about halfway between Bang Saphan Yai and Bang Saphan Noi ☎ (032) 691 058. It is set about 150m back from the beach behind Lola Huts, and large airy bungalows cost 80B with share shower and 100B with private shower. Meals are communal, cheap and tasty.
Lola Huts sits almost on the beach with very basic huts for 100B with shared bathroom. For a meal try **Wa-Ra Seafood Restaurant** near the guesthouses down on the beach.

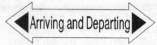 **Arriving and Departing**

To reach the resorts from Bang Saphan Yai by **motorcycle taxi** costs 30B or 50B after dark, but you will need to bargain hard. Alternatively call Karol L's or Suang Luang and they will happily pick you up.

East of Bang Saphan

On the east side of Bang Saphan is a variety of Thai style bungalow resorts and seafood restaurants. Most of the resorts are very similar with prices starting at around 300B, the pick of the bunch is arguably the **Boonsom Guesthouse**, ☎ (032) 691 273, with nice bungalows for 250B. It has no English sign, but is opposite the Tida Karaoke.

A few kilometres further up the beach on the way to Ban Krut is the **Siam Garden Beach Resort** with A/C bungalows at 500B. It is quieter since it is set off the road and has a nicer beach, but it is difficult to find.

Tawee Beach Resort is in a similar location another 2 km further on, is equally challenging to find but it is worth persevering. Basic wooden huts in a pine grove by the beach cost 80B for a single or 120B for a double. If you are looking for a bit of peace and quiet, then this is the place for you. The resort is run by Mr Tawee and his daughter, both of whom speak very good English and love animals. At the time of writing, they had 15 dogs, one of which serves as a receptionist and will show arriving farangs to vacant bungalows! Squirrels run around the kitchen and the hens lay their eggs on the bar so you will not find fresher eggs for breakfast!

A motorbike taxi from Ban Krut station costs 30B at day and 50B at night, or 100B from Bang Saphan Yai. Mr Tawee says if you write to him at Tawee Beach Resort PO Ban Krut 77190 Thailand, and let him know your date and time of arrival, he will pick you up at the station!

North of Bang Saphan

Thap Sakae   ทับสะแก

A small but busy town on the highway, 42 km north of Bang Saphan Yai and some 50 km south of Pratchuap Khiri Khan. The town contains nothing of note and the beaches are pretty grotty. However the total lack of tourists gives the spot a certain charm and there are nicer beaches to the north and south of the main bay. There is only the one place to stay, the **Thalay Inn** which is 2 km out of Ban Thap Sakae and located near the beach. This place has found a great location by a small lake with floating rooms and bungalows for 120B or A/C bungalows in the small garden for 300B. From town it is a 20B motorbike taxi ride away.

Located 15 km further up the highway towards Pratchuap Khiri Khan is the small **Huai Yang National Park** containing a nice seven tiered waterfall which the park is named after as well as various other waterfalls and caves. The park entrance is near the main highway, so jump off the bus, songtheaw or motorbike when you see the sign and walk or hitch from there. Thailand is at its narrowest point here at around only 20 km wide.

Don't judge others on their appearances...

The story behind the flute playing prince and the hideous monster is a well known Thai folk story, which is told to children at school in an effort to impress on them the importance of not judging others by their appearance. The story goes that the prince was in love with a mermaid and would play his flute to the mermaid in an effort to charm her. However, as luck would have it, he charmed the monster instead, who promptly fell in love with the prince. Although the monster was physically hideous, she did have a heart of gold and offered the prince anything in the world to come and live with her so that she could listen to his flute playing, but the bastard ran off with the fishy floozie instead! It is a very sad tale and is well known throughout Thailand, and you may see other sculptures around the country to a similar theme.

South

CHUMPHON PROVINCE

Stretching for over 6,000 sq km this interesting province has enough to keep most busy for at least a few days. Although generally only passed through on the way to Ko Tao, the provincial capital is interesting and serves as a handy jumping off point to some nice beaches as well as a series of impressive caves. The provincial capital, Chumphon lies 460 km south of Bangkok.

CHUMPHON   ชุมพร

This sizeable centre is known as the gate to Southern Thailand but, for most visitors, it is mainly regarded as the closest embarkation point to the beautiful offshore island of Ko Tao. There is however quite a bit to do in the surrounds of Chumphon and if you have time to spare, you could easily spend a few days here.

Orientation

Chumphon is fairly small and everything is within a 15 minute or so walk of each other. The town is more or less bordered by Krom Luang Chumphon Road to the north, Suksamer Road to the east, Porminthra Manka Road to the south and Tha Taphao Road to the west. The railway station is at the northwest corner and the bus station is west on Tha Taphao Road.

Vital Information

Tourist Information is opposite the train station and is a good place to start in town. Infinity Travel opposite and north of the bus station is a second choice, but the staff here are somewhat devious. Considering they are opposite the local bus station, they know little about it, but everything about the mini buses (which they run).

Post Office is in the southeast corner of town on Poraminthra Manka Road just past the intersection with Phisit Phayap Road. It is open Monday to Friday 8.30 am to 4.30 pm and weekends 9.00 am to 12.00 noon.

Banks are found on Poraminthra Manka and Sala Daeng Roads. Refer to the map for details.

Hospital At the intersection of Poraminthra Manka Road and Tha Taphao Road is Wiwarn Private Clinic. The municipal hospital is on Phayarbarn Road, see the map for details.

Police Station is on Sala Daeng Road about five minutes from the train station.

Codes Chumphon's telephone code is (077) and the postal code is 86000.

Cheap Sleeps

Chumphon now has a good range of budget accommodation to suit all tastes.

Sooksamer Guest House at 118/4 Suksamer Road, ☎ (077) 502 430, is the place in Chumphon for a homely, family atmosphere, good food and quiet environment! It is a bit of a walk from the train or bus station, but well worth it. Both singles and doubles with a fan cost 120B. They also hire motorbikes for 200B per day.

Chumphon Guesthouse is down a quiet soi off Krom Luang Chumphon Road. Within the small teak house singles/doubles with shared bathroom go for 80B/120B. The restaurant here is good value.

Mayazees Resthouse on Soi Bangkok Bank off Sala Daeng Road, ☎ (077) 504 452, is friendly offering quiet singles/doubles for 150B/200B and 250B/300B with A/C. Motorcycle hire is available for 150B per day and an international telephone service is also available. Mayazees is run by the sister of 'Chai' at Mother House at Thung Ma Kham and she can arrange transport for you.

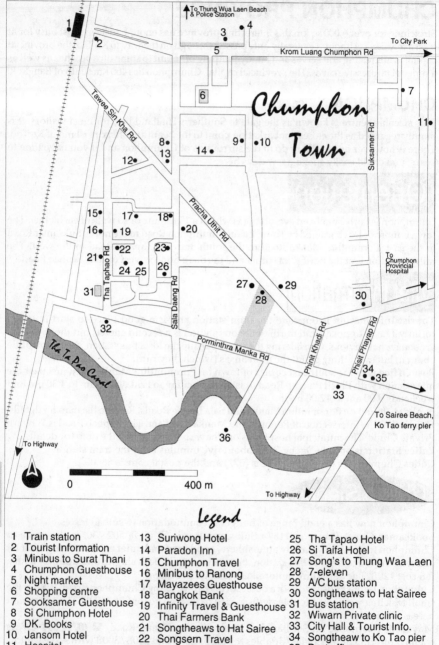

To Thung Wua Laen Beach & Police Station

To City Park

Krom Luang Chumphon Rd

Chumphon Town

Tawee Sin Kha Rd

Suksamer Rd

Pracha Ulhit Rd

Tha Taphao Rd

Sala Daeng Rd

To Chumphon Provincial Hospital

Phinit Khadi Rd

Phisit Phayap Rd

Porminthra Manka Rd

Tha Ta Pao Canal

To Sairee Beach, Ko Tao ferry pier

To Highway

To Highway

0   400 m

Legend

1 Train station	13 Suriwong Hotel	25 Tha Tapao Hotel
2 Tourist Information	14 Paradon Inn	26 Si Taifa Hotel
3 Minibus to Surat Thani	15 Chumphon Travel	27 Song's to Thung Waa Laen
4 Chumphon Guesthouse	16 Minibus to Ranong	28 7-eleven
5 Night market	17 Mayazees Guesthouse	29 A/C bus station
6 Shopping centre	18 Bangkok Bank	30 Songtheaws to Hat Sairee
7 Sooksamer Guesthouse	19 Infinity Travel & Guesthouse	31 Bus station
8 Si Chumphon Hotel	20 Thai Farmers Bank	32 Wiwarn Private clinic
9 DK. Books	21 Songtheaws to Hat Sairee	33 City Hall & Tourist Info.
10 Jansom Hotel	22 Songsern Travel	34 Songtheaw to Ko Tao pier
11 Hospital	23 Bank of Ayudhya	35 Post office
12 Cinema	24 Night market	36 Wat Suphanimit

South

Sureya Hotel on Sala Daeng Road, ☎ (077) 511 144, has large rooms with fan and toilet for 120B. Some rooms are a bit noisy. It is definitely one of the best budget picks in town.
Si Taifa Hotel is further down the road from the Sureya, ☎ (077) 501 690, with rooms starting at 120B. The restaurant downstairs is not bad.
Chumphong Suriwong Hotel also on Sala Daeng Road, ☎ (077) 511 203, has rooms with shower which start at 210B.
Si Chumphong Hotel on Sala Daeng Road, ☎ (077) 511 280, has overpriced rooms for 250B.
Infinity Travel and Guesthouse have devious staff but it is nevertheless popular. Costly and very noisy, small rooms with share shower are 100B and larger rooms cost 120B.

Eat and Meet

If there is one thing Chumphon can boast about it is **great seafood**! Krom Luang Chumphon Road has a lively **night market** and there is another **food market** opposite the bus station. Along Sala Daeng Road there are a few sit down seafood places. There is also a large **fresh produce market** running off Pormintra Manka Road towards the post office. **Infinity Travel** serves generous portions of basic Thai dishes and the **Si Taifa Hotel** has a decent restaurant.

Things to do and Sights to See

Within Chumphon town, there is precious little to see or do except eat, sleep and drink. However the surrounding province boasts over 200 km of beaches and over 30 islands. Some of the beaches are within striking distance of Chumphon whilst others are further afield. See the Around Chumphon section for details.

Arriving and Departing

Air
Bangkok Airways flies from **Bangkok** to **Ranong** (this is the closest airport to Chumphon). There is a new airport under construction at Pathio, 20 km to the north of Chumphon which is due for completion in 1997. Bangkok Airways fly Monday, Wednesday, Friday, Saturday and Sunday and a single fare is 1,980B. THAI Airways also flies to Ranong four times a week.

Train
Chumphon Train Station has the details of all rapid trains which stop at Chumphon listed in English on a large notice board. You can catch slow 3rd class trains to closer destinations such as **Pratchuap Khiri Khan**, **Surat Thani** and **Bang Saphan**, but the buses are generally quicker. You can also catch the faster trains that pass through Chumphon on their way to Surat Thani, but they generally pass from the late evening through to the early hours of the morning.
　　The train to **Bangkok** takes around 7½ hours (depending on the type of train) and costs 172B (2nd class) and 356B (1st class) they leave 10 times a day in the afternoon and evening. The return trains to Bangkok pass Chumphon late in the evening and early hours of the morning. For detailed train timetable information, refer to the end of this chapter.

Bus
Chumphon is an important crossroad between the access to the east and west coasts of southern Thailand and the route to the north to Bangkok. From the local bus terminal (Tha Taphao Road), buses leave to Ranong, Surat Thani and north to Pratchuap Khiri Khan and Bangkok. To **Ranong** it costs 35B taking around 2½ hours, to **Bang Saphan** it costs 35B, to **Pratchuap Khiri Khan** it costs 45B and to **Surat Thani** the price is 60B. Air conditioned buses to **Bangkok** cost 202B (1st class), 157B (2nd class) and an ordinary bus costs 112B.

Minibus

Minibuses depart regularly between 07.00 and 17.30 to **Ranong** for 70B and **Surat Thani** for 90B. See the map for their departure points.

Boat to Ko Tao

If planning a trip to **Ko Tao** from Chumphon, getting there is pretty easy. The midnight boat (yes, midnight) leaves from Ko Tao Boat Pier (Tha Yang), 7 km from Chumphon, and costs 200B taking 6 to 7 hours depending on the weather. The great part about this trip is that you arrive at the island around sunrise to a tranquil and stunning scene. Whilst waiting for the boat there are a couple of restaurants, tourist stalls and a snooker hall near the pier which certainly beats waiting in the foyer of Infinity Travel.

A songtheaw to the pier costs 10B, but they stop running at 6.00 pm, so you can either wait at the wharf for 6 hours or stay in town and catch the minibus from Infinity Travel or your guesthouse later that night for 50B! The other option is to catch the Miami Vice like express speed boat which leaves Chumphon at 7.30 am, costs 400B and only takes around 2 hours depending on weather. It continues onto Ko Pha Ngan and Ko Samui. A songtheaw to the wharf costs 10B. If you are arriving from Ko Tao a mini bus to Khao San Road meets the ferry, leaves at 3.00 pm and arrives in Bangkok at 10.00 pm, costing 290B or else you can get a songtheaw into town from the main road for other connections.

AROUND CHUMPHON

Hat Sairee   หาดทรายรี

One of the closer beaches to Chumphon town, Hat Sairee, has a number of decent seafood places along its shore, although the beach is not spectacular. Before reaching Hat Sairee you will pass **Paradorn Beach** with several upmarket resorts and the **Sweet Guesthouse** which has motel like rooms for 400B with A/C and shower but no restaurant. In Sairee village on the seafront is the **Pool Suway Guesthouse** which has quiet and clean bungalows for 400B with fan and shower and the food here is reasonable. At the far end of the beach at the foot of the Khao Chao Muang Hill is the upmarket **Sairee Lodge**, ☎ (077) 521 212, or Bangkok office, ☎ (02) 260 2303, fax (02) 259 0907, with prices starting at 700B. The complex is nicely located and contains a diving school and combined accommodation and diving packages can be arranged here.

Khao Chao Muang Hill Viewpoint

This viewpoint is on the southern headland which frames the 2 km long beach. Songtheaws from Hat Sairee to Chumphon via Thung Makham go past the entrance. From the entrance it is a short but stiff hike up the hill to the viewpoint itself. The view, particularly of nearby Ko Maphrao is spectacular and there are also some nice walks down the wooded hill to a number of small bays on the other side of the headland.

The viewpoint is about 1 km from the **Krom Luang Chumphon Monument**. This is a monument to a local admiral with an incredibly long name who was the founder of the Thai Navy. The monument is on a rocky headland at the northern most tip of Hat Sairee from where there is a great view of the nearby islands. At the foot of the hill a large naval torpedo boat, the Royal Chumphon, which was de-commissioned on 26 November 1975, has become a permanent attraction.

Thung Makham Yai and Thung Makham Noi   ทุ่งมะขามใหญ่,   ทุ่งมะขามน้อย

Continuing along the road towards Chumphon you will reach the twin bays of **Thung Makham Yai** and **Thung Makham Noi,** separated by a narrow rocky outcrop. Thung Makham Yai contains a small fishing village whilst Thung Makham Noi is deserted and beautiful. These two bays are very calm as they are sheltered all year round. The islands offshore have great coral.

There is only one real budget place around but it is excellent! **Mother House Resort** (also known as) **M.T. Resort** on Thung Ma Kham Noi Beach is a gem. The small bay is secluded and deserted with the bungalows sandwiched between the white sand beach and the wooded hills behind. Huts with fan and shower go for 200B and there is a nice restaurant area on the edge of the beach. The manager, Chai, will organise boat trips to nearby islands for snorkelling for 500B/600B per day which, split between four or five people, is a fair priced day out.

To reach M.T. Resort catch a songtheaw from Chumphon and ask for Thung Ma Khan Noi, the ride will cost 25B and you will be dropped off on the main road. From here it is a 1 km walk down a dirt track to the bungalows. Alternatively call Chai on ☎ (01) 726 0110, from Chumphon and he can arrange transport for you.

Caves and Caving

There are a number of wonderful caves which can be visited in Chumphon Province. Through Tri Star Adventure tours (ask at any guesthouse) you can partake in caving expeditions. These are often not walk through caves but rather some quite challenging climbs involving ropes and other caving equipment. One day tours start at 500B but it is possible to do up to three day tours and if you find a new cave you get to name it!! These tours are generally for small groups of two to four only.

Tham Rubror   ถ้ำรับร่อ

Situated by Wat Thap Charoen (a.k.a. Wat Rubror) is a series of interesting caves including Tham Phra which is the largest and contains a multitude of Buddha images. The biggest and oldest statue is a 6 m high stone Buddha which is rumoured to be over 1,000 years old. Nearby **Tham Ai Teh** is reputed to have been the scene of human sacrifices at one time and it is also thought by locals to contain a hidden treasure map indicating the location of a nearby hoard. This treasure consists of the plentiful offerings made by various wealthy pilgrims to the venerable Buddha image in Tham Phra. Please do not start digging up the cave though as it is a National Heritage Site and the map will be in Thai anyway!

In the same cave system are also **Tham Phet** (Diamond Cave) and **Tham Chang** (Elephant Cave). Several of the caves had electricity installed by the monks so a donation is always appreciated.

To get there take the main highway north from Chumphon for 9 km until you see the sign on the left, then follow the track for 5 km to Wat Rubror. Local buses ply the highway and there are usually motorbike taxis at the junction that will take you the remaining 5 km to the cave for around 20B.

Tham Pee-Sa-Dan

Continuing up the same highway, 15 km from Chumphon, is the English signposted turn-off to Pee-Sa-Dan Cave. A dirt track 3 km long takes you to Wat Pee Sa Dan where, as usual, the local monks have conveniently strung a few light bulbs around the spectacular Tham Pee-Sa-Dan (the English translation of which is 'Strange Cave'). It is not particularly strange, but does have some great stalagmites and stalactites.

The above two caves can easily be visited under your own steam, but there are many other caves in this area, but they are best visited on an organised trip. Ask at Tri Star Adventures for details.

Surrounding Islands

Just offshore from Hat Sairee is a number of islands including **Ko Samet, Ko Mattra, Ko Ngam Ngoi, Ko Thalu, Ko Ka** and **Ko Thong Lang**. It is possible to organise boat trips to these and some other islands from the Infinity Travel in Chumphon. At present only Ko Mattra has accommodation available, but this may change in the future.

Hat Thong Wua Laen

This beach, 14 km north of Chumphon, is much nicer than the beaches around town and is relatively quiet. The various bungalows and resorts mainly cater to Thais, but farangs are always welcome. Thong Wua Laen means 'Plain of the Running Bull' since, as legend has it, hunters were unable to kill any prey in this area. Animals struck by spears or arrows would merely fall over, then get up and run away again. Maybe the hunters in this area were just bad shots and there were a lot of wild animals running around with arrows stuck in their backsides.

Cheap Sleeps

The Chumphon Cabana Resort, ☎ (077) 501 990, Fax (077) 504 442, is a large and very organised resort. It is in a nice spot at the southern end of the beach but the prices are a bit steep. A bungalow with fan and bathroom costs 500B, and with A/C it is 900B. If traffic is low, or you plan on staying a few days, discounts of 20% are available.

Clean Wave Resort is to the north of the Chumphon Cabana and caters mostly to Thais with bungalows starting at 500B.

Opposite and on the beach is the **View Resort and View Seafood Restaurant** which gets good reviews. The restaurant is good, reasonably priced and they have several nice bungalows next door for 350B with fan and shower.

Continuing up the track which runs along the beach is the **Sea Beach Bungalow**, a cheaper proposition, but still nice at 150B for a single, 250B for a double (both with fan and bathroom) and 550B for A/C.

At the northern end of the beach is the secluded **Rim Lae Resort, ☎ (077) 560 119,** where all rooms are A/C and start at 500B though discounts apply for longer stays.

Eat and Meet

All the resorts have restaurants and there are a couple of other **seafood places** along the beach and the occasional **Som Tam and noodle shop** dotted along the track.

Arriving and Departing

To get there, catch a songtheaw from near the market on Pracha Uthit Road. The ride costs between 15B to 20B dependent on how the driver feels.

RANONG PROVINCE

Ranong Province is bordered to the south by Phang Nga Province, the east by Surat Thani and Chumphon Provinces and to the west by the Andaman Sea and Burma. It is Thailand's least populated province and is predominantly mountainous and heavily wooded. Ranong also has the highest rainfall of any Thai province, very green and has a number of waterfalls. Within the province, there are two islands just offshore well worth seeing, Ko Chang and Ko Phayam, as well as Laem Son National Park and the provincial capital Ranong. Parisian visitors may be impressed by the Ranongian Eiffel Tower south of town!!

RANONG   ระนอง

This seldom visited capital is situated at the northernmost point of Thailand's Andaman Sea coast at the junction with Burma. Basically a Chinese town, in Ranong there are more signs in Chinese than Thai. There is also a significant Muslim presence, perhaps created by refugees from Burma. Although there is precious little to see or do within the town, it is a nice place.

In the future, when travel restrictions are reduced (or better still, a change in government occurs), Ranong would be an ideal place from which to explore far southern Burma.

Vital Information

Post Office is on Ruangrat Road about ten minutes walk past the market.

Bank Most of the main banks are along Ruangrat Road and Tha Muang Road. Refer to the map for details.

Hospital is at the northern end of Phoemphon Road, just past the intersection with Kamlungsor Road.

Codes Ranong's telephone code is (077) and the postal code is 85000.

Cheap Sleeps

All the cheap hotels in Ranong are on Ruangrat Road.

Sri Tavee Hotel is probably the pick of the bunch as it has large quiet rooms with good shower and fan starting at 160B, and some English is spoken.

Rattanasin Hotel is further down towards the post office on the corner of Ruangrat Road and Luv Rung Road, ☎ (077) 811 242 This hotel has loads of basic big rooms with shower starting at 100B. The rooms overlooking the street get noisy.

Asia Hotel is located between the market and Tha Muang Road at 39/9 Ruangrat Road ☎ (077) 811 113. Overpriced rooms with shower and fan start at 250B.

Sin Ranong Hotel is opposite the market at 24/24 Ruangrat Road, ☎ (077) 811 454, and for 150B you get a basic room with fan and surly staff.

Jansom Thara Hotel has everything but mini golf. This expensive hotel, ☎ (077) 821 611, has a Thai Airlines office downstairs and also organises ridiculously overpriced tours to Ko Surin.

Eat and Meet

On Ruangrat Road, just past the cinema, there are some **noodle shops** and a **seafood place** with a bilingual menu which does some really special seafood. Between the Sritavee and Asia Hotels is a market which is always a good source of breakfast, lunch and dinner. Also on Ruangrat Road is a number of upmarket **cafes** and **icecream parlours** which make a great escape from the heat. Besides the Thai cuisine, there is also a couple of small **Muslim cafes** doing roti and dahl and also a few **Chinese cafes** and coffee shops.

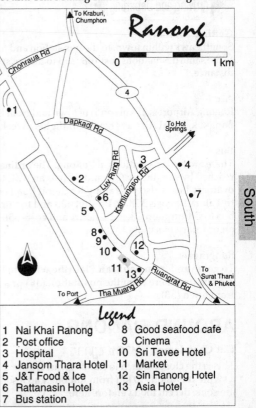

Ranong

0   1 km

To Kraburi, Chumphon

To Hot Springs

To Surat Thani & Phuket

To Port

Chonraua Rd · Dapkadi Rd · Luv Rung Rd · Kamlungsor Rd · Ruangrat Rd · Tha Muang Rd

Legend

1   Nai Khai Ranong
2   Post office
3   Hospital
4   Jansom Thara Hotel
5   J&T Food & Ice
6   Rattanasin Hotel
7   Bus station
8   Good seafood cafe
9   Cinema
10 Sri Tavee Hotel
11 Market
12 Sin Ranong Hotel
13 Asia Hotel

South

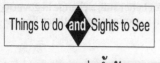

Things to do (and) Sights to See

Hot Springs   บ่อน้ำร้อน

About 1 km east of the Jansom Thara Hotel is a hot spring from where the hotel pipes water for its jacuzzis. There are small floating tables in the river to have a snack on or you can boil some eggs in the springs if you want to. About 8 km past the hot springs is **Wat Hat Som Paen**. A visit to both of these will fill in a few hours if you are waiting for a bus.

Anyone is welcome to use the Jansom Thara Hotel's jacuzzi's so long as there are not too many hotel guests wanting to use them.

Nai Khai Ranong   ไนค่ายระนอง

This building and its surrounding ruins is about 1 km past the post office on Ruangrat Road. To reach them take the turn on the left just after the white walled in enclosure. The building is a shrine/commemoration of King Rama V. The building contains some memorabilia, some really way out photos of the man himself and some interesting photo albums. If you are lucky someone will be hanging around who may explain what its all about. Allow an hour to walk there and back from the Asia Hotel.

◀ Arriving and Departing ▶

Getting Around

Songtheaws within town, to the bus station and to the hot springs cost 5B, a motorcycle taxi to the same destinations cost 10B (15B to the hot springs). Most of the town is within walking distance.

Air

Ranong Airport is 21 km south of town and from there Bangkok Airways flies to Phuket and Bangkok. THAI Airways have four flights a week between Ranong and Bangkok.

Bus

There are two bus stations in Ranong. The ordinary bus terminal is out of town and can be reached by songtheaw (5B) and there is an A/C terminal in the centre of town. Most of the ordinary buses also pass along Ruangrat Road before arriving and departing. A local bus to **Takua Pa** costs 35B, to **Phuket** 60B and to **Surat Thani** 60B. From Ranong town a local bus to **Chumphon** takes 2½ hours and costs 35B. To Bangkok an A/C bus costs 250B and an ordinary bus costs 139B.

Songtheaw

To get to and from **Saphaan Plae** (the wharf to Ko Chang) catch a blue songtheaw if you are heading there from the bus station (5B) or a red one by the market if you are leaving from town (5B).

AROUND RANONG

Hat Chandamri   หาดชาญดำริ

This is the closest beach to Ranong, but is not really worth a look unless you have to have a swim. It is about 10 km from Ranong and a songtheaw will take you there for 5B. There are some decent food vendors here.

Isthmus of Kra คอคอดกระ

The Isthmus of Kra refers to a fairly large area stretching from around Chumphon to as far south as Takua Pa where the land peninsula is at its narrowest. As with the Golden Triangle, this has been localised to one spot which lies 66 km north of Ranong and is the narrowest point in Thailand. A monument close to Route 4 commemorates this point. If you have a photo of yourself walking over the equator, then this is the place for you!

Waterfalls

Being the wettest province in Thailand, Ranong has more than its fair share of waterfalls. **Namtok Ngao** and **Namtok Punyaban** (which is by the highway) are two of the closest to town. Ngao is 13 km south of Ranong whilst the latter is 15 km north. Both are signposted on Route 4 and are reachable by motorbikes or bus, then foot.

Kraburi National Park

A couple of kilometres past Namtok Punyaban heading north is the turn-off for Kraburi National Park (1 km off the road). Kraburi is 58 km north of Ranong and 64 km southwest of Chumphon on Route 4. This is worth mentioning because there is a Thai Military Bank with exchange south of the turn-off to the main road and to the north of the turn-off is the bus station.

KO CHANG เกาะช้าง

This sizeable island sits off Ranong Province in the Andaman Sea. To get there from Ranong is not as straight forward as some of the more popular and established routes to islands further south on Thailand's west coast. All the bungalows offer great sunset views looking towards the large island to the west which is St. Matthews Island in Burma. Rumour has it the Burmese military has a number of military bases on the island, so it may be a while before there are bungalows over there. Also occasional Burmese attacks on fishing boats here have been witnessed from Ko Chang. There is also a number of trails on the island leading to small fishing villages, a shop and the big beach.

Cheap Sleeps

From north to south the resorts are as follows, although there are always new bungalows appearing on the big beach.

Rasta Baby definitely our favourite on the island. Mao and Karla (once a New Yorker now a Ko-Changer!) will rent you a small but practical, nicely located bungalow for 100B. The restaurant here is communal in style with one big dinner and lunch which all are welcome to.

Contex Bungalows on the other side of the bay from Rasta Baby where small A frames cost 100B and the restaurant serves huge portions.

Cashew Resort is one of the biggest and well known on the island. Here bungalows cost 100B (share shower), the people are friendly and the food is very good.

Chang Tong Bungalows have small huts for the usual 100B with share shower.

Saba Jai is quite a way down the beach with very friendly people and the restaurant has a CD collection. The bungalows are nice and high and mosquito nets are provided on the balcony so you can sleep under the stars! Huts with share shower are 100B.

Ko Chang Resort is the longest running on the island and set alone at the rocky outcrop at the south end of the long beach. It has become a bit of a German hippy hang-out recently but they could not be attracted by the food, which is pretty average. Bungalows with shower are 150B. The sunset view from the veranda is spectacular.

South

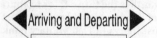

Eat, Sleep, Swim and Boat Trips

There is little to do on Ko Chang but eat, sleep and swim! The snorkelling is not particularly good and the big beach has a lot of black sand through it, but the island is worth visiting nevertheless and the people are wonderful! The bungalows at times do boat trips to Ko Phayam and very occasionally Ko Surin if you can get a group together. A trip to Ko Phayam is well worth doing as the beaches have white sand and the coral snorkelling is quite good. Count on a day trip there, including meals, to cost about 200B per person. The trip takes between 30 to 45 minutes.

If you are feeling particularly energetic, climb the hill at the southern end of the island for a great view of the surrounds.

Arriving and Departing

For a straightforward approach to get to Ko Chang from Ranong, it is a good idea to ask at your hotel and they will write you some directions to give to the songtheaw driver. You need to catch a red songtheaw from in front of the market on Ruangrat Road to Saphan Plae which is the fishing port of Ranong. The ride takes about 15 minutes and costs 5B per person. The songtheaw will drop you by a set of tollgates, beyond which is the fishing port ahead and to your right. Off to the left just before the tollgates is a lane way. If you wander down here, there are offices for most of the bungalow resorts on the island including Contex Bungalows and Rasta Baby.

If you cannot figure out how to get to the port, go to J&T Food & Ice at 258 Ruangrat Road which opens at 9.00 am and tell them you want to stay at Cashew Resort and they will get in radio contact with the resort and organise a boat for you (best to go before 11.00 am.) Someone will then take you to the wharf by car or songtheaw and stick you on a longtail, which will cost 100B (plus the songtheaw fare). Then stay one night at Cashew Resort before moving on to the resort of your choice. Lotus Cafe on Khao San Road in Bangkok can also organise transport to Cashew Resort for you if you so desire.

Once at Saphaan Plaa, you will need to kill some time whilst waiting for the boat to Ko Chang which leaves at midday, costs 100B and the 18 km trip takes about 1 hour. If you prefer to leave earlier you can go directly to the fishing wharf and charter a long boat to Ko Chang for 600B. If there is a sizeable group of you this is a more affordable way to get there. Whilst at the fishing wharf (itself a fascinating place) check out the sea eagles which seem to be as common as seagulls around here.

To get back to **Ranong** from Saphaan Plae (the wharf to Ko Chang) catch a blue songtheaw if you want to go straight to the bus station (5B) or a red one if you want to go into town (5B).

AROUND RANONG PROVINCE

Laem Son National Park   อุทยานแห่งชาติแหลมสน

This terrestrial and Marine National Park includes 15 islands and stretches across 60 km of coastline in both Ranong and Phang Nga Provinces. The park was given Royal decree in 1983 and is Thailand's 12th National Marine Park. Its coast is primarily dense mangroves thus many of its beaches are mainly mudflats, though there are some nice beaches around the National Park office 10 km north of Kapoe and 45 km south of Ranong. **Hat Bang Ben** is a sandy beach by the National Park headquarters and **Laem Son Beach** is another lovely beach 4 km to the north. Park officials maintain that for those who cannot afford to reach the Surin and Similan Islands, Hat Bang Ben is not a bad choice for snorkelling although the coral has been stifled by sediment in the water. Another sub station with amenities exists on **Ko Aow Khao Kwai**.

Many of the park's 15 islands are worth visiting and can be easily visited from Hat Bang Ben. Many of the islands bear witness to human encroachment in the form of logging for boat building. In the past, the only effect on these islands was apparently from the odd boatload of fishermen seeking shelter from monsoon storms. Of these, **Ko Kam Yai** and **Ko Khang Khao** offer very good snorkelling and take less than one hour to reach by boat. Enquire at the park office for details. The birdlife within the park is also reportedly abundant with December to February being the best time for birdwatchers to visit when the park fills with migrating birdlife.

Cheap Sleeps

The National Park office maintains three bungalows and a longhouse at its headquarters and also has one longhouse at Ko Kam Yai. Camping is permitted and tents rented at the park office but, nude and topless bathing is forbidden. If you wish to book accommodation in advance, contact, Headquarters Laem Son National Park, Kapoe District, Ranong Province 85000, or phone the Ranong Office on ☎ (077) 823 255, or at the Reservations Office, National Park Division, Royal Forest Department, Chatuchak, Bangkok, ☎ (02) 579 0529.

PHANG NGA PROVINCE

This small province bordering on the bay of Phuket is home to some spectacular marine scenery. Best known for the karst outcrops spread throughout the bay, a number of trips can be arranged into the bay from either Krabi, Phang Nga or Phuket. A number of sea kayaking operations also run kayak trips in the area. Popularised by the making of a James Bond film, one of the islands has even been named after the man himself, and although the bay can be clogged with tourists at times, if time allows it is still worth visiting. The two islands of Ko Yao Noi and Ko Yao Yai are also in Phang Nga Province although they are best visited from either Krabi or Phuket. Phang Nga is also home to Thailand's most spectacular diving destinations, the Similan and Surin island groups, both of which can be visited from Phang Nga Province.

PHANG NGA   พังงา

Within Phang Nga town, there is little to do (except walk to the post office 2 km away), and the restaurants here are anything but remarkable. Most who decide to stay here do so to do a tour of Phang Nga Bay through Aow Phang Nga National Park. Two main places in Phang Nga do one and two day tours, the Thawisak Hotel and the Ratanapong Hotel. Generally, you tend to visit the same islands: **Ko Pin, Ko Kan** (James Bond Island), **Ko Tapu** (Nail Island), **Ko Talu** and a number of semi submerged caves, then often staying at **Ko Panyi**, a Muslim fishing village. One thing both tours stress is that you visit most of the popular sights (particularly J.B. Island) before 100s of package tourists arrive. Rates vary from 150B to 300B and the tours get rave reviews, especially Sayam's tour who works through the Thawisak Hotel and has an office at the bus station. He has been doing these tours for ten years! Be warned though, do not expect much at Ko Panyi if arriving during Ramadan and always ask for the price before buying anything as the restaurants overcharge savagely.

Orientation

Phang Nga is set upon one very long street, Phetkasem Road. The post office is 2 km out of town towards Phuket. If arriving from Phuket, do not get off the bus until you reach the group of hotels and banks, otherwise you will have a long walk.

South

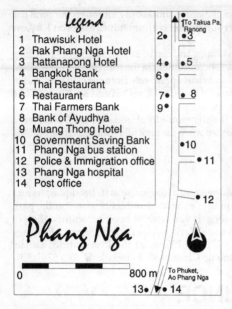

South

Vital Information

Post Office and Telecommunications Centre is about 2 km out of town towards Phuket on the left hand side. Just follow the road!
Banks All the usual banks are dispersed around town. See map for details
Hospital is opposite the post office.
Police and Immigration is about a third of the way to the post office down a lane on the left hand side of the road.
Codes Phang Nga's telephone code is (076) and the postal code is 82000.

Cheap Sleeps

Thawisuk Hotel is run by a crazy old lady and is the pick of the bunch with big rooms with shower and fan starting at 100B. It is also an office of Sayam's boat tours.
Rattanapong Hotel has decent rooms with fan and shower starting at 120B. The restaurant serves passable food from a bilingual menu.
Muang Thong Hotel has friendly staff and rooms with fan and shower for 120B. The restaurant next door is adequate.
Rak Phang Nga Hotel is only for the desperate, and try here only after everything else in town has burnt down! Surly staff will provide you with a room starting at 120B.

Eat and Meet

The only half decent places in town face each other near the Rattanapong Hotel. Both have bilingual menus and similar prices. The one between the Bangkok Bank and the Muang Thong Hotel is arguably the better of the two.

Arriving and Departing

Buses leave from Phang Nga bus station to **Surat Thani** for 50B, **Krabi** for 29B and to **Phuket** for 25B taking 2½ to 3 hours throughout the day. You can flag down buses to Takua Pa (via route 4090) out the front of the Rak Phang Nga Hotel. The fare to **Takua Pa** is 20B and takes about 1½ hours. Buses to **Ranong** can also be flagged down here and cost 40B.

AROUND PHANG NGA

Aow Phang Nga National Park   อุทยานแห่งชาติอ่าวพังงา

This National Park can be both described as a photographers heaven as well as a tourist nightmare. The marine park covers 400 sq km where over 40 islands with sheer limestone cliffs tower out of the year round calm green water. Some reach as high as 300 m and are covered with tufts of forest. Evidence of prehistoric man is painted in some caves — not a bad place to live back then. Now the increasingly common human life seen in these parts is the boatloads of tourists and the occasional Thai fisherman. Millions of years ago the whole region was one of

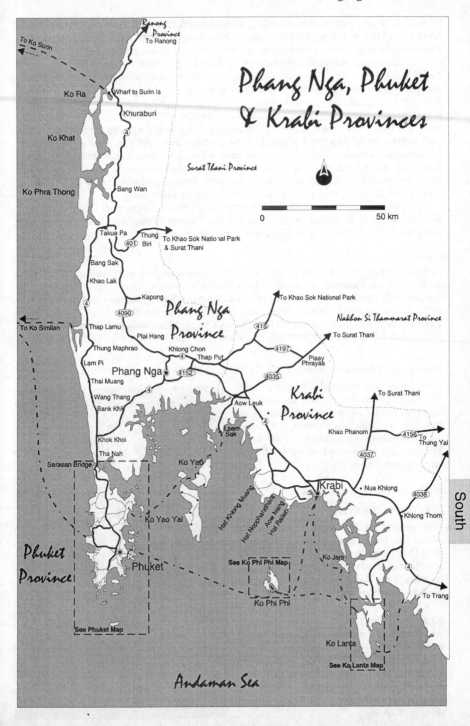

South

the worlds largest barrier reefs extending thousands of kilometres. However natural forces came into play and the earth's movements created the irregular formations, with erosion smoothing the edges, leaving the geography reminiscent of Yunnan in China but with the water.

The common tourist destinations include **Ko Kan** (James Bond Island), and **Ko Panyi** (Sea Gypsy village where a coke costs you 40B and no gypsies live there). If you can somehow organise to get around on your own (try sea kayaking, but it will be expensive) you will be rewarded with exotic beauty. **Ko Phanak** and **Ko Hong** are stunning where hongs (or collapsed cave systems) have been discovered from the air, where worlds of their own exist below sheer cliffs. Caves are worth exploring including **Lod Yai** and **Lod Lek** as well as the cave passages on **Ko Talu** full of stalactites. Beautiful also in their own way are the mangrove forests which you can penetrate through the myriad of established canals. Keep an eye out for the rock painting in Ko Panyi and at the entrance to the Phang Nga River. For those contemplating staying in the park, there are nine bungalows available for rent as well as a few camping sites, but bring your own everything.

The park is 9 km from Phang Nga town and almost 100 km from Phuket. The park headquarters is on Route 4144 which is off Route 4. Visiting by boat is the more popular way to see the National Park and regular tours run from Phuket and Phang Nga.

Caves

Outside of Phang Nga there are a number of caves and waterfalls worth visiting if you have a half day to kill. However you cannot hire motorbikes in Phang Nga so you will need to take a motorcycle taxi there and be prepared to bargain hard! **Suwan Khuha Cave** has a number of Buddha images and is about 15 km from Phang Nga towards the town of Takua Thung. Two caves much closer to town are **Tham Phung Chang** (3 km south) and **Tham Reusisawan** (3 km south). The waterfall, **Namtok Manohra** is around 10 km north of Phang Nga.

Khao Lam Pi National Park   อุทยานแห่งชาติเขาลำปี

This dot of a National Park covers only 72 sq km. It is located on the coast of Phang Nga Province incorporating **Chai Thale Thai Beach** where you can observe sea turtles laying eggs between November and March. The park also has a couple of waterfalls and an assortment of wildlife.

Si Phang Nga National Park
อุทยานแห่งชาติศรีพังงา

This park is a little larger encompassing 246 sq km, but is also out of the limelight after Phang Nga Bay. A couple of waterfalls are the major attractions within the park, **Namtok Tam Nang** falls over 60 m whilst **Namtok Ton Ton Toei** drops around 50 m.

Kapong   กะปง

About one hour north of Phang Nga by bus on route 4090, this quaint town has a number of waterfalls including **Namtok Lam Ra**, 6 km south of town, which may be of interest to some. The landscape in this area is beautiful. Most buses from Phang Nga to Takua Pa pass through Kapong.

View from James Bond Island

TAKUA PA   ตะกั่วป่า

This mid sized town is 160 km from Surat Thani, 169 km from Ranong and around 70 km from Phang Nga. Although there is nothing to see in Takua Pa, it is a good launching point for Khao Sok National Park (see the Surat Thani section) and to some of the western beaches of Phang Nga Province. Due to its positioning, many buses use Takua Pa as a rest stop.

The people here are very friendly and there is only one hotel in town, the **Extra Hotel** which charges a lot for an average room. Rates start at 220B for a room with fan and shower. To get there, leave the bus station, turn right, walk over the bridge and about 100 m further there is an ESSO gas station - the hotel is behind the gas station. Further down the same road is a park with a market. The mixed fruit shakes are 10B and yummy. An A/C bus to **Bangkok** costs 322B.

AROUND TAKUA PA

Hat Bang Sak   หาดบางสัก
Bang Sak Beach is located 14 km to the south of Takua Pa. This long, clean, white sand beach is a nice spot to stop for breakfast on the way to Khao Lak from Takua Pa. The water here is very clear and the surf is generally fairly calm. About 1 km to the north there is the **San Splendid Resort** on Hat Tam Tauree.

Hat Khao Lak   หาดเขาหลัก
Around 30 km to the south of Takua Pa, this lovely beach has a number of cheap places to stay. From here you can also organise trips to the Similan Islands. The beach is split into a number of small bays ensuring privacy, but it is easy to walk from one end to the other in an hour or so. Around the head from the southern end of the beach is Khao Lak National Park. Some of the walks through the old forest here are beautiful. Other than the bungalow food, there are a number of small restaurants on the beach which double up as dive places to the Similan islands.

Cheap Sleeps

From south to north the accommodation is as follows:
On the point, just below the road but with a fantastic view there are some **no name concrete bungalows** which start at 600B.
Khao Lak Resort has the most natural setting with a large range of bungalows starting at 100B with share showers. The staff are friendly and the restaurant is not too bad. Up the beach is another resort which has concrete cottages with no shade starting at 500B though they give a discount for longer stays.
Nang Thong Bay Resort has nicely designed bungalows ranging from 150B to 500B all with shower and fan and the nicest restaurant.
Garden Beach Resort has rooms for 200B and 300B with shower and fan.

Things to do **and** Sights to See

Khao Lak National Park
This 125 sq km park is set on the coast of Phang Nga Province combining peaks reaching 1,080 m, the source of two important rivers, a few impressive waterfalls (Lam Ri, Lam Phraw and Hin Lad) as well as beaches. The park used to be home to a wide range of large mammals and birds, including the tiger, but none have been sighted for some time. The park headquarters is just to the south of Khao Lak Beach.

◀▏**Arriving and Departing**▕▶

A local bus from Takua Pa takes 45 minutes and costs 15B. Buses coming north from Thai Muang etc. will also drop you here. Hitching is good all the way along this route.

Khuraburi   คุระบุรี

Khuraburi is a dot of a town 114 km south of Ranong that has no hotels or anything much of interest but is the closest town to the wharf to the Surin Islands. If travelling by bus, tell the conductor to drop you at the turn-off to the wharf, 8 km north of Khuraburi. From there, you can catch a motorcycle taxi for 10B to the wharf.

Similan Islands National Park   อุทยานแห่งชาติหมู่เกาะสิมิลัน

Like the Surin Islands, the Similans are well renowned for their diving and snorkelling with one of the most diverse underwater worlds that Thailand has to offer. The islands themselves are distinguished by huge weathered granite boulders, evidence of past volcanic action, but the rocks do not exist on land alone. The same structures are evident underwater surrounded by abundant sea life. To the east of the islands they are mostly covered by sand, but to the west the strong currents have kept the ocean rock formations fairly clear of sand. It is also to the west that you can visit the popular 'Burmese Banks', an area which is frequented by large schools of sharks. Around late March and early April experienced divers can swim alongside whale sharks and manta rays. Snorkellers will have to be content with the best snorkelling areas which are off the beaches of Ko Miang, in the channel which separates it from the closest island and in Campbells Bay. Despite its isolation from the mainland the colourful underwater world, reefs and fish populations have, in the past, suffered from dynamite and commercial fishermen who are now banned from the area. Now the region is starting to face tourist pollution and damage instead.

The Similans are located around 80 km west off Phang Nga Province and made up of a number of islands including Ko Bon, Ko Ba Ngu, Ko Similan, Ko Payu, Ko Miang, Ko Payan, Ko Payang and Ko Hu Yong. The park office is located on Ko Miang, and there is a National Park sub station on Ko Similan which is the largest island, but they are otherwise undeveloped. The best time to go to is December to April.

Cheap Sleeps

There are basic bungalows and camping area and restaurant on Ko Miang run by the National Park as well as camping grounds on Ko Ba Ngu and Ko Similan.

◀▏**Arriving and Departing**▕▶

There are a number of departure points to the Similans with Phuket, Khao Lak and Thap Lamu the three most popular. From **Poseidon Bungalows** between Thap Lamu and Khao Lak you can organise by far the most economical tour. They offer 3 day/2 night tours including food and board for 3,300B which is far cheaper than from Phuket or Khao Lak. To get there, catch a bus up Route 4 and watch out for their sign on the highway.

The National Park office in Thap Lamu also runs daily boats out to their office on Ko Miang on a daily basis for between 600B and 800B each way per person which takes between and 3½ to 5 hours depending on weather, contact them on (076) 411 914 to find out when the boat leaves. For a one day tour from Phuket (this is a long day as a one way trip to the islands from Phuket take a minimum of 4 hours!) count on around 2,000B per person. Seatran Travel on Phang Nga Road in Phuket town can arrange tours there, or else you can try the various travel agents in Patong, Karon and Kata. If you decide to travel to the Similans with a travel agent or dive shop, look around as the prices vary tremendously.

Surin Islands National Park   อุทยานแห่งชาติหมู่เกาะสุรินทร์

The Surin Islands are famed around the world for their unspoilt beauty and fantastic diving and snorkelling. Before being declared a National Park, there had been a number of proposals put forward for their use, including the development of a Vietnamese Refugee Camp. Eventually, they became Thailand's 29th National Park on 9th July, 1981. The archipelago is just south of the Burmese border but 60 km offshore from Phang Nga Province and are made up of five main islands. Ko Surin Nua and Ko Surin Tai are the largest islands and are separated by a shallow strait, which is walkable at low tide, but expect to get a little wet. The other islands are quite small and are more islets than islands with the largest being Ko Ree, Ko Elang and Ko Khai.

Turtles lay eggs every year on the Surin Island beaches from December to February and these are collected and raised by National Park staff. If you are found touching them, you will be thrown off the island with a fine. The young turtles are usually released in April for the Songkran festival.

Sea gypsies (*Chao Nam*) live on and around Ko Surin Tai and in April they hold an important festival known as *Loi Reua*, a ceremony honouring their ancestors, which attracts gypsies from Burma and as far away as Malaysia. This is the latest time you would want to go here as from May to November the monsoons make the seas virtually impassable.

Due to their far offshore positioning and the strong prevailing currents in the ocean around them, the water at the islands is particularly clear with visibility commonly reaching 20 m. The east bank of the islands have better coral as it is more sheltered in times of rough seas. The sea itself is particularly abundant in underwater life including lobster, starfish, clown fish, white shark, parrot fish, and many many more. For the walking fans, the islands are quite densely forested and possibilities for interesting walks exist.

Cheap Sleeps

The National Park Headquarters is on the southwest side of Surin Nua where they maintain dormitory style bungalows for 150B per person and a restaurant but it is a good idea to bring some of your own food as that supplied by the Park Office can be quite expensive. Further south is a campground where you can pitch a tent.

Arriving and Departing

Boats leave for the Surin Islands from a wharf about 8 km to the north of Khuraburi and take around 4 hours. Unfortunately the boats are quite expensive and leave in a random fashion. If you are lucky a group tour may be leaving around when you want to go and if this is the case you may be able to get the fare for around 750B to 1,000B per person. However, if there is no group you will need to charter your own boat for around 8,000B.

A good idea would be to visit the wharf and find out from the officials when the next group will be going and to try to co-ordinate with that whilst staying in Ranong, Takua Pa or Khao Lak. Boats only leave from November to May. Around Chinese New Year is a good time to try for tours as the islands are popular with the Thais at this time of year.

Tours also leave from Phuket, usually Patong or Rawai. They are predominately scuba diving trips, but you may be able to jump on board. The trip is 10 hours in a slow boat or 3½ hours in a speed boat.

South

Ko Yao Noi   เกาะยาวน้อย

This island east of Phuket and west of Krabi is very little explored and well off the tourist trail in Phang Nga Province. Boats can be taken from Bang Rong pier in Phuket or from Laem Sak in Krabi Province which has a boat which leaves most mornings for 40B from the south of Thamboke Kharanee National Park. Bungalow accommodation is available on the island at the upmarket **Long Beach Resort** on Hat Klong Jaak with bungalows starting at 650B and a dormitory for 200B. On Hat Sabai there is the **Sabai Corner** with bungalows starting at 100B. The beaches here are OK but nothing amazing. Ko Yao Yai has by far the better beaches.

SURAT THANI PROVINCE

Well known to roving farangs as the gateway to the Thailand Gulf Islands, and by Thais for the commercial importance of Surat Thani city and the historical importance of the town of Chaiya. One of the South's largest provinces at almost 13,000 sq km, Surat Thani stretches from the east coast almost to the Andaman Sea, encompassing a stunning and rarely visited mountainous centre. Opt for the mountainous road between Surat Thani on the east coast and Takua Pa on the west and you will find yourself in a tropical Mae Hong Son.

Â Â Â South of Surat Thani towards Nakhon Si Thammarat is a second mountainous region equally spectacular with summits of over 1,500 m and large expanses of tropical rainforest.

CHAIYA   ไชยา

Chaiya (derived from a contraction of the Thai pronunciation of Srivijaya) is actually one of the oldest cities in Thailand, its foundation dating back to the 8th Century when it was a regional capital and major city in the flourishing Srivijaya Empire. This realm stretched throughout Java, Sumatra, the Malayan peninsula and into what is today Southern Thailand. Historians continue to debate the site of the actual capital, generally placing it in the vicinity of Palembang in Sumatra, though recent evidence suggests that, at least during the later part of the empire, Chaiya itself may have been the fabled capital. The empire began to decline during the 13th Century and Chaiya has remained a small 'backwater' town ever since.

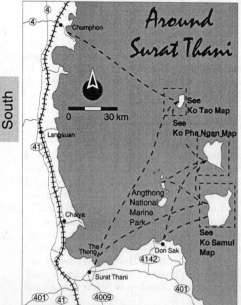

Around Surat Thani

Â Â Â Enough interesting wats remain around the town to warrant a visit though this is probably best done as a day trip from either Surat Thani or Chumphon. The town is also the jumping off point for the nearby Wat Suanmok which is well known for its popular Western attended retreats.

Cheap Sleeps

Chaiya does have one basic hotel, the **Udomlap** which is basic but friendly and reasonably priced at 100B. To reach it, walk down the main commercial street from the market area for about 100 m then turn left before the cinema and wander down there for about 50 m and the hotel is on your right.

For **eating** there are plenty of **Thai restaurants** to munch at plus the market, but no real Western eateries.

Things to do and Sights to See

Wat Phra Mahathat   วัดมหาธาตุ

This is definitely number one on Chaiya's wat list. This beautiful temple dates back to 757 and is the finest Srivijaya structure remaining in Thailand. The central area contains a 24 m high 1,200 year old chedi (restored in 1901) standing in the centre of a pond and contains some relics of Buddha. The chedi and pond are surrounded on four sides by a cloistered courtyard containing almost 200 Buddha images of varying styles and ages. The main shrine has a beautiful wooden roof in excellent condition and the entire wat complex is dotted with ancient chedis amongst bouganvillia and fangipani trees.

Opposite the wat is a **small museum** containing archeological bits and pieces and Srivijaya artifacts. Admission is 10B and it is open 9.00 am to midday and 1.00 pm to 4.00 pm (closed Wednesday and Sunday). A small donation is also required upon entering the courtyard of the wat. The site is around 2 km out of town along the main road and costs 10B by motorcycle taxi from the station to reach.

Four other Srivijaya Period wats can be found in the area, although the above is by far the highlight. The others are **Wat Wiang, Wat Lung, Wat Nop** and **Wat Kaew**.

Wat Suan Mok   วัดสวนโมก

Located 6 km to the south of Chaiya at the foot of Khao Phutta Thong, this forest wat founded by the 'back to basics' abbot Buddhadasa Bhikku in 1932 is a very popular place amongst farangs seeking meditation retreats. Ten day courses are held at the beginning of every month with the emphasis placed on harmony with nature, physical labour, insight and tranquil meditation. Idle chit chat is completely out of place here, this wat and retreat is for the committed only. The 900B fee covers instruction, food and accommodation.

These courses are very popular during high season and often fill up. If you want to do one at that time, you are best to arrive a few days early to reserve a place. Otherwise casual visitors are welcome and the so called 'spiritual theatre' has some fascinating murals.

Ban Phumriang   หมู่บ้านพุมเรียง

Located 6 km to the east of Chaiya, this small Muslim village is well known for its gold and silver brocade cloth which you will see in the road side workshops.

Seaside

To the north of Chaiya are a couple of small **seaside villages**. At **Laem Po** you can unwind on the beach with a beer and a snack. Otherwise go 27 km to the north of Chaiya to **Tha Chana** which has a prettier beach with a view of the Ang Thong Islands in the distance. There is a **budget Chinese hotel** by the central market and plenty of eating places on the beach.

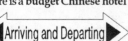
Arriving and Departing

The **orange songtheaw** from No 2 bus station in **Surat Thani** costs 20B and takes 45 minutes to an hour to reach Chaiya. There is also a **train station** and northbound trains from Surat Thani stop here. When leaving, the same orange songtheaw returns to Surat Thani and the blue songtheaws go to Phun Phin railway station.

South

PHUN PHIN   พุนพิน

This small town is 14 km to the west of Surat Thani and this is where **Surat Thani railway station** is. If you are stuck here or spending a night in transit there are a couple of basic cheap hotels opposite the train station. Both the **Thai Fah Hotel** and the **Sri Thani Hotel** have rooms starting at 120B providing eatable Thai and Western food along with tourist information. Around the corner on the main street are plenty of shops, banks, eateries and the first road on the right leads to the **Queen Hotel** which is considerably better than the above mentioned hotels but starts at 180B. If you want something to do while waiting for a train, there is a **small market** off the main street and a **wat** on a hill by the junction of the Chaiya to Surat Thani Road (Just walk past the shops and you will see it).

SURAT THANI (BAN DON)   สุราษฎร์ธานี

Better known amongst the locals as Ban Don (although strictly speaking this refers to the market area only), Surat Thani (also known as Surat) literally means 'City of the Good People' and is an important administrative and commercial centre. Located some 650 km south of Bangkok, this is the first real southern town you will reach travelling down the east coast; the curries are hotter, the locals friendly and there is a noticeable increase in the number of Muslims.

Considering the amount of tourists passing through Surat, very few actually stay in the town or spend more than a couple of hours waiting for a boat or bus. It is a pleasant enough town in its own right, far less touristy than a town such as Krabi and not a bad spot to spend a couple of days lounging around town or to use as a base for day trips to the surrounding area. If you are planning on heading to the Gulf Islands from Surat Thani, savour Surat as it will be the last slice of 'real Thailand' you will see till you return!

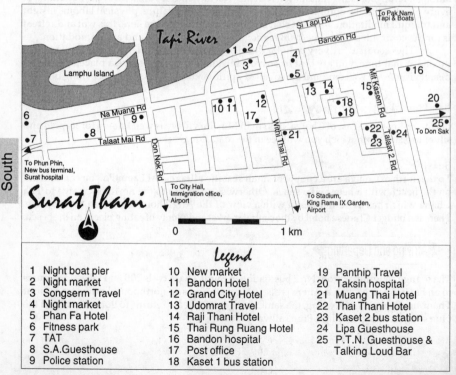

Legend

1 Night boat pier	10 New market	19 Panthip Travel
2 Night market	11 Bandon Hotel	20 Taksin hospital
3 Songserm Travel	12 Grand City Hotel	21 Muang Thai Hotel
4 Night market	13 Udomrat Travel	22 Thai Thani Hotel
5 Phan Fa Hotel	14 Raji Thani Hotel	23 Kaset 2 bus station
6 Fitness park	15 Thai Rung Ruang Hotel	24 Lipa Guesthouse
7 TAT	16 Bandon hospital	25 P.T.N. Guesthouse &
8 S.A.Guesthouse	17 Post office	Talking Loud Bar
9 Police station	18 Kaset 1 bus station	

South

Orientation

Stretched out along the southern bank of the Tapi River, the modern part consists of two long parallel streets containing most of the banks and larger shops whilst the older part, with the market and narrower streets is situated by the river.

Vital Information

Tourist Information The TAT has an office at the western end of Talaat Mai Road.
Post Office is on Talaat Mai Road, near the intersection with Withi Thai Road. The Telecommunications Centre is next door.
Banks Plenty of banks are along Talaat Mai Road, see the map for details.
Hospital The main hospital is on the road out of town en-route to Phun Phin.
Police station is at the intersection of Don Nok and Na Muang Roads. The tourist police are at the TAT office.
Codes Surat Thani's telephone code is (077) and the postal code is 84000.

Cheap Sleeps

Considering the size of the town and the number of tourists passing through, the accommodation situation in Surat Thani is appalling. The rare cheap spots are pretty awful so it becomes relatively expensive to stay here.
Thai Rung Ruang Hotel on Mit Kasem Road off Na Muang Road, ☎ (077) 273 249, has rooms with fan and shower for 310B and A/C rooms for 370B.
Raji Thani Hotel near Talaat 1 Road, ☎ (077) 272 143, has singles/doubles for 240B/260B with fan and shower and 320B/340B with A/C.
Thai Thani Hotel near Talaat 2 Road, ☎ (077) 272 977, is run by the same people as the Raji Thani Hotel and is a large and well run hotel.
Phan Fa Hotel on Na Muang Road, ☎ (077) 272 287, has basic rooms with shower for 170B.
Bandon on Na Muang is popular with farangs and often full. Small rooms with fan and shower go for 150B and larger rooms for 200B. It is noisy, but the restaurant downstairs is good.
Grand City Hotel on Withi Thai Road, ☎ (077) 272 960, has a range of rooms with fan and shower for 200B to 300B.
Muang Thai at the intersection of Talaat Mai and Withi Thai Roads, ☎ (077) 272 559. This is one of the better options in town, is relatively quiet and starts at 200B.
S.A. Guesthouse has no roman script sign and is towards the western end of Talaat Mai Road. The rooms are grotty but relatively cheap at 120B.
Lipa Guesthouse on Talaat 2 Road is an unfriendly, grotty and noisy dump starting at 150B.
P.T.N. Guesthouse is slightly out of town on the road to Don Sak and has very basic noisy rooms on top of the very aptly named 'Talking Loud Bar' which is quite good.

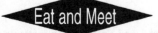

Eat and Meet

What Surat lacks in accommodation, it makes up for with food. Plenty of good cheap restaurants and two lively and very good **night markets** serving excellent seafood and coconut curries. There are also numerous **Chinese and Muslim eating places**. At present Surat is free of bakeries and muesli! Good cheap daytime eating can be had at the **market** by the bus station. The **Talking Loud Bar** is a good place for a night out with Jazz, Soul and draught beer. It also functions as a travel agent and some tour buses leave from here.

Things to do and Sights to See

There is not a lot to do in the town itself, but it is still an interesting place to stroll around for a few hours. The older part of town, between Na Muang Road and the Tapi River is the best area, with narrow streets, numerous old wooden houses and a variety of wats. Otherwise for a quiet walk with interesting views of river life cross over the new bridge and wander through the mangroves. If you are feeling lazy, try Lamphu Island or the fitness park near the TAT Office for lounging around, picnicking or reading a book if you have some time to kill.

Khao Thaphet Wildlife and Nature Education Centre
สถานีศึกษาธรรมชาติและสัตว์ป่าเขาท่าเพชร

Six km along the road to Ban Nasan is the Khao Thaphet Wildlife and Nature Education Station. This is more of a zoo than anything else but Khao Thaphet Hill has a stupa containing Buddha relics and offers some good views of the surrounding area. Take the Ban Nasan bound songtheaw from the market.

Kanchanadit   กาญจนดิษฐ์

This is a monkey training school which you can visit located 13 km from the city centre. Travel Agents in Surat will propose tours otherwise just hop on a songtheaw for Kanchanadit, just do a monkey impression for the driver and he will figure out where you want to go.

Namtok Whipawadi (Namtok Ban Nai)   น้ำตกบ้านใน

Located 38 km from Surat in Don Sak District, this waterfall is worth visiting if you have a few hours to use up. Hop on the songtheaw for Don Sak and ask for *Namtok Whipawadi*. The waterfall is located in a small park and is pretty quiet during the week but can get crowded on weekends.

◀ Arriving and Departing ▶

Air

THAI Airways flies to **Bangkok** at least twice a day for 1,785B. Other prices include **Chiang Mai** 3,115B, **Hat Yai** 1,200B, **Khon Kaen** 2,835B, **Nakhon Si Thammarat** 340B, **Phuket** 485B, **Trang** 495B, **Ubon Ratchathani** 3,180B and **Udon Thani** 3,085B.

Train

There is no train station in Surat Thani, but the train passes through the nearby town Phun Phin, 14 km to the west and a short songtheaw ride away. From here you can catch a songtheaw or local bus to Surat Thani. For detailed bus and train information refer to the timetable section at the end of this chapter.

Bus

Surat Thani has two central bus stations, Kaset 1 and Kaset 2, and a new large bus station out of town on Phun Phin Road which is virtually deserted most of the time. Although most buses will normally do a quick whizz around the new station before leaving or arriving, they tend to go through Surat Thani itself first. As a result of this, by the time the bus reaches the new bus station, it is often already full. Refer to the opposite page for price information.

South

Boat to Islands

Express boats go to **Ko Samui** (2½ hours and 400B) and **Ko Pha Ngan** (3½ hours) leaving Tha Thong pier at 08.00. Another express boat leaves for Ko Pha Ngan at 14.30. The night boat leaves at 22.00 for Ko Samui and Ko Pha Ngan and takes all night for 120B to 200B. If you are continuing to **Ko Tao**, catch the connecting boat from Thong Sala pier on Ko Pha Ngan.

Bus From Surat Thani				
	Hat Yai	**Penang**	**Kuala Lumpur**	**Singapore**
Depart	06.30, 10.30	06.30, 10.30	06.30, 20.00	06.30, 10.30
Arrive	10.30, 14.30	16.30, 20.30	10.30, 06.00	06.30, 06.30

Surat Thani Buses			
Destination	**Depart Surat Thani - Kaset 1**	**Depart Surat Thani - Kaset 2**	**Fare**
Bangkok		N: 07.00, 09.30, 10.30, 11.00	158B
		12.00, 13.00, 14.00, 17.00, 18.00	
		18.30, 19.00, 19.30, 20.00, 20.30	
		A/C: 19.30	285B
Chaiya		Orange songtheaw	20B
Chumphon	N: 05.30 - 15.30 every 30 mins.		60B
	A/C: 09.50, 13.00		70B
Hat Yai and		N: 05.30, 07.30, 09.00, 13.00.	85B
Songkhla		A/C: 06.30, 10.30, 15.00	120B
Khao Sok N.P.		N: As per Phuket (see below)	30B
		A/C: As per Phuket (see below)	60B
Krabi		N: 05.20, 06.10, 07.10, 08.00	60B
		09.10, 10.00, 10.50, 12.50, 13.40	
		14.30, 15.30, 16.30	
		A/C: 07.00, 11.00, 13.30, 16.00	91B
Narathiwat		N: 07.00, 02.00	127B
Nakhon Si	N: 05.30 - 16.30 every 30 mins.		37B
Thammarat	A/C: 06.30, 08.00, 10.00, 11.30	Note: A/C bus departs from	50B
	13.00, 14.30, 16.10	Pan Thip Travel.	
Phun Phin		N: Talaat Mai Rd every 30 mins.	10B
Phuket		N: 05.30 - 15.00 every 30 mins.	77B
		A/C: 06.50, 09.40	130B
Phang Nga		N: 06.00, 08.30, 11.30, 13.00	60B
Ranong	05.00 - 15.30 every 30 mins.		70B
	A/C: 08.30, 12.00, 14.00		80B
Trang		N: 06.40, 08.40	50B
Penang	at 06.30 from Thanaporn Travel by minibus		350B
Kuala Lumpur	at 06.30 from Thanaporn Travel by minibus		650B
Singapore	at 06.30 from Thanaporn Travel by minibus		650B

South

Dodgy Travel Agents...

Some of the travel agents in Surat Thani are amongst the most devious in Thailand. Always be sure to shop around for a good price, and when buying boat tickets, be sure that you have not been sold a ticket on the night boat 'by accident'. One of our researchers was once quoted 1,500B for a minibus ticket to Hat Yai from Surat Thani — thankfully the travel agent does not exist any more... but still be wary.

AROUND SURAT THANI

Khao Sok National Park   อุทยานแห่งชาติเขาสก

Khao Sok National Park located in the extreme west of Surat Thani Province, 109 km from Surat Thani and 45 km from Takua Pa, is one of Thailand's more spectacular National Parks. Declared a park in 1980 it stretches over an area of 750 sq km.

The park topography is rugged limestone outcrops over a mud stone base with some gravity defying rock formations, narrow gorges, caves, waterfalls and jagged peaks, the highest being Khao Sok mountain which reaches 950 m. The park receives a substantial amount of rain for up to ten months a year and the primary, tropical, evergreen forest is particularly dense and lush. The driest time to visit is in December and January. This is the only place in all of Thailand where you can see the famous Rafflesia parasitic flower which can grow up to 80 cm in diameter and it only flowers once a year giving off a very pungent stench.

The park is large enough to support large mammals such as elephants, tigers and bears but poaching has sent them into the deepest parts of the park. Visitors are more likely to spot a huge variety of birds, butterflies, monkeys and reptiles.

Cheap Sleeps

Unusual for a National Park, there is a wide choice of accommodation here including the usual official park accommodation and camping plus a cluster of private resorts around the park office. The variety of accommodation is quite varied ranging from large shared bungalows at the headquarters site to floating huts on Rachabrapah Lake. Enquiries and reservations can be made at the park office.

Star Huts and Restaurant located about 50 m from the main road has only two huts, but they are very nice and cost 150B with fan and shower.

Jungle Huts about another km along the road towards the entrance down a track to the right, this place is situated in a coffee plantation on the banks of a stream and has basic bamboo huts with bath for 80B. This is a quiet and secluded location.

Khao Sok Rainforest Resort Back on the main road some 300 m further on, this more upmarket place has nice huts in a great setting by the stream but they cost 500B with fan and shower. The restaurant is good despite the 'assistant' being a small monkey.

Khao Sok River Lodge opposite the Khao Sok Rainforest Resort, this place has some nice huts but only rents them to German tour groups operating out of Phuket.

Tree Tops is just past the park entrance and visitor centre but they only deal with group tours as well.

Bamboo Huts & **Janpha House** If you follow the track past Tree Tops you will reach these two placesrenting huts at 100B and 150B, and 150B respectively.

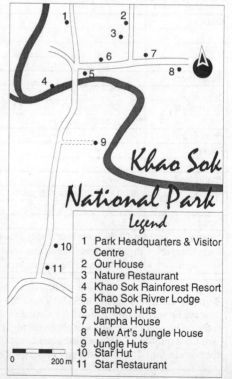

Khao Sok National Park

Legend

1 Park Headquarters & Visitor Centre
2 Our House
3 Nature Restaurant
4 Khao Sok Rainforest Resort
5 Khao Sok Rivrer Lodge
6 Bamboo Huts
7 Janpha House
8 New Art's Jungle House
9 Jungle Huts
10 Star Hut
11 Star Restaurant

0   200 m

New Arts Jungle House a.k.a. **Riverview Jungle Lodge** is further down the same track and has rooms ranging from 300B to 700B all with fan and shower.

Our House is down a track leading to the left after Bamboo Huts and is run by Denis. This place has accommodation in a longhouse for 350B with fan and shower and larger bungalows for 700B. The nearby **Nature Restaurant** has the widest selection of food in the park.

Things to do and Sights to See

All of the above resorts plus the park service offer tours into Khao Sok for overnight camping, rafting and elephant riding. You will definitely need a guide if you plan to visit some of the more distant and inaccessible parts of the park including the spectacular 165 sq km lake and the caves. One of the caves, Tham See-Roo was used by communist rebels until the early 1980s. Tour prices and sights visited vary immensely, so you would be well advised to shop around for the best deal although, if business is slow, you may well be able to tailor the trip to your own desires. **Rachabrapah Lake** was formed by a dam in 1986 which flooded the steep gorges leaving only the peaks. The result of this has been a lake with over 100 islands which is where much of the tourist activity takes place. There are plenty of marked trails which can be followed on your own, particularly into the southwest area of the park where many waterfalls are an easy day hike from the park entrance. The main southwest trail leads 9 km to the waterfall **Namtok Ton Gloy**. Along the way is **Namtok Wing Hin** (3 km from HQ), **Namtok Bang Leap Nam** (4½ km), and **Tang Nam gorge** (6 km). There are two tracks leading off this main trail, one going to the site where the Rafflesia parasitic flower grows, the other to **Namtok Than Sawan**, but prepared to immerse yourself in the river to get to the end. **Namtok Sip-ed Cha** is 4 km north of the park headquarters reached by a trail that follows the Bang Laen River.

Arriving and Departing

Getting Around
From km 109 on the Surat Thani to Takua Pa Road a well signposted road leads off to the park entrance. The turn-off road extends 1½ km to the north along which you will need to either walk of hitch. Dirt tracks lead off this road to the right and left to the various resorts.

If travelling from **Surat Thani**, take a bus bound for Phuket from Talaat Kasit 2. These buses leave regularly, cost 30B for an ordinary bus or 60B for A/C and takes 2½ to 3 hours. This route is spectacular, not unlike a ride through a tropical Mae Hong Son!

If coming from **Phuket**, you may need to go catch a bus bound for Ranong and change at Takua Pa. From **Takua Pa**, take a bus from the bus station heading for Surat Thani getting off at the park turn-off to the park. The ride takes about 45 minutes and costs 20B.

Khlong Yan Wildlife Sanctuary   เขตรักษาพันธุ์สัตว์ป่าคลองยัน

This small park some 50 km south of Surat Thani in Wiphawadi District is famous for the Whipawadi Waterfall. This makes for a nice day trip from Surat Thani by either songtheaw or motorbike, and park accommodation is available. Somewhat confusingly though, the waterfall shares the same name as another in Don Sak District, so make sure you have your songtheaws sorted out.

Kang Krung National Park
This 541 sq km National Park also exists in the area and is dominated by two small parallel mountain ranges. The more popular sites include the 70 km long Khlong Yan, some hot springs and a number of waterfalls. It is possible to hire guides to take you on treks in the park and you can also camp but bring your own equipment.

Tai Rom Yen National Park   อุทยานแห่งชาติใต้ร่มเย็น

This National Park is in the southern part of Surat Thani Province covering 425 sq km. Its appeal, besides the simple fact that it is a National Park, is for frog fans. The park is home to the rare *rana macrodon* mountain frog, which in maturity reaches just under 20 cm in length and weighs a third of a kilogram - you will recognise it by its black dots on a greeny brown coloured skin. Other than this there are a few waterfalls with the best being **Namtok Tad Fa.**

KO SAMUI   เกาะสมุย

Largest, and probably best known of the islands in this area, Ko Samui sits off the coast of Surat Thani in the Gulf of Thailand. The island group consists of almost 80 islands although most visitors only see the three main islands of Ko Samui, Ko Pha Ngan and Ko Tao, with increasing numbers also now visiting the spectacular Ang Thong National Marine Park.

Ko Samui is Thailand's third largest island (after Phuket and Ko Chang), covers an area of just under 250 sq km and is located 84 km from the eastern coast mainland town of Surat Thani. Ko Samui has been a popular tourist destination for many years, hence its infrastructure is quite well developed compared to its nearby counterparts. Transport is made easier by 50 km of sealed roads, and 47 km of dirt roads that lead to sightseeing destinations and local villages. The main town on Ko Samui is **Nathon**.

You are almost guaranteed temperate weather throughout the year at Samui as it very rarely goes outside the 23° C to 33° C range. The hottest months are between February and May and during this season Ko Samui is characterised by warm weather and calm seas. The months with the highest rainfall are between May and October (the fringe months of April and November still get significant rain) and the temperature is still warm remaining between 24° C and 31° C. However this season is often accompanied with rough seas and monsoon rains. The island is quite crowded in summer, but during the monsoon season, the island is fairly quiet, more than compensating for the once a day rains.

Ko Samui has become a very popular destination for travellers visiting Thailand for both short and long holidays. As with any destination, Ko Samui is enjoying both the good and the bad of huge tourist growth. The most popular beaches such as Lamai and Chaweng are dotted with girlie bars, and at times there seems to be a virtual flood of prostitutes. Often little more than a street side bar, these 'girlie bars' can usually be picked out by their names such as Tokyo Rose and Good Friends Bar or by their clientele, usually fat inebriated Western men. Be advised, not all the girls are girls...

The development has definitely marred the island in some places, with Chaweng and perhaps Lamai destined for an increasing number of upmarket accommodation. However there are still many interesting and quiet beaches which are still lined with budget accommodation. Lamai and Chaweng are the two 'nicest' beaches on the island, generally getting the cleanest water and occasional wave, whilst the quieter beaches such as Bo Phut or Mae Nam do not have golden sand and the water is as still as a mill pond. The beaches up this way are much quieter and lend themselves to a more peaceful escape rather than a blaring party.

Many do not appreciate the sheer size of Ko Samui until they see it either from the air or the ferry. If you are catching the ferry, chances are you will be invited to many different bungalows and be enticed by album after album of photos. These serve as a guide, but certainly do not expect the resort to look exactly as it does on film. Nevertheless, these guides are an excellent source for trying to pick out where to stay if you have not already been recommended somewhere by someone you met on your journeys.

As far as farang colonisation is concerned, Bo Phut has a definite Francophile influence, Chaweng has a large British contingent and Lamai is popular with German visitors. In Chaweng and Lamai burglaries and muggings are not unheard of so take care of your belongings.

The following covers Ko Samui in a clockwise direction, beginning in Nathon. The 'Cheap Sleeps' and 'Things to Do & Sights to See' sections follow after a complete roundup of the island accommodation.

Ko Samui

South

Vital Information

Tourist Information There is a TAT office in Nathon at the northern end of town on the seafront road. Virtually every guesthouse on Ko Samui can offer some form of tourist service. The minimarts sell helpful maps of the island with marked points of interest and the occasional walking trail.

Post Office is situated at the northern end of town. There are branch offices in Chaweng and Lamai villages.

Banks At night on the major beaches, mobile exchange vans prowl the street, whilst during the day branch offices will exchange travellers cheques and perform cash advances. There is an ATM in Nathon if your card allows withdrawals abroad.

Legend

1 Chalet B'lows	33 First B'lows, Chalee B'lows	58 Royal Blue Lagoon &
2 Metsai B'lows	& Como's B'lows	Bay View Villa
3 Samui Thong Resort	34 Beach House & Art Pub	59 Comfort B'lows &
4 Chariya Resort	35 Sand & Sea Huts & L.A.	Island Resort
5 Naiphon B'lows	Resort	60 Rose Garden &
6 Blue River Resort	36 Kinaree Resort,	Weekender Villa
7 Axolotl	Secret Garden, Boonlerd	61 Spa Resort & Sukasam
8 Sunbeam B'lows	House & Number One B'low	62 No Name B'lows &
9 Ban Tai Resort	37 Phayom Park Resort &	Tapi B'lows
10 Home Bay B'lows	Sunset Song B'low	63 Paradise B'lows, Amity
11 Co Co Palm Village	38 Pong Petch Servotel &	B'lows & White Sand
12 Phalarm Inn	Big Buddha B'low	64 Nice Resort & Palm
13 Naplarn Villa	39 Big Buddha	Resort
14 O.K. Village	40 Samui Thong Son Resort	65 Sunrise B'lows & Baan
15 Golden Huts	41 Tong Son Bay	Thai Resort
16 Shady Shacks	42 Soleil B'lows, P.S.Villa,	66 Noi
17 Mae Nam Resort	White House Hotel &	67 Chinda, Swiss Chalet &
18 Lolita Resort	Choeng Mon Village	Rocky
19 Moon Hut & Nature B'lows	43 Chat Kaeo Resort &	68 Samui Maria
20 Cleopatra, Seashore &	The boathouse	69 Cosy
Near Seashore	44 Island View	70 Garden Resort &
21 New Lamae Villa	45 Sun Sand Resort	Samui Orchid
22 Paradise & Raindow	46 Phayom Park Resort	71 Wat Samret
Modern Resorts	47 I.K.K. B'low	72 Samui Butterfly Garden
23 Friendly & Rose B'lows	48 Coral Bay Resort	73 Laem Set Inn
24 Silent, Magic View &	49 Papillon, Samui Island &	74 Diamond Villa
S.R. Resort	Matlang Resorts	75 Waikiki Resort
25 Mae Nam Villa & Laem Sai	50 Blue Lagoon, Venus Resort	76 Laem So Pagoda
26 Sunny Resort & Chalee	51 Lazy Wave, Moon B'low &	77 Tan Village B'lows
Villa	Corto Maltese	78 Tan Resort
27 Bo Phut Gh., Sandy Resort,	52 Your Place Resort &	79 Coral Beach B'lows
World Resort & Sala Thai	K.John Resort	80 Coconut Villa B'lows
28 Palm Garden B'lows,	53 Coral Cove Resort	81 Emerald Cove
Calm B'lows &	54 Coral Cove Chalet &	82 Seagull & Pearl Bay
Peace B'lows	Blue Horizon	83 Vastervik & Wiesenthan
29 Chai Had & Samui Euphoria	55 Beverly Hills Resort	84 Copacabana Beach
30 Ziggy Stardust &	56 Samui Silver Beach &	Club
Smile House	Samui Yacht Club	85 Infoo Palace &
31 The Lodge & Boon Huts	57 Little Mermaid Resort	Aran Resort
32 Sandview B'lows &		86 Lipa Bay Resort
Sky Blue B'lows		87 Sawai Home B'lows

Police and Tourist Police Both the police station and the Tourist police are situated in Nathon. The former is on Taweratphakdee Road beside the district office and the latter are on the seafront road beside Samui International Diving. There are also police stations at Chaweng and Lamai village.

Hospital Try Nathon public hospital, ☎ (077) 421 230, or Bandon Inter Hospital with 24 hour service (in Bo Phut), ☎ (077) 245 236, 425 382. Despite rumours to the contrary, a coconut falling on ones head is not the most common form of accidental death on Ko Samui. It is motorcycle accidents involving alcohol and a variety of other substances. Ride safely and always wear a helmet.

Immigration Office The immigration office is 3 km out of Nathon and is easily reached by motorcycle taxi from beside the wharves. Visas can be extended here, but as with many other police related matters on Ko Samui, do not be surprised to be charged a 'surcharge' of another 50B on top of the standard 500B visa extension fee. The process takes around ten minutes, and it helps if you wear clean clothes.

Bangkok Airways office on Ko Samui, ☎ (077) 425 011.
Codes Ko Samui's telephone code is (077) and postal code varies depending on the location on the island: Lamai and Aow Pang Ka 84310, Chaweng, Bo Phut, Big Buddha and Ban Bang Po 84320, Mae Nam 84330 and Ban Bang Makham and Nathon 84140.

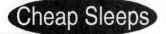
Cheap Sleeps

Nathon   หน้าทอน

Neither interesting nor unpleasant Nathon is basically a 'passing through' sort of town though it is the best place on the island for shopping. There are plenty of restaurants, very little accommodation and no nightlife, but it is not bad for a stroll with numerous old wooden houses remaining, particularly along Ang Thong Road. There are also some reasonable swimming areas a short walk north or south of town. Made up of three parallel streets interconnected by several small roads and alleyways, the main road Taweratphakdee Road contains most of the banks and larger stores whilst the narrower Ang Thong Road has a variety of clothes and silverware shops and the seafront road is mostly travel agents, cafes and bars.
Seaview Guesthouse is the only guesthouse in town, situated on the main street. It has rooms with fan for 150B, with fan and shower for 200B and with A/C for 300B.
Dumrong Hotel, ☎ (077) 420 359, to the north of town has clean rooms starting at 480B.
Seaview Hotel ☎ (077) 421 481, to the south of town. Comfortable rooms cost 300B and 350B.
Win Hotel ☎ (077) 421 500, and **Palace Hotel** are on the seafront and both have comfortable rooms with A/C ranging from 350B to 500B.
Jinta at the southern end of town, just before you reach the Seaview Hotel, has basic concrete chalets for 150B with shower and fan.

Ban Bang Makham   บ้านบางมะขาม

North of Nathon is the 4 km long Bang Makham Bay. Very quiet and practically undeveloped, the beach can be grubby at high tides and muddy at low tide. Nevertheless there are a couple of pleasant budget range resorts.
Chalet Bungalows, ☎ (077) 420 307, this nicely laid our resort has clean rooms for 200B with fan and shower.
Metsai Bungalows, ☎ (077) 421 120, is located at the northern end of the beach and is a particularly friendly establishment with rooms starting at 200B.

Bang Po and Ban Tai   บ้านบางปอ, บ้านใต้

Around the cape moving onto Samui's northern coast is the pretty bay, **Aow Thong Phu**, where there are as yet no resorts. Further north comes the stretching Bang Po Beach. Bang Po is hardly developed with just a handful of resorts though **house lease on a monthly basis** is becoming increasingly popular in this 'unspoilt' area and numerous such establishments are now popping up. Bang Po transforms into Ban Tai after Naiphon Bungalows and after the final set of accommodation (Ban Tai) there is a long stretch of undeveloped coastline, mostly rocky with some **good snorkelling** until you reach Laem Na Pra Lan which marks the beginning of Mae Nam.
Samui Thong Resort is located towards the western end of the beach and has good bungalows for 200B and very large ones for 500B. The Samui Thong Seafood Restaurant is here as well.
Chariya Resort is close to the road and shabbier than the Samui Thong Resort, although the beach here is good. Their huts go for 150B.
Naiphon Bungalows, ☎ (077) 420 124, is further east from Chariya. This ugly mid range resort marks the change from Bang Po to Ban Tai.
Blue River Resort, ☎ (077) 421 357, next off the rank, this resort has a nice garden and beach. The bungalows start at 300B and include kitchen facilities.

South

Legend

1 Customs
2 Tourist A.T.
3 Jin Restaurant
4 Public Health Office
5 Dumrong Hotel
6 Post office
7 Bank of Ayudhya
8 Bangkok Bank
9 New Pier
10 R.T. Bakery & Cafe
11 Spanish Restaurant
12 Bookshop
13 Pier Restaurant
14 Police station
15 Panon Cafe
16 District office
17 Songtheaws to Resorts
18 Seaview Guesthouse
19 Songserm Travel
20 Koh Kaen Restaurant
21 Thai Military Bank
22 'Cafe' Restaurant
23 Pier
24 Rung Thong Restaurant
25 R.T. Bakery & Cafe 2
26 Marco Polo
27 Krung Thai Bank
28 Panthip Travel
29 Will Wait Rest. & Bakery
30 Siam Commercial Bank
31 Clinic
32 A/C buses
33 Thai Commercial Bank
34 Siam City Bank
35 Dentist
36 Siam Mart Dept. Store
37 Palace Hotel
38 Kodak
39 Fuji
40 Thai Restaurant
41 Tourist police
42 Samui Int. Diving
43 Vegetarian Rest.
44 Food market

45 Win Hotel
46 Tangs Restaurant
47 Bangkok Metro Bank
48 Jinta Bungalow
49 Market
50 Thai Farmers Bank
51 Fish market
52 Krua Savoiey Rest.
53 Gospel Church
54 Siam Food Centre
55 Wat
56 Sunset Restaurant
57 Seaview Hotel

Nathon

To Mae Nam

Tawaratphakdee Rd

Angthong Rd

0   150 m

To Lipa Noi

South

Axolotl This interesting and much publicized (in Samui at least) resort is under Italian and German management and offers a variety of courses such as massage, tarot reading, chakra therapy, Tai-chi, bio energetics and various meditation techniques. Prices for the courses vary and the accommodation is in the 300B to 600B range, although you can always stay somewhere cheaper and just pop in for your course. You are also welcome to stay and do none of the courses if that is your preference. This is a great place to relax and there is some coral offshore. Axolotl gets busy in the high season but bookings can be made through either Toci or Sarani on ☎Fax (077) 420 017.

Sunbeam Bungalows, ☎ (077) 421 061, is further along the pretty beach with large huts setting you back 350B.

Ban Tai, ☎ (077) 424 317, this is the last resort on this beach and has decent bungalows that cost 150B.

Mae Nam

Many Mae Nam and Bo Phut residents are of Chinese origin and were former pirates. They were offered land in the area for settlement during the 60s and early 70s by the King of Thailand in return for the cessation of their activities on the high seas. To the pirates it seemed like quite a good deal as the other option was to be blown out of the water by the Thai navy, and they have been living here happily ever since.

The main backpacker scene with budget accommodation is centred in the north and northeast of Samui around Mae Nam, Bo Phut and Bangruk (Big Buddha) beaches and the surrounding coves. The beaches are definitely not as pretty as the east coast beaches, but the development is lower key and the beaches are much quieter.

Mae Nam Beach stretches 5 km from Laem Na Pra Lan in the west to the small rocky headland at the eastern end which separates it from Aow Bo Phut. Most bungalows are a short walking distances from the main road where songtheaw taxi services are frequent. From west to east, the accommodation scene is as follows:

West Mae Nam

Home Bay Bungalow, ☎ (01) 958 9533, this mid range resort is very quiet except during peak season when the prices tend to shoot up. The bungalows are clean and start at 150B for a basic hut and up to 600B for a top of the range bungalow.

CoCo Palm Village, ☎ (077) 425 321, this is very similar to Home Bay Bungalow but has the added comfort of a swimming pool. Prices are the same as at Home Bay Bungalow.

Phalarm Inn This very nicely spread out resort in a nice garden setting has excellent bungalows for 80B to 150B. The staff are very friendly, the only blot in its copy book being a 2 m high concrete wall right around it.

Naplarn Villa Some 100 m back from the beach this place also has a pleasant garden setting and has popular bungalows costing 200B and 250B.

Wat Na Palaan separates the above from the more upmarket resorts of **Harry's,** ☎ (077) 425 477, and **Seafan,** both of which offer very good deals in the low season.

O.K. Village located behind Wat Na Palaan has wooden huts with fan and shower which go for 60B and the bar and restaurant here are good value. The only problem is that to get to the beach you need to walk through the wat, necessitating respectable clothing and thus a big pile of clothes that you will need to leave laying around on the beach while you swim. The next four resorts are very close together, have similar prices and are set in a garden setting. **Anong Villa, Shangri Lah,** ☎ (077) 425 189, **Sunrise** and **Palm Point Village,** ☎ (077) 425 095, all have good bungalows from 100B to 300B, Shangri Lah even has some cheapies for 60B. The beach in this area is quite good.

Golden Huts is a quiet and friendly establishment with huts 50 m back from the beach. Simple wooden huts go for 100B and larger ones for 200B and 300B. The cook here is Italian.

Shady Shacks, ☎ (077) 425 392, next door has similar prices and conditions and the nearby **Mae Nam Resort** starts at 500B.

The western end of the beach is completed by the **Santiburi Dusit** after which a river separates it from the central beach area.

Central Mae Nam

Central Mae Nam kicks off with the **Lolita Resort,** ☎ (077) 425 134, which cannot decide whether it is an upmarket or budget place. Small wooden huts are squeezed between large modern ones and it has a rather ugly and very large new restaurant. Prices here start at 200B.

Koseng 2 Resort Located between Lolita and the Mae Nam pier, this is one of the more popular places to stay but is not one of the cleaner ones. The huts start at 100B and 150B.

Mae Nam Village, ☎ (077) 425 151, to the east of Mae Nam Village, has friendly staff, but the location is not great. Huts are priced at 100B, 150B and 200B.

Mae Nam Beach Bungalows, ☎ (077) 425 060, as equally friendly as the Mae Nam Village, basic huts here go for 60B (no fan or shower) and 100B with fan and shower.

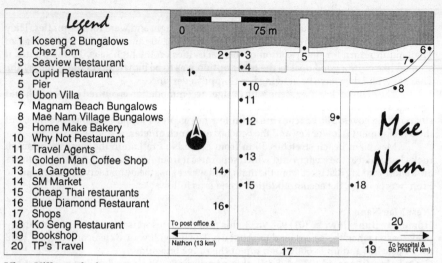

Legend

1 Koseng 2 Bungalows
2 Chez Tom
3 Seaview Restaurant
4 Cupid Restaurant
5 Pier
6 Ubon Villa
7 Magnam Beach Bungalows
8 Mae Nam Village Bungalows
9 Home Make Bakery
10 Why Not Restaurant
11 Travel Agents
12 Golden Man Coffee Shop
13 La Gargotte
14 SM Market
15 Cheap Thai restaurants
16 Blue Diamond Restaurant
17 Shops
18 Ko Seng Restaurant
19 Bookshop
20 TP's Travel

Ubon Villa similar but more cramped than the above, the staff are not as welcoming.

Moon Hut, ☎ (077) 425 247, reached by a track next to the police station, this secluded location has huts on the beach for 100B and 150B.

Nature Bungalows, ☎ (077) 425 201, is just to the east of Moon Hut, where the beach is nice and the huts go for 60B and 80B, but the restaurant is not great.

East Mae Nam

Mae Nam East begins on the other side of the river.

Cleopatra, ☎ (077) 425 486, has a bit of a shanty look to it with various styles of bungalows tightly squeezed together. Prices range from 80B to 180B.

Seashore, ☎ (077) 425 192, is very friendly but the bungalows are ordinary at 80B.

Near Seashore (yes that is the name!) has an attractive garden area and the huts are priced from 80B to 150B and are all with fan and shower.

New Lamae Villa is one of the better ones with a well organised and tasty restaurant. Basic huts cost 80B, nice ones are 150B, 400B for a large hut and 600B for A/C.

Paradise Resort is more upmarket and very popular with Germans, bungalows start at 400B.

Rainbow Modern Bungalows in a garden setting make this not a bad choice. Bungalows go for 100B, 150B and 200B.

Friendly This place certainly lives up to its name. Small huts are 100B and larger huts with fan and shower go for 200B.

Rose Bungalows have nice huts but they are close together for 120B on the beach. Smaller huts back off the beach go for 60B and 100B.

Silent has tiny huts for 70B and larger ones go for 150B, all of them are pretty close together.

Magic View has only five huts which are very nice at 150B.

S.R. Resort has ordinary bungalows starting at 100B.

Mae Nam Villa, ☎ (077) 425 501, at the eastern end of the beach, pleasant though cramped huts go for 80B, 100B, and 150B with fan and shower and larger bungalows cost 300B.

Laem Sai, ☎ (077) 425 133, is much more popular and spacious than Mae Nam Villa and is located in a quiet setting. The bungalows however are not brilliant and the staff here can be pretty unorganised at times. All huts have fan and shower and go for 80B, 100B and 150B.

Who really is a farang then?

Farang is the most common phrase used to refer to foreigners in Thailand. Derived originally from the word Francais, the Thais could not quite get it right and pronounced it instead as farangsay — hence farang — foreigner of western descent.

Ban Mae Nam   บ้านแม่น้ำ

Stretched out along the main road of Mae Nam village are various motorbike hire places, restaurants and shops including a Dutch Diving School, the Golden Dream Pizzeria and the reassuringly named GOD motorcycle hire! In the centre of town a couple of small streets leading down to the pier contain several small shops, a couple of travel agents and various restaurants.

Just to the west of Ban Mae Nam there is a road striking inland. Within a matter of 100 m you are amongst villages watching roosters fight and coconuts being picked. If you are lucky the locals may ask you in for tea and whiskey. The road turns into a dirt track and winds its way up the hill finally reaching the hilltop restaurant (which does a delicious chicken with chillies and cashews) from where the view is superb. The last few 100 m are very steep and getting a motorbike up the deeply rutted trail takes some skill.

Hat Bo Phut   หาดบ่อผุด

A small rocky headland separates Mae Nam from Bo Phut Beach. Hat Bo Phut is wider and definitely prettier than Mae Nam but equally quiet. There is some coral off the rocks at the western end of the beach for snorkelling otherwise the beach is great for just lying around on.

Sunny Resort is spacious and has a nice restaurant, bungalows start at 100B and 150B.

Chalee Villa has bungalows for 100B and 140B but the beach here can get a little grubby.

Bo Phut Guesthouse, ☎ (077) 425 085, is next door and has similar huts with the same prices.

Sandy Resort is set in plush surroundings with pool, fountains and nice garden. If business is slow treat yourself to some luxury with rooms going for 400B, 500B (hot water) and 600B (A/C). In high season these prices double.

World Resort, ☎ (077) 425 355, is very similar to Sandy Resort in both style and price, although it is not as well designed.

Sala Thai, ☎ (077) 425 300, is a bit shabby but cheap and the **Samui Palm Beach,** ☎ (077) 425 494, is even uglier and costs 2,000B per night!

Palm Garden Bungalow, is good value with huts for 80B, 100B and 120B and is run by a French lady. French and Thai food is available although it is not cheap.

Calm Bungalow is nearby and more spacious with huts for 100B or 150B with fan and shower.

Peace Bungalow, ☎ (077) 425 357, is a larger resort, well kept and reasonably priced at 100B with fan, 150B/200B with fan and shower and 500B for A/C.

Chai Had, ☎ (077) 425 196, is run down but very cheap at only 80B.

Samui Euphoria, ☎ (077) 425 098, is an expensive condo type development.

From here on, the road runs parallel to the beach and as a result the beach is dirtier and busier.

Ziggy Stardust, ☎ (077) 425 409, this well known establishment has a very attractive restaurant but the road separates it from the equally smart bungalows. Small huts are 200B, large huts go for 600B and it costs 800B for A/C. This is a popular place to stay and prices can double here in peak season.

Smile House, ☎ (077) 425 361, at the start of Bo Phut village has similar prices and road situation to Ziggy Stardust.

The Lodge, ☎ (077) 425 377, is recommended by many wandering farangs. This mid range hotel starts at 500B, has every comfort you need and is located within Bo Phut village.

Boon Huts, ☎ (077) 425 255, these huts are twenty years old and were the first to be built on Bo Phut. Clean rabbit hutch like rooms go for 50B.

Sandview Bungalows, ☎ (077) 425 432, is shabby and the beach is not so good. Prices are 120B, 200B and 300B.

Sky Blue Bungalows are comfortable and rented on a weekly or monthly basis. Fully equipped rooms go for 4,500B to 6,000B per month.

South

Ban Bo Phut

This small village is calm, being off the main road, laid back and little has changed architectural over time with low wooden houses being the norm rather than the exception. It contains a bank, numerous travel agents, bike and jeep hire and various shops as well as some good value restaurants.

Also in Bo Phut is the **Bandon Inter Hospital** with 24 hour emergency service and brain scans, ☎ (077) 245 236, 425 382.

Hat Bangruk (Big Buddha Beach)   หาดบางรักษ์

East of Bo Phut is Bangruk Bay also known as Big Buddha Beach after the large golden image on an offshore islet which is connected to Samui by a causeway at the eastern end of the bay. This is a preferable place over the previous two bays but the narrower beach can get dirty at times. The sand here is finer than the grittier Bo Phut sand.

First Bungalows, ☎ (077) 425 840, aptly named, this is the first setup at the western end of the beach. There are only four huts which cost 150B, but the First Seafood Restaurant is popular.

Chalee Bungalow is very friendly with bungalows going for 100B with fan and shower.

Como's Bungalows, ☎ (077) 425 210, are priced at 100B, 200B or 500B with A/C.

Beach House, ☎ (077) 425 211, is a bit down the beach from Como's and is popular despite its quite cramped feel. Small huts with fan and shower are 100B and larger ones are 200B. **Art Pub** is next door and has been interestingly decorated...

Sand and Sea Huts have huts for 200B that are clean in fairly well kept grounds.

L.A. Resort in a garden setting — nothing could be further from L.A. than here! Small huts are 150B, larger ones cost 200B and deluxe bungalows go for 400B. All huts have fan and shower.

Kinnaree Resort, ☎ (077) 425 217, **Secret Garden, Boonlerd House** and **Number One Bungalow** are all cheap though close together. **Number One Bungalow,** ☎ (077) 425 466, is the best of the bunch with reasonable bungalows going for 100B and better ones for 200B.

Phayom Park Resort located opposite the post office is cramped with huts going for 150B or 300B with A/C.

Sunset Song Bungalow is friendlier than the Phayom Park and has nice wooden huts in a shaded area for 200B and a good restaurant as well.

Pong Petch Servotel offers low season prices at 300B and 500B for A/C, in the high season these prices double.

Big Buddha Bungalow, ☎ (077) 425 282, has semi-detached wooden bungalows for 300B and 400B with A/C.

Aow Plai   อ่าวปลาย

This is the next bay after Bangruk and is a long, sheltered, west facing bay and so far totally undeveloped. At the end of the bay is Laem Sam Rong, Samui's northern-most point off which sits tiny Ko Sum which has some good snorkelling points.

Aow Thong Song   อ่าวท้องสน

This is Samui's most isolated beach with only two resorts, so it is very quiet but also difficult to reach. Songtheaws will drop you off on the main road (from Nathon take a songtheaw bound for Choeng Mon) at the beginning of a 4 km dirt track with a 'Warning - Bandits' sign at the start of it. Locals say the sign is just a joke.

The **Samui Thong Son Resort** has comfortable wooden huts for 100B (150B in the high season), large chalets for 450B and an A/C chalet for 600B. This is a friendly spot and resident farang Dave organises night fishing and tours of obscure karaoke bars! If this is full, the second resort, the **Tong Son Bay,** has similar accommodation and prices.

Aow Choeng Mon   อ่าวเชิงมน

This pretty beach with fine sand and an offshore island is home to a selection of decent guesthouses and, except for peak season, is pretty quiet.

Soleil Bungalows has wooden huts starting at 150B and 300B for concrete A/C bungalows. There is a nice kiddies playing area by the beach.

P.S. Villa, ☎ (077) 425 160, is spacious with good bungalows all priced at 200B.

Next is the upmarket **White House Hotel** followed by the friendly **Choeng Mon Village Resort,** ☎ (077) 425 372, where wooden huts are 250B with fan and shower, concrete rooms are 350B or 900B for a concrete room with A/C and TV.

Chat Kaeo Resort, ☎ (077) 425 109, has nice wooden huts for 200B and 500B for A/C huts in a shady garden.

Check out the amazing wooden junk shaped chalets next door at the Australian owned **Boat House** although the rates are high enough to sink any ambitions of staying here.

Island View, ☎ (077) 425 080, is nicely spaced out in a coconut grove. Simple A-Frames cost 100B and better huts go for 200B to 300B with fan and shower.

Sun Sand Resort located on the rocky headland overlooking the bay was closed for renovations at the time of research but if prices are kept down it should be a good place to stay.

South of Choeng Mon

A couple of rocky headlands separate Choeng Mon from the next bay. The second bay along contains the upmarket **Phayom Park Resort** (off season prices start at 500B). This is where the east coast proper really starts with a series of undeveloped and attractive beaches. The last beach before Chaweng, **Aow Yai Noi** has a couple of resorts on it, the pick of the bunch being I.K.K.

I.K.K. Bungalow, ☎ (077) 422 482, is very secluded in a great setting with a reef in front. The bungalows go for 200B with fan and shower and the food is good as well although the staff can be a little sour. Further south, opposite the songtheaw station is the upmarket **Coral Bay Resort.**

The southern tip of the beach, opposite **Ko Matlang,** is another popular snorkelling spot and also marks the beginning of Chaweng from where it is more or less built-up for the next 5 km south.

Ban Chaweng

Chaweng village itself stretches out along the main road around halfway between Bo Phut and Lamai. It is a nondescript kind of place, containing a few shops, Thai noodle stalls and cafes, a police station, post office, a wat and a rather out of place gym and squash court. There is only one budget place to stay in the village, the **Samui Holiday Guesthouse**, at the southern end of the village with brick chalets for 200B with fan and shower.

The road by the wat leads to North Chaweng Beach and passes the interesting **Zemthai Village Cultural Centre** which offers courses in cooking, language, massage, yoga, Tai-chi, crystal encounters, magnetic acupuncture as well as jungle hiking tours so there is really something for everyone. The centre is open 10.00 am to 6.00 pm and is closed on Sundays, ☎ (077) 422 282. Skirting Chaweng Lake, the road arrives at the northern end of Chaweng Beach proper.

Hat Chaweng   หาดเฉวง

The most popular location in Samui, the long pretty beach is non stop resorts, upmarket, mid range and budget whilst the parallel road is non-stop bars, restaurants and shops. This place is either paradise or hell depending on what you like doing, but one thing that Chaweng certainly is not is Thailand. Chaweng has been thoroughly colonized and exists entirely for farangs. Most resorts have Thai/Western management, many restaurants have farang cooks and staff and the bars have European DJ's.

Legend

1 Picola Rest.
2 O.P Resort
3 Marco's
4 Samui Cabana
5 Relax Resort
6 Bookshop
7 Samui Country Resort
8 Drop Inn
9 Island Resort
10 Chaweng Royal Beach Resort
11 Chaweng Regent Beach
12 Chaweng Villa
13 Montien House
14 Lotus Rest.
15 Foodstalls
16 Coffee Girls & Coffee Boys Clubs
17 Cheers Beach Bar
18 Bongos
19 The Club
20 Chang Diving
21 Coconut Grove Bungalows
22 Samui Coral Resort
23 In Deep Diving
24 Chaweng Garden Resort
25 Green Mango
26 Fawlty Towers Pub
27 Flamingo Pub
28 Black Jack Pub
29 Baan Chaweng Resort
30 Sheesh Mahal Indian Rest.
31 J.R.s Bar & Bungalows
32 Anchor House Bungalows
33 Post office
34 Royal Thai Cuisine
35 Best Beach Bungalows
36 Samui Royal Beach Resort
37 Anongthai Resort
38 Malibu Beach Resort
39 Chaweng Buri Resort
40 Samui Int'l Diving
41 Magic Light Swiss Restaurant
42 Baan Samui Resort
43 Jah Dub Bar
44 Dew Drop Huts
45 Black Cat
46 Reggae Pub
47 Chaba Samui Resort
48 Siam Commercial Exchange
49 Beach Comber
50 Roll On In
51 Explorer
52 Thai Boxing Stadium
53 The Doors Bar
54 Cheap motorbike hire
55 Silver Sand Resort
56 Viking/Charlies Huts

57 Market
58 Central Bay Restaurant
59 Jazz Junction
60 Princess Village
61 Central Bay Resort
62 Go In-ternet Cafe
63 Central Samui Beach Resort
64 The Terrace Restaurant
65 Sunset Paradise Bungalow
66 Chaweng Resort
67 Thai Farmers Exchange
68 Chaweng Cabana
69 Will Wait Bakery
70 Chaweng Cove Restaurant
71 Poppies
72 Santa Fe Disco
73 Joy Resort
74 Parrot Resort
75 Samui Resotel
76 Munchies
77 Supermarket
78 Sans Souci Samui Resort
79 Eden Seafood
80 Chaweng Garden Resort
81 Ayudhaya Exchange
82 Calypso Diving
83 Bill's Guesthouse
84 Lucky's Home

To Chaweng Town

Chaweng

0   300 m

South

Two kilometres of road runs behind Chaweng Beach. The western side has several sois which are full of bars and numerous dirt tracks on the eastern side run to the beach where all the resorts are. West of the road is a marshy area beyond which a dirt track running parallel to the main drag contains the larger bars such as the Green Mango and the Reggae Club, numerous karaoke bars and the market. Also in this area are several shanty town style developments of corrugated iron and bamboo dwellings where many of the local workers live. Most of the sleazier side of Chaweng is to be found in and around this part of town and the area can appear decidedly squalid in the light of day.

Generally speaking Chaweng starts off in the north at mid range with most of the exclusive resorts to the south. Budget spots are dotted around here and there. From north to south the accommodation is as follows:

North Chaweng
Papillon Resort, ☎ (077) 422 387, located opposite Ko Matlang and run by a friendly guy from Marseilles, this resort has a popular Franco/Thai restaurant and a busy bar. Bungalows start at 400B (500B high season) and large A/C rooms start at 600B (800B high season).
Samui Island Resort, ☎ (077) 422 355, is next and has a range of rooms starting at 250B.
Matlang Resort, ☎ (077) 422 172, Small huts here go for 200B, 300B for a larger room and 500B for a room with four beds. Friendly staff.
Blue Lagoon has new bungalows under construction and some of the older huts are pretty run down but well priced (for the area) at 150B.
Venus Resort, ☎ (077) 422 406, is a pleasant setting has huts for 180B.
Marine Bungalows, ☎ (077) 422 416, has basic huts for 150B and better ones for 300B (if you can tear the staff away from their TV.)
Lazy Wave is nicely laid out and offers large wooden huts for 300B.
Moon Bungalow, ☎ (077) 422 167, the bungalows here are not great and the staff can be a bit of a hassle, the huts are 150B to 300B with fan and shower and 500B with A/C.
Corto Maltese this much touted place is a mid range French run resort. It is very tasteful and very cramped and chances are that Corto Maltese would never have been seen dead in a place like this. (For that matter he would not be seen in Ko Samui at all!)
Your Place Resort has a nice bar but the overall resort is rather cramped. Huts start at 250B with fan and shower and 500B with A/C.
K. John Resort, ☎ (077) 422 116, is quiet and friendly. Large wooden huts start at 150B.

Central Chaweng
From here the beach gets busier, the beach road more built up and the resorts more upmarket. A stretch from the **Samui Villa Flora** (with its neo-Stalinist architecture) to the **Chaweng Regent** contains a dozen upmarket places with the **Tropic Tree** at 300B and the **Relax Resort,** ☎ (077) 422 280, sandwiched in between them at 200B, 250B with shower and fan, 300B with hot water.
Chaweng Villa, ☎ (077) 422 130, is nicely laid out with huts at 350B or 500B with A/C and hot water.
Montien House, ☎ (077) 422 169, charges 400B to 600B for excellent bungalows in a similar setting to the Chaweng Villa.
Lucky Mother this rare cheapie is next door to Montien House with rooms for 100B to 300B.
Coconut Grove follows on from Lucky Mother with plenty of huts between 200B and 300B.
Samui Coral Resort, ☎ (077) 422 143, next door to Coconut Grove has plenty of rooms in the 300B to 500B range.
Chaweng Garden Beach Resort, ☎ (077) 422 265, will rent out very good bungalows for 500B if they are not too busy.
J.R. Bungalows, ☎ (077) 422 238, is a good spot with accommodation starting at 200B.
Anchor House is next south with huts for 180B to 380B but is fairly cramped.
Best Beach Bungalow, ☎ (077) 422 410, is priced at 200B to 250B — reasonable given the location.

South

Dew Drop Hut, ☎ (077) 422 238, is a way further south from Best Beach after a series of luxury resorts. Small huts here go for 150B, large ones for 200B and A/C for 400B. It is a quite shady spot and offers herbal saunas for 100B.

South Chaweng

The next 400 m or do is all luxury resorts until you reach Charlie's Huts.

Charlie's Huts This place is unusual in that basic wooden huts which are well spread out are flourishing amongst the flasher resorts. There used to be several cheapies in this area, including **Viking** and **Thai House**, but they have all been bought out by Charlie's who now run over 200 huts well spaced out over a grassy area. Basic but clean huts go for 80B to 100B with fan or 150B with shower. It has three separate restaurant areas. A word of warning though, Charlie's does get unusually high reports of theft and the police spend a lot of time hanging around so definitely do not smoke anything illegal here unless you are looking for a more permanent stay in Thailand.

From Charlie's heading further south there is only one more budget break, being the very good **Joy Resort** which is quiet and has huts for 150B to 300B and A/C rooms for 400B to 500B. Just off the beach as the road curves to rejoin the main round island route are **Lucky's Home** at 200B for basic accommodation and the cheap **Bill's Guesthouse** with rooms for 60B per person. Further on are a series of mid to up range resorts including **Munchies, White House** and the deceptively named **Chaweng Guesthouse** where rates start at 600B!

Chaweng to Lamai

Chaweng South or Chaweng Noi gets fairly exclusive with **President Samui, Imperial Samui** and **Victoria Park** plus the huge and unattractive **Ponpetch Hotel** all of which have an absolute minimum rate of around 500B per night. The only cheapie around here is the **Chaweng Noi Bungalows** with small basic huts with fan and shower for 80B and 100B. The restaurant here is good and popular with those from the neighbouring luxury resorts. It will be interesting to see how long they will hold out. On the headland is the **Birds Eye View Restaurant** which has excellent views and good food.

Coral Cove   อ่าวท้องยาง

This very pretty small bay is just to the south of the Birds Eye View Restaurant and is home to a handful of resorts.

Coral Cove Resort, ☎ (077) 422 126, this excellent operation is in a secluded setting with some huts on the beach and others along the northern headland. Rates start at 150B to 200B for a wooden hut with fan and shower or 300B for newer concrete bungalows. The staff here are friendly and the food is good.

Coral Cove Chalet, ☎ (077) 422 260, **Blue Horizon, ☎** (077) 422 426, and **Beverly Hills Resort.** These three neighbouring resorts are more mid range than the above with prices starting at around 150B/300B in the low season. All situated on the rocky southern headland, the views are very good, but a walk to the beach often necessitates a steep and rocky climb. Of the three, Coral Cove Chalet is the best situated.

Following Coral Cove, the coast gets pretty rocky in parts, until you reach **Aow Thong Ta Kiaen**, another reasonably small cove but with a couple of rather mediocre resorts. The **Samui Silver Beach** starts at 350B (500B with A/C) and the pretentious but grotty **Samui Yatch Club** with similar prices. On the inland side of the road there is the nicer **Little Mermaid Resort** with comfortable rooms starting at 250B.

Things look up on the large rocky headland which comes next and forms the northern end of the wide Lamai Bay although the resorts around here are a fair walk down a dirt track to reach from the main road. Nevertheless the views are great and there is some good snorkelling in this area. The first place is **Bay View Villa, ☎** (077) 424 246, with basic but well priced huts starting at 100B with fan and shower and next is the pricier but very nice **Royal Blue Lagoon, ☎** (077) 424 086 and the attractive **Green Banana Resort** which starts at 150B.

Further on towards the tip of the headland an as yet unnamed resort is being renovated and as Lamai reaches saturation point, more overflow resorts may open in this scenic area. From here, on heading back west you will reach Lamai Beach proper, albeit the quiet northern tip of it.

Hat Lamai   หาดละไม

Located on the central east coast of Samui, this long beach is Samui's second most popular, and rapidly becoming a popular alternative for the jetsetters for whom Chaweng has become too developed. The long beach has a number of luxurious resorts which are slowly nudging out the more affordable places to stay. However budgeters need not miss out, as, at the time of writing, there were still a whole bunch of cheap sleeps available on the beach and this has allowed it at times to develop a bit of a 'Khao San Road by the sea' feel to it.

Although not as long as Chaweng, Lamai is quieter and it is slightly easier to escape the crowds, but, as always, the beach vendors will still find you. The southern end of the beach is the nicer part and is nowhere near as developed as the central section of the beach. It is also much closer to the **Grandmother and Grandfather stones** for those with a phallic fixation. Towards the northern end of the beach the sand becomes particularly fine and the water reassuringly calm but on the downside there is also a large lagoon here which at night appears to serve as the mosquito breeding centre for the whole island. Nevertheless, the beach up that way is also fairly quiet, especially in the evenings (apart from the whine of mosquitos). It also has a generous selection of palms offering shade, something which is pretty rare on other parts of the beach.

Central Lamai is where all the action happens. This is where the beach is closest to the strip, and as a result parties occasionally spill out onto the sand as the bars forever try to increase their trade. During the day this part of the beach can become pretty crowded and you may get hassled.

If you get an energy spurt and decide to walk the entire length of the beach, count on it taking around 1½ hours without pause. So you can easily fill up a day slowly wandering and sampling the differing cuisines served by the restaurants lining the beach.

Ban Lamai village itself is back on the main road which loops around the bay area. It contains little of interest other than a few shops, cheap Thai noodle and rice stalls, the village wat and **Lamai Cultural Hall** housing various 'cultural' artifacts. The **police station** and **post office** are also located in the village.

On Lamai, budget accommodation is slightly more expensive than on some of the more secluded beaches, but cheaper than that at Chaweng. The cheapest areas are at the northern and southern ends of the beach, as the central area has a lot of mid and high range resorts. A basic room with no shower or toilet costs in the range of 50B to 80B, a bungalow with fan and shower should cost in the range of 80B to 150B and A/C rooms generally start at around 200B to 250B. These prices should serve to give you a rough idea of what you are looking at paying, but in high season when occupation can be almost to saturation, these prices may well jump up. Moving from north to south, the accommodation scene on Lamai is as follows:

North Lamai
Comfort Bungalow, ☎ (077) 424 110, is the first resort on Lamai beach proper and is mid-priced with bungalows with fan and shower starting at 300B.
Island Resort, ☎ (077) 424 202, this large and very well organised resort has plenty of activities laid on and the rooms are clean and comfortable. Rates start at 300B with fan and shower.
Rose Garden, ☎ (077) 424 115, this is a pleasant spot with huts starting at 150B with fan and shower. The neighbouring **Weekender Villa, ☎** (077) 424 116, (not to be confused with the more up-market **Weekender Resort** further down the beach) is pretty run down with old huts starting at 80B and new huts going for 150B.

Spa Resort is under US/Thai management and offers a wide range of traditional holistic health practices, herbal saunas, Thai-chi, yoga, massage, herbal rejuvenation techniques and liver flushes - all of which you could probably do with after a few nights out in Lamai. For a more energetic approach to the island, they organise mountain bike tours through its interior which are strenuous but great fun for 200B per day. They also have an excellent vegetarian restaurant. Bungalows start from 150B per day with fan and shower with larger huts going for 350B to 400B.

Sukasam, ☎ (077) 424 119, is next door and has smart and new bungalows starting at 350B.
No Name Bungalow, ☎ (077) 231 052, is the first in a run of cheapies with basic huts starting at 150B with fan and shower.
Tapi Bungalows, ☎ (077) 424 096, is in a good location, nicely laid out with quiet wooden huts with fan and shower for 100B.
New Hut is very popular with its basic A-frames starting at 60B, with fan and shower for 80B/100B. It also has a good restaurant.
Beers House, ☎ (077) 231 088, and **Wishes Bungalow** are both very similar with huts on the beach going for 130B or 150B respectively. The staff are friendly at both, but the resorts are equally cramped.

Central Lamai

You are now in what makes up central Lamai and the beach is more crowded and the prices are higher.
Lamai Resort, ☎ (077) 424 124, has spacious bungalows starting at 300B/350B.
Sandsea Resort, ☎ (077) 424 026, starts at 500B and marks the beginning of where central Lamai goes well and truly up-market.
Riverside Bungalow and **Platuna,** ☎ (077) 424 138, are separated from the beach by a small rather grotty river but are nevertheless well laid out and priced in the mid range.
Samui Laguna and **Pavillon** are both popular but more expensive than the neighbouring **Utopia,** ☎ (077) 424 151, and **Mui**, both of which are better choices starting at around 200B with fan and shower through to 500B for A/C and hot water.
Samui Resident Resort, ☎ (077) 424 227, has particularly nice bungalows at the same rate as Utopia.
Magic Resort, ☎ (077) 424 229, has bungalows that start at 100B. The restaurant is raised off the ground, good and famous for its 'special omelettes' starting at 200B.
Following **Tannaporn** and **Weekender Resort** is the popular **Coconut Beach**, a low key resort with basic rooms for 100B or with fan and shower for 150B.
Lamai Inn 99, ☎ (077) 424 247, is next with good and clean huts going for 200B, although this price doubles in peak season.
Animal House, ☎ (077) 424 208, this grotty establishment has basic huts for around 100B and is followed by a string of expensive resorts; **Marina Bungalows** (starting at 250B, 400B for A/C) then **Marina Villa, Galaxy** and **Miramar**.
Sea Breeze, ☎ (077) 424 258, is the next cheapie starting at 100B to 200B for well kept huts. Following on from the mid to up-market **Golden Sand** and **Pauhuana** is **Wanderer** which has slightly run down rooms for 100B, 120B and 150B.
Bill Bungalow, ☎ (077) 424 403, this excellent resort costs 500B for a hut on the beach, 150B for a location behind the garden area or 300B on the hill behind.

South Lamai

Paradise Bungalow, ☎ (077) 424 290, is next door and has bungalows for 150B/200B but is not particularly recommended.
Amity Bungalow, ☎ (077) 424 084, is located on the beach far enough from the road so that there is no traffic noise. The staff here are very friendly, and the food is good, making it a popular choice with long term visitors. Rates for bungalows with no shower are 60B on the beach and for rows further away it costs 50B, a bungalow with a fan is 100B and for a

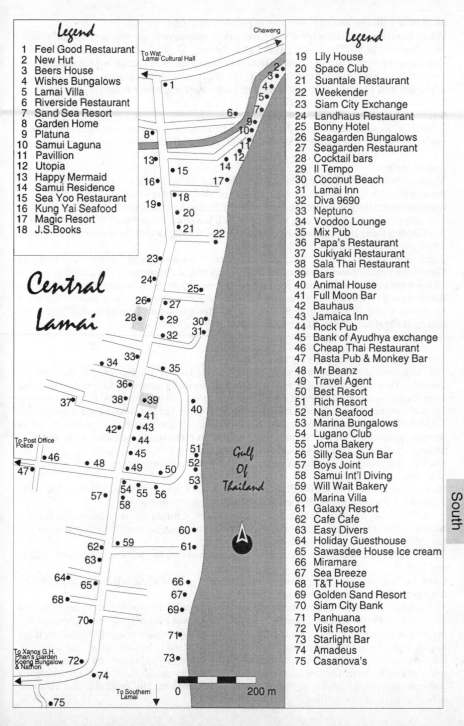

Legend

1 Feel Good Restaurant
2 New Hut
3 Beers House
4 Wishes Bungalows
5 Lamai Villa
6 Riverside Restaurant
7 Sand Sea Resort
8 Garden Home
9 Platuna
10 Samui Laguna
11 Pavillion
12 Utopia
13 Happy Mermaid
14 Samui Residence
15 Sea Yoo Restaurant
16 Kung Yai Seafood
17 Magic Resort
18 J.S.Books

Legend

19 Lily House
20 Space Club
21 Suantale Restaurant
22 Weekender
23 Siam City Exchange
24 Landhaus Restaurant
25 Bonny Hotel
26 Seagarden Bungalows
27 Seagarden Restaurant
28 Cocktail bars
29 Il Tempo
30 Coconut Beach
31 Lamai Inn
32 Diva 9690
33 Neptuno
34 Voodoo Lounge
35 Mix Pub
36 Papa's Restaurant
37 Sukiyaki Restaurant
38 Sala Thai Restaurant
39 Bars
40 Animal House
41 Full Moon Bar
42 Bauhaus
43 Jamaica Inn
44 Rock Pub
45 Bank of Ayudhya exchange
46 Cheap Thai Restaurant
47 Rasta Pub & Monkey Bar
48 Mr Beanz
49 Travel Agent
50 Best Resort
51 Rich Resort
52 Nan Seafood
53 Marina Bungalows
54 Lugano Club
55 Joma Bakery
56 Silly Sea Sun Bar
57 Boys Joint
58 Samui Int'l Diving
59 Will Wait Bakery
60 Marina Villa
61 Galaxy Resort
62 Cafe Cafe
63 Easy Divers
64 Holiday Guesthouse
65 Sawasdee House Ice cream
66 Miramare
67 Sea Breeze
68 T&T House
69 Golden Sand Resort
70 Siam City Bank
71 Panhuana
72 Visit Resort
73 Starlight Bar
74 Amadeus
75 Casanova's

Central Lamai

Chaweng

To Wat
Lamai Cultural Hall

To Post Office
Police

To Xanox G.H.
Phan's Garden
Koeng Bungalow
& Nathon

To Southern
Lamai

Gulf
Of
Thailand

0   200 m

South

bungalow with fan, shower and toilet expect to pay 150B.

White Sand has basic huts for 50B, a particularly extensive menu and very friendly staff.

Nice Resort, ☎ (077) 424 432, **and Palm Resort,** ☎ (077) 424 297, the well placed restaurant here once did some of the best club sandwiches on Lamai, but both the service and the food has slipped downhill a bit. The bungalows are of the concrete variety are adjoining and virtual heat traps if the fan stops working, nevertheless a popular place. Concrete rooms go for 100B to 250B.

Sunrise Bungalow, ☎ (077) 424 435, is next and has functional rooms starting at 250B.

Baan Thai Resort, ☎ (077) 424 317, is behind Sunrise and just off the beach and is not a bad choice with rooms starting at 100B/200B for singles/doubles.

Lamai Strip

If you are fed up with the beach or cannot manage the couple of hundred yards home from the evening drinking hole, there are a couple of places to stay along the Lamai strip.

Garden Home roughly opposite the Riverside Resort has rates starting at 150B.

Lily House opposite Space Club, has rooms with fan and shower for 200B or 350B for A/C.

Sea Garden Bungalows is near the centre of town, set slightly off the main road and is not a bad choice at 150B.

South of the central area down small alleys on the west side of the road are **Holiday Guesthouse** at 200B and **T & T House,** ☎ (077) 424 264, with rooms for 100B, 150B and 200B. At the southern end of the main road where it bends to rejoin the round the island road is the mid range **Amadeus** and then slightly up the hill, **Casanova.** Once around the bend there is a group of cheap guesthouses; **Visit Resort, Xanox Guesthouse, Phan's** and **Koeng Bungalows** which all have rooms in the 80B to 150B range.

Aow Bang Nam Chud   อ่าวบางน้ำจืด

This large bay stretches from Laem Lamai (and its famous phallic rock) in the north to Laem Na Taen almost 5 km to the south. The famous rocks themselves, Grandmother and Grandfather or Hinta and Hinyai are definitely curious and worth a peak if you are passing by. Just past the turn-off for the stones is the **Ko Samui Tourist Association** and **Tourist Police Office.** The southern part of the bay is particularly pretty with huge granite boulders seemingly tumbling down the mountain side with numerous small and sandy coves in between. This is also a pretty good area for **snorkelling.**

Rock Resort is located near the famous stones but it was closed for renovations at the time of writing.

Back on the beach, after the headland is **Noi** which is a cosy spot with basic huts for 100B, 200B to 350B with fan and shower and 400B for larger bungalows.

Next down is a bunch of mid to up-market places, **Chinda, Swiss Chalet** and **Rocky,** whilst on the other side of the road is **Floral** with small bungalows for 100B or larger ones for 150B located in a pretty garden setting.

Samui Maria is a brand new resort at the southern end of the bay and rates start at 400B and higher.

Cosy has basic wooden bungalows set in a coconut grove for 100B. It is then followed by the up-market **Garden Resort** and **Samui Orchid.**

Moving further south around the cape, Laem Na Taen, to the southeast corner of Samui you will find the up-market **Laem Set Inn** and the **Samui Butterfly Garden.** Laem Set Inn organise a variety of watersports and marine activities (you do not need to be staying there to participate) and the snorkelling in this area is supposed to be quite good. The Butterfly Garden also run a glass bottomed boat for reef watching from January onwards for 150B per trip. The Butterfly Garden itself is not particularly spectacular and not really worth the 50B entrance fee. Climb through the jungle on Khao Thale Hill behind it and you will probably see more butterflies.

Hua Thanon   หัวถนน

This Muslim fishing village marks the junction of Route 4169 and Route 4170. It has no accommodation and has remained remarkably untouched and is rarely visited by tourists. The small market here is lively if you arrive in the morning and the village is worth a look since it is just about the only 'traditional' village on the island. Nearby is **Wat Samret** with its famous jade Buddha image.

South Coast

Aow Bang Kao   บ้านบางเก่า

This bay, from Laem Set to Laem So Pagoda to the west, is known as **Aow Bang Kao** and is as yet undeveloped and practically deserted, apart from the small fishing village of Ban Bang Kao. The beach is fine at high tide, but turns rather muddy when the tide is low. The village itself is pleasant with plenty of old wooden houses and hardly a farang in sight; although the 'Land for Sale' signs dotted around here bode ill for the future.

The only accommodation in Ban Bang Kao is **Diamond Villa**, ☎ (077) 424 442, around 1 km west of the village with basic huts for 100B, 150B with fan and shower and 300B for large bungalows. The location is very secluded and very popular.

At the western end of the bay is **Laem So Pagoda**, built right on the beach. The pagoda is not really spectacular but is nicely situated and the boat shaped wat next to it should be interesting when finished. Next door is the **Waikiki Resort** but this is a relatively old resort and was closed (perhaps permanently) at the time of writing. If it does get going again with a new coat of paint, it looks like it would be a good place to stay.

The **offshore reef** is quite close at this point, though at low tide the beach does get too rocky for swimming.

Ban Thong Krut   บ้านท้องกรูด

Around the cape is **Ban Thong Krut** which is the jumping off point for **Ko Taen**. The small village contains a few shops and cheap Thai food stalls. The farang run **Fishing Lodge** has a bar, good restaurant and runs fishing trips, whilst the **Ging Pagaram Restaurant** does excellent and cheap Thai food in a great setting. At the end of the beach are the **Coconut Villa Bungalows** with a variety of accommodation starting at 150B to 200B with fan and shower and up to 400B and 500B for A/C. There is a swimming pool for when the tide is low and a great view.

West Coast

Aow Phan Ka (Emerald Cove)   อ่าวพังกา

One km after Thong Krut on the western side of Ko Samui is the turn-off for **Ban Phang Ka** and the very pretty Emerald Cove. The small village contains the dubious delights of the **Phang Ka Snake Farm**. There is a collection of various reptiles to look at, as well as the twice daily cobra shows where supposed Thai boxers take on king cobras in gruesome combat. Some people enjoy it though. Shows are at 11.00 am and 2.00 pm and run for 1 hour costing 150B. From the village, a dirt track covers the remaining 1 km to Emerald Cove or Aow Phan Ka with its three budget resorts, **Pearl Bay**, **Seagull** and **Emerald Cove.** All have small huts starting at 80B and larger more comfortable bungalows going for 300B.

Phan Ka to Nathon

Continuing along Route 4170, 4 km from Phan Ka is the turn-off for **Ban Taling Ngam**. You cannot miss it as there is an archway supported by two huge concrete elephants spanning the road! Ban Taling Ngam is one of Samui's best preserved villages being off the main tourist circuit and contains a couple of good cheap Thai restaurants, a nice wat and one cafe. Fishing and snorkelling trips can be organised from the cafe.

The coastline along here is in the form of two wide and shallow bays, **Aow Taling Ngam** to the south and **Aow Na Sai** to the north. The village is situated at the northern end of the southern bay, and just to the north of the village are a couple of remote but well sign-posted resorts.

Vastervik has concrete semi-detached accommodation starting at 200B.

Wiesenthan, under Swiss management, has nicer wooden huts with fan and shower for 200B. The road continues along Aow Na Sai to the car ferry pier which is 3 km to the north. The only 'resort' along the way is **Na Sai Garden** with four basic wooden huts for 100B each.

Ban Thong Yang

The car ferry pier is located by the village of Thong Yang and is only worth visiting if you plan to leave the island with or by car, or want some **excellent and cheap Thai food** as by the pier are a couple of excellent curry shops. This is quite a busy spot however few farangs choose to stay here. If you do, there is some accommodation in the area.

Just to the south of the pier is the **Copacabana Beach Club** which (as long as the name does not put you off) is quite a good spot with nice huts in a spacious garden setting go for 200B and up. However the view of the ferry pier certainly is not postcard material.

To the north of the pier, **Infoo Palace,** ☎ (077) 423 066, and **Aran Resort** have large bungalows for 140B and 300B respectively.

At the top end of the beach is **Laem Chom Khram**, a small hillock connected to the mainland by a sand bar and is a good place for **snorkelling**. Around the corner are **Aow Chom Khram Bay** and **Aow Laem Din** which lead back to the starting point of **Nathon**. These two bays are virtually undeveloped, hence very quiet, but like much of the west coast of the island, the beach gets muddy at low tide.

There are a few places to stay, the cheapest of which start with the **Lipa Bay Resort** with rooms with fan and shower for 250B, 350B for a larger bungalow and 450B for the deluxe model. Further north is the secluded **Sawai Home Bungalows** with huts for 200B and large bungalows for 500B.

◆ Eat and Meet ▶

Nathon

Numerous and very similar establishments serve Thai and Western food and they often have bakeries attached such as **R.T Cafe**, **Will Wait** (good bakery) and **'Cafe'**. **Marco Polo** surprisingly specialises in Italian food and there is a small **Spanish restaurant** opposite the R.T. Cafe. Back on the main street **Tang's** has Chinese specialities and sukiyaki and there are several cheaper **Thai places** along the seafront. The **Sunset Seafood** at the southern end of town has a nice garden area.

Mae Nam

Seaview is a well placed and reasonably priced Thai seafood restaurant. **Chez Toms** is a French Restaurant and is equally well placed. Otherwise there are a couple of cheap Thai restaurants as well as **Cupid**, **Koseng** and **Blue Diamond** all which do Thai/Western cuisine and **La Gargotte,** another French restaurant.

Bo Phut

There are **Italian**, **Spanish**, **German** and **French** restaurants in Bo Phut village, so if you are fed up with Thai food, there is a lot to choose from here. Otherwise several **Thai restaurants** do good seafood including the reactively cheap **Oasis**.

Happy Elephant is a Franco/Thai setup and offers fondues (amongst other items) and a nice decor. **Boon** does not look like much but it is very cheap and very good. **Bird in the Hand** advertises no videos or loud music which has got to be a good thing. By the pier are two more traditional and cheaper **Thai restaurants**. Another Franco/Thai restaurant, the **Pink Panther,** is run by Carlo and his wife (who is a great cook) and the prices are reasonable.

Bangruk

Between the Sunset Song Bungalow and Bangruk pier is **Fai's Bar** which is under Hawaiian management. They offer Thai and Western food and drinks and one of the rare cable TV's in the area. Within Bangruk village itself there is the **Blue Banana Bar and Restaurant** which is not bad value.

Choeng Mon

Honey Seafood rounds off the beach and is well situated at the tip of the bay. Seafood prices here are considerably cheaper than in either Lamai or Chaweng.
On the beach is **Otto's Service** with travel agent facilities, diving school, boat tours and overseas calls along with **Otto's Pub and Restaurant**.
New O-Charos Restaurant is on the beach and has cheap seafood.
Phayom Park Restaurant and **Bongoes** have good Thai food and tables in the sand.

Ban Choeng Mon

This minuscule village contains two or three travel agents, a supermarket, more seafood restaurants and a couple of bars, **Jo Jo's** and **Cowboy House Pub**.

Chaweng

Including the resort and bungalow restaurants there are several hundred eating places along the strip, many very similar with the usual Thai/Western menu's, the usual bakeries and the numerous pizza places. You will also find French, German, Italian, Spanish and even Swiss restaurants and plenty of Thai seafood spots.

Some of the commonly recommended places include: Italian; **Cafe Latino, Vecchia Napoli** (cheaper) and **Cafe Cafe**. French; **Papillon** (reasonable prices) and the **Flamingo Pub**. **Mr Beanz Comedy Club** does stuffed baked potatoes!
Most restaurants have menus outside so choosing is fairly easy. Many of the expensive resorts also do good deals on food, so do not be afraid to check them out. **Island Resort Restaurant** in particular gets rave reviews. **Thai Kitchen** has good cheap simple Thai food which otherwise can be a bit of a challenge to find.

Entertainment

The entertainment situation in Chaweng is equally bewildering. German beer gardens, French bistros, English football clubs, video bars and several huge clubs, the best known being the **Green Mango** and the **Reggae Pub** both of which have rave, trance, acid and disco - anything to dance to. **The Doors Pub** has more of a rock emphasis. The newer **Santa Fe Disco** has some wild decor in a high tech, modern, light show setting.

A couple of the more interesting beach bars include the nicely arranged **Bamboo Bar,** next to Venus Resort, which has mats on the sand and a good spot for sundowners, and next to the Lazy Wave is the **Lazy Wave Bar** (quite an imaginative name, don't you think?) which is a small gay bar.

Jazz Junction has smooth jazz and good cocktails but is not cheap, **The Club** has acid jazz, soul and funk in an intimate atmosphere. **Coffee Girls** and **Coffee Boys** is Cabaret.

There is a **Muay Thai boxing ring** near the Reggae Pub, often featuring 'imported' farang boxers!

The **girlie bars** have also arrived in Chaweng but thankfully not to the extent of Pattaya or Patong, so basically there is something here for everyone; rave the night away at the Reggae Pub, drink loads of beer and watch Liverpool play Arsenal, sip cocktails and listen to classical Thai music or ogle bathing costumed lovelies in the karaoke bars. Average drinks prices are 50B for a small Singha or 100B for a small bottle of Mekong Whiskey.

Hat Lamai

You can pick up some good meals on Lamai Beach. A curry and rice will cost around 50B. Seafood is on offer everywhere and is generally good and priced according to what type you get. A large bottle of Mekong Whiskey will cost you around 150B, whilst beer is priced from 35B to 40B (small) and 56B to 70B (large). Some of the restaurants have drugs listed on their menus, such as magic mushrooms and bhang lassis however, as the police continue to crack down on this kind of thing, they are becoming rarer and rarer. One of the easiest ways to eat is on the beach, simply wave at a vendor and have them whip you up a papaya salad or a wide variety of other tasty morsels. For those on a strict budget, the nearby markets are your best bet, although some of the bungalow operations may throw you out if you never eat at their restaurant.

The restaurants along the strip offer a fine variety of both Thai and Western cuisine, although it is difficult to find a place which serves food without with an accompanying blaring video. Dozens of national cuisines are represented amongst the preponderance of seafood and pizza joints and prices are slightly lower than Chaweng. As with Chaweng there are dozens and dozens of restaurants along the strip, most of which display their menus and, in the case of seafood, most of the fresh catches are displayed by the dusty road as well! So wander the strip and see what takes your fancy.

Entertainment

Bauhaus Pub is the pick for those who want to dance or drink the night away. Regular (almost nightly screening) of English, Italian and German football matches guarantee a lively crowd if nothing else. The music is deafening, courtesy of resident UK DJ's, and the drinks are not cheap, but it is nevertheless the choice of many staying at Lamai. Other options include the **Rasta Pub**, **Space Club** and the **Mix Up Pub** amongst many many others. Another option is to catch a songtheaw north to Chaweng where the Green Mango and Reggae Pub draw huge crowds (see the Chaweng section for details). Most of the clubs in Lamai do not get going until pretty late, so the early evening can take on a rather calm appearance with people watching videos, sport, playing pool and so on before heading off to one of the clubs.

Aow Bang Kao

The **Ban Thale Riverside Restaurant** down a dirt track (do not believe the sign which says 500 m, it is more like 1,500 m) at the mouth of a small river is a good place for lunch. Very quiet with a great view, the staff here will lend you a fishing rod so that you can try your luck in the river. The restaurant itself is only a small wooden shack and the prices are cheap.

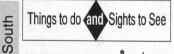
Things to do and Sights to See

Big Buddha   พระใหญ่

Five minutes walk out of town is the famous Big Buddha himself. Not particularly impressive as Big Buddha's go, it is the setting that is unusual on a tiny rocky island some 200 m off the coast. The Golden Buddha and surrounding wat were constructed in the 1970s by monks who conveniently constructed a causeway at the same time so now you can walk over without getting wet. On the island are numerous souvenir shops, seafood restaurants and a bunch of the usual concrete Thai mythological characters such as the sea demon, a flute playing pirate and so on.

Buffalo Fighting

Besides the beach in the Ban Makham area you can be entertained at the **Buffalo Fighting Stadium**. Enquire in town for the fight times and the tickets are 80B for women and 100B for men (men must get more enjoyment for their baht). Buffalo fighting consists of two buffalos fighting each other, no people are involved except in the heated crowd. The fights can be spectacular and are not for the faint hearted.

Herbal Remedies
Around 2 km from Nathon en-route to Ban Makham is the **Garden Home Health Centre**, ☎ (077) 421 311, which is open from 9.00 am to 10.00 pm and offers herbal saunas for 250B and massages for 150B. This place also dispenses herbal medicines.

Monkey Theatre   ศูนย์ลิงสมุย
This 'theatre' is located about 1 km from Bo Phut village and is a good place to avoid unless you would like to take some photos of ill treated animals to send to animal rights groups.

150 Year Old Teak House
A new road runs along the coast skirting Khao Thale to emerge at Ban Thale where you can visit the much touted **150 year old teak house** for 10B.

Go Karts
Instead of whizzing around Ko Samui's roads, try the Bo Phut Go Kart track and weave your way amongst the coconut palms for 250B for ten minutes! There is an accompanying bar and restaurant as well.

Sports
There are many 'holiday' activities that you can get into at Chaweng and Lamai Beaches. These include jet skiing, parasailing, windsurfing (mainly at the northern end of Chaweng) and banana boating. Massages on the beach cost around 100B to 150B for an hour. Many of the beachside resorts have volleyball games in the late afternoon.

Diving — Ko Samui
PADI dive courses can be done out of Chaweng. Sample prices are 7,200B for an open water certificate, 6,500B for an Advanced and 20,000B for Divemaster. A two day beginners course will set you back 3,000B or one day baptisms go for 2,500B. Day trips can also be done to Ko Tao (2,450B), Ang Thong National Marine Park (1,900B) or the Samui reefs for 1,800B, or just take a dive from the beach (600B). If you have your own equipment, expect around a 15% discount.

Ko Samui - Away from the beach
Despite the intense coastal development on Samui, much of the hinterland remains untouched. Some 60% of the island is covered by the **Samui Highlands**, devoid of habitation and roads and pleasantly covered by dense jungle with the highest point being **Khao Thai Kwai** at 635 m. Trails are difficult to follow and hard to find and the terrain is rugged so it can be quite tricky doing much on your own. If you do, take plenty of water and great care not to get lost. Various resorts and travel agents around the island organise trekking and even mountain biking to the highlands at reasonable rates. There is some great scenery, fantastic views and does make an excellent change from laying on the beach.

A couple of waterfalls, **Namtok Hin Lad** near Ban Lipa Yai and **Namtok Namuang** near Ban Thurian are well signposted and easily accessible. One of the best ways to get off the beaten track is to clamber up one of the many streams coming down from the highlands and see how far you get.

The southwest corner of Ko Samui is very untouristed and is also a nice area to wander around on a motorbike or pushbike as it offers plenty of quiet country lanes and traditional villages to explore. Also of note in this area, just off Route 4169 to the southeast of Ban Thurian, is **Wat Khunaram** with its famous mummified monk. He was the former abbot of the wat who died in 1973 aged 79 years old and has been preserved for posterity. Complete with sunglasses he sits in a glass case for all to see, but please no photos. Considering how long he has been dead he is in remarkable condition and all up looks quite curious.

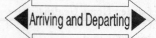 Arriving and Departing

Getting around the island.

Songtheaws

Crimson songtheaws are the easiest and cheapest way to get around Ko Samui. Unusual for Thailand they often drive fast and systematically overcharge farangs. There is not a lot you can do about this except pay twice what the Thais do. Make sure the driver knows where you are going and always check the fare first. Most songtheaws have their destinations on the sides of the roof in English.

Fares vary depending on the length of the trip, the time of day (or night) and can be anything from 20B to 40B. In general the fares from Nathon should be in the order of 20B to Mae Nam and Bo Phut, and 20B to 30B to Big Buddha, Chaweng and Lamai.

Motorbikes

Many people ride motorbikes for the first time in their lives on Ko Samui. Anyone can pick it up after a few hours on a small Honda Dream but go carefully, Samui is one of Thailand's top spots for motorbike accidents and even if you ride slowly, many others do not. The roads here are generally good so people tend to edge a little over the 60 km/h limit. And although it may not seem to be the case, drunk driving, speeding and riding without a helmet are all illegal in Thailand. Hiring a 100cc Honda starts at around 120B to 150B depending on season and length of hire. Trail bikes start at around 200B and jeeps at 500B.

Some motorbikes also serve as taxis to the public. During the evening, the fares may be more expensive. Transport can also be hired using cars, jeeps and mountain bikes.

Air

Ko Samui is accessible through a constant stream of flights by Bangkok Airways. There are six a day from **Bangkok** to Samui, and one a day from U-Tapao. They also fly to **Hua Hin** for 1,640B and **Phuket** for 1,330B.

Train

Daily trains run from Bangkok's Hualumpong and Bangkok Noi railway stations to Surat Thani. From the train, catch a bus or pick up truck to the pier. Refer to the timetable at the end of the chapter for full train details.

Bus

To get to Samui from Bangkok, you have the choice of either A/C or ordinary buses that leave from the southern bus terminal regularly on a daily basis. See the section on Surat Thani for price and frequency details.

Boat
To/From Don Sak

From the mainland at Don Sak, car ferries leave 8 times a day taking 1 hour and 20 minutes between 08.00 and 18.00. The ferry also takes vehicles which are charged according to size. The return ferry service from Ko Samui operates between 07.00 and 17.00. These leave from a wharf to the south of Nathon on Aow Thong Yang.

Gone Fishing...

Looking for something different? Try and get yourself on a fishing boat for a few days to see just how the locals kept themselves busy before the tourists showed up.

To/From Ko Pha Ngan
Boats leave from several locations on Ko Samui for Ko Pha Ngan. From Nathon to **Ko Pha Ngan** (Thong Sala) boats costs 70B with services at 10.30 and 16.30, taking 45 minutes. Boats also leave for **Hat Rin** from Bangruk Beach at 10.30, 13.00 and 16.00 for 60B and take 45 minutes. During the full moon parties, there are numerous 'specials' departing from here. From Bo Phut, Popeye Travel run speedboats to **Thong Sala** at 08.30, 11.30 and 15.00 taking about 15 minutes and costing 200B. From Mae Nam, longtails leave for **Hat Rin** at 09.30 and 11.30, taking 30 minutes and costing 100B per person. Day trips to **Ang Thong Marine Park** can be organised from Bo Phut for 350B including lunch.

To/From Ko Tao
The boat from Nathon to Thong Sala continues onto **Ko Tao** and costs 250B. Occasional boats leave from both Bangruk and Maenam Beaches to Ko Tao and cost 250B. From Bo Phut one day snorkelling trips to Ko Tao can be organised for 1,300B.

Hitching
If you are hitching from Bangkok, take the Thonburi-Pakthaw Superhighway number 35 otherwise known as Phra Ram 2 Road. When you get to the Pakthaw intersection, take a left onto Route 4 which heads for Chumphon and Petchaburi. Once you reach Chumphon, take Route 41 until you get to the Phun Phin intersection, where you need to take a left turn onto Route 401 which heads towards Nakhon Si Thammarat. Next turn left at Route 4142, there will be a sign for Amphoe Kanchanadit at the intersection. Start following the signs for Amphoe Donsak, and when you hit the Donsak intersection take a right towards the ferry pier.

AROUND KO SAMUI

KO TAEN   เกาะแตน

This small island, only a 20 minute long tail boat ride from Ban Thong Krut, could be just what you need if you are fed up with the bustle and commercialism of Ko Samui. No roads, few people and no whizzing motorbikes make Ko Taen a real haven of tranquillity. Most of the island is rocky with one long beach on the eastern side and the small Aow Tok on the western side. There is plenty of **snorkelling** to be done around the island, as on the nearby uninhabited Ko Mat Sum.

Cheap Sleeps

Fishing and coconut farming are the only occupations on the island and most of the inhabitants live in Ban Ko Taen. There are three small resorts on the east coast at Aow Ok. **Tan Village Bungalows**, **Tan Resort** and **Coral Beach Bungalows** all have bungalows in the 60B to 300B range. Before heading out there, be sure to enquire at Ban Thong Krut first to see if they are open. It is highly likely they may be closed outside of the December to March period. **Tan Village Bungalows** is the most organised of the three and can be contacted on (01) 968 4131 and they can also organise transport for you if necessary.

 Arriving and Departing

Boat
A more or less regular boat service leaves from Ban Thong Krut for Ko Taen at 09.00 and 16.00 for 40B. The fishing Lodge in Ban Thong Krut also organises boat trips to the island and is the best place to enquire for up to date information on what is open.

ANG THONG NATIONAL MARINE PARK

อุทยานแห่งชาติหมู่เกาะอ่างทอง

Ang Thong, which means 'Golden Basin', is a beautiful and pristine National Marine Park and Thai authorities are very serious about keeping it this way. It is located in the Gulf of Thailand between the mainland and the islands of Ko Samui and Ko Pha Ngan and exists in and around the archipelago of 42 islands, however not all the islands are part of the National Park. The park is primarily marine covering 102 sq km, with the islands only amassing to 18 sq km. Coral is not extensive due to the high sediment content in the shallow water, but the best viewing is close to shore on the northeast and southwest sides. A variety of forests exist on the islands creating protection for some small mammals, birds and reptiles.

The most beautiful islands in the park, apart from the main island of Wua Ta Lap, are Sam Sao with its rocky arch and panoramic viewpoint, Thia Phlao for its coral and Wua Kan Tang. If visiting by boat tour, you will first visit a small bay on Wua Ta Lap where there is an interesting cave and a vantage point at 400 m above sea level. The climb is quite strenuous but the views of the islands are superb. The second stop is usually at another tiny beach on Ko Mae Koh with a climb to a large and spectacular lagoon which sits in the mountain. Try and get to the viewpoint looking down on to the lagoon which is worth the effort.

Only three of the islands are inhabited; the National Park Headquarters is on Wua Ta Lap, the central island, whilst two other islands have a few very rudimentary houses on them. The National Park Headquarters have bungalows for 400B, 600B and 800B. It is also possible to camp on the beach near the National Park Headquarters. Tents can be hired from the Headquarters which also has toilet facilities.

The trip to Ang Thong is well worth it and can be arranged from travel agents at Surat Thani or from Ko Samui for 300B, though they may try and charge you 450B. The tours leave from three of the island's piers, Nathon, Bo Phut, and Mae Nam, and often if you agree to get yourself to the place of departure, the price will drop to 300B. As the share taxis only cost 20B, this is often the better option. The boat leaves the pier at 08.30 and returns at 17.00, taking almost 2 hours to travel the 31 km. Three companies offer this trip, and if all the boats are full it would certainly detract from the experience. The trips also include coffee in the morning and afternoon and a great lunch.

KO PHA NGAN   เกาะพะงัน

Ko Pha Ngan is the second largest island after Samui in the southern region of the Surat Thani Province. It is located in the Gulf of Thailand, about 100 km from the mainland, and about 15 km from Ko Samui. Ko Pha Ngan covers an area of 168 sq km with 70% of its topography made up of mountainous regions with the remainder comprising of beaches and coconut groves. Over 8,000 people permanently live on the island with the majority of the population concentrated around Thong Sala. The majority of the residents are Buddhist, but you may come across a few Muslims in the village of Ban Tai. It is believed that the first inhabitants of the island were Muslims from Pattani or Malayans from Nakhon Si Thammarat.

If you plan to visit the islands, try to organise your trip for the hot season (January to April). Your other choice is the rainy season from May to December. Either way the temperature is more likely to stay between 20° C and 36° C. October and November can be the worst months to visit with horrendous rainy weather, bad seas, many of the roads are washed away and numerous places are closed. However, the weather is unpredictable and you may be lucky.

Whilst on Ko Pha Ngan you will never be short of a coconut, as together with Ko Samui, they produce over one million coconuts a month, most of which are transported to Bangkok. The coconut fields are spread all over Ko Pha Ngan. You will often see them being collected by a farmer balancing a long bamboo pole with a hook on the end used to detach the coconuts from the tree. There is one word of warning, try not to walk under too many coconut trees, for you have a good chance of getting one on the head.

Orientation

Ko Pha Ngan still retains its island charm with only a couple of paved roads. One is a 7 km road from Thong Sala to Hat Rin, although in December 1996 much of this road was severely damaged by heavy rain. Another road stretches for 11 km from Thong Sala to Chalok Lam and the third runs from Ban Hin Kong to Aow Yao. There are however other dirt roads and numerous walking and mountain tracks throughout the island.

The easiest way to get from one side of Pha Ngan to the other is to signal one of the many passing pick-up trucks or motorbikes. It does not matter if the vehicle is an official taxi or not as many of the locals are keen to make some extra income, and will pick you up if they can. You should not have trouble getting a lift from Thong Sala and a simple wave is all you need to stop any vehicles. Prices depend on the distance travelled, but the minimum is 20B for a truck and 10B for a motorbike. It is possible to hire both motorbikes and mountain bikes from Thong Sala or one of the many enterprising bungalow establishments. Mountain bikes will cost around 80B a day and motorbikes, depending on the type, will start at 120B for the day.

There is also a boat taxi service from Thong Sala to Hat Rin, Hat Yao and Bottle Beach at certain times of the year, which is dependent on weather conditions. The boat taxis will usually meet boats arriving from the mainland.

Vital Information

Most of the services that you may require will be located at Thong Sala town.
Post Office is located a little out of town along the road to Ban Tai and Ban Kai, past the Siam City Bank. It is open from 8.30 am to 4.30 pm.
Money Exchange services operate from 8.30 am to 3.30 pm. There are no ATM's on the island.
Hospital, ☎ (077) 377 034, is open 24 hours but located 3 km from Thong Sala town. There are a few medical clinics around the island that will usually be open from 8.00 am to 7.00 pm.
Police Station, ☎ (077) 377 114, is located about 2 km along the sealed road from Thong Sala towards Chalok Lam.
Tourist Police are located on Ko Samui but can be contacted on ☎ (077) 421 281.
Fax and International Call Service can be arranged through your bungalow or any of the larger travel agents on the island.
Codes The telephone code is (077) and the postal code is 84280.

Cheap Sleeps

It seems that the 'times are a changin'' on Ko Pha Ngan. Wandering around the island, it seems that there are at least as many abandoned bungalow operations on the island as there are new ones. According to the locals, over the past few years tourists to the island have actually decreased.

There are a few contributing factors to this. Many people have probably been put off visiting due to the incredibly high police presence (excuse the pun) and their numerous raids on bungalows. There are often stories of alleged police extortion emanating from Hat Rin in particular. Secondly, alternate islands such as Ko Chang, Ko Lanta and especially Ko Tao are becoming more popular. Ko Tao in particular is receiving hordes of backpackers who, only a few years ago, would have found themselves on Ko Pha Ngan. Thirdly the Full Moon Parties and Ko Pha Ngan in general have simply become too well known and this has served to put off those who were looking for a quiet island (eg. Ko Tao). In the past this used to apply to Ko Pha Ngan in relation to Ko Samui whereas now in fact, per sq km Ko Tao is probably the busiest, Ko Pha Ngan the 2nd busiest and Ko Samui, by virtue of its size the quietest of the three!

South

On the plus side, over the past few years we have seen Ko Pha Ngan become too crowded in places and so a reduction in numbers is probably not a bad thing. The majority of the bungalows are quite simple and very affordable for the budget traveller which is one reason you may stumble across some people that have been there for quite some time. The bungalows are more than likely built of thatch and bamboo, with electricity and running water within easy reach. You often have the choice of a bungalow with bathroom facilities or just a plain hut with no extras. Accommodation will cost you from 50B to 300B in the more popular areas, or even as low as 30B for a bungalow on one of the quieter beaches on the north of the island.

Please bear in mind that many of the bungalow operations make their money on the food rather than the rooms, as a result you will often be expected to eat at their restaurant at least once a day. As mentioned previously it is not unusual at some of the smaller places for people to be kicked out if they have not eaten enough at the guesthouse restaurant.

Accommodation on Ko Pha Ngan - An Overview...

A final note on Ko Pha Ngan's accommodation, basically, upon arrival you have three broad choices regarding where to stay. You can get your navel pierced, graft on a few dreadlocks and head to **Hat Rin**, alternatively go to some totally obscure beach and chill out, or thirdly go to one of the less hectic but accessible 'compromise' beaches.

If you take the first option, then **Serenity** or **Pha Ngan Bay Shore** are the best choices on the sunrise side of Hat Rin. On the western side, **Bird**, **Rainbow**, **Coral** and **Blue Hill** are all good choices, but remember that during the full moon all these places are generally packed.

With the second option, some bays can be very difficult to reach and once you do reach them, you can find yourself pretty much stuck there. If the weather is OK and the longtails are open on the east coast then things are fine. Until January, when the rains have completely stopped access can be difficult if not impossible. Many resorts may be closed in this period anyway. **Coral Bay**, **Mae Hat**, **Hat Salat** and **Thong Nai Pan** are all good choices as long as access is not a problem.

The third option has a lot going for it, in that there are some fine, good value resorts to be found on the south and particularly the west coast. These are also sheltered during bad weather and have relatively good access to the rest of the island. You can get a songtheaw to Hat Rin for a full moon party, make use of the facilities in Thong Sala or hike to some of the more remote bays for the day. **Beach 99** and **Cooky** are recommended at the southern end of **Wok Tum**, and **Chai's** at the northern end. **Rock Garden** on **Aow Chaophao** is good value as is **Ibizi** at **Hat Yao**. On the **south side** try **Lee's Garden**, **Pha Ngan Rainbow** and **Charm**, all good choices.

The following lists the accommodation beginning in Thong Sala and circling the island in a clockwise direction.

Thong Sala   ท้องศาลา
The largest centre on the island, Thong Sala, is most definitely the kind of place you visit only on the way to somewhere else. Packed full of travel agents, book stores, restaurants, cafes and a few places to bed down, Thong Sala is a good place for shopping and organising onward travel but that is about it.
Buakao Inn This excellent establishment situated near the cross roads has singles/doubles for 180B/280B, four people rooms start at 380B and A/C doubles at 390B.
Chai Hotel Large modern rooms start at 250B if you are sick of staying in thatch huts.
Poonam Pattana Guesthouse is a clean and friendly place starting at 150B.
Khao Guesthouse past the market on the way out of town, this guesthouse is pretty good value at 200B with fan and shower or 300B with A/C.

Aow Nai Wok   อ่าวไนวก
To get to this bay walk north out of Thong Sala, cross the bridge and you will be in the hamlet of Ban Nai Wok which sits on Nai Wok Bay. There are a few places to stay here and its convenient location, close to Thong Sala, makes it a good choice if you plan to catch an early boat off the island.
Suan Inn This new establishment is just over the bridge and has a few comfortable bungalows with fan and shower for 150B.
Pha Ngan Bungalows is the first of a group of four places and its bungalows are priced from 80B to 200B.
Charn Bungalows are small, rustic and very cheap at 50B for a small hut with fan and shower.
Siriphun Bungalows has basic huts with fan and shower for 80B or larger bungalows with fan and shower for 250B.
Opposite Siriphun is **Thong Sala Scuba Centre** that also rents out **catamarans**.
The last place to stay on this beach is the very run down **Tranquil**.

Aow Wok Tum   อ่าววกตุ่ม
At the northern end of Nai Wok there is a large rocky headland separating it from the wide bay of Wok Tum. There are a few good resorts perched on the rocks around here although there is no beach proper until you get down into the bay itself. The 2 km stretch of Aow Wok Tum is quite shallow and not really good for swimming as it gets muddy in places and there are

Legend

1 Pier	12 Burger Home	23 Wat
2 Mr Chins Restaurant	13 Buakao Inn	24 Pha Ngan Travel
3 Waiting Time	14 Krung Thai Bank	25 Speedboats to Ko Tao & Samui
Restaurant	15 Food stalls	26 Meeting Point Seafood
4 Planet Scuba	16 Market	27 Sirigun Bakery
5 Fast food	17 Chai Hotel	28 Poonam Patana Guesthouse
6 Dive shop	18 Mountain bike hire shop	29 Siam City Bank
7 Yoghurt Home	19 Vantana Restaurant	30 Cafe De La Poste
8 Fair House Bakery	& bookshop	31 Post office
9 Siam City Bank	20 Khao Guesthouse	32 Mudmai Restaurant
10 Bookshop	21 Clinic	33 Cheap Thai Restaurants
11 Bangkok Bank	22 Back House Seafood	

patches of mangroves along its edge. There used to be a couple of resorts along the beach here, but now the only accommodation available is at the northern and southern headlands.

Beach 99 is one of the top spots on the bay, situated in a beautiful location. Great varnished huts are 80B or 150B with fan and shower.

Cooky is another good choice with basic huts for 70B and 100B with fan and shower.

Porn Sawan is not so new but is a real bargain with rates starting at 40B for a basic hut and 60B with fan and shower.

Bounty is another new addition to this area where friendly staff supply bungalows on the beach for 80B and 70B for those back a row.

Sea Scene have a variety of huts for 80B to 100B.

Darin is an excellent resort with nice huts ranging in price from 60B to 100B.

O.K. Bungalows round things off with views looking right out over Aow Wok Tum. Huts are well priced at 40B, 50B and 70B with fan and shower.

Kiet Bungalows was closed at the time of writing and may or may not reopen.

Following Kiet there is the 2 km stretch of Wok Tum Beach until you reach the northern headland upon which sits another three places to choose from.

Nantakarn has good huts with fan and shower going for 60B.

Chai Bungalows is very friendly place with huts for 50B and their restaurant is good value.

Loyfar is slightly smarter than the previous two and sits on the northern side of the headland facing **Hat Si Thanu**. Huts go for 60B and 80B, the great view is free!

Hat Si Thanu   หาดศรีธนุ

Si Thanu Beach is a wide and calm beach with only a few sets of bungalows. The beach is a little dirty and there is little in the way of shade. The southern end of the beach has a small village with a cafe, two shops and a bike hire place.

Ladda has a collection of six huts within the small village itself.

Seaview Rainbow is a friendly spot with huts for 40B, 60B and 80B all with fan and shower.

Laem Son has rooms starting at 40B increasing up to 80B. The cafe turns into a bit of a trance pub once the sun sets. While the sun is up, you can absolutely bake on the shadeless beach.

Aow Chaophao   อ่าวเจ้าเภา

The beach in this bay is little visited considering its comparative high quality. Plentiful shade and a long stretch of clean fine sand, makes this beach a pleasant place to while away a few days, although the southern end of the beach is badly eroded.

Bovy Resort is furthest south along a very badly eroded strip of beach. It has bungalows in abysmal condition, missing doors, verandahs and some of the roofs are falling apart. If you can handle this it has a degree of rustic charm. Rooms with shower and toilet only cost 50B.

Behind Bovy Resort is **Laem Son Lake**, a freshwater lake which looks like it is off the set of a B grade horror movie. If you are willing to risk what lies in its depths, the water looks tempting, although the mosquitos can be savage around here.

Seetanu is about a ten minute walk north of Bovy and has basic huts for 60B and fan and shower for 100B.

Sea Flower Resort has rooms starting at 60B up to 200B and all rooms have fan and shower. There is half a boat on the beach which has been turned into a bar, which is surprisingly called the Boat Bar.

Haad Chaophao is the most expensive place on the beach with rooms starting at 300B.

Great Bay Resort has rooms with share bathroom starting at 50B and with your own bathroom starting at 80B. The staff here are particularly indifferent.

Rock Garden is located just north of the northern end of the beach and is reached by following the road for 5 to 10 minutes until you come across a sign for Rock Garden. These very secluded bungalows do not offer much of a beach, but some great snorkelling and cost only 50B.

Hat Yao   หาดยาว

Hat Yao is set within a scenic bay between Aow Chaophao and Hat Salat. It offers a larger beach and is considerably more developed than some of the more northern beaches with a supermarket, exchange facilities, a bar on the beach and a telephone service. At the far south of the beach is the Eagle Pub, a ramshackle building which serves to inebriate the clientele. There are around ten bungalow operations at Hat Yao which are generally quite well spaced making this a popular place for those looking for a beach which is not too busy but not too quiet.

Sandy Bay Resort is about two thirds of the way down the beach with the restaurant offering ordinary service, disgusting coffee and very tacky menus. There are a couple of dozen rooms without shower and toilet starting at 50B, those with shower and toilet starting at 80B.

Sandy Bay II has a selection of rooms, all with fan and shower, starting at 200B.

Ibiza has particularly friendly and very hospitable staff. The rooms are large, spacious and very clean. A hut with fan and bathroom starts at 100B. The restaurant here is good and reasonably priced.

Haad Yao is about halfway up the beach with huts starting at 80B with fan and shower.

Silver Beach has basic huts for 50B or larger huts with fan and shower for 100B.

Hide Away Supermarket Guesthouse has a few facilities such as phone, fax, bookswap and supermarket. It is set back off the beach on the other side of the road.

South

Bay View is located to the north of the beach offering great views from the restaurant right down the beach. Many of the bungalows also have tremendous views. Basic huts start at 60B with huts with fan and shower starting at 140B. The restaurant prices are quite reasonable and the food is tasty.

Hat Salat   หาดสลัด

This is a stunning and very isolated location offering good conditions for snorkelling, with a shallow, waveless and clean beach. The walk from Hat Salat to Hat Yao takes around half an hour. The relative seclusion of Hat Salat means that you can get very good and cheap accommodation. There is one old man that offers decent massages on the beach for 100B an hour. **My Way** has about 15 bungalows. A room with a share toilet and shower costs 30B, and 50B for a room on the beach with its own shower and toilet. The food here is also good and cheap. If you agree to go with a tout, expect to pay more, often as high as 50B to 80B respectively. My Way has a small and mostly German bookswap going and supplies a free paper daily. **Salad Hut** is similar to My Way, but the bungalows are closer to each other. Prices are the same, and the restaurant smaller.

There is a small bay between Hat Salat and Hat Yao with just one bungalow set up at the northern end. **Hat Thian** has basic huts starting at 40B without fan or shower and unfortunately has a concrete retaining wall around it to keep it all together. The beach is small and covered in broken coral.

Mae Hat   แม่หาด

Mai Hat is located at the northwest corner of the island, 3 km from Chalok Lam, and about 45 minutes walk from Hat Salat on a not particularly scenic route. Just south of the beach is **Namtok Wang Sai**. Located up a marked trail however this waterfall can be virtually dry in times of little rain. Mae Hat is known for **snorkelling** around the coral reefs off the mainland and out by the islet **Ko Ma**. At low tide it is possible to walk out to Ko Ma along a sand bar. The beach on Ko Ma facing Ko Pha Ngan is quite small and dirty and some dive schools are run off this beach.

The beach at Mae Hat is quite exposed and the wind tends to gust through the channel between the land and the island. The next bay up from Mae Hat, **Thong Lang**, is worth the walk. The beach is nice and small and although it has no bungalows, there are the remains of one from time long past. The **snorkelling** from here is great. The coastal track is difficult through dense bush and often peters out. The best way to get there is to walk back to the road from Mae Hat and take the next track off it to the left. Both routes take about 45 minutes. From the bay the track leads back to the main road, and from here it is only about 10 minutes walk to Chalok Lam Bay.

Wang Sai Resort is at the southern end of the beach and offers nice large bungalows with shower and toilet for 80B. A well placed restaurant also has a comprehensive menu to choose from. They have kept most of the development back from the dunes with some of the huts set on rocks overlooking the bay. There is sometimes a body of water in front of the restaurant which may serve as a mosquito headquarters.

Island View Cabana has many bungalows well spaced and back off the beach a decent distance starting at 100B. The beach is very clean here and it seems they are trying a bit of dune stabilisation. The restaurant is slightly more expensive than others but the food is not bad. The islet, Ko Ma, is directly opposite here. If you want to stay here, transport can be arranged via Back House in Thong Sala.

Mae Haad Bay Resort has basic huts starting at 50B and better, larger bungalows with fan and shower starting at 100B.

Mae Haad has a collection of fairly ramshackle huts starting at 40B, this is probably the poorest choice on the beach.

Crytal Island Garden has similar accommodation to Mae Haad Bay Resort with basic huts starting at 50B and rooms with shower and fan going for 100B.

Chalok Lam   โฉลกหล่ำ

Very bleak and windswept at times, this large bay is home to the biggest fishing village on the island which, weather permitting, is home to over 80 boats. Other than the fishing village there are a few beaches and two resorts on the bay. The western end of the beach is filthy, covered in bottles, trash, broken glass and coconut husks, and the water does not look too inviting either. The centre of the beach is dominated by fishing wharves and the fishing village has a few shops with phone/fax facilities, travel agents, film processing (send away), exchange services as well as a police station and gas station. Opposite Chalok Lam Diving is a **very good cheap pizzeria** run by a Swiss guy. French food is also available and the owner's wife cooks good Thai cuisine. This is a very good spot, although as yet it has no name.

From Aow Chalok Lam you can organise a boat to Bottle Beach or enrol in dive courses. Towards the eastern end is **Khom Beach** set in its own stunning cove. Aow Chalok Lam is located on the north of the island 11 km from Thong Sala and is accessible via a mostly sealed road. The road is not sealed between Chalok Lam and Mae Hat and in the wet season is in appalling condition.

Off the sealed road to the left before reaching Aow Chalok Lam is **Quan Yin Chinese Temple**. This beautiful location overlooks the bay and is a great place for a snapshot. Within the temple there are some ornate decorations and in the main shrine there is a statue of Quan-Yin, the goddess of mercy.

Wattana is located on the western end of the beach and has well spaced bungalows from 60B to 80B depending on position. The restaurant here is good, although the staff are sometimes pretty dismal.

Fanta Resort (no it is not sponsored) on the eastern end of the beach is probably the most popular place to stay in the area with many rooms. Bungalows start at 40B to 80B and there is a volley ball court out front. The restaurant is reasonably priced with a comprehensive menu.

Try Thong Resort built on the rocks at the eastern end of the bay and has basic huts costing 80B to 100B.

Thai's Life has very rustic huts with no electricity (only lamps at night) for 50B per night. To the east of Aow Chalok Lam is **Coral Bay Resort** set on a ridge overlooking **Hat Khom**. It is very quiet and beautiful with bungalows costing 80B to 100B. The snorkelling in the bay is not too bad and this place comes recommended by many people both for its bungalows and the nearby beach. Coral Bay Resort is about a twenty minute walk from Chalok Lam.

Bottle Beach (Hat Kuat)   หาดขวด

Located on the northern side of the island, secluded Hat Kuat is directly accessible by boat from Aow Chalok Lam or via a 3 km hike along a trail from the same place. Once at the beach your efforts will be rewarded with a pleasant and very secluded beach. In the low season the accommodation here closes up. The beach then becomes very dirty as the garbage washes onto the beach and there is no one to clean it up. During the high season the beach is kept fairly clean. There are only two resorts on this beach

Bottle Beach Bungalows has fairly well spaced and roomy huts starting at 80B without fan and share bathroom and 150B with fan and private bathroom. The restaurant here is pleasant.

Bottle Beach II Bungalows offers a similar deal to the other resort, but there are not any rooms with private bath available. The rates were 80B to 100B depending on position.

Aow Thong Nai Pan   ท้องนายปาน

If you want long nice bays without the hassle or crowds of Hat Rin, Thong Nai Pan Bay is for you. Located on the northeast side of Ko Pha Ngan, this beach can be reached in the dry season by songtheaw or motorcycle taxi from Thong Sala or Ban Tai. It is also possible to walk here from Bottle Beach taking about an hour on a not very well defined coastal trail, however the abundance of wildlife along the way makes it well worth it. There are actually two bays here, Thong Nai Pan Yai at the southern end and Thong Nai Pan Noi a little further to the north. The surrounding area offers the opportunity to seek out and explore a number of small coves and beaches waiting to be discovered. In the wet season the road to Thong Nai Pan is virtually impassable. One of our researchers saw motorbike taxi drivers refusing to go there for 500B, and when another driver agreed to go for 200B - all his mates thought he was mad! (The farang must have been crazy as well!!)

Thong Nai Pan Noi is the furthest north of the two bays and tends to get a little more crowded than the southern beach.

Tong Ta Pan Resort is at the northern end of the beach and is set up with lovely wooden furniture, much quieter than the Star Hut. Rooms cost between 100B and 150B. The general setting is nicer at this end of the beach, however the beach is a little dirty.

Honey Bungalow starts at 80B for rooms with share bathroom.

Star Hut is located towards the southern end of Thong Nai Pan Noi. It has around 20 rooms costing between 100B and 150B. The restaurant prepares excellent food.

Panuiman Resort is built on the headland separating the two beaches. It is a modern mid-range resort and is priced accordingly, with the cheapest rooms starting at 300B (600B in the high season). This resort has a 4WD which is by far the best way to try and reach Thong Sala.

Thong Nai Pan Yai is the southern beach and is a better haven for people seeking out particularly cheap beds.

Chanchit Dreamland is the first decent place to stay on Thong Nai Pan Yai with basic huts at 50B with share shower and 100B with private bath and fan.

Pingjun Resort is very similar to Chancit Dreamland with basic huts from 60B to 80B and 100B with fan and shower.

Pen's is the nicest of the bunch on this beach with friendly staff and good huts from 60B to 80B and 100B with fan and shower (150B in high season).

Grouped at the southern end of Thong Nai Pan Yai are a selection of cheapies with nothing between them. **Central** starts at 100B, **Nice Beach** at 60B to 80B, **A.D.View** has nicer huts with fan and shower for 150B and **White Sand** has a full range of huts starting at 50B for no frills through to 500B for most of the mod cons.

Hat Sadet   หาดเส็ดจ

This double beach sits about two thirds of the way up Ko Pha Ngan's eastern side. Little visited by foreigners, the beach in the past has been a real hit with Thai Kings and stones bearing the initials of King Rama V, VII and IX lay around the area. The northern of the two beaches, Hat Sadet is clean and the water is crystal clear. The more southern of the two beaches, Hat Thongleng is both quieter and smaller. The main attraction here (besides the beach that is) is the Than Sadet Historic Park. The river here is about 3 km long and has a number of scenic waterfalls along its length. To wander along the river and swim as you please easily fills a pleasant day trip from your place of lodging.

As at December 1996, the road to Hat Sadet had been completely destroyed by abysmal weather and in the immediate future it looks as though the only easy method of approach will be by boat. During the wet season many (if not all) of the below are closed. Check in Thong Sala before venturing out if you are unsure as to whether they are open or not.

Mai Pen Rai II is at the far northern end of Hat Sadet with basic huts for 50B to 80B.

Silver Cliff is next off the rank with basic huts for 80B and rooms with shower for 150B.

Nids and **J.S. Hut** each have a handful of rooms starting at 50B for no extras through to 200B with private bathroom.

Joke Bar has basic huts for 50B to 80B with share bathroom.

Mai Pen Rai is at the southern end of the bay and has basic huts with share bathroom for around 60B to 80B.

Thaan Wung Thong Resort sits above the beach on the southern headland and has basic huts for 60B to 80B, and 150B for rooms with private bathroom.

Hat Tien   หาดเทียน

This small bay and beach is to the south of Hat Sadet and to the north of Hat Rin and, hiking, you can reach it in an hour or so from Hat Rin. For the less energetic, in high season it is possible to catch a boat there from the western side of Hat Rin. About a ten minute walk to the north of Hat Tien is **Hat Wai Nam** which has no bungalows but does have a waterfall and some great **snorkelling**.

Sanctuary the bungalows here are reasonably priced with the cheapest starting at 40B without a fan or bathroom, and then at 100B for a fan and bathroom. The feeling of seclusion rewards the effort of getting here and, if you are arriving with a lot of luggage, a boat is definitely the best option. They also have a **vegetarian restaurant** which gets good reports. **Hat Tien Resort** is run by the Yoghurt home on Hat Rin and nice wooden bungalows cost 100B.

Hat Khontee

Just to the north of Hat Rin, this small bay has no accommodation but is very nice and secluded. To reach it, walk to the southern end of Hat Rin then follow the trail past Mountain Sea and Serenity Hill to Hat Khon Tee. Allow about 30 to 45 minutes for the walk.

Hat Rin   หาดริ้น

Situated at the southeastern tip of the island, Hat Rin is the name of the tourist village and two bays on either side of an isthmus linking a small rocky peninsula to Ko Pha Ngan proper. To the eastern side is the bay of Hat Rin Nok which is pretty wind-swept for much of the year, and on the other side is the more sheltered Hat Rin Nai. Hat Rin Nok or east Hat Rin is also known as the sunrise side with west Hat Rin logically being called the sunset side.

Once a beautiful isolated peninsula, Hat Rin is now known the world over for its infamous full moon parties. It has non stop bungalows along its two beaches and every available square metre of land in between is covered with travel agents, restaurants, bars and even more bungalows. The only positive side is that, as elsewhere on Ko Pha Ngan, development is generally low key and on a budget level, so there is still more wood and bamboo than concrete and so far no high rise. Aside from the full moon, there is little to do here, the beaches are not the island's best and the nightlife is very tame when compared to that of Lamai or Chaweng on Ko Samui. So wander from cafe to cafe, listen to music, watch videos and stop by the sea every now and then to remind yourself that you really did leave Khao San Road!

The east side is where the full moon beach parties are held, offering a scenic beach perfect for swimming and snorkelling. Due to the popularity of this beach though, it can get quite dirty and at times is packed solid with sunbathers. The waves can get quite large and there are often strong currents, so weak swimmers should exercise caution.

As for the Full Moon Parties themselves, Hat Rim becomes a sweating seething mass of bodies as people pile in from the neighbouring beaches and islands in time to make the festivities. Although considerably tamed down from a few years ago, the parties still attract a big crowd, swollen for better or worse, by undercover and uniformed police. Smokers should exercise particular care at these events unless you want a prolonged stay in Bangkok at the government's pleasure.

For those staying at Hat Rin, the town boasts enough services that, chances are, the only time you will need to venture to Thong Sala is when you are leaving the island. The inland strip is packed with **bars**, **restaurants**, **minimarts**, **exchange offices** and **travel agents**, along with **dive shops**, **tattoo artists** and **book stores**. Virtually every cafe/restaurant on this beach features videos, some starting as early as 11.00 am for those with nothing better to do other than to pretend they are at home. From the travel agents you can organise **visas to Vietnam, India and Nepal** and you do not have to leave your passport. The process is they photocopy your passport, fax it to the relevant embassy, then when you get to Bangkok, you go to the travel agents agent, drop off your passport, wait one day and you get your visa. It is quite a handy service since it usually takes five days to one week to get a visa.

South

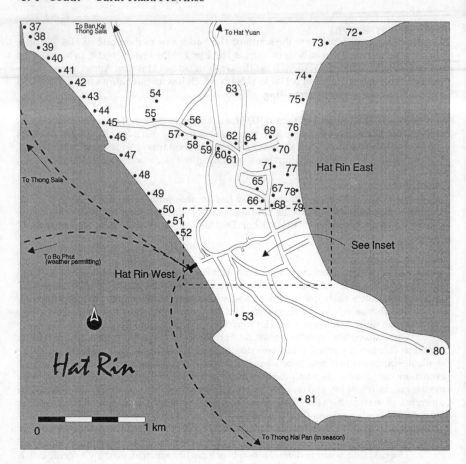

Hat Rin

• 37
• 38
• 39
• 40
• 41
• 42
• 43
• 44
• 45
• 46
• 47
• 48
• 49
• 50
• 51
• 52

To Ban Kai
Thong Sala

To Hat Yuan

72 •
73 •
74 •
75 •
63 •
54
55
56
57
58   59   60   61   62   64
69
76
70
77
71
65
67   78
66   68   79

Hat Rin East

See Inset

To Thong Sala

To Bo Phut
(weather permitting)

Hat Rin West

• 53

• 80

• 81

0   1 km

To Thong Nai Pan (in season)

South

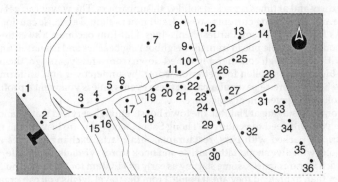

8 •   • 12
• 7   13   14
9 •
10 •   • 25
11 •   26   28
5   6   22   27
1   20   21   23   31
3   4   19   24   33
17   18   29   34
2   15 16   32   35
30   36

Central Hat Rin Inset

Hat Rin's accommodation is broken into three sections, those on the western side, those on the eastern side and then those in between. Generally if you want to be close to the nicer beach and the bigger parties, opt for the eastern side, whilst if you are after a bit of seclusion and a generally quieter stay, head for the western side. The accommodation on Hat Rin is quite over-priced compared to elsewhere on the island, particularly on east Hat Rin behind the beach where the accommodation can get pretty squalid.

Sunrise (East) Side

Here is some of the most expensive accommodation on the island. The prices for accommodation on the sunrise side are generally the same between the bungalow establishments costing from 80B to 100B without shower and 150B with shower. Running from north to south the accommodation is as follows:

Serenity Hill has a range of nice and clean huts starting at 80B and 150B and good restaurant.
Mountain View is on the rocks at the northern end of the bay just before Serenity Hill and has ramshackle huts starting at 80B.
Seaview This is on the most northern part of the beach with basic huts for 80B, huts with fan and shower for 160B and large huts for 300B.
Palita Lodge is a popular but run down establishment with basic huts starting at 80B.
Tommy's Resort The bungalows here are awfully close together and some are in pretty shoddy condition, the whole place could in fact do with a coat of paint. Basic bungalows with share bathroom start at 80B and 150B for a private bathroom.
Pha Ngan Bay Shore Resort has basic huts for 100B and more plush rooms with fan and shower for 250B and 350B. This place was the winner of the 1996 Ko Pha Ngan Tourist Authority Environment Management Competition!

Legend

1 Friendly Bungalows	28 Oi's Kitchen	55 Nee's Bungalows
2 Family House	29 Hat Rin Hill Resort	56 Mama's Family Rest.
3 Lucky Crab Restaurant	30 Harmony Bar	57 Ringo G.H.
4 Outback Bar	31 Bookshop	58 Pino's
5 Bongo Bar	32 Old Lamp	59 Chai House
5 Sand Pizza	33 Anant Bungalows	60 Brown Rice Restaurant
7 Bumble Bee Bungalows	34 Beach Blues	61 La Boheme Restaurant
8 Bumble Bee Restaurant	35 Sea Garden Bungalows	62 Ploy Rin Bakery
9 Krung Thai Bank	36 Paradise Bungalows	63 Thai House Resort
10 Planet Scuba	37 Star	64 Thai House Restaurant
11 Rim Beach Bakery	38 Chop's	65 Police
12 Hat Rin Resort	39 Bird	66 Playhouse Restaurant
13 Chip Buttie Rest.	40 Sunbeach	67 Sunrise Restaurant
14 Cactus Club	41 Sandy	68 Orchid Restaurant
15 Snooker Hall	42 Seaside	69 Yoghurt Home 3
16 Top Gold Restaurant	43 Rainbow	70 Siam City Bank
17 The Shell	44 Coral	71 Pha Ngan Bay Shore Resort
18 Oasis	45 Grammy's Bungalows	72 Serenity Hill
19 Loma Restaurant	46 Crystal Palace	73 Mountain Sea
20 Sand Restaurant	47 Sooksom Bungalows	74 Sea View
21 Sao's Kitchen	48 Palm Beach	75 Palita Lodge
22 Post Office	49 Sunset Bay Resort	76 Tommy's
23 Jonathon Rest & Bungalow	50 Neptunes Villa	77 Drop In
24 Somewhere Else Rest.	51 Dolphin	78 Sunrise Bungalows
25 Ploe Resort	52 Charung	79 Orchid Bungalows
26 Anan Hotel	53 Seabreeze	80 Hua Laem Beach Resort
27 Chang Diving School	54 Pooltrup Bungalows	81 Leela Centre

South

The next few are all one and the same for quality and price with **Sunrise**, **Ploen Orchid**, and **Hat Rin Resort** all starting at 150B for a room with fan and shower.

Anant Bungalows is a slum but at least it is clean. Rooms with fan and shower start at 120B.

Anan Hotel is squeezed between the main road and the beach and is only 50B for a room.

Beach Blues is a bit cramped but not too expensive at 100B to 120B.

Sea Garden This grotty place ends up a little under water when it rains too much but if that does not bother you, the rooms start at 100B to 120B.

Paradise Bungalows is the original source of the full moon parties and is still very popular but it really is nothing special. Huts start at 150B/250B for singles/doubles, all with fan and shower.

Hua Laem Beach Resort is a 10 to 15 minute walk over the rocks where it overlooks the eastern bay and has good huts for 150B. This is a quiet spot with a great view, but can be very windy for much of the year.

Inland places to Stay - Hat Rin

This handful of places really only serves as an overflow when everything on the beach is full to the brim.

Had Rin Hill Resort is opposite Beach Blues and is pretty grotty but well priced at 70B and the restaurant is not too bad.

Royal Garden is next door to the Had Rin Hill Resort and is not great either, at 80B for a basic hut or 150B with fan and shower.

Jonathon at 120B is better value than either of the above mentioned places.

Bumble Bee Hut is popular and relatively quiet at 120B.

Thai House Resort Heading out of town on the hill to the north of town, this brand new place is good value at 200B.

Hill Side About a 15 minute walk from the main strip at Hat Rin, these small basic bungalows are very popular with long term visitors and offer excellent views of the surrounds. Room rates are 60B to 80B depending on position, all with share bathroom.

Ringo Guesthouse, **Nee's Bungalows** and **Pooltrup Bungalows** all have rooms starting at 50B, with **Nee's** being the best kept.

Oasis Bungalows are located near the centre of town but are actually quite secluded. Good huts here are 130B with fan and shower and 250B for a larger bungalow.

Sunset (West) Side

The west side is better for its larger and cheaper selection of accommodation. It is also quieter and the people are generally friendlier. The downside is that the beach only has a thin strip of sand and at high tide becomes only a reminder of a beach. The only significant annoyance is the longtail boats which hug very close to the shore and consequently are quite noisy, although fairly infrequent. The general price for accommodation is 60B to 80B for a bungalow without shower and 100B to 150B with a shower. As you get around the point towards Ban Kai, prices drop to around 50B to 70B without bathroom, and 80B plus with. Running from southeast to northwest the accommodation is as follows:

Lighthouse Resort This is the southernmost resort of Hat Rin and is at the end of a 200 m wooden walkway over the rocks. There are plenty of huts and it is a nice place to chill out. Rates start at 50B or 100B for fan and shower.

Leela Centre situated on the secluded bay of Hat Si Kan Tang where new huts cost 100B and older ones are only 50B. The resort offers meditation, Tai-chi, yoga and zen painting — get the picture! It is certainly very quiet and the otherwise undeveloped beach is great. It is about a 15 minute walk from Hat Rin.

Sun Cliff and **Sea Breeze** are nicely perched on the rocks and each has pleasant wooden bungalows for 50B and 100B with fan and shower. These two mark the end of accommodation on this side of the beach.

Rim Beach is a mid range place located on the southern side of the pier with prices starting at 300B. It also has a nice and spacious A/C restaurant.

Family House starts at 150B to 200B and despite the family atmosphere is pretty grubby.

Friendly and **Black & White** are next and both have rooms starting at 80B and 120B. The beach around this area is a bit dirtier as you are still quite close to the piers.

Dolphin has clean and well sized rooms with fan and shower for 200B.

Charung has basic bungalows with share shower for 70B and is probably the pick of the bunch (along with Neptunes Villa).

Neptunes Villa is a fine establishment with friendly staff who speak good English. All their bungalows have a shower and are very nice. The grounds are well kept and offer great views of the sunset. Rooms here start at 180B with fan and shower.

Sunset Bay Resort has basic rooms for 80B and rooms with fan and shower starting at 150B.

Had Rin Village is slightly off the beach behind Sunset Bay with similar bungalows at the same prices.

Palm Beach is the perfect example of where residents have done their best to turn a patch of paradise into something resembling a squat under a flyover in some run-down suburb of London or Melbourne. They have huge parties every Wednesday night and the rooms go for 50B to 100B.

Sooksum This far out 'resort' has a menu consisting almost entirely of tofu and has rooms going for 60B to 70B.

Crystal Palace has basic concrete ugly rooms for 100B/120B.

Grammy's Resort probably runs intoxication programmes to accompany its quite seedy feel. Basic huts are 50B and huts with fan and shower go for 100B.

Coral is a very nicely laid out resort offering a great menu and herbal detox programmes which you may need after a few nights in Hat Rin. Huts start at 70B or 150B with private bathroom. There is then a group of five resorts all offering similar deals for more or less the same quality rooms. **Rainbow, Seaside, Sandy, Sunbeach and Bird** all have basic rooms starting at 60B with share bathroom. **Rainbow** is best of the bunch, well spread out over a grassy area, closely followed by **Seaside**.

Tiara Palace is rather grotty but fairly separated from the other resorts. Basic huts start at 60B with rooms with shower starting at 150B.

Star has basic bamboo huts perched on the rocks with electricity for 50B.

Ban Kai and Ban Tai   บ้านค่าย, บ้านใต้

Ban Kai and Ban Tai are two fairly small villages located on the southern side of the island between Thong Sala and Hat Rin. Both of these beaches have a smattering of bungalow operations along their length which, thankfully, are spread well apart. The beach along here is nice, although it can get a little thin at high tide and unfortunately when the longtails decide to take a course close to the beach, the noise is not unlike being under a flight path. Of the two villages, Ban Tai is probably the more interesting and has a collection of oddities, such as Ko Pha Ngan's largest tree, a simple walk inland away. Ban Tai is also the only Muslim village on the island and is a low scale fishing village with most of the boats being longtails.

　　　If arriving by songtheaw from Thong Sala, you will need to let the driver know where you want to go as the road stays a fair way inland, so if your desired guesthouse along here is not signposted, you may well miss it.

This moves from east to west taking off from just to the west of where the sunset side of Hat Rin finishes, and ending at Ban Tai.

Blue Hill is a secluded and friendly resort with basic bamboo huts without electricity for 60B.

Bang Son Villa and **Silvery Moon** are both well hidden amongst the rocks and if you manage to find them you will be guaranteed a good stay. Both have simple wooden huts for between 30B and 80B.

Pha Ngan Island This upmarket resort seems a little out of place but is quite well done and has a pool. Off season prices start at 300B and high season begins at 400B.

South

Thong Yang Bungalows is another tricky place to find and the coast gets very steep around here. The huts are a bargain at 50B a night.

Banja has brightly decorated huts which seem to be losing a constant battle with the sea, rain and mudslides. Check it out before it disappears totally. Huts start at 50B.

Beer Huts is next off the rank and is very friendly with a nice restaurant area, but a little close to the road. The huts start at 50B.

Sun Sea has rooms starting at 50B for something basic and 100B/150B with fan and shower.

Golden Beach Resort is set back slightly but has excellent views and is quite secluded. Basic huts go for 50B with bigger bungalows with fan and shower costing 200B.

Green Peace is situated at the foot of the rocks at the end of the bay. This very 'relaxed' place is comfortably small with a pleasant bar restaurant area. All huts go for 50B to 80B and all have shared bathroom. Green Peace organises the increasingly well known black moon parties, with sound systems, live music, fire sculptures, ice sculptures and so on. The average crowd is around 1,000 people, although January can get as large as 2,000. Help in organising it or participation is very welcome. The black moon idea is catching on at several other places on Ko Pha Ngan, Ko Samui and Ko Tao, but Green Peace's parties are the best!

Pha Ngan Rainbow is a large and well organized Australian run spot with basic huts for 50B to 100B and 150B for fan and shower.

Copa Resort is a small German managed establishment with huts for 50B to 100B.

Papillon Resort is run by the same management as the one on Chaweng. This very quiet and low key resort has nice wooden huts for 60B to 80B. French dinners are occasionally shipped over from the Chaweng kitchen!

Lee's Garden is a very popular place with well spread out huts for 40B to 80B.

Pha Ngan Lodge has ten very strange looking bungalows for 60B. It looks like an army base on acid, an eyesore or display of artistic expression depending on your viewpoint, but nevertheless has a very 'relaxed' feel to it.

The next three places are **New Heaven**, **Sabai** and **Jub** all of which have rooms starting at 50B.

Mac's Bay This popular well laid out place has reasonable wooden huts for 40B and 80B for fan and shower. It is popular with long term visitors so it can be quite cliquey, and the food is certainly not brilliant.

Liberty Bungalow is a very small resort which is friendly but pretty basic and is right beside Mac's Bay. Their huts are good though and cost 80B.

Triangle Lodge is not a bad choice with clean huts going for 40B and 80B.

Pink and **S.P. Resort** Of these two the former is pretty rundown at 50B to 80B and the latter has received several bad reports, so maybe just keep on walking.

Ban Tai to Thong Sala

This last area of the island is slowly increasing in popularity as people want to be not too far from the full moon scene but certainly do not want to stay in its midst. There are some really good deals to be had in this area. The following list of accommodation runs from the western side of Ban Tai to just outside Thong Sala. Between Ban Tai and Club Mad there is about a 1 km length of beach with nothing on it but small fishing boats, rotting shell fish and fish bones. If you can put up with the smell, it is a great place for seashells.

Club Mad This well named and funky place is not bad, but is a little on the decrepit side. The rooms are cheap though at only 40B.

Dew Shore is a well maintained, clean and tidy resort with good bungalows for 80B and 120B.

King Bungalows has pretty ugly cluttered rooms starting at 60B to 80B.

First Villa starts at 150B and is just before a small mangrove lined stream which empties into the sea, a popular fishing place amongst the local kids.

Chokana is a well kept resort with something for everyone, starting at 80B for simple clean wooden huts through to 1,000B for deluxe bungalows with A/C and hot water.

Charm Bungalow is a very good and very popular spot, separated from Chokana by a small river and has basic huts for 60B and 80B and concrete chalets for 150B.

Wiang Thai is quite a way past Charm and can be a little tricky to find. It has basic huts for 40B and 80B.

Moonlight, Pha Ngan Villa and **Sundance** are all very similar and close together. Sundance is the most run-down of the three. All have rooms from 40B and 80B.

Petchr Cottage is only a five minute walk from Thong Sala. This quiet place is well laid out and run by Aussie John and his Thai wife. Small huts go for 50B and 70B and larger huts with fan and shower go for 100B. If you are in the area, check out John's excellent Beer Bar, you will not be disappointed!

Eat and Meet

Thong Sala

Apart from the usual bakery and Thai/Western style places to eat near the pier, there are a couple of **cheap Thai restaurants** near the post office. Between Buakao Guesthouse and the Vanttana Restaurant is an **unnamed small Thai restaurant** which is very friendly, does good food and is very cheap with most dishes costing around 20B. **Vanttana** does good vegetarian food and there are several **Thai curry and noodle stalls** near the market. **Mudmai Restaurant** is excellent value for simple Thai dishes such as roast duck on rice for 20B and it also has a variety of ice creams. For something more upmarket try **Back House** which has very good fish and seafood at reasonable prices.

Thong Nai Pan

The restaurant at **Panuiman Resort** does very good, although expensive food. **Dolphin Bar and Restaurant** lists a whole range of 'exotic' items on the menu for those interested and **Chai's Bar** is another good spot. The restaurant at **Star Hut** is another fine choice for good, fast and reasonably priced food.

Hat Rin

Apart from bungalow food there is a fair choice of decent eating spots in Hat Rin. Most of the restaurants along the main drag such as **Drop In, Orchid** and **Sunrise,** have standard Western/Thai food. The cross roads in the centre of town, also known as **'chicken junction',** have some **cheap noodle** and **fried chicken** stands while the lane leading down to the beach has an unnamed restaurant selling **chip butties** and **bacon sandwiches.** Back on the main street **Old Lamp** has a nice sitting area on cushions and a **pool table.** The street linking the two bays has more variety including **The Shell** for Italian, **Sao's Kitchen** for vegetarian, a **burger bar, Sand Pizzeria** and so on. **Golden Terrace Thai Restaurant** has a nice layout by the lake though watch out for the mosquitos.

The track leading out of Hat Rin has some good spots with **Brown Rice** serving Mexican specialities, **La Boheme** for French and **Chai House** and **Mama's Family Restaurant** doing Indian cuisine. **Mama's** in particular is good value with excellent Indian curries for 25B and rotis and chapatis for 5B. **Cafe Hiatus** behind the western beach bungalows is frequently recommended by travellers, it does Thai and Western food and is a better choice than most of the bungalow restaurants.

Entertainment

Outside of the full moon parties there is really not that much nightlife going on in Hat Rin. Most bars tend to close by between midnight and 1.00 am. **Harmony** is probably the liveliest spot and various bungalows operate parties now and then, otherwise just hang out for the monthly extravaganza.

For backpackers, Hat Rin **full moon parties** are now as much a part of Thai tourist musts as trekking in Chiang Mai, diving at Phi Phi and the girlie bars of Pat Pong or Pattaya. In the past an average party in the high season pulled in around 5,000 people,

South

whilst the January one would round up as many as 10,000 people, however in the off season you may be lucky to get more than a few hundred. So get your body painted, stock up on whatever takes your fancy and groove on down but do not plan on getting much sleep. Remember that if you are arriving at Hat Rin on the day before a full moon party, do not expect to be able to get a room. Chances are you will be sleeping on the beach until daylight when the boats carry survivors back to the various beaches on the island, back to Ko Samui, Ko Tao or the ferry pier at Surat Thani.

The party itself is certainly not what it used to be a few years ago. Police, both Thai and foreign, are always around, so be very careful with anything illegal, although in more recent times, the most commonly abused substance at the parties is alcohol.

If you want to check out a different scene, look into Green Peace Bungalows alternative **black moon party.** Apart from this always keep your ear to the ground for anything big that is happening anywhere other than Hat Rin, as the best parties nowadays tend to be moving away from there to gain a wilder feel.

Things to do ◆ Sights to See

Hiking around Ko Pha Ngan

For nature lovers and those who enjoy walking a lot, Ko Pha Ngan has some great opportunities for walks, although there are not well worn trails to follow. This means that trails may at times peter out or disappear completely, so one should exercise care before embarking on any long walks. It is possible to walk all the way around Ko Pha Ngan and during the walk you will find some beautiful coves and beaches along with plentiful wildlife and some great snorkelling opportunities. If you pace yourself well you would not even need to take a tent, as the resorts are well spaced so you could stay in a different one each night. There are only a couple of places where you would need to take main roads and the vast bulk of the walking could be along beaches.

If you were to try to walk around the island, be sure to have a compass, sufficient water, sound footwear, a hat, mosquito repellent and sunscreen as an absolute minimum. Another good thing to have is *V.Hongsombud's Guidemap of Ko Pha Ngan and Ko Tao* on which he has marked some of the trails and distances. If you do get lost, do not panic but rather try to find a vantage point from where you can get your bearings or else find a river bed and follow it to the sea. Do not walk alone and do not walk at night. A suggested route would be in a counter clockwise direction departing from Thong Sala.

Day 1: Depart Thong Sala for Ban Tai and hike inland to see Ko Pha Ngan's biggest tree, a couple of wats and a nice viewpoint, return to the coast and get a room somewhere between Ban Tai and Ban Kai.

Day 2: Depart Ban Kai hike to Hat Rin visiting the lighthouse and mountain viewpoint. Continue to Hat Tien and spend the night there.

Day 3: Depart Hat Tien visiting a series of bays and sleep at Hat Sadet. This is a very long day necessitating over 8 km of at times quite hilly and difficult walks so be sure to leave early.

Day 4: Explore Than Sadet, see stone inscriptions and the waterfall, leave by midday to reach Thong Nai Pan by sun set.

Day 5: Depart Thong Nai Pan arriving at Bottle Beach. This requires some walking along main roads and the track can be a little difficult to follow, but if you do not get lost it will only take around two to three hours.

Day 6: Depart Bottle Beach for Hat Khom and Chalok Lam. The track between Bottle Beach and Hat Kho is some of the most difficult to follow on the whole island. Be sure to leave early to allow you time for when you get lost!

Day 7: Depart Chalok Lam to Mae Hat and then on to Hat Salat.

Day 8: Depart Hat Salat to Hat Yao and Chaophao Bay.

Day 9: Depart Chaophao Bay for a full day of walking (mainly along the beach to Thong Sala). The above is just an example of one itinerary you could follow. If planning to do this in low season be aware that in places such as Hat Salat, Bottle Beach and Hat Sadet everything may be closed, so you may well need to carry more water.

Khao Ra   เขาหรา

This is the highest mountain on Ko Pha Ngan at 627 m above sea level. The summit viewpoint can be reached via a tricky network of trails from Ban Maduawan. The mountain bike hire place in Thong Sala also supposedly organises bike tours to the summit, but the owner seems a little difficult to motivate.

Waterfalls

The waterfalls are quite uninspiring unless you go in the wet season. At other times the trickle of water is not the image that you had in your mind as you made the arduous journey there. There are in fact a few waterfalls along the road starting at Ban Tai that heads north, with the better one being **Namtok Than Prawet**. There is also another called **Namtok Phaeng** which is the biggest and most well known on the island. It is an easy walk off the main road near Ban Maduawan and from the waterfall a trail winds up to a mountain viewpoint.

Thai Boxing

You can still catch some traditional Thai culture in Ko Pha Ngan, however in a somewhat Westernised way. Thai boxing takes place every week at Thong Sala Stadium.

Wat Kao Tam - Meditation Retreat   วัดเขาถ้ำ

This small and attractively laid out wat is on top of a small hill down a dirt track 1 km from Ban Tai. Silence retreats are run here, enquire at the wat for details.

The Big Tree

This huge and very impressive tree is around 1 km from Ban Tai and measures 14½ m around the base of its trunk. It is down the track from Ban Tai which leads to Thong Nai Pan and is just after Wat Boddha.

Full Moon Parties

The main full moon party is held on Hat Rin every full moon.

Mountain Biking

There is a guy at Pha Ngan Batik in Thong Sala who runs mountain bike tours of the island (minimum three people) for 300B. He promises spectacular views, with the tour going to Ban Maduawan and the peak of Kao Ra. You will also visit Namtok Phaeng and lunch is included. He also hires out geared mountain bikes in excellent condition for 80B a day. It is not until you get on a bike that you realise how hilly Phan Ngan is.

South

A night not to miss — The Full Moon on Hat Rin

"I decided to wander down to see what was happening on the beach and was greeted by a chaotic melee of people dancing, drinking, eating, smoking and dancing more. Body painting was to the left and dried squid was to the right. Vendors sold trays of Lipovitam and Red Bull whilst a stand just off the beach sold magic omelettes and speed punch — something for everyone. A friend from Bangkok was setting up his stall of handmade jewellery — All purchases of over 500B got a free bag of grass! Further down the beach, towards Paradise Bungalows hundreds leapt around a twenty foot pole in a bizarre ritual like fashion — made even stranger by the surrounding coloured mist and fireworks. I wandered down the beach, weaving between the fire breathers and stoned drummers. When I reached the end of Hat Rin I climbed up on the rocks and looked back — the beach was alive."

Stuart McDonald

◀**Arriving and Departing**▶

Getting Around the Island
Songtheaw
Weather permitting, it is possible to reach most of the beaches of Ko Pha Ngan by songtheaw and in high season it is also possible to catch a boat to many of the beaches if you so desire. Sample songtheaw fares include: **Hat Sri Thanu** 25B taking 15 minutes, **Aow Chaophao** 30B, **Hat Yao** 50B, **Hat Salat** 40B and **Mae Hat** 50B. During the wet season many of the roads along the west coast are virtually impassable, so do not be surprised if songtheaws refuse to make the trip — even for 200B! **Aow Chalok Lam** is connected to Thong Sala by a sealed road and a motorbike taxi costs 30B. **Thong Nai Pan** can be reached by songtheaw for 60B. In the wet season the ride can be hair raising, if not impassable and as a result many of the resorts close. Enquire in Thong Sala to find out who is open before venturing to this part of the world. **Than Sadet** can be reached by songtheaw from Thong Sala costing 70B and the trip is guaranteed to shake a few screws loose. In the wet season the road is impassable.

The road from Thong Sala to Hat Rin is usually completely sealed however, during the heavy rains of December 1996, many large sections of it floated away. If it is not fixed or you arrive during a torrential downpour, the most straightforward way to reach Hat Rin is by boat. These boats take 10 to 15 minutes, leave from the east side of the pier at Thong Sala and cost 30B (as long as there are at least three people in the boat).

If the road is repaired when you visit, a songtheaw from Thong Sala to **Hat Rin** costs 40B, Thong Sala to **Ban Kai** 20B and Ban Kai to Hat Rin 20B. At low tide it is also possible to walk from Hat Rin to Ban Kai taking around 1½ hours.

Walking
Bottle Beach (Hat Kuat)
If you decide to walk there from either Chalok Lam or Thong Nai Pan, be prepared for a long and at times confusing walk. The walk however is well worth the effort for the abundant wildlife and scenic views. From Aow Chalok Lam walk to the eastern end of the beach then past Coral Bay and follow the road past Hat Khom. From there the start of the trail is fairly obvious and is straightforward to follow for the first kilometre, but the next 2 km are difficult and the track often disappears. If trying this walk make sure you have decent footwear, water and sunscreen and allow about two hours to reach Bottle Beach.

From Thong Nai Pan, take the road out from beside Panviman Resort until you hit the main road and follow it for about 500 m where you reach a turn to the right. Take this turn and follow it to the end of the road then look for the trail and follow it all the way to the beach. This trail goes through some fields of long grass - prime snake territory, so you may want to wear shoes and long pants to reduce the risk of snake bike.

Boat
Weather permitting, there is a longtail from **Hat Rin** to **Hat Tien** at 12.40 costing 30B. Otherwise you can walk there from Hat Rin by starting near the Thai House Restaurant, following a 3 km trail which is marked in yellow paint. It is supposed to be easy to follow, but it is very simple to get lost along the trail so keep an eye out for the yellow paint at all times. **Bottle Beach** can be reached by boat from Chalok Lam, Thong Nai Pan or Hat Rin during high season. The boat leaves Chalok Lam twice daily (weather permitting) at 13.00 and 16.00 and returns at 09.30 and 15.00 for 30B.

To/From Ko Samui
A speedboat leaves for **Bo Phut** daily at 09.30, 12.00, 15.00 and 16.30 and costs 200B for the 15 minute trip. In the reverse direction the speedboat leaves Bo Phut for Ko Pha Ngan at 08.30, 11.30 and 15.00.

Weather permitting, boats run from Hat Rin to **Hat Bangruk (Big Buddha Beach)** on Ko Samui for just 60B. These leave Hat Rin at 09.30, 11.40 and 14.30, take about 50 minutes and are invariably overloaded. However, this is the cheapest way to get to Ko Samui from Hat Rin. In the reverse direction boats to Hat Rin leave Big Buddha Beach at 10.30, 13.00 and 16.00.

To **Nathon** (Ko Samui) there is a boat at 06.15 and at 13.00 which takes 1 hour at a cost of 65B. This boat continues on to Surat Thani, arriving at 10.00 and 17.00 and costs 145B for the full distance. In the reverse direction the boat leaves Nathon at 10.50 and 17.10 arriving at Thong Sala at 11.30 and 17.50.

To/From Ko Tao

To **Ko Tao** there is one boat a day at 12.30 which costs 150B and takes 3 hours. In the high season there is also an express boat which takes only 1½ hours at a cost of 250B. In the reverse direction, the boat leaves Ko Tao at 10.00 arriving at Thong Sala at 11.30.

To/From Surat Thani

There is a direct boat to **Surat Thani** which leaves Ko Pha Ngan at midnight, arrives in Surat Thani at 05.30 and costs 120B. In the reverse direction, the boat leaves Surat Thani at 22.00, arriving at Thong Sala at 03.00. It is possible to sleep fairly well on this boat - as long as the weather is good.

KO TAO   เกาะเต่า

Until fairly recently Ko Tao existed undisturbed, virtually ignored and uninhabited. Used as a stop-over point for fishermen or pirates, it was chosen by the Thai government as a prison site by virtue of its isolation, and past and to the left of the post office concrete foundations of this prison still remain. Some 30 years ago 'squatters' from Ko Pha Ngan arrived to fish and cultivate coconuts. By the time the government realised what was going on, it was too late and the newly established families remained. The current permanent population is now around 600 with as many seasonal workers arriving to work in the tourist trade as there are locals.

Some ten years ago Ko Tao was 'discovered' by Western tourists and the first bungalow operations were constructed. Of these only Taraporn, Rocky and Char remain. By 1990 it was a well established 'quiet' alternative to Ko Pha Ngan and Ko Samui with good snorkelling and cheap bamboo huts. Since then it has exploded with resorts multiplying like rabbits and diving schools growing like mushrooms in the wet season. The most popular beaches such as Sairee and Chalok Ban Kao now resemble miniature versions of Chaweng and Hat Rin with the mixed video, scuba, full moon, chill out, Bangkok Post, real toilet and fruit shake set firmly established. Prices have increased to Ko Samui rates and the bamboo huts are becoming rare as concrete chalets begin to take prevalence. Expect this trend to continue. The old style cheapies continue to survive in the more remote areas to the northwest and southwest and along the eastern coast, however due to the weather conditions, many on the east coast do not open until late in the season.

Ko Tao can be very quiet for much of the year, then it suddenly packs out from Christmas onwards when accommodation of any kind can be difficult to find. Prices on Ko Tao for food are generally high and the distance from the mainland is the most common excuse. Yet many more isolated islands have lower prices than Ko Tao and as usual the locals are often not paying the same rates as the farangs. The diving industry can be held responsible for much of the surge in room rates.

Nevertheless, most of Ko Tao is still well preserved and it is a very beautiful island which probably causes more than its fair share of visa extensions as visitors often decide to stay longer than planned. Unfortunately development does appear to be taking a very worrying direction.

South

Orientation

There is only one place to arrive on Ko Tao, the wharf at Mae Hat. What was once a small village is rapidly sprawling out and becoming increasingly concrete. Upon arrival you will be met by loads of touts who will either put you in the back of a pick-up, motorbike or boat and whisk you off to the resort of your choice.

From Mae Hat two main roads lead off, to the north the road winds along Aow Mae Hat and Hat Sairee before becoming virtually impassable a little way after Eden Bungalows. About 2 km before Eden the road branches off to the right for around a kilometre then splits into two, with the left veer heading to Aow Hin Wong and the right to Aow Mao and Laem Thian. Both of these forks are undriveable and you will need to hike it from where the road splits. To the south of Mae Hat the road goes to Aow Chalok Ban Kao and is sealed that far. Just under 1 km out of Mae Hat the road takes a fork to the left, this fork runs out to Aow Leuk and another kilometre down the road, the road divides again to the left out to Hat Sai Daeng.

You may find that for the more distant destinations such as Hin Wong and Aow Tanoa, a boat is a better and more comfortable option, although it is generally more

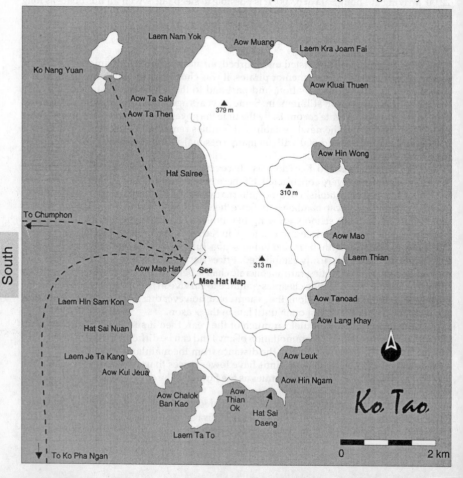

expensive. In the wet season many of the dirt roads become completely impassable and boat is the only way to reach your destination other than on foot. However if the weather is bad the resorts which are difficult to reach often close up, so enquire in Mae Hat before hiring a boat.

Post card material Ko Nang Yuan lies off the northwest point of the island and is easily reached by a daily morning boat from Mae Hat.

Guide Map of Koh Pha-Ngan and Koh Tao by V.Hongsombud is an excellent guide to the island and has many walking trails marked on the map along with points of interest, bungalows and their prices and boat timetables and much much more and is a bargain at 40B. It is available in Mae Hat.

Vital Information

Post Office is on your right as you walk away from the pier on the main road leading up from the wharf at Mae Hat. Telephone offices abound throughout the town.

Banks The exchange offices on Ko Tao take advantage of your relative isolation and the rates are sometimes poor. It is normal for a surcharge to be charged on any credit card transactions. The largest concentration of exchange offices is in Mae Hat. To your right as you walk off the pier is Krung Thai Bank.

Police Station is located between Mae Hat and Hat Sairee.

Hospital Basic medical care is available at the clinic in town. To get there from the wharf take the first right then the first left after Scuba Junction Travel.

Travel Agents abound throughout town and, if you ask, your guesthouse will probably be more than willing to pretend to be one.

Codes The telephone code for Ko Tao is (077) and the postal code is 84280.

Cheap Sleeps

Accommodation on Ko Tao, particularly in high season can become both expensive and hard to get. In the middle of peak season, it is not unusual to spend your first night sleeping on the beach if you want to stay at one of the popular beaches such as Hat Sairee, but this is much less frequent at the quieter beaches. Also in high season, the prices may jump up a little from what you read here. The accommodation on Ko Tao is covered in a clockwise direction starting at Mae Hat.

Aow Mae Hat   อ่าวแม่หาด

This beach is sandy and nice enough to lay around on, but can get a little dirty due to the proximity of town and the prevalent current appears to be north to south. This proximity does however make it a handy place to stay if you need to sort things out in town. Just over the rocky point at the north end is a stone bearing the initials of King Rama V which he carved during a visit to sunny Ko Tao. (*Tales From the Other Side* is certainly not suggesting that you do the same).

The first two places here are actually just to the south of Ban Mae Hat, whilst the remainder head north.

San Si Paradise has something for every budget with basic 80B huts right through to 2,500B family bungalows!

Paell is very close to the village and starts at 100B for a basic hut.

The only accommodation within the village itself is the **Ko Tao Garden Resort** which has rooms starting at 200B. However unless you have some desperate desire to stay in town, we would suggest you venture a little further afield.

Crystal has reasonably priced rooms starting at 80B and the beach is fairly clean but watch out for falling coconuts.

South

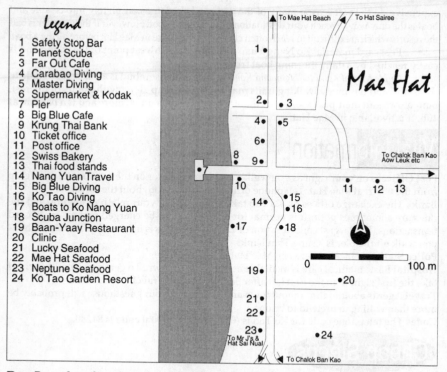

Legend

1 Safety Stop Bar
2 Planet Scuba
3 Far Out Cafe
4 Carabao Diving
5 Master Diving
6 Supermarket & Kodak
7 Pier
8 Big Blue Cafe
9 Krung Thai Bank
10 Ticket office
11 Post office
12 Swiss Bakery
13 Thai food stands
14 Nang Yuan Travel
15 Big Blue Diving
16 Ko Tao Diving
17 Boats to Ko Nang Yuan
18 Scuba Junction
19 Baan-Yaay Restaurant
20 Clinic
21 Lucky Seafood
22 Mae Hat Seafood
23 Neptune Seafood
24 Ko Tao Garden Resort

Mae Hat

To Mae Hat Beach
To Hat Sairee
To Chalok Ban Kao Aow Leuk etc
To Chalok Ban Kao
To Mr J's & Hat Sai Nual

0   100 m

Dam Bungalows have basic huts going for 80B (100B on the beach) and the restaurant is particularly good.

Queen Resort is on the headland above Dam and has rooms for 60B, 80B and 100B and the staff are very helpful.

Tommy Resort is beside Queen Resort with rooms for 150B and cheaper rooms for 60B if you are a diver.

D.D. Resort has huts that start at 100B.

View Cliff Resort lives up to its name with nice view of the surrounds, the rooms here go for 100B and 150B with fan and shower depending on position. (150B to 250B in the high season).

Hat Sairee   หาดทรายรี

This is by far the most popular beach on the island and is one of the nicest. Long and very flat, the beach is great for sunbaking but not so great for swimming as the water is very shallow for a considerable distance out. The sunsets from here are spectacular. Due to its popularity, this beach can be quite a scene, with nightly beach parties complete with thumping techno into the early hours whilst during the day stoned drummers beat away on drums and frolic in the water. It is a nice enough beach, but only the dedicated party lover would want to stay in its midst. If you value your sleep, stay a bit away from the centre of the beach and walk to the party each evening. The beach parties often have large **seafood barbecues** serving punch, and you can either chill out at the low candlelit tables on the beach or put your dancing shoes on for a bit of a jig around the fire.

A.C. 2 Resort is the first on the beach with only six huts, but they are good, starting at 150B with fan and shower (250B in the high season).

Bing Bungalow has a nice selection of bungalows which start at 150B.

Ban Diving Resort has concrete rooms in a pretty garden setting. Small rooms go for 50B or larger rooms go for 80B and 100B with fan and shower.

A.C Resort is one of the more popular places on this beach. Large A frame bungalows start at 150B and the restaurant is justifiably popular, though it would be nice if they could switch off the TV for thirty seconds.

Big Fish Dive Resort is one of the friendlier dive resorts and has well kept bungalows for 100B and 120B with fan and shower.

Koh Tao Cabana is between Big Blue Diving and Scuba Junction with huts starting at 150B and 250B with fan and shower.

SB Cabana was closed at our last pass and has only four huts.

Sai Ree Cottage just to the south of Planet Divers has clean rooms starting at 100B with share bathroom and 150B for private bathroom.

Seashell Resort is a large establishment with small huts for 150B and large ones for 200B.

New Way has huts starting at 100B and though the food is good, you can wait up to two hours for a meal as the management do not seem to want to hire more staff. Nevertheless some love it and some hate it. The bungalows are clean.

Suthep was in a pretty rundown state at our last pass with huts with fan and shower for 200B.

Dance Palace is behind Suthep, a bar and club which is a popular for drinks and dancing.

Simple Life Villa It is this end of the beach that can get pretty wild in the evenings and the noise can be unbearable. This operation has rooms starting at 100B and 150B.

Sunset Buri Resort and Scuba Diving is definitely the luxury place on this beach. Pool, clean good restaurant and equally good rooms start at 300B (more in the high season). The rooms are quite good value given the conditions, but why do people insist on building pools virtually on the beach?

Sai Ree Hut Resort has rooms starting at 100B with shower. They do a great seafood BBQ.

Blue Wind Bakery is very popular and as a result can be particularly difficult to get into. Their bread is good as is the elevated restaurant. The rooms are clean and well placed, perhaps a little close together though. Huts with shower start at 100B.

Golden Cape There is a big break along the beach till you reach these rundown huts for 80B.

Aow Taa Then, Aow Taa Sak and Laem Yaay Nee
อ่าวตาเทน, อ่าวตาศักดิ์, แหลมยายณี

Situated at the northernmost end of Hat Sairee, this collection of bays have little in the way of beach but a lot in the way of solitude. Reached by following the road on and past Hat Sairee, the road is passable by motorbike as far as Mahana and C.F.T. and to walk from there to the centre of Mae Hat takes around 30 minutes.

Silver Cliff is well placed offering good views and a decent dose of solitude starting at 100B.

Sun Sea This friendly place offers great views for only 50B or 100B with fan and shower.

Eden Resort This place is set on the inland side of the road and is a good five to ten minute walk to the beach. The bungalows are basic but have a lot of character and are priced from 50B to 100B according to size.

Sun Lord sits on Aow Taa Sak and has four basic huts for 60B and a few with shower for 150B.

Mahana Bay has a great view of Ko Nang Yuan and is a friendly place to stay. Rooms start at 60B or 100B with shower.

C.F.T. has a strange name and is quite a hike to reach, but the seclusion is well worth it. The huts are perched on the rocks and go for 50B and 100B.

Smiling Garden was closed at our last pass and may or may not reopen.

Aow Hin Wong   อ่าวหินวง

This idyllic bay is set on the eastern side of Ko Tao and is home to two resorts. There is little in the way of beach here, but the snorkelling is excellent and the feeling of isolation is unmatched elsewhere on the island.

Hin Wong Bungalows In our opinion, this is the *best guesthouse in all of Thailand!* run by the particularly friendly family of Mol, Tep, Sahaat and Mom. Once you make the effort of getting here, you will be kicking yourself for not doing it a week earlier. The food is very good and reasonably priced considering it is all lugged from town. The bungalows are well spaced, large and roomy and cost 80B with share bathroom. Very good snorkelling gear is available for hire, but it is expensive, so if you are planning on snorkelling for more than a couple of days, it works out cheaper to buy your own.

Green Tree Resort is set further to the north of Hin Wong. It is a slightly steeper climb up to here but the bungalows are clean and reasonably priced at 80B.

Laem Thian   แหลมเทียน

This secluded bay has a very small beach and some good snorkelling. It is quite an effort to reach, so if you have a lot of luggage catch a boat but be sure to check in town find that it is open. If arriving under your own steam follow the directions to Aow Hin Wong until you reach the split in the road and take the right fork instead of the left. From there it is a gruelling 2½ km walk to the guesthouse!

Laem Thian Resort is very well located with a range of basic huts starting at 50B to 80B.

Aow Tanote   อ่าวโตนด

This scenic beach is strewn with rocks in places and has a small rocky islet off its centre offering some great snorkelling. Sick of snorkelling? Climb onto the islet and sunbake all day! On the track leading down to the bay, and with a great view, is Ko Tao's **only guesthouse**! As yet un-named and under Franco-Thai management, this place is due to open in June 1997 at 60B per room.

Tanote Bay Resort has nice bungalows on the rocks at the northern end of the bay for 100B and 200B with fan and shower.

Bamboo Huts is next door to Tanote Bay Resort, but on the beach with huts going for 80B.

Diamond Beach is cheaper at 60B or 120B with fan and shower.

Poseidon is well organised and very friendly with basic huts for 50B and 100B for rooms with a shower. They have a 4WD and can arrange a pickup from the pier.

Aow Leuk   อ่าวลึก

This pretty bay is not too difficult to reach and has some great snorkelling opportunities. The beach here is not too bad either. The road to get there has some great views and is in not too bad a condition. To walk there from Mae Hat takes around 1 hour, or about 15 to 20 minutes from Hat Sai Daeng.

Aow Leuk is a friendly place with a handful of rudimentary huts going for 80B.

Nice Moon is located halfway between Aow Leuk and Hat Sai Daeng and wins the prize for one of the friendliest places on the island. Good huts go for 150B and it is a 5 minute walk to the beach at Aow Leuk.

Hat Sai Daeng   หาดทรายแดง

Another very nice beach with just the one set of bungalows (and dive shop), the snorkelling here is again very good.

Kiet Bungalow has wooden huts scattered all over the hillside. This is quite an old resort by Ko Tao's standards and some of the huts look it, while others are fine. Huts start at 50B and 150B with fan and shower.

Aow Thian Ok   อ่าวเทียนออก

This very pretty bay is home to a well known family of reef sharks who are much friendlier than the staff at Rocky Resort! The snorkelling is pretty good.

Rocky Resort We have visited this place three times over the last six years and on every occasion here found the staff to have a real attitude problem. The management own the whole bay and seem to spend a lot of time tacking up private property signs when they are not busy perving in your room or into the showers! This is a really creepy place. Basic huts go for 60B to 80B or 150B to 200B with fan and shower. Not Recommended.

Taa Toh Headland (Laem Taa Toh)   แหลมตาโต๊ะ

This peninsula offers some great views of the surrounds and there is a trail which leads to the John Suwan Mountain Viewpoint which would have to have more photos taken from it than anywhere else on Ko Tao. Both resorts on the headland have their own bays and both are very popular since they are pretty quiet and secluded compared to Chalok Ban Kao.
Freedom Beach has clean huts for 150B accompanied by indifferent staff.
Taa Toh Lagoon Bungalow and Scuba Diving has a few huts for 50B otherwise 100B or 150B on the beach with fan and shower. The staff here are equally indifferent.

Aow Chalok Ban Kao   อ่าวโฉลกบ้านเก่า

This is the second most popular beach and the most expensive on the island. It is also an important diving centre. The beach is long, flat and fairly clean, although it can get very crowded. The water is very shallow for a long way out so it is not great for a swim, but more for a lay around. The peninsula to the east of the beach is where the popular photo of Ko Tao is taken with the two beaches splitting off. The sides of this peninsula are also lined with some small bays and beaches and you can hike along it to reach the John-Suwan Mountain Viewpoint if you are feeling energetic.
AUD Resort has rooms with fan and shower for 150B and is reasonably quiet.
New Heaven Dive is located on the rocks and is equally quiet and similarly priced.
Ko Tao Cottage This large, plush resort has nice bungalows on the hill for 500B or on the beach for 600B.
Porn Resort is on the other side of the road and accommodation here starts at 150B.
Carabao Bungalow and Scuba Diving Only contemplate staying here if you plan on going diving with Carabao.
Buddha View has accommodation starting at 200B for non-divers, although we have heard some negative reports about this place.
Sunshine has huts starting at 200B.
Sunshine II The friendly staff make a fresh change and there is no dive school. The restaurant is good and rooms with fan and shower start at 120B. If you really want to stay on the beach, this place is the best choice.
Laem Khlong Getting onto the rocks at the western end of the bay, this well kept and relatively quiet place costs 200B or 250B on the beach with fan and shower, although the staff are not so helpful.

Hat Saal Chao   หาดศาลเจ้า

This small beach is set to the southwest of Aow Chalok Baan Kao and although the beach itself has little to recommend it, the bungalows here are not bad value.
Taraporn and **Viewpoint Bungalows** Taraporn was the oldest remaining bungalows on Ko Tao and has just been taken over by Viewpoint. Rates will stay the same though at 100B for basic huts with discounts available for divers. The restaurant is well priced with excellent views.
Black Rock Bungalows situated behind **Big Bubble Diving** (one of the friendlier, low key dive places on the island) has a couple of basic huts for 50B.
Banana Rock is back on the beach area, behind the road on the hill. This place is friendly, relaxed and rustic and rates are 50B for a basic hut or 100B with fan and shower.
Miramar was undergoing renovation at the time of writing and when it re-opens will probably have nudged itself up into the mid-range.

Aow Kul Jeua   อ่าวกุลเจือ

This secluded bay has a nice beach which is more than long enough to allow you to find a bit of private paradise. The snorkelling offshore is not bad and the best of it is off to your right when looking out to sea.

Sunset Bungalows is the only accommodation on the beach and rates start at 60B. The staff here are particularly friendly, have snorkelling gear available and can dish up some great food.

Laem Je Ta Kang   แหลมเจ๊ะตะกัง

This small cape is home to one resort, Tao Thong Villa. The beach is very small, but the water is very clean around here and snorkelling on both sides of the cape is good.

Tao Thong Villa has a dozen rooms starting at 80B, though you may be able to bargain down the price in low season. The restaurant is small but well set on the cape. The staff (when they are awake) are very friendly.

Hat Sai Nual   หาดทรายนวล

This is actually made up of two small beaches upon which there are three resorts. The beach is clean but quite rocky and there is some good snorkelling around here.

Sai Thong has a collection of rustic huts starting at 50B and sits between the two beaches.

Siam Cookie has only a dozen bungalows but is a great place to stay even though some of the huts are in particularly rustic condition. The decent huts here start at 80B with share bathroom. In low season you could bargain the price down. The restaurant is also good.

Char is the best appointed of the three at the southern end of the beach overlooking the cove and has the cheapest huts, starting at 40B. The staff are friendly and run a good restaurant.

Aow Jan Som   อ่าวจันทร์สม

At the time of writing this beach did not have any bungalows on it, but this may change soon. The beach here is particularly nice and very secluded. It is only a ten minute walk from the southern end of Aow Mae Hat and is well worth visiting for a quiet day of sitting around contemplating your navel.

Aow Taa Saeng   อ่าวตาแสง

This small beach would be quite nice, but unfortunately it catches a lot of floating refuse from Mae Hat, so is not a great place to lay around. There is a **wreck** offshore which makes it a popular diving destination. It is about a ten minute walk from Mae Hat.

Coral Beach is the only resort on this bay with a good range of rooms starting at 80B to 100B for basic bungalows with share bathroom and more expensive if you want a private bathroom.

Inland Places to stay

The vast majority of Ko Tao is unexplored and for good reason. There is not a particularly well maintained network of paths and trails on the island and it is easy to get lost. The only accommodation on the island that is not near a beach are the resorts on the way to the mountain viewpoint on the centre of the island. To get there take the turn-off on the road between Mae Hat and Sairee which then leads up the hillside. These places all have fantastic views but are quite a hike from the beach.

OK View has dingy rooms for 50B or very nice bungalows for 150B (more in peak season).

Mountain is rustic with very basic huts for 50B, but nicely laid out with a cosy restaurant area.

2 Views If you continue up the hillside along a very steep trail you will reach the well signposted 2 Views. Run by a friendly Thai guy and his farang girlfriend they offer Yoga, Tai-chi and meditation courses and have a couple of basic wooden huts which they rent to guests. If you continue along this trail you will eventually end up at Hat Tanote.

Eat and Meet

The very similar collection of seafood restaurants overlooking the beach to the south of the pier are generally good and certainly cheaper than most bungalow restaurants and with a wider choice. Both **Lucky** and **Mae Hat Seafood** are very good. Past the post office is the popular **Swiss Bakery** which is good for apple pie and Earl Grey tea and past this are a string of cheap **Thai eating places** for pad thai, som tam, fried rice and so on. Between Paell and the village is **Mr J's**, an old wooden house which functions as a bar and vegetarian restaurant, travel agent, second hand shop, photo developing service and much much more! It is worth visiting to check out the amazing tree out front.

Things to do and Sights to See

SCUBA Diving

Ko Tao has a number of pastimes to offer, most of which revolve around the water. **Diving** is without a doubt the big industry on the island, with virtually every bungalow able to at least facilitate the organising of dive trips. At last count there were 17 separate dive companies on the island and rumour has it that more people now pass their diving certificates on Ko Tao than anywhere else in Thailand, even Phuket! There are a number of dive shops on the island including Gecko Divers, Ko Tao Divers, Carabao Divers and Big Blue Divers amongst many more.

The water is particularly clear here and there are sheltered spots on one coast or the other most of the year round. The marine life on Ko Tao is varied, but not as varied as the Andaman Coast and the coral is often not as spectacular. What makes Ko Tao's diving popular over nearby Ko Pha Ngan, Ko Samui and the Andaman Sea is the increasingly easy access to the island, reasonably cheap diving along with plenty of accommodation opportunities. For better underwater life get yourself to more spectacular sites such as the Surin, Similan and Tarutao Groups. There is a wreck off Aow Taa Saeng which is popular for diving.

The prices of the dive trips are fairly reasonable, but it is worth shopping around for the best price, program and accommodation deal to suit you. Take your time choosing, chat to the instructors to get a feel for the diving school 'atmosphere'. It is possible to gain certification for the basic PADI certificate as well as more advanced courses and tuition is generally available in English, German, French and sometimes Italian.

Typical prices are Open Water PADI course 6,500B, Advanced 5,500B, Fun Dives: 1 for 700B, 2 for 1,200B, 6 for 3,000B and 10 for 4,500B with one free dive and there are also reductions if you have your own equipment. Some bungalows also offer discounts on accommodation which can make a big difference in total price.

Snorkelling

You do not need to enrol in a dive course or spend a lot of money to see plenty of fish and some pretty coral. Many parts of the island have good snorkelling opportunities which are close to the shore, and most bungalows will either rent or lend you snorkelling gear. Otherwise Mr J in Mae Hat rents decent gear at 40B per day with another 40B per day for fins. If you are planning on doing a lot of snorkelling, most dive shops do sell the gear, but count on around 1,500B for decent mask, snorkel and fins. Try for 2nd hand gear or ask Mr J.

Some good spots include **Hat Sai Nual** and **Aow Kul Jeua** on the south coast, the bays in front of **Rocky Resort** and **Kiet Bungalows**, and if the weather is good **Aow Hin Wong** is also very good. Opposite Kiet Bungalows is **Shark Island** around which you can see some small reef sharks — they are not aggressive but do not hassle them either.

When snorkelling, never step on the coral as you will destroy it and do not take inhabited shells from the water. Just enjoy the visual feast and leave it alone for others to enjoy. The more popular paces to stay such as Hat Sairee, Ban Chalok Ban Kao and Ko Nang Yuan have all been badly damaged from anchor drag, run off from resorts and vandalising tourists.

Fishing

For those more into above water pursuits, it is possible to organise day and night **fishing trips.** The entire southern area of the island is a marine reserve within which fishing is prohibited so be sure to check that you allowed to catch dinner before you throw that line in.

Hiking

There are some great opportunities for **hiking** on the island as there is a wide network of tracks covering much of the island. In the wet season some of the tracks can and do fade off to virtually nothing. Ko Tao is a small enough island that most areas are accessible within a few hours and it is difficult to get lost for too long. Many of the trails are easy to follow and none of the hills are too high.

From Mae Hat try the track that runs along the southwest coast leading around the rocks from Coral Beach to Tha Thong Bungalows then cutting inland to Chalok Ban Kao. Count on some great views and an hour or so on your feet.

For Aow Kul Jeua, Laem Je Ta Kang, Hat Sai Nual and Aow Jan Som the track is well marked in places, but in other areas fades away to virtually nothing. When we walked it, a black dog led us all the way around, so if you are lost, look out for a black dog with white feet who responds to 'Fido'! It is not difficult to lose the track around here, so if you do get lost, try and retrace your steps and if that is no help, head to the water and climb along the rocks till you figure it out. The *Guide Map of Ko Pha Ngan and Ko Tao* by V.Hongsumbud has a rough guide of where the tracks are and is an invaluable asset to have with you. Also wear decent shoes and bring loads of water and sunscreen. There are a lot of snakes in this area so do not step on anything that moves.

From Chalok Ban Kao you can wander around Laem Taa Ton, a cape which has some nice secluded coves and great views from the top, or continue along the coast to Aow Thian O.K. From here it is not far, but a bit of a struggle to Kiet Bungalows taking about 15 minutes. From Kiet, you can either cut back over the hills to the Mae Hat to Chalok Ban Kao road some 1½ km of jungle away or continue along the coast to Aow Leuk. This track is particularly scenic running along the top of the rocks and begins from the top of the ridge amongst the Kiet huts and takes around 15 minutes.

From Aow Leuk a wide track leads up to join the Mae Hat to Aow Tanote 'road' some ½ km away. From here go straight along the concrete road to reach the village or turn right for a pretty ½ hour walk down to Tanote Beach. The final part down to the beach is pretty steep.

From Aow Tanote you have several choices, you can either find a pick-up, bike or boat back to town for 50B or keep walking. Laem Thian is a 30 minute walk away along the coastal trail or if climbing back up from the beach two trails lead inland over the hills. The first takes you the 1 km to the Sairee to Laem Thian track and is not too strenuous but can be a little difficult to follow. The second trail on the right leads up to the viewpoint and 2 Views and is well indicated by coloured arrows on the rocks. The white trail cuts through the jungle and is shorter but more difficult whilst the orange trail climbs gently, taking around 45 minutes to reach the viewpoint. From the top you will have great views of both sides of the island, and only a 30 minute downhill clamber through some great vegetation will have you back in Mae Hat.

Unfortunately the northern part of the island has no real network of trails yet, except for the roads to Aow Hin Wong to the east and Smiling Garden to the west. As development creeps north perhaps a network of trails will open up.

> When chatting to a couple of the locals on Ko Tao about the rapid rate of development on the island and as to whether it is sustainable or not, they replied that there is simply no going back. And the dive shops — well they just grow like mushrooms in the wet season!

South

◀ **Arriving and Departing** ▶

Getting Around on Ko Tao

Songtheaws and motorcycle taxis meet the ferry and can take you to many of the places on the island. For those not easily accessible, boats operate from the wharf at the surrounding beaches. A motorcycle taxi or songtheaw to **Hat Sairee** or **Chalok Baan Kao** will cost 20B each way, whilst the boats to outlying destinations vary according to the number of people on the boat. It is worth asking around at the pier to try to get the best price. To reach **Aow Hin Wong**, you will need to either catch a boat around or hire a motorbike. To walk there from Hat Sairee takes about one hour and is a pretty hard slog. The best way to reach Aow Tanote is courtesy of Poseidon's 4WD, otherwise taxi from Mae Hat will cost 50B as the track is very difficult by motorbike. The easiest way to reach Hat Saal Chao is to catch a songtheaw around to Aow Chalok Baan Kao then walk along the coast till you reach the bay. This walk will involve a little climbing over rocks and, depending on the tide, you may need to cut inland at times. If you reach Gecko Divers and are wondering where you are, Hat Saal Chao is the next bay along. For **Aow Kul Jeua, Laem Je Ta Kang, Hat Sai Nual and Aow Jan Som** there are two ways to reach them, you can either get a boat to take you there or walk. There are no roads down this way, so a songtheaw is out. The track is well marked in places, but in other areas fades away to virtually nothing.

To/From Ko Tao

Ko Tao is only reached by boat from two places, Chumphon on the coast and Thong Sala on Ko Pha Ngan to the south. From **Chumphon** there are two boats daily. A **speedboat** leaves Chumphon at 08.00 daily and costs 400B taking only 1½ hours. The speedboat leaves Mae Hat pier in the reverse direction at 10.30. The other boat is the **slow boat**, this leaves Mae Hat at 10.00, costs 200B and takes around 4 to 5 hours and leaves Chumphon for Ko Tao daily at midnight. Both of these boats are subject to weather conditions, if the weather is bad, neither will leave, so in case you have poor weather, you may want to allow yourself a few days to get off the island.

The second point from where you can reach Ko Tao is **Thong Sala** on Ko Pha Ngan by either speedboat or slow boat. The **speedboat** leaves Thong Sala at 13.00, costs 350B and takes just under 1 hour, whilst a slow boat leaves at 10.30 and midday, takes around 2½ to 3 hours and costs 150B. In the reverse direction, the speed boat leaves Mae Hat at 15.30 and continues on to Nathon and Bo Phut on Ko Samui. This costs 350B to Thong Sala and 450B to Bo Phut. There are two **express boats** heading to Ko Pha Ngan, leaving Mae Hat at 09.30 and 13.30 costing 150B and taking around 2½ hours. There is also an **express boat** to Thong Sala which leaves at 15.00 and costs 200B for the 1½ hour trip.

AROUND KO TAO

KO NANG YUAN   เกาะนางยวน

This small island sits off the northwest coast of Ko Tao and is famed for being the only place in the world where three islands are joined by sandy beaches. There is only the one resort on the island, the aptly named Koh Nang Yuan Dive Resort. If you decide to stay out here, you will generally have the place to yourself, although the beaches are quite small and occasionally the island is somewhat overrun by dive groups. On the southern of the three islands you can hike up to a mountain viewpoint from where an impressive view can be had. **Koh Nang Yuan Dive Resort** The sole establishment on the island has a range of bungalows starting at 200B for basic huts with share bathroom through to over 2,000B for a luxury pad. The restaurant on the island serves OK food, but could certainly do better.

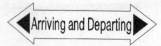
◄ Arriving and Departing ►

The island can only be reached by boat from Mae Hat pier. The boat leaves twice a day, leaving Mae Hat at 10.00 and 17.00 and from Ko Nang Yuan at 08.30 and 16.00. The boat costs 40B for a return trip. There is a policy of no plastic bottles on the island, so if you take any with you, they will be confiscated upon arrival. Drinks in glass can be purchased once you arrive.

PHUKET PROVINCE

Although Phuket is an island, it is connected to mainland Thailand at Phang Nga Province by the Sarasin Bridge and as a result (as well as its natural beauty) it is considerably more developed than any other island in Thailand. It is 885 km south of Bangkok, lying in the Andaman Sea and referred to as the 'Pearl of the South' in tourism literature. Phuket forms an important segment, if not the only segment, of many package tourist's time in Thailand, and since catering to this market, much of the budget accommodation is as good as extinct. The beaches were once some of the best in Thailand but now some would find it difficult to even qualify. If you are looking for unspoilt, beautiful beaches, you may find them much easier to locate elsewhere in Thailand, however there is much to see on Phuket island besides the beaches which make it worth a visit.

Phuket town itself is an interesting place blending Portuguese and Thai architecture, with some good restaurants and reasonably priced accommodation - a rarity on many of the more popular beaches. Phuket Province also has a number of offshore islands worth visiting and it is also one of the departure points to the fantastic Similan Islands. Phuket Province is very wealthy by Thai standards and this is reflected in the decent roads all over the island — a blessing for those tired of substandard Thai roads. In the centre of the island there is one of Phuket's last remaining pockets of rainforest and a Gibbon Rehabilitation Centre, both well worth visiting.

Maps of Phuket make it look deceptively small, but for one to fully explore the island and its many beaches you would want to allow five to six days to do it justice, and a another few days if you wanted to explore some of the offshore islands or visit the Similan Islands. Generally expect to pay more for most things, especially food, than anywhere else in Southern Thailand. If you are intent on staying somewhere like Patong, then double your budget. For great food, try to get to Phuket in late September/early October, just in time to make the Vegetarian Festival. This festival takes place in a number of southern cities, but Phuket is known for being one of the best places for it. The festival runs for nine days and during processions honouring the gods, mediums in trances stick metal rods through their cheeks — quite a sight.

Legend

1 Sirinat National Park	8 Kamala Rooms for rent	16 Jungle Beach Resort
2 Phuket International Airport	9 Charoen Seafood & Bungalows	17 Ao Sane Bungalows
3 Khao Phra Taew National Park	10 Kamala Beach Pavilion	18 Phuket Yacht Club
4 Bang Pae waterfall	11 Phuket Golf Course	19 Samnak Song Nai Han
5 Tonai waterfall	12 Wat Chalong	20 Pornmai Bungalows
6 Amanpuri Resort	13 Sea Gypsy village	21 Siam Garden Resort
7 Pansea Resort	14 Marine Biological Research Centre	22 Viewpoint
	15 Coconut Huts	

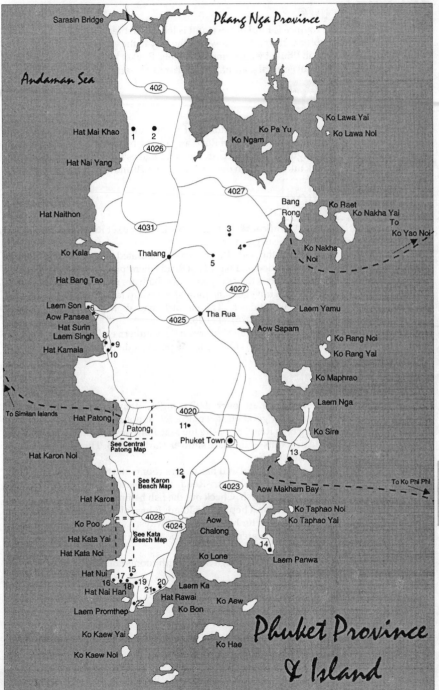

Phuket Province & Island

PHUKET ภูเก็ต

The capital of Phuket Province is Phuket town and is located in the southeast region of the island. Many travellers breeze through the town on the way to the western beaches, but one could easily spend a day in Phuket wandering the streets. Phuket town is also the centre of action during the Vegetarian Festival - one of Thailand's most bizarre and colourful festivals.

Orientation

Although the town sprawls out, for the visitor all of 'importance' is within a confined area centring around Ratsada Road, Thepkasatri Road and Phang Nga Road. It is easy to walk most places, and the Portuguese influenced architecture makes it pleasing to the eye. For those too lazy to walk, a tuk tuk ride within the city limits costs 7B and a motorcycle taxi is 10B.

Vital Information

Tourist Information The TAT office, ☎ (076) 211 036, is on Phuket Road and has a good supply of brochures and they speak good English.
Post Office At the time of writing the post office was being relocated. The old post office is on Montri Road near the main bus station off Phang Nga Road where 'poste restante' facilities are available. Bus stamps were for sale at the new post office. Both are marked on the map.
Banks There are many banks with travellers cheque and Visa Card facilities. Refer to the map.
Hospital Phuket's Adventist Hospital is on Thepkasatri Road about 1½ km out of town.
Tourist Police can be reached on ☎ (076) 212 046.
Immigration Office This is near the public library on the southern end of Phuket Road.
Codes The telephone code for Phuket is (076) and the postal code is 83000.

Cheap Sleeps

Most of the hotels in Phuket town are over 300B a night, often for pretty substandard facilities. There are however a few good budget places left as not all are extinct — yet.
Pengman Hotel is on Phang Nga Road, opposite the Mae Porn Restaurant. This is the best 'bargain' in town. Big, clean rooms with share shower start at 100B. There is a good and very affordable restaurant downstairs. .
Suksabai Hotel is off Thepkasatri Road and has decent rooms starting at 140B and 180B.
Thara Hotel is further north on Thepkasatri Road. It has reasonable rooms for 150B, although none of the staff speak English. Check out the fish behind the reception.
Siam Hotel is closer to town, still on Thepkasatri Road. It has tolerable rooms starting at 150B, with women of dubious character lurking the hallways.
Wasana Guest House is handily located near to the beach bus rank. This hotel starts its rates at an odd 161B a night.
On On Hotel is a large hotel at 19 Phang Nga Street with rooms starting at 200B. It is in a good central location.

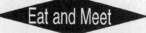

Eat and Meet

Mae Porn Restaurant is opposite Pengman Hotel on Phang Nga Street. This excellent restaurant has an extensive English menu at reasonable prices and friendly staff. The coconut shakes are divine.
Lotus Coffee Break on Phang Nga Street has decent food at decent prices. It is a nice place to catch up on news, but a shame about the surly staff.

Miano Restaurant at 54/10-11 Montri Road has a selection of tasty pizzas and cold beer.
Kanda Bakery This place on the roundabout separating Ratsada and Ramong Roads is great for a meal if you do not mind paying a lot for breakfast.

Rang Hill   เขารัง
Just a short walk from town is Rong Hill from where you can get a great view of the surrounding area. To get there follow Ranong Road to where it meets Patipat Road, turn right, cross Mae Luan Road and follow Ko Sim Be Road all the way until you get there.

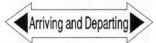

Air
THAI Airways has ten flights a day to Phuket from **Bangkok** for 2,000B. Other flights from Phuket include **Hat Yai** (780B), **Trang** (435B), **Surat Thani** (475B) and **Nakhon Si Thammarat** (690B). Flights connect to places further afield such as **Chiang Mai** (3,455B), **Khon Kaen** (3,050B), **Ubon** (3,295B) and **Udon** (3,300B). Bangkok Airways also flies to Ko Samui twice a day. A number of international charter flights also arrive in Phuket from London, Sydney, Kuala Lumpur, Hong Kong, Penang, Taipei, Seoul, Tokyo, as well as a number of places in Europe including Amsterdam, Brussels, Frankfurt and Vienna. Phuket International Airport is 32 km out of Phuket town.

Bus
Both ordinary and A/C buses can be caught from Phuket to most regional destinations at regular intervals throughout the day. Sample fares are set out below, all being departures from Phuket bus station.

Phuket Buses			
Destination	**Duration**	**Depart Phuket**	**Fare**
Bangkok (VIP)	14 hours	16.00, 17.00	570B
Bangkok (1st Class)	14 hours	17.30	378B
Bangkok (2nd Class)	14.5 hours	08.25, 14.25, 16.20, 17.30	294B
Bangkok Ordinary	15 hours	6 times a day between 06.00 and 18.30	210B
Hat Yai (A/C)	7 hours	7 times daily between 07.30 and 21.30	192B
Hat Yai Ordinary	8 hours	06.20, 07.40, 09.00, 10.20	112B
Krabi (A/C)	3 hours	every 30 minutes 07.00 - 18.30	84B
Krabi Ordinary	4 hours	10.50, 12.50, 14.30	47B
Nakhon Si Thammarat (A/C)	7 hours	07.20, 08.20	129B
Nakhon Si Thammarat Ord.	8 hours	9 times daily between 04.30 and 23.00	80B
Phattalung (A/C)	6 hours	11.00	116B
Phattalung Ordinary	7 hours	08.10	90B
Phang Nga Ordinary	2.5 hours	10.10, 12.00, 13.40, 15.30, 16.30	26B
Ranong (A/C)	5 hours	10.00, 12.00, 15.10	137B
Ranong Ordinary	6 hours	08.00, 11.20, 13.20	76B
Surat Thani (A/C)	5 hours	07.30, 09.00	139B
Surat Thani Ordinary	6 hours	8 times daily between 04.45 and 13.50	77B
Takua Pa Ordinary	3 hours	10 times daily between 06.20 and 18.00	38B
Trang (A/C)	5 hours	every hour 07.00 to 18.30	140B
Trang Ordinary	6 hours	9 times daily 04.15 to 12.20	78B

South

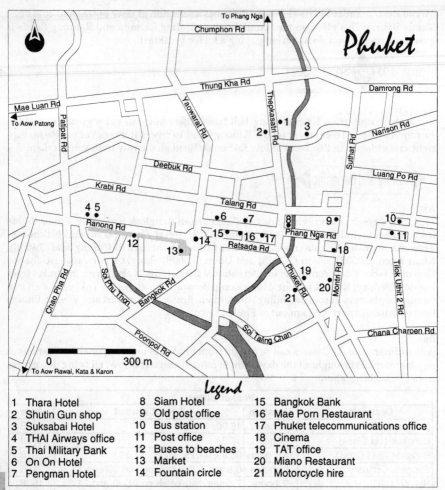

Legend

1	Thara Hotel	8	Siam Hotel	15	Bangkok Bank
2	Shutin Gun shop	9	Old post office	16	Mae Porn Restaurant
3	Suksabai Hotel	10	Bus station	17	Phuket telecommunications office
4	THAI Airways office	11	Post office	18	Cinema
5	Thai Military Bank	12	Buses to beaches	19	TAT office
6	On On Hotel	13	Market	20	Miano Restaurant
7	Pengman Hotel	14	Fountain circle	21	Motorcycle hire

Minibus

Travel agents in Phuket and at the beaches will organise minibuses at inflated prices to the destinations in the table as well as to Ko Samui, Ko Pha Ngan and so on.

Boat

The most common boat arrival point is from **Ko Phi Phi** and fares to and from this island range from 180B to 350B depending on the boat. From the ferry pier it is a 10B to 15B fare by tuk tuk into Phuket town depending on your bargaining ability. It is also possible to travel by yacht to **Malaysia** and sometimes **Sri Lanka** and further afield from Phuket — look out for notices in cafes for details and do not forget your immigration formalities. Boats can be taken from Bang Rong Pier in Phuket to get to **Ko Yao Noi** which is east of Phuket and west of Krabi and is covered in the section on Phang Nga Province.

Getting around on Phuket

Phuket is a large island but it is pretty easy to get around. Tuk tuks cost 7B within the city limits, although they often ask for more. You can also hire out a tuk tuk to a particular beach, however this can be quite expensive unless you can cram in a lot of people. Some of the 'official' chartered rates from Phuket are: Kamala Beach 200B, Karon 130B, Kata 130B, Patong 130B, Phuket Airport 250B, Rawai 90B and Surin 200B.

A far cheaper way of getting to the beaches from Phuket town is by local bus. Unfortunately the buses run only from Phuket town to a particular beach rather than beach to beach (though there are a couple of exceptions - Karon and Katon for example). The buses leave from the market on Ranong Road around every half an hour from 07.00 to 17.00. Fares are as follows: Aow Chalong 10B, Hat Mai Khao 20B, Kamala 20B, Karon and Kata 15B, Naiharn 20B, Nai Yang 20B, Patong 15B, Rawai 15B, Surin 15B, and Thalang town 10B.

Motorcycle
Honda Dreams (often of questionable quality) can be hired all over Phuket Island for between 150B and 250B per day, without insurance. Try and get insurance cover if possible. Exercise extreme caution as the drivers, particularly the foreign ones, on Phuket can be extremely dangerous. Larger bikes and Harley Davidsons can be hired at Patong. A motorcycle taxi within Phuket town should cost a flat 10B.

Hitching
The hitching is very good on Phuket Island, just do not expect any tourists to pick you up. After all, they know you have a hatchet in your backpack. Most of the roads have heaps of traffic, though north of Kamala to Noi Yang the traffic can be nonexistent. From Kata to Patong there are no problems.

Car
Huge road hogging, atmosphere clogging, gasoline guzzling 4WDs can be hired for around 800B to 1,000B with insurance. Make sure you clean the Honda Dreams off the radiator when you return it.

AROUND PHUKET PROVINCE

Beaches
Beaches in Phuket Province fall into three distinct categories. Those occupied by luxury hotels and up market bungalows, those with a mix of middle range places and those with a few budget places left over from the good ole days.

Phuket still has some lovely unspoilt beaches, but now you just have to look a lot harder. Most beaches will have deck chairs and umbrellas, but there are still some caves and small bays with little on them to disturb the natural environment. Take a ride from Rawai in the south to Nai Yang in the north and see what you find. Note that in the monsoon season, many of Phuket's beaches have dangerous riptides, so exercise caution. All of Phuket's best beaches are on the west coast and for simplicity's sake we will start from the south at Rawai Beach and work north all the way to Maikhao Beach.

Hat Rawai   หาดราไวย์
Situated 17 km to the southwest of Phuket town, around the point and to the west of Aow Chalong, this long quiet beach is an ideal place to stay if planning an offshore jaunt to **Ko Hae** (Coral Island), **Ko Bon**, and **Ko Lone**. It is also close to the spectacular cape **Laem Promthep** and **Wat Chalong**. There are a number of nicer beaches also within easy striking distance of Rawai including **Hat Laemkha** to the northeast and **Hat Nai Han** to the northwest.

Rawai is about a 20 minute bike ride from Phuket town or can be reached by bus for 15B, whilst a chartered tuk tuk will set you back 90B.

Cheap Sleeps

Siam Garden Resort is about 300 m towards Nai Han Beach from Pornmae. This upmarket resort has good rooms with fan and toilet starting at 500B and the pool and restaurant here are both great. There are also a few seafood places, bars and snack huts on the beach close to here.
Pornmae Bungalows are about half way down the beach, but set back from the road so it is fairly quiet. Huge bungalows with fridge and fan start at 300B. he restaurant is reasonable.

Hat Nai Han   หาดในหาน

To the northwest of Rawai and separated from it by Laem Promthep, this very nice beach is home to the prestigious Phuket Yacht Club, but do not be put off as there are still some fairly cheap places to stay. Nai Han is also home to **Samnak Song Nai Han** — a monastic centre and one of the main reasons it is still largely underdeveloped. A bus from Phuket town to Nai Han Beach costs 20B and a tuk tuk charter, 130B. To get to Aow Sane and Jungle Beach, you need to wander through the Phuket Yacht Club and follow the dirt road for about 1 km.

Cheap Sleeps

Coconut Huts set on the hill before the entrance to the Phuket Yacht Club. These rustic bamboo bungalows will set you back a mere 100B for great views.
Ao Sane Bungalows are situated in a lovely little cove west of the Phuket Yacht Club. This is a family run operation with rates starting at 250B and 300B. The restaurant is very reasonably priced. The Spanish omelette is yummy.
Jungle Beach Resort is in the bay further west from Aow Sane. This delightful resort's rates range from 400B to 4,500B. There is a big pool, lovely gardens and a quaint little beach.

Nai Beach Lookout

About 5 km north of Nai Han Beach is a dirt track turning off to your left to Nai Beach. The road goes for 2 km and the beach is quite nice. About 1 km further along there is a large lookout with scenic views up the coast to Kata and Karon Beaches. About 1 km further on there is some elephant 'trekking' which you can do - just look out for the signs.

Hat Kata   หาดกะตะ

Of Phuket's highly developed beaches (Kata, Karon and Patong), Kata, 17 km from Phuket town, is probably the quietest and has the best value accommodation. The beach is split in two with Kata Noi to the south and the much longer Kata Yai to the north. Kata Yai is home to Club Med, and Kata Noi has a number of very up-market places as well. The main town of Kata Yai has a number of bars and restaurants but unfortunately it can be quite a challenge to find any decent, cheap Thai places to eat. Both the beaches are nice and the water crystal clear (if you can get to it through all the deck chairs). Kata also has plenty of dive shops and travel agents.

A bus from Phuket town to Kata costs 15B and goes via Karon Beach. A chartered tuk tuk costs 130B.

Cheap Sleeps

Kata Noi

There are only two 'budget' places on this beach, and signs of further up-market development abound. Most of the restaurants here are quite pricey, so if you elect to stay here riding into Kata Yai for food may be your best option.
Katanoi Riviera sits almost behind the large Kata Thani Hotel. Rooms here start at 300B and when the staff are awake, they are very helpful.

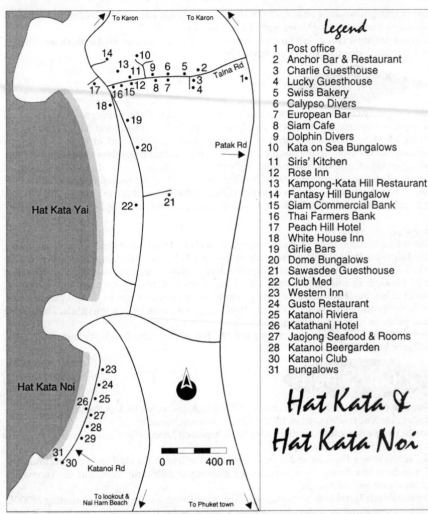

Legend

1 Post office
2 Anchor Bar & Restaurant
3 Charlie Guesthouse
4 Lucky Guesthouse
5 Swiss Bakery
6 Calypso Divers
7 European Bar
8 Siam Cafe
9 Dolphin Divers
10 Kata on Sea Bungalows
11 Siris' Kitchen
12 Rose Inn
13 Kampong-Kata Hill Restaurant
14 Fantasy Hill Bungalow
15 Siam Commercial Bank
16 Thai Farmers Bank
17 Peach Hill Hotel
18 White House Inn
19 Girlie Bars
20 Dome Bungalows
21 Sawasdee Guesthouse
22 Club Med
23 Western Inn
24 Gusto Restaurant
25 Katanoi Riviera
26 Katathani Hotel
27 Jaojong Seafood & Rooms
28 Katanoi Beergarden
30 Katanoi Club
31 Bungalows

Hat Kata & Hat Kata Noi

To Karon   To Karon

Taina Rd

Patak Rd

Hat Kata Yai

Hat Kata Noi

Katanoi Rd

To lookout &
Nai Harn Beach   To Phuket town

0   400 m

Jao Jong Seafood have rooms that start at 300B and the seafood is not too bad.
Katonoi Club is a quiet resort at the end of the road starting at an overpriced 500B, though the staff are nice. The bungalows on the hill charge a starting rate of 600B.

Kata Yai

The bulk of budget accommodation in Kata Yai is intermingled with bars and restaurants along Taina Road. There is also a post office on the main road leading back to Phuket town.
Fantasy Hill Bungalows are probably the pick of the bunch in Kata Yai. This operation is quiet and the staff friendly. Large rooms with shower and fan cost 200B.
Kata On Sea Bungalows are more centrally locate. This nice resort has huge bungalows on the hill above Kata with a great view. All rooms have shower and fan starting at 300B.
Rose Inn is about as central to the strip as you can get. Rooms with shower start at 250B. The staff are rather surly and tend to take out their frustrations on guests.
Lucky Guest House and **Charlies Guest House** are on a soi off the main road. These places offer the stock standard room at an expensive 350B with shower and fan.

Dome Bungalows are a bit away from the centre of town. However this nicely landscaped residence has large bungalows with shower and fan for 300B.

Sawasdee Guest House is a fair way from town. Rooms start at 300B with share shower, but the rate drops to 150B if you stay a week.

Eat and Meet

Unfortunately cheap Thai eating houses do not abound in Kata. Some noodle stalls set up at night, but otherwise get ready to visit Europe with Swiss, German and Italian restaurants. **Kampong Kata Hill Restaurant** is the most popular restaurant in Kata. It is worth visiting just to check out the place, even if you cannot afford to eat there. It comes complete with great staff, awesome decor and enjoyable atmosphere.

There are also bars with satellite TV further up the road - great for catching up with world sport. **The Anchor Bar and Restaurant** is one of the better ones, and the **Voodoo Bar** is not too bad for an evening drink and has great glass topped tables displaying voodoo dolls.

Hat Karon   หาดกะ รน

Karon Beach, 20 km from Phuket town, has the feel of a Thai tourist ghost town. Dilapidated buildings side by side with plush multi-storey hotels, bars and restaurants. The beach here is nice and some sections do not even have deck chairs, though you may have to dodge jet skis, parasailers and windsurfers. Like Kata, there is definitely no oversupply of great places to eat, but there are some good places to sleep. There is some big development going on in the centre of the beach as Karon tries to inject a bit more zest into itself. There is no post office in Karon, the closest is at Kata.

A bus from Phuket town costs 15B and returns via Kata Beach. A chartered tuk tuk will cost you 130B.

Cheap Sleeps

Brazil is on a quiet lane off the centre of the beach and is the pick of the bunch for places to stay. Decent rooms start at 150B and the staff are friendly.

Robin House is about five minutes from the beach on Luang Pho Chuon Road with rooms starting at 250B with shower.

J&J Inn is located nearby and is similarly priced although the staff are quite indifferent.

Karon Seaview Bungalows have rooms starting at 200B and 250B, but the rooms are pretty small and quite ugly.

Crystal Beach Hotel in downtown Karon has rooms with a shower and fan starting at 300B.

Karon Bungalows is perfect if you want a bland, noisy bungalow on the beach. Rooms with a shower start at 300B.

My Friend Restaurant and Bungalow is a popular place on the beach, although quite noisy. Rooms with fan and shower cost 300B.

Prayoon Bungalows is set at the end of a dirt road towards the southern end of the beach. Large quiet bungalows with shower start at 350B.

Guesthouse This no-name dump is up the soi from the Melon Karon Hotel. Rooms with share shower start at 250B, but it really is only for the desperate.

Eat and Meet

Most of the restaurants in Karon offer Western style food, though some of the cafes on the beach do tasty noodles and other dishes. **My Friend Restaurant** is not a bad choice for standard Khao San Road style fare.

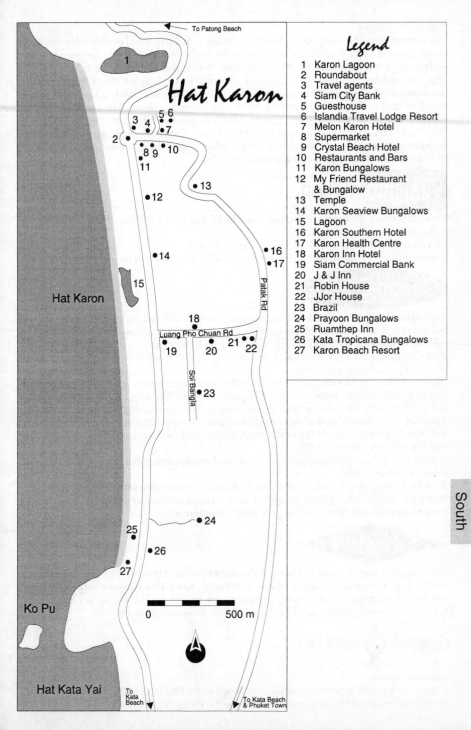

Hat Karon

Legend

1 Karon Lagoon
2 Roundabout
3 Travel agents
4 Siam City Bank
5 Guesthouse
6 Islandia Travel Lodge Resort
7 Melon Karon Hotel
8 Supermarket
9 Crystal Beach Hotel
10 Restaurants and Bars
11 Karon Bungalows
12 My Friend Restaurant & Bungalow
13 Temple
14 Karon Seaview Bungalows
15 Lagoon
16 Karon Southern Hotel
17 Karon Health Centre
18 Karon Inn Hotel
19 Siam Commercial Bank
20 J & J Inn
21 Robin House
22 JJor House
23 Brazil
24 Prayoon Bungalows
25 Ruamthep Inn
26 Kata Tropicana Bungalows
27 Karon Beach Resort

To Patong Beach

Hat Karon

Patak Rd

Luang Pho Chuan Rd

Soi Bangla

Ko Pu

0   500 m

Hat Kata Yai

To Kata Beach

To Kata Beach & Phuket Town

South

Patong   ป่าตอง

The current state of Patong, 15 km from Phuket town, is the result of overdevelopment and desperate and dateless tourists. Do not cross the roads for fear of being rundown by crazy Germans on their Harleys on the wrong side of the road. Beat your way through the beggars, buskers, con men, pick pockets, and prostitutes to find that the only places to eat are overpriced Mexican, German, Austrian, Italian, Australian and Indian restaurants. Head to the beach to be bothered by beach chair renters, parasailing vendors and hair plaiters. The town is a den of sex and sin bars with places aptly named as Red Hot, Kiss Me, I Love You, Exotic Woman and Paradise Girl Bar. Catapulting and go karting are two popular pastimes. If you want to find a noodle bar — good luck. A bus from Phuket town to Patong costs 15B and a chartered tuk tuk is 130B.

Vital Information

Post Office is on the corner of Thaweewong Road and Soi Post Office. It has a full overseas call office and is open until late.

Hospital is on Sawatdirak Road east of Ratuthit Road.

Tourist Police are located on Thaweewong Road, a block north of the post office.

Cheap Sleeps

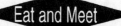

The vast majority of accommodation in Patong is over 300B and for anything less you will not get much. If you are intent on spending time in Patong, you will save a lot a cash by staying in Karon or Kata and riding or hitching up to here even on a daily basis.

Best Guesthouse is centrally located for the crazy nightlife of Patong, but this is not much of a claim. Rooms start at 250B.

Asia Guesthouse is around the corner from Best and rooms with a share shower cost 250B.

Sea Dragon is facing a huge concoction of girlie bars, and has large rooms with shower for 350B. Try to get a room away from the bar side if you want to have any sleep at all.

Charlies on Soi San Sabai is a fairly quiet place (for Patong) with rooms for 300B and 350B.

Suk San Mansion is down the road from Charlies and an overpriced room with shower and fan will set you back 450B.

Nordic Bungalows This inappropriately named establishment has decent and insulated rooms starting at 500B.

KSR Hotel is central located on the beach. Average rooms with shower start at 400B.

Many places on Patong tend to appear and disappear without notice, so have a look around on your arrival, a new 'bargain' may have shown up.

Eat and Meet

There are very few cheap places to eat in Patong and most of them serve Western food such as steaks, pasta and pizza. Those restaurants that do serve Thai cuisine charge exorbitant prices. **Soi Bangla** is about as good a place as any to look for something to fill you up.

S & G Restaurant serves tasty Thai food at fairly reasonable prices.

Things to do and Sights to See

Similan Islands

Patong is a popular launching point for day trips to the Similans. Prices start at 1,600B and the boat takes around three hours each way. See the Phang Nga Province section for details.

South

Flight of your life

Ever felt like being catapulted - well you can finally do this at the Ex-pat Hotel for just 600B, including an 'I did it' T-shirt. It is open from 7.00 pm until late and promises a great view of Patong (for about 2 seconds).

Nightlife

Once the sun goes down, Patong awakens. The only place in Thailand with more girlie bars than Patong is probably Pattaya. Row after row of small bars fill up after dark and bear witness to Thai girls chatting up inebriated Westerners. If this is your scene you may want to read the AIDS section in the introduction to this book. Patong also has a very lively gay scene, concentrated along Sawatdirak Road and towards the Paradise complex on Ratathit Road.

For a full summary of the evening events, take a look at 'Phuket', a free monthly entertainment guide available from most travel agents .

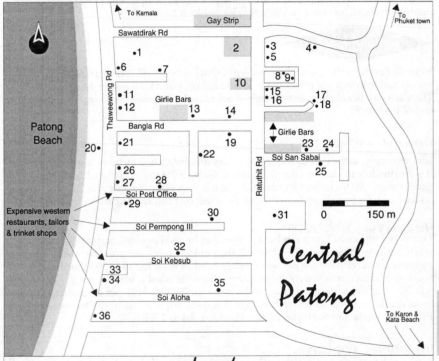

Central Patong

Legend

1	Porn Phateep Guesthouse	13	Sea Dragon Hotel	25 Charlies Guesthouse
2	School	14	Nordic Bungalows	26 Bank of Ayudhya
3	7-eleven	15	Thai Farmers Bank	27 World Gems
4	Hospital	16	PS Guesthouse	28 S &G Restaurant
5	Paradise Corner Guesthouse	17	Catapult	29 Post office
6	KSR Hotel	18	Expat Hotel	30 Viva Mexico
7	Al Vechio Venezia	19	Le Croissant	31 Patong Night Plaza
8	Best Guesthouse	20	Tourist police	32 Oasis Bungalows
9	Asia Guesthouse	21	Patong Beach Hotel	33 Andaman Square
10	Night Food Market		& Disco Banana	34 Paradise Bungalows
11	Siam City Bank	22	Buffalo Steak House	35 Fitness Club
12	Safari Beach Hotel	23	Suksan Mansion	36 Patong Merlin Hotel
		24	Villa Swiss Garden	

Hat Kamala   หาดกมลา

North of Patong and about 10 to 15 minutes by motorbike, this quiet beach forms a stark contrast to the dubious 'high life' of Patong and has some fairly cheap places to stay. Some of the beach turns to mud flats at low tide, but the northern end is particularly beautiful. To Reach Kamala Beach the bus from Phuket town costs 20B, while a chartered tuk tuk is 200B.

Cheap Sleeps

Charoen Seafood is a restaurant in the village of Kamala which rents large twin rooms with shower for 250B and their seafood is not too bad.

In the other half of town (take the left turn by the police station sign and follow the road) you will find that some houses will rent you a room at very reasonable rates. Try 95/1 about half way to the end of the road. These places tend to open and close on a somewhat random basis, so just ask anywhere that looks like it has room.

Eat and Meet

Kamala Beach Pavilion is at the southern end of the beach. This restaurant has good food at reasonable prices and offers an excellent vantage point for a sunset dinner.

There is a number of other mainly seafood orientated restaurants backing onto the northern end of the beach.

Hat Surin   หาดสุรินทร์

Unfortunately, at the time of writing, this very nice beach had no budget accommodation. It is worthwhile to visit on a day trip from Kamala or Patong as the beach has a number of good restaurants to choose from and the water is very clear. You are also allowed to camp on the beach for free. A bus from Phuket town will cost 15B and a chartered tuk tuk is 200B.

Hat Bang Tao   หาดบางเทา

This very long, clear beach has been dominated by the Laguna Complex. The Laguna is worth visiting to see how the other half live, but the rates are over the moon. It is very pleasant if you visit for the day as you only need to walk for 15 to 30 minutes along the beach to reach your own private paradise. When the wind is up, this is a great place for windsurfing and some good gear can be hired for 200B to 300B per hour. Bang Tao also hosts the Siam World Cup Windsurfing Championships. A bus from Phuket town costs 15B (via Kamala and Surin) and a chartered tuk tuk is 170B.

Hat Naithon   หาดในทอน

Between Bang Tao and Naithon there are three beautiful, secluded and completely undeveloped beaches (except for a few deck chair merchants). Naithon Beach itself is a very long, quiet, clean beach with only one resort on it, the aptly named **Naithon Beach Resort**. It has fantastic bungalows with fan and shower starting at a worthwhile 800B, whilst the luxury ones cost 1,200B. The ride from Naithon north to Nai Yang is reminiscent of Vietnamese landscape (for those who have been there). At Naithon Beach Resort the mixed fruit shakes are delicious. A bus from Phuket town to Naithon costs 30B.

Hat Nai Yang and Nai Yang National Park   หาดในยาง

This very long and unspoilt beach stretches for 13 km, south from Sarasin Bridge, and is part of Nai Yang National Park. It was established on 13 July 1981, and covers 90 sq km. There is a 10B entry fee (20B with motorcycle) and the beach is shaded with casuarina trees. There is a reef offshore with good snorkelling and plentiful fish (there is a no fishing zone for the first 5 km offshore). On 13 April every year there is a turtle release festival when baby turtles are released back to the sea by the Fisheries Department. At the same place throughout November to March turtles come here to lay as many as 15,000 eggs. Four different species of endangered turtle frequent the park, however their numbers are still dwindling despite the Fisheries Department involvement.

The National Park office has a number of big bungalows for rent starting at 250B. Camping is also allowed. Route 4026 through to Nai Yang Beach is a very nice and cool ride through large rubber plantations.

A chartered tuk tuk will set you back 250B, whilst the bus fare is 20B. The park headquarters are near Phuket's International Airport, just follow route 4031 or 4036.

Hat Mai Khao   หาดไม้ขาว
This is Phuket's northernmost and largest beach with no real development. The turtle releasing festival also takes place here so it is worth coming up in mid April. Ask at the National Park Office for further details. A bus from Phuket town costs 20B.

AROUND PHUKET PROVINCE

Khao Phra Taew National Park   อุทยานสัตว์ป่าเขาพระแทว
North of Thalang town in the centre of Phuket Island is the turn-off to **Namtok Ton Sai**. The waterfall is nothing amazing but the National Park has some of Phuket's best remaining rainforest.

Gibbon Rehabilitation Centre
This centre is dedicated to preparing gibbons for life in the open rather than in cages. It is estimated that there are more gibbons in captivity in Phuket than in the wild. It is worth visiting and any donations are appreciated. To get there follow Route 4027 north of the heroes monument and take the left turn as marked. Not much further north is **Bang Pae Waterfall**, worth visiting if you are in the area.

Horse Riding
Horse riding is available at Phuket Riding Club, off route 4024 on Chalong Bay.

Bungy Jumping
Tarzano Bungy Jump is in Kathu District to the west of Phuket town on the road to Patong.

Islands
From Rawai Beach you can do boat trips to **Ko Hae** (Coral Island), **Ko Raya Yai**, **Ko Bon** and **Ko Lone** for snorkelling and diving. Shop around as rates vary tremendously. **Ko Siray** is to the east of Phuket town. This interesting island is separated from Phuket by a canal and has some sea gypsy (Chao Nam) villages. Accommodation is available on Ko Siray and there is an upmarket resort on Ko Hae. See Patong section for prices on boats to the Similans, trips start at 1,600B and skyrocket to 15,000B plus for multiple day stays. See Phang Nga Province for details on the Similan Islands.

Canoe and Kayak Trips
From Phuket you can organise to go on either day or overnight trips into Phang Nga Bay. Experienced guides take you through the maze of limestone outcrops, but even more amazing are the hongs (collapsed caves) that are hidden within them. These lagoons are only accessible via sea caves, and a journey through a dark, mystical cave opens up to a sunsoaked world, with plants, animals and marine life oblivious to anything but their own paradise.

South

Arriving and Departing

From Phuket Province to Ko Yao Noi
Boats leave Bang Rong pier on the northeast side of the island. To get there you can catch a bus from Ratsada Road to the pier for 20B. The last bus leaves Phuket at 11.00. Otherwise you can hire a tuk tuk for 200B.

From the pier a few cheap boats leave, but only until 11.00 costing 40B to 80B per person depending on the boat. After 11.00 you need to charter a boat for the trip which will cost 500B or more. There is nowhere to stay in Bang Rong, so its best to make sure you get to the pier on time.

NAKHON SI THAMMARAT PROVINCE

This little visited province on the east coast between Surat Thani to the north, Surat Thani and Phattalung to the south and Krabi to the west is predominantly mountainous with some substantial forest areas, notably Khao Luang National Park. There are also some pretty coastal villages and Nakhon Si Thammarat town itself is not a bad spot to spend a couple of days, so all in all another interesting off beat destination.

NAKHON SI THAMMARAT   นครศรีธรรมราช

Nakhon Si Thammarat was traditionally one of southern Thailand's commercial and transportation hubs. Now this role has now been taken over by booming high rise Hat Yai. As a result Nakhon Si Thammarat is a lot more pleasant than Hat Yai. Quite well set up for tourism, Nakhon Si Thammarat has an excellent transportation network, some good, cheap hotels, plenty of religious sites and loads of great food along with a large and helpful TAT office. The only things missing are the farangs themselves! The city is 780 km from Bangkok and has a population of around 80,000.

Orientation

Long and narrow, Nakhon Si Thammarat consists basically of three or four parallel streets stretching from north to south for several kilometres. The newer and busier part of town with most of the hotels, shops and restaurants is to the north around the train station whilst the older part to the south has the main wats and the museums.

Vital Information

TAT Office is next to the park at the southern end of town, ☎ (075) 356356.
Post Office is on Si Prat Road, near the roundabout at the southern end of town.
Banks There are numerous banks along Ratchadamnoen Road and on weekends the Thai Hotel will exchange cash and travellers cheques.
Police Station is at the southern end of town, by the roundabout.
Hospital There is the municipal hospital opposite the city park or a Christian hospital to the east of the centre of town.
Codes Nakhon Si Thammarat's telephone code is (075) and the postal code is 80000.

> Of the southern Thai cities, Nakhon Si Thammarat is one of the more idiosyncratic. At one stage ruled by a Japanese Samurai, Nakhon appeared to feel a closer connection with its immediate neighbours than the faraway overlords in central Thailand. This influence is displayed in the local Buddhas which exhibit notable Polynesian features.

South

Cheap Sleeps

Most of Nakhon Si Thammarat's cheaper hotels are concentrated in a small area of central town within five minutes walk of the train station. There are no guesthouses as yet but there is a wide choice of budget hotels, but as usual many of the cheapest double as brothels.

Thai Lee Hotel ☎ (075) 356 948, at 1130 Ratchadamnoen Road is probably the best bet, a new very clean hotel with large rooms with fan and shower for 120B. This is a quiet spot with a midnight curfew and a 'no girlies' policy.

Thai Far ☎ (075) 356 727, at 1751 Charoen Withi Road has no roman script sign but is friendly and clean and the rates start at 100B.

Nakmorn Hotel ☎ (075) 356 318, at 1477/5 Yommarat Road is passable at 120B for a room with fan shower, but it can get a bit sordid.

Yaowarat Hotel ☎ (075) 356 089, at 1475 Yommarat Road is very similar to the Nakorn Hotel but starts at 150B and is equally sleazy.

Muang Thong Hotel is by the night market and better value than the above two and starts at 130B for fan and shower.

Bua Luang Hotel ☎ (075) 341 518, at 1487/19 Soi Luang Muang Chamroen Withi Road also has a busy night trade but the rooms are clean and start at 170B.

Montien Hotel on Yommarat Road is a bit more up-market and is the large concrete block by the train station. Rooms with fan and shower start at 220B and A/C rooms start at 360B.

Thai Hotel ☎ (075) 341 509, at 1375 Ratchadamnoen Road is very reasonably priced given the high standard, with singles/doubles starting at 230B/290B and A/C starting at 490B.

Eat and Meet

This is a great town for eating with food stalls and cafes everywhere in the centre of town, with Thai, Muslim and Chinese coffee shops and local specialities. The **night market** on Charoen Withi Road has all the usual goodies and many of the stalls are open all day. The alley between Ratchadamnoen Road and the market has a couple of **good cafes** as well as an **excellent Chinese bakery** and coffee shop.

The alley leading to the so called **'Bovon Bazaar'** has some good **roti** spots as well as a stall selling the local speciality of *Khao Man Gaeng*. This is a kind of very small grained rice, vaguely similar to Basmanti rice, only grown in Nakhon Si Thammarat Province and is served with either a prawn, beef or chicken curry for 12B - delicious! The bazaar itself is a recent development containing a couple of bars and restaurants around a quiet square set off Ratchadamnoen Road. There are also a couple of very good, slightly more up-market restaurants. Do not forget to check out the huge tree in the middle of the square - it must be at least 200 years old. Also in the Bazaar is a farang orientated bar, but without any farangs! It is called **99% Rock** and has, surprisingly, rock videos, beer and an extensive Western menu with everything from pizza to hot dogs and beef stroganoff.

South

Things to do and Sights to See

Walking tour of Nakhon Si Thammarat
The older part of town and most of its sights are a short walk from the centre of town. Start walking south on Ratchadamnoen Road allowing you to nip into the TAT office near the park where helpful and friendly staff can provide you with additional information. There are some moderately interesting handicraft stores in the small street behind it. Jewellery, and particularly silverware, is a local speciality and is relatively cheap.

Carrying on down Ratchadamnoen Road, cross over the canal to see the remnants of the **city wall** and the old northern gate. There is about a 100 m stretch of the impressive city rampart remaining, dating originally back to the 14th Century. This wall once stretched over 400 m from east to west and over 2 km from north to south, which indicates the size and importance of Nakhon Si Thammarat at that time.

Walking south for another 1 km you will reach **Wat Phra Mahathat**, which is Nakhon Si Thammarat's landmark and most famous sight. This wat is indeed very impressive and must be one of the largest and most spectacular outside Bangkok. A beautiful courtyard area contains a 77 m high pagoda/chedi dating (according to the

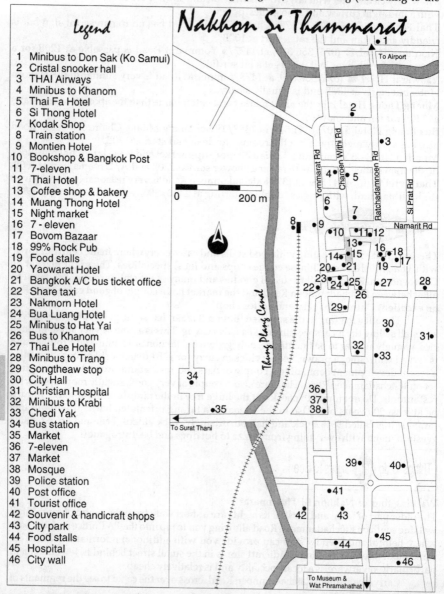

Nakhon Si Thammarat

Legend

1   Minibus to Don Sak (Ko Samui)
2   Cristal snooker hall
3   THAI Airways
4   Minibus to Khanom
5   Thai Fa Hotel
6   Si Thong Hotel
7   Kodak Shop
8   Train station
9   Montien Hotel
10 Bookshop & Bangkok Post
11 7-eleven
12 Thai Hotel
13 Coffee shop & bakery
14 Muang Thong Hotel
15 Night market
16 7 - eleven
17 Bovom Bazaar
18 99% Rock Pub
19 Food stalls
20 Yaowarat Hotel
21 Bangkok A/C bus ticket office
22 Share taxi
23 Nakmorn Hotel
24 Bua Luang Hotel
25 Minibus to Hat Yai
26 Bus to Khanom
27 Thai Lee Hotel
28 Minibus to Trang
29 Songtheaw stop
30 City Hall
31 Christian Hospital
32 Minibus to Krabi
33 Chedi Yak
34 Bus station
35 Market
36 7-eleven
37 Market
38 Mosque
39 Police station
40 Post office
41 Tourist office
42 Souvenir & handicraft shops
43 City park
44 Food stalls
45 Hospital
46 City wall

South

TAT) to 555AD and was restored during the Srivijaya Period. The marbled courtyard also contains numerous smaller chedis, Buddha filled cloisters and, for some reason, a 12 m whale skeleton! There is also an interesting museum housed in a beautiful old temple building and although 20B admission may seem a little steep, there is an incredible range of objects crammed in there. Unfortunately there are no explanations in English and very few in Thai, so it becomes a bewildering array of religious items, weaponry, household objects, pottery and everything else under the sun strewn around or piled up in dingy corners collecting dust! The collection of antique jewellery and Chinese porcelain must be worth a fortune, and the security consists of a wizened old lady with a broom! Be careful not to step on any of the exhibits and a torch for searching through the dark corners would be of use. This is a crazy museum comparable to an ancient Egyptian tomb which has been untouched for thousands of years and it holds everything from stone age goods to recent acquisitions.

Continue down Ratchadamnoen Road for another kilometre or so and you will reach a second, larger but more normal museum, the **Nakhon Si Thammart Museum**. It is much better presented and explained than the wat museum and contains an equally large number of exhibits from various historical periods plus a large folklore and handicraft section. The museum is open Wednesday to Sunday from 8.30 am to 4.30 pm and admission is 8B.

To get back into town, flag down one of the passing songtheaws and for a couple of baht ride back into town.

The older area of Nakhon Si Thammarat is packed with other interesting wats and temples, ask at the TAT office for their suggested walking tour of these sites.

Puppetry
Both Nakhon Si Thammarat and Phattalung are well known for their shadow puppetry. The puppets are cut from buffalo hide then carved intricately into characters from Thai drama stories. Today the shows are becoming increasingly rare but the TAT will be able to point you in the right direction if you would like to see one.

Markets
A very large food market is located near the bus station and further down the same road is an entertaining Saturday cattle market. It is a few kilometres out of town, so hop on a songtheaw and ask for *Taalat Nua-Sat*.

◀ Arriving and Departing ▶

Getting Around
Nakhon Si Thammarat has excellent local and long distance connections. There is a large centralised share taxi stand on Yommarat Road for Hat Yai, Surat Thani, Krabi and Songkhla, and there are various minibus services from around town to the same destinations. There is a huge songtheaw station on Charoen Withi Road with songtheaws leaving every 5 minutes to virtually all conceivable destinations. The main bus station is a 15 minute walk from the centre of town, although tickets can be purchased on Charoen Withi Road by the night market.

South

Air
THAI Airways to **Bangkok** every day for 1,770B as well as to **Narathiwat** (835B), **Phuket** (690B), **Surat Thani** (340B) and **Trang** (560B).

Train
The train station is conveniently located in the centre of town. Refer to the timetable at the end of the chapter for details.

Bus

Buses can be caught from Nakhon Si Thammarat to all over southern Thailand. The chart below lists the more common services.

Nakhon Si Thammarat Buses			
Destination	Duration	Depart Nakhon Si Thammarat	Fare
Bangkok 1st Class	12 hours	17.30, 17.40	400B
Bangkok Ordinary	12 hours	07.00, 08.30, 16.30, 17.30, 18.30	190B
Bangkok 2nd Class A/C	12 hours	17.30, 17.40	266B
Hat Yai A/C	2.5 hours	07.10 to 17.40 every 40 minutes	80B
Hat Yai Ordinary	3.5 hours	05.00 to 16.15 every 40 minutes	55B
Phuket A/C	5.5 hours	06.00 to 16.00 every 30 minutes	150B
Phuket Ordinary	7 hours	04.00 to 10.20 every 30 minutes	93B
Krabi A/C	2 hours	04.00 to 10.00 every 30 minutes	80B
Krabi Ordinary	3 hours	04.00 to 10.00 every 30 minutes	50B
Trang A/C	3 hours	07.00 to 17.00 every 30 minutes	60B
Surat Thani	3.5 hours	06.00 to 16.00 every 30 minutes	52B
Surat Thani Ordinary	3.5 hours	04.50 to 16.20 every 30 minutes	37B
Don Sak (for Ko Samui)	2 hours	07.15 to 11.30	60B
Phattalung Ordinary	3 hours	05.30 to 16.30 every 30 minutes	32B
Songkhla Ordinary	3 hours	05.15 to 15.00 every 30 minutes	47B
Songkhla A/C	2.5 hours	11.35, 13.00, 13.50	72B

AROUND NAKHON SI THAMMARAT

There are plenty of things to see around Nakhon Si Thammarat and it is all made very easy by the particularly efficient songtheaw services.

Khao Luang National Park   อุทยานแห่งชาติเขาหลวง

This park has 570 sq km of jungle covered mountains with some spectacular waterfalls and good hiking. The highlight is **Khao Luang Mountain** itself, south Thailand's highest peak at 1,835 m (see the Khiriwong section for details on climbing the peak). The park has an unfortunate history. In 1988 a huge landslide killed over 300 people with a contributing factor being deforestation. Now logging has stopped, at least in the surrounding area. The park headquarters are situated in Lan Saka District, 29 km from Nakhon Si Thammarat, 3 km off the main road by Karom Waterfall. The visitors centre has a good map of the park and plenty of pretty photos, but unfortunately no information in English. Not much English is spoken here, as few farangs ever visit this area. There is also a small cafe, and large wooden bungalows are available for 400B per night and tents are also for rent.

The park contains some spectacular scenery, a mixture of limestone outcrops and granite massifs with a correspondingly varied flora including tropical rainforest, tropical deciduous, bamboo forest and plenty of giant tree ferns. Locals also claim that the rare Rafflesia flower, supposedly only found in Kaeng Krachan National Park can also be found here. Deer, Tapir and wild cats are amongst the mammals found in the park, although it is too small to support populations of the larger mammals. Several easy hikes from the park headquarters can be done, and the staff may be able to show you around for 200B to 300B per day.

Namtok Karom is 300 m from the park office and is very popular with Thais on the weekends. It is a great waterfall, even for jaded 'namtokkers'. Water cascades from a height of 1,000 m in all, over a series of cliffs and boulder strewn slopes, creating at least ten different levels with some great bathing spots. The lower levels are very popular whilst the higher ones have great views and are rarely visited. However watch out for the voracious leeches. An east trail leads up to the top level where you can follow the river off through the jungle surrounded by giant tree ferns and plentiful bird and butterfly life.

Namtok Phrom Lok is even more spectacular, with three main levels. This waterfall is also very popular during the weekend. It is 26 km from Nakhon Si Thammarat in Khiriwong District. A songtheaw direct from Nakhon Si Thammarat costs 15B.

Namtok Krung Ching is 70 km from Nakhon Si Thammarat and is very impressive. There is also an elephant training school here and park accommodation. A songtheaw from Nakhon Si Thammarat costs 35B and takes 2 hours and will drop you on the main road, then it is a 4 km walk, hitch or motorbike taxi ride to the waterfall.

◀ Arriving and Departing ▶

Direct songtheaws run from Charoen Withi Road to the park entrance which is 3 km off the main road but there are no motorcycle taxis. During the week, if songtheaws are hard to find, walk or hitch to the main road and flag down any bus or songtheaw going back to town.

Ban Khiriwong

This charming village is nestled at the foot of the mountains by a rocky stream and is the departure point for the **ascent of Khao Luang Mountain**. The village is surrounded by fruit orchards and there are some nice hikes around the village and also some waterfalls within walking distance.

Khao Luang rises up from little over sea-level at Khiriwong to 1,835 m, making it a spectacular sight. The peak is often cloud covered. This was one of the last hideouts of the CPT guerillas and it is hard to believe that only 15 years ago, this was the scene of fierce fighting. The Thai government forces pounded the CPT tunnel systems on the peak with fighter bombers, to no avail until the guerillas finally gave up of there own accord following an amnesty offer. It takes at least two days to hike to the peak and back and you will definitely need a guide. Expect to pay around 300B per day for a guide and 300B a day for a porter. English speaking guides will be difficult to find. The hiking can be fairly tough going, but the scenery can be stunning. Note it can get cool in the evenings, so some warm clothing would be an asset.

A good place to try to organise a trek and an interesting spot to stay is at **Mr Nui's house** on the edge of the village by the river. Mr Nui has four basic but clean bamboo huts for 100B per night and will provide breakfast and dinner if desired. Washing is done in the river. Mr Nui is a very friendly guy and organises Khiriwong's Nascent Ecotourism Project but unfortunately speaks no English. Fortunately his son, Art does, so you should have no problems. Ask in the village for Mr Nui, his house is 1 km out of the village and to reach it by motorbike taxi will cost 7B. If you are thinking of staying here, mention it to the TAT office in Nakhon Si Thammarat as they work with Mr Nui and can help to sort things out.

Ban Khiriwong has a small market, a small wat, a couple of shops and a noodle shop by the market. Direct songtheaws from Nakhon Si Thammarat leave from Charoen Withi Road and cost 15B to cover the 23 km.

Nakhon Si Thammarat Beaches

The best and most popular beaches in the north of the province are up around the Don Sak area in Surat Thani Province. **Hat Khanom** is 80 km from Nakhon Si Thammarat and is a pretty beach with a range of accommodation. It is very popular on weekends. If you want to stay here, try **Watanyoo Villa** at **Na Dan Beach** with huts ranging from 120B to 400B. Or on **Nai Phlao Beach** the **Fern Bay** has huts for 300B and both of these places are just to the south of Khanom Beach. Buses from near the Thai Lee Hotel in Nakhon Si Thammarat will drop you at any resort in Khanom you want. **Hat Sichon** and **Hat Ngam** are slightly closer to Nakhon Si Thammarat and are also very pretty. Direct songtheaws from Nakhon Si Thammarat are available and **Hin Ngam Bungalows** has huts for 150B and is a good place to stay.

Namtok Yong National Park   อุทยานแห่งชาติน้ำตกโยง

This park stretches over 200 sq km and apart from the rainforest itself holds quite a few natural sites which are great for waterfall enthusiasts. The sites are predominately made up of waterfalls including **Namtok Khao Men** and **Namtok Nan Pliw** (both reaching 20 m), **Namtok Khlong Jang** (reaching 15 m), as well as others such as the **Namtok Yong** and **Yong Noi**. It is possible to hire a guide at the park headquarters. Camp sites are available but bring your own equipment.

KRABI PROVINCE

Both Krabi and Trang Provinces contain rainforest which remains the habitat for the fortunate Gurney's Pitta. This small, yellow bellied bird was thought to be extinct. In 1986 some were found in this region, but only 13 pairs are known to be alive. For the birdwatcher, the rainforest is a must as it is also home to other feathered rarities. Krabi Province has only two seasons, the hot and the wet, the latter of which stretches from May till December.

What follows is a coverage of many of the main sights in Krabi Province, but for those who want to see the province inside out, there are two indispensable purchases. *Krabi Holiday Guide* by Ken Scott which is available throughout Krabi and covers the area comprehensively and is a bargain at 90B and V. Hongsombud's map, *Guide Map of Krabi* (50B), is also an indispensable source of information on the out of the way sights and features of the province.

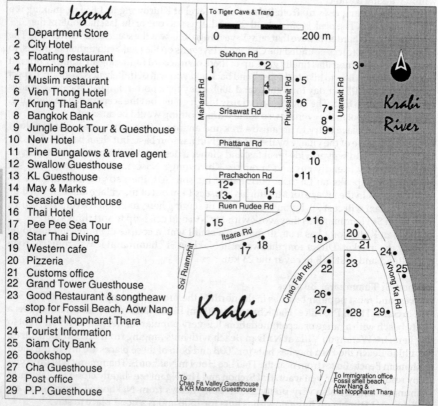

Legend

1 Department Store
2 City Hotel
3 Floating restaurant
4 Morning market
5 Muslim restaurant
6 Vien Thong Hotel
7 Krung Thai Bank
8 Bangkok Bank
9 Jungle Book Tour & Guesthouse
10 New Hotel
11 Pine Bungalows & travel agent
12 Swallow Guesthouse
13 KL Guesthouse
14 May & Marks
15 Seaside Guesthouse
16 Thai Hotel
17 Pee Pee Sea Tour
18 Star Thai Diving
19 Western cafe
20 Pizzeria
21 Customs office
22 Grand Tower Guesthouse
23 Good Restaurant & songtheaw stop for Fossil Beach, Aow Nang and Hat Noppharat Thara
24 Tourist Information
25 Siam City Bank
26 Bookshop
27 Cha Guesthouse
28 Post office
29 P.P. Guesthouse

To Tiger Cave & Trang

0   200 m

Sukhon Rd
Maharat Rd
Srisawat Rd
Phattana Rd
Prachachon Rd
Ruen Rudee Rd
Itsara Rd
Phuksathit Rd
Utarakit Rd
Soi Ruamchit
Chao Fah Rd
Khong Ka Rd

Krabi River

Krabi

To Chao Fa Valley Guesthouse & KR Mansion Guesthouse

To Immigration office Fossil shell beach, Aow Nang & Hat Noppharat Thara

South

KRABI กระบี่

Although it is the provincial capital, Krabi town can be completely explored on foot in about half a day (if that). The majority of travellers tend to breeze through heading for some of the surrounding very scenic beaches or the offshore islands of Ko Phi Phi, Ko Lanta, Ko Jam (Pu) and Ko Si Boya. If you do decide to spend a day or so in Krabi, you will not leave disappointed. The town is just over 800 km south of Bangkok.

Vital Information

Tourist Information Within Krabi town every guesthouse is a travel agent and vice versa. Some of the more popular agents for tours include Jungle Tours, Pine Bungalows Office and the Grand Tower Travel located at the base of the Grand Tower Guesthouse.
Post Office is located on Utarakit Road, opposite the Cha Guesthouse, and it has overseas phone facilities.
Banks They are concentrated along Utarakit Road. Check the map for details.
Immigration Office is on the southern end of Utarakit Road. To extend your visa it will cost 500B for 30 days.
Codes Krabi's telephone code is (075) and the postal code is 81000.

Cheap Sleeps

Although Krabi appears at a glance to have loads of guesthouses and hotels, at times (especially during the high season) it can be a challenge to find a room. Local entrepreneurs are trying to defeat this problem with new places regularly opening up.
Cha Guesthouse Located on Utarakit Road, the rooms are basic but comfortable with fan and share bathroom. The prices range from 60B, 70B and 80B. The staff are very friendly and the food is reasonably priced.
Jungle Book Guesthouse This guesthouse is on Utarakit Road. It has rooms with share bathroom for 60B and also a decent travel agent. It can get a bit noisy, but is a popular travellers' choice.
P.P. Guesthouse is by the water on Khong Kha Street. It has rooms with fan for 70B.
Thong Chai Guesthouse just before Cha Guesthouse, this new place has very small rooms for 80B and one minute single for 60B, all with share shower and fan. The setting is an old wooden house and although it is a little noisy, it is clean and friendly.
KR Mansion and Guesthouse at 52/1 Chao Fah Road, ☎ (075)612 761. Located a little out of town, this multi story hotel has good rooms for 120B and with shower for 180B. The roof top offers good views of Krabi town, is used for sunbathing during the day, and turns into a beer garden at night. This is also a popular choice for accommodation.
Chao Fa Valley Guesthouse at 50 Chao Fah Road, ☎ (075) 612 499, has huge, quiet bungalows with bathroom for 150B.
Seaside Guesthouse is on Maharat Road and has rooms starting at 80B through to 150B.
KL Guesthouse on Ruen Rudee Road, ☎ (075) 612 511, has plenty of rooms for 100B, but indifferent staff. This guesthouse is only for the desperate.
Thai Hotel at 7 Itsara Road, ☎ (075) 611 122, is a bit pricey at 330B with fan, but not a bad choice if all else is full. The staff are very courteous.
Grand Tower Guesthouse at the intersection of Chao Fa and Utarakit Road, ☎ (075) 611 741, is very central which tends to make it a bit busy. Rooms start at 100B with a share bathroom. There is a busy travel agent on the ground floor.
New Hotel at 9-11 Phattana Road, ☎ (075) 611 541, has pretty average rooms for 120B/180B.

Eat and Meet

Krabi has a number of restaurants suitable for those whose palates have tired of Thai cuisine. Pizza places, burger joints and German restaurants can be found throughout Krabi but expect to pay inflated 'tourist prices' for anything ordered.

May and Marks on Ruen Rudee Road, sells all types of European food including a home style English fried breakfast for 65B. The staff are very friendly and can organise a series of 'eco-tours' to the surrounding National Parks.

Floating Restaurant sits on the Krabi River. The seafood served here is quite decent, and it is an enjoyable venue for that late afternoon beer.

Morning Market situated at and around the corner of Phuksathit Road and Srisawat Road. This is undoubtedly the cheapest place to eat in town, with an assortment of local dishes.

Muslim Restaurant is opposite the morning market on Phuksathit Road and serves good Muslim food at very reasonable prices.

Pizzeria is located on Khong Kha Street and serves delicious pizzas but at slightly inflated prices. You even have to fork out to use the bathroom.

Good Cafe on the corner of Chao Fah Road and Utarakit Road, serves good food in a nice setting, although a bit pricey. To make it more enjoyable they have invested in some decent music. Diagonally opposite this cafe is another Western place making pizzas, burgers and other Western goodies.

Evening Market on Prachachon Road is the cheapest place in town for evening meals. Watch out for the hot curries, because they really lay on the heat.

Europa Cafe is on the corner of Soi Ruamchit and Itsara Road and is very popular. Under Danish management, the Western food here is good value.

Many of the **guesthouses** also sell their own cuisine, but prices and quality vary tremendously. Look around and see what you think.

Things to do and Sights to See

Fossil Shell Beach   สุสานหอย

This beach has large and small fossil like formations, but is only really worth visiting if you are particularly bored or have an interest in fossils and/or shells. The shells date back 75 million years to when the area was a fresh water marsh, inundated with crustaceans. Only the ghosts of the crustaceans are left, their fossils covering the beach. Clearly marked songtheaws leave Krabi every 20 minutes or so and can take up to 45 minutes for the 14 km trip as they generally go via Aow Nang. The songtheaw trip costs 20B.

On the road to the Fossil Beach is the **Dawn of Happiness Resort**. This 'eco-friendly' resort runs a series of excellent tours to the surrounding sights including the National Parks, rubber plantations and some of the surrounding islands. They also run Thai cooking classes. The rooms are a bit pricey at around 500B but the variety of courses and pastimes here make the price not unreasonable. The songtheaw to Fossil Beach runs past the resort.

Wat Tham Sua (Tiger Cave)   วัดถ้ำเสือ

This wat is one of the most revered in southern Thailand and is well worth a visit, not so much for the wat itself, but more for the area surrounding it. Upon arrival, to your left, there is a reasonably sized building which has been built into the side of a shallow cave. This building contains all manner of material pertaining to the head monk, including a life-size wax model of him in a glass box. The model is so realistic that at first you may find yourself looking for the air holes which keep him alive! (something straight out of Madame Tussauds)

As you continue past the building you will reach a staircase to your left which virtually leads to heaven. In fact the 1,272 steps lead up to yet another Buddha footprint. The walk is very steep and most smokers can count on at least a couple of cardiac arrests on the way up. Other than the footstep, the view from the top is stunning and worth the climb. If you pass the first staircase, the second is nowhere near as strenuous but is still worthwhile. As you follow the path after the stairs it leads to a series of monk's residences built into the cliff face and then a sizeable cave. After this cave the path meanders through some very nice forest with some huge trees. The serenity and feeling of peacefulness is remarkable. Well worth the trip if for no other reason than to escape the noise and hustle and bustle of urban Thailand.

Occasional songtheaws leave from Krabi town to Wat Tham Sua, cost 20B and take about 15 minutes. A motorcycle taxi to the same will cost 30B, but if you are with a group, it is worth bargaining down one of the yellow tuk tuks to something half reasonable.

Organised Tours
From Krabi, it is quite common to organise tours to destinations far and wide. The one tour we would definitely recommend you miss is the James Bond Island tours for 300B to 350B. This is an absolute tourist nightmare and the 'Sea Gypsy village' has become nothing more than a trinket selling shop with rip-off sub standard seafood restaurant thrown in.

◀ **Arriving and Departing** ▶

Boat
Many visitors either arrive or depart Krabi by boat. From here you can catch boats to Phuket, Ko Phi Phi, Ko Lanta, Ko Jum and Hat Raileh. The fares vary tremendously depending on the type of boat and time of departure, so shop around to try to get the best price. The only destination for which an early departure is recommended is Ko Phi Phi, where in high season, if you arrive on the afternoon boat you will have a lot of difficulty in finding anywhere to sleep. To get to **Hat Raileh** from Krabi longtail boat will cost 40B. The boat will drop you off at West Raileh if the tide is out and East Raileh if it is in. To **Ko Phi Phi** two boats a day leave at 09.30 and 14.30, although in high season there is also a boat at 11.00. The cost is between 100B and 150B and the trip takes a round 2 hours. Shop around for the lowest price. To **Ko Lanta** the boat leaves at 10.30 and 13.30 and costs 130B to 150B. This boat stops over at **Ko Jam** to where the fare is also 130B to 150B!

Bus
Buses go from Krabi to most regional destinations. Sample fares include; Overnight A/C bus to **Bangkok** via Surat Thani 347B and 193B for an ordinary bus, **Nakhon Si Thammarat** 50B (A/C 80B), **Hat Yai** 130B, **Trang** 40B, **Surat Thani** 60B (A/C 91B), **Phuket** by ordinary bus costs only 40B and takes 4 hours, whilst A/C vans cost 150B and take 2 hours and to **Phang Nga** a bus costs 29B.

Buses from Krabi's bus station go to most regional centres including Hat Yai, Phuket, Satun, Nakhon Si Thammarat, Surat Thani and Ranong as well as destinations further afield.

Songtheaw
Songtheaws to **Fossil Beach**, **Aow Nang** and **Hat Noppharat Thara** leave from the corner of and Chao Fah Roads and cost 15B to 20B.

Will Krabi become the next Phuket???
Krabi has been earmarked by the TAT and foreign tourism groups as a future boom centre for tourism. Once Krabi airport is finished, jet setting tourists will be able to fly into Phuket International Airport then get a short hop flight over to Krabi for their holiday escape.

AROUND KRABI

Aow Nang   หาดอ่าวนาง

In the past this was probably a very nice place to stay, but now, with a road running directly behind the beach and some of the accommodation looking quite squalid, it is certainly not Krabi's most beautiful spot. The beach is small, and if you can dodge all the longtails roaring back and forth, the water is pretty clear. The beach is backed by a road which carries just about as much traffic as a major highway guaranteeing that a huge dust cloud sits permanently over the restaurants and beach. The staff in many of the restaurants are surly, probably in permanent bad moods due to the noise of motorbikes 24 hours a day. Surprisingly many of the places to stay here are quite expensive.

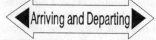

If you have to stay here, some of the more bearable budget places include the following:
Ao Nang Beach is at the northwest end of the strip with rooms for 150B. All the staff appear to have had charisma by-pass operations.
Wanna's Place has bungalows ranging from 150B, 250B, and 300B and more.
Sea Breeze has noisy bungalows starting at 150B. The travel agent is pretty good though.
Gift Bungalow, ☎ (01) 723 1128, Rooms with shower start at 300B.
Orchid has friendly staff with decent and fairly quiet bungalows for 150B.
BB Ao Nang Bungalows start at 200B.
Ya Ya is located further up the road on the left with rooms starting at 350B.
Green Park has bungalows starting at 180B, however absolutely no English is spoken here.

Arriving and Departing

Songtheaws leave from **Krabi** every 20 minutes or so between 06.30 and 18.30 and take about ½ hour for 15B. The songtheaws arrive via Hat Noppharat Hara and return via the turn-off to Fossil Shell Beach.

Hat Khlong Muang   หาดคลอง เมือง

This nice beach has only two sets of bungalows on it. Pine Bungalows in Krabi will arrange free transport out there if you ask. The beach has some nice coral offshore. **Pine Bungalows** have basic huts starting at 60B but the restaurant is a little pricey, so you may want to bring some of your own food. Pine Bungalows have an office in Krabi town from where you can organise free transport out to the beach. The Office is near the intersection of Chao Fa Road and Uttarakit Road, just a little up the hill, in an office called PS Tours Guesthouse and Pine Bungalows, ☎ (075) 611 308 or ☎ (01) 464 4298, for the bungalows themselves. Further up the beach is the **Andaman Holiday Resort**. From here there is a trail which leads north for about another 5 km to some hot springs.

Hat Nopphara Thara   หาดนพรัตน์ธารา

This lovely beach is spitting distance from Aow Nang, but may as well be a world away due to its feeling of isolation and particularly friendly people. It is also commonly visited from Krabi town which is only 18 km away. From where the longtail drops you off, it is a ten minute walk to the waters edge, and from there a longtail will whisk you over the river to the beach. If you are staying at one of the resorts the boat is free, otherwise it will cost you 10B. Along the beach there are only four resorts which are well spaced out and very popular. Often the cheaper ones are full, with people sleeping in hammocks waiting for a vacancy. Nevertheless it is easy to find a quiet spot to soak up the sun and scenery. The beach itself is actually part of the National Park that also includes Ko Phi Phi offshore.

Cheap Sleeps

Andaman Inn, ☎ (075) 612 728 (ext 114), is closest to the pier and is the biggest of the resorts. It is a good place for an evening drink and is open until 4.00 am. Basic bungalows start at 50B, then 150B and 250B.

Emerald Resort, ☎ (075) 611 944 (ext 26), is a very popular place with a pricey restaurant and cocktail bar. The staff speak good English and the bungalows will set you back 120B and 150B. If it is full you can sleep in a hammock for free as long as you eat and drink there.

Bamboo is somewhat of a bohemian joint with very basic bungalows for 40B and 60B.

Sara Cove is the pick of the bunch located up the end of the beach. Here you can stay in huge bungalows with walls that can open out. With a shower these cost 100B. The staff are always very eager to please and this is a setting offering more isolation that the other bungalow establishments.

◀ Arriving and Departing ▶

Same as for Aow Nang, except get off at the wharf or the turn-off to Hat Noppharat Hara. The boat is then free or 10B depending on if you stay or not.

Hat Raileh   หาดไร่เล

Raileh Beach is actually two beaches connected by a trail lined by bungalows and separated by karst rock formations on each side which has made it one of the better known and more notable rock climbing centres of Southeast Asia. Only a few years ago Raileh Beach was touted amongst travellers as a good alternative to Ko Pha Ngan for those who thought Hat Rin was too much of a 'scene'. Unfortunately development at Raileh has made this a past dream, and now virtually every piece of usable land on Raileh has a bungalow on it.

Along with bungalows have come bars, restaurants, video cafes and so many longtails, that at times a swim can be tempting death. Raileh has two main beaches, the west beach and the east. The eastern beach has more rustic and thus cheaper bungalows than the west, but the beach on the east is primarily mangroves and at high tide is virtually non existent, whilst the western beach is nice and sandy with clear water, however due to its being used as a port of sorts for the longboats, it can be very busy.

The coast line around Raileh is some of the most scenic in Thailand — beaches and headland, culminating at Aow Phang Rang. Coming from Krabi the longtails need to dodge numerous sheer karsts that are jutting out of the water reaching as high as 100 m.

Cheap Sleeps

West Raileh is where you will arrive if coming from Aow Nang, and east Raileh if arriving from Krabi. All bungalows here have restaurants, so you can take a pick. If you arrive late in the day all the 'cheapies' may be gone, but do not fret. Due to the very high turnover, it is rare that you will miss out the next day. Raileh is also easily visited from nearby Hat Noppharat Hara which is a much nicer, quieter place to stay. West Raileh is generally quite expensive, so it will be best to head over to east Raileh.

West Raileh

Railey Village, ☎ (075) 611 944, has good bungalows, though placed very close together and starting at 400B, then 600B and 700B.

Sand Sea, ☎ (01) 722 0114, is pretty up-market with their cheapest bungalow at 550B and then moving rapidly up in price.

Railey Bay, ☎ (01) 722 0112, is the best budget establishment on this beach, though the complex is huge, stretching right through to the eastern beach. Its like a bungalow suburb here with row after row of bungalows, precariously close to one another. Rooms here start at 150B, then 300B and 350B.

East Raileh
Railey Bay is more or less the same resort as that on the western beach again starting at 150B. The bar on the 'beach' out front is not bad.
Sunrise Bay has a huge restaurant (yes, and video), rooms here start at 250B, then 400B.
Ya Ya's ☎ (075) 612 728, bungalows here start at 120B with shower outside, and shoot up to 250B if you want your own. Ya Ya is also home to Pra-Nang Rock Climbers - one of the best climbing outfits in town. See things to do and see for details. The bungalows are three storied, and some are actually tree houses. Careful of the top floor bungalows, as the stairs can be quite a challenge if you have been out playing.
Co Co probably has a bit more space than anywhere else in Raileh, but rooms are 150B to 200B. The restaurant is packed at night because it offers an extensive menu which is quite reasonably priced.
View Point has stock standard bungalows for 150B and 250B.
Diamond Cave is named after the cave not far from them. These bungalows go on forever and there are signs of them trying to fit in even more. Prices range from 180B to 600B.

Things to do ◆ and ◆ Sights to See

Two things served to put Raileh on the map, caves and climbing - both of which are still here with the former worth seeing and the later worth it for the adrenaline rush.

Rock Climbing
Raileh is one of the premier climbing locations of Southeast Asia. Most places you look (especially the very high ones) you will see farangs slowly working their way up sheer cliff

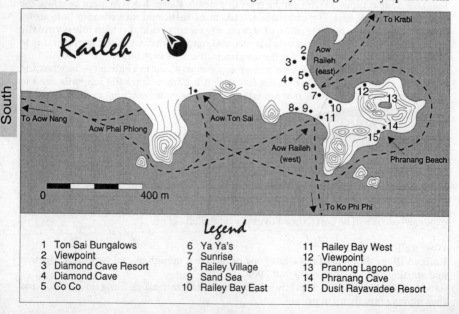

Legend

1	Ton Sai Bungalows	6	Ya Ya's	11	Railey Bay West
2	Viewpoint	7	Sunrise	12	Viewpoint
3	Diamond Cave Resort	8	Railey Village	13	Pranong Lagoon
4	Diamond Cave	9	Sand Sea	14	Phranang Cave
5	Co Co	10	Railey Bay East	15	Dusit Rayavadee Resort

faces. If you are into this, or want to learn, the schools here are very good and the views extraordinary. No climbing gym could ever compete with the scenery. One thing that the climbing staff are worrying about is that since Raileh is still developing as an area for climbers, some of the more unscrupulous climbers are doing so with a 'don't give a toss' attitude. Unfortunately more and more graffiti and garbage is showing up, something this area certainly doesn't need. The limestone rock has been around for a long time and certainly does not need your initials carved into it.

Pra Nang Rock Climbers (not club!)

Pra Nang Rock Climbers is one of the three climbing outfits in town and offers comprehensive climbing courses from half day beginners courses to three day 'hard core' climbing trips. They have been in the area around three years and are very knowledgable on climbing and the surrounds. The staff are very friendly and are around most of the time. If no one is there, leave a message and they will chase you up. In their words Raileh is "a sports climbing area on limestone rock with over 250 bolted routes available". Natural protection climbing is also possible and there is access to a comprehensive range of gear rental and purchases.

Quite often longtail boats will take you to the offshore karsts, hook you into the bolts, and off you go on a free climb. Other climbs are landbound, so you can be belayed from below.

The French grading system is used in Raileh and a guidebook is available showing most of the climbs, though there are always more being added. Routes are also routinely re-bolted. To do a climb with Pra Nang Climbers, a full day including gear will set you back 700B whilst a half day is only 400B. The three day rambo trek comes in at 2,000B. If you need more details, contact Pra Nang Climbers at Ya Ya Bungalows or by fax on 66-75-612914 or PO Box 15, Krabi 81000, Thailand. If you want your correspondence answered, do not mention the word 'club' as they will not reply if you do.

Tham Phet   ถ้ำเพชร

The limestone cliffs surrounding Raileh are riddled with caves, nooks and crannies. One of the best caves which is definitely worth a look is the Diamond Cave. Set to the left of Diamond Cave Bungalows, this cave is very deep and a walkway and stairs have been built to make it more accessible. You will need a torch (a cigarette lighter will definitely not suffice) to see the amazing stalactites and stalagmites of sparkling limestone and the famed golden waterfall. Please do not leave the walkway and climb on the formations as they are fragile and can easily break. Touching the stone will turn it black so try to avoid this. The Diamond Cave is pretty easy to find. Just look out for the sign on East Raileh Beach and follow the trail.

Tham Phranang

This cave is off Phranang Beach and is said to be the home of a princess from a village nearby. She played a vital part in the myths which attempt to explain the incredible natural formations surrounding Krabi. Local fishermen place wooden phalli in the cave in the hope that the then pleased princess will grant them large catches at sea. It is an interesting cave, but not as impressive as Tham Diamond.

Miscellaneous

There is another trail which climbs up the mountain and which houses Phranang lagoon. Along the way there are two viewpoints which offer spectacular views of the surrounds. It is also possible to reach the lagoon by a trail, but you are best to do this in the early morning as it is quite a hard walk. You will see loads of monkeys along this trail.

Beaches

The nicest beach in the area is **Hat Phranang** behind which sits the Dusit Rayavadee Resort. This can be reached by foot or boat from either side of Raileh. **Ton Sai** is the next bay from

Raileh, going towards Aow Nang. It has one set of rustic, basic bungalows for 80B and 120B and you can also camp on the beach. This is quite a popular alternative to Raileh Beach. A boat to Phranang Beach costs 10B from Raileh. **Aow Phai Phlong** is the first beach after Aow Nang and is a pretty place to laze away the day as its a lot quieter than Aow Nang. There are no bungalows on this beach yet. A boat from Aow Nang should only cost 5B to 10B depending on numbers.

Snokelling

The snorkelling on West Raileh, especially around the base of the mountain, is quite good but watch out for the longboats. There is also very basic windsurfing gear for hire but no jet skis. At West Raileh Beach you can hire kayaks for half a day for 250B in calm weather, this would be an ideal way to explore around to east Raileh, and around the headland and island near Aow Ton Sai. On West Raileh there is also one of the most outrageously priced bookstores (new and second hand) we have seen this side of Khao San Road.

◀ **Arriving and Departing** ▶

From **Krabi** you can get a longtail boat all the way for 40B per person with the trip taking upwards of an hour depending on sea conditions. The other way to get there is to take a songtheaw to **Aow Nang** for 20B, then a boat to Raileh for another 20B. Out of season (ie May to September) boats will not round the headland between east and West Raileh. So you may have to walk the last bit.

Aow Leuk   อ่าวลึก

This small town is surrounded by limestone outcrops which are riddled with some excellent caves. There are two guesthouses in town, with the **Aow Leuk Bungalows,** the better of the two, starting at 200B. Aow Leuk is easily reached from **Krabi** by songtheaw (20B) and it makes an interesting day trip.

Khao Phanom Bencha National Park   อุทยานแห่งชาติเขาพนมเบญจา

Translated this park means 'Mountain Praying on Five Points' refering to the five points of the body that touch the ground in both Buddhist and Muslim religious worship. The highest peak within the park reaches 1,350 m, but the mainly Thai patronage usually only visit two waterfalls, **Namtok Huai To** and **Namtok Huai Sad**, both of which are within reasonable distance of the park office. Namtok Huai To originates in the nearby Phanom Bencha Mountains and the water fills eleven pools on its way down. The second waterfall, Namtok Huai Sad, is just over 1 km fro the park office. Other than waterfalls, there is also a series of caves worth mentioning, of these Tham Khao Phung is the most worthwhile and is around 3 km from the park office and contains some impressive stalactites. There are another five caves near Tham Khao Phung.

Despite these natural attractions, the park is still suffering irreversible damage through illegal logging and poaching both of which the National Park authorities are finding it difficult to stop. One of the best ways to visit the park is on an **organised camping tour** which both May and Marks and Dawn of Happiness Resort organise at reasonable costs.

◀ **Arriving and Departing** ▶

The best way to reach the park from Krabi is to do so by hired motorcycle as public transport is infrequent. You could hitch, but if you were planning this, weekends would be the best choice as that is when more Thais would be visiting the park.

Than Bokkhoroni National Park   อุทยานแห่งชาติธารโบกขรณี

This National Park is about 45 km to the north of Krabi town along Route 4 around the town of Aow Leuk. The park is particularly lush and the main swimming pool has been nicely landscaped and is great for a refreshing dip. The swimming pool is actually formed by a collection of streams and although the waterfalls are hardly spectacular, the monkeys surrounding the pool can be.

Besides the pond, the park boasts a collection of caves including **Tham Hua Kalok, Tham Lod Tai** and **Tham Phet**. To visit Tham Hua Kalok and Tham Lod Tai, you will need to hire a boat from Bo Tho pier which will take you along the Ta Prang canal for about ten minutes after which you reach Tham Lod Tai which has a stream running out of its entrance. The cave is only navigable at low tide. Tham Hua Kalok is a little further down the canal and the entrance is set above ground level. Once inside the cavern, the tunnel splits into two with the left branch entering a large cavern, whilst the right branch enters an area which archeologists believe was once inhabited by prehistoric people.

Tham Phet is heralded as Krabi's most beautiful cave. The name *phet* means diamond and as you wander the cave, the glistening walls will explain the basis for the naming. The cave is best reached with a guide from Aow Luk Nua Market which is just under 3 km from the cave.

◀ **Arriving and Departing** ▶

To reach Than Bokkhoroni National Park, head north from Krabi on Route 4 until you hit the intersection with Route 4039 where you take a left and follow it for around 1½ km till you reach the park office. The National Park is well signposted. To reach Bo Tho pier, follow Route 4039 for just under 5 km from the park office turn-off heading southwest and take the right turn down the dirt road to the pier.

KO PHI PHI   เกาะพีพีดอน

At one stage, not all that long ago, Ko Phi Phi Don and Ko Phi Phi Leh were two pristine islands with heavenly beaches and awesome coral at the bottom of clear turquoise seas, but not any more. The Ko Phi Phi - Hat Nopparat National Park officially covers the 2 km Nopphara Thara Beach on the mainland, the Phi Phi islands, Ko Mai Phai (bamboo island) and Ko Yung (mosquito island) as the marine area. Ko Phi Phi Don is included in this National Par but it should be put in the record book of National Park disgraces. Development on Ko Phi Phi Don continues completely unchecked by the National Park Authority. Where you should be able to hear nothing but breaking waves, longboats roar past metres off the beach, bungalows, restaurants and bars line the beaches, which in turn are covered with deck chairs and umbrellas stating, "No travellers please, these are for guests' use only" (but even for guests they cost 20B). Everything costs money here. The diving here is excellent and very competitively priced, but weigh up your accommodation costs before promising yourself a bargain.

Up to 20 yachts crowd the wharf area where the fishing boats look to be virtually permanently moored. No better example of tourism destroying a local lifestyle can be found in all of Thailand. There are generally two boats from Krabi, and if this is your intended destination, we would strongly advise you get to the pier in time. If you miss the morning one in peak season, wait a day and chances are you will be paying 600B a night or sleeping on the beach! The main developed area is between Aow Ton Sai and Loh Dalam. Luckily they tiled a road to separate the dive shops, bars, restaurants, shell shops, clothes shops, exchange offices, travel agents and even Krung Thai Bank (the only National Park branch!), otherwise you could not wade through it all. In the restaurants the food is exorbitantly priced and the service often lack lustre to say the least. All up, if you decide to visit Ko Phi Phi for diving or for the excellent snorkelling, you will be very pleased with your choice. If you visit to meet nice Thais or to have a 'cheap' break away from home, prepare yourself to be rudely disappointed.

Cheap Sleeps

Accommodation on Ko Phi Phi falls into two very distinct brackets. Luxury colossal concrete condos/bungalows and the usual bungalows where anywhere else in Thailand you would pay about half the amount. The touts who congregate around the wharf are some of the most dishonest, deceiving Thais you will ever meet, and just because they say something is full or 1,000B a night certainly does not mean it is even remotely true. As for rude - if you do not have a suitcase on wheels, they just do not want to know you.

Aow Ton Sai   อ่าวต้นไทร

This is the point of arrival from Krabi, Ko Lanta and Phuket. The beach here is not remarkable (any more) and the accommodation on the beach or just off it is considerably overpriced. The best 'budget' bet is near the wharf hence near all the bars and restaurants, and set back from the pier into a maze of sois. If you take a right at the end of the wharf and a left about 50 m down you will reach a group of small guesthouses and bungalows.

Thara Inn is one of the first you will reach with decent rooms with shower starting at 300B. Further on, **Jong Guesthouse, Rimna, ☎** (01) 229 2520, and **Orchid** all have decent rooms with shower for 250B and up. There are a few others around this area that charge similar rates. **Ton Sai Village, ☎** (01) 722 0008, is located at the western end of the beach. This resort was closed for refurbishment at the time of writing.

Phi Phi Cabana Hotel Just keep walking - very expensive.

Chaokah Lodge is back on the beach and has rooms with fan and shower starting at 500B.

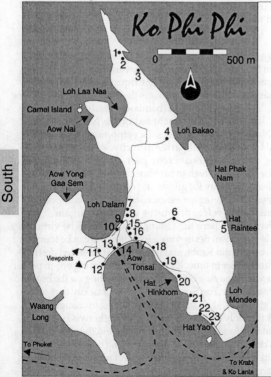

Ko Phi Phi

0   500 m

Loh Laa Naa
Camel Island
Aow Nai
Aow Yong Gaa Sem
Loh Dalam
Viewpoints
Waang Long
To Phuket
Loh Bakao
Hat Phak Nam
Hat Raintee
Aow Tonsai
Hat Hinkhom
Loh Mondee
Hat Yao
To Krabi & Ko Lanta

Legend

1 P.P. International Resort
2 P.P. Coral Resort
3 Phi Phi Palm Beach Resort
4 Pee Pee Island Resort
5 Raintee Huts
6 Viewpoint
7 Viewpoint Resort
8 Parkway Seaside Bungalows
9 Charlie Beach Resort
10 PP Princess Resort
11 Chong Khao
12 Ton Sai Village
13 Pee Pee Hotel
14 Post office
15 Orchid Guest House
16 Thara Inn
    (Jong Guest House nearby)
17 Chao Koh P.P. Lodge
18 P.P. Don Resort
19 Pee Pee Andaman
20 Bay View Resort
21 Maphrao Resort
22 Pee Pee Paradise Pearl
23 Long Beach Resort

Pee Pee Don Resort, ☎ (01) 722 0083, is on the road towards Hat Hin Khon. It has concrete rooms with A/C and shower starting at 500B. The bar/restaurant here is not a bad starting point before heading in to town.

Bay View Resort, ☎ (01) 723 1134, is on the headland where huge and comfortable bungalows start at 1,000B.

Maphrao Resort is at the eastern end of Hat Hinkhom. It is a very reasonable place with bungalows with share shower for 100B, 200B and 300B.

Hat Yao   หาดยาว

P.P. Paradise Pearl, ☎ (01) 723 0484, is a large bungalow operation with a few rustic bungalows with shower on the beach for 200B, but the majority are 350B and over.

P.P. Long Beach, ☎ (075) 612 410, is past P.P. Paradise Pearl and has rundown dirty bungalows starting at 100B, 120B, 150B and up to 600B. The restaurant food is bad, expensive and the staff lack any personality.

Loh Dalam   โล๊ะดาลัม

This nice beach is opposite Tonsai Bay and is way overpriced.

Chongkhao is one of the better places with rooms starting at 200B with shower.

P. P. Marina Resort, ☎ (075) 612196, is concrete insanity with a pool. Best to keep on walking.

Charlie Beach Resort is towards the other end of the beach and is a huge 'scene' with a big bar and restaurant. Rooms start at 300B with shower.

Parkway Seaside Bungalow is past Charlies and here they specialise in unfriendly staff. Rooms with shower start at 550B.

View Point Resort, ☎ (01) 722 0111, is up on the headland and is nicely laid out. Bungalows with showers start at 350B and they do a decent monthly rate.

Hat Raintee   หาดรันดี

Great place to stay if you have the energy to get there. A boat from Ton Sai will cost upwards of 200B, but to walk there with a pack would be quite an ordeal. Follow the signs to the viewpoint from the centre of town, past the viewpoint cafe, then keep going down where you will find:

Raintree Huts have very basic bungalows (no power) for 100B. The beach is very nice and the coral great along with a feeling of isolation. To walk there from Ton Sai Bay will take about an hour - but is worth the walk.

◄ Eat and Meet ◆

All the nightlife goes on in the central madhouse backed by Aow Ton Sai on one side and Loh Dalam on the other. The **Reggae Pub** gets consistently good reports, **Tin Tin Pub** is another good choice. There are loads of Khao San Road style cafes nested in this area, screening movies all day and night, although the sound is often inaudible due to the noise of construction going on around you.

Things to do ◄and► Sights to See

Walks

There are some worthwhile walks for the energetic. From Hat Yao you can walk over to Loh Mondee then up to Hat Raintee, on to Hat Phaknaam (no development there yet), then to Loh Bakao, over the hill to Loh Dalam stopping at Charlies for a beer, then wander back to the wharf and get a boat home. An alternate route is to visit the viewpoint which is excellent and have a chat to Noi who is a great guy.

South

View of Ko Phi Phi from the mountain viewpoint

Diving
One of the main reasons people visit Ko Phi Phi is to do a scuba diving course. Ko Phi Phi and its surroundings boast some of the best snorkelling and diving in Thailand, hence there are many dive shops in and around the area. Prices for a PADI open water certificate with four deep dives and two shallow dives start at between 6,000B and 7,000B, including gear. If you already have your gear and certificate, dives start at around 1,000B a pop. Shop around though as a fair degree of discounting goes on from time to time. One of the more popular places for snokelling is the reef off the coast from Long Beach Resort. The fish life is abundant and you only need to wander in waist deep to be surrounded by fish nipping at you.

Getting Around
There are two ways — boat and foot. With a little effort, all the resorts on the island can be reached by foot, though boat is considerably less taxing on the legs. Some longboat rates are as follows: around the island (300B), half day (500B), full day (800B), from Ton Sai Bay to Palm Beach, Coral and Inter Resorts (300B), from Ton Sai Bay to P.P. Village (200B).

◀ **Arriving and Departing** ▶

Boat
The four points from which you can reach Ko Phi Phi are Krabi, Aow Nang, Phuket and Ko Lanta. **Krabi** is probably the favourite amongst travellers and there are generally two boats a day leaving at 09.30 and 14.30, though on high demand, another boat departs at 11.00. Fares vary from 100B to 150B, so shop around. The trip takes about two hours. Boats leave Ko Phi Phi in the reverse direction at 09.00 and 13.00 and in high season there is a later boat. To **Aow Nang** one boat a day leaves from the beach by the main strip at 08.00 and costs 150B, taking around two hours. In the reverse direction, a boat leaves from Ton Sai Bay at 16.00. To **Phuket** boats run between five and seven times a day depending on the season. The price ranges between 150B and 300B based on the speed of the boat hence the trip ranges from 1½ and 3 hours, arriving at Phuket wharf, a ten minute tuk tuk ride away from Phuket town, costing 10B. From **Ko Lanta** one boat a day leaves from Ban Saladon pier on Ko Lanta (in high season only) for 150B and taking 1½ hours. In the reverse direction, the boat leaves Ko Phi Phi at 13.00.

KO JAM (KO PU) เกาะจำ

This island is about one hour south of Krabi by ferry, just to the north of Ko Lanta. There are only two bungalow operations on the island, both of which are close together and very popular. North of the bungalows, along the beach is **Ban Ting Rai**, a small sea gypsy village from where a track then leads back to Ko Jam village. If you walk south from the bungalows there is a nice small beach at the end of the main beach which is popular with the local pearl divers. Opposite is **Ko Lola** which has some coral worth snorkelling if the water is clear enough. The main beach on Ko Jam is long and the water is clear, but the beach does at times get a bit of sea refuse on it. The villages on Ko Jam are quite conservative and discreet dress is a very good idea — tread lightly!

Cheap Sleeps

Joy Bungalows, ☎ (01) 723 0502, The first to be built on the island, this resort has plenty of basic bungalows for 70B, as well as more up market ones by the water. The restaurant is good but considerably overpriced, however the staff here are friendly. They run a half day boat tour of the island and if sufficient numbers are interested will go to Phi Phi for a day of snorkelling for 200B per person.

New Bungalows Aptly named, this relatively new resort has some great bungalows situated up trees! The one above the bar is the best bargain for only 70B, just pray for quiet nights. The bulk of the bungalows cost 100B plus.

Both resorts on the island have volleyball nets, umbrellas and other beach paraphernalia.

Eat and Meet

Both Joy and New Bungalow have overpriced food. Of the two, New is probably the better choice. In Ko Jam village there are a few shops if you want to stock up on fruit, snacks and drinks. The village itself is quite charming with a Chinese/Muslim mix of people living there. There are a couple of basic cafes which are very pleasant and there are two noodle shops. **Mama's Cooking** is run by a large Chinese lady who understands a few words of English and cooks good, basic food. Down the road from Mama's Cooking is a **snooker hall**.

Arriving and Departing

You can catch a boat direct form **Krabi** en-route to **Ko Lanta**. Unfortunately it costs the same whether you go to Ko Lanta or Ko Jam. The boat sits offshore and longboats ferry the people on to the two resorts. It takes 1 to 1½ hours and costs 130B to 150B (ask around Krabi for the best price). The boat leaves Krabi twice a day at 10.30 and 13.30 from the main pier. You can also get a boat from Ko Jam village to **Ban Laem Kruad** on the mainland and then by songtheaw to Krabi. The boat costs 20B. The boat from Ko Jam to **Ko Lanta** costs an outrageous 100B. The boat passes en-route to Ko Lanta at around 12.00 and 15.00.

South

OTHER ISLANDS

Ko Poda เกาะปอดะ

This island is visible from Aow Nang and Hat Noppharat Hara. There is only one resort on the island with bungalows starting at 600B. It is more economical to visit it on a snorkelling trip from Aow Nang, Hat Noppharat Hara or Raileh. The beach is very nice and the snorkelling very good. You may see some Leopold sharks laying around.

Ko Hua Kwaan (Chicken Island)   เกาะหัวขวาน

This very nice island can be visited in conjunction with a trip to Ko Poda, Ko Si and some of the surrounding rocks. The island is known as Chicken Island as from a certain angle it supposedly looks like a chicken!!

Ko Si

These twin islands have some excellent coral between them and some lively sea life. Both leopard sharks and small reef sharks are seen around here.

◀ Arriving and Departing ▶

Many places run snorkelling trips out to these islands but the price varies from 100B to 350B. Raileh Beach seems to have the best bargains, but look around yourself. Emerald Bungalows at Hat Noppharat Hara seem to be the most pricey at 350B, although this includes lunch.

KO LANTA   เกาะลันตา

Ko Lanta is a long thin island situated southeast of Krabi. Parts of the island are part of Ko Lanta National Park which encompasses over 15 islands in the near vicinity, but many of Ko Lanta's lovely bays and beaches are being developed to cater to the tourist dollar. Much of the land being developed is owned by *Chao Nam* (Sea Gypsies) but some development seems to be creeping into the National Park. Ko Lanta has a number of villages lining both sides and the town of Ban Saladan to the north being the major arrival and departure point. The best beaches line the west coast and they improve the further south you go. Ko Lanta is a popular place to visit for those with young families as the sea is relatively calm and the beaches long and sandy. Many of the bays have good snorkelling offshore and the sunsets all the way down the west coast are stunning.

Nudity is definitely not acceptable here, not matter how secluded you may think the beach or bay is, as many of the villagers are Muslim, so keep some clothes on. Be culturally sensitive, as you did not come to Thailand to press your lifestyle on the locals, but rather try and learn something from the locals, plus sunburn of certain parts of the body really hurts.

Other than beaches, there is also a good **cave** worth visiting and a very nice **waterfall** down by Waterfall Bay Resort. The cave is reached by taking a left turn about 3½ km south of Lanta Coral Beach. Continue up this road for a little over a kilometre, and you will reach a trail off to the right marked to the 'mountain cave'. Follow this trail for about 1½ km or until you reach the cave. It is worth checking out if you are sick of the beach or feel like a bit a variety in your day.

The waterfall is down between the Waterfall Bay Resort and Sea Sun Bungalows. The best way to reach it is to pop into either bungalow both of which have directions on the wall. To walk there from Sea Sun takes around three to four hours round trip and the walk is as beautiful as the waterfall (which is nothing spectacular out of the wet season). Many people have commented that the area is ideal for meditation.

Many of the bungalows will organise boat trips to many of the surrounding islands including **Ko Rok**, **Ko Ngai** and **Ko Muk**. You may also be able to organise fishing trips at some bungalows and there is a diving headquarters in Ban Saladan. The main post office is at Lo Lanta town as is the immigration office.

Rumour has it (according to some bungalow owners) that a bridge is to be built joining Ban Saladan to Ko Lanta Noi.

A final note on Ko Lanta, do not bother to wash your clothes before getting here, as the trip from Ban Saladan to your guesthouse will coat you completely in red dust, so save your washing powder till you leave!

South

Cheap Sleeps

Virtually all of the bungalow operations are on Ko Lanta's west coast. They all have pick-ups which meet the boat at Ban Saladan and ferry you off to your own piece of paradise. Some have touts who work the boat on its way from Krabi and if you agree to go with one, your room rate may jump 10B or so. Otherwise you can choose one of the bungalow pick-up trucks waiting at Ban Saladan and save the 10B. Have a look through their brochures anyway and see what you prefer. Also some of the Muslim run places are dry - no booze except at the beach bar so bear that in mind as well when choosing. From north to south, the bungalows are as follows:

Deer Neck Cabana, ☎ (075) 612 487, set to the west of Ban Saladan, is on the cape to the north of Ko Lanta's busiest beach. It is quite a good spot, very spread out in a pleasant garden area and is very quiet. The advantage of staying around here is that its only a walk to Ban Saladan. Rooms here start at 150B.

Kaw Kwang Beach Bungalows Situated by Deer Neck Cabana, this place is quite cramped and the bungalows are not particularly good value, nor is the food! The staff here are not especially friendly either.

Golden Bay Cottages has large bungalows starting at 200B and a decent restaurant. The beach here is far from postcard material.

Lanta Villa has a large range of bungalows starting at 150B and skyrocketing through to 600B.

Lanta Sunset has close bungalows starting at 200B.

Lanta Royal Beach Resort is quite a mouthful but the restaurant is even better. Bungalows start at 250B.

Lanta Sea House Bungalows here start at 150B and are well placed on the beach.

Lanta Garden Home Bungalows start at 120B and up, making it the bargain of the beach. It is also close to the bars and restaurants towards the southern end of the beach. The stretch between Golden Bay to the south of Lanta Garden Home is where many bars and restaurants take advantage of the great sunsets. Museum Art Bar, Danny's Pizzeria and Shady Garden are just a few of the many.

Aow Phraae   อ่าวพระแอะ
At the north of this bay you have **Memory Sea Beach** with decent bungalows for 80B and 100B.

Lanta Palm Beach This place has bargain priced concrete bungalows with shower for 50B and nicer bamboo constructions (which face the beach rather than the restaurant) for 100B and 150B. The 'Impossible Beach Bar' pumps at night and has great food.
At the southern end of the beach you have the **Rapala**

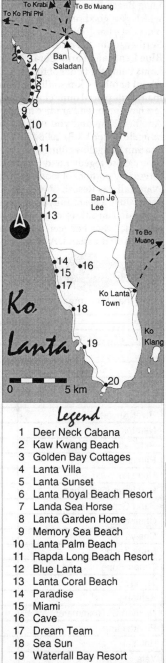

Legend

1 Deer Neck Cabana
2 Kaw Kwang Beach
3 Golden Bay Cottages
4 Lanta Villa
5 Lanta Sunset
6 Lanta Royal Beach Resort
7 Landa Sea Horse
8 Lanta Garden Home
9 Memory Sea Beach
10 Lanta Palm Beach
11 Rapda Long Beach Resort
12 Blue Lanta
13 Lanta Coral Beach
14 Paradise
15 Miami
16 Cave
17 Dream Team
18 Sea Sun
19 Waterfall Bay Resort
20 National Park Headquarters

South

Long Beach Resort and just around the point is the **Relax Bay Tropicana**, ☎ (075) 620 618, which gets good reviews and is particularly popular with German travellers. Both of these places start at 150B.

Further south, the resorts are spread out adding to the secluded atmosphere.

Blue Lanta and **Lanta Coral Beach** are the next two resorts, both starting at 150B with Blue Lanta being the better of the two. The snorkelling around here is quite good.

About another 4 km south are **Paradise** and **Miami Bungalows**. Both are quite cheap with many huts placed quite close together and starting at 100B and 70B respectively. Some travellers have reported **Paradise** having a 'scene' similar to a Californian spring break beach party.

Another 2 km and you will reach the nicely laid out and very quiet **Dream Team** with bungalows for 100B/200B/300B and the nice beach is a mere 50 m walk away.

Sea Sun Bungalows Bungalows are 80B for bamboo and 100B for concrete. The bungalows are a very close together and Bamboo Bungalow D1 is an infested shanty. The restaurant here serves tiny portions of food but the bar on the beach is good value. Lucky the staff are friendly.

Waterfall Bay Resort, ☎ (075) 612 084, is worth splurging a few Baht on. Bungalows are 400B and 600B in a beautifully landscaped garden. The more expensive bungalows have separate rooms and an attic (second storey). This is one of the best places on the island.

Also, the beach between Sea Sun and Waterfall is one of the most secluded and beautiful beaches on the island. A bit of a challenge to reach the sand, but well worth it.

Eat and Meet

Other than the bungalow operations, there are a few good restaurants on the northwestern

Southern Train Line Fares				
From Bangkok	**Fares without supplements (baht)**			
	Class			**Distance**
Station	**1st**	**2nd**	**3rd**	**km**
Nakhon Pathom	54	28	14	64
Kanchanaburi	111	57	28	133
River Khwae Bridge	115	59	29	136
Namtok	168	85	41	210
Ratchaburi	99	52	25	117
Phetchaburi	138	71	34	167
Hua Hin	182	92	44	229
Prachuap Khiri Khan	245	122	58	318
Bang Saphan Yai	296	145	69	393
Chumphon	356	172	82	485
Chaiya	443	212	101	614
Surat Thani	470	224	107	651
Thung Song	550	261	124	773
Trang	597	282	135	845
Kantang	614	290	138	866
Nakhon Si Thammarat	590	279	133	832
Phatthalung	611	288	137	862
Hat Yai	664	313	149	945
Yala	738	346	165	1,055
Sungai Kolok	808	378	180	1,149
Padang Besar	694	326	156	990

beach (the one with Lanta Villa etc). Ban Saladan also has a few good restaurants especially **Sea Side**, but the service can be slow.

Getting Around
Many of the bungalows hire motorbikes for an extortionate 200B to 250B per day and also run pick-ups to Ban Saladan at certain times, rates vary according to the position of the bungalow. Hitching up and down the island is good, but be prepared to get real dirty.

◀ Arriving and Departing ▶

Boats leave for **Krabi** (Chao Fa pier) at 08.00 and 13.00 from Ban Saladan for 150B taking 2 hours. To **Bo Muang** from Ko Lanta town, boats leave at 07.00 and 08.00 for 40B and take 45 minutes. To **Ko Phi Phi** a boat leaves from Ban Saladan at 08.00, taking 1½ hours for 150B. A boat can be chartered from Ko Lanta town to Ko Bubu for around 200B depending on the number of passengers. A long tail from Ban Saladan across the river to Ko Lanta Noi costs 5B per person and they leave regularly all day. From there you can get a motorcycle taxi across the island, then another boat to Ban Hua Hin, from where you can get a local bus to Krabi.

Southern Train Line Timetable												
Type and Class	O,3	R,23	O,3	X,123	X,12	R,23	E,23	R,23	E,23	R,23	S,2	S,2
Train Number	171	45	197	19	11	43	13	41	15	47	983	981
Supplements		A,B		B	B	A,B	A,B	B	B		A	
Bangkok		13.30		14.35	15.15	15.50	17.05	18.30	19.20	19.45	21.55	22.35
Thonburi	07.50		13.45									
Nakhon Pathom	09.27	15.03	14.53	15.54	16.28	17.11	18.30	19.55	20.44	21.07	23.01	23.41
Kanchanaburi	10.55		16.26									
River Khwae Bridge	11.02		16.33									
Namtok	13.00		18.40									
Ratchaburi		15.53		16.46	17.19	18.14		20.44	21.34	21.59	23.38	
Petchaburi		16.35		17.31	18.06	18.59		21.26	22.17	22.40	00.10	
Hua Hin		17.30		18.22	19.02	19.51	20.55	22.19	23.14	23.31	00.49	01.40
Prachuap Khiri Khan		18.42		19.39	21.10		23.36	00.30	00.55	01.57		02.47
Bang Saphan Yai		19.43			22.34					01.58		03.54
Chumphon		21.36		22.20	22.54	00.20	00.40	02.45	03.39	04.05	04.24	05.08
Lang Suan		22.46			01.31			03.50	04.40	05.05		06.02
Chaiya		23.55			02.28			04.55	05.38	06.05		06.47
Surat Thani		00.48		01.23	01.55	03.10	03.45	05.44	06.29	06.57	06.30	07.20
Thung Song		03.12		03.37	04.06	05.27	06.05	08.20	08.54	09.36	08.30	
Trang							07.35	09.55				
Kantang								10.25				
Nakhon Si Thammarat										10.50		
Patthalung		04.39		05.04	05.30	06.56				10.00	09.37	
Hat Yai		06.30		06.50	07.20	08.44					11.05	
Yala		08.14		08.35		10.40					12.25	
Sungai Kolok		10.00		10.20								
Padang Besar						08.00						
Butterworth						12.40						

X=Extra Express, E=Express, R=Rapid, O=Ordinary, S=Sprinter, (123)=Class of train, A=Air Conditioning, B=Sleeping Car

South

Southern Train Line Timetable

Type and Class	O,3	R,23	R,23	X,23	S,2	R, 23	X,23	X,12	R,23	X, 123	D,3	S,2
Train Number		48	42	16	984	46	14	12	44	20		982
Supplements		B	A,B	A,B	A	A,B	A,B	A,B	A,B	A,B		A
Butterworth								13.40				
Padang Besar								17.00				
Sungai Kolok						12.00				15.00		
Yala					16.15	13.52			15.05	16.45		
Hat Yai					17.40	15.55		18.10	17.05	18.40		
Phatthalung					18.44	17.19		19.32	18.35	20.04		
Nakhon Si Thammarat		13.50		15.40								
Kantang			13.15									
Trang			13.44				18.20					
Thung Song		15.07	15.22	16.47	19.55	19.01	19.52	21.15	20.15	21.46		
Surat Thani		17.35	17.50	19.04	21.41	21.10	21.52	23.18	22.19	23.48		11.05
Chaiya		18.11	18.32	19.40		21.47			22.52	02.48		11.37
Lang Suan		19.11	19.35	20.35		22.44			00.04			12.22
Chumphon		20.06	20.49	21.52	00.00	00.11	01.05	02.02	01.23			13.15
Bang Saphan Yai		22.10	22.33						03.01			14.23
Prachuap Khiri Khan		23.17	23.56	00.29	02.15	03.21			04.10			15.12
Hua Hin		01.05	01.38	01.56	03.22	04.40	05.12	05.40	05.54	06.42		16.13
Petchaburi		02.10	02.34	02.52	04.07	05.35			06.50			
Ratchaburi		02.55	03.18	03.37	04.42	06.21		07.20	07.38	08.18		
Namtok	06.10										13.15	
River Khwae Bridge	08.18										15.14	
Kanchanaburi	08.26										15.21	
Nakhon Pathom	10.03	03.46	04.12	04.24	05.23	07.11	07.44	08.12	08.35	09.10	16.47	18.29
Thonburi	11.15										18.10	
Bangkok		05.10	05.35	05.50	06.35	08.35	09.10	09.30	10.00	10.35		19.35

X=Extra Express, E=Express, R=Rapid, O=Ordinary, S=Sprinter, (123)=Class of train, A=Air Conditioning, B=Sleeping Car

THE
FAR SOUTH

Unlike any other area, Narathiwat, Yala, Pattani and Satun are culturally different to the rest of Thailand as Muslims make up the majority of the population in all four provinces. This area, like the far north of the country, has been a hotbed of dissension and strife as those seeking more autonomy from Thailand (if not outright independence) have in the past used violence as a method for getting their message across. Although most of the fighting has died off, the movement is still strong in the provinces, as many feel they have more in common with those south of the border in Malaysia than they have ever had with the rulers in Bangkok.

This area is a big hit with Malaysian visitors who pop over for a weekend in 'liberal' Thailand. The aim of these weekenders can be seen in the hotel occupancy rates. In the provinces of Narathiwat, Pattani and Yala, the hotels average 350% to 400% occupancy daily, indicating that not all Malaysian men visiting are doing so to soak up sun on the beach.

The Far South of Thailand is made up of four provinces, Narathiwat, Yala, Pattani and Satun. We have extended this coverage to the extra three provinces of Songkhla, Phattalung and Trang solely on a geographic basic.

Highlights
Visit the tropical paradise of **Ko Lipe** (Satun Province).
Dive into the **Emerald Cave** on **Ko Muk** (Trang Province).
Kick up your feet on the back veranda of the **Narathiwat Hotel** and just watch life float by (Narathiwat Province).
Explore Phattalung and its little visited but impressive **Khao Poo Khao Ya National Park** (Phattalung Province).
Head out of a veritable Robinson Crusoe Island — **Ko Rok** (Trang Province).

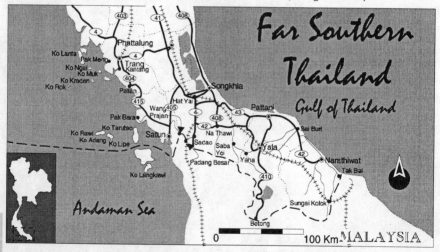

TRANG PROVINCE

Trang's geography is predominantly hilly in the north, coasting down to flat plains towards the sea. Offshore are a number of beautiful islands which are easily visited. The main crops grown in the area are rubber and oil palms, both of which are well suited to Trang's very high rainfall — only February to April is considered to be the dry period in Trang.

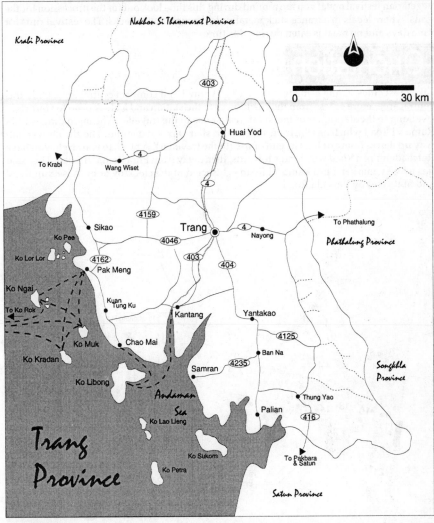

TRANG   ตรัง

Trang would have to be the cleanest city in Thailand - even cleaner than Yala. It has won 'cleanest city of the year' on a number of occasions and it **really is clean**. However, unless you are a big fan of cleanliness, there is little to bring you to Trang except for what lies off the province's coast — islands and loads of them. Despite the islands off its coast, Trang is not a popular Western tourist destination, yet it is an easy place to kill time. It is also the virtual start of one of the rail lines north to Bangkok.

Trang is famed for its locally brewed coffee known as *ko-pii*. It has quite a thick almost malted/chocolate taste when compared to Western brewed coffee and makes a nice change from Nescafé. The main Road on Trang has a number of coffee and cake places which serve Ko-pii and a wide assortment of cakes and pastries. These places are also very popular with local students and hence a great place to meet Thais. Trang town also celebrates the vegetarian festival and if you are around during this time look out for the procession for the gods, where locals in a trance stick metal rods through their cheeks. The festival runs for nine days and no meat is eaten during this time.

Orientation

Like most cities, Trang is made up of a huge sprawl and compact central area. Only this central area, more or less from the clocktower to the station and a block or so to your right (walking to the station), is of much interest or use to the traveller. The main drag is Phra Rama VI Road which has the train station and share taxis at one end. The clocktower half way up marks (more or less) its end of use (to the traveller). A block to your right you have Ratchadamnoen Road which runs towards, then away from Phra Rama VI Road. This road has a lively market. Phra Rama VI Road is bisected at the clocktower by Wisetkun Road and at its end by Ratsada Road.

Trang

0   400 m

Legend

1 Phraya Rasadanupradit	9 Bus terminal	17 Trang Hotel
2 Taxi to Hat Yai	10 Tourist Information Office	18 Clock tower
3 Taxi to Pak Meng	11 Train station	19 Post Office
4 Market	12 Thamrin Hotel	20 Travel agent
5 Cafe and cake shop	13 Post office	21 Market
6 Phet Hotel	14 Cheap telephone office	22 Cafe and cake shop
7 Provincial Office	15 Thai Farmers Bank	23 THAI office
8 Police Station	16 Ko Teng Hotel	24 Buses to Satun & La Ngu

Vital Information

Tourist Information There are a number of travel agents in Trang, including Trang Tour Service at 22 Sathanee Road, ☎ (075) 214 564, Porpon Diving and Libong Beach Resort at 59/1 Taklang Road, ☎ (075) 214 676, and KK Tours around the corner on Sathanee Road. They all offer similar packages, but its worthwhile comparing prices and there are a number of agents, particularly along Pharama VI Road.

Post Office is on the corner of Phra Rama VI and Kantang Roads. It is open from 8.30 am to 4.30 pm and has an international phone service. However a **cheaper place** for calls under three minutes is about two blocks towards the clocktower on the same side of the road. There is a small sign reading long distance calls.

Banks There are heaps of banks in Trang, see the map for details. Thai Farmers Bank is open from 8.30 am to 3.30 pm on Monday to Friday.

Tourist Police are by the train station which doubles as a tourist information office.

Code's Trang's telephone code is (075) and the postal code is 92000.

Cheap Sleeps

Trang has only two really 'cheap' hotels worth considering.

Ko Teng Hotel, ☎ (075) 218 622, is on Phra Rama VI Road and has large rooms starting at 160B. The restaurant downstairs is overpriced and the food is not great. However this is a popular place to stay.

Phet Hotel on Ratchadamnoen Road has rooms that very enormously. Huge rooms with grimy bathroom are 100B or very hot rooms with share bathroom cost 80B. The restaurant serves very generous portions at a bargain price, although there is no English menu.

Eat and Meet

There are a number of **coffee and cake shops** (check map) which serve a wide variety of cakes and pastries. In front of Thai Farmers Bank there is some **night street seating** with decent and cheap food. To the left of the train station is a day market selling heaps of cheap food. Other farangs advise well of **The Boss Club** and **Old Time Pub**. There is a large and interesting **market** on Ratchadamnoen Road.

Things to do and Sights to See

Waterfalls and Caves
Unfortunately to visit all the waterfalls and caves around Trang would cost about 600B to 1,000B if travelling alone. Only dedicated cave or waterfall freaks would be willing to cough up the dough. The travel agents in Trang will organise tours to the southern area of Trang to a couple of waterfalls and two caves and a weaving village. You can put your name on a list at the travel agents and when enough people congregate you can go on the trip. The best way to visit the surrounding caves is by hired motorbike.

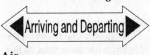

Arriving and Departing

Air
THAI Airways has flights to **Bangkok** daily for 2,005B, **Nakhon Si Thammarat** 560B, **Phuket** 435B and **Surat Thani** 495B.

Train

It is possible to catch the train directly from Bangkok's Hualumpong station to Trang, which is probably a more pleasant trip than the long bus ride. Refer to the end of the Southern Thailand chapter for timetable and price details.

Bus

The local bus from Trang to **Krabi** costs 40B and takes 2½ hours. The bus station is 2 km out of town. From the bus station, both government and A/C buses go to most regional destinations. A tuk tuk to anywhere throughout town costs 5B.

AROUND TRANG

Hat Chao Mai National Park   อุทยานแห่งชาติหาดเจ้าไหม

Created as a National Park on October 14, 1981, this National Park encompasses some nine islands including Ko Muk and Ko Kradan as well as 20 km of coastal beach on the mainland including Hat Pak Meng. The marine section of the park offers protection to the dugong which is an endangered species as well as coral reefs at Ko Kradan, Ko Muk and a number of other islands within the park. The black necked stork which is non existent on the mainland is found on the islands as well as 54 other bird species. Other than the islands, some of the highlights of the park include hot springs at Ban Bor Nam, Chao Mai Cave, Yong Ling and San Beaches.

   The park headquarters are located at Hat Chang Lang just under 60 km from Trang. The ride between Hat Pak Meng and Hat Chang Lang is particularly scenic at times with many of the offshore islands visible although there has been a lot of construction along this stretch. It is possible to hire tents at the National Park office if you want to camp there or stay in one of the park bungalows. The entire strip from Hat Chang Lang to the southern tip of the peninsula at Hat Chao Mai has a number of nice quiet beaches, including Hat Yao and Hat Yong Ling. All of these are best reached by hired motorbike as the public transport is fairly infrequent. If you want to get to the National Park, talk to one of the travel agents in town and they may be able to put you on the songtheaw which takes people to Pak Meng and from there you could either hitch or convince the driver to take you the rest of the distance to the National Park office. As in much of Thailand, on the weekend hitching along this coastal strip is not be too difficult.

   If you have your own transport take Route 4046 from Trang towards Krabi, left on Route 4162 to Hat Pak Meng and follow the beach road for around 7 km to the park headquarters.

Hat Pak Meng   หาดปากเมง

The northern end of this beach is marked by Pak Meng pier, the jumping off point for the nearby islands. The beach itself is nothing special, and there is a lot of road construction going on, especially towards Hat Chang Lang. This beach is very popular with Thais on weekends and as such there are loads of not particularly cheap concrete bungalows generally priced in the 200B to 300B range. The only real reason for staying here is if you miss one of the boats to the offshore islands where the beaches are far nicer and the crowds smaller. As a consolation some great seafood can be had on the beach opposite whichever bungalow you opt for. A songtheaw from Trang to Hat Pak Meng costs 20B. The beach further round at Hat Chao Mai (jumping off point to Ko Libong) is much nicer and accommodation is available there.

KO MUK   เกาะมุก

This is one of the closest, most accessible and hence most popular islands in Trang Province. For some reason it is especially popular with German tourists. There is only one resort on the island, the **Ko Muk Resort**, ☎ (075) 219 499, which is well endorsed with more than its fair share of touts in Trang. The resort has nice bungalows with shower starting at 200B and a restaurant which serves decent food. The touts in Trang will tell you it is possible to visit many islands from Ko Muk, but this is only the case if you have a group of six or more to charter the boat. Ko Muk itself has some interesting sights but the beaches here are far from spectacular. The beach in front of the Ko Muk Resort turns to mudflats at low tide and at high tide is really too shallow for good swimming. We suggest you bring your own snorkelling gear as those provided for free are substandard.

Beaches
Ko Muk Resort runs a free boat to Sabay Beach on the west, the **Emerald Cave** (west) and **Farang Beach** (southwest). Farang Beach is touted as the nicest beach on Ko Muk and it is in terms of isolation. The beach on the south side of the headland off from the Muslim village is also OK though not as sheltered (discreet dress applicable). Sabay Beach is pretty ordinary but is one of the better places on the island to view the sunset.

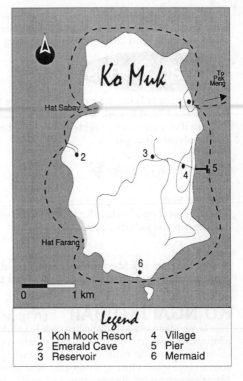

Legend

1	Koh Mook Resort	4	Village
2	Emerald Cave	5	Pier
3	Reservoir	6	Mermaid

Tham Morakot (Emerald Cave)
ถ้ำมรกต
The one 'must' see place on Ko Muk is Emerald Cave. This cave is reached only by boat. You have to swim through a cave for about 80 m during which it is pitch black and damn scary (unless you hire a boat). At the other end you reach a 'cave' which is open to the sky and surrounded by spectacular cliffs. Well worth a look but bring a torch, mask and snorkel. This is definitely not a place for claustrophobics.

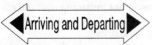

Boat
Boats leave from **Pak Meng pier** at midday costing 60B and take about 1 hour. If you arrive much earlier or later, let the police box know you want to get to Ko Muk and they should be able to call the resort for you and organise a boat over. To get to Pak Meng from Trang, a songtheaw will cost 20B and takes from 1½ hours. From Trang the best place to catch one is at one of the travel agents at 11.00 am, as the songtheaw then does the round.

KO KRADAN เกาะกระดาน
Ko Kradan is further southwest of Ko Muk into the Andaman Sea and most of it is under the jurisdiction of the Hat Chao Mai National Park and is protected, but the coconut and rubber plantations are not. The island boasts beautiful white sand beaches and an exquisite coral reef, as well as good offshore fishing.

To the south of the Ko Kradan Resort, around the bend on the beach is a long reef in very good condition. It is marked by a series of red buoys (which the longtails are supposed

Far South

to anchor to) and is only about 10 m from the shore. The reef abounds in sea life, including large moray eels, and in the deeper waters, sleeping leopard sharks may be seen (but not disturbed unless you do not mind risking a leg).

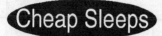

Ko Kradan has only one resort whose prices are far from cheap.

Ko Kradan Island Resort, ☎ (075) 211 391, has large concrete bungalows for 700B with shower! If you stay for six nights or more you can get away with 600B per night. The menu is also extortionately priced.

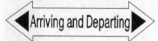

From Ko Muk
Ko Muk Resort runs boats to Ko Kradan when there are enough people for 100B per person and the trip takes about 1 hour.

From Trang
Boats leave from **Pak Meng pier** at around midday and cost 150B. If you cannot make it for 12.00, tell an agent in Trang and they may hold the boat for you.

KO NGAI (KO HAI) เกาะไห

This large island lies to the northwest of Ko Muk and has two resorts. The beaches here are nice but not a patch on Ko Kradan, and there are a number of coral reefs which are quite light on sea life. One of the main attractions for staying at Ko Ngai is that it is possible to do diving courses here while visiting some of the other islands. It is also possible to get boats from Ko Ngai to the surrounding islands including Ko Muk, Ko Kradan, Ko Rok and Ko Lanta.

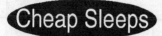

Ko Ngai Resort This is located opposite the pier. Basic bungalows here with share bathroom and small bed start at 150B after which accommodation jumps up to 300B, 400B and 600B. Unfortunately, the resort has built the boisterous and large restaurant (retaining wall and all) on the beach. They also seem to have an acute litter disposal problem. They do organise boat trips to the surrounding islands as well as dive courses and general diving.

Ko Hai Villa is located one beach east of the Ko Ngai Resort and placed at the centre of a very long beach with some decent coral. Bungalows with shower are 300B or you can rent a tent for 150B.

About one third of the way from Ko Ngai to Ko Muk there are two limestone outcrops around which there is some good (though deep) snorkelling with plenty of fish. The deeper water around the limestone peaks is also popular with the locals for fishing.

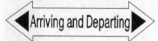

Boat
Boats leave from **Pak Meng pier** at 10.00 am and 2.00 pm and take between 45 minutes and 1 hour to reach Ko Ngai for a price of 80B. One can also reach Ko Ngai from Ko Muk by boat from the Ko Muk Resort. The boat runs only when there are sufficient numbers and takes about 1 hour. Count on paying 100B to 150B (depending on the number of passengers).

Far South

KO ROK

Ko Rok is actually two islands, Ko Rok Nai and Ko Rok Nok. They are part of Ko Lanta National Marine Park. The park office is set on the western island. Other than the park office there is no other building on the islands, no village and thankfully no bungalows (yet). On Ko Rok you are guaranteed pristine beaches and good snorkelling. Ko Rok Nai (western islet) has two very long white sand beaches with some good coral formations offshore. Ko Rok Nok (eastern island) has a smaller white sand beach but around the point to the north is some very good (though sometimes quite deep) snorkelling. The channel between the two islands is also good for snorkelling. Some of the fish, especially towards the point are extremely brightly coloured. Ko Rok is also a favourite with visiting yachties and the occasional dive team.

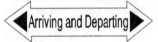
Arriving and Departing

From Ko Muk
Ko Muk Resort runs occasional boats to Ko Rok (weather and numbers permitting) for 250B per person (lunch included). The ride takes around 2½ hours by longboat each way, so bring a pillow.

From Ko Ngai (Hai)
Ko Ngai Resort runs occasional snorkelling and diving trips to Ko Rok. A snorkelling trip costs 300B and leaves at 9.00 am taking between 1½ to 2 hours, depending on the weather.

From Other Islands
The trip from Ko Kradan takes about 1½ hours. For details ask at Ko Kradan Resort.

KO LIBONG   เกาะลิบง

Ko Libong is the largest island in Trang Province and is quite a hit with domestic tourists. The island contains the Libong Prohibited Wildlife Hunting Office which endeavours to protect the islands protected birdlife. The island is home to one resort, the **Ko Libong Beach Resort**, ☎ (075) 214 676, which has an office in Trang at 59/1 Taklang Road. The resort has bungalows with breakfast starting at 250B which are well placed on the west coast of the island.

There are a couple of fishing villages worth visiting and some good snorkelling which together with the nice beaches is enough to keep you more than occupied for a few days at least. The island can be reached from Kantang pier with the boat trip taking about 1 hour and it leaves at noon or it is possible to hire a boat from Hat Chao Mai to Ko Libong.

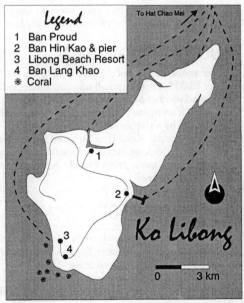

Legend
1 Ban Proud
2 Ban Hin Kao & pier
3 Libong Beach Resort
4 Ban Lang Khao
＊ Coral

To Hat Chao Mai

Ko Libong

0   3 km

Far South

Khlong Lamchan Waterbird Park   อุทยานนกน้ำคลองลำชาน

This bird sanctuary is situated about 300 m off Route 4125 about 10 km from the junction with Route 4. The park is an important breeding and resting place for the local waterbird population and is a scenic enough place to wander around, although you will need a telephoto lens if you are after good photos. A visit here is best combined with a trip along Route 4125 visiting the four or five waterfalls along this stretch of road.

Coming from Trang, the trip is best done by motorbike. Follow Route 4 out of town to the east until you hit the junction with Route 4125 where you turn right. The waterbird park is about 10 km down this road on your right and there are about a half dozen waterfalls down the left hand side of the road which you may want to explore. All the waterfalls are signposted. **Namtok Ton Te**, with a drop of over 100 m is the most impressive and best visited towards the end of the monsoon, when the water flow is at its strongest.

It is also possible to organise trips to all of the above from one of the travel agents in Trang. Price in dependent entirely on the size of the group you can get together and what you want to see.

PHATTALUNG PROVINCE

This relatively small province sandwiched between Songkhla to the east and south, Trang to the west and Nakhon Si Thammarat to the north is landlocked, with the only water lapping its boundaries to the east from Songkhla Lake. The province can be divided into two areas, the mountainous area to the west bordering Trang Province and the flat rice growing area sloping down to the tranquil expanse of Songkhla Lake.

It is a peaceful, rural province with a Muslim minority and is very rarely visited by tourists. It does make a very pleasant 'out of the way' destination and there is enough to see around and outside of Phattalung town to warrant a few days attention. It goes without saying that the locals are very friendly but very little English is spoken around here.

PHATTALUNG   พัทลุง

In the image of the province, Phattalung town, 860 km south of Bangkok with a population of about 85,000 people, is small tranquil and friendly with a couple of interesting sights, no farangs and plenty of good food. The town's population is a mixture of Thais, Chinese and Malays and is set in a very scenic spot. Surrounded by tall limestone outcrops, the landscape is dominated by a particularly large outcrop, Khao OK Thalu which has an unusual hole through the middle. Khao Hua Tack and Khao Khuhasawan lie to the west with Wat Khao Khuhawan overlooking the central area. Phattalung is famed for its shadow puppet shows. The puppets are made from buffalo hide and are now mostly sold to tourists but are attractive nonetheless.

Vital Information

Tourist Information approximately 1 km out of the centre of town down Ramet Road is a small tourist information centre. English is spoken and they distribute all the usual brochures and sell a few handicraft specialities.

Post Office is just to the south of the train station.

Banks Both Thai Farmers Bank and Krung Thai Bank are on Ramet Road and have exchange facilities.

Police Station can be found near the city hall at the western end of town.

Hospital is on Ramet Road at the western end of town.

Codes Phattalung's telephone code is (074) and the postal code is 93000.

Cheap Sleeps

There is not much choice and nothing is very cheap but some of the hotels are still very good value. Most of the old Chinese hotels along Ramet Road have been demolished or closed down.
Ho Fa Hotel, ☎ (074) 611 922, at 28-30 Kuhasawan Road, is a large modern hotel with efficient and uniformed staff. Rooms with fan and shower start at 180B and A/C rooms start at 400B. This place is luxury at low prices.
Thai Hotel, ☎ (074) 611 636, at 14-14/1-5 Disra Sakarin Road (just off Ramet Road) and beside the Bangkok Bank has large clean rooms with fan and shower and the linen is changed daily (now that is luxury!) for 180B or 400B with A/C.

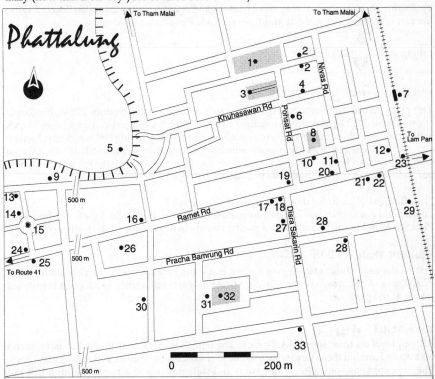

Phattalung

Legend

1	Food market	12	Post office	23	Songtheaws & motorbikes to Lam Pan	
2	Songtheaw station	13	Town Hall	24	Tourist Information	
3	Clothes market	14	Provincial Office	25	Hospital	
4	Haw Fa Hotel	15	Phra Buddha See Mum Muang	26	Wat	
5	Wat Kuhasawan	16	Kodak shop	27	Thai Hotel	
6	Buses to Chai Son	17	Songtheaw, bus stop	28	Cafe	
7	Train station	18	Bangkok Bank	29	City Park	
8	Food stands	19	Krung Thai Bank	30	Food stalls	
9	Police Station	20	Thai Farmers Bank	31	Buses to Nakhon Si Thammarat	
10	Bookshop & Bangkok Post	21	A/C bus to Hat Yai	32	Food stalls	
11	Ice Cream & Beer	22	Minibus to Hat Yai	33	24 hour supermarket	

Eat and Meet

There is an **exceptionally good market** here with very low prices between Pohsat and Nivas Roads. The stalls are open from early morning to late evening selling Muslim rotis and pancakes, Chinese rice dishes, and all the usual Thai dishes. Pad Thai goes for 15B and numerous tasty curries and vegetarian dishes start at 15B. Just point to whatever you want. **Ice cream** and **cold beer** can be purchased at the place with the Walls Ice Cream sign on Nivas Road or the similar spot opposite the train station. There are a selection of good **Chinese restaurants** along Pracha Bamrung Road.

For **nightlife**, the road south of and parallel to Pracha Bamrung Road has several bars, some karaoke style, others with Thai rock and country music. Lam Pan Beach, 7 km to the east of town also is good at night, see the Lam Pan section for details.

Things to do and Sights to See

Wat Khuhasawan   วัดคูหาสวรรค์

This pretty Ayutthaya Period wat is set at the foot of the forested limestone hill with a couple of caves behind it. The main cave contains a variety of Buddha images in various poses. A rock at the entrance to the cave has some royal graffiti on it, carved by roving and wandering Rama's.

There is a smaller cave nearby which is home to several hundred bats which fly out at dusk to fill the Phattalung skies. From beside the cave, steps lead up the hill to a viewpoint, be careful not to trip over the monkeys which are everywhere.

Phra Buddha Nira Rokantarai Chaiyawat Chaturathit

Located in a pavilion by the Tourist Information Centre, this bronze Buddha is also known as Phra See Mun Muang and is worth a peek if you are in the vicinity of the tourist centre.

Khao OK Thalu   เขาอกทะลุ

Just to the east of the station you cannot miss this limestone crag which towers over Phattalung. A trail leads to the top, a bit tricky in parts but a truly great view is for your taking at the peak.

Tham Malai   ถ้ำมาลัย

Although not the most spectacular cave in Thailand, it is a nice walk to reach it and you can hike up and around the cave to where there are some Chinese shrines and more great views. The cave contains some pretty stalactites and stalagmites and a pool, although it is not lighted, so you will need to bring a torch.

This cave complex is situated a few kilometres to the north of the train station. Either follow the railway tracks or follow the road out of town to reach it, any local should be able to direct you. An alternative route is to walk out of town in the direction of Lam Pan for about 1 km until you see a track to the left with a roman script sign marking Tham Malai.

Arriving and Departing

Trains

The train station is at the eastern end of town and has five southbound and five northbound trains a day. Refer to the timetable at the end of the chapter for price and timetable details.

Far South

Buses

Most buses stop on Ramet Road outside of the Bangkok Bank. The main bus station for Bangkok departures is out of town at the junction with Route 4. The bus to **Bangkok** costs 220B for an ordinary bus and an A/C bus leaves at 16.30 and costs 385B. Buses to **Hat Yai** leave every 30 minutes from Ramet Road and cost 30B and a minibus to Hat Yai costs 35B and leave from Ramet Road near the train station. Ordinary buses to **Nakhon Si Thammarat** cost 32B and leave every hour from Ramet Road and buses to **Chai Son** leave from Poh Sat Road and cost 12B.

AROUND PHATTALUNG

Hat Lam Pan   หาดแสนสุขลำป่ำ

Lam Pan Beach on Songkhla Lake is 7 km east of town and is a very pleasant spot for a stroll with snack stands selling tasty local specialities and a string of seafood restaurants to the left on arrival serve reasonably priced food and cold beers, all with deck chairs by the lake. A river joins the lake at this point and a small wooden bridge leads over to the **Lam Pan Resort** which has reasonably priced bungalows for 300B during the week, although weekend and holiday prices are much higher. The beach is a 10 minute motorbike taxi ride for 20B or 10B by songtheaw from the post office.

Ban Saensuk Lam Pan

Just before the beach is Saensuk Lam Pan village with a couple of interesting sites.
Wat Wang is a beautiful old wat housing a 100 year old bot surrounded by Buddha filled cloisters. The bot also contains some attractive murals. You will probably have to ask a monk to open the courtyard doors for you, although the monks can be quite scarce. If and when you find one, there is a small donation box in the main bot. While you are in this area, about 100 m down the road towards the beach there is a beautiful old **courthouse** and the **Governor's residence**. Both of these are just off the main road and are well worth a look.

Ban Chai Son   ชัยสน

This friendly little town around 30 km to the south of Phattalung has some **hot springs**, a **cave temple** and an **interesting wat**. It is set in paddy fields dotted with limestone outcrops. The village itself has a small but lively market, a few shops and cafes and plenty of buses to Phattalung. The 60° C hot springs are around 2 km out of town at the foot of the cliffs and although they are not much to look at, you are welcome to use the hot showers. Next to the hot springs is a stand selling shadow puppets, a good place to buy one if you want to watch them being made.

　　　　Some 500 m further along the cliff face walking back towards Chai Son is a small but **attractive cave temple** containing a large reclining Buddha, some interesting murals and several very old wooden carved figures. The cave curves around where steps lead up to a second entrance further up the cliff. Nuns at the bottom of the stairs will light the lamps for you. In the main cave there is a spring, the water of which is supposed to have healing qualities.

　　　　Further east of Chai Son on the lake side is **Wat Khian Bang Kaew** which is another attractive Ayutthaya Period wat. From Chai Son market a motorbike taxi to here costs 10B.

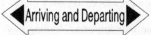

Arriving and Departing

To reach Chai Son from **Phattalung**, direct buses leave from Pohsat Road for 12B and take 20 minutes or get a bus bound for **Hat Yai** for 5B and get off at the turn-off for Chai Son. A motorcycle taxi to the caves and hot springs costs 20B.

Khao Poo Khao Ya National Park   อุทยานแห่งชาติเขาปู่ - เขาย่า

At 700 sq km this is not one of Thailand's smallest National Parks, but it is certainly one of the least visited and least funded, and although the park is mostly situated in Phattalung Province it also stretches into Trang and Nakhon Si Thammarat Provinces. This lack of visitors is a shame, since there is some great scenery and well preserved forest and very helpful park wardens. Mountains reach 1,000 m here and are covered with tropical rainforest. None of the larger mammals are here any longer, but there is still many smaller ones. Encroachment from rubber plantations and hunters are a problem and the limited funds of the park go towards this end rather than accommodation and the visitors centre consists of bare walls. Nevertheless the wardens (some of whom speak English) will be glad to guide you for free to any of the nearby sites which include caves and a spectacular cliff face, Pha Phung, or bee cliff as it is known, which is covered with bees' nests. There are fantastic views from the summit. For longer treks 200B a day is demanded and the park accommodation goes for 200B per night.

From Phattalung songtheaws leave from the market and Bangkok Bank, cost 15B and will drop you off at the turn-off to the park. From here it is a 4 km hitch, walk, hike or 20B motorbike taxi ride to the park headquarters, where food and drink is available.

Thale Noi Waterbird Sanctuary   อุทยานนกน้ำทะเลน้อย

This waterbird sanctuary some 30 km north of Phattalung is one of Thailand's top bird spots and is the largest bird park in Thailand. Nearly 200 species live in this marshy swampy area on the northern reaches of Songkhla Lake. Boat trips can be done here for 150B for 1½ hours and although accommodation is available, you are best to reserve in advance. Enquire at Phattalung Tourist Centre for reservation information.

Songtheaws from the market or Bangkok Bank in Phattalung cost 15B and the park is worth a look for its beautiful and tranquil setting, even if you are not interested in birds.

SONGKHLA PROVINCE

This medium sized province of just over 7,000 sq km is situated on the eastern coast of Southern Thailand and the provincial capital of Songkhla is 950 km from Bangkok. Once known as Singha-la (Lion) by foreign sea traders due to two offshore islands which supposedly look like lions, Songkhla was also once a pirate stronghold but today has quietened down considerably to a quaint fishing town.

SONGKHLA   สงขลา

Though much smaller and quieter than Hat Yai, Songkhla is actually the administrative capital of the province. It is also far less visited than Hat Yai as it is not really on the way to anywhere, which is a shame since it is a very pleasant town with several interesting sights. Unlike the vast majority of Thai towns, Songkhla is actually attractive in itself, situated on a narrow headland separating the gulf of Thailand from *Thaleh Sap Songkhla* (Songkhla Lake). The town is surrounded on three sides by water and contains plenty of parkland, some wooded hills, a couple of beaches and some interesting wats, as well as plenty of quiet streets to wander around. The older part of the city along the western part of the headland shows a heavy Chinese influence, dating from its historic role as an important trading post, whilst the rest of the city is a mix of Thai and Malays with the inevitable Muslim influence found in the southern areas.

The oil industry is important off the coast here, so there is a significant expat community, explaining the presence of several farang bars despite the apparent lack of tourists.

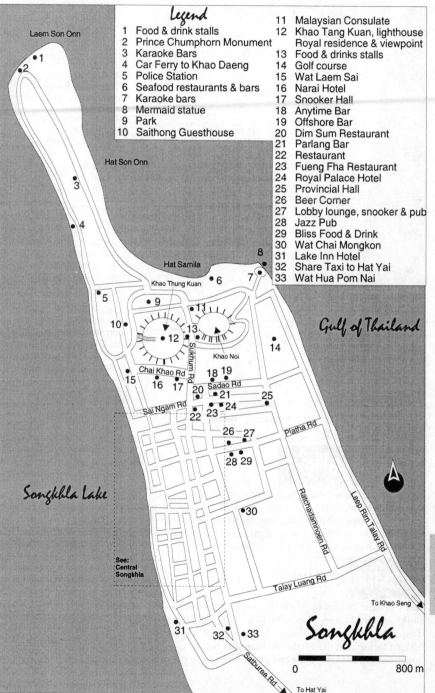

Legend
1 Food & drink stalls
2 Prince Chumphorn Monument
3 Karaoke Bars
4 Car Ferry to Khao Daeng
5 Police Station
6 Seafood restaurants & bars
7 Karaoke bars
8 Mermaid statue
9 Park
10 Saithong Guesthouse
11 Malaysian Consulate
12 Khao Tang Kuan, lighthouse
   Royal residence & viewpoint
13 Food & drinks stalls
14 Golf course
15 Wat Laem Sai
16 Narai Hotel
17 Snooker Hall
18 Anytime Bar
19 Offshore Bar
20 Dim Sum Restaurant
21 Parlang Bar
22 Restaurant
23 Fueng Fha Restaurant
24 Royal Palace Hotel
25 Provincial Hall
26 Beer Corner
27 Lobby lounge, snooker & pub
28 Jazz Pub
29 Bliss Food & Drink
30 Wat Chai Mongkon
31 Lake Inn Hotel
32 Share Taxi to Hat Yai
33 Wat Hua Pom Nai

Laem Son Onn

Hat Son Onn

Hat Samila

Khao Thung Kuan

Khao Noi

Gulf of Thailand

Chai Khao Rd

Sukhum Rd

Sadao Rd

Sai Ngam Rd

Platha Rd

Songkhla Lake

Ratchadamnoen Rd

Laep Rim Talay Rd

See:
Central
Songkhla

Talay Luang Rd

To Khao Seng

Songkhla

Salburae Rd

To Hat Yai

0   800 m

Legend

1   Wat Sai Ngam
2   Smile Inn
3   Buses to Hat Yai
4   A/C buses to Bangkok
5   Bangkok Bank of Commerce
6   Songkhla Hotel
7   Holland House
8   Arom Guesthouse
9   Amsterdam Guesthouse
10 Museum
11 Buses to Ranot
12 Sooksomboon Hotel
13 Sooksomboon 2 Hotel
14 Digital clock
15 Rabiang Thong Restaurant
16 7-eleven
17 P.M.s House
18 Songtheaws to Ko Yaw
19 Queen Hotel
20 Thai Farmers Bank
21 Night market
22 City Hall
24 Market
25 7-eleven
26 Siam Commercial Bank
27 Train station (not in use)
28 Post Office
29 Wat Yang Thong
30 Hospital
31 Arai Restaurant
32 Chinese temple
33 Wat Matchimawat
34 Viengsawan Hotel

Orientation

Ramwithi Road is the main thoroughfare and splits Songkhla in two. On the western side are the narrow lanes, wats and wooden houses of the old town along with the market and main commercial area, whilst to the east on the Gulf side are the newer, wider streets and the administrative buildings. The northern tip of the peninsula has the parkland, the beaches and two hills, Khao Noi and Khao Tung Kuan.

Vital Information

Post Office is located opposite the market by the lake side of town.
Banks are mostly along Ramwithi Road or around the market area, see the map for details.
Hospital is on Ramwithi Road, see the map for its position.
Police Station is at the northeastern end of town.
Codes Songkhla's telephone code is (074) and the postal code is 90000.

Cheap Sleeps

Most cheap hotels are concentrated between Khao Tung Kuan and the market area. The Chinese part of town around Nang Ngarm Road has some older cheap Chinese hotels.

Narai Hotel, ☎ (074) 311 078, 12/2 Chai Khao Road, at the foot of the hill is a pretty good spot run by a friendly family with spacious rooms for 120B with share bathroom. If the family could stop their dogs from running around the house barking crazily and do something about the 10 watt lightbulbs in the rooms, which preclude any recreation which requires illumination, this would be a very good hotel.

Slightly south, by the museum on Rong Muang Road are a collection of guesthouses.

Holland House mainly caters to long term residents rather than backpackers.

Arom Guesthouse this friendly place has double rooms for 150B and a dormitory for 75B. There is also a small cafe and, usefully, bicycles are for rent.

Amsterdam Guesthouse at 15/3 Rong Muang Road, ☎ (074) 314 890, is very popular and is under Dutch management. Singles/doubles are 180B/200B with fan and shared toilet.

Songkhla Hotel just around the corner on Lamsai Road, this place has rooms with fan for 140B and 180B for fan and shower.

Smile Inn is just past the Songkhla Hotel which is a friendly modern hotel with an inexpensive restaurant on the ground floor. Rates start at 200B for fan and shower and 300B for A/C.

Saithong Hotel is further north on the same road, on the other side of the hill. The hotel is a little pricey at 250B but is in a quiet part of town. There is a bar downstairs.

Near the market on Saiburi Road are three hotels very close together.

Queen Hotel at 20 Saiburi Road, ☎ (074) 323 273, starts at singles/doubles 280B/350B all with fan and shower.

Sooksomboon 2 is next door at 14-18 Saiburi Road, ☎ (074) 323 808, and is quite a nice spot and the rates start at 160B.

Sooksomboon Hotel is just up from the Sooksomboon 2 and new A/C rooms start at 400B. If you want to stay in the Chinese quarter of town, try the **Viengsavan Hotel** which is reasonable at 180B with fan and shower. Otherwise cheaper hotels also exist around here for the more adventurous.

Eat and Meet

Good daytime eating is available in the market and night market near the old train station. There are plenty of Chinese cafes off Nang Ngam Road - try **Arai** and some excellent dim sum restaurants on Sai Ngam Road near the Royal Palace. Around the corner on Sukhum Road is an excellent and very popular restaurant doing seafood and standard Thai dishes at very reasonable rates. Across the road, slightly further south, a more basic but equally popular restaurant does even cheaper Thai fare. **Rabiang Thong** is an ice cream, drinks bar which is popular with the local youngsters.

Alternatively stroll up to Hat Samila where at least a dozen identical seafood restaurants and bars await you on the sand's edge with deckchairs and views through the casuarina trees of the waves coming in from the Gulf - good fresh seafood at reasonable prices and good fresh beer for 60B a large bottle. This is a nice spot to while away an hour.

For bars and nightlife there are two main areas, the Sai Ngam/Sadao area with farang type bars such as Offshore, Anytime and Parlang; and Pratha Road with bars such as Bliss, Jazz Pub etc which often have live music and are popular with the local groovers.

Songkhlas Zebra Doves
Something which Songkhla is famous for is its Zebra Doves. You may well see them hanging outside houses in little bamboo cages as they are regarded as both a sign of good luck and prosperity with the best birds worth hundreds of thousands of baht.

Things to do ◆ Sights to See

In a word, plenty! The above mentioned Samila Beach is a hive of activity in the evenings and weekends, the sea is not particularly inviting here but it is nice to look at whilst the adjacent park areas are crowded with picnics, football matches, kite flyers, toddler walkers and farang spotters! On Saturdays and holidays a market sets up behind the seafood cafe selling bric-a-brac, clothes, nibbles, whiskey and so on. All very entertaining.

At the eastern edge of the beach is the Laem Hin Pavilion and Songkhla's famous mermaid statue sitting on a rock. Offshore you can see the two offshore islands of Ko Maeo and Ko Nu which supposedly look like lions...we were unable to find out just how many Singhas this vision requires, although maybe you need to be approaching in a pirate ship to grasp it.

Heading north from Hat Samila is a quieter, long stretch of tree lined beach called Hat Son Onn. This makes a good walk at low tide, as at high tide the beach can be a bit grubby. The parallel road behind the trees is also lined with bars, but is distinctly sleazier than at Samila Beach. Reaching the northern tip of the cape is another popular spot for locals with plenty of snack stalls and benches to sit on and yet more picnicking areas. If you are too lazy to walk here a tuk tuk should cost 5B or a motorbike taxi will cost 10B.

Khao Noi and Khao Tung Kuan   เขาน้อย   เขาตังกวน
These two small wooded hills are situated between Songkhla centre and Samila Beach. The road leading between them has a few *som tam* and drink stalls, deckchairs and loads of monkeys. There is nothing at Khao Noi apart from trees but it is a nice place to wander around. A variety of constructions sit upon the slightly higher Khao Tung Kuan, these include a lighthouse, a shrine and a royal residence built in 1888 for Rama IV by the governor of Songkhla. There is an interesting mix of western, Thai and Chinese architectural styles and an even more interesting view from the top looking over Songkhla Lake on one side and Samila Beach and the Gulf of Thailand on the other. Steps lead up here (only 207) and are located on the west side of the hill.

National Museum
This interesting old Chinese style pavilion was built in 1878 and was formerly the governor's residence. Set in quiet gardens, the pavilion is currently undergoing restoration. The exhibits include various Stone Age items and odds and ends from most historical periods, particularly from the Srivajaya Period when Songkhla first attained importance. Admission is 10B and it is open 9.00 am to 4.00 pm daily except for Monday and Tuesday. Next door is the house belonging to the 16th Prime Minister of Thailand which is a well preserved and beautiful old traditional wooden house. Opposite this is a 50 m stretch of brick wall which is all that remains of the former Songkhla city walls built in 1836 by the governor of the province for Rama III for a cost of 1,600B! The entire wall used to form a rectangle of 400 m by 1,200 m around the city.

Wat Matchimawat or Wat Klang   วัดมัชฌิมาวาส
This attractive old wat in the Chinese district of town was originally constructed in 1590 and demonstrates considerable Chinese influence. The ordination hall contains some great murals and there is even a small museum on the grounds containing further Srivajaya Period items. The museum is open the same hours as the National Museum.

Old Town
While you are in this area of town check out the narrow streets around Nang Ngam and Nakhon Nai Roads. This is the oldest part of town and there are some interesting shops and houses.

Wats
Other wats which may be of interest to wat freaks are dotted around town and include **Wat Chaimongkhon**, **Wat Hua Pom Nai** and **Wat Laem Sai**.

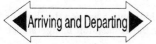
◀ Arriving and Departing ▶

Train
The train station at Songkhla no longer operates.

Bus
There is no central bus station in town, so pick them up at one of the stops along Ramwithi Road. There are also minibuses to **Nakhon Si Thammarat** and **Hat Yai**, but for most destinations outside of Songkhla Province, you are best to go via Hat Yai. Air conditioned buses to **Bangkok** depart from Lamsai Road near the Songkhla Hotel at 07.00, 15.30 and 17.00 for the 14 hour trip which costs 425B (non A/C 236B). Green buses to **Hat Yai** leave every 15 minutes from the top end of Saiburi Road stopping along Ramwithi Road. The trip takes 20 minutes and costs 10B. There are also regular buses to **Nakhon Si Thammarat** and **Surat Thani**.

AROUND SONGKHLA

Kao Seng   เก้าเส้ง
This attractive fishing village and nice beach just 3 km south of Songkhla is a good place to see the brightly painted **Kaw Lae** fishing boats typical of far southern Thailand. Songtheaws leave from the market area in Songkhla, take 10 minutes and cost 8B.

Khao Daeng
This was the original site of Songkhla town, until the King in Ayutthaya burnt it down (This action may have caused the somewhat grovelling nature of later Songkhla governors!) Not a lot remains except for a cemetery and a fort near the road to Ko Yaw. A path leads to the top of the hill from where you will have a fantastic view and very sore thighs. This large wooded hill is directly opposite Songkhla town to the northwest on the other side of the lake, a ferry to here costs 10B and leaves from the north of town or a songtheaw can be taken via Ko Yaw for 12B.

Ban Ko Yaw   เกาะยอ
Seven kilometres from Songkhla via the Tinnasulanon Bridge (the longest in Thailand) this small wooded island on Songkhla Lake is known for its **weaving industry**, its **seafood** and its **folklore museum**.

Just past the bridge is Ko Yaw village with a small market selling locally woven cloth and lots of dried fish - not wildly exciting, but the pretty material is much cheaper here than by the time it gets to the weekend market in Bangkok. There are also plenty of good seafood restaurants between the village and the lake.

Two kilometres further on is the village of **Ban Ao Sai** where you will find the folk museum just before the second bridge on a small hill to the left. The museum is part of the Institute for Southern Thai Studies and is obviously very well financed. It is a large museum with well displayed exhibits and English explanations. There are 17 exhibition rooms containing historical, religious, cultural and folklore displays, so it will take a while to explore but it is certainly fascinating and very informative. If you are in a hurry, the coconut graters and Kris (wiggly knives common in southern Thailand and Malaysia) rooms are recommendations. The museum is set in well tended gardens and has a good view over the lake. There is also a small cafe on the site. Admission is 50B but worth it (30B for Thais!) and the museum is open 8.30 am to 5.30 pm daily.

Far South

On the western end of the island, 5 minutes walk from the museum away from the main road, are some quiet, **cheap seafood restaurants** built on stilts over the lake, looking across the water to the prawn and shellfish 'farms' stretching across the inland sea. This area is very scenic and fried rice with prawns goes for only 25B.

There are plenty of good spots on Ko Yaw for walking, either around the shore or into the hills. **Wat Khao Po** set on the lake side just over the Tinnasulon Bridge is also interesting and has a small market in front.

To get here, songtheaws leave regularly from the market area in Songkhla or along Ramwithi Road for 10B. Red buses bound for Ranot also pass through here and leave from Saiburi and Ramwithi Roads.

Songkhla Lake (Thaleh Sap Songkhla)   ทะเลสาบสงขลา

Actually a lagoon rather than a lake, this body of water extends 80 km north into Phattalung Province and is 20 km wide at its widest point. The lower reaches of the lake are saltwater and are renowned throughout Thailand for their prawns and other seafood, whilst further north the lake becomes freshwater and is an important site for birdlife.

Khao Khut Waterbird Sanctuary   อุทยานนกน้ำคูขุด

One of two well known bird sanctuaries on the lake (the other being **Thale Noi** in Phattalung Province) this sanctuary is situated in Sathing Pra District, 33 km from Songkhla along the road to Ranot and Nakhon Si Thammarat. The sanctuary covers over 500 sq km and has nearly 250 identified species, so take some binoculars. Information available at the visitors centre (closed on Sunday). To see much you will have to hire one of the boats which go for 150B for a 1 hour trip or 400B for a 3 to 4 hour trip including stopovers.

Apart from doing a boat trip there is nothing to do here, except for sitting around in the restaurant or cafe , you cannot really walk anywhere - it really is all water and only of interest to birdwatchers. For the casual visitor Thale Noi is of more interest, although the boat trip here is very pleasant.

To reach here take a red bus bound for Ranot or a songtheaw to Sathing Pra. The ride costs 12B and takes about 45 minutes. The sanctuary is well signposted and around 4 km off the main road - 10B by motorcycle taxi. As there is no accommodation available here, be sure to be out on the main road by 5.00 pm at the latest to catch one of the last buses back to Songkhla.

HAT YAI   หาดใหญ่

Pronounced Hadyai, Hat Yai is in Songkhla Province. Although Hat Yai is only a district of Songkhla Province, it is the province's principal town and the commercial centre of Southern Thailand. For travellers, Hat Yai is an important transportation hub with links to throughout Southern Thailand and into Malaysia. Hat Yai does not have many sites of interest to most travellers, but as far as large Thai towns go, it is not a bad place at all. One reason for spending more than one night in Hat Yai is the food, as many an evening could be spent sampling the wide and varied cuisine available at very reasonable prices.

Orientation

Upon leaving the train station, Thamnoonvitee Road leads east forming the main junction of town. All the action is along Niphat Uthit Roads 1, 2 and 3 which cross Thamnoonvitee one after the other. The main bus station is a 20B ride out of town, but travel agents run minibuses from much closer to town at reasonable prices to virtually everywhere. Most of the travel agents can be found on Niphat Uthit 1 Road within a few blocks of Thamnoonvitee Road.

Far South

Vital Information

Tourist Information (TAT), ☎ (074) 243 747, is on Soi 2 Niphat Uthit 3rd, they are open 8.30 am to 4.30 pm weekdays and 9.00 am to 12.00 am weekends. On weekends, the TAT office is prone to not bother opening.

Post Office On Rattakan Road, about a five minute walk to your left as you leave the train station. This post office is open weekdays and is more convenient than the GPO, although the GPO, which is on Niphat Songkro Road is open seven days (weekends till midday).

Banks The only thing that exceeds the number of banks in Hat Yai is the gold shops. Refer to the maps for their placements.

Tourist Police, ☎ (074) 246733, have two central locations, one by the TAT office on Niphat Uthit 3 Road and the other on the same road past the intersection to Thamnoonvitee Road, though this second office is little more than a kiosk.

Bookshop DK Books has a very good election of English books, guidebooks, and maps. As you leave the train station they are to your right on Thamnoanvitee Road.

Codes Hat Yais's telephone code is (074) and the postal code is 90110

Cheap Sleeps

Cathay Guest House is on the corner of Niphat Uthit 2 Road and Thamnoonvitee Road, three blocks on your right from the train station. The entrance is on Niphat Uthit 2 Road though the ground floor houses Magic Tours. This hotel is pretty popular with travellers and is a good source of information for throughout Thailand and Malaysia. It also has a message board facility, large rooms with shower and fan starting at 160B and the dorm is 60B when it is not full. English is spoken here, and there is a pretty lively night trade going on. Cathay Guest House also provide a small selection of English books for sale.

Weng Aun Hotel is located on Niphat Uthit 1 Road, just past the Muslim Ocha Restaurant, this hotel is the cheapest in town with somewhat grotty rooms for 100B.

Pueng Luang Hotel is near the intersection of Saeng Chan Road and Thamnoonvitee Road, this hotel has nice rooms starting at 170B for a single and 220B for a double.

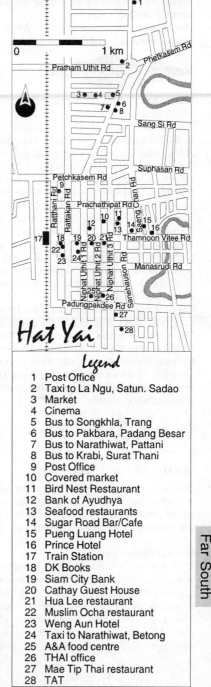

Hat Yai

Legend

1 Post Office
2 Taxi to La Ngu, Satun. Sadao
3 Market
4 Cinema
5 Bus to Songkhla, Trang
6 Bus to Pakbara, Padang Besar
7 Bus to Narathiwat, Pattani
8 Bus to Krabi, Surat Thani
9 Post Office
10 Covered market
11 Bird Nest Restaurant
12 Bank of Ayudhya
13 Seafood restaurants
14 Sugar Road Bar/Cafe
15 Pueng Luang Hotel
16 Prince Hotel
17 Train Station
18 DK Books
19 Siam City Bank
20 Cathay Guest House
21 Hua Lee restaurant
22 Muslim Ocha restaurant
23 Weng Aun Hotel
24 Taxi to Narathiwat, Betong
25 A&A food centre
26 THAI office
27 Mae Tip Thai restaurant
28 TAT

Prince Hotel is quite a walk from the station on Thamnoonvitee Road, has not bad rooms starting at 150B.

Hat Yai has many more hotels, starting at 200B and up and they are concentrated along Niphat Uthit 1, 2, and 3 Roads. Look around and see what you find if these four are full.

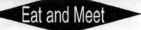

Eat and Meet

Hat Yai has a wide variety of excellent food, including the usual small noodle and rice shops which are along most streets, but some of the best food is in the indoor 'eating lanes' between Niphat Uthit 3 and Sanehanuson Road. Along here you can get fresh crab, lobster, prawns, and other seafood, as well as birds nest soup and the usual dishes.

A&A Food Centre is situated along Niphat Uthit 2 Road, about half way between the Cathay Hotel and the tourist office. The food here is good and everything has been price labelled making it easy to point at what you desire to tantalise your tastebuds.

Mai Tip Thai Food is on Niphat Uthit 3 Road on the corner of Padungphakdee Road. Here they serve reasonable food in a nice setting and it has had really good reviews from many travellers, especially for the curries and vegetarian food.

Beatles Seafood and Bird Nest does good seafood and the **Chinese restaurant** with the Fantasia sign (Hua Lee) above it is very good and popular.

Ocha is a Muslim restaurant and is one worth checking out as it gets rave reviews. This restaurant, as with most Muslim establishments, closes down for Ramadan.

To your right as you leave the train station, there is a **KFC** and **Dunkin Donuts** for those who need a junk food hit.

On your right between Niphat Uthit 1 and Nasatanee Roads, on Thamnonvitee Road, there is a good **bakery**, matched by the other on Niphat Uthit 3 Road at the start of the eating lane. There are also several cheap and good **Muslim places** serving roti and dahl etc on Niyomrat Road between Niphat Uthit 2 and 3 Roads. On Niphat Uthit 1 Road there are good late night **Chinese coffee shops** which serve Jasmine tea and dim sums. **Langma,** this great bar has good live Thai rock most evenings from 9.00 pm onwards. It is on Niphat Uthit 3 Road. There are also some plusher restaurants down towards the Ocean shopping centre, however they also command plusher prices.

Things to do and Sights to See

Wat Hat Yai Nai   วัดหาดใหญ่ใน

This is a large reclining Buddha a few kilometres from the centre of town. Best reached by motorbike taxi for 10B. Underneath the Buddha there is a small shop and museum which is open from 8.30 am to 5.00 pm. Try to visit in the morning as otherwise it is backlit by the sun. The wat is located off Soi 24 Phetkasem Road.

Hat Yai Municipal Park

This park has a rather grotty zoo but is otherwise very nice. It has a lake with a small waterfall and a large fountain where you can hire paddle boats for 30B an hour. There are also the usual snack bars, some excellent restaurants and a very spectacular Bird Park which is open from 8.00 am to 6.00 pm. The huge aviary encloses an entire valley and contains walkways, viewpoints, raised wooden platforms and of course, loads of birds. The park is about 5 km from the centre of town along the road to Songkhla. To get there either catch a songtheaw (10B) or a Songkhla bound bus (4B).

Far South

Bullfights
These are held on the first Saturday of every month from 10.00 am to 3.00 pm. Full details of timing and venues should be gathered at the TAT office. Note: these fights are between two bulls, not one bull and one man.

Things to Buy
There are day and night markets along Niphat Uthit 2 and 3 Roads selling everything from cashews to pineapples, to stereos, to shoes, to batik, to cheap T-shirts and jeans. There is also an indoor strip between Niphat Uthit 2 and 3 Roads which sells handbags, wallets, and so on.

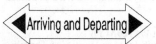

Air
THAI Airlines services Hat Yai with flights to **Bangkok** at least five times a day for 2,280B, to **Phuket** twice a day for 780B and Chiang Mai four times a week for 3,850B. Flights to other areas are as follows: Khon Kaen 3,325B, Narathiwat 420B, Surat Thani 1,200B on Orient Express Air 1,150B), Ubon Ratchathani 3,670, Udon Thani 3,580. Thai International Airways at Hat Yai can be reached on ☎ (074) 245 861. Flights to Kuala Lumpur leave every day except Monday and Wednesday, and there is a minimum of two daily flights to Singapore.

Train
Hat Yai is a major rail junction in Thailand with links south to Sungai Kolok and Padang Besar and to Bangkok to the north. Third class to **Yala** costs 25B and takes 2½ to 3 hours. Hat Yai railway station can be contacted on ☎ (074) 243 706. Refer to the end of the chapter for detailed timetable and price information.

Bus
Hat Yai central bus station is a long way out of town and not really worth the journey unless you have a fascination for bus stations, as buses can be caught closer to town. Thai A/C and normal buses to many regional centres can be caught from near the cinema and they also stop in front of the clocktower. An ordinary bus to **Songkhla** costs 10B and takes about 40 minutes. The easiest way to travel from Hat Yai is to organise it through one of the many travel agents. Magic Travel, below the Cathay Hotel, can organise just about anything and the staff here are very friendly and speak some English. Sample fares are as follows: **Surat Thani** 130B, **Bangkok** 428B (A/C bus), **Krabi** 130B, **Phuket** 200B, **Penang** 200B, **Ko Samui** 220B, **Kuala Lumpur** 250B, **Singapore** 350B. There are many travel agents along Nuphat Uthit 2 Road, all of whom can organise similar deals. For those going to **Betong**, Kinaree Tours on the corner of Niphat Uthit 1 Road and Thamnonvithee Road do minibuses to there for 150B plus all the other usual destinations.

Share Taxi
Share taxis to Songkhla, Satun, Sadao and other destinations leave from in front of the cinema complex on Phetkosen Road, a taxi to **Satun** costs 50B and a taxi to **Yala** costs 40B.

Getting Around
Hat Yai is crawling with tuk tuks whose sole mission in life is to rip off farangs. A better option is the motorbike taxis (they wear numbered vests) who are less unscrupulous than the tuk tuk drivers. Count on paying 5B within the central area and 10B for anything outside the central grid.

AROUND HAT YAI

Khao Nam Khang National Park

Located in Nathawi District, some 60 km and 2 hours from Hat Yai off Route 42, this park stretching over 210 sq km is a good day out from Hat Yai. The park stretches to the Malaysian frontier holding a mountain range honouring the highest peak Khao Nam Khang. The park was also once a base for Malaysian communists who used to hide out along the border regions. One of their camps can be visited within the park and there is a cave and tunnel once used to store equipment and food, although the main attractions are natural. Much of the park is covered in dense forest, reputedly still rich in wildlife. There are a few waterfalls which can be visited as well as Muang Luk Nung, an interesting compilation of boulders. Accommodation is available.

Namtok Ton Nga Chang (Elephant Tusk Waterfall)   น้ำตกโตนงช้าง

Two pronged (hence the name) this seven tiered waterfall is quite large and very nice. There are some nice hikes around the waterfall as well as some pools to cool off in. The waterfall is about 25 km from Hat Yai in Rattaphum District. Songtheaws depart from behind the night market and cost 15B. During the weekend, the waterfall is a popular place to visit amongst the locals and you may need to wait awhile for a ride there. To return, if there are no songtheaws at the waterfall, hitch down the track to the main road (Route 4) and wait for the next Hat Yai bus.

SATUN PROVINCE

This is the southern most province of the west coast of Thailand and is bordered to the north by Trang and Phattalung Provinces, to the east by Songkhla and to the south by Malaysia. The vast majority of the people living in this province are Muslim and this is nowhere more obvious than in the provincial capital of Satun. The province is best known for its offshore islands which form the Ko Tarutao National Marine Park, but also has a couple of other attractions making a visit here well worth the effort.

SATUN   สตูล

Satun Province has been somewhat shielded from the bustling provinces to its east and as a result the capital, Satun, retains a quiet atmosphere and is a pleasant place to hang around. The majority of the locals here are Muslim and the gold topped mosque dominates the centre of town. The one thing which may put it on the travellers map is that you can cross to Langkawi Island and Kuala Perlis (both in Malaysia) by boat from here.

Orientation

Satun is so small you could walk from one side to the other in about 15 minutes. The main roads are Burivanich Road and Satun Thanee Road, both crossed by Samantha Pradit Road just past the centre of town. As you enter from Hat Yai, the main landmark building is the Wang Mai Hotel.

Vital Information

Tourist Centre Satun Tourist centre is on the road opposite Thai Farmers Bank.
Post Office This is on Samantha Pradit Road, just past the Satun Thanee Road intersection. It has EMS and overseas phone facilities upstairs.
Banks Thai Military Bank, Bank of Ayudhya, and Thai Farmers Bank all have branches in Satun, refer to the map for details.

Police Station has a booth on Satun Thanee Road, near to the banks.
Immigration Office is on Burivanich Road, just north of Satun Library.
Codes Satun's telephone code is (074) and the postal code is 91000.

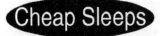

Cheap Sleeps

Udomsuk Hotel At the corner of Sarit Phuminarot Road and Hatthakam Seuksa Road, this is probably the best budget stay in Satun. Rooms start at 120B and the management is very friendly. The hotel also has a nice garden to kick back in.
Rain Tong Hotel Better located than the Udomsuk Hotel, on the end of Samantha Pradit Road, this hotel has big rooms with shower starting at 120B and the management speaks some English.
Satul Thani Hotel on Satun Thanee Road, with its noise outside, this hotel is really only a last resort, with rooms starting at 190B.

Eat and Meet

In the lane between the vacant block (sometimes home to kid's rides) and the Shell station, an **evening market** sets up with a variety of Thai and Muslim food for cheap prices. On Samantha Pradit Road between the Rain Tong Hotel and Burivanich Road there are a few **noodle shops** with the usual fare.

On the above mentioned lane there is some very yummy food, on the vacant block side there are stand up stalls doing **fruit and chicken satay style dishes**, whilst on the other side, there are some sit down stalls making tremendously delicious curries for only 15B. Similar places with similar prices are on Satun Thanee Road opposite the vacant block on the river side of Burivanich Road. Opposite the lot and north of the immigration office there is an open air restaurant that is more pricey. There is also a **vegetarian cafe** on Satun Thanee Road opposite the Melee Supermarket.

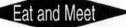

Things to do **and** Sights to See

The only vaguely interesting thing to do in Satun is to wander around the base of the hillock to the northwest of town. At its base there are some small shrines where the monks live, and further around there is a poor fishing village set in the mangroves - quite photogenic. Further still there is a bridge over to another poor village. A bit of a contrast to the centre of town.

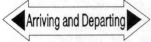

Arriving and Departing

Bus
An air-conditioned minibus from **Hat Yai** costs 40B and takes about 1½ hours, a normal fan big bus costs 28B. There is no central bus station in Satun. There is only a bus depot outside of town. The buses come in to Satun on Satun Thanee Road and leave via Burivanich Road (ie go in a circle) so just stand on Burivanich Road and flag the one you want. An A/C bus to Bangkok costs 427B.

Share Taxis
Share taxis to **Hat Yai**, **La-Ngu** (25B) and **Pakbara** leave from Burivanich Road opposite the Thai Military Bank. Orange songtheaws to **Tammalang pier** leave from just to the south of Thai Farmers Bank and cost 10B, a motorcycle taxi costs 20B.

Far South

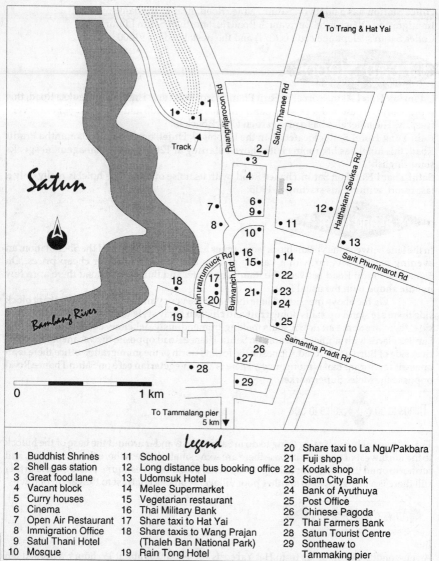

Legend

1	Buddhist Shrines	11	School
2	Shell gas station	12	Long distance bus booking office
3	Great food lane	13	Udomsuk Hotel
4	Vacant block	14	Melee Supermarket
5	Curry houses	15	Vegetarian restaurant
6	Cinema	16	Thai Military Bank
7	Open Air Restaurant	17	Share taxi to Hat Yai
8	Immigration Office	18	Share taxis to Wang Prajan
9	Satul Thani Hotel		(Thaleh Ban National Park)
10	Mosque	19	Rain Tong Hotel

20	Share taxi to La Ngu/Pakbara
21	Fuji shop
22	Kodak shop
23	Siam City Bank
24	Bank of Ayuthuya
25	Post Office
26	Chinese Pagoda
27	Thai Farmers Bank
28	Satun Tourist Centre
29	Sontheaw to Tammaking pier

Boats

Boats to **Kuala Perlis** and **Langkawi Island** leave from Tammalang pier, about 5 km to the south of Satun. Boats to **Langkawi Island** leave at 09.00, 13.00, and 16.00 pm whilst boats coming the other way leave at 07.45, 11.00, and 14.30. A boat either way costs 150B and on occasion the 16.00 boat from Satun may leave up to 45 minutes earlier. Boats to **Kuala Perlis** cost 30B. The boat to Langkawi takes 2 hours. You cannot change money at Tammalang pier so be sure to have some baht if leaving Malaysia and if going the other way remember banks are closed on east coast Malaysia on Thursday afternoon and Friday.

Far South

AROUND SATUN

Thale Ban National Park   อุทยานแห่งชาติทะเลบัน

This picturesque National Park is about 40 km from Satun and was established and opened on 27 October 1980. There are three main habitats within the National Park; tropical evergreen forest, mixed deciduous and mangroves. The park is also abundant in wildlife and has a number of waterfalls and caves worth visiting. The park is suspected to have taken its name for the Malay words *leur* and *ga ban* which describe low lying marshland. It is believed that an earthquake in the past acted to form the present day valley and its many surrounding caves and waterfalls.

The highest point in the park is Khao Gin at 756 m and the total area of the park is 196 sq km. One of the major problems which the park faces is in areas where the park has been deforested and the claylike soil tends to slide after prolonged rain, in turn creating more exposed earth. When the park was originally declared the main role of the staff was one of protection, but now that it is felt the park is fairly 'secure', tourism and education are becoming an important part of the staff role.

The park headquarters can supply you with some information regarding the park and most of the waterfalls and caves are clearly signposted from the park headquarters. None of the waterfalls are stunningly breathtaking, but the lake, right beside the visitors centre, is beautiful and well worth a day trip from Satun for an afternoon picnic.

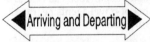

The National Park Authority maintain some nice bungalows which are set upon a large freshwater lake near the National Park Office. The bungalows sleep five people for 1,000B per night and there is a restaurant nearby.

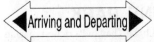

From Satun
Songtheaws leave from nearly opposite the Rain Tong Hotel, some are marked in English either Thale Ban National Park or Wang Prajan. The fare is 20B and takes about one hour. The entrance to the National Park is not marked, but a sealed road runs off to your left just after the 20 km mark towards Wang Prajan. From this turn-off it is a five minute walk to the National Park HQ. Songtheaws returning to Satun can be quite irregular, but it is not difficult to hitch a ride back to Satun. A better way to reach Thale Ban is by hired motorbike as some of the caves are a long distance from the National Park headquarters.

WANG PRAJAN

This **border crossing** to Malaysia is little known to travellers, but is one of the cheapest ways to get another 30 days on your visa. The crossing is about 2 km further north of the National Park turn-off and costs 20B to reach from Satun. There is also a small market here but nothing else. The border is open seven days.

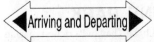

Songtheaws depart from opposite the Rain Tong Hotel, cost 20B and take about 1 hour. These songtheaws can be quite infrequent, particularly in the middle of the day. Early morning is often the best time to try. Hitching to the border is not too much trouble.

LA-NGU   ละงู

This small town marks the junction of Route 416 and the road down to the pier at Pakbara. Most people end up here for a little while as they wait for their songtheaws to coordinate. Importantly, La-Ngu has the **closest bank** to the offshore islands and will exchange travellers cheques and give cash advances. The branch is at the Satun end of town, down a road on your right once you have passed the Sri La Ngu Hotel. La-Ngu does have a bustling market, which is a great place to buy cheap food if you are planning on spending a while on the islands.

Cheap Sleeps

Only really for the desperate, who arrive too late to push onto Pakbara, the **Sri La Ngu Hotel** is about half way between the turn-off to Satun and the share taxi stand from Satun. Passable rooms here start at 120B.

Arriving and Departing

A share taxi from Satun to **La-Ngu** costs 25B and takes about one hour, ask them to drop you at the songtheaw station for Pakbara. From La-Ngu a songtheaw costs 8B and takes about 15 minutes to reach Pakbara wharf. The share taxi stand back to Satun from La-Ngu is almost opposite the stand from Satun, a little further from the Satun turn-off. The local bus from La-Ngu to **Trang** costs 30B and takes between 2 and 2½ hours.

PAKBARA

The beach here is mainly mudflats and pretty dirty. The wharf area is the central 'downtown' and there is a pool hall to keep the bored happy and some good Muslim food can be had at the small market area just before the pier. There are a number of travel agents near to the wharf who can organise tickets to the regional and usual destinations.

Cheap Sleeps

The beach just before Pakbara 'town' is lined with some drab and dreary bungalows generally of the concrete variety.

Marina Bungalows These are the first set of bungalows (coming form the wharf). It has huge rooms in concrete longhouses and concrete bungalows for 150B with shower and fan.

Andrew Tours also have a few rooms for hire in their house. Rates start at 50B per person and they occasionally offer tours of Pakbara's karaoke bars in the evening!

Arriving and Departing

A songtheaw to **La-Ngu** takes about 15 minutes and costs 8B. They leave regularly throughout the day.

KO TARUTAO NATIONAL MARINE PARK

This National Park is made up of 51 islands and is believed to be Thailand's richest marine reserve. The two main groups of islands are the Tarutao group and the Adang - Rawi grouping. Ko Tarutao was once a prison for political prisoners and remains of the prison can be seen today. All of the islands are plentiful in wildlife, with Ko Tarutao in particular having a wide and obvious range of monkeys and birdlife. Dolphins and whales have been sighted in this area, as have turtles. The Thais used to see quite a few crocodiles on Ko Tarutao but they shot the last one twenty odd years ago. Due to weather considerations (ie., the ocean being a stormy angry mass) **no boats run** out to Ko Tarutao, Ko Adang and Ko Lipe from mid May to mid November.

KO TARUTAO   เกาะตะรุเตา

Empty beaches with sand like dust and not a bungalow or person in site is standard on Ko Tarutao. Here the beaches are lined by pine rather than palm trees, and the hills behind are heavily forested, but the most remarkable feature is the silence. Here it is so quiet that you can hear the things which are so quiet you normally cannot hear them (except when the generators come on at 6.00 pm). There are only about a half dozen motorcycles on the whole of the island, and the ferries only arrive twice a day. In fact, probably the loudest thing here are the geckos.

The beaches are nice, although the water off Aow Pante is generally too cloudy for snorkelling and is notorious for its sandflies. This island is great for a couple of days before heading further afield out to Ko Lipe or Ko Adang. The longer walks, particularly to the far end of the island, are really only feasible to visit if you are camping and have your own supplies as the length of the walks limits the day trips to a couple of beaches.

Ko Tarutao has some good possibilities for hiking with some particularly long and strenuous walks available. This is the perfect place for self contained campers to explore the island at their leisure. Some of the trails are clear, others quite badly overgrown. Hopefully the trails will be cleared up in the future.

During the holidays and weekends, Ko Tarutao is a hit with the Thais and it can get a little busy. At this time the boats can get a bit erratic with the regular large boats making the trip as well as smaller dinky boats.

Lone Fisherman en-route to Ko Tarutao

Cheap Sleeps

The National Park Authority runs bungalows, cottages and longhouses about a five minute walk from the park office. The longhouses are ten rooms long, with each room having four beds. One bed costs 80B a night. The bungalows sleep eight people for 800B, and the cottages sleep six for 600B. Camping is also allowed at Ao San and Ao Jak, but you need to bring your own tent. The rates vary with a maximum of 10B.

Eat and Meet

On Ko Tarutao there is only one restaurant, the **Co-op Restaurant** on Ao Pante, between the park office and the longhouses. The food here is more expensive than the mainland, but is generally pretty good and the seafood salad is spicy with a capital S.

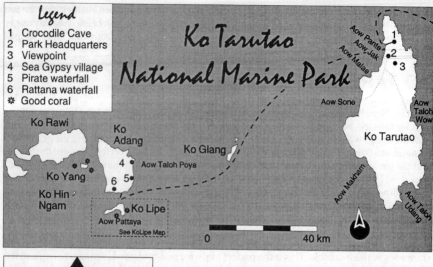

Legend

1 Crocodile Cave
2 Park Headquarters
3 Viewpoint
4 Sea Gypsy village
5 Pirate waterfall
6 Rattana waterfall
✸ Good coral

Ko Tarutao National Marine Park

Things to do and Sights to See

There is a nice hike from the park office to the top of Toh Boo Hill. The walk takes about 20 minutes and the view from the top is very nice, all the way down the beach. As you leave the wharf, take the trail to your left past the Park Headquarters. There is then a sign marked "Toh Boo Nature Trail", "are you here" and the track is easy to follow.

From the pier by the National Park headquarters you can take a boat ride up the river to a cave. You were once able to walk into the cave, but the platform is in a state of disrepair. It is known as the Crocodile Cave, though the last crocodile was shot 20 years ago. To hire a longtail up to the cave and back costs about 200B.

◀ Arriving and Departing ▶

Boats

Boats usually leave from Pakbara wharf everyday at 10.30 and 15.00 and cost 100B each way. You generally buy a return ticket at Pakbara for 200B. The dinky boat takes 1½ to 2 hours, and if the swell is high, expect quite a hairy trip. Returning to Pakbara from Tarutao, the boats leave from the National Park wharf at 9.00 am and 2.00 pm (not Tuesday, Thursday and Saturday), costing 100B.

To Ko Adang and Ko Lipe

Boats leave from the National Park wharf at 1.00 pm on Tuesday, Thursday and Saturday. You can buy the ticket for this boat also at Pakbara and if you buy this ticket and your one to Ko Tarutao at the same time, you should get some discount. At Pakbara, the ticket costs 180B each way, therefore a return for 360B, and the boat takes around 2½ hours from Ko Tarutao to reach Ko Lipe and Ko Adang. Upon reaching the channel between Ko Adang and Ko Lipe, you are ferried by longboat for 20B to either Ko Lipe (various beaches) or Ko Adang.

Ko Lipe Travel Tips
The seas en-route to Ko Lipe can be savage to say the least. It is not unusual for boats around here to sink and those with weak stomachs should consider skipping breakfast if the weather is sour. If the weather is good, don't forget the suncream — you'll need it.

Far South

KO LIPE   เกาะลิเป

If you are looking for a tranquil piece of paradise, Ko Lipe is about as close as you are likely to get. Great snorkelling and some very nice beaches and bays make this a place which becomes very easy to get stranded on.

Besides the lovely beaches and great snorkelling, the people here are also particularly friendly and hospitable. You can do interesting fishing/snorkelling boat trips from here and also organise transport over to the secluded Ko Adang. The shop near the oval and school also have a good book selection and flippers for hire.

Important: There are NO money changing facilities on Ko Lipe or Ko Tarutao except for small amounts of cash. The closest bank for travellers cheques and credit cards is at La-Ngu on the mainland. Make sure you have enough money to last before you leave the mainland. It can be more expensive than you plan as people often stay longer than expected and if the weather is bad boats can be cancelled. Many people who visit Ko Lipe have problems running short of money.

Cheap Sleeps

If you agree to stay five days or more, you should be able to get a discount. On a whole, accommodation is not too cheap on Ko Lipe as there are only three bungalow operations.

Chaolea Resort is on the eastern side of the island with bungalows with shower for 150B and 200B. Offshore there is some very good snorkelling. Chaolea Resort has a good restaurant and has a second branch of the restaurant on Pattaya Beach.

Pattaya Song Resort is without a doubt on the nicest and longest beach on the island and has bungalows at 100B, 150B and 200B. The down side is that the restaurant at Pattaya resort is very small and fills early.

Lipae Resort This large resort has bungalows for 200B to 300B, although they are a bit close together and the restaurant is not very good.

Eat and Meet

All the bungalows have restaurants which use the same menu (with local variations). Prices are higher then the mainland but not excessively. There is a restaurant and general store to the north of Chaolea Resort near the football field and there is also a **restaurant** on Pattaya Beach which is the most popular place on the island.

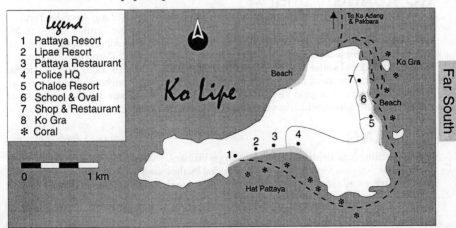

Legend

1 Pattaya Resort
2 Lipae Resort
3 Pattaya Restaurant
4 Police HQ
5 Chaloe Resort
6 School & Oval
7 Shop & Restaurant
8 Ko Gra
✳ Coral

0   1 km

Ko Lipe

To Ko Adang & Pakbara

Beach

Ko Gra

Beach

Hat Pattaya

Far South

Snorkelling

Snorkelling is the top activity on Ko Lipe. Gear can be hired for 100B for a set of mask, snorkel and fins, but they can be difficult to find, so bring your own if you can. The best snorkelling is off the beach from Chaolea Resort, around the northern islet, and around the point with Pattaya Beach to the south. The fish here are often brilliant colours and abundant everywhere you look.

For a pretty walk, it is possible to hike around the entire island of Ko Lipe. If you take your snorkelling gear with you (highly recommended) it will take all day to do the walk. You will find little bays here and there with some brilliant snorkelling. The beach off Chaolea Resort is quite long but gets dirty with the prevailing westerly winds. Pattaya Beach is beautiful and very clean.

Longtails can be hired at Ko Lipe for around 100B per hour - a very cheap price considering how many people you can get in a longtail.

Water Activities

Ko Lipe often catches strong westerly winds, making it an excellent place for windsurfing (but there is no local gear for hire so you will need to bring your own).

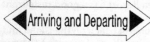

Boat

The boat to **Ko Tarutao** leaves at 9.00 am. However if the swell has picked up, this can be quite a traumatic trip to say the least, and may take up to four and a half hours. On occasion the boats may leave in the afternoon when the wind has died down a bit or they may not leave at all. Do not count on returning to Pakbara from Ko Lipe and/or Tarutao in time to make the connection to Ko Bulon. If the weather slows you down, you will miss the 2.00 pm boat to Ko Bulon as it does not wait. To hire a longboat to Bulon costs 1,200B one way from Pakbara or about 4,000B from Ko Lipe for a direct trip to Ko Bulon. In peak season, boats run a circuit running Pakbara - Ko Tarutao - Ko Lipe - Ko Bulon - Pakbara.

KO ADANG   เกาะอาดัง

The National Park Authority runs the only accommodation on Ko Adang. As on Ko Tarutao, this consists of rooms for four costs 280B, singles 70B. Unlike Ko Tarutao, many of the bungalows are derelict, without roofs etc. There is no shop within walking distance to speak of, though many people do camp here. There is a park entrance fee of 50B and bring as much of your own food and water as you can carry. It is not possible to walk along the coast to the fishing village, so you need to either beat a track through or catch a longboat, although you can climb up the cliffs for a great view of Ko Lipe and surrounds. There are also a number of waterfalls on the island, which can be visited by boat from Ko Lipe.

KO YANG

The snorkelling (and fishing) around Ko Yang is brilliant, without doubt the best in the area. Vast coral outcrops cover the bottom, surrounded by thousands of lively and vivid coloured fish. You are not allowed to stay on Ko Yang and to reach there the cheapest way is to get a group of people together and hire a longboat. Most places on Ko Lipe can organise it for between 600B and 900B for the day. Some offer a seafood lunch while you are there, others to cook all you catch, so shop around and see what you find.

Far South

KO BULON LAE

Situated approximately 20 km from Pakbara pier (about 1 hour by longtail), Ko Bulon forms a halfway point between Ko Lipe and one of the more crowded islands such as Ko Tao. The island has a number of small rocky bays to its north and one long sandy beach on its northeast corner, backing onto the islands most popular resorts, Pansand Resort, and Bulone Lae Resort. There is a very small fishing village to the north on Panka Yai Bay and a number of other sights worth seeing, including a bat cave and a moon sighting platform. There is only one 'real' shop on the island, which is considerably overpriced, so it is not a bad idea to bring some commodities (such as whisky) yourself.

Cheap Sleeps

Pansand Resort This is the flashest and best known of the operations and maintains a high quality, low impact resort. Longhouse beds cost 70B and small A-frame bungalows (suitable for singles or really close couples). Then bungalows (large) jump up to 250B, 600B and 800B. The resort also has a large spacious restaurant. Snorkelling mask and snorkel can be hired for 40B for 4 hours and various boat trips can be arranged from here. The resort also has international phone facilities from 8.00 pm to 10.00 pm and books for sale.

Bulon Lae Resort This resorts' bungalows start at 70B with a double bed, then smallish bungalows start at 100B and large bungalows for 170B (all with share bathrooms). If you plan to stay awhile try for a discount, but if they agree, get it in writing, as the staff here are known to 'forget'. Given the number of bungalows, the restaurant is pretty small and gets very crowded. Also for some unknown reason, the restaurant serves no Thai food before 10.00 am. The bungalows hire snorkelling gear (including flippers) for 80B and also hires spearguns and fishing rods. It is also possible to organise fishing trips and snorkelling trips from here.

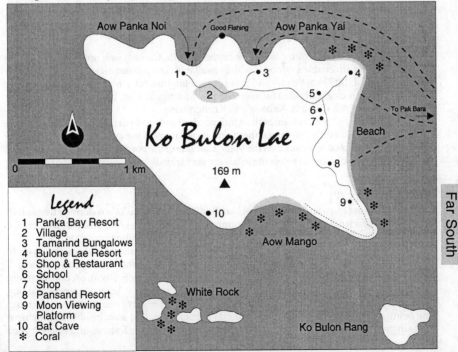

Legend

1 Panka Bay Resort
2 Village
3 Tamarind Bungalows
4 Bulone Lae Resort
5 Shop & Restaurant
6 School
7 Shop
8 Pansand Resort
9 Moon Viewing Platform
10 Bat Cave
✻ Coral

Far South

Tamarind Resort on Panka Yai Bay. This resort is open on an off and on basis. The bay is very rocky and the bungalow operation is by the fishing village.

Panka Bay Resort These nice, well positioned bungalows are about a ten minute walk from the main beach and are very quiet. All bungalows here are 150B with shower and toilet. The bay here is all rocky but the view from the bungalows is very nice. The restaurant has slightly more reasonable prices than the other bungalow restaurants.

Things to do **and** Sights to See

Snorkelling

The beach near the rocks near Bulon Lae Resort has good snorkelling. Also on Mango Bay the snorkelling is said to be good. Bulon Lae Resort offers combined snorkelling and fishing trips to White Rock off Mango Bay as well as four day 'Adventure trips' to the surrounding islands (you sleep on Ko Lipe) but visit Ko Adang, Ko Rawi, Ko Yang and Ko Bulon, and many others for 2,500B all inclusive. They also hire fishing equipment.

On the 'rock' around from Panka Bay there is good fishing - popular with locals. Below Pansand Resort there is a 'moon viewing' platform and a big cave, full of bats. If none of this is of interest, just lie on the beach.

◀ **Arriving and Departing** ▶

Longboats leave from **Pakbara** pier at 2.00 pm for 100B each way and take between 45 minutes to one and half hours dependent on the weather. The boat leaves from Ko Bulon Lae at 9.00 am, check at your guesthouse for details on where it leaves from as they rotate around the island.

YALA PROVINCE

Of the 14 southern Thai provinces, Yala is farthest south, the only one not bordered by the sea, yet good and affordable seafood is widely available. The province itself is 1,440 km from Bangkok by road, 1,055 km by rail, and is very mountainous, offering very little flat land for farming. The province is divided into six districts: Muang, Betong, Bannang Star, Yaha and Raman, with two sub-districts: Kabang and Krongpinang.

In the past, Yala has been both an independent state and part of the adjoining Pattani Province and, as with the other far southern provinces, many of the inhabitants feel they have much more in common with those on the Malaysian side of the border than with their faraway overlords in Bangkok. Nevertheless the locals are very friendly and always keen to be of help.

YALA   ยะลา

Yala is a sprawling town and the capital of Yala Province. The name Yala is derived from a folk word, 'yalor' which means fishing net. Although there is little to see within Yala itself except for Thailand's largest mosque, there are a number of places worth visiting on day trip's.

In the past Yala has been voted as being Thailand's cleanest city, though it is up to the visitor to decide whether this means Yala is clean or if everywhere in Thailand is dirtier!! Yala is also the proud host of the ASEAN Barred Ground Dove Festival, an annual event taking place in March. The event brings feathered friends from many Asian countries including Thailand, Singapore, Malaysia, and Indonesia to take part in dove competitions, the main one being a cooing contest with close to 1,500 participants. You may be able to pick up a bargain prize winning bird which are bought and sold during the festival, and also get your hands on some of the local handicrafts.

Vital Information

Banks All the major bank branches are in Yala. Refer to the map for their location.
Police Station There is a mini police station, ☎ (073) 212 636, on Sirorot Road, opposite Ranong Road and the Thai Military Bank. The tourist police can be reached on ☎ 1699.
Hospital Yala Hospital can be reached on ☎ (073) 212 223.
Codes Yala's telephone code is (073) and the postal code is 95000.

Cheap Sleeps

The cheapest and most convenient hotels in Yala are near the railway station.
Aun Ann Hotel (pronounced Ann Ann), ☎ (073) 212 216, at 32-36 Pipitpakdee Road, is probably the best value in town. Here a clean room without shower, but a fan, will cost only 90B and a room with fan and shower will cost 120B.
Yuan Dong Hotel, ☎ (073) 212 306, at 28-30 Pipitpakdee Road, is two doors down from the Aun Aun Hotel towards the train station. This very basic Chinese Hotel has bargain rooms for only 70B with shared shower and toilet.
Shanghai Hotel, ☎ (073) 212 037, at 34-36 Ratakit Road, has cheaper rooms without shower starting at 80B but they are a little dingy and a few blocks further from the station.
Saen Suk Hotel, ☎ (073) 212 038, at 52/3-5 Ratakit Road, is situated beside the Shanghai Hotel and has basic rooms with shared bathroom for 70B.
Thepwiman Hotel, ☎ (073) 212 400, at 31- 37 Sri Bamrung Road, has nice rooms with fan starting at 130B and is both close to the station and some good restaurants.
Phanfar Hotel, ☎ (073) 212 685, at 348-350 Sirorot Road, about a 15 minute walk or 5B songtheaw ride from the train station is quiet, clean and friendly and has rooms with fan and shower starting at 150B.
Hua Ann Hotel, ☎ (073) 212 771, at 352/1 Sirorot Road, is almost beside the Phanfar Hotel and has similar quality rooms starting at 180B.

Eat and Meet

Yala abounds in cheap places to eat. At night there is a **large food market** on the other side of the railway tracks that is very popular with the locals and has all the usual street fare. **Vendors** also line Rot Fai Road on the station side as well. If you prefer to sit down, there are two standout locations for food, especially seafood and shellfish.
One is the **Yalaresto** on the corner of Pipitpakdee Road and Sri Bamrung Road and the other, the **Sattelite Restaurant** is on the corner of Pipitpakdee Road and Ranong Road. Both of these are very popular local spots, the food is good and they have English menus. Of the two, the Yalaresto is probably the cheaper.
Along Ranong Road there are a number of other **Thai places** serving the usual cuisine, handily displayed, so it is easy to point if your Thai is not up to scratch and the one opposite the Police Box is particularly good value.
There is a collection of popular **Chinese restaurants** along Sri Bamrung Road as well.
There are two other **smaller markets**, both running off Sirorot Road, one at the intersection with Chaleun Thai Road and the other runs almost opposite Prachin Road.
There is also an **ice cream parlour** at the intersection of Ranong and Yala Roads.

Of the four far southern provinces Yala, as a result of its extensive rubber cultivation, is the best off. The milking of the rubber trees is extremely labour intensive as each tree needs to be milked by hand. To do this a small incision is made into the bark of the tree and the sap to drip into a container. This is periodically emptied and the rubber is produced on site.

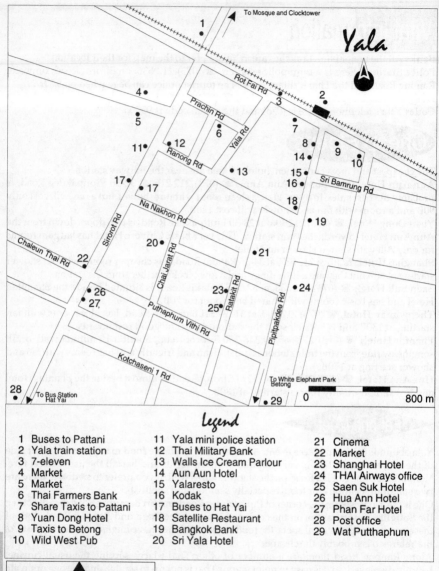

Yala

To Mosque and Clocktower

Legend

1	Buses to Pattani	11	Yala mini police station	21 Cinema
2	Yala train station	12	Thai Military Bank	22 Market
3	7-eleven	13	Walls Ice Cream Parlour	23 Shanghai Hotel
4	Market	14	Aun Aun Hotel	24 THAI Airways office
5	Market	15	Yalaresto	25 Saen Suk Hotel
6	Thai Farmers Bank	16	Kodak	26 Hua Ann Hotel
7	Share Taxis to Pattani	17	Buses to Hat Yai	27 Phan Far Hotel
8	Yuan Dong Hotel	18	Satellite Restaurant	28 Post office
9	Taxis to Betong	19	Bangkok Bank	29 Wat Putthaphum
10	Wild West Pub	20	Sri Yala Hotel	

Things to do and Sights to See

Biggest Mosque in Thailand

This mosque is on Sirorot Road past the railway tracks, about a 10 to 15 minute walk from the station. Other than the fact that it is the biggest mosque in Thailand, there is little reason to visit.

Wat Phutthaphum

Located on Pipitpakdee Road towards Phrupakoi Park, this wat has a pretty good 10 m high golden Buddha in the subduing evil pose.

Phra Buddha Saiyas at Wat Khuhaphimuk (Wat Nah Tham) วัดหน้าถ้ำ
This is one of the most important and most revered sites in Southern Thailand. Wat Nah Tham means 'A temple in front of a cave' and that is more or less what it is. The cave contains an ancient reclining Buddha almost 30 m long and the site is believed to have been established in the year 757. The cave also contains considerable stalactites and in 1986 was voted the most beautiful 'natural' tourist attraction in the Far Southern provinces. Not far from Wat Nah Tham is a cave known as Tham Mued (dark cave) although it is now artificially lighted. The cave contains interesting formations and is probably worth checking out if you go to Wat Nah Tham.

The wat is around 8 km from Yala. To get there, get a songtheaw and ask the driver to let you off at the road leading to Wat Nah Tham along Route 4065 (towards Hat Yai). The ride should cost 5B to 10B and it is about a 10 to 15 minute walk to the site.

White Elephant Field Park สวนสาธารณะสนามช้างเผือก
This pretty park is situated about a 5B songtheaw ride out of the centre of town, along Pipitpakdee Road. It contains the usual collection of plants, ponds and hedge-work animals and makes a pleasant visit from the centre of town if you have a few hours to kill.

Festivals in Yala
Landmark Pole Celebrations - San Chaopor Lak Muang
This festival is held from 25 May to 4 June every year. At this time there are parades, exhibitions and traditional entertainment. This is a very big celebration as the landmark pole is believed to be Yala's guardian spirit and worshipped by the locals.

The construction of the pole, which is located in front of the city hall, was ordered built by King Rama IX, the current King, in 1961. The surrounding area is a garden where many of the locals relax.

Yala Cultural Fair
Generally held around the first weekend in August every year. During this time there are various fruit contests, the highlight of which is definitely the banana eating contest!

◀**Arriving and Departing**▶

Train
Hat Yai train station is located at the northern end of town and can be contacted on ☎ (073) 212 737. Train to **Hat Yai**, third class costs 25B and takes between 2½ and 3 hours. Due to it being a single track most of the way, you sometimes have to wait up to 10 to 15 minutes for a train coming the other way. Trains to Hat Yai leave Yala at 06.30, 11.22, 15.42, 13.50, 14.18, 16.43, 15.05 and 20.59. The train to **Sungai Kolok** is 25B and takes around 2½ hours, though the share taxis are faster. All trains leave on time if they commence at Yala. There is also an advance booking office at Yala train station. For detailed timetable information refer to the end of the Southern Thailand chapter.

Share Taxis
As with most far southern locations, Yala has no central bus station but a number of share taxi stands. The share taxis here are all old Mercedes Benz cars and each carries six people. They are quiet comfortable and once you get going, they are the quickest way to get around. The problem is getting going. Generally, the taxi does not leave until full, so if you are waiting at a bad time (say early to late afternoon), you may wait for over an hour, whilst in the early morning you may not have to wait at all. A way around it is to pay for two seats, then not only is it more comfortable, you get going ASAP (albeit at a higher price). Share taxis to

Betong leave from Rot Fai Road to the right of the train station and take between 2 and 3 hours (depending on the quality of the Merc) for 70B one way. Generally the Mercs stop leaving Yala at 6.00 pm. Share taxis to **Pattani** cost 20B and take 45 minutes and leave from around the train station. Share taxis to **Hat Yai** cost 50B, take 2 hours and leave from a couple of shifting sites in town.

Buses and Vans
Most of the buses through town leave from in front of the train station, although there is no central departure point. A van to **Hat Yai** costs 60B and takes 2 hours, to **Betong** a van costs 50B and takes 2½ hours, to **Narathiwat**, a van takes 2 hours and costs 50B and to **Pattani** the bus leaves every 45 minutes, costs 11B and takes 45 minutes. Air conditioned buses to **Bangkok** leave at 16.00 and 17.00, take 19 hours and cost 460B and the ordinary bus to Bangkok leaves at 14.00 and takes 255B.

AROUND YALA

Yala to Betong
This 138 km trip begins with some limestone scenery, jungle topped crags amongst the rice fields then turns into more rolling hills. The scenery around here is very pretty but it is a pity that there are so many rubber trees at the expense of the dwindling rainforest.

Around 60 km south of Yala you will pass the **Bang Lang Dam**, of which there are good views from the road. Although the dam's main role is a hydroelectric one, the Thais have installed a viewing point for its scenic value.

Buses and taxis stop halfway for refreshment and toilet breaks, then the next point of interest is at the 80 km mark, which is the turn-off for **Ban Sakai**. Four kilometres off the main road, this village is the home to the few remaining **Ngoh** or **Sakai** people.

Formally a nomadic hunting and gathering tribe, they are an aboriginal race with dark skin, frizzy hair and are very small in stature - very similar to other proto-Malay groups still inhabiting parts of Indonesia and the Philippines. Some 20 families live in bamboo houses and are receiving medical and educational assistance from the Thai government. They also receive considerable encouragement to grow rubber plantations, so their nomadic traditional life is more or less at an end.

If you want to visit the village, get off a Betong bound bus when you see the sign for Ban Sakai on the right and walk or hitch the remaining 4 km to the village.

Tham Krasaeng   ถ้ำกระแซง
Krasaeng Cave contains an array of stalactites. This cave and three others within close range (Tham Look Om, Tham Nam Lod and Tham Phra) are located in Banang District, around 8 km from Yala.

Tarnto Waterfall Natural Park   วนอุทยานน้ำตกธารโต
Located at Tham Talu, within a forest reservation, the waterfall falls in nine levels. Take the road from Yala towards Betong, turn off onto a dirt road after about 47 km and follow that for a couple of kilometres.

BETONG   เบตง
Betong is often referred to as the 'town in the mist' although in Malay, Betong means 'bamboo'. It is the southernmost city in Thailand, situated around 140 km from Yala, in a hilly district that borders with Malaysia. Although not a 'hill station' by any standard, the nights here are cooler and the mornings are often quite misty. Almost completely surrounded by rubber plantations, Betong is a good place to see all the rubber being collected and trucked away. It

---

P.U.L.O.(Pattani United Liberation Organisation)
Along with the Kaw Lae fishing boats, this is what Pattani is best known for. This communist inspired movement was formed in the 1950's at the time of the Malayan emergency, to fight for, at best, independence for Pattani, Yala and Narathiwat (collectively known as Pattani), or more recently, a compromise unification with Islamic Malaysia. They have had a variety of bankrollers as time has worn on, from China and Libya in the early days, through to the now defunct U.S.S.R. during the cold war and more recently to hardline Arab states, Iran and radical Islamic groups in Malaysia. However the movement has never really had mass popular support, and with several quite publicized surrenders and amnesties over recent years, activities have declined sharply from their peak in the early 1980's. Isolated incidents still occur, such as the bombing of Hat Yai train station in 1992, though the most recent P.U.L.O. actions have been difficult to distinguish from rural banditry and mafia style squabbling over the rich pickings in border towns such as Sungai Kolok, Betong and Yala.

---

is also a great place to see the Siberian swallow which is the symbol of Betong and hundreds of thousands of these birds migrate here every year, camping on the rooftops and weighing down the electricity cables.

The town itself is quite bustling and can be a very interesting place to walk around as it seems there is always something going on. The people here are generally very friendly and laid back and do not be surprised to be invited off for a drink or meal.

Due to its proximity to Malaysia, Betong has a very multicultural feel to it with the population mix being 50% Muslim, 40% Chinese and 10% Thai. There is also a large recently constructed gold sitting Buddha, a wat behind it which offers good panoramic views and the world's largest mailbox.

Orientation

As you enter Betong, coming from Yala you come down Sukkayang Road. Ahead is the stairs to the lookout and museum. As you cross Tetchinda Road, the market is to your right. The main intersection has the clocktower and to your left (along Rattanakit Road) you reach the Boddhadhiwas Temple, Golden Pagoda and hospital. The cheaper hotels are all to your right.

Vital Information

Tourist Information The tourist office is on Sukka Yang Road, near the stairs up to the lookout and museum.
Post Office is at the western end of Rattanakit Road.
Banks Bangkok Bank is on Sukka Yang Road, Thai Farmers Bank is on Rattanakit Road and Siam City Bank is also on Sukka Yang Road.
Police Station is to the west of the post office on Rattanakit Road.
Immigration Office is opposite the post office.
Codes Betong's telephone code is (073).

Cheap Sleeps

Fah Un Rung Hotel, ☎ (073) 231 403, is at 113/1-2 Chantarothai Road. This hotel is the best value in town with rooms without shower starting at 120B, but the sign on the desk alludes to there perhaps being an hourly rate (condom users receive better service!) The hotel also has a taxi to Hat Yai.

Sea World Long Hotel is off a lane on Tetchinda Road. This hotel has small rooms without shower starting at 160B.

There are a number of other hotels in town, so look around, but most are either over 200B or double as brothels, especially the **Sri Betong Hotel** on Chavachawalit Road and the **Tian Aun Hotel** on Chantarothai Road.

◀ Eat and Meet ▶

Outside the market on Tetchinda Road there are numerous **street vendors** (especially in the evening). On the corner of Rattanakit and Sukka Yang Roads is a large very popular restaurant with good prices. Along Rattanakit Road opposite the taxi stand to Yala there are some **good coffee shops**. There are also cafes along Chavachawalit Road.

Things to do ◆ and ◆ Sights to See

Off Sukka Yang Road, between Rattanakit and Tetchinda Roads, there is a lane with motorcycle hire shops (opposite the Catholic Church). This is a good way to visit the hot springs.

Phra Mahathat Chedi Phra Buddha Dhamma Park
พระมหาธาตุเจดีย์พระพุทธธรรมประกาศ

As impressive as its name, this 40 m high golden stupa is particularly pretty and contains some of the usual Buddha relics. It is located to the west of town along Rattanakit Road.

River Walk

By the small river running through the north of town, there is a small path with occasional sitting areas built over the river. The walk is quite pleasant and unusual at times, as you do get a different view of most of Betong's buildings this way.

Betong Hot Springs   บ่อน้ำร้อนเบตง

These hot springs can hard-boil an egg in 7 minutes! The Thais have set up some nice seated areas around the springs, though the grounds could definitely do with some upkeep! The springs have been built into a pool structure with a walkway to the centre where some of the springs can be seen, though they have been covered with a wire contraption. Do NOT put your hand in the water under the wire (like a silly researcher) as it is extremely hot. The rest of the pond is very warm and there is a second pond where you can dangle your feet (not your socks though) for some supposed mineral medical miracle. The springs are worth visiting if you have nothing better to do. They are situated at a village around 10 km from town. If you go on your own, follow the main road back to Yala for about 4 km, then there is a turn-off and down to your left, there are 3 or 4 signs (all in Thai) pointing the way you go. Follow the road for about another 6 km to Jaroh Parai Village and you are there. Tuk tuk drivers will take you there and to some communist tunnels for 50B to 100B.

Betong Tunnel   อุโมงค์เบตง

Built by the Chinese guerillas in 1976, the tunnel is made up of nine entrances. It is located in the mountains, at a town called Tanoh Maeroh.

Thai Arts and Culture Museum

Atop the staircase this museum holds a small collection of Thai Art and Cultural effects, from all over the country. The view is more interesting than the exhibition.

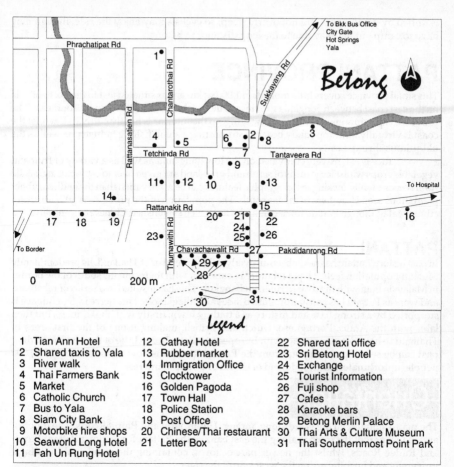

Legend

1 Tian Ann Hotel	12 Cathay Hotel	22 Shared taxi office
2 Shared taxis to Yala	13 Rubber market	23 Sri Betong Hotel
3 River walk	14 Immigration Office	24 Exchange
4 Thai Farmers Bank	15 Clocktower	25 Tourist Information
5 Market	16 Golden Pagoda	26 Fuji shop
6 Catholic Church	17 Town Hall	27 Cafes
7 Bus to Yala	18 Police Station	28 Karaoke bars
8 Siam City Bank	19 Post Office	29 Betong Merlin Palace
9 Motorbike hire shops	20 Chinese/Thai restaurant	30 Thai Arts & Culture Museum
10 Seaworld Long Hotel	21 Letter Box	31 Thai Southernmost Point Park
11 Fah Un Rung Hotel		

World's largest mailbox

Quite a strange location for the worlds largest mailbox, as it seems unlikely that the mailmen in Betong could ever get that busy. Nevertheless, the box is there and still functioning. Constructed in 1924, the mailbox is 3.2 m tall.

Arriving and Departing

Buses and Vans

Vans to **Yala** leave from the intersection of Tetchinda and Sukka Yang Roads, take 3 hours and cost 41B. A van to **Hat Yai** leaves every hour from in front of the Fah Un Rung Hotel and costs 150B, taking 4 hours. Air conditioned buses to **Bangkok** leave from further to the north of this intersection, but before the archway into town. They depart Betong at 14.00 and arrive at Bangkok at 10.00 the next day and cost 520B.

Share Taxi

The quickest way to get to Betong from **Yala** is by share taxi. The fare is 70B one way and takes between two and three hours, depending on the condition of the Mercedes. The road up to Betong is very scenic, passing by and around a lake formed by Bang Lang Dam. The area is dotted by picnic spots and not overly steep, so cyclists may enjoy the ride, though may have to camp out halfway due to the long distance to Betong.

PATTANI PROVINCE

This small province covers little more than 1,000 sq km and is situated just to the north of Yala on the east coast between Songkhla Province to the north and Narathiwat to the southeast. The province is predominantly flat and low lying, so the interior is highly cultivated whilst the coast is virtually non stop sandy beaches supporting a small fishing industry as well as the ubiquitous shrimp farms.

Rice is extensively cultivated on the low lying land as well as a variety of fruit and vegetable crops whilst large areas of scrub and grassland are given over to cattle raising, so the rural scenery, whilst lacking in topographic features can be more varied than the endless rubber plantations seen elsewhere in the far south. The population of the province is 80% Muslim/ethnic Malay, though Pattani town contains a large well established Chinese community.

PATTANI   ปัตตานี

In past history, Pattani has never been an overly willing member of Thailand. Its predominantly Muslim population feels it has a lot more in common with their cousins south of the border in Malaysia than with the distant rulers in Bangkok. This has resulted in a series of rebellions and wars as Pattani has constantly shifted sides and allegiances. This fierce independence is supported by a strong base and history as a trading town, firstly with the Chinese, but then later with the Arabs, Portuguese, Dutch and British, making it one of the first areas of Thailand to have regular contact with European traders. Today little of the historic trading past can be seen. Sprawling out from the Pattani River, it is now a modern city of 40,000 people, unfortunately almost devoid of charm or points of interest.

Orientation

The main commercial areas are along Yarang, Udom Vithi and Phipit Roads. The quietest and oldest part of the town is along the east bank of the Pattani River along Pattani Pirom and Rudee Roads, whilst the newer part of town, containing the municipal buildings, university and hospital are on the west side of the river.

Vital Information

Post Office located on Phipit Road, near the river. Nearby is overseas phone facilities.
Banks All the banks in town, are on Phipit Road, see the map for their positions.
Police Station is located on Pattani Pirom Road between the two bridges.
Hospital is on Decha Road near the provincial hall.
Codes Pattani's telephone code is (073) and the postal code is 94000.

Cheap Sleeps

Palace Hotel at 38 Soi Talaat Tetiwat is near the market and has friendly staff. Clean and comfortable rooms go for 150B with fan and shower or 250B with A/C.
Thai An is a small Chinese hotel at 67 Pattani Pirom Road, ☎ (073) 348 267, which has basic rooms for 100B.
Si Ha Hotel also on Pattani Pirom Road, this place is a slightly better deal than the Thai An and its rates start at 120B.

Santisuk Hotel, ☎ (073) 349 122, at 29 Phipit Road, is the cheapest in town with decent rooms with bathroom for 150B, but at the time of writing had a 'no farang' policy.

Not quite as desperate as the accommodation situation! There is a lively, if uninspired, **night market** down Soi Talaat Tetiwat and there are plenty of small Chinese cafes along Phipit Road between the market and the river.

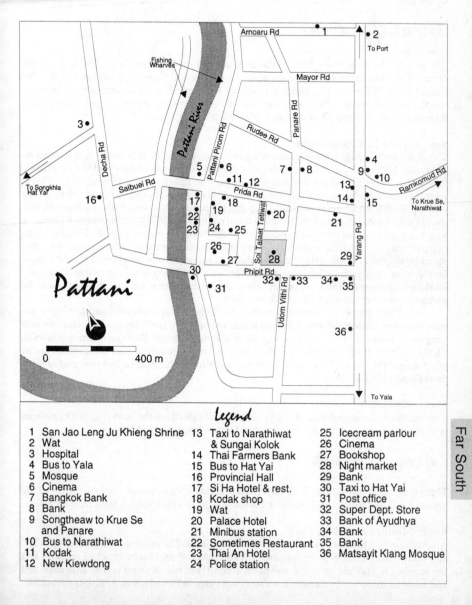

Legend

1	San Jao Leng Ju Khieng Shrine	13	Taxi to Narathiwat & Sungai Kolok	25	Icecream parlour
2	Wat	14	Thai Farmers Bank	26	Cinema
3	Hospital	15	Bus to Hat Yai	27	Bookshop
4	Bus to Yala	16	Provincial Hall	28	Night market
5	Mosque	17	Si Ha Hotel & rest.	29	Bank
6	Cinema	18	Kodak shop	30	Taxi to Hat Yai
7	Bangkok Bank	19	Wat	31	Post office
8	Bank	20	Palace Hotel	32	Super Dept. Store
9	Songtheaw to Krue Se and Panare	21	Minibus station	33	Bank of Ayudhya
10	Bus to Narathiwat	22	Sometimes Restaurant	34	Bank
11	Kodak	23	Thai An Hotel	35	Bank
12	New Kiewdong	24	Police station	36	Matsayit Klang Mosque

Around the corner on Pattani Pirom Road is the small but modern **Sometimes** food and drink spot. The **Si An Hotel** also has a restaurant on the ground floor overlooking the river and it has an English menu which is slightly overpriced, but not too badly.

Turning right onto Prida Road, the **New Kiew Dong** serves reasonable Chinese food whilst on the corner of Prida and Soi Talaat Tetiwat next to the Palace Hotel is the quiet and comfortable **Jong Ah** which serves Chinese and Thai specialities. Further on down the soi between the Palace Hotel and the market there is a **Thai restaurant** which has a good selection of cheap standard dishes. Finally for an ice cream or milk shake, try **Ton Tang Ku** by the cinema on Pattani Pirom Road.

The area by the river along Pattani Pirom Road and the lanes leading off it, is your only chance for a decent stroll, the narrow streets are quiet and there are plenty of old wooden buildings and Chinese style shops remaining, although there is nothing here which you cannot see in Penang or Songkhla for example. Anyway, since you are here, carry on to Arnoaru Road for Pattani town's one and only interesting site.

San Jao Leng Ju Khieng Shrine
The shrine and Chinese temple is interesting to look at and the story behind it is even more so. In the mid 16th Century a Chinese nobleman called To Khieng whilst on a visit to Pattani fell in love with a local girl and married her. He converted to Islam, and being wealthy decided to prove his new faith by constructing a mosque in his new found home. However, his sister Kor Niaw arrived from China to persuade him that his proper place was back home and that he should return with her forthwith. He refused and continued working on his edifice whereupon Kor Niaw cursed the mosque vowing it would never be completed. To Khieng began experiencing certain difficulties in that every time someone worked on the mosque they were struck by lightning. When this still failed to dampen his enthusiasm, she got fed up and hanged herself from a nearby tree. This action finally brought To Khieng to his senses and he stopped working on the mosque as he was overcome with grief. Ever since, all attempts to complete the mosque, known as Matsayit Kreu Se, have failed.

The cashew tree from which she hung herself was enshrined and Kot Niaw has since achieved Goddess status. A festival is held to honour her in February/March every year with processions and the site is now one of the most sacred Buddhist/Chinese sites in Thailand. Visitors of Chinese origin flock here in droves - note the tour bus carpark on the other side of the road. The mosque is about a ten minute share taxi ride to the east of town on the road to Narathiwat.

Matsoyit Klong
This mosque is the second largest in Thailand, five minutes from the market area. The mosque is pretty but unspectacular. If you want to see a good mosque, try Morocco.

Arriving and Departing

There is no main bus station. Both buses and taxis leave from various points, mostly along Yarang Road, and minibuses leave from the eastern end of Prida Road. See the map for details.

Buses, Minibus and Share Taxis
An ordinary bus to **Yala** costs 11B and takes 45 minutes. The minibus to **Narathiwat** is 50B and takes about 1½ hours, the minibus to **Yala** costs 30B and takes about 45 minutes and the minibus to **Hat Yai** costs 60B and takes about 1½ hours. A share taxi to **Yala** costs 20B and takes 30 minutes. To **Bangkok**, an A/C bus costs 464B and a non A/C bus costs 258B.

Far South

AROUND PATTANI

Krue Se Mosque   มัสยิดเก่าที่กรือเซะ

Located in Ban Krue Se, 7 km from Pattani on the road to Narathiwat, To Khieng's famous half built mosque has stood up well to the last four centuries and it is interesting, although not as spectacular as the TAT photos make it look. Next door is the grave of his poor sister, set in a small Chinese garden with a sitting area, well looked after and another popular destination for Chinese and Malaysian tourists. There are plenty of snack bars as well as stalls selling dried fish and giant squid which, to the Malaysian and Singaporean tourists seem like the equivalent of postcards to Westerners. (If you do want a giant, dried souvenir squid then prices are slightly lower here than at the Kor Niaw Shrine in town). To reach the mosque, songtheaws cost 5B from Pattani and you cannot miss the mosque as it is right by the side of the main road.

Beaches

Basically there are two in Pattani Province. One starts by Pattani town and continues all the way to Songkhla and the other runs southeast from Pattani, all the way to Narathiwat, interrupted only by occasional rivers and fishing villages.

Hat Talor Kapor   หาดตะโละกาโปร์

This is the most accessible area from Pattani town. The beach is wide, covered in fine sand and popular with the locals during the weekends. Sheep and goats graze amongst the fruit and snack stalls under the casuarina trees which line the beach. A couple of hundred metres down the beach is the friendly fishing village of **Talor Kapor** which is a good spot to see the famous **Kaw-Lae fishing boats**. These elaborately painted, photogenic boats are the traditional fishing craft for locals along the Pattani and Narathiwat coastline. The water around here is clean, though if you want a dip remember the locals are all Muslims, most have never seen a farang before, so dress accordingly if you do not want to offend or shock them. Note, the local girls bathe fully clothed around here, so when in Rome... A songtheaw from Pattani will drop you at Yaring for 10B and takes about 15 minutes. From here either get a motorbike taxi from the small market for 10B or wait for a songtheaw direct to the beach (weekends only). Yaring has a few shops, cafes, a bank, police station and loads of friendly people.

Panare and Hat Khae Khae   หาดปานเระ   หาดแฆแฆ

Ten kilometres down the coast from Talor Kapor, **Panare** has another nice beach and plenty more fishing boats. A songtheaw to here costs 15B from Pattani. Five kilometres further on is Pattani's most popular and prettiest beach, **Hat Khae Khae,** where the occasional boulder breaks up the otherwise non stop sandy coastline. This spot can get very busy during weekends and there are even a couple of resorts here. During the weekend the resorts are completely overpriced, but if you arrive during weekdays, you should be able to bargain them down to 200B.

Further south Saiburi District has some nice beaches such as **Hat Wasukri** and **Hat Patatimo** and plenty more kaw lae boats. Away from the villages, though more difficult to reach if you do not have your own transport, are some **completely deserted areas of shoreline**.

Namtok Sai Khao   น้ำตกทรายขาว

Inland, this is Pattani's only real point of interest. Relatively small, the waterfall is still pretty and set in a wooded area. The waterfall is located in Khok Po District, some 20 km southwest of Pattani, and songtheaws leave from Pipit road.

Far South

NARATHIWAT PROVINCE

Narathiwat is the easternmost of the far southern provinces and boasts a considerable stretch of fine beaches. The provincial capital, Narathiwat, is a very pleasant town, well regarded for its very friendly people and pleasant setting. The province is bordered to the north by Pattani, Yala to the west, Malaysia to the south and the Gulf of Thailand to the east. There are only two seasons in Narathiwat - the dry and the wet.

NARATHIWAT   นราธิวาส

Narathiwat is the capital of Narathiwat Province, set upon the river and on the east side of the Malay peninsula, 1,473 km south of Bangkok by road. It is a very pleasant and extremely friendly town, that is much quieter and cleaner than Sungai Kolok. The coastal position provides a guaranteed and welcoming fresh sea breeze that is great for lowering your body temperature in the blistering heat of summer. Narathiwat comes from the words 'nara' and 'athiwas' which means a residence of good people.

The province is fairly mountainous with the San Kala Kiri Mountain Range following the border between Thailand and Malaysia.

Vital Information

Post Office has friendly staff. The adjoining overseas phone facility is open all day.
Banks are spread throughout town on both Phupapakdee Road and Phichit Bamrung Road.
Police Station is on the road out of town towards Sungai Kolok.
Codes Narathiwat's telephone code is (073) and the postal code is 96000.
Tip: Opposite the Narathiwat Hotel is a small grocery store run by a young Chinese guy who speaks very good English. He loves to practise it and will tell you anything you need to know about the area and how to get there.
Tip 2: Certain areas of Narathiwat Province outside of the main towns can get a bit dodgy, especially at night time. Many locals will warn you about this, thus it can be a bit risky wandering around outside of the major towns after dark.

Cheap Sleeps

Narathiwat Hotel at 341 Phupapakdee Road, ☎ (073) 511 063. This excellent hotel is popular with travellers and with 21 rooms is 'the' place to stay. For 100B you get a large room , decorated with a dresser and a share bathroom. The old wooden hotel sits out over the Bang Nara River with a verandah with great views where you can comfortably spend a few relaxing hours. The lower floor of the hotel is a brothel, but do not let that worry you as the locals know the difference between a Western backpacker and a Thai prostitute.
Bang Nara Hotel at 274 Phupapakdee Road, ☎ (073) 511 036, has 16 rooms. Like the Narathiwat Hotel, this hotel has quite a lively night trade, but if that doesn't bother you, decent sized double rooms with fan and share bathroom start at 110B. The hotel is not very well signposted and is down a dreary hallway.
Yaowarat Hotel at 131 Pichit Bamrung Road, ☎ (073) 511 148. This large hotel has 42 rooms providing double rooms with a fan starting at 170B. It is much noisier than the other two hotels because it is situated on a main intersection.

Top Hotel!
The Narathiwat Hotel is one of our favourite hotels in Thailand. Although the lower floor is a brothel, the upstairs is well planned with a very pleasant balcony and large communal meeting area. There is a good restaurant downstairs and the staff are very friendly. For those arriving from Malaysia, the Narathiwat Hotel is an ideal introduction to Thailand.

Eat and Meet

Narathiwat Hotel has a small cafe downstairs with OK food but one of the best deals is up past the Thai Farmers Bank on the same side of the road. Here there is a great **Thai restaurant** that does delicious dishes for around 10B. Almost opposite the Bangkok City Bank on Wichit Chaibun Road is **Rat Cafe**, an excellent Muslim cafe where curries and satays are 10B. This cafe is also noted for its wildlife. Rats frolic amongst the tables, weave in and out of the customers and sit under your chair waiting for you to drop a grain or two of rice. The cat is terrified of them but none of the customers in this popular cafe seem to notice.

The **night market** is a bit of a half hearted affair with just a handful of fruit stalls and not much else. The **morning market** though is good value. Opposite the 7-eleven and slightly towards Pichit Bamrung Road is a **good little restaurant** which does excellent fried rice.

Hat Narathat

Along the beginning of Narathat Beach there are about five or six **bars with banana chairs** and light meals. This place is popular with both Thais and Malays during the weekend. The drinks are good but the food is generally chilli laden dynamite to make you drink more and you get about five prawns for 60B. Stick to the deckchairs outside as the bars can get a bit sleazy. The bars are lined up and named accordingly ie., Karaoke 1, Karaoke 2 etc.

Things to do and Sights to See

Hat Narathat   หาดนราทัศน์

This beach is located a couple of kilometres from the centre of town along Pichitbamrung Road. It is a very long beach bordered by a small pine grove with the above mentioned cafes at the beginning. Other than this, the beach is pretty much deserted. The rough golden sand makes the beach enticing, however one look at the water and you may not want to go for a swim, as it is quite murky. Also some of the locals have a habit of burning cable on the beach without cleaning up afterwards. If you were inclined you could camp amongst the pines or further up the beach or you could stay in one of the bungalows available. To reach the beach costs 10B on a motorcycle taxi.

Fishing Village

Located between the beach and Narathiwat town is a small fishing village. The view from the bridge is quite interesting or try taking the road down to the water on your way back to town. Along here you will see craftsmen building intricately painted boats which are unique to this area, although better ones can be seen in Pattani Province.

Mosque

The mosque is located just before the bridge to the beach. It is worth taking a peek if you are headed that way.

Graveyard

The graveyard is opposite the intersection of Pichitbomrung and Pitaklikit Streets. This small graveyard will provide you with a change of pace and way to observe the Thai culture. It is worthwhile to walk around and it makes an interesting contrast to its Western equivalents.

Narathiwat Specialities Festival and Longkong Fruit Fair

Held during 21 to 25 September every year, this festival features boat racing, parades, dove cooing contests and the sale of local handicrafts.

Hat Narathat

Legend

1   Bars
2   Fishing Village
3   Mosque
4   Bus to Pattani
5   Share Taxi to Ban Taba
6   Market
7   Fish market
8   Graveyard
9   Songtheaw to Ban Thon
10   Yaowarat Hotel
11   Siam Commercial Bank
12   Bang Nara Hotel
13   Food vendors/night market
14   Thai Military Bank
15   Market
16   Thai Farmers Bank
17   Royal Princess Hotel
18   Thai International
19   Narathiwat Hotel
20   Clocktower
21   Rat Cafe
22   Minibus to Hat Yai
23   Minibus to Pattani
24   Buses to Sungai Kolok, Ban Taba
25   Post Office
26   Provincial Hall
27   Nangkorn Tong Restaurant
28   Bus & songtheaw stop for Sungai
     Kolok, Ban Taba and Tak Bai
29   Municipal Offices
30   Boat race viewing area
31   Park
32   Police Station

To Ban Thon Airport

Phichit Bamrung Rd

Phupakdee Rd

Bang Nara River

Sophapisai Rd

Chamroonara Rd

Wichit Chaibun Rd

Narathiwat

To Yala

To Hat Manao
Taksin Palace
Tak Bai
Sungai Kolok

0   400 m

Far South

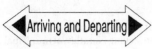

Air
THAI Airways flies to **Bangkok** daily for 2,575B and to **Nakhon Si Thammarat** for 835B.

Bus
If you are arriving from Sungai Kolok, the bus does not necessarily take you to the centre of town, but instead it may drop you at the post office. If this happens, just give a yell and hop off on the main road near the clocktower, thus cutting out a 15 minute walk. The bus to **Sungai Kolok** costs 19B and takes about an hour. If you are going to **Tak Bai**, take the southern road until you reach the signposted turn-off around 33 km south of Narathiwat.

Mini Bus
The mini bus from Narathiwat to **Pattani** costs 50B and leaves from the intersection of Wichit-Chaibun Road and Puphapugdee Road, just south of the Narathiwat Hotel. Minibuses to **Hat Yai** leave from east of the clocktower on Wichit Chaibun Road, cost 100B and take 3 hours. A van to **Yala** costs 60B.

Train
Narathiwat train station is 7 km out of town in the village of Tanyong, a 10B songtheaw ride away. Refer to the end of the chapter for details on prices and timetables.

AROUND NARATHIWAT
North of Narathiwat
Budo-Sungai Padi Mountains National Park
อุทยานแห่งชาติเทือกเขาบูโด-สุไหงปาดี
Located 26 km to the north of Narathiwat on Route 42 en-route to Saiburi and Pattani, this small National Park is situated by **Ba Cho** within a hilly area in the north of the province and is famous for its 60 m high **Bajo Waterfall**.

      From Narathiwat take either a songtheaw for 10B or a Pattani bound bus. Accommodation is available within the park for 200B by the park office in front of the waterfall. The waterfall is pretty, particularly after the rainy season when there is a considerable amount of water cascading down the cliff. Bajo means waterfall in the local Jawi dialect.

Wat Cherng Khao
Five kilometres from Ba Cho on the road from Ba Cho to Raman, this wat contains the body of the former abbot, Luang Phor Daeng, in a glass case. He has been preserved in the glass case since 1979 and the body is in surprisingly good condition.

Wadi Al Husin Mosque   มัสยิด 200 ปี
Also located in Ba Cho District, just off Route 42, 16 km to the north of Narathiwat in the village of Luboh Sawor is this 200 year old mosque. Built out of wood, and combining Thai, Chinese and Malay architectural styles, the mosque is unusual to say the least.

South of Narathiwat
Wat Khao Kong   วัดเขากง
This is a large sitting Buddha, Phra Buddha Taksin Mingmongkol, that reaches a height of 24 m and a width of 17 m between the knees and is decorated with shimmering golden tiles. The Buddha is about 6 km to the southwest of Narathiwat and a songtheaw there costs 5B.

Far South

Hat Manao   หาดอ่าวมะนาว

One of Narathiwat's prettiest and most popular beaches, Hat Manao is easily reached from Narathiwat and is pretty much deserted during the week. Upon leaving Narathiwat municipal district, you will cross over the bang Nara River. The turn-off for Hat Manao, indicated in Roman script, is a couple of kilometres further on, on the left. It is another 3 km down this turn-off to the beach, either 10B by motorbike taxi or a 30 minute walk. During the weekends, songtheaws leave from Narathiwat direct to the beach, try opposite the post office for a ride. At other times, hop on a bus bound for Tak Bai and ask for Hat Manao.

Taksin Royal Palace (Taksinrajanives Royal Palace)   พระตำหนักทักษิณราชนิเวศน์

After the turn-off to Hat Manao, continuing south there is a large forested hill at the southern end of which is situated the entrance to Taksin Royal Palace which was built in 1973 for when the royal family visits the Narathiwat Province. The entrance is quite imposing, difficult to miss and there is a sign in English as well. The modern palace is not up to much, but the grounds are attractive. Take your passport with you since the security guards usually like to keep this while you are wandering around the grounds. Do not worry as they will give it back. The beach in front of the palace is secluded and pretty and you can walk around to Hat Manao from here. The palace is open 9.00 am to 4.00 pm. A songtheaw from Narathiwat costs 10B or you can take a bus bound for Tak Bai or Sungai Kolok.

Tak Bai

This sleepy little town has a post office, bank, police station, hospital and even some accommodation in the form of the Tak Bai Lagoon (starting at 200B, depending on the time of the week).

Wat Choltharasinghey   วัดชลธาราสิงเห

This temple was built to prove that Narathiwat Province was indeed part of Thailand. At the time of construction, Narathiwat Province was part of Kelatan state, Malaysia, and thus under British rule. Following the construction of the Wat, the British relinquished their claim and agreed for the Sungai Kolok and Tak Bai Rivers to be the dividing line. The Wat is situated about a five minute walk from the central market at Tak Bai towards the sea and has some very nicely painted murals. Just follow the English signs, it is quite easy to find.

Ko Yao   เกาะยาว

This small island is about 1 km from Tak Bai and is connected to the land by a bridge over the Tak Bai River. The beach here is quiet and pleasant.

Dan Taba   ด่านตาบา

Another sleepy little town at first glance. All the action goes down on the waterfront where the river separates Malaysia and Thailand. There is a very busy market selling all sorts of stuff and dozens of boats carrying people and goods to and fro. Apart from that, the village is pretty filthy and goats and sheep are wandering all over the place.

◀ Arriving and Departing ▶

From the border crossing office, ferries across the river cost 10B and once on the other side, direct buses head off to Kota Bharu. Dan Taba is 39 km from Narathiwat.

Buses arriving here from Narathiwat and Sungai Kolok arrive in front of the market on the river front and next to the border crossing office. A songtheaw to **Tak Bai** costs 5B, **Sungai Kolok** 12B, and **Narathiwat** 12B. The bus to Narathiwat also costs 12B. The Sungai Kolok to **Bangkok** bus goes via Tak Bai, although you will have a better chance of getting a seat on it if you hop on at Sungai Kolok or Narathiwat.

SUNGAI KOLOK สุไหงโก-ลก

Sungai Kolok is in the Narathiwat Province, located 66 km from Narathiwat town, although there is virtually nothing to do here, it is interesting for its degree of Malaysian influence if nothing else. For many people arriving from Kota Bhara in Malaysia this is their first stop and unless you cross the border late in the afternoon, it would probably be a wise idea to continue on to anywhere else. Even the tourist office in Sungai Kolok says there is precious little to see here except perhaps for **Pa Phru To Daeng** which is Thailand's largest swamp forest. Very few locals speak English in town and the town is very dirty and very sleazy. The one thing Sungai Kolok has going for it is its transportation links — it is easy to get out of here.

Vital Information

Tourist Information Office is next to the passport control centre on the Sungai Kolok River. The staff here are very friendly and speak passable English offering enough brochures to deplete a small forest of its trees.

Post Office is near the intersection of Thetpathom Road and Bussayapan Road.

Bank There are three main banks and exchange offices, mainly along Charoenkhet Road, Thai Farmers Bank charges 13B commission per travellers cheque.

Police Station is opposite the Thai Farmers Bank on Charoenkhet Road, and the **Tourist Police** are by the Tourist Information Office by the border crossing.

Codes Sungai Kolok's telephone code is (073) and the postal code is 96120.

Note 1: Ringits (Malaysian currency) are widely accepted in Sungai Kolok, so if you have not had time to change your money, do not fret.

Note 2: This area and the surroundings are particularly Muslim, so it important that you dress accordingly so as to not offend the locals.

Cheap Sleeps

Sungai Kolok has more hotels than the tourist office has brochures, however most of them are in the 300B plus range. The cheapest hotels are along Charoenkhet Road, between the train and police stations.

Savoy Hotel, ☎ (073) 611 093, at 8/2 Charoenkhet Road has 27 rooms which are mostly large and comfortable with fans and bathroom facilities at 120B. There is a cafe downstairs.

Thailiang Hotel, ☎ (073) 611 132, at 12 Charoenkhet Road has 14 rooms with shower, toilet and fan for 150B.

Asia Hotel, ☎ (073) 611 101, at 4-4/1 Charoenkhet Road has rooms with shower and toilet starting at 200B and a very lively night trade.

Pimarn Hotel at 76-4 Charoenkhet Road, **☎** (073) 611 464, has rooms with fan for 150B.

Thai Liang, ☎ (073) 611 132, at 12 Charoenkhet Road has 14 rooms with either a fan or air conditioning with prices ranging from 80B to 230 B.

On weekends, Sungai Kolok becomes a huge brothel as Malay men come across the border for a bit of action, so it may be a little difficult to find accommodation. There are many hotels with names such as Come In, Honey and Marry and My Love which you pay for by the hour rather than by the night.

Eat and Meet

The cheapest place to get a feed in Sungai Kolok is at the **market** which is located between the train station and Asia Hotel. There is a central covered section which sells everything imaginable and there are heaps of food vendors on the streets bordering it to the north and

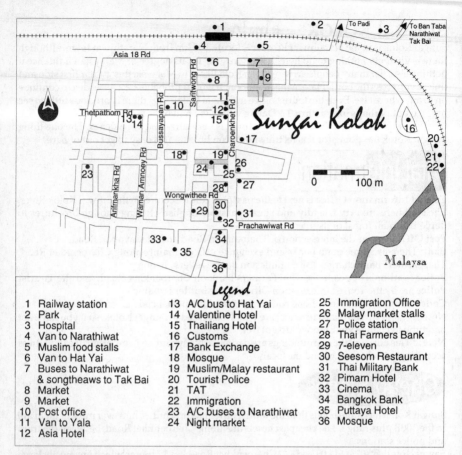

Legend

1	Railway station	13	A/C bus to Hat Yai	
2	Park	14	Valentine Hotel	
3	Hospital	15	Thailiang Hotel	
4	Van to Narathiwat	16	Customs	
5	Muslim food stalls	17	Bank Exchange	
6	Van to Hat Yai	18	Mosque	
7	Buses to Narathiwat	19	Muslim/Malay restaurant	
	& songtheaws to Tak Bai	20	Tourist Police	
8	Market	21	TAT	
9	Market	22	Immigration	
10	Post office	23	A/C buses to Narathiwat	
11	Van to Yala	24	Night market	
12	Asia Hotel			

25	Immigration Office
26	Malay market stalls
27	Police station
28	Thai Farmers Bank
29	7-eleven
30	Seesom Restaurant
31	Thai Military Bank
32	Pimarn Hotel
33	Cinema
34	Bangkok Bank
35	Puttaya Hotel
36	Mosque

south. The **Merlin Hotel** has a decent restaurant which does BBQ and seafood, and the Thai restaurant beside it, **Siam**, is also OK. On the corner of Thetpathom and Charoenkhet Roads is a **Malay restaurant** which does excellent Randang curries for 20B and for **vegetarians**, there is an OK place between the Asia and Savoy Hotels. The road in front of Thai Farmers Bank and at right angles to Charoenkhet Road becomes a lively **street eatery** at night. There are many stalls with tables and chairs on the road.

Things to do ◆ Sights to See

Pa Phru To Daeng   ป่าพรุโต๊ะแดง

The only thing to do here is leave and avoid the prostitutes! But if you insist on staying in the area, the only thing worthwhile to see is Pa Phru To Daeng (Thailand's largest swamp forest). To get there take a motorbike taxi, as it is about 10 km from Sungai Kolok on the road to Tak Bai. The forest is quite abundant in flora and fauna with over 400 kinds of plant life and more than 200 types of animals.

Far South

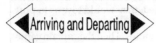

Arriving and Departing

Getting Around
Once you cross the border from Malaysia, it is a ten minute walk or five minute rickshaw ride for 10B to Charoenkhet Road.

Vans and Bus
Air conditioned vans to **Yala** cost 80B and leave every hour (between 06.45 and 17.00) taking 3 hours, to **Hat Yai** they cost 110B, take 4 hours and leave every hour (between 06.00 and 17.00) and to **Narathiwat** they cost 40B, take 1 hour and leave every hour between 07.00 and 18.00. Air conditioned buses leave Sungai Kolok for **Hat Yai** from beside the Valentine Hotel at 2/1 Waman Amnoey Road at 07.00, 09.00, 13.00 and 15.00 costing 98B. Air conditioned buses to **Surat Thani** leave at 08.00 and 12.30 and cost 200B and 256B, taking 10 and 9 hours respectively. The bus to **Narathiwat** leaves from beside the train station and costs 16B, taking 1 hour. To Bangkok an A/C bus costs 533B and a non A/C costs 282B.

Train
Sungai Kolok train station has timetable and price information displayed in both English and Thai. It is possible to pre-book train tickets from here. Refer to the end of the chapter for detailed timetable and price information.

Motorbike
Sungai Kolok is crawling with motorbike taxis which will take you to any regional destination such as Dan Taba, Narathiwat and Tak Bai. You can either find where they hang out in town or flag them down as they pass you. Unfortunately none of the share taxis have signs in English, so it is a bit of a trial and error basis.

Crazy Times on the high seas...
" I had been visiting Ko Bulon Lae off the coast of Satun Province for about a week or so, during which time the weather had been very ordinary so I decided to get the boat back to the mainland and try another island further up the coast where the weather might be better.

The boats that run out to Ko Bulon Lae are nothing flash — just large longtails with a roof if you are lucky. We had about 35 farangs on the boat and about a dozen Thais when the pilot pushed off into what rapidly became strong winds and high seas. Within 30 seconds, everyone on the boat was saturated. The boat was being thrown around as if we were in the super wash cycle in an enormous washing machine

When I prised my eyes open, what had began as amusement and even nervous laughter had degenerated into absolute hysteria. The young lady behind me was being violently ill, the Anglo French couple across from me were popping valium at a rate of knots and the French guy was working his way through his third joint as his eyes flickered around the place — No happy campers on this boat.

Suddenly there was a huge explosion and before we could say *mai pen rai* five times, water started pouring into the boat! Some part of the motor had broken off and gone straight through the bottom of the boat! My worst nightmares immediately manifested themselves — I cursed Steven Speilberg as I debated whether the giant shark would choke on my backpack before it ate me?! We looked at the pilot who made the bailing gesture so we all started to paddle *inside* the boat.

There was only a faint glimmer of land in the distance, certainly too far to swim with my backpack — Oh my God, my notes...I had the last two weeks of research on paper in my pack — my paddling sped up.

Then, salvation. A dive boat full of Thai tourists saw us and within ten minutes they were alongside. As soon as they touched, our boat almost rolled as we all tried to change boats at the same time. NO NO the captain screamed, they would tow us to port and we all should stay in the boat.

Everything was running smooth for the first few minutes. Then the captain came out the back of his boat and asked our driver how much he was going to pay for the tow. A vicious bargaining session took place with a price eventually settled. Then, ten minutes from port the captain came back out and asked for more money. We refused, and the next thing we knew his assistant came out with a machete and cut the rope! We were dumfounded as the dive boat turned around and headed to sea — we never saw them again!

Luckily for us, another boat passed and within 30 minutes we were safe and sound. Ever since then I have carried a plastic (waterproof) sleeve for my notes — afterall, one can never be too careful!"

Stuart McDonald

Malaysia and Singapore						
Type and Class		X,123	M,23	X,23	S,23	X,12
Supplement		A		A		
Butterworth	D	07.30	08.30	15.20	20.30	22.30
Bt Mertajam	A	07.43	08.44	15.33	20.44	22.43
Ipoh	A	10.25	12.12	18.28	00.49	02.12
Tapoh Road	A	11.20	13.40	19.31	02.38	04.57
Kuala Lumpur	A	14.40	17.15	22.40	06.05	06.45

Type and Class		X,123	S,23	X,12	M,23	X,12
Supplement		A				A
Kuala Lumpur	D	14.45	20.45	22.00	08.30	07.10
Seremban	A	17.06	23.10	00.50	10.45	09.20
Segamat	A	19.12	02.29	03.35	13.27	11.14
Johor Bahru	A	21.37	05.48	06.25	17.00	13.42
Singapore	A	22.30	06.55	07.25	18.20	14.40
X = Express train, M = Mail train, S = Slow train, (123) = Class of train, A = Air Conditioning						

Singapore and Malaysia						
Type and Class		X,123	X,12	M,23	S,23	X,12
Supplement		A	A			
Singapore	D	07.30	15.30	08.30	20.00	22.35
Johor Bahru	A	07.55	15.53	08.56	20.27	22.59
Segamat	A	10.29	18.21	12.15	00.27	01.44
Seremban	A	12.22	20.18	14.40	03.35	04.42
Kuala Lumpur	A	14.25	22.45	17.45	06.15	07.05

Type and Class		X,123	S,23	X,12	M,23	X,12
Supplement		A				A
Kuala Lumpur	D	15.10	20.45	22.00	09.00	07.20
Tapoh Road	A	18.01	00.17	01.28	12.41	10.09
Ipoh	A	18.52	01.57	03.10	13.49	11.12
Bt Mertajam	A	21.55	05.52	06.38	17.50	14.13
Butterworth	A	22.20	06.40	07.15	18.20	14.40
X = Express train, M = Mail train, S = Slow train, (123) = Class of train, A = Air Conditioning						

Crossword 3

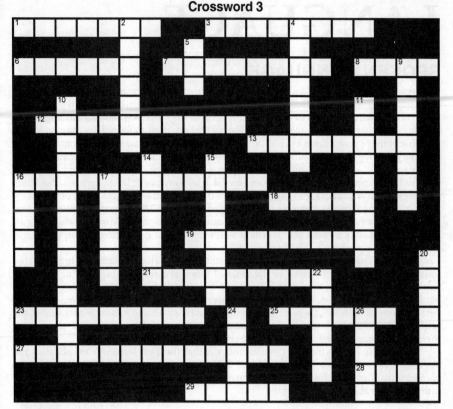

Across

1 Popular alcoholic drink: Mekong _____
3 District on the west side of the Chao Phraya River
6 Muslim temple
7 Type of Buddhism
8 The Rama number of the current King
12 Boat used in special occasions by king
13 Some hotels double as these
16 Animal used on farms
18 Important people's remains are kept in this religious structure
19 Bangkok has too much of this
21 Thailand is located in this part of Asia
23 Bombs planted in the ground
25 King of the Thonburi Period
27 Held once a month on Ko Phangan
28 Wat name translated as the Temple of Dawn
29 Second largest island in Thailand

Down

2 Famous jade Buddha at Wat Phra Kaew
4 Popular form of accommodation
5 Buddhist temple
9 King known as Black Prince from Ayutthaya period
10 Thailand's form of government _____/monarchy
11 Capital of Laos
14 Animal that buries eggs in the sand
15 The majority of the Muslim population of Thailand live in this region
16 Buddhist nuns wear this colour
17 Disease caught from animal bites
20 Popular tourist activity in the north
22 Sport similar to volleyball
24 Home of Aun Sun Suu Kyi
26 Second most popular religion in Thailand

Answers at the back of the book

LANGUAGE

SPOKEN LANGUAGE

The spoken language in Thailand is called Thai and can prove to be relatively difficult to master to the untrained farang. Fortunately the influence of tourism, Western cultures and particularly US involvement in Indochina over the past few decades has introduced the English language to Bangkok and many tourist areas. Thai nationals that are used to foreigners may be able to decipher some of your efforts at Thai, but do not be suprised if those with less contact stare at you like you have an arm coming out of your forehead. Also take laughter as encouragement not as an insult — they are laughing with you. Officially the dialect and script of Central Thailand is the form used in education and media. It is a very poetic language with translation creating colourful images for example, the word fruit can be translated as 'child of wood'.

In the following pages we have provided you with a Thai language section covering phonetics of useful words and phrases so you can attempt to converse in the native tongue. Even if you master a few basic words it will bring you a rewarding and appreciative perspective to your visit to Thailand.

The Thai language made up of five tones using different accents to highlight the required sound, either neutral, or the marked tones of rising, falling, low or high. For instance ma in a neutral tone means *to come*, in a high tone, *horse*, and in a rising tone, *dog*. Similarly, in different tones, *khao* can also mean rice, white, news, knee and mountain. Once you get familiar with the tones, the rest is fairly easy as most basic Thai words are monosyllabic, the sentence structure is simple and the grammar is informal. The most difficult part for foreigners is grasping the tones which are central to the language.

A clue for beginners is to remember is that the Thai language emphasises the beginning of every word. The second half fades away if the word ends in a vowel, or is spoken abruptley if ending with a consonant. Also try and make your Thai words flow rather than breaking it up with gaps.

WRITTEN LANGUAGE

The Thai alphabet originated in 1283, established by King Ramkhamhaeng. The King based it on the ancient Indian Sanskrit and Pali using old Khmer characters. The language continued to develop over the next 700 years until it settled in its current state, showing a mixture of Pali, Sanskrit, Khmer, English, Malayan and Chinese influences.

The main difficulty for understanding the written language is that words immediately follow each other without a space. Spaces only separate sentences. The Thai language itself is very description and poetic, but the lack of rules governing the translation into the Western alphabet, introduces a few problematic areas. The biggest problem facing direct translation letter for letter means that it is quite common to see a variety of spellings for any one word, usually based on its phonetic sound.

Monarchy

Any reference to the monarchy commands the use of a special royal language, called Rachasap. Virtually the same as the the traditional Thai language, Rachasap has a few substantial differences and rules when it comes to the use of nouns and verbs. Add the prefix *phra* to nouns in any referrance to gods, objects of worship, or objects associated with royalty. Additionally, *racha* is also added to replace the word royal, and *chalong* is used to describe personal items. *Song* is added to any verb that anicdotes an action by royalty. When referring to the royal family in general conversation, it is respectful for Thais, and Westerners alike to use the word *phra ong tahn*.

Vowels

a	as in up and Lisa	e	as in ten
aa (ae)	similar to the a in ban	ee	as in deep
ah	as in cart	eh	similar to the a in gate
ai	as in thai and sigh	ehw	eh + w
ao	as in cow		(no equivalent sound in English)
aw	as in saw	eu	as in adieu
aew	aa + w		(no equivalent in English)
	(no equivalent sound in English)	euu	drawn out version of the above
		euua	euu + a
		euuay	euu + ay
i	as in it	o	as in hot
ia	ee + a (as in Maria)	oo	as in food
io	ee + oh (as in mio)	oh	as in go
iw	shortened form of ew in pew	oi	as in boy
	(no equivalent sound in English)	oei	similar to the urry in furry
u	as in foot and put		
ua	oo + a		
uay	oo + ay		
ui	oo-ee		

Initial Consonants

b	as in book	ng	as in sing
ch	as in chip	p	similar to p in top
d	as in dog		(no equivalent sound in English)
f	as in fog	ph	as in pit
g	as in got (often transcribed as k)	r	as in red
h	as in hit	s	as in shed
j	as in jet	t	similar to t in peter
kh	as in cat		(no equivalent sound in English)
l	as in look	th	as in ten
m	as in meet	w	as in wet
n	as in net	y	as in yet
	silent initial consonant		

Tone Markers

a	normal tone
à	low tone
â	falling tone
á	high tone
a	rising tone

Tones

Using tones is not as straight forward as what it would seem. The tone of a syllable is determined by the tone marker, the class of letter the syllable begins with and the type of vowel contained in the syllable. Tones only apply to the syllable in which it is marked and are noted above the first vowel. Its easiest for farangs to master normal toned words first, so once you have your tongue around these, try the others.

Classifiers

The Thai language includes the use of classifiers in each sentence. This is a word that represents the noun which is part of a group with similar characteristics. Examples of classifers include: kohn (for people), rohng (buildings), cha-bap (paper with printing/writing on it), paan (flat and thin objects), lookh (fruit). The list is extensive and beyond the scope of this book. You will be able to get by in Thailand with basic Thai without classifiers, however if you plan to study the language, it is essential you have an understanding of them.

Personal Pronouns

The Thai language has a seemingly endless variety of personal pronouns. The choice of pronoun will depend upon a range of factors, including gender, age and social status. In casual conversation, Thais will often use first names in the place of "I" and "you", and it is not unusual, at least in colloquial speech, for personal pronouns to be abandoned completely. For this reason, and because travellers will already have enough to contend with in their attempts to master the Thai language, pronouns have been omitted from the following translations. Even in their absence you will have not problem making yourself understood using these phrases. If however, you are in a slightly formal situation, or wish to be particularly polite, the safest bet is to use the following pronouns:

phôm	for males
di-chân	for females

Do not forget, however, that even in casual conversation you should always conclude each sentance or phrase with "khrap" if you are male and "kha" if you are female. One its own, this is also used for 'yes'. Alternatively use 'chai' for yes and 'mai' or 'mai sai' for no.

kháp (khráp is used in central Thailand)	for males
kha	for females

Some useful words

Numbers

0	sóon	11	sìp èt
1	nèung	12	sìp sâwng
2	sâwng	20	yèe-sìp
3	sâhm	21	yèe-sìp èt
4	sèe	30	sâhm-sìp
5	hàh	50	hàh-sìp
6	hòk	100	nèung-rói
7	jèt	1,000	nèung-pan
8	pàat	10,000	mèuun
9	gao	100,000	sâan
10	sìp	1,000,000	láhn

Greetings and Civilities

hello/goodbye	sa-wàt-dee
see you later	phóp-gan mai ná
thank you very much	khàwp-khùn mahk
thank you	khàwp-khùn
excuse me	kháw-thoht
OK	oh-kheh

Days of the Week and Time

Monday	wan jan	today	wan née
Tuesday	wan ang-khahn	yesterday	meuua wan née
Wednesday	wan phút	tomorrow	phrung née
Thursday	wan pha-réu-hàt	day	wan
Friday	wan sùk	night	keun
Saturday	wan sâo	this morning	chao née
Sunday	wan ah-thít	morning	cháo
		afternoon	bài

Time

In regard to time, you will make yourself understood if you use the 24 hour clock — this is commonly used in Thailand. The more casual method that Thais use for telling the time is quite confusing to a novice. When stating the time, simply add the words na-le-ga (o'clock) after the number. Eg,

6.00 am (06.00)	hòk na-le-ga
6.00 pm (18.00)	sìp-pàat na-le-ga

Months

January	mok-ga-ra kom	July	ga-rák-ga-da yon
February	gum-pa pan	August	sîng-hâ kom
March	mee-na kom	September	gan-ya yon
April	meh-sâ yon	October	tu-la kom
May	préut-sa-pa kom	November	préut-sa-jìh-ga yon
June	mí-tu-na yon	December	tan-wa kom

For easy reference, the days that have 30 days end in yon, those with 31 days end in kom, and February which has 28 days, ends in pan.

Directions

north	néu-uh	turn right	lée-oh kwâ
south	tai	turn left	lée-oh sái
east	ta-wan awk	go straight ahead	tohng bai
west	ta-wan tohk		

Transport

Where is the . . . ?	. . . yoo thee nai		
aeroplane	khreu-uan-bin	airport	sa-nâhm bin
bus	rót-meh	bus station	sa-thâh-nee rót-meh
train	rót-fai	railway station	sa-thâh-nee rót-fai
car	rót-yon	taxi	rót-tháak-see
ferry	reuua dùan	pier (tha)	thah-reuua
bicycle	jàk-ra-yan (jak-a-yan)	motorcycle	rót-maw-ter-sai
petrol station	pám-nám-man	kilometre	gih-loh-met

Family

mother	khun-maa	father	khun-paw
older brother	phee-chai	older sister	phee-sâo
younger brother	náwng-chai	younger sister	náwng-sâo
daughter	look-sâo	son	look-chai
woman	phoo-yîng	man	phoo-chai
friend	pheuuan	boy/girlfriend	faan

Sights and Landmarks

bay	àow	beach	hàt
canal	khlong	cape	laem
district	amphoe (am-puh)	island	kò
lane	soi	mountain	khâo
museum	phí-phí-tá-phan	pier	tha
river	mae-nám	road	tha-nôn
temple	wát	town	muang
village	ban	waterfall	nám-tòk
province	changwat (jang-wàt)		

Food

Following are a few rules to eating etiquette in Thailand to save offending your host or being classed as another rude farang. Rice based meals are usually eaten with a fork and spoon where the fork is used to shovel the food onto the spoon. The spoon ends up in your mouth (not the fork). Noodle dishes are eaten with chopsticks and spoon, similar to soups, however a soup spoon is the familiar oriental soup spoon. Also remember to ALWAYS leave a small portion of food on your plate. If you're in doubt, watch a Thai eat for a few handy hints on dining Thai style.

Meals

breakfast	a-hân cháo	lunch	a-han glang wan
dinner	a-han kam		

Drink

water	nám	drinking water	nám-dèuum
ice	nám khaang	no ice	mai sài nám khaang
orange juice	nám-som	tea	chah
coffee	gah-faa	milk	nom
beer	bia		

Rice & Noodles

rice	khao	noodles (thin white)	gûay-tîo
fried rice	khao-phàd	noodles (yellow egg)	ba-mèe
sticky rice	khao-nío	noodle soup	kuai-tuaw-nám
steamed rice	khao nun		

Meat — néu-uh

chicken	gài	beef	néuua
duck	pèt	pork	móo
lamb	look gàa	lobster	goong yài

Seafood — ah-hâhn tha-leh

fish	plah	crab	poo
oyster	h ôi	shrimp/prawn	kung

Vegetable — phàk

bean sprouts	thua ngook	cabbage	ga-làm-blee
chillies (small)	prik kii nuu	corn	koa-poht
cucumber	taang-gwa	garlic	gra-thi-am
ginger	khing	lemon	ma-nao
lemongrass	ta-gray	lettuce	pàk-gàt hâwm
mung bean	thua-giao	mushroom	hèt
onion	hûa-hâom	potato	man-farang
spinach	pàk kôhm	tomato	ma-kêuuh-tet

Fruit

apple	aa-puhn	banana	glu-ay
coconut	má-phráo	custard apple	nao-ynàa
durian	thóo-ri-an	guava	fa-rang
jackfruit	ga-nóon	longan	lam-yai
lychee	lin-cii	mango	má-muang
mangosteen	mang-gút	orange (mandarine)	som
papaya	má-lá-gaw	pineapple	sàp-pà-rót

| rambutan | ngó | rose apple | chom-phuu |
| tamarind | ma-gaam | watermelon | taang-moh |

Thai Dishes
Check the food section of the culture chapter for details on some additional Thai dishes.

spring rolls	po-pia thot
hot and spicy lemongrass soup with prawn	tôm yam kung
spicy salad with beef/chicken/pork	lâap néuua/gài/móo
chicken curry	gaang khıaw waan gài
chicken in coconut milk	tôm kha gài
chicken with cashew nuts	gài phat met ma-mu-ang
sweet and sour pork/chicken	phat priaw-waan móo/gài
fried noodles with chicken and peanuts	phat Thai
stir fried bean curd and bean sprouts	phat tao-hu kap thua ngok
red curry with beef/chicken	gaang phet néuua/gài

Flavour
spicy	phèt	not spicy	mai phèt
sour	prıo	salty	kem
sweet	wâhn	bitter	kôhm
delicious	a-ròy		

Cooking method
roast	bıng	barbeque	yahng
fry	tawt	boil	tohm
steam	neung		

Additional Food Words
curry	gaang	bread	kha-n ôm pang
cheese	nu-ee káang	coconut milk	neu-uh ma-prao
egg	kài	omelet	kài jee-oh
chillie sauce	nám prík	fish sauce	nám-plaa
salt	gleu-uh	peanut	thùa-li-sông
sugar	nám tan		

I am a vegetarian	gin jeh	serviette/tissue	gra-tàat-chét-mu
I am hungry	hîw khao	waiter/waitress	kohn duhn tó
I am not hungry	mai hîw	restaurant	ráhn ah-hâhn
Are you hungry?	hîw mái	bill	bin (or check bill)
I am thirsty	hiw nam	receipt	bai ráp ngun

Eating Utensils
fork	sawm	knife	meed
spoon	cháwn	plate	caan
bowl	chaam	cup	thûai

Accomodation
hotel	rohng raam	guesthouse	(sounds a bit like get-hów)
Have you an available room?		mii hûng wâng mái	
air conditioner	kreu-ung tam kwam yen	fan	páht
towel	phâa-chét-tua	hot water	nám ráwn

Shopping

How much? (What is the price?)	thao-rai
Very expensive	phaang mahk
That is cheap	thòok
I have no money	mâi mii ngen lai

Health

ambulance	róht pa-ya-ban	doctor	mu
hospital	rohng pha-yah-bahn	dentist	máw fahn
medicine	yaa	sick	mai sa-bai

Emergency

Help!	chu-ai du-ai	police station	sa-thâhn-nee tam-ruàt
thief	ka-moai	lost	lóhng tang

Post & Telegraph

post office	prai-sa-nee	stamp	sa-taamp
envelope	sawng jòt-má	letter	jòht-mâi
air mail	brai-sa-nee a-gàht	telephone	toh-ra-sàp

Nationalities

I am a/an . . .	pen khon		
Where do you come from?	kun mah jahk ny		
Australia(n)	aw-sà-treh-lia	America(n)	a-meh-rih-gah
Chinese	ciin	England (English)	ang-grìt
France (French)	fa-ràng-seht	Germany	yuh-ra-man
Japan(ese)	yee-pòon	Khmer	gha-meen
Laos	laaw		

Occupation

I am a . . .	a-cheep		
author (writer)	nák bra-pahn	artist	sın-lá-pin
businessperson	nák-thu-rá-kìt	engineer	wí-sa-wa-koon
mechanic	chaang-khruang-yon	salesperson	khon-kai-khun
student (university)	nísìt		

Extra Words

fast	reh-oh	slow	cháh
small	lék	big	yài
hot	ráwn	cold	yen
good	dee	no good	mai dee
more	èek	another (or other)	èun

bank	ta-na-khahn	beautiful	sôo-ai
cigarettes	boo-rèe	delicious	a-ràwai
embassy	sa-tân toot	market	ta-làat
money	ling	visa	wee sah
bathroom (restroom)	hawng nám	toilet	hawng soo-um

Questions and Statements and Small Talk

How are you?	sa-bai dee réu
I'm well	sa-bai dee
I'm not well	mai sa-bai
What is your name?	cheuu a-rai
My name is	cheuu . . .
How old are you?	ah-yú thao-rài
I am (x) years old.	ah-yú . . . pèe
I don't understand.	mai khao-jai
I understand.	khoa-jai
It doesn't matter (never mind)	mai pen rai
Its not a problem	nai mee pan-hah
I like	chawp . . .
I don't like	mai chawp . . .
Where are you going? (Where is it going)	pai nái
Please speak slowly	phûut chá-ch áa nài
Where is the . . .	. . . yòo thee nâi
I am sorry (regretful)	chân sèe-uh jai
Where are you going?	bai nâi
come here	mah nee
go away (get lost!)	pai hái phôn

Chart Index

Bangkok

Central & Eastern bus dep.	151	Malaysia & Singapore train timetable	686
Northeastern bus departures	152	Nakhon Si Thammarat bus timetable	612
Northern bus departures	152	Northeastern train fares	492
Southern bus departures	150	Northeastern train timetable	493
Central train fares	242	Northern train fares	410
Central train timetable	242	Northern train timetable	411
Chiang Mai bus timetable	323	Phitsanulok bus timetable	347
Chiang Mai flights	322	Phuket bus timetable	597
Currency exchange rates	73	Southern train fares	630
Domestic airfares	148	Southern train timetable	631-632
Eastern train fares	306	Surat Thani bus timetable	537
Eastern train timetable	305	Temperature/rainfall chart	64
International airfares	147	Train type/supplementary costs	96
Kanchanaburi bus timetable	194	Vaccinations	87

Photo Index

103	Bangkok temple guardian (SM)	307	Lisu hilltribe woman (DK)
129	Ramakien mural, Bangkok (SM)	324	Yao hilltribe woman (DK)
132	Bangkok temple guardian (SM)	337	Buddha's hand, Sukhothai (SM)
155	Buddha head in tree, Ayutthaya (SM)	349	Praying to Buddha, Sukhothai (DK)
163	Phra Pathom Chedi (DK)	375	Sunset at Sukhothai (DK)
185	Bridge over the River Khwae (DK)	413	Prasat Hin Khao Phanom Rung (SM)
185	Three monks, Suphanaburi (DK)	461	Wat Khaek, Nong Khai (SM)
198	Deforestation sign, Sai Yok NP (DK)	495	Ang Thong Marine NP (SM)
223	Drum maker in Ban Bnag Phae (DK)	528	View from James Bond Island (SM)
243	Water view from Ko Chang (DK)	626	View from Ko Phi Phi (SM)
294	Tree in water, Ko Chang (DK)	661	Rowing boat (SM)
302	Coconut picker, Ko Mak (DK)	633	Kao Lae boat (MO)

Danielle Karalus (DK), Stuart McDonald (SM), Mark Ord (MO)

Language

MAP INDEX

Amnat Charoen	445	Ko Pha Ngan	566	Phitsanulok	344
Aranyprathet	241	Ko Phi Phi	624	Phrae	400
Ayutthaya	168	Ko Ratanakosin	126	Phu Hin Rong Kla NP	347
Bang Saphan Yai	512	Ko Samet	269	Phuket Province	595
Bangkok city	106-107	Ko Samui	541	Phuket town	598
Betong	673	Ko Si Chang	252	Prachuap Khiri Khan	510
Buriram	427	Ko Tao	584	Raileh	620
Central	186	Ko Tarutao Marine NP	662	Ranong	512
Cha Am	501	Krabi	614	Ratchaburi	157
Chachoengsao	176	Lamai (Central)	555	Roi Et	488
Chainat	218	Lampang	334	Sai Yok	197
Chaiyaphum	481	Lamphun	330	Sakhon Nakhon	451
Chanthaburi	277	Loei	472	Samut Sakhon	180
Chatuchak Market	140	Loei Province	470	Samut Songkhram	183
Chaweng	550	Lopburi	228	Sangkhlaburi	205
Chiang Khan	476	Mae Hat	586	Satun	658
Chiang Khong	394	Mae Hong Son	372	Si Racha	248
Chiang Mai city	312-313	Mae Nam	546	Si Saket	435
Chiang Mai old city	316	Mae Sai	389	Si Satchanalai Hist. Park	352
Chiang Mai (Tha Phae)	315	Mae Sariang	369	Silom Road	122
Chiang Rai Province	384	Mae Sot	372	Soi Ngam Duphli	118
Chiang Rai town	387	Mahasarakham	486	Songkhla	647
Chiang Saen	396	Mukdahan	447	Songkhla Central	648
Chinatown & Pahurat	136	Nakhon Nayok	234	Soppong (around)	361
Chonburi	245	Nakhon Pathom	161	Southern Thailand	496
Chumphon	516	Nakhon Phanom	452	Sukhothai	350
Damnoen Saduak	159	Nakhon Ratchisima	420-421	Sukhumvit Road	124
Doi Mae Salong	391	Nakhon Sawan	224	Sungai Kolok	684
Eastern Thailand	244	Nakhon Si Thammarat	610	Suphanaburi	210
Fang	328	Nan	404	Surat Thani	534
Far Southern Thailnad	634	Narathiwat	680	Surat Thani (around)	532
Hat Rin	574	Nathon	544	Surin	430
Hat Rin detail	574	Nong Bua Lam Phu	468	Tak	374
Hat Yai	653	Nong Khai	456	Thailand	10-11
Hua Hin	507	Nonthaburi	164	Thailand flights	94
Kaeng Krachan NP	503	Northeast Thailand	414	Thailand train routes	95
Kalasin	491	Northern Thailand	308	Thailand Provinces	80
Kamphaeng Phet	381	Pai	358	That Phanom	455
Kanchanaburi	190	Pak Chong	416	Thong Sala	568
Kanchanaburi Province	189	Pathum Thani	166	Trang	636
Karon Beach	603	Patong	605	Trang Province	635
Kata & Kata Noi Beaches	601	Pattani	675	Trat	282
Khao San Road	114	Pattaya	257	Trat Province	281
Khao Sok National Park	538	Phang Nga	526	Ubon Ratchathani	438
Khon Kaen	483	Phang Nga, Phuket		Udon Thani	464
Ko Bulon Lae	665	& Krabi Provinces	527	Umphang	377
Ko Chang	290	Phattalung	643	Uthai Thani	221
Ko Lanta	629	Phayao	408	Uttaradit	356
Ko Libong	641	Phetchabun	340	West Banglamphu	116
Ko Lipe	663	Phetchaburi	498	Yala	668
Ko Mak	301	Phichit	338	Yasothon	442
Ko Muk	639	Phimai	424		

INDEX

A

A Hui 478
Ajaan Man 450
Amnat Charoen 444–446
Ananda Panyarachun 24
Ang Thong 215–216
Angkor Wat 15, 424, 428
Anna Leonowens 21
Aow
　Ban Bang Kao 557
　Bang Nam Chud 556
　Chalok Ban Kao 589
　Chalok Lam 571
　Chaophao 569
　Cho 271
　Choeng Mon 549
　Hin Khok 270–271
　Hin Wong 587–588
　Jan Som 590
　Karang 273
　Khlong Phrao 293
　Kiu 272
　Kiu Nanai 272
　Kul Jeua 590
　Leuk 588, 622
　Mae Hat 585–586
　Manao 510
　Nang 618
　Nuan 271
　Phai 271
　Phrao 273
　Phutsa (Thap Thim) 271
　Plai 548
　Taa Then 587
　Takiap 509
　Thian 272
　Thong Nai Pan 572
　Thong Song 548
　Wai 272
　Wiang Wan 273
　Wong Duan 272
Aranyprathet 240
Art periods 48
Ayutthaya 6, 156, 169–174

B

Ban Ahong 462
Ban Bang Bao 294
Ban Bang Makham 543
Ban Bang Phae 215
Ban Bo Phut 548
Ban Chai Son 645
Ban Chiang 13, 415
Ban Dan Kwian 422

Ban Hat Khrai 395
Ban Huak 410
Ban Huay Khrai 391
Ban Kai 577–578
Ban Khiriwong 613
Ban Khlong Son 291
Ban Khong Sawan 469
Ban Pak Thong Chai 423
Ban Phe 266–267
Ban Prasat 13, 423
Ban Sakai 670
Ban Si Than 444
Ban Ta Klang 431–432
Ban Tai 577–578
Ban Thakradan 203
Ban Thong Krut 557
Ban Thong Yang 558
Bang Pa-In 174
Bang Phli 179
Bang Po and Ban Tai 543–544
Bang Rak 105
Bang Saen 246–247
Bang Saphan Yai 511–513
Bang Saray 262–263
Banglamphu 115
Banharn Silpa-archa 25
Baw Sang 321, 325
Beach see Hat
Betong 672
Bophloi 208
Border Entry Points 91
Border Fighting 78
Buriram 426–427
Burma 390

C

Cambodia 244, 285
Canoe and Kayak 235, 607
Caves see Tham
Cha Am 501–502
Chachoengsao 175–177
Chainat 219–220
Chaiya 532–533
Chaiyaphum 479–482
Chanthaburi 244, 275–278
Chatichai Choonhavan 24
Chatuchak Market (B) 140
Chavalit Yongchaiyudh 25
Chiang Dao 321
Chiang Khan 476–478
Chiang Khong 393–395
Chiang Mai 308, 310–323
Chiang Rai 386–388
Chiang Saen 14, 15, 396

Chinatown (B) 105, 135
Chitralada Palace (B) 105
Chonabot 484
Chonburi 244–246
Chong Mek 441–442
Chumphon 515–518
Constantine Phaulkon 18, 230
Credit Cards 77
Crystal Buddha (C) 318
cyclists 414

D

Damnoen Saduak 156, 159
Dengue fever 87
Diarrhoea 86
Diving 626, 561, 591–592
Doi Ang Khang 321
Doi Mae Salong 309, 391
Doi Suthep 321
Doi Tung 391
Druggings 77
Drugs 78
Dusit (B) 105
Dusit Zoo (B) 138
Dvaravati 14, 15

E

Elephant 43, 236, 379, 431
Elephant camp 360
Elephant Roundup 431
Elephant Ctr (Taeng Dao) 329
Elephant Ctr (Baby) 337
Entertainment 141–142

F

Fang 328–330
Festivals
　Bua Tong (MHS) 370
　Buriram Kite Festival 426
　Buriram Regatta 427
　Candle Festival (UR) 440
　Chakri Day 20
　Dragon & Lion (NS) 226
　Lam Duan Flower (SS) 434
　Narathiwats Speciality 579
　Phanom Rung (NR) 427
　Rocket (Ya) 443
　Thao Suranari (NR) 419
　Yala Cultural Fair 670
Fine Arts Department 108
Floating Market
　Damnoen Saduak (R) 160
　Khlong Pho Hak (SSo) 182

Food 85
Foreign Embassies 112–115
Full Moon Parties 78, 584

G

Gems 76, 278
Gibbon Rehab Ctr (Pk) 607
Golden Triangle see *Sop Ruak*
Grand Palace (B) 105, 127

H

Hat Bang Sak 529
Hat Bang Saphan 513
Hat Bang Tao 606
Hat Bangruk 548
Hat Bo Phut 547
Hat Chao Samran 500
Hat Chaweng 549–551
Hat Kai Bae 293–294
Hat Kamala 606
Hat Karon 602
Hat Kata 600–602
Hat Khao Lak 529
Hat Khiriwong 513
Hat Khontee 573–578
Hat Lamai 553–556
Hat Lek 285
Hat Long 295
Hat Mai Khao 607
Hat Manao 682
Hat Nai Han 600
Hat Naithon 606
Hat Narathat 679
Hat Nopphara Thara 618
Hat Pak Meng 638
Hat Puk Tian 500–502
Hat Raileh 619–620
Hat Rawai 599–600
Hat Rin 573–578
Hat Sadet 572
Hat Sai Kaew 252, 270, 292
Hat Sairee 518, 586, 587
Hat Salat 570–631
Hat Surin 606
Hat Tam Pang 252
Hat Tha Wang 252
Hat Thong Wua Laen 520
Hat Tien 573
Hat Yai 652–655
Hat Yao 569–570, 625
Hellfire Pass (K) 198
Hilltribe
  Akha 37
  Lahu (Muser) 35
  H'tin 40
  Hmong (Meo) 34
  Karen 32

Khamu 40
Lawa 40
Lisu 38
Mlabri 41
Padang (long-necks) 33
Yao (Mien) 36
Hilltribe Education Ctr. 389
Historical Parks
  Kamphaeng Phet 383
  Old Sukhothai 309, 352
  Phu Phra Bat (NB) 466
  Prasat Hin Phimai (NR)
  424
  Prasat Muang Singh (K)
  196
  Si Satchanalai (Su) 354
HIV Virus 88
Hospitals 111
Hua Hin 22, 504–508
Huay Xai 393
human sacrifices 519

I

Immigration 108
Internet & Email 71, 110, 327
Isthmus of Kra 523

J

Jim Thompson's House 133
Jomtien Beach 260–261

K

Kaeng Khut Khu 477
Kaeng Loeng Chan 487
Kala Shrine (Lo) 186
Kalasin 490–492
Kamphaeng Phet 382–385
Kamthieng House (B) 135
Kanchanaburi 14, 187–195
Kanchanadit 538–539
Kapong 529
Khao Pha Raet 223–225
Khao Kho 342–343
Khao Khong Chai 223–225
Khao Wang and Phra Nakhon
Kharu 403
Khlong Yai 284–291
Khon Kaen 482–484
Khong Chiam 440–441
Khorat 418–422
Khum Kham 15
Khun Yuam 369–370
Khuraburi 530
Kick Boxing 141
Kings of Thailand

Anantayot 336
Athittayarat 331
Bhumibol Adulyadej 22
Borommakot 19
Boromtrailokant 16
Chai Chettha 460
Chaisiri 382
Chulalongkorn 21–22
Ekathotsarot 18
Maha Thammaracha 17
Mangrai 318–320, 354, 386, 389
Mongut 184
Narai 18, 479
Naresuan 146, 346, 468
Ngam Muang 409
Prajadhipok 22
Rama I 20
Ramathibodi 20
Ramkhamhaeng 399
Suriyamarin 19
Taksin 19–20, 357, 376
Ko Adang 665
Ko Bulon 666
Ko Chang 244, 289, 496, 523
Ko Kham 303
Ko Khlum 304
Ko Kong (Cambodia) 285
Ko Kradan 639
Ko Kut 244, 303–304
Ko Lan 261–262
Ko Lanta 628–631
Ko Libong 641
Ko Lipe 634, 663
Ko Loi 250
Ko Mak 299–303
Ko Mattra 519
Ko Muk 634, 638
Ko Nang Yuan 593–594
Ko Ngai (Ko Hai) 640
Ko Ngam 304
Ko Panyi 526
Ko Pha Ngan 564–583
Ko Phi Phi 623–626
Ko Rok 634, 641
Ko Samet 268, 519
Ko Samui 540–563, 541–563
Ko Si Chang 251–253
Ko Taen 563
Ko Talu 525
Ko Tao 497, 583–593
Ko Tapu 525
Ko Tarutao 661
Ko Wai 244, 298–299
Ko Yao 682
Ko Yao Noi 532–594

Koo Puai Noi 484
Krabi 615–617
Krit Sivara 23
Krue Se Mosque (Pa) 677
Ku Kasing 490

L

La Ngu 660
Laem Ngop 288–289
Lampang 333
Lamphun 321, 330–333
Lan Na 15
Lan Sak 186, 223
Language Schools 110
Laos 395
Leeches 87
Loei 469–473
Lopburi 14, 186, 226–231
Lost Passports & Visas 82
Luang Prabang 14
luggage storing 97
Lumpini Park (B) 138

M

Mae Chan 380–385
Mae Hat 570–571
Mae Hong Son 366–367
Mae Lana 363–367
Mae Nam 545
Mae Sa Valley 325
Mae Sai 390
Mae Salid 372–373
Mae Sam Laep 371–380
Mae Sariang 369–370
Mae Sot 373
Mahasarakham 485–487
Malaria 86
Medical Kit 88
Marijuana. 78
Monkey Theatre (ST) 561
Mountain Bikes 417, 584
Muang Boran (SP) 179
Muang Fa Daet (Ka) 14, 492
Muang Lap Lae 357
Mukdahan 446–448
Museums
  Forensic Medicine (B) 135
  Hariphunchai (L) 331
  Khon Kaen 483
  Ubon Ratchathani 437–440
  Nakhon Si Thammart 611
  Bangkok 132
  Phimai (NR) 425
  Ubon Ratchathani 439

N

Na Yang-Nam Som Forest

Park 467
Nakhon Nayok 233–236
Nakhon Pathom 161–163
Nakhon Phanom 452–453
Nakhon Ratchasima 418–422
Nakhon Sawan 225–226
Nakhon Si Thammarat 608–612
Namtok
  Erawan (K) 186, 201
  Heo Narok (NR) 418
  Heo Suwat (NR) 418
  Nang Rong (NN) 235
  Sarika (NN) 235
  Than Thip (NK) 461
  Thu-Lor-Sue (Ta) 379
  Ton Nga Chang (So) 656
Nan 402–405
Nan Chao 13
Nang Rong 427
Narathiwat 678–681
Nathon 543
National Gallery (B) 134
National Library (B) 110
National Parks Div (B) 108
National Parks
  Ang Thong (NMP) 564
  Aow Phang Nga (PG) 528
  Budo (Na) 681
  Chae Son (Lam) 338
  Chaloem Rattanakosin (K) 208
  Doi Fang (C) 328
  Doi Inthanon (C) 321, 326
  Doi Khun Tan (L) 332
  Doi Luang (Py) 409
  Doi Phu Kha (N) 309, 406
  Doi Suthep (C) 321, 324
  Erawan (K) 201–202
  Hat Chao Mai (Tr) 638
  Hat Nai Yang (Pk) 606
  Hat Wanakorn (PKK) 511
  Huai Huat (SN) 451
  Kaeng Krachan (Ph) 502
  Kang Krung (ST) 540–543
  Khao Chamao - Khao Wong (Ra) 266
  Khao Kitchakut (Cb) 278
  Khao Laem (K) 201
  Khao Lak (PG) 530
  Khao Lam Pi (PG) 528–529
  Khao Luang (NST) 612–613
  Khao Nam Khang (So) 656
  Khao Phanom Bencha (Kr) 622
  Khao Phra Taew (Pk) 607

Khao Poo Khao Ya (Pt) 646
  Khao Sam Lan (Sb) 232
  Khao Sam Roi Yot (Pkk) 508
  Khao Sok (ST) 497, 539
  Khao Yai (NR) 414, 416
  Khlong Lan (KP) 385–386
  Khlong Wang Chao (KP) 386
  Ko Tarutao NMP (Sa) 660
  Koh Thalu NMP (PKK) 513
  Kraburi (Rn) 523
  Laem Son (Rn) 525
  Lan Sang (Ta) 376
  Mae Ping (Lam) 332, 338
  Mae Wong (KP) 385–386
  Mukdahan 449
  Nam Nao (Pb) 343
  Namtok Phliu Khao Sabap (Cb) 279
  Namtok Mae Surin (MHS) 368–370
  Namtok Yong (NST) 614
  Pha Taem (UR) 441
  Phu Chong Nayoi (UR) 441
  Phu Hin Rong Kla (P) 348
  Phu Khao-Phu Phan Kham (NB) 467, 485
  Phu Kradung (Li) 473
  Phu Pha Man (Li) 475
  Phu Phan (SN) 451
  Phu Rua (Li) 474–475
  Phu Sa Dok Bua (M) 449
  Phu Wiang (KK) 485
  Prang Sida (SK) 239
  Sai Thong (Cy) 481–482
  Sai Yok (K) 198
  Si Nakharin (K) 202
  Similan Islands (PG) 530
  Sri Phang Nga (PG) 529
  Surin Islands (PG) 531
  Taksin Maharat (Ta) 376
  Tat Ton (Cy) 481
  Thale Ban (Sa) 659
  Than Bokkhoroni (Kr) 623
  Thap Lan (Pi) 238
  Thung Salaeng Luang (Su) 349
  Wiang Kosai (Pe) 402
Ngam Muang 15
Nong Bua Lam Phu 467–469
Nong Khai 455–459
Nong Pheu 478–479
Nonthaburi 165–166

O

opium 79
Overseas Thai Embassies 83

P

Pahurat (B) 105, 137, 141
Pak Chom 475-476
Pak Chong 415-416
Pak Huay 478-479
Pakbara 660
Palang 329
Palatha 380
Panare & Hat Khae Khae 677
Pangmappa Village 361
Pasang 332
Passport 90
Pathet Lao 23
Pathum Thani 166
Patong 604
Patpong Road 141-142
Pattani 20, 674-676
Pattaya 253-260
Peung Kleung 380
Phae Muang Phii 402
Phan Ka 557
Phang Nga 525-526
Phattalung 642-645
Phayao 407-410
Phetchaburi 497-500
Phetchabun 341-342
Phibun 62
Phibun Songkhram 22
Phichit 339-340
Phimai 14, 423-425
Phitsanulok 14, 17, 345
Phra Buddha Chinnarat (P) 346
Phra Pathom Chedi (Nk) 162
Phra Singh Buddha (C) 318
Phrae 399 - 402
Phraya Chaiyabun 401
Phu Manorom 448
Phuket 596-597
Phun Phin 534
Police 79
Prachinburi 236-238
Prang Ku (Cy) 480
Praphat Charusathien 23
Prasat Hin Khao Phanom Rung 415, 428-429
Prasat Muang Tam 429
Prasat Phanomwan 425
Prasat Ta Meuan 432-433
Pratchuap Khiri Khan 509-511
Pridi Panomyong 22

Prince Ananda Mahidol 22
Prison (Klong Prem) 164
Pua 406
Puppetry 611

R

Rabies 86
Radio 111
Rafting 360, 367, 370, 378
Ranong 520-522
Ratchaburi 156-159
Rayong 265-266
Refugee Camps 287, 375
Renu Nakhon 454
River Khwae 186
Rock Climbing 621
Roi Et 488-490
Royal Barges (B) 134, 154

S

Sa Kaew 238-240
Sa Morakot 238-239
Saen Pu 396
Sai Ngam 425
Sai Yok 196
Sakhon Nakhon 14, 449-450
Samut Prakan 21, 177-178
Samut Sakhon 181-182
Samut Songkhram 183-184
San Jao Leng Ju Khieng Shrine (Pa) 676
San Kamphaeng 321, 325
Sanam Chand Palace (B) 163
Sanam Luang Park (B) 138
Sang Khom 461-462
Sangkhlaburi 186, 203-206
Sao Chaliang 441
Sao Din 406
Saraburi 232-233
Sarit Thanarat 23, 446
Sattahip 263-264
Satun 656-658
Savannakhet 446
Seni Pramoj 23
Si Chiang Mai 460
Si Maha Mariamman (B) 137
Si Racha 244, 248-250
Si Racha Farm 250
Si Saket 433-434
Si Sawat 203
Siam Society (B) 105, 110
Siam Square (B) 105
Silk 432, 465, 480, 485
silver 432, 465
Similan & Surin Islands 496
Similan Islands 604, 605
Singburi 216-218

SLORC 390
Snake Bites 87
Songkhla 18, 646-651
Sop Ruak 399
Soppong 361-362
Sri Lanka 19
Student Card 90
SUA 391
Suan Pakkard Palace (B) 134
Sukhothai 14, 16, 351-353
Sungai Kolok 683
Suphanaburi 14, 208-213
Surat Thani 534-537
Surin 429-431

T

Tak 375-379
Tak Bai 682
Takua Pa 529-537
Tha Li 478-479
Tha Ton 326-327
Thai Boxing 306, 583-585
Tham (Cave)
  Chiang Dao (C) 329
  Davadaeng (K) 199-200
  Phet (Kr) 621
  Erawan (NB) 469
  Krabok Buddhist Monk Sanctuary (NN) 232-233
  Lawa (K) 198
  Lot (C) 362, 365
  Luang (CR) 390
  Morakot (Tr) 639
  Pua Tuub Cave Complex (N) 405
  Rubror (Ch) 519
Thanom Kittikachorn 23
Thap Sakae 514
That Phanom 14, 454
Thonburi 105
Thong Pha Phum 200
Thong Sala 567
Three Pagoda's Pass 207
Thung Kwian Forestry Market 337
Thung Makham Yai and Thung Makham Noi 518
Traditional Medicine and Thai Massage 112
Trat 21, 280-283
Travel Insurance 90
Trekking 77, 79, 308, 360, 366, 370, 378, 392, 406
Tribal Research Inst. (C) 319

U

U Thong 16

Udon Sunshine Fragrant
Orchid Farm 465
Udon Thani 463–466
Umphang 378–379
Uthai Thani 186, 220–222
Uttaradit 356–357
Utthayan Sawan 225–227

V

Vientiane 20
Vietnam 23
Village Weaver Handicrafts
Self Help Project 459
Vimanmek Mansion (B) 128
Visas 81
Vongburi House (Pe) 401

W

Waley 377–379
Wang Prajan 659
Wang Takhrai 235
Wat
  Arun (B) 130
  Benchamabophit (B) 131
  Bovornivet (B) 131
  Bupharam (T) 282–283
  Chamma Thewi (L) 331
  Chiang Man (C) 318
  Chiang Man (C) 321
  Chiang Yuen (C) 321
  Chong Kham (MHS) 367
  Chong Klang (MHS) 367
  Duang Di (C) 320
  Kate (C) 321
  Ku Kut (Lam) 331
  Ku Tao (C) 319
  Lokayasutharam (A) 173
  Maharam (C) 321
  Mahathat (B) 130

Mahathat Worawihan (PH)
  499
Mon (K) 206–207
Nakhon Kosa (L) 230
Nong Bua (UR) 439
Pha That Doi Kong Mu
  (MHS) 367
Phailom (A) 167
Pho (B) 105
Pho (B) 129
Phra Chao Phanan Choeng
  (A) 172
Phra Kaeo (CR) 388
Phra Kaew (B) 127–128
Phra Mahathat (A) 172
Phra Mongkhon Bophit (A)
  172
Phra Narai Maharat (NR)
  421
Phra Phutthabat (LO) 231
Phra Si Ratana Mahathat
  (R) 158
Phra Si Sanphet (A) 172
Phra Singh (C) 318, 320
Phra That Chedi Luang
  (CR) 397
Phra That Chom Kitti (CR)
  398
Phra That Doi Chom
  Thong(CR) 389
Phra That Doi Suthep (C)
  325
Phra That Hariphunchai (L)
  331
Phra That Lampang Luang
  (LA) 336
Phra That Pa Ngao (CR)
  398

Phra That Phanom (NP)
  454
Phu Thawk (NK) 462
Rachanada (B) 132
Ram Poeng (C) 319
Saket (B) 130–131
Sala Kaew Ku (Wat Khaek)
  (NK) 458
Sala Loi (NR) 421
Sothon (Cha) 176
Suan Dawk (CM) 319
Suan Mok (ST) 533
Suthat (B) 132
Tham Mongkon Thong (K)
  193
Tham Sua (Kr) 616–617
Traimit (B) 105, 130
Yai (P) 346
Water 85
Waterfalls see Namtok
Wild Tiger Corps 22
Wildlife/bird Sanctuaries
  Huay Kha Khaeng(UT) 224
  Khao Khut (So) 652
  Khao Thaphet (ST) 536
  Khlong Lamchan (Tr) 642
  Khlong Yan (ST) 540–543
  Phu Luang (Li) 475
  Tha Sadet (AT) 214–215
  Thale Noi (Pt) 646
  Thung Yai Naresuan (K)
    201

Y

Yai Phrik Vipassana Centre
  252
Yala 667–670
Yasothon 442–444

A–Ayutthaya, AT–Ang Thong, B–Bangkok, C–Chiang Mai, Cb–Chanthaburi, Cha–Chachoengsao, CR–Chiang Rai, Cy–Chaiyaphum, K–Kanchanaburi, Ka–Kalasin, KK–Khon Kaen, KP–Kamphaeng Phet, Kr–Krabi, L–Lamphun, Lam–Lampang, Li–Loei, Lo–Lopburi, M–Mukdahan, MHS–Mae Hong Son, N–Nan, Na–Narathiwat, NB–Nong Bua Lam Phu, Nk–Nakhon Pathom, NK–Nong Khai, NN–Nakhon Nayok, NP–Nakhon Phanom, NR–Nakhon Ratchasima, NS–Nakhon Sawan, NST–Nakhon Si Thammarat, P–Phitsanulok, Pa–Pattani, Pb–Phetchabun, Pe–Phrae, PG–Phang Nga, Ph–Phetburi, Pi–Prachinburi, Pk–Phuket, PKK–Pratchuap Khiri Khan, Pt–Phattalung, Py–Phayao, R–Ratchaburi, Ra–Rayong, Rn–Ranong, Sa–Sa Keaw, Sa–Satun, Sb–Saraburi, SN–Sakhon Nakhon, So–Songkhla, SP–Samut Prakan, SS–Si Saket, SSo–Samut Songkhram, ST–Surat Thani, Su–Sukhothai, T–Trat, Ta–Tak, Tr–Trang, UR–Ubon Ratchathani, UT–Uthai Thani, Y–Yala, Ya–Yasothon

GLOSSARY

aow — bay

ban — village

bot (ubosoth) — ordination hall of a temple

Brahma — Hindu God

chedi — a tower containing remains of revered persons (monks, royalty)

CPT — Communist Party of Thailand

DEA — Drug Enforcement Agency (US)

DKBA — Democratic Karen Buddhist Army

farang — colloquial term for foreigners of western origin

hat — beach

I-san — northeast Thailand

khlong — canal

kip — Lao currency

KMT — Kuomintang

KNU — Karen National Union

Lak Muang — city pillar

laterite — porous stone often used by Khmers in the construction of religious sites

lintel — a decorative stone placed above a doorway supporting the upper wall

Mahathat — A chedi which contains relics of Buddha

making merit — A Buddhist practise where one aims to become closer to nirvana by performing good deeds

Mon — kingdom based in southern Burma with some influence in the development of early Thailand

mondop — A pavilion housing religious paraphernalia

naga — A mythical serpent used to guard approaches to holy sites

namtok — waterfall

pali — language of ancient India and the script used for original Buddhist scriptures

phanom — Khmer for mountain or hill

phra — term denoting royal or religious status

PLAT — Peoples Liberation Army of Thailand

prang — Khmer styled chedi

prasat — Khmer temple complex

PULO — Pattani United Liberation Organisation

Ramakien — Thai version of the Indian epic Ramayana

sala — religious meeting hall

SLORC — State Law and Order Restoration Council

soi — lane

SUA — Shan United Army

TAT — Tourism Authority of Thailand

tham — cave

thanon — road

wai — a traditional Thai greeting

wat — Buddhist temple

Crossword 1

Crossword 2

Crossword 3

Riddle Answers

Riddle nèung (Page 46)

You are playing monopoly therefore everytime you land in front of the hotel, you are required to pay the rent.

Riddle sâwng (page 158)

You and two other people were ballooning but were having trouble. The balloon was loosing altitude and heading for the ground at a rapid rate so you had to get rid of some weight. After throwing out the sandbags, still more weight loss was required, so you and the other two drew straws to see who had to jump out of the basket — unfortunately, you got the short straw.

Riddle sâhm (Page 247)

Rub your hands together until they are sore. With the saw, cut the chair in half. Two halves make a whole. Climb through the hole and out of the cell. Yell until you are hoarse then jump onto the horse and ride into town!

704

NOTES

Tales From the Other Side
PO Box Box 743
Hornsby NSW 2077
Australia

email: mcdonald@mail.enternet.com.au
http://people.enternet.com.au/~mcdonald/